SUPER HOUSE

Donald R. Wulfinghoff

Also by Donald Wulfinghoff

ENERGY EFFICIENCY MANUAL

SUPER HOUSE

Design Your Dream Home
for Super Energy Efficiency, Total Comfort, Dazzling Beauty, Awesome Strength, and Economy

Donald R. Wulfinghoff

ENERGY INSTITUTE PRESS

Wheaton, Maryland USA

Super House

**Design Your Dream Home
for Super Energy Efficiency,
Total Comfort, Dazzling Beauty,
Awesome Strength, and Economy**

by **Donald R. Wulfinghoff**

published by:

**Energy Institute Press
3936 Lantern Drive
Wheaton, Maryland 20902
U.S.A.**

301-946-1196

Library of Congress Cataloging-in-Publication Data

Wulfinghoff, Donald.
Super house : design your dream home for super energy efficiency, total comfort, dazzling beauty, awesome strength, and economy

pages cm
Includes index.

ISBN 978-0-9657926-3-9 (alk. paper)

1. House construction – Amateurs' manuals.
2. Architecture and energy conservation.
3. Ecological houses – Design and construction.
I. Title.

TH4815.W85 2015
728'.37 – dc23
2014033581

Printed in Canada

for Nancy

CONTENTS

Warning & Disclaimer   11

Meet Your Design Guide   **12**

Welcome to Your Greatest Adventure!   **13**

STEP 1: PLAN YOUR HOME'S LAYOUT AND STYLE   **17**

Get Organized for the Creative Process   18
Provide for Each Function and Activity   19
   Home Activities Worksheet   **20**
Design Your Rooms and Spaces   26
The Interior Layout   61
Stacking the Living Space   76
   Basic Roof Structures   **78**
Reality Check: the Size of Your Home   86
   How to Lower Your Construction Cost   **87**
Frame or Masonry Construction?   91
Additions to an Existing House   93
Beautiful Exterior Shapes and Surfaces   98
Elegant and Functional Roof Shapes   115
   Roof Styles   **116**
   Snow and Ice Protection Checklist   **125**
Beautiful Roof Surfaces   126
   Roof Surface Comparison   **127**
Ornamental Carpentry: Delightful Icing on the Cake   131
Your Outdoor Environment   135

STEP 2: LAY OUT YOUR GLASS AND SHADING   **139**

Glass & Sunlight: the Minimum You Should Know   140
   Glazing Comparison   **142**
Glass Design 1: Minimize Heat Loss   149
Glass Design 2: Daytime Solar Heating   151
Glass Design 3: Stay Cool in Warm Weather   153
   Tree and Shrub Selection Guide   **156**
Glass Design 4: Daylighting   167
Glass Design 5: Exploit Views & Preserve Privacy   176
Glass Design 6: Ventilation for Health and Comfort   179
Glass Design 7: Beautiful Appearance   180
Glass Design 8: Emergency Escape   181
What If You Want a Space with Lots of Glass?   182

STEP 3: CREATE A SUPER STRUCTURE   185

How Houses Are Built: the Minimum You Should Know   186
Building Codes   205
Super-Structure Design Advance #1: Super-Insulation   207
    Insulation Worksheet   **213**
Super-Structure Design Advance #2: Condensation Protection   224
Super-Structure Design Advance #3: Leak-Free Construction   231
Super-Structure Design Advance #4: Super-Strength   238
    Wind Protection Checklist   **239**
The Ground on Which You Build   244
The Foundation   250
    Foundation Types   **251**
Building a Super-Basement   270
Building Perfect Frame Floors   282
Building Super Frame Walls   289
Condensation Protection for Frame Houses in Cold Climates   299
Insulation and Condensation Protection for Masonry Walls   301
Adding Insulation to Existing Walls   305
Interior Surfaces for Walls and Ceilings   308
Installing Your Exterior Wall Surfaces   308
Your Super-Roof   312
Cool Roofs for Warm Climates   336
Insulation for Interior Frame Walls, Floors, and Ceilings   345
The Wiring and Cable   347
Selecting and Installing Your Windows   350
    Window Selection Guide   **352**
The Entrance Doors   374
    Entrance Door Selection Guide   **376**
Interior Doors and Partitions   385
Garage Doors and Other Large Doors   389
    Large Door Selection Guide   **390**
Skylights   400
    Skylight Selection Guide   **401**
Your Floor Surface Options   405
    Floor Surface Comparison   **406**

STEP 4: PERFECT HEATING, COOLING, AND VENTILATION   413

Main Heating and Cooling Recommendations	414
Heating Equipment Comparison	**415**
Select Your Energy Sources	417
Energy Cost Worksheet	**420**
Hydronic Heating Systems	422
Hydronic Room Heater Comparison	**427**
Builder's Hydronic System Checklist	**440**
Split-System Heat Pumps	454
How Heat Pumps and Air Conditioners Work	**456**
Air Conditioners, Maybe	469
Electric Resistance Heaters	471
Direct-Fired Room and Space Heaters	475
Cooling Without Air Conditioning	480
Using Fans to Reduce Stratification	485
Evaporative Coolers for Dry Climates	486
Ventilation for Health, Safety, and Humidity Control	490
Eliminate the Danger of Carbon Monoxide	495
Limiting Humidity	497
Raising Humidity	504
Efficient Control of HVAC	505
Programmable Thermostat Selection Guide	**506**

STEP 5: YOUR PLUMBING FIXTURES AND WATER SYSTEMS   511

Efficient and Luxurious Plumbing Fixtures	512
Making Hot Water	522
Water Treatment: Pure Water Anywhere	530
Home Water Treatment	**534**
Your Water Pipes	542

STEP 6: YOUR HOME'S LIGHTING   549

How Vision Works	550
Your Lamp Choices	553
Lamp Selection Guide	**554**
Efficient and Comfortable Lighting Layout	564
Selecting and Placing Your Lighting Fixtures	570
Home Lighting Worksheet	**572**
Efficient Lighting Controls	581

STEP 7: SELECT YOUR HOUSEHOLD APPLIANCES   587

 Appliance Efficiency Ratings   588
 Refrigerators   589
 Food Freezers   590
 Conventional Ranges   591
 Electric Induction Ranges   593
 Ovens and Broilers   594
 Microwave Ovens   596
 Dishwashers   597
 Clothes Washers   598
 Clothes Dryers   599
 Room Air Cleaners   600
 Home Electronics   601

STEP 8: GET YOUR HOME BUILT   603

 Working With Your Builder   604
 The Contract with Your Builder   609
  The Super-House Clause   **610**
 The Construction Drawings   612
  Typical Construction Drawings for a Super-House   **613**
 Getting Expert Help   621

LAST LOOK: ENERGY FOR PIONEERS   625

 Heating with Firewood and Other Solid Fuels   626
 Movable Insulation for Windows   646
 Active Solar Heating Systems   649
 Passive Solar Heating   654
 Solar Electricity Generation   658
 Wind Energy   662
 "Zero Energy Houses" and "Going Off the Grid"   663
 Geothermal Heat Pumps and Air Conditioners   664
 Heat Recovery Appliances   669
 Earth Sheltered Construction   670
 Unusual Structures   672
 Rainwater Recovery   674
 Recycling Household Sewage   676

Index   **681**

WARNING & DISCLAIMER

This book is written to inspire, educate, and entertain. It is based on the conviction that it is practical for any motivated person to design a home that is greatly superior to conventional standards of home construction. The book offers a methodical process for designing a superior home, with the understanding that the user will seek appropriate additional knowledge and assistance as needed. This book is not intended to be your sole source of information about any activity.

Designing one's own home is a major achievement that has been accomplished successfully by many lay persons. This book is intended to make that activity better organized, easier, and more certain, while advancing the state of the art. However, all progress involves the risks of pioneering. No book can guarantee success or freedom from problems. This book cannot cover all situations, and the author does not claim to have expert knowledge of all aspects of building design or construction.

The advice given in this book involves subjective judgments that reflect the opinions of the author. The book does not presume to define or to impose standards for home design or construction.

This book is not intended to teach the trade skills that are used in home construction. Where construction techniques are explained, the purpose is to provide orientation so that the reader can communicate effectively with his/her builder, select the best methods, and in various ways, to improve upon conventional home design.

This book is offered with the understanding that neither the author nor the publisher is using it to engage in the professional practice of engineering, architecture, law, or any other trade or profession. Where expert or specialized services are required, those services should be performed by appropriately qualified practitioners.

Home design and construction have safety implications and the potential for consequential damage. The book offers cautions related to various aspects of design and construction, but these cautions are not comprehensive. The ways in which someone may suffer injury are legion and unpredictable. Safety results primarily from the training and licensing of builders and building design professionals, and from building codes.

Great care has been taken to make this book as complete and as accurate as possible for its intended purpose. However, there may be errors in content and typography. Neither the author nor the publisher guarantee the accuracy of any information provided. Furthermore, construction methods and materials change continually, with results that cannot be completely foreseen.

Some of the book's innovative concepts may be covered by patents. It is the responsibility of the user to avoid infringing any patent rights that may exist.

This book is not approved for use by anyone who declines to accept the preceding conditions. If this is unacceptable, return the book for refund.

The author, the publisher, and future readers will be grateful for any suggestions, for identification of any errors, and for bringing the book to the attention of other readers. Please address your comments to the publisher, Energy Institute Press. Thank you!

Meet Your Design Guide

Don Wulfinghoff has a mission to improve the quality of buildings. His *Energy Efficiency Manual* is the world's leading book on energy efficiency in buildings and industry. He taught the first courses on energy efficiency at the George Washington University, in the U.S. capital. His talks have been attended by thousands from around the world. He was introduced on C-Span as "the world's expert on efficiency in buildings" by Congressman Roscoe Bartlett, the respected sustainability sage of Congress.

From the outset, Don recognized the quality of homes as a prime component of human wellbeing, and he has worked to optimize every aspect of home design. He was a pioneer in exploiting the synergy between energy efficiency, comfort, indoor health, structural strength, and fire safety. And, he is emphatic that energy efficient homes must also be beautiful, practical, and economical. He built his own home as a proving ground for several major innovations.

Don is renowned for merging theory and practice in a way that is accessible to people of all backgrounds. Readers applaud his easy, conversational style. As you will see, he doesn't resist droll observations, and he doesn't pull his punches.

Don wrote this book for you. He understands your ambition to have an ideal home, and he wants you to bring that wish to reality. You and he will be spending a lot of time together. So, get ready and enjoy the ride!

WELCOME
To Your Greatest Adventure!

You are about to begin the design of a home that is radically superior to any tract house or custom home that you could buy today. Your home will be precisely tailored to your needs. It will be totally comfortable, exceptionally strong and safe, and beautiful. It will be super-efficient, eliminating most of the heating and cooling costs of a conventional house. It will be immune to the health problems that afflict modern housing.

Your super-home will be economical to build. It makes no compromises with appearance or practicality, so it will have an exceptionally high resale value. It will be a superior investment for the conditions that lie ahead.

If you want to expand or renovate an existing house, **SUPER HOUSE** will show you how to reap the benefits of a super-house design in your project.

Designing your own home or designing an addition to your home may be the most satisfying thing that you will ever do. You will create the perfect environment in which your family will live. And, when later generations live in your creation, they will respect your ability and imagination. No achievement is more enduring.

To achieve these benefits, we will spend several months together as we have fun learning about super-house design. You don't need any prior experience with building a house. All the principles and special techniques that you need to learn are here.

You won't need to become a skilled tradesman, and you won't need to deal with the administrative aspects of construction, such as getting permits. That's because you will hire a professional custom homebuilder or a good remodeling contractor to do the construction. Your contractor will provide the knowledge of the conventional aspects of house construction. This book will teach you enough about conventional construction so that you will communicate effectively with your builder.

Is it really possible for a person with no prior experience to design a home that is far ahead of contemporary residential architecture? It certainly is. We will do it with a step-by-step design sequence that gives you the information you need at just the right times.

Even if your dream home still lies years in the future, start planning it now. Designing your home will be an immensely pleasurable activity for you and your family while you wait for the opportunity to build.

HOW WE WILL DESIGN YOUR HOME

We will design your super-home in a series of eight Steps, which are identified by the color bars on the right side of the pages:

- In **STEP 1**, we design the *interior layout*, the *exterior shape*, and the *architectural style* of your home. Your home will provide space for all your activities, along with a dazzling appearance that suits your taste. This is the most creative part of your design.

- In **STEP 2**, we design the *glass and shading* for your home, providing important lifestyle benefits while minimizing your energy costs. This is one of the most interesting parts of your design, providing a major advance over conventional homes.

- In **STEP 3**, we design the *structure* of your home. We make it super-efficient, exceptionally strong, and resistant to weather, fire, and intrusion. And, we eliminate the common problems of foundations that cause settlement cracks and moisture problems.

- In **STEP 4**, we design your *heating, cooling, and ventilation,* providing total comfort under all conditions. We narrow the choices to two highly efficient types of heating and cooling systems, which we will select based on the climate and energy supply of your location. We eliminate all causes of indoor health problems.

- In **STEP 5**, we design your *water and plumbing* systems, which will provide luxurious bathing, conserve water and water heating energy, and protect against waterborne diseases.

- In **STEP 6**, we design your *lighting*, combining ideal visual quality with energy efficiency.

- In **STEP 7**, we select the best *appliances* for energy efficiency, convenience, and reliability. This Step is especially easy, because we will exploit an established system of appliance efficiency ratings.

- In **STEP 8**, we *get your home built*. We explain how to find the right builder, and how to have an effective relationship with your builder. We show how to get your formal construction drawings prepared by a specialist. And, if you need design help, we will tell you where to find it.

YOUR HOME WILL BE SUPER-EFFICIENT

The superior features of your home will be designed around the central principle of energy efficiency. In a typical climate, your super-efficient house will use only 10% to 20% as much heating and cooling energy as a house of similar size that is built to contemporary standards. For much of the year, your home will be comfortable with no heating or cooling at all. Also, your other energy costs, which include water heating, refrigeration, cooking, and lighting, will be much lower than for a conventional house.

For the first time, **SUPER HOUSE** offers a thorough, fully practical approach to super-efficient home construction. There is no longer any reason to build an ordinary, inefficient house. This breakthrough is based on following five key principles of super energy efficiency, listed in the adjacent sidebar.

Why is energy efficiency so important? The world will soon be a very different place because we are exhausting our supplies of cheap energy sources. The Age of Petroleum will end some time around the middle of the 21st century. Even if we manage to find adequate supplies of new energy sources, their prices will rise to many times present levels. It will not be economical to heat and cool an ordinary wasteful house to the levels of comfort that we take for granted today. However, your super-efficient home will remain comfortable under virtually all conditions.

Your super-efficient home design offers a wonderful bonus. It enhances the other qualities that you want your home to have, including comfort, health, durability, economy, and beauty. For example, when you make the walls thicker to accommodate super-insulation, you will use the greater thickness to make the walls strong, to make them virtually fireproof, and to exploit the sills and wall openings as beautiful stylistic enhancements.

Your super-home will integrate super-efficiency so smoothly that only you and the person who pays the utility bills will know that you have a super-efficient house. Everyone else will think of your home as exceptionally beautiful, interesting, and convenient.

THE INNOVATIONS IN YOUR SUPER-HOME

Your home will have many innovations, ranging from radical improvements to small conveniences. The innovation symbol, shown here, identifies these advances:

 This symbol lets you know where your design is being especially innovative.

Many of these innovations appear for the first time in this book. Others are proven advances that have not yet received the attention that they deserve, such as super-insulation. And, some are important improvements to existing technology, such as heat pumps that can operate well in colder climates.

Equally important is what your super-efficient home *won't* have. It won't need a solar system on the roof or a wind generator in the back yard. It won't need outlandish features, like straw bale walls or sod roofs.

THE FIVE PRINCIPLES OF SUPER-EFFICIENCY

Localize Your Energy Use. You live in one room at a time, so heat and cool all the rooms independently. Design your floor plan to isolate unoccupied rooms and spaces while providing convenient travel between occupied rooms.

Insulate Abundantly and Efficiently. Your home will use much more insulation than a conventional house. Distribute it for maximum effectiveness.

Design the Glass and Shading for Maximum Benefit. Optimize the location, size, and orientation of your glass. Design shading for your glass that optimizes the balance between cooling and heating, and that prevents glare.

Minimize Air Leakage and Control Ventilation. Eliminate air leakage through the structure with improved construction techniques. Provide optimum ventilation for health and comfort with localized fans and air inlets.

Select High-Efficiency Appliances. Use efficiency ratings to select each energy-using item in your home.

You won't have to build your home underground. It won't be a humid greenhouse. You won't need to heat your home with corn kernels or other exotic fuels. Because these concepts are popular and some of them offer future promise, we give them a closer look at the end of the book, in a bonus section titled *Last Look: Energy for Pioneers*.

WHAT WILL YOUR SUPER-HOME COST?

One of the main features of your super-house will be economy. Your home will require no expensive or risky features. Construction cost is less than 10% more than the cost of a well built conventional house. The land cost is the same, so the overall cost premium is typically only a few percent. By careful purchasing and negotiation – which you will learn – you may actually lower your cost below the price of a conventional tract house. Your energy savings will pay for the improved features early in the life of the house.

How do we achieve all these benefits without a big cost premium? The answer is that your home will use only proven materials and equipment. All of your home's advanced construction features are based on skills that conventional builders already have. The big difference is that your design will use conventional materials and skills much more effectively.

USING THIS BOOK FOR ADDITIONS, RENOVATIONS, AND REPAIRS

SUPER HOUSE does not make a big distinction between building a new house and upgrading an existing house. The techniques and materials are the same in both cases. Usually, the only difference is the scope of the project. If an upgrade does require some special methods, they will be explained.

If you are building a major addition, go through the book in sequence, from Step 1 through Step 8. While you are doing that, broaden your perspective to improve the original part of the house. For example, if you are adding new rooms, providing their heating and cooling can be an ideal opportunity to replace the house's original inefficient heating system with a highly efficient system that will serve the entire expanded house.

For a more limited project, use the Table of Contents and the Index to go directly to the parts of the book that apply to your project. For example, if your windows need replacement, the coverage of windows in Step 3 will show you how to achieve the perfect installation.

For every kind of repair or renovation, this book will show you how to do it better, including better energy efficiency, comfort, convenience, and appearance.

We're going to have fun. Let's begin!

STEP 1

PLAN YOUR HOME'S LAYOUT AND STYLE

Step 1 is the broadest and most creative part of your design. We begin with a blank sheet and a vast range of choices. By the end of Step 1, the main visible features of your house – it's size, shape, room layout, and architectural style – will be complete. Your home will have the rooms and spaces to perform all the functions that you imagine. And, it will have a harmonious relationship to your property, your neighbors, and the surrounding environment. To organize this creative process as efficiently as possible, we will follow this sequence:

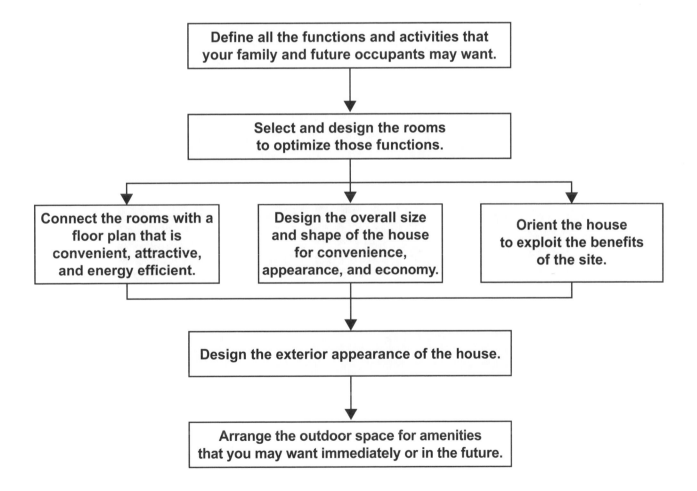

Define all the functions and activities that your family and future occupants may want.

Select and design the rooms to optimize those functions.

Connect the rooms with a floor plan that is convenient, attractive, and energy efficient.

Design the overall size and shape of the house for convenience, appearance, and economy.

Orient the house to exploit the benefits of the site.

Design the exterior appearance of the house.

Arrange the outdoor space for amenities that you may want immediately or in the future.

GET ORGANIZED FOR THE CREATIVE PROCESS

How will you make the creative decisions of your design? They will not spring forth in a flash of inspiration. Instead, they will grow progressively from many ideas. It's an evolving process. You will seek ideas, find them randomly, and put them in order. Every feature and detail that you will want is already "out there" somewhere. You are like an artist who uses ordinary paints and brushes to create a unique masterpiece. Keep your eyes open, and make the entire world your palette.

Create an idea file. Your first official act as the designer is to set up shop for collecting and organizing your ideas. Get a file box and a bunch of folders. Use the idea file to collect and organize your photos, sketches, pages from magazines, catalog sheets, and whatever. If you are designing an entirely new house or a major renovation, start with eight primary folders, corresponding to each of the Eight Steps. Add more folders as you gather material for different parts of your design, using the Table of Contents as a guide to organizing the folders.

Keep a digital camera handy whenever you venture outside. If you have several vehicles, keep a camera in each vehicle. Once you start looking, you will see ideas everywhere. Look at old and new houses. Whenever you see a feature that might be used in your design, take a picture of it. You are not looking for your complete dream home, but for elements that will go into your ideal design, such as a roof shape, some beautiful brick detailing, or a kitchen layout that you like.

Observe construction practices. Stop at building sites and photograph houses as they are being built, as in Figure 1-1. This reveals features that you can't observe in finished houses. You will soon distinguish better building practices from inferior ones. This will build your confidence to discuss the practical details of your home's construction with your own builder.

Make sketches. Expect to make lots of sketches before arriving at your finished design. Sketch quickly. Play with different ideas. Modify things. Start over. Paper is cheap. Mark each sketch with the date and time, and put it into your idea file. Save all your sketches, even doodles that you make on cocktail napkins.

DRW

Figure 1-1. Carry a pocket camera or cell phone camera wherever you go. It is the ideal device for taking notes on every aspect of your home design. Make a special effort to photograph the details of houses under construction.

PROVIDE FOR EACH FUNCTION AND ACTIVITY

The primary purpose of a home is to provide space for all the activities and functions of the lifestyle that you want. So, visualize your home life in the years ahead. What are all the things that you want to do? What will your spouse want to do? What will you want your children to do, and what will they want?

Look into the future, from the time you are a young couple to the time you have hordes of grandchildren visiting your home. Will in-laws or other relatives be moving in? What happens when you retire? And, to maximize the resale value of your home, consider what later owners may want.

This is a revolutionary improvement in home design. Contemporary houses have generic rooms that come from a common menu of room types, such as bedrooms and bathrooms. Their design gives little regard to the activities that the occupants may want to pursue, or to the way that activities occur in related rooms. To remedy that weakness, we will begin your design with a tally of all the functions and activities that your family will want. To do that systematically, use the *Home Activities Worksheet*, which begins on the next page. The *Worksheet* identifies the activities that may occur in a home. For each activity, it suggests various room or fixture options to consider.

An important point is that you can satisfy most functions in a variety of ways, often involving several choices of rooms or features. For example, a living room may be used for many activities, including reading, sewing, playing games, watching television, and lounging on the floor around a heating stove. Not all those activities are compatible. You may try to design your living room to fulfill all those functions, or you may assign some to those activities to specialized

rooms. For example, if you have a large and boisterous family, consider a separate reading room in a quiet corner of the house. Or, you may want to isolate the noisy activities, such as watching television and playing games, in one or more separate rooms.

 Start your design with a complete tally of all the activities that you want your home to accommodate. This is a revolutionary advance in home design practice.

Similarly, the functions should guide the design each room and space. For example, a porch is often included in tract houses as a stylistic feature, with little regard to the functions that a porch may serve. As a result, a typical porch is rarely used. But, a porch may add significant pleasure to your life and add value to the house if it is designed to fulfill its potential. For example, to make the porch a desirable gathering place, design it to be wider than usual. Maybe add an extension that allows a barbecue grill to vent smoke away from the house. If your home has a great view and a season of mild weather, orient the porch toward the view. If you will have a multi-story house in a snowy climate, extend the porch under the eaves to act as a snow shield.

After you have used the *Home Activities Worksheet* to identify all the spaces and features that you need to fulfill your desires, we will design your individual rooms.

Okay. Sharpen your pencil, turn the page, and let's get started.

──── HOME ACTIVITIES WORKSHEET ────

Use this Worksheet to identify all the activities that you want your home to accommodate. For each activity, check the type of space or fixture that you prefer to use. If you desire more than one room or fixture, write the total number in the check box. Account for future changes in your interests and health, and in the size of your family. Consider features that may increase the value of your home to future owners.

For more detail about your space and fixture options, see the descriptions of the individual room types under *Design Your Rooms and Spaces*.

ACTIVITY	ROOMS, SPACES & FIXTURES
SLEEPING & DRESSING	
sleeping, occupant couple (parents)	☑ large bedroom (typically having dedicated toilet and shower)
sleeping, typically other family members and long-term guests	☑ bedroom (typically arranged for shared toilet and shower)
sleeping, supplemental for transient guests	☑ spare bedroom, furnished with conventional bed, bunk bed, or trundle bed
	☐ other room, furnished with sofa bed, daybed, or Murphy bed
	☐ other room, with nighttime space for rollaway bed or futon
dressing and undressing	☒ dedicated space in bedroom
	☐ dressing room
storage, clothing for daily wear	☐ closet, in bedroom
	☐ closet, in dressing room
	☒ walk-in closet
	☒ dresser
	☒ vertical storage module (perhaps as room divider)
	☐ freestanding wardrobe

ACTIVITY	ROOMS, SPACES & FIXTURES
storage, seasonal and occasional clothing	☐ closet, in bedroom
	☐ closet, in dressing room
	☐ walk-in closet
	☐ bed with drawers
	☐ vertical storage module (perhaps as room divider)
	☐ storage chest
	☐ general storage room (with temperature & humidity control)
	☒ coat ~~room~~ closet
storage, linens & bedding	☒ linen closet
	☐ chest in bedroom
	☐ general storage room
TOILET & HYGIENE	
toilet	☒ toilet room
urinal	☐ urinal space, in toilet room
	☐ urinal space, in garage, workshop, etc.
hand washing	☒ toilet room
	☐ laundry tub
	☒ kitchen sink
	☐ basin, in garage
	☐ basin, in workshop
storage, for toiletries, towels, toilet paper	☒ cabinets in toilet rooms
	☐ linen closet
	☐ general storage room

ACTIVITY	ROOMS, SPACES & FIXTURES
BATHING	
showering	☒ shower room ☐ shower in toilet room
bathing or soaking in tub or whirlpool bath	☒ bathtub room ☐ bathtub or whirlpool bath in toilet room
dental care	☑ toilet room
shaving	☑ toilet room
hair styling and drying	☑ toilet room
applying cosmetics	☑ toilet room ☐ makeup table in bedroom or dressing room
clean bathing in hot bath, alone or with others	☑ hot tub (usually outside)
sweat bathing	☐ sauna/steam room
ROMANCE	
preliminary	☐ (commonly off-site) ☐ living room ☐ porch ☐ parlor
consummation	☐ bedroom ☐ dressing room ☐ separate bathrooms ☐ shower ☐ bidet space (in toilet room or bedroom)
FOOD PREPARATION	
meal preparation, routine meals	☑ kitchen
cooking, as an avocation	☐ larger kitchen
meal preparation, large gatherings	☐ larger kitchen ☐ butler pantry

ACTIVITY	ROOMS, SPACES & FIXTURES
food storage, immediate access from kitchen	☑ kitchen cabinets ☑ pantry cabinet or closet ☑ pantry room, adjacent to kitchen
food storage, bulk and long term	☑ pantry room _mud room_ ☑ general storage room ☐ basement storage area ☑ garage storage area
meal preparation, outdoors	☑ portable grill, on porch, deck, gazebo, etc. ☐ masonry barbecue, remote from house
DINING	
dining, informal	☐ eat-in kitchen ☑ dining area adjoining kitchen ☐ breakfast room
dining, formal	☐ dining room ☑ great room ☐ butler pantry
dining, outdoors	☑ porch ☐ deck ☐ gazebo ☐ lawn, perhaps with tent
SOCIAL GATHERINGS	
entertaining guests, small numbers	☑ living room ☐ dining room ☑ dining area adjacent to kitchen ☑ porch ☐ deck
large gatherings	☐ living room ☐ dining room ☑ great room ☐ butler pantry ☐ beverage/serving bar ☑ porch ☐ deck ☐ outside areas, perhaps with tents

ACTIVITY	ROOMS, SPACES & FIXTURES
OCCUPANT INDOOR ACTIVITIES	
family group activities	☑ living room ☑ dining room ☐ game room ☐ outside areas
using computer	☑ office (spare room) ☐ desk in living room ☐ desk in bedroom, for children
reading	☑ living room ☐ sunroom / enclosed porch ☑ bedroom (in bed) ☐ library ☐ reading room
watching television	☑ living room ☐ bedrooms (in bed) ☐ game room ☑ television room (spare bedroom)
children's indoor play	☐ living room ☐ children's bedroom ☐ game room
indoor sports	☐ game room
music, listening and playing	☑ living room ☐ bedrooms ☐ game room ☐ music room (spare bedroom)

ACTIVITY	ROOMS, SPACES & FIXTURES
hobbies, requiring implements	☐ table in bedroom (mainly for children) ☐ hobby/sewing room (spare bedroom) ☐ workshop (in unfinished basement, garage space, or outbuilding) ☑ ~~garage~~ Kitchen desk
home maintenance	☐ workshop (in basement, garage space, or outbuilding) ☑ work space in garage
sewing	☐ sewing room (spare bedroom) ☐ sewing area, in well lighted room
exercise	☐ bedroom space ☐ exercise room ☑ ~~game room~~ garage
illness, contagious	☐ separate bedroom ☑ spare bedroom
infant care	☐ infant bedroom ☐ nursery space in parents' bedroom
smoking	☐ smoking room ☐ porch ☐ deck

ACTIVITY	ROOMS, SPACES & FIXTURES
ADMINISTRATIVE & HOME OFFICE	
sorting mail	☐ entry foyer, with table & wastebasket ☐ office ☐ other daytime room, with desk ☑ ~~dining table~~ *mudroom*
paying bills	☑ office ☐ other daytime room, with desk ☐ dining table
operating a business	☑ office ☐ storage rooms, if needed ☐ workshop (in basement, garage space, outbuilding)
LAUNDRY	
clothes washing and mechanical drying	☑ laundry room ☐ laundry space in garage ☐ laundry space adjoining kitchen
clotheslines & other fixtures for air drying	☐ outdoor, without cover ☐ outdoor, under gazebo or other shelter ☐ porch ☐ sunroom ☐ garage (preferably with screen door) ☑ laundry room (for delicate articles, in dry climate or with dehumidifier)
STORAGE **(except food, clothing, linens, vehicles)**	
in general, providing temperature and humidity control	☐ storage room, in conditioned area of house ☑ "spare bedroom" ☑ cabinets, within various rooms ☑ shelves, within various rooms ☐ storage chests, within various rooms

ACTIVITY	ROOMS, SPACES & FIXTURES
in general, providing protection from extreme temperatures, but exposed to higher humidity	☐ basement
in general, sheltered from precipitation, but exposed to outdoor temperature and humidity	☐ attic ☑ garage ☑ storage building *1*
high security, for valuables	☐ strong room ☐ safe, built into conditioned room
books	☑ bookshelf unit *office*
knickknacks and art objects	☑ bookshelf unit ☐ display cabinet ☐ display table ☐ perimeter shelves
indoor cleaning equipment	☑ broom closet
outdoor equipment & sporting goods (lawn mower, trimmers, ladders, bicycles, skis, horseshoes, etc.)	☑ storage building ☐ storage room, attached to house ☐ garage storage space
flammable and hazardous materials	☐ storage building
CONTACT WITH THE OUTDOORS	
looking at view	☑ living room ☑ kitchen ☑ other rooms for daytime activity ☐ bedroom, if a night view exists ☐ dedicated view room ☐ sun porch / sunroom ☑ porch *front & back* ☐ deck ☐ balcony ☐ widow walk
enjoying breezes and outdoor sounds	☐ porch ☐ deck ☐ gazebo ☐ lawn canopy

ACTIVITY	ROOMS, SPACES & FIXTURES
MOVEMENT BETWEEN LEVELS	
between floors ✗	☐ stairway ☐ chair lift, on stairs ☐ elevator
between garage and main floor	☑ step or stairway (circled)
attic access	☐ attic stairway & doorway (vertical or horizontal) ☐ attic hatch, with integral folding ladder ☑ attic hatch, requiring portable ladder
ENTRANCES & ENTRY FEATURES	
sheltering entrance from rain & snow	☐ entrance canopy ☑ porch ☐ vestibule, exterior ☐ balcony, overhead ☑ recess into house ☑ deep roof overhang ☑ garage entry
blocking wind entry	☐ vestibule, exterior ☑ entry foyer, enclosed by interior doors ☑ garage entry
visual isolation of interior	☑ entry foyer
ready access to clean outdoor clothing	☐ coat room ☑ entry foyer, with coat rack
ready access to dirty outdoor clothing	☑ mud room, with hangers for drying and rack for dirty shoes and boots ☐ entry foyer, with coat drying rack and dirt-proof floor
removal of shoes (if shoes are not worn indoors)	☐ entry foyer, with chair and rack for shoes and slippers ☐ entry vestibule with platform and stowage for shoes and slippers

ACTIVITY	ROOMS, SPACES & FIXTURES
basement outside entrance ✗	☐ enclosed stairwell, with doors at grade and basement levels ☐ stairwell within vestibule or mud room ☐ (undesirable) exterior stairwell, with door at basement level
access from laundry space to clothesline ✗	☐ exterior door providing short path between laundry and clothesline
ENERGY & WATER SYSTEMS	
central heating equipment, gas and liquid fuels (See Step 4 for recommended equipment.)	☐ basement space ☐ equipment room
heating equipment, solid fuels (All solid fuel options have serious limitations. See *Energy for Pioneers*, at the end of the book.)	☐ in-room freestanding stove, with safety zone ☐ fireplace insert, with safety zone ☐ ducted furnace, in fireproof equipment room ☐ ducted furnace, glass front, in occupied room ☐ hydronic boiler, in fireproof equipment room ☐ hydronic boiler, in outbuilding ☑ open fireplace, in wall, with safety zone ☑ open fireplace, freestanding, with safety zone
central cooling equipment	*Not Recommended* (See Step 4.)
central water heater	☐ basement space ☐ equipment room ☑ laundry room ☑ garage (only in warm climate)

ACTIVITY	ROOMS, SPACES & FIXTURES
central water treatment equipment (See Step 5 for recommended equipment.)	☐ basement space ☐ equipment room ☐ laundry room ☐ water supply entry point ☑ garage (only in warm climate)
electrical power switch panel	☑ closet at electrical power entry point
communications wiring/cable connections	☑ closet at wiring/cable entry point

EMERGENCY SHELTER	
shelter from extreme wind, earthquake, air contamination, etc., with NO RISK OF FLOODING	☐ basement emergency shelter, with reinforced direct exit ☐ strong room, with reinforced direct exit
shelter from extreme wind, earthquake, air contamination, etc. with FLOODING LIMITED TO BASEMENT	☐ strong room above grade, with reinforced direct exit

VEHICLES (automobiles, RV's, golf carts, boats, garden tractors, snowmobiles, etc.)	
vehicle parking	☑ garage (attached or detached) ☐ carport ☑ driveway
vehicle turnaround	☑ circular driveway? ☑ backup space
vehicle maintenance	☑ garage (attached or detached), with workbench & storage ☐ carport, with tool storage ☐ level driveway, paved
storage of seasonal vehicles (RV, boat, snowmobile, etc.)	☑ garage (attached or detached) ☐ carport ☐ exterior parking space, with individual covers

ACTIVITY	ROOMS, SPACES & FIXTURES
PETS	
containment, exercise & toilet	☑ indoors ☑ feeding area ☐ litter box, in ventilated room or space ☑ pet run ☐ pet cage (small animals) ☑ fenced property (urban) ☐ outdoors (rural)

OUTDOOR RECREATION	
swimming	☐ permanent in-ground swimming pool ☐ above-ground swimming pool, with entry platform ☐ swimming pool enclosure (for any kind of pool)
communal bathing	☑ hot tub ☐ hot tub annex to swimming pool
sheltered activities (picnics, etc.)	☐ gazebo ☐ lawn canopy ☐ space under trees
outdoor games (badminton, horseshoes, etc.)	☐ lawn area ☐ children's play area, with gym set, etc.

LARGE & SPECIAL ACTIVITIES	
tennis, baseball, etc.	☐ appropriate court
equine and animal activities	☑ barn ☐ paddock ☐ etc.
boat operations	☐ pier ☐ boathouse
aircraft operations	☐ hangar, separate ☐ hangar, part of house

DESIGN YOUR ROOMS AND SPACES

The room is the basic unit of living space. You live in one room at a time. So focus your first design effort on the individual rooms.

A common mistake of architecture is to begin a home design with the outer shell of the house, and then to use rooms to fill the house. Instead, design each room to contain all the functions that you want it to have. Only then, arrange the rooms into floor plans, and ultimately, enclose the rooms with the house structure.

Some rooms, such as the kitchen and the shower rooms, are defined largely by their special features. For such rooms, we will recommend features to consider.

And, we will learn how to enhance certain rooms to make them more useful and versatile, such as a "strong room" or a "cold weather refuge room."

In addition to the usual room types, we will suggest some less common types that may be valuable assets for your home.

We don't cover hallways or corridors here. We will design them later, when we connect the rooms to create your floor plans.

In the following, related types of rooms are grouped together, including their unusual variations.

Bisse Bowman

Figure 1-10. A classic canopy bed.

BEDROOMS

Let's start with bedrooms, because you will spend more than a third of your life in a bedroom for sleeping, dressing, and more memorable activities. For this reason, I recommend making all your bedrooms commodious. Also, bedrooms are important because they are the most numerous rooms in your home, occupying the largest percentage of floor space.

There's nothing really revolutionary to say about bedrooms. Don't make them too big or too small. Provide adequate space for dressing and for amenities. Provide space for a dresser for each occupant, unless you will have a separate dressing room. Every bedroom should have built-in closets of adequate size, about which we will say more.

Many houses have one or more "spare bedrooms," a term used to describe any room that does not have a specific purpose. A spare bedroom may become an office or a sewing room or a storage room. It is prudent to design each such room as an actual bedroom, including a full sized clothes closet. If a "bedroom" is used for almost any purpose other than sleeping, the closet will provide valuable storage.

Bedrooms that are actually used for sleeping by adults should be furnished with conventional beds. Bunk beds are suitable for children who are old enough to use the top berth safely.

To make large bedrooms cozier during cold weather, recover a technique from days of yore. The beds of prosperous people in cold countries included an insulated canopy and curtains on all sides. Such a bed is called a "canopy bed." Figure 1-10 is an example. This style provides an opulent appearance in any climate. For warm weather, the sides are removed to provide cooling air circulation.

If you have occasional overnight guests who exceed the capacity of your regular beds, you can use the following kinds of temporary or movable beds. However, these alternatives are all inferior to conventional beds.

- *Sofa beds* fold into the bottom of a sofa. Because of the compromises needed to make the mattress fold, sofa beds are notoriously uncomfortable. They may even injure persons with sensitive backs.
- *Rollaway beds* generally are narrow, with a thin mattress, to minimize storage space. The bed folds in the middle, so back support at the middle of the mattress is poor. Generally, rollaway beds are acceptable only for children and lightweight adults.

- *Trundle beds* have a flat mattress that is stowed underneath a taller bed on a low platform. The platform rolls out on casters, so it tends to mar the floor surface. The mattress usually is smaller than the mattress of the main bed. The trundle bed interferes with access to the main bed.

- *Daybeds* are small beds, typically with a twin size mattress, that have a back and arms to create the appearance of a deep sofa. A daybed typically is used as an item of furniture for a formal room. It is comfortable as a bed, but it is too deep to be practical for seating. A daybed commonly has a trundle bed or storage drawers underneath.

- *Futons* are mattresses that are laid on the floor at night and are rolled up for storage during the daytime. They can be comfortable for sleeping, with good firmness. However, they are difficult for elderly and disabled persons to use. The sleeper is forced to breathe dust and debris that rises from the floor surface. So, futons are best limited to houses where occupants remove their shoes before entering the house.

- *Murphy beds* are beds that fold up flat against a wall. Typically, they are built into a piece of furniture that looks like a wardrobe when the bed is stowed. A Murphy bed can use any kind of mattress without deforming it, but the mattress must be strapped to the frame. A balance mechanism typically is installed to ease lifting. Although comfortable when sleeping, a Murphy bed is awkward to use and it limits the layout of the room in which it is located. Murphy beds can be very fancy, costing as much as an additional bedroom. Generally, they are used in apartments that have limited floor space.

CLOTHES CLOSETS

Clothes closets typically are installed in bedrooms or dressing rooms. They can also be located elsewhere, primarily for seasonal storage of clothing. Each bedroom should have a closet of ample size. Maximize the width of the closet by having it span the entire inside wall, rather than sharing the wall with another closet for the room on the other side of the wall. *You can never have too much closet space.* A closet that is built into a bedroom is the least expensive type of storage space, and it is the most convenient.

Aside from size, the other important design issue for closets is avoiding mildew. (See the sidebar, *Defeat Mildew,* under the heading, *Limiting Humidity,* in Step 4.) Closets typically are cooler than the rest of a house because they have no heat sources, such as light fixtures or sunlight. This makes them vulnerable to condensation, which promotes mildew. Locate closets where they will remain as warm and dry as possible.

Don't install closets in any rooms that generate moisture, including shower rooms, toilet rooms, the kitchen, and the laundry area. And, keep the doors of closets away from those rooms.

Try to arrange closets so that they have little or no contact with outside walls. Clothing that presses against an exterior wall acts as insulation, making that wall of the closet colder than the inside of the house. Moisture will condense on this cold surface and on the clothing.

It is common practice to build bedroom closets into interior walls between rooms. This arrangement works well. It locates most of the closet surface inside the heated portion of the house, with perhaps only a narrow end against an exterior wall. To prevent mildew at that end, build a ventilated barrier there so that clothing cannot press against the outer wall. For example, you could place a shoe rack at that end. Closet doors should fit loosely or they should have louvers, to allow the closet interior to be warmed by the room it serves.

If your floor plan requires a wide closet against an exterior wall, install the hanger rods far enough away from the wall so that clothing will not contact the wall. Install louver doors, as in Figure 1-20, to keep the interior of the closet as close to room temperature as possible. The idea is to allow air from the inside of the house to circulate between the clothing and the exterior wall.

However, do not install louvered closet doors if you install a closet heater as a defense against mildew. In a humid climate, all closets may need additional steps to avoid mildew. See *Keeping Closets Dry*, in Step 4.

DRESSING ROOMS

A dressing room is a wonderful adjunct for a large bedroom in which adults sleep together. The dressing room maintains privacy and darkness in the bedroom, while allowing light for dressing. It provides for intimate preparations. The dressing room can serve as a passage to the toilet and shower room, isolating their light and noises.

A dressing room can provide a lot of convenient clothing storage. For example, the dressing room in Figure 1-20 has an entire wall of closets. A dressing room typically is furnished with a dresser or two, one or two chairs that are comfortable for dressing, a valet, and a large mirror. An elegant carpet is appropriate.

Dressing rooms were a feature of opulent architecture in the past, and they deserve to be revived. The walk-in closet is paltry in comparison. Unlike a closet, a dressing room has the size, lighting, convenience, and beauty of a primary room.

LINEN CLOSETS

A linen closet serves as the central depot for bed linens for all the bedrooms, and for towels for all the showers and toilet rooms. It is also handy for storing toilet paper, soap, and other clean items. A linen closet should be a clean environment, free of dirt, dust, and mildew.

Linen closets typically are installed where they minimize the distance to the bedrooms. As a result of their handy locations, they tend to fill up. So, make yours bigger than you think you will need. The additional cost is trivial.

A solid door is needed to keep the contents clean, but this blocks evaporation of any moisture that may remain after laundering or after a damp spell of weather. To avoid mildew, locate the linen closet away from any exterior wall and away from doors to shower or bathtub rooms. Other techniques for keeping closets dry are explained under the heading, *Keeping Closets Dry*, in Step 4.

BROOM CLOSETS

A broom closet is a storage space for cleaning equipment, such as brooms, buckets, cleaning supplies, and the vacuum cleaner. Its purpose is to keep the dirt accumulated by these items from spreading to the rest of the house.

Make a broom closet big enough for all your cleaning equipment. Include space for a tall stepstool or an indoor ladder, unless there is convenient space for these items elsewhere. Locate the broom closet for convenience, near the center of the area where the vacuum cleaner is used.

If a house has more than one floor of formal space, provide a broom closet, with a separate vacuum cleaner and stepstool, on each floor. This avoids the drudgery of lugging equipment between floors.

COAT ROOMS / COAT CLOSETS

Coat rooms usually are too small. Often they are located to fill a small dead space in a floor plan, such as the space under a stairway. As a result, the coat room gets stuffed, and everything becomes difficult to retrieve. When guests come, their coats and hats have to be piled on a bed. Make your coat room big enough to serve its purpose conveniently.

The coat room is one of the most frequently used spaces in your home. In addition to sufficient hanger space, provide convenient access to hats, scarves, gloves, overshoes, and anything else that you put on before going outdoors. The key word is "convenient." Lay out the room so that everything is handy. This will increase the size of coat room, but the increase in construction cost will be too small to notice.

DRW

Figure 1-20. A spacious dressing room. Closets cover one long wall of the room. The closets are against an exterior wall, so louver doors are installed to prevent mildew. The view is from the bedroom entrance. The door at left leads to bathrooms. The door at the far end leads to a central corridor.

The location of the coat room requires some thought if occupants and guests use a variety of entrances, including the garage. Try to locate the coat room near the entrance that is used most often.

If you have an entrance that is used mainly for formal occasions, place a separate coat room adjacent to that entrance for use by guests.

If you have a "mud room," furnish it so that it serves as a coat room for your dirty outdoor apparel.

STORAGE ROOMS

Storage is one of the most important functions in a house, and storage space usually is inadequate. A beautiful interior can turn into a dump if it is cluttered with more objects than fit the decor. It is likely that you will accumulate more nice things than you can display or use at one time, but you may still want to keep them. Adequate storage space is the solution to this modern dilemma.

Storage requirements are diverse, so they need planning. The *Home Activities Worksheet* lists various kinds of storage. Divide your storage requirements according to (1) the ease of access required, (2) the need for temperature and humidity control, and (3) whether the stored items are clean or dirty.

> A dedicated storage room is a relatively inexpensive addition that you will increasingly appreciate.

High quality storage is provided within the living spaces by closets, cabinets, dressers, bookshelves, and specialized gadgets, such as umbrella stands and under-bed storage boxes. Less formal storage is available in the basement, garage, attic, and an outdoor shed.

In addition, I recommend that you include a dedicated storage room in your design. Locate this room within the main living space of the house, to make it easily accessible and to protect its contents from extremes of temperature and humidity. A storage room is appropriate for bulky items that often clutter clothes closets, such as holiday decorations, photo albums, hats you rarely wear, boxes of old books, etc.

A separate storage room can also be used for storing vacuum cleaners, brooms, and other bulky cleaning equipment that doesn't belong in linen closets or clothes closets. This is an alternative to a broom closet.

Design the storage room as a spare bedroom, with the appropriate size and location in the house. Include closets of ample size, as for all bedrooms. This allows the room to be converted to a bedroom or some other use if the need arises in the future.

A storage room does not add much to the cost of your house, because it is bare floor space. After the house is built, you can equip it at your leisure with movable storage fixtures. Freestanding shelf units are versatile and inexpensive. You could fill the entire room with them.

Freestanding shelf units and various heavy items that you park on the floor can scuff the floor surface. To protect the floor, cover it with a durable, replaceable surface, such as sheet vinyl or commercial carpeting.

Generally, sporting goods and other dirty items, such as bicycles, skis, horseshoe sets, etc., should be stored in a less expensive space, such as the garage or an outdoor shed.

STRONG ROOM

Where do you put your valuables when you leave the house, especially when the entire family leaves on vacation? The items that you particularly want to protect, such as computers, antiques, and guns, occupy so much space that an ordinary safe can't hold them all. Furthermore, safes are awkward, requiring you to remember a combination or to use a special key.

The solution is to select a room, such as a storage room or a spare bedroom, and to reinforce it to become a "strong room." The room should be located within the conditioned part of the house and above ground, to minimize humidity. You can make an entire room almost as impregnable as a large safe, for less money. Upgrading a room to make it a strong room involves a few easy enhancements: (1) install a strong door, (2) reinforce the interior walls, and (3) eliminate any access to the room from the outside.

> A strong room is the most convenient place to protect your valuables, large and small, at modest cost.

Instead of a conventional interior door, install an exterior-type door, using all the reinforcement techniques that we will recommend in Step 3. Use the same model of high-security deadbolt lock for your strong room that you use for the exterior doors. This allows you to use the same key for your entire house. For added security in case your house keys are stolen, add a second secure lock that has a unique key. Use the second lock when vacating the house for an extended period.

To strengthen the interior walls, start by attaching the interior wall frames strongly to the ceiling, floor, and exterior walls. Use a stud spacing no greater than 16" (40 cm).

*Seperate storage room inside the house?
mudroom?*

Sheath both sides of the strong room's interior walls with plywood, using thicker plywood on the outer surfaces. Nail the plywood to the wall frame using lots of barbed nails, which can't be knocked out. This creates a strong box structure. It will resist attempts to crash through the wall with a crowbar or anything heavier that intruders are likely to use.

Cover the plywood on both sides with gypsum board ("drywall") to resist fire and to match the rest of the house. The plywood sheathing makes the wall thicker than the other interior walls, so lay out the walls to avoid a visible break in the finished wall surface.

To block access from the outside, the most reliable method is to omit windows. Try to locate the strong room so that the absence of a window does not leave an unattractive blank space on the exterior wall. If the room is on an upper floor, you can install a special impact-resistant window, which we describe in Step 3. You might install a small porthole window, but skinny burglars can get through surprisingly small holes. If you install a window, obscure the view of the inside.

In an existing house, if your potential strong room has a window that is vulnerable to intruders, extend the interior wall structure to cover the window opening. You can preserve the exterior appearance by leaving the window itself in place and installing a decorative surface behind the window. Since this decoration will not be accessible for replacement, select a material that will not be degraded during the life of the house by sunlight or moisture.

To resist fire, fill the exterior walls, the interior walls, the ceiling, and the floor with glass or mineral fiber insulation, as recommended in Step 3. To provide additional protection for computer media, papers, ammunition, and other items that are vulnerable to high temperature, install a fire resistant vault in the strong room.

With all these features, a strong room may also serve as an emergency shelter. See the heading, *Emergency Shelter*, below.

THE ATTIC AS STORAGE SPACE

An attic is a large unoccupied space underneath a roof. An attic usually results from a truss roof structure. An attic must be vented to the outside to protect the structure from moisture damage. (We cover roof venting in Step 3.)

If you are building a new house with a truss roof, or if you are expanding an existing house by adding an upper floor with a truss roof, you can design the trusses to make the attic a practical storage area. This opportunity is too easy and too inexpensive to ignore. It requires two design features: shaping the roof trusses to provide a useful amount of convenient storage space, and providing easy access to the attic.

Give the roof enough slope to provide full standing room in the center portion of the attic. This provides an access corridor to shelving that is installed under the lower portions of the roof, as in Figure 1-22.

A roof with a gambrel shape provides considerably more standing room in relation to the roof's ridge height, but gambrel roofs have significant disadvantages. (We will describe gambrel roofs later in Step 1.)

The supplier of your trusses can design them to provide openings for walking upright, to support walkways over the insulation, and to provide attachments for storage shelves. See the sketch in the later sidebar, *Basic Roof Structures*.

Although attic storage space is an inexpensive bonus, its application is limited. An attic must be vented to the outside, so the storage space is exposed to extremes of temperature and humidity. During warm weather, solar heating of the roof surface makes an attic much warmer than the outside air temperature. During cold nights, heat radiation from the roof into the night sky may make an attic space colder than the outside air. The relative humidity inside the attic may remain near 100% for many hours of the year, except in a dry climate.

 Simple modifications to a truss roof can provide a large amount of convenient storage space.

Only certain kinds of articles – such as ceramics – will survive hot, cold, and humid conditions over the long term. Attics can also be used to store items of transient value that are needed only occasionally, such as holiday decorations. But, don't use an attic to store articles such as books, fabrics, paintings, photographs, and steel implements. Even with good packing, they would deteriorate over the long term.

Now ..., step back and think this over. Instead of using a truss roof, use a triangle-frame roof, which is wide open inside. With minor additional cost – for insulation, an interior finish surface, and proper moisture venting – you can use a triangle-frame roof for a larger storage space that is sheltered from outside conditions. For a little more money, you can outfit the space as living space. If you don't need the extra living space right away, you can leave the interior unfinished. And, in the meantime, you have storage space of higher quality.

Access to the Attic Space

If you plan to use your attic as storage space, design easy access into it. You can do much better than the typical small trap door that requires teetering on a ladder. Trap doors with folding stairs are commonly used, but even these tend to be narrow and unsteady. If a healthy octogenarian cannot get into the attic easily and safely, then you need a better entry.

DRW

Figure 1-22. Attic modified to provide extensive storage space. This was done in an existing house. In a new house, the roof slope should be greater to provide a taller walking space.

Unless you are really cramped for space, design a permanent stair that leads to the attic. This sacrifices some space on the floor below, but it is a small amount compared to the useful attic space. Find a location for the attic door and its stair that is convenient and unobtrusive. Make the stairway and the door large enough to allow moving articles into and out of the attic conveniently.

 This improvement on the classic attic trap door makes access much more convenient and safe.

You need a tightly sealing attic door to prevent heat loss during cold weather. However, your stairway doesn't need a stairwell or an upright door. Instead, use a regular hinged interior door, but install it horizontally in the floor of the attic, directly over the stair. In this way, it acts as an elongated trap door. A standard interior door has the right dimensions. Align the stair and the long side of the door with the attic floor joists.

A soft gasket between the door and the frame can block air leaks effectively, with the weight of the door compressing the gasket. Install a balance spring to make it easy to open the door. Attach insulation to the top surface of the door.

To make the attic a secure storage area, install a standard deadbolt lock on the attic door.

TOILET ROOMS

We avoid the term "bathroom" where it can be misleading. Most "bathrooms" are actually toilet rooms, and many have no provision for bathing. Illogically, a toilet room that has no bathtub or shower is often called a "half bath."

Therefore, we will use the term "toilet room" to identify a room whose primary equipment is a toilet and a wash basin. It may or may not have bathing facilities, as we will discuss shortly. We will say "shower room" to identify a room whose primary purpose is showering, and we will say "bathtub room" to identify a room whose primary function is using a bathtub.

The cost of equipping a basic toilet room, without bathing facilities, can be modest. For example, a good conventional toilet costs no more than a fancy dinner. Nice wash basins and cabinets cost even less. Inexpensive sheet vinyl flooring is satisfactory, because a toilet room is not subjected to the extreme wetness of a shower or bath.

We will select the toilets, basins, and faucets in Step 5. Make your toilet rooms perfect by including these accessories:

- a **big mirror-front medicine cabinet** over each basin, to hold the burgeoning variety of medicines, bandages, and sundries that have become available in modern times. *[handwritten: w/elec outlets inside]*

- **a big shelf** over each basin, to hold dental care and shaving items, combs and brushes, a hand soap dispenser, and other items that would clutter the basin and make it awkward to clean.

- lots of other **cabinet space**, including a cabinet behind each toilet, for spare toilet paper, baby wipes, bulk medicinals, etc.

- lots of **drawer space** immediately below the basin, for hair dryers, curlers, and other hardware.

- an **accessory shelf** to hold a radio, small television, and other entertainment equipment.

- an **exhaust fan**, for odor control. We will cover toilet exhaust fans in Step 4.

- a **heater**, if there is a cold season, and especially if the toilet room has a window. A fan-forced ceiling heater usually is the best choice, for quick warm-up. We cover other heating options in Step 4.

- several **electrical receptacles** at convenient locations. Install at least one quadruple receptacle at chest height for powering a curling iron, hair dryer, radio, etc. Locate it to serve the basin and the accessory shelf. Install at least one duplex receptacle about 18" (45 cm) above the floor for installing a night light and powering a vacuum cleaner. Locate this receptacle where the installed night light will not create glare for a toilet user.

[handwritten: bathroom heater]

- *toilet paper holders* that are convenient for toilet users who are seated or standing. Typically, mount the toilet paper holder on a wall adjacent to the toilet, alongside the front edge of the toilet, at a height of about 32" (80 cm) above the floor. Don't install a holder under a countertop or other obstacle.

If a single toilet room serves a bedroom where a couple sleeps, also consider:

- a *double wash basin*.
- *two toilets*, each with a partition.

A more deluxe alternative for a couple is to outfit two separate toilet rooms adjacent to the bedroom. The cost of the extra wall and door is small.

The design of toilet room lighting is especially important for avoiding glare when using the wash basin, and for effective dimming when sleepers use the facilities at night. Step 6 explains the details.

Some toilet rooms are associated with bedrooms and some are associated with daytime spaces. To save space and cost, make some toilet rooms accessible to both. We will cover various nice arrangements under the heading, *The Bedroom Clusters*.

Sewer connections for toilets are big and mostly vertical, so they create an obstacle in any rooms below. You can minimize the obstruction by clustering toilet rooms so that they are served by a common main sewer connection. We will cover this issue when we design your space layout, under the heading, *Locate the Sewer Drains and "Wet Walls" Efficiently*.

Windows and Exterior Walls

If the climate has an extended cold season, it is best to avoid windows for toilet rooms that serve bedrooms. A window will make a toilet room chilly at night, when the heating is turned down. For the same reason, it is desirable to locate the toilet rooms so they have a minimum of outside wall area, but the super-insulation in your walls makes this a minor issue.

If the climate is predominantly warm, try to locate toilet rooms against an outside wall, with a window for light and natural ventilation. This is especially desirable for toilet rooms that are used during the daytime.

Because you want privacy in a toilet room, any window needs to be located so that people outside cannot look in. Or, the window needs obscuring glass. We will design your windows for privacy in Step 2.

Keeping Toilet Rooms Warm

If the climate has a cold season, most toilet rooms should have their own separate heating equipment. A fan-forced ceiling heater provides quick warm-up. If you want to keep the toilet room warm for extended periods, install a quieter kind of heating, such as a thermostatically controlled radiator or floor heating. We cover appropriate heaters in Step 4.

If a toilet room is kept warm for long periods while the surrounding spaces reduce their heating, consider insulating the interior walls, ceiling, and floor of the toilet room. We cover interior insulation in Step 3.

A toilet room may not need its own heating equipment if (1) it is exclusively for daytime use, and (2) it is surrounded by other spaces that are heated during the times when the toilet will be used.

SHOWER ROOMS

A shower room could be a toilet room with a small cabinet-type shower. Or, it could be a large, opulent dedicated shower space with its own walls, doors, and entry area. Or, something in between.

In most home designs, the shower does not get the attention that it deserves. You will spend a lot of hours in the shower. You stand wet and naked in an environment that is radically different from the rest of the house. Making this environment comfortable and safe involves a variety of issues, which we cover here. We will cover the details of the plumbing fixtures in Step 5.

Showers have largely displaced bathtubs as the preferred method of bathing. The main reasons are convenience, safety, and water conservation. If you want to conserve water, you can take a thorough "Navy shower" with only a few quarts (or liters) of water.

Bathtub Showers are Obsolete

Let's begin by eliminating one common shower option, the stand-up bathtub shower. This kind of shower is dangerous for people of all ages, accounting for thousands of deaths and serious injuries each year. Stepping over the tall side of a tub is a balancing act, and the curved, slippery bottom of the tub is a treacherous footing. If you do install a bathtub in your home, don't install any shower fittings with it.

Instead of using tubs for showering, install real stand-up shower spaces that are designed for safety. Entry requires only stepping over a low curb, and the shower floor can be designed to eliminate the risk of crippling falls.

Bathtubs should be limited to use as a luxury accessory for taking an occasional long soak. We will cover this use of bathtubs in our next room type.

Relationship Between Showers, Toilet Rooms, and Bedrooms

A shower often is located inside a toilet room. However, it is more deluxe and convenient to install a separate shower room that is adjacent to a toilet room. Either way, the toilet, wash basin, and cabinets are accessible to the bather. It's also an economical use of space.

There are variations on this theme. When we design your room layouts, you will create clusters that associate shower and toilet rooms with bedrooms. (See *The Bedroom Clusters*, below.) If a bedroom is used on a regular basis, it should have a dedicated shower that is adjacent to a dedicated toilet room.

If a bedroom is intended for a couple, consider installing two separate toilet spaces, both of which have access to a shared shower. Separate toilet rooms provide privacy and avoid interference when both occupants need to use a toilet or wash basin.

If you have a big family or overnight guests, make some of the showers separately accessible from a hallway or other common space, usually through a toilet room. This reduces the total number of showers needed to serve all the occupants.

The Shower Entry

Each shower room needs a dry entry space for undressing and toweling. Most commonly, the entry space is an adjacent toilet room. Less commonly, the shower may use a dressing room or a bedroom as its entry. And in some cases, the shower has its own dedicated entry space, which typically is about as large as the shower itself.

Whatever your entry space may be, provide dry space for standing and for sitting, hooks for hanging a robe and clothing, and racks for an adequate number of towels and wash cloths.

Install a waterproof floor in the entry space, because the bather will drip water on the floor after exiting the shower.

Shower Size

Be generous with the sizes of your shower spaces. The floor area of showers is so small that increasing their size hardly affects your overall construction cost. Showers that are the size of a telephone booth make no sense, except perhaps if you are adding a shower in an existing house that has limited space.

A reasonable minimum size for a shower is 60" (150 cm) long and 36" (90 cm) wide. This is the same length as a conventional bathtub, and slightly wider. Increasing the width of the shower to about 42" (105 cm) makes the shower luxuriously spacious at little additional cost.

For showers that serve a bedroom where couples sleep together, consider making the shower large enough for two shower heads, with individual faucets. Couples don't actually shower together very much, but it's a nice option.

If the shower will be used by a person who has difficulty standing, make the shower large enough for a portable waterproof seat. Showers sometimes have benches built into the wall, but such seating is awkward because the surface is cold and the location is inflexible.

DRW

Figure 1-24. A moderately sized shower that has all the essentials. The sliding glass door has been removed to show the full interior.

Fixture Layout

The basic shower layout shown in Figure 1-24 is convenient, efficient, and easy to build. It includes a shower head with adjustable spray, a temperature sampling spigot near the shower floor, separate hot and cold water faucets, and a diverter valve that routes the water either to the shower head or to the sampling spigot.

There is no compelling reason why the shower head, the faucets, and the floor spigot must be arranged in a vertical group, as is usually done. Instead, you can place the faucets away from the shower head. This makes it easy for the bather to avoid the stream of cold water that first emerges when the shower is turned on.

Similarly, if the shower will be used by a handicapped person, locate the faucets where they can be manipulated easily from a shower chair. For example, you can install the shower head on the end wall of the shower, and locate the faucets and the sampling spigot on a side wall.

min shower   60" x 36"
42" more desireable

Maintenance Access

All shower fixtures need periodic repair. Usually, this can be done from inside the shower space. However, in the longer term, plumbing components inside the wall will need replacement. These components include the bodies of the valves, and the fittings in which the valves are mounted. If no access is provided, the only way to reach these components is to smash through the wall, either inside the shower or through the wall on the opposite side.

Unfortunately, this is a common situation, requiring a major repair. If it is necessary to break through a tile shower surface, you probably won't be able to match the tile properly. If you have a plastic shower enclosure and you can't break through the opposite wall, you have an even bigger problem.

To avoid this problem, provide access to the hidden plumbing components. An older solution that works well is to install an access panel in the wall of the adjacent spaces. However, this limits the layout of the adjacent space. Locating access panels is even more difficult if the plumbing is installed in more than one wall of the shower.

 Mounting all the shower fixtures on a removable panel eases maintenance and avoids the need for access panels in adjacent rooms.

There is an innovative way to avoid this difficulty, while also simplifying the plumbing installation. Install all the fixtures on a removable panel made of a waterproof material, such as stainless steel, Corian™, or marble. The assembly is attached to the inside surface of the shower space, over a framed opening in the wall. A pair of flexible hoses connect the assembly to the hot and cold water systems.

This idea came from an inventor I met who had received a patent for a method of attaching the removable panel to the wall. It goes to show that basic improvements still wait to be discovered.

Triton

Figure 1-25. A "shower tower" that has a lot of spray options. The shower fixtures are all installed on this assembly, rather than inside the shower room wall. Only a single cold water connection and a single hot water connection are needed. This model is mounted directly on the wall. Other models are freestanding columns.

A related commercial product is a "shower tower." This is a column that contains all the shower hardware. An extravagant variety of fixtures may be mounted on the tower, as in Figure 1-25. The tower may be mounted to the surface of the shower wall or between the floor and ceiling. The water connections still require an opening through the wall or floor.

A shower tower will become a breeding site for mildew if it does not provide all-around access for cleaning.

Enclosure Materials

The inside surfaces of a shower room are soaked by the shower spray and by condensation. To protect the structure from this moisture, the surfaces must be waterproof. To resist mildew and to allow mildew to be removed, the surfaces must be non-porous and they must survive scrubbing and cleaning chemicals.

At present, three materials satisfy these requirements for home showers: ceramic tile, plastic composites, and glass.

Ceramic tile is excellent for the walls, ceilings, and floors of showers. Tile can last as long as the house, and it is the most beautiful of building materials, offering almost unlimited variety of appearance.

A tiled shower is a custom work of art. Make a tour of home furnishing showrooms and tile stores to find examples of tiled showers that look attractive. And, search the Internet for examples.

The main caution about tile is the need for skilled installation. Your goal is to hire a tile layer who knows good tile installation techniques and who avoids shortcuts that will cause cracks and leaks. To learn what is needed, buy a book on tile work that includes a thorough explanation of shower room tiling.

Tile shower floors are the most demanding part of a shower because of the preparation needed to support the weight of the bather and to resist water leakage. A waterproof membrane must be installed under the tile surface. The surface must funnel toward the drain. And, building the entry curb requires more special technique. We say more about tile floors in general under the heading, *our Floor Surface Options*, in Step 3.

For safety, use small tiles for the shower floor, with sides no longer than 2" (50 mm). The grout lines between the tiles provide most of the grip for wet feet, and using small tiles keeps the grout lines close together. The tiles themselves should have a rough or textured surface. For the floor of the entry outside the shower, the tiles can be somewhat larger, but they should still have a textured surface.

Tile for the shower walls and ceiling should be smooth for ease of cleaning. They carry no load, so they can be relatively thin and much larger than floor tiles. These tiles can be relatively inexpensive because they are made from weaker clay that is found in countries with lower labor and transportation costs.

Plastic composites provide a variety of options for shower enclosures. One option is a molded enclosure that includes the walls, ceiling and floor. Such enclosures have size limits because the entire assembly must be carried through the doors that lead to the shower.

Larger showers can be created using plastic panels for the walls and ceiling. However, the joints between the panels are vulnerable to leakage and mildew.

Unlike tile, which has almost unlimited life, the smooth surface of a plastic shower will become dull as it ages, and it will eventually crack. To delay the cracking as long as possible, support plastic shower panels firmly against the wall structure.

Prefabricated plastic floor pans are starting to become popular as a substitute for handmade tile floors. They may be used with tile or plastic walls, which overlap the top edge of the pan. They eliminate most of the work and the specialized skill needed to create a good tile shower floor. It seems likely that composite plastic floor pans will become the main type of shower floor, even for tiled showers.

But, it is important to select a plastic floor pan that is very sturdy, and to support it well. Plastic products tend to be flimsy, and a flimsy floor pan will flex, crack, and leak. Replacing the pan would require replacing the overlapping wall as well, which would be an expensive job.

Glass is increasingly used for shower walls that face a toilet room. You could also use glass for the ceiling of an enclosure that is lower than the ceiling height. The shower floor needs to be made of tile or a molded plastic pan.

A wide variety of décor is possible by selecting glass that is clear, tinted, or obscured by etching or embossing. In addition to plate glass, glass block has been used to create some very attractive shower walls.

Similarly, plate glass toilet partitions can be very attractive in toilet rooms that are shared by couples.

Shower Doors

The shower usually is entered through a door that is made of plastic or strengthened glass. Sliding shower doors are an inexpensive standard item. Hinged glass doors usually are custom items that are made as part of a glass partition, as in Figure 1-26. The door and/or partition is mounted on top of a curb.

Don't use fabric or plastic shower curtains. They are growth media for mildew, they are difficult to clean, and they are less pleasant to use than a glazed door.

No shower door that I have found includes a bottom seal that will prevent water from leaking across the curb and rotting the adjacent wall and floor. Leakage tends to concentrate where the curb meets the wall, as in Figure 1-27. Leakage at this point usually can be

GlassCrafters, New Jersey

Figure 1-26. A nicely made hinged shower door.

DRW

Figure 1-27. Typical wall damage that occurs at the lower corners of the shower opening. Careful design and installation of the curb and the shower door bottom rail are needed to prevent this.

prevented by careful caulking with silicone when the door is installed. The door will have to be removed and resealed every ten years or so.

Here's an improvement to conventional shower curbs. Slope the top surface of the curb toward the interior of the shower. This will drain the spray from under the shower door, greatly reducing the tendency of grime and mildew to form there. This obvious solution is rarely used, so ask for it.

> **Slope the curb of a tiled shower toward the inside of the shower. This stops leakage of water to the adjacent floor and reduces the formation of grime.**

By the time you build your house, some manufacturer may offer a shower door with a sloped bottom track that serves the same purpose. Such a track would have to extend over the inner edge of the curb.

One way to minimize leakage under the door is to make the shower so wide that the door is not flooded by the shower spray. This also helps to keep the bottom track clean.

Keep Water Vapor Inside the Shower

Showers and toilet rooms are very different environments. Showers produce a huge amount of warm moisture, which condenses on all the surrounding surfaces. In contrast, toilet rooms usually do not produce enough water vapor to make condensation a problem.

A common problem is that the water vapor from showers floods into the adjacent toilet room. If this happens, the moisture fogs the mirrors and makes all the surfaces in the room damp, risking mildew. It is awkward for one person to use the shower and for another person to use the wash basin at the same time. Similarly, moisture from the shower may cause damage in other surrounding spaces.

To minimize the spread of moisture from your showers, design these features into your showers:

- a *waterproof enclosure*, which could be a plastic shower enclosure, a glass wall between the shower and the adjacent toilet room, or walls that form a separate room for the shower.
- an *exhaust fan*, located where it will divert the water vapor out of the shower and draw air from the surrounding space into the shower. We explain the fan details in Step 4.
- an *opening for fresh air* from the house into the shower. This provides air for the bather and for the exhaust fan. The opening typically is above the shower enclosure or above the shower door. The opening should be no larger than necessary for the needed air flow.

Windows and Exterior Walls

Avoid windows in shower rooms. Warm water vapor condenses copiously on a cold window, causing it to fog, streak, and mildew. The moisture will leak into the wall surrounding the window, causing rot. A window would make the shower room cold between usage, and make it uncomfortable during use.

As a general guideline, install a window in a shower room only if the climate is usually warm enough to allow the window to remain open while the shower is being used. Even in such a climate, this is possible only if the open window does not sacrifice privacy. You might install an attractive louver panel over the window to maintain privacy.

In a location with a severely cold season, try to locate shower rooms so that they have no exterior wall area. However, with your super-insulated walls, this is not a critical issue.

Essential Accessories

Check off these features for each of your showers:

- Plenty of *shelves* inside the shower. You can't have too many. Locate them where the shower spray can't wash over them and melt your soap. Generally, this means placing the shelves in the corners or at the end of the shower opposite the shower head. Accessory shelves located below the shower head will be drenched and become mildew gardens.
- *Grab rails* on the shower walls, installed where they are accessible from any location where the bather may be standing. This is both a convenience and safety feature for all bathers, and an important aid for handicapped persons. The rails are also handy for hanging wash cloths.
- A *low spigot* for testing the water temperature with your foot before turning the shower on your body. Install the spigot high enough to allow filling a bucket for housecleaning purposes, typically about 18" (45 cm) above the floor. An ordinary diverter valve routes water either to the shower head or to the spigot. The diverter valve also allows the water in the pipes to drain after using the shower. You can buy special small spigots for showers, but don't bother. An ordinary bathtub spigot works best. The exception is a spigot installed on a side wall, where an ordinary tub spigot might be long enough to injure the bather's shins.
- A *heater* is important in any climate that has a cold season, when comfort requires heating the shower space to a temperature that is warmer than the rest of the house. We will select the heating for your showers in Step 4.

> **A built-in dehumidifier may be the only practical way to prevent mildew in a shower if the climate is humid.**

- A *dehumidifier* may be the best way to avoid mildew in a climate that is warm and humid. If you decide to install one, build it into the adjacent entry area. We cover dehumidification in Step 4.

BATHTUB ROOMS

We treat a bathtub as a specialty item that is used for occasional soaking, while daily bathing for hygiene is done with showers. The one exception is bathing small children, which is best done in a tub.

I strongly recommend against using any bathtub as a stand-up shower, which is dangerous. Tubs create a slippery footing. Installing grab bars does not eliminate this risk.

Even when a tub is limited to soaking, entering and leaving the tub can be dangerous, especially for elderly and disabled persons. Therefore, it is critical to select a tub, and to arrange it within the room, to minimize the risk of falls. An alternative for disabled persons is to install a "walk-in" bathtub. We cover bathtubs, along with their safety challenges, in Step 5. Here, we will talk about the room.

A bathtub is primarily an esthetic feature, so design the room accordingly. Figure 1-30 is an example. The room should be large enough for entering and leaving the tub conveniently, with space to hang robes and plenty of towels. You may want some shelves for waterproof decorations. A window for daylighting and ambience is worth considering, even though it will stream with condensation when the weather is cool or cold. A colder climate argues for smaller windows. Moisture damage is limited by the fact that you won't use the tub very often.

If you install an old fashioned freestanding tub, provide clearance from the walls on all sides. The modern types of tubs, with water jets and bubblers, are built into a wall or corner. Provide ample space for access to their electrical and plumbing accessories, which require maintenance.

Bathtubs emit warm water vapor, which will condense on cold surfaces. A tub does not throw off water vapor as rapidly as a shower spray, but all the room surfaces will become wet with condensation when the tub is used. Therefore, design the room surfaces to resist damage from moisture. A tiled surface is best. Thick impermeable paint is a less expensive alternative. Don't use sheet wallcovering, which invites mildew and tends to peel.

A lot of water will spill on the floor, so the floor needs to be completely leakproof. To keep water on the floor from seeping under the walls, install a baseboard that seals to the floor.

The ventilation and heating requirements for a bathtub room are similar to those for a shower room. In a humid climate, it may be advisable to build a dehumidifier into your bathtub room, as we recommended previously for shower rooms.

A bathtub filled with water and people is the heaviest object inside your home. Furthermore, there is a big change in weight as the tub is filled and emptied. This causes the floor to flex. Therefore, the floor of your bathtub room needs to be especially strong. Design the floor so that the feet of the tub rest directly over floor joists, or on reinforcements that span between the joists.

Depositphotos

Figure 1-30. An extravagant bathtub room with a view. The adjacent shower eliminates the temptation to use the bathtub as a shower. The extensive tile surfaces are appropriate for this damp environment. The large glass area is satisfactory for a warm climate.

KITCHEN

Kitchens provide more opportunity for design than any other space in your home. In existing houses, kitchen renovations are a common renovation project. Many industries exist to supply the vast variety of appliances, plumbing fixtures, and cabinets for kitchens. Specialty stores for kitchens sell innumerable gadgets.

Nowadays, kitchens serve three purposes. They are a place to cook, a place to eat, and a showpiece to impress your friends. Ironically, as less cooking is done at home, kitchens have become bigger and fancier.

So, how should you plan your kitchen? The main elements are the equipment and gadgets that you want, a convenient layout, and style. Look ahead to Step 7 for help in selecting your major kitchen appliances. Visit kitchen showrooms. When you see a feature that you like in someone's home, take a picture and put it into your idea file. You can buy books that are devoted entirely to kitchens.

Then, step back and take a deep breath. Much of contemporary kitchen design is pointless extravagance. There may be a huge mismatch between your actual needs and current kitchen fads. You may want a kitchen that is appropriate for a 5-star hotel, when in reality your kitchen may be used mainly for heating snacks in the microwave oven. If the grandeur of the kitchen exceeds the cook's ability, it's just wretched excess. Fit the kitchen to the household, including households who will occupy your home in the future.

Unless you have money to burn, don't spend a fortune on trendy, exorbitantly expensive appliances. They are designed to look like "professional," but the best mass market kitchen appliances usually are better.

In your kitchen layout, the main issue is work flow. Consider how people will move within the kitchen, and between the kitchen and the dining areas. For example, if you want a work table or island, don't place it in the middle of the traffic pattern.

The Basic Kitchen

Most kitchens have a basic layout, no matter how fancy they are. The layout consists of a long counter that includes three appliances: a *range with an oven*, a *sink*, and a *dishwasher*. The range is actually a freestanding appliance that matches the counter in height and depth. *Bare counter space* is added between these appliances for food preparation and for washing tableware. In addition, there is a freestanding *refrigerator*, which typically is deeper than the counter, and which requires ventilation space around the sides and top.

All this equipment could be arranged in a line, but that would result in a very long kitchen. To make the kitchen more compact, the counter may have an L-shape, as in Figure 1-33. Or, the counter may be divided into two shorter counters that face each other, creating a "galley kitchen," as in Figure 1-34.

Storage of cookware, tableware, foodstuffs, and other items is provided by two kinds of *cabinets*. "Base cabinets" support the counter, and they typically are 24" (60 cm) deep. Their height is standardized to produce a counter height of 36" (90 cm). Most of their storage space is in drawers. "Wall cabinets" are installed from chest height upward, usually over matching base cabinets. They typically are 12" (30 cm) deep. Most of their storage space is on shelves.

A common option is to have a *separate oven*, installed at chest height in a full-height cabinet. This configuration eliminates the stooping that is needed when using an oven that is part of a range. When a separate oven is installed, a *cooktop* may be installed in the counter, rather than a freestanding range.

FinalArchitecture.com

Figure 1-33. A kitchen in which the major equipment is located along an L-shaped counter. This layout exhibits good ventilation and fire safety.

KitchenMaking.com

Figure 1-34. A galley kitchen.

A *microwave oven* is now virtually a standard appliance. I recommend that you buy a freestanding unit, not one that is built into a cabinet front or into another appliance. Design a handy location for your microwave oven on a counter or shelf.

More Nice Kitchen Features

Among the vast range of kitchen options, here are a few that I consider especially valuable, even for smaller kitchens:

- *Maximum cabinet space.* You can't have too much. Run cabinets all the way to the ceiling. Make a stowage place for a step stool, and use it to put rarely used items on the upper shelves of the cabinets. However, as we will discuss, don't place wall cabinets alongside a range, cooktop, or other fire hazard. An adjoining *pantry* is desirable for storing larger amounts of foodstuffs, as we describe below.

- *Specialty cabinets.* In addition to the usual base cabinets and wall cabinets, you can install a variety of cabinets with special features and functions, such as carousel cabinets for corners and full-height cabinets for brooms and similar tools. Get a complete catalog from the cabinet manufacturer that you expect to use.

- *Open space for three trash cans.* With recycling becoming the norm, you need one can for paper trash, one for metal, and one for other waste. Also, you want more capacity for trash than most kitchens provide. I recommend that you place your trash receptacles in an open space under a counter or alongside a counter, not hidden inside a cabinet. This is because you want the trash cans to be easily accessible, and you want the space around them to be easy to clean.

- *A second microwave oven.* The microwave oven has increasingly become a primary method of cooking, even for heating a cup of water. You may want two microwave ovens for the same reason that you want several burners on your range.

- *Two sinks.* Install one near your dishwasher for pre-soaking used dishes and utensils. Install the other as part of a work area near your range for cooking activities. This avoids filling pots and draining food on top of a pile of dirty dishes.

- *A triple sink* is a practical alternative to separate sinks. A large basin on one side is used for cooking, another large basin on the opposite side is used for soaking and rinsing tableware, and a small basin in the middle is used for soaking utensils.

- *An abundance of electrical receptacles.* Install them along the wall behind all counters, so that the cords for electrical appliances don't sprawl over the counters. Install receptacles behind the refrigerator and microwave ovens. Install at least one receptacle

on an open wall area, about two feet (60 cm) above the floor, for a vacuum cleaner and other service equipment.

- *A work table or island.* Counter space is limited because it takes up a lot of wall area. To supplement your counters, design the layout for a stand-up work table. These can be inexpensive and portable, designed for kitchen use with a cutting board top. Or, install an island, which is less flexible and more expensive. An island allows you to install additional fixtures, such as a sink or deep fryer.

 Building a convenient enclosure for your kitchen water filter makes periodic replacement much easier.

- *Convenient and effective water filtering equipment.* In Step 5, we will select filtering equipment for your drinking and cooking water. This equipment typically requires filter replacement every six months. The usual location for filters, under the kitchen sink, is so awkward that it discourages this important maintenance. Instead, leave space on your counter for a "countertop" water filter that can use the best kind of water filter. Or, install the filter housings and the valves in a cabinet that is located at a convenient height, with room for storing spare filters. This is a novel feature.

Kitchen Layout for Ventilation

Ventilation is a big issue in your kitchen's layout. The kitchen generates a lot of cooking fumes and water vapor. In addition, any kitchen appliances that use natural gas or propane will generate carbon dioxide and some carbon monoxide. You don't want any of that to spread into the rest of the house. Therefore, ranges and ovens have hoods that collect their fumes and expel them to the outside.

If the kitchen has other appliances that generate cooking fumes, such as a deep fryer, each location requires its own hood.

The kitchen ventilation layout should keep occupants comfortable. During warm weather, the hood keeps the kitchen cool by capturing the heat from the appliances and discharging it outdoors.

During cold weather, the ventilation layout is more demanding. All the air that is discharged by the hood must be replaced by an equal quantity of outdoor air. Occupants should not be in the path of that cold air as it travels to the range hood.

For most homes, the easiest and most economical solution is to arrange the kitchen layout so that the range is against an outside wall, and a window is located adjacent to the range to provide replacement air. In this way, no outside air flows across the occupied part of the kitchen. Figures 1-33 and 1-35 illustrate this arrangement.

Range hood

DRW

Figure 1-35. A fairly effective range hood installation. For fire protection, the hood is wider than the range, and the cabinets are kept above the hood. Still, the cabinet bottoms are exposed to a stovetop fire.

If you want to install your range and oven in an island or other interior location, using a window will create a draft that is uncomfortable for people standing between the window and the island. Some commercial range hoods avoid this problem with an outside air supply that is built into the hood. Unfortunately, you may not be able to find a residential unit with this feature. If your climate has a cold season, check for such a hood on the Internet before deciding on a kitchen layout that requires an interior hood.

Don't expect to get kitchen ventilation air from inside the house. Your home will be tightly sealed, so the hood exhaust fan won't get enough replacement air from the rest of the house to work properly. Anyway, you don't want to drag outside air through the house during cold or hot weather.

We will cover the mechanical details of kitchen ventilation equipment under *Kitchen Ventilation*, in Step 4.

Kitchen Fire Safety

Take special care to protect against range and oven fires. A kitchen fire is a leading contender to burn your house down. During the life of your house, a fire on your range or in your oven *will* occur. Design your kitchen to isolate the fire until it can be extinguished.

DRW

Figure 1-36. To further protect the cabinets from a stove fire, matching metal panels are installed under them.

Most kitchen fires start on top of the range, typically because the cook fails to pay attention while a burner is operating. Food is fuel, and it will burn if it gets hot enough. A stovetop fire will grow until it reaches other sources of fuel. Typically, these are nearby wooden cabinets. Also, nearby painted surfaces and wallpaper will ignite. Once this happens, the house is doomed unless the fire is extinguished while it still remains in the kitchen.

A primary defense against a stovetop fire is to deprive the fire of additional fuel. A fire will seek fuel in an upward direction, and then spread sideways. Therefore, keep your range as far as practical from side walls, cabinets, and partitions. Cover the wall behind the range with a fireproof "backsplash" surface. This might be tile, metal, or mirror glass. Figure 1-33 is a good example of these defenses.

It is a bad practice to extend cabinets down alongside the range hood, as you often see. A fire on the range would spread quickly to the cabinets. And, even in normal use, the sides of such exposed cabinets become disfigured by water vapor and cooking fumes.

The range hood is another part of your defense. It keeps a fire from spreading upward, and it has a limited ability to clear smoke out of the kitchen. Select a hood that is wider than the range itself, because stovetop fires spread upward and sideways. In fact, buy the widest model that fits your kitchen plan. This is especially important if you install cabinets above the range hood, as in Figure 1-35.

Smart Space Design

Figure 1-39. A small walk-in pantry

DRW

Figure 1-40. Butler pantry. This one is located to serve as a passage between the kitchen and a formal dining room.

If the bottoms of overhead cabinets are exposed alongside the range hood, install attractive metal panels under the cabinets, as in Figure 1-36. These are simple custom items that any sheetmetal shop can make at modest cost. Your builder can arrange to get them made.

Some range hoods have a fire sensor that automatically turns on the hood fan to maximum speed in the event of a fire. We will cover other selection criteria for your range hood under *Kitchen Ventilation*, in Step 4.

The grease that accumulates in the hood and the discharge duct can be ignited by a stovetop fire, creating a second fire that may ignite flammable materials around the duct. To minimize accumulation of grease, try to arrange the kitchen to keep the ducts short and vertical. The simplest solution is to install the range and oven against an exterior wall, so the hood can exhaust right through the wall.

If you need to install a hood over an island or other interior location, and if the kitchen is directly under the roof, try to route the exhaust duct straight up through the roof to a well designed roof cap.

As a last resort, if your layout requires a horizontal section of duct, slope the duct so that grease will drain back to the range hood. However, grease is sticky, so a lot of grease will still accumulate in the duct.

Install a big fire extinguisher at a prominent location at the kitchen entrance, where you can reach it if the kitchen is filled with smoke. Also, clearly mark the location of the circuit breakers and the gas valve that serve your kitchen appliances. You will need to turn these off immediately to stop the fire.

PANTRY

A pantry is a storage room for food, paper goods, and occasional kitchen equipment. It will save many trips to the grocery store, increase the variety of your cuisine, and allow you to save money by buying in bulk. Figure 1-39 shows a typical small walk-in pantry.

Make your pantry as big as practical. The shelf size determines that actual storage space, so make the shelves deep. A good depth is 18" (45 cm). Freestanding adjustable shelf units are the easiest way to outfit the space efficiently. They are inexpensive.

Locate the pantry where it is convenient from the kitchen, either as part of the kitchen itself or adjacent to the kitchen. In your floor plan, locate the pantry on the route from the entrance where you bring groceries into the house, typically from the garage.

For the sake of appearance, you probably want to build your pantry like a walk-in closet, with a door to hide the contents. However, it may be more convenient to build it as an open alcove that faces into the kitchen.

You can buy pantry-type stowage fixtures that are built into kitchen cabinetry, but they are expensive in relation to the amount of storage space they provide. I don't recommend them.

A large pantry is a convenient location for a food freezer, if you decide to have one. We have more to say about food freezers in Step 7.

BUTLER PANTRY

A butler pantry is a small auxiliary space that acts primarily to supplement the kitchen when serving large gatherings. It may be used for preparing beverages, washing glassware, preparing side dishes, and serving desserts. It has a counter and a sink, and it may have small appliances, such as a microwave oven, toaster, and small refrigerator. It may be the primary place for storing alcoholic beverages, for example, with a wine rack. It may have a limited amount of food storage. Figure 1-40 shows a nice example.

A butler pantry usually is located conveniently with respect to the gathering space, such as a great room or a formal dining room. In some layouts, it may be located as a passage between the kitchen and the gathering space.

INFORMAL DINING AREAS

A big decision is whether to have an informal dining area for everyday dining. Generally, it's a good idea. It saves steps between the food preparation and dining areas. It keeps the cooks in contact with the other members of the family. An informal dining surface typically does not use a tablecloth or cloth napkins, so it requires less maintenance. And, kitchens have become showpieces, so there is no longer a reason to hide the kitchen from diners.

As a result, with families up to about four people, an informal dining space is becoming the primary site for most family meals. Indeed, smaller homes today often forego a separate dining room. You have a variety of options for your informal dining area, including:

- an *eat-in kitchen*, which is a kitchen that is designed to accommodate a dining table, as in Figure 1-43. The dining table may be within the kitchen itself, or it may be located at the perimeter of the kitchen. The kitchen should be arranged so that the table does not impede easy movement within the kitchen for food preparation or dishwashing.

Figure 1-43. A kitchen designed to serve as a primary dining space.

DRW

Figure 1-44. A kitchen with a breakfast bar.

- a *counter* or *breakfast bar*, which typically has food preparation activities on one side and seats diners on the other side. Figure 1-44 is an example. In this arrangement, the eating surface usually is elevated above the adjoining kitchen counter that has the dishwashing sink. This layout is convenient for moving used tableware to the sink and dishwasher, and it has a surface that is easy to clean. This arrangement is best for eating quick snacks in a house that has a separate dining area. It is not satisfactory as a primary dining area, because it accommodates only a few seats and it does not allow the diners to face each other. The elevated surface requires diners to perch on bar stools.

- an *island* within the kitchen, which typically accommodates both dining and food preparation, as in Figure 1-45. The dining experience is similar to a counter, except that an island may be shaped to allow dinners to face each other better.

- a *breakfast room* or *nook*, which is a small room adjoining the kitchen, with enough space for a small dining table. Figure 1-46 is an example. If the space is well designed, it provides a cozy feel.

Any dining area should have nearby storage for the tableware and accessories that are needed by diners. The needed storage may be provided by kitchen cabinets, by drawers in an island, or by a separate piece of storage furniture.

Unless you specifically want an isolated dining area, such as a "breakfast nook," try to arrange your informal dining area so that it can act as an expansion space for the larger dining spaces when you are hosting large groups.

FORMAL DINING ROOM

Despite the trend toward eat-in kitchens, a formal dining room, as in Figure 1-49, remains a desirable space for festive meals.

Unless the size of your home is limited, include a dining room, and err in favor of a larger one. Families grow, you may have a large number of guests, and the dining table may become a preferred location for various activities. Leave plenty of room to maneuver around the chairs and to locate various furniture, such as a hutch and wine rack. A large decorative "buffet" or "hutch" is almost a necessity for a formal dining room. That is where you will store tableware, table linen, candle holders, fancy glassware, etc.

HomeArtBlog.com

Figure 1-45. A kitchen with an island for dining.

DRW

Figure 1-46. A cozy breakfast nook adjacent to the kitchen.

When we design your floor plan, we will suggest positioning the dining room as an "expansion room." This means that it is located where it can be connected with the smaller everyday dining area to produce a well integrated larger dining space.

Similarly, if your home will have a "great room," consider arranging the dining room so that it integrates with the great room when you have large social functions.

Design your floor plan so that you can isolate your formal dining room from heating and cooling when it is not occupied. French doors (attractive hinged doors that are mostly glass) are a particularly attractive way of doing this. You may also want to isolate the dining room from the kitchen area for a formal event. We spell out your door and partition options under *Interior Doors and Partitions*, in Step 3.

DRW

Figure 1-49. A small, well equipped formal dining room.

LIVING ROOM

The "living room" has come to mean the largest room in the house that is regularly occupied, where the family comes together and where individuals can lounge. It is used for reading, watching television, playing games, and other occupant purposes. It is also the primary room for entertaining, unless there is a separate "great room" or other large space for that purpose.

The goal is to make the living room pleasant for all these activities. For reading, you want the room to be cozy, quiet, and well lighted, as in Figure 1-50. However, for watching television, you want the space around the screen to be dark. For entertaining, you want the space to be large.

There are several ways to resolve these competing requirements. One is to have a large living room and to arrange it in zones for the different activities. For example, reading chairs may be arranged next to windows, while the television may be located inside the darkest part of the room. A movable screen may be used to separate different activities, such as darkening the television area.

Consider selecting some of the living room furniture to be easily movable, so that you can change the room quickly from a compartmentalized arrangement to an open arrangement for gatherings.

Another approach is to divide the functions of a living room among different rooms. Activities that require quiet or that make noise may be done in separate rooms, as we discuss next. If large gatherings are a regular part of your lifestyle, and if you can afford a larger house, you may wish to add a "great room,"

DRW

Figure 1-50. A cozy living room where the family relaxes. The door at the rear opens to a large great room, which is used mainly for social functions.

which we will discuss after that. Using separate rooms allows you to make the living room smaller and cozier for family activities or for small gatherings.

In smaller homes, it is common to combine the functions of the living room and the dining room in a single space.

ROOMS FOR ISOLATED ACTIVITIES

The living room is not suitable for occupants who engage in incompatible activities, such as reading and watching television. Therefore, you may want to have one or more rooms for those activities. Examples include a reading room, a television room, a sewing room, and a "den." For children's activities, such as homework and hobbies, it is usual to install a desk or table in the children's bedrooms.

If the room is supposed to be a quiet environment, locate it at some distance from the noisy spaces, including the kitchen, workshop, etc. If the room will be used for noisy purposes, such as practicing music, it should be located away from the rest of the occupied rooms. It is best to locate such activities on a different floor or in a different wing of the house.

Under the previous heading, *Bedrooms*, we said that it's a good idea to design the layout of specialized rooms so they can serve as bedrooms if the original function changes. Make the rooms large enough for bedroom furniture, and provide a full closet. The closet will be useful no matter how the room is used.

GREAT ROOM

Medieval castles and manor houses had huge banquet halls where crowds of courtiers feasted on game and danced the *pavane*. In affluent modern times, the memory of such grand spaces has made the "great room" a feature of larger homes. Figure 1-51 shows one of many possible configurations.

Be clear about why you would want a great room. What's the purpose? Whom are you trying to impress? You might visualize hosting huge parties, but how often will that happen? A large, superfluous fancy room projects an image of *nouveau riche*.

The practical purpose of a great room is large gatherings. It may have a wet bar and other amenities to aid in entertaining. Except for those occasions, a great room is mainly a showpiece that is unoccupied. It is too large to be cozy for individual or family activities. Typically, a house with a great room also has a conventional living room that is used in preference to the great room.

DRW

Figure 1-51. A "great room." It is distinguished by large size and opulent furnishings.

As an alternative for occasional large gatherings, consider increasing the size of your living room. Also, arrange your floor plan so that the living room, the formal dining room, the kitchen dining area, and perhaps the kitchen itself can be opened up to form a connected space. We will learn how to do that.

A great room usually has a tall ceiling, which separates it structurally from the rest of the house. It should be arranged on the floor plan of the house as an "expansion" space. This means that it will be placed outside the daily pattern of movement inside the home. Also, it should be thermally isolated from the rest of the house so that it does not add much to heating or cooling costs when it is unoccupied.

If your home has a grand view that requires a lot of window area to appreciate, a great room may be an appropriate place to put the windows. In a climate with a cold season, rooms with large windows must be designed in a special way to avoid large heating costs. Step 2 covers the details, under the heading, *What If You Want a Space with Lots of Glass?* If you use a great room for this purpose, you can extend the view into the rest of the house by isolating the great room with French doors (hinged glazed doors), perhaps augmented with glass wall panels.

Some architects have started to use the term "great room" to describe a regular living room. This is simply sales puffery.

PARLOR

At the other extreme from the great room is the parlor, or "sitting room." This is a small, heavily decorated room that allows for small formal meetings without cleaning up the rest of the house. It is similar to a living room, but smaller and generally fancier. Figure 1-52 shows an elegant example.

Parlors were once a feature in genteel Victorian homes. Common uses were courtship and ladies' teas, with the room remaining empty most of the time. Under present conditions, the parlor is obsolete, as its functions have moved to the living room and other spaces.

DRW

Figure 1-52. An elegant parlor. This one is located adjacent to the main entrance, so that guests do not have to pass through the rest of the house.

COLD WEATHER REFUGE ROOMS

If your home site has extended periods of sub-freezing weather, consider enhancing the design of one or more of your daytime rooms to act as a cold weather refuge. Such rooms increase your ability to get through a period of cold weather comfortably if energy supplies are curtailed or if energy becomes extremely expensive. To create a cold weather refuge room, accentuate features that minimize its heat loss. Specifically:

- *Minimize the total exterior surface area*, including walls, ceiling, and exposed floors.
- *Use horizontal ceilings of normal height*. Horizontal ceilings minimize temperature stratification inside the room.
- *Insulate the interior walls, ceiling, and floor*, in addition to the super-insulation of the exterior walls. Interior insulation also improves fire safety and noise isolation. (Step 3 covers interior insulation.)
- *Install conventional, well sealed interior doors* between the refuge room and all adjacent spaces.
- *Limit the size of windows.* For daytime rooms, size the windows for daylighting and to provide enough view to dispel cabin fever. (Step 2 covers the sizing and layout of windows.)
- *Maximize the insulation value of the windows.* In particular, consider tandem windows, a novel feature introduced in Step 3.
- *Orient the windows southward,* if they are exposed to winter sun.

These are not fundamental changes to the design of a super-house, but only increased emphasis on certain features that reduce heat loss. You could apply these enhancements to all the rooms in your house. But, the prudent course is to design most of your rooms for the prevailing conditions, not for the extremes.

> **These variations will reduce your heating requirement to an absolute minimum. However, they may cramp your style somewhat.**

Typically, the cold weather refuge rooms would be a well connected cluster consisting of the living room, the kitchen, and an adjoining informal dining area. These provide enough space for all family members, including furniture and amenities to keep them comfortable for extended periods.

For sleeping, you don't need separate refuge bedrooms. The super-insulation of your home will keep everyone snug while sleeping. With a good mattress and comforter, body heat is enough to keep a sleeper warm in the coldest weather. Especially in a larger bedroom, you might want to have a canopy bed, as in Figure 1-10.

LAUNDRY ROOM

Most home layouts don't pay much attention to the laundry area. The laundry gets revenge for this snub by being inconvenient and by having humidity problems. In fact, your laundry room deserves careful design. Here are the main issues to consider, including some improvements over usual practice.

Fixtures and Appliances

Provide enough space for all the items needed to make your laundry efficient. In addition, provide storage for items used in wet activities, such as buckets and sponges for car washing, unless there is adequate storage for them elsewhere. Make room for these items:

- *clothes washer.* A top loading washer sits on the floor. If you have a front loading washer, try to find a model that offers an optional stand to reduce the stooping required to load and unload. You will select your washer in Step 7.
- *clothes dryer.* Consider installing the dryer on a stand to avoid the need for stooping. If you install a stand, build it as a storage cabinet. See Step 7 for the details.
- *sink.* The sink serves for pre-soaking laundry and for other functions not related to the laundry, such as filling buckets. It can also serve as the drain for the washing machine and for a dehumidifier.
- *table or counter for sorting and folding laundry.* It should be about 36" (90 cm) tall, for use while standing. This is the standard height of kitchen counters.
- *table for heavy boxes or jugs of detergent.* This avoids the need for stooping or reaching up for getting the detergent, and it keeps detergent powder dry. Locate it alongside the washer. It should be about 30" (75 cm) tall.
- *ironing board* and *iron*, including space for storing them. The ironing board can be hung on a wall.
- *laundry supplies*, including detergent, bleach, brushes, sponges, etc. Options include a long shelf over the basin, an open storage cabinet, and storage inside base cabinets for the washer and dryer.
- *laundry baskets*
- *dehumidifier.* A dehumidifier is a powerful tool for removing moisture from the laundry and nearby spaces. If you install one, mount it where it can drain into the sink or to the outside through a drip hose. We show how to do this in Step 4.

Don't install a clothesline or drying rack inside the laundry room, unless the climate is always dry. For air drying, make a clothesline accessible in a safe location. We will cover the details shortly.

If your home has an electric water heater, but no basement, the laundry room is a good place to install it. The laundry sink is a handy place to drain the tank for maintenance, and you don't have to build a separate closet for it. However, the laundry room is not a good location for a fuel-fired water heater.

Laundry Location

In most houses that have a basement, you will find the laundry located there. But, the basement is not convenient, and doing laundry there aggravates the natural tendency of basements to be damp. So, put the laundry in a basement only if you are building on a tight budget and you need to minimize the upstairs floor space. (For perspective, note that the main costs for the laundry are the plumbing connections and the appliances, not the raw floor space.)

Convenience. The most convenient location for the laundry room is near the bedrooms and shower rooms, where most dirty laundry originates. Also, try to locate the laundry room near the linen closet and the dressing areas where clean laundry is stored. And, provide convenient access to your clothesline, which may be located in a variety of indoor or outdoor places, as we discuss next.

Another convenient location for the laundry room is adjacent to the kitchen. In this way, the laundry can be done during lulls in cooking. The kitchen already has the needed plumbing connections, ventilation, and a waterproof floor, all of which can be extended to serve the laundry space. A separate drain connection is needed for the washer.

In a compact floor plan, the washer and dryer could be installed in the kitchen itself. These appliances are made with the same height as kitchen appliances. However, I recommend installing front loading washers and dryers on elevated stands for convenience. See Step 7 for the details.

Utility connections. A laundry room needs water and sewer connections. To simplify these, locate the laundry room adjacent to a "wet wall" that provides plumbing connections for a shower room, toilet room, or kitchen. A wet wall also is a good route for a gas connection, if your dryer is fueled by gas.

The washing machine can drain into the sink. This requires the washing machine to be installed next to the sink, and it may interfere with other uses for the sink. Another option is to drain the washing machine into a special wall fitting that also includes the hot and cold water connections for the washer.

Try to locate the laundry room next to an exterior wall, to provide a nearby vent for the dryer. Alternatively, the dryer vent could go up through the roof, but that route is more complicated and it invites air leakage. The duct from the dryer to the outside wall will eventually fill with lint. Install the vent pipe so that it is easy to disassemble for cleaning.

Isolating noise. The washer and dryer are noisy, so locate the laundry room distant from the rooms that require quiet. An ordinary interior door works well to isolate noise. Minimize the gap between the bottom of the door and the floor by installing a "sweep" on the door.

Dealing with Dampness

The laundry space generates enough moisture to invite serious mildew growth. Therefore, design the laundry space to avoid mildew.

The mildew hazard is greatest if you hang any clothing to dry in the laundry space. Resist the temptation to air dry laundry in the laundry room, unless the climate is always dry and the laundry room is well ventilated. Instead, do your air drying in a dedicated clothesline area.

The laundry sink and the washing machine also emit enough moisture to cause trouble. The clothes dryer should not be a problem, because it must be vented to the outside.

If possible, locate the laundry room in a warmer part of the house, as we said previously. The higher temperature lowers the relative humidity.

Ventilation usually is the primary way to remove moisture from the laundry room. In a climate that is usually warm, a window helps with ventilation. However, in a cold climate, a window gets wet from condensation, grows mildew, and rots the wall around the sill. Under those conditions, a ventilation fan is needed. We cover the details of ventilation fans in Step 4.

 A built-in dehumidifier keeps the laundry area free of mildew and it allows garments to be hung in the laundry space for final drying.

You may need a dehumidifier to control dampness in the laundry space, especially if you hang any clothes to dry there. If so, build the dehumidifier into the space so that it circulates dry air effectively, and so that it is out of the way. Step 4 explains how to install dehumidifiers.

Make the floor waterproof, because it will get wet from spills and from the need to mop up detergent and bleach. Vinyl flooring is fine for laundry rooms.

Because a laundry room is a relatively damp space, at least periodically, do not use it to store linens, clothing, or anything else that is vulnerable to mildew. Instead, store such items in closets and other spaces that are located to stay as dry as possible.

← vent location

Laundry Chute

A laundry chute is handy if bedrooms are located on a floor above the laundry room. A chute allows dirty laundry from upstairs to be dropped directly into a basket in the laundry room. Installing a laundry chute requires you to line up the upstairs space with the laundry room below. Also, the upstairs opening should be located conveniently and attractively. The chute should have a cross section that is large enough to allow bulky laundry, such as bedding, to fall easily. Dimensions of 18" by 18" (45 cm by 45 cm) should be adequate.

To block the spread of fire from below, make the chute of unpainted sheetmetal, and provide a tightly closing metal lid at the top. The lid also blocks temperature stratification between the floors. If the chute serves more than one floor, install a lid at each floor.

Install the lid at a height above the floor that is convenient for dropping the laundry into the chute while standing. This also helps to keep unintended objects, like children and their toys, from falling into the chute.

A shop that makes air conditioning ductwork can make a good chute economically. Explain that the chute should not have any seams or edges that could snag the laundry.

CLOTHESLINE AREA

A clothesline is an important appliance. It has no operating cost, and you can maintain it yourself. It is a "solar clothes dryer." Don't scoff, clotheslines are proven technology. As energy becomes scarce, it makes no sense to buy energy for drying laundry when you can do it free. Also, a length of rope is vastly less expensive to replace than a clothes dryer.

Also, a clothesline offers benefits for your clothes. It dries them without high temperatures, so your cotton garments won't shrink, and the elastic in your garments won't be damaged. And, it doesn't turn your fabrics into lint. If the clothesline is exposed to sunlight, the sunlight acts as a mild bleach and sterilizer.

Clotheslines do have shortcomings, which is why powered clothes dryers exist. First of all, it takes time and effort to hang laundry to dry. But, household chores are no longer the burden they once were. In fact, people today need more exercise. Hanging up a basket of laundry will be good for you. If you have children, instruct them to take some time from video games to help with the laundry.

Your "clothesline" does not have to be a long piece of rope, which requires a long space. Instead, you can install a grid of shorter parallel ropes. Or, install a set of hooks for drying laundry on hangers. Or, dry the clothes on clips that hang from pendants. There are many kinds of folding and retracting clotheslines on the market.

An open or screened porch, or a sunroom that has openable windows, is a prime location for clothes drying. In fact, clothes drying is one of several good reasons to have a porch. The covered location protects the laundry from rain and bird droppings. If the space is warmed by the sun, that's even better because the laundry will dry more quickly. If the porch has screens, the laundry will be less obvious to your neighbors.

You can also use a garage for drying laundry, which requires leaving the garage door open. You can maintain a nice appearance and block the entry of birds and insects by installing a garage door screen, as in Figure 1-55.

If you live in a climate that is always dry, you can set up an indoor drying area. In fact, the moisture from the laundry will provide some relief from the dryness. For convenience, you could install your clothesline as part of your laundry space. However, the damp air must move from the drying space quickly to avoid mildew, whether it goes into the rest of the house or to the outside. Before planning to have an indoor drying area, look ahead to *Limiting Humidity*, in Step 4.

If you lack a porch or a dry climate, you can still dry your laundry outdoors. You can greatly improve upon the bare outdoor clothesline by installing a cover to protect the laundry from rain and birds. If you don't want to expose the neighbors to the sight of your laundry, surround your clothesline with a trellis, shrubbery, or other visual screen. For a fancy drying area, you could buy a nice prefabricated gazebo.

No matter where you install your clothesline, make it as convenient as possible. Coordinate its location with the laundry room and with other rooms where the laundry will be folded and stored.

DRW

Figure 1-55. This Florida house has a garage door screen. When the garage door is open, the screen maintains an attractive appearance and blocks the entry of birds and insects. This screen rolls up vertically. Another type is mounted on horizontally sliding panels.

SUNROOM

You may want a sunny space with a lot of glass to escape from cabin fever in winter. Such a space may be called a "sunroom." It can be a nice getaway and it can be an attractive element of style. A sunroom can also be a space to enjoy your grand view, if you have one.

A sunroom is most practical in the middle latitudes, where the climate has a cold season that is extended, but not severe. Because of its large glass area, a sunroom can't be comfortable when it is cold outside.

An alternative to a sunroom is a porch that is fully enclosed with windows. We cover porches below.

In terms of construction, such spaces are relatively simple. Sunrooms often are added to existing houses with little trouble. However, they have important design requirements. We will cover them in Step 2, under the heading *What If You Want a Lot of Glass?*

GARAGE

Automobiles, recreational vehicles, tractors, golf carts, and other vehicles are expensive. Their life is limited largely by exposure to weather. Their enemies are sun, rain, snow, hail, condensation, debris from trees, and salt spray. A garage provides complete protection from these hazards. If vehicles are well maintained, a garage may extend their lives almost indefinitely.

A garage also keeps your vehicles clean. If you use tree shading for your home, a garage is almost a necessity. It will protect your vehicles from bird droppings and from the large amount of debris that some trees shed throughout the year. In winter, you won't have to remove frost or snow from your car. And, a garage protects vehicles from theft and vandalism.

The cost of garage space is less than the cost of the equipment that it covers, and it will protect many generations of equipment. And, the cost of garage space is relatively low compared to other space in the house. So, provide enough garage space for all your vehicles and expensive equipment. Unless your building lot is very tight, make your garage large enough for at least two full sized cars.

Don't install any equipment in a garage that has an open flame. This includes fuel-fired boilers, furnaces, water heaters, and clothes dryers, unless they have "sealed" combustion systems (explained in Step 4). An open flame could ignite fuel fumes escaping from the vehicles.

Don't store flammable and hazardous materials in a garage. Instead, store them in an outdoor shed. You can use the same shed for storing lawn mowers, garden tools, and other outdoor implements. ~~Shed~~ ℞

Provide some daylighting for your garage. The easiest way to do this is to buy a garage door that has windows. Step 3 will cover all aspects of garage doors.

If you want windows in the garage wall, locate them where they will be most effective for your intended purposes, which may be daylighting or exterior appearance. Installing windows higher on the wall enhances their security and light distribution, and interferes less with the storage shelves that tend to adorn garage walls. Step 2 will cover window placement.

You can use a garage to store sporting goods, such as bicycles, skis, horseshoe sets, and other items that are not sensitive to temperature. You can install shelves and cabinets for them along the wall. In warm climates, well pumps and water treatment equipment commonly are installed in the garage. Enlarge the garage to include these items, so they don't interfere with vehicle parking.

A garage can double as a workshop if you add a workbench and appropriate tools. But, you can't build projects and park vehicles in the same space. So, add more space for your workshop activities, or expect to park the vehicles outside while you build your boat or whatever.

As shown in Figure 1-55, a garage door screen allows you to keep the garage door open for daylight and ventilation while blocking insects and a view of the inside.

DRW

Figure 1-56. An attractive detached garage.

Effects on Your Structure and Layout

The garage floor must rest on grade, because of the weight of vehicles. If the house has a basement, the garage floor cannot extend over the basement. Even if the house is built on a slab-on-grade foundation, the garage floor slab usually is separate from the house foundation. Also, it usually is somewhat lower, typically by about six inches (15 cm). This requires a step up into the house from the garage.

If your house has a wooden main floor that is supported above grade (with or without a basement), the ground floor of the house typically is higher than the garage floor by about three feet (about 90 cm). As a result, a short stairway is needed between the garage and the house interior. The height difference works well, as it creates a taller garage space that allows the garage door to be stowed under the garage ceiling.

(You will learn about foundations in Step 3. For the moment, we are covering these points to help you with the space layout.)

Garages commonly have truss roofs because they provide a strong, inexpensive way to cover the large open space of the garage. You can create valuable storage space within the roof structure of a garage if you design the trusses to provide safe walkways and shelves for this purpose. See the sidebar, *Basic Roof Structures*, below. If practical, provide a convenient stairway that leads to this overhead space.

Attached or Separate?

A garage may be attached to the house or it may be separate. The cost is about the same for either choice. For a new house, an attached garage is preferable on most points. It is more convenient. It reduces heat loss from the part of the house that it covers. And conversely, it is warmed slightly by contact with the house. The only disadvantage of an attached garage is the fire hazard to the house from flammable materials that may be located in the garage.

On the other hand, a detached garage usually is preferable if you want to add a garage to an existing house. It can enhance the appearance of your property, as in Figure 1-56. If you are building a new house, you can defer building a detached garage until later, when you can build it without disrupting your home life.

It is increasingly common to create a "mother-in-law" cottage by adding living space to a detached garage.

CARPORT

A carport is a less expensive alternative to a garage. It can be attached to the house, or it can be a freestanding structure, as in Figure 1-57. A carport protects vehicles from sun, rain, snow, hail, falling debris, and from most condensation. Those are the major enemies of your vehicles. Sunlight and rain can be blocked from the open sides of a carport with inexpensive screens, such as vine-covered trellises. So, figure that a good carport can provide most of the protection from these threats that would be provided by a garage.

But, a carport lacks protection against theft and vandalism. If your home is located near salt water, a carport is not effective in blocking salt mist. And, it cannot be heated during cold weather. Because the contents of a carport are exposed to view, you can't use one for storing your lawn mower, bicycles, etc. without creating an eyesore.

How much money does an attached carport save, compared to a garage? Not as much as you may think. If you install a concrete slab, the slab will cost as much as for a garage. And the driveway cost is the same. In a climate where snow does not fall to a significant depth, the roof is somewhat less expensive than the roof of a formal garage. The main saving is the cost of the walls and a garage door.

Carports are common for modest homes in warm climates. They are less common in cold climates. This is mainly because a roof that is strong enough to support a heavy snow load needs strong walls to support it. Add a door to that, and you have a full fledged garage.

Prefabricated steel panel carports are becoming increasingly common because their cost is relatively low, especially if a concrete floor slab is not needed. These are standard items that you can order with almost any desired dimensions. Figure 1-58 is a typical example. You can extend the side walls downward to any desired extent. A rear wall can be installed, and even a front door.

Generally, steel carports are installed by the manufacturer, requiring only a few hours. It's your responsibility to provide a graded surface before the vendor arrives. The whole assembly rests on steel bottom rails, which don't need a foundation. The carport is held in place against wind by long pins that are driven into the ground through the bottom rails.

The kind of carport shown in Figure 1-58 has lengthwise ribs that prevent rain on the roof from draining to the sides. With this kind of carport, ask the installer to slope the roof so that rain will drain toward the rear. Make the front end a few inches (about ten centimeters) taller than the rear.

Steel carports don't look elegant, but they don't have to look shabby either. They are inexpensive and fairly strong. If you are building on a tight

DRW

Figure 1-57. An attractive carport that was added to an older house located in a warm climate.

DRW

Figure 1-58. A typical sheetmetal carport.

budget, one of these carports can serve until you get the mortgage paid. To improve its appearance, leave a discreet space between the carport and the house, and perhaps surround the carport with trellises or shrubbery.

A steel carport can also supplement a garage to provide protection for recreational vehicles, boats, and other vehicles that are too large to fit inside a conventional garage.

Steel carports can last a long time if the sheetmetal is well enameled and if the steel tube supports are heavily galvanized. Exposed support tubes eventually will rust away, starting with the bottom rails. The bottom rails will survive much longer if they are kept clear of the soil. Mount them on a row of pressure-treated timbers or on a row of concrete blocks. Install ventilation spacers between them and the foundation to let the rails dry between rainstorms.

WORKSHOP

You will need a workshop for manly pursuits that produce air pollutants and noise. Isolate these activities from the rest of the house.

Install a door that allows you to move large items in and out. If you use a standard door, buy the widest available, which typically is 36" (90 cm). Install a larger door, such as a roll-up door, if you plan to build large projects, such as a boat. Make sure that the door is airtight, well insulated, and strong. Also, provide a clear path from the shop to the outside.

Ventilation is a major design issue for most workshop activities. To protect your health, install an exhaust fan near the work area and an air inlet that feeds replacement air across the work area. Typically, the fan

is located in an opening similar to a window opening. Other windows in the space provide replacement air. Step 4 covers the ventilation details.

If you expect to do long term projects that involve dangerous air pollutants or a lot of mess, such as spray painting or building things with composite materials, keep your workshop out of the main part of your home. For such work, it is best to leave space on your property to build a separate workshop building. Design the building to be as efficient as possible, consistent with the climate and the amount you will use it. You can defer this until after your home is built.

A garage is commonly used as a workshop, but this interferes with its primary purpose of protecting your vehicles. If you decide to create a workshop in your garage, make the garage as large as practical. It can never be big enough.

To keep a garage workshop from being an eyesore for your neighbors when the door is open, you can install a garage screen door, as in Figure 1-55.

The large garage door provides good ventilation during temperate weather, but not when the door needs to be closed. So, consider a separate ventilation system, as for a basement workshop. If you will be spending a lot of time in the garage during cold weather, insulate the walls and ceiling. Buy a door that is as airtight and well insulated as you can find. A garage door is a huge energy leak, so heating a garage is never efficient.

SPACE FOR THE HEATING, AIR CONDITIONING, AND WATER EQUIPMENT

Your home will need equipment for heating, cooling, water heating, and perhaps for water treatment. The space for this equipment should be just as well planned and just as neatly executed as any other room in your home.

Don't skimp on floor space for your equipment. It doesn't require much, in any event. Lay out easy access to each item of equipment, especially to controls and maintenance access panels. It's ridiculous to see all the equipment for a house jammed into a dark corner of a vacant basement, or squeezed into a tiny equipment closet.

You will complete the layout of your equipment space, or spaces, after you complete Steps 4 and 5. In summary, Step 4 recommends two choices of primary heating equipment, hydronic (hot water) heating or heat pumps. A hydronic system requires space for a boiler and various accessories, whereas the type of heat pumps that I recommend does not require an indoor equipment space.

If you select hydronic heating, your water heater normally uses the same fuel as the heating boiler, and it is installed in the same space. If you heat your home with heat pumps, your water heater probably will be electric, and it can be located in various places. For example, the laundry room is satisfactory for an electric water heater, but not for a fuel-fired water heater.

Hydronic systems, water heaters, and water treatment equipment all contain large volumes of water. The equipment may leak, or it may need to be drained for maintenance. Therefore, include a floor drain that allows the equipment to be drained and serviced without creating a mess.

In a warm climate, an alternative is to install water-containing equipment in the garage, near the exterior door. The garage floor should be sloped so that any drainage flows out the garage door.

If your home has a basement, that is usually the best place to install the equipment. The location of the equipment space within the basement is not critical. Generally, you would locate it to minimize the overall length of the pipes.

A fuel-fired boiler or water heater needs a flue and an outside air intake pipe. High-efficiency gas-fired boilers and water heaters can exhaust through an adjacent wall, but oil-fired equipment requires a flue that extends through the roof. We cover this in Step 4.

SPACE FOR FIREPLACES AND HEATING STOVES

First, a recommendation. Don't be casual about deciding whether to install a fireplace or heating stove. In most houses that have them, they sit idle and waste energy. Even in locations where it may be practical to use wood or other solid fuels for heating, selecting the equipment and working out the installation requires a lot of effort to get it right.

For these reasons, we have placed our discussion of fireplaces and heating stoves under *Heating with Firewood and Other Solid Fuels*, in *Last Look: Energy for Pioneers*, at the end of the book. If you have a yearning for a heating fire inside your living space, read that part of the book before planning the space.

Fireplaces and heating stoves require a significant amount of space within the rooms they serve. Typically, a fireplace should have a fireproof safety zone of about 100 square feet (10 square meters) inside the room. Heating stoves require a somewhat smaller safety zone. The safety zone generally cannot be used for other purposes.

All open fireplaces are major heat leaks when they are not operating. Heating stoves also have a significant amount of heat loss when they are idle. Therefore, any room that has one should also have interior doors to limit heat loss from the rest of the house.

ENTRY SPACES

Many houses have an abrupt transition from the outside to the inside. As soon as you open the front door, you are in the living room. The only transition is a doormat for wiping your feet. In many cases, that's okay.

But, what if your shoes are muddy, or your coat is wet, or you are carrying a dirty snow shovel? Or, you live in a culture where people remove their shoes before entering the house? Or, you want to visually isolate the inside of the house from the entrance? For such cases, you need an additional space to transition from outside to inside. There are several ways to do this.

A *foyer* is a separate space inside an entrance door, usually situated to break the line of sight from the entrance to the main rooms of the house. The main entry foyer creates the first impression of your house for guests, so it should be nicely decorated. The foyer should lead efficiently to the rooms of the house. Figure 1-61 is a dramatic example.

A foyer should have a waterproof floor surface, such as tile, to avoid damage by shoes that are muddy or wet. A coat room should be accessible from the foyer. Leave room for accessories, such as an umbrella stand and perhaps a chair or bench for removing shoes or galoshes.

DRW

Figure 1-61. An elegant foyer that leads efficiently to all the main areas of a two-story house. Doors to the ground floor rooms would minimize stratification of heating.

DRW

Figure 1-62. An attractive entry vestibule. The glass in the door and side windows provide ample light and visibility into the vestibule. The main security door to the house should be inside the vestibule, where it is protected from the weather.

A *vestibule* is a separate space that acts like an airlock between the outside and inside, with an outer door and an inner door. A vestibule performs the functions of a foyer, and it also blocks wind from blasting into the house. Vestibules are found most commonly in cold, windy climates. To get the most benefit from a vestibule, install it at the entry that you use most often.

Normally, a vestibule is built as an extension on the outside of the house, as in Figure 1-62. An outside vestibule is a prominent feature of the exterior of the house. It can be decorated just as nicely as a formal entrance foyer. It can have windows, nice light fixtures, and other refinements.

The outer door of a vestibule usually is located on the first floor level, with the entry stairs on the outside. The outer door and the entry stairs may be sheltered from rain and snow by extending the vestibule roof outward. If the house is built on sloped terrain, the outer door of a vestibule may be located below the first floor level, with the entry stairs inside the vestibule.

To serve its purpose, the vestibule should be long enough so that the door on one side is closed when the other is opened. The space should be large enough for accessories, such as an umbrella stand. A bench is desirable for sitting to remove dirty shoes and for holding groceries and other items that are being brought into the house. The floor should be waterproof.

You don't want the vestibule to be a space where a criminal could lurk. To counter this risk, make the interior of the vestibule visible through both the outer and inner doors. Windows in the sides of the vestibule will help. You might install a light switch for the vestibule outside the outer door, as well as inside the house.

You can also create a vestibule inside the main walls of the house. For example, a foyer that is separated from the rest of the house by a French door acts as a vestibule.

A *mud room* is built like a vestibule, only larger. Typically, it is installed at a rear or side entrance, not at the formal entrance. The name derives from the fact that mud rooms are common on farm houses, where they provide a place to leave muddy boots, dirty coats, snow shovels, etc. Think of a mud room as a dressing room for your outdoor work clothing. Although this is not a fancy application, you can decorate a mud room to make it attractive in a rustic way.

If you need a mud room, try to arrange the floor plan so that the laundry room is nearby. Or, combine the laundry room and mud room, as in Figure 1-63. Because the mud room is a passageway to the outside, this will allow you to carry clothes from your washing machine to your outdoor clothesline.

Figure 1-63. An entrance room that combines the functions of mud room and laundry. can we design ours like this?

A serious mud room should have:

- a floor that is waterproof and easy to clean
- walls that tolerate dings gracefully (e.g., knotty pine planking)
- clothes racks or hangers that keep dirty clothing away from the walls
- a bench for sitting while putting on boots, with a bootjack
- boot and shoe racks that allow wet footwear to dry
- a rack for dirty tools brought in from the outside, installed over a tub for rinsing the tools
- a wash basin or deep sink. ← ?

The wash basin should be located against an interior wall, and the pipes should be routed from a heated space to minimize the chance of freezing the water pipes.

Other types of rooms or spaces can serve as entrance spaces, such as an *enclosed porch*. An *attached garage* or *carport* may serve as the most used entrance, if a vehicle is needed when traveling from the house.

The value of an air lock entrance for energy efficiency has declined since the introduction of modern exterior doors that are airtight and insulated. A vestibule or mud room will not pay for itself in energy savings, but the small savings are a nice bonus in addition to the other benefits. If you are upgrading an existing house, you may be able to add a vestibule or mud room with little difficulty.

To avoid wasting energy, do not install heating equipment in any entrance space.

ENTRANCE COVERS

Entrances are often a major stylistic focal point of a home's exterior. The door itself can be a showpiece. (See the *Entrance Door Selection Guide*, in Step 3.) But, for most homes, the structure that protects the door from weather is a much more prominent feature.

A well designed door should last as long as the house itself. To make this possible, protect all your exterior doors from rain, snow, and direct sunlight. Provide each door with a cover so that rain cannot splash on it and snow cannot pile up in front of it. The cover also prevents water from flowing under the door threshold and rotting the floor.

If the first floor is elevated above grade, usually there will be a short stairway and a porch or landing outside the door. It is best to extend coverage to the stairs to provide safer footing in rain and snow, and to protect the stairs themselves from deterioration.

As a rule, provide an effective cover for each exterior door. The following are the common ways to cover entrances.

Canopies can be an effective and attractive way to protect entrances. Figure 1-64 shows an attractive example. Make sure that the canopy is wide enough, and extends outward far enough, to protect against blowing rain and snow.

Attractive canopies often are added to existing houses to provide protection for a door that was originally exposed to weather.

An *entrance alcove* is similar to a canopy, but with closed sides. Typically, it repeats a particular style theme of the house. Figure 1-65 is an example.

A *vestibule* protects the main security door effectively. The previous Figure 1-62 shows a nice example that was added to an existing house. The outer door typically is protected only by an overhang of the vestibule roof. If the vestibule is outside the main

DRW

Figure 1-64. An attractive and effective entrance canopy that was added to an existing house.

DRW

Figure 1-65. An alcove entrance.

DRW

Figure 1-66. A porch entrance that is accented by a gable that is added to the porch roof.

Figure 1-67. An entrance that is protected by extending a deep roof overhang.

Figure 1-68. An exceptionally attractive recessed entrance. It is deep enough to provide ample protection for the door.

structure, the inner door usually is the prime security door, and the outer door is a less robust unit that is largely decorative.

A covered *porch* can provide excellent protection for an entrance, along with outdoor living space. Figure 1-66 is an attractive example. In a snowy climate, cover the porch steps with a canopy, or extend the porch roof to cover the steps. We have more to say about porches under the next heading.

A *balcony* can protect a door effectively if the balcony is deep enough and if it is located immediately above the door. We cover balconies below.

A *deep roof overhang* can protect a door effectively, if it is not too far above the door. As a rule, the overhang should extend outward by at least half the height of the roof above the bottom of the door. Figure 1-67 is an example. The overhang should be deeper if the location receives heavy snow that can pile up at the level of the door.

A *recessed entrance* locates the door inside a pocket built into the exterior wall, as in Figure 1-68. For a good appearance, the opening should be significantly wider than its depth. Usually, the height of the entrance is limited to the inside ceiling height. In a multi-story house, a recessed entrance could be taller, displacing upper floor space. However, an entrance that is too tall would expose the door to slanting rain, snow, and sunlight.

This method of covering the door complicates the main structure and the interior floor plan. It may be the best choice if the entrance faces a rising slope.

Decks are effective as door canopies only if the deck is waterproof. Typical open wooden decks are not effective.

PORCH

A porch is an outdoor extension of the living space. This apparently simple addition involves a variety of important decisions. The first decision is whether to have one. If you decide to add a porch to your home, you have many design options. Figure 1-71 shows an attractive example.

Visualize the *intended uses* of the porch, and design its shape and location accordingly. You may want one for social gatherings, for solitary reading, or for sitting with your family and talking. If your home offers a pleasant view, a porch may be the best place to enjoy it. A porch can be an ideal location for hanging your laundry to dry. If the climate has a snow season, a porch can be an important safety feature to protect against snow that slides off a tall roof. See the heading, *Snow Protection Under Eaves*, later in Step 1.

The *weather* affects how much a porch will actually be used for lounging. People are uncomfortable with sitting outdoors when the temperature is below about 70 °F (about 21 °C). People also do not like to linger

Figure 1-71. A porch that is large enough to perform a variety of functions, including lounging, social functions, shading of the first floor windows, laundry drying, and protection from roof snowfall.

DRW

Figure 1-72. A screened porch in Florida. Screens are virtually a necessity there. The roof is mesh material, a common choice that provides filtered sunlight. However, a conventional roof is better.

outdoors if the weather is hot and humid, especially when indoor air conditioning is an option.

The **surroundings** of the house largely determine whether a porch would be pleasant for lounging. Quiet and a semblance of privacy are important. For example, you rarely see anyone sitting on a porch that faces a busy street. You can enhance privacy with a fence or shrubbery. In crowded neighborhoods, a balcony that is installed well above the surrounding grade level may provide better privacy than a porch.

Insects, especially mosquitoes, can make a porch too unpleasant to use. In locations where insects are oppressive, fully screened porches are common, as in Figure 1-72.

Shading is important. The porch roof shades the space from overhead sun. A porch that is open to the west is vulnerable to severe glare from the sun in the afternoon and evening. Sunscreens can block the glare, but they also block the view and they are a nuisance to handle.

A porch will have various **accessories**. If the porch will be used for extended lounging, make ample space for large, sprawling chairs, and perhaps a table for serving drinks and snacks. If you want a barbecue grill, the porch should have a convenient location where the smoke can escape freely. A porch in a warm climate may have several ceiling fans, which we cover in Step 4. A porch may have a wet bar, but it probably won't be used much. A hammock may seem appealing, but it would hog a lot of space, so it is better located under a tree.

If you decide to build a porch, exploit it as an element of the home's **exterior style**. Usually, a porch will serve as an **entrance cover**, and it can be valuable as a **shading fixture** for windows. We have more to say about style later in Step 1, and we cover sunlight design in Step 2.

A **"sun porch"** is a porch that is fully enclosed with windows that can be opened for cooling ventilation. A sun porch is a close cousin to a sunroom. If you may want a sun porch, look ahead to *What If You Want a Lot of Glass?*, in Step 2. In a warm climate, jalousie windows provide the best ventilation when the windows are opened. In a cooler climate, windows that close tightly are a better choice. Step 3 provides detailed guidance in selecting windows.

BALCONIES

A balcony is an outdoor extension of the house structure at an upper floor level. Generally, it does not have roof of its own, but it may be covered by a roof overhang or by a higher balcony. There are several kinds of balconies.

One style of large balcony is characteristic of older multi-story houses, as in Figure 1-73. The width of older houses was limited because the weight of upper floors was carried only by the exterior walls, making floors narrow. Exterior balconies provided a connection between different rooms, each of which required an exterior door opening to the balcony.

Another style of balcony is intended to provide an outdoor lounging area at an elevation above ground level, as in Figure 1-74. This type of balcony can be extended from a wall, or it can be built above a lower space. Think of this kind of balcony as an elevated porch. To make it useful and pleasant, design it to have generally the same features that we recommend for porches.

DRW

Figure 1-73. A classic house in Gettysburg, Pennsylvania that uses a balcony above the porch entrance for lounging and connecting adjacent rooms.

DRW

Figure 1-74. A modern house in South Carolina that uses a second floor balcony to provide an ocean view over the surrounding foliage and dunes.

In multi-unit housing, a balcony of ample size should be a standard feature of each dwelling unit that lacks private outdoor space at ground level.

Balconies of the previous kinds can provide a place to lounge on warm nights, escaping insects that concentrate near the ground. Also, they may provide a view that is not accessible from ground level.

Finally, false balconies are sometimes used as a stylistic accent or as an entrance cover, as in Figure 1-75. Such balconies typically are installed below windows, rather than doors, so they are inaccessible. Personally, I don't like fake features that appear to perform a function but don't deliver on their promise.

Any of these kinds of balconies may serve effectively as an *entrance cover* or for *shading windows*.

DRW

Figure 1-75. A false balcony that serves as an entrance cover.

PATIO

A patio is an outdoor extension of the living space that lies on grade level, either adjacent to the house or near to it. The surface typically is paving stones or a concrete slab. Paving stones can produce a beautiful appearance, but they are an uneven surface for lawn furniture, and weeds tend to grow between the stones. The weeds can be controlled with herbicide, if you don't mind chemical warfare.

A concrete slab is more expensive. By itself, it looks drab, but it can be decorated with a layer of paving bricks. Slope a slab for drainage away from the house. If a slab is properly reinforced, it can support columns for an overhead deck or roof.

A patio may be used alone or in combination with a porch or deck. Figure 1-78 shows a historic house in which a newly installed patio and deck integrate well with the original porch.

The issues to consider in designing a patio are similar to those for a porch. The biggest difference is that a patio or deck is exposed to rain and sunshine. Unlike a porch, it is practical to defer building a patio until after the house is built.

A patio is better than a porch for cooking food because it keeps the smoke away from the house. Masonry barbecues are popular, but they are less practical than a portable propane-fired grill. If a patio has a well designed fire pit, it can be pleasant for gatherings on cool evenings.

If you use a patio at night, keep a container of insect repellant handy. Other forms of insect control, such as citronella candles and electric bug zappers, detract from the pleasure of using your outdoor space.

If you plan to use a patio during broad daylight, shade it with trees or with a canopy. It is uncomfortable to linger under direct sunlight.

DECK

A deck is yet another kind of outdoor living space. It is usually built of lumber. It can be built at any desired height or with a combination of heights. A skilled carpenter can make a deck a work of art. Figure 1-79 is a nice example.

Concrete decks can be built, but they are rare. In locations where masonry construction is common, concrete balconies or roof decks are more common.

Like a patio, a deck is a superior location for outdoor cooking because it allows the smoke to blow clear of the house. Also like a patio, a deck needs shade, either from trees, from a canopy, or from an extended roof overhang (if the deck is on the proper side of the house).

DRW

Figure 1-78. A patio that blends well with an existing porch and a newly built deck.

A wooden deck needs periodic rebuilding, which is expensive. Figure the life of a deck as about ten years in a wet or snowy climate, and thirty years or more in a dry climate. Because of environmental concerns, the preservatives presently used for deck lumber are not as effective as earlier kinds.

DRW

Figure 1-79. An attractive deck that adds a large amount of outdoor living space.

To maximize the life of a deck, build it to drain water quickly. In particular, lay the floor boards so that they dome upward as they warp with age. To do this, lay the boards *with the end grain cupped upward, not downward.* This seems contrary to intuition, so a majority of carpenters get it wrong.

A fancy deck is an expense that you can defer into the future. Just make provision for it in your home design.

EMERGENCY SHELTER

Your house may experience a variety of calamities during its life. Hurricanes threaten coastal areas. Tornadoes are a major peril in the central United States, and changing weather patterns may expand the range of tornadoes considerably. Earthquakes are common in many of the earth's most populated areas. Homes that are surrounded by forests or dry vegetation are vulnerable to forest fires. Volcanoes may erupt, releasing toxic gases over a wide area. A nuclear reactor meltdown may spread radiation over a wide area. And that's not all.

If your home site is vulnerable to one or more of these perils, consider building an emergency shelter into your house. An older example is the "storm cellar," widely adopted in tornado regions of the United States from the 19th century onward. These consist of a small underground space, with its own structural walls and with a door that exits directly to the outside.

The first point to make is that you should *build your entire house strongly enough to serve as an emergency shelter.* By exploiting the construction methods and materials that we recommend, you can build a house that is so strong that it will protect you against most of the previous terrors. The construction techniques recommended in Step 3 provide a host of benefits, all of which reinforce each other. Exceptional strength is one of these benefits.

Some hazards are so powerful that no home can protect against them. To avoid those, build your home in a safer location. It is folly to build a home near an active volcano, or to build in a low coastal area that is vulnerable to hurricanes or tsunamis. Millions of people do so, but think hard before joining them. (See the sidebar in Step 3, *Some Places You Just Don't Build*.)

Basement Shelter

A basement shelter provides the strongest defense against forces that may collapse a house or blow it away, especially tornadoes and hurricanes. Basement walls cannot be crushed or blown over.

A basement shelter is less reliable as a shelter against fire. It provides protection from the high temperatures of a surrounding fire, such as a forest fire. It also provides refuge from smoke because smoke tends to rise during a fire. However, if the house itself is burning, a basement shelter would be deadly. It would not block the high temperature of the fire, and it would accumulate deadly gases, such as carbon monoxide. The only safe response to a burning house is to get out of it. For protection from a fire that surrounds the house, equip the shelter with respirators.

A basement shelter is not desirable if the basement can be flooded.

If you are building a new house with a basement, Step 3 recommends reinforced concrete basement walls. It is a simple matter to create a strong emergency shelter by extending the foundation walls into the basement to create a refuge space, as in Figures 1-82 and 1-83. To add an emergency shelter in the basement of an existing house, create a shelter space with a concrete block wall that is tied together with steel reinforcing bars ("rebar"). The wall should enclose a portion of the basement that includes an exterior exit.

The floor above the shelter acts as its ceiling. It can be strong enough if the joists span a relatively short distance across the shelter walls. Secure the floor joists to the shelter walls with anchor bolts that are embedded into the tops of the shelter walls.

To protect against fire, install a thick fireproof layer, such as gypsum board, between the floor joists and the shelter.

The exits from a shelter are critical. You don't want to be trapped inside. Also, it is important to have a quick escape from the poisonous gases that are generated in a house fire. Locate the shelter so that it has direct access to the outside, along with an interior entrance from the basement. The exit door should open inward, so that it cannot be obstructed by wreckage. The door opening should be very strong to avoid jamming the door. Select doors that are fire resistant.

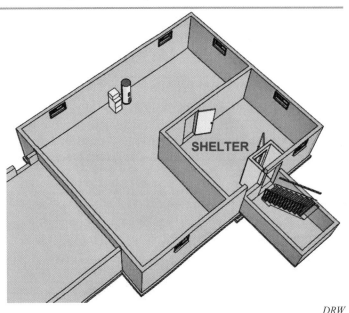

DRW

Figure 1-82. A basement emergency shelter that is completely surrounded by reinforced concrete walls. The walls provide strong support for the joists that form the ceiling. The shelter has direct access to the outside.

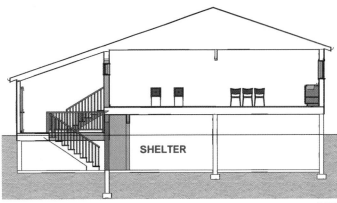

DRW

Figure 1-83. The same shelter as in the previous figure, showing how the stairs to the outside share an entry vestibule with the stairs leading to the main floor.

To enhance escape from a collapsed house and surrounding wreckage, place the exit above grade. This means that you will need a strongly protected stairway from the basement shelter to grade level.

Shelter on a Slab Foundation

If a house is built on a slab foundation, you can create a strong shelter by creating a space with interior concrete walls, as in a basement. Reinforce the ceiling and make it fireproof, as for a basement shelter. Include a strong exterior exit.

If the house has a single floor, the roof structure forms the shelter ceiling. Therefore, it is especially important to attach the roof strongly, as we explain in Step 3. Severe windstorms commonly lift the roofs off houses that are not designed and built specifically to resist wind damage.

If you will have a shelter room that is located above grade, design it to serve double duty as a "strong room," which we recommended previously.

Shelter on a Pier Foundation

Most houses built on pier foundations have frame construction. Attach the upper structure to the piers securely, so that wind cannot lift the house off the foundation. If the house is built on tall piers, brace the piers so that they will not topple.

If your house will have a "strong room" with strengthened walls and ceilings, it can serve double duty as an emergency shelter. Make it large enough for that purpose, and provide a fortified exit to the outside.

Separate Shelters

In earlier times, underground emergency shelters sometimes were built separate from the house. However, it is generally more desirable to create a shelter that is part of the house structure. A separate shelter may not be accessible in time, especially if the hazard is tornadoes, which appear quickly and unpredictably.

Separate underground shelters are dank. They do not benefit from the heating, cooling, and dehumidification inside the house. The entrances tend to be ugly, suggesting something you would find in a horror novel.

You can buy prefabricated emergency shelters that are made primarily of sheetmetal with reinforced corners, somewhat like a cargo container. These are more vulnerable than a strongly built house. If installed inside the house, they may become a trap if the house collapses.

Shelter Size and Amenities

Generally, the size of the shelter depends on the duration of the hazard. If the hazard comes and goes quickly, as does a tornado, the shelter can be small. If the hazard lasts longer, such as an episode of earth tremors (which may extend for weeks), the shelter should be large enough to allow your family to live in it for longer periods. If the hazard may be powerful enough to destroy your home, the shelter gives you a place to live until you can rebuild or find new lodgings.

Any shelter requires some accessories, which vary depending on the hazards and their duration. Make the shelter large enough to accommodate them. Here is a typical list of accessories:

- *portable toilets*, one or more, with an adequate supply of toilet paper, disposal bags, and an airtight trash can.
- *furniture*, at least consisting of folding chairs and folding cots for all occupants. For longer occupancy, add a folding table.
- *drinking water* in strong containers, along with water purification chemicals
- *food* in sufficient quantity, on convenient storage shelves
- *lighting*, including flashlights and candles. A few pounds (or kilograms) of candles can provide lighting for an extended period.
- A *portable stove*. If the house has a basement, select a stove that uses alcohol as its fuel, not propane.
- *plastic sheet* and *duct tape* to seal the house against smoke, dust, and/or radioactive particles
- *tools* to escape through debris, including a chainsaw, pry bars, and jacks
- *medical supplies*
- *respirator masks* to protect against smoke
- a *radio* to receive news, preferably powered by a hand crank as well as batteries

---

✓ *Good work! You have now completed the first big portion of your home design. You have identified all the functions that you want your home to perform. You have selected the rooms and spaces that you want for those functions, along with the major amenities of those rooms. For the rest of Step 1, we will put those features together to create the layout, shapes, and exterior appearance of your house and property.*

THE INTERIOR LAYOUT

Now that you know the types of rooms you want, and how many of them, we will arrange the rooms into a layout, or "floor plan." The main goal of your room layout is to provide pleasant living. A good layout allows convenient travel between rooms, isolates noise, exploits views, provides easy accesses to outside areas, and keeps you comfortable under all weather conditions.

Don't start with a commitment to a particular exterior shape. Instead, let the shape of the house flow from the arrangement of the floor plans. In a manner of speaking, select the box to fit its contents. Later in this Step, we will decorate the "box" with almost any style that you may want.

The interior layout is also a key to energy efficiency. One of the Five Principles of Super-Efficiency is to localize energy use to the rooms that are occupied at any given moment. A good layout makes it convenient to separate the occupied rooms from those that are unoccupied. Convenience and energy efficiency complement each other.

Where do you find your layout ideas? In a few pages, we will explain how to group your rooms in ways that are most convenient and energy efficient. Use the *Home Activities Worksheet* to make sure that you include every room type and activity that you need. Dip into your idea file to enrich your thinking about the appearance and amenities of your layout. For additional inspiration, you may want to sift through some plans books. See the sidebar, *Plans Books*.

Designing the interior layout doesn't apply just to building a new house. Often, it is practical to build an addition to an existing house that offers opportunities for improving the interior layout. We will introduce those opportunities later in Step 1, under the heading *Additions to an Existing House*.

This is the most creative part of your design. Play with the floor plan, creating a variety of layouts. Take your time, and let ideas germinate. Eventually, your floor plan will merge the best features of your various designs.

START YOUR WORKING DRAWINGS

From this point forward, you will create a set of working drawings to embody your design. These are not the formal construction drawings that you will create (or acquire) in Step 8, but a set of less formal drawings that you will use as visual notes to include all the essential features of your design. We call them "working" drawings because you can change them at

PLANS BOOKS

Plans books are essentially catalogs of floor plans, with one or two pages devoted to each plan, along with a sketch or photo of the house exterior. Plans books are sold in most large hardware stores. They don't cost much, so buy a few.

A plans book may help you to get closer to the one special layout that captures all your desires. You probably won't find your ideal layout, but you may find parts of it. Ready-made plans tend to group rooms for convenience, which is a prime issue. If you find a layout that you like, minor adjustments may make the layout energy efficient as well. And, you may find appealing decorative ideas, mainly for the exterior, such as a fancy entrance or roof line.

Recognize the limits of plans books. They tend to neglect some nice features, such as dressing rooms, multiple toilet rooms for master bedrooms, and well planned laundry areas. Plans books generally don't address optimum use of sunlight and other aspects of energy efficiency. They say almost nothing about the structure of the house, and nothing about the HVAC and water systems. The publishers of plans books are trying to sell expensive sets of construction drawings, but those drawing sets generally suffer from the same deficiencies.

any time, and you can create as many different designs as suit your fancy.

To begin, make pencil sketches of your floor plan to work out the approximate size of each room and how the rooms join together. You need a floor plan for each occupied level of your home.

If you are comfortable using a computer, I recommend that you use a home design computer program to make your working drawings. See the adjacent sidebar, *Home Design Computer Programs*. The effort that you invest in learning the program will stimulate your creative juices and reward you with deeper insight into house construction.

The desired end result is a *scale drawing* of your floor plan. A scale drawing is one that is drawn to precise dimensions. You need scale drawings to insure that the rooms provide proper space for their furnishings, to insure that the rooms and connecting spaces fit together properly, and to allocate needed space for walls and other structural components.

HOME DESIGN COMPUTER PROGRAMS

If you are comfortable using a computer, consider using a home design computer program to make your working drawings. A good program offers a big speed improvement in drawing floor plans, compared to using paper and pencil. It automatically creates accurate lines and exact scale as you drag your computer mouse. You can stretch or shrink rooms instantly as you add or relocate the furnishings, with the dimensions changing automatically.

To find a good program, search the Internet for reviews of "home design computer programs." A good basic program costs about twice the price of this book, which is peanuts compared to the value of your home. Some programs are free or very cheap, but the cheaper programs lack features that you will want. Avoid general sketching programs, which lack the automatic features that make it easy to draw a house layout.

The basic level of home design programs are best for making accurate floor plans, as in Figure 1-86. With a typical floor plan program, you begin by outlining the exterior walls of the main floor by clicking and dragging. Then, draw the interior walls in the same way. You can add additional floors with a few keystrokes.

More than that, the best of the inexpensive programs include large libraries of windows, doors, cabinets, appliances, furniture, and other accessories. You select an item from the library, drop it into the floor plan, and drag it to the position you desire. You can customize the dimensions and features of most items.

A typical program allows you to add features in almost any order, which eliminates most of the strain of planning your drawings. As your design grows, you can add, delete, and modify most features easily. You can make endless revisions, and keep copies of each.

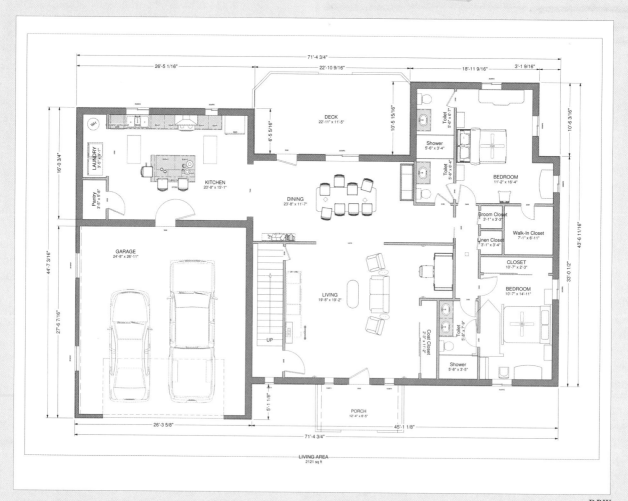

DRW

Figure 1-86. A typical floor layout made with a home design computer program. The labels, dimensions, and furnishings are drawn automatically. It's important to include all the furnishings, because they should determine the room size and shape.

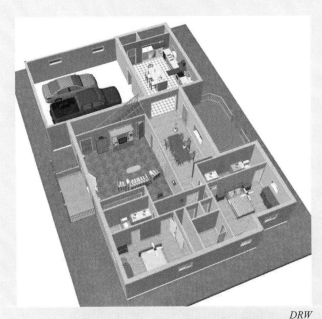

DRW

Figure 1-87. An example of 3-D imaging that can be produced automatically by one inexpensive home design computer program. This is a "doll house" view of the previous floor plan.

The best of the basic programs have the ability to create three-dimensional views of your design from any vantage point, inside or outside. For example, a "doll house" 3-D view shows you each floor plan from above, with the upper structure removed, as in Figure 1-87.

Select a program that gives you this powerful graphic capability. If you fill in all the furnishings and color schemes, the interior views can seem almost photographic, as in Figure 1-88.

The most popular floor plan programs are well organized and they have reasonably clear instructions. A beginner can produce a basic floor plan within a few hours. However, drawing the floor plans and furnishings for a fairly complex, multi-story house may require several weeks as you learn to use the program's features.

The basic level of home design programs have only rudimentary capability to show the exterior shape and features of the house. Some basic programs will add a roof automatically, but with no capability to modify the roof details, such as the shape of the eaves. Certain features, such as stairs and dormers, can be damnably difficult to draw.

If you want a program that draws the roof, foundation, stairs, and structural features more realistically, you need to ratchet up to a more sophisticated mid-level program. A program with this level of capability costs about ten times the price of this book, which is still peanuts. The real cost of this capability is a much longer investment in learning.

For example, the instruction manual for the best mid-level program has over 900 pages. The instructions are well written, but you will encounter snags that you can't figure out. The software company does not provide adequate customer support, so you have to join a user group or pay a consultant to complete drawings of any complexity. To add insult, the reference manual is provided only as a digital file, so you have to spend more than half the price of the software to get your local copy shop to print it.

You would need a still more advanced program to draw all the details that your builder will need, but don't go there. Such a program costs thousands of dollars, plus a steep hourly charge for customer support. Unless you are professionally involved with home design, plan to hire a drafting service to make your detailed construction drawings, as we will explain in Step 8.

Here's the bottom line. Most users of this book will be satisfied with a basic floor plan program that includes 3-D imaging. Those who are more technically inclined will enjoy the capability of a mid-level program, along with the camaraderie of joining a user group to discover the tricks that the manual doesn't tell you. Only design or construction professionals should undertake the cost and difficulty of a top level program.

DRW

Figure 1-88. An interior view of a room layout that is generated automatically by the same computer program.

CAUTION! REAL VS. NOMINAL METRIC DIMENSIONS

Standard dimensions for building materials originated primarily in the United States, using the antiquated English system of measurement. This creates a dilemma for the U.S., Canada, and other countries where builders are struggling to convert to the metric system.

 In the U.S., so far, the old English dimensions are being retained for most building materials. However, in Britain, the common size for plywood sheets is 1220 millimeters wide and 2440 millimeters long. This is approximately one millimeter wider and two millimeters longer than the U.S. standard sheet, which is 4 feet wide and 8 feet long.

In some cases, the old dimensions are being converted to approximate, or nominal, metric dimensions. The conversion is based on the coincidence that one inch almost equals 25 millimeters. (Actually, one inch is 25.40 millimeters). For example, a 4-foot by 8 foot sheet of plywood may be given the nominal dimensions of 120 cm by 240 cm, even though the sheet is actually larger than those metric dimensions.

So, be sure that you know whether any metric dimensions are real or nominal. *In this book, metric equivalent dimensions are nominal, unless stated otherwise.*

If you prefer not to use a computer, make your scale drawings with paper and pencil. Buy a quadrille pad that is at least 11"x17" (about 28x42 cm) in size, a long ruler made of clear plastic, and a good eraser. Select a pad with a grid size that matches the units on your ruler. For example, if you use inches, select a pad that has a quarter-inch grid. You don't need a drawing board or other drafting paraphernalia. Your dining table can serve perfectly well as a drafting table.

Use a soft pencil, which is easy to see and to erase. To save time as you refine your layouts, cut out scaled cardboard templates for furniture, appliances, and the other furnishings that you want. You can trace around these templates quickly.

By the end of Step 1, your working drawings will include your entire space layout and the exterior shape of your home. The additions after Step 1 will be quick and easy, unless you change your mind about your basic design.

Don't be uptight about making changes, including big ones. You don't need to settle on a final design until Step 8. As long as your home design consists of lines on paper, it costs nothing to improve it. Remember, one of your main objectives is to have fun. The more you play with your design, the more fun you will have.

Use Standard Dimensions

As you make your working drawings, take advantage of the fact that most building materials and components are produced in standard dimensions. Lumber studs and joists, plywood sheets, insulation batts, concrete blocks, bricks, shingles, cabinets, kitchen and bathroom appliances, windows, and doors are all made in standard dimensions.

For example, the spacing of floor joists, wall studs, and rafters is keyed to the standard size of plywood sheets. The common spacing of 16" (40 cm) allows a standard sheet of plywood, which is 48" (120 cm) wide, to span three spaces. A spacing of 24" (60 cm) allows a sheet of plywood to span two spaces. Exploiting these dimensions in your design allows most of your plywood to be used without any cutting.

In the U.S., the common ceiling height is about 8 feet (240 cm) because lumber, plywood, and drywall are most commonly sized for this height. A ceiling height of 10 feet (300 cm) is a common alternative, and again, you can find materials sized for this height.

Doors have a standard height of 80" (200 cm), with various standard widths. Windows are less standardized, but they commonly offered in multiples of 6" (15 cm) in height and width.

Kitchen counters in North America have a standard height of 36" (90 cm). Base cabinets, ranges, ovens, and dishwashers are standardized to this height. Kitchen cabinets generally are offered in width increments of 3" or 6" (7.5 or 15 cm). When you design the kitchen walls, be aware of these dimensions to avoid awkward gaps. Appliances that fit into a kitchen counter also come in matching widths.

Refrigerators, washing machines, and other freestanding appliances are less standardized.

You are not limited to standard dimensions, but using them saves a lot of money, makes it easy to buy materials, expedites construction, and minimizes waste.

If you hire an architect to assist in designing your home, be aware that some architects are oblivious to standard materials dimensions and thereby cause the homeowner needless expense and trouble. Discuss this issue with anyone you consider for design assistance. (We discuss the skills of architects and other design advisors in Step 8.)

This book provides both U.S. and metric dimensions. Our metric dimensions usually are "nominal" equivalents, as explained in the sidebar.

SIZE THE ROOMS TO FIT THE FURNISHINGS!

Typical tract houses size their rooms without adequate regard to their functions. Rooms tend to be too small, so that the seller can claim a larger total number of rooms. Even many big, expensive trophy houses are crammed with rooms that are too small to fulfill their functions conveniently or elegantly.

Don't make that mistake. Instead, *size each room to fit its furnishings.* Identify all the furniture and appliances that you will want to fulfill the room's functions. Make each item, such as a bed or desk or bookshelf or washing machine, a focal point of activity. Visualize the surrounding space needed for each activity. Play with the arrangement of the furnishings until you find one that efficiently knits together all the activities in the room.

Only then, finalize the shape, dimensions, and door locations of the room.

LOCATE THE INTERIOR LOAD-BEARING WALLS AND BEAMS

Before you start arranging your rooms, we need to discuss the interior "load-bearing" walls and the "load-bearing" support beams that your house is likely to have. These will impose some limitations on your floor plans.

Load-bearing interior walls and beams are a feature of modern houses. If you look at houses that are more

Figure 1-92. Floor joists attached to the sides of a support beam with steel hangers. When the ceiling surface of the room below is applied, the beam will be hidden from view.

than a century old, you will notice that most of them are fairly narrow, typically about 15 feet (4.5 meters) in width. The reason is that the horizontal timbers that support the floors (called "joists") were limited in length. In the old days, the floor joists spanned from one exterior wall to the opposite exterior wall. This was because the exterior walls were the only walls strong enough carry the weight of the house structure.

Modern houses have become much wider, providing increased interior volume with little additional material. This was achieved by making certain interior walls strong enough to support the inner portion of the house structure. Like the exterior walls, any load-bearing interior walls must be based on a strong foundation.

Typically, a load-bearing interior wall is located near the centerline of the longest axis of the house. This arrangement doubles the practical width of the house. For this reason, modern houses typically are about 30 feet (9 meters) wide. At the same time, a load-bearing interior wall tends to divide the floor plan into halves, with the rooms usually arranged on either side, as in Figure 1-91.

If the house has several floors, each floor must have load-bearing walls or beams that are stacked directly on top of the load-bearing walls and beams of the floors below. Therefore, *you need to coordinate the floor plans of all the levels.*

A load-bearing wall can have doors and wide openings. However, wherever a load-bearing wall has an opening, the top of the opening must include a strong beam that spans across the top of the opening, as in Figure 1-91. (For narrow openings, such as doors, these beams are called "headers.")

If the ceiling joists or the floor joists of the level above rest on top of a load-bearing beam, the beam itself will be visible below the ceiling surface. As an alternative, floor or ceiling joists can hang on the sides of the beam, so that the beam is partially or completely hidden by the ceiling surface. The latter design is becoming more common with the widespread use of steel joist hangers on wooden beams, as in Figure 1-92.

DRW

Figure 1-91. On the right is a typical load-bearing wall. It is placed on the centerline of the house, with rooms on both sides. The wide opening in front requires an overhead beam to support the ceiling joists above. The narrower door openings are capped with "headers" to support the ceiling.

Joist = horizontal structural member used in framing to span open space between beams

In some cases, a beam may entirely replace a load-bearing wall. This is common practice in basements, which typically have a central beam that supports the ground floor. The beam may be steel or wood. It is supported by the end walls of the house and by a series of columns. Each column rests on a foundation that is built into the basement floor slab.

A load-bearing wall limits the *width* of rooms, but not their *length*. So, if you want an especially large room on one side of a load-bearing wall, its longer side will be parallel to the long axis of the house.

However, that is not an absolute limitation. If you want a large room that spans the full width of the house, use the same procedure as in basements. Use a supporting beam for the joists above the room, and support that beam with columns inside the room. The columns will be visually prominent. In formal rooms, they may be decorated with fancy capitals and bases, fluted sides, etc.

A load-bearing wall or beam does not have to be exactly at the centerline of the house. It may be offset so that the floor joists on one side are longer than the joists on the other side. Also, load-bearing walls do not have to be arrayed in a straight line. However, each floor should align its load-bearing walls and beams with those on the floors below and the floors above.

There is one major exception to the need for load-bearing walls. A truss roof structure can be designed economically to span across the entire width of a house. Therefore, the top floor of a house with a truss roof may not need any load-bearing walls. Even so, a load-bearing wall often is used to support the bottom of a truss roof. This arrangement allows the trusses to be somewhat lighter, especially if the trusses are designed to create open attic space for storage.

Maximum Floor Joist Spans

The typical maximum span of solid lumber floor joists is about 15 feet (4.5 meters). The reason is that the depth of a floor joist is proportional to its span. Longer spans require deeper joists, increasing the height of stairs and the overall height of the house. Also, satisfactory solid lumber for deeper joists is difficult to find.

In the 1970's, fabricated floor joist materials, including "I-joist" and other designs, were introduced. (We explain them in Step 3.) These materials make it possible for a floor joist to span about 20 feet (6 meters) with a depth of 12 inches (30 cm).

That is about the maximum free span that you should use in your home, in most cases. Longer spans require deeper joists, which may conflict with ceiling heights. Also, deeper joists need special reinforcements, and they need special bracing to keep them from tipping over.

Despite the limitations in floor joist spans, you can still make the footprint of the house as large as you can afford by adding more load-bearing walls.

ARRANGE THE ROOMS IN GROUPS

As you arrange your floor plan, some room types should be connected to related types fairly rigidly, while other room types can be moved around more independently. Your floor plans will provide the greatest convenience, and your floor plan designs will flow more easily, if you organize your rooms in these groups:

- the *day cluster*, which includes the rooms that are used routinely during waking hours. It includes the kitchen, the everyday dining area, a toilet room, usually the living room, and other rooms regularly occupied during the day, such as an office.
- *expansion rooms*, which may be connected to other rooms in the day cluster for occasional functions. Common expansion rooms are a formal dining room and a great room.
- *bedroom clusters*, each of which includes a bedroom, dressing space, and a conveniently accessible toilet and shower. A toilet room or shower may be shared by different bedroom clusters.
- *independent rooms*, which are occupied or used independently of other rooms, usually on irregular schedules. Examples are the strong room, laundry area, broom closet, and workshop.

If you decide to build a home with multiple floors, work out how you want to divide the rooms and room groups between the floor levels. Look ahead to *Stacking the Living Space*, later in Step 1, which explains the advantages and limitations of multi-level dwellings.

 Arranging your rooms in the clusters recommended here maximizes convenience and energy efficiency.

In a multi-level house, locate the rooms with the heaviest traffic on the ground floor. These rooms include the day cluster, its expansion rooms, and some independent rooms. The master bedroom cluster may be located on the ground floor or on the second floor.

Upper floors usually contain bedroom clusters and some other independent rooms, such as a storage room. A basement typically contains informal spaces, such as a workshop, storage space, and space for the heating and water treatment equipment. But, a well designed basement can also be a good location for formal rooms.

The Day Cluster

The day cluster includes rooms that are used for regular daytime activities, which continue until the occupants go to bed. This group includes:

- the kitchen
- the everyday dining area
- the living room or other room that is the primary location for lounging and family activities
- any other spaces that are used regularly during the day, such as an office or office alcove
- at least one toilet room, which may be shared with a bedroom cluster.

The rooms in the day cluster are heated and cooled to normal temperatures, although their schedules may differ somewhat. There is continual travel between the rooms in the day cluster, so any doors between rooms in this group are likely to be left open for convenience. All the rooms in the day cluster have windows, except perhaps the toilet room.

A good way to start your floor plan is to visualize carrying groceries into the house from the garage. The garage and kitchen should be located close together, with a convenient passage between the two. This passage should contain the food storage pantry, or it should lead to the pantry, which is adjacent to the kitchen or inside the kitchen.

Then, work outward from the kitchen. The kitchen is the most frequently used room in the house, and the occupants travel to and from the kitchen in all directions.

The next space adjacent to the kitchen is the everyday dining area. We covered the options previously. The dining area may be within the kitchen itself, at a counter, island, or dinette table. Or it may be adjacent to the kitchen area, or in a separate dining room.

If there is a separate formal dining room in addition to the everyday dining area, treat it as an expansion room. Locate it with respect to the everyday dining area so that it can act as expansion space to the everyday dining area, if desired. This will allow all dining to occur in contiguous space. Separate the formal dining room with a door or partition that can block air movement.

Adjacent to the kitchen and the dining area (or areas) is the room that your family will use as its primary space for lounging and family activities. Normally, this will be the "living room."

If you want a separate room for larger numbers of occupants, such as a "great room," arrange it as an expansion room on the far side the living room. Separate the two rooms with a door or partition to block air movement, but arrange them so that the two rooms merge into a single space when needed.

Locate at least one toilet room within the day cluster. To economize, locate it so that it can serve one of the bedroom clusters.

If you plan to use any other room on a daily basis – such as an office, a study room, or a separate television room – include it within the day cluster. If you want that room to be isolated from the noise of the other daily activities, or if the activity in that room makes noise, locate it on the far side of the toilet room.

If the climate has a cold season, try to orient the windows in the day cluster southward, especially if the windows are exposed to direct sunlight during the cold season. Windows are useful for collecting solar heat only during hours of sunlight. During short winter days in more northerly latitudes, the sun provides most of its warming after breakfast and before dinner. We will exploit any potential for heating with sunlight in Step 2. Look ahead to there before you get too far into your day cluster layout.

The Expansion Rooms

"Expansion rooms" are rooms that are used to expand the space for gatherings beyond the day cluster. The design goal is a floor plan that avoids splitting a big gathering into groups that cannot interact. This is a common flaw of big, poorly designed trophy houses, where large gatherings overflow into various isolated rooms.

The most common expansion room is a formal dining room, which can be joined with the smaller everyday dining space to form a larger, integrated dining area.

If you have a "great room," arrange the layout so that it can serve as an expansion room. Provide a large opening between it and the living room, the formal dining room, or any other sitting or lounging rooms to create a large, connected space for social functions.

A sunroom or enclosed porch can also function as an expansion room during weather that does not require it to be heated or cooled.

Well placed doors and partitions are an essential part of the design of expansion rooms. They must isolate the rooms from heating and cooling when the rooms are vacant, and they must also connect the rooms conveniently and elegantly when the rooms are used. The heading, *Interior Doors and Partitions*, in Step 3, offers your options.

If your home has expansion rooms for large functions, provide an adequate number of toilet rooms to serve the functions. You can do this by adding a separate guest toilet room, or by arranging one or more of the toilets in the bedroom clusters to serve this purpose conveniently. Or, do both.

The Bedroom Clusters

Make each bedroom in the house the hub of a cluster of spaces that include, for each bedroom occupant: (1) ample closet space, (2) dressing space, (3) a privately accessible toilet, (4) a shower, and (5) a separate wash basin. A bedroom cluster may include a dressing room, which typically substitutes for a bedroom closet. In general, design each bedroom cluster to include all the amenities needed from the time of undressing in the evening to dressing in the morning.

Several bedrooms may share toilet rooms and shower rooms, so that the bedroom clusters overlap. Each bedroom should have direct access to toilet and shower facilities without requiring the occupant to pass through another bedroom or through any occupied space.

A shower may be located in a toilet room or in its own space, a decision that we covered previously under the heading, *Shower Rooms*.

If several bedrooms are connected to a common toilet room and shower by a corridor, isolate the corridor from the rest of the house with a door.

The most convenient arrangement is for each bedroom cluster to have its own dedicated toilet room and shower room. This is commonly considered a luxury that is reserved for a single "master bedroom" suite. But, that arrangement is worth having for each bedroom that is occupied on a regular basis. It avoids the traffic jam that occurs in the morning if several occupants must compete for the same facilities.

Arrange some of the bedroom cluster toilet rooms so that they are accessible from the rest of the house, without guests having to walk through a bedroom to reach them. These toilet rooms will have two doors, one leading to the bedroom and one leading to the "public" space. This dual access reduces the total number of toilet rooms that you will need, while maintaining privacy.

Locate a linen closet on each floor to conveniently service all the bedroom clusters on that floor.

Figure 1-95 illustrates some of these concepts with two bedroom clusters that are located in the bedroom wing of the house whose floor plan is shown in Figure 1-86. Each cluster is designed for a couple. The two clusters are joined by a corridor that can be isolated from the rest of the house by a pocket door. In this way, each bedroom can be isolated from the other areas of the house by two doors.

The upper bedroom cluster in the figure has individual "his and her" toilet rooms on opposite sides of a shared shower. One of the toilet rooms is accessible from the common areas through a second door. Clothing storage is provided by a large walk-in closet and two dressers.

The lower bedroom cluster has a single toilet room that includes a shower and twin wash basins. The toilet room is accessible from the corridor through a second door. Clothing storage is provided by a wide closet and a large "bureau" dresser.

Both bedroom clusters are served by a linen closet that opens to the corridor. The location of the linen closet minimizes exposure to the humidity generated in the showers.

■ Arranging the Rooms Within Bedroom Clusters

Each bedroom cluster can be located independently, except for clusters that share a shower or toilet. Locating a bedroom cluster at some distance from the day cluster, or on a different floor, provides privacy and isolation from noise.

DRW

Figure 1-95. A bedroom wing that contains two bedroom clusters, joined by a corridor that can be isolated from the rest of the house.

People like to sleep at a lower temperature than normal daytime room temperature. In a warm climate, install bedrooms in the coolest part of the house, usually on the north or northeast side. In a multi-story house, lower floors generally are cooler, although night cooling ventilation with outside air can cool upper floor bedrooms effectively (as we will explain in Step 4).

In cool and moderate climates, the east side is a good bedroom location because the morning sunlight will get you out of bed, and the room is shaded during the afternoon. In colder climates, the temperature of the bedrooms is not affected much by their locations. In northern winters, the sun sets long before bedtime.

If the house faces a heavily used street or other source of nighttime noise, place the bedrooms away from that side. Since a view of the outside is relatively unimportant for a bedroom, consider placing the bedrooms on the sides that don't offer much of a view, such as facing adjacent houses.

The shower rooms should have no windows, unless your home is located in a balmy climate. If the climate has a cold season, try to locate the shower rooms to minimize contact with exterior walls. However, with super-insulated walls, this is not a compelling issue.

The toilet rooms typically will have windows if the climate is moderate or warm, but not if the climate has a significant cold season.

The linen closet should have no contact with outside walls. Clothes closets should minimize contact with outside walls.

The Independent Rooms

"Independent rooms" are rooms that have no strong spatial relationship to other rooms. They are usually occupied on an occasional basis. They include the laundry room, storage rooms, game room, sewing or hobby room, and workshop.

Heating and cooling of these rooms should be isolated by a door or partition that allows little air leakage. Independent rooms should not intrude into the traffic pattern within the day cluster or within the bedroom clusters.

Aside from that, locate each independent room wherever it is most convenient. For example, the laundry room might be located so that it separates the day cluster from the master bedroom cluster, while satisfying other laundry room considerations that we considered previously. Refer back to our earlier discussion of room types to help you decide where to place each of your independent rooms.

LOCATE THE SEWER DRAINS AND "WET WALLS"

Toilets, showers, tubs, sinks, washing machines, and dishwashers need sewer drains. Sewer pipe is large and heavy. The layout of sewer pipe is inflexible because the contents must flow downward by gravity. All the sewer drains must connect with a main sewer line that is buried underneath the house. Also, the sewer system needs one or more vent pipes, which rise from the lower sewer pipes all the way up through the house, ending above the roof.

The large sewer pipes that carry solid waste from the toilets should fall straight down to the main line, with perhaps some short and steeply sloped lateral connections. Therefore, arrange the toilets so that their solid waste pipes are lined up to connect with a main sewer line under the house.

Sewer drains that do not carry solid waste, such as those that serve the kitchen and utility sinks, require only a modest slope. They may travel horizontally for some distance, usually between floor joists. These smaller pipes must connect to the main sewer line either inside the house or through underground branch lines.

To minimize interference with the room layouts and to simplify connections, sewer drains may be clustered in a row that is inside an interior wall. This wall is called a "wet wall." It may also contain water supply pipes, gas pipes, and a radon vent pipe. Drain pipes for solid waste and vent pipes for radon require a wet wall that is thicker than other interior walls.

A wet wall should have access panels for installing and repairing hidden pipe fixtures, such as those that serve a shower. A wet wall should always be an interior wall. This minimizes the risk of freezing and avoids interference with the structure and insulation of the exterior walls.

Shower rooms and toilet rooms usually have a wet wall. A wet wall is also convenient for sinks and washing machines. Water, sewer, and gas pipes that serve upper floors usually run through wet walls on the floors below.

A wet wall has two interior sides, so it can serve rooms on both sides of the wall. For example, a shower and toilet room may be located on one side of a wet wall, and the laundry may be on the other side.

If the house has a basement, drains that serve the first floor can be routed directly through the floor into the basement, in a row that is parallel to the floor joists. Under the floor, the smaller drains typically feed into the large toilet drain to minimize clutter in the basement.

If the house has a slab-on-grade foundation, the drain pipes typically rise directly from sewer lines that are buried under the slab.

Water and gas pipes are smaller than drain lines, and they do not depend on gravity. As a result, they do not limit your floor plan in the same way as the sewer drains. Still, try to make these pipe connections as direct as possible. Provide access to repair or replace the pipes, because all pipes eventually leak. (See *Install Pipes to be Replaceable*, in Step 5.)

In most cases, the location of the main sewer line that connects your house to the public sewer system is determined last, by the locations of the house's interior drain lines. However, some terrain and some public sewer systems may dictate the location of the main sewer connection, requiring you to adapt the locations of the interior drains.

SIZE THE INTERIOR DOORS, PARTITIONS, AND CORRIDORS

Your rooms are connected by doors, partitions, and corridors. At this point in your design, the main point about all three is to make them wide enough.

The minimum width of corridors is determined by appearance and by the need to move furniture into rooms through the corridor. On both counts, the minimum corridor width is 36" (90 cm), but this is appropriate only for a compact floor plan. A more attractive and convenient width is 44" to 48" (110 to 120 cm).

See the adjacent box for some door width guidelines. Look ahead to *Interior Doors and Partitions*, in Step 3, for the full menu of doors and movable partitions that are available to you. The minimum width of doors is determined by the use of the room and by handicap access. Wider doors make it easier to move furniture, suitcases, and other bulky objects through the door. Narrower doors are somewhat easier to use, especially when they open into small spaces, such as a toilet room.

Most of the doors in your home will be ordinary hinged swing doors. These are convenient, easy to install, inexpensive, and potentially strong. Wider hinged doors are somewhat less convenient to use and they sweep over more floor space, which may interfere with the layout of smaller rooms.

Hinged interior doors are limited to a maximum width of about 36" (90 cm). If a hinged door may be used by a person using a wheelchair or walker, make it at least 32" (80 cm) wide. With swing doors, the effective opening width is about 2" (5 cm) narrower

doors for bedrooms occupied by one or two persons	**30" (75 cm), without handicap access** **32" (80 cm), with wheelchair access** **36" (90 cm), for rooms with large furnishings**
doors to toilet, shower, and bathtub rooms	**24" (60 cm), with a compact floor plan** **28" (70 cm), without handicap access** **32" (80 cm), with handicap access** **24" (60 cm), connecting between shower and toilet, or between adjacent toilets**
doors to stairways	**32" (80 cm), for basement stairs, if the basement has separate access for large objects** **36" (90 cm), for basement stairs with no alternate access** **36" (90 cm) or wider, for stairs between floors**
doors for walk-in closets	**24" or 28" (60 or 70 cm)**
doors for closets and coat rooms, except walk-in	**almost as wide as the space within, to make all the contents accessible**
doors and movable partitions for opening expansion rooms to related spaces	**as wide as practical**

than the door itself because of the stop strips inside the door jamb and interference with the open door.

MOVING BETWEEN FLOORS

If your home has more than one level, getting from one level to another is a major design issue. You will need space on each level for stairs, and possibly for an elevator. In addition to the stairs themselves, design space to maneuver at the top and bottom of the stairs. And, design a stairwell and door for each stairway to prevent stratification. Use the following as a guide in designing the paths between floors in your home.

Where to Locate Stairs

Convenience should be the primary criterion in deciding where to locate stairs. The location should follow the traffic pattern in the house, which depends on the activities that occur on each floor.

For example, if the upper floor of a 2-story house is occupied mainly by bedrooms, the stairs to the upper floor probably should connect with the access to bedrooms on the lower floor, and with the laundry room.

If the house has a basement that is used primarily for a workshop and for storage, the stairway to the basement may be located separately from the upper floor stairway.

One way to harmonize the stairs with the floor plans is to locate the stairway in a structure at a side of a house. In this way, only the entrances to the stairway need to be coordinated with the floor plans. Also, it is easy to install a door at each floor to prevent temperature stratification, which we explain next. This design may be the only satisfactory choice when adding an additional floor level to an existing house (see *Additions to an Existing House*, below).

If you are designing a grand house with a full-height entry foyer, you might use the foyer as a stair gallery. If the foyer is isolated by doors from each floor, or at least from the upper floors, this arrangement provides effective isolation from temperature stratification. The staircase can be wide and splendid. The access through the front door provides easy access for carrying big items up the stairs.

Prevent Stratification

Stratification is the tendency of warmer air to rise and cooler air to fall, which can cause large temperature differences between floors in a multi-story house. In a climate that requires a significant amount of heating or air conditioning, stratification can cause discomfort and energy waste. During cold weather, heating energy is wasted to keep the ground floor at a comfortable temperature while vacant rooms upstairs are overheated. During warm weather, cooled air drains to a lower floor or to the basement.

Stairs and elevators are the prime path for stratification. (Ducted heating and cooling systems also allow stratification, but we won't use ducted systems in your home.) The solution is to install a well fitted door at all stairs. If your climate requires heating primarily, it is best to install the door at the bottom of the stairs. If your climate requires air conditioning primarily, it is best to locate the door at the top of the stairs. However, this is not a major issue, provided that the stairway is enclosed on at least one level.

Provide a space of at least a few feet (about one meter) between the door and the stairs. This keeps people from tripping over the stairs and gives them space to maneuver, especially while carrying bulky items.

Generally, make the door as wide as the stairs. If necessary, install a double door. Select the doors for ease of use. We cover the choices of interior doors under the heading, *Interior Doors and Partitions*, in Step 3.

Bruno

Figure 1-96. Typical chair lift. A track is bolted to the stair treads and to the lower floor. The chair is powered on the track by an electric motor. Design the stair to provide ample width for normal use alongside the track and around the chair.

Stair Dimensions and Safety

A starting point is to make all your stairs wider than normal. A broad staircase adds a touch of elegance at little additional cost, and makes it easier to move bulky objects between floors. The minimum width for any stair is 36" (90 cm), except perhaps for attic stairs. For formal stairs, where people may be rising and descending at the same time, the minimum width is about 44" (110 cm).

Provide room to maneuver bulky objects on both sides of doors that lead to stairways.

Building codes specify the details of stair construction, such as the rate of rise, the height of individual steps, the height of handrails, etc. Select normal dimensions for the height and width of the steps, with a normal ratio between the two. Unusual stair dimensions invite stumbling.

Install sturdy handrails on both sides of stairs, at exactly the same heights and spacing from the walls. Extend the handrails all the way from top to bottom, so that a person can grasp them before stepping on or off the stairs. Use attachment brackets made of steel or solid brass, not cheap cast metal. Install the brackets at close intervals, and attach them to framing members in the wall. This will protect the user from a bad fall in case one of the brackets should fail. (It happened to me as a result of a cheap bracket.)

Telco

Figure 1-97. Residential elevator. This arrangement wraps the stairway around the elevator, providing a compact use of space. There are many possible designs, including elevators that have fully enclosed cabs and shafts.

Handicap Access

At the time of your life when you are planning your dream house, you and your spouse are probably healthy and athletic. You may never have suffered an injury that limits your motion. You don't mind climbing stairs.

It won't always be that way. Design the house with expectation that you will be lucky enough to get older. Also, plan for visitors who are impaired and for aging relatives who may move in. Make the house convenient for people suffering from the crippling injuries that happen from time to time. Even youngsters break legs.

One way to ease movement between floors is to install an elevator or chairlift. But even with such an aid, it is still best to accommodate the routine needs of a handicapped occupant on the main floor, where all the amenities of the day cluster are located.

Chair Lifts

A chair lift is a motorized chair, or a wheelchair platform, that rides up the stairs on a rail. Figure 1-96 shows the most common type of chair lift.

A chair lift will crowd a stair of normal width. Depending on the design of the chair lift, make your stairs 6" to 18" (15 to 45 cm) wider if you install a chair lift, or if you anticipate that you may install one later.

Chair lifts that use a straight track are relatively inexpensive and easy to install. For a higher price, you can get a stair lift that follows a curved staircase and goes around corners.

Elevators

Many styles of elevators are available for residences. Figure 1-97 shows an example. The cab may be lifted by a cable or by a hydraulic piston. If you are considering an elevator, search the Internet to find what's available. You will have to create space in your structure both for the cab and for the machinery that hoists it.

The floor area of residential elevators is limited, typically to a maximum of about 15 square feet (1.4 square meters). Different models trade off length against width. Select a shape and height that will make it easy to move furniture between floors.

An elevator does not reduce the need for conventional stairs. You still need safe exits in the event that the elevator fails.

To save initial construction cost, you can defer the installation of the elevator. In that case, allocate the space for the elevator and its accessories in an attractive way. For example, in Figure 1-97, design the stairway to provide space for the elevator to be installed later. For a later enclosed elevator, you can use the shaft space beforehand for other purposes, such as closets. Design the floor structure so that the elevator shaft can be cut through the floor without weakening it.

ISOLATE SMOKING

If you will allow smoking inside your home, make it tolerable for non-smokers. If you don't think that is necessary, rising energy costs and complaints from others will change your mind. There is only one reliable way to isolate smoking, which is to have one or more separate smoking rooms. A smoking room used to be a common feature in homes of the gentry, who had the good manners not to impose their smoking on others.

Each smoking room needs to be isolated from the rest of the house by a door, which could be a glass door. For each smoking room, install a quiet exhaust fan that creates a negative pressure to keep smoke from diffusing into the rest of the house. Step 4 covers ventilation design.

In recent years, it has become common to recommend high ventilation rates to clear tobacco smoke out of an entire building. However, this radically increases heating and cooling costs. And it does not work, because tobacco smoke contains materials that adhere to inside surfaces.

Various kinds of filters have been used to trap tobacco smoke in individual rooms, but none works well. Recirculating filters, usually mounted on the ceiling, are sometimes seen in bars and restaurants where smoking occurs. They are big, somewhat noisy, and limited in effectiveness. Ashtrays with self-contained filters work only when the cigarette, cigar, or other weed is placed in the ashtray. They are cheap, but basically hopeless.

COORDINATE THE INSIDE WITH THE OUTSIDE

Your home offers two separate worlds, the interior environment and the exterior. The exterior includes both your own property and the world beyond. Design your home to maximize your enjoyment of all these environments and to connect them effectively. These are the main points to consider.

Exploit Your Views

Stand at your home site and look around. If your home site has a good view in one or more directions, make the view a primary issue in the orientation of your house and its interior layout. It is amazing how often homes miss this opportunity. For example, you can see mansions located on the shores of beautiful waterways with their backs facing the waterway. At the same time, they often have large windows that face in directions with no view.

Even if the view from your property is modest, you should still design your room layout to exploit what you have. For example, you can make almost any back yard into a beautiful setting of trees, shrubbery, a garden, or other features.

Match the views to the rooms where you linger during the daytime, including the living room, the dining room, the kitchen, and perhaps an office. Also, consider the view from exterior living spaces, such as porches, decks, and balconies. In Step 2, we design the locations and sizes of your windows to exploit the view that is available to each room while exploiting the other benefits that windows provide.

At night, you won't have any view from inside the house unless the outdoor scene is lighted and you turn off your interior lights. Window glass reflects the lighted interior of rooms, making it impossible to look outside.

If your home site does have a nighttime view – for example, if it overlooks a city – then consider a porch, deck, or balcony that is accessible from your living room or from another room that you will occupy in the evenings. You may want to situate your bedrooms to exploit a night view, if you can arrange the sight lines from your bedroom windows in a way that preserves privacy.

Many people dream of owning a home located on the shore of a body of water, such as a lake, bay, ocean, or wide river. If you have that dream, and if you have not yet purchased your property, beware of the intense glare and heat of sunlight that can be reflected from water. For a pleasing view from your waterfront property, select a location where the sun will not reflect toward the house when it is low in the sky, especially in the afternoon. See the heading, *Avoiding Glare from Water and Snow*, in Step 2.

If your home has a view that deserves a lot of glass, you need to design your layout in a special way to avoid high heating and cooling costs. For the details, see *What If You Want a Space with Lots of Glass?*, in Step 2.

Relationship to the Street

In most cases, your home makes its strongest impression on visitors when seen from the street. Often, the formal entrance faces the street, but that is not necessary for a good appearance. However, the side of the house that faces the street should have a nice shape, an attractive exterior surface, elegant detailing, and attractive windows. The windows facing the street will be designed in Step 2 to satisfy a variety of considerations.

The street is a source of noise and a source of glare from outside lights. It intrudes on privacy. Therefore, it is usually desirable to orient the interior layout so that the main functions of your home are located away from the street. Also, your outdoor activities typically are on the side of your property that is opposite the street.

Some of your rooms are normally unoccupied. Place them on the street side of the house so that they will act as a buffer against street noise and street light. For example, place closets, storage rooms, guest bedrooms, and the garage on the street side.

Also, you can use trees, shrubbery, or a decorative fence to isolate the house from street.

If your house is close to the street, maintain an attractive geometric relationship to the street and other houses. Usually, one side of the house should be parallel to the street.* If your house is far from the street, orient it to satisfy other requirements, but make the orientation look attractive from a distance.

---

* A notable exception is a block of ornate mansions on Monument Avenue in Richmond, Virginia, all of which are turned with respect to the street by the same angle.

Facing the Neighbors

Consider the relationship of your interior layout to adjacent houses, including houses that may be built later. Don't orient view windows toward neighboring houses. But, don't go the extreme of confronting your neighbors with drab, featureless walls. Even where houses are closely spaced, adjacent walls are still visible.

You can decorate the sides of your house that face the neighbors with shrubbery and clever accents. For example, a trick once used in elegant neighborhoods was to dress up small windows in neighboring walls with a touch of decorative glass, such as stained glass, that provides both light and privacy. It's still a good idea.

We say more about avoiding drab walls in *Alternatives to Excessive Window Area*, later in Step 1.

Locate the Doors Effectively

After you have taken the previous issues into consideration, it's time to locate the exterior doors. The prime issue is convenience in connecting indoor activities to related outdoor activities. For example, if you bring groceries by car, install a door that is conveniently located between the garage, the pantry, and the kitchen.

By the same token, locate all the outside doors where traffic through them does not disturb inside activities. While most houses have a formal entrance, other doors may handle most of the traffic. Make all of them attractive and convenient.

Most houses have a formal entrance that faces the street, but don't feel obliged by this arrangement. Your formal entrance generally leads into the living room, or into a foyer that opens to the living room. If the living room is oriented toward a fine view in the rear, the formal entrance may be on a side of the house, or in back. Design the outside approach to the formal entrance accordingly.

Provide Transition Spaces

Previously, we listed the various kinds of spaces that provide a transition between the inside and outside worlds. These spaces include foyers, vestibules, porches, mud rooms, and various kinds of entrance covers. For each exterior door, select the kind of transition that is most appropriate.

For example, if the climate is snowy or rainy, or if your property is muddy, include an entrance space to allow changing shoes and hanging up wet clothing.

If you plan to have a swimming pool or hot tub, make it possible for bathers to shed their clothing, take a shower, change into swim suits, get towels, and go to the pool without trekking through the house. Ideally, include a changing room in your interior layout, and make it big enough to accommodate all the bathers.

If outdoor activities require equipment, such as horseshoes, badminton gear, or firewood tools, include a convenient place to store the equipment. This might be an equipment room with an exterior door, a vestibule with storage space, or a separate outbuilding.

AVOID BELOW-GRADE DOORS AND WINDOWS

As a rule, do not locate any exterior entrance or any window below grade level, as in Figure 1-99. More generally, do not have any depressions in the soil near your house. Wind currents rapidly fill below-grade spaces with leaves, trash, and dust. The accumulated debris is a haven and passageway for insects and vermin. Drainage of rain water from below-grade spaces requires a separate sewer drain, which is vulnerable to clogging.

DRW

Figure 1-99. Below-grade entrance door. Such entrances collect dirt, leaves, and other debris. They may also collect large amounts of rain, which may flood a basement. A solution for this entrance would be an enclosure over the existing stairwell, with an exterior door and a raised threshold at the head of the stairs.

DRW

Figure 1-100. Extreme condensation on the door frame of a below-grade entrance. The masonry structure was still cold from winter during a spell of humid spring weather.

Openings that are located below grade also invite moisture problems. Things that are located in such spaces will rust or rot. Paint will peel, and mildew will take hold. The structure itself will be attacked. Such spaces are especially vulnerable if they are heavily shaded. Figure 1-100 shows how severe moisture condensation can occur on the shaded part of the structure.

The solution is to fully enclose any below-grade entrance, so that the stairs lead to an exit door above grade. Build the enclosure as an exterior vestibule, with a secure entrance door at the lower level and a lighter door at grade level.

If you want basement windows for daylighting, the bottoms of the windows should be well above grade. If the house is built on a slope, you can place the windows on the low side. Otherwise, raising the basement to include windows will increase the height of the main floor, requiring more steps to enter the house.

CONSIDER THE SUN

Sunlight may be an important factor in the overall orientation and layout of your home. Or, it may not be. It depends on whether you home will be exposed to direct sunlight, and when. The orientation of your glass and shading with respect to the sun is so important that we devote Step 2 entirely to that part of your design. So, take some time to look ahead to Step 2 before you finalize your layout.

Sunlight provides important benefits, and it can also create major problems. Glass is used to let sunlight into the house, and shading is used to keep unwanted solar heat and glare out of the house. As explained further in Step 2, these are important points to consider as you design the layout of your home:

- In a climate that has a cold season, orient the layout so that sunlight can help with heating. Try to locate rooms with larger windows so that their glass faces toward the south. But, note that sunlight is useful for heating only if windows are exposed to direct sunlight at the times when the heat is needed. Winter sun is so low in the sky that it is easily hidden by terrain, trees, and other houses.

- Try to locate the kitchen and breakfast area toward the southeast to exploit warming by morning sunlight, if direct sunlight is available in the early morning.

- In a warm climate, you want bedrooms to stay cool, so try to locate bedroom windows on the north or northeast sides.

STACKING THE LIVING SPACE

The size and cost of your living space is affected by how you stack it, on one level or on several levels. So, let's look at various ways to arrange your living space vertically. At one extreme is a house with all living space on one level, and perhaps some storage space in an attic. The "ranch" or "rambler" style is typical of this arrangement. At the other extreme is a 3- or 4-story "townhouse."

In addition to full floors, we will also exploit the benefit of your roof volume, which provides options for living space, storage space, or vaulted ceilings.

SINGLE- OR MULTI-STORY?

Multi-story houses offer a major advantage in the cost of living space. Upper floors are cheap to build because they add little or nothing to the cost of the foundation, the roof, and the site work. If the foundation is properly designed to resist earth movement, it will be strong enough to support the weight of additional floors. This cost advantage is partly offset by the need for stair space on each floor, along with partitions and doors to block temperature stratification.

A multi-story house provides more living space on a small lot, which is important in locations where building sites are scarce or expensive. Also, building upward may provide other benefits, such as a good view or cooling breezes.

The need to climb stairs is a major lifestyle difference. This may actually be a boon for exercise-deprived urban dwellers. Climbing stairs is probably better than buying exercise equipment that you are not likely to use.

Stairs are a barrier to handicapped persons. This impediment can be overcome with an elevator or chair lift. Still, it is best to provide a bedroom suite for handicapped persons on the same floor where the daytime activities occur.

The floor plans of upper floors are constrained by the need to align any interior load-bearing walls with the load-bearing walls or floor support beams on the floors below. We discussed this previously, at the beginning of your floor plan design.

On balance, multi-story construction usually is a good deal. Consider it, unless there is a compelling reason not to.

DRW

Figure 1-103. A house in Camden, Maine with two successive overhanging floors. It was built this way to overhang a sidewalk to the right.

Overhanging Frame Floors?

If you decide to build a multi-story house, you can economically increase the area of upper floors by extending the floor joists beyond the walls that support them. This works with frame construction, and with frame floors that are built over a lower masonry structure. A good foundation generally has plenty of extra load bearing capacity to carry bigger floors above.

This technique has been used in crowded cities to increase the size of upper floors by extending them over the sidewalk or street, as in Figure 1-103.

Overhanging the second floor has become a common way to increase living space when adding an upper frame floor to an existing single-floor house, as in Figure 1-104. (We explain this further under the heading, *Additions to an Existing House*, later in Step 1.) Also, an overhanging floor on the south side may provide sun shading for the windows below the overhang, as we will learn in Step 2.

When building a new house, the cost benefit of overhanging floors is limited to a relatively small

DRW

Figure 1-104. An overhanging floor created when a second story was added to a single-story house. The adjacent houses show the original configuration.

reduction in the size of the foundation that is needed to support the upper floors. It is simpler to design a foundation that has the same footprint as the upper floors. This also produces a larger first floor and basement.

Overhanging floors were simple to build when floor joists were solid timbers. However, fabricated floor joists ("I-joist") require careful reinforcement to prevent collapse when used with overhanging floors. (Step 3 explains I-joist and its special needs.) This added complication is a reason to avoid overhanging floors, unless they offer some special benefit, such as expanding an upper floor over an urban sidewalk.

ADD A BASEMENT?

In addition to adding space upward, you can also add space downward by building a basement. A basement usually is inexpensive space because the house needs a foundation anyway, and the foundation can be deepened to serve as the basement walls. The bottom of any foundation must extend downward below the frost line, and with frame construction, the foundation should also extend upward at least two feet (60 cm) above grade level. To get enough total height for a living space, just make the foundation a little deeper and/or a little taller. The additional foundation cost is lowest in colder climates, where the foundation must be fairly deep anyway to get below the frost line.

A basement is an ideal location for heating and water heating equipment, making it easy to install the pipes to serve the entire house. Similarly, a basement makes it easy to distribute electrical wiring and gas pipe for the house through the basement.

A unfinished basement provides a large space for storage and occasional activity, such as a workshop. The concrete floor of a basement is well adapted to workshop activities,

If a basement is well protected from moisture and if it is well insulated, the quality of living space in a basement can be almost as good as in the rest of the house. In principle, a basement can be used for most of the functions that occur on the other floors of a house.

One drawback of basements is that windows are unavailable, or they are limited to small sizes high on the wall. I don't recommend basement windows unless their sills are at least one foot (30 cm) above the finished grade level.

During warm weather, basements are cooler than the rest of the house because they are in contact with the deep soil under the house, which remains cool during the summer. This minimizes the need for air conditioning. For example, if you have a business in your home, the basement is a naturally cool location for an office.

Basements also have a tendency toward high humidity, which is caused by their lower temperature and by penetration of water from the surrounding soil. Protecting a basement against humidity and water damage is a major requirement, which Step 3 will cover in detail.

Not all houses should have a basement. The decision depends largely on soil conditions, some of which create serious problems or increase cost. Common obstacles to basements are a dangerous level of radon in the soil, underground water that could rise above the basement floor, terrain that would be dangerously weakened by digging into it, and shallow bedrock that prevents digging. Step 3 explains the details, under the heading *The Ground on Which You Build.*

USING THE ROOF VOLUME

In most parts of the world, the roofs of houses are sloped substantially to shed rain or snow. This results in a large volume of space below the roof that is located above the occupied areas of the house. This under-roof volume is large, often comprising the largest single space in a house. By selecting a particular type of roof structure, you can use this volume to create valuable space in a variety of ways. The sidebar, *Basic Roof Structures*, describes the main types of roof structures that are used in houses today. Use the sidebar to decide which type of roof structure is best for your home.

Most houses around the world have wooden roof structures of various types. Among those, give preference to three types, which are ***truss***, ***beam***, and ***triangle-frame***. Other types of wooden roof structures offer variations of style, but they have significant disadvantages, which may include weaker structure, higher cost, less efficient use of space, and greater vulnerability to leaks.

BASIC ROOF STRUCTURES

There are many ways to build a roof. We cover most structural issues in Step 3, but we need to make a short detour into the basics of roof construction at this point so that you can select the type of roof that is best for your home.

This sidebar looks under the skin of the various roof types to see how they are built. The later sidebar, *Roof Styles*, shows how different styles of roofs look from the outside.

The following are the fundamental types of roof structures that are used for contemporary houses. These structures can be modified or combined to yield a variety of shapes and styles. They can be supplemented with auxiliary structures and accessories, such as dormers, side gables, and skylights.

Truss Roofs

A truss is a lightweight framework of timbers that uses many triangular connections to achieve strength and rigidity. The roof is supported by closely spaced trusses. The roof surface is supported by the top members of the trusses. The bottoms of the trusses act as the ceiling joists for the top floor. Figure 1-106 shows a truss roof being built.

Truss roofs offer these benefits:

- **strength with economy.** Trusses can provide great load carrying capacity with minimum use of materials.
- **clear span.** Trusses can be made to span any desired width. They can provide a clear span from one outside wall to the opposite wall. This allows you to build the uppermost floor of the house without interior load-bearing walls to support the roof. By the same token, the clear span provides unlimited flexibility in locating the interior walls.
- **access for installation and inspection.** The space inside a truss roof remains accessible for installation of wiring, fixtures, and insulation. It allows inspection for damage from moisture and insects.
- **virtually unlimited super-insulation.** The attic space can be designed to accommodate almost any thickness of insulation, allowing a truss roof to have a higher insulation value than other roof types.
- **adaptability to loose fill insulation.** If the floor of the attic space is flat, a truss roof allows the use of loose fill insulation as an alternative to batt insulation.
- **ample space for ventilation cooling.** The large air space above the insulation can be a path for effective cooling ventilation. During warm weather, this reduces heat penetration into the house and extends the life of roofing materials, especially shingles.
- **versatility of shape.** Trusses can be used to produce a roof of almost any shape and complexity, suitable for any style and climate. Figure 1-107 gives examples of various truss designs.

DRW

Figure 1-106. A truss roof being built. It is about to be covered with the sheathing panels that are stacked along the wall. Note the variety of truss shapes needed to create a "hip roof" shape.

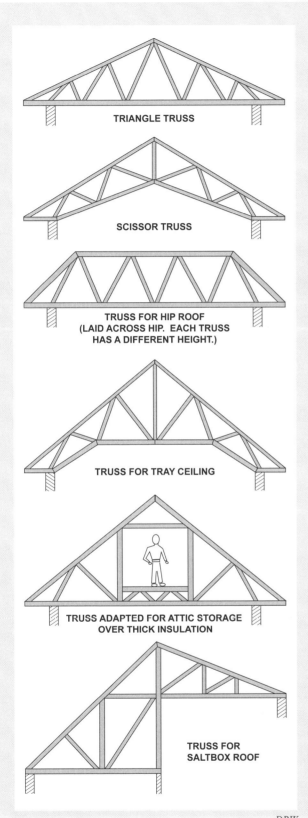

Figure 1-107. A variety of truss designs illustrate the versatility of truss roof construction.

The big disadvantage of a truss roof is that it does not make efficient use of the attic space. For strength, trusses must be fairly tall in relation to their width. The large volume of space within the trusses creates an attic in the finished house, which may or may not be useful. (In this book, we usually limit the term "attic" to mean the space inside a truss roof structure.)

A truss roof must be vented to the outside to protect the structure against moisture damage. Venting exposes the attic to extremes of temperature and humidity. Subject to this limitation, the attic may be adapted to provide a useful amount of storage space, as discussed under *The Attic as Storage Space.*

These days, roof trusses typically are prefabricated in specialized factories. This lowers cost and helps to ensure that the trusses are designed properly. Usually, the home designer tells the truss manufacturer the outer shape of the truss, and an engineer who works for the truss manufacturer designs the size and placement of the truss members.

The truss manufacturer will deliver trusses to the home site using a truck that has a crane to lift the trusses into place. Experienced builders know how to work with truss manufacturers to make this part of the job go smoothly.

Most trusses are spaced at intervals of 16" (40 cm) or 24" (60 cm). If the building will have a sheetmetal or tile roof, the trusses may be spaced at longer intervals, typically 4 feet (120 cm). In this case, the sheetmetal panels are supported by "purlins," which span horizontally across the trusses, as in Figure 1-108.

Figure 1-108. This truss roof uses purlins to support a sheetmetal surface, increasing the distance between the trusses.

Beam Roofs

This book introduces the term "beam roof" to describe a roof whose structure consists of a row of beams, which are supported only at their ends. The beams serve as rafters, which support the upper surface of the roof. Usually, the ceiling of the space below is attached to the bottoms of the beams. Figure 1-109 shows a typical beam roof being built.

Shutterstock

Figure 1-109. A beam roof being built. The beams span between the opposite walls of the house.

Beam roofs have a long history. The flat roofs of Indian pueblos are beam roofs that use poles spanning adobe walls, covered with adobe as a weather surface and cementing agent. Until recently, the flat roofs of the Greek islands used poles spanning between stone walls, with concrete serving as the weather surface and structural binder.

In modern construction, a beam roof is built similarly to a wooden floor, except that it is sloped to shed rain and snow. The roof insulation and the venting space above the insulation are contained within the beam structure.

Figure 1-110 shows common beam roof designs. A beam roof can yield a "shed roof," a gable roof, or a multi-shed roof that includes a clerestory between the roof panels. Other shapes are possible.

Beam roofs can have any slope, but they are most favorable for designs with moderate slopes. A beam roof over a room creates a sloped or "vaulted" ceiling, as in Figure 1-120.

Beam roofs have become more popular in modern homes with the development of wooden I-joists. These allow longer spans than are practical with solid timbers. The strength of a beam and the distance it can span are determined primarily by the

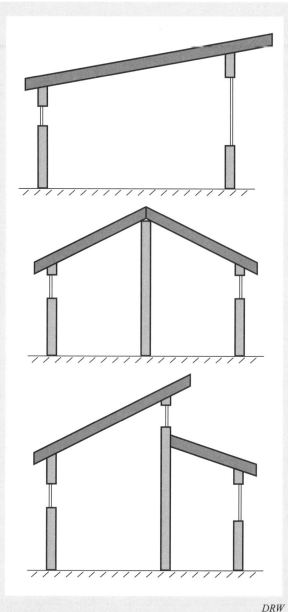

DRW

Figure 1-110. Common beam roof designs. The top is a "shed" roof. The center yields a gable roof. The bottom enables a clerestory window for a rear room.

depth of the beam, which is the distance from the top of the beam to the bottom. For a given roof load, the required depth of beams is proportional to their span.

The depth of the beams may be determined by the span or by the needed amount of insulation. In a super-insulated house, it may be necessary to increase the depth of the beams to accommodate a larger amount of insulation. In a warmer climate, a larger vent space is desirable for ventilation cooling.

The interior of a beam roof becomes inaccessible once the interior sheathing is installed. This makes it is essentially impossible to inspect the interior of a beam roof after the house is completed. Therefore, work out the details of the insulation, venting, insect protection, and other features of the roof before construction. We cover these design issues in Step 3.

By the same token, install any electrical wiring and ceiling fixtures, such as light fixtures and ceiling fans, while the interior of the roof is still accessible.

Triangle-Frame Roofs

We use the name "triangle-frame roof" to describe a roof that is supported by members in the shape of a large open triangle, as in Figure 1-111. This method of roof construction is so common that it does not have a special name in the construction trade. It may be called a "rafter roof" to distinguish it from a truss roof.

The two top members of each triangle are roof rafters. The bottom members serve as floor joists for the space inside the roof and as ceiling joists for the space below. Triangle-frame construction yields a plain gable roof that is usually symmetrical. The rafters generally are steeply sloped. Otherwise, their outward thrust would be excessive.

Figure 1-112. Typical inside structure of a triangle-frame roof, ready to become living space. The useful living space typically is about half the amount on a full floor.

Depositphotos

Figure 1-111. A triangle-frame roof being built over a log house. The vertical framing members at the sides create "knee walls." The horizontal members will create an interior ceiling.

The steep slope yields a large amount of headroom under the roof, making the interior easily adaptable to living space. When the roof is used for living space above a single ground floor, the house is sometimes called a "floor and a half" because the space within the roof structure typically provides about half as much useful space as a full floor.

The side corners of the triangle are not very useful as living space, so they usually are enclosed by "knee walls," which create voids that may be used for storage. The top corner may be cut off to create a horizontal ceiling. Figure 1-112 shows the typical finished structure from inside.

A properly built triangle-frame roof is very strong, and its steep slope sheds snow effectively. Each triangle must be connected strongly at its three corners. The rafters must be deep enough to support the roof load, and the bottom joist must be designed to support the floor and ceiling loads.

Usually, a triangle-frame roof sits on top of a conventional house structure. However, the roof structure can be placed directly on the ground, supported only by a short foundation. This produces an "A-frame" house, which may have one or several floors, as in Figure 1-196. This style of construction was once popular for cottages because of its simplicity and charming shape. However, the interior space layout is not efficient.

A plain triangle-frame roof has windows only in the end walls. Dormers and side gables can be added to a triangle-frame roof to admit sunlight and view through the roof surface, along with a small amount of additional living space. Skylights can also be used to provide sunlight and a limited view, but they are especially vulnerable to leaks if snow accumulates on the roof.

The basic triangle-frame structure is many centuries old, but the addition of insulation has changed its character. As with beam roofs, the rafters must be deep enough to accommodate super-insulation, plus adequate space above the insulation for moisture venting. And, as with beam roofs, routine inspection of the roof structure for moisture or insect damage is impractical after the insulation is enclosed by the interior sheathing.

Gambrel Roofs

A gambrel roof has a cross section that is a five-sided polygon. It has a ridge and two "knuckles," which are breaks in the roof line below the ridge. The gambrel shape offers more living space under the roof than a triangle-frame roof, so a gambrel roof usually encloses the upper story of a two-story house. It typically yields a rustic "barn" appearance on the outside. See Figure 1-200 in the later sidebar, *Roof Styles*.

Gambrel roofs have been built in many ways, because no one method is fully satisfactory. Any gambrel roof design requires compromises between strength, living space, and complexity. Figures 1-113, 1-114, and 1-115 illustrate different methods of construction.

Unlike a triangular roof cross section, the gambrel shape is not stable. A heavy load from above, such as snow, tends to collapse it. A heavy load from the side, such as wind, tends to push it over. Such loads place stress on all five corners. As a result, many older gambrel roofs show a visible sag in the middle, where the roof cannot be supported by the end walls.

In most gambrel roof designs, the end walls prevent the roof from tipping over. Strength is enhanced by using a plywood roof deck, which creates rigid roof panels that resist the tendency of the center portion of the roof to sag.

A gambrel roof offers no compelling advantages, but some serious disadvantages. It has a shallow slope on top, which invites leaks and allows snow to accumulate. It requires dormers to install windows through the roof sides, which increases the complexity and cost of the carpentry. The steep sides make it difficult to install shingles.

Mansard Roofs

A mansard roof has a gambrel shape on all four sides. Figure 1-201, in the later sidebar *Roof Styles*, shows an example. A mansard roof usually encloses the upper story of a multi-story house, and it may also create a short attic above that story.

The mansard design is exclusively an appearance option. Unlike the rustic appearance of most gambrel roofs, the style of a mansard roof is considered to be elegant. The carpentry and detailing are often highly ornate. The eaves may be flared outward to provide wider overhangs and a fancier appearance.

The footprint of a mansard roof usually is a square or a short rectangle. This makes the roof somewhat stronger than a similar gambrel roof. It also constrains the shape of the house and the floor plans.

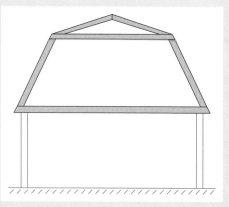

DRW

Figure 1-113. A common gambrel roof structure. The roof is held upright primarily by the end walls. The rafter joints are placed under great stress by side winds and by heavy loads on top of the roof.

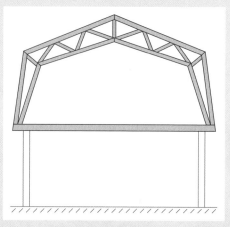

DRW

Figure 1-114. A stronger gambrel roof structure. In effect, it encloses the upper floor in arched trusses. Many variations are possible. The carpentry is complex and space consuming.

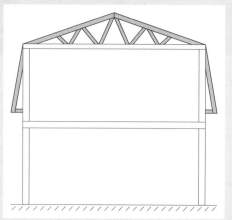

DRW

Figure 1-115. A house that uses conventional "platform" construction, dressed up with a gambrel roof shape. It uses a shallow truss roof and adds sloped sides.

The top of a mansard roof usually has a slope that is even shallower than the top surface of a gambrel roof. To avoid leakage, the top surface roof often uses a special membrane material, which is unattractive and expensive to install.

A mansard roof requires dormer windows to provide daylight and view for the upper floor. The carpentry is complex and expensive.

Flat Roofs

Flat roofs are common in dry climates that use masonry construction. Figures 1-207, 1-208, and 1-209, in the later sidebar *Roof Styles*, show typical examples.

Flat roofs are built on beams that usually are oriented in one direction. The beams are supported by exterior walls, and additional support may be provided by interior load-bearing walls.

Flat roofs made of concrete are common in regions where wooden roof construction is impractical or is more expensive than concrete. Many construction methods are used, based on regional custom. Some are much better than others.

Any "flat" roof should have at least a slight slope for drainage. It can slant toward one edge, collecting the drainage in a gutter. If the roof has a parapet that blocks drainage, slanting the entire roof toward one corner provides drainage at a single point, reducing the area where roof leaks may occur.

The slope of the roof may result in a slightly sloped ceiling below. Or, a level ceiling may be built below the roof, leaving a void space between the roof and the ceiling.

A flat roof on a frame house is a foolish architectural indulgence. It offers no benefit, it invites leaks, and the waterproof surface is ugly.

Flat roofs are advisable only with masonry construction, and only in locations where rain is infrequent and snow is rare.

Later in Step 1, we will design the shape of your roof to provide a beautiful appearance. Your roof structure options allow you achieve virtually any roof shape or style that you want. Make it your design goal to achieve an optimum combination of strength, utility, and beauty.

CEILING HEIGHT AND SHAPE

In the U.S., a ceiling height of 8 feet (about 240 cm) is standard, and a similar height is standard in most countries. This height is fine for most rooms. However, taller ceilings can add grandeur to certain rooms, especially to larger formal rooms. In tract houses, taller ceilings usually are priced as an expensive option. However, they actually add little to construction cost.

In the U.S., ceiling heights up to about 10 feet (about 3 meters) are common alternatives to the normal ceiling height. Wall studs, plywood, and drywall are available in standard 10-foot lengths, which reduces labor cost and waste of materials.

Generally, all the rooms on a given floor will have the same ceiling height. Otherwise, the structure becomes complicated and wasteful. In a multi-story house, the ceiling heights can easily differ between floors. For example, the ground floor may have a ceiling height of 10 feet (3 meters), while the upper floors may have a ceiling height of 8 feet (240 cm).

In a warmer climate, where ceiling fans can be a useful means of cooling and a prominent item of decor, taller ceilings are needed to exploit their appearance and to allow them to operate efficiently. (Step 4 covers ceiling fans.)

In a multi-story house, you can dramatically increase the ceiling height of one room or a group of rooms by eliminating a portion of the floor above. This extends the height of the space to the next ceiling above. For example, this technique is commonly used for large living rooms and full-height entry foyers. The perimeter of the cutaway portion of the upper floor must be supported by beams and columns that transmit the upper floor load to the foundation. See Figure 1-118.

DRW

Figure 1-118. A living room with a mezzanine.

Obviously, this subtracts from the space available on the upper floor.

Not all ceilings are flat, or horizontal. A ceiling can have various shapes, with the options depending mainly on the type of roof structure.

A "cathedral" or "vaulted" ceiling is sloped on two sides, with a ridge along the centerline of the room. Figure 1-119 is an example. This shape usually is achieved by using a scissor truss roof or by using triangular trusses that have their bottom members exposed.

Using a beam roof generally results in a ceiling underneath that is slanted in one plane, as in Figure 1-120.

A "tray" ceiling is a hybrid shape that is flat at the center, but sloped or stepped on the sides. It has that name because it looks somewhat like an inverted serving tray. A tray ceiling may be formed by building soffits or lighting coves around the perimeter of the room. Figure 1-121 is an example. A tray shape may also result from a ceiling that follows the roof rafters up to a certain height, and then becomes horizontal under a partial attic or void.

Gatlinburg Lodge

Figure 1-119. A living room with a cathedral ceiling.

Energy and Comfort Effects of Tall Ceilings

Tall ceilings aid cooling, but they increase the cost of heating. The main reason is stratification, which is the tendency of warmer air to rise to the ceiling and of cooler air to fall to the floor. Stratification occurs when there is a difference in temperature between the inside and the outside.

In the days before air conditioning, fancy houses in warm climates typically had tall ceilings to keep the lower parts of rooms cool, whereas houses in cold climates generally had lower ceilings. In a super-insulated house, heat loss is small, so the effect of stratification is greatly reduced. Raising the ceiling by a foot or two (a fraction of a meter) has a minimal effect on comfort.

In very tall spaces, such as a great room or an entrance foyer that is several stories tall, temperature stratification can become a comfort problem if the space is occupied at both the top and bottom. For example, if a great room has a mezzanine or a loft, the upper level can become significantly warmer than the lower level.

DRW

Figure 1-120. A living room with a slanted ceiling.

Stratification is minimized by good overall insulation of the exterior surfaces. Stratification is magnified by larger glass areas for windows, clerestories, and skylights, all of which have poor insulation value.

Fans can be used to offset stratification in tall spaces, but this technique is not entirely effective. See *Using Fans to Prevent Stratification*, in Step 4.

Depositphotos

Figure 1-121. A tray ceiling breaks up the expanse of ceiling in this large bedroom.

REALITY CHECK: THE SIZE OF YOUR HOME

Now, we are ready to tally the total space that you want to satisfy your desires, and see how that total matches your budget. In the best of cases, you will be able to comfortably afford your entire wish list. But, what if you can't? Don't despair. We will suggest ways to substantially reduce your construction cost. This will include deferring features that you can economically add to your home later.

As a baseline, the minimum floor space for a home for a couple without children is about 600 square feet (60 square meters). This includes a single bedroom, the common appliances of modern countries, modest storage space, and limited space for entertaining guests. For each additional bedroom and its related amenities, add a minimum of 200 square feet (20 square meters). These figures yield living arrangements that are compact. They are more appropriate for apartments than for houses.

The minimum practical size for a detached house is about 1,000 square feet (about 100 square meters). It makes little economic sense to build a house that is smaller. Any house has a fixed minimum cost for land, site preparation, and utilities connections. And, the space requirements of a family generally increase with time.

In many areas, house sizes are much larger than this minimum. In the United States, the average house has about 2,400 square feet (240 square meters) of finished floor space. This allows for several bedrooms, one of which is spacious, a large living room, a separate dining room, and a specialized space, such as an office. These figures do not include an unfinished basement, garage, or deck, which usually are tallied separately.

Houses beyond that size typically have a large number of rooms, including one or more rooms that are very large. For example, a large house may have a "great room" that has the same floor area as a small apartment.

So, how large should your home be? Answer the following questions to reach your decision.

How much total space do you need or want?

You have already taken inventory of all the activities that you want to occur in your home. Calculate the amount of space that you need for each function, add those amounts, and then add another 15% to the sum.

That's your target. Now, let's see if it is realistic.

What size can you afford?

Find out typical costs of construction for custom homes in your area, based on their sizes. You can get this information from builders, from the Internet, and by examining the prices of new homes. Include the cost of the land, insurance, permits, landscaping, paving, and other costs unrelated to the house construction.

If your estimate is uncomfortably high, reconsider your requirements. Don't make yourself "house poor." It will limit your life and cause financial anxiety for the duration of the mortgage.

Be frank with yourself about the size you need. Bigger is not necessarily better. A house can become preposterous if it has a lot of unused space that provides only empty pretense. On the other hand, it makes no sense to build a house that is smaller than you need.

It is common to estimate the cost of a house from its overall size, for example, as dollars per square foot. However, this is only an approximation. These factors also have a large effect on the cost of living space:

- The additional cost of upper floors is typically much less than the cost of a ground floor alone, because upper floors incur little or no additional cost for the foundation or roof. Also, upper floors add nothing to land cost. These factors are largely responsible for the proliferation of 3- and 4-story "townhouses."

- Living space in a basement is less expensive than on the main floors, especially if the site requires a deep foundation. The cost of adding a basement is primarily for a floor slab, drains, and taller foundation walls, plus any fixtures installed in the basement.

- Using triangle-frame roof construction is an inexpensive way to create a large amount of living space within the roof structure.

- Smaller rooms have a higher unit cost than larger rooms because they use more lumber, wall finishing materials, doors, and heating and cooling equipment per unit of space.

- The cost of kitchens, shower rooms, and toilet rooms is much higher per unit of floor space than the cost of other rooms. Their main costs are for piping, wiring, permanently installed fixtures, and waterproof surfaces. The floor space itself is a lesser cost factor for these rooms.

- The cost of unheated garage space is substantially lower than the cost of single-floor occupied space. However, a long concrete driveway leading to the garage is a major cost.

─── HOW TO LOWER YOUR CONSTRUCTION COST ───

☐ For a given amount of floor space, build a multi-story house instead of a single story. But, consider the inconvenience of multiple floors.

☐ Add a basement to provide some of your living space, if your soil conditions allow it. Consider the lower temperature, higher humidity, and limited daylighting of basements, as well as the potential radon hazard. See Step 3.

☐ Use a triangle-frame roof with ample slope so that you can create living space beneath it. Consider the shape limitations of this space and its limited daylighting.

☐ If you build a triangle-frame roof, but you don't immediately need the living space it offers, leave the space unfinished and use it for storage. In that case, insulate the floor of the space.

☐ If you build a basement, but you don't need the living space immediately, leave it unfinished.

☐ Leave the garage unfinished. But, don't make it too small.

☐ Or, leave space for a detached garage, and build it later.

☐ Or, install an inexpensive carport instead of a garage. Arrange the carport so that you can replace it later with a detached garage, or design the house so that you can add an attached garage easily.

☐ Forego a brick veneer, and use a less expensive exterior surface. You can give yourself the option of adding a brick veneer later by adding a "brick shelf" to your foundation, but retrofitting a brick veneer is difficult.

☐ Minimize the number of corners, breaks, and odd angles in the shape of your house, especially in the roof. Use plain roof gables instead of a more complicated shape, such as hip, gambrel, or mansard. Make all corners and breaks useful to enhance your interior room layout and/or to increase the strength of the foundation. However, avoid excessively large, unadorned wall surfaces.

☐ Locate toilet rooms so that they can be shared between bedrooms, and between bedrooms and public spaces. However, install a sufficient number of toilets to provide an alternate during sleeping hours and to avoid conflict during the morning rush. "His and her" toilet enclosures are a worthwhile luxury for couples' bedrooms.

☐ If some of the planned toilet rooms and shower rooms are not needed immediately, "rough in" their plumbing connections and leave them as unfinished storage space.

☐ Don't have a fireplace. Fireplaces are expensive, they waste energy, and they cause discomfort. If you have a reliable source of firewood, consider more efficient wood burning equipment, such as an attractive wood stove. You can install a wood stove later, but create a fire safety zone for it, along with an attractive way to install the flue. See *Heating with Firewood and Other Solid Fuels*, in *Last Look: Energy for Pioneers*, at the end of the book.

☐ Design the interior in a modern style that avoids the need for interior trim carpentry and wallpaper. Painted gypsum wallboard works well for almost any style. You can easily redecorate later by adding wallpaper, crown moldings, chair rails, etc.

☐ Defer exotic countertops. Inexpensive laminate countertops work just fine. You can replace them later with fancier materials.

☐ Use molded plastic shower enclosures of convenient size, instead of building tiled showers. Design at least the main shower rooms so that you can convert them to tiled showers later.

☐ Use ordinary asphalt shingles for the roof, but buy a durable grade. Shingles are available in many colors, and are adaptable to most climates. If you plan to substitute a different type of roof later, design the roof structure to accommodate the change.

☐ Defer the fancy light fixtures, and use attractive budget fixtures. Light fixtures can be upgraded easily.

- ☐ Defer the fancy deck. Design your home to look good without it, but leave space for it in a manner that will blend perfectly with the appearance and function of your home.

- ☐ Defer your outdoor amenities, such as a swimming pool and outbuildings. But, leave space for them in your design.

- ☐ Defer the fancy landscaping. This will also speed your design. Maybe, do the landscaping yourself over the next few years, providing healthful exercise.

- ☐ Do the shopping for appliances, fixtures, and hardware yourself, so your contractor can leave these items out of the bid price. Buy as a "contractor," rather than a "homeowner," as we explain in Step 8. Check prices at discount hardware stores, and on the Internet.

- ☐ Avoid name brand windows, which are overpriced. Use the *Window Selection Guide*, in Step 3, to get the best features.

- ☐ For appliances, plumbing fixtures, and decorative hardware, buy good mass market brands. They can be attractive, efficient, and full of features. They commonly perform better than boutique brands. We will recommend more expensive versions of equipment, such as high-security door locks, where they are needed.

- ☐ For cabinets, buy one of the better mass market brands. Behave like a contractor, and buy them directly from the wholesaler. Get the trade catalogs and learn how to order valuable upgrades, such as strong plywood frames instead of particle board. Select inexpensive door styles, which can be attractive and just as good as the most expensive.

- ☐ Negotiate effectively with your builder. Your best bargaining chips are having a clear, detailed set of drawings and giving the builder confidence that your job will proceed smoothly. We show you how in Step 8.

- ☐ Build during an economic slump, when labor and materials are less expensive. You are more likely to find a good builder who will give your project the attention it deserves. But, don't delay excessively. If the economy is threatened by inflation, build soon to convert your paper money into a lasting asset.

Don't spend more than necessary to achieve the features that you want. If the initial estimate of the cost of your home is uncomfortably close to the limits of your budget, defer some of the deluxe features until after the house is built. For example, if you want a big crystal chandelier for your entrance foyer, install an inexpensive but attractive light fixture to hold its place until your finances improve. See the adjacent sidebar, *How to Lower Your Construction Cost.*

What size is appropriate for the neighborhood and the land value?

If you home will be located in a neighborhood of nearby houses, try to make your house compatible in size with the others. Your home would look strange if it differs greatly in size. This will lower its resale value, whether the house is exceptionally large or exceptionally small. Your real estate tax assessment will be determined largely by the value of the surrounding houses. You benefit from this is your home is large, and suffer a penalty if your home is small.

Land for building homes is becoming increasingly scarce, driving up its price. This fact has contributed to a craze for building houses that are much larger than the owners need, in order to match the cost of the house to the cost of the land. There is some logic to this, but not much. If you build more house than you need or want, all you gain is the hope that you will eventually sell the house for a higher price. In the meantime, you have higher mortgage and tax payments, increased cleaning and maintenance, and a lot of vacant space.

The trend toward larger houses is causing many older houses to be expanded, or to be torn down and replaced with larger houses. If you build in an older neighborhood, consider that you may be surrounded by larger houses eventually.

You can design your home to facilitate an expansion later. However, an expansion will cost a lot more than the same space would cost if it is included in the original house. If the footprint of the house is extended, it is virtually impossible to make a strong structural connection with the original foundation. If you extend the house upward, the house will be vulnerable to weather during the addition. On balance, it is better to make the overall structure big enough for your eventual configuration, and leave some of the space unfinished.

How does size affect your energy requirements?

Rising energy costs and threats of energy shortages motivate people to think about limiting the size of their houses. But, is it really true that smaller houses use less energy?

The answer is not as simple as it may seem. A house consumes energy in two ways: (1) the energy needed to keep the house comfortable and to operate its appliances, and (2) the energy required to build the house and to make its materials.

People are familiar with the first kind of energy – the operating energy – because they have to pay for it every month. Past experience seems to show that the need for operating energy is proportional to the size of a house. But, that is not true of a super-house. Among the Five Principles of Super-Efficiency (introduced at the beginning of this book), three tend to make energy consumption independent of size:

- You can eliminate most energy use in rooms and spaces that are not occupied because your rooms are heated and cooled individually. Groups of rooms that are usually occupied during the same times of the day are clustered together, saving energy. Unoccupied rooms act as insulation for adjacent rooms that are occupied. So, the energy consumption of the house is not determined by its overall size, but by the typical *occupied* area.

- Increasing the insulation of the exterior surfaces compensates for larger surface area. For example, if you double the surface area of a house and also double the insulation value, energy consumption remains about the same.

- You can virtually eliminate air leaks, removing the relationship between building size and air leakage. And, efficient localized ventilation can satisfy the needs of the occupants without regard to the overall size of the house.

So, if you design your home following the principles of this book, you can increase the size of your house without a corresponding increase in its monthly energy bills. A bigger house probably will use more energy, but not much more.

The size of your house does have a big effect on the second kind of energy – the kind needed to make the materials and build the house. This energy is called "embodied" or "embedded" energy. See the sidebar.

How important is embodied energy? In climates that require much heating or cooling, it is less important than the operating energy. For a conventional house in a cold climate, the embodied energy amounts to less than ten years of operating energy. If the house lasts for several centuries, that is a small fraction.

EMBODIED ENERGY: THE HIDDEN ENERGY IN YOUR HOME

The "embodied energy" (or "embedded energy") of a house is the energy that is required to create the materials of the house and to build the house. For example, the embodied energy of lumber includes the energy needed to cut down and transport trees to the sawmill, to cut and dry the lumber, and to transport it to the building site. It also includes the energy used by all the workers who are involved in the production of the lumber.

Building materials differ widely in their embodied energy. Here are some published numbers, expressed in terms of both weight and volume. Look at the relative sizes of the numbers. The units don't matter, unless you are an engineer.

MATERIAL	EMBODIED ENERGY	
	per weight (mJ/kg)	per volume (mJ/m³)
Lumber	2.5	1,400
Plywood	10.4	5,700
Particle board	8.0	4,400
Concrete, poured	1.3	3,200
Concrete block	0.9	2,300
Brick	2.5	5,000
Gravel	0.1	150
Stone, local quarry	0.8	2,000
Gypsum wallboard	6.1	5,900
Shingles, asphalt	9.0	4,900
Glass	15.9	37,500
Carpet, synthetic	150	85,000
Paint	93	117,000
Insulation, cellulose	3.3	112
Insulation, mineral wool	15	140
Insulation, fiberglass	30	970
Insulation, polystyrene	117	3,800
Straw bale	0.24	31
Steel (from ore)	32	251,000
Steel (recycled)	8.9	37,000
Aluminum (from ore)	227	516,000
Aluminum (recycled)	8.1	22,000
Copper	71	631,000
PVC	70	93,600

If you want to study embodied energy further, be forewarned that the subject is complicated. The available information is incomplete, and the numbers are unreliable. Excessive zeal to minimize embodied energy can lead to bad decisions. In particular, don't be lured into using certain "renewable" building materials, such as straw bales and soil. They cannot produce a house that is durable and pleasant. As a reality check, we discuss some of these materials in *Last Look: Energy for Pioneers*, at the end of the book.

Concrete is the largest user of embodied energy in typical houses, even in wood frame houses. This is primarily because a large volume of concrete is needed for the foundation (see Figure 1-123), not because concrete has exceptionally high embodied energy.

Your super-efficient house will use an increased amount of certain building materials – especially insulation – to radically reduce the amount of operating energy that is used over the life of the house. The resulting increase in embodied energy is small in relation to the lifetime saving in operating energy.

All other things being equal, masonry construction has more embodied energy than wood frame construction. However, steel-reinforced concrete is the preferred foundation material for both wooden and masonry houses. And, masonry houses commonly have wooden roofs. Thus, most of the difference between the frame and masonry construction is limited to the walls.

The cost of common bulk building materials is a rough guide to their embodied energy. For example, aluminum roofing material is more expensive than asphalt shingles largely because it requires more energy to make.

Embodied energy is only one of many factors to consider in selecting building materials. Other factors, such as durability, fire safety, and environmental impact, are also important. The materials that we recommend for your home take all the essential selection factors into account, so it is unlikely that other materials will strike a better balance.

DRW

Figure 1-123. Concrete for the foundation of a frame house. Concrete is the largest component of the embodied energy in this house, primarily because of the large volume of concrete that is required. Nonetheless, solid concrete is essential for a good foundation here. Careful design of the forms and the reinforcing steel can minimize the amount of concrete required.

FRAME OR MASONRY CONSTRUCTION?

There are two basic methods of construction for houses — using a wooden frame or using masonry. We will cover the details in Step 3. For a quick comparison, look ahead to *How Houses are Built: the Minimum You Should Know*, at the beginning of Step 3.

In most parts of the United States, in Japan, and in many other countries, wood construction for houses is the norm and masonry is the exception. On the other hand, in many parts of Europe and Asia, masonry is the norm and wood frame construction is rare.

You need to choose the methods of construction at this point because it will affect the remainder of your design in Step 1. Frame and masonry construction offer radically different appearance options. Your space layout is also affected somewhat. For example, you can have overhanging floors with frame construction, but not with masonry. In addition, the choice may have a big effect on energy efficiency, cost, and other qualities of your home.

Start by looking at the prevailing types of construction in your region. Often, these will alert you to factors that you should consider.

These issues tend to **favor frame construction**:

- *Insulation*. Frame construction allows wall insulation to fit easily inside the wall, without requiring extra structure or extra space to hold the insulation. In contrast, masonry itself has poor insulation value, and it may be difficult or impractical to include a high level of insulation in a masonry structure. Insulating masonry structures substantially increases their cost, complicates the design, increases wall thickness, and limits appearance options.

- *Weak terrain and earth movement*. A frame house can be built as a rigid box that keeps its shape even if it is supported only at a few points. For example, a frame house can be built on piers. A well built frame house may topple over in an earthquake, but it will remain intact. In contrast, masonry's lack of tensile strength makes a masonry house more vulnerable to a collapse of the underlying soil or to an earthquake.

- *Expansion and contraction*. Frame construction accommodates the expansion and contraction that occurs with temperature changes, changes in humidity, and aging. In contrast, masonry has no reliable tensile strength, so it tends to crack from contraction that is caused by temperature change and by shrinkage of concrete as it cures.

These issues tend to **favor masonry construction**:

- *Termites and other damaging insects*. Masonry construction is virtually immune to damage by termites and other insects (although some insects can even bore through mortar). In some regions, termites and other insects are such a severe hazard to wooden structures that masonry construction is the default choice. Protecting wooden structures from damaging insects may be impossible, or it may require specialized techniques and continual inspection.

- *Damage from condensation of water vapor*. Masonry structures can be virtually immune from damage by condensation of moisture within the structure, provided that the moisture cannot freeze. In contrast, frame structures are vulnerable to condensation damage. In climates that are warm and humid for extended periods, it is especially difficult to avoid condensation and mildew.

- *Flood damage*. Masonry structures resist flooding damage much better than frame structures. Also, a well reinforced concrete structure has much more resistance to storm surges along a coastline. However, with any kind of construction, flooding will destroy insulation, interior finishes, and furnishings.

- *Thermal lag*. Thick masonry walls act to moderate the temperature inside the house when the days are too hot and the nights are too cold. However, good insulation and effective shading make this benefit unimportant in most climates. See the sidebar, *Can Your House Benefit from Thermal Lag?*

These issues may **favor frame or masonry construction, depending on the circumstances**:

- *Style or cultural preferences*. For example, a California mission style requires masonry construction, while a Queen Anne style requires frame construction.

- *Available construction skills*. If the local builders are unfamiliar with frame construction, it will be difficult to build a good frame house. The same applies to masonry construction, even more so.

- *Resistance to wind damage*. The sheer weight of masonry structures keeps it from flying away, and the thickness of the walls provides rigidity. However, a well designed frame structure can resist wind damage almost as well as a reinforced concrete structure.

CAN YOUR HOUSE BENEFIT FROM THERMAL LAG?

Ancient desert structures with heavy masonry walls and small windows were able to keep their occupants cool during the heat of the day. They also provided some warmth at night. This observation led to the mistaken belief that masonry has good insulation properties. In reality, the insulation value of masonry is poor. However, masonry has the ability to **store** heat from day to night, which results from its great mass.

The storage of heat creates an effect that is called "thermal lag." To understand thermal lag, visualize sunlight striking the outside of a thick masonry wall. The solar heat is absorbed by the outside surface of the wall, whose temperature gradually increases. The higher temperature drives heat deeper into the wall, where more heat is stored. Thus, heat is pushed through the wall by a slowly advancing temperature wave.

When the sun sets, the temperature wave keeps flowing, driven by the temperature differences deep inside the wall. The heat eventually emerges from the inside of the wall, warming the house during the night.

Only thick masonry develops a significant thermal lag. Wooden house structures are too light to store much heat, and they are too thin to develop a useful time lag. In metal structures, heat travels much too quickly to develop a lag.

Should your home's design attempt to exploit thermal lag? It's probably not worthwhile. In order for thermal lag to provide a benefit, three conditions must be satisfied.

First, the climate must be too hot in the daytime and too cold at night, and this pattern must repeat regularly. A daily cycle of hot-and-cold is common on islands and deserts extending from the middle latitudes to the equator, but it is unusual elsewhere. Thermal lag is not useful if the weather stays too cold or stays too warm for several days or longer.

Second, the masonry must be thick enough to create a temperature lag of at least several hours. A thickness of about two feet (60 centimeters) is needed for thermal lag to work well. Such thickness is encountered in multi-story walls made of natural stone. Walls made of poured concrete or concrete blocks are barely thick enough to provide a significant benefit.

Concrete and clay blocks that are made with large cavities have about the same thermal time lag as solid masonry of the same thickness. However, they have reduced heat storage capacity, so they are less able to offset large day-to-night temperature swings.

Third, the masonry must be exposed to the outside and to the interior of the house. And preferably, the exterior surface should be exposed to direct sunlight to store a useful amount of heat for warming at night.

Insulating the exterior surface kills the lag effect by isolating the masonry from the changes in outdoor temperature. Insulating the interior surface isolates the house from the benefit of thermal lag. So, **thermal lag is incompatible with insulation**. In a contest between thermal lag and insulation, insulation usually wins.

Thermal mass **inside** a house can store solar heat if it is exposed to sunlight that enters through windows and other glazing. This is a feature of "passive solar" design, which typically yields more trouble than benefit. (See *Passive Solar Heating*, under *Last Look: Energy for Pioneers*, at the end of the book.) In a house with well designed glazing, the mass of conventional interior surfaces, such as gypsum board, is adequate to exploit the heating of the surfaces by sunlight. It's not worthwhile to increase the interior mass further, unless the glazing is larger than optimum.

• **Maintenance**. A brick or stone wall will require little or no maintenance, except perhaps for touching up the mortar joints every century or so. A well built masonry veneer offers the same benefit for a frame wall. However, lightweight exterior finishes for frame houses require periodic painting or replacement.

• **Cost**. The relative cost of frame and masonry construction depends on the location. When you make a cost comparison between the two, include the differences in the costs of the foundation, the insulation, and exterior finishes. A masonry structure needs an especially strong foundation, and it may still need a frame structure to carry adequate insulation. If either style of construction is uncommon at your home site, scarcity of skills and materials may increase its cost considerably.

ADDITIONS TO AN EXISTING HOUSE

If you own a house and you want more space, you have three choices. You can build a new house. You can trade up to a larger existing house. Or, you can expand the house you own.

Building a new house is the only way to reap all the benefits that this book offers, and it allows you to customize the house exactly as you want. Also, most of the benefits of a super-house, such as a highly efficient heating system, are less expensive to include in a new house than to retrofit to an existing house.

On the negative side of the ledger, the cost of building a larger house typically is much higher than the cost of adding space to an existing house. However, that may not be true if you want a much larger house. In that case, it may be less expensive to buy a piece of land and build your ideal house on it. Or, if land is scarce where you want to live, you might tear down an existing house, and replace it entirely with a larger house. The so-called "teardown" is becoming common in urban areas where little vacant land remains.

The option of trading up to a larger existing house has two major limitations. One is that you probably won't find exactly the room layout and other features that you want. The other is that it will be impractical to add all the super-features in this book to an existing house. And, it will be more expensive to add the features that are possible. Houses everywhere are built to lower standards than this book recommends, so don't expect to trade up to an existing super-house.

This leaves the option of expanding an existing house. In many cases, this proves to be the best choice. Expanding existing houses has been done through the ages. Now that land is becoming increasingly scarce, additions are becoming larger and bolder.

Small additions tend to be expensive in relation to the amount of space added, typically costing several times more than the same amount of space in a new house. However, the situation reverses if you build a large addition. In that case, the cost of the addition is often lower than the cost of moving to a house of the same ultimate size.

For example, in the neighborhood where I live, modest tract houses built after World War II typically are about 1,000 square feet (100 square meters) in size. Many of them have recent additions that double their original size, and in several cases, triple the original size.

A multi-room addition not only will increase the total living space, but it may provide a room layout that is more luxurious. For example, in expanding my house from 1,000 square feet (100 square meters) to 2,400 square feet (240 square meters), I was able to add a much larger living room, a large master bedroom, and a large office. The original master bedroom became a dressing room, and the original living room became the dining room. One of the smaller bedrooms became a sewing room. The original basement is unchanged, but it was extended outward to provide the office. The total cost was much less than the cost of moving to a larger house, which still would not have provided a room layout that I wanted.

Additions often require compromises. For example, in my house addition, it was not practical to add more toilet and shower facilities at reasonable cost. This would have been a serious disadvantage for a larger family.

You can make the addition itself as attractive and energy efficient as a new house, but it is generally impractical to bring the original part of the house up to the standards of a super-house. This is partly compensated by the fact that the addition covers a large part of the exterior surface area of the original house, reducing its heat loss. Also, in a large addition, you can locate the most active rooms within the addition. This allows you to minimize the heating and cooling that is needed for the original part of the house.

For example, in my greatly enlarged house, the present total energy consumption is significantly lower than it was in the original house. And, the original toilet and shower rooms all became interior space, with no cold exterior walls, making them comfortable during cold weather.

The construction techniques for an addition are the same as for building a new house. However, designing a large addition requires additional creativity. For example, you may have to convert some of the original windows into interior doors. The structural connections between the old and new structures are especially important, and it may take some thought to work them out satisfactorily.

Now, let's look at your three options for expanding an existing house: adding an upper floor, adding a horizontal extension, or doing both.

ADDING UPPER FLOORS

It is becoming popular to increase the size of existing single-story houses by tearing off the roof and building upward on the existing walls. The previous heading, *Single- or Multi-Story?*, presents the pros and cons of having a multi-story house.

If the original house has an attic, you may leave the original ceiling in place or you may remove it. Experience seems to teach that you will get better results by tearing off the ceiling along with the roof. This avoids the need to work around the original ceiling joists and the clutter in the original attic. Also, it is easier to install new electrical wiring, thermostat wiring, plumbing connections, etc.

While the roof is removed, it is almost impossible to protect the interior of the house from rain and snow. Therefore, the new structure and roof must be installed quickly. While this is happening, it is best to vacate the house entirely, put vulnerable furnishings into storage, cover everything else, and be prepared to remove any rainwater that accumulates.

Usually, the new upper floor is a frame structure, even if the original walls are masonry. Figure 1-104 shows a typical example of an upper floor addition, flanked by houses of the original height. Figures 1-124 and 1-125 show fancier additions of this kind.

Adding a second story approximately doubles the living space. Often, the floor joists of the new upper floor overhang the original walls by about two feet (60 cm) on one or both sides. This is an easy and inexpensive way to increase the area of the upper floor. However, a stairway must be added, which deducts from the total living space.

The resulting floor plan is typical of most two-story houses. The rooms that are occupied mainly during

DRW

Figure 1-125. Another attractive second story addition.

the daytime remain on the ground floor. Most of the upper floor is occupied by "bedrooms," along with their associated toilet and shower rooms.

Another option is to remove the original roof and replace it with a roof that has a steeper slope, thereby adding living space under the roof. Figure 1-126 shows an example. This approach provides less space than adding an entire floor, and the cost per unit of additional space is higher.

You are not limited to adding one floor level to a house. You could add two or more, provided that you are certain that the foundation and the load-bearing walls can support the additional weight. Building codes may impose additional requirements if a house is taller than two stories, so check that issue if you want to add more than one level.

Usually, it is easiest to expand upward if the original house has *structural* masonry walls, such as concrete block or brick-and-block. When you remove the existing roof, you are unlikely to find nasty surprises that you can't overcome.

If the original walls are frame construction, you may not be able to tell whether they are built strongly enough to support the additional floor and walls. However, it is usually possible to reinforce

DRW

Figure 1-124. An attractive second story addition. The result matches the original style well. The house was originally identical to the one at its left.

DRW

Figure 1-126. Increasing the roof slope to convert a low attic into living space. The house to the right shows the original slope.

the original walls, if needed. To inspect and reinforce the original walls, remove the outer sheathing, one wall at a time. Strengthen the walls, if necessary, by inserting additional structural members. At the same time, maximize the insulation in the wall, as we explain in Step 3.

The exterior sheathing is an important structural component of the wall. If necessary, replace the original sheathing with strong plywood. Figure 1-127 shows an example of such an addition. Step 3 explains how to install exterior sheathing to create a strong wall.

Adding an upper floor is most difficult if the original house has brick veneer walls. The brick veneer makes it difficult to inspect the original walls, and makes it impossible to replace the exterior sheathing. The brick itself should not carry any load in a veneer wall. Unless you are sure that the wall construction is adequate, you

DRW

Figure 1-127. Adding a second story to a house that has frame walls. The original board sheathing of the exterior walls is being replaced with plywood sheathing for additional strength. This modification is in the wrong sequence. The lower walls should have been strongly reinforced before adding the second story.

would have to remove the brick veneer. It's not impossible, but it is a big deal. Certain kinds of brick can be salvaged and reused, while others can't be. The original windows and doors probably would not survive, making it prudent to replace them with better models at the same time you build the addition.

Adding Stairs to an Existing House

You will need a stairway to reach the new upper floor(s). Design the stairway to satisfy the requirements that we explained previously, under the heading *Moving Between Floors*.

Adding a stairway within the original floor plan of an existing house is likely to be awkward. For example, one expansion that I witnessed placed the stairway in the middle of the original living room. Don't do anything like that.

Instead, it is usually best to build a stairway enclosure outside the original footprint of the house, as in Figure 1-128. On the original ground floor, the stairway can connect through an existing door, or a window can be converted into a door.

The stairway structure needs its own foundation. In addition, attach the stairway enclosure securely to the house wall.

EXPANDING HORIZONTALLY

In the past, most additions were attached to a side of the house. This can be done with any kind of original structure. Also, if you are starting with a single-story house, this approach avoids the disadvantages of multiple stories.

Figure 1-129 shows a typical horizontal addition. Figure 1-130 is the addition that I made to my house, in which both the main floor and the basement level were extended horizontally.

The biggest challenge in extending a house horizontally is creating a secure structural connection between the old and new portions of the house. Without this, the addition may settle independently of the house, creating a gap between the two that looks bad, leaks heat, and is an entrance for vermin.

The key to minimizing such future trouble is to build the addition on a firm foundation, going as deep as necessary to rest on solid soil or bedrock. Step 3 explains how to build a good foundation.

If conditions permit, the foundation of the addition should be joined to the foundation of the original house with steel reinforcing rods (called "rebar"). The rebar is drilled and cemented into the original

DRW

Figure 1-128. In this second story addition, the stairway has been placed in a structure outside the original footprint of the house, at the right.

DRW

Figure 1-129. A typical horizontal addition that is aligned with the original ridge line of the house. The addition matches the original style well.

foundation, with ample length extending into the new foundation. The adjoining part of the new foundation should be designed to reinforce the original foundation. This is needed because any settlement of the addition will tend to break the old foundation. This method of connection requires thought. In many cases, connecting the foundations would not be practical.

The walls of the addition should be joined to the walls of the original house as securely as possible. Generally, a strong connection is practical if an addition with frame walls is being added to a house with frame walls or solid masonry walls. Unfortunately, it is difficult or impractical to make a strong connection between between new and old masonry or masonry veneer. In such cases, stability depends entirely on the foundation.

Expanding a house horizontally reduces the exposure of the house interior to weather during construction, compared to adding an upper floor. However, weather is still a hazard. For example, during my house expansion, rain entered the original roof where it had been cut away to connect to the new roof. The rain traveled through the attic, did widespread damage to the ceiling, and (fortunately) drained through the ceiling light fixtures.

A lot of horizontal additions are plain, or even ugly. The most common stylistic mistake is using a shed roof that extends from the original roof. As a rule, design a roof for the addition that matches the appearance of the original roof, typically with a matching gable.

DRW

Figure 1-130. A horizontal addition, perpendicular to the original ridge line, that extends both the main floor and the basement level. Attaching the addition to the original foundation and masonry structure was challenging.

EXPANDING BOTH UPWARD AND OUTWARD

Many homeowners are maximizing the potential of adding space to an existing house by building both upward and outward. Figures 1-131 and 1-132 are two examples. Such aggressive expansion combines the advantages, shortcomings, and construction methods of both approaches.

DRW

Figure 1-131. A house expanded both upward and rearward. The house originally was identical to the one at the left.

DRW

Figure 1-132. Another house expanded both upward and rearward. In this case, only the second floor is extended rearward, with the extension supported on columns. The house originally was identical to the one at the left.

BEAUTIFUL EXTERIOR SHAPES AND SURFACES

Now that we have organized the functions, interior layout, and vertical arrangement of your home, we will create a beautiful exterior for it. This is mostly a matter of *shapes* and *surfaces*.

When you look at a house from a distance, you see large shapes and their colors. The main shapes are the walls, the windows, and the roof. These primary shapes can be enhanced by attachments, such as entrances, porches, and balconies. Most of these are functional, but you can also add shapes that are purely decorative. The first step in creating a beautiful exterior is to organize your home's exterior shapes in a well proportioned manner.

As you get closer to a house, you see the surface textures and the detailing of walls, windows, and roof. You have a large palette of choices for making these surfaces interesting, and you can combine them in many ways.

The combination of shapes and surfaces that create the appearance of a house is commonly called its "architectural style." Let's start there.

YOUR ARCHITECTURAL STYLE

Homeowners tend to begin their planning with a particular architectural style in mind, but that's a mistake. Selecting your architectural style is not the first decision you should make. Instead, it should be one of the last, made after you have considered all the design issues related to the space layout that you want. The architectural style is the wrapping on the package.

Prior to the 20th century, houses tended to have an appearance that was characteristic of the location and the era in which they were built. Such localized appearance has come to be called the "architectural style" of the house. For example, the "California mission" style combined adobe walls with barrel tile roofs. Other combinations of features result in architectural styles with names such as "Tudor," "Georgian," "New England saltbox," or "rancher." Today, architectural styles are much less localized.

The architectural style begins with the exterior shape of the house, which is determined mostly by the number of floors, the appearance of the walls and windows, and by the shape of the roof. The style may also involve attachments, such as deep encircling porches that are a characteristic of southern U.S. coastal houses. It may also involve details, such as cedar shingle wall surfaces, "Palladian" windows, and fancy roof edge trim.

Some styles have significant benefits and/or disadvantages. For example, the New England saltbox style has no overhangs and it uses cedar shingles as siding. Selecting this style sacrifices all the benefits of overhangs, and it incurs a periodic cost for replacing the siding. Some styles require special materials and skills, which may be expensive or difficult to find. For example, the highly decorated Queen Anne style requires a large amount of skilled trim carpentry.

Keep Your Style Consistent

The architectural style is a unifying theme for your home's appearance. Keep the theme consistent. One of the biggest stylistic mistakes is mixing styles that prove to be incompatible.

For example, a wealthy couple hired an architect to design the home in which they expect to live the rest of their lives. The wife likes Moorish architecture, but the husband likes modern architecture. The couple never resolved their differences in taste. The architect listened passively to each spouse in turn. His solution was to add some Moorish detailing to a severe box design with a flat roof. This house was actually built. It is now an ugly blight on a neighborhood of grand older houses.

If you want to have funky features, like a big ornate cupola on your roof, make the rest of the house funky in a compatible way. If your taste is "eclectic," recognize that as a style. It must be consistent, too. In general, it is wise to avoid strange house shapes, such as geodesic domes or other oddities. If you are tempted to go in that direction, see *Unusual Structures*, in *Last Look: Energy for Pioneers*, at the end of the book.

DRW

Figure 1-135. An unfortunately common combination of brick veneer and vinyl siding. The siding betrays the brick as a veneer, which looks cheap when used partially.

DRW

Figure 1-136. A combination of brick and stone veneers, whose appeal is a matter of taste.

Within limits, the interior style is independent of the exterior style. A "modern" interior is compatible with most kinds of exteriors. Interior furnishings, appliances, and surfaces have become so standardized that they can look good in any kind of house.

But, the reverse is not true. An interior that evokes a particular location or time period should be matched with a corresponding exterior style. For example, an interior style based on Colonial furnishings and decor would seem strange in a house with an austere modern exterior.

Be cautious about combining different styles of wall surfaces. For example, many tract houses and even some custom homes use a brick or stone veneer on the front wall, but not on the other walls, as in Figure 1-135. This is supposed to add a touch of class. Instead, it makes the whole house look cheap. It says that you are putting up a false front, literally.

It has become popular to mix brick and stone surfaces. For example, Figure 1-136 is one of many such combinations. Think twice before doing this, because it is non-historical. Hence, it will look fake. Houses originally were built with either brick or stone, but not both. Architects sometimes use some stone as trim for a brick wall, or *vice versa*, but this risks a patchy appearance. Similarly, it is risky to combine bricks of different color and texture. Avoid such combinations unless you can copy the style of an existing house that you like.

Look Good in the Neighborhood

As you select your style, consider the geographic location and the other houses in the neighborhood. For example, a California mission style would look strange in a neighborhood of Colonial houses. The Deep South style with wide porches all around the house is well adapted to warm climates, keeping the interior of the house cool and providing lots of shaded exterior space. The same style would be a misfit in a cold climate.

Consider the appearance of the neighborhood. If it has a consistent theme, such as Colonial or Swiss Chalet, be cautious about departing from that theme. A glaring exception won't be appreciated, and it may turn your house into a white elephant with low market value.

A neighborhood may look good with houses having a diversity of styles, in which case the variety of styles becomes a dominant theme of the neighborhood as a whole. Doing this well requires effective visual separation of the houses. This requires a minimum lot size. Trees and tall shrubbery are effective for separation. If the neighborhood is built on hilly terrain, differences in elevation also create visual separation.

How Energy Efficiency Affects Your Choice of Style

Energy efficiency is compatible with most architectural styles, but not with all. Styles with large areas of windows or skylights cannot be energy efficient if the climate has a cold season. During cold weather, large glass area increases energy cost, causes discomfort, and invites other trouble. Step 2 explains how to get the most benefit from the glass that you use. If you want to have large expanses of glass in a cold climate, efficiency requires you to limit that craving to one or two special rooms, as we will explain.

Your home will have unusually thick insulation for the walls, roof, and floors. In your super-insulated walls, it is easy to exploit the increased wall thickness as an appearance enhancement. In your super-insulated roof, the thickness of the insulation requires some tricks to keep your roof line from looking clunky. Step 3 explains the tricks.

The energy saving approach of this book never requires your home to have unattractive or peculiar features, such as a covering of dirt ("earth-sheltered construction") or a huge greenhouse wall. Those were experimental concepts that failed, and they proved to be unnecessary.

Unusual appearance features are needed only if you decide to pursue certain efficiency concepts to their limit. Probably the only such concept worth considering is a "cool roof" for a warm climate. Step 3 explains cool roofs, including their appearance.

BEAUTIFUL WINDOWS

For centuries, windows have been a primary appearance feature of houses. Their sizes, forms, and placement largely determine the style of the house, and whether the house looks elegant or clunky.

Windows are so important that we devote all of Step 2 to the design of your windows and other glazing. Windows perform five vital functions, one of which is to serve as a primary element of your architectural style. So, as you consider the role that windows will play in your home's style, look ahead to Step 2. Don't select the sizes and locations of your windows until you have coordinated the appearance of your windows with their other functions.

In particular, the total size of the windows is now recognized as a major factor in home energy cost. In the past, the usual practice was to select an architectural style and to size the glass to fit the style. We will take a more efficient approach. Based on the climate and the needs of each room, select the minimum amount of glass that will serve your needs. Windows don't have to be the primary appearance feature of your walls. We will offer other ways to make the exterior of your home beautiful.

Window Shape

For all or most of your windows, the basic rectangular shape is all you need to create a fine appearance. Standard rectangular windows are inexpensive. It is easy to make wall openings for them, and it is easy to install insulation around them. Standard windows offer the most advanced energy efficiency features, not all of which are available with custom windows. Well-made mass production windows are also less likely to develop leaks between multiple panes, and they are less expensive to replace.

That being said, a window with a special shape may provide a nice accent, setting off the rectangular windows. But, use such highly stylized windows with discretion, usually no more than one on a wall.

Circular and elliptical windows can effectively fill a small wall space, typically under a gable end, as in Figure 1-139.

DRW

Figure 1-140. Fanlight window. This style typically is used to fill the apex of a gable end wall, as here.

A "fanlight" is a window that is a segment of a circle, as in Figure 1-140. Semicircular and quarter circle fanlights generally are used at the top of a gable end wall. A semicircular fanlight may also be placed above a door, acting as a transom window. This requires a tall ceiling for the space inside the door.

In some modern home styles, windows with a polygon shape can look good, as in Figure 1-141. Generally, windows with polygon shapes are less expensive to make on a custom basis than rounded windows, and they are easier to install.

Figure 1-139. A fancy elliptical window highlights a dormer of a house that is decorated with extensive filigree.

DRW

Figure 1-141. A window with polygon elements. This shape of custom non-opening window is relatively inexpensive to make.

DRW

Figure 1-142. Palladian window. Generally, it is centered on a gable end wall. Only one window of this style should be used on a wall, and it should be larger than other windows. The structure is weak, because the brick above the rectangular sides lacks support.

Window shapes can be combined to produce a dominant shape in a wall. A common example is a "palladian" window, which uses a semicircular window on top of a wider rectangular window, as in Figure 1-142.

Prior to the mid-20th century, double-hung and casement windows were the only styles that could be opened for ventilation. Both of these styles were tall and narrow, creating a "classic" shape for windows. Unfortunately, the old types allowed considerable air leakage. Modern energy-efficient windows have a different appearance, which may conflict with older architectural styles. For example, a Colonial style does not look authentic with horizontal slider windows.

Positioning the Windows in the Wall

From the inside of a room, the positioning of the windows has major effects on view, privacy, daylighting, and esthetics, which are design issues that we will cover in Step 2. From the outside of the house, the positioning of the windows is important in creating a harmonious appearance.

There are no sacred rules for attractive window placement. However, some arrangements naturally look good, and some don't. The best way to learn is to observe lots of houses, judging whether their window size and placement make the house look attractive. Generally, these guidelines will yield an elegant appearance:

- Use identical shapes and sill heights for most windows at each floor level in a wall. This becomes more important as the number of windows increases.

- If windows are grouped, space them evenly within the group. Set apart windows of contrasting size, either by physical distance or by some feature of the wall, such as a change in surface materials.

- If you install a fancy window as a focal point of a wall, locate the other windows on the same wall in a manner that complements the main window.

- Leave space between the tops of windows and the roof line, including separation from the fascia board or frieze under the roof line.

- Similarly, if the top of a window is decorated with a lintel, arch, or cornice, leave ample wall space above that feature.

DRW

Figure 1-143. A palladian window and a porthole window that are placed elegantly in a gable end wall.

DRW

Figure 1-144. A graceless clutter of windows that misuses several potentially attractive styles.

If you use any kind of stylized accent window as a focal point for a wall, its location is critical. Place it symmetrically, and don't crowd it with other shapes or decorative features. For example, Figure 1-143 shows how a large palladian window and an attractive porthole window are centered in a gable end wall with well balanced spacing.

In contrast, Figure 1-144 shows several potentially attractive windows that look awkward because they are thrown on a gable end wall haphazardly, broadcasting to onlookers that money was spent without taste.

Highlight Your Windows

In centuries past, windows had to be assembled from small pieces of glass, called "lights." A wooden framework of "muntins" held the lights. The muntins gave the glass a characteristic texture. But, modern glass manufacturing technology produces glass in large sheets, so that is how most windows use it.

As a result, muntins are now obsolete. To preserve the classic appearance, it is common to lay fake muntins over the glass. However, it is glaringly obvious that these are fake, especially with double glazing. Also, fake muntins tend to warp away from the glass, making windows look shabby. It's best that we abandon our taste for muntins, even with "classic" architectural styles.

You might use decorative glass for selected windows that do not offer a view. Decorative glass may use colors ("stained glass"), etched designs, or molded patterns. It may be flat or embossed, and it may have high or low light transmission. Figure 1-145 shows a nice example. Decorative glass has not been used much in recent years, but it is making a comeback. The *Window Selection Guide*, in Step 3, says more about decorative glass options.

Studio 66 Custom Design Stained Glass

Figure 1-146. Stained glass transom window over a main entrance.

DRW

Figure 1-147. The windows in this classic Gettysburg, Pennsylvania house are highlighted with contrasting cornices and casings.

Rose Window Stained Glass

Figure 1-145. Decorative glass provides daylighting with privacy for this shower room.

DRW

Figure 1-148. Rectangular windows in a brick wall are nicely accented with arches and wooden shutters.

DRW

Figure 1-149. Rectangular windows in this masonry wall are framed with moldings made from shell concrete, providing a distinctive texture.

Generally, limit decorative glass to individual windows that stand apart from the main view windows. For example, it can be used in a "transom window" over a main entry door, as in Figure 1-146. Or perhaps, use stained glass in a window that is installed halfway up a staircase.

You generally won't use decorative glass in your main windows, but you can accentuate the windows with features that surround them. With frame walls, you can use real or simulated shutters, flower boxes, a painted "frame," and other things. Figure 1-147 shows a classic example.

With brick surfaces, you can use fancy lintels, contrasting brickwork, shutters, and other highlighting. Figure 1-148 shows an attractive example.

With plain masonry surfaces, such as stucco, you can "frame" windows with formed stonework, as in Figure 1-149. Or, use decorative paintwork, as in Figure 1-150.

Step 3 introduces a method of installing windows that makes them easy to replace. (Unfortunately, modern "insulating" windows must be replaced periodically.) This method creates a visible band around the window on the outside wall. (See Figure 3-217, for example.) You can decorate this band with a distinctive color, a pattern, or whatever.

In addition, the thicker walls that your home will use for super-insulation create a nice "window box" interior appearance. This allows you to decorate your deep window sills in many ways. See the sidebar, *Fancy Window Sills*, in Step 3.

DRW

Figure 1-150. The small windows in this stucco wall are emphasized and imaginatively decorated with simple paintwork.

BEAUTIFUL WALL SURFACES

The wall surfaces are one of the three main appearance elements of a house, along with the windows and the roof. There are many ways to make them attractive. Base your choices primarily on appearance, longevity, and cost.

A primary decision is whether you will use frame or masonry construction. This decision fundamentally affects the appearance of the house, and it has other important consequences. Refer back to the topic, *Frame or Masonry Construction?*, before you make your choice.

Lightweight Wall Surfaces

Lightweight surfaces are popular because they are relatively inexpensive, and they can be installed quickly. They require no separate structural support because they are attached directly to the wall.

If you are renovating an existing house, it is practical to change an existing lightweight surface, creating an entirely different appearance.

These are the main types of lightweight surfaces:

- *Clapboard siding* consists of wooden boards that are overlapped horizontally. Figure 1-153 is an example. Clapboard may last for centuries if well protected, but most wood requires periodic painting. This style provides superior rain protection, while providing texture to the wall. It also provides essential moisture venting of the exterior wall surface. Boards can be repaired individually, which is desirable especially because boards near the bottom of the wall tend to decay first.

- *Aluminum clapboard siding* is intended to mimic wooden clapboard siding in appearance. It has good longevity if it is coated with enamel of high quality. It requires no maintenance during its lifetime, but it is vulnerable to dents.

- *Plastic (vinyl) lapped siding* also mimics wooden clapboard. It may have a variety of colors and embossed textures. Longevity is limited because the material becomes brittle from exposure to sunlight.

- *Board-and-batten siding* consists of wide boards installed vertically, with narrow boards (called "battens") to cover the gaps. Figure 1-154 is an example. In comparison with clapboard siding, it is less resistant to rain, and it requires wider boards. Rot near the bottom of the wall cannot be repaired locally.

- *Ribbed metal siding*, with the ribs oriented vertically, mimics wooden board-and-batten siding. The material is similar to sheetmetal roofing. Dents in the ribs stand out unattractively, and they are practically impossible to remove.

- *Cedar shingles* resist insects and weathering. They are rough in texture, cut square, and usually are left unpainted. They change color dramatically, from brown to grey, as they weather. Figure 1-155 is a well rendered example.

- *Decorative wooden shingles* can be shaped to create various appearances. Figure 1-156 is a beautiful example. They require periodic painting, and they will rot in a wet climate unless well protected by overhangs.

DRW

Figure 1-153. Wooden clapboard siding. Wood has been replaced almost entirely by aluminum and vinyl siding, which requires no painting.

DRW

Figure 1-154. Board-and-batten siding. Wooden boards of adequate width are expensive and increasingly scarce. Ribbed metal siding with a similar appearance is vulnerable to dents.

DRW

Figure 1-155. Cedar shingles used as siding. Cedar changes color dramatically with sunlight and rain exposure. It generally is not painted, but it may be treated with a preservative to extend its life and original color.

DRW

Figure 1-156. Decorative wooden shingles. These are used with ornate styles. They can be cut to various shapes.

- *Stucco* is a plaster material. It is inexpensive, and it can be dressed up by using various surface textures, decorative paint designs, false half-timbering, and other things. It is the most common covering for concrete walls, providing excellent adhesion and longevity. Figure 1-157 is an attractive example. Similar materials made for plywood sheathing don't perform as well.

DRW

Figure 1-157. Stucco over concrete walls. Paint color is the most common appearance option.

- *Paint* provides color and limited moisture protection by itself, and it is used as the ultimate surface of most other lightweight surfaces. We will devote a separate discussion to decorating walls with color.

- *Other materials* are sometimes used, usually to provide an exotic appearance. For example, you could cover the walls of your tropical hut with palm leaves.

As a rule, frame construction uses lightweight siding materials, whereas concrete block walls are covered with stucco, brick, or stone. Most of the surfaces that are used with frame walls can be installed on concrete walls, but attaching them securely to masonry is problematic.

The main shortcoming of lightweight wall surfaces is that they are not as durable as masonry surfaces, and they require periodic maintenance or replacement. Roof overhangs multiply the life of all lightweight surfaces by shielding them from rain and sunlight.

For example, cedar shingles may last for a century on a wall that is sheltered by deep overhangs, but they may degrade within a few years on a wall that is not sheltered. (Overhangs provide other major benefits, which we list below.)

Among the modern lightweight siding materials, enameled aluminum has the greatest longevity. It is the most expensive in terms of initial cost, but it is economical in the long term. It also protects the exterior of the wall from external fire.

The main disadvantage of sheetmetal siding is that it retains dents. Don't install it where it is likely to be hit by baseballs, lawn furniture, etc. Big dents can occur where the aluminum is held away from the wall, as with conventional clapboard pattern siding. A crushed metal surface is virtually impossible to restore to a good appearance.

Metal surface materials also interfere with radio and television reception that depends on antennas.

Vinyl plastic siding is popular because it is cheap. It requires no maintenance while it lasts, but it has relatively short life. All plastics lose their strength and become brittle after a few years of exposure to weather. The material becomes vulnerable to cracking from stress at the nails, from baseball hits, etc.

Brick Surfaces

A brick exterior can survive as long as the house, if the brick is well made. Brick is immune to damage by sunlight, and it tolerates wetting by rain. It requires little maintenance or cleaning. Figure 1-160 shows a nice example of a brick house that is attractive without the addition of expensive decorations.

When a brick surface is used with a masonry wall, the combination is called "brick-and-block" construction. If the brick is cemented and interlocked to the concrete block, the brick itself contributes to the strength of the wall. If the brick is not attached in this manner, it is a decorative covering that adds no strength to the wall.

In North America, it is common to add a brick exterior surface to frame construction. This is called a "brick veneer." A brick veneer provides the appearance and longevity benefits of brick as a wall covering, but the brick plays no role in the structure of the house.

There is concern about cracking of brick and mortar joints by expansion and contraction of the walls from temperature changes. These concerns focus mostly on brick veneers, but brick-and-block is also vulnerable. The construction industry is still struggling to define bricklaying procedures to avoid the problem. That being said, you can find buildings that are centuries old with brick walls that are fully intact. We cover the construction issues in Step 3.

Brick walls can be beautiful or drab, and the difference can have little relationship to cost. Beautiful brickwork is mostly a matter of taste and skill. You have to provide the taste, and your mason must provide the skill. Artistic masonry work became almost extinct in the 20th century, but fortunately it seems to be coming back. Make an effort to find the right mason and you will be rewarded with a house that stands out for its beauty.

DRW

Figure 1-160. A beautiful brick house that uses no special types of brick or fancy trim. The key ingredients are a fine sense of style and skilled bricklaying.

■ Kinds of Brick

Most brick is made by baking clay in a kiln at high temperature. The color and strength of the brick is determined by the clay that is used. Most clay brick has a generally brown color, but the shade may vary from reddish to grey. Various surface textures are offered.

The life of clay brick varies with the quality of the clay, the quality of manufacture, and the weather. Good brick may last for several centuries, while brick of lesser quality may erode seriously in one century. Increasingly acidic rain may shorten the life of all masonry. By the same token, protecting brick surfaces under wide roof overhangs may keep brick looking fresh for generations.

Brick color varies from one batch to another. Therefore, your mason should sort through the bricks from all the pallets delivered to your construction site, and lay them out in a pattern that mixes the variations consistently. Not all masons take the initiative to do that, so discuss this with your builder.

Brick can be made with a glazed exterior surface. Like the glazing on pottery, a wide variety of surface colors are possible. Generally, it's best to avoid glazed brick. When glazed brick is new, its appearance can be dramatic. However, the glazed surface will eventually chip off, making the wall look shabby.

Other brick materials merit less consideration. True adobe has a nice appearance for a desert location, but it is not durable. You can get almost the same appearance with a more durable clay brick. Bricks can be cut from natural stone, but they are expensive.

DRW

Figure 1-161. Many older brick buildings, such as this country church, can provide inspiration for elegant brickwork.

Some bricks are made from concrete. These lack the durability of clay brick. Don't use them in the structure of your house. They should be limited to applications such as walkways and patios, where they can be replaced easily. Concrete brick commonly is made with coloring agents, allowing a wide range of colors. The colors will fade unless the coloring agent is a mineral, such as iron oxide.

You may be surprised by the large variety of bricks that are available. To select the brick for your home, start with a search on the Internet to find the larger brick suppliers for your location. Then, visit some of the suppliers and look at their samples.

■ **Beautiful Bricklaying**

The first step in designing a brick exterior is to search for examples to copy. Maybe buy a book or two about decorative brickwork. You are looking mainly for two things, the appearance of the brick itself and the placement of the brick to provide elegant detailing or to break up a large surface.

Many older brick buildings provide examples of beautiful brickwork that you can copy for your home. When you are looking for models, don't limit yourself to homes. For example, many older churches provide good examples, as in Figure 1-161.

Figure 1-162 shows how a simple enhancement to the brick walls of a two-story building added grace with virtually no additional cost.

The key to the beauty of brick is the skill of the bricklayer. A skilled mason can create beautiful surfaces in a variety ways, without using special kinds of brick. For example, the house in the previous Figure 1-160 relies mainly on elegant proportions, nicely curved arches and buttresses, and careful mixing of brick colors.

Brick also has the ability to create beautiful surface textures. The mason can do this with ordinary brick by jutting out courses of brick, or by rotating the bricks in various patterns. Figure 1-163 illustrates a variety of elegant detailing that adds nothing to the cost of the brick.

A brick mason can make clean, straight cuts in ordinary bricks by using a masonry saw. This allows you to use ordinary bricks to create arches, corners of various angles, and various kinds of decoration.

There are special names for different kinds of brick detailing, such as "corbel" and "dentil," but you don't need to know the names to communicate your design to the mason. (He may not know the names, either.) Include detail drawings and/or photographs, as appropriate, in your construction drawings.

Where brick crosses the top of a window, doorway, or other opening, you need either a lintel or an arch. A lintel results in a flat top for the opening. Heavy steel angle is commonly used for lintels. It should be invisible and protected from moisture. Often this is neglected, resulting in rusty lintels that detract from the appearance of the house.

DRW

Figure 1-162. A band of bricks extended from the wall surface elegantly separates the floor levels in this two-story building.

DRW

Figure 1-163. This house in St. Michaels, Maryland, was built in 1883 by Dr. Henry Clay Dodson, the owner of a brick factory. A variety of decorative effects are achieved entirely by placement of the bricks, using no special bricks. How many decorative patterns can you count?

In contrast to hidden steel lintels, pre-cast concrete lintels are a highly visible style element, creating a strong accent against the brick.

Arches are an ancient method of spanning the tops of window and door openings in a masonry wall. Arches provide strong support for the surface above the opening. They require no steel or other lintel, and their appearance can be impressive. The main limitation of arches is that they increase the height of the opening, which conflicts with conventional ceiling heights. To be attractive, an arch should not press against the roof line. Figure 1-165 shows well proportioned arches in a brick wall.

Arches take time to build. The brick must be laid on a temporary support, which the mason must make or purchase. The support must remain in place for several days as the mortar cures.

Figure 1-165. A house with well executed brick arches over its windows. Arches should be used only if there is adequate separation from the structure or decorative features above them.

Natural Stone Walls and Stone Veneers

Stone was once a primary structural material for house walls, as in the houses shown in Figures 1-166 and 1-167. Stone is still desirable as a decorative surface, providing an exterior that is enduring and often dramatically beautiful.

The walls of stone houses are thick. Adding super-insulation makes them very thick. This is not an insurmountable problem, but the entrances and windows become very deep. Because stone is irregular, laying it requires special esthetic sense by the stone mason. If you decide to use stone, find an attractive model to copy.

Stone comes in great a variety of appearance, strength, and ease of preparation. However, stone is expensive to ship, so economy may dictate using stone that is native to your locale. Figure 1-168 shows a modern house that was built with stone that was available on the owner's property.

A stone wall is vulnerable to cracking for the same reasons that cracking occurs in brick and concrete blocks. A strong foundation avoids most cracking. If you examine old stone houses that are built on firm foundations, you may see that a few individual stones have cracked, but the cracks have not spread.

In a real structural stone wall, the stones have wide horizontal sides. In this way, the weight of the wall locks each stone in place and keeps it properly loaded. Now, it is becoming popular to create stone veneers by laying the flat sides of the stones vertically, as in Figure 1-169. This reduces the thickness of the wall and the amount of stone that is needed. However, the stones are no longer locked into the wall in the same secure way.

If a stone veneer is applied in this manner, it is important to install clips to attach each stone to the structural wall. If the stones are held to the wall only by the mortar, rain may enter the mortar joints, freeze, and burst the stone loose from the wall. So-called "lick and stick" application of stone veneer is false economy, and it looks false. Don't do it.

Figure 1-166. This stone house in Frederick, Maryland was built in the late 18th century. It is still intact and attractive because it is built on a firm foundation that can carry the enormous weight of the structure.

Figure 1-167. This stone house was built in the early 20th century. Note the deep entry door opening.

DRW

Figure 1-168. A new stone house built on the Greek island of Naxos. The stone was available on site, avoiding any cost for the materials or shipping. The flat concrete roof is acceptable in this generally dry climate.

DRW

Figure 1-169. A house with a stone veneer. To save cost and reduce wall thickness, the stones are laid vertically. With this method, the stones require strong clips to hold them to the underlying frame structure.

Half-Timbered Walls

Medieval houses and public buildings in northern Europe were built with heavy timber frames that were diagonally braced. The space between the timbers was filled with brick or lath, and covered on the outside with stucco. The structural timbers were left exposed on the outside, and typically were painted with a dark wood preservative. The visible outline of the timbers made the walls attractive. Figure 1-170 is an example.

Wikipedia Commons

Figure 1-170. A 16th-century half-timbered house in Denmark, in which the visible timbers are the actual structure.

DRW

Figure 1-171. False half-timbered deco on a frame house in Idaho. The pattern adds texture that is especially enhancing for a wall that has few windows or small windows.

Because of the cold climate, windows in half-timbered walls often were small. As a result, this style evolved to look good with few windows and small windows.

Half-timbered walls in modern houses usually are faked with boards and stucco over conventional frame walls or over concrete block walls. Figure 1-171 is an example. This surface creates a Teutonic or Swiss

Chalet appearance, and it is relatively inexpensive. To keep the boards from warping and rotting, and to avoid staining the stucco by algae, shelter the surface with ample roof overhangs.

DECORATE WALLS WITH PAINT COLOR

Colored paint can be used to great advantage to decorate woodwork on both frame and masonry houses. It can be used on larger surfaces, such as shutters or entire walls. It can be used to create delicate patterns and highlights. It can be used with relatively plain carpentry, or to highlight fancy trim. Contrasting colors can break up an expanse of wall attractively.

The additional cost is relatively small, compared to painting in a single color. Figures 1-174 through 1-178 show some nice examples. Select colors that age gracefully, to avoid the need for frequent repainting. A shade of white is the most common wall color because it remains attractive. Other colors fade, losing their initial sparkle. Subdued colors, such as pastels and "earth tones," age better than bright primary colors. However, the bold colors of some decorative schemes may be worth the periodic repainting that is required.

During warm weather, lighter colors will help to keep the walls cool during the daytime, especially on walls that are directly exposed to the sun. During cold weather, wall colors have little effect on energy efficiency.

Periodic repainting is the price of keeping paintwork attractive. By the same token, you can change your color scheme when you repaint.

As a rule, don't paint brick or stone. Paint masks the uniquely beautiful texture of well chosen masonry.

DRW

Figure 1-175. A classic house in Pennsylvania that uses bold colors as a primary decorative theme.

DRW

Figure 1-176. A condominium complex in Occoquan, Virginia that uses elaborate color detailing to decorate each unit and to distinguish the units from each other.

DRW

Figure 1-174. A highly ornate house in Maine that uses color to accent the details.

DRW

Figure 1-177. A modest cottage in New Orleans that is enlivened with bright colors.

DRW

Figure 1-178. A row of identical houses in the Florida Keys that are distinguished by contrasting monochrome colors.

ALTERNATIVES TO EXCESSIVE WINDOW AREA

Historically, windows have been the main adornment of walls. However, Step 2 explains that windows are a major challenge to energy efficiency. Therefore, you should budget the size and number of your windows to the minimum needed to satisfy their functions – especially view and daylighting. This reduces their ability to make your walls attractive by themselves.

The imperative for energy efficiency in recent building codes often leads builders to take the brute force approach of deleting windows from entire walls, as in Figure 1-180. These huge, blank expanses are a blight on the appearance of a house. You don't want your home to have any walls that look like that. So, let's consider some ways to make large walls interesting without relying on excessive window area.

Break Up Flat Surfaces with Attached Structures

One way to avoid a long expanse of flat wall is to attach useful structures to it. These are prime candidates, which we discussed previously:

- garage
- carport
- sunroom
- greenhouse
- vestibule
- mud room
- porch
- deck
- patio
- balcony

For example, the house in Figure 1-181 breaks up a large blank wall by adding a small room with a decorative chimney. The house in Figure 1-182 covers a blank wall with a false gable and a deck. The house in Figure 1-183 avoids a large, flat wall with a protruding structure that contains a flue and other equipment.

Such structures usually require the foundation to follow the footprint of the wall. If the house has a basement, Step 3 explains how additional angles in the basement foundation walls can be used to strengthen the walls against soil pressure. Also, the roof design usually follows the wall. This can make the roof line more interesting, but also more expensive to build.

DRW

Figure 1-180. The drabness of this side wall is what we are trying to avoid. Compare it to the attractive appearance of the front wall.

DRW

Figure 1-181. The addition of a room to the side of this house avoids having a blank end wall.

DRW

Figure 1-182. A false gable and a deck keep this house from having a blank end wall.

Enhance Walls with Foliage

Trees, shrubs, and vines can be attractive ways to cover expanses of walls that do not have windows, or that have unattractive blank wall space. Figure 1-184 is an example. Foliage that is planted close to the house is suitable for almost all environments, including tightly packed urban housing.

To decorate a wall, select foliage that is evergreen. It should grow quickly to an appropriate mature size. It should be easy to trim, and it should remain attractive when trimmed. For example, azaleas and rhododendrons are attractive evergreen shrubs that grow well in many locations.

If your climate has a warm season, trees and taller shrubs can play a primary role in shading your home for coolness. Step 2 explains the details.

DRW

Figure 1-183. This long wall is broken up by a structure that contains a woodstove flue and air conditioning equipment.

Vines are controversial as a wall covering. Ivy covered walls have been popular for centuries, but vines grow slowly and unpredictably. And, they may damage masonry and wood trim. If you decide to plant vines, select the species to minimize wall damage. Expect to keep vines trimmed or tied away from windows.

Foliage needs time to grow and it needs periodic trimming. Watering and fertilizing may also be needed, although it is usually possible to find species that minimize these requirements. Look ahead to Step 2 for the full story.

You can defer the design of your decorative landscaping until after your home is built. And then, you can change the smaller plants at will.

Decorate the Walls

Decorative objects or paintwork can break up the drabness of plain wall surfaces. Figure 1-185 is a nice example. Metal stars and other objects that hang on the wall can provide a whimsical appearance. Make sure that the appearance is consistent with your overall style.

Select decorations that will age gracefully, or they will become an eyesore. Ornaments made of steel will corrode, so they need a durable coating. Wide roof overhangs are a primary protection for wall deco.

A "half-timbered" wall surface, which we discussed previously, is another form of decoration that can make a wall attractive, even if the windows are few and small.

DRW

Figure 1-184. Effective use of shrubbery to enhance the appearance of walls. These two houses have mirror-image fronts, but foliage makes the one on the right look much more attractive.

DRW

Figure 1-185. A simple painted decoration dresses up the front of this tropical concrete house. The ample roof overhang will keep the paint fresh for years.

ELEGANT AND FUNCTIONAL ROOF SHAPES

To a large extent, the architectural style of a house is determined by its roof. For example, the dominant feature of a "Tudor" house style is a "hip roof." Likewise, a primary feature of the "Swiss chalet" style is a plain gable roof that is extended far beyond the end wall.

You determine the roof's appearance primarily by selecting its shape, its slope, and its surface covering. The adjacent sidebar, *Roof Styles*, is a menu of attractive shapes.

You can use one or more of the primary types of roof structures to build these shapes. (See the previous sidebar, *Basic Roof Structures*.) For example, a gable roof may have truss construction, beam construction, or triangle-frame construction. Each type of construction produces a different outcome for the interior space, as we learned previously under the heading, *Using the Roof Volume*. So, coordinate the exterior style of your roof with your interior design.

You can decorate a large expanse of roof with well proportioned dormers and side gables, which also provide daylighting and increased living space.

Breaks or staggers in the roof line also provide more interest. But, don't get carried away. Too many breaks in a roofline look fussy, they increase cost, and they may weaken the structure.

You can enhance the appearance of the roof with accessories, including fancy chimneys, filigree work, and other decoration around the perimeter of the roof and along the ridges. Functional items, including skylights and ridge vent monitors, can also highlight a roof. And, the appearance of the roof is affected by trees that grow close enough to shade the house.

In the next few pages, we will cover the design features that determine both the appearance and the functions of a roof. Step 3 will cover the structural issues.

THE ROOF SLOPE

Selecting the roof slope is an important stylistic decision, and it has major functional consequences, including these effects:

- A steeper slope makes the roof a more prominent feature of the exterior appearance. By the same token, it makes the selection of the roof surface more critical to the home's appearance.
- Increasing the roof slope can greatly increase the volume under the roof. For example, in a house of average width, a roof slope of 25° yields an attic space that is almost useless, while a slope of 45° yields a large amount of living or storage space.
- In climates that may experience a significant amount of snow, reliable snow shedding helps to protect the roof from moisture damage. The roof slope must exceed a certain angle in order to shed snow effectively. The angle depends on the surface material and the typical nature of the snow (e.g., wet or dry). We summarize the relationships between roof slope and various roof surfaces under the heading, *Roof Surfaces*, below.
- Increasing the roof slope has only a minor effect on the cost of the roof itself.
- A steep slope limits safe access to the roof for maintenance, especially for cleaning the gutters. If a house has a steep roof, it is essential to provide safe access for gutter cleaning from below the roof. See the later heading, *Roof Access for Maintenance.*

EXPLOIT ROOF OVERHANGS

Wide roof overhangs* are a major asset for most houses. They are rarely exploited adequately in contemporary design. In most locations, wide overhangs are so beneficial that you should give preference to a roof style that looks good with them. Wide overhangs provide these benefits:

- They *protect the underground parts of the house from water intrusion and humidity problems*. This benefit is especially valuable for houses with basements. Maximize the benefit by making the overhangs wide, and grade the surrounding soil away from the house.
- They allow you to *keep windows open for ventilation* during rainy weather.
- They *protect the outer wall surfaces and doors* from deterioration by rain, snow, and sun. However, there are better ways to protect doors, which we cover elsewhere.
- Over walls that face southward, wide overhangs can *block the entry of direct sunlight through windows*. This helps to keep the house cool and prevents glare.
- Wide overhangs are needed to provide *eave vents* that are large enough for effective roof cooling in a warm climate.
- With a brick or stone wall, wide overhangs *minimize thermal cracking* that tends to occur in the upper part of the wall.

---

* A roof overhang may be called a "cornice." More narrowly, "cornice" may refer to the woodwork that encloses the overhanging eaves of a roof. And, more broadly, "cornice" can mean any decorative horizontal structure that overhangs a wall or window.

ROOF STYLES

DRW

Figure 1-190. *Gable roof.* This is the basic shape for most roofs because it is strong and easy to build. Usually, the sides are symmetrical. The eaves can be extended easily to provide wide overhangs.

DRW

Figure 1-191. *Inline staggered gables.*

Separate gables are attached end to end, but offset laterally or in height. The design accommodates spaces of different sizes, such as a garage attached to a house. This style is commonly used to break up a long roof line for the sake of appearance.

DRW

Figure 1-192. *Side gables* provide daylight, view, and additional living space, usually in roofs with triangle-frame construction. The side gables may have the same height as the main gable or they may be shorter. Shorter gables tend to weaken the portion of the roof where they are attached.

DRW

Figure 1-193. *Cross gable roof.* Gables of equal height meet in a cross pattern.

ROOF STYLES

DRW

Figure 1-194. *Dormers* provide increased daylight and view through the sides of a triangle-frame roof. They can serve as clerestories for a beam roof. The width of dormers is limited, to avoid weakening the roof. Dormers can be effective appearance enhancements to break up a large roof surface.

DRW

Figure 1-195. *Gable roof with end wall overhang*, commonly used to provide coverage for an outdoor balcony or deck. Typically yields a "Swiss chalet" appearance. If the overhang is oriented toward the south, it can provide sun shading that adapts to the seasons (as explained in Step 2).

DRW

Figure 1-196. *A-frame roof.* This roof structure encloses the entire house. It may have one or more floors of living space. The rafters function as wall studs, usually resting on a short foundation. Dormers may be added to provide daylighting and view through the roof surfaces.

DRW

Figure 1-197. *Hip roof.* A gable roof that has hips, which are sloped ends, instead of gable end walls. Primarily an appearance feature. For good appearance, the hips generally have the same slope as the main gable. Can be built with truss or triangle-frame construction. Sacrifices valuable attic space. Complicates the carpentry somewhat. Considered to be less vulnerable to wind damage than a simple gable shape, although both styles resist wind damage if they are built strongly.

ROOF STYLES

DRW

Figure 1-198. *Partial Hip roof.* A gable roof that has hips extending downward from the ridge only partially. Usually, windows are placed under the partial hip.

DRW

Figure 1-199. *Dutch Hip roof.* A hip roof that has small gable end walls that rise from the upper portions of the hips. The small gable ends can be used for vents or windows, depending on what is under the roof.

DRW

DRW

Figure 1-200. *Gambrel roof.* Two slopes on each side of the ridge meet along a line called the "knuckle." Has more volume under the roof than a plain gable roof, but the roof is weaker. Various construction methods are used. Stronger designs require more lumber. The eaves are sometimes flared outward to provide wider overhangs and to enhance appearance.

DRW

Figure 1-201. *Mansard roof.* Has a basic gambrel shape on all four sides. Avoids the somewhat barn-like appearance of a gambrel roof. Often highly ornamented, mansard roofs are primarily an expensive appearance option with little other merit. The carpentry is complex. Windows must be installed in dormer structures. The eaves often are flared outward to provide wider overhang. The top surface of the roof has a shallow slope, inviting leakage.

Figure 1-202. *Saltbox roof.* An unsymmetrical gable roof where one side of the roof slopes down to the first floor level, typically at the front of the house. The other side of the roof covers a second story. The interior layout is inefficient. The slope of the higher side is shallower than the slope of the low side, inviting leakage. Characteristic of coastal New England.

ROOF STYLES

DRW

Figure 1-203. *Shed roof.* The simplest kind of beam roof. Unusual for an individual house because the shape is not attractive when viewed from the side. Once common for row houses, where the roof is invisible from the street.

DRW

Figure 1-204. *Overlapping shed roof.* Uses several roof planes, separated by a clerestory or other vertical surface, typically to create a "modern" style.

DRW

Figure 1-205. *Pyramid roof.* Has a square footprint, symmetrical sides, and a fairly steep slope. The sides can have a single slope or variable slopes. A skylight may be mounted at the apex.

DRW

Figure 1-206. *Pagoda roof.* Flared eaves yield an "oriental" appearance. The structure on top evokes a "Polynesian" roof, which originally used a tall central shaft to vent warm air and create a draft.

ROOF STYLES

DRW

Figure 1-207. *Flat roof*, on a Greek island. Typical of Mediterranean regions. Generally, flat roofs should be used only with concrete construction in relatively dry climates. The roof may be used for mounting equipment, such as air conditioners and solar water heaters. It is always sloped somewhat for drainage.

DRW

Figure 1-209. *Flat roof*, in coastal Florida. A flat roof in a wet climate requires a weather surface that is expensive and unreliable.

DRW

Figure 1-208. *Flat roof* on an Italian island, used as a terrace. Sometimes, it may be covered with floor tile. The terrace requires a parapet or railing.

- With a brick or stone veneers, wide overhangs *keep the wall dry enough to avoid the need for weep holes*, which are an entry route for insects.
- During construction, overhangs *protect the interior of the house and the unfinished exterior* from rain.

 Extended roof overhangs and other overhanging structures offer a number of valuable benefits.

We will discuss these benefits in greater detail at the appropriate points.

Most architectural styles can look good with wide overhangs, but not all. For example, a New England saltbox style would not look authentic with extended overhangs. A plain gambrel roof with wide eave overhangs would make the house look like a mushroom.

DORMERS AND SIDE GABLES

Dormers and side gables can be beautiful stylistic enhancements for both the interior and exterior of the house. They attractively break up a large expanse of roof, while providing daylight for the interior. Figure 1-212 shows a house that uses both a dormer and a side gable.

For roof structures that enclose living space – such as triangle-frame, gambrel, and mansard roofs – dormers and side gables can provide daylight to the central portions of the roof. A full side gable can provide a certain amount of additional living space, in addition to daylighting. However, dormers are too narrow to provide much additional living space.

With a truss roof, dormers can provide useful daylight for an attic.

If a room has a vaulted ceiling under the roof, dormers and side gables can be used to create clerestories, providing effective daylight deep into the room. (Step 2 explains how to design clerestories.)

The dormer itself has a roof, which can have a variety of shapes. For example, a dormer that has a gable roof is called a "gable dormer." A dormer with a hip roof is called a "hip dormer." And, a dormer with a shed roof is called a "shed dormer."

Another difference is where the dormer is located on the roof. A dormer that is located uphill on the roof, back from the exterior wall, is called a "floating" dormer. Other dormers have a front face that is an extension of the exterior wall below.

Figures 1-213 through 1-216 show a variety of dormer styles.

Shed dormers inherently cannot match the slope of the roof on which they are installed. They look good only with a limited range of styles, such as steeply sloped antique roof designs. Because a shed dormer must have a shallower slope than the main roof, it may invite leaks and ice dams.

Most dormers have vertical sides, but not all do. Figure 1-217 shows a house that has dormers with and without side walls.

Dormers look simple from the outside, but they can be tricky for a first-time home designer to visualize from the inside. The inside appearance depends on the location of the dormer in the roof and on the method of framing. Figure 1-218 shows the interior appearance of four gable dormers that are arranged in different ways. Further variations in appearance are possible by changing the heights of the dormers, changing the dimensions of the windows with respect to the dimensions of the dormers, and changing the shape of the dormer roof.

Dormers usually look best if their slope and style match the main gable on which the dormers are installed. Mismatched dormers tend to look awkward.

Side gables may differ in appearance from the main gable. Differences in the basic shape and the degree of ornamentation may be dramatic, as in Figure 1-219, but they are stylistically risky.

DRW

Figure 1-212. This house nicely illustrates the difference between a dormer and a side gable.

DRW

Figure 1-213. Dormers with gable roofs. These dormers "float" on the roof structure.

DRW

Figure 1-215. Dormers with round roofs. These dormers are covered with copper sheathing.

DRW

Figure 1-214. Dormers with shed roofs. Because a shed roof must slope downhill, the available window height is greatly reduced.

DRW

Figure 1-216. A dormer with a hip roof. The front face of this dormer is supported directly on the exterior wall.

DRW

Figure 1-217. One dormer has vertical exterior walls, and the other does not.

DRW

Figure 1-219. This house has highly ornate side gables attached to a house with a fairly plain gable roof line. The combination works well here, but it is risky to mix radically different styles.

DRW

Figure 1-218. The inside appearance of dormers. From left to right, the first dormer has its front face resting on the exterior wall. The second dormer "floats" on the roof structure between the exterior wall and the ceiling. The front face of the third dormer rests on a low interior "knee wall." The front face of the fourth dormer rests on a taller knee wall. The roof of the fourth dormer is built above the ceiling line. The three dormers on the left have gable roofs. Different dormer roof shapes (round, shed, etc.) can yield different interior appearances. Alternatively, any dormer can be built with a flat ceiling, yielding a rectangular opening.

AVOID WEAK ROOF SHAPES

A roof must support an enormous weight and it must resist strong winds. Total roof collapse is rare, but if you observe many older houses, you will see that roof sagging is common. You want to design a roof that will not sag at all over its lifetime. We will cover the details of roof construction in Step 3. At this point, enhance the strength of your roof by selecting a strong roof shape.

The three main residential roof types – truss, beam, and triangle-frame – are easy and economical to build strongly. Other roof shapes that enclose living space – such as gambrel and mansard – are inherently weaker. If you select a relatively weak roof shape, it can be reinforced to make it adequately strong, but this requires extra lumber, extra complication, and a sacrifice of some living space.

A roof can be weakened by dormers and side gables that are not designed properly. Step 3 explains the limitations on the size and the position of dormers and side gables that you should observe to maintain the strength of the roof.

ACCOMMODATE SUPER-INSULATION, VENTING, AND RADIATION BARRIERS

In most climates, the roof insulation of your super-house will be extra thick. In a warm climate, your roof may need extra depth to accommodate a heat radiation barrier and an open ventilation path for cooling air. The structural modifications are easy, but you don't want your roof to look clunky.

Step 3 covers these aspects of roof construction. Take a look ahead for ideas on how to provide the needed space in an attractive way. Wide overhangs help to accommodate the needed depth. A steeper slope also helps.

If you plan to use ventilation for cooling your roof in a warm climate, the eaves, the ridge, and/or the gable ends may have very large vents. These will be a prominent feature of your roof, so reconcile them with your roof style. See *Roof Cooling by Ventilation*, in Step 3, for the details.

ROOF ACCESS FOR MAINTENANCE

Not enough attention is given to providing safe access to the rooftop. This is an important design issue. Someone will have to climb on your roof periodically for maintenance. If not you, roofing professionals and gutter cleaners will need to go there. They have equipment that gives them access to any roof. However, if you make it easy for them, you will pay less for their services.

 Designing easy and safe access to your roof from inside the house will ease gutter cleaning and make repairs less expensive.

Gutter cleaning is the most frequent maintenance requirement. If you shade your house with trees – which I recommend for many locations – your gutters may have to be cleared several times each year. Decide whether you will clean the gutters from below or from the roof itself, and provide access accordingly. If the roof has a safe slope and a surface that tolerates human weight, it may be easiest to clean the gutters from above. A solid roof deck with conventional shingles is a satisfactory walking surface. Roof tile and sheetmetal roofing that is installed over purlins generally are not.

If the roof is not too high above the ground, plan one or more locations around the perimeter where you can erect a ladder for safe access to the roof, preferably where the edge of the roof is closest to the ground. If you will be doing your own gutter cleaning, consider attaching a permanent bracket near the roof edge to hold the top of the ladder securely without pressing on the gutter.

If the roof is high above the ground, you have an opportunity for innovation by providing safe access to the roof from inside the house. If you want to maintain a traditional roof style, you can provide access to the roof through a dormer. Build an attractive platform at the base of the dormer, with a safety rail.

The dormer will need a tall window that opens completely, such as a casement window. If access is through an attic, consider installing a louver door in the dormer, along with easy access to the attic, as we discussed previously. A louver door in a dormer will look unusual, but less so in a warm climate.

If your architectural style allows a more creative appearance, you might build a structure that provides access to the roof from an interior stairway. A decorative "widow's walk" is a classic example of this.

Safety must be the prime concern when providing access to the roof for work or pleasure. The roof slope is a dominant issue. If the slope is too steep for safe walking, it's probably better to leave all work on the roof to professionals.

ROOF LAYOUT TO AVOID SNOW DAMAGE

If your home will be built in climate that may have a significant amount of snow, dealing with snow becomes an important aspect of your roof design. Snow causes condensation damage to the structure, major water leakage into the house at ice dams, leakage into skylights and other roof features, and possible roof collapse from the weight of the snow. Use the adjacent *Snow and Ice Protection Checklist* to design your roof and its surroundings to avoid damage that is commonly caused by snow and ice.

In Step 3, we will cover the features in the checklist that protect the roof itself from damage by condensation and ice dams. The main defense against this damage is to design the roof to shed snow quickly. We previously learned how the roof slope and the selection of the roof surface affect snow shedding.

Snow Protection Under Eaves

The "eaves" of a roof are the lower margins of the sloped surfaces, where rain and snow fall from the roof. Snow tends to slide off abruptly, as an avalanche. This can be dangerous, especially if the eave is high above the ground. Therefore, design effective protection for areas under the eaves that may be occupied by people.

One effective solution is to build a structure under a tall eave that protects people. A porch is ideal for this purpose. The porch roof usually is limited to a shallow slope, so cover it with metal panel roofing to hasten snow shedding, if practical.

Any other low structure, such as a sunroom that extends for the length of the eave, serves the same purpose.

Another solution is to lay out the area under tall eaves so that people cannot occupy the danger area. For example, plant shrubs or a flower garden under the eaves, with plants that will survive the impact of the falling snow and burial under snow.

Make all eave overhangs wide enough so that snow that falls from the roof will not pile up against the walls. When a large amount of snow melts, it soaks the ground for an extended period. For the same reason, grade the surrounding soil away from the walls.

Snow fences and other devices are used to hold snow on the roof until it melts. I recommend against them, as well as anything that tends to hold snow on a roof. The heading, *Protection from Snow and Ice*, in Step 3, explains the reasons.

SNOW AND ICE PROTECTION CHECKLIST

☐ Plan the space under tall eaves to eliminate a hazard from falling snow and ice. Keep these areas inaccessible. For example, isolate them with shrubbery. Or, install a porch, sunroom, or other structure to protect persons below the eaves.

☐ Don't install snow guards or snow fences on the roof. Let the snow slide off into the protected space below.

☐ Make the roof steep enough to shed snow before a large amount accumulates.

☐ If appropriate, consider a smooth roof surface, especially sheetmetal. This reduces the slope needed to shed snow.

☐ Install widely overhanging eaves to keep snow from piling against the walls.

☐ Minimize roof shapes that cause sliding snow to jam in place, especially near the bottom of the roof. Snow is blocked at the valleys between gables and at the tops of dormers. It is also blocked by flues, vents, and other protrusions from the roof.

☐ Don't install skylights. Use dormers or side gables to bring daylight through a triangle-frame roof. Use clerestories to bring daylight through a beam roof.

☐ If practical, orient the roof so that most of the roof surface is exposed to direct sunlight for several hours during the day.

☐ Insulate the roof from interior heat, to minimize ice dams.

☐ Ventilate the underside of the roof deck just enough to keep it cold, for the purpose of minimizing ice dams. Don't bring in large amounts of outside air that will carry moisture to condense under the roof deck.

☐ Install the gutters well below the edge of the roof, so snow can slide over them.

☐ Insulate flues, vents, and ducts where they pass through the roof structure, to prevent ice dams. Use fireproof insulation around hot surfaces.

☐ Use an extra thick, self-adhering underlayment under the roofing surface, instead of ordinary "roofing felt." Overlap it generously to create a layer that is impermeable to water penetration. This is most important for the lower portions of the roof, where ice dams form.

☐ Use moisture-resistant lumber and plywood for vulnerable parts of the roof deck.

BEATIFUL ROOF SURFACES

The thin outer surface of the roof is what does the roof's main work. It provides the protection against weather, it dominates the appearance of the roof, and it is the largest variable factor in roof cost. In warm weather, it is a significant factor in comfort and energy efficiency, because the roof surface alone determines the amount of heat that the roof collects from the sun and that it rejects to the sky. It is the only part of the roof structure that should need replacement during the life of the house. And, the choice of the roof surface determines how often it must be replaced.

The roof is the largest visible surface of your house. Make it look good in its own right, and match it to the overall style of the house. The roof surface becomes even more prominent if the roof has a steeper slope.

Selecting the roof surface is much more critical than selecting the wall surfaces, because the roof is the primary barrier between your home and the forces of nature. Fortunately, you have a fairly broad menu of roof surface choices that reconcile appearance with the other important characteristics that a roof should have.

Over the centuries, many materials have been used as roof surfaces, from palm fronds to exotic metal alloys. At the present time, three types have taken over most of the roofing market. These are **composition ("asphalt") shingles**, **sheetmetal panels**, and **ceramic tile**. A fourth type, **metal shingles**, is an old roofing material that has returned recently with an updated appearance.

Table 1-1, *Roof Surface Comparison*, explains the main selection factors of these four surfaces. Generally, start with the climate. If your home site has a substantial amount of snow, use a steep roof slope to shed the snow, or if you want a shallower slope, use a metal panel roof.

If you are building on a budget, the next factor is cost, and this will argue strongly in favor of composition shingles. On the other hand, if you can afford to be extravagant, you might consider either ceramic tile or metal shingles. The other factors in Table 1-1 may be more or less important, depending on your situation. For example, if your home is surrounded by forest, a metal roof increases resistance to a forest fire.

If you are re-roofing an existing house, you may want to change the roof surface. Your options are limited by the original roof structure. Changing to a metal panel roof would be impractical or expensive unless the original roof surfaces are flat. Changing to a tile roof requires an exceptionally strong roof structure.

COMPOSITION SHINGLES

Invented in 1901, composition shingles soon became the most common type of roof surface in the U.S. and many other countries. They are commonly called "asphalt" shingles because the weather resistant material is a tarry petroleum product. It is soaked into a fibrous mat and coated with mineral grit. Originally, shingles used a mat that was made of wood or paper fibers. Today, almost all shingles use glass fiber fabric as a base for the asphalt. Therefore, this newer kind is also called "fiberglass" shingles.

In the past, asphalt shingles were available only in a limited range of dark, uniform colors. Now, they are also available in a range of lighter colors and they offer various tonal patterns, as in Figure 1-222.

A caution is to select colors that will age well. In wet climates, black algae grows on asphalt shingles, especially if the roof is shaded. Algae growth is not very apparent on dark grey shingles, but it may mar the appearance of brighter or patterned colors.

DRW

Figure 1-222. An attractive asphalt shingle roof.

Composition shingles are the least expensive practical roof surface. They can provide good protection against weather in all climates, except for climates with extreme wind or cold.

Composition shingles are vulnerable to leaks from capillary action because of the close contact between the layers of shingles. To minimize this, a minimum slope is needed so that the weight of the water keeps it flowing downhill. A slope of about 18° is the minimum to shed rain, and steeper is better if the climate has rainy spells.

The gritty surface of composition shingles tends to hold snow. To shed snow reliably, shingles require a slope from 45° to 60°.

There are several situations where you might not want asphalt shingles. One is a snowy climate where you don't want the steep roof slope that asphalt shingles need to shed snow. Another is a hot climate where you want a cooler roof surface. In locations that are vulnerable to wildfires, the shingles may ignite in a hot surrounding fire.

Table 1-1. ROOF SURFACE COMPARISON [Note 1]

	Composition Shingles	Sheetmetal Panel	Metal Shingle/Tile	Concrete & Clay Tile
Cost (% of nominal construction cost) [Note 2]	Least expensive. 0.5 to 1.5%.	1.5 to 2.5% for coated steel and aluminum. Up to 6% for exotic alloys and coatings.	2 to 4.5% for steel and aluminum. 3 to 6% for copper.	Most expensive. 5 to 10%.
Service Life	15 to 40 years, depending mainly on climate and shingle temperature.	20 to 50 years for materials with good coatings. [Note 3]	Aluminum promises 50 years or longer, but too early to verify. Coatings are the limiting factor.	50 years to centuries, depending on material and climate.
Climate Limitations	Very tolerant, but vulnerable to extreme wind and extreme high temperature.	None.	None.	Best in consistently warm or arid climates. Vulnerable in climates with substantial snow, blowing rain, intense wind.
Appearance Options	• Many colors available, but with underlying asphalt appearance. • Matte finish. • Individual shingles are monochrome. • Patterning is possible by mixing colors.	• Individual panels are monochrome. • Many colors available. • Glossy appearance until surface is weathered. • Standing seams provide texture. • Minimal decorative options.	• Mimics many styles of tiles and shingles, including various surface textures.	• Many colors. • Various shapes. • Earthen to glossy finish. • Patterning is possible by combining colors.
Ease of Installation & Repair	Easy and quick.	Relatively easy, but concealed attachments require careful placement.	Relatively easy and quick, but requires special techniques.	Requires specialized knowledge and a fine touch. Repair may be difficult.
Leak Resistance	Good, but declines toward end of life. Requires good underlayment to resist ice dams.	Excellent, with concealed attachments. Standing seam may leak at ice dams.	Good, but may leak at ice dams without underlayment.	Generally good, except in strong wind. Requires underlayment to resist ice dams.
Slope Requirements	Nominal 18° minimum, with good underlayment, to avoid rain leaks. 45° to 60° to shed snow.	Nominally at least 10° to avoid rain leaks. Nominally at least 30° to shed snow.	Nominally at least 15° to avoid rain leaks. Perhaps 40° to shed snow, depending on tile shape.	At least 15° with interlocking tile. At least 23° with most other types. Snow increases slope requirement.
Fire Resistance	Combustible. Vulnerable to ignition by an adjacent fire.	Best. Resists exterior ignition, quenches fire from below.	Good for exterior fire, but not as effective as flat panels for quenching fire in roof deck.	Fair. Openings between tiles feed air to fire in the roof structure.
Weight	Moderate. 2 to 4 lb/sf (10 to 20 kg/m²)	Light. 0.4 to 0.7 lb/sf (2 to 3.5 kg/m²) for aluminum. 0.8 to 1.5 lb/sf (5 to 8 kg/m²) for steel.	Light. 0.7 to 1.2 pounds/square foot (3.5 to 6 kg/m²) for aluminum	Heavy. 7 to 20 lb/sf (35 to 100 kg/m²)
Resistance to Damage	Superior resistance to impact and walking. Good resistance to wind.	Good resistance to impact, wind, and walking if fully supported by deck. Otherwise, vulnerable to hail, falling limbs, walking on surface.	Unsupported raised metal is vulnerable to dents and crushing.	Vulnerable to falling branches, walking, extreme wind. Porous tile cracks from freezing.
Reflectivity	3 to 30%	5 to 75% for coated metal, depending on color. Ca. 60% for unpainted galvanized.	5 to 75% for coated metal, depending on color.	10 to 80%, depending on color and surface treatment.
Emissivity	Up to 90% is available in all colors, but may be substantially lower.	80 to 90% with most coatings, all colors. ca. 25% for unpainted galvanized.	80 to 90% with most coatings, all colors.	85 to 95%, depending on type of tile and surface treatment.

Notes:
[1] The comparisons assume the best conventional materials and adherence to recommended installation practices.
[2] To provide a common basis of comparison, the costs are based on percentage of construction cost per unit of floor area, for typical houses. However, more expensive roofing is likely to be used on a more expensive house, lowering the percentage of actual construction cost.
[3] Service life is for factory-fabricated panels, which are superior to site-fabricated panels.

SHEETMETAL PANEL ROOFING

Sheetmetal panel roofs were once limited to industrial buildings and barns. Now, they are becoming common for homes, offering superior performance in some respects. Figure 1-223 shows a typical installation.

A good sheetmetal roof is considerably more expensive than composition shingles. Increasingly, houses are using a combination of the two. Shingles are used for the steeply sloped main roof, while metal panels are used for the shallow roof slopes over porches and shed dormers. Figure 1-224 shows a typical combination.

Metal panels have long unbroken surfaces from top to bottom, providing excellent protection against water penetration. A well installed metal roof is almost impervious to rain leaks, and it can be installed with a shallower slope than other roofing materials. To shed rain, a sheetmetal roof requires only enough slope to keep wind from blowing rain uphill through the overlap between the panels and into the ridge vents.

A sheetmetal panel roof would be a prime choice if you want good snow shedding without a steep slope. As with other roof surfaces, the minimum slope for reliable snow shedding depends on the winter temperature and the nature of the snow.

Sheetmetal has a less formal appearance than other surfaces. This becomes more apparent with steeper slopes. Sheetmetal roofing of good quality is now available in a selection of colors that give it a less industrial appearance. The quality of the coating is a dominant factor in longevity. Quality varies widely, so shop carefully. Aluminum has the longest life and the highest cost. The best factory-fabricated panels probably are substantially better than panels fabricated on site from flat stock.

Plain, unpainted galvanized steel is the original type of metal roofing, but the homely appearance of bare galvanized metal limits it to rural or historical applications, as in Figure 1-225.

With steel roofing, eventual rust is the limiting factor in the life of the roof. The main deterrence to rust is a zinc (galvanized) coating. The zinc is slowly consumed, so the life of the zinc coating is proportional to its thickness. Therefore, select roofing metal that has the heaviest galvanized coating.

The main driving force for rusting is rain or melting snow, which activates the chemical reaction between atmospheric oxygen and iron. Acid in rain and roof debris hastens rusting. The tendency to rust is proportional to the time the roof is wet. That is mostly a matter of weather, which you can't change. You can delay the penetration of water to the metal surface by selecting the most durable paint or enamel coating.

With light colored coatings, a metal roof surface can be substantially cooler than asphalt shingles of any color. Metal provides superior protection from external fire, such as a fire in a surrounding forest.

Adjacent panels usually are joined with raised seams, called "standing seams," that provide good rain protection and a distinctive appearance, as in Figure 1-223. Panels may have additional lengthwise ribs between the seams to provide more texture to the roof's appearance. These ribs also stiffen the panels if they are installed over purlins with long gaps in support.

Metal panels can also be attached with screws, as in Figure 1-225. To minimize rain leakage, the screws are

DRW

Figure 1-223. An attractive sheetmetal roof. This type has "standing" seams, which provide a texture to the roof's appearance. Standing seams are superior for leak protection.

installed through the tops of ribs in the panels. Today, the screws have rubber washers. However, the washers will disintegrate after several years of exposure to sunlight and heat. Unless first cost is a dominant issue, don't use this method of installation.

The long panels of a metal roof expand and contract by a considerable amount in the temperature extremes of the roof environment. Aluminum panels expand more than steel panels. The fastening method should accommodate this motion for the life of the roof. Specify this in your design.

Drumming of rain on a sheetmetal roof can be noisy if the metal panels are installed on purlins. The noise may annoy nearby neighbors, but it is unlikely to be objectionable from inside a well insulated house. If a sheetmetal roof is securely fastened to a plywood deck and underlayment, rain noise probably is comparable to that with other roof surfaces.

DRW

Figure 1-224. A house that uses composition shingles for the main roof and sheetmetal for the porch roof. The sheetmetal allows snow to shed more easily from the shallow slope of the porch roof.

DRW

Figure 1-225. A galvanized sheetmetal roof on a Key West "conch" house. It is attached with screws and rubber washers through the tops of the ridges. The rubber washers deteriorate in a few years, allowing a small amount of leakage.

CLAY AND CONCRETE ROOF TILES

Clay and concrete roof tiles offer longevity and attractive appearance, which comes at an elevated price. Tile is especially favorable for hot climates because it is not harmed by high temperature. Also, a tile roof vents through the top surface, which keeps the roof cooler and aids in protecting the structure against moisture damage.

The weight of roof tiles is much greater than the weight of other roof surfaces. Tile may require a stronger supporting structure than other roof surfaces, adding to the already high cost of tile. To avoid rain leaks, the roof slope should be at least 18° to 23°, depending on the shape of the tile. Shedding snow reliably requires a slope from 45° to 60°.

The least expensive roof tiles are simple concrete "barrel" tiles, which are best limited to warm climates to avoid freezing damage. These typically look plain. At the other extreme, some enameled clay tiles can be beautiful, as in Figure 1-226.

Roof tiles come in many shapes, with various methods of attachment. Barrel tile and other loosely overlapped styles tend to stay cooler, but they are more vulnerable to blowing rain and wind damage. Many tile designs are interlocking, which improves their wind resistance, but also makes them difficult to replace individually. Some tiles overlap fairly tightly, like wooden shingles. All tiles are vulnerable to leaks from capillary action.

Selecting the best tile roof for a home involves more decisions than selecting composition shingles or metal panels. If you are considering a tile roof, invest time to learn more about your options. Start by visiting the Web sites of tile manufacturers, and read the installation instructions for tiles that look attractive to you. The installation manuals will tell you how the roof must be designed, how to get a reliable installation, and how difficult repairs will be.

METAL "SHINGLES" AND "TILES"

Metal "shingle" or "tile" roofing is sheetmetal that is formed into the shapes of shingles or tiles. The material usually is installed in multi-"shingle" sheets of various sizes. Figure 1-227 is a typical installation. The sheets can be installed on purlins, similarly to the installation of flat metal panels, avoiding the need for a solid roof deck.

Metal roof panels can be embossed to mimic the appearance of all common types of roof coverings, including various shapes of tile, asphalt and cedar shingles, and slate. Their appearance can be varied further with different surface coatings, which can be any color or combination of colors. Some even offer an embedded granular surface. An attractive, antique appearance is available with sheetmetal roofing that is embossed to give it the appearance of old tin ceiling tiles, as in Figure 1-228.

Why would you install a metal imitation of another type of roof covering, instead of the real thing? The usual reasons are durability, and perhaps lower cost. Metal shingles are available in aluminum, coated steel, copper, and exotic alloys, some of which may have a much longer life.

DRW

Figure 1-226. Attractive enameled tile roof. Most roof tiles have a basic barrel shape, as here.

Compared to ceramic tiles, metal "tiles" are much lighter, much quicker to install, and they provide a more secure weather barrier if they have a good attachment system.

Price ranges widely, with the most expensive metal roofing costing as much as good ceramic tiles. Generally, price is proportional to longevity.

Depositphotos

Figure 1-227. Sheets of metal "tiles" mimic the appearance of a ceramic tile roof.

DRW

Figure 1-228. An embossed metal roof. This is a characteristic of historical houses and churches in older neighborhoods of the American South.

HISTORICAL ROOF SURFACES

A variety of other roof surface materials have been used over the centuries, including *slate*, *wooden shingles*, *thatch*, and *sod*. Today, these materials are historical relics. Compared to modern roofing materials, they impose penalties in the form of higher cost, shorter life, dampness, vermin infestation, and/or fire hazard.

You would select one of these roof surfaces only if you want to indulge a taste for their historical appearance. If you do, be prepared to pay a high price to install them properly. Do more homework with unusual roof types, and good luck. We won't discuss them further.

ORNMENTAL CARPENTRY: DELIGHTFUL ICING ON THE CAKE

To make your home stand out as exceptionally beautiful or interesting, you can use a variety of ornamental carpentry. Without changing the basic structure, adding decorative trim can turn a plain house into a work of art. Ornamental carpentry can be a great enhancement to both new and existing houses.

One disadvantage of wooden trim work is that it must be painted manually, which is painstaking work. The paint must be renewed at timely intervals because exposed wooden trim is vulnerable to rot. All wooden trim should be protected from rain and snow by ample overhangs.

Figures 1-231 through 1-239 are a sampler. Gather more examples for your idea file as you look around. You probably will find the majority of attractive examples on older houses. Ornamental carpentry almost died out during the 20th century, as emphasis shifted toward mass production housing. Fortunately, it is now experiencing a revival, as homeowners seek ways to distinguish their homes.

Carpentry trim may be attached to the wall or roof, or both. It can break up the stark line between the roof and the walls, and it ties the two together in a beautiful way.

DRW

Figure 1-231. Fine "stickwork" in Key West.

DRW

Figure 1-232. Ornate porch filigree and gable end trim in Key West.

Ornamental carpentry can be inexpensive, but it is also opportunistic. For example, if a local carpenter loves to do "stickwork," you may be able to decorate your home elegantly with stickwork at modest cost. But, if such a craftsman is not available locally, even a fortune won't buy you good detailing of that kind.

Nowadays, there are likely to be carpenters, bricklayers, stone masons, stained glass artists, and others in your vicinity who have special detailing skills and who are anxious to showcase them. You need to find these craftsmen by asking on the local contractors' grapevine. Or, if you see a house with decoration that you like, ask the homeowner who did the work.

DRW

Figure 1-233. A gingerbread house in New Brunswick, Canada.

DRW

Figure 1-234. Another gingerbread house in New Brunswick.

DRW

Figure 1-235. Eave trim for a small cottage in Key West.

DRW

Figure 1-236. Astrological signs decorate a porch.

DRW

Figure 1-237. A highly ornate turret house in Frederick, Maryland.

DRW

Figure 1-238. Filigree on a country porch is achieved primarily with carefully drilled holes.

DRW

Figure 1-239. This ornate roof trim is achieved by varying the orientation of the shingles and by using ridge ornaments.

Architects use a private vocabulary to describe decorative features, with names such as "pendentive," "finial," "dentil," etc. You don't need to know those fancy words. When you find the right craftsman, communicate your ideas with pictures. You will soon pick up any special terms that you need.

Don't Overdo It

The previous pages contain many examples of attractive exterior decoration. These range from simple adornments around windows to ornate gingerbread. A key point is that each of these examples is consistent and well placed.

Exterior decoration is the frosting, not the cake. Don't overdo it. It is art. It requires talent and taste, including a sense of proportion and limits. If you use a variety of decorations, make sure that each kind is compatible with the others. We have given you an extensive menu of ways to decorate the exterior of your house. Don't order too many items from the menu, or your house will suffer from stylistic glut.

YOUR OUTDOOR ENVIRONMENT

An ideal home has a rich outdoor environment as well as an indoor environment. Using the previous *Home Activities Worksheet*, identify the outdoor activities and facilities that you want to accommodate on your property. In addition to your own interests, consider activities for your children and your guests and later owners of your home.

Even a small backyard can be a fine environment for barbecues, badminton, or pitching horseshoes. You probably will want a storage shed. A somewhat larger lot can accommodate a swimming pool. If you have even more space, you might want to leave space for a garden, a tennis court, an archery range, or whatever.

A nice thing about your outdoor facilities is that you can delay designing them until you have built your house, moved in, and gotten comfortable. The main point now is to locate your house on your property so that you can later position your outdoor facilities properly with respect to the house.

PRESERVE YOUR SITE'S NATURAL ASSETS

If the property for building your home has not been cleared yet, Mother Nature may provide you with valuable assets in the form of trees and shrubs. While you are considering the location and orientation of your house and its outdoor amenities, take advantage of those assets.

It's a tragedy that mass production homebuilders bulldoze beautiful groves of trees into fields of mud, leaving empty and uninteresting landscapes for years after the houses are occupied. There is no excuse for this. Only the space for your house and its outdoor amenities needs to be cleared. Lines for water, sewer, electricity, and gas require only narrow trenches, which can be routed clear of trees and other features that you wish to preserve. A smart builder recognizes that this lowers site preparation costs, including measures to limit runoff of mud.

Trees are important for shading as well as for beauty. Tree shading is so important for cooling in warm weather that Step 2 offers it as a main component of your design for controlling sunlight. Saving the mature trees around your home overcomes the biggest limitation of tree shading, which is the long time required for trees to grow.

Make a copy of the plat for your property and indicate all the trees, shrubs, creeks, and other features that you may want to preserve. For example, if your property has azaleas or rhododendrons that you find attractive, fit them into your landscaping plan.

Also, mark the trees and shrubs that you want removed. Construction is the best time to remove them because the needed equipment is already there. Removing trees and shrubs later would be much more expensive.

Other features of your property may affect the location and orientation of your house. For example, you may be able to build a dam across descending terrain to create a nice pond.

OUTBUILDINGS

Outbuildings can be a great asset. Most homes should have a nice storage building for lawn mower, bicycles, flammable and toxic materials, and other items that you should not store inside the house. If your home does not have an attached garage, you might have a carport or a separate enclosed garage. You might want a separate workshop for big, noisy, or dirty projects. Or, a playhouse for children. Or even a complete lodging facility, such as a "mother-in-law cottage." Out in the country, you might have a barn or stables.

Plan the size, location, and orientation of each outbuilding so that it will complement your house and enhance the overall appearance of your property. Leave ample space for each outbuilding. Err on the side of making them larger. If you look inside many storage buildings and garages, you find them overflowing.

The design of each outbuilding is a condensed version of the design of your house. When you are ready to design the outbuildings, your experience will take you quickly to the features in this book that you should include in your outbuildings.

As you plan the utilities for your house, make it easy to provide electricity to your outbuildings. Typically, you will extend wiring from the house to the outbuilding through a trench. If an outbuilding will be heated and pipeline gas is available, make provision to extend the gas line to the outbuilding.

SWIMMING POOL AND ENCLOSURE

Almost everyone wants a swimming pool. You can use a pool comfortably in any location that has a sunny season. But, make a sober judgment about whether to install one for your home. As with fireplaces, people tend to overestimate how much they will actually use a swimming pool. A pool is expensive and it requires continuing maintenance, whether you use it or not.

Anthony & Sylvan Pools

Figure 1-240. An attractive swimming pool, properly placed in an unshaded location on the south side of the house. A hot tub joins the side of the pool.

Locate the pool at a minimum distance from the house. Any leaks in the pool will wet the soil around your house, potentially causing trouble. Also, moisture from the pool surface will raise the humidity in the vicinity of the pool. As a rule of thumb, separate the pool from the house by a distance that is several times the depth of the pool's nearest side.

Installing a pool involves important decisions about the size, location, and method of heating the pool. First of all, consider the way that the pool will be used. Will it be mainly a place for children to frolic during the summer vacation? Or, will serious athletes use it for lap swimming? Should it be shallow for safety, or deep for diving?

Most people spend more time lounging around a pool than actually swimming in it. Lounging space greatly enlarges the footprint of the pool area.

Like any living space, your pool area should be designed to provide comfortable temperature and controlled sunlight intensity.

In a climate that gets cool, a glazed pool enclosure may extend your home's swimming season. However, the improvement may not be great. The limiting factor is the large amount of condensation on the inside surface of the enclosure during cooler weather. An enclosure further increases the footprint required.

Direct sunlight helps to keep your pool clean. The sterilizing power of sunlight is a primary tool for keeping mildew under control. This is especially important if the pool has an enclosure, because the inside of the enclosure will remain damp for long periods.

Therefore, locate your pool so that all parts of it will be exposed to direct sunlight for much of the day. If the pool is near the house, place it on the south side, as in Figure 1-240. At the same time, coordinate the locations of the pool and your shade trees to avoid shading the pool and dropping tree debris on the pool.

Unless your climate is always warm, install a pool cover that is easy to operate. The cover will keep the pool water warm, minimize evaporation, and keep debris out of the water.

■ "Indoor" Swimming Pools

Can you install a pool inside a house? Sure, if you can afford to spend a small fortune for it. For example, the YMCA has indoor swimming pools. However, their buildings are designed around their pools. They require unusual features to protect the structure, including continuous operation of humidity control equipment. An indoor pool is a feat of engineering. If you are determined to have a pool inside your house, start by finding an engineer who has the specialized experience and skills to design the pool environment properly.

The main challenge of an indoor pool is that the water in the pool is warmer than the inside of the house. Therefore, vapor rising from the pool will condense all over the interior surfaces. Even worse, if the vapor can penetrate into the structure, it will condense inside the structure, causing progressive damage. The cooler the climate, the worse the problem.

In principle, it is possible to avoid damage by confining the water vapor to the pool space. However, this is difficult in practice. It requires an unbroken impermeable barrier, such as fully tiled walls or a separate glass wall surrounding the pool. In addition, an indoor pool needs a lot of energy to lower the humidity around the pool. Without lowering the humidity, the pool area will be covered with mildew and all the metal fittings, such as light fixtures, will corrode.

A pool cover can save a lot of energy and minimize moisture problems when the pool is not being used. It provides no protection when the pool is being used. Mechanized pool covers are easy to use, but expensive.

Because an indoor poor does not benefit from the sterilizing power of sunlight, it will need regular and thorough cleaning. An indoor pool is more practical in a house that has a domestic staff.

If you really must have an "indoor" swimming pool, it is best to enclose it in a separate structure, with its own foundation. You can match the exterior appearance of the shell to the exterior appearance of the house, and you can build a matching passage between the two.

HOT TUBS AND SPAS

A hot tub, or "spa," gratifies a peculiar impulse to crowd into hot water with people you barely know. Most hot tubs are not actually used much, because the vision is more attractive than the reality. However, a hot tub is a relatively inexpensive indulgence. The freestanding variety doesn't occupy much space, and it can be moved. See Figure 1-241.

As a rule, hot tubs belong outside, even in cold climates. For people who like hot tubs, scurrying through freezing outdoor temperatures wrapped only in a towel seems to be part of the pleasure. The hot tub should be located near an entrance to a nearby toilet room or dressing room where bathers can dry off and get dressed. Since everyone may exit the tub together, this space needs to be large.

An outdoor hot tub needs to be protected from freezing. Design the installation in a way that protects the plumbing.

If a hot tub is placed indoors, it has the same moisture problems as an indoor swimming pool, only worse. The higher temperature of the water causes hot tubs to emit water vapor at a much higher rate. That's why you rarely see a hot tub indoors.

The indoor whirlpool bath is basically a smaller version of a hot tub, but it is drained after each use. This makes it possible to clear out the water vapor and allow the space to dry, as with showers and bathtubs.

Vanguard Spa

Figure 1-241. Hot tub. To complete the vision, add three guys and a case of beer.

STEP
STEP 2

LAY OUT YOUR GLASS AND SHADING

> **NOTE TO READERS IN THE SOUTHERN HEMISPHERE**
> To keep the discussion simple, compass directions are stated with respect to locations in the northern hemisphere. For locations in the southern hemisphere, simply substitute "south" where the text says "north," and *vice versa*.

Now, we are ready to select the locations and dimensions of the windows, skylights, and other glazing for each of the spaces that you designed in Step 1.

Glazing is powerful stuff. It performs five essential functions in a home. At the same time, glazing is a major threat to energy efficiency, and it can cause discomfort if it is located and sized carelessly. As a result, your glazing design needs to juggle more factors than any other aspect of your home design. Enjoy the challenge. If you design your windows optimally, your home will be exceptionally efficient, comfortable, and elegant.

Shading should be an integral part of glazing design. Shading keeps occupants comfortable in warm weather with a minimum of cooling cost. And, it makes daylighting pleasant and glare-free.

We lay the groundwork for your glazing design by explaining the five functions that glass performs and the four major types of home glazing. The sun is the source of daylight and solar heat, so we will get to know the sun's behavior. To make it easy for you to deal with all the issues of glazing design, we will cover those issues in a logical sequence.

At the end of this Step, you will learn how to preserve the energy efficiency and comfort of your home if you want to have a large area of glass to enjoy a special view.

We will use the term "glazing" to mean all the parts of your house that transmit light, including windows, skylights, light pipes, glass doors, etc. We will use the terms "glass" and "glazing" interchangeably, unless there is a reason to make a distinction.*

---

* Architects have a fancy name for glass or glazing. They call it "fenestration," which is a superfluous term that we won't use.

GLASS & SUNLIGHT: THE MINIMUM YOU SHOULD KNOW

FIVE REASONS WHY HOUSES HAVE GLASS

Windows were first invented to provide *daylighting*. The houses of our ancient ancestors were dark places. Limited sunlight entered through the entrances and through the smoke vents for the fires that were used for cooking and heating. The Romans introduced glass for daylighting during the first century BC. Small skylights were blown in the same way as bottles and other glassware. These provided good lighting because they could face upward into the weather, unlike the fragile oiled paper and thin animal skins that were also used to admit sunlight. Today, glass is virtually the sole source of daytime lighting for houses.

Glass that is reasonably clear and flat was developed by the Romans during the second century AD. This glass allowed people to enjoy a *view* of the outdoors without exposing themselves to the elements. Later, small panes of glass were assembled into larger windows using wooden frames. Wealthy homeowners radically increased the sizes of their windows to exploit their vistas.

Next, builders adapted framed windows so that they could be opened. This made windows the primary means of *ventilation*, primarily for cooling houses during warm weather, but also for clearing air pollutants. Windows are virtually ideal for ventilation because they are located throughout the house, so they can effectively channel air flow through the parts of the house where ventilation is desired. Windows can easily be fitted with insect screens, providing ventilation without pests.

As windows became essential for the previous functions, they also became an important aspect of houses' *appearance*. Windows are now a basic element of every architectural style. In fact, this function has become so dominant that it tends to overshadow the other functions, often to their detriment.

When windows became large enough to admit copious amounts of daylight, it was discovered that sunlight provides a significant amount of *heating* during the daytime. By the 17th century, this effect was exploited deliberately, primarily in palaces and the homes of the wealthy. Houses added "sun rooms" to be islands of light and warmth during winter days. During the latter half of the 20th century, the formalized use of glazing for "passive solar heating" was introduced as a way to reduce heating cost.

Your glass design will optimize all five of these functions, as well as making improvements in several other ways.

FOUR KINDS OF HOME GLAZING

There are four modern forms in which glazing may be used in a house: *windows*, *clerestories*, *skylights*, and *light pipes*. Each has its own benefits and limitations, summarized in Table 2-1, *Glazing Comparison*. We will learn how to use each type most effectively.

Windows are the most common kind of home glazing. In fact, most homes use windows as their only kind of glazing. However, windows provide very unbalanced daylighting in large rooms, and they cannot provide daylighting in interior rooms. Clerestories and skylights can provide good daylighting for rooms under vaulted ceilings. Skylights can also provide daylighting through truss roofs, but at the cost of complicating the roof structure. Light pipes offer an easy source of daylighting through truss roofs.

THREE KINDS OF SUNLIGHT

We use glass in homes because it admits sunlight, including the view of the outside world that is illuminated by sunlight. The sun emits radiation in a broad and continuous spectrum of wavelengths, or frequencies*, which is shown in Figure 2-1. The particular wavelength of sunlight determines how sunlight affects people, and the wavelength also determines how glass behaves toward sunlight. Three regions of the sun's wavelength spectrum have different behaviors, which we need to understand.

Visible light lies near the end of the solar spectrum that has the shortest wavelengths. It contains about 35% of total solar energy. Glass is highly transparent to visible light. Human eyes are very sensitive to light, so only a small amount of solar energy is needed for vision. Bright sunlight delivers about 200 times more energy than you need to see comfortably. All visible light becomes heat when it is absorbed, for example, by the furnishings inside your home.

* Here is all the science you need to know. (1) Light travels across empty space at a constant speed, called "c". (2) All the characteristics of light result from a single variable, its wavelength or frequency. Wavelength and frequency are the inverse of each other. (3) For visual purposes, light is usually described in terms of its wavelength. Frequency is commonly used in scientific formulas. (4) Light travels as individual packets of energy, called "photons." (5) The energy of a photon is directly proportional to the light's frequency, or inversely proportional to its wavelength.

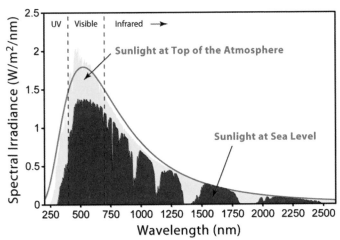

adapted from Wikipedia Commons

Figure 2-1. The spectrum of sunlight. The sun emits energy like a big incandescent lamp filament. The solid line is the emission of an ideal filament at a temperature of 9,480 °F (5,250 °C). The blue curve is the sunlight that reaches sea level after being filtered by the atmosphere. The most intense sunlight is in the visible spectrum, but a large amount of sunlight is invisible heat. The notches in the solar spectrum are caused mainly by absorption of sunlight by atmospheric water vapor, except that the ozone layer absorbs most of the sun's ultraviolet emission. A small fraction of the heat radiation is absorbed by atmospheric carbon dioxide.

Infrared light is invisible sunlight that has frequencies lower than the frequencies of visible light. ("Infrared" means "below red," in terms of frequency.) The infrared wavelengths contain about 60% of total solar energy. Glass is transparent to most of these wavelengths. This component of sunlight delivers heat to the inside of your home, but it does not help vision. The infrared component of sunlight may be useful or it may be a problem, depending on whether you want to heat your home or to keep it cool.

Ultraviolet light consists of the highest frequencies of sunlight, which are invisible to human beings. ("Ultraviolet" means "above violet.") It contains only about 3% of solar energy. However, the individual photons of ultraviolet light have enough energy to destroy chemical bonds. Therefore, this part of sunlight bleaches fabrics, causes skin cancer, and destroys vinyl siding. By a lucky coincidence, window glass absorbs most ultraviolet light, although glass still passes enough ultraviolet light to cause slow degradation of curtain fabrics and other organic materials.

(There is one other kind of radiation that will influence your glazing design. This is "heat" radiation that comes from your own body and from the interior surfaces of your home. It is like sunlight, but the wavelengths are much longer and the radiation is much weaker. This low-temperature radiation is completely absorbed by glass, but coatings can be applied to glass to reflect it.)

HOW THE SUN MOVES THROUGH THE SKY

The sun moves through the sky in a predictable pattern that repeats on a daily and yearly basis.* Understanding solar motion is the basis of several important aspects of your glazing design. You need this knowledge to exploit solar heating during cold weather, to shade your glazing against unwanted heat during warm weather, and to create effective daylighting. It also is important for optimizing the benefit of your views. So, let's get familiar with the sun's motion.

The apparent motion of the sun through the sky results from the way that the earth moves with respect to the sun, as shown in Figure 2-2. The earth rotates around its own axis every 24 hours, creating the impression that the sun swings through the sky every 24 hours. Because of the direction in which the earth rotates, the sun "rises" toward the east and "sets" toward the west.

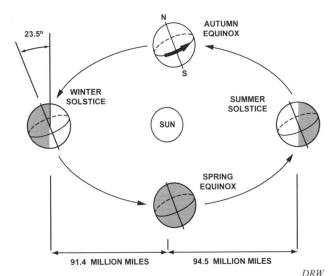

DRW

Figure 2-2. The motion of the earth around the sun. The tilt of the earth's axis is the dominant factor that determines seasonal changes in climate and daylighting. The closer distance to the sun during the northern hemisphere winter slightly offsets the effect of the axis tilt, whereas the opposite is true in the southern hemisphere.

---

* Today, few architects or homebuilders understand the sun's motion, which is one reason for the high air conditioning costs and poor daylighting of modern buildings. In many "primitive" societies, people had an accurate understanding of the sun's daily and seasonal motion. Typically, they used this knowledge for timekeeping, navigation, and religion. Some of those civilizations, such as the pueblo peoples of the American Southwest, also used their knowledge of solar motion to improve home construction. If that sun-oriented society had developed glass windows, it would have been interesting to see how they employed glass for its various purposes.

TABLE 2-1. GLAZING COMPARISON

FUNCTION	WINDOWS	CLERESTORIES	SKYLIGHTS	LIGHT PIPES
Best Applications	• All climates. • All structures.	• All climates. • At the top of a tall wall. • Dormers in a sloped ceiling, with beam roof construction.	• Climates with minimal snow and without frequent rain. • In sloped ceiling, with beam roof construction.	• Climates with minimal snow. • Rooms under truss roof.
View	• Highly adaptable to available views.	• Limited view of sky or trees.	• None.	• None.
Privacy	• Most windows require interior privacy shades. • Tall sills may provide privacy, depending on exterior terrain.	• Provide privacy, except from elevated exterior vantages.	• Provide privacy, in most cases.	• Complete privacy.
Daylighting	• Poor lighting geometry, concentrated near windows. Most light falls on floor. • Entry of direct sunlight can cause intense glare. • Easy to modulate intensity with interior shades.	• Superior to windows in distribution of daylight. • Can provide daylighting to spaces not facing the sun. • Orientation determines sunlight intensity and variation with time of day. • Difficult or impractical to control intensity.	• Superior to windows and clerestories in positioning and distribution of daylight. Intensity less variable with time of day. • Broad light distribution with beam roofs, narrower distribution with attic roofs. • Difficult or impractical to control intensity.	• Optimal positioning and distribution of daylight. • Limited lighting capacity. • Impractical to control intensity.
Ventilation	• Optimum locations for cooling ventilation. • Can provide restricted air flow for air quality ventilation.	• Can provide ventilation at high points for cooling. • Awkward access for opening.	• Some skylights are openable for ventilation, at increased risk of water leakage. • Awkward access for opening.	• None.
Esthetics	• Important element of style, inside and outside.	• Pleasant and visually effective daylighting. • Some shapes add interest to large ceilings. • Some exterior shapes are attractive, and some are drab.	• Pleasant and visually effective daylighting. • Add ceiling texture. • Clash with decorative roof surfaces.	• Minimal esthetic value. • Clash with decorative roof surfaces.

Energy Efficiency	• Poor insulation value. • Typically, responsible for most heating and cooling energy use. • Passive heating may provide net heating gain, only in moderate mid-latitude climates. • Saves daytime lighting energy.	• Poor insulation value, worse than vertical glazing. • Saves daytime lighting energy. • Typically, heating and/or cooling energy losses exceed lighting energy saving, except in mild climates.	• Ineffective because of small size, light loss, and covering by snow.	• Poor insulation value. • Saves daytime lighting energy. • Increases heating and cooling energy, typically by small amounts.
Passive Solar Heating	• If facing south, vertical orientation of glass is favorable for capturing low winter sun. • Ineffective if not exposed to direct sun for large fraction of day. • Usually requires extended roof or other structural features for exterior shading against summer sun. • Heat is delivered low in the room, which is optimum.	• If facing south, vertical orientation of glass is effective for capturing low winter sun. • Can provide heating to rooms on sides of house away from the sun. • If facing south, easy to adapt roof line to shade from summer sun. • Heat is delivered high in the room, which aggravates stratification.	• Generally not desirable for solar heating because of difficulty in controlling heat gain during warm weather. • Skylights sized for daylighting are too small for solar heating. • Sunlight is blocked by snow.	• Similar to windows.
Problems	• Eventual failure of seals in multiple-glazed windows, requiring periodic replacement of glass or entire window assembly.	• Constrains roof structure, floor plan, and room layout. Requires tall ceiling geometry. • Same maintenance problems as windows. • Overhead location allows cold drafts to fall into the space from the glazing. • Awkward to clean.	• Vulnerable to water leakage. • Vulnerable to hail and falling objects. • In cold weather, may drip condensate into room and on surrounding trim. • Eventual failure of seals around frame and between panes. • Plastic glazing deteriorates from sunlight. • Troublesome to install through a truss roof. • Awkward to clean.	• Similar to small skylights, except less prone to water leakage and easier to install through truss roofs.

As seen from the surface of the earth, the sun appears to rotate around the axis of the earth's rotation. This axis points toward the North Star (whose official name is Polaris) in the northern hemisphere, and toward an opposite location in the southern sky.

The axis of the sun's rotation through the sky is tilted with respect to the horizon. The angle of tilt depends on your "latitude." The latitude of a location on the earth is its angular distance north or south of the equator, expressed in degrees.

The motion of the sun through the sky differs greatly from lower (southerly) to higher (northerly) latitudes. For example, Figure 2-3 shows how the sun moves across the sky at Miami, Florida, located at a latitude of 26°. Figure 2-4 shows how the sun is seen at Anchorage, Alaska, located at a latitude of 61°.

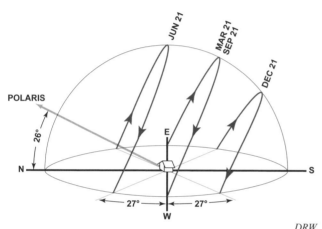

DRW

Figure 2-3. The seasonal paths of the sun through the sky of Miami, Florida. The sun rises and sets quickly, and arcs high overhead during most of the year.

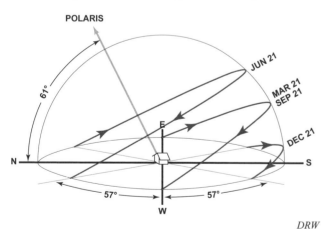

DRW

Figure 2-4. The seasonal paths of the sun through the sky of Anchorage, Alaska. The steep slant of the sun's paths results in long twilights. The grazing angle of sunlight results in low temperatures. The locations of sunrise and sunset move far around the horizon as the seasons change. The very short sun paths during winter result in very low temperatures

Exploiting the sun's motion for the benefit of your home starts with this key fact: ***the slant of the sun's path with respect to the vertical is equal to the latitude.*** For example, Sydney, Australia is located at latitude 34° south, so the sun's path at Sydney is slanted 34° from the vertical.

In addition to its 24-hour rotation, the earth also swings around the sun once a year. If the earth's axis were perpendicular to its path around the sun, this would make no difference in the sun's apparent motion. However, Figure 2-2 shows that the axis of the earth's rotation is tilted about 23.5° with respect to its path around the sun.

Because of this tilt, the sun's path shifts toward the north or south by a small amount every day. Over the course of a year, this north-south motion shifts the path of the sun laterally from one part of the sky to another, as shown in Figures 2-3 and 2-4.

SUN POSITION CHARTS

A sun position chart is an accurate diagram that shows when sunlight will shine on your house, and from which directions. It shows the position of the sun at all times of the day and at all times of the year. A sun position chart is the same for all locations at the same latitude. Figures 2-5, 2-6, and 2-7 show sun position charts for the latitudes of 20°, 40°, and 60°, respectively. These charts are in "polar" format, which is the easiest to understand and the easiest to use.

Sun position charts show the position of the sun by using two coordinates, "elevation" and "azimuth." The "elevation" is the number of degrees that the sun is above the horizon. The "azimuth" is the lateral position of the sun over the horizon, measured in degrees from true north.

Azimuth is marked on your sun position chart with compass coordinates. This is a 360-degree circle, measured clockwise from north. North is 0°, east is 90°, south is 180°, and west is 270°.

The chart also shows the time at each solar position. The time is expressed as the hours between sunrise and sunset. Hour 12 is centered at true south, where the sun is highest in the sky.

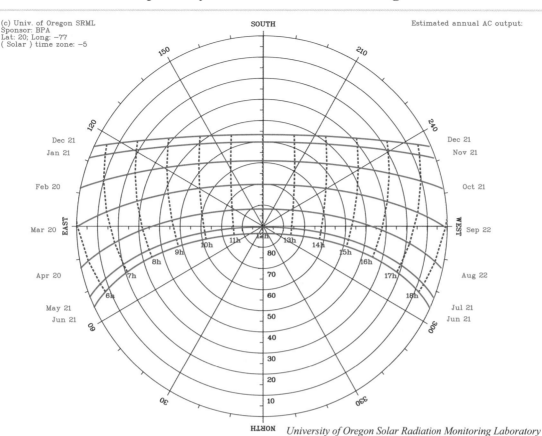

Figure 2-5. Sun position chart for latitude 20°, in "polar" format. Note that south is up, north is down. This is the latitude of Mexico City and Hilo, Hawaii.

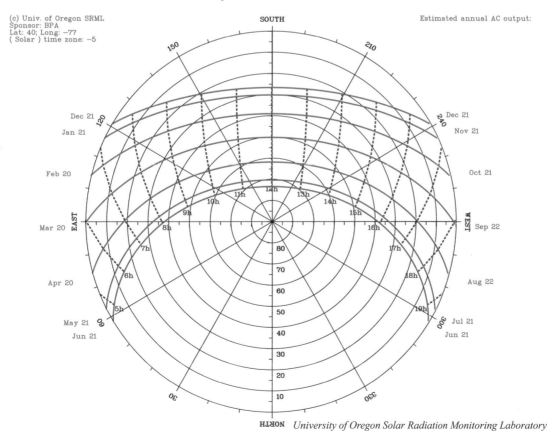

Figure 2-6. Sun position chart for latitude 40°. This is the latitude of Philadelphia (USA), Madrid (Spain), Ankara (Turkey), and Beijing (China). A large fraction of the world's population lives near this latitude.

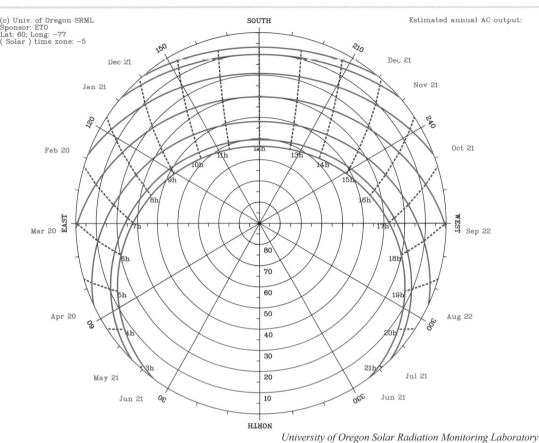

University of Oregon Solar Radiation Monitoring Laboratory

Figure 2-7. Sun position chart for latitude 60°. This is the latitude of Oslo (Norway) and Saint Petersburg (Russia).

WHAT TO LEARN FROM SUN CHARTS

Take a few moments to study the sample charts. They will give you a wealth of insight. Take away these points:

- *The arc of the sun's path through the sky is centered exactly over the direction of true south.* This true in every location and at all times of the year. The sun is always highest when it is due south.

- *The sun's path is slanted from the vertical by an amount that is equal to the latitude.* For example, at a latitude of 40°, the sun's path is slanted 40° from the vertical.

- *The slant of the sun's path through the sky remains constant throughout the year.* That's because the slant of the sun's path is determined by the latitude, which does not change.

- *The sun's daily path shifts toward the north in summer, toward the south in winter.* The sun's path reaches its extreme northern limit at the "summer solstice" (June 21), and its extreme southern limit at the "winter solstice" (December 21). The sun literally "rises in the east" and "sets in the west" only on two days each year, the "spring equinox"

(usually March 20) and the "autumn equinox" (usually September 22).

- *The sun is higher in the sky in summer because the sun's path moves northward in summer.* This is one reason why it gets warmer in summer. (Near the equator, this is not exactly true.)

- *The sun's daily path is longest in summer, shortest in winter.* The sun remains in the sky for a longer time as its path gets longer. This is another reason why it gets warmer in summer. At higher latitudes, the sun travels far around the horizon during summer, whereas it remains near the southern horizon during winter.

- *The sun remains entirely in the southern half of the sky during the colder six months from September 21 to March 21.* During the warmer six months, from March 21 to September 21, the sun rises and sets in the northern half of the sky, but it moves into the southern half of the sky during the middle of the day.

- *The noontime sun at the summer solstice is 47° degree higher than the noontime sun at the winter solstice.* This difference is twice the tilt of the earth's axis (23.5°). The difference is smaller near the equator (below latitude 23.5°) and at arctic latitudes (above 66.5°).

- *The seasonal differences in the length of the day increase greatly with latitude.* That is the main reason why locations at higher latitudes have greater seasonal differences in temperature.

(If you live in the southern hemisphere, exchange "north" and "south" in the previous statements.)

GET YOUR OWN SUN POSITION CHART

You will need a sun position chart to design the glass for your home. To get a chart for your location, do an Internet search for "sun position chart." There are several free sources. At this time, my favorite source is the Web site of the University of Oregon Solar Radiation Monitoring Laboratory:

www.SolarDat.UOregon.edu/SunChartProgram.html

To create your chart, you will need to input some information. The only input that matters is your latitude, which you can find easily on the Internet. If asked by the program, select the time as "local solar time." The program may ask for your longitude, time zone, or other data, but those inputs will not affect the appearance of the chart.

Get your chart in "polar" format. Make a bunch of copies to play with.

DRW

Figure 2-8. Using a protractor at the building site to survey the angular height of obstructions to direct sunlight.

MAKE A SUN & VIEW SURVEY OF YOUR HOME SITE

A sun position chart tells you the location of the sun in the sky, but the sun may be hidden by obstructions that surround your building site. To identify and locate those obstructions, you need to make a survey at your building site. The purpose is to record the location of every large object that may block direct sunlight to your house or to particular parts of your house.

Another important purpose is to locate all the views that you want to have from the house or from particular rooms in the house.

Making the survey is easy, and it will give you valuable insight about your building site. All you need is the sun position chart for your latitude, a compass, and a "protractor" for measuring vertical angles.

The protractor can be inexpensive, but you will have to shop for it. It may be called a "bubble level protractor," "digital level," "inclinometer," "slope finder," or other name. Figure 2-8 shows a typical protractor. The key point is that you want it to indicate angles from the horizontal or vertical.

A more elegant way to make your azimuth and elevation observations is to use a surveyor's transit, which includes a compass. You can probably rent one locally.

Using the protractor or transit, measure the elevation of the obstructions, as in Figure 2-8. Mark your observations on the elevation lines of the sun chart. Then, mark the azimuth of all views that you want to see from your house. Figure 2-9 shows a typical sun & view survey.

Since your compass is magnetic, you need to correct for the difference between *true* and *magnetic* directions. This difference is called "magnetic variation." It changes with location. The difference may be large enough to degrade your solar heating and solar shading design if you don't account for it. For example, magnetic variation is about 17° in Seattle, Washington. The error can be even greater at northern locations in Europe and Asia.

So, make an Internet search for "magnetic variation map" to find the correction for your location. In the U.S., the line of zero variation is centered approximately on the Mississippi River. To the east, true directions are to the right of the compass needle. To the west, true directions are to the left of the compass needle.

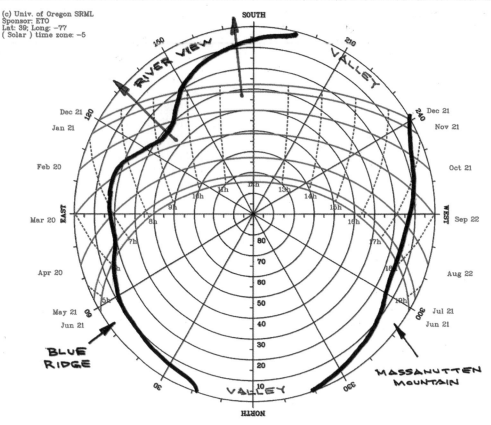

DRW with University of Oregon Solar Radiation Monitoring Laboratory

Figure 2-9. Typical sun obstruction and view chart. This chart is for a location in the Shenandoah Valley of Virginia that is adjacent to the Blue Ridge mountains. During the cold months, the sun is blocked from the east until late morning. During the warm months, the sun is blocked only during early and late daylight hours.

 Now, you are an expert on glass and sunlight! Let's use your knowledge to design your home's glazing.

GLASS DESIGN 1: MINIMIZE HEAT LOSS

Glazing is the biggest route for heat loss from your home during cold weather. That's because of the poor insulation value of glass. The best conventional windows have insulation values that are only about one-tenth of the appropriate insulation values for walls and ceilings in a cold climate.

The poor insulation value of glass causes discomfort as well as wasting energy. The glass itself is a cold surface, even when the sun is shining through it. The air inside the house cools by contact with the glazing, creating a draft of cold air that pools on the floor. Also, the cold surface absorbs heat that is radiated from people's clothing and exposed skin, creating a sensation of "radiating cold."

Windows and other glazing are energy holes in your home. If your home is located in a climate that has a significant cold season, minimize the size of those holes. The design principle is: *make your windows and other glazing no larger than necessary to satisfy your needs*.

In addition, select your glass for maximum insulation value, which is covered in the *Window Selection Guide*, in Step 3.

It is especially important to minimize the area of glazing in your bedrooms and in other rooms that are used at night and in the early morning. Heat loss through glass during long winter nights can make those rooms uncomfortably cold. Fortunately, you don't need much glass in those rooms for view, and only a small amount for daylight.

Before the era of cheap energy, cultures located in colder climates built their homes with smaller windows. As energy becomes expensive and scarce, we need to return to this understanding.

How much glass do you need? Daylighting requires only a small amount of glass for each room. The size of windows that you need for ventilation cooling depends on the climate, with larger windows being needed only in climates that have an extended warm season.

Glancing ahead, we see that the largest amount of glass area is needed to exploit a good view, if you have one. That glass is needed only in the rooms where you will be enjoying the view. Windows are also a major factor in a house's exterior appearance, but we learned in Step 1 how to dress up the exterior without using a lot of glass.

What if you really want a large amount of glass because you have a panoramic view or because you want to bask in sunlight during winter or just because you like the idea of a space with lots of glass? You can create such a space, but you will have to accept some compromises in your space layout if you want to keep your home super-efficient and comfortable. We will show you how to do it at the end of this Step.

DRW

Figure 2-11. Useless glass. All the windows in this house have been obscured to provide privacy. They contribute only heat loss and discomfort during the extended cold season. Why do architects repeat these mistakes?

REDUCING WINDOW HEAT LOSS IN EXISTING HOUSES

In existing houses, the most common way to reduce window heat loss is to replace the present windows with better models. Replacing windows is expensive. However, if the windows are single-pane or leaky, it is worthwhile. Step 3 covers the selection and installation of windows, which are done the same way in new and existing houses.

In many cases, you can also install supplemental windows in tandem with the existing windows. This may allow you to double the insulation value of conventional windows. See *Installing Tandem Windows*, in Step 3.

In many existing houses, it is practical to reduce excess window area. For example, the house in Figure 2-11 has far too much window area for the climate in which it is located. It would be practical to replace most of the windows with decorative insulating panels, leaving only windows that actually perform the useful functions of providing view and daylighting.

In houses with a more abstract style, it is usually possible to make such a change without diminishing the overall appearance of the house. If the house has a more classic appearance, it is more challenging to eliminate excess window area. In such cases, your best option may be to install insulating panels inside selected windows. Decorate the outward facing sides of the panels so they look attractive when seen through the window.

If your existing windows have you living in a fishbowl, modifying the windows will also improve your privacy. We cover the details later, under the heading, *Glass Design 5: Exploit Your Views And Preserve Privacy*.

MOVABLE WINDOW INSULATION: STILL A WISH

In principle, there is a way to substantially reduce the heat loss of windows during cold weather. That is to install removable insulation over the windows during the dark hours when windows don't provide any benefit.

In fact, many kinds of movable insulation have been tried, but none is practical enough for mainstream application. For that reason, I don't recommend movable insulation yet. However, in a location where the winters are long and cold, you may want to try movable insulation for your windows on a custom basis. If you are skilled and daring, see *Movable Insulation for Windows*, in *Last Look: Energy for Pioneers*, at the end of the book.

GLASS DESIGN 2: DAYTIME SOLAR HEATING

We just advised you to minimize your glass area to reduce heat loss during cold weather. However, glass can also contribute a significant amount of heat during the daytime. Think of how your car warms up when you park it in a sunny location. If your climate has a cold season, use your glass as much as possible to assist in heating your home.

The maximum amount of energy that a window can collect from direct sunlight is about 240 BTU's per hour per square foot (750 watts per square meter). This maximum occurs when the sky is clear, the window azimuth faces the sun, and the sun is about 30 degrees above the horizon. Under these conditions, the heating effect of sunlight through a window of average size is roughly the same as that of a small portable electric heater.

During cold weather, any sunlight entering through your glass provides a free heating bonus. However, most worthwhile heating comes from direct sunlight, which has about ten times more energy than indirect sunlight. The sun's path is centered at due south, so follow this design principle if your house is exposed to direct sunlight, and if you want the heat:

① **Concentrate the glass toward the south as much as possible.**

② **Concentrate the glass in rooms that are used during the daytime, to maximize the heating benefit and to exploit view and daylighting.**

Orienting your glass toward the south is worthwhile only if your home will be exposed to direct sunlight during cold weather. Indirect sunlight – from a clear sky, or from clouds, or reflected from surrounding terrain – has approximately the same intensity from any direction.

Aiming your glass toward the south can be a big design commitment. It may require you to adapt your room layout, the shape of your house, and perhaps the design of the roof. It may have a major effect on the appearance of your house and your views. So, the first thing to consider is whether orienting your glass toward the south is worth the trouble.

CHECK THE SOLAR HEATING POTENTIAL OF YOUR HOME SITE

From the data that you previously collected about your home site, identify the months when the daytime temperature lingers below 50 °F (10 °C). Check your weather data to see how many hours of clear skies you have during those months. This will tell you whether the local climate justifies orienting your windows toward the south.

You also need to know whether your home would be exposed to direct sunlight during those months. The sun survey that you prepared for your home site will tell you this.

Don't be surprised if much of your winter sunlight is obstructed by trees, terrain, and other buildings. The sun remains low during winter. For example, look at Figure 2-6, the sun position chart for latitude 40°. At this latitude, the mid-winter sun rises only 27° above the horizon at noon, and it spends only about 7 hours per day at elevations higher than 10° above the horizon.

Windows on upper floors may be able to capture more direct sunlight than windows on lower floors by looking over barriers to direct sunlight, including terrain and adjacent houses.

HOW CRITICAL IS WINDOW ORIENTATION?

How accurately should the glazing face toward the south? Again, look at the sun position chart for latitude 40°. During deep winter in the mid-latitudes, the path of the sun is confined to an arc that extends only about 60° horizontally on each side of true south. If you want to collect solar heat all day, the glazing should face within about 30° of true south. As the glazing is turned further away from true south, the effective window area for collecting sunlight falls substantially.

Orienting your windows somewhat toward the southeast will help to warm your home in the morning, after it has lost heat all night. However, the sun rises late in winter, so solar heating won't help you to get out of bed or warm your breakfast room.

There is a special case where window orientation is more critical. Most climates with a cold season also have a warm season, when glass exposed to the sun would overheat the room. If a wall is oriented fairly precisely toward true south, you can design fixed exterior shading that will admit direct sunlight during cold weather, but exclude it during warm weather. We will learn how to do this soon, when we design your shading.

SHOULD YOU INCREASE GLASS AREA TO EXPLOIT "PASSIVE SOLAR" HEATING?

Direct sunlight brings much more heat through a window than the window loses by conduction at the same time, even during very cold weather. Therefore, it is tempting to increase the size of your south-facing windows to get more free heating for your home. This general idea is called "passive solar heating."

Should you increase the size of your south-facing windows? The answer usually is no. At most, you might increase the glazing area of your daytime rooms by a modest amount, but even then you should be prepared for a dose of extra analysis and design work.

As a general rule, minimizing glass area to reduce heat loss is more important than using the glass to collect sunlight. Minimizing glass area saves energy and improves comfort at all times. In contrast, increasing glass area for solar heating works only when the window is exposed to direct sunlight, and large glass area can create serious discomfort during both cold and warm weather.

Passive solar heating enjoyed a surge of interest in the 1970's, and a number of houses were built specifically to push this concept forward. Unfortunately, most of these attempts yielded houses that are ugly and uncomfortable. Passive solar heating looks simple, but it is full of pitfalls. If the concept interests you, read *Passive Solar Heating*, in *Last Look: Energy for Pioneers*, at the end of the book.

GLASS DESIGN 3: STAY COOL IN WARM WEATHER

Now that you know how to design your glass to minimize heating costs during cold weather, we will see how to avoid discomfort and high cooling costs during warm weather. Glass lets unwanted heat into the house in two ways – by conduction of heat from the outside air and by radiation of sunlight through the glass.

Heat conduction through glass is the lesser evil during warm weather. To minimize it, follow the same principles that we used previously to reduce heat conduction during cold weather. Namely, keep the glass area as small as practical and select glazing that has the highest available insulation value. The area of the glazing is less important in warm climates than in cold climates, because the average temperature differences are smaller. Still, budget your glass area in each room to the actual needs of that room.

Direct radiation of sunlight through unshaded glass is the biggest source of unwanted solar heat. For example, if 100 square feet (10 square meters) of glass is exposed to direct sunlight, it can create a cooling load of about 20,000 BTU per hour (6 kilowatts).

The prime defense against unwanted heat from sunlight is well designed shading. During warm weather, all the glazing in your house should be shaded. One exception is small skylights and clerestories that are installed for daylighting, but you have to be careful even with them.

 Well designed shading is the most important window feature for minimizing cooling cost and staying comfortable during warm weather. It also helps to create glare-free daylighting.

In an existing house, it is usually uneconomical to change your windows just to reduce cooling cost. But, adding effective shading for your windows is an important improvement if they are exposed to much direct sunlight.

During the warm season, the sun spends considerable time shining on all sides of the house, so the glass on each side must be shaded. This is true at all latitudes, as you can see from Figures 2-5, 2-6, and 2-7.

Indirect sunlight that is reflected from the outside environment can also bring unwanted heat into your home, although much less than is carried by direct sunlight. Your shading design should give you almost complete control of both direct and indirect sunlight.

If our only goal were to keep direct sunlight from entering through the glass, we could simply cover each window with a shade that blocks any part of the sky where the sun may travel. However, we also want your windows to provide a view of the surroundings and to provide nice daylighting. To achieve all these purposes, each window or each side of the house must be shaded in a distinct way. This makes shading one of the most interesting and creative parts of your design.

To achieve optimum shading, you can select from three main methods, individually and in combination: *foliage*, *external window shading fixtures* that are attached to the house, and *internal window shades*. Each has advantages and limitations. These are the highlights:

- If you can surround a house with mature trees, they can provide all the shading you need. However, trees take years to grow, so you can't achieve this benefit immediately unless you can build your house within an existing grove of trees. Foliage of all kinds requires a lot of maintenance.

- Fixed external shading fixtures may be able to provide all the shading that you need on the south and north sides of the house. However, they cannot completely shade east and west sides without interfering with the view.

- Internal shading fixtures can block direct sunlight through glass that faces in any direction. However, interior shading devices interfere with the view, and they must be adjusted continually to minimize the interference. A significant amount of heat still gets into the house from the space between the glass and the interior shade. Most windows use interior shading fixtures for privacy as well as for shading.

Before we get into the details of each type of shading, let's make one important point. The need for shading changes continuously with the hour of the day and with the season of the year. Therefore, *select your shading methods to adapt to the motion of the sun with as little action by the occupants as possible*.

It would be ideal if your shading would adapt itself automatically to these changes. In fact, there are two powerful methods of shading that offer this ability. One is shading with deciduous trees, the kind that shed their leaves in winter. The other is installing fixed external shading for windows on the south side of the house. We will cover both in detail.

DRW

Figure 2-13. A neighborhood that is almost totally shaded by deciduous trees.

TREES AND SHRUBS FOR SHADING

Using trees and shrubs for shade is as old as humanity. When air conditioning became economical, tree shading fell into the background, but we should restore it to the status of a primary cooling technique. For brevity, we will say "foliage" to mean "trees and shrubs."

A major advantage of tree shading is that it can shade large areas of the house, not just individual windows. This is especially important for the roof, which can become quite hot in direct sunlight. Beyond that, tree shading can create a cool micro-climate around the entire house, and even on a large part of your property. See Figure 2-13.

Shorter trees, planted closer to the house, can provide shading for specific portions of the house, as in Figure 2-14.

Trees and shrubs can create a wonderful esthetic environment. Visualize your house and its environs entirely shaded by a grove of trees. There are few locations where you would not want them. Certain foliage can grow well even in heavily paved urban areas.

Foliage blocks over 90% of the solar energy falling on it. The incoming sunlight is either reflected or absorbed by the foliage. Much of the absorbed sunlight powers photosynthesis, and solar heating of the foliage is carried away by wind. Shading the

ground around the house reduces reflection of sunlight into the house.

And, there's more. Trees actually lower the temperature of the air by evaporation from the leaves. This may lower the temperature in the vicinity by 3 to 6 °F (2 to 4 °C). Thus, the air under a tree canopy may be noticeably cooler than the air under a gazebo or a shade tent.

How to Use Foliage for Shading

Trees and/or shrubs can shade all sides of a house. Select the appropriate shapes and locate them effectively with respect to the glass. Your sun position chart shows where the foliage needs to be placed.

For example, look at Figure 2-6, the sun position chart for latitude 40°. First of all, the chart tells us that you need to block sunlight broadly on the east and west sides of the house. We see that the sun rises and sets within a band that extends from about 30° north of the east-west line to about 30° south of the east-west line.

During the morning and afternoon, when the sun is low in the sky, you need dense foliage close to the ground to block the low sun. Or, you could plant taller shrubs or short trees at some distance from the house, so you preserve the view of the nearby property.

In all warm climates, the sun remains fairly high in the southern sky during the middle of the day. Therefore, you could plant tall trees to shade the south side. Their trunks would not obstruct low angles of vision. You can plant one or more trees on the south side in a pattern that connects their shadows with the shadows of lower foliage on the east and west sides.

DRW

Figure 2-14. . The palm trees on the west side of this Key West house effectively shade the second floor rooms from the heat and glare of the afternoon sun.

In a climate that is always warm, select trees and shrubs that are evergreen. If the trees or shrubs have leaves, the leaves should not shed on a seasonal basis. Magnolias and photinia are good examples. Fortunately, many attractive evergreen species are native to warm climates.

For a climate with both hot and cold seasons, plant deciduous trees, rather than evergreens. If you select the trees properly, most of their shading will cease before the weather becomes cold.

Deciduous trees can drop a lot of debris. Take this into account as you plan your property's layout, particularly where vehicles and other equipment may be parked under the trees.

Advantages of Shading with Foliage

In comparison with the other methods of shading, trees and shrubs offer these advantages:

- Trees can shade large areas, not just individual windows. They can shade all or most of the house, and they can shade large areas of the property surrounding the house. A grove of trees can create a cool micro-climate. Tree shading is the only practical way to keep the roof surface cool.
- Deciduous trees can lower the surrounding temperature by a few degrees, by a process that is essentially evaporative cooling.
- Properly selected deciduous trees adjust shading to the seasons. They provide virtually total shading during the warm season. When cold weather arrives, they shed their foliage, allowing sunlight to warm the house.
- A tall tree canopy can shade effectively in all directions with little obstruction of the horizontal view.
- Shrubs are especially advantageous when shading in the east and west directions, where the sun is low in the sky. This is because they can be planted at a distance from the house, preserving a view of the property adjacent to the house.
- Foliage is a major element of beauty for your house and property.
- Shrubs and some trees can serve as a privacy fence.
- Foliage damps noise.
- Tree layout for shading is relatively easy to design.
- Foliage is relatively inexpensive to buy and to plant, unless it has grown to large size.
- Some trees and shrubs will provide you with plentiful fruits or nuts, provided that you are willing to compete for these goodies with birds, squirrels, and various blights.

Problems of Foliage

Offsetting the virtues of foliage for shading are these shortcomings:

- Even the most rapidly growing shade trees and shrubs require several years to grow to a useful size. Some shade trees and shrubs can be purchased large enough to provide shading immediately or in a greatly reduced time. However, large trees and shrubs are expensive.
- Trees and shrubs have a limited life. Species that grow rapidly tend to have short lives, although this is not true for all.
- Trees can die prematurely from diseases and attack by parasites. Certain leafy species are vulnerable to foliage loss from insects, such as gypsy moths, that feed specifically on those species.
- Trees shed a variety of debris at different times of year, along with the droppings of birds and tree-dwelling animals. At certain times during the growth cycle, a car parked under a tree may become shabby within a day or two.
- Trees and shrubs require repetitive and tedious maintenance. If debris from trees can fall on the roof, gutter cleaning may be required several times per year, which may be difficult, dangerous, or expensive. Tree trimming is a further cost.
- Trees are vulnerable to lightning and wind, especially as they age. Falling limbs and trunks can cause major damage to the house, to parked vehicles, and to electrical and communications lines. Trimming or removing a potentially dangerous tree is a big expense.

Select the Best Species for Each Location and Use

After you have worked out the locations and shapes of your foliage, the next step is to research all the good and bad habits of each species that you are considering. Does it drop branches in windstorms? Does it drop a lot of debris over the course of a year? Does it emit a lot of pollen that causes allergies? Use the *Tree & Shrub Selection Guide* to help you select the shade trees and shrubs that have the best characteristics for your home.

How can you select trees and shrubs that will grow quickly and prosper at your location? My best advice is to ***favor trees and shrubs that you observe to be flourishing around your home site***. If you see trees and shrubs growing well in many sites similar to yours, your odds are much better than with trees that you don't see growing in your vicinity. And, you can observe their good and bad habits firsthand.

Look carefully. Many trees and shrubs are sensitive to local differences in soil properties, sun exposure, water supply, and drainage. For example, willows prosper at the edge of a creek or lake, but they may not

TREE & SHRUB SELECTION GUIDE

☐ Evergreen or Deciduous

For trees that shade the house from above, select evergreen species if the climate is always warm. Select deciduous trees if the location has both warm and cold seasons.

For low shrubs and short trees that you want to maintain privacy and to block the glare of the sun when it is low in the sky, select evergreen species. These also maintain a nice appearance throughout the year.

☐ (for Deciduous Plants) Proper Timing of Leaf Growth and Shedding

The tree should grow a well developed canopy by the beginning of the cooling season, and it should shed all its leaves near the beginning of the heating system.

Not all deciduous trees shed at the best times. For example, some species of oaks keep their dead leaves through the winter, and shed them only when new leaves push the dead ones loose in spring.

☐ Appropriate Shape

Select trees with shapes that will provide effective shading for the areas that you want shaded, while providing either an unobstructed view or privacy from inside the house.

The shape of a tree may be distorted severely by surrounding trees. For example, tulip poplars spread widely when they stand alone, but they will not grow branches in the direction of adjacent trees. When close to other trees, they grow tall and scraggly.

☐ Rapid Growth

You want the trees to grow as quickly as possible to minimize discomfort and use of cooling energy. Trees will block desirable views until they grow tall enough for the lower branches to be pruned above the sight lines.

The growth rate may depend heavily on the environment. For example, a pecan tree grows rapidly in Georgia, but slowly in Maryland.

☐ Longer Life

Tree life ranges from 20 years to 1,000 years. The more rapidly growing trees tend to have shorter lives, but the correlation varies. If your trees won't survive as long as your house, at least select them to live as long as you will.

Long life is not important for rapidly growing trees or shrubs that you plant as a stopgap until more permanent trees can grow to adequate size, usually farther away from the house.

☐ Ability to Flourish at the Site

Make sure that the tree is adapted to the conditions at the exact planting site, including exposure to sunlight, soil moisture, and soil properties. Otherwise, the tree may require watering, fertilizing, or other frequent tending.

☐ Roots That Don't Cause Damage

Roots can penetrate foundations, lift sidewalks, and destroy pavement. Check for radius of the root system and its tendency to cause damage.

☐ Roots That Remain Below the Surface

Roots that grow on the surface can interfere with lawn mowing, and can make the space under the tree unusable.

For example, magnolias will grow in shallow soil. But, if they are forced to do so, their roots form a large ropy mass on the surface that is unsightly and that is incompatible with grass.

☐ Wind Resistance

Some trees survive high winds by sacrificing branches, which is dangerous. Some trees topple easily in high winds. Resistance to toppling depends on soil conditions and local geology as well as the tree species. Any tree is unstable if it is forced to grow in a thin layer of soil.

☐ Minimum Shedding of Debris

Trees can shed a remarkable amount of material. This is particularly objectionable if the debris can collect in gutters or on things that you want to keep clean.

For example, tulip poplars shed a sequence of different kinds of debris through the seasons. At different times, they shed leaves, twigs, seed pods, petals, pollen, and a resinous spatter that makes cars filthy.

As a rule, evergreen species drop much less debris than deciduous species. However, some evergreen species drop more debris than others.

☐ Compatibility with Surrounding Vegetation

All trees have some effect on surrounding shrubbery, decorative plantings, and grass. Select your shading plants to be compatible with your other plants.

☐ Resistance to Disease and Parasites

All species are susceptible to unpredictable blights, but some are known to be vulnerable to recurring infestations. These may kill the plant or destroy its foliage.

For example, mulberries and certain other species are vulnerable to periodic infestation by gypsy moths, which strip the foliage and may kill the tree.

☐ Edible Fruits and Nuts

Some trees and bushes that are suitable for shading also provide free food. You will have to fight for it with birds, squirrels, worms, and blights, all of which will be attracted by the treats.

The fruit can become a nuisance when it falls, so be careful where you plant. For example, walnuts grow in pods that contain a large amount of material that stains badly.

☐ Resistance to Air Pollution

Some trees are more vulnerable than others to air pollutants, including smog, acid rain, ozone, etc. This matters especially in urban areas.

☐ Minimum Allergy Potential

Even if you don't have allergies now, some of the occupants of your home are likely to develop them later. Avoid trees that are notorious for triggering allergies.

This has become a regional problem in some places. For example, foliage planted in Arizona by immigrants from other climates now cause the same kinds of allergies that people once went to Arizona to escape.

grow well on ground that is slightly higher and drier. For help in learning about local growing conditions, check with your local agricultural extension service or with a local arboretum.

If you can't find suitable species that are native to your locale, you have a wide range of choices from elsewhere. The big question is how well a foreign species will prosper on your property. If you have a local arboretum or public garden, you can check with them. However, be conscious that they know how to keep imported plants healthy, and you probably don't.

You can also work with a good landscaper who knows trees. However, don't get committed to a species that requires continual tending by a professional. Don't believe the claims in nursery catalogs, including the biggest ones. They speak with forked tongue, and their products may be inferior to stock that is grown locally.

If you will be shading with evergreens, distinguish between two major kinds. One kind has needle-like leaves. Examples are pine, fir, and juniper. The space under the tree accumulates a brown carpet of dead needles, which choke out other vegetation, for better or worse. This kind of evergreen comes in many shapes. As a rule, they favor direct sunlight and they are not aggressive about spreading into other trees.

The other kind of evergreen has broad leaves. Examples are magnolias, photinia, and rhododendron. These have much less leaf fall than deciduous plants, and they generally don't shed as much of the other kinds of debris. In the middle latitudes, your choices are somewhat limited, because Mother Nature finds it difficult to design broad leaves that can survive freezing temperatures.* In the tropics, there are many species of leafy evergreens, some of which provide copious amounts of tasty fruit.

Plan for Growth

The main shortcoming of foliage is the time that it takes to grow. For this reason, you may want to plant temporary foliage at the same time that you plant permanent trees and shrubs. The temporary foliage is selected for rapid growth, and it is planted close to windows that need shade. Permanent trees and shrubs are planted farther away from the house, where their locations will be optimum at maturity. When the permanent foliage has grown to an adequate size for shading, you can remove the original foliage, which may be crowding the house by this time.

If you will be building on a site that is already wooded, you can avoid the delay in growth by exploiting the existing foliage as much as possible. Don't lose this resource to the builder's bulldozer. In fact, existing

---

* For example, rhododendrons act as an outdoor thermometer because their leaves curl up to stay warm when the temperature is below freezing. On a cold morning, you can gauge the temperature fairly accurately by observing how tightly the leaves have curled overnight.

large trees may be so valuable that you may want to adjust the location and orientation of your house to accommodate them. We discussed this in Step 1, under the heading, *Preserve Your Site's Natural Assets.*

Leave room for growth! A common mistake is planting trees and shrubs too close to the house and its outdoor amenities, including the driveway, sidewalks, swimming pool, etc. Little saplings become great big trees, which are huge structures that weigh many tons. You can't move them. You don't want thick tree trunks right outside your windows. The roots may damage the substructure, adjacent sidewalks, etc. Tree limbs may block the driveway.

Professional landscapers make this mistake as well as amateurs, so don't delegate responsibility for the layout. Determine the size and shape of the mature tree or shrub, and space them accordingly.

Try to keep trees from overhanging your neighbors' property. Otherwise, you will have a dispute at some time in the future.

Avoid interference with power and communications wires. Utility companies perceive trees as a hazard to their lines, and they usually have authority to prune them drastically, without regard to appearance or to the energy saving intentions of the homeowner. Underground power wiring on your property is one way to minimize interference, although underground wiring is vulnerable to freezing, flooding, and root damage.

Select your species and locations so that you can prune your growing plants to maintain desirable views. As the plant grows, it obstructs higher views, but you may be able to trim lower limbs to preserve the view underneath.

EXTERIOR SHADING FIXTURES

The best place to block solar heat is outside the house. Once heat is absorbed inside the house, getting rid of it requires cooling energy. External shading fixtures can be designed to block all direct sunlight, typically reducing solar heat by 80% to 90%. In comparison with foliage, shading fixtures have the advantage that they are available as soon as the house is occupied, and they can be tailored specifically to the geometry of the glazing.

External shading can be done with anything that casts a shadow over the glass during warm weather. It's best if you can exploit parts of the house's structure, such as roof overhangs. These are designed to withstand the elements, and they may cost little extra. Similar structural elements, such as false eaves, may be added to provide shading.

Where the structure itself cannot provide adequate shading, you can install specialized shading devices, such as awnings and louver panels. These devices s are just as exposed to the elements as your roof, and they need to maintain a good appearance for many years. As a result, durable exterior shading devices are not cheap.

We begin this explanation of exterior shading with a quick summary of how to use it on different sides of the house. Exterior shading for glass that faces toward the south is an important special opportunity that we cover in greater detail. Then, we review the various kinds of exterior shading that you may want to consider.

Overview: How to Use Exterior Shading

The design goal is to keep all windows in shadow during warm weather, while minimizing interference with the view. Start your design with the sun position chart for your latitude. (Instead, if you are using a home design computer program, it may be able to display shadows at all times of the day and year. However, most basic programs lack this ability.)

Different faces of the house favor different shading methods. For each window, select an appropriate type of shading fixture, minimizing conflict between shading and any view that the window may provide. Then, adjust the dimensions of the fixture to the orientation and shape of the window.

Shading against high sun is relatively easy. You can use essentially anything that projects out above the window, such as a roof overhang, a balcony, or an awning.

However, when the sun is low in the sky, it "looks underneath" overhanging shades. Exterior shading alone cannot reconcile view and shading on east and west sides.

You can use fixed exterior louvers or louver panels to block the low sun on the east and west sides, provided that your view is limited to a downward angle. For example, exterior louver panels may be satisfactory for the upper floor of an urban townhouse, where the desirable view is of the street below. Otherwise, you probably will use interior shading and/or exterior shrubs to supplement any exterior shading.

As odd as it may seem, you should also shade glass that faces toward the north. Look at a sun position chart, and you will see that the summer sun spends the early morning and late afternoon in the northern half of the sky. This is true at any latitude. Furthermore, the sun travels farther into the northern sky at locations in higher latitudes.

Northern sunlight strikes the north side glass at a grazing angle, from a relatively low angle. This requires shading features that are oriented vertically alongside the glass. For example, tall shrubs planted alongside a north-facing window can shade the window adequately.

The most beneficial application for exterior shading is over windows that face toward the south. So, let's examine that situation more closely.

Important Special Case: Shading for South-Facing Glass

A large fraction of the world's population lives in climates that have both hot and cold seasons. For example, over half of the States of the U.S. have climates that cause homeowners to spend large amounts of money for both heating and air conditioning.

In these climates, exterior shading can provide a unique advantage when it is used with south-facing glass. The shading can block direct sunlight completely during the warm season, and the same shading can allow full sunlight to enter during the cold season.

To understand how this works, let's look at the sun position chart for 40° latitude (Figure 2-6). On the longest day of the year, the sun rises to a maximum elevation of 74° above the horizon. On the shortest day of the year, the sun rises to only 27° above the horizon.

The diagram in Figure 2-15 shows the effect of these seasonal changes on the shading of a south-facing window. The diagram shows that the window can be fully exposed to sunlight during the coldest season, and fully shaded during the warmest season.

What's really interesting is how this shading remains effective throughout the day. During the winter season, the sun remains in the southern sky, so the sun can look underneath the overhang all day.

However, the reverse is true during the summer season. The sun wraps around the horizon during the morning and afternoon hours, so it cannot look underneath a south facing overhang during the hours when it is low in the sky. The wide overhang casts a longer shadow when the sun strikes the south face from the side. The net result is that the sun's shadow is shortest at noon, and becomes deeper in the morning and afternoon.

To exploit this south-facing geometry, you have to figure out the shadow pattern for the window at different times of the year. To do this, get the angles of the sunlight from your sun position chart. Then, lay out the window and the shading fixture on a sheet of graph paper, similarly to Figure 2-15. You want to arrange the layout so that the shadow of the sun always falls below the window during the warm months, and the shadow falls above the window during the cold months.

The shading fixture must extend well beyond the sides of the window. Otherwise, the sun would look underneath the shading fixture when it is in the eastern or western part of the sky. You can achieve effective shading with any wide structure that overhangs the window, such as a roof overhang, a false eave, an overhanging floor, a long awning, a ledge, etc.

In order for exterior shading to behave in this favorable manner all day, the orientation of the glass and its shading must be close to true south, say, within 15° or so. If the window faces toward the southeast, it will be exposed to summer sun in the morning. If the window faces toward the southwest, it will be exposed to summer sun in the afternoon and evening.

Previously, we recommended that a home in a climate that has a cold season should concentrate its glass area toward the south as much as practical. Now, by adding exterior shading over the south-facing glass, you get control of sunlight that is close to optimum all year.

Roof Overhangs

Roof overhangs provide a number of important benefits, which are listed under the heading, *Exploit Roof Overhangs*, in Step 1. Overhangs have no substantial disadvantages, except that they are incompatible with certain traditional architectural styles. If you design deep overhangs for your roof, get the most benefit from them as shading devices. Figure 2-16 shows how a roof overhang can shade windows.

As with all exterior shading, a roof overhang is most effective for a wall that faces toward almost true south. Otherwise, shading is effective for only part of the day.

Extended Gable End Overhangs

If a gable end wall faces south, as in Figure 2-16, extending the roof's gable end overhang can provide almost ideal shading for the south wall throughout the year.

This geometry provides improved shading during the early and late hours of the day because the downward sloping roof surfaces are more effective in blocking low sun. Also, the wall does not have to be

DRW

Figure 2-16. Shading by wide roof overhangs. The latitude is 39°, and the picture was taken in May. The wall to the left faces south, so the overhang will be able to shade the second floor windows almost completely for the duration of the day. The wall to the right faces east, so the overhang cannot provide shade during the early morning.

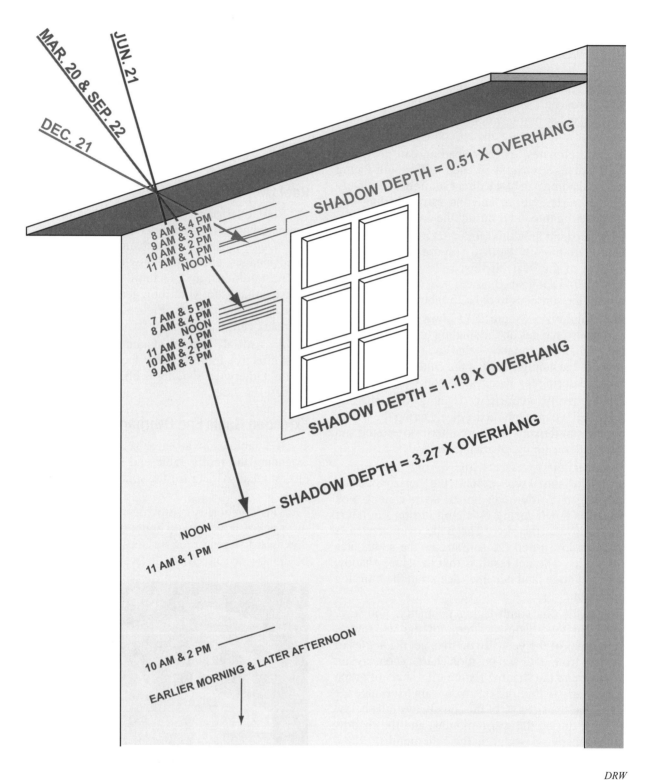

SHADOW DEPTH = 0.51 X OVERHANG

SHADOW DEPTH = 1.19 X OVERHANG

SHADOW DEPTH = 3.27 X OVERHANG

DRW

Figure 2-15. Exterior shading of a window on a south-facing wall, at latitude 40°. The window is shaded at all times during the warmest months. The window is exposed to direct sun during the coldest months. The lines to the left of the window indicate the bottoms of the shadows at the times indicated. The depth of the noon shadows is expressed as a multiple of the depth of the overhang. To provide shading in the morning and evening hours, the shading overhang must extend well beyond the sides of the window.

DRW

Figure 2-17. False eaves on a Florida house. At this sun angle, approximately half of the window area is shaded.

as precisely oriented toward true south as for the other types of exterior shading. Even if the wall is turned as much as 30° from true south, it is still practical to shade the entire wall during the warm months.

This shading geometry is especially valuable in the mid-latitudes and higher, where there are both extended warm and cold seasons. During the warm season, when the sun is high in the southern sky, the gable overhang can shade a relatively large amount of glass throughout the day. During the winter season, the lower winter sun can illuminate the windows for solar heating.

Exploiting the full advantage of an extended end wall overhang requires careful design of the shading angles. It also requires strong carpentry to support the overhang, which we will cover in Step 3.

False Eaves

To shade the windows of lower floors in a multi-story house and to provide the other benefits of roof overhangs, you can design false eaves for the lower floors that match the style of the roof. Figure 2-17 shows an example.

Floor Overhangs

Step 1 explained that overhanging upper floors are a relatively inexpensive way to gain additional living space. An overhanging floor can also serve as a shading fixture for windows that are located below it. However, for structural reasons, it is not desirable to extend a floor overhang very far.

The shadow pattern of a floor overhang is similar to that of a roof overhang. A floor overhang can shade the windows of a lower floor, while the roof overhang shades the windows of the top floor. As with other horizontal shading features, floor overhangs can provide shading throughout the day only if the wall faces almost true south.

Porches and Balconies

A porch roof or a balcony can be an especially effective shading device for the windows below it. Figure 2-18 is an example. The shadow pattern is deep and wide, while most of the view from the windows is preserved. In any orientation, a reasonably deep porch or balcony provides shading for most of the day.

However, as with all horizontal shading, a porch or balcony cannot provide *complete* all-day shading unless the wall faces toward the south. During the warm months, the sun rises and sets in the northern sky, so that not much sunlight leaks underneath a wide porch or balcony that faces south. At higher latitudes, low sun during the winter months will reach part of the window area, providing useful heating.

Awnings

Awnings are most effective on south faces, and they can provide fairly good shading of windows that face east and west. Awnings shade most of the window area because they extend downward over the upper portions of the windows. By the same token, awnings block an upward view.

A common mistake is making awnings the same width as the window, which allows an excessive amount of sunlight to enter from the sides, as in Figure 2-19. The trick is to make awnings substantially wider than the windows, as in Figure 2-20. If windows are clustered closely, use a single awning to shade all of them.

Fabric awnings can be attractive when new, but they begin to look shabby after several years. This makes them expensive in relation to their benefit.

DRW

Figure 2-18. A house that uses both a porch and a balcony for effective shading.

DRW

Figure 2-19. An awning that fits a window narrowly allows a certain amount of direct sunlight to peek under its sides. While most of the solar heat is blocked, the entering sunlight can still cause glare.

Metal awnings, usually made of enameled aluminum, can last for decades. However, they have a somewhat cheap appearance, and their sparkling surface becomes dull after a few years.

Louver Panels

Exterior louver panels are used for shading windows in warm, sunny climates. They are sometimes called "Bahama shutters" or "Bermuda shutters." They are hinged at the top, so they can be adjusted to change the shading and the view. See Figure 2-21. They are popular in some hurricane-prone locations because heavier versions can serve double duty as security and storm shutters.

DRW

Figure 2-21. Louver awnings. The louvers block sunlight completely at this sun angle, while preserving some downward view through the louvers.

DRW

Figure 2-20. One solution is to make the awning wider than the window. This is more practical and more attractive if a wide awning can shade several windows.

Louvers limit the view to a downward direction, so they are commonly used for the upper floors of houses, where they provide a view of the street level. Unlike most awnings, louver panels are open at the sides. To keep sunlight from entering at the sides, select panels that are considerably wider than the window. Subject to this requirement, louver panels can provide effective shading on most sides of the house, except northerly orientations.

Louver panels are easy to install, but covering many windows with them can become expensive. They are made of wood, plastic or aluminum. Enameled aluminum is the best choice.

Louvered Shutters

Louvered window and door shutters are popular in warm, sunny countries. They provide complete shade from direct sunlight, while admitting cooling breezes. Figure 2-22 shows a typical example.

Because the louvers are fixed, they generally are made with a complete overlap to exclude direct sunlight at all times of day. This geometry eliminates most view when the shutters are closed. It also limits the amount of indirect daylighting that can enter.

Shutters with adjustable louvers are also available. They operate like jalousie windows, except that the slats are opaque. Figure 2-23 shows an example.

Their shading performance is similar to that of venetian blinds, but the louvers are outside the window. This keeps more heat outside the house. As with venetian blinds, the slats interfere with the view.

DRW

Figure 2-22. Window and door shutters on a Greek island. These shutters are fixed, allowing cool sea breezes and keeping the rooms dimly daylighted. View through the shutters is minimal.

DRW

Figure 2-24. Fixed shutters cover an entire wall of a house in Key West.

DRW

Figure 2-23. Adjustable louver shutters in Italy that are installed outside openable windows.

For openings that face south, adjustable louvers don't need much adjusting. With openings that face east or west, louvers must be adjusted throughout the day to balance shading and view. Louvers are not desirable for windows that face toward the north.

To adjust exterior louvers, you need to open the window. This tends to limit them to warmer climates. Also, insect screens interfere with adjusting the louvers, so that movable insect screens are required.

Fixed Louvers

Fixed louvers are sometimes the best way to shade a particular part of the house, such as certain windows or a side of a deck. For example, Figure 2-24 is a louvered wall for one side of a house. Fixed louvers can provide effective shading for any orientation, but they limit the view.

Louvers require careful selection of the blade width, slant, and spacing. On the south side, the blades should be horizontal. For the north side, the blades should be vertical. For other wall orientations, the louvers may be mounted at a slant.

Custom louvers are a specialty item, so you may have to search to find someone to make them for you. In the past, louvers were made of wood, which required periodic repainting. Today, you probably would want louvers made of aluminum with an anodized or enamel finish.

DRW

Figure 2-25. A translucent patterned roller shade provides diffuse light and looks attractive. However, it becomes a source of glare if sunlight shines on it directly.

INTERIOR WINDOW SHADING

Unwanted sunlight can be blocked with a variety of interior shading devices.* This category of sun shading is the most versatile. It can be used with windows of all types and orientations. It can provide privacy. It can darken the room. It is adjustable for different conditions. It is protected from wind and precipitation, so it can be inexpensive, lightweight, and easy to install. It does not require much design; simply select the best type of shading device for each window or room.

These benefits come with penalties. All types of interior shading interfere with the view while they are blocking direct sunlight. And, they require repeated adjustment as the sun moves.

Interior shading is the least efficient method of rejecting solar heat. That's because interior shading allows the solar radiation to penetrate through the glass into the house. An interior shading device is efficient only to the extent that it can reflect the sunlight back out of the house before the radiation is converted to heat.

Some interior shading, such as reflective roller shades, can reflect about 70% of solar heat back through the window. Other interior shading, such a dark draperies, blocks as little as 20% of the incoming

_____

* Architects call these devices "window treatment," along with anything else that decorates the interior of a window. Many architects view them primarily as decor items, giving little attention to selecting them to perform their functions well.

Figure 2-26. A dramatic use of wood venetian blinds to match the woodwork of this elegant window daybed.

heat, even though it blocks most of the visible light. All the solar energy that is absorbed by the shade turns into heat. Most of the absorbed heat enters the room, mostly by convection.

Roller Shades

Roller shades are the most effective kind of interior shading for blocking the heat of sunlight. They provide complete privacy and darkness when desired. They are also the least expensive and the easiest to install. Their one big disadvantage is that they block the view when in use. A partially opened roller shade is only partially effective for shading.

Roller shades can reject as much as 70% of the sunlight that strikes a window. To achieve this, select a shade that has a highly reflective outer surface, and install the shade close to the window. For best heat rejection, the outward face should be stark white or have a mirror finish, which is somewhat garish.

Plain roller shades look cheap both inside and outside. You can dress them up with stripes or other texture. Decorative hems, fringes, and tassels help to provide a fancier appearance.

You can buy roller shades that combine a highly reflective outward face with various colors and textures of interior faces, such as a linen surface. Such combinations typically are "blackout" shades, which means that they are completely opaque.

You can select roller shades that are slightly translucent to provide a low level of diffuse daylighting and to keep the closed shade from looking bleak. For example, see Figure 2-25.

Be careful about doing this, though. If a shade is too transparent, it becomes a bright surface when it is illuminated by direct sunlight. In most cases, you are safe if the transparency is only a few percent, which is about as transparent as two or three sheets of newspaper.

However, if an occupant must face a roller shade for an extended period – for example, while working at a desk – that shade should be completely opaque.

Venetian Blinds

Venetian blinds are the only common kind of interior shading that can block direct sunlight while preserving some view and avoiding glare. Manufacturers offer a wide range of styles and colors. Figure 2-26 is an attractive example.

A fully closed venetian blind blocks sunlight almost as well as a roller shade. To block solar heat most effectively, the blades must be light in color.

Venetian blinds do have annoying deficiencies. They are difficult to clean, and they are vulnerable to damage. The cords tend to be balky. They require you to look through the slats, except when you pull them up.

The slats of venetian blinds are made of metal, wood, or plastic. Narrower slats have become more popular in recent years. However, narrow slats are weaker and they require closer spacing, which provides a less desirable view and makes the blind more difficult to clean.

For windows that face south, venetian blinds don't need much adjusting to maximize the view. One setting may provide satisfactory shading all day. With windows that face east or west, venetian blinds must be adjusted as the sun rises and sets.

Vertical Louver Blinds

Vertical louver blinds are similar to horizontal venetian blinds, but the slats hang vertically by gravity, as in Figure 2-27. They have the same kinds of stringy controls, which allow the slats to be rotated and retracted.

Most vertical blinds dangle loosely, with no connection at the bottom. They should not be used when windows are opened, because wind will blow the slats around.

Generally, vertical louver blinds are less desirable than horizontal venetian blinds. Individual slats tend to get out of alignment, and it is not obvious how to fix them. Vertical slats are useless for sun control on south facing glass, and they require more daily adjustment on east and west faces than horizontal blinds.

Despite their annoyances, vertical blinds may be your best kind of interior shading for windows that face northward. From April to September, the sun rises and sets in the northern half of the horizon, so it can shine directly through north facing windows in the morning and afternoon. Vertical louvers can block this low sun effectively.

DRW

Figure 2-27. Vertical louver blinds. The blinds on the rear wall face north, where they are appropriate. The blinds on the right face east, where horizontal blinds would be better.

Depositphotos

Figure 2-28. Typical draperies. Sheer curtains are drawn over the French doors at center and right.

Draperies and Curtains

Draperies can give rooms a formal appearance that is compatible with older decorating styles, as in Figure 2-28. They can be installed on a track of any width to cover an entire wall or a group of windows.

Draperies are much less effective for blocking solar heat than roller shades and venetian blinds. Even if the fabric has a relatively light color, the folds of the fabric trap sunlight.

Most draperies are opaque. To provide daylight along with privacy, interior decorators often install separate translucent curtains behind their draperies. These sheer curtains provide a view of the outside that is hazy, at best. Unfortunately, these diffusing curtains create strong glare when sun shines on them. Also, when the room is lighted at night, the sheer curtains allow voyeurs to see into the room.

Draperies have another disadvantage if you use baseboard heaters or any other type of heater that emits heat near the wall. Draperies trap the heated air against the windows, increasing heat loss through the windows and reducing heating of the room. This can waste a lot of heating energy.

To solve this problem, if you install draperies, install a deflector above the baseboard heaters to divert the heated air flow toward the interior of the room. Step 4 covers this simple technique. With this arrangement, the drapery cannot fall entirely to the floor, but must end above the deflector.

Combinations of Interior Shading

Often, it may be desirable to install more than one kind of shading device for a window to adapt to different conditions of cooling, solar heating, daylighting, and privacy.

For example, Figures 2-29 and 2-30 show a combination of a translucent roller shade and an opaque roller shade in the same window opening. The translucent shade provides a pleasant ambience for the room when it is used socially. The opaque shade blocks glare for someone working at the desk. The deep window openings of a super-insulated wall make it especially easy to install multiple shading devices.

It is easy to install double shades in the deep window openings of super-insulated walls, providing great adaptability.

You can also use combinations of interior shading to adapt to changes in the season. For example, for the warm season, you could install highly reflective roller shades close to the glass. For the cold season, you could also install dark curtains to convert sunlight to heat while blocking glare. Using conventional drapery hardware, install attractively patterned, semi-opaque curtains several inches (about fifteen centimeters) inside the wall surface so that they heat the room by convection and radiation.

DRW

Figure 2-29. A translucent shade produces pleasant room lighting. However, it also produces troublesome glare for someone working at the desk. The glare is debilitating when sunlight shines directly on the shade.

DRW

Figure 2-30. An opaque shade eliminates the glare problem. However, it is less attractive. It leaves the window looking dark, especially if lowered completely.

GLASS DESIGN 4: DAYLIGHTING

Daylighting has been the primary method of illuminating indoor activities since the invention of glass. Daylighting also is one of the most important esthetic features of your house. It gives occupants a sense of connection with the daily and seasonal rhythms of nature. It bathes the inside of daytime rooms with beautiful light that brings out the colors and textures of the furnishings. It can be used to highlight certain parts of a room. And in bedrooms, it provides a natural wakeup call.

Does daylighting save energy, compared to electric lighting? With energy becoming more expensive, daylighting may cut a welcome amount from your electricity bill. However, the benefit will be relatively small, especially because Step 6 will make your electric lighting as efficient as possible.

If you are not careful, increasing your glass area for the sake of daylighting may increase your heating and cooling costs more than it saves in lighting costs. Fortunately, the human eye is very sensitive. On a clear day, about one percent of the sunlight that falls on a house would be sufficient for illumination if it could be distributed efficiently. In the real world, you will need more glass than that, but daylighting still requires relatively little glazing.

Design your daylighting to provide good coverage of the room and to avoid glare. Tailor the daylighting of each room. For example, a dining room usually should have more subdued daylight than a living room. You won't want to move your activities from day to night, so plan your daylighting to be compatible with your artificial lighting. For example, plan a location for your favorite reading chair where you will have both daylight and artificial light that are optimized for reading.

Most of your daylighting will be done with windows. But in addition, you have the options of clerestories, skylights, and light pipes. Each of these requires its own design approach, which we will cover individually.

SUNLIGHT INTENSITY AND GLARE

A direct beam of sunlight is approximately one hundred times too bright* for most indoor activities. Try reading a newspaper in direct sunlight, and you will be blinded. If a beam of raw sunlight falls where it creates a bright patch in the room, it will be unpleasant.

"Glare" is the name for uncomfortable brightness within the field of vision. Glare interferes with vision not only because of excessive light intensity, but also by creating excessive contrast between light and dark parts of the room. In order for vision to be comfortable, the different parts of a scene should have approximately the same level of brightness, within a ratio of about 10:1. If there is an area of glare within the room, the sensitivity of the eye will diminish to accommodate that area, making it more difficult to see everything else.

To avoid glare in daylighting, keep direct beams of sunlight from entering the room, or at least from striking visible surfaces in the room. You can do this by arranging the geometry of your glass and shading to block direct sunlight. Or, you can use interior shades to block direct sunlight. Or, you can use glazing that diffuses sunlight, a technique that generally is limited to skylights. Or, you can use various fixtures inside the room to intercept the beam of sunlight.

Indirect sunlight – light from the open sky, not from the sun itself – provides good daylighting quality. It has the right intensity, and it is nicely diffused.

This is not to say that you should banish direct sunlight from all rooms. For example, there is nothing wrong with direct sunlight entering bedrooms and other unoccupied rooms during the day, as long as the climate does not require air conditioning.

As a rule, don't attempt to block glare by using tinted glass or mirror glass. It can't work well, for the reasons explained in the *Window Selection Guide*, in Step 3.

USING WINDOWS FOR DAYLIGHTING

Table 2-1, *Glazing Comparison*, summarizes the advantages and disadvantages of windows compared to other methods of daylighting. As the table shows, windows are far from ideal for daylighting. They are vulnerable to glare, and light distribution into the interior of the room is poor. Both these limitations arise because windows are located low in the wall in order to provide a view of the outside landscape.

Despite their limitations for daylighting, a compelling reason to use windows for that purpose is that you will have them anyway. View generally requires more glass area than the other window functions, so the glass area of windows is ample for daylighting. Also,

---

* Here are some brightness numbers using "lux," a unit that expresses the intensity of visible light that shines on a surface. Direct sunlight provides an illumination of about 60,000 lux. An overcast sky typically provides 5,000 to 15,000 lux. In comparison, young persons can read comfortably with an illumination level as low as 200 lux. Elderly persons may want 500 lux. Highly detailed work, such as sewing, may require 1,000 lux or more. People may get headaches from extended exposure to indoor illumination higher than about 2,000 lux.

windows can be fitted with inexpensive and convenient manual shades to control glare and unwanted solar heat.

For smaller rooms, windows may provide all the daylighting you would want. For better daylighting coverage in larger rooms, you can supplement the windows with clerestories, skylights, or light pipes. However, in climates that have extended hot or cold seasons, artificial lighting is usually the most economical and efficient way to supplement the daylighting that is provided by windows.

Improving the Daylight Coverage of Windows

The intensity of daylight from windows falls off rapidly with distance from the window. For this reason, in the days before electric lighting, people sat near windows to perform activities that require relatively strong illumination, such as reading and sewing. Your reading chair today probably is located next to a window.

The ability of a window to project daylight into a room is determined mainly by its height above the surfaces that you want to illuminate. Daylight that is adequate for background illumination (but not for reading or other detail work) will penetrate approximately two to three times the height of the windows above the surfaces being viewed.

For example, let's say that the tops of the windows are eight feet (2.4 meters) above the floor, and you want to illuminate table tops that are two feet (0.6 meters) tall. The difference in height is six feet (1.8 meters). Multiply this by two or three, giving a penetration of about 12 to 18 feet (3.6 to 5.4 meters) into the space.

Increasing the ceiling height allows you to install taller windows for better daylight penetration. This is a major stylistic decision for both the interior and exterior appearance of the house.

Increasing the total size of the windows also increases heat loss. To limit the glass area, raise the sill heights to a level that provides privacy while maintaining good sight lines for the available view.

If a room has a long exterior wall, install windows at intervals along the wall to improve daylight coverage. The individual windows can be narrowed to reduce heat loss.

Avoiding Glare from Windows

To avoid glare while maintaining the outdoor view, use exterior shading to keep direct sunlight from entering the windows. You can use the same exterior shading methods that we introduced previously to block unwanted sunlight in a warm climate.

If you rely on interior shading to block glare, avoid materials that are translucent enough to become a source of glare themselves. For most windows, select shade materials that are nearly opaque.

USING CLERESTORIES FOR DAYLIGHTING

Everyone is familiar with windows and skylights, but what's a clerestory?

A *clerestory* (or *clearstory*) is a vertical window or a group of windows that is located above normal window height for the purpose of providing daylight and/or solar heating.* Clerestories can also be used for ventilation. The distinction between ordinary windows and clerestories is mainly a matter of height above the floor level.

Clerestories generally require a beam roof structure to provide light distribution to the space below. They can be installed anywhere in the roof or wall structure that provides a high elevation for the glass. Locations include high side walls under shed roofs, gable end walls, dormers, and roof monitors. Figures 2-33 through 2-39 show a variety of clerestory arrangements.

These examples do not include clerestories that are installed in dormers. The reason is that clerestory dormers look exactly the same as dormers that bring light into the space enclosed by a triangle-frame roof.

Table 2-1, *Glazing Comparison*, summarizes the advantages and disadvantages of clerestories. In comparison with windows, clerestories can provide better penetration of daylight into the interior of large rooms. Some configurations have the unique ability to bring sunlight into rooms that are located on the side of the house opposite the sun. And, their height and size gives them an advantage in collecting sunlight for heating.

In comparison with skylights and light pipes, clerestories have other important advantages. They use conventional window components, which have much longer life than skylights and light pipes. They avoid the leaks that plague skylights, and they are immune to hail and other falling objects. And, the fact that the glass is oriented vertically lowers its heat loss compared to glazing that is installed horizontally or on a slant. This reduces condensation on the glass and reduces falling drafts of cold air.

On the negative side of the ledger, clerestories limit your home's design. You have to adapt the room layout and the roof structure to take advantage of them. They require tall ceilings, which limits your ability to use the space under the roof as living space. If you want to use clerestories, include them in your space planning in Step 1.

---

* Clerestories were first used in large public buildings to bring light down from the upper parts of tall spaces. They were used about 2,000 years ago in Roman basilicas, and later in large churches. In the 19th century, clerestories became common in civil buildings with tall interior spaces, such as railroad stations. Clerestories rarely appeared in houses until the 1970's, when some houses included them to provide passive solar heating.

DRW

Figure 2-33. Clerestory windows along the top of the high wall under a shed roof. This style is effective for daylighting, but austere in appearance.

DRW

Figure 2-36. The clerestory windows in this gable end wall are well shaded by a deep roof overhang. The result is diffuse daylighting with little solar heat gain. This is efficient for a warm climate, but not for a cold climate.

DRW

Figure 2-34. A house in the Florida Keys with clerestory windows that provide ventilation as well as daylighting. This arrangement provides daylighting for the rooms at the rear of the house.

DRW

Figure 2-37. This house has two sets of clerestory windows. One is between the roof planes. A triangular clerestory is located over the main windows in the side wall.

DRW

Figure 2-35. The upper clerestory, between the two roof planes, provides daylighting for the rear of the house. The clerestory over the front porch provides daylighting for the front of the house.

DRW

Figure 2-38. Clerestories created by extending the roof rafters beyond the ridge. These create a somewhat bugeyed appearance.

DRW

Figure 2-39. Clerestory windows in a roof monitor provide daylighting from all directions.

Where to Use Clerestories, and Where Not To

Clerestories are best for daylighting rooms that are large, that are used frequently during daylight hours, and that do not require darkening. They are especially effective for the parts of a room that are distant from windows. Living rooms and great rooms are prime candidates, along with large kitchens. They can also feed light into interior rooms that lack windows, by using walls of partial height. However, partial-height walls provide no privacy against sounds and smells.

Avoid clerestories for rooms that you may want to darken during the daytime, such as bedrooms. Clerestories are usually inaccessible without a ladder, so it can be difficult to operate interior shading devices to shut out the light when you don't want it.

Don't use clerestories for rooms that get damp, where condensation on the glass would damage the surrounding structure.

Clerestories are relatively easy to build into a beam roof or triangle-frame roof, or in the wall underneath a beam or truss roof. However, clerestories are impractical to build as part of a truss roof unless you are willing to make the trusses visible inside the living space.

A clerestory must be installed well above normal lines of sight, or it wouldn't be a clerestory. So, the room requires an exceptionally tall ceiling. In a cold climate, tall ceilings suffer some temperature stratification. If your location has a cold season, don't create a tall ceiling just for the sake of having a clerestory. Instead, if you will have room with a tall ceiling for other reasons, then consider a clerestory for daylighting and solar warming.

Making Clerestories Attractive

Many of the recently built houses that use clerestories have a clunky appearance. It doesn't have to be that way. There are several ways to include clerestories in your design elegantly.

An attractive design, which is compatible with a classic exterior styles, is to install clerestories in dormers or in side gables that open into a vaulted ceiling. From the outside, the appearance is entirely conventional. A dormer provides a narrow rectangular opening. A full gable can mount a large triangular window.

A more modern style can use clerestories that are installed in the gable end wall of a beam roof, as in Figure 2-36. The structure is easy to build because the clerestory is built into the gable end wall as a conventional window.

Another modern style is a wide row of clerestory windows located in the break between the roof planes of a multi-shed roof, as in Figures 2-34, 2-35, and 2-37. This style risks an industrial appearance, which can be muted by extending the upper roof panel over the windows.

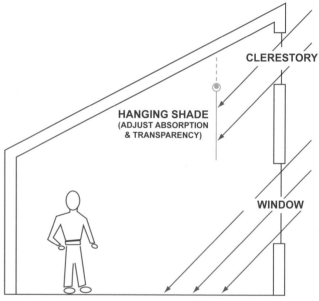

DRW

Figure 2-40. A shade blocks direct sunlight coming through a clerestory. A material that absorbs sunlight acts as a radiant heater. A reflective material spreads daylight over the interior surfaces on the clerestory side. A diffusing material spreads daylight throughout the space, but risks being a source of glare itself. Using more than one shade, perhaps in different positions, can accommodate seasonal variations in heating requirements and in the angle of the incoming sunlight.

Orientation, Climate, and Shading

Think of clerestories primarily as light fixtures, not as windows. Place them where they will illuminate the room effectively. Design the compass orientation and the shading of your clerestories to be consistent with the climate and the interior room layout.

If the climate of your home site is always mild or warm, your latitude is fairly close to the equator, so the sun follows a high arc through the sky. This makes it desirable to orient your clerestories toward the north or toward the south. For both orientations, you can design exterior shading for your clerestories that will block direct sunlight at all times. To do this with any of the methods of installing clerestories that we described previously, extend the roof beyond the top and sides of the glass. Refer to the previous heading, *Extended Gable End Overhangs*.

Or, completely shade the house with evergreen trees.

If the climate of your home site has both warm and cold seasons, and if the roof is exposed to direct sunlight during winter, orient a clerestory toward the south. Extending the roof over the top and sides of the clerestory, as described previously, exploits solar heating in winter and blocks it in summer.

An east-facing clerestory provides intense illumination in the morning, and little during the rest of the day. Conversely, a west-facing clerestory provides intense illumination before sunset.

If the space layout allows it, you can use a "monitor" clerestory that faces in different directions to provide more consistent daylighting throughout the day. A monitor that is installed on a roof ridge faces in opposing directions. Figure 2-39 shows an example that faces in four directions.

Glazing and Diffusion

Generally, clerestories should use clear glass. The reason is that diffusing glass becomes a glaringly bright surface when direct sunlight strikes it. A clerestory usually is within the normal field of vision, so the glare from diffusing glass would be severe. Also, a diffusing surface would look unattractive from both outside and inside. Clear glass may provide a limited view of the sky, surrounding trees, and higher surrounding terrain.

This leaves the need to diffuse direct sunlight that enters through the clerestory. First, use your sun position chart to determine where the sunlight will fall inside the room. In general, you want to prevent a direct beam of sunlight from creating a bright glare spot on a wall or floor.

An effective way to diffuse direct sunlight is to intercept the beam with a diffusing material, such as a hanging shade that is made of a decorative fabric. Figure 2-40 illustrates an example. The shade can be selected to reflect a desired amount of light from the front side, to transmit a desired amount of light, and to absorb the rest. All absorbed light will warm the shade, making it act as a mild heating surface. Reconcile this with the climate of your home site.

Another way to diffuse the beam is to arrange the interior geometry so that sunlight falls on a relatively dark diffusing surface, such as a tapestry, an interior stone wall, or a stone floor. But even with dark surfaces, room occupants should generally be facing away from the daylighted surfaces. Furthermore, avoid an overall color scheme that is dark. In Step 6, we will recommend that you keep your interior colors as light as possible to minimize lighting cost.

Glazing Area and Distribution

A clerestory that is exposed to open sky can provide pleasant illumination with a glazing area that is about 3% to 5% of the floor area that the clerestory is intended to illuminate. If the clerestory is shaded by trees or other features, it must be considerably larger to provide a given level of daylighting.

If the climate is fairly mild, clerestories may provide a saving in lighting cost that offsets the increased cost for heating and air conditioning.

If your climate has an extended cold or hot season, limit your overall glass area to the minimum that will satisfy your requirements, as we discussed previously. Decide how to divide your glass area between the windows and the clerestories. For example, if a grand view is your primary justification for glass, concentrate your glass area in the windows that provide the view. If daylighting is your primary requirement, shift more of your glazing area to the clerestories.

USING SKYLIGHTS FOR DAYLIGHTING

Skylights excel for daylighting. They generally are used in combination with windows, although they can provide dramatic daylighting for a space without windows, such as an interior toilet room. The daylighting provided by skylights can be a wonderful esthetic feature, highlighting parts of a room, such as an island in a kitchen. Skylights also add shape to the ceiling.

Unlike windows, skylights generally are limited to the single function of daylighting. In most cases, they can't provide a useful amount of view, ventilation, or solar heating.

Skylights have a big weakness, which is a tendency to leak. Skylights are exposed to the elements, where they are drenched by rain and may be buried under snow. As a result, a small installation defect or a defect in the skylight itself may allow a leak that can damage the roof structure. The damage may remain invisible until it is severe. Avoiding water damage requires special care in selecting and installing skylights.

Skylights are easy to install in beam roofs and in triangle-frame roofs. When installed in a truss roof, each skylight requires a light shaft, as in Figure 2-43. This is a structure that is built inside the attic to channel the sunlight through the attic from the skylight to the ceiling below. Light shafts complicate the roof carpentry and they interfere with movement through the attic space.

Think of skylights as light fixtures that are attractive, but expensive and temperamental. They save electric lighting cost, but in climates that are cold or hot, this saving is likely to be cancelled by increased heating and/or cooling cost.

Step 3 will explain the details of buying and installing skylights. At this point, we will discuss whether, where, and how to use skylights for daylighting.

Where to Use Skylights, and Where Not To

Use skylights only where their daylighting advantage outweighs their shortcomings. The balance depends primarily on the room type and the climate.

Skylights are best in rooms that are large, that are used frequently during daylight hours, and that do not require darkening. They are especially effective for parts of a room that are distant from windows. Living rooms, large dining rooms, and large kitchens are prime candidates. They can be pleasant for toilet rooms, but don't use them in shower rooms.

Avoid skylights in rooms that you may want to darken during the daytime, such as bedrooms. You can buy skylights with shading devices, but these are awkward to use and difficult to repair.

Don't put skylights in rooms that get damp, where condensation on the skylight would damage the surrounding structure.

With respect to climate, skylights are most satisfactory in mild and warm climates. Avoid skylights if the weather is rainy, because skylights are a common source of roof leaks. This warning applies until manufacturers develop skylights and mounting hardware that reliably prevent leaks.

Skylights are less suitable in locations that have heavy cloud cover for a large fraction of the time. Clouds typically reduce solar illumination by a factor of five to ten, and you would have to increase the size of your skylights accordingly. If the climate remains mild, you can tolerate the larger skylight size.

Skylights don't belong in cold climates, where they act as an energy hole in your insulated structure. Because skylights are installed on the roof, low winter sun does not illuminate them efficiently. In northern latitudes, there are few hours of daylight during the coldest months. In climates with snowfall, skylights tend to create ice dams, which cause leakage and progressive damage to the roof and ceiling.

To avoid physical damage to skylights, do not install them in climates where heavy hail is likely. Also, avoid them if the roof is within range of falling tree limbs. Falling leaves and other debris will collect above skylights, rotting there and causing eventual leaks.

If you have a beam roof and you want to supplement the daylighting from your windows, consider clerestories instead of skylights in a climate that is unfavorable for skylights.

DRW

Figure 2-43. A living room that is nicely daylighted with two skylights. The skylights themselves are not visible here. They are located at the top of a box structure that passes through the attic and connects the roof to the interior ceiling.

Figure 2-44. Typical skylight exterior appearance.

Skylights are a visible feature of roofs. They have the best appearance with fairly plain roof surfaces, as in Figure 2-44. With such surfaces, the skylights may accent the roof. However, if a roof has a decorative surface, especially fancy tiles, skylights will clash with the roof style.

Layout and Size

Think of skylights as light fixtures. Place them where they will illuminate the room effectively.

With a beam roof or a triangle-frame roof, the light distribution into the room can be fairly broad. Select diffusing glazing to distribute the light, or install a separate diffuser below the skylight.

With a truss roof, sunlight travels through a deep light shaft. Relatively little of the room area is exposed to the skylight itself, and most daylighting occurs by reflection from the surface of the light shaft, as in Figure 2-43. For this reason, the inside of the light shaft usually is painted flat white.

The ceiling opening of the light shaft does not have to be the same size as the skylight. For example, the ceiling opening may be widened in one or both dimensions to improve light distribution.

Don't overdo the size or number of skylights. Don't try to illuminate a large room with a single skylight. In a room with a low ceiling, don't make individual skylights larger than about three square feet (0.3 square meters). In a large room with a tall ceiling, use skylights no larger than about 6 square feet (0.6 square meters).

In mid-latitude climates, the skylight area in any room should total no more than about 3% to 5% of the floor area in that room. This size provides a pleasant level of illumination. The saving in electric lighting cost is balanced against increased cost for heating and air conditioning.

It is asking for trouble to increase skylight area further. Too much skylight area overheats the space and may create glare. Brochures for skylights may show pictures of houses that have batteries of skylights grouped close together. That's a serious mistake. You might as well live in a greenhouse.

Even in a mild climate that needs no heating or cooling for most of the year, 8% of floor area is about the maximum. This much skylight area can easily overheat a space. If you use this much skylight area, the outdoor climate should be cool enough to allow you to use outside air for cooling, and the room should be designed to exploit outdoor ventilation. On sunny days, large skylights yield a bright "garden" type of atmosphere. If you choose this level of illumination, you may need a shaded area within the room for comfortable reading.

If skylights are shaded by trees, they must be considerably larger than skylights that are exposed to direct sunlight, to provide the same amount of daylighting. However, larger area creates increased heating cost. Also, skylights under tree cover are vulnerable to falling limbs.

If you insist on having skylights in a cold climate (which I don't recommend), keep them small and locate them where the sun can shine on them directly for the largest number of hours. The south slope of a roof is best.

Some new types of skylights offer translucent insulation that reduces winter heat loss. These skylights must be larger to provide a given level of daylighting. The *Skylight Selection Guide*, in Step 3, gives the details.

Avoid Glare

Skylights can cause two kinds of glare. The worst is the glare of a direct beam of sunlight through clear glass. The beam produces a glaring bright spot where it falls, and not much lighting elsewhere. You can avoid this kind of glare by diffusing the light beam.

The simplest way to diffuse the light is to select skylights that have diffusing glazing. This usually provides the most satisfactory illumination, spreading the light fairly uniformly in all directions. The *Skylight Selection Guide*, in Step 3, explains how to select the right glazing.

However, the bright diffusing surface of a skylight creates a second kind of glare. A skylight with a diffuser looks approximately like a big fluorescent light fixture. It is too bright for comfort if you look at it directly.

Fortunately, human beings evolved to be comfortable with the sun overhead. To exploit this advantage, locate your skylights well above normal lines of sight. For example, if you have a room with a sloped ceiling, install the skylights as high in the ceiling as possible, consistent with good light distribution.

Another method of diffusing direct sunlight is to splash the beam across a diffusing surface that is above normal lines of sight. If there are parts of a room where the skylights would be too visible, you can install attractive screens to block the line of sight to the skylights. For example, decorative fabric hangings can be effective. This is the same trick that we used to block glare from clerestories, as shown in the previous Figure 2-40.

With a truss roof that uses a light shaft, the skylight glazing may be clear or diffuse. Clear glazing gets more daylight into the room, but glare occurs if the sun can shine straight through the light shaft. In more northerly latitudes, it is practical to orient the light shaft to block any direct sunlight from entering the room. Reflection from the walls of the light shaft spreads sunlight into the room.

Minimize Heat Loss and Condensation

Conventional skylights have exceptionally poor insulation value, for reasons explained in Step 3. Because of this, skylights may sweat badly at night during cold weather. The condensation can harm the surrounding structure and trim, and it may drip on the floor. To minimize these problems, select skylights that have features to minimize condensation and its effects. The *Skylight Selection Guide*, in Step 3, explains these features.

USING LIGHT PIPES FOR DAYLIGHTING

Light pipes are alternatives to skylights. Increasingly, vendors are calling them "tubular skylights." Localized daylighting is the only function they perform.

A light pipe is a thin metal tube that has a highly reflective interior surface. The tube carries the sunlight through an attic space, as shown in Figure 2-47. A dome or other transparent cover on the roof allows sunlight to enter the tube. The light is reflected down the tube to a diffuser that is installed in the ceiling of the room.

Table 2-1, *Glazing Comparison*, summarizes the advantages and disadvantages of light pipes. Their main appeal is that they are much easier to install in truss roofs than are skylights. The diameter of the pipe is small enough to fit between the roof rafters and the ceiling joists. No special framing is needed.

From inside the room, a light pipe looks similar to an electric ceiling fixture, as in Figure 2-48. The exterior dome of a typical light pipe is shown in Figure 2-49.

Solatube

Figure 2-47. Diagram of a light pipe. Its main virtue is easy installation through a truss roof.

DRW

Figure 2-48. A light pipe as seen inside a room. In bright sunlight, the diffuser surface can be glaringly bright.

Most residential light pipes have a maximum diameter of about 14" (35 cm), which allows them to fit within the standard spacing of ceiling joists. This small size does not allow a light pipe to illuminate a large area. Such small light pipes are most appropriate for small spaces, such as a toilet room or hallway. The tube should be kept short and straight to minimize loss of light.

Larger light pipes are starting to make an appearance. These cannot fit inside the standard spacing of roof rafters and ceiling joists. Therefore, they require special framing, as for skylights. These larger sizes can provide useful daylighting for a larger room, and they have less light loss.

Light pipes do not add the same texture to the ceiling line as skylights, and their light is less pleasant. Under bright sunlight, the diffuser can have a glaring appearance. The heat loss through a light pipe is similar to the heat loss through a skylight of the same size.

Since a light pipe is installed through the roof, it has a potential for roof leakage. However, the fact that the roof fitting is round reduces the risk.

The transparent dome of a light pipe is made of plastic. The portion that is exposed on the roof will fail after a number of years, requiring replacement.

Someone figured out that a dome shape is unnecessary if the roof is oriented toward the southern half of the sky. As a result, some manufacturers offer a light pipe that has a flat glass cover, as in Figure 2-50, which may be almost flush with the roof surface. The glass is not harmed by sunlight, so this type of light pipe may last a long time. However, the flush mounting probably is more prone to leakage, especially if there is snow.

DRW

Figure 2-49. The exterior of a light pipe with a plastic dome. The plastic is eventually destroyed by sunlight.

Velux

Figure 2-50. A light pipe with a flat glass cover, which will last indefinitely. The flush design is less obtrusive than a dome, and hence is more suitable for installation in this slate roof.

GLASS DESIGN 5: EXPLOIT VIEWS & PRESERVE PRIVACY

In Step 1, you selected the overall orientation of your home and its room layout to exploit your views. Now, lay out your windows to exploit those views. Of the various functions of glass, view of the outside is the one that provides the greatest pleasure, and it usually requires the most glass area. But, glass area conflicts with comfort and energy efficiency, as we have seen. So, exploiting your view deserves clever design.

Let's start with a reality check. Dramatic views that merit big windows are rare. More likely, you will have a nice view of some general vista, such as surrounding lawns or distant hills. Or, in an urban environment, you outdoor view may be limited to a pleasant patch of greenery behind the house. At night, you won't have any view from inside the house unless the outdoor scene is lighted and you turn off the interior lights.

However, if you are fortunate to have a view that deserves a lot of glass, consider a special space from which to enjoy it. This is especially desirable if your climate has a substantial cold or hot season. In that case, design your special space as we discuss later, under the heading, *What If You Want a Space With Lots of Glass?*

WINDOW LOCATION AND SHAPE

The basic design approach is to locate the windows between the occupants and the desirable views outside. Depending on the climate and the nature of the view, you may decide to install a single large window or a succession of smaller windows to "sample" the view.

If the occupants will be enjoying the view mostly while seated, sketch the furniture in the viewing rooms so that you know where the outward looking chairs will be located. If you place a chair near a relatively small window, you can achieve a relatively wide view. However, if you want the view to be visible from a large area of the room, that will require more glass.

A panoramic view does not necessarily require big windows. For example, if you have a view of the ocean, a lake, or distant hills, you may want a wide expanse of windows, but they don't need to be tall. On the other hand, if your view faces a back yard with tall trees, your viewing windows may be tall and narrow.

The height of the window sills is governed by your downward view. In a house on a hillside, windows facing a downhill view should have low sills. But, if your living room windows face a large deck, raise the sill height and don't waste window area for a view of the deck floor.

DRW

Figure 2-55. Tall window sills provide effective daylighting for this bedroom while maintaining privacy. The tall sills also allow furniture to be placed beneath the windows.

SIGHT LINES TO PRESERVE PRIVACY

Consider view and privacy together when designing each window. Light travels through windows in both directions. If the occupants can look out, people outside can look in.

In many houses that have windows designed without regard to privacy, the occupants are forced to achieve privacy by permanently obscuring the windows, as in the previous Figure 2-11. Such windows contribute nothing except higher heating and cooling costs.

The sill height of the windows usually is the most important factor in privacy. Your eyes are in your head, so a tall sill allows you to see the outside view while preventing an outsider from seeing the lower parts of your anatomy. To preserve modesty, make the window sills high enough so that a person standing outside cannot tell whether a woman inside the house is nude or is wearing a sun dress. Consider tall sill heights especially for bedrooms and related rooms where occupants may be undressed. Figure 2-55 shows a bedroom window layout that provides good privacy with tall sill heights.

 Tall window sills are often the best way to provide privacy, especially where they can also maintain view and daylighting.

If you can eliminate the need for privacy shades by using tall window sills, view and daylighting are always accessible. You can leave the windows open at night for ventilation. And, in bedrooms, sunlight coming through the windows makes it easier to start the day.

DRW

Figure 2-56. Tall window sills may create a large expanse of exterior wall, as here. Therefore, consider shrubbery or other deco to cover the lower portions of the wall.

Windows on upper floors provide more reliable privacy, and they can do so with somewhat lower sill heights.

For rooms on the ground floor, the height of the foundation has a big effect on privacy. For example, let's say that you select a tall sill height of five feet (150 cm) for your bedroom windows. If the house has a low slab-on-grade foundation, a Peeping Tom can still look into the bedroom if he is standing directly outside the window. In contrast, if the house has a foundation that elevates the floor three feet (90 cm) above grade, the window sills will be eight feet (240 cm) above grade, too tall for Tom.

The slope of the surrounding terrain also has a big effect on privacy. If the terrain slopes downward from the windows, privacy is enhanced. On the other hand, if windows are below the surrounding terrain, the windows will need privacy screens.

DRW

Figure 2-57. The window design of this house provides little privacy because the bottoms of the windows are at floor level. Without curtains or other privacy screens, the occupants have chosen to live in a public showroom.

DRW

Figure 2-58. The same house as in the previous photo. The occupants have made a virtue of their exposure by decorating the house interior so that it can be admired from the street.

Tall window sills leave the outside wall with a lot of bare surface. For example, see Figure 2-56. Use shrubbery or other wall decoration to avoid a drab exterior appearance.

Installing louver panels over windows is another way to achieve privacy, especially where a tall sill height is insufficient or impractical. Louvers limit the view to a downward direction. They may be the best choice in a warm climate where a window is used for ventilation, as for a toilet room or shower room.

Windows sacrifice privacy most seriously at night, when indoor activities are most intimate and when a lighted room is entirely visible from the outside. Compare Figures 2-57 and 2-58.

GLARE FROM WATER AND SNOW

Some of the most spectacular views are over bodies of water, such as a river, lake, or ocean. However, reflection of sunlight from the water's surface can steal the pleasure from such views. The reflected glare of the sunlight can be blinding. And, during warm weather, it adds a blast of heat.

Glare over water is especially troublesome because the reflection of sunlight is within the normal vertical field of vision. Tourists may flock to watch a sunset over water at some distant beach, but you won't want to do it many times at your home on the shore.

When the surface of the water is flat, glare is most objectionable when sunlight strikes the water at a grazing angle, generally less than 30°. However, if the water has waves, even small ones, uncomfortable glare will occur at higher sun elevations, as in Figure 2-59.

At tropical and sub-tropical latitudes, where the sun arcs high in the sky all year, a water view toward the north or south is mostly free of glare. A view toward the east or west is intolerable when the sun is low in that direction.

In more northerly latitudes during winter, the sun remains within an arc that ranges from southeast to southwest. The sun is low in the sky all day, so glare reflected by water can be uncomfortable from any direction within this arc.

Reflection from snow can be even more intensely blinding than reflection from water. The geometry of the problem is similar.

It is difficult to create shading to block this glare because you are dealing simultaneously with the glare of the sun itself above the horizon and with its reflection below the horizon. About the only practical option is some kind of opaque screen, which blocks the view when the screen is needed.

The best time to deal with reflected surface glare is before you buy your property. Consider the direction of the view over the water, and the times when you want to exploit it. Get a sun position chart, and highlight the directions where the sun is lower than 30° above the horizon. Standing at the property, you don't want any of those directions to be over a large body of water.

DRW

Figure 2-59. Sun glare on the Chesapeake Bay in the mid-afternoon, facing southwest. This glare is mainly from small waves. Later in the day, glare from the low sun will be blinding. During warm weather, the heat reflected from the water is oppressive. If you want a glorious view over water, build on a lot that faces water toward the north. Or, in lower latitudes, a view toward the south or southeast is also acceptable. Otherwise, your only salvation is to block your view in the afternoon and evening, when you will want it the most.

GLASS DESIGN 6: VENTILATION FOR HEALTH & COMFORT

In virtually all homes, the ventilation air enters through glazing that can be opened. Ventilation is needed to maintain good air quality and to provide cooling air flow during warm weather. Ventilation to maintain air quality requires only small openings. Ventilation for cooling requires large openings.

Generally, windows are the most effective type of glazing for both purposes. The *Window Selection Guide*, in Step 3, explains which types of windows are best for both kinds of ventilation.

You could install skylights or clerestories that are openable for ventilation. As a rule, avoid openable skylights, because they have an increased tendency to leak. Clerestories, if they are well protected from rain, may be effective for ventilation in a climate that is always warm. For example, see Figure 2-34.

Glazing plays a secondary role, or no role, in other ventilation requirements, such as providing combustion air for heating appliances. We will discuss those applications separately.

VENTILATION FOR COOLING

Outside air ventilation is a comfortable substitute for air conditioning whenever the outside air is cool and not humid. Cooling occurs in two ways. One is replacing warm interior air with cooler outdoor air. The other is "wind chill" effect, which is cooling of skin that occurs when air movement increases the evaporation of moisture from the skin.

Cooling ventilation works well at night, even in warm climates, because the outdoor environment cools quickly by radiation into the night sky. (See the sidebar, *The Sky is Cold*.) For this reason, bedrooms benefit the most. Daytime cooling ventilation is limited to weather that is mild.

Cooling ventilation that depends on outdoor breezes requires larger window openings. But, don't enlarge the windows just for ventilation. This would increase your heating cost in cold weather and increase your air conditioning cost in sunny weather.

Even a relatively small window can provide comfortable cooling when aided by a fan. The fan is installed in an attic or in some other central location where it can draw outside air through any room that has open windows. Step 4 will explain how to install fans in a way that is quiet and efficient.

To make the best use of ventilation cooling, arrange the windows on opposite sides of the room so that outdoor breezes will force air through the room. Or, if you will install a cooling fan, arrange the room so that occupants are located between the windows and the cooling fan (which typically draws air through a hallway).

VENTILATION FOR AIR QUALITY

In most homes, windows are the prime source of ventilation air that is needed to eliminate pollutants from the interior. In certain rooms – especially the kitchen and the workshop – you need large volumes of ventilation air for short periods of time, generally to provide air for an exhaust fan in that space. Locate windows in those spaces so that they clear out the contaminants quickly without dragging a lot of outside air through space that does not need ventilation.

The rest of the house needs only a low rate of ventilation to maintain air quality. Natural movement of air within the house may provide all the ventilation that is needed for some rooms. To provide more outside air, you can open a window slightly. The location of the windows in such spaces is not critical.

For energy efficiency and comfort during extreme weather, windows that are opened for air quality ventilation should allow fine adjustment of the opening. Small slider windows, especially horizontal sliders, satisfy this requirement.

In Step 4, we will design the ventilation that is needed to protect health in each part of the house, under the heading *Ventilation for Health, Safety, and Humidity Control*. Look ahead to there to help you decide where to locate the windows for air quality ventilation.

THE SKY IS COLD

Why does the earth cool down so quickly after sunset? The reason is that the sky is very cold. The cold sky acts as a "negative campfire" that seems to radiate coldness toward the earth. This effect can be surprisingly strong at night.

When you look up at a clear sky, you are looking into outer space, which has a temperature that approaches absolute zero. Everything on the surface of the earth radiates heat into that cold void. Fortunately for life on earth, the atmosphere captures much of that heat and radiates it back down to us. (This process is the famous "greenhouse effect.") As a result, the temperature of the sky, as seen from the surface, looks much warmer than deep space, but the sky is still much colder than the surface of the earth.

If the climate is dry and clear, the effective temperature of the sky is colder than the air temperature at ground level typically by 70 to 80 °F (38 to 44 °C). You can measure this yourself by pointing an inexpensive remote reading thermometer at the sky. (Don't point your gadget at the sun, which may ruin it.)

This difference in temperature remains fairly constant, both night and day, winter and summer, as long as the sky is clear. Contrary to intuition, the sun does not change the sky temperature during the day. The sun covers only a tiny part of the sky, and the temperature of the rest of the sky remains cold.

During the daytime, heat radiation from the sun is much stronger than the cooling radiation into the sky. So, for example, a roof surface may become much warmer than the surrounding air. However, at night, radiation of heat into the sky can cool an exposed surface to a temperature that is considerably lower than the surrounding air temperature. That's why your car windshield may be covered with frost in the morning, even though the air temperature did not fall to freezing.

Cooling by radiation is greatly reduced when the sky is hazy or cloudy. With cloudy skies, the sky temperature is approximately equal to the temperature of the atmosphere at the cloud base. With typical clouds, the temperature difference between the surface and the sky ranges from 20 °F to 40 °F (from 11 °C to 22 °C). At these smaller temperature differences, radiation cooling becomes much less significant.

The sky has little cooling effect on objects that are shielded from the sky. That's why dew may form overnight on an exposed lawn, but not on lawn that is covered by a canopy. Similarly, if a roof is heavily shaded by trees, it does not experience much radiation cooling.

GLASS DESIGN 7: BEAUTIFUL APPEARANCE

The glazing of your home serves as an important element of style, both inside and outside. In Step 1, you already made the primary decisions about the role that windows will play in the appearance of your home. You developed those decisions further as you incorporated the previous issues into your glass design. Now, go back to Step 1 and review all your options for making the windows beautiful.

Making clerestories attractive involves a separate set of issues, which we covered previously when we designed clerestories for daylighting.

Skylights don't have much potential for decorating the exterior of a house, although they can help to create a beautiful environment inside.

GLASS DESIGN 8: EMERGENCY ESCAPE

Windows may be your only route of escape in an emergency, especially from fire. They are most important for this purpose in bedrooms, where the interior paths to the outside may be blocked by fire or smoke before the occupants awaken. For this reason, each bedroom should have at least one window that has an opening large enough for escape, with easily openable glass and an easily removable insect screen.

For bedrooms that are high above ground, install a compact escape ladder at a designated escape window in each bedroom. Figure 2-61 shows a typical escape ladder. If the window sill is high above the bedroom floor, hang a folding step stool on the wall adjacent to that window so that occupants can get over the sill easily.

X-IT Products

Figure 2-61. A typical fire escape ladder. This is essential for each occupied bedroom on an upper floor.

WHAT IF YOU WANT A SPACE WITH LOTS OF GLASS?

What if your home site has a panoramic view that demands a wall of glass to let you see it all? What if your house is situated in a forest and you want to be able to look upward into the trees to watch the birds and squirrels frolic? What if you just want to have a lot of exposure to the outside?

Well, that will require a lot of glass. We have emphasized that large glass area normally conflicts with energy efficiency. So, what can you do?

 If you want a space with lots of glass, be able to isolate it from the rest of the house.

The answer is to concentrate all that glass into a single room and to isolate that room thermally from the rest of the house. Figures 2-62 and 2-63 are attractive examples.

Unless the climate is always mild, your heavily glazed space should not be one that is used for daily activities, such as the living room or dining room. It is a place to visit, not a place in which to live. It should be arranged as an "expansion room" or an "independent room," as defined in Step 1.

Because of cold drafts that fall from large glass surfaces, no glassy space can keep people comfortable for long periods during cold weather. For warm weather, a large fraction of the glass area should be openable, allowing the space to be cooled by breezes.

The most efficient glassy space has no heating or air conditioning equipment, so it is usable only on a seasonal basis. A "sun porch" is typical of this type. Another kind of glassy space is used only occasionally, but at all times of the year, so it needs heating and/or cooling equipment. A "great room" or a "sunroom" has these characteristics.

Don't have a lot of glass just for the sake of having it. Figure out your reasons and design accordingly. For example, if you want the glass to take advantage of a great view, locate the glass to optimize the view, as explained previously. If you want glass as a style feature, consider the alternatives to glass that we suggested in Step 1.

LIMIT HEATING AND AIR CONDITIONING

You can't heat a heavily glazed room economically. If your space is used seasonally, don't install heating equipment in it.

If you must have heating equipment in the room, make it entirely independent of the heating for the rest of the house. (We will design independent heating for all the rooms in your house, so this is not a fundamental change.) This avoids the risk that turning on the heat in the rest of the house will also turn on the heat in the glassy space.

The glass makes the space vulnerable to freezing when it is vacated, so don't install plumbing fixtures or other equipment that is vulnerable to freezing. Or,

DRW

Figure 2-62. A Maryland house with a heavily glazed space that is isolated from the rest of the house. This kind of space typically is called a "sunroom."

DRW

Figure 2-63. A Maine house with a glass-enclosed porch, oriented toward a seaside view. During balmy weather, the porch windows can be opened for cooling breezes. Or, the deck on top of the porch can be used.

install isolation valves in the water supply to the glassy space, and drain the plumbing during unoccupied periods.

Try to cool the space during warm weather using methods that use no energy or little energy. Shading the space is the essential first step. Take advantage of breezes by making the glass openable. If the climate is warm most of the time, consider jalousie windows. They open almost completely, they don't intrude into the space, and they don't require muscle to operate. However, jalousie windows have severe air leakage. If your climate has a cold season, install sliding or hinged windows.

Ceiling fans (covered in Step 4) provide comfortable air circulation if breezes are inadequate.

SHADE THE GLASS APPROPRIATELY

Shade all glazing in a manner that is appropriate for the climate. The fact that a space is called a "sunroom" or "sun porch" doesn't change the shading requirements. Don't mistake your sunny room for a greenhouse. It's a place for lounging, not for growing vegetables. In a climate that has a warm season, take special care to design the shading so that direct sunlight enters the space only during cold weather.

Unless you have an unusual location that calls for an upward view, don't use a greenhouse roof for your glassy space. It would create intolerable glare. Instead, install a conventional roof that matches the rest of the house.

If your location has a cold season, try to arrange the shading so that sunlight can heat the space during that season. However, even in a cold climate, the occupied area of your heavily glazed room should have adequate shade from direct sunlight, which is too bright for comfort.

INSULATE THE JOINING WALLS OF THE GLASSY SPACE

Unless the climate is always mild, insulate the wall between the glassy space and the rest of the house, following the insulation guidelines in Step 3. The glassy space normally is vacant and unheated during cold weather, so the occupied portion of the house will lose heat into it.

Do this whether your glassy space is an "exterior" type of structure, such as a sun porch, or an "interior" room, such as a great room. For example, to insulate a great room from the rest of the house, you may have to increase the interior wall thickness to accommodate the recommended amount of insulation.

Use a door, or doors, to isolate the glassy space from the rest of the house. To extend the view into the adjacent rooms while the doors are closed, use "French doors." These are hinged doors that have large glass panels. Get doors that have good weatherstripping, along with glass panels that have the best available insulation value.

You can increase the view through the glassy room even further into the adjacent parts of the house by installing glass panels in the interior walls. However, all glass has poor insulation value, so don't make this glass any larger than necessary to show off the view. If you install such panels, get them made with the best insulation value that is available.

OTHER INSULATION FOR A GLASSY SPACE

Even if your glassy space does not have heating or cooling equipment, you should still insulate the roof. This will extend the season during which the space is comfortable. In cold weather, the ceiling will not create a cascade of cold air. In warm weather, roof insulation keeps the ceiling from radiating heat into the space when the roof is heated by sunlight.

If the space has a large amount of opaque wall area, and especially if it has heating equipment, it may be advisable to insulate the walls. If the space has a floor that is exposed to outside air, it may also be appropriate to insulate the floor.

Use the *Insulation Worksheet*, in Step 3, to calculate the amount of insulation that is appropriate for your glassy space.

STEP 3

CREATE A SUPER STRUCTURE

We will now design the physical structure that encloses the space layout that you created previously. This structure is what protects you from the forces of nature. It largely determines your comfort and your energy costs. As we design your structure, we will stress energy efficiency, strength, and longevity.

Your super-home will be built using mostly conventional construction materials and practices, so we will start with a quick tour of conventional home construction. Then, we will introduce four important design advances that apply throughout the structure. Armed with that knowledge, we will optimize each part of the structure individually, from the foundation to the roof.

This Step is the longest of the Eight. That's because there are several good ways of building a house, and we will cover the best options for different situations that may exist at your home site. In addition, we will introduce a number of valuable innovations.

We will get through this Step easily because we break it down into bite sized pieces. Remember, it's not your job to become an expert builder, but to apply to your design the advanced features that turn a conventional house into a super-house.

How Houses Are Built: The Minimum You Should Know

The construction of your super-house will be mostly conventional. It will use well-proven materials and mostly standard construction methods. So, let's spend a few moments to get familiar with the fascinating subject of house construction.

Knowing about house construction will add to the fun of planning your dream house. It will build your confidence in dealing with your builder. If you decide to hire design assistance, understanding construction will help you to express your desires more effectively. And, you will save money by being an educated client.

House construction has become highly standardized. That is mostly good. It allows a small number of workers to erect the frame of a house within a few days, and it allows small teams of specialists, such as plumbers, electricians, and drywall installers, to install the interior components within a few more days. Standardization of components provides economy and reliability in construction, and it still allows almost unlimited variation in architectural style.

To get the most benefit from this overview, visit construction sites to observe how houses are built. If you can, follow the construction of a few houses from the foundation to completion, so you see how the pieces fit together. House construction is logical and easy to understand. You will be pleased at how quickly you learn the process.

We will introduce important innovations into the design of your structure. This quick tour will provide you with a baseline for understanding how your super-home differs from conventional homes. And, if your builder sees that you understand basic construction, he will be comfortable in making the changes to his own past practices that your design introduces.

Houses are built from the ground up, so let's begin our tour of construction practices at the bottom.

THE UNDERGROUND STRUCTURE

Today, most houses use concrete construction at grade level and below. ("Grade" is builder language that means the top of the finished soil level.) Concrete or stone is needed where the house contacts the soil to resist destruction by moisture and by insects.

If the climate allows the ground to freeze, the foundation usually must extend below the frost depth to prevent "frost heaving" (which we explain later). If the foundation supports a frame structure, the foundation is extended well above the surrounding soil level to protect the wood from contact with the soil.

The foundation must support the structure at every part of its footprint. This may be done with a continuous foundation that supports the outer walls of the house, with concrete or masonry piers, or with a combination of the two. For example, common North American practice is to support the outer walls with a continuous perimeter foundation, and to support interior load-bearing walls with columns and a center beam.

Soil has limited ability to carry the weight of a house. Therefore, unless the house is built on solid bedrock, the bottom of the foundation rests on a broadened concrete base that is called a "footing." Figure 3-1 shows how the soil is excavated in preparation for making the footings.

The main footing follows the outline of the outer walls. Individual footings are created for columns that support the structure inside the outer walls. Additional footings may be laid for exterior stairs, porches, and so forth. Figure 3-2 shows the completed footings for a house.

If the house has a basement, the basement walls are built next. A poured concrete wall resting on a good footing can produce an excellent foundation with great strength. Before the concrete is poured, wooden or steel forms must be erected to hold the concrete, as in Figure 3-3.

Figure 3-4 shows how concrete is pumped into forms using modern equipment. Figure 3-5 shows the completed foundation wall. Once the footings are completed, a well organized crew can erect a complex foundation in two or three days.

The thickness of underground walls is determined primarily by the need to resist buckling by soil pressure. The parts of the wall that are farther below grade need to be thicker. However, to simplify construction, poured concrete foundation walls typically have the same thickness from top to bottom.

Prior to the use of poured concrete foundations for houses, foundations commonly were built from stones. Later, concrete blocks or cinder blocks were used, and they are still used as a cheaper alternative to poured concrete. Concrete blocks have hollow cores, reducing the amount of material required. And, forms are not required. However, the resulting foundation is weak. It is prone to sidewise buckling from soil pressure. It is vulnerable to cracks at the mortar joints, which are caused by uneven settling of the soil under the footing. The cracks and the hollow cores of the blocks admit water, radon, and insects from the surrounding soil. Therefore, we consider concrete block house foundations to be obsolete and unsatisfactory.

DRW

Figure 3-1. Excavation for foundation footings. The soil has been excavated and flattened to bring the entire lower floor below the frost depth. Trenches are then dug for the footings. In this loose soil, the trenches are lined with boards. Steel reinforcing rods are supported within the trenches to strengthen the footings. In addition, five holes have been dug to act as forms for individual footings for columns that will support the interior structure of the house.

DRW

Figure 3-2. Completed footings. Grooves along the centers of the footings act as keyways to prevent the foundation walls from being pushed off the footings by soil pressure. This foundation also has four individual footings to support interior columns. Only one was poured when the picture was taken.

DRW

Figure 3-3. Forms being erected for a poured concrete foundation for a house with a basement. The metal panels are held in position by steel strips that connect the panels. These strips remain embedded in the wall, where they will rust and expand unless the wall is well sealed against moisture. Steel forms are reusable. Plywood forms are also commonly used. They are braced externally, which requires more labor.

DRW

Figure 3-4. Concrete being poured into the forms for basement walls. A concrete pumping truck feeds concrete through an overhead pipe that ends in a flexible hose. The hose is guided by the man in the blue shirt. The man on top of the wall to his left is leveling the top of the concrete. A train of concrete delivery trucks supplies the pumping truck. This allows the entire foundation to be poured in a few hours. An older method is filling the forms in separate batches from individual delivery trucks. For foundations that use less concrete, the concrete may be mixed on site.

DRW

Figure 3-5. A completed poured concrete foundation. This is for the same house as in Figure 3-2, and the picture was taken only two days later. The brick pattern in the concrete is created by the metal forms. The exterior sheathing should overlap the top of the foundation to block air leakage, but the brick pattern prevents an airtight seal between the sheathing and the foundation.

Underneath the house is a network of pipes that are needed to discharge sewage by gravity. Figure 3-6 shows how these pipes are laid. These pipes may pass underneath the footings, or they may pass through the foundation wall or footings.

Pipes for water and conduits for electrical wiring may also be buried under the house. However, if the foundation wall is deep, they are usually passed through the foundation wall, below the frost depth.

Natural gas supply pipes are kept outside the footprint of the house, so that a leak in the gas mains cannot enter the house and cause an explosion. Usually, the gas meter is also located outside the foundation. The gas pipe that serves the house from the meter may enter through a basement wall, or near the edge of a slab foundation.

Additional excavation around the house may be needed for septic fields, oil tanks, or other specialized requirements.

After the basement walls are built, a concrete slab is poured to form the basement floor, as in Figure 3-7. The slab is poured over a bed of gravel. The slab is reinforced with a mesh of steel wire and perhaps with reinforcing bars. The gravel commonly is covered with a plastic sheet to block underground water and radon. In a cold climate, insulation may also be laid over the gravel, but this practice may cause the slab to crack.

A perimeter foundation supports the outer walls of the house and the outer ends of the floor joists. In most modern houses, the floor joists do not span across the entire width of the house. Instead, the interior ends of

floor joists are supported by support columns and beams. Figure 3-9 shows a typical steel beam installation. Support columns for beams rest on individual footings, as shown in Figure 3-6. Interior supports may also be installed to support heavy localized loads on upper floors, such as a brick fireplace or a spa tub.

Another method of supporting interior loads is to build a frame wall to carry the weight of the upper structure down to the floor slab, as in Figure 3-10. With this method, the load that is carried must be relatively light, or the floor slab must be reinforced where the wall is built on it.

Basement walls are insulated with insulation that is placed on the outside or inside surfaces of the walls, or both.

Basements are vulnerable to damage from water that enters through cracks and openings in the foundation wall and the floor slab. To keep water away from the basement, a waterproof surface is applied to the outside of the basement wall. If the soil may be wet, good practice is to surround the foundation with gravel to bypass water to a level below the foundation. Additional measures include drain pipes around the footing, and perhaps a sump pump. Underground moisture protection continues to be a weakness of contemporary house construction, so we will explain how to do it correctly.

If the house does not have a basement, a relatively short foundation wall may be built on footings to support the outer structure. This short foundation is called a "stem wall."

DRW

Figure 3-6. Sewer pipes that will soon be covered by a concrete floor slab. The larger pipes are for toilets. Smaller pipes may be used for sink drains. The sewer line also requires one or more small vent pipes, which rise through interior walls all the way through the roof. The two large round objects in front are footings for interior columns.

DRW

Figure 3-7. The concrete floor slab. The two small holes in front are for steel support columns that rest on the buried concrete footings shown in Figure 3-6.

DRW

Figure 3-9. Steel support beam. The ends of the beam are supported by the foundation walls, and the center is supported by a steel column that rests on one of the buried footings shown in Figure 3-6. A wooden timber is bolted to the top of the beam to act as a pad. The bottom of the column has been completely embedded in concrete.

DRW

Figure 3-10. Installing a steel beam to span the top of a wide passageway through a wooden load-bearing wall. Each end of the beam is supported by a steel column. This wall is located at the basement level. It will support the floor joists of the level above.

DRW

Figure 3-12. Florida concrete house built on piers to survive flooding from hurricanes.

DRW

Figure 3-13. An attractive house that uses a rock formation as its foundation, on the Greek island of Naxos.

Alternatively, a house without a basement may be built on concrete piers, as in Figure 3-12. Pier foundations commonly are used if the soil is soggy, or to raise the house where a risk of flooding exists, or to build on a slope, or to avoid the danger of radon in the soil.

If a house is elevated above the soil level by a stem wall or piers, the space under the house is called a "crawl space." This space normally is vented to the outside. Therefore, the lower floor of the house is exposed to outside temperatures, and it should be insulated accordingly.

If the building site has solid bedrock at or near the surface, the bedrock itself can serve as the foundation, or as the footing for a concrete foundation. Figure 3-13 shows a house that is built directly on bedrock.

Especially in warmer climates, and in locations with weak soil, the foundation may be a continuous slab that rests directly on the soil. This type of foundation is called a "floating slab." It acts as its own huge footing, allowing it to support a house on very weak soil. However, in cold climates where the slab does not extend below the frost depth, protecting a floating slab against frost heaving and perimeter cracking requires methods that are controversial.

Steel reinforcing bars (commonly called "rebar") are an essential part of all modern concrete foundations. They are needed because concrete and other masonry lack resistance to tension forces. Unfortunately, rebar often is installed in a manner that does not fully exploit its intended benefit.

WOOD FRAME CONSTRUCTION

In most parts of North America and in some other regions, wood "frame" construction is the prevailing type. The name derives from the fact that the portion of the house above ground level is built on a wooden frame.

In a well built frame house, the structure forms a strong box. It can tolerate soil settlement, earth tremors, and high winds without suffering cracks or misalignment.

Most types of masonry foundations support the lowest wooden floor (the "ground floor") above grade in order to protect the wooden structure from moisture and insects in the soil.

However, if the house has a slab-on-grade foundation, the concrete slab itself is the ground floor. The wooden walls and upper structure rest on the slab. This type of foundation places the wooden structure close to the soil level, where it is vulnerable to damage from moisture and insects. Protection involves various methods, none of which are fully reliable.

Platform Construction

In North America, most modern frame houses are built using a method called "platform" construction. All floors above the masonry foundation are built like platforms. The walls of each level rest on the platform below, and the next higher platform rests on those walls. A multi-level house is like a layer cake of alternating floor platforms and walls. Figure 3-15 shows the basic structure.

Platform construction is economical, it makes good use of materials, and it easily accommodates the super-features that you will want in your home. Platform construction is versatile. In a multi-level house, each floor can have a separate outline. Virtually any shape of floor plan is possible. A common example is that an upper floor overhangs the floor below it. A split-level house can be created by staggering the floor levels.

Platform construction begins by laying "sill plates" along the top of the concrete foundation, as in Figure 3-16. The sill plate is a thick board that is attached to the foundation with bolts. It is the connection between the foundation and the lowest floor platform. In strong construction, steel connectors attach the platform to the sill plates.

The next step is to lay the floor joists, as in Figure 3-17. The floors derive their weight carrying capacity from "joists" that span from one side of the floor to the other. The outer ends of the floor joists rest on the sill plates, and are attached to them. The inner ends of the joists rest on beams or load-bearing walls that were erected under the floor, as we saw in Figures 3-9 and 3-10.

Until recently, floor joists were thick wooden boards placed on edge. However, fabricated wooden beams are now replacing solid timbers, providing flatter floors and allowing longer spans. The most common kind of fabricated floor beam is "I-joist," as shown in Figure 3-17. Its name derives from the fact that it has the cross section of an I-beam.

The floor platform is enclosed by "rim joists" or "band joists," as shown in Figures 3-18 and 3-19. The rim joists rest on the sill plates. They are especially important because they support the weight of the walls and the structure above them. The ends of the floor joists are held in position and prevented from tipping by a rim joist. This rim joist also supports the edge of the floor surface between the joists.

I-joists cannot adequately support heavy wall loads. Therefore, if the floors use I-joists, a stronger kind of joist must be substituted for the outer joists that rest along the sill plates. Various kinds of rim joists are used for this purpose, and we will cover them in greater detail.

Modern houses usually are so wide that a single joist cannot span its width. Therefore, floor platforms usually are supported along their centers. If the house

DRW

Figure 3-15. "Platform" construction for a wood frame house.

has a basement, a strong horizontal beam, which may be steel or lumber, supports the inner portions of the ground floor platform, as we saw in Figures 3-9 and 3-10. The inner portion of the beam rests on columns in the basement. The columns transmit the weight of the center of the house to the earth through individual piers or footings, as shown in Figure 3-6.

After the floor joists and rim joists have been installed, the "subfloor" is laid over them, as in Figure 3-20. The subfloor is the top surface of the platform. It is called the "subfloor" or "underlayment" because the visible finished floor surface (carpet, tile, hardwood, etc.) is laid over it. The best subfloor material is real plywood. If a plywood surface is attached to straight joists with glue and nails (or screws), the resulting floor is strong, level, and quiet.

Unfortunately, chipboard and similar cheaper materials are being substituted to reduce cost. At the same time, subfloors are being made thinner, resulting in floor surfaces that are weak and yielding.

Once the floor platform is complete, the exterior and interior walls are erected on it. The subfloor is a large, flat surface, so it is ideal for assembling parts of the wall. Often, an entire wall is assembled on the floor, and the wall is then lifted into position, as in Figure 3-21.

Frame walls are made of vertical wooden members called "studs." The studs usually rest on horizontal members called "sole plates" or "bottom plates." The bottom plates hold the bottoms of the studs in position, they distribute the weight carried by the studs, and they provide a nailing surface for the interior and exterior wall sheathing. Similarly, the tops of the studs are joined by horizontal members called "top plates."

The walls are built with framed openings for the windows and doors, as in Figure 3-21. "Headers" are installed at the tops of these openings to carry the weight of the structure above the openings. The bottoms of window openings are horizontal timbers called "sills." Headers and window sills are supported by shortened vertical members called "jacks," "cripples," or "trimmers."

After all the wall panels are built, they are joined at the corners. When the next floor or the roof is added, the result is a rigid box that can be enormously strong. To achieve the potential strength of the structure, the connections between the wall panels, the floor platforms, and the roof must be as strong as these components. Strong connections are easy to make in frame construction, but they are often inadequate in practice, making the house vulnerable to wind, earth movement, and sagging.

After the wall frames are built, they are covered with rigid exterior sheathing, as in Figure 3-22. In addition to creating an airtight wall, the sheathing also is an important structural component. It provides rigidity to the wall, preventing it from tipping sideways. (You can see old frame houses and barns that have collapsed sideways because they lacked adequate diagonal bracing in their walls.)

The sheathing also reinforces the wall studs, adding to the load carrying capacity of the wall. And, the sheathing serves as the base for lightweight exterior finish surfaces, such as siding or shingles.

Plywood is the strongest and most reliable sheathing material, but it is being replaced in cheap construction by chipboard and similar materials. It is bad practice to use any kind of insulation board as sheathing, although this has become a common way of increasing the insulation value of walls.

The exterior sheathing may be attached to the wall frame before or after the wall is erected. Installing the sheathing beforehand adds rigidity to the wall segment as it is being erected, improving safety and keeping the

DRW

Figure 3-16. A "sill plate" being installed on the foundation. This is the first step in platform frame construction. The sill plate is anchored to the foundation with bolts that are embedded in the concrete. The pink strip between the sill plate and the foundation is "sill sealer." It prevents air leakage through the gap between the lumber and the concrete.

DRW

Figure 3-17. The floor joists being installed on the foundation. The outer ends rest on the sill plates. The inner ends rest on beams and/or load bearing walls that were built as interior parts of the foundation. These floor joists are made of composite "I-joist" material, which is now prevalent. However, some houses still use the older style of solid timbers, which have both advantages and disadvantages.

DRW

Figure 3-18. Rim joists, as seen from above, before the platform surface is installed. The rim joist in front joins the ends of the floor joists. The rim joist at left is designed to support the heavy wall load. It is made from a series of closely spaced support blocks.

DRW

Figure 3-19. Rim joists, as seen from below, after the platform surface is installed. At the far end, blocks should be placed alongside all the I joists to carry the load of the rear wall. However, some of these blocks are missing.

DRW

Figure 3-20. The "subfloor" being installed. It consists of sheets of plywood or cheaper material. To make the floor rigid and stronger, and to avoid squeaks, adhesive is applied between the subfloor and the floor joists, as shown here.

DRW

Figure 3-21. Wall framing. Usually, carpenters assemble wall sections using the subfloor as a flat working surface. Then, each wall section is lifted into position, as shown here. Temporary braces hold the first wall sections upright, as with the wall on the right.

DRW

Figure 3-22. Exterior wall sheathing. The best material is plywood, but cheaper materials, such as the chipboard used here, are becoming common. Some of the sheathing may be nailed to the wall frames before the walls are erected, to keep the wall frame from tipping sideways.

DRW

Figure 3-23. The roof structure is placed above the finished walls. This house has a truss roof. The trusses were prefabricated at a factory and were lifted into place with a crane. The trusses will be covered with a plywood deck, which provides a structural connection between the trusses and supports the roof weather surface.

DRW

Figure 3-24. A completed frame house. This is the same house shown in Figures 3-6 through 3-10, and in Figures 3-16 through 3-21.

joints tight. However, doing so also prevents the bottom of the wall from resting properly on the platform, and it leaves gaps between the bottom of the wall and the floor platform. A reasonable compromise is to attach a narrow sheet of sheathing to the frame to keep the wall square during erection, and to install the rest of the sheathing afterward.

If the house has more than one floor, the second floor platform is placed on top of the first floor walls. If the house has three floors or more, construction continues in the same way.

The centers of upper floor platforms usually are supported by interior "load-bearing" walls. The load-bearing wall on the first floor is located above the steel I-beam (or a wooden beam) in the basement. A load-bearing wall on the second floor is located above the load-bearing wall on the first floor. And so forth, if the house has more levels.

After the top floor walls are completed, the roof components are lifted into place, as in Figure 3-23. This is covered with a sheathing, usually plywood or a cheaper substitute. The sheathing connects the rafters together, and it acts as structural support for the roof weather surface, which may be asphalt shingles, metal panels, ceramic tiles, or other materials.

Once the house is "under roof," the windows and doors are installed in the wall openings, and the exterior wall surfaces are installed. This provides protection from the weather, so that finishing the interior can proceed. The surrounding terrain is graded and vegetation is planted to hold the soil, yielding a house that is ready for furnishing and occupancy, as in Figure 3-24.

Figure 3-25 is a diagram that summarizes the components of platform construction. All the components play important roles. Seemingly small improvements in the way that the frame is built can provide big improvements in strength and energy efficiency. As we move through Step 3, we will refer to this drawing to make sure that each component is installed in the best way possible.

Insulation and Surfaces for Frame Walls

The insulation for the walls is installed from the inside. In a cold climate, the inner surface of the insulation is covered with a "vapor barrier," which also covers the ceiling insulation. Then, the interior sheathing is attached to the walls and ceiling. The insulation and vapor barrier are critical elements of a super-house, but they are poorly understood by the construction industry. So, an upcoming part of Step 3 is devoted to understanding them thoroughly.

The most common interior surface used today is gypsum board, also called "drywall." Gypsum board is an effective fire retardant, it dampens noise, and it provides a good base for interior paint and other decoration.

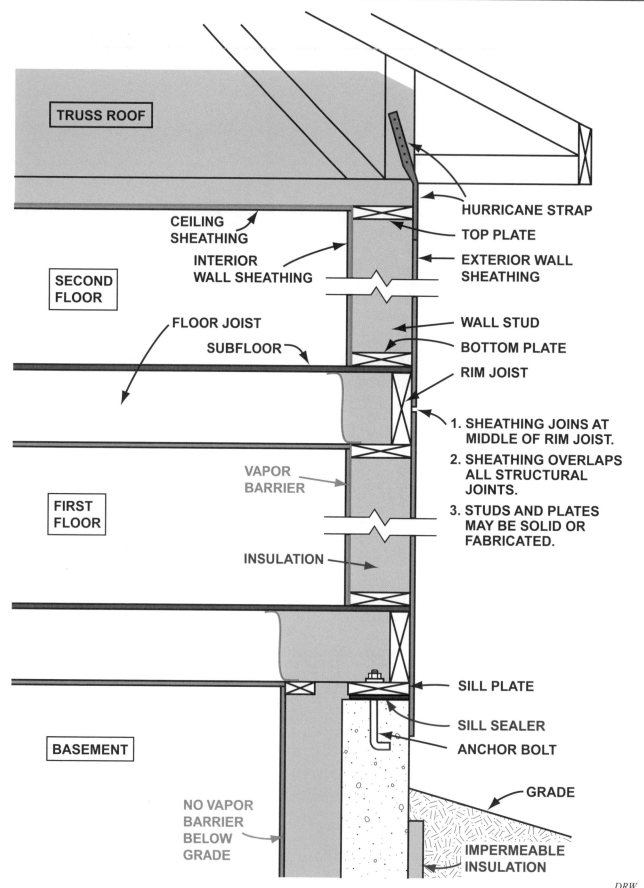

TRUSS ROOF

HURRICANE STRAP

TOP PLATE

EXTERIOR WALL
SHEATHING

CEILING
SHEATHING

INTERIOR
WALL SHEATHING

SECOND
FLOOR

WALL STUD

BOTTOM PLATE

FLOOR JOIST

SUBFLOOR

RIM JOIST

1. SHEATHING JOINS AT
   MIDDLE OF RIM JOIST.

2. SHEATHING OVERLAPS
   ALL STRUCTURAL
   JOINTS.

VAPOR
BARRIER

3. STUDS AND PLATES
   MAY BE SOLID OR
   FABRICATED.

FIRST
FLOOR

INSULATION

SILL PLATE

SILL SEALER

ANCHOR BOLT

BASEMENT

GRADE

NO VAPOR
BARRIER
BELOW
GRADE

IMPERMEABLE
INSULATION

DRW

Figure 3-25. The components of super-insulated platform construction, from the foundation to the roof. The details are important for achieving superior strength and energy efficiency.

OLDER FRAME CONSTRUCTION METHODS

Prior to the middle of the 20th century, most multi-story wood frame houses were built with "balloon frame" construction, as shown in Figure 3-15. This method uses long wall timbers that extend from the foundation to the roof. The ends of the floor joists on each side of the house rest on a horizontal timber that is set into the wall timbers. Balloon frame construction creates strong walls because the walls are made of continuous pieces of lumber. However, platform construction can be just as strong if the connections between the floors and the walls are made properly.

"Post-and-beam" construction is an earlier method that uses heavier wall timbers, or posts, that are continuous from the foundation to the roof. The posts are connected by heavy horizontal beams using pegs or mortise-and-tenon joints that require considerable skill and time to complete. Today, this method is still used for building fancy barns and other buildings to display the craftsmanship involved.

A nostalgic market for these older methods remains, but platform construction is better adapted to modern building materials, especially to lumber and plywood of standardized dimensions. Platform construction is quicker to build and it uses shorter pieces of lumber, saving cost. It is less susceptible to uneven floors and crooked walls. It provides strong nailing surfaces for the edges of the interior and exterior sheathing, which are lacking in balloon frames. It is more resistant to fire because each platform blocks the upward movement of fire inside the wall cavity. And, by the same token, it blocks convection inside the walls.

Mantiques Modern, New York

Figure 3-26. A model of "balloon frame" construction, showing the tall wall timbers.

The outsides of the walls receive an exterior finish that largely determines the appearance of the house. The exterior finish is not structural, but it is important for protecting the wall structure. We covered your exterior surface options in Step 1.

The most common type of lightweight exterior surface consists of overlapped horizontal boards, or other materials that mimic their appearance. They may be made of wood, aluminum, or plastic. Many other types of siding, such as wooden shingles or stucco, can work well.

Or, a frame house can have a heavy exterior surface of brick or stone. This type of surface is called "masonry veneer" because the masonry is just a covering. The masonry is essentially independent of the frame wall, and it provides no structural benefit. Because of its weight, the masonry must rest directly on the concrete foundation.

MASONRY CONSTRUCTION

"Masonry" means concrete, concrete block, brick, or stone.

In masonry construction, the weight of the roof and above-grade floors is carried by masonry walls, rather than by wooden walls. In North America, the term "masonry construction" usually is limited to the foundation and the exterior walls, while the interior walls, the upper level floors, and the roof usually are wooden structure. In many other regions of the world, houses are built entirely of masonry, including the interior walls, all the floors, and the roof.

Masonry has only one kind of strength, the ability to resist crushing. Without getting too technical, we say that masonry has great "compression strength." In fact, a masonry wall gets stronger as more weight is placed on it, up to a point. However, unlike wood or steel, masonry has little "tensile strength," which is resistance to pulling. Masonry will not crush under normal loads, but it will easily crack or buckle if it is loaded unevenly or if it is subjected to water penetration and freezing.

Masonry construction requires an especially strong foundation. This is because masonry is heavy and it lacks tensile strength. The weight of each part of the wall transmits downward to the foundation almost independently of the rest of the wall. If a part of the foundation can sag, everything above it will sag also, and cracks will occur. You can see this in many masonry buildings.

Insulating masonry walls is not as simple as insulating frame walls. Masonry itself has poor insulation properties, and builders have not mastered the techniques of using the best types of insulation with masonry walls. As a result, many houses with masonry walls are poorly insulated.

Concrete Block Structural Walls

In the United States, most masonry walls above grade are made of hollow concrete or cinder blocks combined with a decorative outer facing of brick, stone, stucco, paneling, or just paint. Figure 3-27 shows a typical North American house that uses concrete block walls.

Structural concrete blocks have holes (called "cores") to save weight and material, but the concrete walls of the blocks (called "webs") are fairly thick. The webs and cores are oriented vertically, so that the blocks can carry the weight of the structure above.

Concrete block walls can be reinforced with steel rods ("rebar") to resist high winds and earth tremors, and also to brace underground walls against soil pressure. The rods are placed through the holes in the blocks and are held in place by mortar. The strength of this kind of wall is greatly inferior to the strength of a steel-reinforced poured concrete wall. However, if an above-grade concrete block wall is well supported from below, it may perform well.

Concrete blocks have little insulation value. Furthermore, the vertical orientation of the holes allows strong convection inside the wall. In all but the mildest climates, a concrete block wall requires separate insulation.

In "brick-and-block" construction, a outer face of brick is connected to the inner block wall. Some methods of making this connection improve the overall strength of the wall. Other methods create two essentially independent walls, with the brick outer surface being relatively weak.

In some regions, it is common to use solid blocks made of clay or adobe, instead of cored concrete blocks. Some of these are attractive enough that they do not require an outer finish surface.

Concrete Frames with Filler Blocks

In much of Europe, Asia, and Central America, a house structure commonly begins with a steel-reinforced concrete frame that includes supporting columns, concrete floors, and often, a concrete slab roof. See Figure 3-28. In North America, this design usually is found only in hurricane zones.

The walls are enclosed by filling the spaces in the concrete frame with lightweight blocks. In the U.S. the filler blocks typically are concrete, as in Figure 3-12. Elsewhere, the filler blocks typically are made of terra cotta or other clay, as in Figure 3-29. These blocks are divided into many cavities by thin walls, and the blocks are laid so that the cavities are oriented horizontally.*

This type of construction cannot be insulated well, except with exterior insulation. The heavy concrete supporting frame has minimal insulating value. It conducts heat between the inside of the building and exterior surface. If clay filler blocks are used, their many narrow cavities and their horizontal orientation yield a small but significant insulating value for the wall surfaces.

Walls of this type typically have an exterior finish of stucco, but other finishes may be used.

Natural Stone Walls

Walls and foundations made of natural stone were once prevalent in locations where suitable stone was available nearby. The results could be beautiful and durable, as you can see in many historic houses.

However, the need to trim each stone individually and to fit the stones together requires much more labor than building with concrete blocks and other materials that have standard dimensions. Stonework also requires special skill. As a result, houses with real stone walls have become a rarity. They continue to be built in some locations where usable stone is available locally and other building materials are expensive, as in the Greek islands. Figure 1-168, in Step 1, shows an example.

Like all masonry, stone has little insulation value. To preserve its exterior appearance, a stone wall must be insulated from the inside. The combination of the stone and the insulation results in a wall that is very thick. The doors and windows should be designed to be attractive in such walls.

---

* Clay or terra cotta filler blocks are too weak to support much load beyond their own weight. They are fragile, and should not be used as a structural element. In countries where I have observed clay blocks used in walls, a significant fraction break even before they are installed.

DRW

Figure 3-27. Typical concrete block house construction in the warm sourthern United States. The concrete blocks rest on a slab foundation, whose perimeter almost solely keeps the walls intact. The walls may be covered with a variety of decorative surfaces.

DRW

Figure 3-28. Typical modern house construction in Greece. The entire concrete frame is reinforced by steel. The walls will be created with non-structural filler blocks. The houses in the background are complete.

DRW

Figure 3-29. A Turkish apartment building in which the concrete structural frame is being enclosed with clay filler blocks. Balconies are created by extending the reinforcing steel beyond the outer walls.

THE ROOF

After the walls are built, the structure is covered with a roof. For most of the world's houses, the roof is a frame structure. This is true for all wood frame houses, and for most houses that have masonry walls. There are three basic methods of building a wooden roof structure, and each of them has variations. They were covered in the sidebar, *Basic Roof Structures*, in Step 1. We will have more to say about improving your frame roof, later in Step 3.

A house with masonry walls may have a roof that is made of concrete or other masonry, rather than having a wooden roof. Concrete roofs are prevalent in climates that are warm and generally dry, and in locations where wood is vulnerable to termite destruction, and in regions that are visited by hurricanes. For examples, houses with flat concrete roofs are prevalent around the Mediterranean coast and in the Caribbean islands.

BUILDING CODES

Where do the various tradesmen who will build your home get their knowledge? A small fraction have attended trade schools, but most get their education primarily on the job. They learn by observing others and by following the instructions of foremen. That kind of informal training is not sufficient to achieve the high standard of home construction that presently prevails in most advanced countries.

The current level of quality in home construction was achieved largely through the development of building codes. A building code is essentially a catalog of mandatory minimum acceptable practices. Around the beginning of the 20th century, engineers began to formulate minimum standards for home construction that incorporated the experience of previous generations of builders.

By standardizing building practices, building codes served as an important educational tool for builders. This helped to ensure that builders did a generally good job in the areas covered by the code. Building codes arrived just in time to help builders deal with historic developments in house construction, including electricity, indoor plumbing, automatic heating systems, and the use of concrete and other new building materials.

Building codes arose in response to concern about safety and sanitation. Early codes focused on structural integrity to prevent collapse, on electrical and fire safety, and on the handling of sewage to prevent the spread of infectious diseases. Because building codes aspire to maintain safe conditions throughout the life of the house, they indirectly enhance the durability of the house.

As time went on, the initial success of building codes led them to broaden their requirements beyond concerns related strictly to safety and health. By the late 20th century, building codes made a big leap to include requirements for energy efficiency. And now, some codes attempt to cover construction practices broadly. For example, some building codes go so far as specifying methods of attaching roof shingles.

In North America, the dominant building code for houses is the relatively new *International Residential Code* (IRC). Despite the name, the IRC is oriented primarily toward North American building practices.

The IRC regulates structural strength, fire safety, electrical safety, safety of combustion equipment, plumbing requirements, ventilation, and other areas. The IRC imports the electrical requirements of the long established National Electrical Code. The IRC also includes an imported energy efficiency code that is the latest of many attempts to mandate energy efficiency in buildings.

The introduction to the IRC states that it "... was created to serve as a complete, comprehensive code regulating the construction of single family houses, ... duplexes ... and townhouse units ... The IRC contains coverage of all components of a house or townhouse ... It has been said that the IRC is the complete cookbook for residential construction. ..."

Most of this is true. The requirements of the IRC are encyclopedic, and often extremely detailed. The IRC has extensive tables of specifications for many methods of construction and many kinds of materials. Many methods and features are illustrated with detailed drawings. However, the IRC is not a "cookbook" in the sense of providing a linear set of instructions for building a house.

The IRC gives specifications for alternative construction methods, but it does not indicate the relative merit of the different methods. This can be misleading, because some of the methods are greatly preferable to others, including some methods that are obsolete or ill-advised.

Building codes are works in progress. Their requirements are compromises that reflect the collective wisdom, prejudices, and misconceptions of the people who write them. Building codes change frequently, sometimes incorporating requirements that have not been well proven or well thought out. We will point out some code mistakes as we come to them in the related parts of your home's design.

A building code establishes minimum standards. To achieve the level of super-performance that is possible, we will design important aspects of your home to higher standards than codes require. And, we will make improvements in your home that are not covered by building codes.

Who enforces the building code? Generally, it is the building permit office of your local jurisdiction. It is the responsibility of the builder to satisfy the requirements of the code, it is not your responsibility as the homeowner.* In principle, you don't even have to know that the building code exists.

However, it is valuable for you to have a copy of your local building code, especially if you are building an entire house or doing a major renovation. Even if you refer to the code only a few times, its price will be money well spent. Builders treat the building code as their rulebook, so it will help you to understand what guides the builder's thinking. By the same token, it helps to have the code on hand when you are discussing important details of your design with your builder.

You can request specific deviations from the code, which may be granted if you can provide a good reason for your request. As a rule, a deviation is most likely to be granted if it is made on your behalf by an engineer.

Virtually all modern countries have building codes. But, many local jurisdictions don't enforce them, because they lack the staffing or skills to do so. For example, surveys have shown that most parts of the United States do not enforce their building codes entirely, especially the more complex parts, such as energy efficiency requirements. If that is true of your location, you should still require your builder to satisfy the code, along with the other requirements of your design. You will write that provision into your contract with the builder, which we cover in Step 8.

✓ **That's the end of our primer on conventional house construction. From this point forward, we will build upon those conventional techniques to turn conventional house design into super-house design. Before we get into the specifics of designing the structure of your super-house, we will introduce four advanced design principles that you will apply throughout the structure.**

---

* The law varies among jurisdictions, but here is the common practice in the United States. A homeowner may act as his own designer, but the design must satisfy code requirements. In jurisdictions that actively enforce the building code, the designer must submit the construction drawings for review. In any jurisdiction, the builder is held responsible for satisfying the code, so the builder generally will examine the homeowner's drawings to make sure that they comply. A home designer who works for a fee, such as an architect, is legally responsible for meeting code requirements, along with the builder.

SUPER-STRUCTURE DESIGN ADVANCE #1: SUPER-INSULATION

One of the Five Principles of Super-Efficiency is fully exploiting the benefits of insulation. Your home will have much more insulation than a conventional house, and the insulation will be distributed efficiently. Certain parts of your house, especially the walls, will have a greatly enlarged share of the insulation. Figure 3-30 shows the difference between the old and new approaches to insulating a house.

 Super-insulation is one of the keys to the supreme efficiency and comfort of your home.

This improved method of insulation has been called "super-insulation." Successful super-insulated houses have been built since the 1970's, and they prove that the concept works. Super-insulation will radically reduce your heating and cooling costs, and it will keep you comfortable all year.

Is super-insulation economical? This is a subject of continued argument. Generally, tract home builders want to use as little insulation as possible to lower their home prices, but this is false economy. In any case, insulation is inexpensive compared to the overall cost of a house. A survey by the National Association of Homebuilders showed that the cost of insulation for current conventional homes is less than 2% of the total construction cost.

Our recommendations more than double the amount of insulation, but they don't double the cost. The reason is that largest cost of insulation is for labor, and increasing the amount of insulation material does little to increase the labor cost. Modifying the structure to accommodate super-insulation also will not greatly increase your total construction cost.

Even conventional practice has been tending toward increased insulation, driven by rising energy costs and increased awareness of energy depletion. I believe that the recommendations that you will calculate with the *Insulation Worksheet* are close to optimum for the conditions that lie ahead. Others, including the U.S. government, are now recommending similar values. (That being said, don't follow current U.S. government recommendations. They are unbalanced, being based on obsolete assumptions about construction methods.)

HOW INSULATION PERFORMANCE IS RATED

The insulation performance of construction materials is expressed by "R-value." "R" stands for "resistance" to heat flow. If you go to a hardware store to buy insulation, you will see this rating displayed on the package, for example, as "R-7" or "R-19."

R-value is defined by this formula:

$$\text{Heat Loss} = \frac{\left(\begin{array}{c}\text{surface}\\\text{area}\end{array}\right) \times \left(\begin{array}{c}\text{temperature}\\\text{difference}\end{array}\right)}{\text{R-value}}$$

So, for example, doubling the R-value of a wall cuts the heat loss through the wall in half. Obviously, bigger R-values are better.

The R-value of a material is proportional to its thickness. For example, glass fiber batt insulation has an R-value of approximately 3 per inch. Therefore, a batt that is thick enough to fill a 3.5" stud wall is rated as R-11.

Every material has an R-value, not just insulation. For example, in a frame wall, there is a separate R-value for each layer that makes up the wall, including the interior sheathing, the insulation, the exterior sheathing, and the exterior surface material. The total R-value of the wall is the sum of the R-values of all the layers.

In a super-insulated house, most of the R-value of the outer structure is provided by the insulation. In contrast, many older houses lack wall insulation, so the R-value of their walls depends entirely on their structural materials.

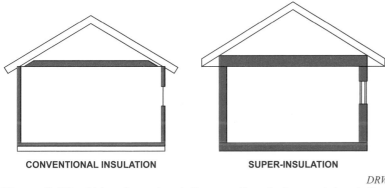

CONVENTIONAL INSULATION   SUPER-INSULATION

DRW

Figure 3-30. Old and new insulation practice. In the past, insulation was limited by the structure. In a super-house, the structure adapts to an optimum amount and distribution of insulation.

Table 3-1. R-Values and RSI of Insulation and Building Materials

Material	R-Value per inch (U.S.)	RSI per cm (Metric)
Mineral wool, loose fill	ca. 2.5	ca. 0.18
Mineral wool, batt [1]	2.9 to 3.8	0.20 to 0.27
Glass fiber, loose fill	ca. 2.5	ca. 0.18
Glass fiber, batt [1]	2.9 to 3.8	0.20 to 0.27
Glass fiber, board	3.8 to 4.2	0.27 to 0.29
Cellulose, shredded paper, new	ca. 3.3	ca. 0.23
Straw bale	ca. 1.4	ca. 0.1
Extruded polystyrene	3.6 to 5.0	0.25 to 0.35
Polystyrene bead board	3.7 to 4.0	0.26 to 0.28
Polyurethane foam board [2]	ca. 5.5	ca. 0.38
Polyisocyanurate foam board [2]	ca. 5.5	ca. 0.38
Polyicynene foam	3.6 to 4.0	0.25 to 0.28
Silica aerogel (experimental)	ca. 10	ca. 0.7
Perlite	ca. 2.7	ca. 0.19
Vermiculite	ca. 2.3	ca. 0.16
Lightweight "insulating" concrete (expanded mineral or foam bead aggregate)	0.2 to 2.0	0.014 to 0.28
Concrete, sand or gravel mix	0.1	0.007
Concrete block or cinder block	0.15 to 0.3	0.01 to 0.02
Brick	0.2	0.014
Plywood	1.2	0.08
Pine lumber	1.2	0.08
Acoustical tile, typical	ca. 2.5	ca. 0.18
Fiberboard sheathing, typical	ca. 2.5	ca. 0.18
Air, film on vertical glass [3]	0.7	0.05
Air, film on ceiling, in winter	0.6	0.04
Soil, typical	0.1 to 0.3	0.007 to 0.02
Snow	ca. 1	ca. 0.07

Notes:

1. Higher density provides better insulation because commercial batt insulation has less than optimum density.

2. Aged, expanded with pentane.

3. The attached air layers are fragile. This value is for a protected air layer, such as the interior of a multi-glazed window.

Table 3-1 lists typical insulation values for the common types of insulation, along with the insulation values of common building materials for comparison.

In the United States, R-value presently is calculated using English units. In most other countries, it is calculated using metric units, so the numbers are different.

R-values using English units are written in the form "R-30", for example. Metric values increasingly are written in the form "RSI 5.3", for example. The "SI" following the "R" stands for "Standard International," which is the worldwide format for metric units. The relationship between the two is:

RSI = 0.176 x R-value,
for the same thickness

For example, glass fiber batt that is 10" (25 cm) thick is rated R-30 in English units and RSI 5.3 in SI units.

Be aware that R-values of certain kinds of insulation may be wildly exaggerated. This cheating happens most commonly with materials that use a reflective surface, such as window films and foil-faced bubble wrap. The insulation materials that are available today have real R-values that range from 2 to 7 per inch (RSI from 0.15 to 0.5 per centimeter).

R-value does not imply resistance to air leakage. It is a common mistake to use insulation as caulking material to plug envelope leaks. All types of fibrous and porous insulation are poor at blocking air leakage.

R-value is not the only thing that matters about insulation. Insulation has many other important characteristics, including fire resistance, moisture permeability, resistance to vermin and physical damage, cost, and other factors. The insulation recommendations in this book take these factors into consideration.

RECOMMENDED INSULATION VALUES

The *Insulation Worksheet*, which is located at the end of this heading, makes it easy for you to select the insulation values for your home. To use the *Insulation Worksheet*, follow this simple procedure:

① Get two numbers for your home site, the "heating degree-days" and the "cooling degree-days."

② Use these two numbers as input to the Insulation Worksheet to get the recommended R-value for each component of your home's structure.

Fill out the *Insulation Worksheet* before you continue into the design of your structure. The R-values that you calculate will determine the dimensions of most major parts of the structure, and they may even affect the shape of some parts, especially the roof. You can update the *Worksheet*, if needed, as you complete your design.

The recommendations produced by the *Insulation Worksheet* apply to new construction. When renovating an existing house, install insulation as close to these values as practical.

To save paper and avoid confusion, we will use only Fahrenheit temperatures and Fahrenheit-based degree-days to calculate your insulation requirements. Then, if you want to express your insulation values in RSI, simply use the previous conversion factor from R-value to RSI.

Where to Find Degree-Days for Your Home Site

The climate of your home site dictates the amount of insulation. We express the climate in terms of "degree-days," which are explained in the sidebar, *Understanding Degree-Days*.

There are two kinds of degree-days, one for heating and one for cooling. For the reasons explained in the sidebar, you may be able to use published heating degree-days, but it is unlikely that you can use published cooling degree-days. Therefore, if your climate has a warm season, expect to calculate your own degree-days using a calculator that is available on the Internet.

To find a degree-day calculator, do a search for "heating degree-day calculator," and you will find several Web sites that offer free calculators that are easy to use. Use the search words, "heating degree-day," not just "degree-day." Otherwise, most of the Web sites that you encounter will be devoted to agriculture and insect control. Their degree-day data are not suitable for heating and cooling calculations.

You need to find a calculator that allows you to calculate both heating and cooling degree-days, and that allows you to specify a separate "base temperature" for each. As this is being written, two good sites are **www.DegreeDays.net** and **www.WeatherDataDepot.com**.

The Web site calculator will ask you for the geographic location of your home site. If the calculator does not have temperature data for your location, select an available location that has similar weather.

The calculator should ask you to specify the base temperatures for heating and for cooling, separately. Use these values:

• base 65 °F, for heating degree-days

• base 73 °F, for cooling degree-days

It is critical to use these base temperatures because the *Insulation Worksheet* is based on them. Using different base temperatures will result in large errors.

A good degree-day calculator will give you the option to use weather data that are averaged over several years. Use this option. It compensates for changes in the climate from year to year.

For perspective, Table 3-2, *Degree-Days of World Cities*, gives heating and cooling degree-days for a range of worldwide locations, using our recommended base temperatures.

And for more perspective, Figure 3-31 is a heating degree-day map of the United States. It shows how climate can vary drastically over small distances, especially in mountainous areas and near large bodies of water.

UNDERSTANDING "DEGREE-DAYS"

Degree-days are a standard way of reporting temperature data for a specific location in a form that is useful for making heating and cooling calculations. The degree-days for a location are calculated from temperature measurements that are made at that location over a long period of time. National weather agencies, such as the U.S. National Weather Service, calculate degree-days for many locations and publish them. Or, a degree-day calculator (usually available free on the Internet) can give you the degree-days for any location that has the needed temperature data.

The concept of degree-days is simple: multiply the temperature difference between the outside and the inside (in degrees) by the length of time (in days). For example, for a month of 30 days, if the outside temperature remains 20 degrees below the inside temperature, that month has 600 heating degree-days.

Unfortunately, calculating degree-days for the real world is more complicated. The previous example is unrealistic because the outside temperature changes throughout the day. For that reason, degree-days usually are calculated from hourly temperature readings, and a daily average temperature is calculated. Various methods are used to calculate the daily averages, giving somewhat different results.

There are two versions of degree-days, "heating degree-days" (HDD) and "cooling degree-days" (CDD). HDD are calculated for outside temperatures below the indoor temperature, and CDD are calculated for outside temperatures above the indoor temperature.

Degree-days provide information only about temperature. They do not provide information about other weather factors that affect energy requirements and comfort, especially sunlight intensity, humidity, and wind. Therefore, *this book uses degree-days only for estimating insulation requirements*. That's because the need for insulation is approximately proportional to the difference between the outside and inside temperatures.

To deal with the other weather factors, we give you specific guidance about related construction features. For example, to deal with sunlight intensity, we recommend appropriate sizing and shading of windows.

Base Temperatures

There is another complication in calculating degree-days. In reality, degree-days are not calculated from the actual inside temperature, but from an assumed "base temperature." For heating degree-days (HDD), the base temperature is lower than the daytime inside temperature. That's because heating is not needed until the outside temperature falls somewhat below the inside temperature.

The actual base temperature varies with conditions, but to make calculations practical, a base temperature of 60 °F or 65 °F is commonly assumed. *This book assumes a base temperature of 65 °F for heating degree-days.*

Similar logic is used for cooling degree-days. *This book assumes a base temperature of 73°F for cooling degree-days.* That base temperature was selected after extensive analysis so that the *Insulation Worksheet* will provide consistent R-value recommendations.

The assumed base temperature has a big effect on the number of degree-days. For example, a base temperature of 65 °F yields 4,016 HDD for Washington, DC, whereas a base temperature of 55 °F yields only 2,245 HDD. Thus, using the wrong base temperatures to calculate degree-days will result in selecting the wrong insulation R-values.

Limitations of Degree-Days for Calculating Energy Requirements

Some people use degree-days as a shortcut method of calculating the total heating and cooling energy requirements of a building. This may work moderately well for estimating heating energy requirements, because the outside temperature is the dominant factor in heating. However, *cooling degree-days are unsatisfactory for estimating cooling energy requirements*. That's because the need for cooling is driven largely by sunlight and humidity, which do not relate directly to the outside temperature.

Table 3-2. Degree-Days of World Cities (5-year averages)

Location	Heating (base 65 °F)	Cooling (base 73 °F)
UNITED STATES		
Albuquerque, NM	4,180	780
Anchorage, AK	10,340	0
Aspen, CO	9,140	80
Atlanta (Dekalb), GA	3,090	870
Boston, MA	5,640	320
CALIFORNIA (N to S)		
Sacramento	3,010	820
San Francisco	3,280	50
San Jose	2,670	350
Los Angeles	1,530	200
San Diego	1,490	130
Chicago, IL	6,350	420
Denver, CO	6,020	400
FLORIDA (N to S)		
Jacksonville	1,750	1,120
Gainesville	1,500	1,420
Orlando	810	1,500
Tampa	630	1,880
Ft. Myers	460	2,080
Miami	230	2,060
Key West	80	2,420
Houston, TX	1,460	1,790
Kansas City, MO	5,140	660
Las Vegas, NV	2,010	2,560
Minneapolis, MN	7,470	400
New Orleans, LA	1,580	1,260
New York, NY	4,460	540
Oklahoma City, OK	3,460	1,200
Phoenix, AZ	1,100	3,290
San Juan, PR	0	2,970
Seattle, WA	4,900	110
Tucson, AZ	1,810	1,940
Washington, DC	4,030	780

Location	Heating (base 65 °F)	Cooling (base 73 °F)
CANADA		
Montreal	7,860	170
Saskatoon	10,900	110
Toronto	6780	210
Winnipeg	10,530	140
LATIN AMERICA		
Lima	490	200
Mexico City	1,870	200
Santiago, Chile	3,400	400
Sao Paulo	670	500
AUSTRALIA		
Sydney	1,310	360
EUROPE		
Athens	2,350	860
Hamburg	5,860	70
Istanbul	3,350	530
London	4,840	50
Madrid	3,870	710
Moscow	8,470	160
Oslo	8,750	30
Paris	4,870	120
Rome	3,290	530
Zurich	6,060	130
ASIA		
New Delhi	720	3,420
Hong Kong	430	2,130
Mumbai	5	3,520
Riyadh	710	4,250
Singapore	0	3,300
Taipei	480	1,970
Tokyo	2,810	580
AFRICA		
Cairo	660	1,980
Johannesburg	2,200	220

ANNUAL HEATING DEGREE DAYS
BASED ON NORMAL PERIOD 1961-1990

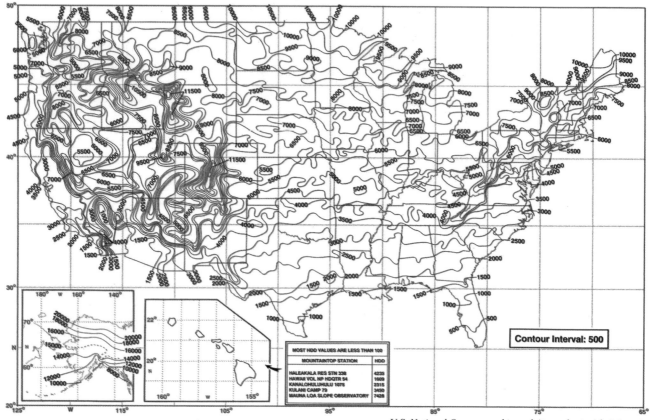

U.S. National Oceanographic and Atmospheric Administration

Figure 3-31. Heating degree-day map of the United States. The map neglects to state the base temperature, which is essential information. Extreme local variations occur in mountain regions.

Accuracy and Assumptions

A huge benefit of super-insulation is that it acts as an insurance policy against large changes that may occur in the future, including:

- *climate change*. Weather may change widely over a span of years or centuries. The *Insulation Worksheet* accounts for changes that may be reasonably expected during the life of the house, which we assume to be a minimum of two centuries.

- *energy sources and their costs*. From our current vantage point in history, it seems likely that new energy sources will emerge during the life of the house. But, it is folly to predict which ones will become practical, and what their costs will be. It is certain that today's major energy sources are being depleted, but we can't predict the trend of depletion or prices with any accuracy.

- *heating and cooling equipment*. The *Insulation Worksheet* assumes the best efficiencies that are available with current heating and cooling equipment. Future changes in heating and cooling efficiency are not predictable.

For simplicity, the *Insulation Worksheet* does not account for local variables, such as:

- *weather characteristics other than temperature*, such as wind and cloud cover. Other recommendations of this book deal with such local variations. For example, our emphasis on preventing air leakage makes wind a minor factor. Our window shading recommendations account for window orientation, solar intensity, etc.

- the *sunlight absorption characteristics* of exterior surfaces. The *Worksheet* assumes average values for common surface materials.

- the *orientation of exterior surfaces with respect to the sun*. The *Worksheet* assumes average exposure to sunlight.

- *house size*. We discussed the effect of house size on energy consumption in Step 1.

The *Insulation Worksheet* assumes that the other recommendations of this book will be followed. For example, if you build in a location that has a warm season, the *Worksheet* assumes that your roof design will keep your roof insulation as cool as practical.

INSULATION WORKSHEET

(Notes 1, 2)

HOW TO USE THIS WORKSHEET:

1) Find the heating degree-days (HDD) and the cooling degree-days (CDD) for your location from a source explained in the text. Be sure that the HDD have a base temperature of 65 °F and that the CDD have a base temperature of 73 °F.

2) Identify the components in the Worksheet that are used in your home design.

3) For each component, use your HDD in the red tinted column and your CDD in the blue tinted column to get R-values for heating and cooling, respectively.

4) Add the R-values from both columns and write the sum in the last column, unless stated otherwise. The value in the last column is the recommended insulation value for each house component.

5) If your design has an insulated component that is not included in the Worksheet, estimate a reasonable insulation value from similar components in the Worksheet.

6) Refer to the Notes at the end of the Worksheet for brief explanations of the multiplication factors. Refer to the text in Step 3 for greater detail, for general assumptions in the recommendations, and for the insulation materials and methods that apply to each component.

7) When selecting the actual insulation, select available R-values that are closest to the values derived from the Worksheet. In case of doubt, select the next larger size. Similarly, when designing the components that hold insulation, such as stud walls, select dimensions that are standard or easy to use.

8) – **FOR METRIC USERS** – The Worksheet calculates R-values (in English units) using Fahrenheit-based temperature data. To avoid repetition and confusion, we do not have a worksheet that uses Celsius-based units. If you desire to calculate RSI (metric) insulation values, use this Worksheet with Fahrenheit-based HDD and CDD, and then convert the resulting R-values to RSI.

My location is:	HDD: _____ (base 65 °F)	CDD: _____ (base 73 °F)	
INSULATED COMPONENT	**HEATING** Multiply HDD	**COOLING** Multiply CDD	**TOTAL R-Value**
ROOF, Truss (heavily vented for cooling)	by **.008** = _____ (Note 3)	by **.008** = _____ (Notes 4, 5)	= _____
ROOF, Truss (typical venting, primarily for moisture protection)	by **.008** = _____ (Note 3)	by **.012** = _____ (Notes 4, 6)	= _____
ROOF, Beam or Triangle-Frame	by **.007** = _____ (Note 3, 8)	by **.008** = _____ (Notes 4, 7, 9)	= _____
ROOF (primary roof structure, over non-occupied space, without built-in heating or cooling) • Example: garage covered by primary house roof.	= 0	= 0	= 0

ROOF
(top-surface deck insulation for supplemental roof, over seasonal enclosed living space without built-in heating or cooling)
• Example: enclosed porch with large, openable windows.
	if HDD < 1,000:
	= 0
	if HDD ≥ 1,000:
	= R-5
	(Notes 12, 13)
		= 0
		except, for comfort, if CDD > 1500 and roof is heavily exposed to sun:
		= R-5
			Higher of HDD or CDD:
			= _____

ROOF (top-surface deck insulation for supplemental roof, over outdoor living space) • Example: open porch.	= 0 except, if climate is snowy or rainy: = R-5 (Note 13)	= 0 except, for comfort, if CDD > 1500 and roof is heavily exposed to sun: = R-5	Higher of HDD or CDD: = _____
EXTERIOR WALL, Frame **(insulation in wall cavity)** (Notes 14, 15)	by .005 = _____	by .005 = _____	= _____ (Notes 14, 15)
EXTERIOR WALL, Masonry **(typical finished concrete block exterior, with interior insulation)**	by .005 = _____	by .0035 = _____ (Note 16)	= _____ or highest practical (Note 17)
EXTERIOR WALL, Masonry **(heavy masonry, exposed exterior surface, with interior insulation, in warm desert climate)** (Note 21)	by .005 = _____	by .0025 = _____	= _____ or highest practical (Note 17)
EXTERIOR WALL (enclosing non-occupied space, without built-in heating or cooling) • Example: garage covered by primary house roof.	= 0	= 0	= 0
EXTERIOR WALL (for seasonal enclosed living space without built-in heating or cooling, heavily glazed) • Example: enclosed porch.	= 0	= 0	= 0
BASEMENT WALL (exterior below-grade insulation)	by .002 = _____ (Note 22)	= 0	= _____
BASEMENT WALL (interior insulation)	by .003 = _____ (Note 23)	by .002 = _____ (Note 24)	= _____

INTERIOR WALL, Frame or Masonry (between living space and unconditioned attached structures) • Examples of unconditioned structures: garage, carport, enclosed and open porches.	by .005 = _____	by .003 = _____	= _____
INTERIOR WALL, Frame (separating "day cluster" from "bedroom clusters," "expansion rooms," and "independent rooms," and enclosing shower rooms) (Note 25)	**if HDD < 4,000:** = 0 **if HDD ≥ 4,000:** = Fill wall cavity. (Note 15)	= 0	= _____
INTERIOR FLOOR & CEILING, Frame (separating "day cluster" from "bedroom clusters," "expansion rooms," and "independent rooms," and enclosing shower rooms) (Note 25)	**if HDD < 4,000:** = 0 **if HDD ≥ 4,000:** by .0015 = _____	= 0	= _____
INTERIOR WALL, Masonry (between interior living spaces)	= 0 (Note 26)	= 0 (Note 26)	= 0
FLOOR, Frame (over vented crawl space and over open, shaded soil)	by .005 = _____	by .002 = _____ (Note 31)	= _____
FLOOR, Frame (overhanging an exterior wall or area exposed to sunlight)	by .005 = _____	by .003 = _____ (Note 32)	= _____
FLOOR, Frame (over normally unheated basement) (Note 25)	**if HDD ≤ 3000:** = 0 **if HDD > 3000:** by .0012 = _____	= 0	= _____
FLOOR, Basement Slab	**if HDD ≤ 2500:** = 0 **if HDD > 2500:** by .0015 = _____ (Note 33)	= 0 (Note 34)	= _____

FLOATING SLAB FOUNDATION, Perimeter (for protection against frost heaving, perimeter cracking, and heat loss)	if HDD ≤ 1000:
	
	= 0
	
	if HDD > 1000:
	
	by .004 = _____
		= 0	= _____

FLOATING SLAB FOUNDATION, Floor (for comfort, above or below the slab)	if HDD ≤ 2500:
	
	= 0
	
	if HDD > 2500:
	
	by .002 = _____
	
	(Note 33)
		= 0
		
		(Note 34)
			= _____

WINDOWS & CLERESTORIES	if HDD + CDD < 1000: **double glazing, plain** if HDD + CDD = 1000 - 3000: **double glazing, enhanced** if HDD + CDD > 3000: **as high as practical** (Note 35)		
SKYLIGHTS	if HDD + CDD < 1000: **double glazing, plain** if HDD + CDD ≥ 1000: **as high as practical**		
WINDOWS, CLERESTORIES & SKYLIGHTS (for unoccupied spaces, without built-in heating or cooling)	= minimum	= minimum	= minimum

EXTERIOR ENTRANCE DOORS (Note 36)	if HDD ≤ 1500:
	
	= minimum
	
	if HDD > 1500:
	
	= as high as practical
		if CDD ≤ 2500:
		
		= minimum
		
		if CDD > 2500:
		
		= as high as practical
			Higher of HDD or CDD:
			
			= _____

GARAGE DOORS & LARGE DOORS (for normally unoccupied spaces attached to house)	if HDD ≤ 2500:
	
	= minimum
	
	if HDD > 2500:
	
	= **R-5 to R-10**
		= minimum	**Higher of HDD or CDD:**
			
			= _____

GARAGE DOORS & LARGE DOORS (for spaces in which informal activities occur occasionally)	if HDD < 400:
	
	= minimum
	
	if HDD = 400 – 3000:
	
	= **R-5 to R-10**
	
	if HDD > 3000:
	
	= as high as practical
		if CDD ≤ 2500:
		
		= minimum
		
		if CDD > 2500:
		
		= **R-5 to R-10,** without air conditioning
		
		= as high as practical, if air conditioned
			Higher of HDD or CDD:
			
			= _____

NOTES:

1. The recommendations are based primarily on analysis of successfully built super-insulated houses, in locations ranging from 4,000 to 11,000 heating degree-days. Recommendations for milder climates, and for cooling, were extrapolated from the heating degree-day data and from experience in such locations.

2. The insulation values yielded by the Worksheet apply to the insulation material itself, not to the overall insulation value of the structure. The Worksheet takes into account the insulation value of the structure, which is significant mainly in mild climates.

3. For heating, roofs are insulated more heavily than walls because: they comprise a large, unbroken surface, which is more economical to insulate; they are exposed to extra cooling by radiation into the night sky; and to a lesser extent, because warmer air inside the house rises to the ceiling surface.

4. For cooling, roofs are insulated more heavily than walls because: they comprise a large, unbroken surface, which is more economical to insulate; they are exposed to extra heating by solar radiation; and, roof structures trap solar heating against the upper insulation surface.

5. A heavily ventilated truss roof has an interior temperature that remains near the outside air temperature.

6. The space inside a truss roof with smaller vents sized primarily for moisture protection will be substantially warmer than the outside air, during daylight. This increases heat flow through the insulation.

7. The small moisture venting space of beam and triangle-frame roofs does not allow good ventilation for cooling of the insulation during warm weather. Improved cooling ventilation requires a ventilation fan and special framing, which generally is limited to rectangular roof panels. See *Cool Roofs for Warm Climates*, in Step 3.

8. It is less economical to increase insulation for heating in a beam or triangle-frame roof than in a truss roof. In a very cold climate, consider using a truss roof instead.

9. It is less economical to increase insulation for cooling and to provide adequate cooling ventilation in a beam or triangle-frame roof than in a truss roof. In a very warm climate, consider using a truss roof instead.

12. Such spaces typically are heavily glazed, which limits the ability of the roof insulation to provide comfort in colder weather.

13. In climates that have significant snow or cold rain, insulation installed above the roof deck protects the roof structure against condensation damage.

14. Generally, frame wall insulation should be entirely within the wall cavity. In most climates, the selected R-value determines the wall thickness, which can be increased without limit at modest cost.

15. The insulation should completely fill the wall cavity to exploit the benefit of fire protection.

16. Concrete block with an exposed exterior surface has a small thermal lag, which reduces the insulation requirement in warm climates. See the sidebar, *Can Your House Benefit from Thermal Lag?*, in Step 3.

17. The thickness of interior insulation adds to the thickness of the masonry, which may result in an unacceptably thick wall, especially in a climate that has a very cold season.

21. A climate that alternates between hot days and cold nights is needed to exploit the thermal lag of heavy masonry. See the sidebar, *Can Your House Benefit from Thermal Lag?*, in Step 3.

22. Even in mild climates, the soil temperature typically lingers below the inside temperature. Therefore, some exterior insulation is recommended to minimize condensation inside the basement wall. This condensation protection is not needed in consistently dry climates.

23. In a mild or predominantly cold climate, install the interior insulation at the same thickness from top to bottom. It is assumed that the basement has limited occupancy, making less insulation economically optimum.

24. In a predominantly warm or hot climate, install the interior insulation only from the top of the basement wall to a short distance below grade level. The insulation blocks heat entry above grade, while the lack of insulation below grade allows the surrounding soil to keep the basement cool. The lower cooling R-value accounts for the added insulation value and the thermal lag of the masonry wall.

25. Insulation of interior walls, ceilings, and floors provides several benefits. See *Insulation for Interior Frame Walls, Floors, and Ceilings*, in Step 3.

26. Interior masonry walls typically have perforated blocks, which have adequate insulation value for this purpose.

31. The insulation requirement is reduced because the exterior surface radiates heat toward shaded, cool soil.

32. The bottom surface of the insulation is warmed somewhat by radiation and convection from below.

33. The moderating effect of warmer soil temperature under the house, and the insulation value of the soil itself, reduce the need for floor insulation.

34. The soil below the slab is virtually always cooler than the desired indoor temperature.

35. If a house is insulated properly, its glazing accounts for the largest amount of heat loss. For this reason, install glazing with the highest R-value that is technically and economically practical. Options include triple glazing and tandem double-glazed windows. Also, look for new developments that improve glazing R-value, such as vacuum-insulated glass.

36. Resistance to intrusion should be the primary criterion for selecting entrance doors. Resistance to air leakage is the most important energy efficiency and comfort criterion. Insulation value is a secondary criterion because entrance doors have a small surface area.

INSULATION MATERIALS FOR HOUSES

"Insulation" is anything that blocks the movement of heat.

Okay, what is "heat"? It is the random thermal jiggling of the molecules in matter. Heat flows through matter when molecules with more energy bump into molecules with less energy. This process of heat movement is called "conduction."

It is possible to block all heat conduction by creating an empty zone that has no matter. This is the principle used in a thermos bottle, which has a double-walled shell with vacuum inside. Unfortunately, nobody has yet invented a cheap and reliable vacuum container for large surfaces, such as the walls of a house.

The next best thing to vacuum is a gas, in which the molecules are far apart and don't bump into each other very often. Virtually all home insulation uses a gas as the insulating material. Air is the most common gas used in insulation, because it is everywhere. The big limitation of using air for insulation is that it moves easily, and it carries heat when it moves.

Fortunately for insulation, air has a tendency to form a thin, sticky layer on the surfaces of solid materials. Common porous insulation exploits this stickiness to keep air from moving. Such insulation has a lot of surface area with small air spaces, so that all the air inside the insulation can stick to a nearby surface. The shape of the solid material does not matter much. For example, some insulation is made from fibers, other types are made from granules, some is made from shreds of paper. However, the sticky forces that hold air in porous insulation are weak. For this reason, all porous insulation must be protected from wind and drafts.

Another method of keeping an insulating gas from moving is to enclose it in bubbles. This is the principle of plastic foam insulation, as well as some less common materials, such as foam glass and neoprene insulation. Using closed bubbles offers an additional advantage, which is the ability to use gases that have better insulation value than air.

Good insulation contains so little solid material that most heat conduction occurs through the gas. Still, heat loss through the solid material is significant. For this reason and to reduce cost, manufacturers minimize the amount of the solid material. That's why all good insulation is light in weight.

There is another way that heat moves, which is by radiation. When the molecules in solid matter bump into each other, they get excited and radiate energy. This radiated energy is another form of heat. Heat radiation inside insulation is not a big factor, because the radiation is captured inside the insulation itself. However, heat radiation between windows and the inside of a house is more important, as we will learn when we select your windows.

Now that we understand the concept of insulation, let's look at the types of insulation that are used in houses.

Glass and Mineral Fiber Insulation

"Glass" fiber insulation is made from melting a mineral, such as silica sand, and spinning it into fine fibers. Glass fiber insulation is presently the dominant type for wood frame buildings. Its overwhelming advantage is fire safety. The material itself will not sustain a fire, and if it is installed properly, it will deter the spread of fire through a wooden structure. Beyond that, it has reasonably good insulation value and it is relatively inexpensive. It is fairly easy to install, but installation requires more care than it usually gets.

"Mineral wool" or "rock wool" is similar to fiber glass, but it is made from a broader range of materials, such as basalt rock, limestone, or boiler slag. Its insulation value is similar to that of fiber glass. Typically, it looks dirtier. The choice between the two is mainly a matter of availability and price.

All fiber insulation has one big disadvantage, a lack of resistance to the flow of air or water vapor. To keep wind and drafts from blowing heat through fiber insulation, it must be enclosed. To block the flow of water vapor into fiber insulation, it must be supplemented with a separate "vapor barrier."

The hard, brittle glass or mineral fibers are a safety hazard during handling. They can penetrate eyes and skin, and there is suspicion that they may cause lung disease if they are inhaled. After installation in the house, the material is harmless unless it is disturbed.

Fiber insulation is available in the form of batts, loose fill, and semi-rigid boards. Each type is applied in different way.

■ Batts

A "batt" is a blanket of glass or mineral fibers that is made to a controlled width and thickness. The fibers are held together by a small amount of adhesive. Batt insulation is available in a variety of widths to accommodate common joist and stud spacings. Batts are also available in a wide range of thicknesses.

In most locations, glass and mineral fiber batts are the best all-around insulation for frame walls, floors, and ceilings. Batt insulation is also a prime choice for insulating the interior of masonry walls, as we will explain. The material usually is packaged in compressed rolls, as in Figure 3-35. Batts can easily be cut to the

Figure 3-35. Glass fiber batt insulation, as usually packaged.

Owens Corning

desired length with scissors, an electric carving knife, or similar tools.

Batts are available in three styles. One is without a backing sheet, as in Figure 3-35. Another has a paper backing sheet that is impregnated with a tar-like moisture retardant, as in figure 3-36. And, a third type adds an aluminized coating to the backing sheet. Each of these types has its proper application, and it is important to know where to use each kind. Using the wrong kind can cause serious moisture trouble.

The backing sheets on batts have two functions. One is to hold the batt securely in place between wall studs, roof rafters, or floor joists. The other function is to serve as a vapor barrier.

The paper backing sheet has tabs on each side, about one inch (25 mm) wide. The tabs should be stapled to the face of studs, rafters, and joists, as in Figure 3-36. This provides secure positioning and a well overlapped vapor barrier. Unfortunately, builders often fail to use this valuable feature, so you need to discuss it with your builder.

Aluminum foil backing is also supposed to improve insulation value during cold weather by reflecting heat radiation from the interior of the house back into the house. For reasons that are rather technical, foil backing provides no significant benefit in a wall that is completely filled with insulation.

Plain batts, without a backing sheet, are needed where moisture must vent through the insulation. This includes the upper layers of attic insulation, as in Figure 3-37, and basement wall insulation.

Johns Manville

Figure 3-36. Glass fiber batt being installed in a frame wall. Note that the tabs of the backing sheets are overlapped properly, creating an unbroken vapor barrier.

Certainteed

Figure 3-37. Proper installation of batt insulation in an attic. The upper layer or layers must have no vapor barrier, so that moisture can vent into the attic space. The crisscrossed arrangement of the batts provides optimum resistance to heat leakage along the joists and between the batts.

In the United States, the width of batts is determined by the common spacings for studs and joists, which are 16" (400 cm) and 24" (600 mm). The thickness of common timber studs and joists is 1½" (38 mm), so most batts are made narrower than the stud spacing

COMPRESSING FIBER INSULATION

Contrary to what you might expect, the R-value of glass and mineral fiber insulation is higher (for a given installed thickness) if the material is compressed somewhat more densely than it is supplied. This is because the cost of the material leads manufacturers to produce batts that are less dense than is optimum.

For example, if you design your walls to hold 10" (25 cm) of insulation, install two layers of "R 19" insulation, each of which is nominally 5.5" (14 cm) thick. This compresses the batts slightly. But, don't overdo it.

By the same logic, don't expand or fluff fiber insulation to make it thicker. That would result in a net loss of insulation value.

Fiberboard insulation is already compressed more tightly than batts. As a result, it has slightly higher R-value, even though it contains more solid matter.

to account for the stud thickness. The actual width of batts used with 16" (400 mm) spacing is 15" (375 mm). Insulation used with 24" (600 mm) spacing is actually 23" (575 mm) wide. These dimensions are still one half inch (13 mm) wider than the actual space between the studs. The small extra width provides a snug fit for the batt, and it provides for some misalignment of the studs.

However, not all studs and joists are thick. I-joist, which we will explain later, has now become the primary material for floor and ceiling joists. It uses thin plywood for most of its surface. Therefore, batt insulation that is used with I-joist should have the same width as the joist spacing. For example, if I-joist spacing is 24" (600 mm), use insulation batts that are a full 24" (600 mm) wide.

Not all insulation manufacturers offer full-width batts. Your builder may need to make a special order to get them. Search insulation manufacturers' Web sites to find the right batt dimensions for all the applications in your home.

If you want a higher insulation value than is possible with a single layer of batts, simply install two or more layers of batts. For example, if your walls will have cavities that are 8" deep, you can install one layer of batts with a nominal thickness of 5½" (R-19) plus one layer of batts with a nominal thickness of 3½" (R-11). That adds up to 9", rather than 8", which is okay. Compressing batts slightly will actually improve their insulation value, because batt insulation is manufactured with a density that is lower than optimum. See the sidebar.

■ Loose Glass and Mineral Fiber

Glass and mineral fiber insulation is also available in the form of loose material that poured or blown into place, as in Figure 3-38. Loose fiber insulation is used primarily in attics over flat ceilings, where it is cheaper to install than batts. It does an excellent job of filling cavities around the ceiling joists. However, if you select loose fill insulation, your ceiling design will need dams to keep the insulation from falling into places where it doesn't belong, such as bathroom ceiling heaters.

Getting glass and mineral fibers into your eyes or lungs is dangerous, so installing this material requires protective clothing, goggles, and a respirator. Even getting glass fibers on any exposed skin is unpleasant. By the same token, using loose fiber insulation makes an attic undesirable for storage or for other purposes.

For these reasons, *I recommend against using loose glass or mineral fiber insulation*. Instead, use batts.

Owens Corning

Figure 3-38. Loose glass fiber insulation being blown into an attic. This requires protective clothing, including effective protection for eyes and lungs.

■ Fiberboard

Finally, fiber insulation is available in the form of semi-rigid boards. The fibers are packed more densely, requiring a larger amount of binder for the fibers. The material has a slightly higher insulation value than the same material in the form of batts or loose fill. Fiberboard insulation usually is attached to flat masonry surfaces, such as the inside of a concrete block wall, as in Figure 3-39, or to the underside of a concrete roof.

You may be able to find fiberboard insulation that is bonded to a variety of finish surfaces, such as gypsum board, plywood, and plywood substitutes. Such combinations provide a handy way of insulating and finishing masonry surfaces at the same time.

Knauf Insulation

Figure 3-39. Attaching semi-rigid insulation to the interior of a concrete block wall. It is important to attach the insulation snugly. This illustrates one of several methods.

Cellulose Insulation, a Problematic Option

"Cellulose" insulation usually consists of shredded waste paper that is treated with chemicals. It is used most commonly in the form of a loose fill material, as in Figure 3-40.

The most common application for cellulose insulation is in attics, where it is poured from bags or blown into place with a hose, as in Figure 3-41. The material is not considered to be particularly dangerous to handle, but the installer should wear a dust mask.

Cellulose insulation became popular during the 1970's as a way of recycling waste paper. It can be cheap, and it has good insulation value. Also, recycled paper has low embodied energy.

Unfortunately, cellulose insulation has a variety of problems that offset its virtues. It settles more than other types of loose insulation, losing perhaps 20% of its depth over time. The recycled paper is a fire hazard, it degrades and promotes mildew when wetted, and it is food and nesting material for vermin.

Cellulose insulation depends on additives to minimize these weaknesses. For example, borax may be added to retard fire, and other chemicals may be added to discourage vermin. Quality varies widely among different manufacturers, and cellulose has gained a reputation for trouble. That is a pity, because cellulose is especially attractive for its low embodied energy and low cost.

The settling tendency of cellulose insulation tends to limit its use to attics, where extra insulation can easily be installed to compensate for settling.

WeatherShield Insulators

Figure 3-40. A typical sample of cellulose insulation. It consists of shredded paper, with additives.

If you decide to use cellulose insulation for an attic, it is essential to install dams in the ceiling framing to keep the insulation from spilling into eaves, passages for vents and flues, ceiling light fixtures, ceiling heaters, and other places where it can cause trouble.

Don't use cellulose insulation in ordinary frame walls, where it would settle and leave an uninsulated band at the top. If you want to use cellulose insulation in a wall, you need to open the top of the wall cavity to the attic, so that additional insulation can fall into the wall from the attic to compensate for settling. We explain the design under the heading, *Insulating Walls with Cellulose Insulation*, later in Step 3.

Cellulose has been used for under-floor insulation. This requires an enclosed box structure to hold the material in place.

Freedom Solar Energy LLC

Figure 3-41. Cellulose insulation being installed by blowing. It can also be poured from bags. Then, it is raked to a uniform depth.

Figure 3-42. Plastic foam board insulation for a foundation. It is installed on the outside of the foundation, as it should be. The insulation should be covered with a reliable water barrier, and the soil should be kept dry.

Plastic Foam Board Insulation, Only for Fire-Safe Applications

Plastic foam insulation created a revolution in the construction industry because of its high R-value, low moisture permeability, and ease of installation. Plastic foam has high R-value because the insulating gas is completely encapsulated, preventing its movement by convection, wind, or pressure differences. The walls of the foam bubbles are thin, which limits conduction through the solid material.

Most plastic foam is installed in the form of rigid boards, which are easy and safe to handle. They have almost no weight, they can be cut easily with a box knife, and they do not irritate eyes or skin. The foam can be bonded to structural and finish materials, such as plywood, chipboard, and gypsum board.

Now, the bad news. All plastic foam insulation produces large amounts of deadly smoke in a fire. A great deal of effort has gone into making plastic insulation fire retardant, and some types can resist small fires. However, all plastic foam materials are made from petroleum, and all of it will burn or emit smoke if it is surrounded by a hot fire.

For this reason, it is prudent to avoid using plastic insulation in all parts of the house that can burn. As a rule, plastic foam insulation is safe only if it is buried outside a foundation wall, as in Figure 3-42, or if it is used to insulate the outside of a masonry wall, where it will be covered by an inflammable surface of stucco or metal.

Covering plastic foam insulation with a non-flammable material, such as gypsum board, may buy time to evacuate a burning house, but this practice cannot keep the plastic from igniting. In a big fire, plastic foam insulation melts, runs out into the fire, and then ignites.

Unlike insulation that is made from mineral materials, plastic foam insulation has a life that is short in relation to the life of the house. Within a few years, the R-value of foam insulation declines because the insulating gas leaks through the thin walls of the bubbles, to be replaced by air. Eventually, all plastic foam disintegrates.

There are several types of plastic foam board insulation. For foundation insulation, the only kind that you need to consider is *extruded polystyrene*, which has the best resistance to water penetration.

Note the word "extruded" in the name. This distinguishes extruded polystyrene from *expanded polystyrene*, which is commonly called *beadboard*. Beadboard is made by melting foam beads together to form rigid boards or other shapes, such as coffee cups. Beadboard becomes crumbly as it ages and is less resistant to long-term moisture penetration.

Polyurethane and *polyisocyanurate* foam boards are used for insulation that must operate at higher temperatures, typically on a roof. Both have somewhat better R-value than extruded polystyrene, but they are more expensive and less resistant to moisture penetration.

Insulation to Avoid

The following are some other types of insulation presently being used in houses. I don't recommend them, because better options are available.

Wet sprayed cellulose is a slurry of cellulose material mixed with a glue. When the slush dries, it becomes rigid, like *papier mache*. It can be applied to any orientation, including overhead. It's an interesting product, but it is very messy to apply. It shares most of the weaknesses of dry loose cellulose, except that it does not settle. It encapsulates electrical wiring, ducts, and other fixtures, which makes maintenance and additions difficult.

Sprayed plastic foam is an alternative to foam insulation boards. It promises quick installation. However, it cannot be applied thickly enough to provide a high insulation value. For applications such as exterior insulation of masonry walls, a better alternative is to use foam board insulation and cover it with a weatherproof surface.

Urea formaldehyde foam was used for a period of time to insulate the walls of houses by injecting it into the closed wall cavities. The results were sometimes disastrous. Unless the ingredients were mixed precisely, the insulation released formaldehyde – a dangerous chemical – into the house. This method of insulation fills the walls with a solid block of foam, making it impossible to run wiring later. There have been attempts to resurrect this material with promises that the same problems won't recur. Don't believe it.

Perlite and *vermiculite* are mineral insulations that are made by expanding granules of the materials to make them light and porous. Their R-value is relatively low in relation to their cost. They offer no advantages when used alone. However, they are used to make "insulating concrete," which can be valuable for floor slabs and flat roof decks.

Loose *plastic foam beads* have been used for some insulation applications, such as filling the cavities in concrete block walls and making lightweight concrete. I can't think of any application for the material in a well designed house.

Soil, *straw bales*, and other *"natural" materials* have been used as insulation. Despite the low cost of the materials themselves and their apparent ecological benefits, they are not viable insulation materials for a house that is designed to have a long life. We weigh the advantages and disadvantages of these materials in *Last Look: Energy for Pioneers*, at the end of the book.

We will recommend the best kind of insulation for each part of your home. If you are tempted to try something else, avoid any insulation material that can serve as food or nesting material for vermin, or that can be damaged by occasional wetting, or that emits noxious gases. Don't use insulation that can kill occupants in a fire or hasten the spread of fire.

Beyond that, use each type of insulation in a way that is consistent with its properties. For example, if the insulation can settle, don't use it in an enclosed wall cavity. If the insulation is permeable to air, protect it from wind and drafts.

ENFORCE GOOD WORKMANSHIP

Bad insulation workmanship is one of the worst deficiencies in house construction today. If you visit tract house developments, you will see that batt insulation is simply stuffed into place, with little regard for filling the cavity. Backing sheets are rarely attached properly. Figure 3-45 is an example.

Sloppy installation like this robs the wall of a large part of its insulation value. Don't let it happen to your home. Good installation costs nothing extra in materials, and it requires little extra in labor. Resolve this issue with your builder before you sign the contract.

> **Monitor the installation of your home's insulation to achieve a perfect job.**

Also, plan to be at the construction site to enforce good practice when the insulation is installed. Fortunately, the insulation is installed during two short periods of construction. The first is placement of the insulation outside the foundation and under concrete slabs, which occurs early in construction. This insulation is installed by the masonry subcontractor.

The rest of the insulation in your home is installed after the structure is completed. The insulation for the walls, floors, and roof usually is installed as one activity, typically requiring one or two days. This insulation may be installed by the carpenters or by a separate insulation contractor.

Insulation workmanship is commonly so poor that some concerned homeowners install their own insulation. You might consider this if you are physically fit, if you can spare a few days, and if you are not afraid of working on ladders and scaffolds. However, that's not realistic for most homeowners.

DRW

Figure 3-45. Badly installed insulation. This sloppy installation robs a significant fraction of the benefit of the insulation. Also, the contractor obviously did not coordinate the electrical wiring with the insulation.

SUPER-STRUCTURE DESIGN ADVANCE #2: CONDENSATION PROTECTION

A house is immersed in the water vapor that is contained in the atmosphere. In addition to the vapor coming from the outside, water vapor is generated inside the house from bathing, cooking, dishwashing, laundry, hanging clothes to dry, decorative plants, breathing and sweating by occupants, operating humidifiers, and using evaporative cooling.

Water vapor is not a hazard by itself. It is a fairly inert gas. But, big trouble happens if water vapor can condense into liquid water inside the structure of the walls, ceiling, or floor. Liquid water helps the oxygen in the air to rusts nails and steel fittings. Moisture nourishes microorganisms that rot lumber. It degrades the R-value of the insulation. It promotes mildew on all surfaces.

Condensation damage inside a house structure can occur in most geographic locations, but some climates are especially vulnerable. Condensation problems have increased dramatically in housing since the introduction of air conditioning, humidification, and airtight construction. Therefore, you need to design the structure of your home with particular care to avoid damage from condensation.

The subject of moisture condensation damage is still poorly understood in the building industry, so it is especially important that we understand it as we design your home. We begin by learning the basic process of condensation, which is explained in the sidebar, *Why Water Vapor Condenses*. Then, we will learn how moisture condenses and causes damage in a house structure.

HOW WATER VAPOR CONDENSES IN A HOUSE STRUCTURE

Condensation will occur inside the house's structure if three conditions are met:
(1)   water vapor can move into the structure,
(2)   water vapor can concentrate there, and
(3)   the temperature of the air inside the structure is below its dew point.

Water vapor moves into the structure by diffusion. This simply means that water molecules move randomly from a region where they are concentrated to a region where they are less concentrated.

Colder air has less ability to hold moisture than warm air. So, in cold weather, the outside air usually contains less water vapor than the air inside the house. As a result, water vapor tends to migrate toward a region of lower temperature.

Putting these facts together reveals how moisture condenses inside the insulated wall of a frame house when it is cold outside. Figure 3-50 shows what happens. Assume that the air inside the house contains a lot of water vapor from internal sources. Assume that the inside surface of the wall is leaky to water vapor and that the outside surface blocks water vapor. The wall is insulated with fiber insulation, which allows the water vapor to move freely.

As the water vapor moves outward through the insulation, it encounters progressively lower temperatures. At the point where the temperature of the insulation and/or the structure equals the dew point temperature of the air, the water vapor starts to condense. Vapor continues to condense from that point outward, so that the entire outer portions of the structure and the insulation become wet.

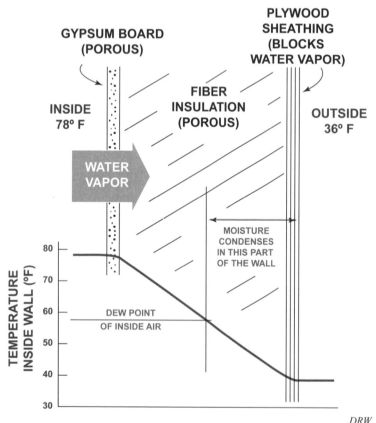

DRW

Figure 3-50. How water vapor can destroy a wall during cold weather. If humid indoor air can pass through the inner surface of a wall, it will condense in the colder outer portions of the wall. The condensation of the water vapor creates a reduced pressure that draws more vapor into the wall, so that the wall is increasingly soaked. The culprit is a combination of a porous interior surface and an impermeable outer surface. **The solution is to make the interior surface less permeable to water vapor than the outer surface.**

WHY WATER VAPOR CONDENSES

Molecules tend to stick to each other. That's why they clump together in the form of liquids and solids. But, some molecules have a weaker tendency to stick, and that's why they remain free in the form of gases. Water molecules have a relatively weak attraction to each other, and even less attraction to the other molecules in air (nitrogen, oxygen, argon, etc.). As a result, air at normal temperatures may contain a substantial amount of water vapor, typically about one percent by weight in moderate weather conditions.

A "vapor" is a gas that is close to condensing into a liquid. The water in air generally is considered to be a vapor. Two related conditions can make water vapor condense into liquid water: *low air temperature* and *high concentration of water vapor* in the air.

(1) air temperature. The molecules in air collide ceaselessly. The air temperature is a measure of their energy. At higher temperatures, water molecules crash into each other too violently to stick. If two water molecules do stick, they are soon knocked apart by another molecule. However, as the temperature drops, the water molecules become sluggish. They stick together in clumps before they can be knocked apart, and the clumps grow to become microscopic droplets of water. This process is "condensation."

(2) concentration of water vapor. When air contains relatively little water vapor, a water molecule mostly collides with molecules of the other gases. Water molecules have almost no tendency to stick to those molecules. However, as the concentration of water vapor increases, it becomes more likely that molecules of water will encounter each other and stick together. Above a certain concentration, the water vapor condenses. That concentration depends on the temperature.

You can see how condensation works after sunset on a humid day. As the earth cools, air close to the ground is cooled by contact with the earth. When the air temperature falls to a certain point, the water vapor condenses into water droplets, which appear as fog or dew.

Two common terms are useful for describing the tendency of water vapor to condense. **Dew point temperature** is the temperature at which condensation occurs. Higher concentration of water vapor raises the dew point temperature.

Relative humidity is the amount of water vapor in the air, expressed as a percentage of the amount that would cause the vapor to condense at that temperature. For example, 1,000 grams of air at 78 °F (25 °C) has a maximum moisture capacity of 20 grams (about 2% by weight). If the actual moisture content is only half that amount, or 10 grams, we say that the relative humidity is 50%.

To prevent condensation, we must keep the air above its dew point temperature. Or, said in another way, we must keep the relative humidity of the air below 100%.

The condensation of the water vapor in the cold part of the wall reduces its concentration in the air. This causes still more water vapor to diffuse into the colder part of the wall, where that vapor condenses also. This process continues as long as the outside remains cold, so the outer part of the wall and the wall insulation become soaked.

Observe that we can have an endless flow of **water vapor** into the wall, even though there is no overall movement of **air**. An airtight exterior sheathing will do nothing to reduce the rate of condensation. In fact, it will make the condensation worse by concentrating the water vapor in the wall.

Let's create an example that has numbers. Assume that the inside temperature is 78 °F (25 °C) and the outside temperature is 36 °F (2 °C). Further, assume that the indoor relative humidity is 50%. From looking at a chart*, an engineer sees that the dew point temperature of the indoor air is 57 °F (14 °C). This is about halfway between the indoor and outdoor temperatures. Since the temperature inside the wall insulation falls uniformly from inside to outside, the temperature inside the insulation falls to the dew point about halfway through. So, the outer half of the insulation is colder than the dew point temperature. Therefore, condensation will keep the outer half of the insulation wet, along with the outer part of the wall structure.

This example is a worst-case situation because water vapor can get into the wall from the warm side, but it can't escape on the cold side. Unfortunately, this situation has become common in modern houses that have walls sheathed with panels of plywood to make them strong and airtight. The gypsum board interior sheathing and the fiber insulation inside the walls are porous enough so that water vapor flows through them easily. However, the plywood exterior sheathing is fairly resistant to water vapor. Thus, airtight walls can become traps for moisture, resulting in condensation during cold weather.

Old houses tended not to suffer from condensation damage. Their exterior wall surfaces were so leaky that moisture generated inside the house could escape to the outside before concentrating enough to condense. This experience gave rise to a modern myth that houses must "breathe," which continues to deter progress in energy efficiency. We should build airtight houses, but we should build them in a way that keeps water vapor from concentrating inside the structure. The climate of your home site dictates how to do this.

---

* This chart is called a "psychrometric chart," and you don't have to be an engineer to use one. If you want to learn more about humidity, get a psychrometric chart and play with it. One axis of the chart is temperature, and the other is the amount of water in the air. Using only those two fundamental properties of air as a framework, the chart is densely packed with information about moisture. You can find free psychrometric charts on the Internet.

CONDENSATION PROTECTION STRATEGY: (1) KEEP WATER VAPOR OUT, (2) LET IT ESCAPE

If we think about the previous example, we can see that condensation occurs because water vapor is able to travel from the inside of the house into the wall structure. The water vapor can't escape while it is still a vapor, so it concentrates there until it condenses. Unfortunately, modern walls greatly increase the difficulty of venting moisture to the outside because both plywood and masonry exterior surfaces obstruct the flow of water vapor.

We compensate for this by installing a "vapor barrier" on the inside (the warm side) of the wall. If we keep water vapor from entering the structure, the problem disappears. Vapor barriers are a primary tool in protecting houses from condensation damage, so we will get to know them well. With modern vapor barriers, we can get close to the ideal of blocking water vapor completely.

Venting is the partner of the vapor barrier. It is a route of escape for any water vapor that gets into the structure. Venting is located on the cold side of the structure to allow moisture to escape before it concentrates enough to condense. *The ideal condensation protection strategy is to block water vapor on the warmer side and to vent it from the colder side*. Vapor barriers and venting are the *yin* and *yang* of condensation protection.

In some climates, such as Florida's, we should not use a vapor barrier. That's because water vapor flows outward through the structure during cold weather and inward during warm weather. In those climates, the only way to protect the structure is to rely entirely on venting. The structure must be able to vent moisture toward both the inside and the outside.

A VERY SHORT COURSE ON VAPOR BARRIERS

A "vapor barrier" can be any material that is effective in blocking water vapor. The effectiveness of a vapor barrier is relative. It must block water vapor from entering the structure more effectively than the structure keeps the vapor from escaping. For example, in old houses, the accumulated paint on the interior walls was an adequate vapor barrier because the exterior surfaces of the walls were so leaky.

When fiber batt insulation became available, a paper backing was made available on one side of the batts to act as a vapor barrier. The vapor resistance of the paper was improved with a thin coating of tarry material or aluminum foil. However, the paper backing on fiber insulation may not be an adequate vapor barrier for modern houses, because airtight plywood exterior sheathing retards water vapor almost as much as the paper backing.

Today, the most effective vapor barrier is an unbroken layer of polyethylene plastic film. It is installed over the inside surfaces of the wall and ceiling insulation. (A separate vapor barrier typically is not used with insulation that is installed under plywood floors.)

The vapor barrier also performs an important additional function of blocking air leakage at the inside surfaces. This is especially important for the ceiling under the roof, because the ceiling structure has no exterior surface to block air leakage.

A well installed vapor barrier also helps to prevent water penetration into the house from rain leaks. However, this is a mixed blessing because the vapor barrier may channel leaks into the roof, wall, and floor structures, where serious damage may occur before it is discovered.

The effectiveness of a material in blocking water vapor is measured by its "perm" rating (which stands for "permeability."). This is the rate of water vapor penetration through a surface. A rating of one perm is defined as a specified rate of water vapor flow through a surface of standard area when a relative humidity difference of 50% exists across the surface.

Note that a higher perm rating indicates a higher rate of water vapor penetration, and hence a lower resistance to water vapor. A good vapor barrier has a low perm rating.

Perm ratings were developed in the U.S. using the old inch-pound system of units. In this system of units, *a material is arbitrarily considered to be a "vapor barrier" if it has a perm rating lower than about one perm*. Don't be misled by this. Use perm ratings only as a relative guide.

There is also a metric, or "SI", perm rating. One U.S. perm equals 57 metric (SI) perms.

Table 3-3, *Perm Ratings of Building Materials*, lists the ratings of the most common building materials that affect moisture penetration into the structure. The perm rating of a material generally is inversely proportional to its thickness. For example, the perm rating of concrete that is four inches thick is one fourth the perm rating of concrete that is one inch thick. Correct for this when you use Table 3-3.

It is not always desirable to install a vapor barrier. So far, we have been talking in terms of the direction of water vapor flow from the warm side of the structure to the cold side. But, in many parts of the world, the warm and cold sides reverse from summer to winter, or from day to night. If the warm periods are long and humid, a vapor barrier that is designed for a cold season becomes a moisture trap. For such climates, we will

Table 3-3. Perm Ratings of Building Materials

MATERIAL	Perms [1]	SI Perms [1]	MATERIAL	Perms [1]	SI Perms [1]
VAPOR BARRIER MATERIALS:			extruded polystyrene, 1" (25 mm)	0.4 – 1.2	20 - 60
polyethylene film, 0.006" (0.15 mm)	0.08	5	expanded polystyrene (beadboard), 1" (25 mm)	2 – 6	110 – 300
aluminum foil, 0.001" (0.025 mm)	0	0	polyisocyanurate, 1" (25 mm)	26	1500
aluminum foil backing for fiber insulation, typical	0.5	30	polyisocyanurate, 1" (25 mm), with foil face	0.05	3
kraft insulation backing sheet, asphalt coated	3 – 30	170 – 1700	**ROOF SURFACES:**		
STRUCTURAL MATERIALS:			roll roofing, "55 pound"	0.03 – 0.08	1.8 – 5
plywood, exterior, ¼" (6 mm)	0.7	40	"tar paper"	1.5 - 4	80 – 230
plywood, interior, ¼" (6 mm)	2	110	**PAINTS and WALLCOVERINGS:**		
oriented strandboard, 7/16" (11 mm)	0.7 – 4	40 – 230	vapor barrier paint	0.5 – 2	30 – 110
fiberboard sheathing, light asphalt coat, ¾" (18 mm)	7	400	vinyl-acrylic paints [2]	3 – 10	170 – 600
			latex paints [2]	3 – 10	170 – 600
concrete, 1" (25 mm)	3	180	vinyl wallcoverings, conventional	0.05 – 1	3 – 60
cored concrete block, U.S., 8" (200 mm)	2.4	140	perforated vinyl wall coverings applied to gypsum board [3]	1 – 20	60 – 1100
clay brick, U.S., 4" (100 mm)	0.8	45			
gypsum wallboard, ½" (13 mm)	20 – 50	1100 – 2800	**HOUSE WRAP MATERIALS:**		
gypsum wallboard, painted with latex paint [2]	1 – 4	60 – 230	Spun bonded polyolefin, Tyvek™	58	3300
			Polypropylene non-woven, Typar™	12	700
gypsum wallboard, with aluminum foil backing	0.06 – 0.28	3.6 – 16	Perforated polyethylene, typical	6	350
INSULATION MATERIALS:			**STILL AIR,** 1" (25 mm)	120	6800
mineral wool, 4" (100 mm)	30	1700			

Notes:

1. These data come from various sources, and they are subject to wide variation.

2. Paint that is applied to a porous material, such as gypsum board, is absorbed to create a thicker dried layer than paint on a non-absorbing surface, so it produces greater resistance to water vapor.

3. Permeability depends strongly on the types of adhesive and primer used to attach the covering.

not use a separate vapor barrier. Instead, we will rely on easy venting of water vapor toward both the outside and the inside.

If the climate makes a vapor barrier desirable, the perm rating for the warm side should be much lower than the perm rating of the cold side. So, start by finding the perm rating of the components on the cold side of the insulation. Then, select a vapor barrier for the warm side that has a much lower perm rating, perhaps by a factor of five or more. For example, Table 3-3 shows that polyethylene sheet has a much lower perm rating than plywood exterior sheathing, so polyethylene is an appropriate vapor barrier for a frame wall that is sheathed with plywood.

It's worth knowing that some plastic foam insulation can act as an effective vapor barrier. Extruded polystyrene has the lowest perm rating among the common types of insulation. It has about the same perm rating as plywood. Such insulation always keeps the moisture on the warm side, where it will not condense. This would eliminate the need for a separate vapor barrier, except for one frustrating fact. At present, all plastic foam insulation creates toxic smoke in a fire. Therefore, in my opinion, it has no place in wood frame construction. It should be limited to exterior insulation of masonry walls.

DIFFERENT CLIMATES REQUIRE DIFFERENT CONDENSATION PROTECTION

Modern house design is still struggling to prevent the condensation damage that is associated with new construction materials and methods. There is not yet sufficient understanding that condensation protection must be tailored to the climate. *Methods that are essential in one type of climate may cause serious trouble in a different climate*.

We avoid trouble by identifying the type of climate at your home site, and designing your home accordingly. These three types of climates require different kinds of condensation protection:

- climates that are mainly cold or moderate in temperature
- "semi-tropical" climates, which may be either warm or cold for extended periods
- "tropical" climates, which are usually warm and humid.

"Desert"* climates are a fourth kind of environment that generally does not require condensation protection.

---

* Technically, the term "desert" describes a region that has little precipitation, regardless of its temperature. For example, central Alaska is classified as a desert, even though it is cold. A house in a cold, dry climate can still suffer condensation damage if a large amount of water vapor is generated inside the house. In this case, the protective measures are the same as for other cold climates.

These climates are very dry, or "arid," so there is not enough water vapor in the atmosphere to condense at the indoor or outdoor temperatures.

You can ignore the headings below that do not apply to your location.

Condensation Protection in Cold and Moderate Climates

We define cold and moderate climates as climates where the outside air temperature usually is lower than the inside air temperature. If the outside temperature becomes warmer than the inside temperature, such periods are brief and the outside temperature does not remain much higher than the inside temperature. Such periods would include summer daytime hours.

In North America, for example, moderate and cold climates prevail from the middle latitudes of the United States northward through Canada.

When the climate is cold, the condensation hazard arises from moisture that is generated inside the house, mainly from showers, baths, cooking, and laundry. We use the basic two-part defense of (1) blocking the flow of water vapor into the structure from the inside of the house and (2) allowing any water vapor that gets into the structure to vent to the outside.

To block the flow of water vapor into the structure, you typically need to install a vapor barrier on the interior side of the wall and ceiling insulation. Common interior sheathing materials – especially gypsum board – are very permeable to water vapor. With these materials, you need a separate vapor barrier. We will explain the vapor barrier installation in detail when we design your structure. (See *Condensation Protection for Frame Houses in Cold Climates*, later in this Step.)

With wood frame construction, an especially impermeable vapor barrier is needed on the interior of the walls because the outer sheathing of plywood resists venting of water vapor. Indeed, plywood qualifies as a marginal vapor barrier itself, so the actual interior vapor barrier must have a much lower perm rating than plywood.

With masonry construction, a good vapor barrier is needed if the insulation is installed inside the wall. This is because masonry also resists venting of water vapor. However, if you select exterior impermeable foam insulation for your masonry walls (not an ideal choice), no separate interior vapor barrier is needed.

Most cold and moderate climates have periods of warmer weather. In some locations, these warm spells are also humid. At these times, water vapor tends to flow from the outside toward the interior of the house. If the interior is cooled, this could cause condensation inside the structure. However, brief periods of warm, humid weather are unlikely to cause a problem. Also, the plywood outer wall sheathing slows the flow of water vapor into the walls.

Condensation Protection in Humid Sub-Tropical Climates

Climates that are classified as "sub-tropical" are primarily warm, but they have a season lasting as long as several months that may be cold enough to require home heating. The cold weather temperatures typically remain above freezing.

If a sub-tropical climate is also humid, protection against condensation is especially challenging. Such conditions occur in the southeast United States, including all of Florida and much of the territory that borders the Gulf of Mexico. Such conditions also prevail in much of Southeast Asia, southern Japan, eastern Australia, and southeastern South America. Smaller areas occur in the northern Mediterranean and around the Black Sea.

The key point about this kind of climate is that water vapor flows into the structure from both the outside (during warm weather) and the inside (during cold weather). Because of this, it is important to *avoid creating any vapor barriers in the structure*. An interior vapor barrier would trap moisture inside the structure during warm weather, and the moisture would condense on the cooler interior side. An exterior vapor barrier would trap moisture during cold weather, and the moisture would condense on the cooler exterior side.

Mildew infestation has become epidemic in humid sub-tropical climates as a result of air conditioning and the use of impermeable interior wallcoverings. Water vapor passing through the wall from the outside is stopped by the wallcovering and condenses on the cool interior surface. The condensed moisture stimulates mold to feed on the organic wallcovering, the adhesive, and any organic components of the wall structure. Figure 3-51 shows a typical example.

So, don't decorate interior surfaces using impermeable materials, such as conventional vinyl wall coverings. Mildew infestation is widely associated with such materials. Instead, use interior finishing materials that are porous, such as special perforated vinyl that is intended to allow the venting of water vapor. Various fabrics can also be used. These materials should be attached with a special adhesive that is permeable to water vapor.

Because we can't use vapor barriers, we can't block the entry of water vapor into the structure. Instead, condensation protection depends entirely on making it easy for the vapor to escape from the structure before it condenses. *The prime defense is to vent the structure toward both the inside and the outside*.

Also, favor construction materials that resist condensation damage. Masonry is relatively immune

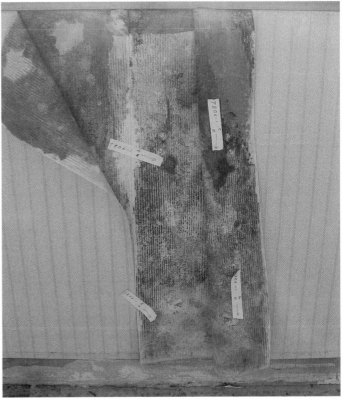

Philip R. Morey, PhD

Figure 3-51. Severe mold infestation behind vinyl wallcovering in New Orleans. The mold destroys the adhesive, the wallcovering peels away from the wall, and the interior space is exposed to intense mold contamination. Four tags indicate the locations of samples taken for laboratory examination.

to condensation, and it resists termites and other insects. For lumber construction, cypress and other moisture-resistant species have largely been depleted, and they are being replaced by pressure-treated lumber and plywood.

During warm weather, moisture vents into the inside of the house. You have to get rid of this moisture to avoid discomfort and mildew inside the living space. Step 4 will explain how to remove moisture from the inside of the house. In brief, install appropriate ventilation for rooms where moisture accumulates. During weather that is humid and mild, operate a dehumidifier. During weather that is hot as well as humid, running an air conditioner will lower the humidity.

If your home will use masonry construction, you have another option. It is to use impermeable foam insulation that is installed on the outside of the exterior walls or on top of a concrete roof. Foam insulation acts as its own vapor barrier, so that water vapor cannot migrate from a warm, humid side to a cold side. Unfortunately, plastic foam insulation is not safe for installation in a wooden structure or inside a masonry structure.

Condensation Protection in Tropical Climates

A "tropical" climate is one that remains warm (or hot) and humid for much of the time. Home heating is never required, or only rarely. Tropical climates dominate the equatorial regions of South America, Central America, Africa (except its desert regions), and south Asia.

In tropical climates, condensation problems are always caused by the flow of water vapor from the outside toward the inside. These problems have become much worse because of air conditioning, which cools the interior of the structure and promotes condensation there.

With high humidity on the outside and air conditioning on the inside, condensation in tropical climates is the mirror image of the situation in cold climates. The solution is to install a vapor barrier, or an impermeable exterior sheathing, on the outside of the structure. The vapor barrier should entirely surround the structure that encloses the living space, including the walls, the ceiling insulation, and the underside of exposed floors that are insulated.

Another possibility is using impermeable foam insulation, which acts as its own vapor barrier. However, such insulation is combustible, so it is safe only if it is installed externally on a masonry wall or on top of a concrete roof.

With all types of structures, the materials for the interior surfaces should be porous, or permeable, so that any water vapor that gets into the structure from the outside can vent easily into the interior. Select interior finishing materials such as fabric or perforated vinyl, which should be attached with a special permeable adhesive. A thin coat of latex or acrylic paint is probably acceptable.

Avoid interior surface materials, such as conventional vinyl wallcovering, that have a low "perm" rating. In humid climates, vinyl wallcovering is frequently associated with severe mildew infestation behind the wallcovering. The mildew attacks the adhesive, which causes the wallcovering to peel off and expose the interior to health problems and further infestation.

Water vapor that vents to the interior of the house must be removed, or it will accumulate enough to condense. Air conditioning will protect the walls and ceilings as long as the climate is hot. If the outside becomes cooler but remains humid, you need a dehumidifier to keep the inside dry. Step 4 explains how to limit humidity inside the house.

SUPER-STRUCTURE DESIGN ADVANCE #3: LEAK-FREE CONSTRUCTION

Preventing air leakage is one of the Five Principles of Super-Efficiency. In the past, air leakage was responsible for about one third of the total heating energy needed by houses. Today, it is possible to virtually eliminate air leakage, and that is what we will do in your home. Sealing your house against air leaks also prevents entry of outside humidity during warm weather. And, good sealing blocks insects, many of which can squeeze through tiny clearances.

You may have heard that the airtight construction of modern houses is responsible for health and condensation problems, but that is not true if you build the house correctly. See the sidebar, *Can a House be Too Airtight?*

We bring up the issue of air leakage early in the design of your home's structure because a house has many places where unwanted outside air can intrude. To organize our airtight design, let's group the leakage sites this way:

- *the long joints in the structure*. These extend all around the exterior walls, between the foundation and the ground level floor, between the wall studs and the floors, between the roof and the top of the walls, and at corners. To block air leakage, we use effective sealants between the components as the house is built, and we overlap the joints completely with the exterior sheathing.

- *penetrations through the structure for pipe, wiring, flues, and vents*. Blocking leakage at these sites requires a combination of techniques. We make the penetrations as small as possible. We secure the pipe, wire, or vent to keep it from moving within the hole. And, we use appropriate sealants. For flues and vents, we use special fittings at the penetrations.

- *gaps between wall openings and doors and windows*. We use careful carpentry to minimize the size of the gaps and we use effective sealants. In the case of windows, we can block leakage by installing windows that have finned frames.

- *leakage through windows and doors*. These leaks are caused by poor quality or by failure of the weatherstripping. For windows, we minimize leaks by careful selection of the weatherstripping and by selecting window styles that minimize leakage. For doors, we install the doors strongly to prevent sagging, and we install effective weatherstripping.

- *leakage inside the structure*. Air can travel through cavities within the insulation. Even if outside air is blocked from entering the structure, such cavities allow internal convection to bypass the insulation. We eliminate this convection by installing the insulation carefully to completely fill the insulated space.

The goal is to block air leakage in a manner that will survive for the life of the house. Modern homes often are fairly airtight when new, but they become leaky within the first decades of their lives. Therefore, we introduce improvements to make the house airtight

CAN A HOUSE BE TOO AIRTIGHT?

Airtight house construction has been common for less than half a century, and it is still misunderstood by builders and architects. Airtight construction was introduced to enhance energy efficiency at about the same time that indoor air quality problems and mildew became popular issues. This led to a fallacy that energy efficiency causes health problems, and it reinforced the vague old notion that a house must "breathe" (whatever that means).

Airtight construction is not inherently unhealthful. But, it does increase the possibility of health and condensation problems if the house is not designed and built properly. An airtight house can concentrate cooking fumes, tobacco smoke, organic vapors from building materials, radon from the soil, carbon monoxide from combustion equipment, and other health hazards. Moisture from showers, laundry, and other sources can cause mildew and structural damage.

Each of these hazards requires its own protective measures, which this book explains in detail. Localized ventilation is used to remove pollutants and moisture that originate in individual spaces, such as the kitchen and showers. Appropriate foundation construction blocks the entry of radon.

An airtight exterior surface for the walls creates a potential problem of moisture condensation inside the walls during cold weather. An effective vapor barrier on the interior surface of the walls counteracts this tendency. A vapor barrier also keeps organic vapors from construction materials (such as plywood) out of the occupied space.

For most of the house, where no offensive contaminants are generated, the air volume usually is so large in relation to the number of occupants that natural circulation keeps the air pleasant. Opening windows can freshen the air in these spaces.

In urban areas, the air inside a house often is cleaner than the outside air. Under those conditions, airtight construction and properly localized ventilation minimize the hazards of outdoor pollutants.

permanently. Some of these improvements overlap (literally as well as figuratively), creating a structure that is super-airtight. We will apply these improvements to individual parts of the house as we go through Step 3.

Creating a permanently airtight house is not difficult, and it does not require special materials. However, it does require new procedures as the structure is being built. You should cover these procedures with your builder before signing the contract. Also, plan to inspect the construction to make sure that your improved procedures are followed.

MINIMIZE THE SIZE OF HOLES AND GAPS

When a house is being built, it is necessary to make holes in the outer structure for windows, doors, pipe, wiring, vents, and flues. After these items are installed, gaps remain around the edges of the holes. If these gaps are not sealed, they can radically increase heating and cooling cost, and they may also cause significant discomfort. The amount of air leakage into a house is roughly proportional to the total size of all the unsealed gaps.

During the 20th century, the introduction of pipe and wiring into houses created many more gaps. Electricians and plumbers typically made holes much larger than necessary, and left them unsealed. And, the introduction of prefabricated door and window assemblies created large new gaps around doors and windows.

In the past, gaps were filled with a variety of common materials, including mud, mortar, wool, and other materials that might be available. After World War II, the plastics industry developed new kinds of caulking and weatherstripping, which promised to seal all these gaps easily. Unfortunately, it was a false promise.

All organic sealing materials will lose their elasticity and adhesion early in the life of the house. For the latter part of the life of a house, a gap that is sealed by organic materials depends on the dried-out residue of the sealant to fill the gap and to remain in place. This residue can be adequate only if the gaps are small. Generally, caulking materials cannot provide a reliable seal for gaps that are wider than about one eighth of an inch (about three millimeters).

So, the first step in sealing penetrations effectively is to avoid excessively large or irregular holes. For example, where a pipe passes through a concrete wall, the builder should use a hole saw to cut through the wall, rather than knocking out a block with a chisel. The diameter of the hole saw should be only slightly larger than the diameter of the pipe. In addition to

providing a more reliable airtight seal around the pipe, this provides a neater appearance.

The usual problem in this example is that the subcontractor who installs the pipe does not use the proper equipment to make a neat hole. To avoid this problem, make all the necessary holes in advance. For holes in masonry, include the locations and sizes of all the holes in your drawings. This allows the masonry contractor to make the holes by inserting appropriate forms in the wall as it is built. (For round holes, the forms may be cardboard tubes, empty plastic bottles, or anything else of the appropriate diameter.)

Electrical wiring may create a lot of holes in the structure that usually are not sealed well. We will show how to stop these leaks under the heading, *The Wiring and Cable*.

DRW

Figure 3-54. A lack of proper air sealing along the top of the foundation. The daylight is entering through various air leakage paths.

Platform construction includes series of long joints that extend all around the exterior walls, between the top of the foundation and the ground level floor, between the wall studs and the floors, and between the roof and the upper wall, as shown in Figures 3-15 and 3-25. All these joints can be major paths for air leakage if they are not sealed effectively.

Figure 3-54 shows an example of such a leaky joint above the foundation.

To minimize the size of these gaps, erect the wall framing before attaching the exterior sheathing. This allows the weight of the studs to push the bottom plate of the wall against the subfloor, so that the sealant between the two (which we will explain shortly) needs to close only a very thin gap. Then, attach the sheathing in the way that we learn next.

USE OVERLAPPING JOINTS TO BLOCK AIR LEAKS

The use of plywood in modern house construction greatly reduced air leakage by creating large, unbroken surfaces. The plywood itself is impermeable to air leakage. Equally important, if the plywood sheets are installed to overlap the long joints in the structure, the combination of overlapping exterior sheathing and the proper use of sealants makes the wall structure very airtight.

Using overlapping joints from the foundation to the roof also gives the structure enormous strength. It provides great security against damage from wind, flooding, and earth movement. We will explain this further when we design the outer wall sheathing.

Overlapping the long joints requires sheathing plywood that is extra long. For example, if the interior ceiling height is 8 feet (240 cm), use exterior sheathing that is 10 (300 cm) feet long. This is a standard size for plywood, but the builder may need to make a special order to get it.

Such overlapping joints make the best use of caulking materials. They provide a large surface area for the caulk to adhere. The joint can be nailed down, leaving little or no gap to be filled. Overlapping joints protect sealants against sunlight and oxidation, which are the main enemies of sealants.

Windows with finned frames create an overlapping joint that can completely eliminate air leakage between the frame and the surrounding wall. We will cover the details later, when we select your windows.

Where molding is used to cover gaps in the structure, as between a door frame and the surrounding wall, install the molding so that it creates an overlapping joint that is nailed down securely at each side. We will cover the details later, when we design your doors.

APPLY ADHESIVES AND SEALANTS BETWEEN THE COMPONENTS

The carpenters should apply the appropriate caulking material or structural adhesive between the mating surfaces of joints *as each part of the structure is built*. The key is to apply the sealants *between* the mating surfaces of the components before they come together.

You can't make the structure airtight after construction by going around with a caulking gun and trying to push caulk into cracks. If you try that, the caulk will dry out and fall off in a short time.

For example, Figure 3-55 shows the right and wrong ways to create a seal where the edges of adjacent plywood sheets meet on a stud or other structural member.

 Applying sealants during construction, rather than afterwards, helps to produce a structure that is permanently airtight and exceptionally strong.

At structural joints, there is another important point about sealing against air leakage. Using construction adhesive properly between the mating surfaces of the joints substantially increases the strength of the structure. This helps to avoid sagging and interior surface cracks as the building settles, and it makes the building more resistant to windstorms and earth movement. Construction adhesive is similar to the caulk that is used for air leakage sealing, and it is just as effective for blocking air leakage when it is used appropriately.

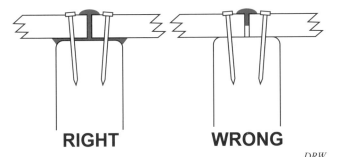

DRW

Figure 3-55. In order to grip effectively, an adhesive must completely coat the mating surfaces of a joint. Similarly, a sealant must be captured inside the joint. Sealant that is forced into an existing joint from the outside will shrink, crumble, and fall out of the joint.

Habitat for Humanity

Figure 3-56. Construction adhesive being applied between floor joists and the plywood subfloor. Note the extended caulking gun, which avoids the discomfort of kneeling.

Work with your builder to make sure that the sealing is done properly. The challenge is that you are changing the workflow of the carpenters. Carpenters take pride in working fast. To seal the structure as it is being built, they have to pause, lay down their nail guns, pick up caulking guns, and apply ribbons of sealant to the components before joining them.

Speed has become a mania with carpenters after the introduction of nail guns. Today, many carpenters resist using any other tool. You will have to make sure that your carpenters are just as proficient with caulking guns as with nail guns.

It is a good idea for the builder to assign a single individual to apply the caulk or construction adhesive to each component immediately before installation, as in Figure 3-56. All this sealing does not add much to the labor cost, because the parts of the structure that require sealing usually are assembled in a few days.

Caulking guns that are powered by batteries or compressed air are now available. They are almost a necessity for the large amount of sealing that super-tight construction requires. They distribute sealants more uniformly than manual guns, and they minimize waste.

Make sure that your builder has enough caulk of the proper kinds at the construction site, along with enough caulking guns. If your builder understands this issue, he will buy the appropriate sealants by the case.

SELECT THE BEST SEALING MATERIALS FOR EACH APPLICATION

There are two general groups of sealing materials for houses, *caulk* and *construction adhesive*. Hardware stores have entire aisles of sealants and adhesives that block air leakage. The reason for all that variety is that different sealing jobs require specialized materials. And, there may be several materials that you can use for a particular application. Sealing materials account for only a tiny fraction of the cost your home, so get the best.

Caulk is used to fill small gaps. Two important characteristics of caulk are flexibility and adhesion. These allow the caulking material to compensate for small movements, such as expansion and contraction from temperature and humidity changes. However, flexibility and adhesion disappear with age.

Caulks are used for several purposes, in addition to blocking air leakage. They block water leakage in showers, baths, basins, kitchen counters, and other places. And, they are used for decorative filling of gaps, as between a wash basin and the adjacent wall. Select a caulk that is appropriate for the application.

Caulks are made from variety of materials. All use organic materials to provide adhesion and flexibility. The organic components have limited life. Oxidation destroys them slowly, and sunlight destroys them rapidly. Inorganic materials may be added to provide bulk and longevity. For example, "putty" and "glazing compound" are thick caulking materials that contain mostly mineral filler.

Construction adhesive is similar to caulk, but it is formulated to act as a glue, helping to hold assemblies together. It also acts as a sealant, but only for tight joints where the gap is minimal. It is not as flexible as sealants.

In frame construction, use construction adhesive where the exterior sheathing is attached to wall framing, both for air leakage sealing and for increased strength. Also, use it where the subfloor is attached to the floor joists, both to avoid squeaks and to strengthen the floor. Special kinds of construction adhesive are used for drywall, paneling, and some other materials.

No kind of sealant or adhesive has long-term strength by itself. The strength of the joint should be provided primarily by metal fasteners, including nails, screws, bolts, and specialized connectors.

All caulks and construction adhesives eventually become dry and brittle, but they continue to seal narrow gaps against air leakage if the gap is filled with the material. Construction adhesive continues to provide friction for joints, which keeps the components from sliding past each other. (In engineering terms, this increases the "shear strength" of the joint.)

Silicone is primarily a caulking material and sealant, not an adhesive. It is the best material available for most caulking applications, except with concrete. It has the longest life, the greatest elasticity, and it adheres well to most construction materials, including glass. It is most resistant to ultraviolet decay. It cures to a rubbery consistency. It is expensive, but worth it. You won't use much if you minimize the size of the gaps.

The most common variety of silicone, which has a vinegar smell while it is curing, attacks concrete and non-stainless metals. For use with those materials, get the "neutral curing" type of silicone, which is even more expensive.

Pure silicone is clear, and it cannot be painted. You can buy silicone that is tinted in a variety of colors.

Urethane is used for both caulk and construction adhesive. It can be painted, and it adheres exceptionally well to most construction materials, but not to glass. It is the best material to use with concrete. As a caulking material, it is second best to silicone in most other respects.

To caulk items where the item itself or the sealant may need to be replaced, such as a clothes dryer vent, use silicone instead of urethane. Old silicone caulk can

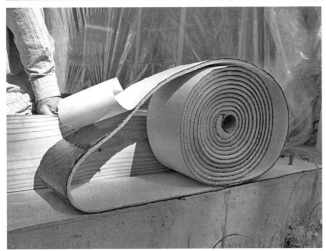

Protecto Wrap

Figure 3-57. "Sill sealer" being installed. Sill sealer closes the gap between the top of the concrete foundation and the bottom the frame wall. The material shown has two layers. The black layer is dense, adhesive, and durable. The lighter layer is plastic foam, which has relatively short life. In time, the foam will collapse and the black material will do most of the sealing.

Demand Products

Figure 3-58. "Backer rod" being pressed into a gap. The material is lightweight closed-cell foam plastic.

Demand Products

Figure 3-59. Backer rod used as a base for a more permanent sealant.

be removed cleanly, providing for reliable resealing. The same is not true of urethane and other sealants.

Acrylic and *latex* are inferior in most respects to silicone and urethane. Their primary advantage is cheapness. Don't use them.

There are combinations of these caulking materials, such as "siliconized acrylic," that promise to provide the best features of the basic types, usually to lower the cost. There is no general way to predict how well these hybrid sealants will perform.

Gap filling foam is applied with a small nozzle from a pressurized can. The foam expands into the gap, making it easy to seal larger, irregular gaps. The best foam is polyurethane, but all foam has a limited life, after which it crumbles. Most foam has little flexibility, unlike the best caulks. One valuable application is around the inside of window frames, where it blocks condensation on the frame and the surrounding structure.

Cement mortar is commonly used to fill larger gaps in masonry, for example, where a vent passes through a concrete block wall. If mortar is mixed and applied properly, it will last as long as the house. This is a major advantage over organic sealants. Mortar holds tightly to pipe that passes through a gap, so the pipe layout should allow for expansion and contraction.

Pre-formed gaskets are made for a variety of specialized applications. Every frame house that is built on a concrete foundation needs special gasket strips for sealing the gap between the top of the foundation wall and the bottom of the frame wall. This is necessary because the top of the foundation is always irregular to

some extent. The material should remain resilient for several decades, and it should remain intact for the life of the house. Figure 3-57 shows how it is installed.

Inexpensive gaskets are made to seal the gaps between electrical receptacles and the surrounding wall, as in Figure 3-198. You may find special gaskets for other parts of the structure. Gaskets made of plastic materials will disintegrate early in the life of the house, so use them only where they are easily replaceable.

Backer rod is a pre-formed sealing material made of closed-cell plastic or rubber foam. It is usually cylindrical in shape, and is available in a variety of diameters. It is used to fill wide gaps of fairly constant width, as in Figure 3-58. It is stuffed into the gaps manually and it is held in place only by friction, so the sides of the gap must be roughly parallel. Typical applications are the gaps between door frames and the structure, and between pipes and smooth holes cut in masonry with a hole saw.

Like all organic materials, backer rod has limited life. Generally, it is used to provide a temporary backing when filling a large gap with mortar, plastic foam, and other filler or sealing materials that have longer life, as in Figure 3-59.

Weatherstripping is pre-formed material that is made specifically for sealing the movable gaps of doors and windows. We discuss it further when we design your doors and windows.

Specialized sheetmetal and rubber seals for plumbing vents and flues are needed to block air leakage through the large gap between vents and flues and the surrounding structure. We cover these later, under the heading, *Block Air Leakage at Flues and Plumbing Vents*.

Fiber insulation is not an air sealing material, and it is a mistake to use it for that purpose. Air and water vapor flows through it easily.

Protect the Sealant

Where pipe or wiring passes through a gap, lay out the pipe or wiring so that it does not place stress on the sealant. Physical movement will eventually break the seal. Once the seal is broken, further movement will enlarge the gap.

Pipe that changes temperature, especially flue pipe and hot water pipe, can expand and contract enough to break a seal. To avoid this, include one or more right angle bends that allow the pipe to flex easily without creating stress on the sealant. For example, Figure 5-16 shows right angle bends in a flue pipe and a water pipe that pass through a basement wall.

Where electrical wiring passes through holes that should be sealed, tightly secure the wiring on each side of the hole. We cover the details later, under the heading, *Block Air Leakage Around Wiring*. See Figure 3-197.

Sunlight will destroy any organic sealant within a few years. Therefore, install some sort of cover over any exposed sealant.

AVOID CONFUSION: AIRTIGHT CONSTRUCTION VS. CONDENSATION PROTECTION

There is a lot of confusion about the relationship between airtight construction and moisture protection, so let's clarify. As you design the structure of your home, you will find that there is a big overlap between features that make the structure airtight and features that prevent condensation. But, confusing the two functions can cause big trouble.

The purpose of airtight construction is to block the flow of *air*, specifically air flow *through* the structure, because air leakage carries heat out of the house.

The purpose of condensation protection is to prevent the flow of *water vapor*, specifically the flow of water vapor *into* the structure, where the water vapor may condense and damage the structure.

Air and water vapor do not flow in the same way, so the two functions are not the same. Blocking air leakage is primarily a matter of eliminating gaps and voids in the structure, as we just discussed. Blocking water vapor requires the techniques that we discussed before that, primarily involving a "vapor barrier" that encloses the entire interior of the house.

A vapor barrier must have an exceptionally low "perm" rating. For example, polyethylene plastic vapor barrier has a perm rating less than 0.1 (6 SI perms). In contrast, air leakage can be blocked effectively with conventional construction materials that have much higher perm ratings. For example, bare gypsum wallboard blocks air leakage, even though it may have a perm rating as high as 50 (3,000 SI perms).

Vapor barriers can serve double duty to block air leakage because any surface that blocks water vapor will also block air movement. However, a vapor barrier is applied to only one side of a wall, roof, or floor, so it cannot protect against air leakage within the structure.

You should not use any vapor barrier in a climate that is warm and humid, for the reasons that we discussed previously. In such a climate, block air leakage by using structural materials that are sufficiently permeable to water vapor to avoid condensation.

Confusion about air leakage protection and vapor barriers has been increased by the introduction of "house wraps." These have become so widespread that we need to take a critical look at them.

"HOUSE WRAPS": USEFUL OR SNAKE OIL?

These days, especially in North America, it has become common practice to cover the wall sheathing with a "house wrap," sometimes called an "air barrier." House wrap is a paper-like material that is stapled on the outer wall sheathing of a house, as in Figure 3-60. It is later covered by the finish surface.

House wraps are promoted as a barrier to air leakage. In theory, they act like a windbreaker jacket, blocking air flow through the structure, but letting water vapor pass through.

Unlike a vapor barrier, house wrap material has microscopic pores that allow water vapor to pass through the material relatively easily. The material specifically should ***not*** act as a vapor barrier, and it would cause condensation damage if it did so. By definition, house wrap materials have high permeability to water vapor.

House wraps are an example of a notion that gains widespread popularity without anyone really understanding the need for it. Unfortunately, even some building codes now require house wraps. The truth is that *a house wrap is superfluous if you build your walls with plywood exterior sheathing, or with some other sheathing that creates an unbroken surface*. Such a wall is already the most airtight part of the structure because it has both exterior and interior sheathing, plus a vapor barrier.

Virtually all air leakage through modern walls occurs at the openings that surround windows and doors, and at penetrations for electrical wiring and pipe. These leaks are not effectively blocked by house wrap, but by sealing methods that are specific for those openings (which we cover in the relevant places).

And ironically, house wrap material generally is not used in the roof structure or under exposed floors, which lack the double sheathing between inside and outside that is characteristic of walls.

Are there useful applications for house wraps? If you build your house with an exterior wall sheathing that consists of individual boards, a house wrap would protect the outer portion of the wall insulation from air currents that leak between the boards. If the structure is well built, including a good vapor barrier, the benefit would be small, but perhaps significant. A house wrap is likely to be more valuable if your are renovating the leaky walls of an old building.

There is some concern among engineers that a house wrap may cause damage by acting as a vapor barrier on the wrong side of the wall. This would depend on the particular product, the climate, and other factors. Perm ratings and resistance to liquid water penetration vary widely. If the perm rating is at the low end of the range, a house wrap might cause condensation damage during cold, wet weather. If a wall has been soaked by flooding or a roof leak, a house wrap may impede the drying of the structure.

But for most situations, my opinion is that house wraps are useless rather than dangerous.

DRW

Figure 3-60. "House wrap" installed on a house that does not need it.

SUPER-STRUCTURE DESIGN ADVANCE #4: SUPER STRENGTH

The structure of a house requires strength to support its own weight against collapse, to resist sagging, and to resist impact from falling objects, such as tree limbs. It should also resist damage by soil settling, which creates cracks in the interior finish and exterior masonry, and may break the structure. A house should be strong enough to resist wind damage, including the intense winds that may be caused by tornadoes and hurricanes. And, a house should be able to survive earthquakes.

Today, most houses are built too weakly to defend against all these perils. Hardly any house collapses of its own weight, and sagging roofs are becoming less common. However, the other perils routinely damage or destroy houses.

Recently, there has been a decline of strength in newly built homes. A growing emphasis on cheapening construction has led to structures that are increasingly flimsy. Your super-home will reverse this trend with an emphasis on superior strength that will enable your home to survive and to remain free of defects for its entire intended life span.

Your home's design will strengthen it against all the perils of soil settlement, wind damage, and earthquake. The increase in construction cost will be small because improving resistance to each peril improves resistance to all of them. Another bonus is that the same features that make a wall strong also block air leakage, as we learned previously. And, we will exploit the thickness of super-insulated frame walls to make the walls even stronger.

Hurricanes, tornadoes, and earthquakes are not just local threats. As we will see, a large majority of all houses are endangered by one or more of these perils. And, soil settling is a condition that threatens houses almost everywhere. So, let's start there.

RESISTANCE TO SETTLING

Soil settling is uneven compression or collapse of the soil under the foundation. Settling occurs underneath most homes, unless they are built on bedrock. Settling usually is gradual, causing damage that may not appear for years.

A strong foundation is the defense against soil settling. All your life, you have heard the proverb about building on a firm foundation. This wisdom originated from centuries of experience with inadequate foundations. Nothing is sadder than seeing a beautiful old stone building that has a large fracture in a wall. Or, a grand old frame house that has slumped, forcing windows and doors out of alignment, turning the floors into ramps, and causing the roof to droop.

DRW

Figure 3-63. Someone's dream castle that fell to ruin because it lacked a good foundation. You can tell from the windows and other components that this house was still fairly new when it became derelict.

WIND PROTECTION CHECKLIST

ROOF (See *Roof Design to Resist Wind Damage*.)

☐ Select a roof shape that minimizes wind pressure, but reconcile the shape with other considerations, such as roof venting and usable attic space.

☐ Use an appropriate "hurricane strap" to attach each rafter to the wall on which it rests. For greatest strength, use hurricane straps that wrap over the top of the rafter and extend below the wall top plate to connect each rafter directly to a wall stud.

☐ Attach the roof deck to the rafters with nails of appropriate size. Space the nails as specified by building codes for hurricane-prone regions. Drive each nail into the center of the rafter.

☐ Reinforce gable end walls to prevent them from blowing outward at the top or bottom. (See *Reinforcing Gable End Walls*.)

☐ Attach roofing materials with the most secure methods available.

FRAME WALLS

☐ Use an ample number of anchor bolts, embedded deeply in a poured concrete foundation, to secure the sill plate. (See *Installing the Lower Floor on the Foundation Wall*.)

☐ Use plywood exterior wall sheathing as a connector across all structural joints below the roof. Use an ample number of nails to attach the sheathing to each side of structural joints. (See *The Exterior Wall Sheathing*.)

☐ If the exterior sheathing cannot create strong connections between certain parts of the structure, install appropriate steel connectors between those parts.

☐ Design the corners to resist interior wind pressure that tends to separate the walls at the corners. Adapt the corner design to the types of studs used. (See *Strong Corners*.)

MASONRY WALLS (See *Masonry Construction*.)

☐ Use a steel-reinforced poured concrete frame. Secure masonry filler blocks within the concrete frame using rebar.

WINDOWS & EXTERIOR DOORS

☐ Install hurricane-resistant windows. These provide continuous protection, in contrast to storm shutters, which block the view and must be installed manually in advance of a storm. (See *The Windows*.)

☐ Install hurricane-resistant doors. (See *The Entrance Doors*.)

☐ Install hurricane-resistant door locks. (See *Door Locks*.)

☐ Install a garage door that is heavily reinforced against wind damage. Make sure that the garage door frame and rails are strongly attached to the house wall. (See *Garage Doors and Other Large Doors*.)

INTERIOR DOORS & OPENINGS

☐ Install a strong door, with a strong lock, between the garage and the interior of the house.

☐ Install strong doors or hatches, with strong latches, at all entrances to attics.

☐ Avoid installing an attic entrance inside the garage or in any other space that has a large door or window. If an attic access is needed in such a space, create a very strong attic door and frame, with a strong automatic latch.

Depending on soil conditions, even a relatively new house can suffer settling damage if it lacks a good foundation. Figure 3-63 is an extreme example. In many new houses, cracks appear in the walls within a few months. These are all signs of an inadequate foundation.

With the construction methods that are commonly available today, damage from soil settling should never happen. We will explain foundations in detail so that you can make your home virtually immune to settling damage.

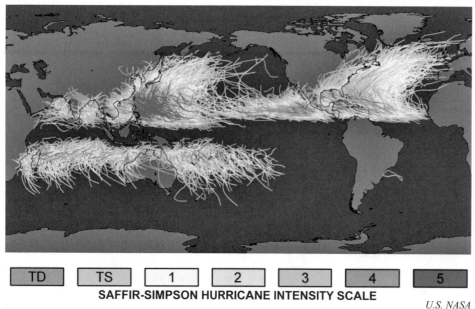

| TD | TS | 1 | 2 | 3 | 4 | 5 |

SAFFIR-SIMPSON HURRICANE INTENSITY SCALE

U.S. NASA

Figure 3-64. Hurricane tracks around the world, from 1860 to 2006. "TD" means "tropical depression". "TS" means "tropical storm."

RESISTANCE TO WIND DAMAGE

Most contemporary home construction plays the odds that a house will not be hit by a severe windstorm, omitting critical reinforcements that would enable the house to survive if a windstorm does hit. But, the probability of wind damage during the life of your home is greater than you may realize. You don't have to take that gamble. We will design your home to stand up to the most severe winds, including hurricanes and tornadoes.

Protecting against severe wind damage is still a relatively new and specialized area of knowledge. In principle, your contractor should know about it. However, unless your home site is located in a recognized hurricane or tornado area, even a capable contractor may not know the best methods.

So, if your local building practices and your local building code don't provide adequate guidance, where do you get it? In my opinion, the State of Florida building code is presently the gold standard for wind protection. This code evolved after a series of hurricanes in the 1990's broke records for devastation in Florida, and also broke many insurance companies there. Florida engineers studied the damage intensively, and in a series of evolving codes, construction practices were defined that have proven to minimize storm damage.

Even if your home is located in Kansas or Costa del Sol, there is no reason why you can't follow the provisions of the Florida code for wind protection. It turns out that protecting a house from wind is simple and inexpensive, so why not do it?

The Florida code is based on the *International Residential Code*, which we described previously, but supplements it extensively for wind protection. Your builder should be intimately familiar with the parts of both codes that apply to your home.

The *Wind Protection Checklist* summarizes the main points of wind protection. These points derive from building codes and from further thinking about wind protection. As we progress through Step 3, we will cover the items in the *Checklist*.

How Wind Destroys a House

When wind destroys a house, the destruction usually begins by lifting off the roof. This makes it easy for the wind to blow the walls over. Even if the walls stand, the interior is ravaged by wind and rain. By the same token, if the roof stays on the house during a windstorm, the house is likely to escape serious damage.

In the past, roof construction depended mainly on the weight of the roof to keep it from flying off the house. However, a hurricane or tornado can create a lifting force that is several times the weight of the roof. The lifting force may exceed 100 pounds per square foot (about 500 kilograms per square meter).

This lifting force is the result of a pressure difference between the inside and the outside of the roof surface. If windows or doors fail, wind blows into these openings, creating a pressure inside the house that is much higher than the outside pressure above the roof.

The worst case is the failure of a garage door. The large area of the garage entrance allows wind to create high pressure inside the garage, which will lift the roof above the garage. Once the roof is partially exposed, wind can quickly remove the rest of it. Alternatively, if the garage has a hatch that leads into an attic roof, the pressure can travel into the attic through the hatch, and blow off the entire roof.

High pressure inside the house can be created by a hurricane or by a tornado. In addition, a tornado can also remove a roof by creating a low pressure above the roof. The center of a tornado has a very low pressure. If a tornado passes over a house, the low pressure can suck the roof off like a vacuum cleaner.

Wind damage to the rest of the house occurs because of weak connections, usually at the tops, bottoms, and corners of walls. If a house is not well anchored to its foundation, the entire house may be blown off the foundation. Internal wind pressure tends to break walls apart where they join at corners.

The force of extreme wind on a house is not a steady push. In addition to the high wind pressure, eddy currents form around the house that create strong shaking forces. The shaking tends to hammer the structure apart.

Hurricanes

Hurricanes are a danger to populations living near coastlines in tropical to middle latitudes around the world, as shown in Figure 3-64. For example, more than half the population of the United States lives in areas that are vulnerable to hurricane damage, from either wind or flooding.

Hurricanes are born in warmer ocean waters near tropical latitudes. Tropical oceans absorb vast amounts of solar energy, which evaporates vast amounts of water. Water vapor is lighter than air, so it rises. The rotation of the earth causes the rising moist air to rotate in a circular pattern, creating wind. As the water vapor rises to cooler altitudes, it gives up its energy by condensing into clouds, which feeds more energy into the winds.

The rotating weather system begins as a mild "tropical depression." It gains energy as it travels over warm water. Depending on the weather over the ocean, the tropical depression may die out, or it may grow to become a Force 5 hurricane.

The storm travels in a direction that is guided by the rotation of the earth, by ocean currents, and by other factors. A hurricane travels at relatively low speed, ranging from 10 to 30 miles per hour (16 to 50 kilometers per hour). This usually provides days of warning for people to board up their homes or to evacuate, but not enough time to strengthen a house that is weakly built.

A hurricane can cause devastation over a vast area, along a path that may stretch more than a thousand miles (1,600 kilometers). For example, in the Atlantic Ocean, hurricanes are born west of Africa. They travel westward, gaining energy. By the time a hurricane reaches the Caribbean Sea, it may devastate one island nation after another, then enter the Gulf of Mexico or turn northeast to travel along the Atlantic coast of the United States. Where a hurricane crashes into the mainland, it may cause heavy damage before dying out perhaps hundreds of miles inland.

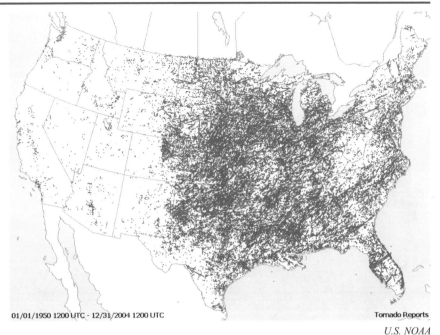

01/01/1950 1200 UTC - 12/31/2004 1200 UTC   Tornado Reports

U.S. NOAA

Figure 3-65. Reports of tornadoes in the United States, from 1950 through 2011. Sparser reports in the mountainous and desert areas are partly due to fewer people living there to make reports. The moral of this story is that tornadoes can be expected almost anywhere, not just in Tornado Alley.

A hurricane traveling over land is dissipated by the friction of the land surface and by the lack of warm moisture to feed it. High wind speed generally does not extend inland more than about 100 miles (160 kilometers). However, a hurricane may cause heavy rains hundreds of miles inland by circulating moist ocean air over the land mass.

Tornadoes

Tornadoes can create the highest wind speeds that occur in nature, causing almost total devastation over a narrow track, typically a few hundred yards (a few hundred meters) wide. A tornado typically travels several miles (several kilometers) before dissipating. Although the area of destruction of an individual tornado is much smaller than the track of a hurricane, tornadoes occur much more frequently.

Tornadoes are spawned by strong thunderstorms, and they may occur anywhere that thunderstorms occur. They develop rapidly, providing little or no warning of their approach, especially at night.

The United States suffers far more tornado damage than the rest of the world. Tornadoes occur virtually everywhere in the continental United States, although they are reported far more often east of the Rocky Mountains, as shown in Figure 3-65. Tornadoes also occur throughout Europe, in various parts of east Asia, in New Zealand and eastern Australia, and in southeast Africa.

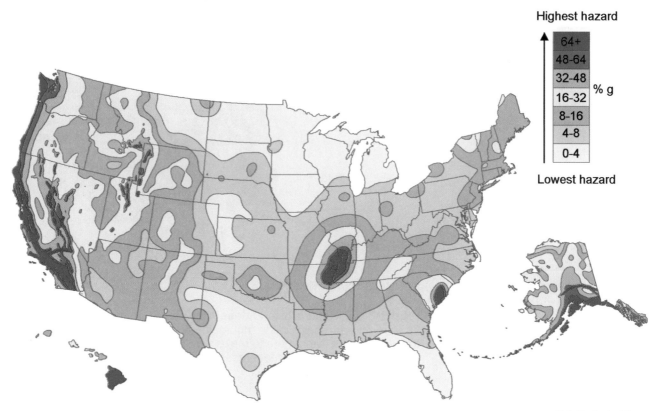

Highest hazard

64+
48-64
32-48   % g
16-32
8-16
4-8
0-4

Lowest hazard

U.S. Geological Survey

Figure 3-66. Historical danger of earthquakes in the United States.

At present, wind-resistant house design is used mainly in regions that are notorious for hurricanes or tornadoes, especially the Midwestern part of the United States that is called Tornado Alley. However, wind causes extensive damage even outside these areas. Furthermore, weather patterns change, and your house is being designed to last for centuries. Therefore, make your house fully resistant to wind damage, even if your region has not been visited by severe winds within recent memory.

RESISTANCE TO EARTHQUAKES

Earthquakes are quick, violent movements of the earth. An earthquake occurs when stress that has been building up in the earth's crust is suddenly released by slippage between adjacent geological formations. The region of slippage is called the "epicenter." It may be located anywhere from the surface of the earth to many miles down. The earthquake may cause damage within a geographical region that extends from several miles (or kilometers) to hundreds of miles (or hundreds of kilometers) from the epicenter.

The release of energy at the epicenter travels outward as a series of waves that travel through the ground. Earthquake waves come in several types. Some travel along the surface, while others follow a more direct path from the epicenter. The waves travel at different speeds, and they combine in different ways as they travel.

A severe earthquake typically lasts from a fraction of one minute to several minutes. During that time, the damage is done by shaking the entire structure, with a frequency that typically ranges around one cycle per second. The shaking is a combination of vertical and horizontal motions. The main quake may be preceded by small tremors. It is usually followed by smaller quakes that are called "aftershocks."

The defense against earthquakes is to build the entire house very strongly. Anything that is not secured, from the walls to the teacups, will be shaken loose. Experience shows that lumber and reinforced concrete can withstand the strongest earthquakes, while weaker materials, such as adobe and concrete blocks, may fail. The survival of the building depends mainly on strong connections that hold the components together during the shaking.

It is feasible and practical to build a house that will remain intact through an earthquake, even if the house is tipped over by a considerable angle. Protecting the below-ground structure against earthquakes is similar to the defenses against soil settling. Protecting the above-ground structure against earthquakes is similar to the defenses against hurricanes and tornadoes.

So, design your home to resist all these hazards together, as you will learn to do.

Where Earthquakes Occur

Damaging earthquakes occur much more widely than you might expect from watching the news or documentaries. Figure 3-66 shows that serious earthquake hazards range across the United States from the entire West Coast to the marshy coast of South Carolina. Earthquakes are common in the many areas around the world where tectonic plates meet. In the U.S., the steady northward sliding of the Pacific tectonic plate is responsible for continual quakes along the West Coast and in southern Alaska. Earthquakes are common near volcanoes, as on the island of Hawaii, near Mt. Vesuvius in Italy, and in many other heavily populated locations around the world.

Severe earthquakes sometimes occur in areas that have no previous history of earth movement. For example, the Missouri earthquakes of 1811-12 were the most powerful recorded in North America. Geologists still lack a convincing explanation of why earthquakes should occur in that region.

Okay! You have learned the important principles of building a superior structure. From this point forward, we will be using that knowledge to design the structure of your own home. As we do so, keep in the mind the "200-Year Rule":

THE 200-YEAR RULE

Design your home to endure for at least 200 years without any significant degradation of comfort, economy, or structural integrity. Your are building an asset that can easily retain its value for generations. In addition to creating a financial legacy, you are creating a testament to your foresight, skill, and style. Your house will be ready for the much higher energy prices of the future and for major changes in climate that may occur.

The principle is simple. *Each component of your home should either (1) last at least 200 years, or (2) be easy to replace.* For example, we will design every part of your main structure to remain intact for centuries. On the other hand, contemporary windows fail within a few decades, so we will install them in an improved way that makes them much easier to replace.

If 200 years is too far beyond your personal time horizon, consider that a 200-year house also provides short-term benefits. For example, most houses suffer from settlement cracks within a few years, but a 200-year house will not. All the edges will remain straight and the surfaces will remain flat. You won't discover roof rot the first time you replace the shingles. Your floors won't squeak or sag. Repairs will be easy when you (or your descendants) do need to make them.

A 200-year house won't cost much more than a flimsy tract house. It is the product of excellent design and workmanship, not expensive materials or exotic technology.

THE GROUND ON WHICH YOU BUILD

We begin the design of your home by considering the ground on which you will build it. The ground under your home is its ultimate foundation. It's not just dirt, but a material that has a variety of important properties. Those properties vary widely from one location to another. For example, the ground will determine whether you should have a basement.

In case of doubt, hire a local soils engineer to examine the soil of your home site. To design your foundation well, you need to know the ground under the exact footprint of your foundation. The following are the most important issues to investigate.

RADON: THE FIRST CONSIDERATION

The danger of radon in soil is one of the most important safety issues in house construction. Radon was not recognized as a serious health hazard until 1984, when a nuclear power plant worker in Pennsylvania triggered a radiation monitor with contamination brought from his own home.

A system for protecting homes from radon was quickly developed, and it works well if it is installed properly. The key questions for you are whether your home site has a radon hazard, and if so, what you should do about it.

What is radon? It is one of the 92 naturally occurring elements that you learned about in chemistry class. Radon is a chemically inert gas, but it is radioactive. Radon is a product of the radioactive decay of uranium, so it occurs in soil wherever uranium ore is present. Uranium is surprisingly widespread. In most locations, uranium is not concentrated enough for making bombs or reactor fuel, but it is often concentrated enough to create dangerous levels of radon.

Once radon forms from uranium, it tends to travel toward the surface. Being chemically inert, it does not form compounds with other materials in the soil that would hold it in place. Instead, it travels easily through soil and through cracks in rock formations. Also, it is soluble in water, so it can concentrate in underground water sources and travel with them into dwellings.

Radioactivity causes cancer. It is believed that breathing radon is second only to smoking as a cause of lung cancer. The main hazard is not the gas itself, which clears out of the body quickly. The main hazard is the decay products of radon. Radon has a short half-life – only 3.8 days – so radon in your lungs is likely to decay into dangerous radioactive particles that can lodge in the lungs.

Some of these particles decay further by emitting alpha radiation, which is especially destructive to the DNA of cells, causing cancerous mutations. The radioactive decay products of radon also attach to dust in homes, and the dust may be inhaled.

If you are building a new house in a location that has a radon hazard, design it to minimize the hazard. If you have an existing house, find out whether you have a radon problem. If so, you can take steps to reduce the hazard. We will explain the methods later, under the heading, *Radon Mitigation for Foundations*. For now, we want to know whether you have a problem.

How Radon Enters Houses

Radon can enter your home by a variety of routes, which are summarized in Figure 3-70.

Radon is driven out of the ground by the enormous pressure of the soil. If radon gets to the surface, it diffuses into the atmosphere and is blown away. However, if a house gets in the way of the rising radon, it will enter the house through any gaps in the foundation and floor slab. Gaps may occur at entry points for underground pipes and wiring, between a basement floor slab and the surrounding wall, and through any concrete block wall that is below grade.

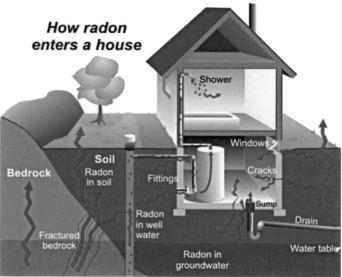

Natural Resources Canada

Figure 3-70. How radon enters a house.

Such gaps worsen as the house ages. Also, a weakly made foundation wall or floor slab may crack, creating more gaps.

If your home requires a sump pump to remove surrounding ground water that leaks into the house, an ordinary sump system becomes a point of entry for radon that is dissolved in the ground water.

And, if your water supply comes from a well in ground that contains uranium, the water may contain high levels of radon. The most dangerous exposure to radon in well water occurs in showers, which release the dissolved radon into the shower space.

Thus, most houses are potential radon traps. The exception is houses that are raised above the ground on pilings or on a foundation that allows air to flow freely underneath the house. Even these houses may be vulnerable to radon in well water.

Building a house over a "crawl space" may increase or decrease the radon hazard, depending on the design of the crawl space. A foundation with a crawl space has no concrete slab to block the flow of radon out of the soil under the house. If the crawl space is well isolated from all living space and if it is very open to the outside, radon will vent to the outside before it finds a way into the house. However, if the vents are small, radon will accumulate in the crawl space and some will enter the house. Fully enclosed crawl spaces, which have no vents, act as radon traps that maximize the danger of radon.

The radon hazard at any given home site may fluctuate widely. Any condition that makes the surface of the surrounding soil less porous will increase the tendency of radon to enter the house. For this reason, the radon hazard increases when the surrounding soil is soaked by rain, or freezes, or is covered by snow.

During cold weather, the warmer air inside the house tends to rise, sucking radon into the house from the bottom. Even worse, houses are closed in cold weather, so that the radon is trapped inside the house.

Test Your Home Site for Radon

The U.S. Environmental Protection Agency recommends that all home sites should be tested for radon, regardless of location. An individual site test is needed because the hazard can be very localized. One house may have a serious radon problem, while the house next door does not. Dangerous radon levels have been found in most parts of the United States, and in many other parts of the world.

A radon test of a building site is relatively inexpensive. You can do the test yourself, using a one-time test kit that is widely available from hardware stores and other vendors. The test kit is simply a canister of gas absorbent, which you remove from a sealed package. Place the canister in the test location for a specified period of time, then seal it and send it to a testing laboratory in the mailer that comes with the kit.

To perform the test, dig a hole inside the footprint of your foundation, suspend the canister in the hole from a piece of plywood, and pack soil around the plywood

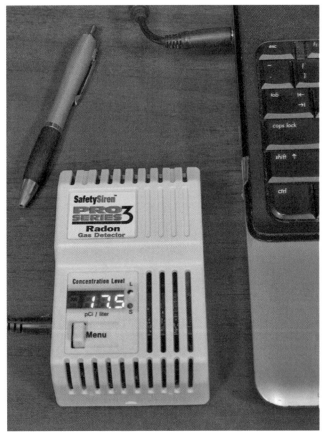

DRW

Figure 3-71. Continuous-reading radon detector. The instrument indicates an elevated radon level in this room.

to form a seal. After the designated time has elapsed, send the canister to the laboratory. If the radon risk is significant in the region of your home site, or if the soil is not uniform, test several holes. If you excavate for a basement, repeat the radon test in the bottom of the excavation.

The site test can't guarantee that radon won't become a problem in the future. The radon hazard may change during the life of the house because of movement in the earth underneath the house. Also, radon may leak into your home through local crevices in the soil that escaped the site test.

Therefore, unless you are certain that radon is not a hazard at your home site, design your home to minimize radon entry.

Continue to test for radon after your home is built. Buy a continuous-reading radon detector, which you can move around to various parts of your house. Figure 3-71 shows a typical unit. A reliable detector is one of the least expensive accessories for your home. If you plan to remain in your present home, get a detector of this kind to determine whether you need to take remedial action.

WATER IN THE SOIL

Most soil contains significant amounts of water. Water in the soil around your foundation can come from two sources, "ground water" and rain that soaks into the soil. When you evaluate your home site, consider both. Ground water is a factor that you can't change. It will determine the kind of waterproofing that your foundation needs, and even whether it is advisable to have a basement. You can minimize rain soaking into the soil around your house by sloping the soil around your house to drain water away.

DRW

Figure 3-72. Winter ice shows where ground water is emerging from different strata of the underground rock formation. If a house is built into this hillside, it will be a challenge to keep the below-grade portions of the house dry.

"Ground water" means water that is underground, but shallow enough to cause trouble for the underground parts of a house. Ground water may be found anywhere, even in deserts. It's an unavoidable aspect of geology. Rain water soaks into the ground until it comes to an impermeable layer. Then it flows along the top of that layer. Ground water accumulates above underground layers of rock, clay, or other impermeable soil. These layers may be irregular. Underground water flows downhill over the layers until it encounters an opening, such as a basement. You can see this behavior in road cuts, which often display water cascading out of the ground at several levels, as in Figure 3-72. Or, the water stays underground and forms an "aquifer." Ground water may also rise into the house from an aquifer that is under pressure.

Ground water is a bane of basements. If you have ground water that rises high enough in the soil to flow into a basement, reconsider whether to have a basement. Water surrounding your basement will try to enter, like water surrounding the hull of a boat. Wet soil can erode concrete and concrete blocks. "Chalking" of basement walls, where the interior surface of the wall crumbles and breaks away, is a common effect seen in portions of basement walls that are soaked by ground water. Even worse damage occurs when water soaks into concrete and rusts the steel reinforcement. This can destroy your foundation over the long term, as we discuss later.

If water penetrates to the interior of the basement, the resulting dampness will rust and rot materials. It will make the basement useless for most functions. It creates an area of high humidity that can cause trouble for the rest of the house. Mold and mildew will proliferate, destroying furnishings and creating health problems.

If ground water is close to the surface, it can even penetrate into a house that is built on a slab on grade.

But, don't panic. Underground water is a matter of degree. A small amount of underground water is not a serious obstacle to adding a basement. Good waterproofing practice, combined with the use of a dehumidifier, can keep your basement dry. We will learn both techniques.

When you are surveying your home site for ground water, the first thing to know is whether ground water ever rises to the level of your foundation. If so, your foundation will require more elaborate waterproofing than if the water level stays well below your foundation. A large amount of ground water may make a basement impractical.

The depth of ground water may be consistent over a large area, or it may vary locally. The depth varies with rainfall, the level of adjacent bodies of water, and other factors. Unless you are sure that the soil at your home site is dry, test the ground water depth at your home site.

BEDROCK OR NOT

Most types of ground under a house will shift substantially during the life of the house. The one exception is bedrock. Bedrock is a stable, solid rock formation that is not likely to move or to crack during the life of the house. A bedrock formation typically is much larger than the footprint of the house. The bottom of the bedrock formation should extend below the frost line to be useful as a foundation.

Bedrock is a stable base for a house, although it is difficult or impossible to shape. Bedrock acts as both the footing and the rigid base of a foundation, making it satisfactory to use concrete blocks or natural stone to elevate the foundation to the height needed, as in Figure 3-13.

In many locations, bedrock is too deep to be accessible. How deep should you be willing to dig to reach bedrock? That's an economic question. Ask your contractor how much it would cost, and in comparison, the cost of a good poured concrete foundation that rests on the soil above the bedrock.

Shale and other highly fractured rock formations are not as good as solid bedrock. If your home site has such a rock formation, consider whether the formation is likely to remain stable. For example, shale on a hillside or shale that transmits a lot of ground water is not likely to be stable in the long term. Loose rocks embedded in soil, no matter how large they are, do not have the stability of bedrock.

SOIL STRENGTH AND STABILITY

What if you can't build your foundation on bedrock? Then, you will build on soil, adapting the design of your foundation to the soil's characteristics. The key is to judge the amount of soil movement that may occur, and to design the foundation accordingly.

The soil under any house will settle irregularly over time. All soil is compressible to some extent. The earth's crust is constantly moving, creating tremors that shake the soil. Tremors are also created by nearby road traffic and other disturbances. Flowing underground water, perhaps far below the foundation, undercuts the soil and causes it to collapse locally. If the water table under a house becomes depleted, the ground probably will settle.

Soil is fluid, which means that it will flow away from pressure. Soil varies widely in its strength, which is related to how tightly the particles in soil are bonded to each other. Some soils are so strong that they will not flow under the weight of a properly designed foundation. Other soils, such as sand, are so weak that they have no ability to support a house reliably. The general way to deal with weaker soil is to create a broader base, or footing, to distribute the load at the bottom of the foundation.

Another important factor is the presence of cavities in the soil. Any type of soil will eventually flow into the cavities, undermining your foundation at various points. Cavities exist in all reclaimed land, in soil that has underground water currents, and in many rock formations. The general way to deal with voids is to

have a foundation that includes an adequate "shear wall," which we will explain shortly. The shear wall is able to span local weaknesses of the soil, but it cannot compensate for soil that is weak everywhere.

An increasingly common situation in densely populated areas is building on landfill. Landfill is spongy and filled with cavities, unlike soil that has settled over millions of years. As land for house construction becomes scarce, it is increasingly likely that your home site will include landfill or even an old dump site, even where you may not expect it.

In principle, you can dig through fill dirt and find good foundation soil underneath it. The question is, how deep is the good soil? An experienced builder can tell the difference between old landfill and original firm soil. Reclaimed spoil feels spongy when you stamp on it, whereas firm soil does not. If your builder is experienced, he can judge the quality of your soil as he digs the foundation trenches. However, that is too late to be designing your foundation.*

How can you determine the properties of your soil? You have to judge whether the local knowledge by builders and code officials is credible. In case of doubt, hire an engineer to survey your soil, including its strength, water content, water depth, and distance to bedrock. The engineer will tell you how much support your foundation will need.

FROST DEPTH AND FROST HEAVING

Water expands when it freezes. If wet soil underneath the foundation can freeze, it will lift that portion of the foundation, and the house above it. This is called "frost heaving." The resulting stresses are likely to break the foundation and the house structure unless the foundation is built very strongly.

Frost heaving requires two conditions. First, the soil under the foundation must fall to the freezing temperature. Frost heaving does not occur in warm climates. Second, there must be so much water in the soil that it fills the empty pores in the soil when it freezes. If that happens, the soil mass can only expand upward.

The most reliable way to avoid frost heaving is to extend the base of the foundation below the frost depth or "frost line." This is the greatest depth at which the soil may freeze. Excavating to place the footing below the frost line is common practice in locations that have a freezing season.

---

* When digging the foundation trench for an addition to my house, we discovered that the site was landfill, full of voids and trash. At the corner where we began to excavate, solid soil was four feet [MF] (about one meter) below grade. By the time we got to the other end of the wall, solid soil was thirteen feet [MF] (four meters) below grade. Fortunately, my masonry contractor tenaciously followed the original terrain, resulting in a very deep foundation. Without it, the addition would now be tipping away from the original house. Don't get caught by such a surprise. If poor soil is discovered when you dig the foundation trenches, your builder may not be as conscientious as mine, and your house may be built on unstable soil that your foundation is not designed to handle.

Therefore, you need to find out the frost depth for your home site. This depends primarily on the average annual temperature. For example, in most of the mid-latitudes, the frost depth typically is a few feet (about one meter) or less. In northern Minnesota, it presently averages about five feet (1.5 meters).

Over the life of the house, the climate may change enough to lower the frost depth considerably. Building codes may specify a particular frost depth, but that is only approximate and only for the near future.

The amount of moisture in the soil is the other factor that determines whether frost heaving will occur. If the soil above the frost line is fairly dry, any moisture in the soil can expand into pores in the soil when it freezes, instead of forming a solid frozen mass that expands as a whole.

To avoid frost heaving, the soil must be well drained. There must be no "water table" or layer of water in the soil above the frost line. Any soil or gravel that is flooded with ground water will heave if it freezes.

In order for the soil to drain well, the soil above the frost depth should have a large fraction of empty space, or pores. The spaces allow any water to drain to a level that is too deep to freeze. At the same time, porous soil provides more space to absorb any ice that forms.

For example, frost heaving will occur in damp clay. However, frost heaving will not occur in clean gravel, provided that there is no water layer that exists above the frost depth.

Soil moisture is especially important when using a foundation that does not extend below the frost depth. The most common foundation of this type is a "floating slab," which requires special protection against frost heaving that we will cover under the heading, *Slab Foundations*.

SURFACE WATER DRAINAGE

Select a building site where rainwater can drain away from the house. It is folly to build on a lot where your house would be at the bottom of a local basin, unable to drain rainwater. The foundation would soon become waterlogged, creating serious water problems inside the house. A basement would be unusable.

If your home is located on a slope, you may need major earthwork to divert rain runoff from the uphill side. In some cases, it may be necessary to build a retaining wall on the uphill side. It is expensive to build a wall that can resist toppling against soil pressure. But, whatever the cost, don't stint on drainage to keep surface water away from your house.

You may be able to use an underground pipe to drain rainwater to a lower side of the house. This method is less desirable than surface drainage. You need to have a permanent right of way for the pipe and for the surface drainage where the pipe discharges. And, clogging of the inlet or the pipe itself could leave the house flooded.

SINKHOLES

In some areas, rock strata near the surface are thin and they have been undermined by water that dissolves the rock layer from below. The ground may collapse without warning into the void below, creating a deep hole called a "sinkhole." Sinkholes occur only in certain locations, but they are catastrophic. They can break the foundation of a house, or swallow a house whole.

The state of Florida is especially notorious for sinkholes. Parts of the state are cratered with sinkhole lakes, looking from the air like a World War I battlefield. The sinkholes are caused by collapse of the limestone surface rock into underground rivers, which fill the holes with water. New sinkholes appear periodically, and old ones get bigger. There is a suspicion that pumping of water from wells is accelerating the process. Many houses have been destroyed by a sinkhole that forms after the house is built, as in Figure 3-73.

If you build in an area that is vulnerable to sinkholes, it is best to use a strongly reinforced floating slab foundation to distribute the weight of the house and to span local collapse under the house. That won't save the house if a sinkhole forms, but it gives the occupants a better chance of escape.

Figure 3-73. Life in certain parts of Florida. Come home from work to discover that your house has fallen into a hole.

SOME PLACES YOU JUST DON'T BUILD

 Sometimes, a dream location for a home should remain a dream. There are places where no practical type of construction can survive. The only smart decision is not to build there, despite what other people do. Builders may get permits to build houses in stupid places, and some will do so if they can find gullible customers. So, don't be gullible.

Perhaps the most common mistake is building on a flood plain, which is anywhere that water can rise enough to flood a house. The usual cause of catastrophic flooding is concentration of heavy rainfall in a nearby river or stream, which may simply widen or may break through a dam or levee. However, in flat terrain, rain alone may flood a widespread area. Or, a hurricane may push seawater over shallow coastal terrain.

It may be practical to build on a flood plain if you elevate the house above the highest predictable water level. One method is to build the house on a tall pier foundation. Another is to build an earth platform for the house that is tall enough to rise above flood waters. Otherwise, this is what you can expect:

Figure 3-76.

Building near the edge of steep terrain is risky unless you are sure that you have a stable rock formation underneath. When weak soil is sloped, it is just a matter of time before the slope will collapse. The collapse will occur if the soil becomes waterlogged by rain or by an overflowing river, or if the slope is undercut by a nearby body of water. The worst case is soil that consists mainly of silt, as in this case:

Figure 3-77.

The sea or a meandering river may invade deeply into a shoreline consisting of weak soil. For example, shoreline erosion occurs rapidly along the sandy banks of Cape Cod and North Carolina. But, it does not occur along the coastline of Maine, most of which is sold rock. This is what happens eventually to a shoreline that consists of silt or sandy soil:

Figure 3-78.

In some active volcanic areas, people rush in to build houses and entire subdivisions on freshly hardened lava fields. Meanwhile, lava from the same volcano is destroying other houses nearby, as is happening to this house in Hawaii:

Figure 3-79.

THE FOUNDATION

Now, we are ready to begin the design of your home's structure. We start with the foundation, which supports everything else. Mankind has invented various kinds of foundations, at least one of which will allow you to build a house reliably on almost any kind of terrain. Now that we know the soil conditions of your home site, we are ready to select the kind of foundation that is best adapted to those conditions.

There are four prevailing types of foundations for houses. The names are not standardized. We will call them *shear wall* foundations, *block* or *stone* foundations, *floating slab* foundations, and *pier* foundations. Table 3-4, *Foundation Types*, summarizes the characteristics of the main foundation types.

A house may have more than one of these basic types. A common example is using a shear wall foundation under the exterior walls, and pier foundations under the supporting columns for interior load-bearing walls.

Also, different types of foundations can be used for the same purpose. For example, if you need to build your house above ground to protect against radon, you may use a pier foundation or you may choose a shear wall foundation that has large vent openings.

More specialized kinds of foundations are used in challenging environments. For example, *friction pilings* are used in boggy ground and in shallow water, where it is impossible to dig deep enough to find stable rock or soil. In arctic regions, specially insulated foundations are needed to avoid melting the permafrost under the house.

The foundation is the most technical part of your home's structure. It requires specialized knowledge, equipment, and skills. These should be provided by your builder and by his concrete contractor. But mistakes, obsolete practices, and harmful shortcuts are still common in building foundations. So, it is your job to make sure that the best practices are followed. In the following pages, we will explain the aspects of foundation design that you should know. And, we will recommend improvements over conventional practice.

Your contractor should be able to follow all these recommendations. But in case of doubt, seek design help from an engineer who has experience with residential foundations, especially with the soil of your home site.

---

* Shear forces are forces that are applied in opposing directions. Scissors work by applying shear forces. When the soil under a foundation subsides locally, gravity pushes downward on the portion of the wall above the gap, while the firmer soil pushes up on the adjacent portions of the wall. A weak wall will fracture where these opposing shear forces meet. When engineers design structures, they exploit the fact that all the forces on an object can be broken down into three types: tension, compression, and shear.

SHEAR WALL FOUNDATIONS

A shear wall foundation is a continuous wall made from poured concrete that is reinforced by embedded steel rods. This is the best kind of foundation for most soil conditions, but not for all. Shear wall foundations are superior to concrete block or stone foundations in all respects, except cost.

On typical soils, the shear wall rests on a footing that is wider than the thickness of the shear wall itself, to reduce pressure on the soil and thereby reduce settling. Shear wall foundations are mostly buried, but typically extend above grade level far enough to support the ground floor. The previous Figures 3-1 through 3-5 show how a typical shear wall foundation is made.

This type of foundation can be used with almost any terrain, including steep slopes. It offers reliable support for the house on all soils, except on soil that is sandy or so weak that the entire foundation may sink into the ground. A shear wall foundation can produce either a crawl space or a basement under the house, depending on the depth of the foundation. A basement requires additional design features, which we will cover.

We call this type of foundation a "shear wall" because its outstanding characteristic is its resistance to the "shear" forces* that occur when the soil settles unevenly underneath the foundation. Each part of the shear wall is strong enough to carry a large fraction of the weight of the house, and it is able to span localized soil collapse under parts of the footing.

This kind of foundation is exceptionally strong, like a bridge girder. It can support frame, masonry, and masonry veneer walls. A well designed shear wall foundation resists all forces that tend to crack or collapse the foundation, including soil pressure from the outside.

How tall should a shear wall foundation be in relation to its length? The answer is somewhat arbitrary. It depends on the thickness of the wall, the amount of steel reinforcement, the weight of the house structure, and other factors. A practical figure is to make the height of the foundation at least 10% of its longest width. This makes efficient use of concrete and steel. For example, if one side of the house extends 50 feet (15 meters), make the shear wall under that side at least 5 feet (1.5 meters) tall.

Reinforced concrete basement walls are shear walls that are very tall in relation to their length. This makes them extremely strong as a foundation.

Table 3-4. FOUNDATION TYPES

Type	Advantages	Disadvantages	Where to Use
Shear Wall	• The strongest type of foundation, resisting all normal destructive forces. • Deep shear walls can serve as walls for below-grade living space (basement or walk-out). • Unbroken surface, in combination with effective sealing and waterproofing, resists entry of ground water, radon, and insects.	• Expensive. • Requires specialized skills and equipment for pouring concrete. • Vulnerable to corrosion of steel reinforcement, if water penetrates the concrete. • Lacks sufficient footing area for very weak soil.	• The best choice in most locations. • Not needed if continuous bedrock is accessible. • May not provide adequate footing area on weak soils. • Less appropriate than pier foundation for steep grade.
Block or Stone	• Relatively inexpensive. • Deep foundations can serve as walls for below-grade living space (basement or walk-out).	• Vulnerable to cracking caused by movement of soil below foundation. • If used as basement walls, vulnerable to buckling by soil pressure. • Vulnerable to water, radon, and insect intrusion at joints and cracks. • Lacks sufficient footing area for very weak soil.	• Use only on bedrock, or as an above-grade extension of a shear wall foundation. • Do not use below grade where radon or groundwater is a serious problem.
Floating Slab	• Allows building on weak soil. • Relatively easy to build. • Resists entry of radon and below-grade insects.	• Requires level terrain, or terrain that has been filled or graded to a level surface. • Vulnerable to frost heaving. • Vulnerable to perimeter cracking in cold weather. • Difficult to insulate well. • No living space below grade.	• Best for weak soil. • Best for soil or rock layer vulnerable to local collapse. • Over wet soil, build on an elevated berm. • In colder climates, special steps are needed to prevent frost heaving. Perimeter cracking may be difficult or impossible to avoid.
Pier	• Relatively inexpensive. • Easy to build. • Easily adaptable to irregular and sloped terrain. • Avoids water intrusion. • Requires no waterproofing, except to protect steel reinforcements. • Avoids radon intrusion if freely vented. • Easy to install shields that block insects and rodents.	• Cannot support masonry walls or masonry veneers. • By themselves, provide no resistance to uneven settling of the piers. • Provides no below-grade living space. • Exposes the lower floor to outside temperature, requiring insulation of the floor. • Requires special protection against freezing of pipes between the house and ground.	• Good for steep or irregular terrain. • Good for locations with a radon hazard. • Must rest on bedrock, or on a continuous grade beam that connects all piers. • On wet soil, build piers on a grade beam and adequate footing.
Friction Piling	• Works in wet and underwater soil where bedrock is not accessible.	• Limited life. • Uneven settling.	• Limited to frame structures designed to resist sagging, usually in marine or marshy environments.

Strong Foundations Use Concrete and Steel

Several centuries before Christ, the Romans developed concrete in essentially its modern form, and they applied it to building construction in modern ways. Concrete has the compression strength and durability of other masonry materials, with the advantage that it can be molded to the desired shape and size. These characteristics make concrete the preferred form of masonry for foundations.

Like other masonry materials, concrete has virtually no reliable "tensile" strength, which is resistance to pulling apart. This may not be obvious, because a brick or a stone or a rock stratum in a mountain may seem to have great tensile strength. However, all masonry materials are vulnerable to cracking, and when that happens, they lose all tensile strength.

This means that a concrete foundation will support the heavy weight of a building, but only if all parts of the foundation are kept under compression. However, unless the foundation rests on bedrock, settling of the soil under the foundation will change the load on parts of the foundation from compression to tension.

For example, if the soil under the center of a wall settles, the center of the foundation is bent downward by the weight of the building. The footing at the bottom of the foundation is now subjected to a force that pulls it apart, creating a crack that travels up through the house wall, as in Figure 3-82.

Similarly, if the soil under the corner of a building settles, the top of the corner foundation is placed under tension. This will eventually cause a rupture in the wall as the corner settles, as in Figure 3-83.

In the mid-19th century, concrete structures were given tensile strength by embedding steel reinforcing bars in them. Today, steel reinforcing bar, or "rebar," is an integral part of most concrete structures. Steel wire, usually in the form of a welded mesh, is also used to reinforce concrete slabs.

Steel has high tensile strength and it bonds well with concrete, so the combination of steel and concrete can produce a structure that resists all forces. But, not all steel is equal. If your soil has moisture problems, consider rebar and wire that is galvanized to resist rusting. See the sidebar, *Better Reinforcing Steel*.

It's not your job to be an expert about the technical aspects of concrete work. This is an area of specialized knowledge that concrete contractors generally understand. However, your foundation is so important that you want to be sure that it is built as well as possible.

In case of doubt, hire an appropriate engineer to help you with the specifics of your foundation design, or at least to check the contractor's design. The charge for this should be small.

Our next topic is a significant improvement to conventional practice that you should discuss with your builder and include in your construction drawings.

Orient the Rebar for Greatest Strength

The usual practice with rebar is to install a simple grid of horizontal and vertical rods. This pattern is appropriate for the top, bottom, and corners of a shear wall. However, the rest of the reinforcing steel – covering most of the area of the wall – should be installed diagonally. This is because the shear wall needs reinforcement primarily to resist diagonal cracking forces that occur when soil subsides unevenly underneath the foundation.

 Placing rebar diagonally in the center portions of a poured concrete foundation provides the maximum shear strength.

Figure 3-82. Fracture of a house wall that is caused by collapse of the center portion of the foundation. This is an example of the weakness of concrete block foundations.

Figure 3-83. Fracture of a house wall that is caused by collapse of a corner of the foundation.

BETTER REINFORCING STEEL

Steel reinforcement that is used for concrete has a catastrophic weakness that many builders still fail to recognize. The steel itself may act as a time bomb that eventually destroys the concrete. If soil is wet, moisture will penetrate a concrete foundation and rust the steel. Rusting steel expands. It will eventually burst the concrete around it, destroying the foundation's strength. The result is similar to the cracking of masonry by freezing water.

The vulnerability of steel-reinforced concrete depends on water conditions in the soil. In soil that is always dry, steel that is encased in concrete will not rust enough to cause trouble. Concrete is alkaline, which causes a stable protective iron compound to form on the surface of the rebar or wire. However, if the concrete becomes wet, impurities in the concrete or steel cause corrosion. This danger is particularly severe if the concrete contains any salt, or if salt is in the environment, as along a seashore or from road salt. In extreme cases, the foundation may be destroyed within a few years.

The problem begins before the concrete is poured. Rebar and wire rusts if it is exposed to rain during construction, and the rust is embedded in the concrete.

The life span of steel reinforcements can be greatly extended by protective coatings. If rebar is selected properly, it can survive soil moisture for the full life of your house, which is at least several centuries.

Ancient Roman engineers embedded iron reinforcing bars in lead, a system that keeps many Roman structures standing to this day. Today, using lead would violate environmental regulations. The best modern alternative is galvanizing, which means that the rebar or wire is heavily coated with zinc. Zinc is a tough coating, and it extends galvanic protection against corrosion to all parts of the rebar, even if a local area of the steel is exposed.

Use galvanized rebar or wire in any part of the foundation that may be wetted. Water in concrete will wick upward, like water in a sponge. Therefore, it is prudent to use galvanized steel even for parts of the foundation that are above grade level.

Your builder may think that using galvanized steel in your home is radical, but take the long view. Foundation damage from rusting rebar will occur in many houses during their lifetimes. Don't let your house be one of them.

Plastic coatings for rebar are now offered, but they provide no galvanic protection, so the steel is vulnerable to rusting anywhere the plastic coating is penetrated or chips off. Also, the plastic coating prevents a tight grip between the concrete and the steel, so it compromises the purpose of the rebar from the start.

Glass fibers and other fibers are now being used to strengthen concrete. A benefit is that the fibers do not rust. So far, fiber reinforcement has been limited to non-structural applications, such as decorative wall panels. It remains to be seen whether fiber can become an alternative to steel reinforcement.

Installing the rebar diagonally in the center portion of the foundation wall makes the foundation stronger than the same weight of steel that is installed vertically and horizontally. Stated differently, you can get the desired strength with less steel. Installing rebar diagonally is unusual, so work with your builder to get it done most effectively. Also, make sure that your drawings show the optimum rebar pattern.

The Corners

In a shear wall foundation, each wall is strong individually. But, it is the corners that hold each wall upright. To make the entire foundation strong, the individual walls should be connected strongly at the corners. To make strong corner connections, rebar is bent at right angles and placed horizontally in the corners.

Where the foundation has outside corners, soil pressure pushes the walls together at the corners. However, if the foundation has inside corners, soil pressure tends to break the walls apart at the corners. You can see this in many retaining walls, as in Figure 3-103, below. Therefore, the steel reinforcement must be especially strong at inside corners.

If a house has a plain rectangular footprint, a shear wall foundation is very resistant to localized soil settlement. Each wall is a continuous beam, and the corners hold the beams together. However, if the foundation has additional corners, it becomes less rigid. In most cases, this won't matter. However, it might be an issue if the soil is very unstable. We explain how to deal with this situation under the heading *Add Corners to Strengthen Basement Walls*, later.

The Footing

The footing is a wide pad of concrete that is poured where foundation walls and supporting columns will be located, as in Figure 3-2. The footing becomes the bottom surface of the foundation.

The purpose of a footing is to distribute the weight of the house on the soil below. Therefore, adapt the width of the footing to the soil. Soil that is loose requires a wider footing than soil that sticks together. Footings are the least expensive part of your foundation, so don't skimp on them. Your masonry subcontractor should know the appropriate footing dimensions for your location.

A good footing begins with a good trench. The trench should be deep enough to reach bedrock or firm soil. If the trench is not dug down to firm soil, or if loose soil is allowed to drop into the trench before the concrete is poured, the footing will rest on weak soil.

Reinforce the footing lengthwise with rebar, as in Figure 3-84. The rebar keeps the footing from cracking if soil subsides locally under the foundation.

"Capillary Breaks" and Water Barriers

Concrete has a strong tendency to act as a wick for water. Water in a concrete structure may travel upward several stories. The absorbed water creates moisture problems all the way up.

The volume of water that is carried upward is much greater in concrete block structures than in solid concrete. The reason is that concrete blocks and their mortar joints are very porous, providing a large internal surface area for water to climb.

The wicking behavior of concrete results from "capillary" action, which is the tendency of a liquid to climb up a solid surface by attraction between the molecules of the liquid and the molecules of the solid.

In home construction, a "capillary break" is anything that blocks water from contact with masonry. The most common capillary break is polyethylene plastic sheet. Also, waterproof coatings are commonly applied to the outside surfaces of foundation walls.

Plastic foam insulation board can also act as a capillary break, if it is applied properly. A layer of clean gravel acts partially as a capillary break by creating a gap between a concrete slab and moist soil below it. Water does not wick through gravel as readily as it does through concrete.

A "water barrier" is just what the name implies. It is a material that keeps water from entering the structure. For all practical purposes, water barriers are also capillary breaks. However, the converse is not true. Some capillary breaks, such as a gravel bed, do not serve as a water barrier or as a vapor barrier.

The soil surrounding the foundation may be wetted by underground water sources, rain, melting snow, irrigation, or other sources of water. These conditions

Concrete Forms Services

Figure 3-84. Rebar properly placed to strengthen a footing. Note how the rebar for the side footing is well connected to the rebar of the main footing.

are likely to occur around the foundations of most homes, if only occasionally. Therefore, the drawings of foundations in this book usually include capillary breaks or water barriers.

A Perfectly Flat Top Surface

The top surface of the foundation wall should be flat, straight, and smooth. The first floor above grade will rest on the foundation wall. If the foundation wall is not flat, there will be gaps between the foundation and the bottom of the floor platform. These gaps are paths for air leakage and insect entry. If gaps leave the floor locally unsupported, cracks will occur in the inside wall sheathing as the weight of the structure pushes the walls down into the gaps.

This is the responsibility of the concrete contractor. When finishing the top surface, he should use a laser level. Local deviations from flatness should be less than one quarter inch (less than 6 millimeters). The entire top surface of the foundation should be at the same height and should be straight within one half inch (within about 12 millimeters).

PARTIAL-HEIGHT SHEAR WALLS

If you plan to have a basement that is only partially buried, you can save money by limiting the poured concrete portion of a shear wall foundation. The bottom portion of the foundation is built as we described previously, with poured concrete and steel reinforcement. This part extends upward at least a foot (30 cm) above grade level. It provides resistance to soil pressure from the side. Because it is a continuous surface, unbroken by mortar joints, it also blocks water, radon, and insects. As recommended previously, the height of the poured concrete portion of the foundation should be at least 10% of the foundation's length.

Above that level, you can continue the wall with concrete block. Aside from saving money, this makes it easy to create openings for windows, fans, furnace flues, dryer vents, etc. In contrast, it is difficult to make openings in steel-reinforced concrete.

Make a strong connection with the concrete block by extending rebar upward from the poured shear wall. The blocks are placed over the rebar, and the rebar is bedded in mortar inside the concrete blocks. To do this, the concrete contractor needs to line up the vertical rebar with the holes in the concrete blocks.

BLOCK OR STONE FOUNDATIONS

Until recently, the most common type of foundation has been made of concrete blocks, cinder blocks, and other types of formed masonry, as in Figure 3-85. To many builders, "foundation" means a concrete block foundation.

A block or stone foundation may have the same outline as a shear wall foundation, but it is fundamentally weaker because it lacks tensile strength. Because of its lack of shear strength, a block or stone foundation should be used only if it can rest directly on bedrock, so that little shear strength is needed.

Figure 3-85. A typical concrete block foundation.

Unfortunately, the relatively low cost of concrete and cinder block foundations causes them to be used on soil that will shift over the life of the house. This misuse of block foundations has persisted for a long time. Avoid it.

Builders may try to strengthen a concrete block wall by inserting rebar vertically through the holes in the blocks and cementing the rebar in place. This helps, but not much. The vertical bars provide no strength for the vertical mortar joints between the blocks. These joints will still fail under the shearing loads that are created by soil settlement.

Some builders try to compensate for the weakness of a block or stone foundation by creating a heavily reinforced footing, a sort of poor man's shear wall. This is only marginally effective, because a footing does not have enough depth to support the wall. If soil settles under the footing, the weight of the wall above will eventually break through the footing.

SLAB FOUNDATIONS

A slab foundation is a one-piece concrete raft on which the house is built. It is sometimes called a "floating slab" or a "slab on grade." A properly designed slab can support frame or masonry wall construction. For example, the house in the previous Figure 3-27 is built on a floating slab.

A floating slab acts as a huge footing, so it is favored where the soil is weak or unstable, such as sandy soil, landfill, or terrain that is vulnerable to sinkholes. Although a floating slab foundation may seem simple, it requires specialized skill to make it strong and economical. It requires well designed steel reinforcement and capillary breaks, as for shear wall foundations.

A floating slab is poured on level terrain, or on terrain that has been filled or graded to a level surface. In locations where flooding occurs, it may be built on a raised earth platform. The top of the slab should be at least a few inches (at least 10 centimeters) above the finished grade level. This slight elevation deters penetration of rainwater or snowmelt into the house, and it makes the bottoms of the walls accessible for protection against insects.

The soil must be excavated skillfully to give the slab its correct thickness profile, as in Figure 3-86. Simple forms are used to define the perimeter. Depending on soil conditions, a plastic sheet water barrier, a gravel bed, and/or rigid insulation may be laid under the slab. Well placed steel bar and wire reinforcement is needed to provide tensile strength. All the concrete is poured at the same time, without expansion joints.

The weight of the house is carried by the exterior walls and by any interior load-bearing walls. These push the slab downward where the walls rest, while the pressure of the soil pushes the slab upward everywhere. However, soil may settle locally under the slab, so the slab has no support in those places. The slab design should provide strength against all the downward forces on the slab and it should provide support anywhere that soil may settle under the slab.

Concrete is expensive. To make a large slab strong with a minimum of concrete, the underside of the slab may be designed in a waffle pattern, which creates a grid of supporting beams, which may be called "grade

DRW

beams." This requires careful excavation of the soil and careful placement of the reinforcing steel, as in Figure 3-86.

Don't confuse a slab foundation with an interior floor slab that rests freely on the soil, independently of the foundation. A floor slab, as commonly used in basements and garages, is not attached to the foundation, so it carries none of the weight of the outer walls. Its design is usually simple, although it may need reinforcement for localized interior loads.

Slab foundations are most common in warm climates. A floating slab foundation invites trouble if the climate has a cold season, and special features are needed to make the foundation satisfactory. The additional design issues for cold climates are *frost heaving*, *perimeter cracking*, and *comfort insulation*. Figures 3-87 and 3-88 illustrate methods of dealing with these issues, which we will now cover.

Pavement Services

Figure 3-86. A well designed slab foundation being poured. Note the vapor barrier laid over the soil, the steel reinforcement, and the pattern of excavation. The resulting waffle pattern on the underside of the slab supports the slab surface strongly with a minimum of concrete. This foundation is for a warm climate. It provides only minimal protection against frost heaving.

Protection Against Frost Heaving

Under the previous heading, *Frost Depth and Frost Heaving*, we explained "frost heaving" and how to avoid it. In cold climates, avoiding frost heaving is a particular challenge for slab foundations because the entire slab acts as a footing that terminates above the frost depth. If frost heaving can occur, it will easily lift the house and it is likely to break the slab.

For this reason, it was long believed that slab foundations should not be used in cold climates. More recently, the pendulum has swung in the opposite direction, with various authorities claiming that slab foundations can safely be built in almost any climate. Various techniques for avoiding frost heaving have been proposed. Some of these methods seem sound, while others depend on hopes that I consider to be unrealistic.

The key to using a slab foundation in a cold climate is preparing the base under the slab so that frost heaving cannot occur at any temperature. We do this (1) by building the slab over base material that is porous, and (2) by keeping the base material dry.

During very cold weather, some water vapor will rise from the soil below the frost line and it will freeze within the base material. But, the limited ice that forms can expand into the pores of the base material. As long as the volume of ice is less than the pore space in the base material, frost heaving does not occur.

The base material may be gravel, sand, or porous soil. However, these materials should not be mixed. Otherwise, the finer materials will fill the gaps in the larger materials, defeating the purpose. If layers of different materials are used, they should be separated by plastic sheet or by "filter fabric," depending on the foundation design.

The porous base material must extend well below the lowest frost depth that may occur during the life of the house. This is to allow any water that gets into the soil to drain down below the frost depth.

Keeping the base material dry is the biggest challenge for a slab foundation in a cold climate. During the coldest weather, the base material that lies above the frost depth will be cold enough to freeze any water that gets into it. Therefore, if any substantial amount of water can penetrate into the base material, frost heaving will occur.

Ground water that exists above the frost depth makes it virtually impossible to keep the base material dry. Even a gravity drain to lower terrain will not work, because the drain itself will freeze. *Therefore, the presence of shallow ground water at the building site in a cold climate virtually prohibits using a slab foundation*.

If the soil is free of ground water sources, it is still necessary to keep rain, snow melt, irrigation water, or any other source of water from soaking into the base material. To do this, we need to create an "umbrella" to keep water from soaking down into the base material. The components of this underground umbrella are shown in Figures 3-87 and 3-88.

Starting at the bottom, the umbrella includes a rain barrier of heavy plastic sheet that is attached securely to the sides of the slab. At the base of the slab, the plastic sheet extends outward and downward to below the frost depth.

This barrier must survive for the life of the house. It is protected by the layer of soil that is placed above it. Even so, it is unlikely that a plastic sheet will remain fully intact for centuries. So, this is an Achilles heel of the slab foundation.

The next part of the umbrella is grading the soil downward and away from the foundation. For maximum protection against frost heaving, the grading should continue downward until the surface is lower than the frost level below the house. The ideal is to build the house on a raised platform of dry, porous soil or gravel.

If this is not possible, the grading should extend outward for a distance that is several times the frost depth. It may be necessary to do extensive earthmoving to keep the surrounding terrain from draining toward the foundation.

Finally, wide roof overhangs will minimize the amount of rain and snow melt that soaks into the soil that surrounds the foundation.

■ Don't Depend on Perimeter Insulation

If you search for information about building a slab foundation in cold climates, you will encounter the claim that you can prevent frost heaving by installing insulation around the slab, extending either downward or outward. The idea is that heat from inside the house will keep the soil under the foundation from freezing if perimeter insulation is used to keep the heat from escaping.

This is probably a false hope. During the life of the house, it will be unheated for periods that are long enough to allow the soil under the slab to freeze.

There is another flaw in the logic. In a cold climate, the slab will be insulated to keep the interior floor warm. The same insulation will keep the interior of the house from warming the soil below the slab.

And finally, the insulation is likely to decay or to become saturated with water during the life of the house.

At best, using perimeter insulation is a supplement to the basic technique of using porous base material and keeping it dry.

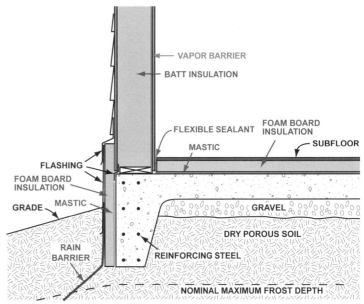

Figure 3-87. Slab foundation for climates that freeze the ground below the slab, using above-slab floor insulation. The main defense against frost heaving is building the slab on porous soil and/or gravel and keeping the soil dry. The soil and gravel below the slab are isolated from the heat of the house interior, so they will linger at freezing temperatures. This house uses frame walls with batt insulation. The exterior foam insulation plays a minor role in keeping the floor warm and in reducing thermal stress in the slab perimeter.

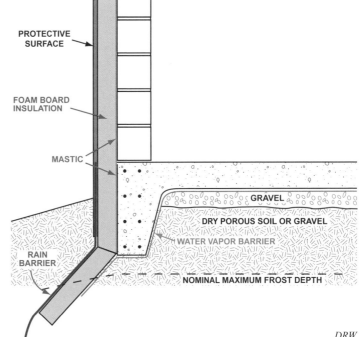

Figure 3-88. Slab foundation for climates that freeze the ground below the slab, using only perimeter insulation. The prime defense against frost heaving is building the slab on porous soil and/or gravel and keeping the soil dry. The soil and gravel below the slab may freeze when the house is vacated for long periods. This house uses concrete block walls. The insulation is a continuous layer, from the top of the wall to the bottom of the slab perimeter. The insulation keeps the house warm and minimizes thermal stress in the slab, but it is not a reliable defense against frost heaving.

Protection Against Perimeter Cracking

A floating slab foundation is one big piece of concrete that has no expansion joints. This creates a problem if the weather causes the perimeter to become much colder than the interior of the slab. The warm center of the slab will push outward on the shrinking perimeter with great force, creating stresses that may crack the perimeter. Cracks in the perimeter of the slab are especially bad because the perimeter carries the heavy wall loads.

Several methods can help to protect the perimeter against cracking:

- Install strong steel reinforcement around the perimeter.
- Use welded wire mesh reinforcement to equalize the temperature within the slab.
- Install ample insulation around the perimeter to contain heat that comes from the inner area of the slab and the soil.

None of these defenses has been proven to be reliable over a period of centuries, which is the intended life span of your house. So, the survival of a slab foundation in a cold climate is still a matter of hope and faith.

Comfort Insulation

Concrete has very poor insulation value, so a concrete foundation slab acts as a path for heat loss from the interior of the house directly to the soil under the foundation and to the soil surrounding the foundation.

If the climate is warm most of the time, a slab foundation requires no insulation. The interior portion of the slab is kept warm by the relatively high deep soil temperature of warmer regions. Carpets may provide all the insulation that is desirable, and the somewhat cooler floor surface is welcome during warm weather.

In a climate with a cold season, insulation is needed to keep a slab floor warm enough for comfort. The interior of the slab is cooled by lower deep soil temperatures, which can approach freezing in very cold climates. (See Figure 3-111, below, for a map of deep soil temperatures.) Several methods of insulating slab foundations are used, because no single method is ideal for all applications. With any of these methods, select the appropriate insulation R-values by using the *Insulation Worksheet*.

■ Method 1: Insulate the Top of the Slab

The most comfortable and energy efficient way to insulate a slab foundation is to install rigid foam insulation on the top surface of the slab, as shown in Figures 3-87. The floor insulation meets the wall insulation, creating an unbroken blanket of insulation inside the room. (This applies to frame wall insulation, and to masonry walls that are insulated from the inside.)

The insulation needs a protective top surface. For example, you can buy foam board insulation that is laminated to plywood, which can serve as a subfloor for the finish surface, such as carpet.

This method does not waste energy in warming the soil below the house. By the same token, the insulation isolates the slab from the heat of the house interior, so there is less stress that tends to break the foundation perimeter during cold weather.

I usually recommend against any kind of plastic foam insulation inside a house. However, the fire and smoke hazard of foam board lying directly on a concrete slab is greatly reduced.

This method keeps the slab cold, so any moisture that gets underneath the floor insulation will condense on the top surface of the slab. This condensation may freeze, breaking loose the insulation. And, water below the insulation will infest the slab surface with mildew. Therefore, it is important to attach the insulation to the floor slab with an unbroken coat of waterproof mastic. Also, the gap between the floor insulation and the walls should be sealed with a flexible sealant, such as silicone.

■ Method 2: Insulate the Perimeter of the Slab

Another method of comfort insulation is to surround the slab perimeter with foam board insulation, as shown in Figures 3-88. If the climate does not experience very cold winters, perimeter insulation can provide adequate comfort.

The insulation should extend below the perimeter of the slab, and deeper is better. The insulation should also extend upward along the wall to overlap the wall insulation or to join with it.

As we have learned, the soil must be kept dry to prevent frost heaving. Dry soil is also important to keep the insulation intact. All plastic foam insulation will eventually become waterlogged and useless if it stays wet.

Because the floor slab is not insulated, keeping the floor comfortably warm is limited by the deep soil temperature. Heat from the house that escapes through the slab will slowly warm the soil underneath the house. However, in climates with an extreme cold season, a lot of heat will still escape by conduction into the cold deep soil and under the perimeter insulation.

■ Don't Place Insulation Under the Slab

A widely promoted method of insulating a slab foundation is to install rigid foam insulation underneath the slab. Usually, the advice is to place insulation board around the perimeter of the slab, typically extending inward for a few feet (about one meter) or so.

This method is badly flawed from a structural standpoint. Foam insulation will eventually yield under the weight of the slab. However, the perimeter carries the weight of the exterior walls and most of the weight of the roof. If the perimeter insulation sags while the inner portion of the slab is supported by soil, there will be intense leverage along the inner edge of the insulation. This could break the slab later in the life of the house.

A solution to this problem is possible, but probably not practical. It is to place insulation of equal thickness under every part of the slab. For this method to work, no part of the slab should rest directly on the underlying soil or gravel. Also, the insulation should sag evenly throughout the life of the house. This seems unlikely to happen.

PIER FOUNDATIONS

A pier foundation uses individual piers to support the structure of the house at spaced intervals. See Figures 3-89 and 3-90. Pier foundations are used almost exclusively with frame houses, which can be built to span the distance between the piers. Pier foundations are inexpensive because they require little material and they are easy to build.

Each pier is independent of the others, so piers will settle individually on soil, causing distortion or cracking of the house structure. For this reason, a pier foundation is best on bedrock. If bedrock is not accessible, the piers can be built on a strong, continuous "grade beam" that provides a common base for the piers. See the sidebar about grade beams.

Piers carry only compression loads, so they can be made of any strong masonry. In regions of high winds, piers should include steel connections that extend from the earth to the house to resist lifting the house off the piers.

A pier foundation produces a crawl space underneath the house. The crawl space itself needs certain design features, which we will cover.

Tall Piers

Piers are an economical way to build on steeply sloped terrain, and on ground that consists of heavy boulders or irregular rock formations. Piers are also commonly used to elevate houses above flood levels.

Piers that are tall and slender should be built in a way that keeps them from tipping over. In concrete house construction, piers may be an integral part of a concrete structure, connected by steel reinforcement, as in Figure 3-91.

If this arrangement is not possible, tall piers should have strong cross bracing. If possible, keep the cross bracing above ground for longevity. Galvanized steel rods are a good choice for most locations, except that they are not attractive.

DRW

Figure 3-89. Pier foundation for a house in Key West. The piers rest on solid coral limestone, so they will not settle individually. Steel rods embedded in the piers, shown on the right, are cemented into the limestone, anchoring the piers. Heavy steel brackets are embedded in the piers to hold the upper structure against the hurricanes that visit the region.

DRW

Figure 3-90. This house now sits on the foundation shown in Figure 3-89.

A house built on tall piers may have partial walls between the piers to create a storage space or garage. If these walls are connected strongly to the piers, they can act as cross bracing.

DRW

Figure 3-91. A typical Florida Keys house built on tall piers to stay above hurricane floods. The space under the house is commonly used as a carport and general storage area. A lightweight screen of perforated blocks or other material is often installed between the piers for privacy, security, and appearance.

THE HEIGHT OF YOUR FOUNDATION

With wood frame construction, the foundation should be tall enough to keep the wooden structure well above the surrounding grade level. This is to keep rain and melting snow from entering along the top of the foundation. Also, the joint at the top of the foundation is a favored entry point for ants, termites, and other insects. Having a raised foundation makes it easier to inspect for insects and to apply insect shields and pesticides.

Because the first floor is raised above grade, most houses need outside stairs or a ramp to enter the house. If you have a garage, its floor will be near grade level, so you probably will need interior stairs between the garage and the rest of the house.

If you will have a basement, design any basement windows so that their sills are well above grade. Don't use window wells, which collect debris and become entry paths for vermin.

If your house will be built over a crawl space, make the foundation tall enough to provide reasonable access to the underside of the floor. We will discuss this further, under the heading, *Stem Wall Foundations and Crawl Spaces.*

A slab foundation with masonry walls can be closer to grade level because masonry is much less vulnerable to damage by water. Still, you want to keep the joint between the slab and the bottom of the wall above grade, because this joint is a path for water and insects to enter the house. As a guideline, make the

top of the slab at least six inches (about 15 centimeters) above the finished grade level at all points. Typically, a single step or a shallow ramp suffices to enter the house.

■ Allow for a Drainage Slope

The height of the foundation should allow you to build up a sloped surface against the foundation for draining water away from all sides of the house, as in Figure 3-92.

When the house is first built, the soil that is backfilled around the foundation can settle enough to create a trough, so build up the soil enough to compensate for this. Make the slope wide enough to carry water at least a few yards (a few meters) away from the house. In this way, the slope will blend nicely into the surrounding terrain.

In any climate that has much rain, use wide roof overhangs in your roof design to keep the top of the soil dry around the foundation. At the same time, exploit the overhangs for their other important benefits, which are summarized in Step 1 under the heading, *An Elegant and Functional Roof.*

A common source of moisture trouble is the house's own gutters draining near the foundation. Locate downspouts so that the runoff goes away from the house, preferably on a downhill side. Increase the slope of the soil under the downspouts. If the runoff is useful for watering nearby shrubbery, trees, and lawn, grade the soil appropriately and locate the downspouts for this purpose. Plant shrubbery beyond the ends of the roof overhang, where it can be watered by rain.

GRADE BEAMS

A "grade beam" is a horizontal concrete beam, reinforced with steel rods to provide shear strength. It can be used for various purposes. It is commonly used at grade level or underground, where it acts as a reinforced footing or a partial shear wall foundation.

For example, a grade beam can be used to reinforce the front edge of a garage floor slab. If you want to build a pier foundation on weak soil, you can install a continuous grade beam to support the piers.

Despite the name, grade beams are also used above grade. For example, grade beams are sometimes installed to span between the tops of piers to support masonry walls.

DRW

Figure 3-92. Soil built up alongside a basement wall to keep the basement dry.

RADON MITIGATION FOR FOUNDATIONS

Most houses have foundations that tend to act as radon traps, channeling radon from the earth into the house. To compensate for this tendency, a family of techniques have been developed for keeping radon out of the house. Collectively, these protective measures are called "radon mitigation." They should be part of your foundation design. Radon mitigation that is designed properly for a new home is very effective, and it adds little to construction cost.

Also, radon mitigation can rescue most existing houses that have a radon hazard, although the protection is not as complete as you can achieve in new construction. The cost of a retrofit radon mitigation system may be fairly modest, for example, less than the cost of replacing an air conditioning system.

While radon mitigation can be very effective, I would advise you to forget about having a basement if the ground under your home site contains large amounts of radon. In such a location, build the house entirely above ground, with the entire underside being freely vented to the outside. Or, if the climate is warm, build on a floating slab foundation, with special attention to sealing the gaps in the slab.

We will cover the basic principles of radon mitigation so that you can discuss

the details with your contractor. If your soil contains radon, find out whether your builder understands radon mitigation adequately. If not, you or your builder will need to hire a specialist. Be sure to get your advice from a genuine expert, and be sure that a specialist is not biasing his advice to sell you an excessively expensive mitigation job.

If your home will need radon mitigation, read a book that explains the critical details.* A warning: I have found that much of the radon mitigation information on the Internet is dubious or dangerously incomplete. This includes information published by government agencies.

Here, we will design the underground structure of your home to repel radon. In Step 5, we will provide defenses against radon in your water supply.

The Basics

Radon mitigation is based on the following three principles, which are illustrated in Figure 3-94.

(1) Block radon from entering the house. Ideally, there should be an unbroken barrier between the soil and the interior of the house. The main surfaces of this barrier are the floor slab(s) and the underground walls. If the house is built over a crawl space, it has no floor slab. In that case, the lower floor must serve as a radon barrier, or a barrier must be installed under the floor.

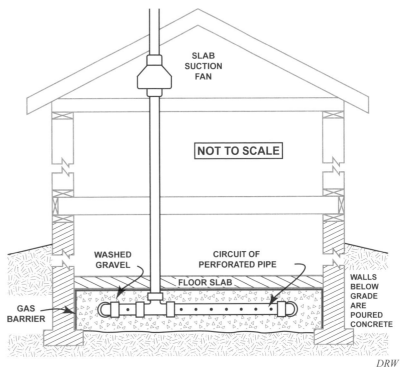

DRW

Figure 3-94. The basics of radon mitigation. The structure of the house blocks the entry of radon, and a vent system makes the pressure under the house lower than the pressure inside the house. An effective radon mitigation system is often no more complicated than this diagram.

---

* A good choice is *Protecting Your Home from Radon: a Step-by-Step Manual for Radon Reduction*, by Douglas L. Kladder. The book is well organized, well illustrated, and easy to read. It covers important details thoroughly, and it offers practical advice to ease installation. Like most authorities, it recommends venting the radon at roof level, about which I am skeptical.

Solid concrete floor slabs and solid concrete walls are effective vapor barriers. However, they must be designed well to avoid cracking. Cracks in concrete are virtually impossible to seal.

Avoid concrete block underground walls. They are highly porous to radon, especially at the mortar joints. Also, if narrower blocks are laid on top of wider blocks in the underground portion of the foundation, there will be a large gap where the width of the blocks changes. Radon can flow easily through the hollow interiors of the blocks from the underground portions of the wall to the living space inside the wall.

Add a gas barrier under the floor slab and on the outside of basement walls. The gas barrier typically is polyethylene plastic sheet, about 8 mils or .008" (0.2 mm) thick. The builder must be careful to seal the joints between the plastic sheets and to avoid puncturing the plastic.

This gas barrier is identical to the barrier that is recommended for keeping ground water from penetrating slabs and basements. So, the same barrier materials perform double duty.

All gaps and joints require careful sealing. These include the underground pipe penetrations for water, sewer, and gas; all penetrations for electricity, television cables, etc.; and, the long joints between the floor slab and foundation walls.

Design the methods of sealing to last for the life of the house. This means that sealants should be replaceable in a reliable manner. For example, the joints between a basement floor slab and the foundation wall must allow the slab to float independently. This requires a flexible seal, and no flexible sealing method will last as long as a house.

(2) Vent the pressure that forces radon into the house. Radon wants to leak into the house because the pressure of radon in the soil is greater than the air pressure inside the house. Installing a vent pipe that connects the underside of the slab to the outside, as in Figure 3-94, allows the radon to escape to the outside more easily than entering the house.

Under the slab, the radon needs an easy path to reach the vent pipe. This path is created by laying a bed of gravel under the slab (and ***under*** the plastic sheet). The gravel should be ***large*** and ***washed***, so that radon will travel easily through the gaps between the stones.

For even better venting, embed a circuit of perforated pipe in the gravel, typically around the perimeter of the slab, and connect this circuit to the vent pipe.

The vent pipe can connect to the gravel bed in several ways. The most common is through a hole in the floor slab, connected to a pipe that rises inside the house.

You can keep the radon vent pipe outside the house by routing it underneath the footing, and then up. Or,

if the footing is about one foot (30 cm) or more below the slab, you can install the vent pipe through a hole in the foundation wall between the slab and the footing. Figure 3-95 shows an example.

Because the soil contains moisture, water will condense in the radon vent pipe. Allow the water to flow back to a point from which it can drain into the soil or into a foundation drain. Be careful not to create any low points in the vent pipe that could fill with condensed moisture and block the vent.

At this time, standard practice is to extend a radon vent pipe above the roof, like a plumbing vent. I am skeptical about this. Radon gas is much heavier than air, and it has a strong tendency to stay low. A vent that exits above the roof is a tall hurdle for the radon to cross. Unless the vent includes a continuously operating exhaust fan, it seems that radon will accumulate in a tall vent pipe, increasing the pressure that forces the radon into the house.

Also, the vent pipe will fill with cold outside air during cold weather, when the radon hazard is greatest. The cold air is heavy and it will increase the pressure under the slab, tending to force radon into the house.

Therefore, it seems more reasonable to install a vent pipe that discharges to the outside at the lowest practical level. If you do this, locate the discharge as far as possible from any doors, windows, or other openings, and aim it in a safe direction. Install the discharge over a downslope, if practical. Install a bird screen at the outlet.

If you do install a pipe that vents at roof level, route it inside the house. A tall exterior pipe and fan is not attractive. Also, a tall exterior pipe will condense a lot of moisture, which will flow back toward the fan and into the foundation. However, that may be your only choice if you are adding a radon vent to an existing house.

(Don't take any radon mitigation recommendations as gospel. Experience is still being gained, and some of the "conventional wisdom" may be less than ideal.)

(3) Use an exhaust fan to create suction under the slab and/or inside buried walls. Radon vents alone cannot keep all radon from leaking into the house, because the vents may not be the path of least resistance for all radon rising from the soil.

The effectiveness of a vent pipe system may be greatly improved* by installing an exhaust fan in the vent system, as in Figure 3-94. With a fan, the vent system acts like a vacuum cleaner that sucks radon out of the soil before it enters the house. The vacuum extends to gaps in the underground structure, so that radon is sucked out of the house, rather than flowing into the house.

Radon removal fans are designed specifically for this purpose. They create relatively high suction at low

DRW

Figure 3-95. A radon vent installed through the foundation wall, between the basement floor slab and the footing. Figure 3-96 shows the finished system.

DRW

Figure 3-96. Radon vent fan system, exhausting away from the house at grade level. This is less common than exhausting with a tall vent at roof level. The choice between the two depends on the surrounding terrain and adjacent houses.

flow rates. They are designed to resist the moisture condensation that occurs in radon vents. They typically have vertical suction and discharge connections to drain condensate through the fan housing, as in Figure 3-96. A range of suction pressures and flow rates are available. Typical residential radon fans require 15 to 150 watts.

If the fan is installed properly, it does not make much noise. It generally is inaudible inside the house. Most of the noise occurs at the discharge of the radon pipe. In close quarters, it may be desirable to install a muffler there. Such mufflers are standard items.

The suction fan usually operates continuously, so it will require replacement every few years. Typically, the fan is installed with standard rubber pipe couplings, which makes installation and replacement easy. This installation method also minimizes noise from the body of the fan.

Even if you don't think you need a suction fan, make a portion of the vent pipe accessible to install one later. After you complete the house, monitoring your radon level may show that a fan is desirable.

Pipe and Fan Size

Radon venting systems for houses typically use plastic pipe with a nominal inside diameter of 3" (75 mm) or 4" (100 mm). Most residential radon fans and other system components are designed for these pipe sizes.

Radon fan characteristics are listed on their manufacturers' Web sites. When selecting a fan, the contractor must choose the right flow capacity and the right suction pressure. The energy consumption of the fan is proportional to the air flow rate multiplied by the suction pressure. So, don't choose a fan with an excess rating for either.

Most of the gas that is moved by the fan will be air that leaks into the system from gaps in the slab and underground walls. This air leakage determines the pipe size and the air flow capacity of the fan. Building the underground structure of your house as we recommend

---

* My house, which was built before the radon hazard was recognized, had an elevated level of radon in the basement. I installed a radon vent under the floor slab and leading into the surrounding concrete block wall, which was the main culprit. Before installing the fan, passive venting lowered the radon level only by about half. Adding the fan lowered the radon level to less than 5% of the original level, so the radon level is now below the threshold that the U.S. EPA recommends for taking corrective action.

will minimize the air leakage. However, in a system that is retrofitted to an existing house, a large amount of air leakage into the system may be unavoidable.

In terms of volume, the radon gas itself seeps from the earth at a low rate, even in the worst of cases. Therefore, contrary to intuition, the radon level itself is not a factor in selecting the pipe size or the fan.

If you install a bed of clean, washed gravel under the slab, radon will flow to the fan easily. This minimizes the fan suction rating that is required.

Monitor the System's Performance

The ultimate check on the effectiveness of your radon mitigation measures is a continuous radon detector, such as the one in Figure 3-71. Install one in the most vulnerable part of the house, typically a basement, and monitor its readings. For the first year, keep a log to record how the readings change with the weather.

Any radon removal system that has a fan should also have a "manometer," which is a simple device for measuring small pressure differences. In a radon removal system, it senses the suction on the intake side of the fan. Figure 3-97 shows how a manometer is installed.

The manometer tells you how well the fan is matched to the system, and it can also indicate trouble in the system. In the best case, the suction indicated by the manometer will be near the center of the fan's pressure operating range.

RadonAway

Figure 3-97. A radon suction gauge, called a "manometer." This inexpensive device mounts easily anywhere on the radon suction pipe leading to the fan. It verifies the performance of the system.

If you design the radon vent system for a new house properly, successful operation of the system is virtually certain. Your radiation monitor should verify this. If suction pressure is lower than you expect, and if the radiation level is safe, you can save energy by substituting a fan that has a lower pressure rating.

If you retrofit a radon vent system to an existing house, the manometer will tell you how efficiently the system is working. If the suction pressure is at the low end of the fan's operating range, it means that a there is a high rate of flow through the fan. This may mean that air is leaking into the foundation. For example, if you have a concrete block wall that extends below grade, air may leak into the wall from the outside and inside of the house and flow down into the underground suction space.

Air leakage into the foundation may keep the fan from developing sufficient suction under the slab. This is a likely explanation if your radon level continues to be unsafe. In that case, find the leakage paths and block them as best you can. If the radon level still remains high, install a fan with a larger air flow (not suction pressure) capacity.

If the suction pressure is at the high end of the fan's operating range, it means that radon is not flowing to the fan easily. If the radon level does not fall to a safe level, a fan with greater suction pressure (not flow capacity) may be required. Or, you may need to install additional suction points.

If the fan suction sometimes rises considerably, along with a drop in flow, it probably means that the suction paths are waterlogged as a result of rising ground water. If you design your foundation properly to deal with wet soil, this won't happen.

Install a reliable method of indicating fan failure. The fan itself probably will be installed in a location where you won't usually see it or hear it. So, install the manometer where you will see it easily.

If that is not practical, have your contractor install an electrical air flow sensor to trigger an alarm if flow stops. The flow sensor can be installed anywhere in the suction side of the vent pipe that is not vulnerable to freezing.

Avoid Freezing and Condensation Damage

A radon venting fan sucks water vapor out of the soil. In cold weather, the water vapor will condense in portions of the radon vent system that are colder than freezing temperature. Enough ice may form to block the vent pipe.

To minimize this risk, keep as much of the radon venting system as possible within the heated portion of the house. In an extremely cold climate, where ice may clog an exposed section of pipe, you can install electric heating tape along the pipe to melt the ice.

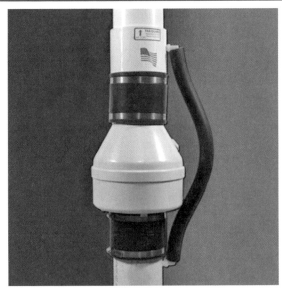

RadonAway

Figure 3-98. A condensate bypass that protects the radon suction fan. The collar fitting above the fan collects any condensate that drains down the inside wall of the pipe. The rubber hose bypasses the condensate around the fan and back to the soil under the house.

Slope all pipe uphill, with no local low points in the pipe. In this way, any condensation that forms inside the pipe will drain back to the soil below the house. If the discharge pipe from the fan is long, condensation that drains back may damage the fan. To prevent this, install a special fitting that bypasses condensate around the fan, as in Figure 3-98.

Avoid "Backdrafting"

The exhaust fan of a radon venting system creates a suction under the slab. If the slab and adjacent walls have leaks into the interior of the house, interior air will be sucked into the radon vent system, creating a reduced pressure inside the house. "Backdrafting" is a word that radon specialists invented to describe this condition.

Backdrafting may create a hazard from carbon monoxide if you have any fuel-fired heating equipment, such as a boiler or water heater, that has a conventional flue. Backdrafting also increases the cost of heating and cooling costs by sucking air out of the house. And, it increases the cost of operating the radon fan itself.

A well built house will not have serious backdrafting, because the interior of the house is isolated from the soil. Indeed, the first defense against backdrafting is to completely seal the underground structure of your house. We will design the understructure of your house to keep out both ground water and radon, so this will also prevent backdrafting.

Backdrafting is most likely to be a hazard if you install a radon vent system in an existing house. In particular, foundations and basement walls built with concrete blocks make it difficult to prevent backdrafting, because the porous nature of concrete blocks makes them a conduit that transmits the suction of the radon system to the interior of the house. Correcting the problem can be tedious, requiring the sealing of many gaps and surfaces.

Step 4 recommends boilers and water heaters that have sealed combustion systems, i.e., their combustion air intakes and their flues are not open to the interior. *Such equipment cannot create a hazard even if backdrafting occurs.* If you select fuel-fired heating equipment, this is one of several reasons to select equipment that has a sealed combustion system.

The suction created by backdrafting is too weak to create a hazard with fuel-fired equipment that is served by their own exhaust fans, such as gas ranges and gas ovens. Also, backdrafting does not interfere with ventilation of toilet rooms and other spaces that are served by exhaust fans.

Use a Sump Pump System for Radon Venting

If the soil of your home site contains underground water, you need to take special steps to drain the water away from your foundation. We cover the details under the later heading, *Drain Underground Water Away from the Foundation*.

If the water cannot be drained downhill by gravity, your home will need a sump pump system. This is similar to a radon venting system. A bed of gravel is laid underneath the floor slab, leading any ground water to drain into a tank, or "sump," that is installed below the floor slab. A pump removes the water from the sump.

A sump pump system is so similar to a radon venting system that you should design it to serve both purposes. Radon in the soil will tend to follow the drainage path for underground water into the sump. However, with an ordinary sump system, the sump is vented to the basement, so it is a major entry point for radon into the house. To keep the radon out of the house, install a sump assembly that has a special airtight cover. The cover should include a pipe fitting that allows it to be connected to a radon vent pipe and fan. Figure 3-99 shows an example.

In an existing house, it is fairly easy to convert a conventional vented sump to a radon venting sump by installing an airtight cover that has the needed pipe fittings, along with airtight electrical connections to the sump pump.

Install a permanent sign on the sump cover to warn occupants that the cover must be kept closed and sealed to keep radon out of the house.

Basement Systems of West Virginia

Figure 3-99. A sump pump that is designed for radon removal. The key difference is that the cover of the pump well is tightly sealed. One pipe discharges the water from the sump, and the other is connected to a radon suction fan. This system has a battery backup for the sump pump.

STEM WALL FOUNDATIONS AND CRAWL SPACES

A common way to build a house is to use a "stem wall" foundation. A stem wall is a short perimeter wall that may be made of poured concrete, concrete blocks, or stone. The purpose of the stem wall is to elevate the wooden lower floor of the house above the soil to protect the floor from rot and insects.

Until about a century ago, most houses were built on stem wall foundations, typically using stone. Figure 3-85 shows a recent stem wall foundation that is built with concrete blocks. Unless the stem wall rests on bedrock, it extends below the frost depth and it has a footing.

The strength of a stem wall foundation depends on the material used. If it is made with steel-reinforced concrete, the stem wall becomes a shear wall, and it is very strong. If the stem wall is made with concrete blocks or stone, it is vulnerable to soil settlement.

A stem wall foundation creates a space between the wooden floor and the ground. This space is called a "crawl space" because it usually is so short that a person must crawl to enter it. A house may have a partial crawl space. This is common with houses that have a split level design.

A crawl space may also be created underneath a short pier foundation, as in Figure 3-90.

In some situations, building over a crawl space is a preferred method of construction, or the only available choice. Such situations include soggy ground, a location that is prone to flooding, soil with a significant radon content, immovable rock, or sloped terrain.

However, building over a crawl space invites trouble. The bottom of the crawl space is bare soil, which allows moisture and radon to approach the house structure from below. For this reason, crawl spaces should be liberally vented to the outside. If a stem wall foundation is used, it must have ample openings to vent moisture and radon, as in Figure 3-85. Generally, more venting is better.

The necessary venting exposes the underside of the house to outdoor temperature and humidity. So, design the floor and the crawl space to prevent condensation damage, air leakage, and radon penetration. Protection against these hazards requires three measures:

1. *Vent the crawl space liberally.*
2. *Make the house floor airtight and vapor-tight.*
3. *Keep moisture and radon from rising out of the ground under the house.*

Even with all three protective measures, a crawl space may be a source of trouble if the climate is persistently warm and humid, or if the ground under the house is wet.

Make the Floor Airtight and Vapor-Tight

If a floor is built over a vented or open space, the floor itself is the primary barrier to air leakage, water vapor, and radon. Therefore, take special care to make the floor airtight. (See the later heading, *Building Exposed Frame Floors.*)

The climate dictates the best way to install the vapor barrier, as with the walls and ceilings. If the climate is predominantly moderate or cold, the floor itself is the only vapor barrier that is needed, and the insulation under the floor is vented directly to the outside. Conversely, if the climate is always warm, install a durable vapor barrier on the underside of the floor joists, enclosing the insulation. In that case, any moisture that gets into the floor structure vents through the floor into the house.

The most difficult case is a climate where the climate has extended periods of both warm and cold weather, especially if the warm weather is humid. We will visit that situation at the end of this discussion.

Don't install any heating or cooling ducts under the house. All ducts are leaky to some extent. An exhaust fan operating anywhere in the house will draw moist air, radon, and mold spores from under the house into any duct leaks. This is one of several reasons why I recommend against any kind of heating or cooling system that uses ducts. (See the sidebar, *Why You Don't Want Central Forced-Air Heating and Cooling*, at the beginning of Step 4.)

Block Moisture from the Ground

Before construction begins, grade the surface under and around the house so that rainwater cannot flow under the house. If necessary, build up the soil so that it is well above any ground water level that may occur. Make the surface slightly domed, so that rain and snow will drain away from the underside of the house.

If the surrounding terrain tends to be wet, such as in marshes and low lying coastal areas, try to build up the surface under the house using soil that is relatively impermeable. "Clay" soil is generally good, if a source is available.

Unless the soil remains dry, lay a durable plastic moisture retarder sheet over the ground below the house and cover it with layer of gravel, oyster shells, or other ballast. The ballast keeps the moisture retarder sheet in place and protects it from the degrading effect of sunlight. The moisture retarder should be a special material that is made for the purpose, not just hardware store polyethylene. Search the Internet for material that meets the appropriate ASTM Standard for ground vapor retarders. Buy material that is thicker than the minimum recommendation, so that it will last longer and resist puncturing during installation.

Don't leave loose soil exposed under the house. Because of the absence of sunlight and moisture, no plants can grow to hold soil in place. Exposed soil would dry into dust and blow away, as well as inviting burrowing animals.

The solution is different if the house is built over sloped terrain, such as a hillside. Build a dam on the uphill side of the house, with a drain channel to divert rainwater around the house. Grade the soil that is under the house to drain any water downhill.

Installing the moisture retarder on sloped ground is difficult because any ballast covering would slide off. If the space under the house is very open and if the ground is dry, it's probably safe to omit the moisture retarder. If the climate remains cool or cold, the higher temperature inside the house helps to protect the floor from condensation. But, if the climate has a wet season, or if ground water wets the soil under the house, secure a moisture retarder sheet to the soil, and expect to replace it every few years because of its exposure to sunlight and physical damage.

Radon Mitigation for Crawl Spaces

If a house must have a crawl space, the primary means of radon protection is to make the crawl space wide open, so that any radon emerging from the soil will be wafted away into the surrounding atmosphere.

A common technique used by builders and radon mitigation contractors is to cover the soil with plastic sheet and install a vent pipe or fan to suck radon from under the sheet, as in Figure 3-100. In operation, this technique is similar to burying radon vent pipes under a concrete floor slab.

For this technique to work well, a layer of clean gravel must be placed over the soil and the suction pipe. The gravel acts as a path for the radon to flow to the vent fan. Buy gravel that is rounded, so that it does not tend to puncture the plastic sheet.

If the plastic sheet is laid directly on the soil, it will collapse tightly against the soil when suction is applied, and radon will escape into the crawl space around the

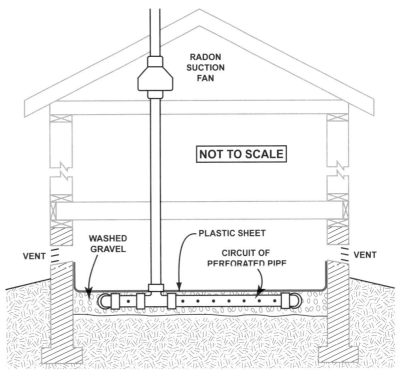

DRW

Figure 3-100. Radon mitigation for a crawl space. The key elements are (1) heavy venting of the crawl space, (2) airtight sealing of the floor structure, (3) a porous gravel bed surrounding the suction pipe, and (4) tight sealing of the plastic sheet. The gravel bed is needed to maintain a path for radon between the soil and the fan. It keeps the plastic sheet from being sucked flat on the soil, which would block the flow of radon to the fan.

edges of the plastic. Neglecting to install a gravel bed is a common mistake, so put the gravel bed on your construction drawings and check that it is installed.

Even with the gravel installed properly, this method is unreliable in the long term. The life of the plastic sheet is a small fraction of the life of the house. Reliable sealing the edges of the sheet is virtually impossible, so radon can leak into the crawl space around the edges and at seams. The plastic sheet is likely to be torn by people or animals entering the crawl space. And, the fan will eventually fail without being noticed.

So, the ultimate defenses against radon in a crawl space must be ample venting of the crawl space and tight sealing of the floor above it.

The same principles apply to an existing house that is built over a crawl space. Test the crawl space for radon. If the level is higher than the outdoor level, take corrective action. If the vents are small, enlarge them. Carefully seal any air leaks in the floor above. Cover the soil with a vapor barrier as effectively as possible. And, if those actions do not lower the radon level completely, install a radon suction system.

Make the Crawl Space Accessible, or Even Useful

Try to avoid creating a crawl space that actually requires crawling. If practical, make the crawl space tall enough so that it is tolerably convenient to install floor insulation, repair pipes, inspect for termites, etc. Also, create a maintenance entrance that is easy for people to use.

Consider raising the house so that the space underneath becomes useful. For example, houses in many coastal locations are elevated to protect against flooding from storms. In such cases, it is common to use the space under the house as a carport or storage area, as in the previous Figure 3-91. The same technique can be used to provide a safe elevation for a house that is built on a flood plain.

Keep Out the Critters

Low crawl spaces are prime living space for a host of animals ranging in size from insects to large furry creatures, such as raccoons. A low crawl space is so attractive that some animals will seek entry aggressively. If you don't want these rude guests, install strong fencing or screens to block the openings.

If a crawl space is tall and very open, it does not provide a safe haven for animals. As a result, most animals larger than insects will not nest there. This eliminates the need for any kind of enclosure or screens.

If your locale has subterranean termites, build the entire crawl space in a way that makes it easy to install termite shields and to inspect for termite tunnels.

Protect the Pipes from Freezing

A crawl space is fully exposed to outdoor temperatures. If the climate has freezing temperatures, minimize the exposure of water and sewer pipes within the crawl space, and protect them from freezing. Unfortunately, there is no completely reliable way to do this. See *Freeze Protection for Your Home Water System*, in Step 5, for the best methods.

Similarly, protect any gas pipe that passes through the crawl space. The gas supply may contain some water, which can freeze and block the gas supply.

BUILDING AN EXPOSED FLOOR IN A HUMID CLIMATE OR OVER WET GROUND

In a climate that is humid, a floor that is built over a vented space invites condensation damage to the lower structure of the house. There is no way to escape this problem. The reason is that the underside of the house receives almost no solar heating, and it faces the cool, shaded soil underneath the house. Especially during the daytime, the underside may be much cooler than the outside air and surroundings. If the relative humidity is high, moisture will condense on the underside, where it will rot the wooden structure and rust iron nails and fittings.

When the inside of the house is cooler than the outside – especially, when using air conditioning – damage can extend more deeply into the structure. Then, water vapor may penetrate through the insulation and condense in the upper part of the floor structure, perhaps creating mildew that infests the floor structure.

When the inside of the house is warmer than the outside, the warmth of the house protects the upper part of the floor structure by lowering the relative humidity there. However, if the floor is well insulated, this protection does not extend to the lowest part of the floor structure.

A vapor barrier that is installed on the underside of the house would protect the floor against condensation during warm weather. However, if the weather turns cold, the vapor barrier will be on the wrong side of the insulation, and moisture will condense on the lower parts of the insulation and floor structure.

If the ground under the house is wet, moisture damage may be greatly accelerated, even in cool weather. Figure 3-101 shows how overwhelming the problem can be. From the end of the warm season until the end of the cold season, the ground is often warmer than the outside air temperature. A large quantity of water can evaporate from wet soil and diffuse to the underside of the house, which is a colder surface. The moisture condenses there and does its damage.

If you can't keep the ground under the house dry, then build the understructure of the house as for a marine environment. Think of the house as being built over water. Build the floor structure with pressure-treated lumber, heavily galvanized nails, and heavily galvanized steel components, such as rebar and joist hangers. And, don't expect the house to survive as long as it would in a dry climate.

The challenge of protecting an exposed floor in a humid environment is so great that we need to consider a compromise with fire safety, which is to insulate the floor by installing impermeable foam insulation board on the underside of the structure. Impermeable insulation acts as its own vapor barrier, so that moisture cannot reach a cold surface. If done properly, this method of insulation could avoid condensation under all weather conditions. At present, extruded polystyrene is the most practical material. Unfortunately, all plastic foam insulation burns in a fire, so I can't recommend this solution with enthusiasm.

DRW

Figure 3-101. Crawl space of a new house built over swampy ground. Plastic sheet was laid over the ground, but water has seeped to the top of the plastic. A house wrap material has been stapled to the underside of the floor. This is exactly the wrong kind of material for the job, because house wrap is intended to be permeable to moisture. Aside from that, the material soon tore loose. Before the house was built, the site should have been graded to drain water away from the foundation.

BUILDING A SUPER-BASEMENT

In Step 1, you decided whether or not to have a basement. If you decided to have one, we will now design it to be top quality living space. Even if you intend to use your basement for informal purposes, such as storage or a workshop, you should design it as if it were going be used as a regular living space.

The basement walls serve as the house's foundation, so they should be designed to satisfy the foundation requirements that we covered previously. To create a perfect a basement, your design should:

1. Withstand soil pressure.

2. Protect the interior from ground water and radon.

3. Insulate the basement walls and floor appropriately for the climate.

Current construction practice often is deficient in dealing with these three issues, so we will emphasize the areas where your design needs to make specific improvements.

BUILD THE BASEMENT WALLS TO WITHSTAND SOIL PRESSURE

A basement is a hole in the ground that is isolated from the surrounding soil by the basement walls. Soil is not a rigid solid, but a fluid that will eventually exert enormous pressure on the basement walls. Because the soil pressure is applied only to the outer sides of the walls, it acts to break the walls inward.

The failure of a basement wall from soil pressure may not occur until long after construction. Because of this, builders may fail to understand how strongly a basement wall must be built.

Fixing a broken foundation wall is expensive and never entirely satisfactory. The cause of this grief is a fundamental fact that builders have not fully absorbed, which is that soil is a fluid.

The Pressure of Soil

Soil is a fluid.

Yes, it's true. Soil is a fluid that flows very slowly, so it's movement is noticeable only over long periods, ranging from months to decades. The flow will continue unless it is stopped by a structure that is strong enough to resist it.

Like an any fluid, soil exerts pressure. But, full pressure does not develop immediately. When you build a basement, the space outside the basement wall is backfilled loosely with soil or gravel. At first, the weight of the backfill is largely self-supporting. But over time, the backfill gradually settles into the space outside the wall like a wedge. Earth tremors, traffic on adjacent roads, walking on the soil, and precipitation shift the soil particles and compact them, causing each particle to push outward on the others.

The ultimate pressure on the wall depends on the weight of the soil and on its depth. Soil weighs about three times more than water, so it eventually exerts a pressure that is about three times greater than the pressure of water at the same depth. For example, at a depth of six feet (two meters) below grade, soil can exert a pressure of 500 pounds per square foot (about 2,500 kilograms per square meter).

Because of this great force, even a shallow wall will eventually be toppled by unbalanced soil pressure if it is inadequately supported, as in Figure 3-103.

In a climate with a cold season, expansion of the soil by freezing may also exert pressure against basement walls. This pressure is applied to the wall from grade level down to the frost line. However, if you follow our recommendations for gravel backfill and foundation drainage, freezing of the soil will not apply pressure directly to the basement wall. Instead, any water coming from the soil will expand into the spaces in the gravel as it freezes.

DRW

Figure 3-103. Soil pressure is powerful, although it acts slowly. Even with limited depth, soil pressure is toppling both sides of this retaining wall. Soil pressure has fractured the wall near the corner, which is typical where unbalanced soil presses against the inside of a corner.

How Soil Pressure Breaks Basement Walls

In centuries past, an underground building foundation was a stack of stones that was wide in relation to its height, and correspondingly heavy. The combination of thickness and weight kept the foundation from toppling over. Such "rubble" foundations (so named because the stones might be built up without much regard to fit) could last indefinitely, as you can see in many old houses. This is because such wide, heavy foundations keep all the stones under compression. Masonry is strong and happy when it is compressed.

However, rubble foundation walls are leaky and unattractive, and they require a large amount of stone. In modern times, they have been replaced by thinner basement walls that use far less material and are quicker to build. Unfortunately, thinner underground walls are vulnerable to breakage in ways that did not endanger rubble walls.

A thin (i.e., modern) basement wall can fail in two general ways. One is that soil pressure can push it over, or topple it, as illustrated dramatically in Figure 3-103. Another way that thin basement walls fail is by bulging inward, or buckling. The outer face of the wall is always under compression, but if soil pressure increases past a certain point, the wall bends inward and the inner surface comes under tension. Masonry alone does not have reliable tensile strength, so the inner surface cracks, and the cracks spread across the wall. The broken wall can now buckle inward.

A wall that is being tipped inward by soil pressure will tend to break near grade level, separating from the portion of the wall above grade level. A wall that is being buckled by soil pressure will tend to break at a lower level, where the pressure is greatest. However, a concrete floor slab resists the pressure effectively, which is an important structural role for the floor slab. That is why buckling generally starts at some level between the floor slab and grade level. From examining many basement wall failures, it appears that both modes of failure are common.

Basement walls that are built with concrete blocks are especially prone to failure. Almost all the basement wall failures that I have seen involved concrete block walls. A concrete block wall is essentially a stack of loose blocks, with the mortar acting mainly as a filler. Mortar joints have virtually no tensile strength, and neither do the blocks themselves. It is mainly the weight of the house that holds a block wall together. If the wall is too far below grade level, or if the wall is too thin, or if the house structure is light, the soil pressure will eventually push the blocks inward.

Also, as we discussed previously, concrete block foundations are weak in general, with little resistance to cracking if the soil under the foundation settles or collapses.

How to Design Strong Basement Walls

As we mentioned previously, it's not your job to be an expert about the technical aspects of concrete work. However, when it comes to basement wall design, there are still myths and misunderstandings that may undermine (literally) the quality of your basement walls, which are also the foundation of your house.

So, we will cover a number of issues about the strength of your basement walls that you should discuss with your builder and spell out in your construction drawings (which you will get made in Step 8). In case of doubt, hire an appropriate engineer to check your basement wall design.

What kind of basement walls should you have? The answer usually is easy and certain. By far the best way to withstand soil pressure is to build the underground portions of your basement walls using steel-reinforced poured concrete. Build your basement walls as a shear wall foundation, using the methods that we discussed previously.

I cannot imagine any situation where it would be advisable to build a basement wall with concrete blocks. Reinforced concrete is greatly superior in strength, and it is a much better barrier to water and radon.

How thick should a reinforced concrete basement wall be? The thickness of concrete needed in a basement wall depends on the height of the soil that creates an unbalanced pressure on the wall. In practice, that height is the distance from the floor slab to the grade level outside the wall.

If you ask builders in North America, most probably would say that 8" (20 cm) is an appropriate thickness for a reinforced concrete wall. And in many cases, that is a good number. It assumes that the basement wall is no more than 8 feet (240 cm) tall, and that the portion of the wall that is exposed to soil pressure is even shorter.

However, the strength of your basement walls is critical, and concrete is expensive. So, base the wall thickness on a reliable authority, such as the tables in the *International Residential Code* (IRC). There is a tradeoff between the wall thickness and the amount of steel reinforcement. The IRC contains tables that specify how your builder can make this tradeoff. In case of doubt, make the walls thicker.

If the wall has a brick shelf, a common practice is to increase the thickness of the wall to support the brick shelf. The typical width of brick is 4" (10 cm), including the mortar joint. So, if the wall thickness would otherwise be 8" (20 cm), the total wall thickness then becomes 12" (30 cm). This adds a lot of concrete, so it usually makes more sense to narrow the top of the wall to provide space for the brick shelf. For example, if the wall adjacent to the brick shelf is 6" (15 cm) wide, the wall below the brick shelf becomes 10" (25 cm) wide.

If your house will have concrete block walls above grade, the top of the basement wall (not including any brick shelf) should be at least as wide as the concrete blocks.

However, it is not necessary to make the foundation wall as thick as a super-insulated frame wall. That's because only the outer part of our super-insulated wall design carries the weight of the structure. (We will explain this under the heading, *Fabricated Wall Studs for Colder Climates*.)

How should the rebar be installed? The key to resisting soil pressure is to give the wall tensile strength on its inside surface. Remember that concrete itself is strong only in compression, and steel reinforcement is needed to resist tension. The stress that tends to break the wall occurs at the inner surfaces of the large, flat central portions of the wall, and at the top edge. Therefore, in these areas, *the concrete contractor should place the rebar toward the inside surface of the wall*.

The rebar that is located in the central portions of the wall should be installed diagonally, for the reasons explained when we discussed shear wall foundations. The diagonal orientation braces the wall both vertically and horizontally. To resist buckling from soil pressure, the wall needs vertical bracing. To resist bowing, the wall needs horizontal bracing.

At the bottom of the wall, the builder should install horizontal rebar near the center of the wall thickness. This is to strengthen the wall against settlement of the soil underneath the footing. The rebar in the footing performs the same function. However, if the wall is poured separately from the footing (the usual practice), the wall itself needs reinforcement along its bottom edge.

At the corners, bend rebar into right angles and place it horizontally inside the wall to keep the corners intact.

Some concrete contractors know how to exploit the strength of rebar most effectively, and some don't. The main point is to locate the rebar strategically at the places where the tensile load on the concrete is greatest.

Does the distance between corners matter? Yes, it does. A wall cannot tip inward at a corner, but it can do so between corners. So, the top of the wall tends to bow inward horizontally between the corners. This tendency increases with the distance between the corners.

One solution is to make the wall thicker for greater distances between corners. Unfortunately, the *International Residential Code* does not seem to recognize this issue, so it does not relate wall thickness to the distance between corners.

Another solution is to add more corners to the basement wall. We'll discuss that next.

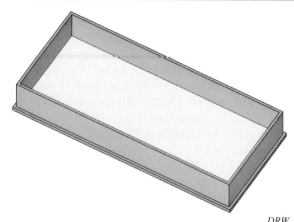

DRW

Figure 3-104. A rectangular shear wall foundation provides excellent protection against irregular settling of soil under the footing. However, the long walls are susceptible to toppling by soil pressure from the side.

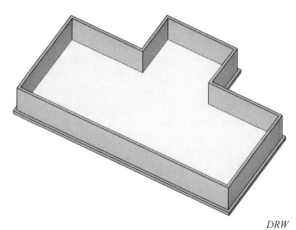

DRW

Figure 3-105. Adding corners shortens the length of the wall segments and buttresses them against both toppling and buckling. However, the wall is no longer a continuous beam from one end of the house to the other, which somewhat increases susceptibility to soil settling under the footing.

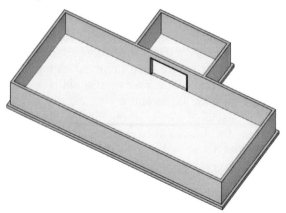

DRW

Figure 3-106. A basement wall design that combines the strengths of the previous two designs. The long wall is still a continuous beam, with a continuous footing below the opening and a header above it.

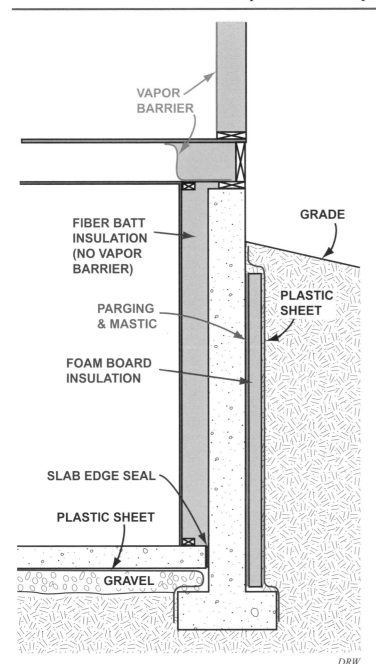

VAPOR BARRIER

FIBER BATT INSULATION (NO VAPOR BARRIER)

PARGING & MASTIC

FOAM BOARD INSULATION

SLAB EDGE SEAL

PLASTIC SHEET

GRAVEL

GRADE

PLASTIC SHEET

DRW

Figure 3-107. Protection of a basement from water and radon in the soil, in a location where ground water is not a problem. The exterior and interior basement wall insulation is appropriate for a cold climate.

■ Add Corners to Strengthen Basement Walls

Previously, we observed that soil pressure may cause a basement wall to fail by tipping the wall inward or by pushing through it (buckling). You can strengthen your walls against both kinds of failure by adding more corners to the walls.

A basement wall is flat, which is a shape that does not resist soil pressure efficiently. By building corners into the footprint of the house, we can stiffen the basement walls, as shown in Figures 3-104, 3-105, and

3-106. The additional corners strengthen a wall in two ways. They brace the wall, and they reduce the length of the individual wall segments.

To see how well this works, use a sheet of paper as a model for a basement wall. Make some folds in the paper, as in Figure 3-105, and you will see how dramatically the corners stiffen the sheet.

Corners may also provide an appearance enhancement for the house by breaking up large, flat wall surfaces, as we recommended in Step 1.

Can you make a basement wall thinner if you add corners or other kinds of buttressing? We don't know. The *International Residential Code* does not recognize corners as a factor in wall thickness. If a basement wall is exceptionally long, buttress it in some reliable fashion, preferably with corners. Otherwise, simply follow the thickness requirements of the building code.

KEEP OUT WATER AND RADON

As we discussed previously, under *Water in the Soil*, basements need protection from water in the surrounding soil. The water comes from rain that soaks into the soil and from underground sources ("ground water").

The goal is not just to keep water out of the interior of the basement, but to keep the entire underground structure dry. Water that penetrates the wall can freeze and crack the concrete. Water will rust the steel reinforcements, causing them to swell and crack the concrete. If water continually seeps through a wall and then evaporates, the concrete will become powdery and weak in the wet areas.

Homebuilders should know how to protect basements from underground water, but actual building practice often is deficient. The principles and methods are easy to understand. The key points are:

1. ***Make your walls, foundation, and floor slab resistant to water penetration.***
2. ***Grade the soil around the house to shed rainwater and snowmelt away from the house.***
3. ***If there is underground water near the basement level, drain it away from the foundation.***

Blocking water entry into your basement also blocks radon. Coordinate your moisture protection features with the "radon mitigation" features that we covered earlier.

Figures 3-107 and 3-108 summarize the main features that we will discuss for protecting your basement against water and radon. The Figures also show the basement insulation, because water protection and insulation are done together.

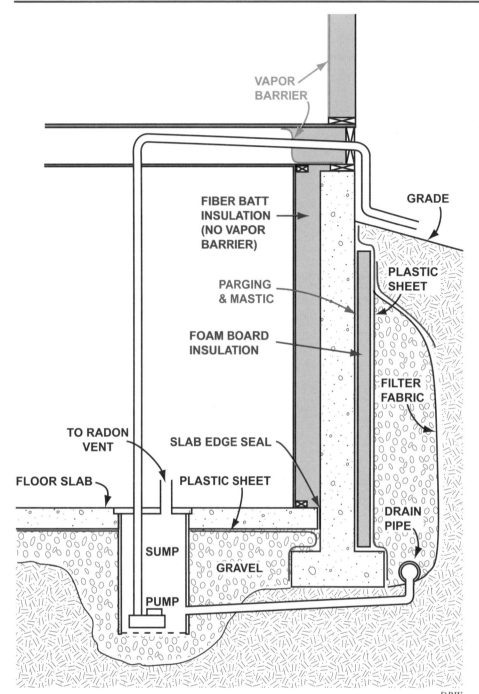

DRW

Figure 3-108. Protection of a basement from water and radon in the soil, in a location where ground water exists at or near the basement level. The footing drain may empty to lower terrain, if low surrounding terrain is available. Otherwise, the drain must empty into a sump system, as shown here. The exterior and interior basement wall insulation is appropriate for a cold climate.

(1) Waterproof the Underground Surfaces

Water can seep into the basement through crevices in the basement walls and the floor slab, and through the joints between them. Water can also penetrate slowly through an intact wall and floor slab, eventually soaking them.

Therefore, the first step in keeping your basement dry and free of radon is to cover the entire underground surface of your walls and floor with an impermeable layer, making your basement like a boat hull. Design this waterproof barrier to last for the life of the house.

(You can buy "waterproofing" paint that is applied to the inside surface of a basement wall. Such paint is worse than useless. It dams water inside the wall structure, damaging the wall. The only desirable way to keep water out of a basement is to block it on the outer sides of the walls and the floor slab.)

At this time, the best impermeable surface is polyethylene plastic sheet, at least 8 mils (0.2 mm) thick. It is available in very wide sheets, and it is easy to install. But, it is fragile. The tradesmen must be careful to avoid puncturing the plastic during all the activity involved in building the basement. The quality of this material varies, and you want the best available. Search the Internet for material that meets the appropriate ASTM standard for "underground moisture retarder." Make sure that your builder uses this material.

Sealing between adjacent sheets of plastic is important to prevent water penetration. Overlap the sheets generously, fold them over, and use tape to hold them in position. The soil and gravel outside the walls will hold the water barrier and the insulation in place after the completed foundation is backfilled.

Make sure that the critical details are included in your construction drawings. Your builder might think that you are going overboard in your zeal to create a perfect basement, but don't be dissuaded. Good waterproofing creates a basement that is dry and cozy. Inadequate waterproofing will leave you with a basement that is infested with mildew and undesirable as a living space.

Wrap the plastic sheet tightly around all pipes and conduit that enter the house from below grade. Secure the plastic to the pipes with strong strapping tape. The concrete walls and the floor slab will maintain these seals after the concrete is poured.

To cover the exterior surface of the wall, make the wall smooth by hammering off any protrusions from the surface. Fill any holes (usually, from air bubbles in the concrete) with a reliable patching material.

(On concrete block walls, a thick coat of cement is applied to the entire underground surface. This process is called "parging." It compensates for the porous nature of concrete block and mortar joints. But, you don't want to use concrete block for any underground application.)

Then, apply a thick coating of waterproofing "mastic" to the outside surface. Attach the exterior insulation board over the mastic.

Finally, apply another coat of mastic over the insulation board, and cover the insulation board with the polyethylene sheet. Select a mastic that has a long underground life and that is harmless to the insulation and to the plastic sheet.

Before pouring the concrete floor slab, install a flexible sealing strip between the floor slab and the foundation wall. The seal should be as deep as the thickness of the slab. The purpose of the sealing strip is to allow the floor slab to rest on the earth below, independently of the foundation walls or footing. This allows the soil to settle under the house without creating stresses in the floor slab that would eventually crack it.

The floor slab is laid over a bed of gravel. Plastic sheet is laid on the gravel before the concrete is poured. At this point, there is a great danger of puncturing the plastic by the gravel and by the reinforcing steel as the contractors walk over the surface. Make sure that your concrete contractor takes pains to protect the plastic sheet.

(2) Divert Surface Runoff Away from the Basement

All basements are threatened by water that enters the soil from the surface, either from rain or from melting snow. The solution is simple, at least in principle. It is to establish a slope away from the house on all sides. The slope should drain away to terrain that is below the level of the footing, or to a storm drain.

This protection begins when you select your building site, as explained previously under the heading, *Surface Water Drainage*. Use the topography to drain rain away from your house. If the topography is not favorable for this, you will have to spend money for earthmoving to create satisfactory local drainage. If you are building near a steep slope, this may include an expensive retaining wall.

Wide roof overhangs are an effective way of keeping basement walls dry. Design yours to be as wide as possible, consistent with your architectural style and the other benefits that overhangs provide. (For a reminder of those benefits, see *Exploit Roof Overhangs*, in Step 1.)

After the foundation is completed, build up the soil around the house to create a slope that is away from the house at all points, preferably for a distance of several yards (several meters). We covered this under the previous heading, *The Height of Your Foundation*.

As we mentioned in the same place, your gutters play an important role in keeping the soil around your house dry. Arrange them and their downspouts to convey rain away from the house as effectively as possible.

There is another reason to keep the soil around the house as dry as possible. If the surface soil is soaked with moisture, or if it freezes, it becomes a cap that blocks the escape of radon from the soil into the atmosphere. With that path blocked, the radon has a greater tendency to enter the house.

(3) Drain Underground Water Away from the Basement

Virtually all terrain contains a source of water at some depth. That's why you can usually get water from a well, if you drill deep enough. However, such underground water sources do not threaten your basement unless the water level approaches the level of your footing, or worse, is above the footing level.

A large fraction of home sites are free of shallow ground water, and the soil allows any water in the soil to percolate down to a depth that is safely below the foundation. In such locations, it suffices to create a waterproof barrier for the basement, as we described previously. Any surface water that soaks into the soil will bypass the basement on its way downward.

So, the first step in protecting the basement from underground water is to determine the depth of the ground water. We covered this earlier, under the heading *Water in the Soil*. After you determine the shallowest depth of the ground water at your home site with certainty, you will know whether or not your foundation needs a drainage system.

If your home site does have ground water at or near the foundation level, you need a drainage system to get rid of it. We said that you should waterproof a basement like the hull of a boat. In reality, you won't be able to waterproof your basement that well. Ground water is pressurized by the weight of the soil above it. If the water reaches the foundation under pressure, it is very penetrating.

A foundation drain should remove ground water before it reaches the level of the basement floor. Preferably, it should also remove water before it rises to the level of the footing, although this is not always practical. This is done by surrounding the footing with a ring of perforated drainage pipe, as in Figure 3-109.

DRW

Figure 3-109. Gravity drain for the outside of a basement wall. Water can flow by gravity to lower terrain surrounding the house. This installation shows some common defects. The pipe should be installed alongside the footing, rather than resting on top of it. The backfill should be entirely clean gravel, but mud has already fallen on top of the drain pipe, restricting future drainage into the pipe. This common type of drain pipe is flimsy.

Use thick-wall perforated pipe instead of the flimsy pipe that is commonly used. The cheap pipe would eventually collapse under soil pressure. Connect the pipe sections with proper pipe fittings. Don't leave the adjacent ends of the pipe open, as is the common practice, because this allows the pipe to fill with gravel and dirt. Slope the pipes all around the foundation toward a common discharge point.

The pipe is covered with gravel, which also separates the basement wall from the surrounding soil. The gravel acts as a passage that conveys any water in the soil to the pipe. The key point here is that you

should use gravel to backfill around the foundation, not the soil that was excavated to create the basement. Use the original soil elsewhere to grade your lot, or truck it away.

The empty spaces in the gravel act as a drain between the soil and the foundation. The spaces are important, not the gravel itself. Therefore, the gravel should be fairly large and rounded, to maximize the size of the spaces. Specify gravel that is washed. If dirty gravel is used to backfill the foundation, water that flows through the gravel will wash the dirt loose, and the dirt will plug the drainage path.

Similarly, as ground water flows out of the soil and into the gravel, it will carry soil into the gravel. To minimize this, install "filter fabric" or "filter cloth" between the soil and the gravel, as in Figure 3-108. Initially, this will allow the water to drain into the gravel, while blocking the soil. After a period of time, the filter fabric will become plugged with soil, and it will block both soil and ground water.

Therefore, it is important to install the filter fabric so that it directs ground water away from the foundation. To make this work properly, grade the top surface of the gravel so that the top surface of the filter fabric slopes away from the wall. As the final touch, cover the top of the gravel with plastic sheet to divert water away from the wall.

Now, what happens to ground water after it flows into the drain pipes? If water merely accumulates at the bottom of the foundation, a foundation drain is useless. The drain pipes and gravel around the foundation are only the first part of an effective drain system. The water in the pipe and the gravel bed must be removed, either by gravity or by a sump pump.

■ Using a Gravity Drain

A gravity drain is the simplest and most reliable way to drain ground water from a foundation. It consists of one or more pipes that connect the foundation drain to lower terrain surrounding the house, where the ground water is discharged above grade or into a storm drain. Figure 3-109 is an example.

Unfortunately, most houses can't use a gravity drain. The problem is that water flows only downhill. In order for a gravity drain to work, the footing must be located above some adjacent terrain. You need to own adjacent property that is below the level of your foundation drain, or you need a permanent right of way to drain on someone else's downhill property. This favorable situation occurs only if your house is built on a slope or near a slope.

All the drain pipes must be sloped continuously downward. And, the pipes must not collapse during the life of the house. If the pipes collapse or become clogged, the basement will be surrounded by a pool of water.

■ Using a Sump Pump

What if your home site does not allow a foundation drain to empty by gravity? In that case, your basement needs a sump pump system. Figure 3-108 shows how it is installed.

A boat needs a bilge pump to expel water that leaks through the hull. Similarly, a basement that is surrounded by ground water needs a pump to get rid of water that cannot drain by gravity. In houses, the bilge pump is called a "sump pump." The "sump" is a pit that you create under the floor slab, serving the same purpose as the bilge in a boat. It is a collecting point for water that seeps into the foundation drain system and into the space below the basement floor slab.

The sump pump must be accessible for maintenance, so the sump usually is installed in the basement floor. Since the foundation drain is on the outside of the wall, a connecting pipe must pass through the foundation wall, or under the footing, to connect the foundation drain with the sump.

The sump is a small round tank that typically is installed to a depth of several feet (about one meter) below the basement floor. The sump is surrounded by the gravel that is installed below the floor slab. The bottom of the sump is open to the gravel, allowing water below the slab to flow into the sump. Also, the bottom of the sump must lie below the level of the foundation drain pipe, so that the foundation drainage will flow toward the sump.

A float-activated pump is installed inside the sump to remove the water that accumulates, like the bilge pump of a boat. Typically, the sump pump discharges to the ground outside, which must be sloped away from the house. The sump pump could also drain to a storm sewer, if one is accessible nearby. But, a sump pump should not discharge into a sanitary sewer.

A conventional sump system is potentially a dangerous entry for radon, because it collects radon in the same way that it collects ground water. If the sump is vented into the basement, any radon in the soil or ground water will enter the basement.

Fortunately, you can easily turn this liability into an asset by making the sump pump a part of your radon venting system, as we previously discussed under the heading, *Use a Sump Pump System for Radon Venting*. This is a primary issue in your radon protection, so don't overlook it when you design your foundation drainage.

If your basement could flood during an extended power outage, consider a sump pump with a battery backup, which is now widely available.

Some houses use a sump system that drains only from beneath the floor slab, and not from a drain outside the foundation. This is false economy. If water can accumulate under the floor slab, it will also back up around the outside of the basement wall and cause a wet basement.

INSULATING THE BASEMENT

Insulating a basement is different from insulating the rest of the house. In a climate with a cold season, a basement should have insulation both inside the living space and buried outside the basement wall, and perhaps under the floor slab.

The exterior insulation for the basement wall is installed together with the exterior waterproofing. It is installed by the masons who build the basement wall or by the contractor who installs the exterior waterproofing.

The exterior basement wall insulation ends slightly below grade level. An exception is a house that has masonry walls with exterior insulation. In that case, the exterior insulation extends all the way up to the roof.

The interior insulation is installed later, after the basement walls and the floor slab are finished. The interior insulation usually is installed by the carpenters or by the people who install the insulation in the rest of the house.

A good doctrine of basement insulation has not yet been adopted by the homebuilding industry. Therefore, we will cover the critical design issues.

R-Value Recommendations

Use the *Insulation Worksheet* to calculate the appropriate R-values for your basement insulation. Assume that the basement will be used as living space, and insulate it accordingly. As a minimum, insulate the outside of the walls, which must be done as the basement is built. If you plan to leave the basement unfinished initially, you can add interior wall insulation later.

The Insulation Must Vent Moisture Into the Basement

A small amount of water will find a way to leak into any basement wall or floor slab. The only way to get rid of water in the below-grade portions of the basement walls and floor slab is to allow it to evaporate into the basement. Your basement design should facilitate this evaporation. Remember that water causes problems only when it is in the liquid state.

To allow moisture to vent through the interior wall insulation, use glass or mineral fiber insulation, which is permeable to water vapor. By the same token, do not use any vapor barriers on the inside of the basement walls. Avoid any waterproof paint or other impermeable material.

Any water in the underground portion of a concrete foundation or wall – especially if it is built with concrete block – tends to wick upward into the above-grade portion of the concrete. To get rid of moisture from the above-grade portions of basement walls, design the walls to allow the moisture to vent both to the inside and to the outside. Do not cover the above-grade portions of basement walls, either inside or outside, with anything that acts as a vapor barrier.

Allowing moisture to evaporate into the basement is only half the battle. The other half is getting the moisture out of the basement, or keeping it from condensing. Step 4 explains how to do both.

Insulation Outside the Basement Underground Wall

In any climate with a cold season, insulating the outside surface of the underground basement wall provides several advantages. Exterior insulation keeps the wall warm, so any water that seeps into the wall does not freeze. The greater warmth of the wall helps to turn water into vapor, so it will not cause water damage by the time it emerges into the basement. Exterior insulation that extends below the level of floor slab insulates the slab from heat loss to the colder soil surrounding the house.

Figure 3-107 shows how the outside of a basement wall is insulated if the soil surrounding the basement is does not have ground water. Figure 3-108 shows additional requirements for installing the insulation if the soil has ground water.

There is no insulation material that is perfect for underground use. The best available today is "extruded polystyrene" foam board. It has high insulation value and it is reasonably economical. Most important, it has the best resistance to moisture penetration among the various types of foam board insulation.

Don't confuse *extruded* polystyrene, usually the best choice, with *expanded* polystyrene, which is often called "beadboard." The latter is a cheaper type of insulation, which is also used for making disposable items, such as coffee cups. It is vulnerable to moisture penetration, and it crumbles.

Use a specific brand of insulation that is certified by a responsible independent organization for underground use. Even extruded polystyrene does not pass muster in all locations. For example, in locations with termites, the insulation may require additives to repel the insects.

The R-values (RSI) that you calculate with the *Insulation Worksheet* determine the thickness of the insulation. Get tongue-and-groove insulation boards, which provide a tighter seal against water leakage.

The builder should make the exterior insulation fit snugly against the basement wall. If water gets between the insulation and the wall, the only place for it to go is into the wall. As we advised previously, make the wall flat before you install the insulation board by knocking off any concrete or mortar that protrudes from the wall. Then, apply a thick coating of waterproofing "mastic" to the outside surface. Stick the insulation board to the wall with the mastic, and use the mastic to seal the joints between the boards. If you use more than one layer of insulation board, stagger the joints.

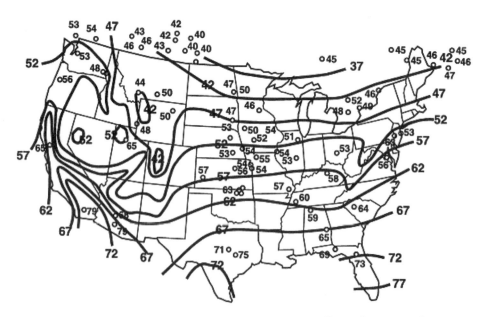

Virginia Department of Mines, Minerals, and Energy

Figure 3-111. Soil temperatures at a depth of 30 feet [MF] (9 meters), for the continental United States and southern Canada, in degrees Fahrenheit. These temperatures remain essentially constant. Rising closer to the surface, the soil temperatures increasingly vary with the seasons.

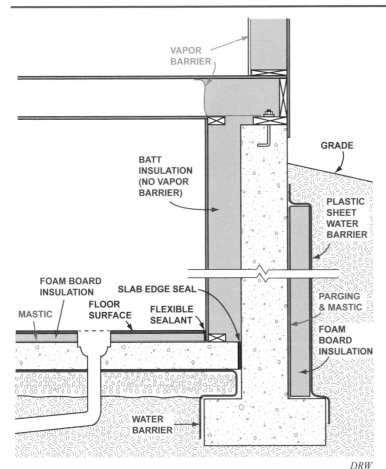

DRW

Figure 3-112. Basement floor insulation placed above the slab. Every basement should have a floor drain for the occasional flooding that will occur, and the floor should be sloped toward the drain.

Mastic that uses organic solvents will attack the insulation and the plastic sheet. Therefore, your builder needs to select a mastic that does not attack the insulation or the plastic sheet that will cover it. Talk to your builder about this. If necessary, do the research to find the right product.

All plastic foam insulation is permeable to moisture over the long term, so cover the outside of the insulation board with polyethylene sheet, as advised previously. If there is ground water in the surrounding soil, the insulation must be protected from waterlogging by a foundation drainage system.

The exterior basement wall insulation usually ends slightly below grade level. Terminating the insulation below grade protects the top of the insulation from damage by lawnmowers and other impacts, and it offers a better appearance. Also, soil pressure helps to hold the insulation against the wall, so that a gap will not form at the top of the insulation that would admit rain and allow heat loss by convection.

Additionally, wide roof overhangs help to keep rain from penetrating behind the insulation.

Generally, extend the exterior insulation all the way down to the top of the footing, even if the footing is well below the frost line. If the foundation is deep, specify insulation that is rated to support the maximum soil pressure.

Don't install insulation below the footing. The footing must rest on solid soil.

Insulating the Basement Floor

A basement floor slab is a large surface, so its temperature tends to dominate the temperature of the basement. A concrete slab has virtually no insulation value, so an uninsulated basement floor will approach the temperature of the soil underneath the house. If your house is located in a colder climate, insulate the basement floor slab, as well as the walls. This improves comfort and helps to avoid mildew.

Whether to insulate the basement floor slab depends primarily on the temperature of the deep soil under your house. This temperature tends toward an annual average of the above-ground temperature for that location. The deep soil temperature varies little with the seasons, unlike the temperature of the shallow soil surrounding the house. Figure 3-111 is a map of deep soil temperatures for the United States and lower Canada.

■ Method 1: Insulation Above the Floor Slab

If the climate makes it desirable to insulate the basement floor, one method is to install the insulation on top of the slab, as shown in Figure 3-112. This method is the most comfortable because the floor insulation joins the interior wall insulation, creating an unbroken blanket of insulation surrounding the space. It is the most energy efficient because it does not waste energy heating the soil below the slab. And, it avoids the potential cracking of the slab that may occur with under-slab insulation.

I usually recommend against any kind of plastic foam insulation inside a house. However, the fire hazard of foam board lying directly on a concrete slab is small.

The top surface of the insulation must be protected from floor traffic. For example, you can get foam board insulation that is laminated to plywood, which can serve as a base for the finish flooring, such as carpet.

This method of insulating a basement floor can be done at any time after the house is built. And, it works well for existing houses.

However, basements are vulnerable to flooding from clogged drains, corroded water pipes, broken appliance hoses, etc. Insulation and flooring that is installed above the slab is a mess to dry out if it floods. This makes it especially important to install floor drains

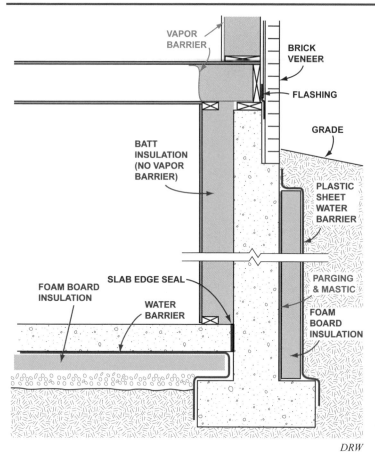

VAPOR BARRIER

BRICK VENEER

FLASHING

GRADE

BATT INSULATION (NO VAPOR BARRIER)

PLASTIC SHEET WATER BARRIER

FOAM BOARD INSULATION

SLAB EDGE SEAL

WATER BARRIER

PARGING & MASTIC

FOAM BOARD INSULATION

DRW

Figure 3-113. Basement floor insulation placed below the slab. To minimize stresses that would crack the slab, the entire underside of the slab should rest on the same thickness of insulation. For the same reason, the edge of the slab should not rest on the footing. The figure also shows how a brick veneer is built on a "brick shelf" in the foundation wall.

in the basement, and to slope the basement floor toward the drains.

This method keeps the slab cold, so any moisture that gets underneath the floor insulation will condense on the top surface of the slab. Water below the insulation will infest the slab surface with mildew. Therefore, it is important to attach the insulation to the floor slab with an unbroken coat of waterproof mastic. Also, the gap between the floor insulation and the walls should be sealed with a flexible sealant, such as silicone.

■ Method 2: Insulation Underneath the Floor Slab

Another method of insulating a basement floor is to place the insulation under the floor slab, as shown in Figure 3-113. This must be done as the basement floor is being built, immediately before the slab is poured.

If you decide to insulate the slab from underneath, install the same thickness of insulation under the entire floor slab, not just under the perimeter. There are two reasons to insulate the entire floor. One is that the entire slab suffers heat loss to the deep soil.

The other reason is that limiting under-slab insulation to the perimeter of the floor risks cracking the floor slab. You are building your house to last for several centuries, but plastic foam insulations have unknown longevity. At some point in the future, the insulation will weaken. If the entire slab has the same cushion of insulation, the slab can settle uniformly. However, if only the perimeter of the slab is supported by insulation, the perimeter of the slab will lose support as the insulation deteriorates. With the rest of the slab resting on firm soil, the slab will tend to crack along the inner edge of the insulation.

At present, extruded polystyrene is the best insulation to use under a floor slab. It is the same type of material recommended for exterior wall insulation. It is available in various densities. Select an appropriate density to support the weight of the slab and the load on top of it.

Insulating the Interior of Basement Walls

The best insulation for the interior of the basement wall is glass or mineral fiber, in the form of batts or fiberboard. It has superior fire safety and it allows free venting of moisture from the wall into the basement. Select the appropriate R-values by using the *Insulation Worksheet*.

Do not use any vapor barriers with interior basement insulation, as this would prevent moisture from venting into the basement. By the same token, avoid impermeable interior finishes, including thick coats of paint.

■ Method 1: Batts on Framework

This method of insulation allows for virtually any desired R-value to be installed. It provides secure support for batt insulation. It also provides secure support for any desired interior surface finish, such as drywall. It provides a good way to extend basement window openings into the living space. And, it creates a well protected channel at the bottom of the wall for electrical and communications wiring.

Begin by erecting a wooden framework inside the masonry wall, similar to an ordinary stud wall, as in Figure 3-114. The framework attaches to the floor and to the ceiling, not to the masonry wall. The framework typically uses 2-by-4 lumber, which is 3.5" (87 mm) deep, regardless of the thickness of the insulation that is used.

Use pressure-treated lumber at least for the bottom member that rests on the floor slab. In an existing house that may have basement wall leakage, it is prudent to use pressure-treated lumber for all the framing that is below grade level.

DRW

Figure 3-114. Framework for installing batt insulation against a masonry wall. The batts are held by friction between the studs, the wall, and the finish surface. You can accommodate any insulation thickness by adjusting the distance of the framework from the wall. The water supply pipe under the window should have been extended to the inside of the insulated wall to avoid freezing.

If the climate requires only a single layer of batt insulation, leave a minimum gap between the framework and the concrete wall to keep any moisture in the wall from contacting the lumber.

If the climate is colder, locate the framework inward and use two layers of batts. First, install one layer *horizontally* between the framework and the wall, snugly filling the gap. Then, install batts *vertically* within the framework, as in a stud wall. This eliminates any gaps or air leakage between the batts or between the batts and the framework.

For example, assume that the *Insulation Worksheet* recommends 5.5" (14 cm) of batt insulation for the basement. Install the framework 2" (5 cm) from the wall. Then, install one layer of 2" (5 cm) thick batts horizontally between the framework and the wall. Next, install 3.5" (87 mm) thick batts vertically within the framework.

Attach the framing for any windows and doors to the wall openings, and extend the framing inward to connect with the insulation framework and the interior finish surface. And finally, attach the interior finish surface to the framework.

■ Method 2: Rigid Fiberboard

If only a limited thickness of insulation is needed, you can use rigid glass or mineral fiberboard insulation instead of batts. This method eliminates the need for a wood frame.

The previous Figure 3-39 shows the method. As a practical matter, this method is limited to the thickest fiberboard insulation that is available, which may be about 4" (10 cm).

The fiberboard attaches directly to the masonry wall with special fasteners. It should contact the masonry wall snugly. The fiberboard can be covered with any porous decorative material, such as fabric.

Before installing the fiberboard, make sure that the surface of the wall is flat and free of protrusions, such as mortar hanging out of the wall.

You may be able to buy fiberboard that is bonded to a porous finish surface, such as gypsum board. Porous interior finishes generally have no resistance to moisture damage or mildew, so your basement must be designed to keep the interior finish absolutely dry.

In mild and predominantly cold climates, install the interior insulation at the same thickness from top to bottom.

In a predominantly warm or hot climate, install the interior insulation only from the top of the basement wall to a short distance below grade level. The insulation blocks heat entry above grade, while the lack of insulation below grade allows the surrounding soil to keep the basement cool.

BUILDING PERFECT FRAME FLOORS

Having designed the foundation, we now continue the design upward. The next component is the frame floors. You will be using "platform construction" for your wooden floors, as shown in Figures 3-16 through 3-20. Each floor consists of a grid of parallel "joists" that are surrounded by a frame of "rim joists." The top surface of the floor is plywood, which is rigidly attached to the joists. The resulting box structure is strong and versatile. And, it is easy to run wiring, pipe, and duct between and through the joists.

If you have a basement and if you will be using frame wall construction, your first wooden floor will rest on top of the basement wall. If your above-grade walls will be masonry, they continue upward from the foundation, and wooden floors are set into the walls.

(If your home will have totally concrete construction, including the floors, you can skip this whole discussion.)

WOODEN I-JOIST, A MATERIAL YOU NEED TO UNDERSTAND

Until a few centuries ago, the floor joists of most houses consisted of logs. The top surfaces of the logs were leveled with an adze to make the floor moderately flat. Later, sawmills allowed logs to be cut into rectangular lumber. Floor joists could now be cut to identical dimensions, greatly improving the flatness of floors.

By the 20th century, lumber dimensions became standardized. To use timber most efficiently, floor joists became narrow and deep, essentially thick boards

Universal Forest Products
Figure 3-117. Construction of I-joist. The top and bottom "flanges" may be made of solid wood or a long stranded composite. The "web" that joins them may be plywood or an inferior material made of glued wood fragments.

placed on edge. In the U.S., a joist width of 1½" (37 mm) became standard. The depth of joists became standardized in increments. In the U.S., nominal dimensions of "2-by-8" and "2-by-10" became prevalent for floor joists, with a standard spacing of 16 inches.

Even with these advances, solid wood floor joists still have weaknesses. As lumber dries, it warps and shrinks. Knots located near the edges of joists weaken them. If a builder is not careful in selecting and placing lumber joists, the floor will be irregular and it will have local weak spots. Gaps between the joists and the floor surface cause squeaks and creaks.

The cost of solid joists has risen as trees big enough to provide solid joists become scarce. At the same time, houses have increased in size, requiring joists that are longer and deeper. In large sizes, solid lumber joists are heavy and difficult to handle.

The lumber industry has responded by offering various designs of fabricated floor joists that use less lumber, keep their shape better, and can be made in greater lengths. In house construction, one clear winner has emerged in the competition between these designs. The winner is the wooden I-beam, which is now used widely for floor joists and as roof rafters.

Wooden I-beams are commonly called "I-joists." Because of their composite construction, I-joists stay straight, creating an exceptionally flat floor or roof surface. I-joists are light in weight because the lumber is concentrated where it is needed for strength.

Figure 3-117 shows how I-joist is fabricated from three pieces. The top and bottom timbers of the joist are called "flanges" or "chords." The flanges typically are smaller than a standard "2-by-4." The flanges carry the bending load of the joist, and they serve as attachments for the floor, ceiling, and roof sheathing.

The center portion of the joist is called the "web." The web is a strip of plywood or other material that is glued into grooves cut into the top and bottom flanges. The web typically is about 3/8" (9 mm) in thickness. The web holds the flanges at their precise spacing and keeps them straight. The connection between the top and bottom flanges provides the joist's resistance to bending. And, the web transmits the weight of the floor or roof from the top flange to the bottom.

For a given flange size, the load carrying capacity and the stiffness of the joist depend mainly on the distance between the top and bottom flanges.

Builders order I-joists from the factory, specifying the desired dimensions. The factory can make I-joist in virtually any length by splicing the flanges and the webs with long overlapping glue joints.

ADHESIVES IN CONSTRUCTION

 Adhesives now have a major role in the manufacture of building materials and for joining parts of the structure. Adhesives can be helpful, and they can also be a weakness. A basic problem is that organic adhesives have much shorter lives than a house, so they should not be used for primary structural strength. Adhesives are weakened by loss of their volatile components and by exposure to oxygen, heat, and sunlight. Pick up a piece of plywood or chipboard that has been lying outside for a few months, and you will see that the material is already coming apart.

For a strong and leak-free house, use adhesives properly and avoid materials that depend on adhesives for long-term strength. Consider these cautions in your design.

1. Strength. *All long-term strength should come from mechanical fasteners.* These include nails, screws, or bolts, depending on the requirement. Steel fittings will last for the life of the house if they are protected from moisture. Moisture resistance can be greatly improved by using galvanized fasteners and fittings, where necessary.

To benefit from adhesives in construction, the trick is to use mechanical fasteners so that they will compensate for the long-term weakening of the adhesives. For example, the layers in plywood are held together over the long term by the nails or screws that are used to install the plywood.

Recently, plywood is being replaced by composite materials that are much more dependent on adhesives. These include "chipboard," "oriented strandboard," and other materials that are made of inferior lumber or wood fragments. *These materials cannot be held intact by mechanical fasteners when the adhesive fails, and therefore they may fail during the life of the house.*

Some composite structures, such as I-joist and laminated arches, are held together by their shape and by the load applied to them, so they may remain strong over the long term *if they are properly designed and properly applied.*

2. Strengthening Joints by Friction. The friction created by adhesives prevents sliding between surfaces, which greatly increases the strength of a joint to sidewise forces. For example, if "construction adhesive" is used where plywood is nailed to lumber, the adhesive creates friction between the two surfaces over an area that is much larger than the area of friction created by the nails alone. Even old and weakened adhesives provide useful friction in joints, *provided that the mechanical fasteners still hold tightly.*

3. Sealing Against Air Leakage. Adhesives and sealants have similar materials and properties, and some products are used for both purposes. For example, using "construction adhesive" when nailing exterior sheathing to a frame wall blocks air leakage at the joints. Old, weakened adhesives can continue to block air leakage *if the gaps are small and rigidly secured by mechanical fasteners.*

I-joists are not foolproof. In particular, they cannot carry heavy concentrated loads, which would buckle and collapse the thin web. Using I-joists requires special techniques to deal with this weakness. If your builder fails to use I-joist properly, your structure may be impaired seriously.

In addition, there is an important caution about I-joist and any other structural materials that are made with organic adhesives. In those materials, the adhesives determine the ultimate life of the material. See the sidebar, *Adhesives in Construction.* Unfortunately, plywood webs are now giving way to cheaper chipboard material. These materials depend entirely on glue to hold the wood fragments together. I suspect that the glue may deteriorate sufficiently within the lifetime of the house to dangerously weaken the structure.

I have found no credible research to indicate the ultimate life of I-joist under different conditions of temperature and humidity. In my own home, I built a major addition using I-joist for the floor joists and

roof rafters. After 30 years, I detect no deterioration in the floor joists, which are kept cool and dry. However, portions of the roof rafters that I uncovered for repair after 25 years had become brittle.

Select I-Joist with Strong Flange Material

The top and bottom flanges of I-joists are more fragile than solid timber joists. They are relatively small in cross section, and as prime lumber becomes scarce, manufacturers increasingly use composite wood that is made from wood fragments joined by adhesives. Such material is more brittle than solid wood, especially when it ages. Driving a nail that is too large through a flange is likely to split it, ruining the strength of the beam.

To minimize this risk, buy I-joists that use solid lumber for the top and bottom flanges. Even then, the relatively cross section of the flanges makes them vulnerable to splitting.

Use Appropriate Fasteners and Connectors

When attaching interior sheathing materials, such as floor sheathing or gypsum board, use appropriate screws instead of nails. Screws provide a good grip with less tendency to split the flanges. For roof sheathing, use slender nails, no larger than necessary. Get secure attachment by increasing the number of nails.

To connect I-joist to other structural components, such as rim joists, use special nails, hangers, and connectors that have been developed for the purpose. Manufacturers of I-joists offer this special hardware. Your builder should order the correct hardware for the particular joists that your home requires.

Reinforce I-Joist at Support Points

I-joists are designed to carry distributed loads, as occur on floors and roofs. However, I-joists cannot carry heavy concentrated loads, because the load would crush or buckle the thin web of the joist. Concentrated loads occur anywhere a wall rests on an I-joist, or where an I-joist rests on a wall or other support.

Expect that many of the I-joists in your house will need reinforcements. Your construction drawings should show all the reinforcements in detail. This will allow your builder to install the reinforcements in a production line manner. Your builder should do this before the joists are installed.

Manufacturers of I-joists may (or may not) provide instructions for reinforcing them when used as joists and rafters. Unfortunately, construction crews widely disregard the instructions, resulting in a structure that may start to fail even as the house is being built. The proper installation of I-joists is a major issue between you and your builder.

For example, where a floor joist rests on a lower wall, with an upper wall directly above, install solid lumber blocks alongside the joists to transmit the weight of the upper structure. Without such reinforcement, the weight of the upper structure will eventually crush the web of the joist.

The reinforcements must be exactly the same height as the joists. For example, use pieces of 2-by-6 lumber with the grain oriented vertically. Attach the reinforcements to the joists with nails or screws, not with adhesive.

In many cases, it is necessary to reinforce the web itself to keep it from buckling. This occurs where a floor is cantilevered over a wall, where the end of the joist rests in a joist hanger, and where hurricane straps are attached. Reinforce the web by bolting a piece of solid lumber to it, extending between the two flanges. *Do not rely on adhesives for this*.

Pre-Cut Holes for Pipe and Electrical Wiring

Before the floor joists are installed, have the carpenters use hole saws to cut neat holes in the webs to provide passage for wiring and pipe perpendicular to the joists. Cut the holes in measured positions along the joists, so that they will line up when the floor is built, as in Figure 3-118. This will speed the installation of wiring and pipe, make the installation neater, and reduce the temptation of the electricians and plumbers to weaken the joists by cutting holes through the flanges.

Make the holes about 3" (75 mm) in diameter for wiring, somewhat larger if you plan to run pipe through the holes. Locate the holes just above the bottom flanges, so that wiring and pipe are installed low in the joist space, making installation easy. This also provides room for insulation in the upper part of the joist space, in cases where floor insulation is desirable.

TrusJoist

Figure 3-118. A neat example of using pre-cut holes in joists. Holes for pipe and wiring would be much smaller than for air ducts, which you generally should avoid.

Show the locations of the holes on your construction drawings, so that the electricians and plumbers will know to use them. Provide extra holes for wiring that may be added in the future. As more wiring is added in later years, this preparation will avoid a rat's nest of wiring crisscrossing the underside of the floor.

 Precut holes in the webs of I-joists for neat wiring and pipe installation with less labor, and to avoid cutting into the flanges.

Some I-joist manufacturers offer joists that have reinforced openings for running wiring, pipe, and duct. Exploit this option, if it is available. Other manufacturers offer joists with knockouts, but these tend to make ragged holes.

Don't Use I-Joist as Rim Joists!

"Rim joists" are the timbers that form the perimeter of a frame floor, as shown in Figures 3-18 and 3-19. In frame construction, the rim joists support the weight of the outer walls, which in turn carry the weight of the upper portions of the house. Thus, rim joists carry vastly more concentrated weight than the inner floor joists.

You can't use I-joist for the rim joists. That's because the thin web (center portion) of an I-joist would collapse under the weight of a wall if it were used as a rim joist.

Therefore, I-joist floor construction requires special rim joists that precisely match the height of the joists and that stay straight. These rim joists usually are wider than old style solid lumber, so they resist tipping over and they provide a broader base for carrying the wall load.

DRW

Figure 3-119. A rim joist fabricated from short support blocks.

Suitable rim joists may be laminated from layers of solid wood. This kind is strong, reliable, and easy to connect with the ends of floor joists.

Another kind of rim joist is built from short blocks of lumber, as in Figure 3-119. These are less expensive than solid rim joists. Because air can flow through this kind of rim joist, the exterior sheathing should overlap it completely, and the sheathing should be nailed along the top and bottom members of the rim joist to provide full strength.

Increasingly, rim joists are being made of composite wood substitutes, i.e., glued wood fragments. Such material will become brittle with age, but it may survive if it is sandwiched between the structures above and below it. See the previous sidebar, *Adhesives in Construction.*

Most I-joist vendors offer rim joists that have compatible dimensions. Generally, your builder will order the rim joists from the same source as the I-joist.

FLOOR JOIST SPACING

The standard floor joist spacing is 16" (nominal 40 cm). This provides adequate support for heavy furniture and other loads that rest between the joists. A standard sheet of plywood is 96" long (nominal 240 cm), so a single sheet of plywood will span six joists.

The floor joists of an upper floor act as the ceiling joists for the rooms below. A spacing of 16" (nominal 40 cm) provides adequate support for heavy ceiling surfaces, such as drywall, that are attached to the bottoms of the joists.

DEPTH OF FLOOR JOISTS

The correct depth of floor joists (the distance from the top surface to the bottom surface) depends on the span of the joists. Longer spans require deeper joists, almost proportionally.

If you use I-joist, the manufacturer will provide a table that allows the builder to order joists of the correct depth. For example, for an interior floor with a span of 15 feet (4.5 meters), the manufacturer may recommend a depth of 10" (25 cm).

If you use solid timber joists or rafters, you can get the appropriate depths from tables in construction handbooks. Or, make an Internet search for "depth of floor joists" to find a reliable source of information.

You can use narrower joist spacing as an alternative to increasing joist depth. However, this approach usually is uneconomical.

If you have any doubt about the joist dimensions, hire an engineer to calculate them for you. See *Getting Expert Help*, in Section 8, for suggestions in hiring an engineer.

All the joists in a frame floor usually have the same depth, to keep the framing design simple. If one portion of a floor has an exceptionally long span, that portion of the floor may have deeper joists than the rest of the floor, and it will require a separate supporting structure. Also, the ceiling below the floor will be lower than elsewhere.

THE SUBFLOOR

The "subfloor" (sometimes call the "underlayment") is the structural sheathing of a frame floor, which is nailed or screwed to the joists. It is called the "subfloor" because the floor's decorative and wearing surface (carpet, tile, vinyl flooring, hardwood strips, etc.) is attached on top of it.

Select real plywood for your subfloors, not a cheaper substitute. The cheaper materials are weaker, they are brittle, and they have a large amount of adhesive that emits potentially harmful vapors into the house. See the previous sidebar, *Adhesives in Construction.*

Your builder should lay a ribbon of "construction adhesive" along each joist before attaching the sheathing with nails or screws, as in Figure 3-56. The adhesive creates a friction bond between the sheathing and the joists that eliminates relative motion between the surface and the joists. This eliminates squeaks for the life of the house, and creates a floor that is exceptionally strong.

The builder needs to be careful when installing the plywood on I-joist. The top flanges of I-joists split easily, destroying the strength of the floor. Avoid this by using screws or special nails that are designed to avoid splitting the flanges.

Use tongue-and-groove plywood that is a full ¾" (18 mm) thick, even though thinner flooring has become common. This will keep the plywood from yielding noticeably between the joists. Also, this thickness is needed to provide a sufficiently stiff base for hardwood flooring, parquet, or ceramic tile. Don't try to achieve the same effect by building up separate sheets of plywood. It isn't nearly as stiff.

INSTALLING THE LOWER FLOOR ON THE FOUNDATION WALL

The lowest frame floor sits on top of the foundation. But, it doesn't just sit there loosely. You have to attach it to the foundation in a special way, for two reasons. One is to keep the floor, and the rest of the house, from blowing off the foundation in a windstorm or sliding off the foundation in an earthquake. The other reason is to seal the long gap that exists between floor and the foundation against air leakage and insect entry.

All the wall components are connected strongly by the exterior sheathing, as we will explain under the heading, *The Exterior Wall Sheathing.* The first step in making the connection is to attach a strong timber along the top of the foundation with anchor bolts. This timber is called the "sill plate." The floor platform is built on the sill plate. The exterior sheathing overlaps the sill plate, and is nailed to it. Figure 3-25 shows the details.

The anchor bolts for the sill plate are set into the concrete when the foundation wall is poured, as in Figure 3-120. Make sure that you have plenty of them. They are cheap, so cost is not a factor. There are well defined procedures for installing anchor bolts, and your builder should know them.

In regions that are especially vulnerable to windstorms or earth movement, steel straps or other connectors may be installed to connect the sill plate to the rim joist of the floor platform and to the wall structure above the platform. The sheathing is installed over these connectors, and it continues to play an

important structural role. It makes the wall stiff, securing it against small movements even better than the steel straps, which have long spaces between them.

Use pressure-treated lumber for the foundation sill. This protects against condensation damage and insect entry.

To seal the gap between the foundation and the sill plate, use "sill sealer," a special sealing material that comes in long strips. Sill sealer also acts as a cushion to push the sill plate upward into contact with the rim joists. The best sill sealer is dense and gummy. You may have to search for it, because good sill sealer is being replaced by a cheap material that is similar to bubble wrap. (See the previous Figure 3-57.) The cheap material would deteriorate early in the life of the house, allowing the gap to re-open.

Builders also commonly use fiber insulation for sealing the sill, but don't allow it. Air will leak through any fiber material.

To complete the seal between the sill plate and the rim joists of the floor platform, lay a thick ribbon of caulk on the sill where the rim joists rest on in.

The exterior sheathing covers all the gaps. To complete the seal, lay a ribbon of caulk between the bottom of the sheathing and the side of the foundation wall. You need extra-long sheets of plywood for this. Use plenty of nails to hold the sheathing snugly to all the wall components, starting along the sill plate. Termites, ants, wasps, and other pests can squeeze through any gaps that you leave here.

DRW

Figure 3-120. Anchor bolts embedded at the top of a concrete foundation wall. The tabs inside the wall held the concrete forms together when the concrete was poured. They will be knocked off.

BUILDING EXPOSED FRAME FLOORS

If the underside of a floor is exposed to the outside (directly or through a vented crawl space) or to an unheated space, the floor becomes a potential path for air leakage into the house. Therefore, an exposed floor should be built with the same attention to avoid air leakage as you give to walls.

Also, in both a cold climate and a warm climate, the floor needs to function as a vapor barrier. Fortunately, the perm ratings for plywood and other flooring materials are low enough so that the floor can act as its own vapor barrier. If the floor has an impermeable surface, such as vinyl sheet flooring, this material will also act as the vapor barrier.

To make an exposed floor both airtight and vapor-tight, use tongue-and-groove subfloor sheathing, and caulk the entire length of the joints. Where sheets of subfloor join over the floor joists, use construction adhesive between the subfloor and the joists, as for other frame floors.

One troublesome exception is building over wet ground, where it may be necessary to select among unreliable alternatives to protect the underside of the house against condensation. For that situation, refer to the earlier heading, *Building an Exposed Floor in a Humid Climate and Over Wet Ground*.

Do not install a separate vapor barrier between the subfloor and the joists. It would interfere with the important adhesive and friction connection between the two.

INSULATING FRAME FLOORS

If a frame floor is exposed to the outside, the exposed portions need to be insulated. Calculate the appropriate R-values (RSI values) with the *Insulation Worksheet*. Here are the installation details.

Insulating the Rim Joists

If your home uses platform construction, the floors will have rim joists that are exposed to the outside. To insulate the rim joists, fill the cavity adjacent to the rim joist with the same batt insulation used in the walls. See Figure 3-25.

Installing an effective vapor barrier requires a method that is easy but somewhat unusual. Before inserting the insulation into the cavity, staple polyethylene sheet to the top plate of the wall below. Then, insert the batts. Finally, wrap the plastic sheet up and around the interior surface of the batts and staple it securely to the bottom of the floor above.

Insulating Overhanging Floors

Insulating an overhanging floor is simple. Consider the overhang to be a portion of the wall that is turned horizontal. In a climate with a significant cold season, fill the space between the floor joists with batt insulation, as in Figure 3-122. The insulation should extend outward to fit snugly against the rim joist, and it should extend inward to completely overlap the insulation in the wall below.

Cover the inner end of the insulation with a vapor barrier of polyethylene sheet. Before inserting the insulation into the cavity, staple the edge of the sheet to the top plate of the wall below. After the batts are inserted, wrap the sheet around the end of the batts and staple it to the bottom of the floor above.

The plywood subfloor above the overhang is sufficiently impermeable to act as a vapor barrier for the overhang.

The depth of the floor joists determines the maximum R-value of the insulation. For most climates with a cold season, this works out well, because a typical overhanging floor joist is about 8" to 10" (20 to 25 cm) deep. This is a reasonable insulation thickness for most climates. Floor overhangs comprise a small fraction of the total insulated surface of a house, so it's not necessary to be more exact.

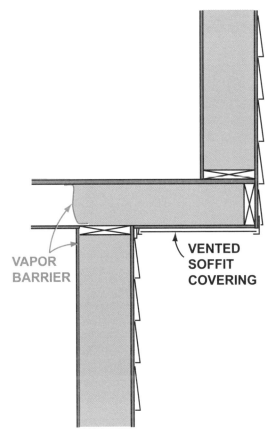

DRW

Figure 3-122. Insulation and vapor barrier for an overhanging floor. Basically, treat the overhang like a horizontal wall section.

Before installing the insulation, secure any wiring in the joist spaces to the sides of the joists with cable staples. This is important to keep the wiring from interfering with the insulation.

The underside of the overhanging floor has a lightweight sheathing to support the insulation. Typically, this is covered with a decorative material that is weatherproof. The covering should be vented to allow moisture venting, just like the walls. Perforated soffit covering is a standard item that serves this purpose attractively. (A "soffit" is the exposed underside of a roof or floor overhang.) Figure 3-123 shows this material.

INSULATING A FLOOR BUILT OVER A VENTED SPACE

Any floor built over a crawl space or a vented foundation should be insulated if the climate has a cold season. Calculate the appropriate R-values (RSI) using the *Insulation Worksheet*. As a practical matter, the maximum amount of insulation that can be installed in a floor is limited by the depth of the floor joists. A typical floor joist is about 8" to 10" (20 to 25 cm) deep, which allows ample thickness for most climates. In colder climates, simply select deeper floor joists to accommodate more insulation.

Insulating a frame floor is similar to insulating a frame wall with fiber batt insulation, except that the insulation is horizontal. The insulation is placed snugly between the floor joists.

Insulation has weight, so it must be held in place securely. The weight of the insulation tends to create a gap between the top of the insulation and the bottom of the floor. This gap might be a path for heat loss if the gap is open to the outside. Therefore, it is important to keep the insulation snug against the bottom of the floor.

The easiest way to support the insulation is to fill the full depth of the joist spaces with insulation, and to attach a continuous supporting cover to the bottom of the floor joists that will remain intact for the life of the building. The cover should protect the insulation from wind, but in most climates it does not need to be airtight.

The insulation should not have a vapor barrier, and the supporting cover should allow moisture to vent. An impermeable cover would act as a vapor barrier on the wrong side of the insulation. Perforated soffit material is good for this application. Thin plywood is satisfactory, but its permeability to water vapor is low. "House wrap" material is sometimes used, but it is not durable.

One major exception is building over wet ground, which may require an impermeable sheathing under the floor. See the earlier heading, *Building an Exposed Floor in a Humid Climate and Over Wet Ground*.

DRW

Figure 3-123. Perforated soffit material that vents moisture while protecting the sheathing and blocking insects.

BUILDING SUPER FRAME WALLS

Next, we continue your design upward by designing super-insulated frame walls for your home. These will rest on the wooden floors that we just completed, or they will rest direcly on a slab foundation. Building super-insulated frame walls is similar to building conventional frame walls, and it is almost as easy.

A highly visible difference is that we will increase the thickness of the walls to accommodate super-insulation. Super-insulated walls provide a number of important bonuses, in addition to superior comfort and energy efficiency. The fact that the walls are completely filled with non-flammable insulation makes them resistant to fire. The rigid structure and the insulation make the walls impervious to noise. Your walls will be much stronger than conventional walls, so your home will be almost immune to damage from earth movement and wind. Also, your interior wall surfaces won't develop settlement cracks.

Thicker walls create a nice "window box" interior appearance. See the sidebar, *Fancy Window Sills*.

If your home will have masonry walls, we will cover their design after we finish with frame walls.

STUD DIMENSIONS AND SPACING

The thickness of the wall is determined by the width of the vertical framing members, which are called "studs." The dimensions and spacing of your wall studs are major engineering decisions because they determine the strength of your house. The dimensions and spacing are specified by the building code for your region. It is the builder's responsibility to satisfy the minimum requirements of the building code, so ordinarily the homeowner is not involved in specifying the studs.

However, you can't leave that issue to the builder of your super-home. The reason is that the width of the wall studs determine how much insulation you can place in your walls, and you will use a lot more insulation than is used in conventional houses.

For approximately the last century, house framing in the United States has relied almost exclusively on standardized "two-by-four" wall studs. These are actually 3½" (87 mm) wide, creating a wall cavity that provides only 3½" (87 mm) of space for insulation. This is too narrow for the amount of insulation that we recommend for most climates.

For example, for the climate of Chicago, the *Insulation Worksheet* recommends wall insulation of R-34 (RSI 6.0). With glass fiber insulation, this requires a wall cavity that is approximately 11" (28 cm) thick.

So, we will explain how to select the dimensions and spacing for your wall studs. As with all the other innovative aspects of your design, make sure that your stud design is shown clearly in your final construction drawings. And, discuss it with your builder before construction commences.

FANCY WINDOW SILLS

In a house with super-insulated walls, the depth of the wall creates wide interior window sills, typically as wide as a shelf. This creates a great opportunity for decor. You can dress up the window sills with flower pots or knickknacks, as here:

DRW

Figure 3-124. A waterproof window sill in a super-insulated frame wall.

You can even sit in your windows, if the sills have the right height. Or, put your cat bed there.

Instead of using lumber or plywood for the sills, consider a waterproof material, such as Corian®, stone, or tile. This is common practice for windows in masonry walls, and you can do the same in a frame wall.

These materials are attractive, dimensionally stable, and immune to damage from the condensation that forms on windows during cold weather. If you search among your local kitchen fabricators for pieces of material left over from making kitchen counters, you may be able to make your fancy sills at bargain prices.

Some of the synthetic materials are slightly flexible and they resist cracking. Corian® is a leading example. It can be cut with a table saw. A fancy edge can be shaped with a router.

For windows in a shower room or other wet space, slope the sill slightly toward the interior to drain any water or condensation.

Minimum Strength Requirements

The *International Residential Code* (IRC) is the leading building code for home construction in North America. To make life simple for builders, it bases stud selection on several standardized lumber dimensions. It also limits selection to two standard stud spacings, which are 16" (40 cm) and 24" (60 cm).

Stud selection depends on the load that the wall must carry. For example:

- In a single-story house, where the studs support only the roof and ceiling, the walls may use 2-by-4 studs placed at 24" (60 cm) intervals.
- If the wall supports an upper floor, in addition to the roof and ceiling, the IRC requires 2-by-4 studs to be spaced at 16" (40 cm) intervals. Or, the wall may use 2-by-6 studs placed at 24" (60 cm) intervals.
- If the wall supports two upper floors, the IRC requires 2-by-6 studs to be spaced at 16" (40 cm) intervals.

There may be additional requirements. For example, if the house is very wide, and if it uses a truss roof that spans from one outer wall to the opposite wall, the heavy roof load may require larger studs or a narrower stud spacing for the outer walls.

If the wall carries an exceptionally heavy local load, use multiple studs at that point. For example, this is done alongside a wide window or garage door, where the studs carry the weight of the structure above the opening.

If your builder is not certain about the stud spacing that is needed (or about any other structural issue), hire an appropriate engineer to calculate the requirement for your home. Be sure that the engineer understands the reasons for your stud design.

Preferred Stud Spacing

If either the 16" (40 cm) or 24" (60 cm) stud spacing will satisfy the strength requirement of your walls, the wider spacing usually is the better choice. Wider spacing reduces the number of studs that are required and allows the use of wider insulation batts. Both factors reduce labor cost somewhat. Also, using fewer studs reduces the heat loss through the material of the studs themselves.

On the other hand, the narrow spacing may be more desirable if it allows you to rest roof rafters, which normally are spaced 16" (40 cm) intervals, directly on top of the wall studs. This may save lumber at the top of the wall. We will discuss this tradeoff shortly, under the heading, *How the Wall Supports the Structure Above.*

A narrower stud spacing makes the exterior sheathing more rigid, which may be important if you use a surface finish, such as stucco, that is vulnerable to cracking. However, you can compensate for the wider stud spacing by using thicker exterior sheathing.

SOLID WALL STUDS FOR WARM AND MILD CLIMATES

In some mild climates, you can satisfy the insulation thickness recommendations of the *Insulation Worksheet* by using "2-by-6" timbers for the wall studs. These timbers have an actual width of 5½" (138 mm).

To allow even more insulation, you can use "2-by-8" timbers for the studs and plates. These have an actual width of 7½" (188 mm).

Solid lumber is not practical for studs wider than about 8" (20 cm), which are needed in colder climates. Where a greater thickness of wall insulation is recommended, we will offer a different type of stud construction.

 Cutting notches for wiring in the bottoms of solid studs makes the wiring easier to install and avoids interference with the insulation.

If you use solid lumber wall studs, have the carpenters cut notches for wiring in the bottoms of the studs before they are installed. The notches line up to form a tunnel for the wiring, which lies along the floor or along the bottom plate, if there is one. This minimizes interference with the insulation.

Locate the notches at the centers of the bottom surfaces of the studs. The notches should keep the wiring at least two inches (50 mm) away from the inside and outside surfaces of the studs. This protects the wiring from the nails and screws that are used to attach sheathing, and it preserves enough surface area at the bottom of the studs to carry the wall loads.

This method eliminates the need for the electrician to cut holes in the studs. This small preliminary effort by the carpenters will save a lot of effort by the electricians, and it will be much easier to install the insulation perfectly.

FABRICATED WALL STUDS FOR COLDER CLIMATES

In colder climates, the amount of insulation that is recommended by the *Insulation Worksheet* requires unconventional wall studs. If the insulation requires a stud width greater than about 8" (20 cm), ordinary lumber becomes too heavy to handle, it wastes material, and it has an excessive tendency to warp and distort the structure. Also, solid studs create a relatively wide path for heat loss through the lumber, which is a significant issue in cold climates. And, wide boards of decent quality are becoming scarce and expensive.

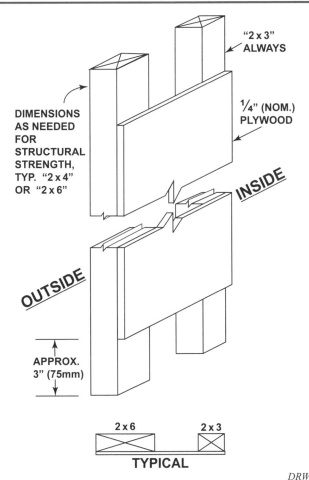

"2 x 3"
ALWAYS

DIMENSIONS
AS NEEDED
FOR
STRUCTURAL
STRENGTH,
TYP. "2 x 4"
OR "2 x 6"

¼" (NOM.)
PLYWOOD

INSIDE

OUTSIDE

APPROX.
3" (75mm)

2 x 6   2 x 3

TYPICAL

DRW

Figure 3-125. An easily fabricated stud design that is adaptable to any thickness of insulation. The outer member carries all the structural load, and it is sized accordingly. The inner member is primarily an attachment for the inner wall sheathing. The thin plywood "web" that joins the two members strengthens the wall and keeps it straight. Electrical wiring and other cables are easy to route through the protected spaces below the webs, avoiding interference with the insulation.

Therefore, for thicker walls, I recommend the fabricated stud design in Figure 3-125. Each stud uses separate outer and inner members. The two members are joined by a strip of thin plywood, called the "web." You can think of this stud design as a conventional stud that has an extension to make it wider and stiffer.

The outer member carries all the weight of the structure above it. It generally has the same dimensions as the corresponding stud for a conventional house. Typically, it is a 2-by-4 (nominally 37 mm by 88 mm) or a 2-by-6 (nominally 37 mm by 140 mm). For a very tall house, the outer members for the lower floors may be larger.

The inner member generally is a 2-by-3 (nominally 37 mm by 63 mm). It serves as a mounting for the interior sheathing and for the electrical connection boxes for light switches, receptacles, etc. It carries no structural load.

OLDER STUD DESIGNS FOR SUPER-INSULATED WALLS

Earlier designs for wide super-insulated walls used separate inner and outer studs separated by a gap, as here:

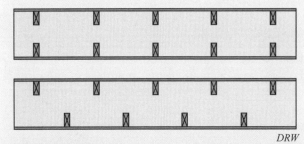

DRW

Figure 3-126.

These designs are sometimes called "double wall" or "double stud" construction. They accommodate any desired amount of insulation, but they make it awkward to install batt insulation snugly. They lack the major improvement in strength and stiffness that results from connecting the inner and outer studs.

The logic behind the gaps in double-stud construction is to minimize the conduction of heat through the studs. However, the thin plywood used for webs in our recommended stud design adds only a negligible amount of heat loss.

💡 **This stud design for thicker walls is easy to fabricate. It is stronger and straighter than earlier stud designs used in super-insulated walls.**

The connecting web is thin plywood, typically ¼" (6 mm) thick. Make the webs about six inches (15 cm) shorter than the timbers, and attach them so that they end about three inches (about 7.5 cm) from the top and bottom of the studs. This creates a tunnel along the floor between the inner and outer members that is ideal for routing electrical wiring through the walls.

The overall width of the studs determines the amount of insulation that you can install in the wall. You can make the studs as wide as you desire by adjusting the width of the webs. Making the studs in this manner gives the wall great stiffness and strength. The walls will remain perfectly straight, which is not achievable with solid lumber studs or with other stud designs that have been used for super-insulated walls in the past (see the adjacent sidebar).

Understand the logic of these studs. The weight of the house from the roof to the top of the foundation is carried through the outer members of the fabricated studs. To support the load reliably, the outer members are held straight by the webs and by the exterior sheathing.

The load must be applied uniformly across the top and bottom surfaces of the outer member. This makes it important to cut the top and bottom surfaces square, and to make all adjacent studs exactly the same length. (The same applies to conventional studs.)

The inner member of the studs should carry no load, except to hold the interior sheathing. To keep any of the structural load from transferring to the inner members of the studs, cut the inner members slightly short, so that they have a small clearance at the top and bottom. Clearances of about 1/16" (about 2 mm) are appropriate.

Your carpenter can easily fabricate these wide studs at the construction site. The webs are glued and nailed to the wide sides of the outer and inner members. A flat frame floor is an excellent place to assemble them on a mass production basis. A carpenter and two helpers can fabricate a set of studs for a medium sized house in one day. To speed the process and to maintain uniform dimensions, the carpenters should nail jig blocks to the floor to keep the components aligned while the studs are assembled.

RESTING THE WALL ON THE FLOOR BELOW

In conventional platform construction, the bottoms of the wall studs rest on a horizontal board that is called a "bottom plate" or "sole plate," as shown Figure 3-25. The bottom plate performs several functions:

- It acts as a cushion to distribute the weight carried by the studs to the floor sheathing and to the rim joist below it.

- It provides a nailing surface for the bottom of the interior sheathing.

- It provides a nailing connection near the bottom of the exterior sheathing, which is also nailed to the bottom plate, the rim joist, and/or the foundation sill plate.

- It connects the bottom of the wall studs during construction. Carpenters often assemble the wall panels on the floor, and then lift them into position.

With our wider fabricated wall studs, use separate bottom plates under the outer and inner members. The widths of the bottom plates should be same as the widths of the stud members.

HOW THE WALL SUPPORTS THE STRUCTURE ABOVE

First, let's assume that the roof is resting on top of the stud wall. The weight of the roof is carried to the wall by the roof's rafters or trusses. If the rafter spacing is the same as the stud spacing, the simplest way to support the roof is to place the rafters or trusses directly above the studs.

If the wall uses solid wood studs, it can have a single horizontal "top plate" that spans the tops of the studs, as in Figure 3-25. If the wall uses our wider fabricated stud design, both the inner and outer members will have their own top plates.

The top plate performs these functions:

- It acts as a pad to distribute the roof weight to the tops of the studs.

- It provides a nailing surface for the top edges of the interior and exterior sheathing.

- It holds the tops of the studs in position as the wall is being assembled.

- It encloses the top of the wall to block heat loss by convection into the space above.

- It can reduce water leakage into the wall from roof leaks.

- A different top plate design is needed if the rafters or trusses rest between the studs, so that the weight of the roof does not rest directly on the tops of the studs. It is common practice for carpenters to deal with this situation by doubling the top plate. However, this solution is relatively weak, allowing the top plate to sag somewhat.

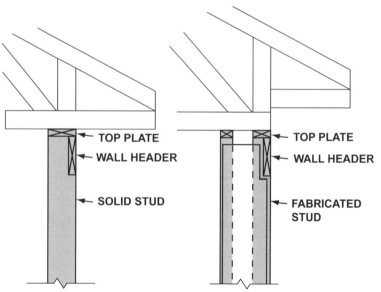

DRW

Figure 3-127. Wall headers for a wall with solid studs and for a wall with fabricated studs. Wall headers avoid the need for the rafters to be placed directly above the studs, and they make it unnecessary to build separate headers for window and door openings.

A stronger solution is to install a "header"* underneath the top plate, as in Figure 3-127. The header is a strong board, such as a 2-by-8, that is laid on its side. When oriented this way, the header acts as a deep beam that can carry a heavy roof load.

The header rests in notches that are cut on the outer sides of the studs. This requires careful carpentry to insure that all the notches align.

If the wall is supporting an upper floor instead of a roof, both of the previous options still apply. If the footprint of the floor above matches the footprint of the wall, the rim joist of the floor above can rest directly on the top plate. The rim joist acts as its own header, so the stud wall below does not require a header.

If a floor overhangs a wall, and if the joists of the overhanging floor do not rest directly on the wall studs, then the wall requires a header to support the overhanging joists.

If a header is deep enough, it can span several normal stud spaces. This is one way to carry the overhead load across a wide window or door opening, which we discuss next.

WINDOW AND DOOR OPENINGS

Figure 3-128 shows the conventional method of creating window and door openings in a frame wall that supports the roof. Each opening uses a header to transmit the roof weight to the studs alongside the opening. The header keeps the rafters above the opening from collapsing into the opening.

This old fashioned design is strong, but it consumes a lot of lumber for headers, for duplicated studs, and for "jacks." We can save much of this lumber by using a continuous header along the top of the wall, as in Figure 3-129. The continuous header carries the roof load to the studs along the entire wall, eliminating the need to build a separate load-bearing header for each opening.

It's probably best to use a continuous wall header for a wall that has several window and/or door openings. The depth of the header is dictated by the roof load and by the greatest distance that the header must span.

With either method, partial wall studs are installed above and below the openings where the edges of the sheathing meet. These partial studs are needed to attach and connect the sheathing panels. When the exterior sheathing is installed, it is nailed all around the openings, making the framing of the openings strong and rigid.

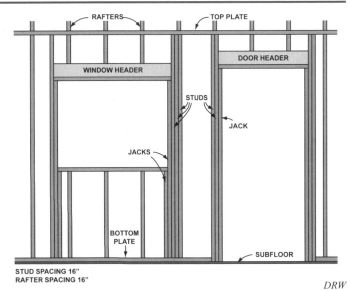

STUD SPACING 16"
RAFTER SPACING 16"
                                                    DRW

Figure 3-128. Conventional framing of window and door openings, using an individual header for each. The structure is strong, but it may require considerable duplication of lumber to align the studs with the roof rafters.

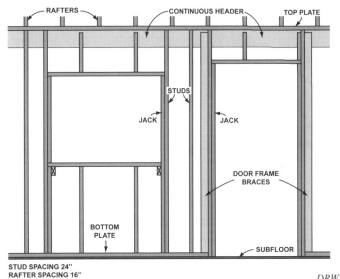

STUD SPACING 24"
RAFTER SPACING 16"
                                                    DRW

Figure 3-129. More economical framing of wall openings that saves lumber and minimizes heat loss through the wall framing. Using a continuous wall header makes the rafter spacing independent of the stud spacing, which avoids the need to duplicate studs and to make individual headers. Also, lumber is saved by allowing a wider stud spacing. Jacks under the window sill have been replaced with supports that are bolted to the adjacent timbers. Figure 3-222 shows the door frame braces in cross section.

The interior surfaces of the window openings are covered with finish lumber, drywall, or some other attractive material. Use a fancy, durable surface for the window sills, as recommended in the previous sidebar, *Fancy Window Sills.*

---

* In general, a "header" is a strong beam that spans the top of an opening, usually a door or a window. The header transmits the weight of the structure above to the sides of the opening. In frame construction, headers usually consist of thick boards that are placed on edge. A header is also called a "lintel." In masonry construction, a lintel usually is a steel support with an angle or channel cross section, or a concrete bar that is reinforced internally with steel rods.

Later, we will introduce some innovations for the framing of door and window openings that improve security and provide other benefits. For doors, preview the heading, *Installing Exterior Doors in Frame Walls*. For windows, preview the headings, *A Better Way to Install Finned Windows* and *Tandem Windows: a Big Energy Saver*.

STRONG CORNERS

Frame walls need strong corners. The challenge is not carrying the weight of the structure, but resisting destruction by windstorms. As we learned previously, under the heading *Resistance to Wind Damage*, a windstorm may create a high pressure inside the house if the wind enters through a failed window or door.

The walls themselves can resist wind pressure because the studs are oriented with their long sides perpendicular to the internal pressure. However, the total wind pressure on adjoining walls tends to push the walls apart at the corners. Therefore, you need strong corner connections.

DON'T CUT CORNERS AT THE CORNERS!

With thick, super-insulated frame walls, special design and careful assembly are needed to make the corners as strong as the rest of the structure, especially to resist damage by windstorms.

In frame construction that uses 2-by-4 wall studs, the usual method is to build a corner post by nailing several 2-by-4's together. Figure 3-132 shows one of several variations. It yields a strong corner connection, provided that (1) the corner post is nailed together strongly, (2) the exterior sheathing is strong, and (3) the sheathing is nailed strongly to the corner post in a way that holds the post together.

Unfortunately, this simple method is not practical for thick, super-insulated frame walls. A solid corner post would consume a large amount of lumber, it would be very heavy, and it could not be insulated. Instead, we can use the designs in Figures 3-133 and 3-134. The method is the same whether the walls use solid studs or fabricated studs. The key feature is using strong steel brackets at the inside of the corner. This is where wind pressure exerts the greatest force to separate the walls.

This design is novel, so you need to cover the details with your builder. A lot of carpenters seem to think that nails are the only kind of fastener for lumber, but this part of the structure needs strong bolts that cannot be pulled out by the shaking of a windstorm. The nuts need appropriately sized washers and lock washers. Once the sheathing is installed, the bolts become inaccessible for the life of the house.

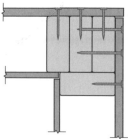

DRW

Figure 3-132. One way of building a strong corner for a wall with narrow studs. Strong sheathing and proper nailing are essential for a strong connection. Only the nails for the sheathing are shown. Additional nails hold the corner post together.

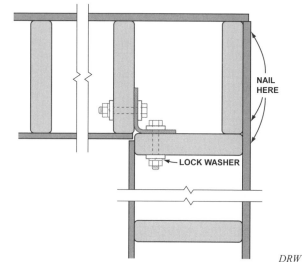

DRW

Figure 3-133. Horizontal cross section of a strong corner for frame walls that use wide solid studs. The key feature is using strong steel brackets to hold the inside of the corner intact. The width of these studs is 7.5" (19 cm), which is about the practical maximum for solid studs.

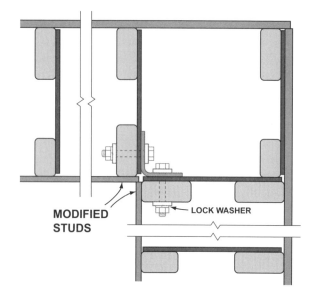

DRW

Figure 3-134. Horizontal cross section of a strong corner for frame walls that use fabricated studs. Two of the studs are modified slightly to provide strong attachments for the brackets. The width of these studs is 10" (25 cm). This design adapts to any wall thickness.

The brackets must be strongly made. They should be attached with bolts made of good steel.* They should be spaced vertically at intervals from top to bottom. The stress on the brackets depends on the wind force and on the area of the walls that are attached to the corner. In case of doubt, hire an engineer to calculate the dimensions that are appropriate for the wind hazard.

Don't forget to insulate the corners! This corner design creates a hollow box structure. Insulation needs to be installed inside the box before it is enclosed. The builder should have insulation available when the corners are built, even though the rest of the wall may be insulated much later.

THE EXTERIOR WALL SHEATHING

The exterior wall sheathing is not just a covering, but a major structural component of your house. It is just as important as the studs and joists, and it needs to last as long. The exterior sheathing should perform these functions:

- ***Strengthen the wall***. The weight is carried primarily by the wall studs, and plywood holds the studs straight, keeping them from warping or collapsing.

- ***Diagonal bracing***. Plywood keeps the wall from tipping sideways ("racking"). Plywood sheathing is more effective for this purpose than old-fashioned diagonal braces. Strong sheathing also keeps the wall from deforming, or drooping, if the foundation support fails. (This is especially important for additions or renovations to existing houses, which may have weak foundations.)

- ***Strong structural connections between the walls, the floor structures, and the foundation***. To achieve this benefit, the sheathing panels must be long enough to span across all the joints in the structure (as shown in Figure 3-25).

- ***Blocking air leakage through and around the wall***. The sheathing should cover the leaky joints between the foundation, the walls, the rim joists, and the corners.

- ***Protect the wall insulation*** from moisture and from exterior air currents that would degrade the R-value (RSI) of the insulation.

- ***Be a reliable base for attaching the exterior weather surface***. Siding materials are attached to the sheathing by nails or screws. Plywood of adequate thickness is needed to hold the fasteners against wind, vibration, and thermal expansion of the siding.

DON'T USE FOAM INSULATION BOARD AS SHEATHING

In an effort to satisfy the energy efficiency requirements in building codes, many builders adopted the practice of using plastic foam board or fiber insulation board for the exterior sheathing.

Don't let your builder do this. It produces walls that will fail. Insulation board has minimal strength for resisting sidewise loads, which is the main structural purpose of sheathing. Nails cannot hold it securely. It is unsatisfactory as a nail base for siding. The material is so fragile that it is commonly broken during construction, allowing big air leaks into the wall. In a fire, foam insulation board creates large amounts of toxic smoke.

Foam board insulation acts as a vapor barrier. Any vapor barrier must be installed on the warm side of the wall to avoid moisture damage to the structure. But foam board used as exterior sheathing is on the cold side, inviting moisture damage.

Finally, plastic foam insulation is expensive. It would cost no more to increase the thickness of the walls and to use less expensive fiber insulation.

Why don't builders avoid all these problems by simply making the walls thicker and adding more insulation inside the walls? Probably because they are creatures of habit, and using foam board sheathing allows them to continue to use 2-by-4's for framing.

- ***Be a strong base for mounting exterior fixtures***. Plywood of average thickness can hold the weight of lamps, flag poles, deco, and other fixtures. However, heavier fixtures should be attached directly to the framing, through the sheathing.

To make sure that your home actually achieves all these benefits, work with your builder to install the wall sheathing properly. Here are the main points.

Avoid Plywood Substitutes

At this time, there is only one exterior sheathing material to consider, which is real exterior-grade plywood. Only real plywood satisfies all the essential functions of the sheathing.

Avoid plywood substitutes that are made of wood particles, such as "oriented strand board," "particle board," "chipboard," and other types. They are made from scraps left over from the lumber milling process, or from wood that is not suitable for making real

---

* Get "Grade 5" bolts for this application. Ordinary hardware store bolts are cheaply made and they have no guarantee of strength. Grade 5 bolts have a specified strength that is ample for critical connections in house construction. They are marked with three radial lines on the head. I have found that you can get them economically at farm supply stores. For example, Tractor Supply Company sells them by the pound.

plywood. The wood pieces in these materials are held together with glue. The glue will fail in the long term, allowing the sheathing to disintegrate. See the previous sidebar, *Adhesives in Construction*.

Under no circumstances should you use plastic foam board or fiber insulation board as exterior sheathing. See the sidebar.

Select the Appropriate Sheathing Thickness

If you sheath the entire wall in plywood, plywood as thin as ¼ " (6 mm) will provide all the structural strength that is needed, as long as the sheathing is well attached to the wooden frame.

If the sheathing will be covered by a masonry veneer, so that nothing is attached to the sheathing, a plywood thickness of ¼" (6 mm) is satisfactory.

If the outer surface covering, such as siding or shingles, is attached to the sheathing itself, the plywood should be approximately ½" (12 mm) thick. This is the minimum thickness that can provide a reasonably good grip for the nails or screws that attach the siding. Also, this thickness is needed to keep the wall surface visually flat between the studs, especially if you use the wider stud spacing of 24" (60 cm).

If you want a stucco exterior finish, thicker sheathing is needed to keep the stucco from flexing and cracking.

In locations where severe winds occur, even thicker plywood may be desirable to resist penetration by

DRW

Figure 3-135. Missed opportunities to enhance the strength of these walls. The sheathing panels are too short to connect with each other at the rim joist, or to cover the joints at the foundation sill. Instead, separate strips of sheathing are used to fill the spaces between the panels. As a result, the sheathing cannot create a strong connection between the floors. Also, the gaps between the sheathing panels are aligned with the structural joints, allowing air leakage along those joints. The particulate sheathing used here is inferior to plywood in strength and longevity.

flying objects and to provide a stronger nail base for the siding. For example, ¾" (18 mm) pressure-treated exterior sheathing is the norm in the Florida Keys, which is a hurricane target.

Extend the Sheathing Over Foundation Sills and Rim Joists

If you examine photographs of neighborhoods that have been destroyed by windstorms, you sometimes see a single house standing intact amidst the rubble. That house survived where the others failed largely because its exterior sheathing was installed properly. We will achieve that same strength in your home.

 Use long exterior sheathing panels that join continuously from the foundation to the roof. This provides a radical improvement in strength at little additional cost.

The key is to install the sheathing so that it functions as a strong connector between the foundation, the wall components, the floor structures (rim joists), and the roof, as in Figure 3-25. In so doing, you can make your house highly resistant to hurricanes, tornadoes, and earth movement. In addition, this simple improvement makes the entire wall airtight, as we explained previously. These major benefits add virtually nothing to the cost of your home.

Begin by locating the bottom of the sheathing somewhat below the foundation sill plate. Nail it to sill plate, then to the rim joist, to the studs, to the top plate, and if there is an upper floor, to the rim joist of the upper floor.

Continue this pattern all the way up to the roof. If the house has more than one level, locate the joints between the sheets of plywood near the middle of the rim joist for each floor. A solid rim joist is an ideal connector for the sheathing, providing strong nailing and a large surface that can be caulked against air leakage. The finished wall will have no exposed gaps.

This strong pattern of sheathing requires sheets of plywood that are taller than the interior ceiling height to account for the thickness of the floor structures and to extend below the foundation sills. For example, in the United States, you can order plywood sheets that are ten feet (nominal 3 meters) tall, which is satisfactory for the standard floor height of eight feet. Taller ceiling heights require corresponding longer sheathing panels.

This good construction practice is not unknown, but it is sadly uncommon. Instead, when you examine frame houses under construction, you commonly will see the bad practice that is illustrated in Figure 3-135. Don't let your builder make this mistake.

Attach the Sheathing Strongly

Exploiting the strength of plywood sheathing requires *lots of nails*. An individual nail holds the sheathing only over a small area. The number of nails, not the plywood itself, is the limiting factor in the strength that the sheathing contributes to the wall. The builder should space the nails closely, following standards that are specified in building codes and in handbooks of frame construction.

Nail the sheathing securely to all the studs, sills, and plates that are covered by the sheet, not just at the edges of the plywood. To do this right, the carpenters should make chalk lines on the sheathing to mark the centerline of each stud. This adds only a few minutes to the wall construction. Nailing at the edges of the plywood sheet is relatively weak, because stress on the wall tends to tear the edges loose. Therefore, the carpenters should use a larger number of nails at the edges.

 Using construction adhesive in combination with proper nailing enhances the strength and rigidity of the wall.

To increase the effectiveness of the nails, the carpenters should lay a ribbon of construction adhesive everywhere that the plywood sheets contact the frame. This includes all the studs, the upper and lower "plates," and the rim joists. The adhesive enhances the strength of the nails, but *adhesive cannot provide long-term strength by itself.* See the previous sidebar, *Adhesives in Construction.*

Using construction adhesive for the exterior sheathing is not standard practice. Agree to this with your builder, and have an enforcer at the construction site to make sure that it gets done.

INSULATING EXTERIOR FRAME WALLS

After your frame walls have been erected, and the house is under roof and protected from the weather, the wall insulation is installed from inside the house. Earlier, under the heading, "Super-Structure Design Advance #1: Super-Insulation," you selected the type and dimensions of the wall insulation. Those decisions determined the design of your walls. If you use batt insulation, your wall design is conventional, except for the wider studs. If you use cellulose insulation, your walls require a special design.

Super-insulation for frame walls uses standard insulation materials, but you will use more of it. Good installation workmanship is critical, and it is important to buy insulation that fits into your walls precisely. These are the issues that you should cover in your design and that you should monitor during construction.

Batt Insulation for Frame Walls

We have introduced the main kinds of insulation that are used in houses today. Glass fiber and mineral fiber batt insulation generally are the best choices for frame walls. They provide the best combination of efficiency, economy, and freedom from problems. Glass fiber is the type of insulation that is most commonly used in frame houses today.

All fiber batt insulation has a thermal resistance of about R-3 per inch of thickness (RSI 0.2 per cm). This value is what determines the thickness of your walls. For example, if you want to install insulation with an R-value of 36 (RSI 6.3), the wall cavities need to be 12" (30 cm) deep.

The only other contender for super-insulated walls is cellulose. Its main advantage is low embodied energy, but its limitations keep me from recommending it over glass fiber batt insulation. For the reasons, see *Cellulose Insulation, a Problematic Option*, earlier in Step 3.

If you do decide to insulate your walls with cellulose insulation, take pains to protect your home against its weaknesses. You will need to design your attic and wall structures in a special way, as described in *Insulating Walls with Cellulose Insulation*, below.

Don't be tempted to use plastic foam insulation in the walls (or in any other part of the house that may be exposed to fire). It will kill your family in a fire, and it has other major drawbacks.

■ Fit the Batts Precisely

The main rule for insulating walls is that *the insulation must fill the wall cavities completely.* Gaps allow convection, which undermines the value of insulation in the part of the wall where the gaps occurs.

When installing batt insulation, it is tricky to insert the batt completely into the cavity. A good method is

DRW

Figure 3-136. Insulating a thick wall that uses fabricated studs. First, fit insulation (colored orange) into the gaps between the inner and outer members of the studs. Then, install the main batts (colored pink).

to use a long trowel to tease the edges of the batts past the friction of the stud surfaces, making sure that the far corners of the batts extend completely into the corners of the wall cavity.

Order batts that are exactly the right width. If the batts are too narrow, even by a small amount, they will leave gaps at the sides of the wall cavities. If the batts are too wide, they will wrinkle and create gaps. (We discussed batt dimensions earlier, under the heading, *Glass and Mineral Fiber Insulation*.)

With our fabricated stud design, there is a gap between the outer and inner timbers that needs to be filled with insulation, as shown in Figure 3-136. Use unfaced batt insulation that is 1½" (38 mm) thick. Cut it into strips that are wide enough to fill the gaps, and insert it into the gaps. Then, insert the main batts into the wall.

Manufacturers now offer batts up to 12" (305 mm) in thickness, which minimizes the need to use multiple layers of batts inside the wall. You may find the thickest batts cataloged as attic insulation, not wall insulation. Don't worry, it's the same material.

Batts are sold in lengths that are just right for the wall cavity if the ceiling has a standard height. For other ceiling heights, cut batts to fit. A big pair of scissors is the main tool that the installer needs. Cut the batts carefully, so they are about a half inch (about 12 mm) longer than the height of the cavity. This will compensate for the tendency of the batts to sag under their own weight. You want the batts to remain snug even against the top surface of the cavity.

■ Use Backing Sheets Correctly

To insulate frame walls in a climate that has a cold season, use batt insulation with backing sheets that face toward the inside of the house. Staple the tabs to the inside edges of the studs. If you use more than one layer of batts to fill the wall cavity, only the layer against the inside wall should have backing sheets.

When the tabs of adjacent sheets are overlapped, they form a continuous vapor barrier for the entire wall. However, in a cold climate, you will also install a much better vapor barrier after all the insulation is installed, as explained previously.

If the climate is warm and humid, use batts without backing sheets. Without a backing sheet, batts are held in position by friction alone. Make sure that the batts are wide enough and long enough to stay in place.

Insulating Walls with Cellulose Insulation

If you decide to use cellulose as wall insulation, your are going into territory where few have gone before. First of all, your house needs to have an attic roof. You need to design the attic and the walls in a special way so that every part of the wall is open to the attic at the top. The wall is filled with the cellulose from the attic. This allows cellulose insulation in the attic to fall into the wall cavity to compensate for settling. In effect, the attic serves as a refill hopper for the walls.

The walls are filled with cellulose after the wall is enclosed. Therefore, the wall cavities must be open from top to bottom, with no obstructions to prevent filling by the cellulose. Some portions of the wall are inaccessible for filling from above, as under window openings. Fill these spaces with fiber batt insulation before enclosing the wall.

Cellulose will leak through any wall openings. Therefore, take special care to keep cellulose from leaking around electrical receptacles, wiring, pipe, and anything else that penetrates into the wall cavity. For example, use "airtight" electrical connection boxes.

Another way to install cellulose is in the form of a wet sprayed material that is held together with glue. It is sprayed into the wall cavity before the interior sheathing is installed. We mentioned it previously, without enthusiasm.

CONDENSATION PROTECTION FOR FRAME HOUSES IN COLD CLIMATES

We learned the basics of condensation protection under the previous heading, *Super-Structure Design Advance #2: Condensation Protection*. For frame walls and ceilings in climates that are primarily cold, we now need to explain the details of the vapor barrier and the venting techniques.

If your home is located in a sub-tropical or tropical climate, we don't need to add anything to the previous discussion.

For cold weather, the key elements are a reliable vapor barrier on the inside of the structure and a path for venting moisture from the inside of the structure to the outside. There are many options for vapor barriers, but we will narrow the choices to one primary method that is easy, inexpensive, and reliable.

If your house will have a floor whose underside is exposed to outside conditions, design the floor to act as its own vapor barrier, as we explained under the previous heading, *Building Exposed Frame Floors*.

THE WALL AND CEILING VAPOR BARRIER IN FRAME CONSTRUCTION

First, let's be clear about one point. We need a separate vapor barrier for the inside of the wall and ceiling surfaces because common interior sheathing materials – usually gypsum board – pass water vapor easily. If you use an interior surface finish for the walls and ceilings that is very impermeable, you may not need an additional vapor barrier.

See Table 3-3, *Perm Ratings of Building Materials*, for interior surface finishes that you might use as an alternative to a separate vapor barrier. If the climate is predominantly dry, even a few coats of impermeable paint may suffice as a vapor barrier. However, don't gamble on this. In case of doubt, install a reliable vapor barrier. For walls, the interior surface must block water vapor more effectively than the outer plywood sheathing.

Plastic Sheet Vapor Barrier

The most effective vapor barrier material for the insides of walls and ceilings is polyethylene plastic sheet. This material is highly resistant to moisture penetration. If you select the best quality material, it can last as long as the house when protected from sunlight inside your walls and ceilings. It is inexpensive, transparent, and easy to handle. It is available in wide widths, which speeds installation.

The polyethylene is installed after the framing carpentry is complete and after the insulation has been installed. It is installed before the interior sheathing, and before the window and door trim.

The plastic sheet is attached with a staple gun to the wall studs, to the top and bottom plates, and to the ceiling joists. The builder should attach the vapor barrier in a way that creates a completely unbroken surface over the walls and the ceilings. Overlap sheets by at least one foot (30 cm). Tape overlapped edges to hold them in place until the interior sheathing is installed.

After the vapor barrier has been installed and before the interior sheathing is installed, standing inside the house is like being inside a huge balloon, as in Figure 3-139.

Polyethylene sheet comes in various kinds. You want the kind that has the greatest longevity. The cheap stuff at the hardware store is not what you want. Take the initiative to find polyethylene that meets the appropriate ASTM standard for insulation vapor barrier. The Internet is the easiest way to identify the right product.

Select polyethylene film that is at least "6 mils" thick, which means .006" (0.15 mm) thick. That minimum thickness should guarantee the life of the material, and it should resist damage when it is being installed. Thinner plastic sheet tears easily and it is more difficult to handle.

The tricky part is installing the vapor barrier in corners. ***Leave plenty of slack at all corners*** so that the plastic does not interfere with installing the interior wallboard. If the plastic takes a shortcut across the corners, the wallboard cannot fit into the corners. The

DRW
Figure 3-139. A perfectly installed polyethylene vapor barrier in the author's home.

installers will deal with this annoyance by cutting the plastic along the entire corner. If that happens, it's the end of your vapor barrier. This is so important that you should be present when the vapor barrier is installed.

The protection of a vapor barrier must extend into the window openings. Usually, the function of the vapor barrier will be performed by the wood or plywood that is used to finish the surfaces of the window opening. Therefore, don't use gypsum board or other porous material to frame the window openings, except as a finish surface.

It is not necessary or desirable to extend the plastic film far into the window openings. Instead, simply extend the plastic around the edges of the rough opening and staple it into place. The edges will be covered by the finish lumber for the window opening. The details depend on the manner of installing the windows, which we will learn later.

Use the same general method with the wall openings for doors and skylights.

Extend the vapor barrier down to the floor, and staple it to the bottom plate of the wall. The caulked joint between the wall's bottom plate and the subfloor is the lower boundary of the wall vapor barrier.

Polyethylene sheet is slippery. Therefore, ***don't install it between any components that should be joined with adhesive or a friction contact***. In particular, you need to attach the gypsum board or other interior sheathing to the wall and ceiling framing with an ample number of screws, because construction adhesive won't work with a polyethylene vapor barrier.

For the same reason, don't extend a polyethylene vapor barrier between a door frame and the wall opening. Door frames should have a friction contact with the adjacent wall to resist impact, as we will explain later. Similarly, don't install a plastic vapor barrier between floor sheathing and floor joists, because these should have an adhesive joint to maximize strength and to avoid squeaks.

Alternatives to Plastic Sheet

Using a plastic sheet vapor barrier for the walls and ceiling is unnecessary if the interior surface materials are impermeable, creating an unbroken interior surface. Recognizing this, the construction industry has introduced condensation protection systems that seek to eliminate the need to install a separate vapor barrier. These systems use special impermeable interior sheathing, such as gypsum board with an aluminum foil vapor barrier.

In principle, these newer systems can work well. But, to install them, a number of separate operations must be accomplished as the sheathing is installed. They typically require specialized gaskets and connecting vapor barriers to seal the joints between the individual panels. Some joints require caulking as the interior sheathing is installed.

These alternative systems slow the pace of construction, and builders hate that. As a result, it is likely that such a vapor barrier system will be installed imperfectly, allowing moisture to leak into the structure through gaps.

In contrast, using large sheets of plastic film for the vapor barrier allows the entire installation to be accomplished at one time, separate from the other construction steps. No specialized skills or materials are required. A couple of ladders and a few staple guns are the only tools required. The only precaution is to leave ample slack in all the corners to allow the interior sheathing to be installed without breaking the vapor barrier.

MOISTURE VENTING IN FRAME CONSTRUCTION

With airtight construction, any moisture that gets into the wall structure must vent through the plywood exterior sheathing. Unfortunately, plywood is not as permeable to water vapor as we would like for the exterior surface. Furthermore, the plywood sheets are sealed tightly to the wall structure with adhesive. Therefore, it is essential to have an especially impermeable vapor barrier on the inside of the wall. Any moisture that gets into the wall despite the interior vapor barrier must vent to the outside through the exterior sheathing.

Then, the moisture must get through the exterior finish surface that provides weather protection. Siding materials that are impermeable to water vapor, such as aluminum or vinyl plastic, should have small vent holes along the undersides of the laps. Check for this before you buy the siding.

A masonry veneer can block water vapor that vents through the frame wall. Fortunately, there is a gap between the exterior sheathing and the masonry veneer that typically is about one inch (25 mm) wide. The gap should extend to the top of the veneer, and ***it should not be covered***. Moisture that vents into this gap must be able to escape freely to the outside. Typically, the gap opens into the overhanging roof structure, which is vented to the outside. Put this detail in your construction drawings.

Venting of moisture from the ceiling insulation is easy, because the top of the insulation is uncovered and vapor is free to vent to the outside through the roof structure. We will have more to say about roof venting when we cover the roof design.

If the underside of a floor is exposed to the outside or to a vented crawl space, any surface below the insulation should be more permeable than the interior floor surface. For example, if you want to install a decorative sheetmetal skin under an exposed floor, use the kind that is perforated for moisture venting, as in Figure 3-123.

INSULATION AND CONDENSATION PROTECTION FOR MASONRY WALLS

Super-insulation for masonry walls is more difficult than for frame walls. No method of insulating masonry offers the same combination of simplicity, economy, longevity, and efficient use of space as super-insulation in frame walls. Designing the insulation for masonry walls requires you to make compromises, especially in colder climates, where a large amount of insulation is desirable.

Various methods of insulating masonry walls have been developed. There are methods of installing insulation on the interior side of the masonry, on the exterior side, and inside gaps between the structural wall and a brick covering. In addition, masonry walls can be made of lightweight "insulating" concrete.

For your home, we have narrowed the choices to two methods of interior insulation and one general method of exterior insulation. Begin your design with the *Insulation Worksheet*, which recommends the amount of insulation for masonry walls.

These three methods apply to upgrading existing masonry walls, as well as to new construction. They are accomplished in generally the same way for both situations.

INTERIOR INSULATION FOR MASONRY WALLS

Insulating a masonry wall from the inside offers these advantages:

- *unlimited R-value*. The installation can be installed to any thickness desired. If the climate is cold, interior insulation is the only practical choice.

- *permanence*. The insulation is protected from weather, so it can have unlimited life.

- *quicker warm-up and cool-down*. The insulation isolates the interior of the room from the mass of masonry in the wall. Without the interior insulation, the mass would absorb a considerable amount of heating or cooling energy before reaching the desired temperature.

- *exploiting the thermal delay effect of masonry*. The mass of the structure is exposed to outdoor temperatures, so it can moderate daily hot-to-cold temperature cycles. See the previous sidebar, *Can Your House Benefit from Thermal Lag?*

If the house has wooden floors, it is possible to heavily insulate the entire wall area. However, if the house has concrete floors that extend to the outer wall surfaces, as in the various designs shown in Figures 3-12, 3-27, 3-28, and 3-29, interior wall insulation cannot block heat loss from the floors to the outside walls. In a cold climate, this heat loss may create discomfort in the portions of the floors adjacent to the exterior walls.

For a given wall R-value, a masonry wall will be substantially thicker than a frame wall because the insulation thickness adds to the thickness of the masonry. For fire safety, interior insulation is limited to non-flammable glass or mineral fiber insulation. The R-value of fiber insulation is limited to about 3 per inch (RSI about 0.07 per centimeter), so a super-insulated masonry wall for a colder climate will be very thick.

The window and door openings will have an unusually deep appearance, although they can still be designed attractively. In warmer climates, where masonry construction is more likely to be your best choice, the overall thickness of the wall will be less dramatic.

Two common forms of fiber insulation, batts and fiberboard, may be applied to the inside of masonry walls. The methods of installation are similar to the methods that we covered previously for insulating the insides of basement walls. One major difference is that above-ground masonry walls in a cold climate will use a vapor barrier on the inside surface.

Method 1: Batts on Framework

This method of insulation lets you install virtually any desired R-value. It provides secure support for batt insulation. It also provides secure support for any desired interior surface finish, such as drywall. It provides a good way to extend window openings into the living space. And, it creates a well protected channel at the bottom of the wall for electrical and communications wiring.

Begin by erecting a wooden framework inside the masonry wall, similar to an ordinary stud wall. The framework attaches to the floor and to the ceiling, not to the masonry wall. The framework typically uses 2-by-4 lumber, which is 3.5" (87 mm) deep, regardless of the thickness of the insulation that is used. See the previous Figure 3-114.

For example, assume that the *Insulation Worksheet* recommends 9.5" (24 cm) of batt insulation. Install the framework 6" (15 cm) from the wall. Then, install one layer of 6" (15 cm) thick batts *horizontally* between the framework and the wall. Next, install 3.5" (87 mm) thick batts *vertically* within the framework. This results in snugly fitting insulation, with no air leakage paths between the batts or between the batts and the framework.

Framing for the windows and doors is attached to the masonry wall openings. The interior of the openings extend inward to connect with the insulation framework and with interior finish surface.

Install the interior vapor barrier, if the climate makes a vapor barrier advisable. And finally, attach the interior finish surface to the framework.

Method 2: Rigid Fiberboard

Another method of insulating a masonry wall is to install rigid fiberboard insulation directly on the wall, as in Figure 3-39. The main limitation of fiberboard is the available thickness, which limits this method to milder climates. You may be able to buy fiberboard that is bonded to a variety of interior finish surfaces, including gypsum board, plywood, and other materials.

The most important installation issue is achieving a snug, permanent attachment of the fiberboard to the masonry. Various methods of attaching fiberboard to masonry are used, some better than others. Special broad-head masonry nails are commonly used, but some types fail to hold properly. Make sure that your builder selects a type of fastener that will remain secure.

Before installing the fiberboard, make sure that the surface of the wall is flat and free of protrusions, such as mortar hanging out of the wall.

Framing for the windows and doors is attached to the masonry wall openings, with the interior of the framing extending inward to connect with the interior finish surface of the wall.

Vapor Barriers and Venting
for Masonry Interior Insulation

The method of moisture protection for the wall depends on the climate, as we learned previously. (See *Super-Structure Design Advance #2: Condensation Protection*, at the beginning of Step 3.)

If the climate has an extended cold season, and if it does not have an extended season that is warm and humid, install a vapor barrier on the interior side of the insulation. In other climates, do not install a vapor barrier. If the climate is predominantly warm, the masonry of the wall will act as an adequate vapor barrier, blocking water vapor from the outside.

If the primary structure of the wall is concrete block, and if you insulate the wall with interior fiber insulation and a polyethylene vapor barrier, water vapor can vent through the concrete block. The perm rating of concrete block is not very high, but it is much higher than the perm rating of polyethylene.

In a warm, humid climate, vapor must be able to vent to the inside. It is especially important to avoid interior surface finishes that block venting of water vapor to the inside.

Masonry is easily wetted by liquid water, which wicks through the wall toward the interior of the house. Ample roof overhangs are your primary aid for keeping a masonry wall dry.

Do not install a vapor barrier on any wall that is below grade, for the reasons explained previously when we designed the basement insulation.

EXTERIOR INSULATION FOR MASONRY WALLS

If you install insulation on the outside of the wall, you will use some kind of foam plastic insulation. This method applies to new houses and to existing houses with plain masonry walls.

Installing foam insulation on the outside of the wall offers these advantages:

- *effective condensation protection*. Certain foam insulation – especially extruded polystyrene – is so impermeable that it can act as its own vapor barrier. When the interior of the house is being heated, installing the insulation on the outside keeps the entire wall warmer than the dew point. When the interior is being cooled, the low permeability of the insulation keeps moisture in the outside air from getting into the wall structure. If installed properly, foam insulation also shields the wall from rain soaking.

- *more complete blockage of heat loss*. Exterior insulation can cover the entire area of the wall, so it blocks any heat that escapes into the wall structure from floor slabs, interior walls, chimneys, etc. The insulation can be extended below grade to any desired depth.

- *ease of installation*. All types of exterior insulation can be installed quickly on any wall that consists of flat surfaces. The insulation does not have to work around interior walls and floors. It does not require a separate vapor barrier or venting provisions.

Exterior insulation also has these major limitations:

- *long warm-up time*. If the insulation is placed on the outside of a masonry wall, the interior of the house is exposed to the mass of the masonry. Masonry has a large heat storage capacity. If the masonry has cooled while the space is vacated, or while the temperature has been lowered overnight, it will take a relatively long time for the temperature of the masonry to return to normal indoor temperature. While that is happening, the surrounding cold surfaces may cause discomfort. The heating system can warm the air in the space quickly, but a higher space temperature is needed to compensate for the colder surfaces.

- *limited R-value*. Depending on the type used, exterior insulation is limited to a thickness that ranges from less than one inch (25 mm) to a maximum of about three inches (75 mm), which corresponds to a maximum insulation value of about R-15 (RSI 2.6). However, this limitation is not absolute, and thicker insulation is certainly possible.
- *limited life*. Exterior insulation materials will not last as long as the house. Plastic foam insulation will eventually crack, and then crumble to powder. Expect several replacements during the life of the house, at least until more durable insulation is developed.

In most cases, the best exterior wall insulation is foam plastic boards, such as extruded polystyrene or polyisocyanurate. Plastic foam insulation can also be applied to vertical surfaces by spraying.

We have warned against using plastic insulation in any part of your house that is not buried. The outside of a masonry wall above grade is a possible exception. The risk of a fire igniting the plastic over a concrete wall is acceptably small, unless there are aggravating circumstances.

Installing exterior insulation properly requires a series of steps, as shown in Figure 3-143 for a typical system. The first goal is to keep the insulation pressed snugly against the wall's exterior surface. Otherwise, outside air will penetrate into the space between the insulation and the wall, leaking heat to the outside. Therefore, installation begins by applying a continuous layer of "mastic" to the wall. Mastic is a thick adhesive

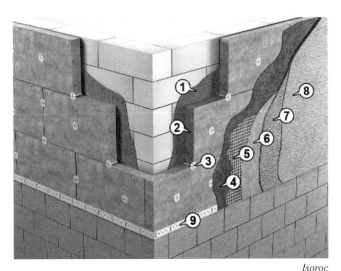

Isoroc

Figure 3-143. Typical exterior insulation of a concrete block wall. Component 1 is a layer of mastic, whose primary function is to prevent convection between the insulation and the wall. Component 2 is the insulation. Component 3 is a system of reliable mechanical fastening, essential for holding the insulation in place. Components 4 through 8 protect the insulation from moisture penetration and mechanical impact.

and sealant. Seal each insulation board to the adjacent ones with the same mastic.

A tight seal between the insulation and the wall is also important because the insulation is acting as the vapor barrier for the wall.

Snug installation requires a method of attachment that will remain secure for the life of the insulation. Only mechanical fasteners have adequate longevity. Plastic insulation becomes weak and brittle with age, so install it in a manner that keeps it physically intact over its useful life.

The insulation must be protected from sunlight and impact. You may be able to buy insulation that is bonded to a plywood nail base, to metal siding, and to other materials. These combinations speed installation, and they allow you to achieve a variety of exterior appearances. For example, you can create a stucco exterior by using glass fiber mesh with the foam boards and then applying stucco over the mesh.

Prevent Air Leakage at the Top of the Wall

The exterior insulation blocks heat conduction through the wall. However, exterior insulation may allow heat loss by convection and air leakage if the wall assembly is not designed and installed properly.

The entire wall structure contains air that is warmed from the inside. The air must be kept from leaking to the outside. The top of the wall is the most serious leakage path because the warm air tends to rise by convection to the top of the wall. If the top of the wall is not sealed, convection will carry the heated air to the outside through the roof eaves.

Figure 3-144 shows three vertical paths for convection inside the wall:
- between the exterior insulation and the concrete wall
- inside the hollow cores of the concrete blocks, if hollow blocks are used
- between the concrete wall and the interior finish.

Eliminate the convection path between the insulation and the concrete wall by installing the insulation snugly against the wall, as in Figure 3-143.

If your wall is made of hollow concrete blocks that have vertical holes, the holes act as chimneys for air currents. There is no practical way to eliminate these currents. They reduce the R-value of concrete block, but this is a minor issue because the block contributes little to the total insulation value of the wall.

It is important to have unbroken mortar joints in the concrete block wall. Gaps in the mortar joints allow air to leak from the inside of the blocks to any gaps between the block and the exterior insulation.

To keep the air inside the blocks from escaping at the top, the top course of concrete blocks should be solid "cap blocks," as shown in Figure 3-144. These are the same as regular concrete blocks, except that they don't have holes. Cap blocks are available in

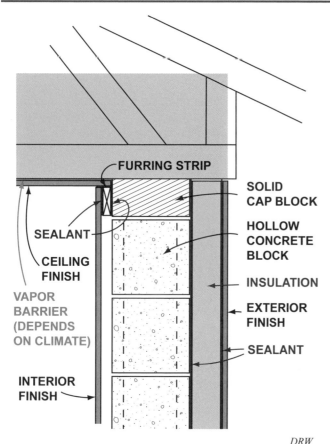

FURRING STRIP

SOLID CAP BLOCK

HOLLOW CONCRETE BLOCK

INSULATION

EXTERIOR FINISH

SEALANT

SEALANT

CEILING FINISH

VAPOR BARRIER (DEPENDS ON CLIMATE)

INTERIOR FINISH

DRW

Figure 3-144. Critical sealing for a concrete wall with exterior insulation. The goal is to create an unbroken barrier against convection through the top of the wall by sealing across all the interior components. Also, an unbroken sealing surface is needed on the outside of the concrete block wall, which is vulnerable to gaps.

various heights, from the full height of the cored blocks to shorter fractional heights. Any height suffices for preventing air leakage.

The interior finish surface, such as gypsum board, typically is attached to the wall with vertical furring strips. This creates a large convection space between the interior finish and the concrete wall. Again, we want to keep the air in this space from escaping at the top. To do this, install a horizontal furring strip at the top of the wall. The furring strip needs to be caulked liberally to the wall and to the interior finish, as shown in Figure 3-144.

Also, the ceiling sheathing should be installed so that it extends all the way to the concrete wall, creating an unbroken seal to the ceiling.

The exterior insulation, which is impermeable, acts as a vapor barrier for the wall. The ceiling should be insulated with non-flammable fiber insulation, which does not act as a vapor barrier. If the climate calls for a ceiling vapor barrier, install it above the ceiling surface, as for any wooden roof.

Moisture Protection for Exterior Insulation

Because the exterior insulation is impermeable, any moisture that gets between the insulation and the wall will be trapped there, causing possible structural damage, mildew, and insect infestation. Such problems have been reported with exterior masonry insulation.

To prevent these problems, keep moisture from getting into the wall. Design the roof so that no rain leakage can enter the top of the wall. Also, use ample roof overhangs to keep the outside of the wall dry, so that rain cannot enter through breaks in the insulation.

Allow water vapor inside the wall to vent before it condenses. Masonry walls with exterior insulation must vent to the inside of the house. The interior surface of the wall should not act as a vapor barrier. In this respect, the wall is similar to basement walls.

In response to moisture problems, some manufacturers of exterior masonry insulation have developed complex vent channels between the insulation and the wall. Avoid these methods, because they allow convective heat loss between the insulation and the wall. Also, the channels are avenues for termites and other insects to invade the wall.

ADDING INSULATION TO EXISTING WALLS

In the United States, many houses built before about 1975 – or even later – have no wall insulation. In many other countries, wall insulation continues to be sporadic. Fortunately, it is often practical to add insulation to the walls of an old house. Reliable methods are available for both frame and masonry walls. However, you need to avoid certain methods of retrofit insulation that can cause big trouble.

Preventing condensation damage is an important issue when adding insulation to existing walls. See the preceding headings about condensation protection in frame and masonry walls.

INSULATING EXISTING FRAME WALLS FROM THE OUTSIDE

One way to insulate an existing frame wall is to remove the outer skin of the wall to expose the wall cavities, fill the wall cavities with insulation, and reinstall the outer skin. In favorable situations, this is almost as simple as it sounds. Figures 3-147 through 3-149 show a successful project of this kind.

DRW

Figure 3-148. The old, leaky single-pane casement window has been replaced with a double-glazed horizontal slider window. The stud spaces are filled with glass fiber batt insulation.

DRW

Figure 3-147. Insulating an old frame wall from the outside. The clapboard and fiberboard outer sheathing have been removed, exposing the uninsulated wall cavity.

DRW

Figure 3-149. The original weak sheathing is replaced with plywood, which will be covered with aluminum siding.

The insulation material is glass or mineral fiber batt. Insert it snugly into the stud spaces, using the same technique that we described previously for insulating frame walls. The only difference is that you are inserting the insulation from the outside, rather than from the inside.

 Adding wall insulation to an existing frame house from the outside may be easier than it looks, and doing so may provide an opportunity to strengthen the wall.

In a climate where it is appropriate to install a vapor barrier, buy batt insulation that has an aluminized backing sheet. Fold the tabs of the backing sheets alongside the batts, and make sure that the backing sheets are installed snugly against the interior surface of the stud spaces.

The vapor barrier created this way is not as vapor-tight as plastic sheet, but in most cases, the foil vapor barrier on the insulation should suffice. However, the new exterior sheathing will retard venting of moisture from the wall. In case of doubt, increase vapor resistance by covering the inside surfaces of the walls with an impermeable material, which might be a thick coat of paint. If that is not practical, you can make small vent holes in the exterior sheathing. If the holes are located away from the parts of the panels that are nailed, the holes will not reduce the strength of the sheathing.

In a climate where a vapor barrier is not desirable, install insulation batts that do not have backing sheets.

As you remove the original sheathing, nail temporary cross braces to the exposed studs. The reason is that the original exterior sheathing may have acted as a cross brace to keep the wall from tipping sidewise ("racking"). If temporary braces are not installed, removing the exterior sheathing transfers all the racking load to the interior wall surface. The wall may then settle, and the interior surface may be damaged.

This is an ideal opportunity to straighten a wall that has fallen out of alignment because the foundation has settled irregularly. This occurs in houses that have weak foundations. The procedure is to jack up the wall from the settled portions of the foundation, strengthen the wall with strong new sheathing, and fill the newly created gaps between the foundation and the bottom of the wall. This is a messy job, likely to create cracks in the interior surfaces and carpentry joints that must be repaired.

In any case, installing a strong exterior sheathing will keep the wall from settling in the future. Strong sheathing turns the wall into a rigid panel. Follow the procedures for selecting and installing the sheathing under the previous heading, *The Exterior Wall Sheathing*.

If the original weather surface consists of large pieces, such as clapboard, it may be practical to reuse it. If so, mark each piece systematically so that it can be reinstalled in its original location. Decide beforehand whether you want to do this, because it will take special care to remove the original material without damaging it.

Alternatively, you may want to upgrade the exterior wall surface. For example, you might replace old painted clapboard with the best grade of aluminum siding to reduce future maintenance. Or, if you yearn for a fancy exterior, you can select a surface that is as dramatic as you like.

This retrofit method cannot super-insulate a wall. The thickness of the insulation is limited to the width of the existing studs. However, if the wall originally had no insulation, filling the available stud space with insulation can make a dramatic improvement in comfort and it can substantially lower heating cost. If the climate does not have an extended cold season, this is likely to be the best compromise for an existing house.

ADDING EXTERIOR INSULATION TO EXISTING MASONRY WALLS

See the previous heading, *Exterior Insulation for Masonry Walls*. The installation issues are the same as for a new house.

With an existing masonry wall, it is important to make sure that heat cannot leak out of the top of the wall by convection. In many houses with uninsulated masonry walls, the tops of the walls are not adequately sealed against air leakage. It may be difficult to seal the walls adequately on a retrofit basis.

ADDING INSULATION TO THE INTERIOR OF WALLS

You can insulate an existing frame or masonry wall by installing insulation inside the original wall. There are two ways of doing this. One is to attach rigid insulation board to the inside surface of the wall. The other is to build a wooden framework inside the original wall, and use the framework to hold batt insulation.

These two methods are largely the same for frame or masonry walls. They are accomplished in the same way in an existing house as in a new house. However, in a new house, you would consider them only for masonry walls. We cover the details under the headings, *Insulating the Interior of Basement Walls*, above, and *Interior Insulation for Masonry Walls*, below.

This pair of methods has disadvantages in an existing house. Both sacrifice floor space, because the additional thickness of insulation intrudes into the room. And, both involve somewhat elaborate carpentry to extend the window openings inward.

Adapting to existing window and door openings is the most awkward part of these methods. It will simplify the job if you can get rid of windows that are not serving a useful purpose for view, daylighting, or ventilation. If so, see the previous heading, *Reducing Window Heat Loss in Existing Houses*, in Step 2.

If the climate makes it desirable to install an interior vapor barrier, install a vapor barrier in the same way as for a new house.

UNDESIRABLE METHODS

Various other methods of adding insulation to walls have been tried. For frame walls, they consist of injecting various insulation materials into the stud spaces through holes drilled in the outside or inside wall surfaces. For masonry walls, they consist of attempts to fill the holes in concrete blocks or to fill the space between concrete block walls and an exterior veneer. Such methods have proven to be unsatisfactory.

Granular insulation, such as foam pellets or cellulose, cannot completely fill the wall. In frame walls, the insulation usually cannot be injected from the top of the wall, so an uninsulated layer remains at the top. The material tends to snag on wiring, fire stops, and nails, leaving large voids. In masonry walls, it snags on extruded mortar, and it does nothing to reduce heat loss through the webs of the concrete blocks. The insulation material tends to leak out of wall penetrations, such as for electrical boxes.

Various kinds of foam insulation have been tried, sometimes with disastrous results. For example, urea formaldehyde foam releases formaldehyde fumes that have made some houses uninhabitable. Foam has difficulty in filling voids. The solidified foam encases electrical wiring, making it impossible to repair wiring or to run new wiring. And, foam insulation emits toxic smoke in a house fire.

Interior Surfaces for Walls and Ceilings

Now that we have completed the structure of the walls and filled them with insulation, we are ready to enclose the walls with an interior surface. This surface is not structural. Its primary purpose is to provide an attractive interior appearance, including the ability to hold decoration, such as wallpaper and pictures.

Gypsum board, widely known as "drywall" or "sheetrock," is by far the most common interior surface for frame walls and ceilings, and for masonry walls that have interior insulation. You can't go wrong by selecting it for most of your interior surfaces.

Gypsum board is an excellent barrier to the spread of fire. It creates an attractive surface when painted, and it holds wallpaper well. It will last for the life of the house. And, it is relatively inexpensive.

Gypsum board is heavy. Its mass makes it effective for blocking noise from the outside, or between rooms. For even better noise blocking, you can buy gypsum board that consists of double sheets, with an air gap between them.

In warm, damp climates, where mildew is a serious threat, gypsum board provides adequate venting of moisture, but it should not be covered with impermeable paint or wall coverings in such climates.

The mass of a gypsum board interior can store a significant amount of heat, which is a design issue for cold climates that we discuss at appropriate points.

Gypsum board has little strength by itself. Indeed, it can support little more than its own weight. And it is crumbly, like chalk. For this reason, make sure that your builder fastens it securely, using plenty of screws to hold it to the structure. This is especially important for ceilings. You don't want heavy gypsum board crashing down upon you during an earth tremor or if a tree falls on the roof.

If you use gypsum board for ceilings, select the thickness to avoid visible sagging between the trusses or rafters. Buy a brand that is reinforced to improve its strength. This is done with strong fibers embedded in the material, and by using facings that have tensile strength to hold the board together.

There are other practical choices for your interior surfaces. These include inexpensive paneling, decorative lumber, corkboard, and many other possibilities. Typically, these are selected to provide a distinctive appearance. Compare their benefits and disadvantages on the basis of the issues that we covered previously.

For rooms where the walls may be wetted by water or condensation, such as shower and bathtub rooms, install an interior surface that resists wetting. Most interior surfaces, including gypsum board, are damaged by moisture. A tile surface generally is best. Refer to our previous discussions of shower and bathtub rooms, in Step 1.

Installing Your Exterior Wall Surfaces

In Step 1, you selected the exterior surfaces for your walls. Now, we are ready to build them. For any type of wall, we have to provide venting of water vapor that comes through the wall from the inside of the house. Also, there needs to be a path for evaporation of moisture that penetrates into the wall from leaks or rain splatter. For brick and stone exterior surfaces, we have additional requirements to support the weight of those surfaces.

LIGHTWEIGHT SURFACES

Most lightweight surfaces are easy to install directly on the exterior wall sheathing. The main caution is to provide for adequate venting of water vapor from the cold side of the wall. If the surface material is impermeable, there must be a method of venting vapor around the material or through it. As we explained before, interlocking aluminum and vinyl siding should have small vent holes on their underside surfaces. Check for this before you buy the material.

Do not caulk any kind of siding. The siding should shed rain, but it should pass water vapor freely.

Long pieces of siding, especially aluminum, may change in length by a fraction of an inch (about one centimeter) as the outside temperature changes. For this reason, the siding has elongated nail holes to allow the siding to slide over the nails as it expands and contracts. The installer must leave space under the nail heads to allow the siding to expand and contract freely.

BRICK VENEER OVER FRAME WALLS

Brick has been used to build walls for centuries. Brick has also long been used as a filler for walls in wooden beam and concrete structures. A relatively new application for brick is using it as a separate covering for a frame wall. This kind of covering is called a "brick veneer." Brick veneers can be very attractive, they can last as long as the house, and they require little maintenance.

However, experience has shown that large brick veneer surfaces have a tendency to crack. At first, it was assumed that cracks were caused by settlement of the foundation, and this is probably the most common cause. However, it was later recognized that thermal expansion and contraction can also cause cracking. So, if you opt for a brick veneer surface, design it to avoid cracking from both causes.

Also, design a brick veneer to expel any water that gets between the veneer and the frame wall.

Solutions for these problems are still being worked out by the construction industry. If you decide to use a brick veneer, spell out the critical details in your drawings and discuss them with your builder. The following are the main design issues.

Foundation Support

A brick veneer is a separate freestanding structure that is supported only at the bottom and by the corners of the veneer. Any break in the foundation will crack the veneer. To avoid cracking, the veneer must rest on a reinforced concrete shear wall foundation, which we covered previously.

The foundation needs a modification to carry the veneer, which is a "brick shelf" or "brick ledge" on the outer side of the foundation wall, as shown in Figure 3-152. The brick shelf should be located below the top of the foundation, so that any water that enters the gap between the brick and the frame wall can drain away from the frame wall to the bottom of the masonry veneer.

Height Limit and Wall Ties

Structurally, a brick veneer is a narrow stack of bricks. The width of common bricks varies from about 3.5" (87 mm) to about 4" (100 mm). The stack has little sidewise support against tipping or buckling. The only effective support for a brick veneer is the corners. The farther the bricks are from a corner, the less support they have against toppling.

For this reason, brick veneers are limited in height. Two stories is a realistic maximum, although building codes may allow somewhat taller veneers. In any location that is prone to strong earth tremors or strong winds, a brick veneer is a gamble.

Figure 3-152. A brick shelf on the outer side of the foundation.

"Wall ties" are commonly used between a frame wall and a masonry veneer to provide sidewise support against wind loads. Building codes generally require them. Wall ties usually take the form of thin steel strips or various shapes of wire loops. One end is nailed to the outside of the frame wall. The other end is buried in a mortar joint of the masonry veneer.

It seems to me that wall ties between a brick veneer and a frame structure are a delusion. A frame wall expands and warps in ways that are very different from the expansion of the brittle masonry veneer, so the two components cannot be tied rigidly to each other. In fact, wall ties for brick veneers are made flexible to accommodate the differences in movement. And anyway, in a moist climate, the steel strips will rust away during the first century of the house's existence.

Expansion and Contraction

A brick veneer expands and contracts as the outdoor temperature changes. In recent years, there has been concern that this may be responsible for cracking of masonry surfaces. This tendency becomes critical when a brick wall exceeds a certain size. It is also related to the climate, the shading of the house, and other factors. For example, cracking is most likely to occur in a large brick wall that receives a lot of warming by sunlight.

Damage occurs because the upper portion of the veneer is free to expand outward, whereas the lower portion of the veneer is held in place on the foundation by the weight of the wall above. As a result, the upper brickwork is pushed outward at the ends of the wall, typically breaking the mortar joints in a stair step pattern.

The construction industry now proposes vertical expansion joints as a solution. These are supposed to be installed at intervals of 20 to 30 feet (5 to 9 meters) for flat wall surfaces. This is now common practice in large commercial buildings with brick surfaces. Also, it is recommended that an expansion joint be installed near one side of an inner or outer corner.

I am skeptical about the value of expansion joints for smaller buildings, such as single-family houses. Expansion joints divide the wall into separate structures, and placing expansion joints near corners forfeits the valuable strengthening that corners provide. Indeed, corners are the only effective supports for a brick veneer above the foundation. Expansion joints are unattractive, spoiling the massive appearance that a brick surface is supposed to create. And, they are an entry for insects.

Unfortunately, protecting brick veneers from thermal cracking is still an open question. If you are interested in a brick veneer, study older houses that have them, and use your best judgement. A brick veneer probably will be okay if you avoid very long surfaces, if you build the veneer on a firm foundation, and if you protect the joints from freeze cracking.

Wide roof overhangs keep the brick dry, which avoids freeze cracking. Also, wide overhangs shade the upper part of the wall, where thermal cracking seems to occur primarily. Add these to the list of benefits provided by roof overhangs.

Water Drainage

There is a gap between the brick veneer and the frame wall, typically about one inch (25 mm) wide. It is conventional doctrine to require "weep holes" at the bottom of this gap to drain any rainwater that may penetrate through the brick. For the same reason, weep holes are placed in the bottom course of bricks where they are supported by a lintel over the top of a window or door.

A common way to create weep holes is to omit the mortar between adjacent bricks at intervals along the lowest course. For example, see Figure 3-153. Other methods include drain tubes or fabric wicks that are installed in the mortar joints. All weep holes are vulnerable to plugging by mortar debris that falls into the bottom of the gap.

The assumed need for weep holes clashes with the reality that they are a highway for insects to enter the house. And, insects may plug the weep holes after laying eggs inside the structure. Various kinds of weep hole materials have been produced to screen against insects.

In the real world, weep holes are commonly omitted from the masonry veneer walls of houses. This may be done deliberately to block insects or just out of ignorance of the drainage issue. In my opinion, the practical solution is to omit weep holes and to use wide roof overhangs to keep the wall from being soaked by rain. Any water that gets behind a brick veneer should evaporate into the space between the veneer and the wall. This space should be vented to the outside at the top of the wall.

BRICK-AND-BLOCK WALLS

A brick surface that is used with a concrete block wall is called "brick-and-block" construction. The brick and the block can be laid in an interlocking pattern that reinforces the wall. This results in a characteristic appearance from the outside, as in Figure 3-154.

This method construction requires the brick and the block to be laid together. This is a slow process that requires special skill. Interlocking the brick and block probably makes the brick surface less vulnerable to cracking from thermal expansion.

Bricks expand slightly after they are made. In contrast, concrete blocks shrink significantly for a period of months after manufacture. If these two materials are joined tightly in a brick-and-block wall, these changes in relative size may break the brick, the block, and/or the mortar joints. A precaution is to use concrete blocks that have been aged.

Another method of joining brick to concrete blocks is to use strong wall ties, as in Figure 3-155. Unlike the flimsy wall ties used between a frame wall and brick veneer, these wall ties are heavy and rigid. They span between adjacent mortar joints in the brick and block.

Ordinary steel wall ties expand when they rust, breaking the wall apart. Wall ties made of stainless steel are now available, and this material should be used if the wall cannot be kept dry for the life of the building.

DRW

Figure 3-153. A "weep hole" created by omitting the mortar between two bricks. It is intended to drain any water that accumulates on top of the steel window lintel.

DRW

Figure 3-154. Two of these rows of brick are turned perpendicular to the others, with their ends showing. The inner ends of the bricks are sandwiched between courses of the concrete block inner wall.

STONE VENEER OVER FRAME WALLS

A stone veneer is similar to a brick veneer. The stones generally are wider than brick, requiring a wider supporting ledge on the foundation. The greater width of stone provides a more stable veneer that is less vulnerable to cracking.

The stone veneer should stand up entirely on its own. A frame wall cannot lend support to a stone veneer, no matter how the stone is installed. A stone wall or veneer is strong only if the stones are sandwiched in place by the weight of the stones above. The mortar acts as a cushion and a seal between the stones.

It may be tempting to lay the stones with their flat sides upright, supporting the stones with mortar and some wall ties attached to the frame wall, but don't do it. An even worse practice is attaching the stones to a wall with mortar alone. This so-called "lick and stick" method is an accident waiting to happen. The stones will eventually break loose from thermal expansion and from freezing of moisture in the joints.

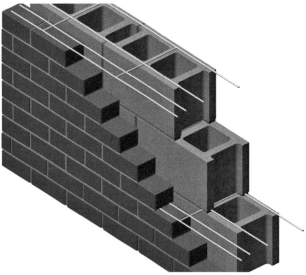

Wire-Bond

Figure 3-155. A method of supporting a brick veneer. Heavy welded wire mesh spans between the mortar joints of the brick and block courses. This method provides lateral support for the narrow brick veneer, but not much strengthening of the concrete block.

STONE VENEER OVER CONCRETE WALLS

A stone veneer can be laid over a concrete or concrete block wall in the same way as with a frame wall, with the stones held in place primarily by their own weight.

Alternatively, it is possible to lay a stone veneer with the stones flat against the concrete by using strong stainless steel wall ties to hold the stones upright. This method requires less stone than laying the stones flat, but it is less reliable. I don't recommend it.

Your Super-Roof

Finally, we will top off the design of your home's structure by designing the roof. You have already selected your roof type (or types) in Step 1 to make the best use of the volume of the roof structure and to make the roof a primary component of your home's appearance. Here, we will design the structure your roof to emphasize the details that will make your roof superior to conventional practice.

Your roof deserves a lot of attention because it performs a number of important functions. It shelters the house from rain and snow, it blocks air leakage, and it holds the insulation for the top of the house. The underside of the roof structure acts as the ceiling of the living space below. In a warm climate, an efficient roof acts as a sun shade for the house and it keeps the top surfaces of the insulation cool.

At the same time, the roof must resist powerful forces that seek to destroy it. A roof may support an enormous weight, and it must be correspondingly strong. The roof's own structure and covering weigh at least 5 pounds per square foot (25 kilograms per square meter), and a roof with a heavy tile surface may weigh 30 pounds per square foot (150 kilograms per square meter).

In a climate where snow may fall, the weight of snow adds to the strength requirement of the roof. For each foot (30 cm) of depth, the additional snow load is about 15 pounds per square foot (75 kilograms per square meter).

Extreme winds, from tornadoes and hurricanes, impose different loads on the roof. In contrast to the previous gravity loads, wind tends to lift the roof off the house. Wind loads require strong connections between the roof and the rest of the house. Similar structural connections are needed to resist earth tremors.

Those loads are distributed over the roof surface. In addition, the roof must withstand localized loads, such as falling tree limbs and people doing repair work. And, the roof is vulnerable to water leakage, condensation, insect attack, sunlight, fire, and hail.

To perform all its functions, the roof has these components:

- the *weatherproof exterior surface*, which may be shingles, tiles, sheetmetal, or other materials
- a *waterproof barrier* between the exterior surface and the roof deck, which commonly is called the "underlayment." Some roof surfaces, especially sheetmetal panels, may not use an underlayment.
- the *roof deck*, which provides local support for the weather surface and the underlayment. The roof

deck may be made with plywood or spaced boards. Sheetmetal panel roofs may not rest on a continuous roof deck, but instead may span between "purlins." The roof deck or purlins also tie the roof structural members together.

- the *supporting structure*, which consists of trusses or beams. "Rafters" are the timbers that support the roof deck. With a truss roof, the rafters are the top members of the trusses. With a triangle-frame roof, the floor joists that connect the bottom ends of the rafters are a part of the roof structure.

The roof encloses the insulation, which rests on top of the ceiling. The roof structure must have vent paths located above the insulation. Venting is needed to protect the roof structure itself, the house structure below, and the insulation. Especially in a "cool roof," the roof may have other components, such as a heat radiation barrier.

Mankind has been learning to build roofs for thousands of years. You can find individual roofs in some parts of the world that have endured for many centuries. However, all contemporary roof construction methods are less than one century old. In addition to providing new benefits, they also have new weaknesses. The construction industry has not yet recognized all these weaknesses and developed reliable solutions to them. Also, poor construction practice can weaken any kind of roof.

In the following, we will cover the design issues that are important for making your roof strong and durable. A good builder will know how to deal with most of these issues, but we introduce some important innovations. Make sure that your builder respects all of the following issues that apply to your roof.

ROOF DESIGN TO RESIST WIND DAMAGE

The previous heading, *Super-Structure Design Advance #4: Super-Strength*, pointed out that large areas of the United States and the rest of the world are vulnerable to windstorms that are severe enough to wreck a house. We learned that the destruction of a house by wind usually begins with a wind pressure that is strong enough to lift the roof off the house.

So, we have to keep the roof attached to the house. Fortunately, this is remarkably easy, inexpensive, and reliable. The main improvements are "hurricane straps" and improved nailing. Also, if your roof will have gable end walls, your design will need to reinforce the end walls to keep them from blowing outward.

"Hurricane Straps"

After the rafters have been set in place, and before the roof deck is installed, a galvanized steel strap or connector is used to hold down each rafter at the point where it rests on the wall.

These connectors are commonly called "hurricane straps." Many kinds are available, each of which connects adjacent components in a slightly different way. Figure 3-158 shows some common types.

With a given type of construction, several types of hurricane straps may work, but some are better than others. Perhaps the strongest kind of hurricane strap is shown in Figure 3-159. It wraps over the top of the rafter, so the strap will hold even if the rafter splits. Also, the strap drops down far enough to attach directly to the wall stud, bridging across the wall top plate. This keeps wind from pulling the top plate off the wall. (Properly installed exterior sheathing also keeps the wall components connected.)

The same benefits can be achieved by using a simple long strap, but it requires tricky bending by the carpenter. Steel connectors designed for the purpose are cheap, and they save labor cost. Make sure that your builder uses the strongest kind.

The steel straps themselves will not fail from the force of a windstorm. However, if they are not installed properly, the nails may pull out. The straps should be attached so that the nails are perpendicular to the pulling force of the strap. Also, the straps should be long enough so that several nails can hold the strap to each member.

The proper technique is to nail the strap to the strongest part of each member. The carpenters should avoid nailing near the edge of a wooden member. If a nail is driven too close to the edge of a member, it will split the wood and the pulling force of the strap will release the nail. Also, the nails should not be spaced too close together.

Securing the Roof Deck and Surface

Even if the roof rafters are held down securely, the lifting force of a windstorm may tear the roof deck from the rafters. The defense is using lots of nails, of the proper size, to fasten the roof sheathing to the rafters. This is where the carpenters can use their favorite toy, the nail gun, to good effect.

The only difference from conventional practice is the spacing of the nails. To find the appropriate nail sizes and spacing, use the Internet to look up the Florida hurricane protection code, which probably provides the most advanced guidance for protecting wooden roofs from wind damage.

The carpenters should be careful to drive the nails through the center of the rafters. This requires drawing

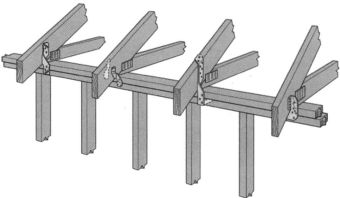

Simpson Strong-Tie

Figure 3-158. A variety of connectors used for holding roof rafters against wind forces.

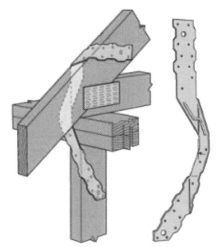

Simpson Strong-Tie

Figure 3-159. A rafter connector that is especially strong because it wraps over the top of the rafter and bridges across the top plate to attach to a wall stud.

a line on top of the sheathing to mark the centerline of the rafter below. This takes a little extra effort, but it is essential. A nail that splits the edge of the rafter has no holding power.

Once the roof deck is secure, the next step is to secure the roof surface material. Each type of roof surface – shingles, metal panels, and tiles – has its own techniques for resisting wind.

For asphalt shingles, use special nails that have large plastic washers. Staples, which are now the favored method of attaching shingles, will pull through a shingle that is being lifted by wind. Another defense is to buy shingles that have strong fiber reinforcement, making it more difficult for the shingles to tear loose from the nails or staples.

Figure 3-160. Conventional gable end wall construction. This is similar to the construction of a stud wall, except that the shape is triangular. The connections at the top and bottom edges should be reinforced to resist wind damage.

For metal roofing, there are various kinds of attachments. Select "standing seam" roofing that has a strong, invisible attachment to the roof deck. Perhaps most important, secure the bottom edges of the panels so that wind cannot get underneath them. The best way to do this is to make the panels about two inches (50 mm) longer than the roof deck. Using a sheetmetal bender, bend the excess length downward and screw it to the edge of the roof using stainless screws.

Roof tiles depend mainly on their weight to resist wind. I am not aware of any reliable method of attaching tiles that resists extreme winds. That being said, it takes very severe wind to lift heavy ceramic roof tiles.

Reinforcing Gable End Walls

When a strong wind blows against a house, a sloped roof surface offers less resistance than a vertical surface, such a gable end wall. For this reason, houses that are built entirely with hip roofs have suffered less hurricane damage than houses with gable roofs.

The greater damage to gable roofs usually is caused by a failure of the gable end wall. High pressure inside the attic and low pressure outside combine to push the gable end outward. Loss of the gable end leaves the roof and the wall below the gable end unsupported.

This does not mean that you should avoid building a gable roof. You can reinforce a gable end wall to make it just as resistant to wind as any other roof shape. It's just a matter of knowing how to do it.

The gable end is a triangular wall section. It should be built in the same way as a frame stud wall, as in

Figure 3-160. The studs of the gable end should have their wide dimension perpendicular to the wall surface for maximum strength, as shown. In this way, the studs themselves will survive any wind pressure.

The slanted top plates of the end wall should be fastened securely to the studs. The bottoms of the studs should be attached securely to the top plate of the wall below. Use the exterior sheathing of the end wall as a connector across all the joints in the wall, using plenty of nails. This is the same way that we use the exterior sheathing of the other walls to tie the wall components together.

So, what makes a gable end wall more vulnerable to wind damage? It can fail in three ways, each of which has its own solution.

(1) In a truss roof, the carpenters may make the mistake of using one of the trusses as an end wall. However, a truss has little resistance to sidewise bending. Unlike a properly built end wall, the truss members are not oriented to resist sidewise wind pressure, and there are few members that span between the top and bottom of the end wall. High winds can easily break a truss that is mistakenly installed as an end wall.

The defense against this weakness is to build the end wall properly, as shown in Figure 3-160.

(2) The roof deck (usually plywood) holds the top of the gable end wall. If the roof attachment breaks, pressure inside the attic pushes the top of the gable end outward, and the gable end will tip over like the flap of an envelope.

The defense against this failure is to use strong roof sheathing as a connector between the top of the gable end wall and the adjacent roof rafters. Use lots of nails to hold the sheathing to the top of the gable end wall and to the rafters.

If the roof has a deep overhang over the gable end, "lookout rafters" rest on the top of the gable end wall, as in Figure 3-164, below. The roof deck is nailed to the tops of the lookout rafters. To keep the lookout rafters from separating from the end wall, wrap a hurricane strap around each lookout rafter and nail it to the inside of the wall studs, as shown in Figure 3-164.

(3) In a frame house, the triangular gable end wall sits on top of a rectangular wall. Low pressure on the outside of the wall pulls both walls outward. This breaks the joint between the two walls. Once this joint separates, both walls are likely to be sucked off the house.

The solution is to brace the bottom of the triangular gable end so that it cannot bow outward. There are various ways to do this. Figure 3-161 shows a method that is strong and simple. It uses plywood and lots of nails to connect several of the ceiling joists that are closest to the gable end. The plywood extends across the width of the end wall. The combination of the plywood and the ceiling joists creates a horizontal beam that cannot bend outward or inward.

Steel straps hold the bottoms of the end wall studs to the plywood and the ceiling joists. The steel straps should be wrapped around the studs in the same way that hurricane straps wrap over the tops of rafters.

"Blocking," or cross bracing, is used between two adjacent ceiling joists to prevent the joists from tipping over when a windstorm pulls or pushes on the gable end wall.

Bracing the bottom of the gable end has become a standard practice in hurricane regions. Insurance companies in those regions may substantially lower their premiums if such features are installed.

In an existing house, end wall bracing is almost as easy and inexpensive as in a new house, provided that the attic space adjacent to the end wall is accessible.

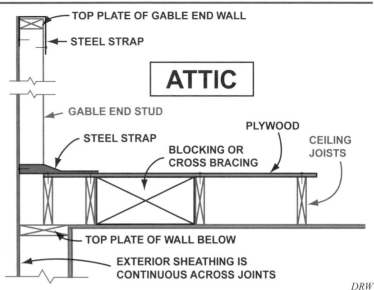

DRW

Figure 3-161. Strong reinforcement for a gable end wall that prevents the wall from bowing outward during a windstorm. This method is easily adapted to an existing house.

A CRITICAL IMPROVEMENT IN TRUSS CONNECTIONS

Today, most roof trusses are made to order by specialized factories. Therefore, you can expect the trusses to be adequately engineered and to meet building codes. However, I believe that there is a serious flaw in modern trusses, which is the current method of joining the lumber pieces.

Large forces occur at some of the connections between the truss members. For this reason, the lumber members are joined by metal plates, commonly called "connector plates," "truss plates" or "gusset plates." Since the 1960's, almost all prefabricated residential trusses have been held together with one type of connector plate. This type lacks a standard name, but it is sometimes called a "tooth plate."

A tooth plate is a relatively thin piece of galvanized steel that is punched to created a large number of short teeth that stick out from the plate. At the truss factory, the lumber members are laid in position, and tooth plates are pressed into the lumber across the joints, yielding the kind of connections shown in Figure 3-162.

This method of making trusses is so easy and cheap that it seems too good to be true. And, it probably is. I don't doubt that tooth plates have been tested extensively, and that they can provide adequate strength when a truss is new. But, what happens after a century? Nobody really knows.

DRW

Figure 3-162. Tooth plates that hold truss members together. The large plate on the right front holds two bottom members together against very strong tension. The smaller plate on the left front supports unbalanced roof loads and the weight of the bottom member.

The thin teeth can rust enough to disintegrate. And, after the structure is shaken by decades of wind and earth movement, it seems that the teeth may eventually pull out. The result could be abrupt and catastrophic collapse of the roof.

In fact, there have been reports of tooth plates rusting away in less than ten years, causing roofs to collapse. To date, these failures have occurred in especially corrosive environments, such as barns in humid environments. While not typical of most houses, these early failures reveal the weakness of tooth plates.

You can tell that truss manufacturers are worried about tooth plates coming loose because they may drive a few staples through the holes to attach the plates better. In my observation, this is an afterthought that is done almost randomly, and it seems almost useless.

The solution is to use truss connections that are stronger than tooth plates. One alternative is to use thicker connector plates that are attached with nails that are long enough to pass through most of the thickness of the lumber.

 Improve the connections in your roof trusses to prevent a roof collapse in the future.

At joints that are subjected to strong pulling forces, even stronger connections are needed. Use pairs of connector plates or pairs of timbers that are bolted through the truss members. The connector should extend well beyond both adjoining ends. This avoids splitting the wood, and it exploits the friction between the connectors and the truss members.

If you can't find a truss manufacturer who will build your trusses in this manner, one alternative is to have your builder install reinforcements over the tooth plates before the trusses are installed.

In an existing building, you can use this same method to reinforce trusses in place.

STRONG FRAMING FOR ROOF OVERHANGS

Deep roof overhangs provide a number of important benefits for most houses. (See *Exploit Roof Overhangs*, in Step 1.) However, deep overhangs require proper carpentry to avoid sagging or collapse.

All overhangs must be able to carry the same weight as the main part of the roof, including the roofing materials, snow, people, and falling tree limbs. Because an overhang is supported only on one side, it must be built as a strong cantilever to carry these loads. Overhangs need separate framing techniques for the eaves, the end walls, and the corners.

It is easy to build strong overhangs at the eaves (the lower edges of a sloping roof). Simply extend the

DRW

Figure 3-163. Weak method of building a gable end overhang. The short blocks that support the overhang are easily pushed down. This is about the maximum overhang that is permissible with this method.

rafters outward to form the overhangs. The rafters are easily strong enough for any reasonable overhang.

It takes more elaborate carpentry to build strong overhangs that extend beyond gable end walls. Short end wall overhangs typically are made using the method shown in Figure 3-163, by nailing wooden blocks to the end wall. This method is acceptable only if the overhang extends no more than about 150% of the height of the blocks. Weight on deeper overhangs could easily pull the nails loose and tip the overhang downward.

For beam and triangle-frame roofs, a strong method of making end wall overhangs is shown in Figure 3-164. The overhang is built using rafters that are placed over the end walls perpendicular to the main rafters. Such rafters are called "lookout" rafters. A better name might be "balanced" rafters because they are balanced on the end wall. Visualize a heavy snow load on the roof. You want the weight on the outer ends of the lookout rafters to be no greater than the weight on the inner ends. Therefore, ***lookout rafters should extend inward by at least the same length that they extend outward***.

The inner ends of the lookout rafters are attached to the last main rafter. If the overhang is wide, double the last rafter and connect the lookout rafters strongly to the doubled main rafters.

DRW

Figure 3-164. A strong gable end overhang. The "lookout rafters" are balanced on the end wall. This method allows long overhangs. Each lookout rafter is secured to the gable end wall with a hurricane strap that is wrapped over the top.

To support each corner of a deep roof overhang, use a diagonal balance rafter that extends out to the corner. The outer end of this diagonal connects with the ends of the "fascia" boards for the eave and the gable end. The fascia boards are primary strength members for the corners of overhangs.

(Fascia boards are the boards that you see under the edges of a roof. See the roof pictures in Step 1 for a sampling. In addition to supporting the outer edges of the roof deck, they also hold the gutters and they provide a finished appearance to the roof perimeter.)

Another way to support a long gable extension is to use large brackets that are attached to the gable end wall, as in Figure 3-165. This method can be used with any kind of roof construction The brackets tend to bend the wall at the points where they are attached. Therefore, the wall needs to be reinforced at these points.

The brackets are prominent visual features, so consider ways to decorate them. For example, heavily decorated roof brackets are a characteristic of the "Swiss chalet" style.

DRW

Figure 3-165. A gable end overhang that is supported by wall brackets. The wall should be reinforced where the brackets are attached. The ends of these brackets extend beyond the roof edge, where they will rot if they are not covered against weather.

CRITICAL CONNECTIONS IN TRIANGLE-FRAME STRUCTURES

A triangle-frame roof structure can be very strong because it is a triangle. In order for the triangle to hold together under the forces that attack a roof, all three corners of the triangle must be connected strongly. In addition, if the bottom of the triangle-frame – which usually acts as a floor – is made of more than one piece, then the separate pieces must be joined strongly.

All these connections must be made with bolts of adequate size and strength. Some carpenters make a religion of using nails for everything, but this is not a job for nails.

If you use solid lumber members, you can bolt them together using overlapping joints or by using galvanized steel straps where the timbers butt together. The straps should be at least 1/8" (3 mm) thick.

If you use I-joist members, reinforce the webs of the I-joist at the connection points. Then, join the members with steel straps. Also, reinforce the joists at the points where they rest on the walls that support the roof.

If you are building an A-frame house, the rafters typically rest on short concrete side walls. You need to connect the bottoms of the rafters so that their outward thrust does not topple the side walls. Usually, an

A-frame house connects the bottoms of the rafters with the joists for the ground level floor.

If your A-frame house will have a concrete floor, install reinforcing steel across the slab. Otherwise, the outward thrust of the rafters will eventually break the floor. If the rafters rest on short walls that are built on the slab, use additional reinforcing steel to rigidly connect the walls to the floor.

BUILD STRONG DORMERS

In Step 1, you saw how dormers look from the outside and from the inside. Competent carpenters know how to build dormers properly, but you have a number of design options to consider. So, we'll give you a quick lesson in dormer construction to speed you through this part of your roof design.

The first issue is preserving the strength of the roof. Installing dormers requires cutting through rafters, so the primary method of maintaining roof strength is to keep the dormers narrow. You can observe that most dormers are the width of two rafter spaces, so that only one rafter is cut away to make a hole for the dormer. For example, if the rafter spacing is 24" (60 cm), the dormer inside dimension usually is about 46" (115 cm). As a result, dormers don't provide much additional living space.

The right kind of framing is needed to support the dormer itself, and to support the portions of the roof that lie above and below the dormer opening. The sides of the dormer, along with most of the dormer's weight, are supported by rafters. Figure 3-166 shows the general arrangement.

DRW

Figure 3-166. Framing of a dormer. This is a "floating" dormer, which is supported entirely by the rafters. The top of the roof opening for this dormer is rectangular, so it will have a flat ceiling. The dormer roof, which remains to be added, could have a variety of shapes.

A horizontal header at the top of the roof opening spans between the intact rafters on each side of the dormer. This header supports the bottom of one or more rafters that are cut off above the dormer. The same technique can be used to support the portion of the roof below the dormer. When a dormer is supported entirely by the rafters in this manner, it is called a "floating dormer."

Another method is to support the bottom of the dormer, and the cut rafters below the dormer, on a "knee wall." This is a short interior wall that transmits the weight of the front of the dormer to the floor joists. Figure 1-112, in Step 1, shows how knee walls are built in a triangle-frame roof.

A knee wall creates a triangular void space, which may be used for storage. Take care to insulate this portion of the roof properly, and to seal it against air leakage.

A third method is to rest the front of the dormer on the top of the exterior wall. This brings the dormer farther forward, and lower, than the other two methods.

Each of these construction options results in a different interior appearance. See Figure 1-218, in Step 1, for a comparison. The dormer may have a flat ceiling, in which case the interior opening will be rectangular. Or, the dormer ceiling may follow the shape of the dormer roof.

RAFTER DEPTH IN BEAM AND TRIANGLE-FRAME ROOFS

For adequate strength, the depth of the rafters is determined by load on the roof and the length of the span. If you use I-joist for the rafters, the manufacturer will provide a table that allows you to order joists of the correct depth. If you use solid timbers, you can get the appropriate depths from tables in popular construction handbooks. Or, make an Internet search for "depth of rafters" or similar search words.

Your super-house may need rafters that are deeper than needed for strength alone. In a cold climate, the rafters may need additional depth to accommodate super-insulation, along with a space above the insulation for venting moisture. In a warm climate, the rafters may need extra depth for the insulation, for cooling ventilation, and perhaps for a heat radiation barrier. We cover these issues below, under *Cool Roofs for Warm Climates*.

If you have any doubt about the rafter dimensions, hire an engineer to calculate them for you. See *Getting Expert Help*, in Section 8, for suggestions in hiring an engineer.

CAUTION WHEN USING I-JOIST AS RAFTERS

We have explained why I-joist has become a preferred material for floor joists. I-joist offers the same advantages when used as roof rafters. However, when used as rafters, the material is subject to higher temperatures for long periods. This will degrade the adhesives more quickly. (See the previous sidebar, *Adhesives in Construction*.) This makes it especially important to avoid I-joist that is made with composite materials (glued chips or strips). The top and bottom flanges of the I-joist should be solid lumber, and the webs should be true plywood.

I-joist rafters encounter the highest temperatures in beam and triangle-frame roofs, which restrict the ventilation that cools the roof deck. In my home, I used I-joist to build a large beam roof for an addition. After 25 years, it was necessary to repair some damage at the ridge of the roof, allowing me to inspect the I-joist there. The adhesive was still intact, but the wood had become quite brittle.

The highest temperatures will occur in the top flange of I-joist rafters, which contact the hot roof deck. In beam and triangle-frame roofs, the bottom flanges lie at the bottom of the insulation layer, which is the coolest part of the roof. Fortunately, the integrity of the bottom flanges is most important for carrying the roof load.

With any kind of roof that uses I-joist rafters, make a special effort to provide cooling ventilation to extend the life of the I-joist. The same cooling will also extend the life of asphalt shingles.

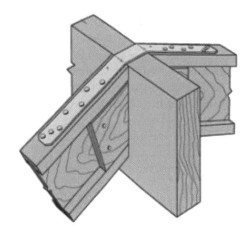

Simpson Strong-Tie

Figure 3-167. Using a steel tie strap to hold opposing roof beams or rafters together at the top.

In contrast, truss roofs do not use I-joist, and they can be well ventilated for cooling. More generally, any roof structure that uses solid timbers exclusively is probably immune to weakening by high roof temperatures.

SECURE ROOF BEAMS AT EACH END

In a beam roof, each beam must be secured strongly to the walls that support it at each end. Use steel "hurricane straps" at each end, not just nails. Connections at both ends are needed to keep the roof from sliding downhill and to keep it from flying away in high winds. Conversely, the roof beams act as connectors between the tops of the walls, keeping the walls upright and straight, and creating a strong box structure.

If you use I-joists for your roof beams, make sure to reinforce them properly at the points where structural connections are attached and where they rest on their supports, as we discussed previously under the heading, *Wooden I-Joist, a Material You Need to Understand*.

If the ends of beams meet at a ridge, connect the ends with strong galvanized steel straps that are nailed properly to the top flange, as in Figure 3-167. Or, bolt long connecting straps to the webs of the opposing joists.

AVOID COLLAR BEAM ROOF CONSTRUCTION!

Collar beam construction is a cheap way to build a plain gable roof. Only a fraction of the rafters are tied together to prevent collapse. Boards called "collar beams" tie these rafters together at an intermediate height, as shown in Figure 3-168.

DRW

Figure 3-168. The inside of a collar beam roof. The roof is supported by horizontal boards that join only a fraction of the rafters. The roof is vulnerable to sagging and collapse unless the ends of the rafters are strongly connected to the ceiling joists, and the ceiling joists are strongly connected to each other.

These rafters support the ridge beam like the legs of a sawhorse. In turn, the ridge beam supports the tops of the remaining rafters. The lower ends of these rafters merely rest on the outer walls, and nothing prevents them from splaying outward, except perhaps a few nails into the ceiling joists.

Sooner or later, the unsupported portions of the ridge rafter will sag because the weight of the roof creates enormous outward thrust on the rafters. The entire roof is vulnerable to collapse. Unfortunately, this type of roof construction has been fairly common in the past, and you may still find it today. Avoid any suggestion to use this construction method on your house.

If you have an existing house with a collar beam roof, strengthen the roof. For example, if the ridge is above a load-bearing wall, you can support the ridge with closely spaced column jacks that rest on the ceiling joists above the load-bearing wall. At the same time, attempt to correct any sagging that has already occurred. This is dangerous work, so get a skilled contractor to do it.

ROOF SUPER-INSULATION

The roof insulation comprises the largest single part of your home's super-insulation. Your roof design should provide adequate space for it.

The basic geometry of roof insulation is the same for all the common types of wooden roofs. The insulation is always installed flush against the ceiling of the space below, and it overlaps the tops of the exterior walls. It should rest snugly against the bottom of the roof structure.

The top of the insulation is exposed to the interior of the roof structure. Any moisture that gets into the insulation must be able to evaporate upward into the roof structure and to escape to the outside through vents.

Use the *Insulation Worksheet* to calculate the amounts of insulation to install. The roof insulation is the largest continuous area of insulation in the house, and it is easy to install if the roof is designed properly. This makes the roof insulation especially economical, so don't skimp on it.

The *Insulation Worksheet* recommends larger insulation values for the roof than for the other parts of the structure. The roof insulation is especially important because it is subjected to the largest differences between the indoor and outdoor temperatures. During cold weather, roof cooling by radiation into the sky increases heat loss. During warm weather, roof heating by the sun during the daytime may double or triple the flow of heat into the house through the roof.

For wooden roof structures, the best insulation practices for cold weather are the same as for warm weather. Here is the recipe for the best possible roof insulation:

- *Select the best kind of insulation.* For truss, beam, and triangle-frame roofs, this usually is glass or mineral fiber batts. For roof structures with horizontal bottom members, cellulose insulation is a secondary choice.
- *Select the optimum amount of insulation.* Use the *Insulation Worksheet.*
- *Design the roof structure to accommodate the thickness of the insulation and the appropriate venting.* We will cover venting for moisture control and venting for cooling, each of which involves different techniques.
- *Design retainers to hold the insulation in place.* Retainers position the insulation where it is needed to block heat loss, to avoid fire hazards, and to maintain free vent paths.
- *Install the insulation carefully.* With batt insulation, take care to place the insulation snugly against the interior surface and to avoid convection paths around the sides of the batts. Snug fit also makes the insulation a powerful barrier to fire.

To achieve perfect roof insulation, we will cover some critical details that tend to be ignored or to be done poorly. The details for truss roofs are somewhat different from those for beam or triangle-frame roofs, so we will cover them separately. After that, we will deal with insulation that is installed above a roof deck.

Insulating Beam and Triangle-Frame Roofs

Batt insulation for a beam or triangle-frame roof usually is installed from below, after the roof surface is in place. The batts are inserted between the rafters in the same way they are inserted between walls studs.

However, be careful that the batts are not pushed up into the vent space on top of the insulation. This is in contrast to wall insulation, which should completely fill the stud space.

If electrical wiring is installed in a beam roof, secure it along the sides of the rafters before the insulation is installed, to minimize interference with the insulation.

If an interior vapor barrier is required, it is installed over the inside surface of the roof, after the insulation is installed. We described the vapor barrier installation previously.

■ The Best Insulation for Beam Roofs

The only kind of insulation to use in a beam roof is glass or mineral fiber batts. A sloped beam roof needs the rigidity of batts to hold the insulation together as it is installed and to keep it in place once the insulation is installed. Also, you want the fire safety of inorganic fiber and its resistance to moisture, vermin, and settling.

If your house has frame walls, this is the same kind of insulation at that you use in your walls.

If you use I-joist for your roof beams, select batts that are about one inch (25 mm) wider than batts that are sized to fit between ordinary lumber joists. (If your walls use fabricated studs, this is the same width that you use in your walls.) The batts should fit snugly on each side. Any gap along the sides of the batts will allow a lot of heat to bypass the insulation by convection. Make sure that your builder orders the correct widths.

The bottom layer of batts should have a paper backing with side tabs. Staple the tabs to the bottom sides of the rafters. The tabs keep the insulation from falling out of the ceiling before the main vapor barrier and the interior sheathing are installed. Also, they keep the batts from sliding downhill inside the roof. If you need more than one layer of insulation, the upper layers should have no backing sheets. They will be held in place by friction until you install the bottom layer.

■ Insulating the Eaves

Extend the roof insulation outward so that it fully overlaps the insulation in the wall below, as in Figure 3-171. The outer end of the insulation should rest snugly against retainer boards, which locate the ends of the batts properly. The retainers also keep wind from blowing underneath the bottoms of the batts. To block wind completely, caulk the bottoms and sides of the retainer boards to the adjacent structure.

Make the retainer boards no higher than the tops of the insulation batts. The gap above the retainers is needed for moisture venting and for ventilation cooling of the roof.

Install screens to keep insects and birds from entering the eave space. If the climate has a warm season, make the screens as large as possible because they interfere with cooling air flow.

■ Insulation Barriers Around Hot Equipment

Make sure that the insulation cannot block the needed cooling of any heat-generating equipment that is installed in the ceiling or that passes through the ceiling. If such items are covered or surrounded by insulation, they may be damaged or they may become hot enough to start a fire. The most common hazards are recessed incandescent light fixtures, ceiling-mounted space heaters, and flues.

The solution is to design barriers around such equipment to keep the insulation away from them.

Whenever possible, avoid equipment that is built into the ceiling, such as recessed light fixtures. In addition to creating a break in the ceiling insulation,

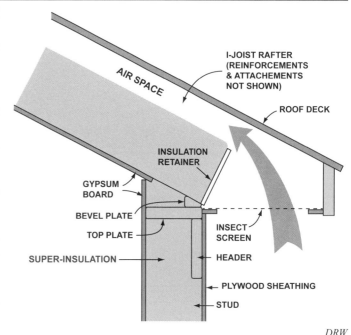

DRW

Figure 3-171. Eave insulation and ventilation for a beam roof located in a mild or warm climate. For ventilation cooling, make the area of the insect screens as large as possible because the screens obstruct air flow.

they create air leaks. If your house will need a flue that passes through the roof, we explain elsewhere how to seal it against air leakage.

Insulating Truss Roofs, Attics, and Voids

One of the main advantages of a truss roof is that you can install an almost unlimited amount of insulation in it. If the roof is well designed, installing the insulation is easy. For the same reasons, increasing attic insulation is often a valuable energy efficiency upgrade for an existing house.

The insulation for a truss roof usually is installed from inside the attic space, after the ceiling surface is attached to the bottoms of the trusses. Both batts and loose fill insulation are satisfactory, but loose fill can be used only if the bottoms of the trusses are horizontal.

The main exception would be insulating an inaccessible void space, which would require installing the insulation from the outside, before installing the enclosing surface. As a rule, design your roof so that it has no void spaces.

If the climate requires a vapor barrier to be installed on the underside of the insulation, staple it to the bottoms of the trusses before the ceiling surface (usually drywall) is attached to the bottoms of the trusses. Thus, the vapor barrier will be in place by the time the insulation is installed. (See the previous heading, *The Wall and Ceiling Vapor Barrier in Frame Construction*.)

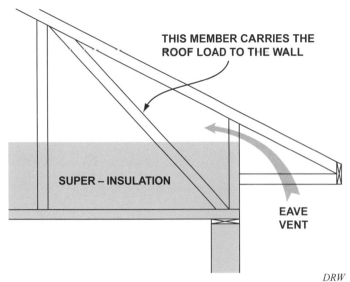

Figure 3-172. The eave end of this truss is modified to provide clearance for attic super-insulation. This feature is often called an "energy heel." It raises the overall height of the roof. If the attic uses eave vents, still more height is needed to allow outside air to pass between the insulation and the roof deck.

■ Design the Trusses for Super-Insulation

Figure 3-30 shows the difference between conventional insulation and super-insulation in a house that has a vented attic. Super-insulation is thicker, so it requires more space in the attic. Providing this space is a simple matter of elevating the roof to provide clearance for the insulation. To do this, design the trusses to include a so-called "energy heel," as shown in Figure 3-172.

If the roof uses eave vents, additional clearance is needed between the insulation and the roof deck. This allows moisture and/or air to flow through the gap between the two, as shown in Figure 3-172. Without the gap, the eave vents would be isolated from the attic space, making them useless.

 Include walkway supports in your truss design to make the attic useful for storage and to protect thick insulation.

If eave vents are used primarily to vent moisture, the required clearance is small, as we will discuss under the heading, *Moisture Venting for Truss Roofs, Attic Spaces, and Voids.* If eave vents are used for ventilation cooling of the roof, the opening between the insulation and the roof deck must be large, as we will discuss under the heading, *Ventilation Cooling for Attic Roofs.*

You can see from Figure 3-172 that deep attic insulation favors wide roof overhangs. The overhang allows the roof surface to drop down toward the top of the wall and the windows, avoiding an awkward blank wall space above the windows. Overhangs offer

other important benefits, which we listed under the heading, *Exploit Roof Overhangs*, in Step 1.

Another way to provide space for super-insulation and to increase eave venting is to give the roof a gambrel shape, which has sides that are almost vertical. However, it is rare to find a gambrel-shaped attic. The increased volume under the roof is too enticing to use as enclosed living space, rather than as a vented attic.

Protect the insulation from activity inside the attic. Otherwise, the insulation will be crushed, and someone is likely to cause damage by stepping on the ceiling of the space below. Design your trusses to support walkways above the insulation, as shown in Figure 1-107, in Step 1.

Aside from installing and protecting the attic insulation, make the attic space large enough so that people can enter it easily to install the insulation, wiring, and ceiling fixtures. Provide ample headroom, at least for getting from one part of the attic to another. Easy access promotes good workmanship and lowers labor cost.

Your attic will be used for storage, whether you plan to or not, so provide an ample amount of accessible storage space in it. While you are at it, you can design your trusses to include supports for storage shelves. Refer back to *The Attic As Storage Space*, in Step 1.

■ Insulating with Batts

Usually, the best insulation for a truss roof is glass or mineral fiber in the form of batts. You want its fire safety and its resistance to moisture, vermin, and settling. Batts are easy to remove individually, for example, to clear work space for installing an electrical fixture on the ceiling.

The batts do not need backing sheets. In climates where a vapor barrier is desirable for the ceiling, a continuous vapor barrier was previously installed from below, before the interior ceiling surface was attached to the trusses. Be careful not to puncture this vapor barrier when laying the insulation. (Installing the vapor barrier is different when adding insulation to an existing house, as we discuss below.)

To achieve the recommended R-value for colder climates, install the batts in layers. The top of the first layer should match the top of the ceiling joists. (In a truss roof, the ceiling joists are the bottom members of the roof trusses.) The next layer is laid across the joists. This crisscross arrangement minimizes convection leakage between the batts and the joists.

The key to perfect batt insulation is careful installation. The batts are inserted between the ceiling joists in the same way that wall insulation is inserted between walls studs.

It's like tailoring. The tools are a big pair of scissors and a long trowel. The goal is to prevent voids between the insulation and the ceiling below. The scissors are used to cut the batts to fit around truss members and around obstructions, such as electrical boxes, recessed light fixtures (avoid them), and ceiling heaters. Cut the batts where necessary to allow wiring to pass through it. Use the trowel to slide the sides of the batts all the way down to the ceiling surface.

If an attic or void space is not easily accessible for installing the insulation, it becomes necessary to install the insulation from below, as with a beam roof. You won't be able to crisscross the batts across the ceiling joists, which is essential if multiple layers of insulation are required. For this reason and others, try to avoid a roof design that creates inaccessible voids.

■ Insulating with Loose Fill

If the attic has a horizontal floor, you have the alternative of installing loose fill insulation. Loose fill is favored by contractors because it is inexpensive to install. Also, it avoids gaps around truss members.

However, loose fill falls into spaces where it does not belong, such as vented eaves and flue chases. It may block proper venting of hot equipment. If you select loose fill, it is especially important to build barriers to keep it where it belongs.

Cellulose loose fill insulation is widely used in attics, despite having serious drawbacks. See our previous discussion, *Cellulose Insulation, a Problematic Option.*

Chopped glass and mineral fiber loose fill insulation avoids most of the weaknesses of cellulose insulation. However, those materials are dangerous to inhale, and they are unpleasant to handle. The fibers tend to get into skin and eyes. For those reasons, I don't recommend glass or mineral fiber in the form of loose fill. Instead, use those materials in the form of batts.

■ Insulating at the Eaves

Extend the ceiling insulation outward so that it fully overlaps the insulation in the wall below, as in Figure 3-25. If necessary, install retainer boards to keep the insulation from pushing too far out into the eaves and blocking air circulation from the eave vents.

■ Insulation Barriers Around Hot Equipment

Make sure that the attic insulation does not block the cooling that is needed by heat-generating equipment that is installed in the ceiling or that passes through the ceiling. If such items are covered or surrounded by insulation, they may be damaged or they may become hot enough to start a fire. The most common hazards are recessed incandescent light fixtures, ceiling-mounted space heaters, and flues.

The solution is to design barriers around such equipment to keep the insulation away from them. This applies to both batt insulation and loose fill. In the case of loose fill, the barriers need to extend well above the top of the insulation.

Whenever possible, avoid equipment that is built into the ceiling, such as recessed light fixtures. In addition to creating a break in the ceiling insulation, they create air leaks. If your house will need a flue – which can be avoided with most of our recommended types of heating equipment – we explain elsewhere how to seal it against air leakage.

Adding More Insulation to an Existing Truss Roof

In existing houses, increasing attic insulation is a common energy efficiency upgrade, for good reasons. This improvement can make the entire house more comfortable while significantly reducing heating and cooling costs. Adding insulation is fairly easy if the attic space is accessible. As a do-it-yourself project, the cost is low in relation to the benefit.

Installing additional insulation in the attic of an existing house follows the same procedures as for insulating a new house. However, installing the vapor barrier is different. If no vapor barrier was originally installed (a likely situation), it is necessary to remove any existing insulation and lay a vapor barrier over the exposed ceiling. There are two ways to do this.

The easiest method is to install batt insulation that has a vapor barrier backing, typically aluminum foil. The backing is placed face down, against the ceiling surface. Any additional insulation should have no vapor barriers. This method allows some leakage of water vapor between the batts and the ceiling joists.

A more complete barrier is provided by laying polyethylene plastic sheet across the attic floor and laying the insulation on top of the plastic sheet. If you choose this method, it is important to provide slack at the bottoms of the joist spaces, so that the insulation can completely fill the joist spaces. This method provides a bonus of additional protection against small roof leaks.

On balance, I prefer the easier method, which is installing batts with vapor barrier backings. Any small amount of moisture that leaks around the backing sheets into the attic can vent easily to the outside. Condensation damage is unlikely if the insulation is installed snugly.

Insulating Concrete and Flat Roofs

We will start by repeating that flat roofs of any kind, including concrete, are generally unsatisfactory unless the climate is warm and dry. Also, a "flat" roof should never be literally flat, but should have some slope to drain rain.

Concrete roofs and other flat roofs can be insulated from above, from below, or in the middle. All the current methods have limitations. The best choice depends primarily on these factors:

- the climate
- the available construction materials
- whether you want the roof to support loads, such as walking, air conditioning equipment, etc.

If the climate is always warm, the insulation can be attached to the underside of the roof deck. No vapor barrier is used, so the insulation can vent any moisture that penetrates through the roof. Glass or mineral fiber insulation board is a good choice because it can be attached directly to the underside of the roof slab with concrete fasteners.

Installing the insulation under the roof deck allows you to use the top of the roof as a deck for occupant activities and for mounting equipment. Installing the waterproofing is easier and less critical.

However, it is not prudent to install insulation under the roof if the roof surface can cool enough to condense moisture on the underside of the deck. Even in mild weather, night sky radiation or cold rain can cool the roof deck considerably.

If you must install a concrete roof in a climate that can be damp, it is better to install foam board insulation on the top of a roof slab. The best types of above-deck insulation are *polyurethane* and *polyisocyanurate*. The latter has a somewhat higher insulation value, and it is more expensive. Both types are rated for the high roof temperatures that can occur in hot climates. (Polystyrene, which is the best choice for underground insulation, may not survive the high temperatures of a roof deck.)

Both types are available in sheets that are several inches (50 to 100 mm) thick. The high R-value of foam insulation yields an insulation value from R-10 to R-30 (RSI 1.8 to 5.4), depending on type and thickness. This is not super-insulation, but it is adequate for mild climates. For colder climates, you may be able to get thicker insulation as a special order, or you can install the insulation in layers.

The most challenging part of installing above-deck insulation is protecting the insulation and the roof structure from rain and snow. This requires an unbroken layer of impermeable material that is installed so that it will divert all rain and snowmelt to drains. Above-deck insulation is a trap for water leaks, because the flat roof deck cannot drain any leakage. Water that surrounds the insulation will eventually soak it, cancelling its insulation value. Also, water will soak into the roof deck, eventually destroying it.

Therefore, the top surface must be sloped sufficiently to keep any pools from forming. The only reliable way to drain rain from the roof is to slope the roof slab itself. You can buy insulation board that is tapered to shed rain, but eventually some rain will leak through it and the water would pool between the insulation and the roof slab.

To support walking loads, select insulation with a density that is high enough to carry the weight. Manufacturers offer various densities for this purpose.

ROOF VENTING FOR MOISTURE PROTECTION

Any roof needs adequate venting as a defense against moisture damage within the roof structure. Water gets into the roof in the following ways:

- *roof leaks*. Occasional leaks of rain and melting snow are a fact of life. Leaks occur because of defects in the roofing material and the underlayment. They occur through unsealed nail holes, around broken shingles, through defective skylight flashing, and from the action of ice dams. We will explain how to install the roofing material and the underlayment to minimize leaks. And, we will soon explain how to minimize snow melting and ice dams.

- *water vapor that enters the roof through the vents*. If the roof surface is cold, and if the outside air is warmer and moist, air may enter through the roof vents and condense in the roof structure, especially on the underside of the roof deck. Snow that lingers on a roof causes the worst condensation damage, as we will explain later. During humid weather, condensation occurs on a nightly cycle, as the roof surface cools by radiation into the night sky.

- *water vapor rising from the basement and crawl spaces*. Vent pipes and flues are surrounded by spaces between the pipes and the interior structure of the house. Similar gaps exists around wiring that rises from the main electrical panel into the attic or roof space. The moisture level is high in basements and crawl spaces where the pipes and electrical wiring originate. If the gaps are not sealed, they become a major source of moisture into the roof structure. We will explain the methods of sealing these gaps.

- *water vapor from the house interior*. A good vapor barrier, of the kind that we have designed, blocks this source of moisture. Without a good vapor barrier, water vapor will diffuse from the interior of the house into the roof. This tendency increases as the roof gets colder.

A small water leak through the roof surface can cause localized damage to the roof structure, the insulation, or to the ceiling below. A larger leak will find its way into walls and rot the wall structure, damage the roof and wall insulation, and possibly find its way into the interior of the house. It will damage gypsum wallboard and most other materials. If a good vapor barrier is installed, leaks may persist unseen, soaking the insulation. A leak may travel across the vapor barrier, draining into the adjacent wall.

Water that enters the roof in the form of vapor can damage large areas of the roof, especially the roof deck. When the humidity in a roof rises to a certain level, it will condense on the coldest part of the structure, mainly the underside of the roof deck. In all but the driest climates, the interior of a roof is likely to experience brief episodes of condensation. If condensation is slight, it will evaporate harmlessly after sunrise and exit through the roof vents. Persistent or heavy condensation will eventually destroy a roof deck.

Venting is the standard method that is used to keep water out of a roof structure. It is accomplished with openings from the interior of the roof structure to the outside. In principle, venting keeps water vapor from accumulating enough to condense into water. (See the previous sidebar, *Why Water Vapor Condenses*.) If a small amount of liquid water leaks into the roof, the water can evaporate and escape to the outside before it does much damage.

Heating of the roof space by the sun is the main force that keeps the relative humidity low inside a roof structure and that drives evaporation of any water leakage or condensation. Solar heating is very effective for lowering humidity during the daytime, but it provides only residual protection at night.

Roof venting is a subject that is not well understood within the building industry. A minimal amount of venting is necessary, and too much venting can cause serious damage to a roof under certain circumstances. So, let's learn how to get the most benefit from venting while minimizing trouble.

Roof Venting is a Compromise

The main issues with vents are their locations and their sizes. Water vapor should be able to diffuse to vents from anywhere within the roof structure and exit to the outdoors. Only small openings are needed to vent moisture under normal conditions.

Roof venting is a two-edged sword that can cause moisture damage as well as minimize it. The purpose of roof venting is to provide an escape path for unwanted water vapor that gets into the roof structure. Unfortunately, roof vents also admit water vapor from the outside. For this reason, moisture damage to a roof may be concentrated near the vents. If you store items in an attic, they are more likely to be damaged by moisture if they are located near the vents.

Building codes typically specify roof vent size as a fraction of the roof area that is ventilated. For example, some U.S. model codes require one square foot of ventilation opening for each 150 to 300 square feet (15 to 30 square meters) of attic floor area. These requirements are largely arbitrary, but they may be a reasonable compromise in many locations.

DRW

Figure 3-173. Typical gable end vent for moisture venting. The vent size and placement are appropriate for a mid-latitude climate. Cooling of the roof and attic is limited.

The vent size needed for moisture venting is too small to provide adequate cooling ventilation during warm weather, when roof cooling by ventilation is desirable. Roof ventilation that is designed for serious cooling of the roof, which we cover later, requires much larger vent openings. Therefore, roof venting is a compromise, except in a climate that is always warm or always dry.

Should you design bigger or smaller roof vents? These are probably the best compromises:

• If the climate commonly has snow that can linger on your roof, make the vents relatively small. This is to minimize condensation under the roof deck.

• If the climate has extended periods of cool, rainy weather, keep the vents fairly small.

• If the climate has an extended warm season, without much weather that is cold and rainy, make the vents as large as practical. In this case, the benefits of cooling ventilation are the deciding factor.

With truss roofs, you have wide latitude in selecting the size of vents, including extremely large vents for natural ventilation cooling. In beam and triangle-frame roofs, vent size is limited. It can be adequate for moisture venting, but not for good roof cooling.

Moisture Venting for Truss Roofs, Attic Spaces, and Voids

Attics provide an essentially unlimited amount of vent space above the insulation, except near the eaves. This makes it easy for any moisture to escape from the insulation. Once the moisture gets into the attic, it has to continue to the outside or it will cause trouble inside the attic. There are three paths that you can create for moisture to escape to the outside: (1) gable end vents, (2) vents at the ridge or near the top of the roof, and (3) eave vents.

Figure 3-174. Typical metal ridge vent, partially installed. Ridge vents are installed over a slot that is created by cutting back the roof sheathing at the ridge. Moisture escapes through perforations in the undersides of the metal cover.

DRW

Figure 3-175. Typical roof top static vents for a truss roof that has only a short ridge. In the warm climate of these Florida houses, several vents are installed to increase air flow for roof cooing.

These three paths can be combined to provide complete venting coverage of the entire attic area, or to increase cooling of the attic in warm climates.

Gable end vents are easy to install, provided that the roof has gable end walls, as in Figure 3-173. Gable end vents generally are installed at each end of a roof. In a snowy or rainy climate, it is desirable to limit the vent size. In such locations, place gable end vents about midway between the roof deck and the top of the insulation. In a warm climate, gable end vents can be greatly enlarged to enhance cooling of the attic.

*Ridge vent*s are installed along the top of the roof, as in Figure 3-174. They are effective for moisture venting of roofs that have long horizontal ridges. To provide an opening for venting, the roof sheathing is cut back at the top. For structural reasons, this type

of vent generally cannot be installed on sloped ridges, such as the ridges on hip roofs. Currently available residential ridge vents have limited ventilation area, which limits them to venting for moisture protection, rather than for cooling of the attic space.

Static roof vents are another path for venting near the top of the roof. The vent is a simple metal cover for a hole in the roof sheathing, as in Figure 3-175. This type of vent is commonly seen on houses that use trusses to create a hip roof, which is not adapted to long ridge vents. Static vents are easy to install, and they do not interfere with the structure. The vent can have various shapes, but a round housing provides superior resistance to rain leaks.

Any desired number of vents may be installed, the primary limitation being appearance. Using this type of vent can offer a much larger opening than is offered by conventional ridge vents. As a result, this type of vent is common in warm climates.

Eave vents can be used wherever eaves overhang the exterior wall. Figure 3-172 shows how an eave vent works. If eave vents are installed along the entire length of the eaves, they provide good moisture venting of the side portions of the attic. Eave vents generally are used in combination with top vents and/ or gable end vents.

Moisture exits through the underside of the eave, where rain cannot enter. In most houses, the underside of the eave has a decorative horizontal cover, as in Figure 3-176. This cover is called a "soffit," which is a term used to describe the underside of any overhanging house structure. The soffit must be perforated or screened to allow the moisture to pass through.

If your roof design uses eave vents, make sure that the insulation is not squeezed against the sides of

DRW

Figure 3-176. Typical soffit covering for eave vents. This is a decorative metal or plastic material that includes perforations or screens to permit air flow, while blocking birds, insects, and other intruders.

Figure 3-177. Typical attic insulation that is jammed against the underside of the roof sheathing. This makes eave vents almost useless. The solution shown here is to attach plastic vent channels to the sheathing to connect the eave vents with the attic space. The channels create a passage that is adequate for venting moisture, but not for cooling the attic space. These channels are flimsy plastic. Aluminum would last much longer.

the roof deck, as in Figure 3-177. This would isolate the eave vents from most of the space in the attic.

A contemporary solution is to attach plastic vent channels to the sheathing, as shown in the figure. The channels create a passage that is adequate for venting moisture. Common channel material is cheap plastic that probably will disintegrate early in the life of the house. Instead of plastic, use aluminum channels. If you can't find aluminum vent channels, use aluminum soffit material for the purpose. Or, design the roof structure so that the insulation is kept away from the underside of the roof deck.

If you use loose fill insulation in the attic, make sure that the insulation does not fall into the eaves and clog the vents. To avoid this problem, you need to design dams at the attic perimeter to hold the insulation in place.

For cooling an attic in a warm climate, eave vents must have a much larger opening area than is required for moisture venting, and the gap between the insulation and the roof sheathing must be much larger. We will learn how to design a roof this way under the heading *Ventilation Cooling for Attic Roofs*.

Moisture Venting for Beam Roofs and Triangle-Frame Roofs

The inside of a beam roof consists of a series of long, narrow rectangular spaces formed by the beams, the roof deck, and the ceiling surface. The inside structure of an insulated triangle-frame roof is similar. The insulation lies on the ceiling. The venting path for water vapor is the air space between the insulation and the roof deck. The ridge vent and the eave ends of the insulation spaces (Figure 3-171) are the only places where openings to the outside can be placed.

As a general guideline for moisture venting, select the depth of the rafters to allow a vent space of about 2" (5 cm) above the top of the insulation. If the beams are longer than about 20 feet (6 meters), increase the height of the vent space by about 1" for each additional 10 feet (25 mm in height for each additional 3 meters in length).

When installing the insulation, be careful not to obstruct the vent space by shoving the batts too far up between the rafters. The way to avoid this blockage is to select batts with the proper thickness for the rafters, and to attach the batts properly at the edges.

If you will be installing a heat radiation barrier to create a "cool roof" (see *Cool Roofs for Warm Climates*, below), it will require even more space above the insulation. Plan for this when you select the depth of your rafters.

If a beam roof has a ridge where the beams meet, as in the second sketch in Figure 1-110, a continuous ridge vent is the easiest and most effective way of venting the top ends of the beam spaces.

At the bottom ends of the beam spaces, don't allow the insulation retainers or any other components to block venting. For example, use perforated soffit material, as in Figure 3-176.

All vent openings require sturdy screens to block insects, birds, and other potential intruders.

Moisture Venting for Insulation Installed Above Roof Decks

If your roof design uses impermeable foam insulation that is installed on top of a roof deck, you have to live with the fact that moisture venting remains an unsolved problem. The space between the insulation and the deck cannot be vented to the outside, because this would allow outside air to bypass the insulation.

The only correct way to vent the space between the insulation and the roof deck is toward the inside. I can imagine various ways of doing this, but none of them is easy or conventional.

In principle, the need to vent the space under the insulation could be avoided by a creating a perfectly watertight barrier to prevent moisture penetration through the insulation. However, in the real world, it is almost impossible to create such a perfect barrier using materials that are appropriate for a house.

PROTECTION FROM SNOW AND ICE

In a snowy climate, one of the most important aspects of your roof design is to resist moisture damage caused by snow, especially by snow that lingers on the roof. We need to cover this because snow damage is underestimated and misunderstood, and because some snow protection measures increase moisture damage.

Lingering snow causes serious damage in two ways. One is by rotting the underside of the roof deck and rusting the nails and other steel fasteners. The other is by creating "ice dams," which can cause major leaks into the roof structure, the walls, and the inside of the house.

The *Snow and Ice Protection Checklist*, in Step 1, summarizes all the techniques that we recommend for dealing with snow in roof design. In Step 1, we focused on the shape and surroundings of the roof. In this Step, we cover structural features that protect the roof against snow damage.

Let's start by understanding how snow can damage a roof.

Snow Maximizes Condensation Damage

Snow that sits on a roof keeps the roof deck cold. When snowfall is followed by warmer weather, humid air flows through the roof vents and water condenses on the underside of the roof deck. An enormous amount of water can condense in this way as long as the snow remains, soaking the deck structure and rafters. Plywood is especially vulnerable to wetting. The moisture also rusts nails and other steel fasteners. Severe condensation can drip into the insulation and down to the ceiling and walls.

We explained that roof venting is a balance between allowing unwanted moisture to escape and bringing unwanted moisture into the roof structure. With a layer of snow on the roof, even small roof vents will allow moisture to enter in amounts that can rot the roof structure. Water inside the roof evaporates very slowly when it is cold. Standing snow can condense water under the roof deck much faster than the water will evaporate. At night, there is no solar heating to aid evaporation, and the snow cover prevents much warming to aid evaporation during the daytime.

Snow Causes Ice Dams

"Ice dams" are a source of serious water damage. They are caused by lingering snow. If the upper part of the roof deck becomes warm enough to melt the bottom of the snow layer, the melted snow flows down the roof surface and then freezes into ice at a lower, colder portion of the roof.

The ice forms a growing dam that blocks the drainage of other melt water. The water backs up behind the dam until it submerges a row of shingles or tiles. From there, the water soaks the roof deck and leaks through nail holes and joints in the roof deck. Even a moderate layer of snow can generate enough water behind an ice dam to flood the roof structure, the ceiling below, and the outer walls.

The underside of a snow layer may melt and cause an ice dam for several reasons. When snowfall is followed by weather that is warmer than freezing temperature, the warmer air flows through the roof vents and melts the snow from underneath. Also, sunshine may penetrate the snow layer and warm the roof surface enough to melt snow. And, if the roof is poorly insulated, heat escapes from the inside of the house and warms the roof deck.

The most severe ice dams commonly form above unheated roof overhangs, where the roof deck crosses over the outer wall. Depending on the roof slope, water may back up several feet [MF] (up to one meter). An important part of the defense is to install an unbroken waterproof underlayment over this portion of the roof. We cover the details under the heading, *The Roof Underlayment*, below.

Skylights and chimney penetrations melt snow locally, creating local ice dams below the penetration.

If snow can pile up on the roof, it may create or aggravate an ice dam by keeping that portion of the roof colder. Snow piles up where it is blocked, as by snow fences and skylights. If snow funnels to a point from several directions, it will pile up. For example, this happens where snow slides toward the valley where two adjacent gables or dormers meet.

Snow that slides off skylights piles up below them, as in Figure 3-178.

Ventilating the underside of the roof is widely recommended to keep the underside of the roof cold, so that the snow layer will not melt and form ice dams. However, this poses a dilemma, because ventilation also brings humid air underneath the roof deck, causing condensation damage.

Design the Roof to Shed Snow

To minimize condensation damage and ice dams, design the roof to shed snow quickly. We did this in Step 1. A steep pitch and a smooth surface are the characteristics that shed snow. Table 1-1, *Roof Surface Comparison*, lists the roof slopes needed to shed snow with various kinds of surfaces.

When most of the snow has slid off, sunlight and wind are more able to remove the remaining snow. Even if a small amount of snow remains, the potential for damage is greatly reduced.

Avoid Snow Guards and Snow Fences

In climates where snow may accumulate on a roof, it is common to install snow guards or snow fences to hold the snow on the roof until warmer weather melts the snow. This is done primarily to protect people, vehicles, shrubbery, etc. from harm by the falling snow and ice. Snow guards and snow fences perform this function well, being able to hold a blanket of snow that is much higher than the snow guard or fence itself.

Unfortunately, snow guards also maximize the damage that snow can cause, including condensation and ice dams. Snow guards can hold a thick layer of snow on a roof for a long time after the air temperature rises enough to initiate both problems. For this reason, I recommend that you avoid snow guards. To protect people from snow and ice that fall from tall eaves, design the outside area under the eaves as recommended in Step 1.

One advertised benefit of snow guards is keeping snow from piling up on the ground alongside the walls. However, if the snow is forced to pile up on the roof instead, the weight may collapse the roof. Ironically, one manufacturer of snow guards advises customers to shovel the snow off the roof if the snow guards allow snow to accumulate excessively. To minimize snow piling against walls, design wide roof overhangs.

DRW

Figure 3-178. Snow piled up below large skylights, creating the conditions for an ice dam. Covers have been added to the tops of these skylights to prevent roof leaks there.

THE ROOF DECK

The roof deck is the permanent part of the roof structure that supports the replaceable weather surface. The roof deck must be strong enough to support the combination of its own weight, the surface material, and people working on the roof. The roof must also support the maximum weight of snow that may occur. If the house is surrounded by trees, the deck should be strong enough to survive falling limbs.

The roof deck is an important structural element. It keeps the rafters straight and it increases the stiffness and load carrying ability of the roof. With a truss or triangle-frame roof, the roof deck acts as a brace to keep the rafters from tipping sideways, called "racking."

However, it is not the job of the roof deck to keep the roof from sagging. This is accomplished by designing the walls to support the roof properly and by proper design of the beams or trusses.

There are several common kinds of roof decks. Select the type of roof deck that is appropriate for the roof surface material. Beyond that, local construction practice prevails. For example, in the United States, plywood roof decks have become standard. Let's look at the main characteristics of your roof deck choices.

Plywood and Plywood Substitutes

Plywood sheathing, as in Figure 3-182, has become the most popular kind of roof deck in many parts of the world. It can be used with most kinds of surface materials. It is quick and easy to install. It contributes strength to the roof. And, it provides an unbroken surface for installing a waterproof underlayment, which is essential for minimizing leaks.

The main shortcoming of plywood roof decks is vulnerability to rotting from roof leaks. This is caused by the lack of venting between the plywood and the roof covering. The best available solution is to install

a reliable waterproof "underlayment" over the plywood to keep it dry.

Because plywood decks cannot vent moisture, don't use them with wooden shingles, thatch, and other materials that decay with moisture. Experience shows that such materials warp and rot when placed on a surface that does not allow venting from underneath.

If a plywood deck is appropriate for your roof, use real plywood, not one of the cheaper substitutes made from wood chips or strands. A roof deck is subject to extremes of moisture and temperature that will destroy the adhesives in these materials within a fraction of the life of the house.

Select a plywood thickness that is adequate to prevent sagging between the rafters and to provide a secure "nail base" for attaching the roof surface. Use a full ¾" (18 mm) thickness, which is adequate for rafters that are spaced 24" (60 cm) apart.

Use "H"-shaped metal clips to hold the edges of the sheathing in alignment between the rafters. The tiny gaps created by the H-clips are useful for venting moisture at the edges of the plywood. Don't use tongue-and-groove plywood on a roof. The grooves would trap leaks and rot the wood.

Don't use construction adhesive to secure the roof sheathing to the rafters. Portions of the roof sheathing may have to be replaced during the life of the house because of moisture damage, and adhesive would risk damaging the rafters when the sheathing is replaced.

■ Plywood Decks in Wet Conditions

Plywood must stay dry. Observe how quickly a piece of plywood will come apart if it is exposed to wet weather. The thin plies absorb water quickly, swell, and break apart. If you want to install a plywood roof deck in a location that is vulnerable to wetting, consider using plywood that is made for wet environments. It may be called "marine grade" or "pressure treated." Its adhesives resist moisture better, and treatment chemicals resist rot. Not all types of moisture-resistant plywood are equal, so do your homework before buying the material.

In a climate where ice dams may form, use moisture-resistant plywood for the parts of the roof that are vulnerable to ice dams. (See the previous heading, *Protection from Snow and Ice.*) This practice is unusual and it adds a little cost, so cover it in your construction contract.

All plywood in damp locations should be installed with heavily galvanized nails. In the long term, it is the nails that will hold the plies together at the edges.

Figure 3-182. Plywood roof sheathing. It offers several advantages over older board decking, but it cannot vent leakage through the roof surface, making it especially vulnerable to water damage. Therefore, it requires especially effective protection against leaks.

DRW

If you use a plywood roof deck in a wet climate, using moisture-resistant plywood may be the only way to minimize long-term damage.

Spaced Boards

Before the introduction of plywood, boards with gaps between them were the most common type of roof deck. Figure 3-183 shows how this kind of roof appears from underneath.

This type of deck is still worth considering. If water gets between the roof weather surface and the roof deck, warming by the sun will evaporate the moisture, which then escapes through the gaps to the underside of the roof deck. From there, the water vapor escapes through the roof vents. Experience shows that this kind of roof deck is less vulnerable to localized rotting from leaks than plywood roof decks.

This type of roof deck can be used with virtually all surface materials. If the roof surface consists of composition shingles or tiles, the boards must be spaced to match the dimensions of the roofing materials.

The boards should be narrow, typically about 6" (15 cm) wide. The narrow width is necessary to shorten the vent path and to minimize any surface irregularity that results from warping of the boards. The gaps between boards created by natural variations in shape generally are wide enough for venting. It should be possible to see through the gaps when the boards are installed. The gaps should not be wider than about a quarter inch |(6 mm), or they would allow the underlayment to sag into the gaps.

The boards must be well seasoned, to avoid warping after installation. Warping pulls nails loose and lifts the surface material, creating leaks and a wavy surface. The wood should be a resinous species, such as pine, that resists brief wetting.

The narrow boards provide only limited strengthening of the roof against sidewise collapse, or "racking." The design of the roof will determine whether other features are needed to provide adequate racking resistance. For example, it may be necessary to install diagonal braces under the rafters.

Purlins

Purlins are narrow supports, typically made of "2 by 4" lumber, that span across rafters.* They are used with sheetmetal, tile, and thatch roofs that are installed without a water barrier underlayment. Figure 3-184 shows a typical purlin roof structure.

For sheetmetal panel roof surfaces, the gap between purlins is determined by the weight bearing capacity of the unsupported sheetmetal. The greatest load on the surface is likely to be the weight of people working on the roof. Walking on the roof requires a gingerly step to avoid damaging the sheetmetal.

Purlins are inexpensive and quick to install. They provide good venting of the underside of the roof surface. However, they provide little resistance to racking. Therefore, a truss roof with purlins also requires diagonal bracing of the underside of the rafters. The lack of racking resistance makes purlins impractical with a triangle-frame roof.

DRW
Figure 3-184. A purlin roof used to support a sheetmetal surface.

DRW
Figure 3-183. Roof decking that consists of spaced boards. This kind of roof deck was standard before plywood decking appeared, and it still has some merit.

---

* The term "purlin" can also mean a strong beam that supports rafters from underneath. This method of construction typically is used in narrow houses, such as row houses, where the purlins span between the masonry walls.

DRW

Figure 3-185. Tongue-and-groove roof decking, from underneath. The appearance is appropriate for this rustic cabin. Any insulation must be installed on top of the deck.

Tongue-and-Groove Decking

Tongue-and-groove decking consists of thick planks that typically have several mating tongues and grooves on each side to create strong joints between adjacent timbers. The timbers typically are 2 to 6 inches (50 to 150 mm) thick, so they can span exceptionally wide rafter spacing.

Almost always, a tongue-and-groove roof deck is chosen so that the bare bottom surface can provide a rustic decorative theme, as in Figure 3-185. Any insulation must be installed on top of the deck.

Typically, the insulation would be rigid foam board that is laminated to a plywood top surface. The insulation value that can be achieved with this method is limited. The installation must be done skillfully to avoid convection and water seepage between the insulation and the roof deck.

If wooden shingles are used to maintain the rustic appearance, skilled installation is needed to keep water from accumulating between the shingles and the deck, which would rot both.

Concrete Roof Decks

A concrete roof acts as its own deck. The roof must be sloped enough to drain rain and snowmelt reliably from all portions of the roof.

A weather surface is needed to prevent rain penetration, freeze damage, and rusting of the reinforcing steel by water penetration. In a climate with a wet season, the weather surface requires periodic maintenance. In a warm, dry climate, a tile surface or a coat of paint may be all that is needed.

THE ROOF UNDERLAYMENT

The roof underlayment is an impermeable layer that is installed on the roof deck before the exterior weather surface is installed. The purpose of the underlayment is to provide additional protection against roof leakage by acting as an unbroken water barrier between the weather surface and the roof deck. Underlayments are a modern addition to roofs, which became essential with the introduction of plywood roof decks.

What Causes Roof Leaks

Shingles, tiles, and most other surface materials have some tendency to leak, for the following reasons.

Capillary action, which is the tendency of water to fill narrow gaps, can cause water to move sideways or even uphill between shingles, tiles, and other overlapping surfaces. Capillary action is especially strong with asphalt shingles, because the layers are tightly overlapped, so leaks may follow unexpected paths. Tiles, wooden shingles, slates, and other overlapping materials are less vulnerable to capillary action.

Blowing rain enters under the bottoms and sides of roofing materials with open or irregular shapes, such as ceramic tiles, wooden shakes, and slate.

Roofing nails are a path for leakage. They penetrate into the roof deck, and usually go entirely through the deck. The heads of nails are hidden under the surface material, but capillary action or ice dams can lead water to them. The water will try to follow the nail down through the deck.

Breakage of shingles, tiles, slate, and other individual pieces of roofing material creates leakage where the coverage is lost.

Ice dams can cause major leak damage if snow lingers on the roof. Ice dams back up melted snow underneath shingles, tiles or other roof surfaces, so that the water flows through any holes or joints in the roof deck. See the earlier heading, *Protection from Snow and Ice.*

Underlayment Materials

Underlayment material is a fibrous sheet that is impregnated with a tarry substance to block water and to seal nail holes. The material comes in rolls that typically are three feet (90 cm) wide.

Underlayment materials differ primarily in their thickness and strength. As a rule, thicker and stickier is better. The material should be strong enough to resist tearing during installation.

Absolute Roofing, Twin Lakes, Minnesota

Figure 3-186. A course of heavy, sticky "leak barrier" roofing is installed at the bottom of the roof, which is most vulnerable to ice dams, and around the valleys of the gable. Lighter "roofing felt" is used for the higher portions of the roof.

"Tar paper" is the lightest and least reliable underlayment. "Roofing felt" uses a thicker layer of paper, glass fibers, or bonded plastic fibers to hold a larger amount of the water resistant material.

These materials do not stick to each other, so the layers do not form an unbroken surface where they overlap. The installer can create an unbroken surface by using a sealant at the overlaps, but this is not a reliable method. Instead, use wide overlaps. If the roof has a shallow slope, an overlap of half the roll width may be advisable. In any case, follow the instructions supplied with the material.

A recent improvement is a thick underlayment that has adhesive properties. This material has been given the name "ice barrier." The material sticks to the roof deck, which eliminates voids where water can collect and rot the deck. The material also sticks to itself, so that overlapped layers form an unbroken barrier. It seals well to the shingle nails.

Because of its stickiness, "leak barrier" material requires some care to install properly. So, monitor the installation if you select it. The material has a plastic release sheet that keeps the material from sticking to itself on the roll. The release sheet must be removed in the right way as the material is applied. The stickiness increases with temperature, and it is best to apply it in reasonably warm weather.

Because leak barrier material is more expensive than ordinary "roofing paper," it is commonly limited to the most vulnerable parts of the roof. These include the lowest part of the roof, valleys, and the borders around dormers and skylights. Figure 3-186 shows a typical roofing installation that combines both heavy and light underlayments.

Selecting the Underlayment

To summarize what we learned previously, the following factors determine whether an underlayment should be used, and the type that should be selected.

The type of roof surface. Asphalt shingles and roof tiles should be backed up with an underlayment. The underlayment must be supported by a continuous roof deck, or by boards with narrow gaps.

A sheetmetal roof supported by purlins does not use an underlayment.

An underlayment should not be used with roof surfaces that can rot, such as wooden shingles and thatch. This is because the underlayment makes it impossible for wet material to dry out by venting through the interior of the roof structure. Such roof surfaces should be installed over a well vented deck.

The roof slope. A steep slope counters capillary action and blowing rain, and thereby protects the roofing nails from exposure to water. It provides quicker shedding of rain and snow, minimizing the volume of any leaks. Therefore, a steeper roof can use a lighter underlayment.

Because an underlayment should not be used with roof covering materials that can rot, a steep slope is required with those materials.

A *plywood roof deck* requires an underlayment because it is especially vulnerable to rotting from leaks in the outer weather surface. Asphalt shingles and sheetmetal lie flat, so any leaks would be trapped against the plywood deck and rot it. With an underlayment, leaks are trapped between the weather surface and the waterproof underlayment instead, and solar heating may eventually evaporate the moisture to the outside.

The use of underlayment with a plywood roof deck is a mixed blessing. Any water that manages to get between the underlayment and the plywood will be trapped there, inevitably rotting the plywood. Therefore, if you select a plywood deck, consider an adhesive "leak barrier" underlayment, and make sure that it is installed perfectly. By sticking directly to the plywood deck, this kind of underlayment eliminates gaps where water can accumulate.

If snow can accumulate on the roof, an ice dam is likely to form. When that happens, the underlayment becomes the primary barrier to leakage. Therefore, if your roof can accumulate snow, install an "ice barrier" underlayment on any portion of the roof where an ice dam may form. See the previous heading, *Protection from Snow and Ice*.

The building code. It may specify the minimum weight of the underlayment, usually based on the slope of the roof. It may also have special requirements for protection against ice dams.

INSTALLING THE ROOF SURFACE

Step 1 presented the types of roof surfaces that merit consideration for a modern roof. Table 1-1, *Roof Surface Comparison*, summarizes their essential characteristics.

If your roofing contractor has done a good job of installing the underlayment, the rest of the installation is likely to proceed smoothly. As with every part of construction, the key is to get properly trained people to do the work.

Composition shingle can be installed well by any good roofing contractor, and by most good carpenters. At least in the United States, the shingles have a standard shape and dimensions, and they are installed in a standard way. However, there are differences between shingles, and the installers should follow the instructions on the package.

One caution is to insist that the shingles be installed with special shingle nails, which have a very enlarged head. And, in windy locations (almost everywhere, at times) use extra shingle nails. Contractors who sacrifice quality for speed use staple guns to install shingles. Don't allow this. Staples will not hold shingles as securely as shingle nails.

The other kinds of roof surfaces – metal panel, metal shingles, tile, and historical types – each require specialized installation skill. They should be installed by contractors who specialize in them. Make sure that your builder knows the installation details well enough to enforce a top quality installation.

DRW
Figure 3-187. The "chase" that surrounds this flue extends from the attic to the basement. If the large space surrounding the flue is NOT needed for supplying air to fuel fired equipment in the basement, it should be sealed at the top with a metal collar that extends to the surrounding framework.

BLOCK AIR LEAKAGE AT FLUES AND PLUMBING VENTS

Plumbing vents and flues originate inside the house, typically in the basement or on the lowest floor. They rise through the house structure and the roof space. There is a gap of significant size that surrounds vents and flues where they rise through the house. If this gap is not closed off, it can be a major pathway for air leakage between the house interior and the interior of the roof. These gaps are invisible in the finished house, so they can cause trouble without raising suspicion.

This leakage path creates two problems. One is that air leaking into the house wastes heating energy and causing discomfort during cold weather. The other problem is that moisture from the interior of the house can condense inside the roof structure during cold weather, causing moisture damage.

The solution is simple to describe, but somewhat tricky to accomplish. It is to install a seal around the vent or flue at the point where it enters the roof structure. This needs to be accomplished after the roof structure is finished, but before the insulation is installed.

Not all builders seal these gaps properly, and some builders simply leave the gaps open. Make a note on your construction drawings to close these gaps at the same time that the vents and flues are installed.

In an existing house, check for effective gap seals around all your vent pipes and flues.

Air Leakage Around Flues

First of all, this is not an issue for your home unless you have a conventional flue that rises through the interior of the house and up through the roof. Step 4 explains that a flue through the roof is unnecessary if you install heat pumps, or if you install high-efficiency heating equipment that uses a gas fuel.

Your super-house will require a conventional flue only if you burn oil or a solid fuel. Also, it is needed if you burn natural gas in an old style non-condensing furnace or boiler. To understand how such a flue should be designed, refer to *Eliminating the Danger of Carbon Monoxide*, in Step 4.

Conventional flues have a large diameter, so they usually are enclosed in a shaft that is called a "chase," as in Figure 3-187. The chase usually is built in the same way as other interior walls. There is a clearance between the flue pipe and the walls of the chase, typically two inches (5 cm) or more from the flue on all sides. The clearance keeps the surface of the flue away from the combustible structure. (Modern flue pipes have multiple walls, so their outside surface remains fairly cool. However, if the inner wall of the pipe burns out in a flue fire, the outer wall may become dangerously hot.)

The top of the chase typically ends at the floor of an attic. The bottom of the chase typically is located above the heating equipment. The gap between the flue and the chase may be left open, so that you can look from the attic down into the basement or wherever the heating equipment is located. In that case, the gap is a direct path for leakage of outside air into the house.

With older types of heating equipment, and with some modern types, the gap between flue and the chase serves as the primary path for bringing outside air to the heating equipment for combustion. *Before deciding whether to seal this gap, determine whether any of your heating equipment requires this source of outside air*.

If you need the space between the flue and the chase to serve as a combustion air inlet, that space is exposed to outside air temperatures. Therefore, insulate the walls of the chase like any exterior wall.

If you upgrade an older house by installing modern heating equipment, all of which has "sealed" combustion systems, you can safely seal this gap and stop the leakage of outside air into the house. But, only in that case.

If you no longer need the old flue, the easiest way to seal the chase against entry of outside air is to remove the flue pipe where it passes into the attic. Then, simply nail a sheet of plywood over the hole, using caulk between the plywood and the attic structure. Finish the job by placing some insulation on top of the plywood. This will keep the inside surfaces of the chase warm.

If you choose to retain the old flue pipe, seal it tightly at the bottom. In addition, install an air leakage barrier around the pipe at the top of the chase, where it opens into the attic or other roof space. Typically, the air barrier is a split sheetmetal plate that fits the flue pipe snugly. The center of the plate has a circular cutout for the flue pipe, and the outside of the plate is a rectangle that fits the top of the chase. The installation must allow for vertical expansion and contraction of the flue pipe. This requires metal-to-metal seals. You can't use caulk to seal around the flue pipe.

Air Leakage Around Plumbing Vents

If you look at almost any house, you will see small pipes sticking up from the roof. Those are vents for the plumbing system, commonly called "vent stacks." When water and sewage falls through the house's drains, it acts as a piston that pushes down the sewer gases in the pipes. The plumbing vents allow the displaced sewer gases to vent harmlessly to the outside. Without the vents, the pressure on the sewer gases would force them into the house through other drains.

Plumbing vents usually are connected to the lowest sewer lines. From there, the vent pipes rise to the roof, usually through walls. The vent pipe emerges from the top of the wall and passes through the insulated part of the roof. The space between the vent pipe and the surrounding structure is a pathway for air leakage. During cold weather, the cold air above the roof insulation is heavy, so it will fall into the house around the vent pipe if possible, emerging through any openings where the pipe passes through a wall or floor.

To block this air leakage, seal the gap at the top, where the pipe enters the roof space. The vent pipe expands and contracts lengthwise as the temperature changes, so the seal should allow for this movement. This solution is the same as for leakage around flues, except that plumbing vents are smaller and easier to seal.

With an attic roof, where the seal is accessible, a rubber seal wraps around the pipe and is nailed to the top of the attic floor framing. This seal is similar to the weather seal that is visible on top of the roof, except that it is split so that it can be installed around the pipe. The rubber won't last for the life of the house, so install the seal in a way that makes it easy to replace. The seal is hidden under the roof insulation after the insulation is installed.

With a beam roof, the vent pipe passes from the wall to the roof in a way that does not provide access after the roof is completed. So, you have one chance to seal the gap for the life of the house. To do that, create a narrow box to enclose the pipe where it passes through the roof, and pack the entire box tightly with fiber insulation around the pipe. This seal won't be airtight, but it will be good enough.

Cool Roofs for Warm Climates

If you touch a roof surface that is exposed to the sun, you may be surprised by how hot it is. Hot surfaces are one of the hallmarks of modern roofs. Common roofing materials absorb a majority of the solar heat that falls on them, and their impermeable nature prevents cooling by circulation of air through them. In contrast, traditional roofing materials, such as wooden shingles, remained relatively cool.

As air conditioning has become a major cost in warm climates, awareness that modern roofs are hot has made "cool roofs" a hot topic. But, just how important are they? If your roof is super-insulated, why should you care about the roof temperature?

The answer is that heat flow through insulation is proportional to the temperature difference across the insulation. If the average temperature difference doubles, it's like eliminating half your insulation. In fact, a hot roof can double or triple the daytime temperature difference across the ceiling insulation. Keeping your super-insulation as cool as possible can reduce your air conditioning energy consumption during a hot day by a few hundred watts. Also, a cool roof will improve your comfort when you are not using air conditioning.

But, let's be clear about this. *The insulation is by far the most important feature that blocks solar heating through the roof.* All the other features of a "cool roof" serve only an auxiliary function, which is to reduce the temperature difference across the insulation. An effective "cool roof" keeps the temperature of the outer surface of the roof insulation near to the temperature of the outside air. A super-insulated roof that is "cool" offers a relatively small advantage compared to a super-insulated roof that is not "cool," and it offers that advantage only during warm weather.

If a "cool roof" lowers your cooling cost during warm weather, will it increase your heating cost during cold weather by depriving your home of solar roof heating? Yes, but very little. Solar heating of roofs is not a big factor in winter, when the days are short and the sun remains low in the sky. And, heat radiates from the roof deck to the insulation only weakly when the roof deck is at winter temperatures.

So, tailor the "coolness" of your roof to the location of your home. In a predominantly warm climate, design a "cool roof" using techniques that are economical and reliable, which we will learn. If your home is located in a climate that is primarily cool or cold, there is no value in a cool roof.

If you live in a climate that has both warm and cold seasons, limit your cool roof design to the most economical techniques. In that climate, you don't have to agonize about fine tuning the coolness of the roof, because the super-insulation under the roof minimizes both cooling and heating requirements.

Bear in mind that some roof warming is always good. Many buildings that are centuries old have their original roof structures, even though the surface materials may have been replaced many times. This remarkable endurance owes largely to warming of the roof surface by the sun, which lowers the relative humidity throughout the roof structure.

Warming the roof deck by only a few degrees above the outside air temperature is sufficient to banish condensation. In addition, solar warming helps to evaporate water that enters from small leaks, so the wetness does not linger long enough to cause rot. Fortunately, almost any roof surface – even a "cool" surface – is warmed enough by daytime sunlight to provide this protection.*

Finally, remember that heavy shading of the roof, especially by trees, is the most effective method of keeping a roof cool. Shading of your entire house will keep the roof temperature close to the outside air temperature. But, before committing to tree shading, go back to Step 2 and review its limitations and challenges.

ELEMENTS OF A COOL ROOF

A "cool roof" is not a specific design, but a design goal, which is to keep the top of the ceiling insulation as cool as possible. Your design can approach that goal by using one or more of these three techniques:

1. *Select a roof surface that stays cool in direct sunlight.* The technique offers a significant benefit with all roof types, and it may cost nothing. The effect of roof surfaces on cooling is poorly understood at present. We will learn how to make the most effective choices.

2. *Ventilate the space between the roof surface and the insulation.* This technique affects the structural design and appearance of the roof structure. It has the greatest potential in a truss roof. Roof ventilation has long been used for cooling, but rarely to its full potential.

---

* For example, consider damp weather when the outside air temperature is 68 °F (20 °C) and the relative humidity is 100%. If solar heating increases the temperature of the roof deck by 9 °F (5 °C), it lowers the relative humidity on the underside of the roof deck to 74%. This is more than adequate to prevent condensation.

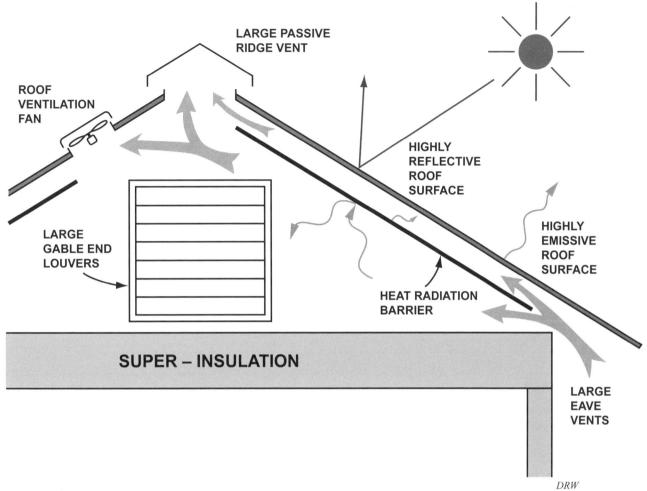

Figure 3-189. The elements of a "cool roof."

3. ***Block heat radiation from the underside of the roof surface to the ceiling insulation.*** This technique is relatively new and unproven, using a heat barrier material that is installed under the roof deck. The material is inexpensive. Installation is easy in a truss roof. It may interfere with insulation and cooling air flow in a beam or triangle-frame roof.

The elements of a cool roof are illustrated in Figure 3-189. Let's examine them at a level of detail that will allow you to design an outstanding "cool roof."

COOL ROOF SURFACES

The roof surface is the hottest part of the roof because it is directly exposed to the sun's heat radiation. It is the front line of defense against solar heat because a majority of solar energy can be blocked here. The color and other properties of your roof's surface material determine how far the roof's temperature can rise. By paying attention to your options when selecting your roof's surface, you can lower the roof temperature over a wide range, at no additional cost.

The temperature of a roof surface is the net result of three competing forces, (1) heating by sunlight, (2) cooling by radiation of the roof's heat into the sky, and (3) conduction of heat between the roof and the surrounding air.

At the beginning of a clear day, heating by the sun greatly exceeds radiation from the roof, so the roof temperature rises. Later in the day, the roof temperature reaches the point that the heat input from the sun is balanced by the combination of heat radiation from the roof and heat conduction to the surrounding air.

Table 3-5, *Maximum Solar Temperature Rise of Roofing Materials*, shows how hot a roof can become if it is heated by maximum sunlight and if there is no wind. The numbers represent a worst case that does not occur often. However, the relative sizes of the numbers are a valuable guide for selecting your roof surface materials.

If direct sunlight is blocked, the heating effect of the sun is reduced to a small fraction of the heating by direct sunlight. This happens if the house is heavily shaded by trees. Cloud cover also greatly reduces roof heating. So, don't go to extremes to achieve a cool roof if you will have tree shading, or if your climate is usually cloudy during warm weather.

Table 3-5. Maximum Solar Temperature Rise of Roofing Materials

ROOF SURFACE	Temperature Rise, °F	Temperature Rise, °C
NON-CONDUCTING SURFACES, BY COLOR:		
Bright white, smooth	15	8
White, rough surface	35	19
Light (pastel) colors	15 - 55	8 - 31
Gray, 50% reflectance	52	29
Deep colors	79 - 83	44 - 46
Black	90	50
MATERIALS:		
Asphalt shingles, all common colors	72 - 90	40 - 50
Aluminum sheetmetal, white enameled	25 - 40	14 - 22
Aluminum sheetmetal, bare	48	27
Galvanized steel sheetmetal	55	31
Concrete tile, off-white coating	20	11
Concrete tile, light beige coating	30	17
Concrete tile, pink or grey coating	40	22
Concrete tile, light brown coating	50	28
Concrete tile, red, uncoated	71	39
Clay tile, red	58	32
Aluminum-pigmented roof coating (flat roof)	50 - 65	28 - 36
Built-up roofing, gravel ballast (flat roof)	61 - 83	34 - 46

NOTES:
- These data were developed by the U.S. Department of Energy in 2000.
- The data indicate the temperature rise above the adjacent air temperature.
- The data assume full sunlight nearly perpendicular to the surface.
- The data assume that wind is absent. Wind has a strong cooling effect.

Roof heating by the sun is also limited by wind. If your home is located in a region that has steady winds during warm weather, the wind will substantially reduce the temperature of any roof surface.

A Bit of Theory to Help You Select Roof Surfaces

Table 3-5 may provide all the information you need to select your roof surfaces for coolness. However, it's helpful to know a little theory to increase your confidence that you are making the best choices.

When the sun shines on any surface, the temperature rise is determined by the balance between two surface properties of materials, called "reflectivity" and "emissivity." Roofing materials do not advertise these properties directly, so we need to know how to judge them in order to select our roofing materials for coolness.

Reflectivity is the fraction of light falling on a surface that is reflected. Table 1-1, *Roof Surface Comparison*, gives the range of reflectivity that is available with modern roofing materials.

Usually, you can judge the reflectivity of a roof just by looking at it. Light colors have high reflectivity, and they make the roof cooler. Dark colors have low reflectivity, and they make the roof warmer.

However, it's not entirely that simple. About 60% of solar energy arrives in the form of invisible light, mostly in infrared wavelengths (called "near infrared") that are fairly close to the visible wavelengths. The color of a roof tells you how it reflects visible light, but not the infrared light. Fortunately, the infrared reflectivity usually is about the same as for visible light.

Some coatings have been developed for roofing materials to reflect infrared sunlight more strongly than visible light. However, these are used mainly to reduce the high temperatures associated with dark roof colors, so they don't apply if you want to create a seriously cool roof.

Emissivity is equally important, but less obvious.* It is the ability of a warm body to get rid of its heat by radiation. Emissivity is a ratio that compares the heat radiation from a real surface to the heat radiation from an ideal surface of the same temperature that radiates at the maximum rate.

Differences in emissivity can make a big difference in roof temperature. For example, a white painted surface in direct sunlight is fairly cool, whereas a shiny metal surface is too hot to touch. What's going on? The answer is that the white painted surface has high emissivity, whereas the metal surface has low emissivity. In other words, the metal surface can't radiate its heat very well.

Most paints and coatings have high emissivity, usually over 0.9. As a result, a painted steel roof may be much cooler than a galvanized roof, even though the galvanized roof has equal reflectivity. In order to maximize emissivity, the coating must be fairly thick, over about 0.006" (0.15 mm). The paint on some metal roofing is too thin to fully mask the low emissivity of the metal underneath.

In general, bare metal surfaces have low emissivity, so they become hot in sunlight. Smooth metal surfaces, such as polished aluminum and electro-galvanized roofing, have emissivities below 0.1. Hot-dipped galvanized surfaces, which are rougher, range from 0.2 to 0.3.

Be aware that paints containing metal powder have much lower emissivities than ordinary paints, in the range of 0.2 to 0.5. Therefore, metallic paints create hot surfaces. Ironically, aluminum roof paint was introduced to reduce solar heating. This was before the subject of emissivity was understood by the paint industry.

Asphalt shingles can have high emissivity, but don't take that for granted. Some of the granular material used to coat shingles has low emissivity.

Also, you can't make assumptions about the emissivity of ceramic roof tiles. Some porcelain and earthenware tiles have emissivities that exceed 0.9, while other clay tiles have emissivities below 0.4. Concrete tiles typically range from 0.6 to 0.9. Some tile manufacturers may be able to tell you the emissivities of their products, but many won't know.

The emissivities of gravel and gritty minerals vary widely. Gravel roofs are notoriously hot.

At night, the reflectivity of your roof does not matter, because there is no sunlight to reflect. However, its emissivity is still important. Emissivity can lower the roof temperature well below the surrounding air temperature. The sidebar, *The Sky is Cold*, in Step 2, explains why this happens.

Avoid a Glaring Appearance

To achieve a very cool roof surface, you would need a stark white surface. This is available on sheetmetal roofing and on some coated tiles. However, a bright white roof clashes with most house styles, and it is likely to create glare that is unpleasant to onlookers. Also, it is difficult to keep a white surface clean. Unless you are trying to mimic the white architecture of the Greek islands, settle for a roof color that is not stark white.

---

* If you want to know the science of emissivity, here's the basic story.

(1) The surfaces of all materials emit electromagnetic radiation, also called "heat" radiation.

(2) The intensity of the radiation is proportional to the fourth power of the temperature of the surface, so a small increase in temperature produces a large increase in the amount of heat that is radiated.

(3) Heat energy is radiated across a spectrum of wavelengths that has the shape of a skewed bell curve. A lot of energy is emitted at wavelengths much longer than the peak wavelength. Relatively little energy is emitted at wavelengths much shorter than the peak wavelength.

(4) The peak wavelength is inversely proportional to the temperature of the surface. So, hotter surfaces emit shorter wavelengths.

(5) The surface of the sun emits an enormous amount of radiation because it is very hot. The wavelengths are short, with about 40% being in the visible spectrum.

6) A warm roof emits very little heat by comparison, and the wavelengths are much longer, so you can't see this radiation.

(7) Not all surfaces emit radiation equally well. In physics language, a surface that radiates heat at the maximum rate is called a "black body." That odd name was coined by the famous scientist Max Planck, and it has mystified science students ever since.

(8) By definition, a black body has an emissivity of 1.0. Many roof materials have emissivities that exceed 0.9, but some have emissivities lower than 0.2

ROOF COOLING BY VENTILATION

When sunshine warms the roof surface, air inside the roof is heated by contact with the underside of the roof deck. If there is no air movement within the roof structure, the heated air soon fills the roof structure and heats the insulation by conduction. You can keep the insulation cooler by venting the heated air to the outside. The exhausted air is replaced by outside air.*

Cooling a roof by ventilation requires continuous and rapid replacement of the air in the roof structure. Research shows that wind, rather than convection, is the main driving force for ventilation cooling. In locations with mild winds, the roof requires big ventilation openings.

For perspective, think of a camping tent that is exposed to the sun in a warm climate. When all the flaps are closed, the tent becomes stifling. Opening small flaps reduces the temperature a lot, but the inside is still uncomfortable. Breezes can cool the tent to a comfortable level only if the tent has large openings on all sides.

As a design target for most locations, ventilation cooling needs openings that total at least 10% of the roof area, and more is better. Both the inlets and outlets should be large, because the smaller of the two limits the flow rate.

Right away, this tells us that *ventilation cooling can work well only for truss roofs or for other roofs that have a large space above the insulation*. In beam roofs and triangle-frame roofs, the roof deck is close to the insulation, so the air between them heats quickly. And, the narrow space retards air flow.

At present, you rarely see ventilation cooling used effectively, even for truss roofs. A roof that uses ventilation cooling will have a novel appearance because the ventilation openings will be very large. If you decide to exploit ventilation cooling, endeavor to design the ventilation openings in a way that is consistent with your desired architectural style.

Ventilation Cooling for Attic Roofs

With a truss roof or other kind of attic roof, you can create large cooling vent openings in three possible locations: (1) gable end walls, (2) the eaves, and (3) the ridge or top portion of the roof. The gable end walls and the eaves serve as both entry and exit points for cooling air, depending on the direction of the wind. The top of the roof is mainly an exit point.

The main design issue is to provide inlet and outlet openings that are large and properly placed. Wind is the primary driving force, not convection, unless the air is still. The roof needs vents that face in all directions, so that wind can enter on one side and exit on the opposite side.

You can supplement wind as the driving force for roof ventilation by using a fan to draw air through the roof. If your roof is well insulated, a fan is not likely to be economical. We will discuss roof fans briefly, along with magical turbine ventilators.

■ Gable End Wall Vents

If the roof uses a simple gable shape, the end walls can have large openings for cooling ventilation. For example, see Figure 3-190. Indeed, the entire gable end can be a ventilation louver. In that case, the roof is similar to a shelter tent with screened ends.

DRW

Figure 3-190. A gable end wall vent in Key West that is large enough to provide significant attic cooling. In this hot climate, it would have been even better to make the entire gable end a large triangular louver, which would have doubled the opening area.

Gable end walls are the easiest places to install cooling vents, requiring no modification of the roof design, except that you must select a roof style that has gable ends. (That means, for example, that you can't select a hip or a mansard roof style.) Gable ends have a large potential opening area, exceeding 10% of the roof area with typical roof shapes.

The main caution with gable end vents is to install louvers that will block blowing rain.

Even with large gable end vents, it is still desirable to install vents at the eaves and the top of the roof.

---

* The outside air also cools the underside of the roof deck. However, this benefit tends to be overestimated. Most cooling of the roof deck occurs at the top surface, by the combined effects of wind, convection, and heat radiation into the sky.

■ Eave Vents

To use eave vents for cooling an attic, you need to design a large air passage between the outer corners of the insulation and the roof deck. You can achieve this by adjusting the truss design to provide more clearance above the insulation at the eaves. (See the previous heading, *Insulating Truss Roofs, Attics, and Voids*.)

If the roof has wide roof overhangs, it is easy to install large vents underneath them. Such vents are completely protected from rain and snow. The necessary bird and insect screens can be made reasonably attractive. However, roof styles that lack wide overhangs cannot provide much cooling with eave ventilation.

Eave vents provide the strongest ventilation when the wind blows perpendicular to the wall. On the upwind side, wind pressure against the wall moves air up into the eave vents. On the downwind side, wind creates a slight suction that draws air out of the eave vents.

Eave vents are limited in their opening area. If a roof has generous overhangs, eave vents may be as large as 5% of the roof area, but most roofs will have a significantly smaller percentage. Use insect screens that restrict air flow as little as possible. Decorative vented soffit material, as in Figure 3-176, restricts air flow too much to allow very effective ventilation cooling through the eaves.

■ Ridge Vents

The primary value of a ridge vent is to serve as an *exit* for air that is moved by wind pressure into eave vents and gable end vents. Ridge vents are not very effective as *entry* points for wind, because wind tends to skip over a ridge vent.

By releasing the air that is heated under the roof deck, the ridge vent minimizes contact between the insulation and the heated air. A full-length ridge vent is desirable in combination with both eave vents and gable end vents. A ridge vent is most valuable for cooling when wind is absent.

At present, the main shortcoming of commercially available ridge vents is that they have limited opening area. They are designed for moisture venting, and they are almost worthless for cooling. You need to search to find a ridge vent that has enough opening area to allow the heated air in the attic to escape easily.

The largest opening area that I have found in a residential ridge vent is about 30 square inches per foot of length (about 600 square centimeters per meter of length), as shown in Figure 3-191. This is typically less than 1% of the roof's surface area. However, it is large enough to provide significant venting of attic air,

FAMCO

Figure 3-191. Cutaway section of a metal ridge vent with a relatively large opening area. The black rain cap is attached to the grey base, which has vent louvers punched into its top. The louvered portion of this model is 8" (20 cm) wide.

provided that cooling air can flow freely into the attic through eave vents and/or gable end vents.

To achieve a larger ridge opening, you could design a custom "roof monitor." It could be built as part of your roof. Or, it could be made of heavy aluminum, in which case it would be built by a sheetmetal shop.

A roof monitor would dominate the appearance of the roof. It could be attractive, but it would be a novelty, and thus a daring stylistic feature. In a windy climate, it probably would not be worth the effort. On the other hand, if the climate is hot and the air tends to be still, a large ridge vent can significantly reduce the air temperature inside an attic roof, especially if you can't install large gable end vents.

■ Roof Top Static Vents

Another way to increase cooling air flow through the top of the roof is to use the kind of roof top static vents shown in the previous Figure 3-175. If you use enough of them, you can get as much air flow through them as through a large roof monitor. However, the resulting appearance would not be classic.

■ Roof Cooling Fans

With a truss roof or other type of roof that has a vented attic, you can circulate cooling air through the attic by using a roof cooling fan (often called a "powered roof ventilator"). Installing a roof cooling fan is most likely to be worthwhile in an existing house, if the existing vent openings are not large enough to

DRW

Figure 3-192. An attic cooling fan installed at a good location, near the center of the ridge. Outside air enters the attic through gable end vents and through the eave vents.

allow ample cooling by natural ventilation. Figure 3-192 shows a typical installation.

If you optimize an attic roof for natural ventilation, it is unlikely that a roof cooling fan will provide enough additional benefit to pay off. With super-insulation and the other features of a cool roof, solar heating of the roof increases air conditioning energy consumption by only a few hundred watts. A fan with sufficient capacity for cooling requires about the same amount of energy. And, it requires maintenance.

Still, if you want to add a fan to an attic roof, it is easy to do. Install the fan somewhere near the center of the roof, as high as practical. When the fan operates, it will draw air through all the vent openings.

If an existing house has gable end wall vents, another option is to install a propeller fan behind one of these openings. When the fan is running, it draws air through the other vent openings. When the fan is idle, air can easily flow past the propeller in either direction. This method avoids the need to make a hole in the roof. However, be careful not to install the fan where it will blow into a prevailing wind.

For convenience in installation, try to find a satisfactory fan unit that has an integral thermostat, which usually has the temperature sensor located inside the fan housing. The thermostat senses the temperature of the air that emerges from the roof at that location. If you can't find a fan with an integral thermostat, install a separate thermostat to control the fan. Place it near the center of the attic area, on the bottom of a rafter near the ridge.

Set the thermostat to start the fan at about 100 °F (38 °C). Operating the fan to achieve a lower attic temperature is a waste of energy.

A *solar powered roof fan* is another option to consider. The solar cells that power the fan are mounted on the cover, so no electrical connections are required.

The fan's output is proportional to the intensity of the sunlight, so it is well matched to the solar heating of the roof. The unit should have a built-in thermostat to prevent operation during cold weather.

The power of a solar powered roof fan is feeble. If the solar array on the fan has an effective area of one square foot (about 0.1 square meter), its maximum power output is only about 20 watts, and cheap units have less power. This won't move much air. You could improve ventilation by installing several solar powered fans.

■ Turbine Ventilators (for Believers)

How about turbine ventilators, as in Figure 3-193? They require no power, which keeps them in fashion among believers in perpetual motion machines. The idea is that warm air rising from the attic by convection will cause the turbine to spin, and the spinning turbine will pull air out of the attic.

DRW

Figure 3-193. Turbine ventilators. They offer no advantage over well designed static vents.

In still air, convection actually does spin the turbine. However, the turbine does nothing but impede the escaping air. If the wind is blowing, it will spin turbine ventilators like a pinwheel. Unfortunately, the wind tends to push the air back into the attic. Conventional turbine ventilators offer no significant benefit, they look ugly, and they tend to squeak.

There is a newer kind of wind-driven turbine ventilator that works better. It has a rotating drum with exterior vanes that are designed to spin the drum. Inside the drum are vanes oriented in the opposite direction, which actually suck air out of the roof. However, if there is enough wind to operate this device, it is no more effective than well designed static vents.

Ventilation Cooling for Beam and Triangle-Frame Roofs

In a beam or triangle-frame roof, the narrow passages between the roof deck and the insulation restrict air flow, making the top surface of the insulation considerably warmer than the outside air temperature. This makes beam and triangle-frame roofs inherently less "cool" than truss roofs.

You have only limited opportunity to improve the ventilation cooling of a beam and triangle-frame roof. You can't increase the space between the roof deck and the insulation very much, because this would make the rafters impractically deep. In a warm climate, make the vent openings at the eaves and ridge as large as possible, and accept whatever cooling they provide.

In principle, it is possible to install a fan to increase cooling air flow through the roof. However, this would involve construction methods that are awkward and unconventional. The methods that I have considered would interfere with static cooling. And, they would work only if the roof has a ridge that extends along the entire length of the roof.

Instead of using a fan, increase the amount of insulation and the size of the ventilation gap above the insulation as much as practical.

In a very warm climate, the practical limitations on the amount of insulation in beam and triangle-frame roofs, along with difficulty of ventilating them for cooling, argue in favor of using a well ventilated truss roof instead.

HEAT RADIATION BARRIERS

A typical roof deck has minimal insulation value, so the underside of the roof deck may be much warmer than the outside air or the air inside the roof structure. A hot roof deck radiates heat toward the ceiling insulation. This radiation may be the primary way in which solar heating of the outer roof surface transfers to the insulation.

You could block this downward radiation from the roof deck with any opaque material, such as a sheet of paper. However, if the blocking material itself becomes warm, it will radiate heat toward the insulation. We can block the heat radiation more effectively by using a material that has low emissivity, because such material also reflects heat well. It works in a manner similar to the "low-E" coatings used in windows (which we will explain when we select your windows).

So, a low-emissivity surface that faces the underside of the roof deck will block heat radiation from the roof deck and reflect it back to the roof. At the same time, a low-emissivity surface that faces downward toward the insulation will not radiate much heat, even if it is warm.

Aluminum foil is an inexpensive material that has the desired properties of high heat reflection but low heat emission. Foil is too fragile to be installed by itself, so some manufacturers offer heat barrier material consisting of aluminum foil that is bonded to a stronger carrier sheet, such as the papery material that is used for "house wraps." This barrier material comes in big rolls, and it can be attached with a staple gun. Figure 3-194 shows a typical installation.

Buy radiation barrier material that has foil on both sides. Also, select barrier material that has perforations for moisture venting. Otherwise, the impermeable barrier material would trap moisture against the underside of the roof deck.

 "Heat radiation barrier" is a new component for cool roofs, providing a limited benefit at minor cost. It may shorten the life of shingles.

Select the most durable barrier material that you can find, so it will survive as long as the house, i.e., for centuries. This is especially important for beam roofs, where the radiation barrier becomes inaccessible after the roof is completed.

Infrared radiation barrier material for roofs is a specialty item, so you probably won't find the best material in your local building supplies store. And don't expect your builder to be familiar with it. Search for it on the Internet using words like "radiant barrier for roofing" or "infrared barrier for roofing."

You can buy roof sheathing that has a layer of foil attached to its bottom surface to reduce its heat emission downward. This method is less effective than a separate radiation barrier that is located between the roof deck and the insulation. Don't use both, because foil attached to the roof sheathing would reduce the effectiveness of a separate barrier.

How to Install a Radiation Barrier

The radiation barrier can block heat effectively if it is installed almost anywhere between the roof deck and the insulation. For best results, it should be installed at least one inch (25 mm) away from any other surface, including the surface of the insulation.

In an attic roof, the radiation barrier should work well if it is stapled to the underside of the rafters, as in Figure 3-194. This method is convenient, and it creates little interference when using the attic as a storage space. It minimizes settling of dust on the surfaces, which interferes with the performance of the material. This method of installation makes the barrier easy to remove and replace for roof repairs.

By reflecting heat back to the roof deck, a radiation barrier makes the roof deck hotter. This may shorten the life of the wooden roof deck and organic roofing

Figure 3-194. Radiant barrier material stapled to the bottoms of the rafters in an attic. The gaps left along the top and bottom of the material allow air to circulate between the barrier material and the roof deck. This minimizes overheating of the roof deck and roofing materials. The warm air rising behind the radiant barrier should be vented through a ridge vent. Replacement cooling air should be able to enter from gable end vents and/or eave vents.

surfaces. Therefore, do not allow the radiation barrier to block air circulation along the underside of the roof deck. An effective ridge vent is especially desirable to release the air that is heated under the roof deck. Also, it becomes more important to select a roof surface that is as cool as practical.

In a beam or triangle-frame roof, the radiation barrier is installed from below, before the insulation. If you use I-joist for the rafters, staple the radiation barrier securely to the top flanges of the I-joists.

You may see other installation methods recommended by manufacturers of barrier materials, such as laying the barrier material directly on the insulation. Don't use these methods if they violate any of the requirements that we have discussed.

RETROFIT A COOL ROOF ON AN EXISTING HOUSE?

Is it worthwhile to retrofit a "cool roof" on an existing house? It depends.

The ceiling insulation is the most important factor in a cool roof. If the amount of insulation does not yet meet the recommendations of the *Insulation Worksheet*, adding more insulation is the place to start.

If it is time to renew the roof surface, select the replacement material to be as cool as practical. This can lower the roof temperature at no additional cost. However, it is not economical to replace an existing roof surface just to improve coolness.

A truss roof with gable end walls provides the most opportunity for improving ventilation cooling. With this kind of roof, you can make the gable end vents very

HEAT RADIATION BARRIERS FOR COLD WEATHER: NOT WORTH THE TROUBLE

A heat radiation barrier that is installed between the roof deck and the ceiling insulation will block some radiation heat loss during cold weather. Heat radiation from the surface of the insulation is reflected back to the insulation rather than being absorbed by the roof deck. At night, heat radiation from the roof into the sky may make the roof surface considerably cooler than the air inside the roof structure, increasing heat loss by radiation.

However, this effect is so small that it barely matters. At the low temperature of the insulation surface in cold weather, heat radiation is feeble. Most heat is lost from the top surface of the insulation by convection, not by radiation.

For maximum effectiveness during cold weather, a radiation barrier would be installed between the living space and the ceiling insulation, rather than above the insulation. In this way, heat from the living space would be reflected back into the living space. The principle is similar that of "space blankets" and "low-E" window coatings. More heat is reflected because the temperature of the living space is much higher than the temperature of the outer surface of the insulation in winter.

Installing a radiation barrier in this manner requires a gap between the living space and the bottom of the insulation to make the radiation barrier reflect properly. This gap would risk heat leakage by convection. Various roof "systems" seek to exploit this principle, but they are a carpenter's nightmare.

large, up to the full size of the end walls. Compared to vents that are sized for venting moisture, such large vents will make the attic much cooler.

With a truss roof, or with any kind of vented attic, you can install one or more static vents near the top of the roof. To make these effective, you will also need generously sized eave and/or gable end vents.

A truss roof also allows you to attach a heat radiation barrier to the bottoms of the rafters fairly easily. However, a heat radiation barrier increases the temperature of the roof deck, which will shorten the life of asphalt shingles. Therefore, install a heat radiation barrier only if you provide good cooling ventilation through the truss structure.

If you have an existing beam or triangle-frame roof, you can increase cooling ventilation by installing a ridge vent that has a large open area, and by maximizing the size of the eave vents. This won't provide enough ventilation to make the roof "cool," but it may lower the insulation temperature by a significant amount.

INSULATION FOR INTERIOR FRAME WALLS, FLOORS, AND CEILINGS

We have completed the insulation of the exterior walls, floors and roof. In addition, you may want to insulate some of the interior walls, ceilings, and floors. Doing so may provide significant benefits in energy savings, fire protection, and noise isolation. Consider these benefits as a package. While each benefit alone may not justify insulation between interior spaces, the combination of the three may be compelling.

If you insulate an interior wall, completely fill it with insulation. Partially insulating a wall won't save much material cost, it will save nothing in labor, and you will lose much of the fire protection benefit. Install interior insulation in the same way as for exterior frame walls and floors, except that you will not use vapor barriers.

 Insulating the interior partitions is an unusual practice that can provide three important benefits.

Insulating the floor over a basement or other unheated space will save heat and make the floor more comfortable. The underside of a basement floor usually is crowded with pipe and wiring. To make it easy to install the insulation, install the wiring and pipe low in the joist spaces to make room for the insulation under the floor surface. See the previous heading, *Pre-Cut Holes for Electrical Wiring and Pipe*.

Should you insulate your interior walls? And if so, which ones? Let's consider the potential benefit of insulation for …

… Energy Conservation

One of the Five Principles of Super-Efficiency is isolating energy use to the rooms that are occupied. In Step 1, you designed efficient layouts for the "day cluster" of rooms, the "bedroom clusters," the "independent rooms," and the "expansion rooms." In climates with a cold season, installing insulation in the walls, ceilings, and floors of these rooms and room clusters maximizes the energy efficiency of these layouts.

Interior insulation is most valuable if it is installed around rooms that may be unoccupied for long periods, if those rooms also have exterior walls. For example, if you have a formal dining room that is not used routinely, insulate the walls that separate it from the rest of the house. Also, insulate the walls that separate spare bedrooms from the parts of the house in daily use.

The width of standard interior framing, which is 3½" (about 82 mm), generally is sufficient for interior insulation. However, in a colder climate, you may need wider studs to accommodate the interior insulation for a large, usually unoccupied room that has an exterior wall. For example, you might use wider interior wall studs for a "great room" that has a lot of exterior wall area.

… Fire Protection

Non-flammable insulation has a powerful ability to quench fire or to delay its spread. Interior insulation could make the difference between a fire that damages a single room or that destroys the entire house. Insulation is not presently recognized as a primary fire prevention tool, but it should be.

As they taught you in elementary school, fire needs fuel, air, and ignition temperature. The wood in a frame structure is fuel. But, filling the structure with non-combustible insulation blocks the flow of heat and air inside the structure. If gypsum board is used as the sheathing on an interior wall or ceiling, the combination of the insulation and the gypsum board surrounds the wood with a fire resistant barrier.

A wall that is filled with insulation will not allow fire to climb inside the wall itself. The insulation acts as a "firestop." An insulated wall also blocks the spread of fire from one room to adjacent rooms on the same level.

Insulating interior floors is also important because fire spreads aggressively in an upward direction. The hot gases created by the fire are much lighter than the surrounding air. Fire tends to spread to the ceiling by climbing up a wall, fueled by paint, draperies, and other furnishings. Insulation in the floor above slows the spread of fire to the upper floors and/or to the roof.

... Noise Reduction

Any wall, ceiling, or floor surface acts like the diaphragm of a loudspeaker, transmitting noise to or from the structure. Therefore, insulating interior walls and floors also improves noise isolation. However, insulation is secondary for this purpose. Mass is the most effective barrier to noise, especially for the lower frequencies that tend to be the worst annoyance in residential environments. (Think of your teenager's "music.")

Gypsum board sheathing is heavy, so it provides excellent sound deadening. With gypsum board sheathing on your walls and ceilings, the additional benefit of fiber insulation may be minor.

If noise isolation is important for a room or for a group of rooms, install special sound-attenuating gypsum board on the walls and ceilings of those rooms. This material consists of double sheets that have an air gap between them. The air gap interrupts the mechanical vibration that transmits sound through the structure. For floors, carpet is an effective sound attenuator.

THE WIRING AND CABLE

The wiring and cable of a house acts as its nervous system, providing its electrical power, telephone and television service, intercoms, doorbells, and other services not yet invented. We will call all this the "wiring," even though it may be fiber optic cable or something else.

Electrical wiring involves potentially deadly hazards. Improper electrical wiring can cause fire and electrocution. It can also cause lesser trouble, such as corrosion of pipes. Fortunately, these dangers are recognized in advanced countries, where there are rigorous requirements for the training and licensing of electricians. Also, electrical practice is guided by a very detailed code. (In the U.S., this is the *National Electrical Code*, which is also part of the *International Residential Code*.) If you deal with a reputable contractor, you can be reasonably certain that the electricians will install your wiring safely.*

Similarly, communications cable usually is installed by specialists from the telephone company or the television cable company, so you can also be reasonably certain that it will be installed properly.

Therefore, this part of our discussion can be brief. However, one consistent failing of both electricians and cable installers is that they tend to be oblivious to non-electrical problems that they cause. Electricians commonly install wiring in a manner that interferes with installing the insulation, and they make a lot of holes that create air leaks. In the worst case, electricians weaken the structure by drilling big holes through strength members.

Good electrical wiring can be a thing of beauty, but many electricians route wiring in a manner that is incredibly sloppy. So, we introduce some improvements that will prevent those problems, at least with the help of a little supervision. We'll start with a valuable convenience feature.

Install Receptacles for Convenience

Install electrical power receptacles at close intervals in all rooms. Space receptacles on walls about four feet (120 cm) apart. The cost is minimal and it avoids a lifetime of using extension cords and receptacle extenders. A fraction of your receptacles will be blocked by furniture, so you want plenty of extras.

Install receptacles at a convenient height, rather than down near the baseboards. A height of 18" to 24" (45 to 60 cm) above the floor is ideal. You will love the ease of plugging in appliances and light fixtures, especially if you have a back injury or other disability. By the same token, the electrician will love the ease of connecting the wiring.

 Install the electrical receptacles at a height that does not require awkward stooping to reach them.

An alternative to individual receptacles is to install surface-mounted strip receptacles, which provide access to power everywhere along the wall. They are probably not attractive enough for a formal room, especially at the receptacle height that I recommend, but they may be perfect for a workshop or for a hobby room.

In the kitchen and toilet rooms, install plenty of receptacles over counters. In a large workshop, install receptacles above head height on stalks that descend from the ceiling.

Don't install receptacles in the floor. Dirt will fall into them. If liquid is spilled into a receptacle, it becomes dangerous. And, no matter where you put floor receptabcles, they will interfere with the legs of a table or chair.

Connect the receptacles and the built-in lighting fixtures on separate circuits. In this way, an overload or failure of a receptacle cannot shut off the lights. Similarly, divide the receptacle and lighting circuits so that no single circuit covers a large area alone.

Install an adequate number of receptacles around the outside of the house at convenient locations. These will be welcomed for operating hedge trimmers, automotive tools, portable griddles, holiday lights, and other uses. Locate outside receptacles in weatherproof boxes, preferably in protected locations.

Install outdoor receptacles on separate circuits, so they can be turned off at the circuit breaker panel without affecting the interior circuits.

How to Route the Wiring

Most wiring is completed before the insulation is installed. A major improvement in your super-home is installing the wiring in a way that does not interfere with the insulation.

The fabricated studs that we use for thicker super-insulated walls include passages for the wiring at the floor level, so the electrician can run the wiring through them easily and quickly. Don't let the electricians (or

---

* In most of the U.S., and in some other countries, homeowners can install their own wiring. However, the wiring must conform rigorously to the electrical code, and the wiring generally must be inspected and approved. If you want to install your own wiring, in either a new house or an existing house, be sure that you know what you are doing. Large hardware stores generally offer well illustrated books on home electrical wiring.

the plumbers or anyone else) cut into the outer members of the studs, which are the strength members that carry the weight of the house.

If you use plain lumber studs, remember that your carpenters are supposed to cut notches in the bottoms of the studs to form a passage for wiring.

Also, as we recommended previously, your I-joist manufacturer or your carpenters should pre-cut holes in the webs of your floor joists to provide neat and easy wiring through the floors.

Route wiring tightly along studs and joists so that it does not interfere with insulation.

Make sure that all electrical connection boxes are mounted on the studs securely and straight, with the proper protrusion through the drywall or other interior sheathing. Otherwise, cover plates will not fit properly and fixtures mounted on the boxes will not be secure.

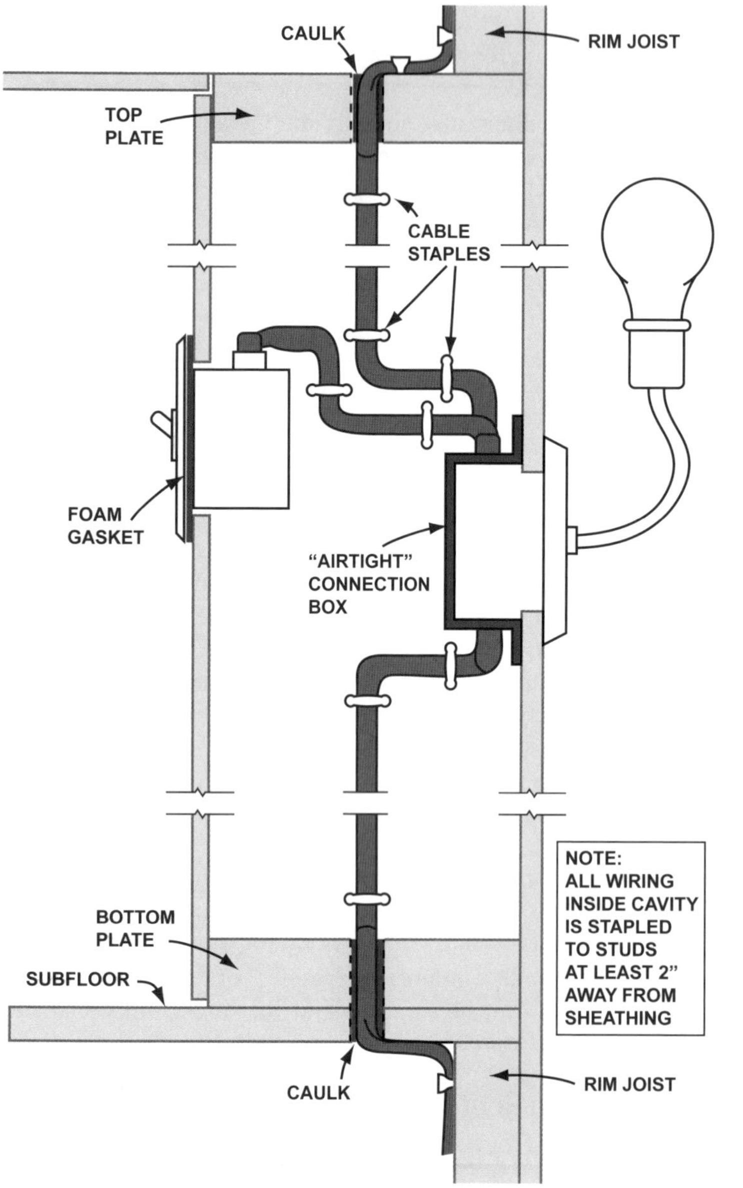

Block Air Leakage Around Wiring

Your electrical wiring and other cabling will require a lot of holes in your structure. For example, consider the wiring for a porch light, as in Figure 3-197. The inside wiring starts at the circuit breaker box in the basement. It penetrates upward into the outer wall through a hole in the bottom plate of the wall. Inside the wall cavity, the wire connects to the indoor switch at a junction box that is mounted through the interior sheathing. It also passes into a box that is mounted through the outer sheathing. If the light is controlled from more than one location, the additional wiring may run through the attic by way of a hole in the top plate of the wall.

Thus, to serve one light fixture, a wall cavity may have holes that lead to the outside, to the inside, to the basement, and to the attic. If the holes are not sealed properly, they can be a major source of air leakage into the house and through the wall structure.

It is practically impossible to make a good seal around wiring where it passes through a thin surface, such as plywood, because the sealant cannot attach to enough surface area to resist movement of the wiring.

So, we need to run wiring through holes in a way that allows the holes to be sealed reliably. Follow these steps, as shown in Figure 3-197:

- Make wiring holes as small as possible, so the wiring fits snugly.
- Make the holes in thick material, such as a top or bottom plate or rim joist. However, do not make holes in the flanges of joists or studs. If it is necessary to make a hole through sheathing or other thin material, use an "airtight" connection box that is attached to the sheathing securely.
- Staple the wire on both sides of the hole to prevent movement that would knock the sealant out of the hole.
- Inject sealant using a nozzle that is small enough to distribute the sealant entirely around the wires and through the entire length of the hole.

DRW

Figure 3-197. Proper installation of wiring in an exterior frame wall. The main issues are avoiding (1) air leakage, (2) interference with the insulation, (3) weakening of the structure by penetrations, and (4) wiring damage by nails and sharp edges. Wiring holes are always drilled through thick members, for reliable sealing. Staples are always attached to thick members.

Secure all electrical wiring along the sides of insulated cavities so that it creates no interference with the insulation.

Your job, as the homeowner, is to make sure that your builder educates the electricians to use these procedures. The prevailing practice of electricians is to run the wiring in any way that is quick and convenient for themselves. In place of this sloppy practice, *require your electricians to install the wiring in a way that does not weaken the structure, does not cause air leakage, and does not interfere with the insulation*. Write this into your contract with the builder.

"Airtight" connection boxes for the exterior sheathing of a frame wall are still a new product. Good ones may be difficult to find, so expect to search. Even this type of box is not truly airtight unless caulking is applied where the wiring passes into the box.

To get wiring through masonry, the best practice is to install a short length of metal conduit through the wall. The conduit is cemented into the masonry at both ends. End fittings are installed on the conduit to protect the wiring from the sharp edges of the conduit. Caulk the wiring where it is held by the end fittings.

If you need to install an electrical box on the outside of a masonry wall, use a special box that has a fitting to accept the end of the conduit.

■ Gaskets for Indoor Switch and Receptacle Covers

The inside of your house will be peppered with electrical switches and receptacles. Each of these has a gap between the electrical connection box and the interior wall finish. If the wall has an inside vapor barrier, the vapor barrier is penetrated at each of these fixtures. The cover plates for the receptacles and switches don't block air leakage well, because they don't fit tightly against the receptacle or switch, and they don't fit snugly against the wall surface.

A simple, inexpensive solution is to install plastic foam gaskets under the cover plates of switches and receptacles that are mounted in outside walls. Such gaskets are standard items that are cut to fit the most common receptacle and switch patterns. Installing them requires virtually no effort. See Figure 3-198.

DRW

Figure 3-198. Gasket that stops drafts at wall penetrations. The foam gasket at left is inserted over the receptacle, where it is held in place by the cover plate.

Well done! You have now completed the design of your home's structure. In the rest of Step 3, we will select the components that fit into the structure: the windows, doors, skylights, and floor surfaces.

SELECTING AND INSTALLING YOUR WINDOWS

By this point, you are fully aware of the importance of your home's windows. In Step 1, we introduced windows as an important element of style. In Step 2, you learned that windows perform many other important functions, and you learned how to design the layout and shapes of your windows to optimize all those functions.

Now, the time has come to select and install the windows themselves. We're going to select all the best features of modern windows and we will make some important improvements in the way that your windows are installed.

Modern windows offer a large variety of valuable features, including some that became available only recently. To select the features that are best for your home, use the *Window Selection Guide* on the following pages.

Almost all of this discussion applies equally to new and existing houses. The selection issues for windows and the recommended methods of installation are generally the same.

Contemporary Windows are Short-Lived

Years ago, I was sitting in the upstairs room of a pub in the old city of York, England. The room hung over a narrow, winding street below, and my elbow was resting on the sill of an open casement window. Gazing at the window, it occurred to me that the glass and mullions were probably hundreds of years old. Being protected by a wide roof overhang, that window might survive many more years.

But today, window technology is in a transitional state. In order to reduce the terrible heat loss of windows, double or triple panes are now the norm. However, despite decades of attempts, no one has found a durable method of sealing the edges of multiple-glazed windows. As a result, most multi-glazed windows become fogged and unsightly within a period that averages about 20 years.

Thus, a modern home needs to replace its windows about as often as its roofing shingles. Expect to deal with that fact as you select and install your windows. This will require some improvements over past practice, which you will learn.

PRELIMINARY WINDOW RECOMMENDATIONS

The *Window Selection Guide* offers you a rich menu of options. Unfortunately, your window choices are so extensive that they may be overwhelming. So, here are some preliminary recommendations to speed you toward the best window selections for your home.

■ Opening Style

The *Window Selection Guide* illustrates all the common ways that windows can open. For most windows and for most architectural styles, my own preference is for horizontal sliders. They offer a good combination of convenience, durability, and energy efficiency.

However, if your home requires windows that are tall and narrow, single-hung (vertical slider) windows are probably your best choice, despite their annoyances.

Other styles may be best for specialized applications, such as jalousie windows for an enclosed porch.

■ Frame Material

Until recently, my recommendation would be to buy windows that have sturdy aluminum frames, and to replace the glass when the seals fail.

Alas, the realities of the market have led me to a different viewpoint. Good aluminum windows with easily replaceable glass have virtually disappeared. Cheap vinyl windows now dominate the market. Being cheap and waterproof gives plastic frames the edge over other available frame materials.

Unlike other frame materials, plastic frames last no longer than the glazing seals, if that long. Instead of leaving the frame in place and replacing the glass, the practical approach now is to replace the entire window assembly, frame and all.

Plastic window frames are elastic, allowing their shape to distort enough to allow air leakage and to make it difficult to open and close the windows. To compensate for this, some windows have metal stiffeners inside the plastic frame. Try to get this feature.

■ Method of Installation

An important improvement in modern windows is the addition of mounting fins to the frames. The fins speed installation and they create a virtually airtight seal between the window frame and the house wall. With plastic window frames, they also help to keep the frame straight. So, favor finned frames over the older types.

Finned windows are difficult to replace if they are installed in the usual way, with the fins covered by the wall's exterior surface. Therefore, use the innovative method of installing windows that is introduced below, under the heading *A Better Way to Install Finned Windows*.

■ Energy Efficiency Features

By far the most important factor in reducing heat loss through a window is the number of glass panes. Because of weight limitations, double or triple glazing is generally the maximum for openable windows. Triple glazing is an expensive specialty feature that requires an especially strong frame.

Instead of triple glazing, I recommend installing tandem double-glazed windows. This is perhaps the most valuable innovation of this book. It is explained below, under the heading *Tandem Windows: a Big Energy Saver*. If your home site has a cold season, I strongly recommend that you try tandem windows.

"Low-E" coatings and "insulating" fill gases are two features that have become standard in all but the cheapest windows. Although these features are much less important than the number of panes, they are probably worth a small additional price.

■ Resistance to Damage and Intruders

Windows have been the weakest points in protecting houses from windstorms. Their weakness has also made them preferred entrances for criminals. A new category of strong windows, introduced at the beginning of the 21st century, greatly reduces these vulnerabilities. Consider them for your home. The details are explained in the *Window Selection Guide*.

■ Buy Quality, Not Brand Name

Don't waste your money on fashionable window brands. The higher price of "premium" brands mostly goes into marketing and higher profit.

Buy for features, not for brand name. This is especially true of windows with plastic frames. Many manufacturers are capable of producing plastic-frame windows that are as good as the plastic-frame windows of the big-name manufacturers. The *Window Selection Guide* tells you what to look for when you select a manufacturer.

WINDOW RATINGS

Windows in many countries have performance ratings. In the United States, use the Energy Performance Ratings developed by the National Fenestration Rating Council (NFRC). The NFRC is a certification organization that was established by U.S. window manufacturers, with support from the U.S. government. Participation in the program by manufacturers is voluntary, and most major manufacturers participate. Manufacturers assign their own ratings using NFRC testing procedures. Random verification is performed by the NFRC.

The NFRC rating system is spreading to other countries. Ratings may be expressed in English or metric units, depending on the country.

The NFRC Energy Performance Ratings cover a variety of characteristics, not just energy efficiency. Different products may receive ratings for different characteristics. At present, these are the most common ratings:

- *U-Factor* is the tendency to conduct heat, averaged for the entire window assembly. U-factor is the inverse of R-value. Smaller numbers are better. This is usually the most important rating for selecting windows.

- *Condensation Resistance (CR)* is a number from 0 to 100 that provides a relative rating of the resistance of the window to forming condensation on the interior surface during cold weather. Higher numbers are better. The CR rating is calculated from the lowest interior surface temperature on any part of the glass or frame. It is especially useful as an indication of the effectiveness of thermal breaks in aluminum frames.

- *Air Leakage (AL)* is the volume of air that leaks through the entire window assembly, per unit of area, under standard test pressure. AL ratings have units, but it is most useful to compare them on a relative basis. Smaller numbers are better. This factor applies only to new windows, and it gives no indication of the ability of the window to remain airtight as it ages.

- *Solar Heat Gain Coefficient (SHGC)* is the fraction of solar energy falling on the total window assembly that eventually enters the house as heat. SHGC is expressed as a number between zero and one. It includes both sunlight that shines directly through the glass and heat that passes into the house by conduction as a result of warming of the window components by sunlight. High SHGC is desirable in cold climates, and low SHGC is desirable in warm climates. For windows with clear glass, differences in SHGC are minor.

WINDOW SELECTION GUIDE

USAGE ISSUES

Let's begin our selection of the windows with the characteristics that matter to the people who will use them, including the people who will clean them and the people who will see them as part of the house's appearance.

☐ Size and Shape

Windows that open are rectangular, unless you can spend a fortune for a custom shape. If you have a wall where you want to install a non-rectangular window, you can combine a rectangular openable window with a fixed window of another shape.

Manufacturers offer some standard fixed windows with non-rectangular shapes, especially involving half circles (called "fanlights"). Be careful about using such shapes. One or two may be a nice accent, but don't overdo it. They complicate the wall framing, and they may be difficult to replace or to repair in the future.

All or most of your windows will be standard items that have prefabricated frames. For those, it is important to know the exact dimensions of the part of the frame that fits inside the wall opening. The gap between the window frame and the wall opening should be less than one half inch (12 mm or less) in width and height. This is necessary for easy installation, strong support of the window, and reliable sealing against air leakage.

In the past, window dimensions were fairly standard, so carpenters could build the window openings before the windows were bought. Unfortunately, this is no longer true. After you identify the window models you want, check the catalogs for a drawing that shows the exact dimensions. Or, order the windows before you build the walls, if you have a safe place to store them during construction.

Fixed windows without frames are made on a custom basis, so you can get almost any dimensions or shape that you want. Polygon shapes are especially easy to make because they have all straight edges. But, avoid acute angles, which are vulnerable to breaking off. Segments of circles and other curves can be made by glass shops having the appropriate equipment. To reduce cost, talk to the fabricator about designing the shapes and sizes of your windows to minimize waste of glass when the window is made.

Openable windows are limited in size by the weight of the glazing. Triple-glazed and intrusion-resistance glazing is heavy, limiting openable windows to smaller sizes. The maximum practical size depends on the method of opening.

☐ Fixed or Openable?

Should your windows be fixed or openable? Make this decision for each window individually, but avoid an unattractive patchwork of different window types. Common reasons to select *openable windows* are:

- Cooling ventilation during warm weather. This requires fairly large openings.
- Ventilation for air quality. This requires only a small opening.
- During warm weather, openable windows can quickly vent moisture from a damp space, especially a shower room or a toilet room.
- Occupants can talk to people outside the house through an opened window.

Common reasons to select *fixed windows* are:

- Fixed windows costs less, because the frames are much simpler. However, a mass market openable window may cost less than a custom fixed window.
- Double and triple glazing is practical in much larger sizes than in openable units.
- Fixed glass without a frame can be made in non-rectangular shapes at modest cost.

In the past, openable windows were a major path for heat loss during cold weather. But today, the best windows have little air leakage, typically less than the ventilation needed for good air quality. Sealing against air leakage is achieved with effective seals (weatherstripping), well designed latches, and rigid frames.

So, make a window openable if it is useful for ventilation or for communication to the outside. Otherwise, use fixed glazing. For example, fixed glass may be best for clerestories and for other glazing that is used primarily for daylighting and passive heating.

WINDOW SELECTION GUIDE

☐ Styles of Openable Windows

For your openable windows, you have a range of style options, which are summarized in the following chart, along with the issues to consider in making the choice.

Air leakage has been a major comfort and energy efficiency issue with windows for as long as openable windows have existed. Today, most styles of openable windows are capable of sealing tightly when they are closed, but this quality comes at a cost premium with some designs. Double-hung windows are especially difficult to seal reliably.

Any kind of window in which more than one pane or sash is moved by a single actuator invites air leakage. The extreme case is a jalousie window, which is limited to climates and applications where air leakage matters little.

Beware of windows that require actuators with gears and linkages. These are usually made of cheap metal that wears out quickly. If your window style requires an actuator, select a window model that allows the actuator to be replaced easily. Even so, replacement parts won't be available throughout the life of the house.

An important innovation that we suggest for colder climates is installing two complete window assemblies in a wall opening, one inside the other. (See *Tandem Windows: a Big Energy Saver*, in Step 3.) If you use that technique, you need to select opening styles that work well together. It is not necessary for both windows to be the same type. For example, the inner window could be a slider model, and the outer window could be an awning model. To avoid condensation on the outer window, the inner window must be able to maintain tighter sealing against air leakage than the outer window.

☐ Ease of Cleaning

Unless the windows are easily accessible for cleaning from the outside, favor window styles that allow you to clean the outer surfaces from inside the room.

Hopper, inward-swinging casement, and tilt-turn windows are easy to clean from the inside,

It is virtually impossible to clean an outward-swinging casement window or an awning window from the inside.

If you install horizontal or vertical slider windows, select models that make it easy to remove the moving sash, or to tilt it inward. Otherwise, you won't be able to clean the outside surface of the moving sash from inside the room.

If you plan to clean your windows from the outside, arrange the landscaping around your home for easy access to the windows.

☐ Internal Shading Devices

Some windows with double glazing include adjustable shading louvers between the panes of glass. Reject this feature. In principle, it provides slightly more efficient shading than a separate shade installed inside the window. However, the internal shading mechanisms will fail long before the rest of the window. Repair will be difficult or impossible. The linkage that operates the louver must pass through the frame, making it impossible to fill the window with insulating gases.

Window Lingo

Here is some window language that we will be using.

- A "pane" is an individual sheet of glass in a window. It may also be called a "light."
- A "sash" is a part of a window assembly that consists of one or more "panes" or "lights" that are held by top, bottom, and side pieces.
- If a "sash" contains several panes, the pieces that join the panes are called "mullions."
- The complete window assembly consists of one or more "sashes" that are held in a "frame," which is attached to the wall opening.
- In a fixed window, the "sash" and the "frame" usually are the same. In a window that can open, the movable glass is held in one or more separate "sashes" that slide or are hinged within the "frame."

WINDOW SELECTION GUIDE

Champion Windows

Figure 3-201. Horizontal Slider (Glider)

Two sashes, one of which slides horizontally to overlap the other. Provides straight-through ventilation. Popular in North America.

PRO: Easy to manipulate. Easy to position for minimum ventilation during cold weather. Movable sashes can be removed for cleaning from inside the room.

CON: Window usually has unsymmetrical appearance because the movable sash has slightly smaller glass area.

Pella Windows

Figure 3-202. Vertical Slider (Single-Hung)

Two sashes, a movable lower sash that slides up past a fixed sash. Provides straight-through ventilation.

PRO: Appearance somewhat similar to historic double-hung windows. The narrower shape allows windows to be installed within one or two stud spaces, and in narrow dormers.

CON: The weight of the movable sash is held in place by friction, making the sash difficult to manipulate. Or, balancing hardware is used, which invites trouble. Weatherstripping is prone to greater leakage and wear than with horizontal sliders. The outer surface of the movable sash cannot be cleaned from the inside. The appearance may be unsymmetrical because the movable sash has slightly smaller glass area.

Nu-Prime of Memphis

Figure 3-203. Double-Hung

Two movable sashes, each of which can slide vertically, overlapping each other. Provides straight-through ventilation. Generally obsolete, except where historic appearance is needed.

PRO: Historic appearance. Able to draw ventilation air through the top and/or bottom of the window. The narrow shape allows window to be installed within one or two stud spaces, and in narrow dormers.

CON: Complex weatherstripping is prone to air leakage and wear. The weight of the movable sashes is held in place by friction in frame, making the sash difficult to manipulate. Or, balancing hardware is used, which invites trouble.

WINDOW SELECTION GUIDE

Figure 3-204. Casement (Outward Swinging)
deedsdesign

Sash is hinged on the side, and swings outward. Blocks wind coming from hinge side. Requires an actuator to hold the window in position. Sashes may be installed in facing pairs, or as side units with larger fixed windows.

PRO: Entire window area is openable.

CON: Difficult to adjust for minimum ventilation during cold weather. Outer surface cannot be cleaned from inside. The actuator eventually wears out. Prone to air leakage unless the frame is very stiff and the weatherstripping is well designed.

Home Crafts Inc
Figure 3-205. Casement (Inward Swinging)

Sash is hinged on the side, and swings inward. Does not require an actuator. Sashes are often installed in facing pairs to reduce their width.

PRO: Entire window area is openable. Easy to clean from inside.

CON: Intrudes into room. Conflicts with blinds and curtains. Without actuator, cannot hold position for minimum ventilation during cold weather.

DRW
Figure 3-206. Awning

Sash is hinged on top, and swings outward. Partially blocks wind. Requires an actuator to hold window in position. Often installed as a lower unit in combination with a larger fixed window.

PRO: Provides partial protection from rain when open.

CON: Outer surface cannot be cleaned from inside. The actuator eventually wears out.

WINDOW SELECTION GUIDE

Flickr

Figure 3-207. Hopper

Sash is hinged at the bottom, and swings inward. Deflects wind upward. Often installed as a lower unit in combination with a larger fixed window.

PRO: Provides some protection from rain when open. Easy to clean from inside.

CON: Intrudes into the room, interfering with curtains and shades. Corners of frame are a possible hazard. Without actuator, cannot hold position for minimum ventilation during cold weather.

Natural Windows

Figure 3-208. Combination Hinged (Tilt-Turn)

Sash opens inward, hinged either at the edge or at the bottom, depending on how a 3-position handle is turned. Deflects wind upward or sideways.

PRO: Easy to clean from inside.

CON: Intrudes into the room, interfering with curtains and shades. Corners of frame are a possible hazard. Most designs limit the sash opening. Most designs do not allow positioning for minimum ventilation during cold weather. Requires a complex actuator, which is likely to become troublesome.

Breezway Louver Windows

Figure 3-209. Jalousie (Louver)

Numerous overlapping horizontal panes, similar to a venetian blind, are operated by a common actuator. Individual panes may be clear, obscured, or opaque. Widely used in warm climates, and as a wind and rain screen for unheated porches.

PRO: Maximum ventilation. Fully adjustable opening and wind deflection. Good protection from rain while open. With opaque panes, can serve as a venetian blind. Easy to clean from inside.

CON: High air leakage, therefore not suitable for heated or cooled spaces. Requires many linkages, which loosen and wear out.

WINDOW SELECTION GUIDE

THE GLAZING

Now, let's look at the glass itself. Window glass is almost completely unaffected by the environment, so it can last longer than the house. It is now available with a large menu of variations.

Window glass is made by only a few large manufacturers, all of whom produce glass of excellent quality. The glass manufacturer determines the basic properties of the bulk glass, including its clarity, thickness, strength, tint, etc. The glass manufacturer also applies coatings that alter its visual and energy properties, including low-E, spectrally reflective, or mirror coatings. The following are the products that come from the glass factory.

☐ Plain Glass

The main application for plain, unmodified glass is in single-glazed windows, in applications that are not exposed to storm damage or forced entry. The main option for plain glass is its thickness.

Plain glass is also used in multiple-glazed windows, but such windows increasingly have coatings applied to the glass.

☐ Impact-Resistant Glass

Window glass shatters easily, so manufacturers have tried various methods to strengthen it. The oldest method is to increase the thickness, which also increases weight. Various methods of heat treatment may strengthen the glass or make it less dangerous when it breaks.

Starting in 2002, a major new choice entered the market, which is glass that is modified to withstand severe impact. This material arose in response to the Miami-Dade County (or ASTM) standards for resistance to windstorms and intrusion.

Most windows that satisfy these standards use laminated glass. Laminated glass is made from an outer sheet of "strengthened" glass that is bonded to an inner sheet of "tempered glass" by a layer of strong, flexible plastic. Under heavy impact, the exterior glass shatters into pieces with sharp points, but the glass sticks to the plastic layer, so that the window is not penetrated. The interior glass breaks by crumbling into small pieces that are much less dangerous if they break loose.

The life of impact-resistant glass is determined by the life of the plastic reinforcing layer. From experience with automotive glass, we can expect it to last at least several decades before it separates and interferes with vision. So, impact-resistant glass in house windows probably will last as long as the glazing edge seals, and perhaps longer.

Impact-resistant glass is heavy. For example, laminated glass that meets the Miami-Dade County standard has two glass sheets, each of which is 0.25" (6 mm) thick. This weighs about 7 pounds per square foot (34 kilograms per square meter). Frames must be specially designed to carry the weight of the glass and to make it easy to operate openable sashes.

In windows with multiple glazing, an outer pane of impact-resistant glass can be combined with an inner pane of ordinary glass.

Various plastic materials are used for glazing, but their limited life makes them unsuitable for main windows. Polycarbonate plastic is commonly used in storm windows and storm doors because it is light and strong. (I don't recommend either storm windows or storm doors.) Very thick plastic, such as used in bank teller windows, was once an option for intrusion-resistant windows, but laminated glass is preferable for its hardness, clarity, and longer life.

☐ Diffusing Glass

"Diffusing" glass is used to distribute light broadly in a fairly uniform pattern. Diffusion may be achieved by etching or grinding the glass surface, by molding tiny prisms into the surface, or by mixing diffusing material, such as a white pigment, into the glass.

Diffusing glazing is desirable in skylights to provide broad light distribution and to break up beams of bright sunlight. It has an intensely bright appearance inside the room when it is illuminated by direct sunlight, so it should be located outside normal sight lines. Therefore, it does not belong in windows or clerestories.

WINDOW SELECTION GUIDE

☐ Obscuring Glass

"Obscuring" glass is used to provide privacy, especially for toilet room, shower room, and basement windows. Most obscuring glass reveals the shape of objects near the glass, but not of objects farther inside the room. It is an option to consider if you want daylight, but you can't provide adequate privacy by raising the sill height.

Obscuring glass is created by giving the glass an irregular surface, which may be in the shape of waves, flutes, pebbles, ferns, or whatever. These act as lenses or prisms, bending the image through the glass into random fragments. When illuminated by direct sunlight, obscuring glass has a sparkling appearance from inside the room.

☐ Decorative Glass

Decorative glass is used to create windows that serve primarily as decorations, which benefit both the interior and exterior of the house. It provides privacy and some light, but no view. It may use colors ("stained glass"), etched designs, or molded patterns. It may be flat or embossed, and it may have high or low light transmission.

☐ Darkening Glass

Darkening glass is used to reduce the light intensity of a view that is excessively bright, like wearing sunglasses. If your home looks out on an exceptionally bright scene, such as a seashore or lake that reflects sunlight into the house, darkening glass may be desirable for windows facing in that direction. Typically, you would select a light transmission of about 20% for such applications. The penalty is that such glass minimizes the view at night. Tinted glass and mirror glass are the two main options for darkening.

Don't try to use darkening glass to reduce the intensity of sunlight for daylighting inside the house. It won't work. The illumination level of direct sunlight is about 60,000 lux (a unit of light intensity). In comparison, desirable room lighting is about 100 to 500 lux. As a result, the glazing would have to be almost opaque, like welder's goggles. Glass with such a low transmission would make the view of the outside almost black. From the outside, such windows would look like the windows of a drug dealer's limousine.

Tinted glass works by absorbing sunlight. It is created by mixing a dye with the glass while it is still molten. The color can be selected. Neutral gray or blue-gray generally are best for vision. Distinctive colors are stylistically risky and may be visually annoying.

Tinted glass is warmed by the sunlight that it absorbs. Some of this heat moves into the house by conduction and by radiation. This effect is greatest with single-pane windows, and much less with double-pane windows where only the outer pane is tinted.

Tinted glass is especially vulnerable to thermal breakage. Tinted glass can become quite hot if the sun can shine on it directly. The exposed glass expands as it warms. The glass at the edge of the window remains cool inside the frame. The resulting stress may crack the glass. The risk of breakage increases with the size of the window.

Also, the difference in expansion between the treated and clear panes in multi-glazed windows also places stress on the edge seals, leading to early seal failure.

To avoid breakage, tinted glass should be permanently shaded from direct sunlight by the structure of the house. If this is not possible, tinted glass should be tempered and it should be protected in other ways, such as by using dark frames.

Mirror glass reflects sunlight, rather than absorbing it. It is made by applying a thin layer of metal to the glass, which is thin enough to pass the desired amount of visible light. The reflecting layer is fragile, so it must be used on an inside surface of a multiple-pane window.

Mirror glass makes your windows look like mirrors from the outside, which gives the house an odd appearance. Some reflective metals give the window a distinctive color. At night, the windows also look like mirrors from the inside.

The coating on mirror glass absorbs a fraction of the sunlight that falls on the window. As a result, mirror glass is vulnerable to thermal breakage in the same ways as tinted glass, but the risk is less severe.

WINDOW SELECTION GUIDE

☐ Low-E Coatings

During cold weather, the objects inside the house, including people, are warmer than the surfaces of the glazing. Therefore, a person's body radiates more heat* toward the glass than the glass radiates toward the person. The glass absorbs this heat, much of which is lost to the outside by conduction. The loss of body heat by radiation is strong enough to make a person near a window feel cold even if the air is at normal room temperature. A window in cold weather has been described as a "negative campfire."

"Low-E" (which stands for "low emissivity") coatings on windows reduce this effect. Low-E coatings are microscopically thin metal films. The film has two essential properties. One is the ability to reflect low-temperature heat radiation, rather than absorbing it. The other is to inhibit the radiation of heat from the surface of the glass, hence its name. This occurs because smooth conducting materials have low "emissivity," which is the tendency of a warm surface to radiate away its heat. For example, the emissivity of an aluminum film is about 0.08. By comparison, the emissivity of ordinary glass is 0.84.

A low-E coating can work in two different ways, depending on its location in the window. If the coating is applied to an outward facing surface, it inhibits the radiation of heat from the glass toward the outside. This causes the glazing to become warmer and to radiate more heat back into the house. If the coating is placed on an inward facing surface, it reflects heat coming from the room back into the house.

Ideally, a low-E coating should be located on the innermost surface of a window, so that room heat is reflected back into the room. However, this is not practical because the coating is too fragile to survive ordinary window cleaning. So, residential windows use low-E coatings only inside sealed multiple-glazed units.

In a double-glazed window, the low-E coating can be located on either of the two inside surfaces. If it is located on the outer side of the gap, it reflects heat radiation back toward the inner pane, which absorbs the heat. If the coating is located on the inner side of the gap, its low emissivity keeps the warmer interior glass from radiating its heat across the gap. Both approaches yield about the same benefit. Only a single coating can be used inside the gap, because two coatings would work against each other.

Triple glazing can benefit from two low-E coatings. The coatings usually are placed on the outward facing surfaces of the two inner panes.

As the purchaser, your main concern is whether the windows you buy have coatings of high effectiveness and that they are installed properly inside the window. The coatings are invisible, so you can't tell by looking. The only practical way of ensuring good low-E coatings is to buy your windows from a reputable manufacturer. Read the manufacturer's product literature, and order carefully.

So, how much benefit do low-E coatings provide? Manufacturers may claim that low-E coatings increase the effective R-value of double-glazed windows by about 50%, and the R-value of triple-glazed windows (with two low-E coatings) by about 65%. In most climates, these are wild exaggerations.

The reason is that the benefit of low-E coatings depends on the temperature difference across the window. The standard testing method assumes a temperature differential of 70° F (39 °C) across the window. In the parts of the world where most people live, such a large temperature difference occurs only rarely. The benefit declines rapidly as the temperature difference diminishes. Low-E coatings don't provide much benefit in a warm or mild climate.

As a practical matter, low-E coatings are now commonly included as a standard feature of multiple-glazed windows, so you may not have to decide whether the get them with your windows.

Low-E coatings do not affect the appearance of glazing. They reduce the overall transparency of the glass by a small amount, but not enough to be noticed. They are not "spectrally selective," a feature that is covered next.

Low-E coatings interfere with the adhesion of the seals between multiple panes. The window fabricator must be sophisticated enough to remove the coating around the edges of the glass where the seal will be located.

---

* All material objects radiate heat energy, even though they don't seem particularly "warm." The heat radiation from objects near room temperature is called "infrared." Unfortunately, the same word is also used to describe heat radiated by very hot bodies, such as the sun or a lamp filament. The difference is the wavelength of the radiation. The short-wavelength infrared radiation in sunlight passes easily through glass, while the long-wavelength infrared radiation from objects near room temperature is completely absorbed by glass.

WINDOW SELECTION GUIDE

☐ Heat Filtering Coatings

Heat filtering glass is used to reduce solar heat radiation through windows. It uses a series of thin coatings that are tuned to reflect the invisible infrared wavelengths of sunlight, while passing most of the visible light. The best coatings can cut the total heat input from sunlight by about 40%. This type of glass looks clear, or it may have a slight blue-green tinge. The fragile coatings must be located on an inside surface of a multiple-pane window.

Heat filtering glass is for climates that are usually warm. During cold weather, heat filtering glass becomes a liability, reducing the ability of sunlight to contribute to heating.

If the shading for a house is well designed, heat filtering glass will provide only a small benefit. During warm weather, your shading will block all direct sunlight and much indirect sunlight from entering the window. Therefore, heat filtering glass is limited to blocking about half of the heat energy of the remaining indirect sunlight. Unless the window area is large, this is a small amount of energy.

However, if the climate is warm and your view demands a large glass area in certain rooms, heat filtering glass may be a good idea for those rooms. Such glass still needs effective shading to block most of the solar heat and to eliminate glare.

Heat filtering glass has the fancy name of "spectrally selective glass." It is not yet offered in mass production residential windows. However, it may become an option by the time you buy your windows, and it is available now for custom windows.

Older and cheaper types of spectrally reflective glass have less ability to discriminate between visible light and infrared heat radiation. Also, they have an annoying green tint. If you decide to get spectrally reflective glass, get the type that has the sharpest filtering ability.

All spectrally selective coatings act as low-E coatings, but not necessarily *vice versa*. Few people – including window salesmen – understand either, so don't be misled by claims that low-E windows are "spectrally selective."

Heat filtering coatings do not reduce visual glare, because they are designed to pass most visible light.

THE COMPLETE WINDOW ASSEMBLY

The manufacturer whose name appears on the window is a fabricator who buys the glass and other components, and assembles them into a complete window that is ready to be installed. The fabricator has the greatest influence on the quality of the window. The fabricator buys the glass in bulk, cuts it to size, and prepares the cut pieces for assembly by finishing the edges and cleaning the glass.

For windows with double or triple glazing, the fabricator assembles the cut sheets into sealed units by installing edge seals. The fabricator fills the space between the panes with a dry gas to prevent condensation. That gas may be air, nitrogen, or an "insulating" gas, such as argon or krypton. The frame material may be made by the fabricator or purchased in bulk, but the fabricator determines the details of the frame design.

All those steps are critical, but how do you know that they have all been followed? *Generally, your best assurance of quality is a long warranty that is provided by a manufacturer who is likely to stay in business long enough to honor the warranty*. Many window fabricators are local or regional. If you are buying from a nearby fabricator, try to visit the factory to judge their workmanship and to see whether they have the special equipment needed to make superior windows.

There is a market for high quality windows and a bigger market for cheap windows. Some of the biggest manufacturers produce windows for both markets, so you can't shop by brand alone. The thermal performance of a cheap window may be almost as good as that of a high quality window, but only for a short while. Cheap windows have a high failure rate, and their average life before requiring total replacement is relatively short. In contrast, the frames of the best windows may last indefinitely, while the sealed glazing and the weatherstripping may last for several decades before requiring replacement.

The following are the aspects of the complete window assembly that you should consider.

WINDOW SELECTION GUIDE

☐ Number of Panes

The number of panes is the most important factor that determines the insulating value of a window. Even the best windows have R-values that are only a small fraction of the R-value of a well insulated wall. So, efficiency always argues for the greatest number of panes that is practical. However, increasing the number of panes increases cost, increases the probability of seal failure, and makes larger windows more awkward to open for ventilation.

Glass itself has only minimal insulating ability. *Most of the insulating value of a window comes from a thin layer of air that sticks to the glass by weak molecular attraction*. This air layer, if it is well protected, has an R-value of about 0.5. A single sheet of glass or plastic glazing has two air layers, so a single-glazed window has a maximum R-value of about 1.0. In practice, the R-value is lower because much of the outside layer is blown away by wind. Even the inside layer may be dissipated by drafts from heating and air conditioning equipment.

Using multiple panes increases the number of air layers, and it provides protection for the air layers between the panes. For this reason, double glazing provides more than twice the R-value of single glazing. Typical R-values are 0.9 for single glazing, 2.0 for double glazing, and 3.0 for triple glazing. These figures are for plain glass with air between the panes.

Unfortunately, three panes of glass is the practical upper limit for sealed glazing units at the present time. Even with three panes, windows become heavy and it becomes more difficult to manufacture reliable seals between the panes. Large areas of triple glazing are practical for fixed glazing, but weight limits the size of openable windows.

You can do better than triple glazing by using a pair of conventional double-glazed windows units that are installed in the same wall opening, as explained under the heading, *Tandem Windows: a Big Energy Saver*. This method allows you to exploit all the efficiency improvements being offered in double-glazed units, including low-E coatings and insulating gases. The main shortcoming of this method is some awkwardness in opening and cleaning the windows.

To increase the number of surfaces with minimum additional weight, some manufacturers offer windows in which one or more films of transparent plastic are suspended between two panes of glass. The films can have low-E coatings, and the windows can be filled with insulating gases. This seems like a good idea, but at the time this is written, it is too early to know how long the plastic films will last. The outer glass protects the films from the main enemies of plastic, which are ultraviolet light and oxidation. When you are ready to buy your windows, search the Internet to see whether this technique has become practical. It may be worth a gamble if the glazing or the windows are easily replaceable.

☐ Insulating Fill Gases

The space between the panes of multiple-glazed windows originally was filled with air or dry nitrogen. Now, other gases may be used because they provide better insulation value than air. In general, the insulating value of a gas improves with higher molecular weight. Argon and carbon dioxide are somewhat heavier than air, and krypton is much heavier. Various estimates assert that argon will increase insulation value by 4% to 12%. The improvement provided by krypton is higher, but not well documented.

Carbon dioxide and argon are relatively cheap, but krypton is rare and expensive. The gas should be relatively inert so that it does not react with the seals and desiccant in the window frame. The safest choices are the true inert gases, which include argon, krypton, and xenon.

There are two cautions when buying windows with special fill gases. One is the question of whether the manufacturer has actually used the advertised fill gas. You are depending on the integrity of the manufacturer. There is no practical way for you to check this, unless you visit the fabricator.

The second caution is the effectiveness of the seals between the panes. If they fail, the insulating gas will leak out, to be replaced by air and water vapor.

☐ Separation Between Panes

You may hear various claims about the best gap between the panes in a sealed window. If the window uses air or nitrogen between the panes, the optimum separation is about one half inch (about 13 mm). Insulation value degrades rapidly as the gap gets smaller, because of direct conduction through the air. Insulation value also declines with larger gaps, but more slowly. This is because larger gaps allow convection currents to form, which circulate heat between the panes.

If the spaces between the panes are filled with a heavy insulating gas, the optimum separation narrows in proportion to the insulation value of the gas. For example, the optimum gap for a window with krypton gas is about 3/8" (9 mm).

☐ Glazing Edge Seals

In virtually all multiple-glazed windows made today, the space between the panes is hermetically sealed. The seal prevents condensation on the inner surface of the outer pane. This would occur in cold weather because the outer pane becomes cold enough to condense moisture that leaks from the interior of the house. If an insulating gas (argon, krypton, etc.) is used between the panes, a hermetic seal is needed to retain the gas.

Today, almost all multi-glazed windows use a seal that is made as shown in Figure 3-212. The panes are separated by a spacer. The spacer is hollow, and it acts as a canister for a small quantity of desiccant, which absorbs any water vapor that is trapped between the panes when the window is fabricated. If you look between the panes of a double-glazed window, you will see that the spacer has tiny holes to expose the desiccant to the interior space.

The panes are held together by a continuous band of polymer sealant around the outside of the spacer. The life of all organic sealants is limited, even though the glazing and some frame materials have virtually unlimited life. Therefore, *the edge seal determines the life of the window*. When it fails, typically in 10 to 30 years, moisture enters the space between the panes. This causes permanent fogging and streaking.

The specific sealants that are used, the preparation of the glass, and the quality of the manufacturer's workmanship are major factors in seal longevity and reliability. For example, if the glass has a coating (low-E or whatever), the coating must be removed from the edge of the glass where the seal is applied. Good window fabricators will do this properly, whereas some fabricators may skip this step, causing the seals to fail within a few years.

Other methods of sealing multiple-glazed units have been tried, but none have proved to be practical. For example, some windows were made by fusing the edges of the panes together. This provided a permanent seal, but the units were too vulnerable to breakage from stresses in the glass. So, be wary of any new sealing methods.

Shutterstock

Figure 3-212. The aluminum spacer for this double glazed window is a perforated tube that is filled with moisture absorbing material. The panes are held together by a thin band of adhesive sealant outside the spacer. This sealant is the limiting factor in the life of the window.

If you buy custom made windows without frames, the glass should be fabricated so that the seals are recessed between the panes by a fraction of an inch (a few millimeters) so that the window rests on the glass, not on the seals. The window fabricator should know how to do this, but it is a feature that you should examine, if possible. The weight of the window should be supported evenly by all the panes of glass. If the window has an odd shape, lessen the load on the bottom of the glass by making the bottom edge straight and fairly long.

☐ Frame Materials and Durability

An openable window is a somewhat complex device that includes glazing, seals, weatherstripping, insect screens, latches, and actuators. In addition to holding all this together, the frame design mostly determines the appearance of the window, its ease of operation, and its resistance to air leakage.

Fixed windows (windows that do not open) have much simpler frames. Usually, you can buy fixed windows with frames that match the appearance of openable windows.

Fixed windows don't need factory frames. You can buy fixed glass without a frame, in which case your builder creates a simple frame as the glass is

━━━ WINDOW SELECTION GUIDE ━━━

installed. This is an option to consider primarily for fixed windows that are large or non-rectangular. You can get unframed glass with all the energy saving features of prefabricated windows, including double and triple glazing, low-E coatings, etc.

The most common frame materials are aluminum, wood, vinyl, and fiber-reinforced plastic ("fiberglass"). Plastic is also commonly used to make guides and other inserts in aluminum frames. The most expensive wood frame windows offer thin plastic coating over the wood, avoiding the need for painting.

Enameled aluminum frames can endure for the life of the house, and they do not deform. Aluminum can be anodized to hold any color or to hold enamel. The big weakness of aluminum is high heat conduction, which must be compensated by a "thermal break" that is built into the frame. If a home is located near a corrosive environment, such as salt water, aluminum is not a good choice for window frames.

The corners of aluminum frames generally are joined with clips and screws. If properly designed, these metal-to-metal connections will maintain a tight corner indefinitely.

If you buy aluminum framed windows, avoid frames that use exposed plastic inserts as window guides or whatever. They turn a highly durable window into one that is vulnerable to damage.

A wood frame is susceptible to rot and warping. Even so, you can find windows with wooden frames that are centuries old. If you want a highly authentic historic appearance, especially with double-hung windows, wood may be your only choice.

Modern wooden windows are no longer entirely wood. They have become complex composite structures, in which lumber is used for stiffness and mounting, while plastic and metal is used for weatherstripping and often for other functions, such as guides for openable sashes. The frame may have plastic or metal mounting fins.

Wood must be painted or coated to survive the elements. Expensive wood windows commonly have a plastic coating, but any plastic has limited life. Wood warps over time, so the wood for high quality windows is selected to minimize warping. In addition, the frame may be fabricated from multiple layers of wood to minimize warping.

Wood frames are joined by nails, screws, or staples. They all allow some degree of loosening over time, so special joinery is needed to keep the corners intact. Only the best wood windows have durable corners.

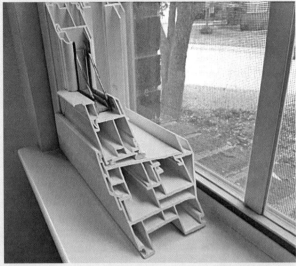

Simonton Windows

Figure 3-213. The inside of a typical vinyl window frame. The frame is divided into many cavities to improve the thermal insulation value of the frame and to allow the flexible plastic to support the heavy glass.

A vinyl frame will become brittle and crack early in the life of the house. Its practical life is about the same as the life of the glazing seals, i.e., about 20 years on average.

The corners of plastic frames may be joined by clips or by fusing. Both methods can be satisfactory, but mechanical fastening of plastic frames may produce sloppy corners.

All plastic frames, including fiber-reinforced plastic, will flex under their own weight. They depend on the wall structure to support them and keep them in alignment. To overcome the tendency of plastic frames to sag, they should be installed with well designed integral mounting fins. Some manufacturers stiffen vinyl windows with aluminum or steel inserts.

Aluminum and plastic frames are made from extrusions designed to provide rigidity with minimum material. These frames are mostly air cavities surrounded by thin walls. The extrusions can be quite complex, because they perform a variety of functions. They guide movable sashes, they provide attachment for the weatherstripping, they include provisions for mounting in the window opening, they minimize heat conduction, and they drain condensation. Figure 3-213 shows a cross section of a vinyl window frame.

WINDOW SELECTION GUIDE

In general, thicker frame sections are better, and also more expensive. Cheap windows have frame sections that are too thin, so the window frame will eventually sag, leak, and break. Any exposed edges of aluminum or plastic should be especially thick, because they are vulnerable to breakage from the force of opening and closing, removing sashes for cleaning, etc.

If you can find one, examine a cross section drawing of the frame that includes the thicknesses of the components. Also, examine the corner connections. All good manufacturers should be able to provide these details. Often, you can get the drawings from the manufacturers' Web sites.

☐ Thermal Breaks for Metal Frames

Aluminum has one major weakness as a frame material, which is high heat conduction. In cold weather, indoor heat is absorbed by the exposed interior surface of the frame and the heat is lost to the outside through the exterior surface of the frame. The most effective way to minimize this heat loss is to include an insulating "thermal break" between the inner and outer portions of the frame. Figure 3-214 shows how a thermal break is built into an aluminum frame. Make sure that all your aluminum windows have this feature.

In effect, a frame with a thermal barrier consists of two frames, an outer unit and an inner unit. The two units are joined by the thermal barrier, which is a plastic material that has a narrow cross section. If the thermal barrier is poorly designed, the frame could split apart eventually.

The plastic thermal barrier has much lower thermal conductivity than aluminum, but it is still not a very good insulator. Therefore, aluminum frames tend to sweat more than other frame materials during cold weather, unless the climate is dry. Deal with this by using a sill material that is not harmed by condensation that may drain to the sill.

☐ Mounting Method

Prefabricated window assemblies are available with two types of frames. The frame determines how the window is installed in the wall opening. One type of frame has a plain rectangular shape that has been used for centuries. The other is a newer design that uses frame fins for mounting the window.

The older rectangular style is mounted inside the window opening. The window is held between inner and outer "stop strips" that are butted against the window frame. The weight of the window rests on the bottom of the wall opening, and the window receives little support elsewhere.

The window assembly must be smaller than the wall opening. This leaves a gap between the two. The window is held in the opening by narrow shims, which leave most of the gap open. Air leakage between the frame and the wall is blocked by the stop strips and by caulking that is applied between the stop strips and the frame.

Because this style of window frame sits inside the window opening, it needs an exterior sloped sill to drain rain toward the outside. Many prefabricated window assemblies include the sill as part of the frame.

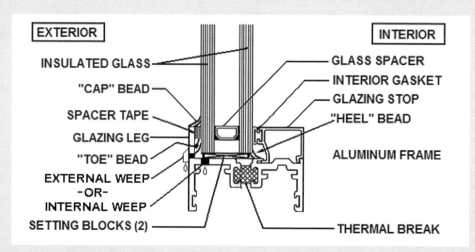

Alwin Windows

Figure 3-214. Construction of an aluminum window frame, showing the critical thermal break.

WINDOW SELECTION GUIDE

A newer frame design uses a continuous mounting fin that surrounds the frame, as in Figure 3-215. The fin lies flat on the outside sheathing of the wall. The window is attached by driving nails or screws through the fin and the outer sheathing into the strong lumber of the wall opening.

Frame mounting fins are a major improvement. They make it easy to create an airtight seal around the window, simply by laying a ribbon of caulk between the fin and the wall. They support all parts of the frame against distortion and sagging. They speed installation by eliminating the need to install stop strips. And, this frame design avoids the need for an outside window sill.

With metal or plastic frames, the fin can be an integral part of the frame extrusion. With wooden windows, mounting fins are uncommon because they are awkward to include. However, some manufacturers offer wooden windows that have a plastic or aluminum mounting fin attached. Aluminum is okay, but think twice before ordering wooden windows with plastic accessories. Wood has a long service life, but plastic does not.

If you buy windows with mounting fins, check the thickness and strength of the fin. On many plastic windows, the fins are so flimsy that they don't even survive installation. They must be strong because they support the weight of the window.

At the same time, check that the fin is attached strongly to the main part of the frame. In cheap windows, it is common for the fin to be molded as part of a flimsy outer face that is attached weakly to the heavy part of the window.

Mounting fins make it difficult to replace the windows later, if the fin is covered by siding or brick veneer. We introduce a new method of installing windows that is quick and easy. See the heading, *A Better Way to Install Finned Windows*.

The finned frame design has a minor efficiency drawback compared to windows that are installed inside the wall opening. A portion of the frame hangs outside the opening, where its uninsulated surface loses heat to the surrounding air. Also, this method of installation creates a shorter path for heat loss through the outer portion of the wall opening. This factor is less important than avoiding air leakage, where finned windows excel.

Figure 3-215. A mounting fin on a plastic window frame. This side of the window is inserted into the wall opening from the outside. Then, the fin is nailed or screwed to the outer surface of the wall.

☐ Weatherstripping

"Weatherstripping" is the combination of frame components that block air leakage between the fixed and movable parts of an openable window. The best modern windows have radically reduced air leakage compared to the windows of a century ago. Most of the improvement is due to the development of effective weatherstripping that is integrated into the design of the windows.

Awning, hopper, and casement windows have relatively simple seals that are squeezed between the openable sash and the fixed frame. To achieve reliable sealing, these window styles require a very rigid frame because the latching force works against the pressure of the seals, tending to distort the frame. With larger windows, it becomes difficult to prevent air leakage unless the window uses multiple latches, which are awkward.

Windows that slide horizontally and vertically have weatherstripping that creates little stress on the frame, so these windows do not need to built as heavily. However, double-hung windows are especially difficult to seal effectively.

As part of your window shopping, examine the weatherstripping design. All edges of movable sashes should be tightly sealed. The sealing system should accommodate any looseness in the tracks and hinges, and the latches should not pull the sashes away from the weatherstripping. The motion of opening and closing should not stress the weatherstripping. The weatherstripping should not be vulnerable to damage while the window is open.

☐ Ability to Replace the Glazing and Weatherstripping

Windows have two components that will fail in a matter of decades. One is the weatherstripping in openable windows. The other is the seals between multiple glazing. If these components cannot be replaced individually, then you or later occupants will have to replace the entire window assembly.

Weatherstripping in modern windows generally is a custom design that locks into the frame. Only the original manufacturer or glazing specialists are likely to have the proper replacement material. Some manufacturers design their weatherstripping to be easily replaceable, and others do not. Favor those that do.

Glazing seals can be replaced only by removing and replacing the glass as a unit. Whether this is practical depends on the frame material and frame design.

With plastic frames, the frame material will be greatly deteriorated by the time that glass and weatherstripping need replacement. Furthermore, the strongest plastic frames are fused at the corners, preventing replacement of the glass. So, make it easy to replace the entire window assembly, using the method that we introduce under the heading, *A Better Way to Install Finned Windows*.

With wooden frames, the situation is similar. The frames of energy-efficient wooden windows are so complex that it is probably impractical to take them apart to replace the glass.

Aluminum frames can last as long as the house, and they are expensive. For this reason, select aluminum frame windows for easy replacement of the glass and weatherstripping. Some models allow this, and some don't.

WINDOW SECURITY

Until recently, windows have been the Achilles heel of the protection that a house should provide against weather and crime. Now, we may be at the beginning of a revolution in window security. In 2002, after a decade of hurricanes that devastated Florida, building code officials in several Florida counties created standards for strengthening windows and doors.

The most radical requirements were enacted by Miami-Dade County, in Florida. These resulted in the development of an entirely new class of windows that have a degree of toughness that hardly anyone would have thought possible.

Although the original motivation was resistance to hurricanes, it was soon recognized that the same improvements make windows much more resistant to burglary. The construction industry outside Florida has not yet recognized the significance of these changes, but we will use them to maximize the security of your home.

At this time, impact resistance standards for windows are still novel. Unless you live in the coastal areas of the southern United States, don't expect to find a good selection of strong windows locally. Fortunately for those who live elsewhere, a growing number of manufacturers produce windows that meet the Miami-Dade County standards. The Internet is the quickest way to find them.

Florida is a warm climate, so the first impact resistant windows were not designed for energy efficiency. Fortunately, some manufacturers now produce multi-glazed versions for cold climates.

The main feature of intrusion-resistant windows is the laminated breakage-resistant glass described previously. The window frame also is strengthened. The heavy weight of the glazing makes it challenging for the manufacturer to produce an openable window that moves easily while maintaining security and tight air sealing.

━━━━━━━ **WINDOW SELECTION GUIDE** ━━━━━━━

☐ Miami-Dade County and ASTM Impact Standards

The Miami-Dade County standards do not specify the details of window construction, only the hazards they must resist. There are two standards, "large-missile resistant" and "small-missile resistant." The former requires a stronger window, and it is the standard you should seek for the best practical security.

The test for "large-missile" resistance consists of hurling 2-by-4 timbers at a window like spears. The timbers weigh 9 pounds (4 kg), and they hit the window at a speed of 50 feet per second (55 km/hr). The test is repeated at least twice, striking the center of the glass area and striking the frame. The window must not suffer significant penetration, although the glazing may fracture. After the impact tests, the same window must survive 9,000 cycles of positive and negative wind loads, simulating the shaking of a hurricane or tornado.

The window must also satisfy criteria for resistance to air leakage, water leakage, wind pressure, and forced entry.

The Miami-Dade standards have now been adopted as standards by the American Society for Testing and Materials (ASTM), so they have become a worldwide standard for high-security windows. There are separate ASTM standards for resistance to forced entry and for resistance to impact.

☐ Resistance to Intrusion

Most houses should have intrusion-resistant windows, even if the neighborhood presently seems safe. Crime will wax and wane over the life of the house, and criminals increasingly probe into previously safe neighborhoods. Windows should be intrusion-resistant if they are accessible from the outside, even if access requires a ladder. Intrusion-resistant windows cost perhaps twice as much as regular windows. Even so, they account for a relatively small fraction of the cost of a house.

 Storm-resistant windows can also provide major security against intruders, if they are selected properly.

Resistance to burglary is a matter of degree. For adequate protection, you probably want windows that meet the Miami-Dade County (or ASTM) "large-missile" standards. Even these windows are not as secure as strongly installed doors, but they are no longer an inviting weakness.

To maximize resistance to entry, consider more than the glazing. Select strong window locks, preferably with key locks. Select strong frames. And, consider the method of removing sashes from the frame, so that an intruder cannot lift the sash out of the window opening.

☐ Resistance to Storm Damage

If you home is located in a region that is visited by hurricanes and tornadoes, select your windows for resistance to storm damage. Ruptured windows threaten the entire house by allowing wind pressure to enter the interior. The interior pressure combines with aerodynamic forces on top of the roof to lift the roof off the house. With the roof gone, the interior of the house is exposed to wind and water, and the walls may collapse as well.

The main hazard to windows is not wind pressure itself, but debris that is picked up by wind and thrown at high speed. Windows that satisfy the Miami-Dade County (or ASTM) "large-missile" standard are now the most reliable defense.

Storm shutters were the original defense against windstorms, and they can still supplement storm-resistant windows. However, storm shutters are not a good primary defense. They block the view when they are installed. They can be removed by burglars. And, they are a nuisance to install, remove, and store. Where tornadoes are the threat, occupants may not receive timely warning to install storm shutters.

- *Visible Transmittance (VT)* is the fraction of visible sunlight falling on the total window assembly that enters the house as light. VT is expressed as a number between zero and one. The VT includes the effects of blocking of sunlight by the frame, tints, glass absorption, etc. High VT is desirable for daylighting. For windows with clear glass, differences in VT are minor.

- Other ratings, such as impact resistance, may also be available for certain windows.

These ratings are available for the windows of all participating manufacturers on the NFRC Web site (**www.NFRC.org**), and often on the manufacturers' Web sites. The relevant ratings for each window are placed on labels attached to the windows at the factory, so you can verify the ratings when they arrive at your home.

The most valuable aspect of the NFRC ratings is that they apply to the entire window assembly, not just to the glass. The main weakness of NFRC ratings is that they tell you nothing about characteristics such as durability, ease of use, or long term performance. For example, a window with a good NFRC leakage rating may have weatherstripping that wears out quickly.

For characteristics where a rating system cannot provide effective guidance, you need to examine those characteristics yourself. That's why you should use the *Window Selection Guide* to select your windows.

A BETTER WAY TO INSTALL FINNED WINDOWS

In the past, when windows had only single glazing, they might last as long as the house. And if a pane was broken, it could be replace individually. But today, multiple-glazed windows have a limited life because their seals fail within a few decades. And, especially with plastic frames, the entire assembly needs to be replaced by the time that the glass fogs. Therefore, *treat your windows as an expendable commodity and make it easy to replace them*.

Unfortunately, the old methods of installing windows still persist. Typically, after finned windows are attached to the exterior sheathing of a frame wall, the builder covers the fins with the exterior finish material or with a masonry veneer. This practice makes it difficult, messy, and expensive to replace the windows.

Therefore, we introduce a better way of installing finned windows to make replacement easy. The key is to avoid interference with the exterior wall finish. Figure 3-216 shows the details.

First, install the finned window against the outer wall in the usual way. The builder should apply a ribbon of caulk to the outer perimeter of the top and sides of the wall opening before inserting the window. This creates a seal against air leakage and a secondary defense against rain entry.

However, the builder should not caulk the bottom of the fin to the wall. Instead, install washers between the fin and the wall where nails or screws attach the bottom of the frame. This creates a small gap where any moisture that gets between the window frame and the wall can vent to the outside.

Then, after the fin is fastened to the wall, inject foam insulation between the frame and the inside of the window opening. Use a good quality of gap sealing foam that is applied with spray cans. After the foam hardens, trim it to the inner edge of the frame with a razor knife. Cover the exposed edge of the foam with molding.

 Installing removable trim around finned windows makes periodic replacement much easier.

The foam insulation has two functions. It keeps heat from short circuiting around the edge of the frame and through the fin. And, it acts as a vapor barrier, keeping indoor moisture from reaching the coldest outer part of the window opening and condensing to cause rot and mildew.

Finned windows don't need outside sills, and they take up only a small part of the inside of the window opening. Take the opportunity to exploit the insides of the window openings, especially the bottom surfaces or sills, as accents for your rooms. See the previous sidebar, *Fancy Window Sills*.

The main innovation here is to cover the fin with decorative trim that is easily removable when the window needs to be replaced. The fin cover can be made of anything attractive, such as a wood or plastic molding, perhaps with a distinctive color. Make it an appearance enhancement for the house, highlighting your windows.

The exterior wall finish butts to the removable trim. To prevent rain leakage into the wall, install a rain flashing around the window frame.

Figure 3-216 shows a wooden wall. For a masonry wall, build a wooden frame inside the wall opening, and install the windows using the same method. Figures 3-217 and 3-218 show how this looks in a masonry wall installation.

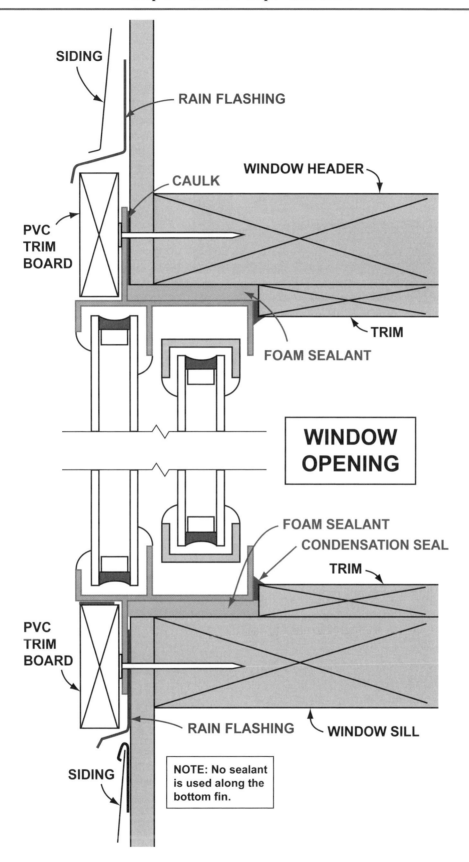

SIDING

RAIN FLASHING

WINDOW HEADER

CAULK

PVC
TRIM
BOARD

TRIM

FOAM SEALANT

WINDOW
OPENING

FOAM SEALANT

CONDENSATION SEAL

TRIM

PVC
TRIM
BOARD

RAIN FLASHING   WINDOW SILL

SIDING

NOTE: No sealant
is used along the
bottom fin.

DRW

Figure 3-216. Installation of a window that has a finned frame. The window is attached to the outside wall in the usual way by nailing through the fin. However, instead of covering the fin with the exterior finish, cover the fin with a removable decorative trim. This allows easy replacement of the window without the need to remove or deface the exterior wall surface. PVC plastic trim board is a good material to use for the fin covering because it is durable and waterproof. The design of the rain flashing is important. At every point, the window installation must prevent rain from getting to the frame wall. The components should overlap so that any water drains toward the outside.

DRW

Figure 3-217. Exterior of an aluminum window that has a finned frame. The window can be replaced easily by removing the trim that covers the fin.

DRW

Figure 3-218. The interior of the same window. The frame fin is attached to the wooden frame that is bolted to the masonry wall opening. The deep sill that spans the masonry wall and the interior wall insulation serves as an attractive shelf for deco items.

This method of installation is simple, but special care is needed to keep air from leaking between the window frame and the wall opening. Mass production windows without fins often include some kind of weatherstripping around the outside of the frame, or there may be a channel where you can insert rope-type weatherstripping. Examine this feature carefully. If the supplied weatherstripping cannot fill the gap between the window frame and the wall opening reliably, or if the weatherstripping looks flimsy, you must design and install the inner stops to block air leakage.

Caulk the inner stops to the wall opening, because they will be part of the air leakage seal. But, don't caulk the bottom of the exterior stop to the wall opening. Any moisture that gets between the window frame and the exterior stop should be able to vent to the outside.

Seal the window frame to the inner stop with a bead of silicone between the frame and the stop. Apply the silicone to the surface of the stop before pushing the frame into place. Seal the outer stop to the frame in a similar way, but *do not caulk the bottom of the stop*. Leave that gap open as a vent path.

If the window does not have a finned frame, the outside of the window opening needs a sloped, weatherproof sill to keep rain from getting into the gap between the bottom of the window and the bottom of the wall opening. Some unfinned windows include an outside sill as part of the assembly.

This method of installation makes the windows easy to replace by removing the exterior stops. Don't forfeit this benefit by overlapping the outside of the window frame with the exterior wall surface.

INSTALLING WINDOWS WITHOUT FINNED FRAMES

Windows that have frames without mounting fins are installed in the old fashioned way. Any good carpenter knows how to do it. The window is inserted into the wall opening and is held in place by "stop strips" that butt firmly against the inside and outside of the window frame. For a masonry wall, build a wooden frame inside the wall opening and install the windows using the same method.

INSTALLING UNFRAMED GLASS

If your design needs windows with custom shapes, you will get them from a local glass fabricator. Custom windows can be single-, double-, or triple-glazed. They can have all the energy saving features of other windows, which are covered in the *Window Selection Guide*. The installation procedure is almost the same as for a framed window without mounting fins.

To avoid local stress on the glass edge or the glazing seals, rest the bottom of the glass on a pad of hard rubber, heavy felt, balsa wood, or similar yielding material. The pad should be perfectly flat.

TANDEM WINDOWS: A BIG ENERGY SAVER

For homes in colder climates, here is a new way of reducing heat loss that uses conventional windows: *install two standard windows in the same opening, one outside the other*. Two double-glazed windows in the same opening provide the insulation value of quadruple glazing, along with all the efficiency features that are available in modern windows.

Tandem windows are practical with a super-insulated thick wall that is appropriate for a colder climate. You can use windows with or without frame fins, or a combination of the two. The outer face of both windows should face toward the outside. Otherwise, the locking hardware would not be accessible.

 Tandem windows are a major advance for cold weather comfort and energy efficiency, allowing you to double the insulation value of your windows using conventional windows and easy installation.

For windows with fixed glass, you might even install two triple-glazed units to achieve an even larger reduction of heat loss.

This is one of the most important innovations that this book offers. It is almost entirely novel, which means that you should be extra careful in using it. I have confidence that this method will work well because long experience with storm windows shows us how to avoid potential problems. (I don't recommend storm windows, for the reasons given in the sidebar.)

These are the design issues to consider when using tandem windows:

• Separate the inner and outer window units as much as practical to make it easy to operate and clean the windows.

• Coordinate the types of windows on the outside and inside. They don't have to be the same type, but they must be compatible to allow easy operation and cleaning. Also, the inner window must be more airtight than the outer window to avoid condensation on the outer window.

• Having so many panes of glass may create some loss of clarity. Also they may create some unusual reflections of indoor lighting when it is dark outside. However, these effects are not likely to be troublesome.

• You can use the space between the windows as a decorative display case. But, you can't put plants in there, or anything else that emits moisture.

Tandem Windows With and Without Frame Fins

For the outer window of a tandem pair, select a window that has a finned frame. A finned outer window will leave more space between the pair, in addition to providing the other advantages of finned frames. Install the outer window as we recommended previously, under the heading, *A Better Way to Install Finned Windows*.

For the inner window of a tandem pair, use either an unfinned window or a finned window. Figure 3-219 shows both arrangements.

If you use an unfinned interior window, install it inside the wall opening, using stop strips in the old fashioned way. There will not be enough space for a conventional window sill facing the interior of the room. Instead, frame the interior of the window opening with molding.

For greater separation between the windows in a tandem pair, you could install a finned window on the interior wall surface, as in Figure 3-219. This results in an unusual interior appearance. Window manufacturers

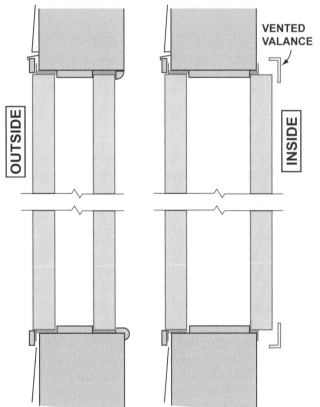

DRW

Figure 3-219. Two methods of installing tandem windows. The installation on the left looks more conventional from the inside. The installation on the right uses a finned window on the inside wall, which provides more space between the windows and also creates an unusual interior appearance.

place the mounting fins close to the outer side of the frame to minimize protrusion of the window beyond the outer wall surface. But by the same token, if you install a finned window on the inside wall, it will protrude far into the room, typically by about 2" (5 cm).

If you decide to be so stylistically daring, don't use molding around the exposed portion of the window frame. Moisture would condense between the molding and the window frame during cold weather, which would lead to mildew infestation around the frame.

Instead, you can dress up the inner portion of the frame by surrounding it with a vented valance or other decoration. Room air should be able to circulate freely between the decoration and the frame.

Select the Window Styles for Compatible Opening

If you install tandem windows that open for ventilation, select models that make it easy to operate the outer window from inside the room.

With slider windows, make sure that the latches of the outer window are located where they are easily accessible through the inner window. If you use a casement or awning outer window, both the security latch and the actuator of the outer window should be easily accessible when the inner window is opened.

You can combine different opening styles, as long as they are compatible with each other. For example, the inner window can be a slider, and the outer window can be an awning style.

Make Window Cleaning Easy

Make it easy to clean the surfaces of the two windows that face each other. If the window is not easily accessible from the outside, also make it easy to clean the outer surface of the window from inside the room.

With horizontal and vertical sliders, make it possible to reach between the two windows by providing an adequate space between them. Using finned windows with finned frames on both the inner and outer wall surfaces provides the maximum separation. One sash of the inner window should be easily removable from the inside.

If the window is so large that it is not possible to reach entirely into the space between the windows, both sashes of the inner window should be removable. If the window is not accessible from the outside, one sash of the outer window also should be removable.

If the outer window is a casement or awning style, it must be accessible for cleaning from the outside.

Check the weatherstripping design of all movable or removable sashes to ensure that both windows will remain airtight. Don't select a leaky window design for the sake of ease of operation or cleaning. This would defeat the purpose of installing tandem windows.

Prevent Condensation Inside the Outer Window

During cold weather, tandem windows are susceptible to condensation on the inside of the outer unit. This happens if water vapor from the inside of the house can leak past the inside window. Condensation spoils the view, streaks the glass, and promotes mildew around the frame. Fortunately, condensation is easy to avoid. ***The key is to make the inside unit more airtight than the outside unit***.

Condensation occurs when the concentration of water vapor against a cold surface becomes too high. (See the previous sidebar, *Why Water Vapor Condenses*.) Therefore, select the inside window unit to be as airtight as possible, so that it keeps water vapor inside the house from reaching the colder outer glazing.

You may have to create a tiny moisture vent *under* the outside window. The vent allows any water vapor that leaks past the inner window to escape to the outside before it reaches a concentration that causes it to condense.

If vent holes are needed, make them small enough to block the smallest insects. Or, install a screen over the vent hole. You could drill two or three small vent holes at the bottom center of the outer window frame, using the smallest drill available. Locate the vent holes so that they will not be blocked by the stop strips, caulking compound, molding, or anything else.

The vent for the outer window unit causes only a minor loss of efficiency because it is very small and because it is located below the outer window. The air between the two window units is warmer and lighter than the outside air, so it will not flow downward through the vent.

STORM WINDOWS: A POOR CHOICE

A storm window is an inexpensive, lightweight window that is intended to supplement a main window. Storm windows are sold as an assembly, with a removable sash installed in a frame that has air leakage seals. If installed in a reasonably airtight frame, a storm window increases the total R-value by about 1.0 to 1.5 (RSI 0.18 to 0.27).

Storm windows are an older method of reducing the conductive heat loss and air leakage of regular windows. They generally are not a good choice for a new house. If your climate is too cold for double-glazed windows alone, consider using tandem double-glazed windows for your openable windows. For fixed windows, consider sealed triple glazing.

Commercial storm windows are designed for installation outside the main window. If water vapor leaks through the main window from the interior of the house, the vapor tends to condense on the storm window, blocking vision and creating a mess. To avoid condensation, a storm window usually has small vent holes at the bottom of its frame.

If the main windows are openable, the storm windows usually are removed during warm weather for cooling ventilation, so they require handling and storage space. You can buy openable storm windows, but they are so flimsy and leaky that they are almost worthless.

If you want to upgrade the leaky windows of an existing house at minimum cost, you can avoid condensation by installing supplemental glazing *inside* the original windows. You might even install conventional windows inside the existing window to create tandem windows. Adding interior glazing to an existing house usually requires some carpentry and refinishing to create a tight seal around the window opening.

THE ENTRANCE DOORS

The entrance doors are the doors that protect your home. Most exterior doors are entrance doors, except for doors that are installed to protect the actual main door, as with a vestibule. Some entrance doors may be inside the house, as between the garage and the house. If you build a "strong room" inside your home (see Step 1), its interior door has the same security requirements as an entrance door.

Typically, one of the entrance doors serves as a formal entrance, and the others are plain. However, all your entrance doors should satisfy a minimum set of requirements. In selecting and installing your entrance doors, two of these requirements are main themes: security and energy efficiency.

Resistance to forced entry is the most important quality of an entrance door. Unfortunately, burglars know that crashing through a door is often the easiest way to get into a locked house. (Police and firemen prefer the same route.) This is because doors have several points of weakness, and because doors typically are weakly installed in the wall openings. By selecting your doors carefully and by using the improved methods of installation that we will explain, you can make your doors very resistant to assault.

The other theme is energy efficiency. The best doors are highly airtight, unlike older doors which wasted a lot of energy by air leakage. The insulation value of doors is limited, but this is a minor concern because doors comprise only a small fraction of the surface area of a house.

To select each of your entrance doors, use the adjacent *Entrance Door Selection Guide* as your main guide. With the *Guide* in hand, visit hardware stores and showrooms that have display models you can examine, and check the Web sites of manufacturers.

Another selection tool is the NFRC Energy Performance Ratings for doors. However, these are less useful than the NFRC ratings for windows, which we described earlier. Most doors are rated only for U-Factor and Solar Heat Gain Coefficient (SHGC). For doors, these criteria are relatively unimportant in comparison with air leakage. And, the NFRC door ratings do not cover security or durability.

Most of this discussion about doors applies to existing houses as well as to new construction. It is practical to upgrade the doors of an existing house to make them much stronger and more energy efficient than typical door installations.

Installing Exterior Doors in Frame Walls

Until the mid-20th century, the doors of houses were attached directly to the walls. As a result, the door attachment could be as strong as the wall itself. Unfortunately, in the pursuit of lower cost and faster construction, it has now become commonplace to install prefabricated door-and-frame assemblies. This is a big setback for security, as explained in the adjacent sidebar.

In your super-strong home, we will reject prefabricated door assemblies for the exterior entrances, and we will return to the older practice of attaching the exterior doors directly to the wall structure. This involves carpentry that is mostly conventional. However, we will exploit the greater thickness of your super-insulated walls to strengthen the attachments for the locks and hinges, as we will explain later.

The price for this greatly increased security is maintaining precise dimensions when your builder makes the wall opening and the door frame, so that you can use a strong door of standard size. The key is total contact between the frame and the wall opening, leaving the bare minimum gap around the door that is needed to allow smooth opening and to install weatherstripping. *No shims are allowed*.

Figure 3-222 shows a strong, simple way to install doors in a super-insulated wall, using solid studs or fabricated studs. The figure illustrates features that greatly strengthen door and make it airtight. We will cover those features under the headings that follow.

Installing Exterior Doors in Masonry Walls

The door frames for exterior doors in masonry walls are similar to those for wooden walls, as shown in Figure 3-222. The door is attached to a wooden frame, which should be bolted securely to the masonry wall. The specific method of attaching the frame to the masonry depends on the nature of the masonry and on the method of insulating the wall.

Thresholds

Most entrance doors have a threshold, which is a thick strip of wood or an aluminum extrusion that is attached to the floor under the door. Thus, the threshold becomes the bottom of the door opening.

Thresholds are used because the bottom of the door must be able to swing over carpets and mats located in the path of the door. This requires a large gap under the door, and the threshold fills this gap when the door is closed. Figure 3-223 shows the relationship of the door to the threshold.

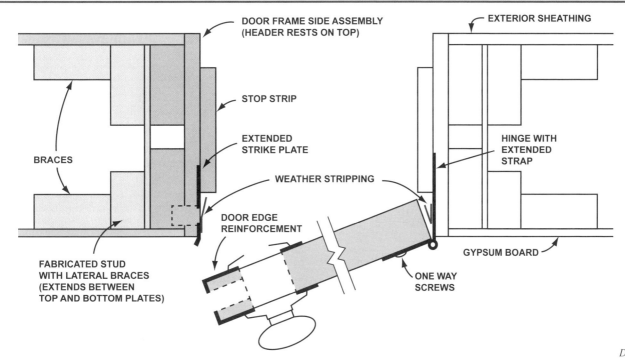

DRW

Figure 3-222. A strong exterior door installation in a super-insulated wall. For strength and convenience, prefabricate the colored assemblies. Their positions can be adjusted when making the wall opening to create a perfect fit for the door without using shims. Use nails, screws, and glue to maximize rigidity and minimize warping.

Also, the threshold acts as a dam to keep rain from blowing under the door. However, if the threshold is exposed to rain, moisture that gets between the threshold and the floor can rot the floor. The primary protection against rain should be a deep shelter for the door, which you designed in Step 1.

When installing the threshold, seal it to the floor with a ribbon of silicone sealant along the outside edge. Also, seal the sides of the threshold to the sides of the door opening.

Weatherstripping

Doors are potentially a major source of air leakage because they require clearance on all sides to allow the door to open and close easily. The gaps also accommodate a limited amount of shifting of the frame as the house ages, and a certain amount of sagging of the door on its hinges. To block air leakage through these gaps, install effective weatherstripping around all four sides of the door.

M-D Building Products

Figure 3-223. Door threshold and sweep. The sweep is a brush or flexible strip that rests against the side of the threshold when the door is closed, forming an airtight seal along the bottom of the door. This threshold is wood, but aluminum is a better choice because of its resistance to rot.

Frost King

Figure 3-224. Typical V-seal weatherstripping. It works well for the sides and top of doors. It is easy to install and to replace, and it accommodates shifting of the door inside the frame.

ENTRANCE DOOR SELECTION GUIDE

☐ Size and Opening Style

The great majority of entrance doors are single swing doors, with good reason. This style is able to combine convenience, resistance to air leakage, strength, and economy.

In the U.S., the prevailing size for mass production exterior doors is 36" (nominal 90 cm) wide and 80" (nominal 200 cm) tall. This is the width of the door itself, not the opening size. For those desiring a taller door, a standard height of 96" (nominal 240 cm) is offered by some manufacturers.

Makers of custom wooden doors offer any reasonable width or height that is desired, along with curved tops. Custom dimensions and features will make a door much more expensive.

DRW

Figure 3-226. A double door that adds a touch of grandeur to a main entrance.

The standard width of 36" (nominal 90 cm) is appropriate for most exterior doors. Virtually all modern furniture and appliances are designed so they can pass through this width. A wider door would be awkward to use and it would place too much stress on the hinges, causing it to sag.

Double swing doors are used for grand entrances. They should look grand from the inside as well as the outside. For example, see Figure 3-226. Double doors also serve as freight entrances for large objects, such as the Louis XIV armoire that you bought at the auction. Don't forget to design the interior doors, stairs, and passages to be large enough to pass those large objects. Go back to Step 1 and check this.

Under most circumstances, only one of the two doors is actually used. For security, this style requires the usually fixed door to have strong bolts at the upper and lower corners that mate with a strong "strike plate" (a steel plate with a hole, fastened by screws) in the door header and in the floor, respectively. The moving door locks into the fixed door.

This arrangement is considerably weaker than a single door that locks into a wall opening. That is an inherent penalty of double doors, and it should make you think seriously about whether you want to have a double door.

Residential doors generally swing inward. This protects the open door from weather, and it keeps the hinges and the weakest part of the frame inside the house. (Doors in commercial buildings usually are required to swing outward.)

Don't use sliding glass doors as entry doors, even in mild climates. They waste energy, they are an avenue for burglary, and they are awkward to operate. Avoid sliding glass doors even in safe locations, such as an entrance to a balcony. Instead, install a regular door, perhaps with adjacent windows for view. In a safe location, it's okay to install a fairly large glass panel in the door. Plan the sight lines to avoid excess glass, as you would for windows. You don't need to see the floor of a balcony or porch.

☐ Materials and Insulation Value

Wood remains the most common material for doors. A well made wooden door can last for centuries if it is kept dry and protected from sunlight. Wood is strong and economical. It offers relatively easy installation of hardware, and it can be made in many styles. Wooden doors can be decorated beautifully by selecting an attractive wood or veneer, using wood or glass panels, or carving.

Wood has limited insulation value. A solid wood entrance door has an insulation value of about R-2 to R-3 (RSI 0.35 to 0.5), which varies with thickness,

ENTRANCE DOOR SELECTION GUIDE

use of panels, and the weight of the wood. Denser wood has lower R-value. You may be able to find a wood door that has an insulating foam core, which will increase the R-value considerably.

Wood is vulnerable to warping, which interferes with good air leakage sealing. However, reliable weatherstripping is now available that accommodates warping.

Mass production wood doors increasingly use plastic coatings and attachments. Avoid these because the plastic has much shorter life than the wood.

Following the pattern set by the window industry, some doors are now made primarily of vinyl and "fiberglass," which is plastic reinforced with fibers. Their only merit is low cost. Avoid them as materials for exterior doors, although they may be satisfactory for some interior doors.

"Steel" doors have thin steel sheetmetal inner and outer surfaces installed over a wooden frame and an insulating foam core. Similar doors use aluminum surfaces instead of steel. Because of the foam core, this type of door has the lowest conduction heat loss. Foam-filled exterior doors have long-term insulation values from about R-7 to about R-12 (RSI 1.2 to 2.1). Steel doors can use magnetic weatherstripping, which is very effective while it lasts.

If you buy a steel door, make sure that the steel has a "hot dipped galvanized" coating. "Electrogalvanized" coatings are thinner. Even with a galvanized coating, it is essential to keep a steel door well painted to avoid rust. Aluminum is not vulnerable to rust, but it is more vulnerable to dents.

So, what material should you select? If your climate has a cold season, install doors that have insulating cores. Such doors are not all equal. Check the NFRC ratings for R-value, and inspect the weatherstripping for reliable long-term sealing.

In a damp location, try to find a good door that has an aluminum exterior face. Wood is far less desirable in a damp location, and steel should be avoided.

If you want a dramatic main entrance, splurge on a beautiful wood door. Be sure that it is made strongly, and design an entrance cover that will protect it from weather.

☐ Strength

If the door frame is built strongly, the door itself can become the weakest security link, allowing a determined intruder to crash through it.

The strongest doors have single-piece interior and exterior surfaces of plywood, steel, or aluminum.

A wooden door with inset panels is relatively weak. It is made of vertical members, called "stiles," and horizontal members, called "rails." In a panel door, only the stiles on the two sides are continuous from top to bottom. The rails are glued to the stiles, and these joints are weak points. The rails should be fairly wide to strengthen these joints. The decorative panels are held by slender grooves in the stiles and rails, so they can be knocked out of the door.

It is possible to buy decorative wooden doors that have special reinforcing features, but examine such features critically. Be prepared to pay a high price for a decorative wood door that is strongly built.

☐ Glazing In and Around Doors

As a general rule, minimize glazing in any entrance door because glazing weakens the door. To identify visitors, install a peephole or an intercom or a video camera. Or, locate a window to provide a view of the entry area from a convenient and secure location.

If you want glass in a door because you like the appearance, keep it small. For privacy, install obscuring decorative glass high in the door. Or, install a "transom window" above the door. This is a window that matches the width of the door and is mounted directly above it, with matching decor.

Door glazing is offered with most of the energy-saving features that are offered for windows, including low-E coating and insulating gas. However, the area of glass in an entrance door is so small that multiple glazing is the only feature that matters much.

If you do want glazing in a door, consider how easy it will be to replace the glass. The seals in double glazing will fail after a few decades, making the glass streaky. Unusual glazing shapes will be expensive to repair.

ENTRANCE DOOR SELECTION GUIDE

A current fad is installing narrow windows alongside an entry door to provide a wider appearance, as in Figure 3-227. Prefabricated door units may even include such windows. This arrangement greatly weakens the door frame on both the lock side and the hinge side. Also, it makes the inner door handle vulnerable to access by breaking the adjacent glass.

Attractive wall decor alongside the door is a better way to create a wide entrance. If you want light and view, install regular windows at a safe distance from the door.

☐ Weatherstripping for Prefabricated Door Assemblies

Prefabricated door-and-frame assemblies are greatly inferior in strength to entrance doors that are installed as we recommend. However, the convenience of prefabricated door assemblies makes them attractive for non-secure applications, such as the secondary door of a vestibule, or for a door that opens to a secure area, such as a balcony.

If you select prefabricated door-and-frame assemblies, the weatherstripping is built into the assembly. There are several effective systems, and new methods are devised from time to time. Judge this detail carefully, because it is the most important energy saving feature of the door.

Examine whether the weatherstripping will remain effective if the door and frame get out of alignment. All doors tend to sag as they age.

Examine whether all the weatherstripping can be replaced. This includes the weather seal between the threshold and the bottom of the door. The bottom seal should be installed on the door, not on the threshold, where it would be damaged by people walking across it.

If the original weatherstripping cannot be replaced, any substitute weatherstripping probably will be awkward to install and less effective.

DRW

Figure 3-227. Don't install windows alongside your entry doors. It gives intruders easy access to the inside of your door locks, and it weakens the door mounting.

The first step in creating reliable weatherstripping is to stabilize the gap between the door and the frame. The strong construction of your super-house will keep the frame from shifting. To keep the door from sagging inside the frame, select strong hinges and install them properly. Design the clearance on each side of the door to be compatible with the kinds of weatherstripping that you will use.

For the top and both sides, use the kind of weatherstripping shown in Figure 3-224. It is usually called "V-seal" or something similar because it has a "V" cross section. On the hinge side, the door edge pinches the seal against the frame. On the lock side and the top, the door compresses the seal in a sliding motion. This kind of weatherstripping is easy to replace, it accommodates warping of the door, and it does not interfere with easy latching of the door locks.

Today, most V-seal is made of plastic, and it is attached with an adhesive backing on one side of the "V."

Another kind weatherstripping is a strip of spring bronze. The inside edge of the strip is nailed to the door frame with small bronze nails. The rest of the strip has a slight angle or curvature. This part of the strip is compressed as the edge of the door slides over it. Bronze will last much longer than plastic.

To block air leakage between the bottom of the door and the threshold, install a "sweep" along the bottom of the door. This is a brush or plastic strip that is installed on the side of the door bottom, as in Figure 3-223. The sweep seals against the side of the threshold when the door is closed.

A different type of bottom seal is a flexible plastic strip or tube that is installed on the underside of the door, where it is slides over the top of the threshold when the door is closed. This type requires a fixed

DON'T INSTALL STORM DOORS

Storm doors are a nuisance. Imagine holding bags of groceries and unlocking the main door while the storm door is being slammed by the wind.

Storm doors are supposed to reduce air leakage. But, they are vulnerable to damage from rough handling and wind. So, they get bent out of alignment and hang open, which defeats their purpose. Instead of using storm doors, select your primary doors to be airtight and durable. If you live in a climate that tempts you to install a storm door, install a vestibule instead.

Storm doors are also supposed to protect your expensive main door from rain. But, what protects the storm door itself? It is smarter to protect your doors from the weather with an entryway that protects both the door and people standing outside the door. See Step 1 for a rich menu of effective entryway choices

AVOID PREFABRICATED DOOR-AND-FRAME ASSEMBLIES FOR ENTRANCES

Prefabricated door-and-frame assemblies have become popular because they are inexpensive and quick to install. The door is already attached to the frame by the hinges, the weatherstripping is installed, and the door is drilled to receive the locks. Some manufacturers also include the lock hardware and other accessories in the assembly.

Unfortunately, prefabricated door assemblies are too weak to consider as entrances to your house. Their basic weakness is that the wall opening must be oversized to allow the door assembly to be inserted, leaving a gap between the frame and the wall opening. A few shims are used to bridge the gap, and the frame is nailed through the shims into the wall. This results in a weak attachment of the door, making it vulnerable to physical impact and shifting. Also, the gap is a major path for air leakage.

Aside from that fundamental weakness, prefabricated door assemblies tend to be flimsy. The frame lumber is thin, the hinges are weakly installed, and the lock hardware is cheap.

You could overcome some of this vulnerability by carefully shimming all around the frame and by substituting better hardware. But even then, the assembly would not be as strong as attaching a good standard door directly to the wall structure. Instead, build all the door frames for your entrances from scratch, and exploit all your opportunities to strengthen the door and the frame.

clearance between the threshold and the bottom of the door. It is more difficult to install and to replace, and it has a shorter life.

Avoid a bottom seal that is installed on top of the threshold. This location is exposed to damage. It may be impossible to replace the seal without replacing the entire threshold.

Door Molding

Molding is decorative trim that covers gaps and rough edges between the door frame and the wall. In the past, molding was the primary defense against air leakage between the door frame and wall opening. We use better methods to block air leakage, but we should still exploit the molding as an additional barrier. Make sure that the molding is installed snugly against the frame and the adjacent wall. Use a ribbon of sealant between the molding and the wall, and between the molding and the door frame.

DOOR LOCKS

You will buy your locks and other door hardware separately from the doors themselves. For entrance doors, buy the most secure locks that are available. The extra cost in trivial in relation to the benefit.

With the locks available today, the best arrangement is a combination of two locks for each entrance door: a latching lock for convenience and a deadbolt lock for ultimate security. This arrangement is the most common, so you can easily find or order all the lock hardware you need.

Let's discuss your options.

Latching Locks

Latching locks are the most common type. Figure 3-229 shows a typical assembly.

The latching lock engages itself when you push the door closed. The bolt of the lock has an angled face that is pushed inward by the edge of the "strike plate," a steel plate that is installed in the door frame. When the door closes fully, spring pressure pushes the bolt into a hole in the strike plate. To open the door, the bolt is retracted by turning the knob or handle. A key lock is located in the outside knob or handle. The main advantage of latching locks is convenience. You can set them to lock automatically whenever the door closes.

Latching locks are relatively weak. The bolt must be short so that it can pass over the strike plate. If an intruder kicks the center of the door, the door may bow enough to pull the bolt out of the hole in the strike plate. A blow with a hammer can knock off the knob or handle, taking the key lock with it. With the knob gone, it is easy to retract the bolt with a screwdriver.

The bolt of a simple latching lock can be retracted by forcing a blade or a flexible piece of plastic between the door and the frame to lift the angled surface of the bolt out of the strike plate. To prevent this, latching

DRW

Figure 3-230. The deadlatch on a latching lock. When the door is closed, the deadlatch is depressed by the strike plate. This prevents the bolt from being retracted by jamming a tool against it.

locks on exterior doors commonly have a "deadlatch" feature, shown in Figure 3-230.

The hole in the strike plate allows the bolt to enter, but not the deadlatch. When the deadlatch is held in the depressed position by the strike plate, it prevents the bolt from retracting except by turning the indoor knob. This feature requires careful alignment of the lock and the strike plate.

DRW

Figure 3-231. A deadbolt lock, above the latch lock, that has both outside and inside lock cylinders. A tapered housing surrounds each cylinder to deflect hammer blows. The tapered housing rotates freely, so the cylinder cannot be twisted off with a wrench.

Figure 3-229. Typical latching lock. Either of the round knobs may be replaced with a lever handle.

SEGAL SURFACE-MOUNTED DEADBOLT LOCKS

In 1912, a New York City policeman named Samuel Segal invented a deadbolt lock that has a bolt that moves vertically, locking into a pair of rings on the strike plate. The locked bolt cannot be separated from the strike plate by impact on the door or by jimmying with a crowbar. The outer lock cylinder is entirely recessed within the door stile, so it is well protected against attack by a hammer or wrench.

Another important advantage is that the lock does not weaken the door edge, and actually reinforces it against impact from outside. The entire body of the lock is installed on the inside surface of the door, except for a hole that houses the outer lock cylinder.

The special strike plate is provided with the lock. Unfortunately, current models do not have a large attachment area, and it would be difficult for the builder to reinforce the strike plate. This makes the frame attachment the weak point of this type of lock. The best you can do is to install the strike plate on a frame of solid, thick lumber so that the screws attaching the strike plate can penetrate deeply into the frame.

You can buy Segal deadbolts with high-security cylinders. To protect the lock from being unlocked from the inside, order a double-cylinder model. The indoor cylinder is mounted on the surface of the lock body, so it is more vulnerable to physical attack than the outer cylinder.

You may not be able to buy keyed-alike cylinders that fit both Segal locks and other kinds of deadbolts. Therefore, if you want the convenience

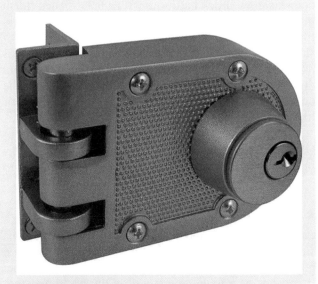

Figure 3-232. A Segal deadbolt lock.

of keyed-alike locks, you may have to select Segal locks for all your exterior and high-security doors.

To prevent a Segal lock from being physically removed from the door by an intruder inside the house, the lock body must be installed with special hardened one-way screws. If you use those, the lock will remain for the life of the door, even though you may want to remove it later.

The Segal deadbolt has faded in popularity, probably because it does not look elegant. The lock does make the door look fortified, which it is. But aside from that, the security that it provides is compelling.

Deadbolt Locks

A deadbolt lock provides greater security than a latch lock because it uses a long bar (the "bolt") to engage the door frame. Its strength comes primarily from the length and toughness of the bolt.

A lock cylinder operates the bolt from the outside. The cylinder must be well protected because it protrudes beyond the door. The cylinder may be mounted in a strong housing that resists the force of a hammer or the twisting of a pipe wrench. The best deadbolts have a variety of features to protect the cylinder, such as a tapered and freely rotating housing that cannot be twisted off. Figure 3-231 shows a strong deabolt lock.

A key is needed to operate a deadbolt from the outside. From the inside, the deadbolt may be opened by a "thumb-turn," which is a small lever or knob.

For greater security, you can install a second inside cylinder in place of the thumb-turn, as in Figure 3-231. In that way, a thief who enters through a window cannot open the door to carry out large objects. He can steal your jewelry and other small items, but he can't clean out your furniture and appliances. (Protecting the door from the inside also requires other features, which we explain elsewhere.)

There is another, older type of deadbolt lock that deserves more attention than it gets today. This is the Segal deadbolt. It is a stronger type of lock that has several important advantages over ordinary deadbolts, and no serious drawbacks. See the sidebar.

Knobs and Handles

The exterior lock hardware is exposed to rain and condensation. Lock hardware with a brass plated finish may corrode or develop a rough appearance. To avoid this, consider exterior lock hardware that is made of stainless steel, bronze, or chrome plated brass. It does not look as elegant as polished brass, but it is more durable. You can buy locksets that are stainless on the outside and brass on the inside. Solid brass exterior hardware will last forever, but it requires polishing.

If a member of the household has a weakened grip, as from arthritis, use sturdy lever-type door handles instead of round knobs. They make it much easier to open doors.

■ Handlesets

Latching locks and deadbolts may be combined in a single fixture called a "handleset." This is a decorative presentation that typically is used for a formal entrance. It consists of a fixed handle with a thumb trigger that operates a latch lock, in combination with a separate deadbolt. Commonly, only the deadbolt has a key lock. The lack of a separate key lock for the latch is a major deficit. Figure 3-233 shows a typical handleset.

There are other ways to combine latches with deadbolts. For example, a type of lock commonly used for hotel rooms operates a latching lock and a deadbolt with a single key.

Lock Cylinders and Keys

Today, most door locks use a mechanical cylinder that is turned with a key. Electronic locks are starting to replace mechanical lock cylinders, primarily for convenience. However, key locks are highly reliable, whereas most electronic locks require a key lock as a backup against failure. So, unless you really want to avoid using keys, you might as well stick with mechanical cylinders as your primary type of lock.

That being said, cylinder locks are vulnerable in three ways: (1) brute force can break the cylinder loose and expose the bolt to operation with a screwdriver or other simple tool; (2) an intruder can pick the lock; (3) an unauthorized person can copy the key. The best locks are highly resistant to all three threats, so buy the best.

If you install double-cylinder deadbolts, you must leave a key in each inside cylinder as long as the house is occupied. Otherwise, the locked deadbolt makes it impossible to escape from the house in the event of a fire. (For this reason, some fire safety codes forbid double-cylinder locks.) If you leave the house for an extended period, remove all the interior keys and hide them.

Order extra keys when you buy the locks, because it is a chore to get copies of keys for highly secure locks. If you use double-cylinder locks, remember that

A CHEAP LUXURY: KEYED-ALIKE LOCKS

A really nice convenience is being able to open all the locks around your home and property with the same key. Or, with the same pair of keys, one for the latch locks and one for the deadbolts. To get this feature, order your locks to be "keyed alike." ("Master keyed" means something else, which you don't need.)

Buy extra keys and a couple of extra matching locks for the future, because it is troublesome to match a high-security lock later. In this way, if you later build a tool shed or an addition to the house, or if you decide to lock an interior door, you can still use the same keys for everything.

The usual practice has been for deadbolts to have high-security keys and cylinders, while latch locks have cheaper keys and cylinders. Recently, sets of deadbolts and latches with common keys have become available, so that you need to carry only a single key. Such sets are desirable only if they have very secure cylinders.

you need to keep a key in each inside cylinder while the house is occupied.

Also, buy a few spare cylinders, and order all of your cylinders to be "keyed alike." See the sidebar, *A Cheap Luxury: Keyed-Alike Locks*.

Keypad and Electronic Locks

Electronic locks that are operated with a keypad, an access card, or some other electronic trigger may become commonplace because they eliminate the need to use a house key. Figure 3-234 is a typical keypad lock.

An electronic lock needs to be just as secure as the best mechanical lock, or it will become the weak link of your door security. Furthermore, electronic locks still need a mechanical key to operate the lock in case the battery or the electronics fail.

"Biometric" locks are now entering the home market. These operate by recognizing a fingerprint, the retina of your eye, or some other unique part of your anatomy. Figure 3-235 shows an example. It's a brave new world.

STRENGTHEN THE DOOR

We have designed a strong mounting for your entrance doors in the wall openings, and we have selected the strongest door locks. To complete the design of your strong entrances, we will now strtengthen the door itself and its attachments to the locks and frame.

Figure 3-233. Typical handleset.

Baldwin

Figure 3-235. A latch lock that works by recognizing your fingerprint. Stick your finger in the hole.

Yale

Figure 3-234. Deadbolt lock activated by a keypad. A mechanical cylinder lock is included in case the keypad fails.

Install Reinforced Strike Plates

The area of the door frame where the strike plate is installed is vulnerable to impact. The strike plate absorbs all the force of an impact on the lock or the prying force of a crowbar, and it transmits the force to the door frame. The best way to reinforce the locking edge of the door frame is to install an extended strike plate for the locks, as in Figure 3-236. An enlarged strike plate distributes the force farther up and down the frame, and farther toward the strong center of the door opening.

You can buy a variety of strong strike plates, the taller and wider the better. They are inexpensive, easy

to install, and invisible when the door is closed. The part of the strike plate that extends beyond the edge of the door is hidden under the stop strip. To install the strike plate, use long screws that penetrate deeply through the lumber of the wall opening, joining the frame securely to the wall.

Reinforce the Door Edge at the Locks

Most locks greatly weaken the portion of the door that surrounds the lock because of the holes that must be bored into the stile. (A stile is a vertical strength member of the door. Each side of the door has a stile.) An effective way to protect the door edge from breaking at the locks is to install a closely fitting metal plate that wraps around the edge of the door, as in Figure 3-237. The plate should be matched to the particular locks being used. The plate can be plated with brass or chrome to prevent corrosion, or it can be stainless steel.

This enhancement is inexpensive and easy to install on the door, but it may interfere with the door frame and the weatherstripping. If the metal is not inset into the door, you will need a type of weatherstripping that accommodates the thickness of the metal. If possible, order this kind of reinforcement from the factory as an integral part of the door.

Another method of protecting the door edge is to select a lock that has a long faceplate. The faceplate spreads the force of an attack along a greater area of the door edge. This is less effective than a wraparound plate. Anyway, such locks are unusual.

DRW

Figure 3-236. Reinforced strike plate for a deadbolt. The inner row of screws holding the strike plate are several inches long, extending deep into the timber frame, which is bolted with lag screws to the opening in a concrete wall.

If you use a Segal deadbolt lock, it is unnecessary to reinforce the door edge. The Segal lock itself helps the door to resist impact. See the previous sidebar, *Segal Surface-Mounted Deadbolt Locks*.

Use Extended Hinges

An intruder usually will attack the lock side of the door. However, if the lock looks strong, he might decide to attack the hinges. The hinge side of the frame is inherently stronger than the lock side. This is because most exterior doors have three or four hinges to distribute impact on the door. And, the hinge sides of the frame and door edge are not weakened by boring holes for lock hardware.

To strengthen the attachment of the hinges to the frame, use screws that penetrate deeply through the frame and into the lumber of the wall opening.

To further strengthen the hinges, use hinges that have a longer strap along the wall opening, as in Figure 3-222. The deeper door opening of a super-insulated wall makes it possible to use this kind of hinge. The longer strap allows the screws to be farther from the edge of the frame, so that a heavy blow will not split the edge of the frame. Figure 3-238 shows two hinges of this kind.

A burglar can easily remove a door from inside the house by pulling the pins out of the hinges. To prevent this, select hinges that have non-removable ("captive") pins. Also, install locks that require a key to be opened from the inside.

For maximum resistance to impact, select hinges that attach to the inside surface of the door, as in Figure 3-222, rather than to the edge of the door. In this way, the hinge supports the door edge against impact, rather than tending to split the edge of the door. A weakness of this method is that the screws are accessible to an intruder who gets into the house by another route and wants to use the door to get out. To defend against this weakness, use "one way" screws to attach the hinge to the inside of the door.

Figure 3-237. Door edge reinforcement plate. It may require some fitting to the door and the frame. Taller reinforcement plates are available that accommodate both the deadbolt and knob lock.

Figure 3-238. Door hinges with an extended strap that can provide stronger attachment to the door frame.

INTERIOR DOORS AND PARTITIONS

Interior doors historically have been used to provide privacy, to block noise, and to keep informal rooms out of sight of the formal rooms. In a super-efficient house, interior doors and partitions also perform the important function of isolating heating and cooling to occupied rooms. In Step 1, you designed the layout of your interior doors. Now, we consider your full range of options when selecting each door and openable partition.

When we speak of a "door," we may be referring to one of two characteristics that determine the type of door. One is the physical panel of the door. For example, when we say "louvered door," we are referring to a panel that has louvers. The other defining characteristic is the method of mounting the panel or panels. For example, when we say "pocket door," we are referring to a mounting method. Where necessary, we will cover both characteristics as we review your interior door options.

Hinged (swing) doors are inexpensive and easy to use. Most have a wooden panel that consists of two thin plywood faces over a lightweight core. Most of the rooms in your home will have this kind of door to provide privacy and to isolate heating and cooling. In many homes, this is the only kind of interior door that is used.

Although most swing doors have a solid panel, a swing door can use almost any kind of rigid panel.

Swing doors can seal tightly at the top and sides because the door mates with the frame. As a result, they muffle noise well. Their insulation value generally is adequate for interior isolation of heating and cooling.

Hinged doors have a gap at the bottom. To block air leakage and noise there, install a "sweep" at the bottom. The sweep may take the form of a brush or a soft plastic strip. A sweep won't work over carpet, so arrange your flooring design to avoid carpeting under the paths of doors. A sweep will eventually mar the surface of a wood or composition floor, so adjust the sweep to leave a small clearance over such surfaces.

Swing doors are limited to a width of about 36" (90 cm), which is ample for most purposes. A double hinged door can be used to create a wider opening, up to about 72" (180 cm).

French doors are swing doors that have a large amount of glass. They provide the ability to block noise and air leakage while maintaining a view between rooms. They can be an elegant decor feature in themselves. If you have adjacent attractive spaces that are used together only occasionally, consider French doors to separate their heating and cooling. For

Simpson Door Company

Figure 3-241. A pair of French doors used to isolate the heating and cooling of a dining room while maintaining a visual connection to the adjacent space.

example, Figure 3-241 shows how French doors can be used effectively.

French doors are commonly installed in pairs, providing a maximum opening of about 72" (180 cm). The visual opening can be increased even more by installing matching glass wall panels adjacent to each side of the doors. Design the room layout so that the doors can open flat against the wall or side panels.

Originally, the glass in French doors was composed of many small panes or "lights" that were held in place by a grid of slender wooden "muntins." This created an attractive appearance. But today, the glazing in French doors consists of a single sheet of glass (or double glass). Muntins offered as options for modern French doors are obviously fake, and they look cheesy. Better decoration of the glass is provided by tasteful etching, or by using delicate overlays, or by using grooves embossed around the perimeter of the glass. French doors are available with double glazing and other features to minimize heat conduction.

All kinds of double swing doors have a gap where the two doors meet, in addition to the gaps at the bottom. Classically, this vertical gap was closed with a strip

DRW

Figure 3-242. Louvered doors between a bedroom and a dressing room.

DRW

Figure 3-243. A pocket door that isolates a bedroom wing from the rest of the house. This style of door mounting avoids interference with the bedroom hallway and with the entrance door on the left.

(called an "astragal") attached to one of the doors. This is awkward because it requires the two doors to be opened and closed in sequence. Modern doors offer a flexible rubber seal to avoid this annoyance.

Louvered doors provide a visual screen while allowing free flow of air and moisture. They can be hinged, as in Figure 3-242, or they can slide on a track.

Louvered doors do not block sound, and they are only partially effective in blocking dust. In appropriate applications, they help to avoid mildew in closets. They can also be used for visual privacy doors between related rooms, such as a bedroom and an adjacent dressing room, as in Figure 3-242.

In the days before air conditioning, louvered bedroom doors were used in warm climates to allow ventilation for cooling at night. They can still be used this way, in combination with a night ventilation fan, as we will explain in Step 4.

Pocket doors are doors that slide into a cavity ("pocket") in the wall, rather than swinging on hinges. A pocket door is a method of installation, in which any desired style of interior door (including a glazed door) is suspended from an overhead track with rollers.

A pocket door is commonly used in a location where a swing door would interfere with movement or where a swing door would take up desirable wall space. Figure 3-243 shows a good application for a pocket door. Another benefit is that pocket doors do not interfere with carpeting on either side of the opening. And, a pocket door saves a few square feet (a fraction of a square meter) of floor space because it does not sweep over any floor space around the door. A double pocket door, with wall cavities on both sides of the opening, can provide a very wide opening.

The wall that encloses a pocket door requires special design. The pocket must be slightly deeper than the width of the door, so it must extend into two or three normal stud spaces. This requires special wall framing. The sides of the pocket are weak, so this part of the wall cannot carry a structural load.

Pocket doors allow more air leakage than hinged doors because the clearances around the door cannot be sealed very well. They are somewhat awkward to use, requiring fingertips to pull the door out of the pocket. Removing a pocket door for maintenance or replacement may require removing some woodwork around the door opening.

Sliding doors are suspended from an overhead track, similar to the track used for pocket doors. The difference is that the door is mounted on the outside of the wall, so that no special wall framing is required. Any style of door can be used. Figure 3-244 shows a nice example.

DRW

Figure 3-244. An interior sliding door with glazing.

Avoca Ridge Ltd

Figure 3-245. An attractive set of sliding doors for a closet.

A sliding door of any width can be used, and double doors can slide in both directions. The opening width is limited only by the amount of wall space available for stowing the opened doors. The track typically is hidden by a valance.

On the negative side, this method of installation allows a relatively large amount of air leakage. And, it provides only minimal security.

Panelfold Doors

Figure 3-246. A folding door used as a partition between spaces. When the door is closed, glass panels maintain a visual connection between the spaces.

LTL Home Products

Figure 3-247. An attractive folding closet door.

Sliding closet doors use several overlapping panels that are installed inside the wall opening, as in Figure 3-245. They do not intrude into the closet or into the room, so they are useful in rooms that are cramped by furnishings. This method of installation keeps the panels inside the door opening, so that no extra wall space is needed alongside the opening. However, the individual panels must be shuffled to get from one part of the closet to another. Closet doors typically use lightweight panels, but any type of door may be used, such as ordinary interior doors or louvered doors.

Folding doors or *folding partitions* are mounted on an overhead track, and they hang clear of the floor. They can have any number of panels, which are hinged together, as in Figures 3-246 and 3-247. They can open to any desired width. If the ceiling is horizontal, a folding door can be suspended from the ceiling, creating a full-height opening. They do not block air leakage as well as hinged doors.

Closets are a common application for folding doors. Unlike sliding closet doors, they can provide almost full-width access to the closet interior. Closet doors typically are installed in pairs, for a total of four folding panels, as in Figure 3-247. This particular configuration is called a "bi-fold" door. Folding doors intrude into the room when the door is opened, but less than a swing door.

Accordion doors are made in the same way as folding doors, except that the individual panels are narrower. As a result, the open door intrudes less beyond the door opening. This makes them desirable for closets, as in Figure 3-248. They may be the only practical option for very wide indoor openings, as commonly seen in banquet halls. If desired, they can be mounted on a curved track. The panels can be decorated in various ways, including glazing. Accordion doors do not block air leakage very well.

Shutter Shack

Figure 3-248. A typical accordion door.

GARAGE DOORS AND OTHER LARGE DOORS

First, a recommendation – make your garage doors as wide as practical. If you plan to have a garage that is wide enough for several vehicles, install a single wide door instead of separate doors for each parking space. At some point, you or someone else will want to build something inside the garage that will not pass through a single-car garage door.

This recommendation reflects my own pleasure in building things like boats and airplanes. You may not have the same interest, or your home may be located in an urban area where you could not move a big object out of the garage. And, a wider door opening complicates the design of the structure. But, think about it. You won't be able to widen the door later.

For a garage door of any size, *stress energy efficiency and strength*. Energy efficiency makes it practical to heat the garage during cold weather, at least occasionally. Strength provides resistance to forced entry. In a location that is vulnerable to windstorms, it also protects the entire house from damage. You can achieve efficiency and strength in combination with other desirable traits, such as appearance and safety features.

To select your garage doors and any other large doors that you may need, follow the adjacent *Large Door Selection Guide*. With the *Guide* in hand, find houses where you can examine doors that have been installed. Also, check the Web sites of manufacturers.

THE DEFAULT CHOICE: SECTIONAL GARAGE DOORS

One type of garage door has become dominant, which simplifies your selection decision. This type is commonly called a "sectional" door. It consists of panels, or sections, that are hinged together horizontally. The door rises vertically in a track and stows under the garage ceiling, as in Figure 3-251.

The main advantages of the sectional garage door design over other designs are:

• It is fairly easy to open manually, and it can be balanced to remain in any position.

• It does not intrude into the garage or toward the outside when it is being opened or closed.

• A powered opener is easy to install.

• It places little load on the house structure, so the opening requires no reinforcement.

The popularity of the design has created the additional virtues of relatively low cost, a vast selection of appearance options, availability of repair parts, and a large number of contractors who know how to install the door properly.

On the other hand, the sectional design is not well adapted to energy efficiency, primarily because the use of a track and multiple sections invites air leakage. However, the popularity of the design has allowed manufacturers to invest the attention needed to minimize this shortcoming. As a result, you can probably achieve energy efficiency with a sectional door that is as good as you could achieve with a less common and more expensive type.

For most homes, the sectional door is the most satisfactory kind. However, there are reasons why you might want a different kind. So, let's see what else is available.

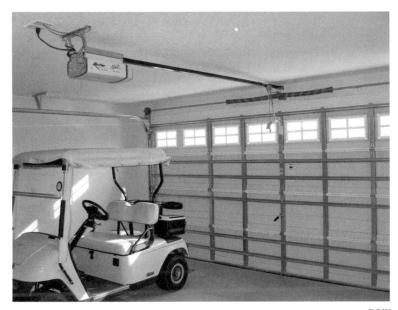

DRW

Figure 3-251. Sectional garage door. The bar across the top has a wound spring that balances the weight of the door. This door has horizontal reinforcing bars to resist wind damage.

LARGE DOOR SELECTION GUIDE

☐ Size

Residential models of sectional garage doors are commonly available in widths up to about 20 feet (6 meters), which is ample for two parking spaces. Commercial sectional doors are available in widths up to 40 feet (12 meters), with limited decorative options.

If you need a door that is wider than about 20 feet (6 meters), consider other types. Bi-fold doors work well for widths up to about 40 feet (16 meters), and hydraulic doors can be even wider. Sliding doors have no width limit.

Most door types are available in heights that are sufficient for practically any application.

☐ Sealing Against Air Leakage

Blocking air leakage is the biggest energy efficiency challenge for a garage door. Examine the sealing methods for the top, the bottom, and the sides, all of which may be different. With sectional doors, also examine the method of sealing between segments.

Sectional doors and roll-up doors ride in tracks at the sides of the door opening. The basic design is very leaky, so you need to be sure that effective seals are included in the model you buy. The seals must compensate for looseness between the rollers and the track, while minimizing resistance to opening and closing. The top and side seals are attached to the door opening, and the door slides past them. The installer needs to position these seals properly to get good sealing.

If you need a larger door, bi-fold and hydraulic doors have the potential to seal tightly. However, to achieve this potential, the door needs a mechanism to clamp the door uniformly against the frame.

All doors need an effective bottom seal to accommodate irregularities in the floor. For doors that move vertically, this usually takes the form of a large, hollow tube of flexible plastic that conforms well to irregularities in the floor surface. For doors that swing on side hinges, the bottom seal usually is a brush that is attached to the face of the door.

Door seals eventually wear out from flexing and abrasion, so select a door with seals that will be easy to replace in the future.

In addition to examining the design of the door, try to find a credible rating for its air leakage. For example, some garage doors may have an NFRC rating for air leakage.

Sliding doors, which may be needed for a very wide opening, are difficult to seal against air leakage, especially if they have more than two panels.

☐ Insulation

Garage doors have a lot of surface area. If the climate can be cold, an insulated door will probably pay for itself if you heat the space even occasionally. And, by eliminating a large cold surface, it will make the space more comfortable. Even if you don't heat the space, an insulated door will keep the space somewhat warmer by trapping heat from the ground and from the adjoining part of the house.

Any mass-produced insulated garage door will have an advertised R-value. Look for a credible rating that validates the claim of the manufacturer. For example, some garage doors may have NFRC ratings for R-value.

Uninsulated garage doors have minimal insulation value, ranging from R-1 to R-2 (RSI 0.2 to 0.4). Typical insulated sectional doors have insulation values from R-5 to R-15 (RSI 0.1 to 2.6). Well insulated models are thicker than poorly insulated ones. Polyurethane insulation is better than polystyrene for this application.

Sectional, roll-up, and lightweight panel doors are insulated by injecting foam between the inner and outer panels during manufacture. This produces panels that are rigid and well insulated.

Hydraulic doors and outward-swinging bi-fold doors may have panels with integral foam insulation, or fiber batt insulation may be installed separately. Either method can insulate well, but batt insulation is less neat, more vulnerable, and invites condensation damage.

If the climate has a cold season and you want windows in the door, select windows with double glazing.

☐ Appearance

The large, blank surface of a garage door is an appearance challenge. Garages that are attached to houses appeared only during the 20th century. Prior to then, carriages and early automobiles were kept in separate buildings. For this reason, a garage door is not an original feature of any classic architectural style.

LARGE DOOR SELECTION GUIDE

Manufacturers of residential garage doors have attempted to compensate for this by offering a variety of decorative styles. The most common technique is to break up the surface into smaller shapes, using the same basic techniques as for formal entrance doors. The most common shapes are embossed "panels" and windows. Check the Web sites of garage door manufacturers for their stylistic offerings.

Recently, it has become popular to make sectional doors look like "carriage house" doors, which were hinged at the sides. Such doors include false hinges, latches, and other hardware. Such fakery is stylistically risky, and this fad may seem *gauche* after it dies out.

Wider doors are more difficult to blend into the appearance of a house because of their large ratio of width to height. You can reduce this ratio by using wall decorations above the opening to increase the apparent height of the door opening. For example, a long arch over the door opening is effective for this purpose. Plan for this in the design of the wall structure above the door opening.

DRW

Figure 3-253. A sectional garage door that has stiffeners to resist hurricane winds.

☐ Durability

Most popular garage doors have steel sheetmetal surfaces over a steel frame. Aluminum surfaces are also available. If the door is insulated, the insulation is enclosed between two sheetmetal skins. If the insulation is foamed in place when the door is made, the insulation bonds to both skins, forming a rigid box structure with greatly increased strength and resistance to dents.

In most climates, the tendency of steel to rust is the limiting factor in the life of the door. The main deterrence to rust is a zinc (galvanized) coating. The zinc is slowly consumed by the chemical action that causes rust, so the life of the zinc coating is proportional to its thickness. If you have a choice, select a door with a heavier galvanized coating on all the steel components. Or, select a door with aluminum skins. For metal surfaces, select the most durable paint or enamel that you can find.

A metal door will last much longer if it is kept dry. Use a wide overhang to keep rain off the door.

Normally, avoid doors that have plastic components, such as vinyl panels, because plastic is vulnerable to the ultraviolet light in sunlight and to oxidation by the atmosphere. However, if the atmosphere is corrosive – such as near a seashore – consider a door with a vinyl plastic exterior surface, even though it won't last many years. This may be the best choice if the climate does not require insulation, so that the door is relatively inexpensive to replace.

Favor a door that uses standard components for the parts that wear out, such as hinges, rollers, and weatherstripping. This allows you to maintain the door far into the future.

A wooden garage door is an expensive boutique item that can be very attractive. It can be strong, but it will not be durable unless the structure of the house keeps it dry at all times.

——————— **LARGE DOOR SELECTION GUIDE** ———————

☐ Wind and Impact Resistance

If your home is located where hurricanes or tornadoes may occur, select a garage door that is well reinforced to resist wind. This is especially important for garages that are attached to houses. If a storm blows out a garage door or distorts the door sufficiently to let wind into the garage, the resulting pressure inside the house can blow off the roof. In fact, it has been discovered that garage door failure is a major cause of roof loss in windstorms.

(For more about this, see *Resistance to Wind Damage*, under the major heading *Super-Structure Design Advance #4: Super-Strength*, in Step 3.)

For this reason, you can now buy garage doors with strong wind reinforcements as a feature. However, the effectiveness of the reinforcement in different models varies widely.

For sectional doors, the reinforcements generally consist of stiffening bars that span horizontally across the door, as in Figure 3-253. The reinforcements may look daunting, but they are well worth the small space that they occupy.

A much less desirable design is reinforcing wide sectional doors with a removable vertical bar that supports the center of the door from top of the frame to the floor. The homeowner must install the bar when danger is imminent, and the door cannot be used while the bar is in place. This method is greatly inferior to permanent reinforcements, and it is virtually useless against tornadoes, which may strike without warning.

☐ Resistance to Intruders

A garage door is just as attractive to burglars as any other door in the house. A garage door can be breached by crashing through it, by prying it open at the sides, or by finding a way to open the lock.

To stop a brute force attack, the door and its attachments to the wall opening must be physically strong. If a garage door is reinforced to resist wind, it will also resist forced entry more effectively. Sectional doors and roll-up doors resist forced entry well because they are secured to the side tracks by many rollers. The tracks must be bolted strongly into the wall opening.

Electronic remote controls and keypads make it impossible to open a lock by brute force.

Any garage door is vulnerable from the inside. A burglar can get into a garage by entering from the house. To block that avenue of attack, install a double-cylinder deadbolt in the door between the garage and the house. The same door will deter a burglar from entering the house through the garage.

☐ Counterbalances

Garage doors that open upward usually have springs to balance the weight of the door. Some doors are balanced by counterweights. However, no balancing system eliminates all the effort needed to operate the door, so check how well this feature works for the doors that you consider. If the door does not have a powered opener, the door should be balanced so well that an older child or an impaired adult can open and close the door.

The ability to open the door manually matters even if your garage doors have powered openers. If the opener fails, you don't want your car and other equipment to be trapped in the garage.

With sectional and roll-up doors, it is easy to arrange springs to balance the weight of the door almost perfectly. As a result, the door will stay in any position.

The most common counterbalance for a sectional door uses a "torsion" spring that is wrapped around a shaft. The shaft is mounted across the top of the door opening, as in Figure 3-251. The shaft also has a drum at each end. Each drum winds a cable that is attached to a lower corner of the door. As the door is lowered, the cables turn the shaft and winds up the spring.

An even simpler arrangement uses a pair of "extension" springs that are attached to the lower corners of the door with cables.

Balance springs break after a period of usage, and when they do, they release a large amount of energy. The advantage of the torsion spring arrangement is that the broken pieces are wrapped around the counterbalance shaft, where they can do no harm except making an alarming noise. If extension springs are used, they should have a retainer wire that runs through the center of the spring. The wire keeps pieces of broken spring from flying into the garage.

If counterweights are used, they should be installed inside a fixed tube, so the weights will be confined inside the tube if the supporting cable breaks.

LARGE DOOR SELECTION GUIDE

☐ Powered Openers

If a smaller garage door is balanced well, it can be opened and closed manually. However, powered garage door openers have become as common as electric car windows. They are inexpensive and convenient. The force they can apply allows you to adjust the weatherstripping for a tighter fit, which reduces air leakage. So, go ahead and get this feature. Larger and heavier doors – especially bi-fold doors and hydraulic doors – require powered openers.

These days, most garage door openers include a radio remote control that you can carry in your car. In addition, the door should be controlled by a key lock or an electronic keypad on the outside of the door and by a similar control inside the garage.

For most garage doors, the opener is an electric motor that pulls the door open with a chain, a reinforced rubber belt, or a screw shaft. A newer type of opener works by turning the counterbalance shaft. Any of these can be satisfactory. The opener for most residential sectional doors is easy to replace separately from the door.

There is a frustratingly obvious flaw in the way that most garage door openers attach to sectional doors, as in Figure 3-251. The opener is designed to connect to the top of the door at the center. But, when the door is in the closed position, the opener pulls mainly inward, not upward. The resulting bending force can distort the top panel so that it fails to seal properly.

One solution is to buy a hurricane resistant door, which has a reinforced top bar that will keep the door from bending. Another remedy is to buy an opener that attachcs to the door at the sides, rather than at the center. Unfortunately, you may not be able to find an opener that offers this option. Still another solution is to buy an opener that functions by turning the counterbalance shaft, which lifts the door at the sides.

☐ Safety Features

Any powered door is an item of machinery that is inherently dangerous. Remote control increases the risk that operation by one person will cause injury to another person, to an animal, or to vehicles.

There is no perfect safety device for a powered door except vigilance by the operator. However, a powered door should have a safety device that turns off the opener if a person or object enters the path of the door. A common safety device is a light beam aligned across the bottom of the door path. If the light beam is interrupted, the power is turned off. Another safety feature that is common on larger commercial doors is a movable bottom edge with a switch that turns off the motor if the edge encounters an obstruction.

Garage doors have other hazards. Fingers can be pinched or broken between the panels of a sectional door, or between the rollers and frame, or in other moving parts. Some sectional doors are designed to keep fingers out of the joints between panels.

☐ Windows in the Door

Most styles of garage doors are now offered with optional windows. For example, see Figures 3-251, 3-260, 3-262, and 3-263. Windows provide useful daylighting, and they may improve the appearance of a plain door.

For greater security and privacy, install any windows high in the door, above head level, and select obscuring glass. A high position provides the best daylighting.

The size, shape, and position of the windows depends on the type of door. The windows usually are rectangular, but they may be mounted in frames that give the appearance of various shapes. The glazing may be tempered glass, acrylic plastic, or polycarbonate plastic. You can select transparent or obscuring glazing, plain or decorated.

Some garage doors offer windows with an array of energy saving features, such as low-E coatings. Select these features based on your climate, the size of the windows, and whether the garage is heated.

Examine whether the windows are replaceable. If necessary, ask the dealer whether replacement windows are offered.

OTHER KINDS OF GARAGE DOORS

Roll-up doors are made of many horizontal sections. The sections are narrow, so that the door can roll up on a spool that is mounted over the door opening. See Figure 3-254.

Roll-up doors have only one advantage over sectional doors, which is that the roll-up door does not block the garage ceiling while the door is open. For this reason, roll-up doors are used in some garages that have lifts for vehicles. If you want to mount clotheslines in the garage, a roll-up door will not interfere.

In order for a roll-up door to work, the door must be thin, which makes it impossible to insulate the door well or to provide bracing against wind and impact. Because the sections are narrow, requiring many joints, it is difficult to resist air leakage. The narrow sections do not offer the same opportunities for decorating the exterior surface as other types of garage doors do. Windows in the door are limited to narrow slits.

Side-hinged (also called *swing* or *carriage house*) doors are the oldest kind. As shown in Figure 3-255, they swing outward, so the terrain outside the door must slope slightly downward. Today, they offer no significant advantages.

There is one exception. If you plan to build the house or garage yourself, a hinged door is easy to make with basic tools, and it can be well insulated.

Side-hinged doors exert a large force on their hinges. The hinges must be strong, and they must be attached strongly to the side of the wall opening. By the same token, the side of the door frame must be well braced to support the door in all its positions.

Figure 3-254. A typical roll-up door. The door is raised and lowered by pulling on the loop of chain that turns the pulley below the door spool.

Figure 3-255. Side-hinged garage door.

Figure 3-256. Tilt-up garage door.

Tilt-up doors (also called "*up-and-over*" doors) have a single panel. They are guided in a track at each side so that they rise and tilt backward as they open. See Figure 3-256. Their virtues are the simplicity of the door panel, potentially low air leakage, and the ability to be well insulated. Smaller models can be operated manually. They have disappeared from America, but they still seem to be available in Britain and Australia.

The bottom of a tilt-up door swings outward through the door opening when the door is opened. This requires the door width to be coordinated closely with the width of the door opening. This can make it tricky to seal the sides of the door against air leakage. The upper part of the door intrudes into the space when the door is in a partially open position.

Single-panel doors are similar to tilt-up doors, in that they have a single panel. However, the entire door remains within the garage space as it is opened, riding on a track similar to that used for sectional garage doors. This makes it relatively easy to fit the door to the opening. If installed properly, the door can seal against air leakage fairly well when closed. They main disadvantage of this type is that it intrudes a greater distance into the space when it is being opened or closed. For whatever reasons, this type seems to have vanished.

DOORS FOR VERY WIDE OPENINGS

What if you need a door that is even larger than a typical garage door? If you have a large lot, you may want a barn or a storage building for farm equipment. Or, if you live in an airport community, you may want an aircraft hangar. For such cases, you have several choices.

Sliding doors are a common choice, primarily because of their low cost and virtually unlimited size range. Sliding doors consist of full-height panels that ride on overhead tracks. By installing parallel tracks, any number of overlapping door panels can be used to cover an opening of any width.

The panels can be light because they are supported along their top edge and they hang like a curtain. As a result, large sliding doors can be opened and closed manually. The hardware is simple and standardized. It is widely available, especially in rural areas. The door panels usually are built on site from lumber, and they are covered with a sheetmetal or plywood outer surface. Figure 3-257 shows an example.

The overhead tracks must extend beyond the sides of the door opening so that the panels can clear the door opening. If there is not enough wall space alongside the door opening for this, an outrigger is built outside the building to carry the tracks. This creates a distinctive appearance.

The main weakness of sliding doors is difficulty in sealing against air leakage. If the door has only two panels that butt against each other, moderately tight sealing is practical. The sides of the door must be clamped against the wall with hardware that is available for this purpose. The top and bottom of the door are sealed with curtain-type sweeps. The joint between the two panels uses a tongue-and-groove seal.

If the door has more than two panels, sealing is more challenging. In this case, each panel must be sealed against the next with clamps and overlapping seals. These make the door much more awkward to open and close.

Hydraulic doors consist of a single panel that is built on a steel frame and is covered with sheetmetal or plywood. It is hinged at the top and opens outward. The panel is lifted upward by a pair of hydraulic pistons, one at each side. The pistons are driven by a hydraulic pump, so the door depends on electricity to operate. The bottom edge of the door is kept straight by a full-width truss, which may be mounted inside or outside the door. Figure 3-258 shows a typical example.

DRW

Figure 3-257. Large sliding door. It is suspended under a track, and it can easily be opened and closed by hand. Outriggers carry the track beyond the width of the building.

DRW

Figure 3-258. Hydraulic door. It is operated by pistons at the sides of the door. The mechanism is simple, but the opening must be reinforced to resist the leverage of the open door. A motor is required.

DRW

Figure 3-259. Bi-fold door. It is operated by a system of cables and pulleys. A motor is required.

Bi-fold doors consist of two panels, hinged horizontally in the middle. See Figure 3-259. The panels have steel frames, which are covered with sheetmetal or plywood. The door is lifted open by steel cables that run through a series of pulleys. An electric motor winds the cable on a winch.

Both hydraulic doors and bi-fold doors can be airtight and heavily insulated. Both create a strong force on the door frame that tends to tip the frame outward when the door is open. The wall structure needs to be reinforced to resist this force.

Most buildings that use one of these large doors will have a separate conventional door for quick entry. As an alternative, you can install a conventional door in any of these larger doors.

THE GARAGE DOOR OPENING

The garage door opening is more than just a big hole in the wall. Its width creates special requirements to carry the weight of the door and the weight of the structure above the opening. The force of wind acting on the large surface area of the door also stresses the structure. You will save money and avoid structural problems if you select your door and design the door opening to minimize the need for expensive strengthening. These are the main issues to consider.

Design the Opening for the Door

When you design the wall opening for your garage door, consider how the weight of the door is carried by the structure and how wind will apply pressure on the door opening. Design the door frame to make it easy to install the door assembly, including the features that block air leakage. Get the door installation manual from the manufacturer to see how the door mates with the wall opening, and design the opening accordingly.

The common sectional garage door rides in a track. When the door is closed, its weight is easily carried by the floor slab. When the door is fully open, its weight is carried by the garage ceiling structure. When the door is partially open, its weight is carried by the top of the door opening and by the ceiling structure. The strongest load comes from the pressure of high winds on the door, which is transmitted to the sides of the wall opening through the track.

Sliding doors are carried by the top of the door opening and by any track extensions (outriggers) that are installed. The opening must be designed to carry the door's weight, typically by installing the door in a gable end, as in Figure 3-257. High wind can create a powerful thrust that is transmitted from the door to the track. The top of the opening should be braced against this thrust, typically with diagonal braces that extend horizontally to the bottoms of several roof trusses.

A bi-fold door is heavy. Its weight is carried by the top of the door opening. In addition, the door exerts a strong outward tipping force on the door frame when it is open. When the door is closed, wind can create a powerful thrust on the top and sides of the wall opening. To resist these forces, reinforce the top of the door opening and brace the wall against tipping.

A hydraulic door requires similar bracing of the wall opening. In addition, the hydraulic pistons create a strong bending force on the sides of the door frame where the pistons are mounted. You can minimize this force by installing the pistons as low as possible.

Minimize the Weight that Rests Above the Opening

With some wall designs, the top of the garage door opening is supported by the structure above the opening. With other wall designs, the top of the door opening must support the weight of the structure above it. Design your home in the former way, and avoid the latter.

A good way to build the garage is to place it under its own roof gable, and to place the garage door in the gable end wall. The bottom of the outermost truss is reinforced to serve as the top of the door opening. The house in Figure 3-260 illustrates this common arrangement.

This design is strong and simple. It works well because a truss provides great rigidity with little weight or cost. Furthermore, the end truss can be designed to provide strong support along the entire width of the door opening.

A similar idea applies if the garage door is located below an upper floor in a frame wall. But, this situation is challenging because the edge of the floor above the garage dangles over the garage door opening. To support that part of the floor, use strong plywood outer sheathing above the door opening, and connect it securely to the rim joist of the floor. In this way, the frame wall acts as a truss to carry the weight of the

DRW

Figure 3-260. A garage door installed in a gable end wall. This method of installation is structurally simple, and it provides strong support for the top of the door opening.

DRW

Figure 3-261. This garage door opening requires an exceptionally strong structure to carry the weight of the brick veneer above it. Otherwise, the brick will eventually crack.

upper floor and the weight of the wall above the garage door opening.

To make this work, the sheathing must be attached securely to the rim joist of the floor above the garage door opening. This requires a strong rim joist, strong sheathing, complete overlap of the rim joist by the sheathing, and lots of nails. Builders usually don't think of sheathing as being a primary structural component, but it is. (Refer to the previous heading, *The Exterior Wall Sheathing*, under the topic, *Building Super Frame Walls*.)

Now, we come to the undesirable situation where the top of the garage door opening must support a substantial amount of weight. Figure 3-261 provides an example of this situation, where a tall masonry veneer rests on top of a wide garage door opening.

In general, masonry should not rest on top of a wide opening. The reason is that masonry has no reliable tensile strength. It can only add weight to the door opening, it cannot provide support.

In such cases, the top of the garage door opening requires a strong beam to support the load above it. A steel lintel or a wooden header for the door opening can be strong enough, but both steel and wood are

more flexible than masonry. Therefore, the lintel or header must be grossly oversized to make it stiff enough to support masonry.

(If the beam is made of wood, it usually is called a "header." If it is made of steel, it usually is called a "lintel." A garage door header or lintel acts like a bridge. The size and strength that it needs are proportional to the door width and to the weight that bears down on top of the opening.)

Any kind of garage door opening must transmit the weight of the structure above the door to the sides of the door opening. In well built houses, you will see that the sides of garage door openings are reinforced to carry this weight.

The sides of the door opening must rest on a foundation that is strong enough to carry the weight. A "grade beam," which is a continuation of the foundation that is buried under the door opening, is generally the best solution.

Block Air Leakage and Rain

The bottom of the garage door opening should be perfectly level from side to side so that the weatherstripping at the bottom of the door will seal tightly to the floor.

To block entry of rain, slope the garage floor under the door slightly toward the outside.

If the local topography causes rain to run toward the door, grade the driveway outside to create a "swale" or trough across the front of the door to carry rain around the house or to a storm drain.

Make the Opening Attractive

A wide rectangular garage door opening tends to create an industrial appearance. You can subdue this tendency in various ways. One is to create attractive trim above the opening that blends the long straight line of the header, as in Figures 3-262 and 3-263.

Another method is to decorate the door itself with fancy windows, painted designs, or other deco that breaks up the bland expanse of the door. Figure 3-264 provides an example.

Figure 3-262. Attractive curved trim above the garage door blends the wide opening into the overall style of the house.

Figure 3-263. Dramatic trim above this garage door subdues its wide appearance.

Figure 3-264. A curved opening and a painted scene avoids a plain appearance for this garage door. The painting is a vinyl film decal. A variety of decals for garage doors are commercially available.

Skylights

In Step 2, you designed the layout for any skylights that you may wish to install. To select your skylights, use the adjacent *Skylight Selection Guide*, which covers the options that are offered with commercially available skylights.

SKYLIGHT RATINGS

In the United States and some other countries, skylights are assigned ratings to help you distinguish the quality of different models. The NFRC Energy Performance Ratings for skylights are similar to the NFRC ratings for windows, which we described previously. Despite the name, the NFRC ratings cover a variety of characteristics, not just energy efficiency. Refer to our previous explanation of the NFRC window ratings to understand the corresponding skylight ratings.

ROOF FRAMING FOR SKYLIGHTS

In a beam roof, installing skylights is simple. Make a hole in the roof between the rafters, install two headers to form a rectangular frame, and install the skylight using conventional methods to avoid water leaks.

In a truss or attic roof, you need to build a light shaft between the trusses to carry daylight from the skylight to the ceiling of the room. The light shaft needs to be insulated as well as any other part of your ceiling. Make sure that the shaft does not make it difficult to install insulation or wiring in any part of the attic.

AVOID LEAKS

Roof leakage around skylights is a common problem that you need to confront. Every part of the connection between the skylight and the surrounding roofing material is a potential site for leaks. The top side of a rectangular skylight is an especially vulnerable area. Round skylights may be less vulnerable.

A skylight is less likely to leak if it has a one-piece mounting all around, with welded seams. Not all skylights are made this way. That's because seamless mountings create a lot of dead space in shipping boxes, making them more expensive to ship and taking up more space in the warehouse. So, search for this feature.

Also, give priority to all the features in the *Skylight Selection Guide* that minimize leakage.

Install your skylights on curbs that have appropriate height for the amount of rainfall or snowfall in your location. The curb should rise above the deepest snow that can accumulate on the uphill side of the skylight. If the skylight is far below the top of the roof, snow that slides off the uphill portion of the roof will build up against the skylight.

SKYLIGHT SELECTION GUIDE

☐ Skylight Types

The most durable kind of skylight is essentially a glass window with an aluminum frame that lies over the roof opening, as in Figure 3-270. Like windows, the skylight may have multiple glazing, it may be fixed or openable, and it may have the full range of energy saving features that are offered by windows. In addition, some skylights offer translucent insulation between double glazing, which improves R-value but reduces light transmission.

Another type of skylight uses domed plastic glazing that is held in place with a metal frame. Figure 3-271 is an example. To improve insulation value, two domes are used, one inside the other. This type is prone to leakage around the frame.

Contrary to intuition, the domed shape of the glazing provides no advantage. The plastic glazing becomes brittle with sunlight exposure, so the skylight has a lifespan that is limited to a few decades. This type is now largely superseded by flat glass skylights.

Round skylights, as in Figure 3-272, are becoming available. These probably have better resistance to leakage at the roof connection because the round shape diverts water around them.

The plastic glazing limits the lifespan of the dome, but the domes typically are designed to be easily replaceable. The cylindrical curb should be well insulated, typically with foam insulation between an inner and outer metal shell.

You can buy skylights with other top shapes, such as cylinders and pyramids, but these shapes generally are limited to larger sizes that are used in commercial buildings. Such shapes offer no advantages, and they multiply the risk of leaks through exposed seals.

☐ Size

Skylights are available in virtually any size you would want. The most common models have widths to fit within standard rafter spacing.

Step 2 explains how to select the area of your skylights for good daylighting, to avoid excessive heat loss in cold weather, and to minimize heat gain during warm weather.

DRW

Figure 3-270. Typical flat glass skylights. The lack of elevated curbs makes the skylights more vulnerable to leakage.

DRW

Figure 3-271. A skylight of domed plastic, held in an aluminum frame. This unit has two domes, one inside the other, for improved insulation value.

DRW

Figure 3-272. A round skylight. This one has a double dome, improving its insulation value. The cylindrical body should be well insulated. The curb height here is adequate only for limited snowfall.

SKYLIGHT SELECTION GUIDE

☐ Curbs, Flashing, and Water Deflectors

A skylight may be attached directly to the roof sheathing with clips, in which case it is called "deck mounted." A deck mounted skylight may be satisfactory if the roofing material is thin, like shingles and sheetmetal, and if the climate is dry.

For climates that have any amount of rain or snow, and with thick roof coverings like tile, the skylight should be mounted on a "curb," as in Figure 3-273. A curb is like the sides of a rectangular box that elevates the glazing above the roof surface. Curbs may be built separately as part of the roof structure, or they may be integral with the skylight. Integral curbs, including flashing, are the best choice. Prefabricated curbs typically are offered with heights from 4" to 6" (10 to 15 cm). This is not tall enough for heavy snow, but then, you should not install skylights in snowy climates.

Skylights should also have integral "flashing,"

DRW

Figure 3-273. Skylights with taller curbs, which reduce the risk of leakage around the top of the skylight during deep snowfall.

which is a wide flange that fits under the surrounding roof covering. This feature helps to resist leaks between the skylight frame and the roof deck. It also serves as an easy method of attaching the skylight to the roof deck.

Until recently, virtually all residential skylights have had rectangular frames. This shape makes skylights easy to make and to install. However, the upper end of the skylight acts as a dam for water and snow. Leaks are likely to begin here. Roofers have never figured out a foolproof way of making a

watertight connection around a rectangular skylight. Other things being equal, a narrower skylight is less likely to leak.

By the time you read this, you may be able to buy rectangular skylights that have an upper side deflector to divert rain and snow to the side. (This feature, called a "cricket," has long been used with rectangular chimneys.)

☐ Materials and Longevity

The main glazing materials for skylights are glass or polycarbonate plastic. Glass lasts indefinitely, but the sealing materials that are needed with glass skylights have a limited life, perhaps 10 to 30 years. Plastic glazing has a similar life span.

All skylights have limited longevity, so select them for easy repair or replacement. For example, if you select skylights that have plastic domes, select models for which the domes can be replaced easily and repeatedly far into the future.

Skylights are exposed to impact from anything falling out of the sky, including hail, broken branches, fruit, drug shipments, etc. Glass should be impact-resistant. In a double-glazed skylight, the top glass should be "tempered" and extra thick. The bottom pane usually is laminated, consisting of two thin sheets of glass with a plastic sheet at the center that holds the glass together if it breaks. This is important for keeping shards of broken glass from falling into the house.

The strength of glazing is determined by the material and by its thickness. Plastic glazing is much less dangerous than glass if it breaks.

The main frame materials are aluminum and wood. Aluminum frames have a very long life if the alloy is selected properly and if it is properly coated. Enamel applied over an anodized surface is the most durable coating.

Wooden components may last for centuries, but they must be totally isolated from weather and moisture leakage. Wood that is exposed to the inside of the house must be painted. Plastic coatings over wood will eventually peel, so avoid them.

The seals in skylights are rubber-like materials that have limited life. Sealing materials exposed to sunlight and the elements will endure no longer than a decade or so. Therefore, the frame design should protect all sealing materials from exposure, and should provide a safe bypass for water that leaks through aged seals.

SKYLIGHT SELECTION GUIDE

University of California

Figure 3-274. A skylight that can be opened for ventilation.

☐ Fixed or Openable Glazing

Openable skylights are widely available. Figure 3-274 is typical. The glazing is hinged at the top, and usually opens only by a small angle, so the glazing always remains sloped downward. Despite their popularity, skylights that open generally are not desirable.

The main appeal of openable skylights is to provide ventilation for cooling during warm weather. This is mostly an illusion. During warm weather, the air inside the house is cooler than the air outside. Therefore, air pools inside the house, rather than rising to the outside. Also, skylights are not well situated for cross ventilation.

Openable skylights become less airtight as they age, leaking air to the outside during cold weather. They need to be opened and closed with long rods, or dangling cords, or electric motors that have remote controls. All of these are a nuisance, and the actuators are likely to fail early in the life of the house.

If you would like ventilation through a triangle-frame roof, install dormers with openable windows, rather than skylights.

☐ Frame Construction to Prevent Leaks

With window-style skylights, rain that drains off the glazing must cross the lower end of the frame, which forms a small trough. The glazing seal will eventually fail at this point, allowing rain to leak through. The frame should be designed so that any leakage through the glazing seals will follow the inside of the frame and drain to the roof on the downhill side of the frame.

The other predictable location for leaks is around the base of the curb. Careful installation of the roofing material is required to prevent leaks there. Integral flashing will help considerably, but it cannot guarantee against leaks. Preventing leaks around the base of skylights is in the hands of the roofing installers.

To be sure that skylights will bypass leaks as well as possible, try to examine a cross section of the frame, as you did for your windows.

☐ Insulating Features

Skylights have higher heat loss than similar windows. Hidden away in the engineering literature is the fact that the heat loss through glazing approximately doubles when the glazing is installed in a horizontal or steeply slanted orientation, compared to glazing that is installed vertically.

For conventional skylights, the primary way to reduce heat loss is to increase the number of panes. Triple glazing is unusual in skylights, but you can find it.

With conventional glass skylights, the insulating features offered by manufacturers are the same as for windows, namely, multiple glazing, low-E coatings, spectrally selective coatings, and insulating gas. Multi-glazed glass skylights have the same kinds of edge seals as windows.

Since skylight frames are made of aluminum, they need effective thermal breaks. These are made in the same way as for windows. If the skylight has a curb, the curb needs good insulation also.

Some manufacturers offer skylights with translucent insulation placed between the inner and outer panes. So far, these offer no net advantage, because light transmission is reduced by about the same fraction as the heat loss.

☐ Protection Against Condensation

Because of their poor R-value, skylights produce more condensation than windows. They may sweat profusely even when windows do not. Because of their overhead location, condensation may drip directly into the room. If the skylight is mounted on a slant, condensation may flow downhill on the surface of the glazing to damage the surrounding framework and trim.

SKYLIGHT SELECTION GUIDE

The tendency of skylights to sweat is increased by the fact that moist air from cooking, washing, bathing, and humidifiers is warmer than the surrounding air, so it tends to rise to the skylights. Also, water vapor itself is lighter than air.

The best defense against condensation is not to install skylights in cold climates. If you do, get the best insulation value for the glazing and frame. Unfortunately, ordinary skylight glazing lacks sufficient insulation value to prevent condensation, unless the climate is dry. Aluminum frames need effective thermal breaks, but even these will not stop condensation during cold weather.

Well made skylights have condensation gutters that are an integral part of the frame. Located at the underside of the frame, the gutter collects condensation that forms overnight and holds it until warming by sunlight and home heating evaporate the water. Condensation gutters provide relief only from condensation that flows into them. They can't protect against condensation that drips directly off the glazing.

☐ Diffusing Glazing

In Step 2, you learned that the light from skylights must be diffused in order to be pleasant and useful. The easiest and most efficient way to diffuse sunlight is by using diffusing glazing in the skylight itself.

If the skylight has double glazing, only one pane should be diffusing. The diffusing pane will reflect and absorb a significant amount of light. If you want to minimize the heat that is brought into the house, select the outermost surface as the diffuser. If you want to keep as much heat as possible inside the house, select the innermost surface as the diffuser.

If the major manufacturers of glass skylights do not offer diffusing glass, keep looking. You will be able to find it somewhere. Plastic skylights commonly offer diffusing glazing as an option, but generally you don't want plastic glazing.

If you select skylights that have translucent insulation between the panes, the insulation will diffuse sunlight adequately.

☐ Tinted Glazing

Avoid tinted glazing, it is illogical. If the tinting is needed to reduce light intensity, then the skylight is too big. Tinted glazing does not diffuse direct sunlight. To diffuse sunlight, use diffusing glazing.

☐ Integral Shading Devices

If you have designed the house properly, your skylights generally should not need any shading devices. If a skylight needs shading to reduce daylight intensity, then the skylight is too big or the sunlight is not properly diffused. Don't install skylights in rooms that need shading for privacy or to darken the room.

Some skylights include adjustable shading louvers between the panes of glass. The internal shading mechanisms will fail long before the rest of the skylight, and repair will be difficult or impossible. Such gadgets require penetration through the window seal, inviting condensation inside the unit.

Some skylights have fabric curtains below the skylight, on runners. The fabric can't last long in the presence of strong sunlight, and repair is likely to be difficult.

Shading devices need to be operated with long rods, or dangling cords, or electric motors that have remote controls. All of these are a nuisance, and the actuators are likely to fail early in the life of the house.

YOUR FLOOR SURFACE OPTIONS

Now, we will complete your home's structure by installing the visible wearing surfaces on the floors. There are no innovations here, but consider all the important issues. To help you select your floor surface, Table 3-6, *Floor Surface Comparison*, summarizes the advantages and disadvantages of the floor surfaces that you are most likely to want. We will also summarize the key selection and installation issues for each of these floors.

You can find other kinds of flooring, but they generally offer little benefit. For example, bamboo is now offered as a "green" floor surface, but it is actually a boutique item that may not wear well. Fake wood flooring is now made from recycled plastic, but it looks insipid and its durability is doubtful.

There is one tricky issue that you need to work into your overall floor design. Different types of floor surfaces have different thicknesses. These range from fairly thin for sheet flooring to very thick for ceramic tile. You don't want the surface height to change from one room to the next, so try to equalize the total thickness of the floor in all adjacent rooms. Otherwise, you will need to install a threshold between rooms, which invites stumbling.

With wood floor structures, the usual way to equalize the height of floor surfaces is to install an extra layer of plywood under thin flooring materials, as in a kitchen that uses sheet flooring. With concrete floors, you can apply a layer of material that is designed specifically for leveling and adjusting the height of concrete floors.

Avoid slippery floor surfaces anywhere. Any portion of a floor will get wet at some time, so select all flooring to resist slipping when wet. Floor tiles should be relatively small, and they should have a textured surface. Smaller area rugs that cover smooth floors, such as hardwood, should have non-skid bottom surfaces or they should be laid over a non-skid mat.

HARDWOOD STRIP FLOORING

With wooden floor structures, hardwood strip flooring is often the best floor surface for formal rooms. Figure 3-280 is a nice example. A hardwood floor can be enhanced by inlays of contrasting wood and by stenciling. For these enhancements, you need to find a craftsman with the appropriate skills.

Hardwood is inherently attractive, it lasts for the life of the house, and it is easy to clean. But, it is vulnerable to denting by furniture and to scuffing by shoes. As a

Shutterstock

Figure 3-280. An attractive hardwood strip floor.

result, area rugs are almost always used to protect areas of wear. The combination of rugs on a hardwood floor can be very attractive, and it ages gracefully.

The hardwood is laid over a subfloor. Pre-finished hardwood flooring is becoming common. It eliminates the need for staining and varnishing the wood. Care is needed to avoid chipping the edges when this flooring is cut.

Unfinished hardwood may be sanded after installation to remove small differences in height between adjacent strips. Then, the wood may be stained to any desired color. The wood should be covered with several coats of urethane varnish, which hardens the surface and seals the pores of the wood so that it will not absorb dirt.

Nowadays, hardwood flooring has tongue-and-groove sides, which eliminate gaps and reduce squeaks. The strips are attached by nails driven through the sides of the strips into the subfloor, so the nails are invisible. In cheaper installations, only adhesive is used.

Squeaking has been a historical annoyance of hardwood floors. It is caused by rubbing between the hardwood strips and the subfloor. You can eliminate squeaks by making the floor structure perfectly flat, as it is with I-joists and plywood subfloors. Start with hardwood that is properly dried, so that it will not warp.

Table 3-6. Floor Surface Comparison

Floor Surface	Advantages	Disadvantages
Hardwood Strip (*usually used with area rugs)	• Lasts for the life of the house. • Inherently attractive. • Easy to sweep.	• Squeaks if floor structure and installation are not perfect. • Needs rugs to protect traffic areas. • Needs refinishing at long intervals.
Hardwood Parquet (*usually used with area rugs)	• Inherently attractive. • Long life. • Range of style options. • Easy to sweep.	• Needs rugs to protect traffic areas. • Needs refinishing at long intervals. • Usually attached with cement, requiring repair at long intervals.
Wall-to-Wall Carpet (*may be accented by area rugs)	• Warm to bare feet. • Absorbs sound. • Many texture and style options. • Relatively inexpensive. • Hides defects in floor.	• Easily stained. • Difficult to clean. • Retains dirt and allergens. • Needs replacement at long intervals.
Sheet Flooring	• Waterproof. • Easy to clean. • Many appearance options. • Skid-resistant surfaces available. • Yielding surfaces available.	• Slippery when wet. • Easily scuffed or scratched. • Needs replacement at long intervals.
Composition Floor Tile	• Easy to clean. • Easy to install. • Many appearance options. • Skid-resistant surfaces available.	• Slippery when wet. • Vulnerable to moisture penetration. • Easily scuffed or scratched. • Individual tiles curl and break loose when adhesive ages.
Ceramic Floor Tile (*may be used with area rugs)	• Lasts for the life of the house. • Durable surface. • Inherently attractive. • Vast range of style options. • Waterproof.	• Grout lines and non-skid surfaces are laborious to clean. • Cold to bare feet. • Requires rigid supporting surface. • Skilled installation is critical.
Terrazzo (*may be used with area rugs)	• Lasts for the life of the house. • Durable surface. • Waterproof.	• Slippery when wet. • Cold to bare feet. • Requires special skill to install.
Concrete Paint	• Many color options, allowing unlimited designs. • Easy to clean. • Easy to repair and touch up. • Seals surface against oil and water. • Prevents dusting of concrete. • Inexpensive.	• Limited life. • Needs skilled application for more elaborate designs. • Slippery when wet. • Hard, cold surface.
*Area Rugs	• Warm to bare feet. • Unlimited style options. • Easily moved and replaced. • Absorbs sound. • Easily removed for cleaning.	• Skid on smooth surfaces, need non-skid backing or mat. • Easily stained. • Expensive to clean. • Retain dirt and allergens.

The subfloor should be thick enough so that it does not yield under the weight of traffic. The final touch is to use adhesive to attach the hardwood to the subfloor, in addition to the nails.

Installing wood flooring on a concrete slab is problematic. There are procedures for it, but none of them seem reliable, especially in the face of moisture. If the slab lies on grade, moisture penetration is likely, at least in spots. Moisture will warp the wood and infest it with mildew.

HARDWOOD PARQUET

A hardwood parquet floor can be a dazzling accent. Parquet comes in several styles and wood species, so you can use different parquet in different rooms. But don't overdo it. Parquet has an opulent appearance that goes best with large formal rooms, as in Figure 3-281.

DRW

Figure 3-281. Parquet floor in a living room.

Don't use it in relatively plain rooms.

Parquet is installed as square tiles, typically one foot (30 cm) on a side. The tiles have tongue-and-groove sides, which makes them relatively easy to install. Usually, they are attached with adhesive only. This is a weakness because adhesives eventually deteriorate. Edge nailing, as used for hardwood strip flooring, is generally impractical because parquet tiles are thin.

Most parquet tile is offered with a surface finish. For example, teak parquet typically has an oil finish or light varnish that requires cleaning and oiling at long intervals. Darker woods may have a durable urethane finish.

Parquet generally is applied over a wooden subfloor. Installation on other surfaces is risky. Some manufacturers claim that parquet can be installed on a concrete slab and other surfaces, but those surfaces would have to be rigid, flat, and perfectly dry at all times.

WALL-TO-WALL CARPET

Wall-to-wall carpet is popular because it offers a combination of benefits. It is warm and soft, it absorbs noise, it is available in many styles and textures, it does not require a special subfloor material, and it can be inexpensive (or just plain cheap).

When installed over a wooden subfloor, it is usually attached at the edges. This makes the carpet easy to replace. When installed over a concrete slab, carpet is attached with an adhesive.

Wall-to-wall carpet is limited to floors that do not become wet or very dirty. Typical locations are bedrooms, living rooms, and offices. Don't lay carpet on a floor that may become damp, such as a floor slab in a house built on wet ground. Mildew would quickly infest the carpet and ruin it, creating a health hazard in the process.

Generally, favor carpet with a shorter pile. This makes it easier to clean. If you want a fluffy carpet for lounging on the floor, buy a separate area rug or a bear skin to lay on top of the main carpet.

Deeply entrenched dirt, stains (such as from pet urine), and mildew require replacing the carpet.

SHEET FLOORING

Sheet flooring is a plastic material that comes in wide rolls. It is available in a multitude of patterns. It is waterproof and easy to clean. With a wooden floor structure, sheet flooring is cemented to the subfloor. With a concrete floor, it is cemented directly to the slab. Expect good sheet flooring to last several decades before it starts to look scuffed and the adhesive fails.

Sheet flooring is the preferred choice for kitchens, and it is a good choice for toilet rooms that do not have a shower or tub. It can provide a finished appearance for a concrete slab floor. Figure 3-282 shows a kitchen application.

Armstrong

Figure 3-282. Attractive vinyl sheet floor for a kitchen.

DRW

Figure 3-283. Ceramic floor tile that provides both a beautiful accent and a fireproof surface around a wood stove.

When purchasing sheet flooring, the most important characteristic is durability. The material is vulnerable to scuffing and to damage from falling tools, spiked golf shoes, and such. The pattern is printed on the top surface, and it will fade after years of exposure to direct sunlight. The better grades offer a surface that is tougher than the base material, and it is impermeable to dirt. To reduce the risk of slipping if the floor gets wet, the surface of some sheet flooring is roughened and "grout lines" in a tile pattern may be recessed.

Some sheet flooring is made extra thick and cushiony to reduce fatigue from standing. It is doubtful that this actually works, and the spongy nature of the material makes it more vulnerable to damage. A more practical solution is to buy a rubber fatigue mat to lay on the floor.

DRW

Figure 3-284. A variety of ceramic tiles are used for the floors, walls, and ceiling of a shower room.

COMPOSITION FLOOR TILE

Composition floor tile is made of material similar to sheet flooring. The main difference is that the material is cut into small squares, or tiles. Its only advantage is that it is less awkward to install than sheet flooring. Because of the exposed edges, composition tile does not create a waterproof surface. Also, the exposed edges will eventually curl as the adhesive fails.

Composition tile is a compromise that offers no benefits worth pursuing. Sheet flooring or ceramic tiles are better choices.

CERAMIC FLOOR TILE

Ceramic tile is perhaps the most beautiful and the most durable floor surface that you can install. Figure 3-283 shows an area of tile that accents a living room while acting as a fireproof zone around a wood stove. Figure 3-284 shows tile used in a shower room, where separate kinds of tile are used for the floor, walls, and ceiling of the shower itself, and for the outside floor.

Don't install ceramic tile where it would be exposed to both wetting and freezing. Such conditions would break the cement attachment, and perhaps break the tile itself.

The main factor in achieving a great tile floor is the competence of the installer. Tile work requires both artistic sense and knowledge of the preparation needed to provide a firm base for the tile. Unfortunately, only a fraction of people doing tile work understand the requirements of the art, and the rest leave disappointment in their wake.

Therefore, if you are considering a tile floor for any part of your home, you have more homework to do before you can select your tile layer. Well illustrated books about tile are available at hardware stores. They spell out the important differences between the types of tiles, they explain the essential preparation work that tile requires, and they give you a host of appearance ideas.

TERRAZZO

Terrazzo is an option to consider for formal rooms that are built on a concrete floor slab. It consists of attractive minerals that are embedded in cement or, more recently, in a resin. The minerals can be almost anything, such as pebbles, pieces of fossilized rock, colored glass beads, and various combinations. What you see is mostly the cross sections of the embedded material, outlined in cement. Such floors can be beautiful, creating a mosaic effect. The pattern may be random, or it may be a detailed figure. See Figure 3-285.

Creating a terrazzo floor requires exceptional skill and specialized equipment. The installer lays the cement base so that it will bond well to the concrete. Small embedded material may be mixed with the cement, while larger material must be laid into the cement while it is wet. After the cement hardens, a rotary grinder is used with successively finer grit to create a flat, polished surface.

You must be sure that the underlying slab will never crack, because if the slab cracks, the terrazzo will crack also and it will look ugly. Cracks in terrazzo are almost impossible to repair in an attractive way.

Terrazzo is expensive. Unfortunately, you won't know how well your terrazzo floor turns out until the grinding and polishing are completed. If you are disappointed, you probably won't be able to improve it.

Terrazzo is a cold, hard surface, so you would supplement it with area rugs unless the climate is always warm. Terrazzo is thick, so using it adjacent to other surfaces, such as floor tiles, requires building up the other surfaces.

Unlike ordinary tile floors, terrazzo has no grout lines and it is very smooth. This makes it especially dangerous if the floor can get wet.

Terrazzo tiles are an alternative to a continuous terrazzo floor. They are made in the same way as a terrazzo floor, so they are thick. Their main advantage is that you know how the floor will appear before it is installed. At their best, terrazzo tiles can look almost as good as a continuous terrazzo floor. Terrazzo tiles are laid in the same way as other floor tiles, except that the tiles butt together without grout spaces. Because of this, the edges of the tiles must align perfectly. This requires a flat, rigid base.

Here's my recommendation. If you are covering a concrete slab, use ceramic tile instead of terrazzo. Tile gives you a broader range of appearance options, its appearance is predictable, it requires less skill to install, and individual tiles can be replaced if they crack.

Figure 3-285. Corner detail of an exceptionally attractive terrazzo floor. The technique used here is framing the random pattern of the pebbles with tile mosaics.

CONCRETE PAINT

If a space has an exposed concrete floor slab, you can dress it up considerably by using concrete paint. Newer polymer paints can be durable. They keep the concrete from dusting, and they seal the surface against water and oil. Still, the surface remains hard and cold.

Most commonly, paint is used for garages, driveways, concrete patios, and informal spaces, such as a workshop. Concrete paint would be an unusual choice for a formal room, but see Figure 3-286. Concrete paint may be the best way to dress up a concrete slab that is subject to moisture penetration, which would destroy other floor coverings. To prevent scuffing of the paint by furniture, use coasters or pads. With a reliably dry floor, you can use area rugs.

The appearance of a painted concrete floor is limited mainly by your imagination and the artistic ability of the painter. With nothing more than masking tape and a few colors, you can create a floor design that is much more interesting than a bare monochrome. Stencils for painting a wide variety of patterns on a concrete floor are available from several sources.

If you have the opportunity to decorate a concrete floor, start by studying the various techniques of preparing the concrete surface and protecting the paint.

AREA RUGS

Area rugs are used in combination with other floor surfaces, as in Figure 3-286. They make it practical to use other flooring materials, such as hardwood or tile. They provide warmth and softness, and they prevent damage to the main floor from concentrated furniture loads, scuffing of shoes, etc. They can be a powerful esthetic feature, providing color, texture, and shape to the room decor.

In comparison to wall-to-wall carpeting, area rugs provide a much broader variety of patterns and themes. With a few rugs, you can create or highlight almost any room style, from Persian to Pueblo. Area rugs can even be attractive accents over wall-to-wall carpeting. They are easy to replace or to remove for cleaning.

The main disadvantage of area rugs is their tendency to skid over a smooth floor. A small area rug without a non-skid backing will eventually cause a nasty fall unless the rug is anchored by heavy furniture. Even large area rugs can skid at the edges. Some area rugs are available with an integral non-skid bottom, but generally not elegant ones. For those, you will need to cut non-skid material to fit between the rug and the floor. This is a nuisance, and it is not entirely reliable.

Royal Design Studio Stencils

Figure 3-286. A stenciled design decorates the concrete floor of a bedroom in Morocco.

STEP 4

PERFECT HEATING, COOLING, AND VENTILATION

Your home will keep you comfortable under all weather conditions. We designed the structure to keep you comfortable with a minimum of energy. However, the structure can't always do the job alone. In most climates, it needs help from equipment that the construction industry calls "comfort systems." These systems perform heating, ventilation, and air conditioning, so they are also called "HVAC systems."

Today, the HVAC industry offers a daunting menu of equipment choices. Fortunately, we can narrow the choices to two heating and cooling combinations that are best for most homes. We will decide which one is best for you. Then, we will explain the critical features of your system so that you can make sure that it is installed flawlessly.

After that, we select special heating and cooling equipment for certain rooms. We learn how to provide cooling at low cost by using ventilation, and in some locations, by using evaporative coolers. We design the ventilation throughout the house for health and odor control. And, we select the most effective and economical methods of controlling humidity.

If you are renovating an existing house or just replacing worn out equipment, your best choices usually are the same as for a new house.

Until late in the 19th century, the only comfort systems in houses were fireplaces and heating stoves. These were replaced by steam heating, and then by a rapidly growing variety of other heating equipment. These innovations improved comfort and convenience radically. The cost of heating remained stable because the new equipment improved the efficiency of fuel burning and because a greater variety of fuels became available.

Central forced-air heating became the norm in much of the world, but it can now be replaced with heating that is safer, more comfortable, and much more efficient. In this Step, we will recommend just the right kind of heating for each room in your home.

Until the middle of the 20th century, keeping a home cool during warm weather was limited to shading the home from sunlight and waiting until nightfall, when outside air ventilation could be used for cooling. Mechanical air conditioning equipment changed that, making it possible to cool the inside of a house independently of outside conditions. Window air conditioners were the first common type of cooling equipment for home use, following by central air conditioning, and now by "split-system" air conditioners.

Home cooling added a large new cost to the household budget. In many population centers, the cost of cooling now exceeds the cost of heating. We will greatly lower your air conditioning costs by selecting the most efficient type of system, and by using it most effectively.

Also, we will learn to optimize older methods of cooling that use air circulation fans. These can provide comfortable cooling during much of the warm season, especially at night.

In dry climates, evaporative cooling is a less expensive alternative to air conditioning, but it has major shortcomings. We will learn where to use it and where not to.

In moist climates, air conditioning provides a benefit of lowering humidity as well as lowering the temperature. However, air conditioning is unsatisfactory for lowering humidity when the climate is humid but temperatures are moderate. For those conditions, we will use dehumidifiers to control humidity. In addition, we will use dehumidifiers to supplement air conditioning, improving comfort while lowering cost.

Ventilation is important for health, odor control, natural cooling, and venting of moisture from damp spaces. We will use a combination of ventilation fans and outside air intakes to optimize each of these functions throughout your home.

MAIN HEATING AND COOLING RECOMMENDATIONS

We will begin with your biggest HVAC decision, which is selecting the best combination of primary heating and cooling equipment. For the great majority of geographic locations, one of these two heating/cooling configurations is best for the main parts of a house:

• **a fuel-fired "hydronic" system for heating, and single-room split-system air conditioners (or heat pumps) for cooling**

or

• **single-room split-system heat pumps for both heating and cooling.**

The main difference between these two configurations is the method of heating. Both configurations use the same kinds of heat pumps (or air conditioners) for cooling.

The choice between the two is determined primarily by the climate of your home site and by the energy sources that are available there. Hydronic heating usually is the best choice in climates that have an extended cold season. They can use any kind of fuel, but they are not appropriate if electricity is your only heating energy source. Heat pumps may be the best choice in climates that do not experience very cold weather, especially if natural gas service is not available at the home site.

Heat pumps have the unique advantage of providing both heating and cooling. In locations where heat pumps are suitable, they provide heat from electricity much more economically than electric resistance heating. In some cases (depending on location and the future of energy supplies), they may have lower energy cost than heating equipment that uses fossil fuels. Unfortunately, heat pumps have significant disadvantages that keeps them from being a good choice in colder climates.

If you are upgrading an existing house, either of these two recommended systems is relatively easy to retrofit, in most cases. If you replace an existing forced-air system with a hydronic system, the boiler and its accessories can be installed in the same space where the original furnace was located. The system pipes are much smaller than the original air ducts.

Split-system heat pumps and air conditioners are relatively easy to add to most existing houses. An appearance challenge is to hide the refrigerant pipes from view, which can be done with a variety of decorative tricks.

Table 4-1. HEATING EQUIPMENT COMPARISON*

SELECTION ISSUE	FUEL-FIRED HYDRONIC	HEAT PUMPS	ELECTRIC RESISTANCE	DIRECT-FIRED SPACE HEATERS
Heats and cools?	No.	Yes.	No.	No.
Energy source and energy cost	Can use any energy source that is available at the home site.	Electricity. Provides heat at a fraction of the cost of electric resistance heating.	Electricity. The most expensive method of using electricity for heating.	Usually natural gas or propane. Larger units may burn oil.
Favorable applications	Primary heating in colder climates.	Primary heating in locations that are warm enough for efficient operation, if a gas fuel is not available at lower cost.	Supplemental heating for small spaces, especially shower and toilet rooms.	Heating for informal spaces that are used occasionally. Sealed-combustion units are satisfactory for living spaces.
Installation cost	Boiler is moderately expensive. Fuel oil and propane require tanks. Most room heating equipment is inexpensive.	Each system is fairly expensive, and several systems may be needed for an entire house. But, saves the cost of separate cooling equipment.	Least expensive heating equipment, by far.	Less than heat pump, more than hydronic room heater.
Isolation of heating to individual spaces.	Very good. Has small system losses.	Almost ideal. Inside units are designed for individual spaces.	Ideal. Units are designed for individual spaces.	Ideal. Units are designed for individual spaces.
Thermal comfort	Very comfortable. Various kinds of room heating units can be selected to optimize comfort.	Good during milder weather. Lower heating air temperatures can be uncomfortable during colder weather. Indoor air distribution requires compromise between heating and cooling.	Baseboard convectors provide uniform, low-intensity heating. Fan-forced heaters provide more intense, localized heating.	Air discharge is warm and strong, localized to vicinity of heater.
Noise	Convection heaters are silent. Fan-forced heaters are audible. Boilers are fairly quiet.	For the best units, noise is fairly low, both inside and outside.	Convection heaters are silent. Fan-forced heaters are audible.	Moderate. Sound level varies among models.
Maintenance requirements	Gas-fired boilers need only minimal maintenance. Oil-fired boilers require periodic cleaning. Room heaters require little or no maintenance.	Heat pumps last 10 to 20 years in normal usage. Occasional filter and coil cleaning are needed.	Convection heating units last indefinitely. Fan-forced heating units last for decades.	Gas-fueled heaters have long lives, require repair at long intervals. Oil-fired heaters also require periodic cleaning.

*Notes:
• Central forced-air furnaces are not included. They are undesirable in comparison with the equipment in the table, for virtually all applications. The reasons are covered in the sidebar, *Why You Don't Want Central Forced-Air Heating and Cooling*.
• Floor heating is available with hydronic systems and with electric resistance heat. Hydronic floor heating is treated as a type of hydronic room heater. Electric floor heating is treated as a type of electric resistance heater.

WHY YOU DON'T WANT CENTRAL FORCED-AIR HEATING OR COOLING

 You may wonder why we don't recommend central forced-air heating as an option for your home, even though it is the most popular type of heating in North America. The reason is that forced-air heating has serious deficiencies when it is used to serve multiple rooms. When a central air system is also used for air conditioning, even more problems arise.

Heating and cooling cannot be limited to individual spaces. Both furnaces and central air conditioners require air flow that remains within a narrow range, which is sized for the entire house. You can't reduce the air flow very much without causing unstable operation of the furnace or freezing the inside coil of the air conditioner. This defies one of the prime principles of energy efficiency, which is heating or cooling each room independently.

A central system cannot provide good temperature control of individual spaces. Only the area where the central thermostat is located has accurate temperature control. In modern houses, the ducts are too small because they are threaded through the narrow walls and floor joists of the house. The small ducts and their tight turns resist air flow, creating uncomfortable temperature differences between rooms.

An air return path is needed, which limits privacy and transmits noise. The air supplied to each room must return to the furnace, so doors must be left open. Or, grilles must be installed in interior doors or walls.

In multi-story houses, ducts increase air temperature stratification from floor to floor. The supply and return ducts connect all the rooms of the house. During the periods when the furnace or air conditioner is not running – which is most of the time – warm air will rise through the ducts and cooler air will fall. As a result, the upper floors will always be warmer than the lower floors.

When cooling the house, the ducts act as drains to the lowest point in the system. The denser chilled air falls into the floor registers instead of staying in the room, wasting a significant amount of cooling energy. Typically, the air falls into the furnace in the basement, where it leaks into the basement through the air filter opening.

The ductwork wastes energy. Duct leaks waste heated and cooled air into the walls and other idle spaces. Ducts and their fittings resist air flow, which increases the fan energy. And, heat escapes from the metal walls of the ducts by conduction. Running ducts through attic spaces is especially wasteful, leaking heated or cooled air to the outside.

Ducts create health hazards. If you look inside a heating duct that is a few years old, you will want to stop breathing. Ducts are traps for every bad thing that floats around in the air, including dust, allergens, and microorganisms. It would be fine if all those contaminants remained in the ducts, but they break loose and they may periodically enter the living space at high concentrations. Also, if there is a basement or other damp area where mold grows, the duct system will transport the mold spores throughout the house.

If the duct system is used for air conditioning, the cold outside surfaces of the ducts will sweat, causing mold and mildew around the ducts.

Forced-air systems have air filters, but ordinary filters block only large dust particles. You can install high-efficiency filters, but this requires a powerful fan to overcome the resistance of the filter. Only certain models of furnaces have fans that are powerful enough for this. In any case, you have to change the filters regularly, which is messy.

Ducts waste space. The main ducts from the furnace clutter the basement ceiling. If ducts of adequate size are used, they require special enclosures (called "chases") where they pass through the living space.

A furnace can leak combustion gases into the house. The furnace has a thin metal heat exchanger that separates the combustion gases from the air that circulates through the house. If a leak develops in the heat exchanger, the combustion products – including carbon monoxide – will mix with the air you breathe.

Well..., if central forced-air heating has all these problems, why is it still used? Because a furnace can warm the air in a house quickly, and because the same system can be used for both heating and cooling. But, these benefits are no longer unique to central systems. It's time for builders to shed obsolete habits and to learn the benefits of the improved heating and cooling systems that this book recommends.

Even though you choose one of these two configurations as the main comfort system for your house, heating of some rooms may be done better by other kinds of equipment. The most common example is using electric resistance heaters for supplemental heating of toilet and shower rooms. Electric heaters may be best for small spaces that are used only occasionally, such as a basement work bench. A fuel-fired air heater may be best for a single large space, such as the garage, that needs to be heated quickly. We will cover these and other kinds of heaters and their applications.

Table 4-1, *Heating Equipment Comparison*, highlights the main differences between hydronic systems, heat pumps, and two other kinds of heating equipment that you may want to use for special rooms.

In mild climates, especially in smaller homes, some secondary types of heating equipment may serve adequately as your primary heating equipment. We will point out those types when we come to them.

We specifically recommend that you avoid central forced-air heating, even though it is presently the dominant type of heating in the U.S. The sidebar, *Why You Don't Want Central Forced-Air Heating or Cooling*, explains why.

SELECT YOUR ENERGY SOURCES

Selecting your energy sources is the first decision in designing your comfort systems. Your choice will affect your comfort, your energy costs, and the way you build your house. Your energy sources will determine which types of systems you can install, and *vice versa*.

Don't leave this decision to your builder. It's not his job to know how to compare energy costs. And, don't select your energy sources just because they are used by other houses in the neighborhood.

In most of the developed world, four sources of energy are used for houses: electricity, natural gas, propane/LPG, and fuel oil. If your house is located in a remote area, you may also contemplate heating your home with wood, coal, or some other solid fuel.

In virtually all cases, electricity will be one of your energy sources. In much of the world, you will also use one other energy source for heating applications. That's because electricity is usually the most expensive energy source for heating.

Look to the future as you select your energy sources. You are building your house on the eve of a historic change in energy supply. The era of abundant oil and natural gas will end some time around the middle of the 21st century, early in the life of your house. The following is a quick introduction to the likely future of your possible energy sources.

Electricity

Electricity is available almost everywhere because it is needed by all modern household appliances.

But, electricity is usually the most expensive heating energy source. That's because most electricity is made from other energy sources. Today, most electricity is made by a process that involves burning fossil fuels. For reasons that are unavoidable, making electricity by burning fuels is a wasteful process, typically recovering only about one third of the energy of the original fuel. In addition, making electricity requires expensive generation equipment and distribution equipment.

Therefore, electricity that is made by burning fuels is always much more expensive than the fuels themselves.

Coal is a much less expensive fuel than oil or gas, so electricity made from coal can be competitive with oil and gas as the latter become scarce. However, coal burning is a prime source of carbon dioxide in the atmosphere. This issue will inhibit coal burning in the future, and it will raise the price of electricity produced from coal. Nuclear energy is another source of electricity that is less expensive than oil and gas, but it is limited in availability and it is beset by safety concerns.

Hydroelectric power is inexpensive. Unfortunately, hydroelectric resources are limited, so they can provide only a small fraction of present electricity consumption. Groups fight political battles to decide who gets this cheap electricity. If you live near a big hydro dam or if you are lucky enough to be a part of a politically favored group, you may be able to look forward to inexpensive electricity until the next political battle redistributes this bonanza.

Electricity can be made from "alternative" energy sources, such as wind, sunlight, and tides. However, electricity made from such sources probably will be much more expensive than present energy sources. The reason is that alternative sources – especially sunlight – have low energy density, so they are expensive to collect.

The cost of electricity for heating depends on whether you use resistance heating or heat pumps. Resistance heating is very expensive because the electricity itself is the heat source. In contrast, heat pumps have the ability to multiply the amount of heat that is delivered compared to the amount of electricity that is used. Because of this multiplying effect, the cost of using heat pumps may be competitive with the cost of heating by burning other available fuels.

Natural Gas

Natural gas is a versatile and desirable heating fuel. It is used for home heating, water heating, cooking, clothes drying, gas grills, gas fireplaces, and so forth. It is usually the best choice of heating fuel, assuming that the climate is cold enough to require much heating.

Natural gas has a number of important advantages over other fossil fuels, and no significant disadvantages. Also, the equipment that uses natural gas has several important advantages, which we will explain when we discuss heating equipment.

Natural gas is delivered directly to homes by underground pipelines. If your climate and requirements are appropriate for natural gas, investigate whether your home site is located within range of a natural gas pipeline. If there is a local natural gas utility, ask whether they serve your neighborhood. If not, ask whether they would extend their service to your home site. This can be a decisive issue in selecting your type of heating system.

In the past, natural gas was the most economical home heating fuel. This is changing, though. The appeal of natural gas is causing the earth's remaining supply to be consumed rapidly. Abundant natural gas from wells probably will be exhausted by the middle of the 21st century.

A new source of natural gas, called "shale gas," is producing significant amounts. Shale gas seems likely to extend the supply of natural gas for a number of years. However, the potential supply is uncertain and it is undoubtedly overstated by promoters. Current methods of extraction may pollute underground water supplies, and there are other environmental concerns.

In the short term, countries can import natural gas from other countries that have excess gas to sell. For example, Europe presently depends on Russia for much of its natural gas. If countries are located on the same land mass, they can transfer gas by using pipelines, which is an inexpensive method of shipment. For example, the U.S. imports gas by pipeline from Canada and Mexico.

Natural gas can also be transported by ship. Natural gas must be cooled to a very low temperature for shipment, converting it to "liquefied natural gas" ("LNG"). Because of limitations in shipping capacity, LNG probably will not be able to serve a large fraction of the gas needs of large populations.

Natural gas is safer than other gas fuels, including propane and LPG, because it is lighter than air. As a result, small gas leaks do not accumulate in basements and other depressions. To alert occupants to leaks, gas companies put small amounts of a foul smelling additive in the natural gas supply.

A synthetic substitute for natural gas can be made from coal, and this is likely to be a response when real natural gas runs out. This gas can be distributed through the same gas pipes that are presently used for natural gas, and it can operate the same heating equipment. However, converting coal to gas is a desperation measure that is wasteful and bad for the environment.

Propane and LPG

Propane is an alternative heating fuel to consider if you can't get natural gas service. Sometimes, propane is called "liquefied petroleum gas" ("LPG"). The latter name also is used for a mixture of fuel gases, usually propane and butane.

Propane offers the same efficiency and maintenance advantages as natural gas. It can be used in condensing boilers and furnaces, eliminating the need for a chimney. Most types of equipment that burn natural gas can be adapted to burn propane.

Unlike natural gas, propane is heavier than air. Propane that leaks can accumulate in a basement or other space that is below grade. At certain concentrations, it can explode. It can also suffocate.

Propane is delivered to homes by truck, in liquid form. Propane is easy to store as a liquid by keeping it under moderate pressure in lightweight tanks. The tank may be located above ground, or it may be buried. A typical propane tank is not very large, so it can be camouflaged easily with an attractive structure or hedge.

Propane is a risky choice from the standpoints of price and availability. It is a byproduct of natural gas and petroleum production. Therefore, the supply is dependent on continued oil and natural gas production.

Propane is expensive to transport. It usually moves long distances by railway tank cars rather than by pipeline. For this reason, propane may be cheap near the wells, but expensive in locations that are far from oil or gas production. By the same logic, propane is more likely to become scarce as the distance from the source increases.

Fuel Oil

Fuel oil is the most common home heating fuel in colder locations where natural gas service is not available. Oil has no advantages over natural gas as a home fuel, and it has some significant disadvantages. Its main appeal is that it is available by truck almost everywhere that it is needed.

Oil-fired water heaters are available, but fuel oil cannot be used for cooking, clothes drying, individual room heating, and other small heating applications. Those applications need another source of energy, usually electricity or propane. Oil-fired heaters require conventional flues and chimneys, unlike high-efficiency gas-fired heating equipment. They also require more maintenance.

Fuel oil is relatively safe. It does not have a strong tendency to emit vapors that concentrate enough to be dangerous. If oil leaks, the vapors are smelly. Oil vapors are much heavier than air, so they accumulate in basements and other low points.

The oil storage tank should be large enough so that you can purchase a season's worth of oil when the prices are lowest. A fairly large, highly efficient house that is located in a cold climate should burn no more than several hundred gallons (one or two thousand liters) of oil during the year. In most jurisdictions, the oil tank can be located above ground, inside or outside, or it can be buried.

Natural petroleum probably will become depleted during the 21st century. Its price will rise drastically but irregularly as that time approaches. Synthetic substitutes for petroleum can be made from coal. It is hoped that petroleum can be supplemented or replaced by liquid fuels that are extracted from large deposits of "oil shale," "tar sands," and other proposed sources. However, the practicality of these sources remains to be seen. Any petroleum replacements will be more expensive, and producing them will bring new environmental problems.

Petroleum is the primary energy source for transportation. Regions with large populations – China, India, and southeast Asia – are becoming prosperous, so vast populations are demanding their first automobiles, along with trucks, aircraft, and other forms of transportation. The competing need for petroleum by transportation will cause heating oil prices to rise severely well before natural oil supplies are exhausted.

Solid Fuels

Burning solid fuel is generally much less convenient or comfortable than using the previous four energy sources. For that reason, I don't recommend any solid fuel as a prime choice. However, in certain locations, you may want to burn wood as a primary or secondary fuel, or it may be desirable to burn coal. For those special cases, we cover solid fuels at the end of the book, under the heading, *Heating with Firewood and Other Solid Fuels.*

COMPARE HEATING ENERGY PRICES

For your heating applications – including space heating, water heating, and cooking – consider the relative prices of all your available energy sources. This comparison should be a big factor in your choice of energy sources and your choice of equipment.

Unfortunately, the prices of different energy sources are stated in different units. For example, in the U.S., electricity may be priced in cents per kilowatt-hour. Natural gas may be priced in cents per "therm" (a unit that equals 100,000 BTU) or dollars per thousand cubic feet. Fuel oil and propane usually are priced in dollars per gallon.

To make it easy for you to compare energy prices, use the adjacent *Energy Cost Worksheet*, which has two steps:

- Step A converts the prices of your available energy sources to a common basis of comparison. The *Worksheet* uses dollars per million BTU as the common basis.
- Step B adjusts for the efficiency of the equipment based on its energy source. For example, equipment that burns natural gas can extract more energy from the fuel than equipment that burns oil or coal. In the case of heat pumps, the *Worksheet* also adjusts for changes in efficiency with climate.

Let's do an example, using the *Energy Cost Worksheet*. We start with natural gas, which you would use in a high-efficiency condensing heating boiler. Your local gas cost is quoted as $0.70 per therm. In Step A of the *Worksheet*, multiply this by 10 to convert this to a raw energy cost of $7.00 per million BTU. In Step B, multiply this by 1.1 to account for heat loss from the system. This yields a final cost of $7.70 per million BTU.

Next, consider using fuel oil in a high-efficiency, non-condensing hydronic boiler. Your local price is $3.00 per gallon. In Step A of the *Worksheet*, multiply this by 7.2 to convert this to a raw energy cost of $21.60 per million BTU. In Step B, multiply this by 1.3, yielding a final cost of $28.08 per million BTU.

Finally, consider electricity, which you would use in heat pumps. Your price of electricity is $0.10 per kilowatt-hour. In Step A of the *Worksheet*, multiply this by 293 to convert this to a raw energy cost of $29.30 per million BTU. In Step B, multiply this by a factor of 0.6 if the home site has a fairly cold winter. This yields a final cost of $17.58 per million BTU.

ENERGY COST WORKSHEET

Step A: Convert all energy prices to the same units.

For:	multiply dollars per	by	to get raw cost in $ per million BTU
electricity	kilowatt-hour	293	=
natural gas	therm	10	=
	cubic foot	970	=
	cubic meter	27	=
No. 2 fuel oil	U.S. gallon	7.2	=
	liter	27	=
propane	U.S. gallon	11	=
	liter	32	=
coal	U.S. ton	.05 (variable)	=
	metric tonne	.045 (variable)	=

Step B: Calculate the end-use energy cost.

For:	used in	multiply raw cost by	to get final cost in $ per million BTU
electricity	electric resistance heater or water heater	1	=
	high-efficiency heat pump in mild climate	0.3	=
	high-efficiency heat pump in climate with extended warm and/or cold season	0.4 to 0.7	=
	heat pump water heater	0.4 to 0.6	=
	conventional electric range	1.4	=
	electric oven	1.1	=
	microwave oven	1.8	=
natural gas and propane/LPG	high-efficiency condensing boiler, furnace, or water heater	1.1	=
	good non-condensing boiler, furnace, air heater, or water heater	1.3	=
	gas range	2.5	=
	gas oven	1.1	=
No. 2 fuel oil	high-efficiency, non-condensing boiler or water heater	1.3	=
coal	well designed hydronic boiler or furnace	1.6 to 2.5	=

(Since we are working with an accuracy of only two significant digits, we should round off these estimates to $8 per million BTU for natural gas, $28 per million BTU for fuel oil, and $18 per million BTU for heat pumps.)

Comparing these three energy sources, we see that natural gas would be your most economical source of heating energy, if it is available. If natural gas is not available, you probably would select heat pumps if the climate is temperate enough for them to work well. You would select fuel oil only if the climate is too cold for satisfactory operation of heat pumps.

Don't base any major decisions on small differences in these numbers. If the differences in cost between your energy options are small, it is more important to focus on the likely trends of these costs in the future.

Where to Find Energy Prices

To get energy prices for your home site, contact local energy suppliers. These include the local electric company, the gas company, propane suppliers, and fuel oil dealers, as appropriate. There may be more than one supplier for each source energy. If so, get prices from several retail suppliers.

For electricity, be aware that most electric utilities add charges to your monthly bill, in addition to the cost of the electricity itself. This raises your average cost. Also, electric utilities offer discounts for special terms of service. For example, see the sidebar, *Two Ways to Lower the Cost of Electric Water Heating*, in Step 5.

For a broader perspective, you can get regional prices from the Internet. In the U.S., the Energy Information Administration (EIA) maintains a Web site that gives regional prices for all major energy sources. The EIA Web site also provides historical prices, which are useful for perspective on how the costs of different energy sources have been changing.

Now, you are able to decide which heating and cooling systems are best for your home. Next, we will learn how to design the two major recommended heating systems, hydronic systems and split-system heat pumps.

If a hydronic system is not the best choice for your home, skip the following explanation of hydronic design and go to the explanation of heat pump design that follows it.

HYDRONIC HEATING SYSTEMS

Fuel-fired hydronic heating is one of two prime types of heating that I recommend for a super-house. In colder climates, it usually is the best choice. However, it is not applicable if electricity is your only practical energy source.

A hydronic heating system uses circulating hot water to heat your house. The water is heated in a central boiler, and it is distributed through pipes to heating units that are located in each room.

Hydronic systems have major advantages, and no serious shortcomings. (See Table 4-1, *Heating Equipment Comparison*, for a summary.) They are comfortable, quiet, and efficient. The heating units in each room can be controlled individually. By avoiding the use of ducts, hydronic systems avoid the health hazards that are associated with forced-air systems. The boiler is compact and fairly easy to install. The water pipes are easy to install, especially if the boiler can be installed in a basement. Because each room is controlled separately, each room can have an optimum type of heating unit.

Hydronic systems require the contractor to install a larger number of different components than other types of heating systems. Also, the relationship between the components is important. Unless the contractor fully understands this kind of system, he is likely to make installation mistakes that will cause exasperating problems. Therefore, it is especially important to select a heating contractor who is well qualified with residential hydronic systems. See the sidebar, *Contractor Skill is Critical*.

To make sure that your hydronic system is perfect, we will now go through the design and installation in a step-by-step sequence. Review these steps with your contractor. We cover a lot of detail here, and it's all necessary. Even professional plumbing handbooks and training manuals still fail to distinguish the best methods of installing hydronic systems from methods that are trouble-prone or obsolete. We have extracted the best information from the chaff, yielding a hydronic design that is clear and easy to follow.

Don't confuse hydronic systems with old-fashioned steam heating systems. Steam heating suffers from poor temperature control, noisy radiators, and equipment failures that are difficult to diagnose. Steam heat was a great improvement over fireplaces, but it is now obsolete.

CAUTION!
CONTRACTOR SKILL IS CRITICAL

Hydronic systems have a larger number of separately installed components than other types of heating equipment. The components are fairly simple to install, but the installation details matter! A hydronic system that is installed properly will operate perfectly for the life of the house, requiring only a minimum of maintenance. However, seemingly minor oversights may cause baffling problems and early equipment failure.

This is a matter of skill, not cost. Hydronic heating is the norm for homes in Europe and in much of Asia, but it is still unusual on the American continent. In the U.S., hydronic heating is common for office buildings. However, the equipment and techniques that are appropriate for commercial buildings don't transfer well to houses. You need a heating contractor who understands residential hydronic heating.

Recent years have seen fundamental improvements in residential hydronic equipment and piping practices. Even if a contractor has long experience, he may not be clear about the best methods to use. To solve that problem, this book focuses on one best hydronic design. Make sure that your contractor follows it.

To find a capable residential hydronic heating contractor, extend your search beyond your neighborhood. Check any contractor's references with other homeowners who have used that contractor to install a hydronic system. Also, the contractor certification program that we introduce at the end of Step 8 may lead you to a capable heating contractor.

HYDRONIC DESIGN (1): ZONE THE HOUSE

In the language of the HVAC trade, a "zone" is a part of a building that has common heating and cooling requirements. In designing your hydronic heating system, create a separate zone for each area that has individual heating requirements. ***Generally, each room should be a separate heating zone***. This is true even if rooms are open to each other, such as a living room and an adjacent dining room.

Each zone should have its own heating units and its own thermostat. Don't try to cut cost by grouping more than one room into a single heating zone. It's false economy. You would save little money, and you would sacrifice comfort and energy efficiency.

In Step 1, you laid out your interior walls, doors, and partitions to localize your heating and cooling to individual spaces, so this part of your heating system design is already complete!

HYDRONIC DESIGN (2): CALCULATE THE ROOM HEATING REQUIREMENTS

Now, you need to calculate how much heating capacity is needed for each zone, or room. You can leave this part of the job to your heating contractor, or you can hire an engineer.

Or, you can easily make the calculations yourself. By this point, you already know all the concepts. Beyond that, it's just arithmetic using two simple formulas. Knowing how to make the equipment size calculations will assure you that your systems are adequate to their task.

The heating requirement for each room is the sum of three different heating requirements:

1. heating needed to compensate for heat lost to the outside by conduction through the walls, ceiling, and floor
2. heating needed to warm outside air that enters the room by leakage or by ventilation fans
3. extra heating that is needed to warm a room quickly after it has been allowed to cool down.

If you are going to calculate your rooms' heating requirements, here is how to calculate the numbers.

(1) Heating Capacity to Offset Conduction Heat Loss

Heating equipment puts heat energy into the room to replace the heat that leaks out of the room. To maintain a desired temperature, the rate of heat input must equal the rate of heat loss. In your super-home, most heat loss will occur by conduction through the room surfaces. Therefore, start by calculating the rate of conduction heat loss from each zone at the coldest time of the year.

Conduction heat loss is directly proportional to the surface area of the zone that is exposed to the outside. Also, it is directly proportional to the temperature difference between the inside and the outside. And, it is inversely proportional to the R-value (RSI) of the exterior surfaces of the zone. Putting these three facts together, we get the Conduction Heat Loss Formula.

Use the *Conduction Heat Loss Formula* for the heating equipment of each zone. You need to plug three numbers into the formula. Here's where to find the numbers:

- Get the area of the exterior surfaces of the zone from your drawings.
- To get the maximum temperature difference between inside and outside, you need to find the "design heating temperature" for your home site. This is approximately the minimum typical temperature that occurs during winter. It is available on the Internet. For example, if you live in Duluth, Minnesota, search for "Duluth winter design temperature." Also, every HVAC engineer has this information on his bookshelf.
- Get the R-values for your exterior surfaces – the walls, ceiling, floor, windows, skylights, and doors – from the *Insulation Worksheet* that you filled out in Step 3.

Use consistent units, either English or metric. In English units, heat loss is stated in BTU's per hour (BTUH), surface area is stated in square feet (ft^2), temperatures in degrees Fahrenheit (°F), and R-value in BTUH per ft^2 per °F.

(In metric (SI) units, heat loss is stated in kilowatts, surface area in square meters (m^2), temperatures in degrees Celsius (°C), and RSI in kilowatts per square meter per °C.)

Apply the formula separately for each room surface where heat may be lost by conduction. This includes any outside walls, the windows, any skylights, any

---

CONDUCTION HEAT LOSS FORMULA

$$\text{Maximum Heat Loss} = \frac{\left(\begin{array}{c}\text{total exposed surface area}\\\text{of the zone}\end{array}\right) \times \left(\begin{array}{c}\text{difference between room temperature}\\\text{and the lowest outside temperature}\end{array}\right)}{\text{average R-value of the exposed surface}}$$

OUTSIDE AIR HEATING FORMULA (English Units)

$$\text{Air Heating Rate in BTU/Hour} = 1.08 \text{ X} \left(\begin{array}{c}\text{ventilation rate in} \\ \text{Cubic Feet per Minute}\end{array} \right) \text{ X} \left(\begin{array}{c}\text{difference between room temperature} \\ \text{and the lowest outside temperature, in °F}\end{array} \right)$$

OUTSIDE AIR HEATING FORMULA (Metric Units)

$$\text{Air Heating Rate in Kilowatts} = 0.0012 \text{ X} \left(\begin{array}{c}\text{ventilation rate in} \\ \text{Liters per Second}\end{array} \right) \text{ X} \left(\begin{array}{c}\text{difference between room temperature} \\ \text{and the lowest outside temperature, in °C}\end{array} \right)$$

---

ceiling exposed to the outside (via the roof), any floor exposed to the outside, and any doors. Then, add all the heat losses for the room.

Be sure to include the heat loss through any interior wall or floor that has an unheated space on the other side. For an unheated space that is primarily above ground, such as a garage or enclosed porch, assume that the minimum temperature in that space may be as low as the minimum outside temperature. (That's why it's important to put insulation in interior walls that face unheated spaces.)

For heat loss to an unheated basement, assume that the temperature of the unheated basement may fall to the deep soil temperature under the house. You can find the deep soil temperature for your geographic region in Figure 3-111 or on the Internet.

(2) Heating Capacity to Offset Air Leakage and Ventilation

In the past, air leakage was a major cause of heat loss from houses. Fortunately, you can build your house with so little air leakage that you don't need to calculate it separately. However, you still have to provide enough heating capacity for the outside air that you bring into the house for ventilation during cold weather.

Use the adjacent *Outside Air Heating Formula* to calculate the amount of heating energy required for ventilation. If the output of your heating equipment will be rated in BTU's per hour, choose the English version of the formula. If you use metric units, use the metric version of the formula.

Get the ventilation rates for the formula from the fan specifications. You may find this information in the literature that came with the fan. Or, you may need to look up the air flow rate in the manufacturer's catalog or Web site.

The ventilation air for a particular space may not be heated entirely inside that space, but at least partially in other spaces where the ventilation air passes through. For example, if a shower room exhaust fan draws air from the interior of the house, outside air enters the house elsewhere and it cools the spaces that it passes through. This adds to the heating requirement of those other spaces.

However, the additional heating requirement for the other rooms usually is not large enough to matter. Let's look at the usual spaces where this issue arises.

Showers typically don't add to the heating of surrounding spaces, even though they need to clear out large volumes of water vapor after each use. When drying out a shower room during cold weather, the relative humidity inside the house is low, so moisture in the shower will evaporate quickly into the rest of the house without the need for outside ventilation. The shower exhaust fan operates only for the duration of the shower, and your shower heating equipment generally will have plenty of spare capacity to compensate for it.

The *kitchen* needs outside ventilation air primarily to carry cooking fumes into the range hood. To minimize discomfort, the outside air should preferably come through a window that is adjacent to the range hood, as we previously discussed in Step 1, under the heading, *Kitchen*. Most of this air flows directly to the hood, so it does not add much of a heating requirement to the occupied parts of the kitchen. Also, the range and oven are major heat sources for the kitchen when the ventilation fan is operating. So, usually you will not need extra heating for the ventilation air.

If your *workshop* has a large ventilation fan for activities such as painting or welding, you can't afford to heat the quantity of ventilation air that is needed to keep the workshop environment healthy. For such activities, supplement the workshop heating by wearing a pair of insulated coveralls during cold weather.

(3) Extra Heating Capacity for Quick Warm-Up

You will turn off the heating in unoccupied rooms to save energy, so their temperature will drift down during cold weather. Also, when your family goes on vacation during cold weather, you will turn off the heating to the entire house, except perhaps for a minimum needed to protect against freezing. When you return, the structure of the house will be cold. You want enough heating capacity to bring the house back to a comfortable temperature fairly quickly, regardless of the outside temperature.

Similarly, you will use temperature setback every night. For example, you may set the programmable thermostat in your bedroom to turn off heating during sleeping hours. Then, you want your bedroom to warm up quickly just before you arise.

So far, we have calculated the capacity that your room heaters need to offset heat leakage to the outside. With this capacity, the room heaters can maintain room temperature under the coldest weather conditions, but they cannot raise it under those conditions. Therefore, the room heaters need additional capacity to quickly restore the temperature of a room that has been allowed to cool down.

This extra heating capacity is needed both to heat the air in the room and to warm the surrounding surfaces. Air has little mass, so it can be heated quickly. The room surfaces, which typically are gypsum board, have a large mass. The room will not be fully warmed until this mass is warmed. Your super-efficient house will have as much interior mass as a conventional house. Therefore, the room heaters will need about the same warm-up heating capacities as in a conventional house.

As a rule of thumb, the additional warm-up heating capacity in most rooms should be about 40 BTUH per square foot (120 watts per square meter) of floor area. (Note that we are now talking about floor area, not exposed surface area.)

Shower rooms and toilet rooms need faster warm-up, so these rooms need greater heating capacity in relation to their size. If a large amount of mass is exposed to the inside, such as an interior brick wall or a huge stone fireplace, additional heating capacity is needed to warm the room quickly.

■ Larger Capacity Improves Boiler Efficiency

It is better to *err toward larger room heating capacity*. Increasing the size of almost any kind of room heater unit adds little to its installed cost. In addition to providing quicker warm-up, larger heating capacity allows a hydronic system to operate with lower water temperature, which improves the efficiency of the boiler. (We explain this under the heading, *Water Temperature Reset*, below).

Note that the system water temperature must be high enough to serve each room heating unit in the house. Therefore, to reap the efficiency benefits of reduced system water temperature, increase the size of your room heating units consistently.

Your contractor may be surprised by your desire to have ample heating capacity, because an obsolete belief remains that "oversizing" is inefficient. See the sidebar. In reality, increased capacity is a valuable benefit that costs little.

"OVERSIZING" IS NOW A MYTH

There is a general belief among builders that "oversizing" a heating system will make it inefficient. That was true for some older kinds of equipment, and it is true for some current types of heating equipment that we don't recommend. However, it is not true for the kinds of primary heating and cooling systems that we recommend for a super-efficient house. In fact, increasing the capacity of hydronic room heaters allows the system water temperature to be reduced, which increases the boiler's efficiency.

HYDRONIC DESIGN (3): SELECT AND INSTALL THE ROOM HEATERS

Hydronic systems offer a variety of heater types, allowing you to select a type that is best matched to each room. Table 4-2, *Hydronic Room Heater Comparison*, summarizes your choices, along with their relative advantages and limitations.

Let's get familiar with the main types of hydronic room heaters and the key issues about installing each type. Then, it's up to you to select the best heater for each room, and to make sure that your contractor installs the heaters as we explain.

Hydronic Baseboard Convectors

Baseboard convectors usually are the best choice for most formal rooms and spaces. In appropriate rooms, they are almost ideal heaters, providing exceptional comfort. They are simple, inexpensive, and completely quiet, with no moving parts to wear out. Figure 4-10 shows a typical installation.

A baseboard convector consists of a water pipe that is wrapped in heat conducting fins. It is surrounded by a partial enclosure that guides the flow of air through the fins. The assembly is attached to the wall near the floor, just high enough to allow room air to enter the convector from below. Figure 4-11 shows the interior of a typical unit.

A desirable enhancement is to install the return water pipe inside the housing and above the heating element, as in Figure 4-12. By allowing any air bubbles to rise into the return pipe, this arrangement helps to avoid trapping of free air inside the heating element.

Baseboard convectors are often called "baseboard radiators." The name is incorrect. The finned heater pipe cannot radiate heat into the room, because it is hidden behind an enclosure. Almost all heating is by convection, which is much more comfortable than heating by radiation would be.

Baseboard convectors are low and long, and they generally are installed along a large portion of the exterior walls of a room. This style of convector is the most common type in North America. For most rooms, it is superior to the narrow, taller styles of radiators and convectors that are common elsewhere (and which we cover next).

■ Advantages

Baseboard convectors are exceptionally comfortable. Their long, low shape provides superior heating coverage by turning much of the exterior wall from a cold surface to a warm surface. The rising blanket of warm air opposes the downward flow of cooler air from the exterior wall and windows, preventing cold downdrafts.

Convectors are free of hot blasts because they change temperature fairly slowly and smoothly. They are totally silent. They require no filters and they can be cleaned easily with a vacuum cleaner.

Because they are low and long, convectors sweep up the layer of coolest air that settles on the floor, bringing warmer air down to floor level.

Convectors are inexpensive to buy and they are easy to install, resulting in low labor cost. They require only small holes in the floor for the water pipes to connect with the boiler. They have no moving parts, so they will last forever if the system water is treated properly to prevent corrosion and scaling.

A baseboard convector can safely use very hot water, which allows the room to warm quickly. That's because the hot water pipe is inaccessible inside the fins and the enclosure. Other styles of convectors do not have this protection from burns.

Mestek

Figure 4-10. A room with hydronic baseboard heating. The window at right has draperies, which would obstruct heat output when they are closed. The draperies should end above the baseboard units, and an air deflector should be installed under the draperies to guide the heated air to the inside of the room.

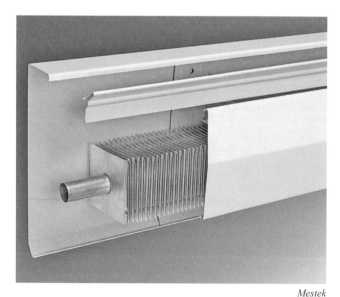

Mestek

Figure 4-11. The inside of a hydronic baseboard convector. This is simplicity itself. There are no moving parts and no noise. It is easy to clean. The main requirement is to provide easy air flow into the bottom of the unit and to allow the heated air to rise easily into the room.

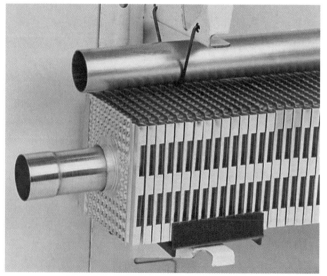

Mestek

Figure 4-12. A hydronic baseboard convector that includes the water return pipe inside the enclosure. This arrangement helps to avoid air trapping that would reduce the heating capacity of the unit. It may also simplify the piping installation by allowing the supply and return water connections to be made at the same end.

Table 4-2. HYDRONIC ROOM HEATER COMPARISON

HEATER TYPE	FAVORED ROOMS	RELATIVE ADVANTAGES	RELATIVE DISADVANTAGES	OBSTACLES TO USE
Hydronic Baseboard Convectors	• Most rooms with sufficient perimeter area that offers free air flow	• Silent • Very comfortable • Inexpensive • Little interference with most furniture	• Slower warm-up than fan-forced units [1]	• Obstructions to air flow along exterior wall, e.g., counters, shelves • Draperies extending to floor • Obstructions in baseboard area, e.g., plumbing
Hydronic Radiators	• Shower and Bath Rooms • Kitchen • Foyer	• Fit limited wall space • Decorative designs available • Stainless materials available • Available as heated towel racks	• Limited heating capacity • High temperature of exposed surface • Less comfortable heating	• Insufficient wall space • Hazard from high temperature • Draperies
Hydronic Fan-Coil Units	• Rooms with limited clear space along exterior walls	• High heating capacity in relation to size • Rapid warm-up [1] • Same unit can be used for heating and for hydronic cooling.	• Fan noise • Institutional appearance	• Insufficient wall space
Hydronic Floor Heating	• Rooms where people walk barefoot or lie on the floor • Spaces occupied below normal room temperature, e.g., garage • Large spaces with limited insulation, e.g., garage	• Silent • Invisible • Warm walking surface • Lower water temperature improves boiler efficiency (only with a dedicated boiler).	• Slowest warm-up [1] • Expensive • Difficult to repair • Heat loss to underside of floor • Complicates hydronic system	• Carpeting or rugs that cover large parts of the floor

NOTES:

[1] When a cold system is first started, the warm-up delay occurs mostly in the boiler and the piping. The mass of the boiler, the water in the system, and the materials of the piping must be warmed before the room heating units can produce heat at full output. This delay typically is less than ten minutes. Floor heating has a significantly longer delay.

And, the low profile minimizes interference with curtains and furniture.

I discovered another dramatic benefit of baseboard convectors when I was called to investigate mildew problems in a large housing complex. The apartments previously had been heated with an old baseboard convector system, but this system was replaced with heat pumps. Many tenants reported severe mildew that commenced when the change was made. The investigation revealed that the baseboard convectors had deterred mildew growth that otherwise would have occurred for a variety of reasons.

There are several reasons for this anti-mildew effect. Baseboard convectors warm the cold surfaces where moisture commonly condenses to promote mildew, as on window frames. The warm air from the convectors has low relative humidity, which prevents mold from growing. And, baseboard convectors continuously sweep up the cold air layer on the floor, which usually is the region of strongest mildew growth.

■ Limitations

Baseboard convectors can't be used everywhere. The room must have a sufficient length of exposed baseboard area to install the heaters. If the room has an exterior wall, the heaters should be installed on the exterior wall.

Convection is a weak force for moving air. Therefore, air must be able to flow upward from the convector freely, and air must able to return to the convector freely along the floor. Generally, there is no conflict with furniture that has legs, such as chairs and side tables. However, convectors should not be installed behind tall bookshelves, cabinets that extend to the floor, counters, or benches that extend to the wall. Convectors should not be used if draperies must extend to the floor.

For these reasons, baseboard convectors usually are not appropriate for kitchens, libraries, workshops, and other spaces where it is not possible to provide easy air flow through the convectors.

Also, baseboard convectors usually are not the best choice for shower and toilet rooms, where they would run afoul of base cabinets and plumbing connections. For these rooms, consider the narrow style of convector that we will cover next.

Convectors need high water temperature to stimulate convection that is strong enough to achieve full heating output during the coldest weather. With a condensing boiler, the high water temperature eliminates much of the efficiency advantage of the boiler. To minimize this efficiency penalty, get a boiler that adjusts the water temperature to the weather, a feature that we will explain.

■ Capacity and Water Temperature

The maximum capacity of a baseboard convector depends mainly on the length of the single finned pipe inside the baseboard enclosure. The heating capacity typically is 500 to 1,000 BTU's per hour per foot of length (0.5 to 1.0 kW per meter of length).

The heat output of a convector also depends on the system water temperature, which is variable. Residential systems are designed to produce peak output at a water temperature of about 220 °F (104 °C). Heat output drops to half at a water temperature of about 160 °F (70 °C).

The heat output of convectors may seem weak, but it is usually ample. Consider the extreme case of a room with double-glazed windows that are 10 feet (3 meters) tall. When the outside temperature is 0 °F (-18 °C), the heat loss from the windows is about 350 BTU's per hour per foot (0.35 kW per meter) of window width. This is much less than the heat output of an equivalent length of baseboard convectors.

In a super-insulated room, baseboard heaters need to occupy only a fraction of the length of the room's exterior walls. Still, you should provide ample capacity to provide quicker warm-up of a cold room. Also, increasing the convector capacity reduces the water temperature that is needed, which improves boiler efficiency.

■ Where to Locate Baseboard Units

The American style of baseboard convector is sold in a variety of lengths, typically from 2 feet to 8 feet (60 cm to 250 cm). The units can be connected end-to-end to produce any desired heat output. The unit may include an integral return pipe, as shown in Figure 4-12, so that the supply and return water connections can be made at the same end of the baseboard.

As a rule, install baseboard units under the windows, especially under the larger ones. This blocks the cold drafts that fall from the windows.

Don't install convectors on the interior walls of rooms that have exterior walls. This would induce air flow in the wrong direction, creating a cold draft down the exterior walls and along the floor.

Space is required under the convector to allow air to flow into the unit. This gap usually is built into the mounting hardware, speeding installation. The top of the enclosure typically is about one foot (30 cm) above the floor.

Design the height of your electric power receptacles, telephone jacks, etc., to provide ample clearance above the convectors. As we noted when you laid out your electrical wiring in Step 3, installing these items higher than usual is a wonderful convenience feature.

Brochures for baseboard convectors typically show a continuous line of convectors along the exterior walls. This is unnecessary, except in the coldest climates. In a super-insulated house, the heat output from relatively short convectors is sufficient to create uniform warmth throughout the room.

However, if you want the appearance of a continuous baseboard installation, you can buy the enclosure separately from the finned pipe, along with end caps, corner fittings, and other finish items. The finned pipe may occupy only a fraction of the length of the enclosure.

■ Avoid Heat Trapping Against Windows and Walls

The warm air from the convector rises along the wall. If a drapery is installed above the convector, the drapery will trap the warm air against the wall, or worse, against window glass, as in Figure 4-13. When this happens, the air is slowed down, the drapery blocks heat flow into the room, and the higher temperature at the wall and window surfaces increases heat loss to the outside.

The solution is to shorten the draperies so that they end above the convectors, and to install an air deflector between the convector and the drapery, as in Figure 4-14. Alternatively, reconsider your decision to install draperies.

The same trapping of the heat from baseboard convectors can occur with roller shades or venetian blinds that are hung from the wall and project into the interior of the room. The solution is to install the shades or blinds inside the window opening. In this way, the window sill acts as an air deflector and the warm air from the convector will bypass the window.

(Installing blinds and shades close to the glass also makes them more effective for rejecting unwanted solar heat during warm weather, and for blocking cold drafts from the windows during cold weather.)

■ Use Parallel Connections for Long Exterior Walls

Heating water enters one end of the convector and cools as it travels through. Therefore, the inlet end of the convector provides the most heat, and the outlet end provides the least. The difference is not important for a short convector. However, if a long convector installation is needed for a long exterior wall, the difference in heat output from one end of the room to the other may be significant if all the convector units are installed in series. The uneven distribution of heat could reduce comfort, especially if the room has a lot of glass area.

In a room that has a long exterior wall, divide the water supply to the convectors to create shorter groups that are piped in parallel. Or, if separate convectors are placed under windows that are spaced far apart, provide a separate parallel connection for each convector.

DRW

Figure 4-13. Drapery blocking a convector in Germany. When the drapery is closed, much of the heat goes outdoors through the glass, rather than into the room.

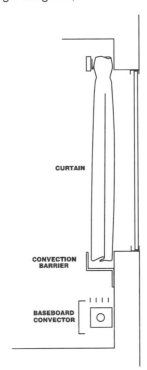

DRW

Figure 4-14. Air deflector for baseboard convectors. This simple, inexpensive fixture eliminates the large heat loss that occurs if the heated air from the convector rises into the space between curtains and windows.

Hydronic Radiators and Narrow Convectors

In much of the world outside North America, hydronic heating is done with convectors that are taller and narrower than American baseboard convectors. Figure 4-15 shows a typical example. Commonly, these are made of one or more hollow flat plates, in which the hot water is circulated. However, a convector can have almost any shape, as long as it has sufficient surface area.

Such units are commonly called "radiators," even though they function primarily as convectors. They do emit some heat by radiation because their outer surface is exposed to the room.

The capacity of a hydronic radiator is limited by the low temperature at which it must operate to avoid creating a burn hazard for the occupants. Also, if a unit is mounted somewhat high on a wall, it cannot suck the cold air layer from the floor and warm it.

Certain styles of hydronic radiators can provide heating in rooms where baseboard convectors would not be practical. In particular, they are the most appropriate kind of hydronic heater for shower rooms and toilet rooms. Figure 4-16 is a typical example.

Hydronic radiators usually are made of painted steel, which rusts quickly in the presence of water and urine. If you want to install hydronic heating in a wet space, try to find a unit that is made of corrosion resistant material.

Some manufacturers offer models that are especially elegant in appearance, so they can be used as an element of decor. For example, the fancy hydronic radiator in Figure 4-17 also serves as "towel warmer."

DRW

Figure 4-16. Hydronic radiator with a self-contained thermostat, installed in a toilet room in Germany. The heat from the radiator tends to turn off the thermostat, so response is slow and temperature control is crude.

Hudson Reed

Figure 4-17. A fancy hydronic radiator that is commonly called a "towel warmer." The unit has limited surface area. When it is covered by a towel, its heat emission is further reduced.

A hydronic radiator can be made in virtually any shape into which tubes can be bent.

Heavier units should be supported by the floor, but many newer models are light enough for wall mounting. Similarly, the water connections can come through the floor or through the wall.

DRW

Figure 4-15. Typical hydronic room heater, in Germany. The front face of the unit heats largely by radiation. In addition, the multiple vertical passages provide considerable heating by convection.

Hydronic Fan-Coil Units

As the name implies, a "fan-coil" unit is a heating unit that consists of a coil and a fan. It is mounted in an enclosure that has an outlet at the top and an inlet at the bottom. The finned coil is folded within the enclosure to provide a large heating area, and the fan forces a large volume of air through the coil. As a result, a fan-coil unit has a large heat output in relation to its size. Figure 4-18 shows a typical unit.

Fan-coil units presently are uncommon in single-family homes. They require an electrical connection in addition to the plumbing connections. They have a certain amount of fan noise, and the cabinets take up wall space. Still, consider fan-coil units for spaces that need to be warmed quickly and for spaces that need a lot of heat output from a small unit. For example, you might install one in a home office that is packed with furniture that would interfere with baseboard convectors.

Some fan-coil units are designed to be installed in an equipment closet. This kind of unit heats an adjacent room through a short duct and a grille.

If you install more than one fan-coil unit in a room or zone, pipe heating water to each unit separately.

Figure 4-18. An attractive hydronic fan-coil unit.

Mestek

Hydronic Floor Heating

Hydronic floor heating circulates heating water through tubing that is embedded in the entire floor surface or that is attached to the underside of the floor. In this way, the surface of the floor becomes the room heater.

Floor heating can be installed in concrete slabs and in wood frame floors. It can be installed under tile, hardwood, and dense synthetic materials, such as vinyl and linoleum, all of which conduct heat adequately.

Despite claims to the contrary, it is not prudent to install floor heating if the surface will be covered with carpets, carpet pads, or extensive rugs, all of which insulate the room from the floor heating system. The heat from the water tubing should be able to reach the visible floor surface without overheating the floor material itself.

Floor heating is often called "radiant" heating, which is incorrect. The water coils warm the floor by conduction, and the floor then warms the bottom layer of air in the room – and occupants' feet – by conduction. Finally, the warmed air rises into the space by convection. Radiation from the floor is minor, and it primarily warms the ceiling.

■ Where to Use Hydronic Floor Heating

There are few applications in typical homes where floor heating provides a compelling advantage over other kinds of hydronic heating. As a rule, floor heating may be an option to consider for certain individual spaces, not as a primary method of heating your home.

For formal rooms, one advantage of floor heating is that it is completely invisible in the room, except for the thermostat. It creates no physical or esthetic interference with furnishings. Also, it is completely silent, a benefit that it shares with convectors and radiators.

Floor heating provides good comfort in rooms with tall ceilings because it tends to cancel stratification. The advantage is greatest if the room is poorly insulated. In your home, that would occur only if you choose to build a special room that has a lot of glass. (See *What If You Want a Space with Lots of Glass?*, in Step 2.)

Bathroom floor heating is a deluxe application that is more expensive than other methods of warming a bathroom. The heating is very pleasant, and it helps to dry the floor after a shower or bath. However, floor heating warms a bathroom much more slowly than a ceiling-mounted electric forced-air heater. If cost is no object, you could install both kinds of heating in the same room.

Another application is a space where the floor would be especially cold without floor heating. The prime example is a garage with a concrete floor where occupants use the garage as a workshop. The floor slab tends to be cold because of air leakage into the space through the garage door, and because of heat loss to the soil under the slab. In such a chilly environment, the warming of feet by floor heating is especially welcome.

For most room applications, floor heating is a "boutique" feature. It tends to be popular because future homeowners have an idealized vision of it, even though they may have little actual experience with floor heating and have never compared it to baseboard heating.

The appeal of floor heating seems to come from a vision of lying on a warm floor in front of a fireplace during a howling blizzard, or of walking barefoot in comfort across a warm tile floor. If either of those situations has strong appeal for you, then consider floor heating.

Beyond that, the vision of cozy warmth in a cold environment is a mirage, because a super-insulated house won't be a cold environment. No matter what the weather is outside, your home will be warm and snug, so a heated floor would add little to your comfort.

■ Disadvantages

Floor heating limits your floor coverings. Carpets, carpet pads, and rugs act as insulation, preventing the heat from entering the room and forcing the heat into the space below. Attempting to warm the surface through the carpet may cause the water temperature to rise excessively, overheating the floor structure. The adhesives in plywood will dry out and the wood itself will become brittle. Thermal expansion and contraction of floor materials, such as tile, may cause them to break loose.

Floor heating has the slowest warm-up time of any kind of hydronic heating. When a cold room is first heated, it takes a long time for the floor structure to warm up. The delay is increased because the heating water temperature is limited to a much lower temperature than is used in other kinds of hydronic heaters. The warm floor produces only weak convection to warm the room air and the surfaces of the room.

Well, how about the "uniform" heating that floor heating claims to provide? In fact, the temperature across a properly installed floor is fairly uniform, but that is a limited virtue. For best comfort, heating should be applied where it leaks out of the room, at the exterior walls.*

Repairs are messy and expensive if the tubing is embedded in the floor surface, whether it is wood or concrete. If a leak occurs in the floor, a lot of damage can occur before the leak is discovered, and then the floor surface must be removed to repair the leak. Pipe of any kind has a life that is only a fraction of the life of the house, so the floor will have to torn out repeatedly to renew the system. More likely, floor heating will be abandoned the first time it needs a major repair.

The tubing is vulnerable to mishandling and damage while it is being installed. For example, if the plumber's apprentice kinks the tube while taking it off the roll, the tube will eventually fail at that point.

Floor heating complicates the piping layout and temperature control, as we shall see. This invites mistakes in installing and repairing the system.

Floor heating is usually more expensive than using other types of hydronic room heaters. This is especially true if the hot water tubing is embedded in a concrete floor, or if the tubing is installed in channels within a wooden floor. However, installation cost is much lower when using the "staple-up" method of installing the tubing underneath a wooden floor, especially when the floor is located above a basement.

■ Energy Efficiency

Floor heating is advertised as being especially energy efficient, but it's not. It has some energy advantages and some disadvantages.

One efficiency advantage is reduced temperature stratification inside the room. Floor heating warms the floor structure directly. Then, the floor warms the air in the lower part of the room, where the people are. The low temperature difference keeps the air from shooting toward the ceiling, where it can't keep anyone comfortable. This advantage is greatest in rooms with tall ceilings. With ordinary ceiling heights, the advantage is small.

Another efficiency advantage is the low water temperature needed for floor heating. The efficiency of high-efficiency condensing boilers is improved significantly if the boiler can operate at lower water temperatures. To exploit this advantage, you need a separate boiler to serve the floor heating. This might be practical if you have a big house with a lot of floor heating. Otherwise, the boiler temperature will be determined by other hydronic heating equipment (such as baseboard convectors) that requires higher temperatures.

---

* In a room with a horizontal ceiling that has heat loss to the outside, cooled air falls from the ceiling in localized drips, not as a uniform layer. Therefore, the uniform heating of the floor is not a benefit. If the ceiling is slanted, air cooled by the ceiling tends to flow down along the ceiling to the lower wall, where it falls to the floor.

An efficiency penalty of floor heating is that the heat from the heating coils flows downward as well as upward. If your floor is built on grade or over a basement, the underside of the floor will be especially cool, so more of the heat will flow downward. To minimize this heat loss, the underside of any heated floor should be heavily insulated.

Floor heating also uses more pump energy than the other types of hydronic heating. Because the water temperature is lower, the zone pump must deliver a larger volume of water and it must be pumped through a long maze of tubing. Also, to maintain stable floor temperature, the pump must operate continuously, wasting energy in recirculating the heating water.

■ Floor Temperature and Heating Capacity

Because the floor is a large heating surface, it needs to be only a few degrees warmer than the air temperature in the room. Typical floor temperatures during cold weather are 5 to 15 °F (2 to 8 °C) higher than the room temperature. The floor and the room environment would be uncomfortable if the floor were much warmer than this.

Floor heating systems typically are designed for a maximum heat output of 15 to 50 BTUH per square foot (0.07 to 0.25 kW per square meter). This is ample to maintain warmth in a well insulated room.

■ How Floor Heating is Installed

Floor heating is promoted with the promise that it provides uniform warmth across the floor. To make that promise come true, the installer must divide the floor piping into multiple pipe circuits. Each circuit must be short enough so that the water in the end of the circuit still remains warm. In addition, the tubing in each circuit should be arranged in a hairpin configuration, so that the cooler water in the return half of the hairpin is adjacent to the warmer water in the outbound half. All the pipe circuits for the room should be connected in parallel.

With a frame floor, the most common method of installing hydronic floor heating is to attach the water tubes to the underside of the floor sheathing. This method is popular because it does not require special floor construction, so it relatively expensive. The water tubing usually is attached to a grid or to metal clips that are stapled to the bottom of the floor sheathing, as in Figure 4-19. Hence, this type of installation is called "staple-up."

With this method of installation, the heat from the coils must pass through the entire floor structure. Unless insulation is placed underneath the tubing, more heat will flow into the space below the floor than into the space above.

Hydronics Heating Systems LLC

Figure 4-19. Hydronic heating coils installed under a frame floor. The plastic water tubes are held by metal clips that are stapled to the subfloor. This method of installation is called "staple-up."

Another method for frame floors is to install the water tubing in special subfloor sheathing that has pre-cut grooves for the tubing. The grooved sheathing is then covered with the finish flooring.

With a concrete floor, hydronic floor heating is most commonly installed by burying the tubing in the slab. The tubing must be laid out carefully to achieve a reasonably uniform floor temperature. A popular method for laying out the water tubing is to install it on a plastic base that has nubs to hold the tubing in the desired pattern, as in Figure 4-20. The plastic base

Figure 4-20. Hydronic heating coils that will be embedded in a concrete floor slab. The red water tubing is held between the nubs in the grey plastic base, a method that provides rapid installation with accurate spacing. Even this small room requires two water circuits to achieve reasonably uniform floor temperature.

HYDRONIC CEILING AND WALL HEATING

Hydronic coils can be embedded in ceilings and walls to provide heating. Ceiling systems are truly "radiant," whereas wall heating is both radiant and convective. These methods of installing hydronic heating are fraught with difficulty. They offer no significant advantages, so we won't consider them.

can also be used to shape the underside of the slab to maximize strength with a minimum amount of concrete.

Another method for concrete floors is to add a supplemental floor on top of the slab, and install the tubing inside the supplemental floor. Various kinds of supplemental floors are offered for use with concrete slabs.

With any type of installation, the hydronic tubing in the floor must be closely spaced to achieve adequate heat output and uniform floor temperature. In larger rooms, the tubing should be installed in several parallel circuits that are relatively short, so that the heating water in each circuit does not cool too much.

Unfortunately, the piping installation instructions in plumbing manuals and manufacturers' literature are often unsatisfactory. We will have more to say about the special piping and pumping arrangements that are needed for floor heating.

HYDRONIC DESIGN (4): SELECT THE BOILER

The boiler is the heart of your hydronic system. The market offers you many choices. Modern hydronic boilers are small and quiet. They are nothing like the monsters that lurked in the basements of old buildings.

Don't leave the selection of your boiler to your contractor. Contractors typically select equipment on the basis of price and immediate availability. Many don't have the time or interest for investigating the features of equipment. Your contractor will be happy to leave the shopping to you. Choose your boiler in the following sequence:

(1) Select the fuel.

(2) Find a complete list of efficient boilers that burn the selected fuel, within the size range you need. We will tell you how to find this list on the Internet.

(3) Narrow your search to boilers that have the highest energy efficiency.

(4) Consider other desirable features.

Buy your boiler from an established manufacturer. This will give you a meaningful warranty and a source of repair parts. Be wary of offbeat models with unusual design features that may have unexpected weaknesses. The best current models are so good that little opportunity for improvement remains.

The type of fuel affects the features of the boiler, and it may limit how the boiler can be installed. So, let's sort our boiler options by fuel type, and see their advantages and limitations.

Boilers Fueled with Natural Gas

Boilers that are fueled with natural gas have several important advantages over boilers that are fired by other fuels, and no significant disadvantages. Gas-fired boilers are compact, typically about the size of a dishwasher. They are quiet. They don't need fuel storage tanks. You can install one almost anywhere that is convenient.

Natural gas provides the highest fuel efficiency when it is burned in a "condensing" boiler. First introduced in the 1980's, condensing gas boilers typically have peak efficiencies over 90%, which is the highest efficiency of any fuel burning equipment. A condensing boiler is the only kind to consider if you are burning gas. The sidebar explains how they work. Figure 4-23 shows a typical installation, with a typical mistake.

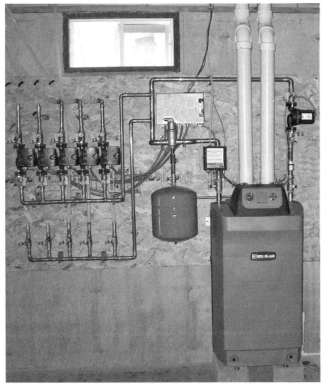

Weil-McLain

Figure 4-23. Gas-fired condensing boiler installation. The primary loop pump is installed incorrectly. See Figure 4-24 for the correct layout.

A condensing gas-fired boiler does not need a conventional chimney. The exhaust gases are clean and cool, so you can vent them through the nearest wall using a plastic pipe. Avoiding the cost of a chimney may offset the higher cost of the boiler. Also, the cool flue pipe does not require a gap around the pipe for fire safety. Eliminating this gap eliminates a major path for air leakage into the house.

You probably won't have to clean the insides of your boiler during its lifetime. The minor residue that occurs from burning natural gas tends to flake off the boiler's heating surfaces. This is an important benefit because any soot that accumulates on a combustion surface retards the flow of heat into the water and increases the amount of heat that is wasted to the flue.

What happens to the water that condenses out of the flue gas? It drains to a small tank, from which a small pump sends it to a sewer drain periodically. Make sure that your plumbing design includes a convenient drain for the condensate.

Most condensing boilers offer another important benefit, which is not inherently related to their condensing feature. It is the ability to bring combustion air to the boiler directly from the outside through a pipe, so the entire combustion system is isolated from the interior of the house. An installation of this kind is called a "sealed" system. These days, all boiler installations should have sealed combustion systems.

HOW CONDENSING BOILERS AND FURNACES WORK

Fossil fuels are compounds of carbon and hydrogen. When a fossil fuel is burned, the hydrogen in the fuel joins with oxygen in the air to become water vapor.

The water vapor in the exhaust gas contains two kinds of heat. One kind of heat, called "sensible heat," makes the vapor hot. The other kind of heat, called "latent heat," is the energy that is needed to turn liquid water into water vapor. With natural gas, the latent heat represents about 10% of the original fuel energy.

In conventional non-condensing boilers and furnaces, the exhaust gas is kept hot to prevent condensation of the gas in the flue, which would corrode a conventional steel flue. As a result, the water vapor escapes up the flue, taking away its latent heat. The high exhaust temperature also wastes some of the sensible heat of the fuel.

In contrast, a condensing boiler operates with a much lower exhaust temperature. It accomplishes this by using a much larger metal surface (called the "heat exchanger") that separates the combustion gases from the water. The larger surface allows the boiler to remove more of the sensible heat from the exhaust gas. In turn, this cools the exhaust to the point that some of the water vapor condenses on the heat exchanger, giving up its latent heat.

To avoid corrosion by the condensed water vapor, the heat exchanger is made of stainless steel or another metal that resists corrosion. Also, the entire flue is made of ordinary plastic pipe, which is immune to corrosion. This is possible because of the low exhaust temperature.

Condensing boilers and furnaces have another feature that improves efficiency. The combustion gas passages inside the heat exchanger are narrow, in order to extract the maximum amount of heat. As a result, the boiler or furnace needs a small fan to force combustion air through the heat exchanger. The fan turns off when the boiler is not firing, so there is little circulation of cold air through the boiler.

When a conventional gas boiler is not firing, the heat in the boiler causes cold air to circulate through the boiler by convection. The air takes heat out of the boiler water and discards it up the chimney. This "standby loss" can waste as much as 10% of the fuel input, but it is minimal in condensing boilers and furnaces.

A sealed combustion system avoids the energy waste of bringing combustion air through the house. It minimizes the risk of carbon monoxide getting into the house from a defective burner. And, the boiler is quieter because the burner noise is isolated from the interior of the house.

Boilers Fueled with Propane or LPG

Most boilers that burn propane are originally designed to burn natural gas, and they are adapted to propane with a modified burner. The manufacturer modifies the burner, or the heating contractor does it with a kit that is provided by the manufacturer.

A condensing boiler will have somewhat lower efficiency when burning propane, but it's not a big difference.

A propane-fired boiler has a big limitation that does not occur with natural gas. As we discussed previously, propane gas is heavier than air, so any leaking propane will accumulate at low points in the house. This is a serious restriction if your home will have a basement or other below-grade space.

Boilers Fueled with Oil

Modern oil-fired boilers are compact, not much larger than gas-fired units. They are clean, safe, and fairly quiet, so you have flexibility in finding a place to install one. For safety and ease of maintenance, install the boiler where any leaks between the oil tank and the boiler can be cleaned up easily. Check your building code about installation requirements, and make sure that your contractor follows the installation instructions completely.

Oil-fired boilers need periodic cleaning of the heat exchanger to maintain efficiency. Fuel oil leaves soot on the heat transfer surfaces of the boiler when it burns. Soot is an insulating material, so it restricts the flow of heat from the combustion gases into the heating water. As soot accumulates, more and more heat is diverted out the flue.

Unlike gas-fired condensing boilers, oil-fired boilers should not be vented through a side wall. Any oil-fired boiler should have a conventional flue that exhausts above roof level. Oil contains many contaminants, especially sulfur, and the exhaust from burning oil is acrid and somewhat sooty. Wind may circulate the exhaust around the outside of your home near ground level, where it might enter open windows or make outdoor activities unpleasant. Oil smoke may also stain nearby surfaces.

If you decide that oil is your best heating energy source, try to get one with a "sealed" combustion system. The sealed system offers the same benefits that we described previously for gas boilers. It has no disadvantages, it saves energy, it is a valuable safety feature, and it is the easiest method of supplying combustion air to your boiler.

■ Condensing Oil-Fired Boilers: Doubtful Advantage

A few oil-fired boilers are on the market that offer a condensing heat exchanger to improve energy efficiency. These operate on the same principle as condensing gas-fired boilers. However, the efficiency advantage of condensing oil-fired boilers is smaller than with gas.

Some manufacturers of condensing oil-fired boilers claim efficiencies as high as 92%. This is lower than the efficiencies of the best gas-fired condensing boilers. The maximum efficiency of conventional (non-condensing) oil-fired boilers is about 85%, which is higher than the efficiency of conventional (non-condensing) gas-fueled boilers.

The reason for the smaller advantage of oil-fired condensing boilers is that oil contains less hydrogen than natural gas. Hence, it produces less water vapor when it burns. The water vapor in the exhaust gas is the source of the efficiency advantage of condensing boilers.

Maintaining high efficiency depends on keeping the heat exchanger well cleaned. But, compared to cleaning a conventional oil-fired boiler, it may be more difficult to clean the heat exchangers properly because the passages are smaller and the interior layout of the boiler is more cluttered with equipment.

Ease of cleaning should be a deciding factor in selecting any oil-fired boiler. To see the cleaning procedures for any model, download its maintenance manual from the manufacturer's Web site.

The condensate from oil firing may be very acidic because of the sulfur in fuel oil. Therefore, the condensate must be passed through a cartridge of alkali material to protect the sewer pipe. The cartridge is small and inexpensive, but it is critical. Make sure that it is installed so that it can be replaced easily.

If you are considering a condensing oil-fired boiler, make an effort to select a model that has gained a good reputation in service. The limited range of models suggests that it has been difficult to produce a practical unit. On balance, if you must burn oil as your heating fuel, I can't recommend a condensing model with any enthusiasm.

Boilers Fired with Solid Fuels

Most home boilers will be fueled with gas or oil. You would consider a solid fuel – wood, coal, refuse-derived pellets, corn kernels, etc. – only for unusual situations. If you are interested in a boiler that uses one of these fuels, see *Heating with Firewood and Other Solid Fuels*, in *Last Look: Energy for Pioneers*, at the end of the book.

Calculate the Boiler Size

The heating capacity that your boiler needs is the sum of the heating capacities of all the hydronic heating units, which you calculated previously, multiplied times a fraction that is called the "diversity factor." The diversity factor accounts for the fact that you will not heat all the rooms simultaneously. Your super-efficient house is zoned so that heating can be shut off in vacant spaces, so the boiler will be heating only the rooms that need heat.

In a smaller, fully occupied house, the diversity factor is close to 1.0. In a large house, with a lot of rooms that are simultaneously unoccupied (such as spare bedrooms, a great room, recreation room, den, etc.), the diversity factor may be as low as 0.5.

However, don't risk undersizing the boiler. There is no efficiency penalty if you err in the direction of excess capacity. The price of a high-quality residential boiler does not increase much if you select the next larger size.

Select High Efficiency

After you have decided which fuel your boiler will use, find the models that have the highest efficiency ratings. The place to go is the Energy Star Web site, **www.EnergyStar.gov**. (We explain the Energy Star rating system in Step 7.)

The Energy Star listing covers all gas- and oil-fueled boilers sold in the United States that have an Annual Fuel Utilization Efficiency (AFUE) rating of 85% or better. The listing gives the manufacturer, the type of fuel, each model number, and its AFUE rating. Narrow your search to models that have the highest AFUE ratings for your fuel type.

Credible efficiency ratings for boilers that burn solid fuels generally are not available. Select a solid-fuel boiler for efficiency by examining the design of the boiler, which we cover under *Heating with Firewood and Other Solid Fuels*, at the end of the book.

Other Features for Boilers

Once you have identified the most efficient boiler models, look at their other features. Major boiler manufacturers offer a full range of literature on their products, which ranges from superficial sales brochures to detailed installation manuals. They offer most of this information for download from the Internet.

You will find that the more efficient models generally offer a variety of features, including a dizzying variety of control options. Here are the main options to consider, either to select or to avoid.

■ Water Temperature Reset

Water temperature reset is a control feature that automatically lowers the temperature of the heating water from the boiler as the outside temperature increases. ***This is an essential feature for hydronic heating systems.*** Make sure that your boiler has it.

Why is it desirable? First of all, it significantly improves the efficiency of the boiler. The high advertised efficiency of condensing boilers occurs only when the water temperature returning to the boiler is very low, around 60 °F (15 °C), which is too cold to be useful. In contrast, if the water temperature is set for 210 °F (99 °C), the maximum efficiency of the boiler drops to about 80%. At a return water temperature of 130 °F (54 °C), the best condensing boiler can provide an efficiency of only about 88% to 90%.

Higher system water temperature is needed only during colder weather. Lower water temperature at other times allows more of the latent heat in the combustion gases to be captured from the flue gas.

Boiler efficiency is improved even more because less frequent cycling reduces the loss of efficiency that occurs at the beginning of each firing cycle. Lower water temperature also reduces heat loss from the distribution pipes. Thermal stress on the boiler is reduced, which increases boiler life.

Water temperature reset also improves temperature stability in the rooms. The heat output of convective room heaters depends strongly on the water temperature. During milder weather, lowering the heating water temperature causes the heating units to respond more gradually, providing more stable room temperature.

Water temperature reset is a standard control option of most high-efficiency boilers. It requires installing a small temperature sensor on the outside of the house, which connects to the boiler controls with a small wire.

■ Boiler Turn-Off During Warm Weather

The outside air temperature sensor that is used by the water temperature reset control should also turn off the boiler when the weather becomes warm enough that heating is not needed. Without this control feature, the boiler may waste a certain amount of energy to keep itself warm during warm weather.

However, this feature may be redundant. The boiler should be controlled so that it does not fire unless a room thermostat calls for heating.

■ Time Controls

Boilers with fancy controls usually include an option to turn the boiler on and off according to a variety of time schedules. Generally, this feature is superfluous. Time control of heating should be done by the thermostats in the individual rooms. The boiler needs to remain available to heat any room on demand.

■ System Leak Detection

If the system leaks water, more water has to be added to replace the lost water. Impurities that harm the boiler and lower its efficiency enter the boiler along with the water that replaces leakage. If the entire hydronic system remains free of leaks, the boiler will last almost forever.

To alert the homeowner to the presence of leaks, some high-efficiency boilers include a feature that indicates when water is being added to the system. This may work in a variety of ways. For example, one model indicates the length of time that the water supply valve is open.

The best way to monitor water loss from the system is to use a special "system feeder," which we will explain later. A good feeder unit will warn about system leakage, so that leak monitoring by the boiler becomes redundant.

■ Domestic Water Heating

This is an option that you probably don't want. Most high-efficiency boilers offer controls that allow the boiler to heat domestic water by circulating hot water from the boiler to a separate water heating tank. However, this method of heating domestic water offers no significant benefit, and it has a number of drawbacks, which we will explain in Step 5.

Instead, install a separate water heater, selecting from the menu that you are offered in Step 5.

HYDRONIC DESIGN (5): THE OPTIMUM SYSTEM LAYOUT*

Unlike other modern kinds of heating, a hydronic heating system must be assembled from a number of different components. This book recommends one specific hydronic system design that makes the best use of modern system components. This design can be comfortable and efficient for the life of your home. It requires no adjustments to achieve perfect operation, and it requires very little maintenance. Make sure that your system follows this design precisely.

A caution in this part of your design is to avoid bad hydronic installation practices that persist in the heating trade. Many different hydronic piping arrangements are shown in plumbing handbooks and training manuals. Most of these arrangements are obsolete, and some are just plain wrong. For example, troublesome hydronic fittings such as "diverter tees" and "balancing valves" are unnecessary in well designed modern hydronic systems, but many heating contractors still use them.

The following discussion won't make you a heating contractor. That's not your job. We won't talk about the routine aspects of hydronic system installation, such as pipe sizing. The purpose of this discussion is to help you communicate with your heating contractor about the critical details that will make your system flawless. It's your home, so don't accept any lame excuses for installing the system in a way that is less than perfect.

System Layout for Most Homes

Figure 4-24 shows the hydronic system layout that is best for most applications. *The positions of the components are important. Make sure that your hydronic system is laid out this way!* The adjacent *Builder's Hydronic System Checklist* will help your contractor to install your system properly.

The main feature of the system layout is that it has two kinds of water loops, "primary" and "secondary." Each loop has its own circulating pump. The single "primary" loop circulates water through the boiler and the system accessories, but not through the house. Multiple "secondary" loops serve each heating zone of the house independently. All the secondary loops tap heating water from the primary loop.

---

* Dan Holohan, top practitioner and scholar of hydronic heating, is the inspiration for many of the ideas and much of the emphasis in our design of hydronic systems, especially the parts that explain how to keep air out of the system. Contractors who want to be sure of installing hydronic heating properly should study Holohan's little masterpiece, "Pumping Away," which is available through his Web site, **www.HeatingHelp.com**.

The primary loop includes several accessories that keep free air out of the water and keep the system filled with properly treated water. These accessories are (1) the expansion tank, (2) the air separator, (3) the vent, and (4) the system feeder. All of these should be connected to the same point in the primary loop, as shown in the diagram. We will discuss these accessories in greater detail, below.

The arrangement in Figure 4-24 is for room heating equipment that operates with high water temperature. This includes the kinds of hydronic room heaters that most houses will use, such as baseboard convectors.

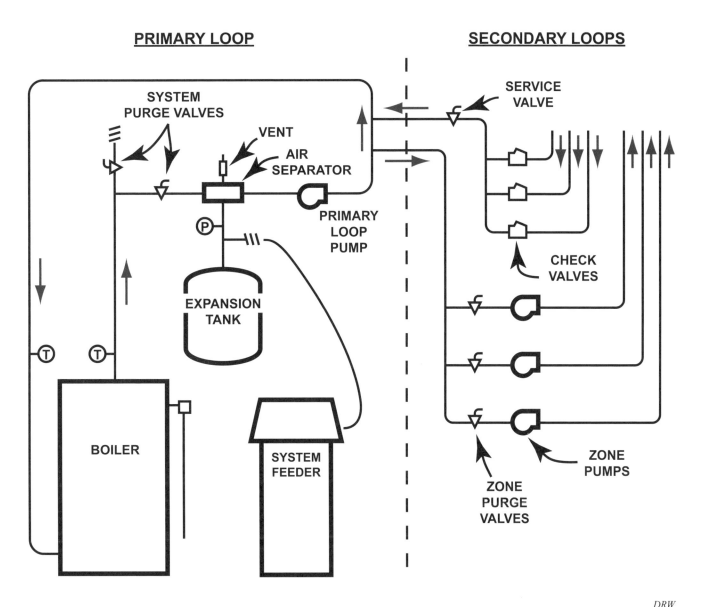

DRW

Figure 4-24. This is the best layout for most hydronic heating systems. The "primary" loop circulates water through the boiler, removes air from the water, and maintains the system pressure. Each room or heating zone is served by an independent "secondary" hot water loop that taps hot water from the "primary" loop. This arrangement provides maximum comfort and energy efficiency, with minimum trouble. The system has no components that require tricky adjustments. All the components shown here are clustered in the equipment space. The zone pumps and return pipes should be arranged in a vertical stack, as shown, for most effective purging of air.

BUILDER'S HYDRONIC SYSTEM CHECKLIST

OVERALL SYSTEM

☐ Use a primary/secondary system layout.

☐ Install all pumps with their shafts horizontal.

☐ Maintain a minimum pressure of 5 psi (35 kPa) at the highest point in the system by setting the appropriate pressure at the system feeder. Coordinate the system pressure with the expansion tank air charge so that the expansion tank is approximately one quarter filled with water when the system is cold. In most cases, the initial air charge of 12 psi (83 kPa) that comes from the factory is correct. Do NOT change it without good reason.

☐ Diligently eliminate all leaks. In case of doubt about the tightness of a connection or fitting, replace it.

PRIMARY LOOP

☐ Control the boiler and the primary loop circulation pump to operate only when one or more of the zones requires heating.

☐ Install a temperature reset control to adjust the boiler output temperature based on the outdoor temperature.

☐ Connect the (1) air separator, (2) air vent, (3) expansion tank, and (4) system feeder together, at the boiler outlet.

☐ Install the boiler circulating pump with its suction side connected to the outlet of the air separator and discharging toward the secondary loops.

☐ Make sure that the expansion/pressurization tank is large enough to accommodate the thermal expansion and contraction of the entire water volume in the system. You can't make the tank too big.

☐ Install the expansion tank vertically, with the water connection at the top or at the bottom. Installing the connection at the bottom makes the diaphragm last longer, and should always be done with larger tank sizes. Installing the connection at the top helps to eliminate air bubbles from the tank, and is acceptable for smaller tanks. Installing the tank sideways is never acceptable, as it will cause early failure of the diaphragm.

☐ Install a hydronic system feeder unit to pressurize the system and to provide treated makeup water. Do NOT install an automatic refilling connection from the house water system, because this invites flooding of the house and incorrect pressurization of the system.

☐ Make the common pipe between the primary and secondary loops 6" to 12" (15 cm to 30 cm) long. Install it as part of a longer straight run of pipe.

BUILDER'S HYDRONIC SYSTEM CHECKLIST

SECONDARY LOOPS

☐ Install a separate zone circulator pump for each heating zone. Yes, this will require as many pumps as zones.

☐ Install the zone pumps to discharge away from the boiler and toward the zones.

☐ Control each zone pump individually with the room (or zone) wall thermostat.

☐ Attach the zone circulating pumps to a vertical manifold. Attach the zone return pipes to another vertical manifold, in the same sequence. This aids purging of the system when it is first filled.

☐ Install a check valve with a weighted seat (also called a "flow control valve") at the return end of each secondary loop. The check valve prevents backflow into the zone when the zone pump is turned off. The weighted seat prevents convection of hot water into idle circuits.

ROOM HEATING EQUIPMENT

☐ Connect all individual heating units in parallel, NOT in series.

ADDITIONAL, FOR BASEBOARD HEATING

☐ Divide long runs of baseboard heating units into shorter runs to provide more uniform temperature distribution. Connect the shorter runs in parallel.

☐ Install the return pipe of baseboard convectors above the supply pipes to minimize air trapping inside the finned heating elements. The easy and attractive way to do this is by using baseboard units that have integral return pipes located above the fin tubes.

ADDITIONAL, FOR FLOOR HEATING

☐ Divide the floor piping of each zone into multiple hairpin loops, each of which is short enough to remain warm along its entire length. In each loop, route the cooler return water adjacent to the hotter supply water. Connect the loops in parallel. This arrangement creates a uniform temperature across the floor.

☐ Install a water temperature limit switch near the inlet to the floor coils. Set the temperature to protect the floor materials from overheating. Connect the limit switch to turn off the zone pump only.

☐ If the primary loop operates at a higher water temperature (which is necessary to serve most other types of hydronic heaters), design the floor heating loops to limit their water temperatures as appropriate for the floor materials.

Primary-Secondary Pumping: the Key to Good Performance

Our recommended layout uses a pumping design that is called "primary-secondary." The essence of this piping layout is that it uses one water circuit (called the "primary loop") to circulate water through the boiler, and additional water circuits (called "secondary loops") for the heating zones.

The water flow in each loop – the primary loop and each secondary loop – is entirely independent. The rate of water flow in each loop is determined entirely by its own small circulating pump.

Your heating contractor should understand that using individual loop pumps – instead of valves – to control the water flow to each heating zone is energy efficient and trouble-free. It can eliminate all the vexing problems of older hydronic systems. This design eliminates "balancing" valves that are difficult to adjust and that cause poor heating performance. *If a primary-secondary system is designed properly, there is nothing that requires adjustment, either during installation or afterward.*

An efficient hydronic system needs lots of little pumps. For example, if your home has eight heating zones (one for each major room, usually), your hydronic system will have eight zone pumps, plus one more pump in the primary loop. These pumps are small, inexpensive, and easy to install. Heating contractors seem to have an urge to reduce the number of pumps, typically by using one pump to serve several zones. Don't fall for this, it will degrade your system.

The Primary Loop

Let's start with the primary loop, which contains the boiler and most of the system accessories. The purpose of having a separate primary loop is to maintain continuous circulation through the boiler whenever any part of the house needs heating. This avoids large, abrupt differences in temperature between the outlet and the inlet of the boiler. Such fluctuations damage the boiler. It is especially important to avoid them with small, high-efficiency boilers that contain little water mass to damp out temperature changes.

Protecting the boiler from rapid temperature changes is so important that manufacturers of high-efficiency boilers typically insist on primary-secondary pumping. And, to make sure that the contractor gets the point, some manufacturers include the primary circulating pump as part of the boiler package.

Continuous circulation also improves efficiency by minimizing the time that the boiler spends at its maximum firing rate, when it is least efficient. (Whenever a boiler first starts firing, it must operate at its maximum output.)

The primary pump consumes only a small amount of energy because the primary loop is short and the pump does not have to overcome much resistance to water flow. To save energy, the boiler controls should turn off the boiler and the primary loop pump when none of the heating zones requires heat.

The Secondary Loops

Next, let's look at the secondary loops, which distribute the heating water to the individual rooms or zones. Each zone loop is fully independent of the others. Each loop has its own pump. The zone thermostat controls the room temperature by turning the pump on and off.

This method of control is simple, inexpensive, and energy efficient. It provides almost perfect isolation of rooms that don't need heating. Pumping is efficient because each pump operates only when its zone needs heating. The pump accounts for only a small fraction of the energy needed to heat the zone. Furthermore, much of the energy consumed by the pumps is converted to heat in the water.

If a single zone has more than one heating unit, pipe all the units in parallel and supply them with one zone pump. For example, you might subdivide the baseboard convectors along a long exterior wall into parallel groups, for the reasons that we covered earlier.

Connecting Secondary Loops to the Primary Loop

Finally, look at the connection between the primary loop and the secondary loops. This is a short length of pipe that the loops have in common. This short piece of pipe is important. It provides just the right amount of water from the boiler to each secondary loop. No valves or other control devices are needed, and there is nothing to fail. The simplicity of this method of distributing the heating water flow is one of the main reasons why primary-secondary pumping is such a good system.

This connection is foolproof if it is installed properly. The common pipe should be installed as part of a longer straight run in the primary loop. Generally, the common pipe should be between 6" and 12" (between 15 cm and 30 cm) long. If the common pipe is too long, it may allow the primary pump to apply pressure to the secondary loops. If the common pipe is very short, it may allow secondary loop water to short circuit from the discharge point back to the inlet of the loop without passing through the boiler first.

This connection seems almost like magic to heating contractors who don't understand it. They want to complicate the system with unnecessary flow control gadgets that will cause trouble. Don't let that happen.

Limit Water Temperature for Hydronic Floor Heating

Under the previous heading, *Hydronic Floor Heating*, we explained that the water temperature for floor heating is much lower than it is for other types of hydronic heating equipment. Floor heating has a maximum allowable temperature, which depends on the floor materials. For tubing installed in a hardwood floor, some authorities state that the water temperature should not exceed 85 °F (29 °C), to avoid drying and warping the wood. The highest water temperatures may occur in concrete slabs, where the maximum is about 120 °F (49 °C). In contrast, other hydronic heating equipment, such as baseboard convectors and fan-coil units, may operate with water temperatures as high as 200 °F (93 °C).

If a hydronic system is used only for floor heating, and only for one kind of floor, simply limit the boiler output temperature to the maximum allowable floor water temperature. For example, this situation would be typical for a house built on a concrete slab that uses floor heating exclusively.

However, if a hydronic system uses high-temperature heating equipment in addition to floor heating, the situation becomes more complicated. The boiler output temperature must be high enough to serve all the heating equipment, but this temperature is much too high for the floor heating. In that case, the secondary loops that serve the floor heating must be designed in special way to limit the water temperature to the floors.

The secondary loop design in Figure 4-25 limits the water temperature for floor heating. It mixes the hot water from the primary loop with the cooler water that returns from the floor heating circuits. A thermostat regulates the mixing valve to keep the water supplied to the floors at a fixed temperature. The temperature of the room is controlled by the room thermostat, which turns the circulating pump on and off.

If a hydronic system serves both high- and low-temperature heating equipment, there is an energy efficiency penalty if you have a condensing boiler. The lower water temperature of floor heating makes a condensing boiler more efficient, but the need to serve high-temperature heaters prevents the boiler from exploiting this advantage. If the system serves mostly floor heating, the higher boiler operating temperature may increase energy consumption by as much as 10%.

If your home is large and if you want to have a lot of floor heating, you can avoid this efficiency penalty by installing two separate hydronic systems, one for the floor heating and one for the high-temperature heaters. This arrangement incurs the cost and space of an additional boiler and its accessories. However, it will save energy for the floor heating, and it may save a certain amount of piping cost if the boilers are installed in different locations.

Any floor heating system should have a high-temperature limit switch that stops the zone pump if the zone water temperature limit is exceeded. This protects the floor from excess temperature that could occur if a thermostat or mixing valve malfunctions. The switch is installed ahead of the inlets to the floor tubing, where it can detect excessive temperature before the water reaches the floor.

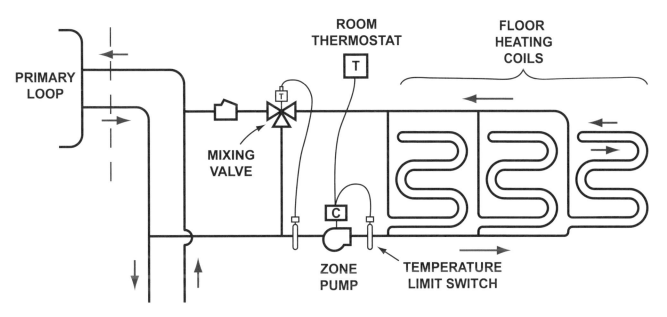

DRW

Figure 4-25. Secondary loop layout for spaces that use floor heating. To limit the floor temperature, the mixing valve mixes hot water from the primary loop with the cooler water that returns from the floor heating. The room temperature typically is controlled by turning the zone pump on and off.

HYDRONIC DESIGN (6): INSTALL THE BOILER, SYSTEM ACCESSORIES, AND PIPE

In Step 1, you set aside a space in your home for the boiler and its accessories. Now, let's organize that space to provide a perfect hydronic system installation and to make every item in the space accessible for maintenance.

Your domestic water heater probably will be installed in the same space as your heating boiler. Also, if you have any large water treatment equipment – such as a water softener – you may wish to install it adjacent to the heating equipment.

The common feature of all this equipment is that it contains a lot of water. Therefore, the space should have an ample floor drain to allow draining the equipment for maintenance and to avoid flooding the space if there is break in the water supply to any of this equipment.

To understand how the hydronic system should be installed, think of it in three groups. The first group consists of the boiler and its accessories:

- the boiler
- its pressure relief valve
- the flue
- the combustion air supply pipe

The second group consists of system accessories that are attached to the primary loop. Referring to Figure 4-24, these are:

- the primary loop pump
- the air separator
- the system air vent, which is attached to the air separator
- the pressurized expansion tank
- the system feeder
- a pressure gauge, located near the pressurized expansion tank
- a temperature gauge for the boiler supply water
- a temperature gauge for the boiler return water
- a system purge valve.

The third group consists of the accessories for the individual zone (secondary) loops, which should be installed on a supply and a return manifold. The accessories for the secondary loops are:

- the zone pumps, preferably mounted on the secondary loop supply manifold, which is a vertical pipe that is connected to the primary loop
- the zone check valves, preferably mounted on the secondary loop return manifold, which is another vertical pipe
- valves for isolating individual secondary loops for purging and maintenance, preferably installed on the supply and return manifolds

- for zones that require regulated water temperature (usually for floor heating), mixing valves that mix primary loop water with zone return water
- for zones that have a maximum allowable water temperature (usually for floor heating), a high temperature limit switch that can stop the zone pump.

Again, we are explaining these items primarily for the benefit of your heating contractor. Your job is to make sure that your contractor understands them, so that he can install them properly.

Be especially vigilant as the hydronic system hardware is installed. Trouble that occurs in hydronic heating systems usually can be traced to mistakes made by the heating contractor when installing the system. The installation of the pipe, pumps, and system accessories involves a number of critical details that may not be obvious to every heating contractor. With the knowledge that you will gain in the next few pages, you may prevent an installation mistake that would cause your system to misbehave in the future.

The Flue and the Combustion Air Supply

If your boiler allows you to install a sealed combustion system (as I strongly recommend), it will be connected to the outside with two pipes, one for combustion air and one for exhaust. In most cases, it will be most convenient to run these pipes through a nearby exterior wall. Simplify the wall penetration by using a "coaxial" wall fitting, in which the outside air intake surrounds the flue pipe. Figures 4-26 and 4-27 show a coaxial wall installation.

The flue pipe from the boiler to the exterior wall should run almost horizontally, but not quite. The water vapor in exhaust gas continues to condense in the flue pipe, especially where the pipe is cooled by the surrounding air intake pipe. The amount of water is small, but if it flows toward the outlet, enough may freeze at the outlet during cold weather to block the exhaust. To avoid this, slant the flue pipe slightly upward as it travels toward the wall. In that way, condensed water flows back to the boiler's condensate drain.

Block any air leakage around the pipes at the wall penetration. The outer surfaces of coaxial vents for condensing boilers remain cool, so you can seal them tightly to the house structure without fear of creating a fire hazard. Make the smallest possible hole in the wall or roof, and fill the gap around the pipe with a rubber seal, or with caulking that will remain pliable. Mortar can be used to seal around a pipe that passes through a masonry wall.

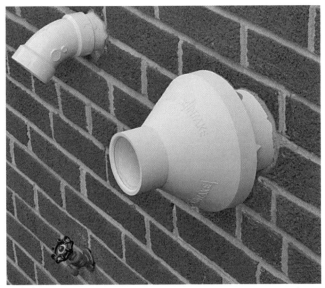

DRW

Figure 4-26. Combined exhaust and outside air intake for a high-efficiency gas-fired hydronic boiler. The exhaust is from the center pipe. Outside air enters behind the conical portion of the fitting. The smaller exhaust to the left is for a direct-vent gas-fired water heater.

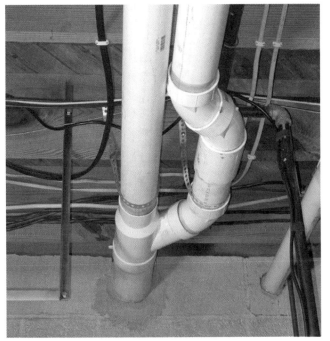

DRW

Figure 4-27. Inside view of the sealed combustion system wall penetration. The exhaust pipe is on the left, and the outside air intake is on the right.

If your boiler is fueled with oil, the flue gas will be smelly and slightly sooty, so the flue should exit vertically above the roof. How you design the flue depends on whether your oil-fired boiler can provide a sealed combustion system. If the boiler can provide a sealed system, the combustion air intake may surround

the flue or it may come from a different direction, through an exterior wall.

If you cannot install a sealed system, be careful to install the flue in a manner that avoids the entry of flue gases into the house. For the critical issues, refer to *Eliminating the Danger of Carbon Monoxide*, toward the end of Step 4.

Prefabricate the Loop Components

As you can see from Figure 4-24, a hydronic system has a number of pieces. Putting the pieces together is the heating contractor's job, not yours. However, a well organized installation is less likely to have mistakes, and it is easier to understand and maintain in the future. And, it is more pleasant to look at. So, talk with your contractor about the arrangement of your "boiler room" hardware.

A capable heating contractor will assemble the components in his shop and bring the entire assembly to your home, ready to install with just a few pipe connections. Alternatively, the contractor can buy the primary loop components piped up and ready to be hung on a wall. Figure 4-28 shows a typical assembly. (The system feeder, another important accessory for the primary loop, is installed separately.)

It is also possible to buy pre-assembled supply and return manifolds for the secondary loops, as in Figure 4-29. Installing the zone connections in a vertical stack makes it easier to purge the system prior to its first operation, as we will explain.

The arrangement of the two figures shows how the secondary loop manifolds are connected to the primary loop. As you can see, the connected assemblies look similar to the diagram in Figure 4-24.

Keep Free Air and Water Vapor Out of the System

Free air is responsible for most trouble in hydronic systems. The hydronic system is filled with water that comes from the domestic water supply. This water contains dissolved air, perhaps lots of it. As long as the air remains dissolved, it does not interfere with heating. However, if the air comes out of the water as a free gas, it will keep the heating units from working at full capacity and it will cause strange noises.

We stressed that your heating contractor should lay out the system exactly as shown in Figure 4-24. Why are we being so fussy about this? Because that arrangement keeps free air out of the system most effectively.

After hydronic systems were first introduced, it took engineers and heating contractors a while to understand the problems caused by free air. They could not see how the water flowed through the system. However,

Figure 4-28. A pre-assembled primary loop accessory package. The boiler output connects to the upper connection on the right side, and the boiler return connects to the lower connection on the right side. The bottom left connection goes to the secondary loop supply manifold, and the bottom right connection goes to the secondary loop return manifold.

Figure 4-29. Pre-assembled secondary loop supply and return manifolds for four heating zones. This is where all the zone pipes come together to connect with the primary loop. The individual zone pumps are installed on the supply manifold, which is in the rear, with the top connection at left. The return pipes connect to the manifold in front, with the top connection at right. The green box controls power to the pumps in response to the zone thermostats. For perfect comfort and efficiency, a typical house needs 6 to 12 secondary loops.

they developed an intuition that air was somehow causing constipation in their systems. They called this "air binding." What is this strange phenomenon? It is simply the trapping of free air inside heating units.

Air can't stop water from flowing through the system, as some people believe. Instead, free air occupies space that reduces contact between the water and the metal surfaces in the heating units. If the water passages inside a heating unit are occupied by air instead of water, that part of the unit becomes ineffective. Figure 4-30 shows an example.

Two conditions cause dissolved air to come out of the water in the form of a free gas: *low pressure* and *high temperature*.

To see how lowering pressure releases dissolved gas, open a bottle of soda pop or champagne. The resulting froth occurs because you have lowered the pressure in the container, allowing the dissolved gas (carbon dioxide, in both cases) to emerge from the liquid.

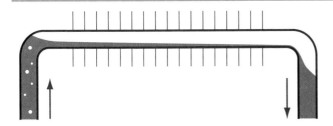

DRW

Figure 4-30. "Air binding" of a heating unit. If dissolved air becomes free inside a hydronic system, it will float to a nearby high point. If a heating unit is located at a high point, air will displace water inside the unit, reducing the surface area that is heated by the water. Here, the fins of the heating coil have little contact with the hot water.

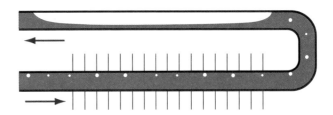

DRW

Figure 4-31. Avoiding "air binding" in a baseboard convector. The trick is to locate the return water pipe above the finned heating element. This allows any free air inside the heating element to rise into the return pipe, where it will eventually flow to the system air separator. Here, the fins of the heating coil are almost completely in contact with the hot water.

You can see the effect of increasing temperature by watching a pot of tap water that is being heated on a stove. Long before the water reaches boiling temperature, you will see bubbles of air being driven from the water on the heated bottom of the pot.

The water temperature in a heating system is highest at the outlet end of the boiler, so air tends to appear there. For that reason, the air separator is installed right after the boiler outlet, where it can intercept the air before the hot water flows to the heating units.

The water pressure is lowest in the highest points of the system. Also, any air that comes out of the water at the high points tends to be trapped there by buoyancy. The combination of these two effects is the prime cause of "air binding" in heating units. For this reason, it used to be standard practice to install air vents on the heating units of upper floors.

However, air vents on heaters are a source of trouble. They may eventually stick in the closed position, in which case they cease to work. Or, they may start to leak water around the outside of the heating units, which makes a mess. Modern hydronic systems avoid the need for individual vents on heating equipment. They do this by keeping the amount of dissolved air in the system so low that it will not emerge from the water as free air.

The system layout in Figure 4-24 needs only a single vent, which is mounted on the air separator. The air separator eliminates excess air before it is distributed to the heaters. And, the pressurization tank maintains enough pressure in the upper part of the system to keep air from coming out of the water.

Low pressure can occur on the suction side of pumps, if they are installed in the wrong place. This can draw air out of the water, causing the pump to "air bind." However, our recommended layout connects the suction side of all pumps to the outlet of the pressurization tank, which holds the pressure constant. Therefore, the pumps can only increase their discharge

pressure. This raises the pressure in the heating circuits, which keeps air from emerging.

The same problems that are caused by free air can also be caused by water vapor. Both are gases, and both can displace water. Water vapor will form inside the system for the same reasons that free air will appear: *low pressure* and *high temperature*.

And, *the solution is the same*. The way to prevent water vapor from forming is to maintain sufficient pressure in every part of the system to prevent the water from turning into vapor. The job of maintaining adequate pressure is shared by the pressurization tank and the system feeder, which we will explain in greater detail.

Free air and water vapor also cause knocking and gurgling noises. Water in a completely filled system flows silently. However, free air in the system breaks up the water flow into slugs. When a slug of water encounters an abrupt turn inside the piping or inside a heating unit, the slug hits the downstream surface like a bullet. If there are big air gaps in the water stream, the slugs of water can build up speed and make loud knocks when they hit. If the water contains a froth of smaller bubbles, the broken-up water stream makes a gurgling sound.

■ The Return Water Should Flow Upward

In hydronic heating units, the water should enter at the bottom and exit at the top. In this way, any air bubbles float out the top and return to the air separator, which is installed near the boiler.

In hydronic baseboard units, where the finned pipe is horizontal, install the return pipe above the finned pipe. Figure 4-31 shows how it's done. Compare this to Figure 4-30.

As shown in the previous Figure 4-12, manufacturers of baseboard units offer a return pipe that is mounted above the finned tube, inside the enclosure.

■ Water Velocity Removes Air

A few small air bubbles traveling along with the heating water will do no harm. However, it is essential to keep the bubbles moving with the water stream so they will reach the air separator before they combine into big slugs of air. Water velocity is the key. If the pumps and pipe are sized properly, the water velocity inside the narrow passages of the heating units will be high enough to sweep out any free air.

In the secondary heating circuits of Figure 4-24, the pumps always provide full flow through the heating units whenever they are running. When a zone pump is not operating, the water in the loop cools and dissolves any free air.

The Air Separator and Vent

The air separator is part of the primary loop, where it typically shares a connection with the expansion tank and the system feeder, as in Figure 4-24.

The air separator is a simple device that causes air to come out of the water, and then collects it. The most common type of air separator is simply a large chamber that slows the water velocity, causing bubbles to emerge. The air is trapped behind a baffle in the separator, where it flows upward into an air vent.

The air vent usually is a separate piece of equipment that screws into the top of the separator. The air vent has a float valve that allows the air to leave the system without letting any water escape.

Why are the air separator and vent installed separately? Because there are different designs for each. Also, air vents commonly are installed alone at the high points of hydronic systems.

One of the advantages of our recommended systems is that they don't need air vents on the individual heating units. However, air must be driven out of the system somewhere. That place is the outlet of the boiler. The water is hottest there, driving the most air out of the water. The air separator should be the first thing that any free air encounters after leaving the boiler.

The Expansion/Pressurization Tank

Every hydronic system needs an expansion tank. The expansion tank performs two essential functions:

- It accommodates the change in water volume as the system changes temperature. Water may expand as much as four percent from its cold state to its maximum temperature in a home heating system.

- It maintains adequate pressure throughout the system. Pressure keeps the water from boiling inside the system, and it keeps dissolved air from coming out of the water.

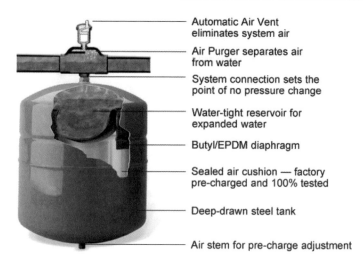

Automatic Air Vent eliminates system air

Air Purger separates air from water

System connection sets the point of no pressure change

Water-tight reservoir for expanded water

Butyl/EPDM diaphragm

Sealed air cushion — factory pre-charged and 100% tested

Deep-drawn steel tank

Air stem for pre-charge adjustment

Amtrol

Figure 4-32. Cutaway diagram of a typical hydronic system expansion tank. The diagram shows the correct location with respect to the air separator and vent. In this installation, the tank dangles below the air separator, with the water on top of the rubber diaphragm. This arrangement allows any air bubbles in the tank to escape easily. However, larger tanks require the water connection to be at the bottom.

In old hydronic systems, these functions were performed by a vented tank located above the highest heating unit in the system. This method was simple and reliable, except that it could be awkward to find a location for the tank at a sufficient height within the house. If the tank was located in an unheated space, such as the attic, it could freeze and burst.

To avoid this difficulty, a modern hydronic system usually has a closed, pressurized expansion tank. Figure 4-32 shows its essential features.

A pressurized expansion tank itself is simple, but installing it properly requires knowledge that not all heating contractors have mastered. Therefore, we will spell out the details.

In a closed expansion tank, a pressurized bubble of air acts like a spring, absorbing the expansion and contraction of the system water, and maintaining the system pressure. The best kind of closed expansion tank uses a rubber diaphragm to separate the air bubble from the water. The diaphragm keeps the water from absorbing the air. This type of expansion tank is called a "diaphragm tank" or "bladder tank." An older type of closed expansion tank that lacks a diaphragm is still around, so be careful to avoid it.

A properly installed diaphragm tank will be trouble-free for years. But, it does have a service life that is only a fraction of the life of the house. In time, a closed expansion tank fails by losing its air charge. The most likely route is through a crack in the diaphragm, which will develop after years of flexing. Then, the air charge will dissolve into the water. Also, air may escape through a defect in the tank itself, typically a leak in the air valve or a pinhole leak in the tank caused by rust.

How do you know if the expansion tank has a leak? The pressure gauge installed in the primary loop will drop below its proper setting. This indicates a leak somewhere in the system, or a loss of the air charge.

■ Selecting the Tank Size

Make sure that the expansion tank is big enough. Oversizing the tank is harmless, but undersizing causes trouble. In case of doubt, select the next larger size. It won't cost much more.

If the tank is undersized, expansion of the water when the system is operating will raise the system pressure until the safety valve (called the "relief valve") blows open and dumps water from the system. This loss of water and its continual replacement will cause trouble.

When the system is turned off, an undersized expansion tank will empty completely as the water cools and shrinks. The fully expanded diaphragm will prevent the air charge from pressurizing the water. If that happens, shrinkage of the water will create a vacuum in the system. The vacuum will draw air into the system through the air vent.

So, how big should the tank be? The contractor should calculate the size from the fact that the water volume in a hydronic system can change by four percent. The tank should be at least one quarter full when the system is cold, and it should be about half full when the system is at maximum temperature. In other words, one fourth of the tank volume represents a four percent change in system volume.

Therefore, *the expansion tank should have a volume that is at least sixteen percent of the total volume of water in the system.* Your heating contractor should calculate the system water volume from the length and diameter of all the pipes and heaters, plus the volume of water inside the boiler.

■ Installing the Expansion Tank

Ideally, a diaphragm expansion tank should be installed so that the air chamber is on top of the diaphragm, with the tank supported on a base and the water connection at the bottom. In this way, the diaphragm is lifted uniformly by the water.

In any other orientation, the water applies an uneven stress on the diaphragm, shortening its life. However, it has become commonplace for smaller, residential sized expansion tanks to be installed with the water connection at the top, as in Figure 4-32. Tank manufacturers approve this installation for smaller

tanks, with a maximum capacity of about 14 gallons (53 liters). This orientation allows any air bubbles in the tank to escape easily to the air vent.

Any other tank orientation is destructive to the diaphragm, and is not approved for tanks of any size. Make sure that your heating contractor installs the tank properly.

■ Setting the System Pressure with a Closed Expansion Tank

Residential expansion tanks usually are shipped by the manufacturer with an air charge pressure of 12 psi (82 kPa). *The contractor should not change this pressure by adding or removing air from the tank.* Fiddling with the air charge pressure is likely to allow free air to form in the heating water.

Even some writers of installation and training manuals fail to understand how the expansion tank works, and they mislead heating contractors into "adjusting" the expansion tank pressure.

Before the system is filled with water, the expansion tank is full of air. After the system is filled with water, the contractor should use the system feeder, which we explain next, to apply pressure to the system. *The pressure that is applied to the system should approximately double the original air pressure of the expansion tank,* to about 24 psi (164 kPa). Doubling the pressure at the tank squeezes the air charge in the tank to approximately half the tank volume. This is the desired condition, allowing the water in the system to both expand and contract.

Let's review this critical point. When the system is first put into service, the system is pressurized so that the pressure *measured at the expansion tank* is double the original air charge pressure. To make this adjustment possible, a pressure gauge is installed at the inlet to the expansion tank.

Why do we want the pressure at the expansion tank to be 24 psi (164 kPa)? In short, because we want to maintain enough pressure in every part of the system to keep the heating water from boiling, and also to keep any dissolved air from coming out of the water. Let's see how we arrive at that number.

The heating water pressure is lowest at the highest point in the system. Keeping the water from boiling requires a minimum pressure of 5 psi (35 kPa), so that is the minimum pressure that we need at the top of the system. However, the expansion tank usually is installed near the bottom of the system, because that is where the boiler and the circulation pumps are located. The weight of the water column above the expansion tank increases the pressure at the level of the tank.

If the pressure is 24 psi (164 kPa) at the bottom of the system and 5 psi (35 kPa) at the top of the system, the difference is 19 psi (129 kPa). This pressure difference corresponds to a water column height of 44 feet (13 meters). This is approximately the height of a mansion that is four stories tall, with the expansion tank installed in the basement.

Thus, by filling the expansion tank to a pressure of 12 psi (82 kPa), the manufacturer makes it possible for the tank to be used in almost all single-family houses or condominiums. The contractor gets the expansion tank to operate properly without doing any math or making any adjustments.

If your building is taller than four stories, be certain that your hydronic system contractor knows how to provide adequate pressure at the top of the hydronic system. To do this, the contractor must increase the air pressure in the expansion tank by an appropriate amount *before filling the system*, and then double that pressure at the time the system is filled.

Another solution is to install the boiler, the expansion tank, and other primary loop components on an upper level of the house, less than 40 feet (12 meters) below the highest point in the hydronic system.

The System Feeder

What maintains the pressure in your hydronic system after it is filled and operating? This question is important because the volume of water in the system will shrink over time. Venting air when the system is started will reduce the water volume. Also, water may eventually escape from the system at corroded pipe connections, failed pump seals, and other leaks.

If the system loses a small amount of water, the water in the expansion tank will replace it. However, *the expansion tank can't maintain the system pressure once the water in the expansion tank is used up*. As the system loses water beyond this point, the system pressure will drop, and troubles will begin as air comes out of the water.

Eventually, a vacuum will form in the system whenever it cools. This will draw more air into the system at any points of leakage.

 The system feeder is an essential new component that offers several important benefits for a hydronic heating system.

A common method of replacing water loss and maintaining system pressure is to connect the hydronic system to the house water system. This works because the water supply system in most locations has a pressure that is high enough to provide the needed system pressure.

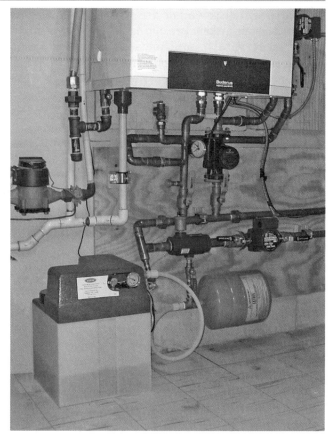

Axiom Industries

Figure 4-33. "System feeder" for a hydronic system, located at the lower left. A larger tank, capable of holding all the system's liquid, would be better. The boiler is mounted on the wall, above all the accessories. The round grey expansion tank is mounted improperly. It should be installed upright. The flexible connection should be a metal-braided hose.

However, *this common practice is a recipe for disaster*. If the system develops a major leak, the water supply system will continue to feed the leak, creating serious water damage. In the longer term, if the system has slow and invisible leaks, the antifreeze will eventually be diluted to the point that a system rupture from freezing becomes likely. And, any special water additives – such as chemicals to prevent corrosion of aluminum boilers – will be diluted out.

So, how should we maintain pressure in the system to avoid free air? The answer is to install a recently developed system accessory that is called a "system feeder." It consists of a storage tank, a pump to fill the system from the tank, and a system pressure switch to control the pump. See Figure 4-33. The system feeder is essential, so make room for it next to your boiler.

The antifreeze and anti-corrosion chemicals are mixed with the water in the system feeder's tank, so that water added to the system always contains the proper amount of additives. If the system needs to be drained for maintenance, draining to the tank avoids a mess and saves all the additives for reuse.

The pressure setting of the system feeder is what determines the system pressure. The pressure needs to be set as we explained previously. If the system pressure falls below the proper setting, the system feeder pump draws water from the feeder tank and adds it to the system until pressure is restored.

The tank typically is made of transparent plastic, with water level markings. If the feeder adds water to the system to compensate for leaks, the tank level drops, warning the homeowner that water is being lost. Some manufacturers may offer an alarm that warns of falling water level.

If the system develops a serious leak, water damage is limited to the amount of water that is contained in the feeder tank. Also, the feeder eliminates the possibility of polluting the public water system with your hydronic system's chemicals. This eliminates the need for a "backflow preventer" in the pipe from the house water supply.

The system feeder's tank should be large enough to drain fluid from the system when repairs are needed. Typically, the amount of fluid removed is only a small fraction of the total system volume. For example, one manufacturer offers two residential sizes, 7 gallons (25 liters) and 17 gallons (65 liters). A smaller unit can be hung on a wall, if desired.

The Pumps and Check Valves

The small pumps used in home hydronic systems are called "circulators" in the trade. These centrifugal pumps are small, inexpensive, and quiet. Figure 4-29 shows typical units.

The location of the pumps in the system is important for keeping free air out of the system. Install the primary loop pump with its suction side connected to the air separator, and the discharge facing toward the secondary loops. This location lowers the pressure in the air separator, helping to remove air, and it increases the pressure in the secondary loops, helping to suppress air.

One quirk of most residential circulators is that they should be installed so that their shafts are horizontal. This is to keep the weight of the shaft and impeller from wearing out the end bearings. The pump housing can be installed in any orientation around the horizontal shaft.

Each secondary loop pump should be installed so that it discharges into the beginning of its loop. In this way, the pump will increase the pressure in the loop, which helps to suppress free air.

Each secondary loop has a "check valve," which prevents the water in the loop from flowing backward when the loop pump is turned off. The check valve is needed for two reasons.

When some loop pumps are operating but others are not, the pressure at the outlet end of the active loops tends to push water backward into the idle loops. This would waste heating energy in the idle zones. The check valves on the idle loops prevent this.

Also, when a secondary loop is idle, the cold water in the loop tends to fall by gravity into other parts of the system that are filled by warmer, lighter water. This creates a slow circulation through the idle loop. The check valve has a weighted disk that is heavy enough to block this weak convection force. (A valve that performs only this function is called a "flow control" valve. If your contractor selects and installs the check valve properly, a separate flow control valve is not needed.)

The check valve can be installed at either the inlet or outlet end of the loop. It's slightly preferable to install the check valves at the outlet end. In this way, air bubbles carried into the return manifold by the active loops will not float into the idle loops.

Routing the Heating Water Pipe

Coordinate the installation of the pipes for the hydronic system with the installation of the pipes for the house domestic water system. Especially, route the pipes so that they will be easily accessible for repair. Refer to *Install Pipes to be Replaceable*, in Step 5.

The hydronic system is a closed system, and the water in it is treated to deter corrosion. Therefore, if the pipes are copper, they should last indefinitely. If the pipes are plastic, all bets are off.

Installing hydronic system pipe is easiest if the boiler is located in a basement. This allows the horizontal distribution pipes to be attached to the bottom of the first floor. The branches that serve the first floor usually can rise directly through the floor to the heating units.

For heating equipment on upper floors, the water pipe usually will rise through interior walls. If those walls are insulated, which is desirable in many cases (see Step 3), install the pipe along the walls studs to minimize interference with the insulation. However, do not fasten the pipe to the studs, which would make it impossible to replace the pipe.

Route the pipes away from all spaces that are not well insulated, such as the garage, crawl space, or attic. Also, route the pipe away from exterior walls. This reduces dependence on anti-freeze to protect the system when it is turned off, and to prevent freezing in pipes that serve individual rooms where the heating is turned off. Anti-freeze slows water flow in the system, and it reduces heat transfer in the heating units. Therefore, you don't want to use more than is necessary to protect your system.

Hydronic System Insulation

All hydronic system pipe should be insulated where it passes through unheated or partially heated spaces, such as an unoccupied basement. Use preformed foam insulation that is sized to fit the pipe exactly. Get the highest R-value that is available. Place the split in the insulation at the bottom of the pipe. Tape the joints in the insulation with long-lasting tape that is made for the purpose.

Where the pipe is attached to a structural member, such as a floor joist, use pipe hangers that provide sufficient clearance to avoid interference with the preformed pipe insulation. Include instructions for hanging and insulating pipe in your construction drawings.

It is not necessary to insulate pipe that is located entirely inside its own zone. In that case, the bare pipe acts as part of the heating unit for the room.

However, the pipe should be insulated if it could lose heat outside the space. For example, if the pipe runs through a concrete slab on grade, some heat from the pipe would be lost to the earth below the slab and to the outer wall. In that case, insulate the pipe.

Insulation does not protect pipe against freezing. It only reduces heat loss while the system is operating. If water is not flowing inside a length of pipe, the water inside the pipe will cool to the surrounding air temperature within an hour or so, even with the best insulation.

Freeze Protection for Hydronic Systems

Hydronic systems use an antifreeze solution in the water to protect the system against freezing. The type of antifreeze depends on the boiler. The boiler manufacturer will be specific about the type and concentration to use. Follow these instructions precisely.

This protection is needed because some parts of your hydronic system may fall below freezing temperature, even if the entire system is located within the insulated shell of the house. For example, a baseboard convector that is installed in an unoccupied guest bedroom may fall below freezing temperature if the room is well isolated from the rest of the house. If the house is shut down for a winter vacation, the entire system may be subject to freezing temperatures.

Freeze protection eventually fails if your system leaks and is then refilled with plain water. In time, the antifreeze solution will become diluted enough to freeze. To minimize this risk, install a system feeder to replenish your system as we described earlier, rather than refilling the system directly from the house water supply.

Treating the System Water Against Corrosion

In addition to using an antifreeze solution, all hydronic systems should have some kind of water additive to prevent corrosion and deposits in the system. The types and amounts of additives depend on the quality of your water supply. They also depend on the metals in the system.

Boilers with aluminum heat exchangers are especially vulnerable to corrosion. They need protection with chemicals that are specifically formulated to protect the aluminum in the boiler.

When you first fill the system and when you refill it after maintenance, follow the manufacturer's instructions for treating the water. This procedure is sure to be forgotten if the system is refilled in later years. Therefore, make a copy of the water treatment instructions, get it laminated for durability, and attach it to the system feeder.

HYDRONIC DESIGN (7): PURGE THE SYSTEM BEFORE STARTUP

After your brand new heating system is installed, the big day comes when it is filled with water and put into operation. This is the climax of your good design. Here's how your contractor should fill your system.

The system initially is full of air, so the first step is to get all the air out of the system and replace it with water. This is called "purging." The layout in Figure 4-24 anticipated the need for purging. That's why it has the valves labeled "system purge valves" and "zone purge valves."

The system feeder, an important accessory that we explained previously, is a great aid in purging the system. The system feeder mixes the appropriate water treatment chemicals with the entering water, so put the proper amount of chemicals into the system feeder.

To get started, attach a drain hose to the purge valve above the boiler, open the purge valve, close the valve between the boiler and the air separator, and close all the service valves that are installed ahead of the zone pumps.

Then, open the service valve for the lowest zone pump (if the pumps are installed in a vertical stack, as we recommend). Operate the system feeder until water appears at the purge valve. Turn off the system feeder, and close the zone service valve. At this point, the entire secondary loop served by that pump is filled, the primary loop is filled, and the boiler is filled.

Next, open the service valve for the second lowest zone pump. Start the system feeder again. This time, the system feeder will be pushing the air in that zone through the already filled primary loop and boiler. You will see a lot of bubbles coming out of the purge valve. When the bubbles stop, turn off the system feeder, and close that zone service valve.

Continue in this manner until the air has been removed from all the zones. With this procedure, the water and air always move in the same direction, which is the same direction that the water flows when

TIP: MINIMIZE AIR WHEN FILLING THE SYSTEM

When filling an empty hydronic system, use hot water from the home's water heater, fed through the system feeder. The high temperature of the hot water and the turbulence of pouring the water into the system feeder will drive off much of the dissolved air. This will reduce the time needed for the system's air separator to get rid of any free air.

the system is operating. The air is consistently pushed toward the purge valve, so it is scrubbed out of any nooks and crannies of the system.

Then, close the purge valve and open the valve between the boiler and the air separator.

The last step is to raise the system pressure to its working pressure. The pressure is applied by the system feeder.

At this point, the water still probably contains a substantial amount of dissolved air, along with a small amount of free air that remains after the purging process. When the boiler is fired for the first time, the high temperature in the boiler will drive air out of the water. The air separator and vent remove most of this air. The rest is swept through the system by high water velocity and returns to the air separator, where more of the air is removed.

A well designed hydronic system that is purged properly will be free of air problems from the first moment it operates. It will continue to remove small amounts of air as it operates for the first few weeks or months.

The purge valve can remain closed until the system must be drained for some later repair. That may not happen for half a century. Valves deteriorate when they are never used, so put a conspicuous tag on the purge valve indicating that it should be opened and closed every three months. Keep a gasketed cap on the hose connection in case the purge valve starts to leak.

That completes the design of hydronic heating systems. Next, we will learn how to design the second of our two major HVAC system choices, split-system heat pumps.

SPLIT-SYSTEM HEAT PUMPS

Split-system (or "ductless") heat pumps are one of the two main types of HVAC systems that I recommend for a super-house. They are best adapted to climates that are moderate or warm. They should not be used for primary heating in a climate that has a prolonged cold season.

A unique advantage of heat pumps is that they can provide both heating and cooling. Therefore, if you select heat pumps as the primary heating for your home, design them for effective cooling also. By similar logic, I recommend using heat pumps instead of single-purpose air conditioners in any climate where heating may be needed, even if you have a different kind of primary heating system.

The adjacent sidebar explains how heat pumps work. For a comparison of heat pumps to other heating equipment, see Table 4-1, *Heating Equipment Comparison*. Figures 4-37 through 4-40 show how split-system heat pumps look from inside the rooms. Figures 4-41 and 4-42 show how they look from outside the house.

The following pages will explain the essential features of heat pumps and they will give you guidance for the best possible installation. These same issues apply to air conditioners. An air conditioner is simply a heat pump that lacks the ability to provide heating.

Installing heat pumps and air conditioners is relatively easy for a qualified contractor, but installation involves critical details that must not be overlooked. Therefore, we will cover the issues that need particular attention. Discuss those issues with your contractor. It's your home, so don't let anyone make it less than perfect.

Advantages of Heat Pumps

Heat pumps have these important advantages:
- They provide both heating and cooling.
- Electricity is the only energy requirement for heat pumps, so they avoid the cost of gas lines or fuel tanks, fuel odors, and explosion hazards from fuel leakage.
- Heat pumps don't need a flue or chimney, so they lower the structural cost and avoid a major air leakage path. (This benefit is not unique. Condensing boilers and furnaces can vent through a side wall. Electric resistance heaters need no venting.)
- Compared to electric resistance heating, heat pumps use from one half to one fourth as much electricity, providing a major operating cost advantage over resistance heat.

Shortcomings of Heat Pumps

On the negative side of the ledger, heat pumps have serious limitations. Understand these limitations before you decide whether to install heat pumps in your home. If you decide to install heat pumps, design your installations to minimize these adverse characteristics:

- The heating capacity of heat pumps degrades as the outside temperature falls. Unlike fuel-fired heating equipment, heat pumps suffer in performance when you need heating the most. At an outside temperature of 17 °F (-8 °C), a typical heat pump loses about 40% of the heating capacity that it has when the outside temperature is 47 °F (8 °C).

- Typical heat pumps cease to provide heating at outside temperatures between 0 °F and 17 °F (-18 °C to -8 °C), depending on the model. Below that temperature, you need alternate heaters, which might be electric resistance or fuel-fired. (Some recently introduced models, which we discuss below, can operate at lower outdoor temperatures.)

- The air discharge temperature into the room drops along with the outside temperature. When the outside temperature drops below freezing, the discharge from a heat pump may be lower than body temperature, creating an uncomfortable wind chill if the air falls on a person. The discomfort has gotten worse because manufacturers design their heat pumps for lower discharge temperatures to improve their efficiency ratings. (Some recently introduced models can maintain higher air temperatures during cold weather, but the air is still much cooler than with other types of heaters.)

- Air distribution within the room is a compromise between heating and cooling. The interior units should be located high in the room for efficient cooling and to minimize drafts. The high mounting location is not efficient for heating.

- The energy efficiency of heat pumps deteriorates as the outside temperature drops. At temperatures below about 36 °F (2 °C), the need to defrost the outside coil lowers efficiency even more. At a temperature of 17 °F (-8 °C), the efficiency of a typical heat pump drops by about 40% compared to operation at 47 °F (8 °C).

- Heat pumps have a compressor that wears out more quickly than other kinds of heating equipment, typically in 8 to 15 years of normal use. Replacement is expensive.

- Heat pumps need outdoor equipment. The outside units and their connecting pipes don't look pretty, and their installation requirements tend to make them visible. (However, the same is true of all air conditioners, so this is not an additional disadvantage in climates that require cooling.)

- A heat pump creates fan noise inside the room. The noise level varies among models, and the best units have become fairly quiet.

- The outside unit contains the compressor and a fan, which are sources of noise and vibration. The noise level of the best current outside units is much lower than in the past.

Heat Pumps are for Warmer Climates

The previous list of shortcomings paints a somewhat grim picture of heat pumps, especially when compared with the comfortable and consistent heating performance of hydronic heating, our other recommended type of primary heating system.

Most of the shortcomings of heat pumps become inoffensive in climates that remain relatively warm. If the weather at your home site rarely dips below freezing, except for a few dark hours in winter, consider heat pumps as a candidate. However, if the winter climate frequently dips to temperatures below freezing, you won't find heat pumps very satisfactory.

A special kind of heat pump, called a "geothermal" heat pump, suffers less loss of capacity, efficiency, and comfort during cold weather. This type extracts heat from the soil or subsurface water rather than from the outside air. However, geothermal heat pumps presently have serious limitations that prevent them from delivering the benefits that they promise. For the details, see *Geothermal Heat Pumps and Air Conditioners*, in *Last Look: Energy for Pioneers*, at the end of the book.

■ A Cold Weather Breakthrough?

Around 2010, a major heat pump manufacturer introduced a design that claims to maintain full heating capacity down to an outside air temperature that is much lower than for conventional heat pumps. This line of heat pumps claims to operate down to a temperature of 5 °F (-15 °C) at full heating capacity. The same models claim to operate at outside temperatures as low as -13 °F (-25 °C), but with reduced capacity.

This equipment also claims to maintain a comfortable indoor discharge temperature of 110 °F (43 °C) at an outside temperature of 5 °F (-15 °C). If these claims are true, this is a major breakthrough that greatly expands the range of heat pumps into colder climates.

Other manufacturers are now producing split-system heat pumps that are designed to operate better at lower outdoor temperatures. By the time you read this, it is likely that a variety of cold-climate heat pumps will be available. Also, the equipment will have more user experience, which is always important to check when selecting equipment.

 A newly introduced heat pump design greatly improves heating capacity and comfort – but not efficiency – in cold climates.

So, if your home is located where the outdoor temperatures dip below freezing for extended periods, check out models that are designed for lower outdoor temperatures. Check the specifications carefully, and find reviews of the equipment by users who have gone through a cold season with the models that you are considering.

But, note this. The improvement relates to heating capacity, not to energy efficiency. All heat pumps suffer a progressive loss of energy efficiency as the outdoor temperature declines. This is dictated by the laws of physics, so no design improvements can overcome it. ("Geothermal" heat pumps exist primarily because they promise to avoid the efficiency limitations of low outdoor air temperature.)

Heat Pumps Perform Better in Super-Insulated Houses

Super-insulation lessens the comfort shortcomings of heat pumps. Super-insulation keeps the inside surfaces of rooms warm, creating a cozy feel even during the coldest weather. As a result, the drafty air distribution of heat pumps and their low supply air temperature are less likely to cause discomfort.

That being said, it is still important to locate the indoor units of heat pumps so that their air discharge does not blow directly on occupants.

Heat pumps in a super-insulated house will operate for fewer hours each year than they would in a conventional house. This means that the equipment will last longer, and you won't have to listen to it as much.

HOW HEAT PUMPS AND AIR CONDITIONERS WORK

As its name implies, a heat pump is a device that *moves* heat, rather than converting heat from some other energy source. Typically, 50% to 80% of the heating energy that is delivered to the inside of a house by a heat pump is taken from the outdoor environment, where it is free.

Normally, heat flows from a region of higher temperature to a region of lower temperature. If you hold a flame under one end of a metal rod, the heat will flow from the hot end toward the cool end. In the same way, during cold weather, indoor heat flows through the structure of a house toward the outside.

The unique characteristic of a heat pump is its ability to make heat flow in the opposite direction, from a cooler region to a warmer region. In a manner of speaking, a heat pump "pumps" heat uphill toward a higher temperature, against its normal tendency.

How does a heat pump perform this magic? Figure 4-36 shows a simplified heat pump. It uses a substance called a "refrigerant" that circulates between the inside and the outside of the house. The refrigerant changes from a liquid to a vapor, or vice versa, in different parts of the system. The process absorbs heat from the cold outside air and delivers that heat to the inside of the house at a higher temperature.

A heat pump exploits two facts that you may remember from chemistry class. One fact is that compressing a gas (or vapor) makes it hot, and letting a gas expand makes it cool. The other fact is that it takes a lot of energy (called "latent heat") to change a liquid to a vapor. Conversely, the vapor gives up that same amount of heat when it condenses into a liquid. A refrigerant is a material that has a large latent heat, and it can change from liquid to vapor within the operating temperature range of the heat pump.

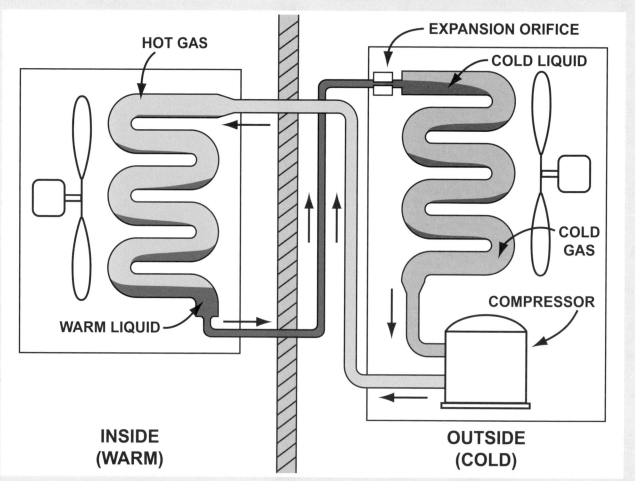

HOT GAS

EXPANSION ORIFICE

COLD LIQUID

COLD GAS

COMPRESSOR

WARM LIQUID

INSIDE (WARM)

OUTSIDE (COLD)

DRW

Figure 4-36. A simplified heat pump. This heat pump extracts heat from the outside air and moves it into the house. Most real heat pumps can move heat in both directions, so they can provide both heating and cooling.

HOW HEAT PUMPS AND AIR CONDITIONERS WORK

Let's start at the compressor in Figure 4-36, and follow the refrigerant as it flows through the heat pump:

(1) The compressor compresses the refrigerant vapor, making it hotter than room temperature. The compressor discharges the vapor to a heat transfer coil located inside the house.

(2) A fan blows house air through the inside coil, which warms the air and cools the refrigerant vapor. As the vapor cools, it condenses into a warm liquid, giving up its large amount of latent heat and providing most of the warmth. The liquid refrigerant drains to the bottom of the coil.

(3) The liquid refrigerant is forced through the "expansion valve" by the discharge pressure of the compressor. The expansion valve is a small orifice that is located at the inlet to the outdoor heat transfer coil.

(4) The outdoor heat transfer coil is at low pressure because it connected to the suction side of the compressor. At the outlet of the expansion valve, the liquid refrigerant encounters this low pressure. This causes a fraction of the liquid to flash into a vapor. The reduction in pressure makes the vapor cold. At the same time, the evaporation absorbs a large amount of energy from the remaining liquid, making the liquid colder than the outside air.

(5) The liquid and vapor flow through the outside heat exchange coil. A fan blows outside air through the coil. The outside air is warmer than the very cold refrigerant inside the coil, so heat flows from the outside air into the refrigerant. The higher outside air temperature causes the liquid refrigerant to change to a vapor, absorbing a large amount of latent heat from the air.

(6) The refrigerant vapor flows to the compressor, and the cycle repeats.

A heat pump needs electricity to operate the compressor, the fan for the inside coil, and the fan for the outside coil. The compressor uses most of the energy. The compressor's need for energy increases along with the difference in temperature between the inside and the outside. Therefore, a heat pump will use more energy to heat a house during cold weather than it will during mild weather.

Also, the heat pump's heating capacity drops as the temperature difference increases. Below a certain temperature, the efficiency and capacity of the heat pump drops so much that it cannot operate effectively. For this reason, ordinary heat pumps are not used in very cold climates.

The simplified heat pump in Figure 4-36 moves heat only from the outside to the inside. Most real heat pumps include a "reversing valve" that can swap the connections of the compressor to the inside and outside coils. In this way, the heat pump can either heat or cool the house.

The electricity used by the compressor ultimately becomes heat inside the refrigerant. This heat is delivered to the warm side of the system, along with the free energy that comes from the cold side. For this reason, a heat pump is more efficient when heating a house than when cooling it.

An "air conditioner" is a heat pump that is designed only to pump heat from the inside of the house toward the outside. It lacks a reversing valve. Other than that, there is little difference in construction between an air conditioner and a heat pump, and little difference in manufacturing cost.

HEAT PUMP DESIGN (1): ZONE THE HOUSE

In the language of HVAC, a "zone" is a part of a building that has distinct heating and/or cooling requirements. In general, each room should be a separate zone. In Step 1, you laid out your rooms to make it possible to localize your heating and cooling efficiently, so this part of your design is already complete!

Each zone should have its own indoor heat pump unit. Resist the temptation to heat or cool more than one room with a single indoor unit. It's false economy. You will save little in construction cost, and you will pay later with reduced comfort and higher energy costs. Air does not travel well between rooms that are separated by a wall, even if a door between the rooms is left wide open. You might use a single inside unit to serve two spaces that have no partitions between them, such as a living room and adjacent dining area. But, in case of doubt, install an inside unit for each space.

Very large rooms may have more than one zone. For example, a "great room" may have a separate zone for a television viewing area, the area around a fireplace, or an area near large windows.

HEAT PUMP DESIGN (2): CALCULATE THE ROOM HEATING REQUIREMENTS

In the previous discussion of hydronic heating systems, we showed how to calculate the capacity of room heating units. Use exactly the same method for calculating the heating capacity of heat pumps (or any other heating equipment).

When you select the heating capacity of your heat pumps, base your choice on the coldest outdoor temperature at your home site. Remember that heat pumps lose capacity as the temperature drops.

Err on the side of larger heating capacity for each room unit. Extra heating capacity is good, contrary to a widespread myth among contractors and engineers. Here's why:

- A larger heat pump will warm a cold room more quickly.
- If you use supplemental heating for very cold weather that is more expensive than operating your heat pumps, increasing the heat pump capacity will reduce the fraction of your heating that is performed by the more expensive supplemental heating.
- A larger heat pump will run for fewer hours, which extends the life of the equipment.
- Larger models may offer more desirable features than smaller units.

HEAT PUMP DESIGN (3): CALCULATE THE ROOM COOLING REQUIREMENTS

If your home is located in a climate that has a significant heating season, as in most mid-latitude locations, the required heating capacity probably will determine the size of your heat pumps. Cooling requires less heat pump capacity than heating in such locations.

For a climate where cooling dominates, it is easy to calculate the cooling capacity of the heat pumps (or air conditioners). Simply use these capacities:

- In a warm climate, use 18 BTU per hour per square foot (60 watts per square meter) of floor area for the above-ground rooms that you want to cool.
- In a climate where cooling is needed only occasionally, and for rooms located below grade with little solar input, use 12 BTU per hour per square foot (40 watts per square meter) of floor area.

These capacities are ample for a super-efficient house. They will easily handle the heat that leaks into the room from the outside, and they provide quick cool-down of a warm room.

You may need a more elaborate calculation of cooling capacity only for a room that may have an exceptionally high cooling load. For example, you might have a big room that you intend for large social functions that involve dancing, a lot of lighting, and food warming equipment. Also, more capacity will be needed if you allow a lot of direct sunlight to enter the room.

In those special cases, to calculate the cooling capacity for a room, add all the sources of heat that may occur simultaneously. Then, add 50% more to cool down the room from its unoccupied temperature. See the sidebar, *Cooling Loads*, for the heat produced by common residential heat sources.

The smallest efficient heat pumps and air conditioners have capacities of about 9,000 BTU per hour (2.6 kW). This is more than ample for a small room. Don't worry about "oversizing" heat pumps or air conditioners. The capacity of the unit has little effect on energy efficiency. Also, the life of a heat pump or air conditioner depends on the number of hours that the unit actually runs. Therefore, a larger unit will last longer.

■ Cooling the Room's Thermal Mass

To a large extent, the cooling capacities of your heat pumps are determined by the thermal mass of the room. Imagine that the cooling in a room has been turned off for several days during warm weather, so the room becomes warm. When you turn on the heat pump, it first cools the air in the room. It can't complete this job until the interior surfaces of the room and the outer surfaces of the furnishings have been cooled.

COOLING LOADS

If a room has an exceptionally large cooling requirement, calculate the cooling capacity by adding all the individual cooling loads in the room. Then, add 50% to the total for cooling down a room that is already warm. Here are typical cooling loads that you can use:

- one person, talking: 500 BTU per hour (150 watts)
- one person, dancing vigorously: 1,500 BTU per hour (450 watts)
- maximum solar heat through an unshaded window or skylight: 200 BTU per hour per square foot (650 watts per square meter) of glass area
- maximum solar heat through a shaded window: 40 BTU per hour per square foot (130 watts per square meter) of window area
- heat entering through walls and ceiling: minor (in a super-insulated house)
- lights and other electrical equipment: Add the wattage of all equipment in the room that will be used during warm weather. (To calculate the heat energy in BTU's, multiply watts by 3.4 to get BTU per hour.)

The mass of the air and the interior surfaces is independent of the outside climate. For this reason, the recommended cooling capacities in cooler climates are almost as large as for cooling in warm climates. The air conditioning bill for your super-efficient house will be much lower than for your neighbors who have conventional houses, but your cooling equipment probably won't be much smaller.

■ Cooling Capacity for Dehumidification

A heat pump (or air conditioner) extracts moisture from the air because the moisture in the air condenses on the cold coil. The condensed moisture drips off the coil, and it is removed by a drain. The moisture gives up heat when it condenses (its "latent heat"), and this heat must be removed by the heat pump.

This additional cooling load is included in our recommendations. In a climate that is humid, a large fraction of a heat pump's energy requirement goes to lowering humidity.

Unfortunately, using a heat pump (or air conditioner) to lower humidity can cause serious mildew problems in a humid climate. This is especially likely when the temperature is mild but the humidity is high. For example, this is a common condition in New Orleans and around the Gulf of Mexico. In such a climate, use an air conditioner to lower the temperature, and use a dehumidifier to lower the humidity. We will learn how to control humidity later in this Step.

HEAT PUMP DESIGN (4): SELECT THE BEST HEAT PUMPS

Now that you know the heating and cooling requirements of each zone, select your heat pumps. Split systems offer different types of indoor units, and you will select the best type for each room. If your home is located in a cold climate, you will also select supplemental heaters for your heat pumps.

Then, use the Internet to search for models that have the highest energy efficiency, the lowest noise level, and the most useful control features. After you have narrowed your choices to a few, read their equipment manuals to learn about their details. Take advantage of the fact that major manufacturers distribute their detailed manuals free on the Internet. The glossy brochures don't provide enough information.

Don't let your contractor select your heat pumps. Contractors tend to take whatever is available at their favorite wholesaler. They don't have the time, or often the skill, for dealing with the issues that are important to you. Focus your search on the best available models, not the cheapened "builders' models" that manufacturers produce for the low-bid market.

Select Split-System Heat Pumps

I recommend only one kind of heat pump for normal residential use. This is the "split-system" heat pump that is designed for heating and cooling individual rooms. This type is also called "ductless," to distinguish it from central systems, which need ducts. This type of heat pump provides maximum efficiency and comfort because it allows you to localize your heating and cooling to the individual rooms that need it at any given time.

Avoid whole-house heat pumps, which are disqualified by a host of serious shortcomings that are summarized in the previous sidebar, *Why You Don't Want Central Forced-Air Heating and Cooling.*

A split-system heat pump uses two separate components. Each room or zone requires a separate inside unit. In addition, the system requires an outside unit, which may operate one or more inside units. There are various kinds of inside units, the most common of which are shown in Figures 4-37 through 4-40, below. Typical outdoor units are illustrated in Figures 4-41 and 4-42.

Originally, each inside unit required its own outside unit. Split systems for a house with many rooms required a phalanx of outside units, which created an unattractive appearance that was difficult to camouflage. But today, you can buy split-system heat pumps that allow a single outside unit to serve a large number of inside units, each of which can operate independently.

WARNING! SELECT A PROVEN MODEL

When properly selected and installed, heat pumps provide comfortable heating and cooling without problems. However, the heat pump market is now being flooded with cheap units from manufacturers in various countries that lack a commitment to quality. Resist the temptation to buy this inferior equipment. While heat pumps are now commonplace, the details of their design and materials matter. Operating life may be short, and repair parts may be difficult or impossible to find. Claims for efficiency, quietness, and other desirable characteristics may be bogus.

Even worse, some heat pumps can cause serious moisture problems, including widespread mildew and leakage of condensate into the structure of the house. I have been called to investigate such problems, which occurred even with new heat pump models produced by a well known global manufacturer. The brand name alone did not insure good performance.

The best defense against trouble is to buy your heat pumps from a manufacturer who has a good reputation and long experience with the kind of heat pump that you want to install. Check the installation details before you buy to make sure that the model has no troublesome installation requirements.

Local product support is important. Even a good model is a bad risk if the manufacturer lacks a strong presence in your region.

LG

Figure 4-38. A heat pump indoor unit for a home office. Note the cast iron radiator, which probably has been retained for comfort during cold weather.

You probably will be able to heat and cool your entire home with one or two outside units.

The best split-system heat pumps are quiet, efficient, easy to install, and user-friendly. However, there is some bad equipment on the market, even from major manufacturers (see the sidebar). It is your job to winnow the best models from the chaff.

Types of Inside Units

You have a choice of various types of inside units for split systems. They are grouped by mounting location. As you choose between the types, place your emphasis on comfortable and efficient air distribution. Consider both heating and cooling, which have different air distribution requirements. In addition to appearance, the type of indoor unit may affect noise level and control options.

■ Wall-Mounted Units

For all or most rooms, the wall-mounted type of indoor unit is probably your best choice. It is by far the most common type for residential applications. Figures 4-37 and 4-38 show typical wall-mounted installations.

LG

Figure 4-37. A typical wall-hung indoor unit for a split-system heat pump.

Ease of installation, with translates to lower cost, is the main reason for the popularity of this type of indoor unit. Mounting the unit on a wall is almost as easy as hanging a picture. A mounting plate is provided with the unit, which is attached to the wall with a few screws. Then, the inside unit is simply hung on the mounting plate.

The preferred location for a wall-hung unit is on an exterior wall. Then, the connections to the outside unit require only a small hole in the wall. The inside unit is designed so that the hole is behind the unit, making the connecting pipes and wires invisible from the inside. No modifications to the structure are required.

Wall-mounted units discharge air in a horizontal direction that is generally perpendicular to the wall. The units have adjustable vanes that allow you to adjust the discharge to the right and left, but only over a limited range. To avoid uncomfortable drafts, plan the location of wall-mounted units with respect to the furniture layout in your room.

Wall-mounted units have vanes that can adjust the direction of discharge up and down over a wide range, from horizontal to steeply downward. The best units have automatic vanes that raise or lower when the unit changes between heating and cooling.

When the unit is cooling, water will condense from the coil. This water drains from the unit by gravity through a small hose. Usually, the hose passes through the wall and drips on the ground outside. Arrange this drainage so that it does not cause a problem.

■ Recessed Ceiling Units

Some inside units are designed to be installed in the ceiling, where they are almost flush with the surface. The visible part of the unit typically is a square that is two to three feet (60 to 90 cm) on a side. The air typically discharges outward in all four directions, but some models provide an option to block one or two of the directions. Figure 4-39 is an example.

This type of inside unit generally is limited to larger rooms, where it offers the potential for broad air distribution, primarily for cooling. The ceiling should be at least 9 or 10 feet (almost 3 meters) tall to exploit this potential without creating uncomfortable drafts. The air distribution pattern is considerably less effective for heating, compared to a wall-mounted unit.

Ceiling-mounted units typically require at least one foot (30 cm) of vertical space above the ceiling surface. The unit could fit into the joist space of the floor above, provided that the floor joists are exceptionally deep. Commonly, the ceiling is dropped to accommodate the unit.

The unit could also project into an attic. It should not be installed in a beam roof. Any penetration through the envelope of the building invites air leaks.

Daikin

Figure 4-39. A heat pump indoor unit that is recessed into the ceiling. This style offers improved air distribution for cooling in some room layouts. It may also be desirable for a decor that requires bare walls. It is not preferable for heating.

In general, this type is more complex to install than wall-hung units.

Draining the condensate usually requires a built-in pump, which makes a busy sound when it operates.

■ Surface-Mounted Ceiling Units

Indoor units that hang below the ceiling are used mainly in restaurants and in similar spaces that require a large cooling capacity. Usually, a ceiling-suspended unit is installed at one end of the room so that it blows across the room, as in Figure 4-40. The air discharge pattern is not well adapted to heating.

The main advantage of this design is that it saves wall space and it does not intrude into the ceiling, except for the connecting pipes.

You might consider a ceiling-suspended unit for cooling a large room that has a horizontal ceiling. A unit of this type could also be installed in a large space that lacks a finished ceiling, such as under the trusses of a garage or a workshop building.

Draining the condensate requires a built-in pump.

■ Enclosure-Mounted Units

Some inside units are designed to be installed inside an enclosure, such as an equipment closet that is adjacent to the room or rooms that are being served. Short stubs of duct connect from the unit to supply and return grilles in the wall of the enclosure.

Mitsubishi

Figure 4-40. A heat pump indoor unit that is suspended below the ceiling. This mounting location is effective primarily for cooling, as in this flower shop.

This mounting option rarely provides an advantage, unless you are keen to hide the indoor unit. If the room has enough wall space for supply and return air grilles, it also has enough space for a wall-mounted or a ceiling-mounted inside unit.

These units typically are used to heat and cool several rooms, with the enclosure being located between the rooms. However, it is generally not a good idea to do this, because it violates the important principle of localizing heating and cooling to individual spaces.

Heat Pump Supplemental Heaters

If your home is located in a climate that has extended periods of weather below freezing temperature, conventional heat pumps will need some form of supplemental heat. This is to compensate for the loss of capacity and low discharge temperature that heat pumps suffer during cold weather.

The supplemental heat usually will be some form of electric resistance heat, but it does not have to be. Don't lose sight of the fact that using electric resistance heat in any form forfeits the efficiency advantage of heat pumps. For heating during very cold weather, a fuel-fired supplemental heater may be more economical than electric resistance heating. However, if you have other economical heating options, you probably would not be using heat pumps in the first place.

Most heat pumps with supplemental heaters – either internal or external – are designed so that the supplemental heater turns on when the heat pump can no longer satisfy the entire heating requirement. This point is reached when the outside temperature falls to the point that the compressor must operate continuously.

As the temperature drops further, the compressor and the supplemental heater will operate together. At very low outside temperature, the compressor will turn off completely, leaving all the heating to the supplemental heaters.

■ Integral Resistance Heaters

The most common form of supplemental heat is electric resistance heating elements that are installed inside the heat pumps. The resistance heater is located on the discharge side of the inside coil. This method of supplementing heat pump output is simple and inexpensive. It provides much warmer heating air during the coldest weather, when the air discharge from unaided heat pumps can become uncomfortably cool.

The addition of resistance heating coils does not change the installation procedure for the heat pump. All the controls are installed at the factory, so your heating contractor does not have any additional installation work. And, you have no additional design work.

Unfortunately, some of the most desirable heat pump models do not include an option for internal supplemental heaters.

■ Separate Supplemental Heaters

If you examine the electrical connection panel of most good split-system heat pumps, you will find a terminal that is labeled "auxiliary heating" or "aux." or something similar. The purpose of this connection is to control supplemental heating equipment that is separate from the heat pump. The method of control is the same as for the internal electric heaters that we just described.

There are several reasons why you might want to install an external supplemental heater:

- The heat pump model that you want does not offer an internal heater as an option.
- External heaters offer greater heating capacity, which may be desirable for warming a cold room quickly.
- External heaters, such as baseboard heat, provide superior comfort.
- You can use a fuel-fired room heater to supplement the heat pump, to gain high heating capacity and high air temperature.

For most rooms, electric resistance baseboard heating would be the most desirable supplemental heating for a heat pump. In a climate that gets very cold, you might also consider a high efficiency propane-fired wall heater. (We assume that natural gas is not available, or you would not be using heat pumps for heating.)

DUAL-FUEL HEAT PUMPS: NOT A GOOD CHOICE

A "dual-fuel" heat pump consists of a heat pump and a fuel-fired forced-air heater that are packaged together. The heater normally is fueled by natural gas or propane, and it requires all the accessories of a combustion heater, including a flue and fuel supply pipes. If the unit serves more than one zone, it also needs air distribution ducts, which you want to avoid.

A dual-fuel heat pump is an awkward compromise. It is difficult to imagine a situation where it would be a good choice. As heat pumps, dual-fuel units are less desirable than ordinary split-system heat pumps. The gas heating that is provided by a dual-fuel heat pump is less desirable than a hydronic gas heating system in comfort and energy efficiency.

In general, combination appliances of any kind are a poor idea. They have more parts to fail, the unit is heavier and bulkier, and it will be difficult to find people to repair it.

Cooling Efficiency Ratings

Many factors determine the efficiency* of heat pumps and air conditioners. Fortunately, you don't have to know about those factors to select an efficient unit. Most countries have laws that require efficiency ratings for heat pumps and air conditioners. By selecting the models that have the best ratings, you narrow your search quickly.

In the United States, all air conditioning units are rated for efficiency using a certification system established by the U.S. air conditioning industry. Similar ratings have been developed by other countries.

In the U.S., the original rating for cooling efficiency was the Energy Efficiency Ratio (EER). This rating is based on continuous operation at standard temperatures. It is still used for window-type air conditioners and other types that operate as auxiliary units.

The EER rating does not relate well to the way that heat pumps and air conditioners are actually used, so it has been replaced by the Seasonal Energy Efficiency Ratio (SEER) for the types of air conditioners that provide primary cooling for a house. The SEER is the average EER of a heat pump or air conditioner when it is operated in accordance with a standard testing schedule that represents typical home usage.

A SEER rating of 10 is a typical minimum value that is allowed in developed countries. A SEER rating of 13 to 16 is good for a small split system. At present, a SEER of about 20 is the highest being claimed by any major manufacturer.

EER and SEER ratings are expressed in units of BTU's per watt-hour. BTU's are obsolete in metric countries, which use "coefficient of performance" (COP) instead. This is defined as cooling energy output divided by the energy input, with both the output and the input measured in watts.

To get the COP of a heat pump or air conditioner, divide the EER or the SEER by 3.413.

In order to earn higher SEER or COP ratings, manufacturers have redesigned their air conditioners and heat pumps in ways that may reduce their ability to remove humidity. In the worst cases, some heat pumps (and air conditioners) have very little ability to lower humidity, and they may even cause humidity problems.

So, be aware that a high SEER rating does not mean that a unit will perform better than a unit with a somewhat lower SEER rating, especially for lowering humidity. Unfortunately, there is no easy way to separate the dehumidification performance of a heat pump from its cooling performance. By the time you read this, there may be reviews on the Internet or in other places that test the dehumidification performance of different models. Check for this characteristic before you buy your heat pumps.

Heating Efficiency Ratings

A heat pump will have two separate efficiency ratings, one for cooling and one for heating. In the United States, the heating rating is called the Heating Seasonal Performance Factor (HSPF). The HSPF is defined in a way that is similar to the SEER.

Since a heat pump operates in the same way whether it is heating or cooling, why are two different ratings needed? The answer is that the temperatures used to test for the two ratings are different. (See the sidebar, *Beware of Rating Temperatures!*) The efficiency of any heat pump falls dramatically as the difference between the inside and outside temperatures increases. Typical heating operation involves larger temperature differences than typical cooling operation, so the heat pump generally operates less efficiently when heating. Also, the HSPF rating includes the energy consumption of supplemental resistance heating elements that may be installed in the unit.

An HSPF rating of 7 is a typical minimum value that is allowed in developed countries. An HSPF rating of about 9 is good for a split system. At present, an HSPF of about 10 is the highest being claimed by any major manufacturer.

---

* Among technical people, the term "efficiency" is not used for heat pumps. Strictly speaking, "efficiency" refers to converting energy from one form to another, whereas heat pumps move heat energy without changing it. However, to keep the discussion simple, we will pretend that we don't know the difference.

The HSPF is stated in units of BTU's per watt-hour, the same units used for SEER ratings. These units are obsolete in countries that use the metric system. Metric countries typically use a "heating coefficient of performance" ("heating COP") for heating operation, in addition to the "cooling COP" that is used for cooling operation. The seasonal heating COP is equal to the HSPF divided by 3.413.

In order to earn higher HSPF ratings, manufacturers have redesigned their heat pumps in ways that lower the temperature of the warm air discharged into the room. This risks discomfort, especially when the outside air temperature is below freezing. However, you can't necessarily get relief by buying a heat pump with a lower HSPF.

In order to minimize discomfort from low discharge temperature, select a heat pump that is designed specifically to maintain a higher discharge temperature during cold weather. See the previous heading, *A Cold Weather Breakthrough?*

■ Where to Find Efficiency Ratings

To find the SEER and HSPF ratings for virtually every model of heat pump or air conditioner that is made or sold in the United States, visit the Energy Star Web site, **www.EnergyStar.gov**.

On the Energy Star Web site, find the link to the database maintained by the Air Conditioning and Refrigeration Institute (ARI), which is the most complete list of heat pump and air conditioner ratings in the world. You can search this database by type, size, manufacturer, etc. The search will yield a ranked list of all models that fit your requirements.

The ARI database may not cover models intended for sale outside the United States. However, the best models sold in the U.S. are probably the best models sold anywhere. Be sure that a model offered in your country is exactly the same as the U.S. model. Make sure that each digit in the model number is the same.

Noise Ratings

Minimizing noise is an important selection feature, for both the inside and outside units. The noise level of a unit is indicated by its "sone" rating. Look for low sone ratings for the individual inside and outside units. The best split systems are much quieter than heat pumps of years past. They do not interfere with conversation or listening to most kinds of entertainment.

The compressor makes most of the noise. Therefore, in split systems, the compressor is located in the outside unit. "Scroll" compressors are substantially quieter than the older reciprocating compressors, and they are now standard in better models.

BEWARE OF RATING TEMPERATURES!

The efficiency and the capacity of heat pumps and air conditioners are affected strongly by the inside and outside temperatures. Therefore, efficiency and capacity ratings are meaningless unless these temperatures are specified. Be sure to use the same rating temperatures when making comparisons between different models.

In the U.S., the Air Conditioning and Refrigeration Institute (ARI) has established standard rating temperatures for different types of air conditioners and heat pumps. If you get ratings from a reliable database, such as the ARI Web site, all the ratings will be based on standard temperatures.

However, if you see ratings in a manufacturer's brochure, you may be seriously misled by ratings that are based on less demanding temperatures. Fudging the rating temperatures is a trick used by some manufacturers – even major ones – to make their equipment look better than it is.

Control Features

Many split systems offer remote controls, similar to television remote controls. This is because the inside unit usually is mounted high on the wall, where it is awkward to reach.

Manufacturers exploit the electronics in their controls to provide a variety of nice features. These may include:

- a timer that turns off the unit after a selected interval
- a feature that slowly raises the cooling temperature so you will not get too cold when sleeping
- the ability to change the discharge vane settings remotely
- and, other options.

Strangely, the glossy sales brochures may fail to present valuable features of a model. Perhaps those features might seem too technical for average homeowners, or maybe the marketing department doesn't understand them. To find out about all the features and how they work, download the owner's manuals or installation manuals from the manufacturers' Web sites.

HEAT PUMP DESIGN (5): INSTALL THE INSIDE UNITS

The way you install the inside units has a major effect on comfort. It also affects the appearance of the house, energy efficiency, system cost, and the ease of installation and maintenance. We will now cover the installation methods that will give you the best performance. We assume that you will use wall-mounted inside units, unless stated otherwise.

There are important installation issues that we don't cover, because your contractor should know how to deal with them. Detailed instructions are included in the equipment shipping cartons. Your heating contractor should follow all those instructions meticulously. To be sure that happens, read the instructions yourself.

Place the Units for Good Air Distribution

Find locations for the inside units that distribute both heating and cooling effectively throughout the room, but that do not create drafts were people are likely to be sitting, sleeping, or lingering.

When the heat pump is cooling, the dense chilled air is discharged horizontally or at a shallow downward angle, above the heads of occupants. When the heat pump is heating, the air is discharged downward at a fairly steep angle and at high velocity to overcome the tendency of the warm air to rise toward the ceiling. In either case, the air should not discharge directly on occupants. The chilled air is too cold to be comfortable, and the heated air is too warm to be comfortable (or in cold weather, the heated air may be too chilly for direct contact).

As we discussed previously, most indoor units lack flexibility for occupants to adjust the direction of the air discharge. So, you need to envision where future occupants will be located within the room.

In rooms with normal ceiling heights, install the inside units close to the ceiling. In rooms with tall ceilings, the unit's air discharge generally should be no higher than about 8 feet (2.4 meters) above the floor, so that heated air will reach the lower level of the room. This height will also improve cooling efficiency by allowing warmer air to stratify to a level above the inside unit.

Condensate Drainage

When the inside unit is cooling the room, moisture from the air condenses on the cold surfaces of its coil. This water is collected in a pan that is installed under the coil, and that pan has a drain connection. Most commonly, the condensate is drained through a hose that passes through an outside wall and drips on the ground outside. Alternatively, the condensate could drain to a sewer, but that would require some awkward piping.

If the hole in the wall for the refrigerant pipes is located below the level of the inside unit's drain pan, the condensate pipe usually passes through the same hole. Otherwise, the condensate pipe may pass through a lower hole.

Make sure that the drain hose is installed so that it drains downward along its entire length. If this is not possible, you will need to buy an inside unit that has a built-in condensate pump. This feature may not be available in a wall-mounted unit.

If the condensate is allowed to drip on the ground outside, it may create a mud puddle near the wall, especially during humid weather. To prevent this, use a splash block under the outlet of the condensate hose, or use a longer hose that carries the condensate away from the wall. Slope the soil away from the wall.

Install the Room Thermostats Properly

Most indoor units now have remote controls, like the ones used for television sets, that allow you to set the room temperature. With this arrangement, the actual room temperature usually is sensed at the inside unit itself, not at the remote control. Therefore, the location of the remote control does not affect the temperature setting. Most models include a wall mounted holder for the remote control that can be installed anywhere that is convenient.

On the other hand, if the controller for the indoor unit is mounted permanently on the wall, the temperature may be sensed at the controller. In that case, install the controller on an indoor wall or on a well insulated portion of an exterior wall, where it is never exposed to direct sunlight or to the air discharge from the unit.

Make Cleaning Easy

The inside units have filters that should be cleaned periodically. So, install each unit where you can reach the filter easily and safely. And, don't install anything under the unit that would make it difficult to reach.

HEAT PUMP DESIGN (6): INSTALL THE OUTSIDE UNITS

The way you install the outside units can affect the energy efficiency of the system, the appearance of the house, outside noise, the longevity of the system, and the ease of installation and maintenance. Figure 4-41 shows an example that is ideal. The following suggestions will help you to find an optimum location for each outside unit.

DRW

Figure 4-41. Two outdoor units for split-system heat pumps. The installation here provides excellent air flow and protection from debris. These units are so quiet that they are barely audible from the other end of the deck.

Shaded for Cooling, Sunny for Heating

The air on the sunny side of a house is warmer than the air on the shaded side. This is because the soil and the house surfaces are warmed by the sun, and these surfaces warm the air nearby.

Therefore, if you install a heat pump or air conditioner in a climate that is usually warm, try to install the outside unit on a side of the house that is well shaded. This will improve cooling efficiency and reduce running time. The benefit won't be great, but it is worth exploiting.

By the same logic, if you install a heat pump primarily for the purpose of heating, install the outside unit in a sunny area on the south side of the house. Most of your winter heating will occur when the sun has set or is low in the sky. So, try to install the outside unit in an area that can store heat from the sun. An example is a brick patio exposed to the sun.

If your climate has both a cold season and warm season, it is best to install the outside unit on the east side of the house. In that location, it will be exposed to the sun in the morning, when most heating occurs. It will be shaded in the afternoon, when most cooling occurs.

More important is where *not* to install the outside unit. Never, never install an outside unit inside an attic, no matter how well ventilated the attic may be. The inside of any attic is much warmer than the outside air, so the cooling efficiency, capacity, and service life of the system would be severely degraded. For the same reasons, don't install an outside unit on top of a roof. The hot surfaces of the roof create a blanket of hot air during the daytime.

Provide Easy Air Flow

The installation instructions for the outside unit usually state minimum clearances in each direction from the unit, but try to do better. Place the unit sufficiently far away from any wall so that the air entering the unit does not need to make a tight turn. Try to provide a completely free path for the fan discharge, as in Figure 4-41. This will reduce the tendency of the discharge air to recirculate back into the inlet. If you install the outside unit behind a decorative screen or enclosure, make sure that the enclosure does not obstruct the air that enters or leaves the unit.

Install Clear of Debris

If possible, install the unit above ground at a height where leaves, grass clippings, and dust will not be sucked into the unit by the fan. Obstruction of the outside coil reduces the system's efficiency and capacity. If the unit has to be located near foliage or other loose material, install it on an elevated stand. Or, install the unit on the side of a masonry wall, as in Figure 4-41. Doing this will keep the unit operating efficiently, and it can virtually eliminate the need to clean the outside coils.

Figure 4-42 shows a row of outdoor units that are hidden behind a screen of decorative shrubbery. This installation requires continuous tending to keep the units from being clogged by debris.

DRW

Figure 4-42. These heat pump units serve separate apartments in a guest house. The shrubbery hides the equipment from view, but debris will quickly clog the coils unless the units are cleaned continually.

Minimize the Noise

Heat pumps and air conditioners have the potential to create an annoying level of outside noise. The outside unit contains the compressor, which vibrates. Minimizing the compressor noise is mostly a matter of installing the outside unit on a rigid surface that cannot vibrate. Installing the unit on a concrete slab is excellent. Or, you can install it on a heavy concrete or masonry wall, as in Figure 4-41. However, don't install an outside unit on a frame wall, which will vibrate like a drumhead.

If you install the outside unit properly, you won't be able to hear it operating inside the house. Fortunately, the outside units of modern split systems are much quieter than older central air conditioners, so they are less likely to annoy neighbors. Still, take care to install the outside units in locations that minimize radiation of noise toward your neighbors. This will give you a stronger case when you need to complain about their noisy habits.

HEAT PUMP DESIGN (7): OPTIMIZE THE CONNECTIONS

To complete your perfect heat pump installation, we need to optimize the connections between the inside units and the outside units. Each inside unit must be connected to an outside unit. Each connection consists of a small insulated pipe for warm liquid refrigerant and a somewhat larger insulated pipe for cold refrigerant vapor. The connection also includes a thin control wire, and it may include an electrical power wire.

Where these pipes and wires pass through a wall, they usually are wrapped in a bundle that is less than 3 inches (75 mm) in diameter. The bundle may also include the condensate drain tube that goes from each inside unit to the ground outside or to a sewer drain.

These connections are more important than they may seem. They influence the energy efficiency, appearance, and longevity of your heat pumps. The following guidelines will give you the best possible installation.

Make the Connections Short and Level

Longer connecting pipes lower the efficiency and the capacity of a split-system heat pump. This is because the pipes restrict the flow of the refrigerant, and because longer pipes suffer greater heat loss to the surroundings.

Manufacturers specify the maximum allowable lengths for the connecting pipes. Get this information from the manufacturer's Web site before you decide where to locate the inside and outside equipment. The maximum allowable lengths are a compromise with efficiency. Keep your pipes as short as possible to improve efficiency.

The manufacturer's specifications will also tell you the maximum allowable height difference between the inside and outside units. The reason is that the compressor must consume more energy to pump the refrigerant against gravity.* So, don't mount the outside unit (which contains the compressor) very far above or below the inside units.

The shortest connection is possible with a system that has a single inside unit that hangs on an exterior wall. Typically, the outside unit is on the opposite side of the wall, so the connection is short.

At the other extreme, some split systems have very long connecting pipes so that one outside unit can reach a number of indoor units anywhere in a house of typical size.

---

* Also, there are reasons that relate to the compressor's lubricating oil. Most refrigerants dissolve the compressor oil and carry it through the system. The maximum height difference is limited so that the oil can get back to the compressor from the low points in the system.

However, this may not be advisable. Instead, it may be better to install two or more split systems on opposite sides of the house. This provides better efficiency, and the installation generally is simpler.

Hide the Connections from View and Weather

The connecting pipes and wires aren't pretty, so try to hide them, both inside your home and on the outside.

Also, protect the connections from weather and sunlight. The pipes are insulated with plastic foam insulation that is covered with a plastic wrapping. Sunlight attacks the plastic and can destroy it within a few years.

So, anticipate the need for concealing the heat pump (and air conditioner) connections when you design the structure.

If practical, hide the connections inside a part of the structure that is accessible. For example, in Figure 4-41, the connecting pipes and wires pass under the deck and then through the "chimney" structure that is located behind the two outside units.

You can get plastic and metal covers to hide pipes that are installed along an inside or outside wall. Such covers look better then exposed pipe, but they are still rather drab.

Figure 4-43 shows a pipe cover that runs along the top of an inside wall. For a deluxe appearance, build decorative covers along the top of the wall, as in Figure 1-121 in Step 1, and run the connections inside the coves.

On an outside wall, pipe covers can further conceal and protect connections that are hidden behind shrubbery.

Keep the Pipes Inside Conditioned Space

Try to minimize the length of connecting pipe that is exposed to outdoor temperatures. During cold weather, the temperature of the hot gas pipe on the outside typically is about 70 °F (40 °C) higher than the outside air temperature. During warm weather, the cold gas pipe on the outside is colder than the outside air by a similar amount. This large temperature difference causes the pipes to lose a lot of heat in relation to their size.

Keep the Hot and Cold Pipes Separated

There is a large temperature difference between the hot and cold refrigerant pipes. Therefore, even though each is insulated, keep them apart by a fraction of an inch (about one centimeter).

It is necessary to bundle the pipes tightly where they pass through the exterior wall, but not elsewhere. Air conditioning contractors are in the habit of bundling the two pipes together along their entire length. Ask your builder to avoid this practice.

DRW

Figure 4-43. The rectangular enclosure along the top of the wall hides the refrigerant pipes that connect this heat pump inside unit to the outside unit. The pipe runs along the inside of the wall because several indoor units are connected to a common outdoor unit.

Routing Long Connections

If your heat pump system has several inside units that are connected to a single outside unit, some of the connections will be fairly long. In the extreme case, some of the connections may need to be routed all the way across the house. Here are several ways to route these long connections, in order of preference:

- Route the pipes along the inside walls. Cover them with a valance or place them inside a fancy cove. Keeping the pipes inside the house minimizes heat loss and greatly extends the life of the insulation.

- If you have an accessible attic, route the connections entirely underneath the ceiling insulation, with no gaps that are open to the attic space. Fasten the pipes to the ceiling joists so that they do not interfere with the insulation. With batt insulation, cut a tunnel through the batts so that the pipes do not dislodge the batts.

- Route the pipes inside well ventilated roof soffits. This requires coordination with the design of the eaves. The pipes are invisible and well protected, but they are exposed to outside temperatures.

- Route the connections along the outside wall, and cover them with metal or plastic covers that are designed for the purpose. If possible, hide the covers with shrubbery. This is most acceptable if the climate is mild and if the pipes are protected from rain by wide overhangs.

Don't route the pipes inside any walls, or through an inaccessible ceiling, or through an inaccessible roof, such as a beam roof. The pipes would be very difficult and expensive to repair.

That completes the design of a primary heating and cooling system based on split-system heat pumps. To complete your home's HVAC design, we will now cover your options for auxiliary heating and cooling, ventilation for cooling and air quality, control of humidity, and HVAC controls.

AIR CONDITIONERS, MAYBE

An "air conditioner" is simply a heat pump that lacks the ability to pump heat in both directions. It is useful only for cooling a house, not for heating it. When you select your cooling equipment, the first question is whether you should select an air conditioner or a heat pump.

Usually, it is worth the small additional cost to select heat pumps instead of air conditioners. If you will use hydronic heating or another type of fuel-fired heating as your primary heating system, using heat pumps instead of air conditioners provides a valuable back-up source of heating. The heat pumps can provide heat if your primary heating system fails, or if the fuel for your hydronic system becomes scarce, or if your fuel becomes so expensive that it is cheaper to heat with your heat pump.

This assumes that you will be using split-system heat pumps instead of split-system air conditioners. In this case, the price difference is small. However, for specialized applications where an inexpensive "window"-type air conditioner is satisfactory, it may be much less expensive to install an air conditioner instead of a heat pump.

SPLIT-SYSTEM AIR CONDITIONERS

Whether you decide to install air conditioners or heat pumps, the type that you want is a "split system." This type is better than other types of room air conditioners, and it is much better than central air conditioning.

Split systems have now become the standard for residential air conditioning in most parts of the world, although the United States is lagging. Split-system air conditioners are used for individual houses, multi-family houses, and for individual apartments in large apartment buildings. They are widely used for individual rooms in hotels and motels.

Split-system air conditioners are almost identical to split-system heat pumps in appearance and installation. In fact, some manufacturers offer the same basic package either as a heat pump or as an air conditioner. They look almost the same on the outside and on the inside. They have almost the same efficiency, capacity, and other characteristics as the corresponding heat pumps. As with heat pumps, some manufacturers offer split-system air conditioners that can serve several rooms independently.

Residential split-system air conditioners are also called "ductless" systems because typical units discharge directly into the room. This distinguishes them from central air conditioners, which need ducts. (This name is a bit confusing, because old-fashioned window-type air conditioners also have no ducts. To add further confusion, split systems for commercial buildings commonly do use short ducts.)

To install split-system air conditioners, go to the previous discussion of heat pump installation and follow those instructions. Capacity calculations, efficiency ratings, etc., are exactly the same. Simply ignore the parts about heating.

"WINDOW" AIR CONDITIONERS

After World War II, the window air conditioner became the first type to be widely installed in houses. This type is the least expensive, and it is easy to install in windows. But, it suffers from noise, air leakage, and crude appearance. The compressor is located within the package, so this type suffers from vibration. Hence its nickname, "window shaker."

Window-type air conditioners may be an appropriate choice for informal spaces where cooling is desired only occasionally. Examples are a basement or garage workshop, an outbuilding, or a vacation cabin in a northerly location.

Despite the name, it is best to install a window-type air conditioner through a framed hole in the wall, not in a window. Installing through a wall preserves the view through the windows, makes it easier to seal against air leakage, reduces noise, and allows you to optimize the location of the unit for comfortable cooling. Because a wall is much more massive than a window, the vibration of the unit is damped better. Figure 4-44 shows a well executed installation.

Mounting in a wall opening usually employs a metal sleeve that forms the sides of the opening. Sealing between the sleeve and the wall requires finesse. Sealing between the air conditioner and the sleeve requires gaskets that may be awkward to install.

Mounting in a window tends to be very leaky. It is difficult to achieve a reliable seal against the window frame, and the partially open window is a major leakage path that is especially difficult to seal.

Air leakage can also occur through the interior of the air conditioner. The inner (evaporator) and outer (condenser) equipment is separated by a sheetmetal divider, which has penetrations for pipes and wires. Limiting air leakage during cold weather may require a temporary airtight covering over the outside of the unit that is installed seasonally. This may be difficult to install, and it is not pretty.

CENTRAL AIR CONDITIONING: NEVER

By the 1970's, whole-house air conditioning had become a standard feature in warmer climates. This was a serious setback for energy efficiency because central air conditioning systems can't target cooling to individual rooms.

As air conditioning spread farther north, it was installed in central forced-air heating systems. This saved the cost of a separate duct system, but it increased energy waste and aggravated the existing problems of forced-air heating systems.

In summary, avoid central air conditioning. For the reasons, see the earlier sidebar, *Why You Don't Want Central Forced-Air Heating and Cooling*.

MultihousingDepot

Figure 4-44. Attractive installation of a window-type air conditioner. Installing the unit through a wall is much better than installing it in a window. The unit should be installed as high on the wall as practical, while retaining easy access to the controls and the filter. This provides better air distribution and minimizes drafts.

ELECTRIC RESISTANCE HEATERS

Electric resistance heaters may be the best choice for a limited number of applications. Table 4-1, *Heating Equipment Comparison*, compares electric resistance heaters to other heating equipment. Calculate the relative operating cost of electric resistance heaters by using the *Energy Cost Worksheet*.

Electric resistance heating seems almost ideal. It is clean, it requires no flue or fuel storage, and it has no explosion hazard. Electric heaters are inexpensive. They are small and unobtrusive, so they don't get in the way of furnishings. They can localize heating to the areas where you need it. Installation is easy, without pipes or ducts. Some kinds of electric heaters are completely silent. And, resistance heaters are virtually 100% efficient (see the sidebar).

Then, why is there any other kind of heating? Because, in most locations, the cost of electricity is much higher than the cost of other sources of heating energy. Only a small fraction of the earth's population live in locations that favor electric resistance heating as the primary method of heating.

In colder locations, the cost penalty of resistance heating is so great that most homes will use fuel heating instead. In moderate and warm climates, heat pumps are an alternative that always provides lower heating cost than resistance heating. And, heat pumps also provide cooling.

But, resistance heat still has a place for supplemental heating in certain rooms, even when fuel-fired heating or heat pumps are the primary heating source for the house.

Shower and bath rooms are the most common applications for resistance heat. If you are naked and wet, you would like the temperature of the room to be warmer than the rest of the house. A fan-forced electric heater, usually installed in the ceiling, can warm a shower room quickly.

Resistance heaters may also be a good choice for spaces that are used only occasionally, such as guest bedrooms. This is most likely if you use heat pumps for the rest of the house, because heat pumps are much more expensive and cumbersome to install.

Electric heaters are excellent for supplemental heating of localized areas, not necessarily an entire room. For example, you might install an electric radiant heater over the work bench in your garage for occasional jobs during cold weather.

Use the following menu of electric heaters to select the best kind for each application in your home.

THE ENERGY EFFICIENCY OF RESISTANCE HEATING

Don't bother looking for efficiency ratings for electric heaters. You won't find any. All electric resistance heating units are virtually 100% efficient. That means that they convert all the electrical input energy into heat where you need it. No waste, no chimney.

But, if resistance heaters are so efficient, why is resistance heating usually so expensive? That's because making electricity from fuel is inefficient at the power plant. Hydroelectric generation is efficient, but there is not enough of it to serve more than a small fraction of humanity.

The efficiency advantage of resistance heating within the house partially offsets the higher cost of electrical energy. But not by much, because high-efficiency fuel-fired boilers and heaters can deliver more than 80% of the original fuel energy.

FAN-FORCED BATHROOM CEILING HEATERS

Fan-powered ceiling heaters are usually the best choice for supplemental heating of toilet rooms and for the entry area of showers, where you want to quickly make the space warmer than the rest of the house. The small size of the space allows the heater to warm it quickly. Ceiling heaters don't get in the way of other fixtures, and they don't get splashed by water.

Bathroom ceiling heaters can be installed as a combination with an exhaust fan and/or a ceiling light, as in previous Figure 1-24. Both the heater fan and the exhaust fan are noisy, because they must force air through small passages. In larger bathrooms, it is better to provide a separate exhaust fan for the shower.

Ceiling heaters are recessed into the ceiling. Therefore, they must be installed properly to avoid heat loss through the ceiling insulation and to avoid the risk of a fire in the ceiling.

Bathroom-type ceiling heaters are not practical for other spaces. They are too noisy, they require a large ceiling penetration, and their restricted air flow limits the volume of air that they can heat.

Qmark

Figure 4-45. Electric baseboard convector.

ELECTRIC BASEBOARD CONVECTORS

Electric baseboard convectors (commonly called "baseboard radiators") are usually the best choice for rooms in which they can be installed properly. They are silent, unobtrusive, inexpensive, and easy to install. See Figure 4-45.

They consist of a straight electric heating element wrapped in fins, with a partial enclosure that attaches to the wall just above the floor level. Installation requires only small holes for the electrical power and thermostat wiring. The thermostat usually operates by turning the unit on and off.

Convectors circulate air only by convection, which is a weak force. To work well, convectors should be installed along the bottom of an exterior wall. Room air should be able to flow through them easily.

In certain rooms, this can't be done. For example, baseboard heaters won't work well in a room that has shelving or cabinets or benches along the wall. Therefore, you probably won't use them in the kitchen, garage, or workshop.

Baseboard convectors may provide supplemental heating for shower rooms and toilet rooms, but they are slow to warm the space. To avoid rusting from moisture and urine, they need corrosion resistant enclosures.

Electric baseboard heaters generally have a capacity of about 850 BTUH per foot (800 watts per meter) of unit width. They are available in various lengths, which can be ganged together for any total length that you would need.

For example, a bedroom room with 12 feet (3.7 meters) of exterior wall could have a heating capacity as high as 10,000 BTUH (3,000 watts). That's more than ample for a well insulated room.

Try to center baseboard units under windows, especially the larger windows in a room. This maximizes comfort by opposing the cold downward drafts that windows create.

Space is required under the convector to allow air to flow into the unit. This gap usually is built into the mounting hardware, speeding installation. The top of the enclosure typically is less than one foot (30 cm) above the floor.

Design the height of your electric power receptacles, telephone jacks, etc., to provide ample clearance above the convectors.

Electric baseboard heaters are vulnerable to heat trapping by draperies and blinds. The solution is to install a deflector above the convector that discharges the heat toward the inside of the room. This is the same technique that is used for hydronic baseboard heaters, as shown in Figure 4-14.

FAN-FORCED WALL HEATERS

Fan-forced electric wall heaters are available for use in formal spaces. Figure 4-46 is an example. The fans in these units make a certain amount of noise, but less than typical bathroom ceiling heaters.

A shortcoming of all localized electric heaters is weak heat output, which is limited by the capacity of normal electrical circuits. In the United States, single residential circuits have a maximum capacity of 20 amperes, so a standard 120-volt circuit limits the heater

Qmark

Figure 4-46. Electric wall heater.

to a capacity of about 7,000 BTU per hour (about 2 kW). This is fairly feeble for heating a larger room. Output can be doubled by installing a heater that is designed to operate at 220 or 240 volts.

WALL- AND FLOOR-MOUNTED ELECTRIC RADIATORS

Electric wall-mounted and floor-mounted radiators look virtually the same as wall-mounted and floor-mounted hydronic convectors. For example, see Figure 4-15. A manufacturer may offer the same style of convector in both hydronic and electric versions. Both heat in the same way. They have generally the same comfort benefits and limitations.

ELECTRIC FLOOR HEATING

Electric floor heating is similar to hydronic floor heating in its benefits and in most of its shortcomings. To save ink, we won't repeat the application information.

The major advantage of electric floor heating over hydronic floor heating is simpler installation. All the floor needs is a connection to electricity. Electric floor heating uses resistance heating cable, which maintains the same temperature along its length, so the entire floor is heated by the same amount. And, electric heating can't leak.

To speed installation, the cable typically comes attached to a mesh backing that maintains the proper spacing of the wires. Figure 4-47 shows this method of installation.

With wooden floors, the heating cable can be installed underneath the floor using the "staple-up" method. Or, the heating cable can be installed between the subfloor and the finish floor.

With a concrete floor, the heating cable is buried in the concrete. Or, especially in existing houses, it can be installed between the concrete floor and the finish surface.

With all kinds of floor heating, the heat travels downward as well as upward. Therefore, the underside of the floor must be well insulated.

CEILING RADIANT HEATING

Ceiling radiant heat is similar to floor heat. The entire ceiling is covered with a grid of resistance heating wire, which is installed between the ceiling joists and below the ceiling insulation. The disadvantages of this type of heating usually outweigh its benefits. It is usable only in warm or mild climates, where its shortcomings are tolerable.

SunTouch

Figure 4-47. Electric floor heating cable being laid. The cable is mounted on a mesh that maintains proper spacing and speeds the installation. The cable will be embedded in concrete, which conducts heat and forms a base for the floor surface.

On the positive side, ceiling heat is quiet and uniform. The distribution of heat is unimpeded by carpets or furnishings. Also, ceiling heat requires no visible equipment inside the room (except the thermostat), which makes it appropriate for austere interior decoration styles.

On the negative side, ceiling heat must operate at low temperature. Otherwise, it would beat down on the heads of the occupants and create serious temperature stratification within the room. Because ceiling heat must operate at low temperature, it warms a room slowly. This makes it unsuitable for rooms that need quick warm-up, such as bathrooms, kitchens, and work rooms.

Because ceiling heat is overhead, it cannot offset cold drafts that fall from the windows. Even if the windows are not oversized, they will contribute to temperature stratification by creating a layer of cold air on the floor.

Ceiling heat wastes a certain amount of energy by upward conduction and convection through the ceiling insulation, especially if the heating coils are installed in an attic or beam roof. Therefore, it is essential to install ample insulation above the heating elements and to install the insulation carefully.

Like floor heat, ceiling heat must be built into the structure of the house. This makes it difficult to repair. Also, it is vulnerable to wiring damage from ceiling penetrations and modifications to the attic. The insulation of the heating wire will last for only a fraction of the life of the house. Eventually, it will crack and disintegrate, creating a safety hazard.

Finally, ceiling heat is more expensive to install than baseboard units.

Stelpro

Figure 4-48. Typical electric unit heater. This model allows the unit to rotate on its bracket, and it has vanes to guide the air discharge up or down.

ELECTRIC UNIT HEATERS

A "unit heater" is a compact fan-powered heater that is hung on a bracket from the ceiling or a wall, so it avoids conflict with furnishings or equipment. Figure 4-48 shows a typical model.

Electric unit heaters are inexpensive. They warm the air quickly, subject to the limitation of their capacity. They are easy to install, requiring only an electrical connection.

Unit heaters look industrial, so you won't use them in finished rooms. They are used mainly in informal spaces, such as a garage or workshop. In larger spaces, they can provide localized heating.

HEAT LAMPS AND RADIANT HEATERS

Radiant heaters warm people and objects directly, without first heating the air. This makes them appropriate for outside locations such as sidewalk cafes, where the air cannot be enclosed for economical heating.

However, radiant heaters are not a good choice for any heating application inside a house. Radiant heat flows in a line of sight from the heater. A person is broiled on the side facing the heater, and is cold on the other side.

Bathroom heaters using infrared heat lamps installed in the ceiling were once popular. However, a fan-forced ceiling heater is much more comfortable.

ELECTRIC BOILERS AND FURNACES

There are hydronic heating boilers and forced-air furnaces that use electric resistance heating elements instead of a fuel flame. Such equipment offers no advantage over other kinds of electric heating, except perhaps in unusual circumstances.

PORTABLE ELECTRIC HEATERS: DANGER!

Some houses located in mild climates are built without heating equipment. For occasional heating, they rely on portable electric heaters. This is false economy. Portable heaters are a notorious fire hazard. They can start fires by tipping over or by coming in contact with flammable material. Their power cords are vulnerable to fraying and to broken strands of wire.

 Portable electric heaters are a serious fire hazard.

A portable heater typically uses most of the capacity of an electrical circuit. As a result, hot spots commonly occur at receptacles and in frayed power cords. Using a portable heater for a long period, such as heating a bedroom overnight, increases the risk of a fire because a hot spot anywhere in the circuit may have time to heat surrounding material to burning temperature.

Instead of using portable electric heaters, install safe, permanent heaters. Most types, such as electric baseboard heaters, are inexpensive. You can afford to install them even if they will be used only a few days per year.

DIRECT-FIRED ROOM AND SPACE HEATERS

A direct-fired space heater is an option to consider for a limited number of situations, usually as a supplement to primary heating with a hydronic system or with heat pumps. Table 4-1, *Heating Equipment Comparison*, compares direct-fired space heaters to other heating equipment. There are several different types of direct-fired room heaters, which we will explain individually.

Direct-fired heaters are relatively inexpensive in relation to their heating capacity, especially in larger sizes. The air is heated directly by the flame through a thin heat exchanger, so heating air is supplied more quickly and at higher temperature than is possible with hydronic heating or a heat pump. Individual room heaters efficiently localize heating to the room, which is a prime requirement for energy efficiency.

The typical application for an auxiliary direct-fired heater is a large, informal space that is heated on an occasional basis, such as a garage or a basement workshop or a separate workshop building. A direct-fired heater can warm a cold space quickly. It has no water pipes or other components that are vulnerable to freezing when the space is unheated.

If heat pumps are your primary method of heating, but you have occasional spells of very cold weather, you might use direct-fired room heaters in some of your formal rooms to supplement your heat pumps. This is a way of dealing with the loss of heating capacity and efficiency that occurs with heat pumps during cold weather. Unlike heat pumps, fuel-fired heaters always warm the room with air that is supplied at a high, comfortable temperature.

You might use fuel-fired room heaters as the primary source of heating in a climate that has only occasional periods of cold weather. Or, in a cold climate, fuel-fired room heaters may be an economical choice for a smaller, less formal house, such as a vacation house or cabin.

Fuel Options

Most direct-fired room heaters burn natural gas or propane. Oil is satisfactory only for larger, furnace-type heaters. Use the *Energy Cost Worksheet* to determine the most economical fuel at your location.

Fuel Leakage to the Interior

Each direct-fired heater requires a connection to its fuel supply. The pipe should be installed in a way that makes it easy to fix the leaks that occur occasionally at fittings. If a pipe is installed behind finished surfaces without regard to access, a small leak can be expensive to fix.

Gas seepage at pipe joints is an increased health concern in a highly efficient house that is tightly enclosed during cold weather. Such seepage typically does not create a risk of explosion or suffocation, because the quantity of gas is small. However, some people seem to have adverse reactions to gas, or at least to the impurities or additives in gas.

Fuel oil leakage also tends to be minor, and small quantities of oil leakage do not create an explosion hazard. However, fuel oil leaks have a pungent odor.

Venting

"Venting" a fuel-fired heater means exhausting the products of combustion. "Vented" heaters discharge the exhaust to the outside. "Unvented" heaters discharge the exhaust into the room. All fuel-fired heaters in your home should be vented to the outside.

If fuel-fired heating equipment vents through a wall, exhaust from the unit can enter the house through a nearby window that is opened. The warm exhaust gases will tend to float upward, but any wind can make them flow sideways. For this reason, building codes and manufacturers' installation instructions generally specify a minimum distance between the exterior vent and any windows or other openings.

Venting is simple if the intake/exhaust of the heater is above grade level. If the heater is installed in a room below grade, extensions are available for the exhaust and outside air intake.

Even today, you can buy gas-fired room heaters that exhaust directly into the room. This is permitted, or at least overlooked, because gas fuels burn cleanly. However, such heaters still pollute the room air with carbon dioxide, carbon monoxide, and small quantities of products that result from the burning of impurities and additives in the fuel. If the room is airtight, these pollutants are likely to rise to a dangerous or unpleasant concentration. As the heater becomes starved for combustion air, it produces even more carbon monoxide, which worsens in a deadly spiral.

You can still buy unvented kerosene room heaters. These are even worse than unvented gas-fueled heaters. It's amazing that they are still allowed.

Unvented portable fuel-fired heaters have limited application for occasional heating of large, leaky structures. An example is heating a barn for a square dance.

Sealed Combustion

In addition to venting exhaust to the outside, some direct-fired heaters are able to draw their combustion air directly from the outside through a pipe. Such heaters are said to have a "sealed" combustion system. A sealed combustion system provides three important benefits:

- It avoids the need to drag outside air through the occupied space. By the same token, a sealed combustion system is compatible with airtight house construction.

- It eliminates the possibility of combustion gases being forced out the heater and into the house. Without a sealed combustion system, wind pressure on the house and the flue, or the operation of an exhaust fan, may cause exhaust fumes to flow backward through the flue and into the house.

- It eliminates the possibility that the flame inside the heater will ignite explosive fumes in the surrounding space, such as fumes from a gasoline spill in the garage.

It's generally a good idea to buy a heater with a sealed combustion system, if an appropriate model is available. The only exception would be a heater for a leaky space that contains no fire or explosion hazards.

Cozy Heaters

Figure 4-51. A high-efficiency gas-fired wall heater. Its sealed combustion system makes it safe for enclosed spaces. The unit is conspicuous, and its fan is audible. The low air discharge of the floor-mounted installation tends to pick up dust from the carpet.

GAS-FIRED WALL HEATERS

Direct-fired wall heaters are practical for both formal and informal spaces. Their name derives from the fact that they are designed to be mounted against an exterior wall for the purpose of exhausting the flue gases through the wall. This method of venting allows only clean gas fuels to be used, i.e., natural gas, propane, or LPG.

Wall heaters come in a variety of shapes, including tall-and-narrow, boxy, and baseboard styles. They protrude into the room typically from 6 to 18 inches (15 to 45 cm), depending on the style. Efficient models are offered in capacities that can heat most well insulated rooms quickly. Figures 4-51 and 4-52 show typical units.

Most direct-fired heaters use a fan for air circulation. These heaters typically discharge from the bottom, minimizing stratification and warming the floor locally. They have audible fan noise.

Some direct-fired heaters operate by convection, avoiding the noise of a fan. These units discharge from the top. Their heat distribution is more localized, and they do not warm the lower portion of the space as effectively as fan-forced heaters.

I have heated my well insulated office with a gas-fired wall heater for 30 years, and it has been entirely satisfactory. Its only drawback is the noise of the fan while the unit is operating. Newer units may be quieter than mine.

Cozy Heaters

Figure 4-52. A wall furnace that is tall and narrow. The unit has a fan, and it discharges near the floor.

Energy Efficiency

As this is being written, the best direct-fired wall heaters are claiming efficiency (AFUE) ratings of about 80%. This is somewhat lower than the typical efficiency of a hydronic system that uses a condensing boiler.

The market does not yet offer a menu of direct-fired wall heaters that use the principle of condensing water vapor out of the flue gases (like high-efficiency boilers and furnaces). If such heaters become available, they could theoretically provide somewhat better efficiency than a hydronic system.

Installation

You can find a wall heater model to mount at any convenient height. The discharge air has a temperature of about 160 °F (about 70 °C), so don't install the unit where it would blow over people. If the unit discharges at a downward angle, a discharge height of about two feet (60 cm) works well. This height allows you to maneuver a vacuum cleaner under the heater.

Most wall heaters are designed to rest on the floor, with the air discharge at the bottom. This tends to raise dust off the floor. With such a unit, I recommend mounting it on a wall bracket or on a floor stand to raise the air discharge above the floor. Check with the manufacturer before doing this, unless the installation manual shows you how to do it.

Installation on the exterior wall is very compact. The heater typically exhausts directly through a hole in the wall behind the heater, using a short flue duct to connect the heater to an exhaust cap that is mounted on the outside of the wall. The same fitting may also serve as the inlet for the heater's combustion air, which travels to the heater around the exhaust pipe. Figure 4-53 shows how a combination pipe is installed.

This method of installation provides a "sealed" combustion system, which has the important benefits that we learned previously.

FORCED-AIR FURNACES

Don't use a forced-air furnace as the primary heating system for your home. (The earlier sidebar, *Why You Don't Want Central Forced-Air Heating and Cooling*, explains why.) However, if you use a furnace to heat only a single large space, its most serious disadvantages disappear. It offers an easy way to install large heating capacity.

Forced-air furnaces are available in many models, for both gas and oil fuel. They generally are made for whole-house heating, so most models are too big for

Cozy Heaters

Figure 4-53. Combination exhaust and combustion air intake for a high-efficiency wall heater. This model requires a hole through the wall that is only 3.5" (9 cm) in diameter.

rooms of normal size. A forced-air furnace may be the best heater for a large, informal space, such as a basement, garage, or outbuilding. The installation may have no ducts at all, with the heated air discharging directly out of the furnace. Or, ducts may be installed to distribute the heated air within the space.

If the furnace will operate for a large number of hours and if the fuel is gas, select a high-efficiency condensing model. A furnace with a sealed combustion system can be installed almost anywhere within the space. This is an essential safety feature if the space may contain flammable vapors, such as from gasoline spills.

The exhaust of a condensing furnace is so cool that it can be ducted to the outside through an exposed pipe, so the furnace can easily be located far from an exterior wall. Similarly, the combustion air supply can be brought to the furnace with a lightweight pipe.

Forced-air furnaces are covered by the Energy Star rating system, which makes it easy to find the most efficient models. Most condensing gas furnaces have AFUE ratings that exceed 90%, and these all have sealed combustion systems. Non-condensing models have efficiencies in the range of 70-80%, and they usually don't have sealed combustion systems.

The best conventional oil-fired furnaces have efficiencies that approach 80%. You can get condensing oil-fired furnaces, but I don't recommend them. They probably won't be kept clean enough to maintain their rated efficiency.

High-Efficiency Furnace Filters

Forced-air furnaces have filters, which usually are installed in a slot at the return air opening. In the past, these filters were capable of blocking only fibers and larger dust particles. Their main purpose was to prevent accumulation of dirt on the furnace heat exchanger and on the air conditioning coil, if one was installed.

Starting around the beginning of the 21st century, home furnace filters with radically improved filtering ability became available. These can protect the occupants as well as the equipment. You can find furnace filters that are made to cover different classes of pollutants, based mainly on the size of the pollutant particles. In order of decreasing particle size, these pollutants include dust and lint, dust mites, mold spores, pollen, pet dander, smoke, bacteria, and viruses.

It would be desirable for furnace filters to have a standardized rating system that indicates their effectiveness for blocking the various types of particles. I have seen such rating systems over the years, but they faded from use. Today, it is likely that the rating you find on the package is a relative number that is used by an individual manufacturer. More useful is the description of the types of particles that the filter claims to block.

There is a big problem with filters that block the smaller particles. They severely restrict air flow through the furnace. Only certain furnace models have sufficient fan power to overcome their resistance to air flow. Therefore, if you need a furnace for an application that requires filtering of the smaller particles, be sure to select a model that has adequate fan power.

The filters with the highest filtration ratings may simply not work with most furnaces. I learned this from experience when a modern furnace developed a high-pitched whistle. Replacing the filter with one having a lower filtration rating solved the problem. The less restrictive filter reduced the length of time required for the furnace to heat the space.

If the furnace uses ducts to distribute air within the space, the furnace filter will slow the accumulation of dirt inside the ducts. Still, if the ducts are shaken or bumped, some of the accumulated dirt breaks loose and enters the space.

DRW

Figure 4-54. Gas-fired unit heater installed in a large workshop. This unit exhausts through an adjacent wall, but draws combustion air from inside the space. The flame is open to the inside atmosphere.

GAS-FIRED UNIT HEATERS

A unit heater is a compact, inexpensive fan-powered heater that is hung by a bracket from the ceiling or a wall. The bracket allows the heater to be aimed in any direction. The heater consists of an array of burners, a simple heat exchanger, and a fan. Unit heaters are made in many sizes. They look industrial, so you won't use them in formal rooms. See Figure 4-54.

The flames and the fan make a certain amount of noise. Some unit heaters exhaust to the outside, and some are unvented. All unit heaters draw combustion air from the space. This exposes the inside of the space to the flame in the heater. Therefore, a unit heater should not be used where explosive vapors may exist, as in a garage.

The main advantage of unit heaters is low cost. You might install one in an informal space that is used occasionally, such as a separate workshop building, provided that the space is free of fire or explosion hazards.

Unit heaters generally are not rated for efficiency.

GAS-FIRED RADIANT HEATERS

A gas-fired radiant heater works by heating a ceramic surface so hot that the surface glows intensely, emitting heat mostly by radiation. See Figure 4-55.

Generally, this is an option to avoid. Heat radiation does not warm the air in the space. In principle, this makes radiant heating efficient because the heat is focused directly on the occupants. However, radiant heat is not comfortable. You broil on one side, while your other side stays cold.

To lessen the broiler effect, some radiant heaters offer an optional circulation fan. When the fan operates, the heater operates in a hybrid manner, emitting heat by radiation and also warming the room air.

Some fuel-fired radiant heaters are vented and some are unvented, but all draw combustion air from the space. This exposes the room air to the flame. Therefore, do not install this type of heater in a space where flammable vapors may occur.

GAS-FIRED FIREPLACES

A gas-fired "fireplace" is a space heater that is contrived to look like a wood-fired fireplace. The gas flame heats ceramic "logs," which then radiate heat into the space. A gas fireplace avoids the major annoyances of a real fireplace, such as the need to remove ashes and the need for a large safety zone. But, it's a fake. Some people like them, anyhow.

Gas fireplaces are much less efficient than other gas-fired room heaters because they vent through an open chimney. They suffer from most of the efficiency penalties of real fireplaces. For the details, see *Heating with Firewood and Other Solid Fuels*, in *Last Look: Energy for Pioneers*, at the end of the book.

Cozy Heaters

Figure 4-55. A gas-fired radiant heater. The intense heat radiation from the unit can be moderated or supplemented by an internal fan that distributes warm air. This unit vents to the outside, but all radiant heaters of this kind take combustion air from inside the space.

Cooling Without Air Conditioning

Before air conditioning became available, people did not submit passively to the heat of summer. In addition to designing the structures of their houses to stay cool, they used two methods of mechanical cooling that are still important. One is to exploit outside air for cooling at night. The other is to circulate inside air over the occupants.

These classic cooling methods won't entirely replace air conditioning in warm climates, but they can greatly reduce cooling cost. The two methods apply to different situations, which we will explain.

In dry climates, another method of staying cool is to exploit the cooling effect of evaporating water. Evaporative coolers are a cheaper alternative to air conditioners, and they generally provide less comfort. We will examine their advantages and limitations.

NIGHTTIME COOLING WITH OUTSIDE AIR

For relief from summer heat in the past, people would wait for the sun to set, open all the windows, and wait for cool night air to circulate through the house. This works because the surface of the earth cools quickly at night by radiating its heat into the sky. (See the sidebar, *The Sky is Cold*, in Step 2.) Within a few hours, the cool outdoor surfaces have cooled the layer of air next to the earth, making the outside air suitable for cooling.

Bringing the cool air into the house requires a breeze, but adequate breezes often are lacking. So, by the 1950's it became popular to install a ventilation fan to draw outside air into the house. The fan not only increases the flow of cool air into the house, it allows the occupants to concentrate the cooling in rooms where cooling is desired at night, typically the bedrooms. If the breeze is directed over the beds, it can produce wonderful comfort even on a sultry night.

Ventilation is directed to the occupied rooms by opening the windows in those rooms. The most efficient way to control the intensity of the breeze is to adjust the speed of the fan.

Typically, the fan is installed in the attic, as in Figure 4-58, so this type of fan came to be called an "attic fan." It is also known as a "whole house" fan, which is a name that misses the point. You don't want to ventilate your whole house, just the rooms that are occupied at night.

Attic fans were popular for a only a short period before they were displaced by air conditioning.

Figure 4-58. A typical attic fan installation, as seen from inside the attic. The fan is mounted on top of the ceiling joists. A damper is installed below the fan to prevent attic air from falling into the house when the fan is not running. The damper usually is flush with the ceiling.

However, the principle remains valid. Outdoor ventilation fans are inexpensive, quiet, and comfortable. With energy costs rising, it makes no sense to operate air conditioning when cool air is available right outside your bedroom windows.

The Fan

Nighttime ventilation fans should be *big* and *slow*, so they will run quietly. The fan typically has a diameter of 30" to 36" (75 cm to 90 cm). This size is big enough to cool several bedrooms. Usually, the fan is driven by a belt for slow rotation and quiet operation.

Get a fan that has several speeds, with a wide speed range. This will require a more expensive motor, but it is worth the effort to find one. An efficient fan uses from 100 to 800 watts, depending on the size of the fan and the speed you select. At bedtime, all you want is a gentle breeze over the beds, which requires little energy.

Better Temperature Control

To optimize comfort and efficiency, control the fan with two thermostats. Install one in the air flow path from the spaces that are being cooled. For example, install it in the corridor that serves the bedrooms. Select a thermostat that has a manual switch to turn off the fan when the house is not occupied.

The other thermostat senses the outside temperature, and it prevents the fan from running when the outside temperature is too high for cooling. Without this thermostat, the fan would run all day if you forget to turn it off, bringing heat into the house. The setting of this thermostat does not change. Install it anywhere that is convenient, with the outside temperature sensor being connected through a small hole in the wall.

 Installing two thermostats for the outside air cooling fan offers perfect nighttime comfort.

For a really deluxe installation, install a fan whose speed is continuously variable. Control it with an inside thermostat that adjusts the fan speed to the inside temperature. This may require some custom controls that will be novel to the electrician.

Where to Install the Fan

A cooling fan can be installed satisfactorily in various locations. Consider these factors to select the best location:

- Install the fan where it will minimize the noise level inside the house.
- The fan opening is large. Install the opening where it will not be unsightly.
- Locate the opening where it will not be an entry for vermin.
- Design the opening so that it can be sealed easily and tightly against air leakage during the heating season.

If your home has an attic, the attic usually is the preferred location. It keeps the fan invisible and quiet. The attic insulation and rafters act as an effective muffler, minimizing noise both inside and outside the house.

Installation is easy. Simply insert cross pieces between the joists to form a box, and mount the fan assembly on top of the box. The fan diameter is larger than the space between the ceiling joists, but there is no need to cut any joists, because the air will flow around them. The damper usually is installed on the ceiling surface. Its frame covers the rough edges of the opening.

To minimize noise, install the ceiling opening at a distance from the rooms being cooled. Mount the fan firmly to avoid vibrating the ceiling surface. Don't use the attic access hatch for mounting the fan.

If you don't have an attic, but you do have a basement, consider mounting the fan in the basement wall. Basements are good sound absorbers and their masonry walls will not resonate from the vibration of the fan. Because you don't want to make a very large hole in the basement wall, the fan typically is somewhat smaller and faster than an attic fan. If you have a workshop in your basement that requires an exhaust fan, as in Figure 4-72, the same fan can serve as a night cooling fan. Both functions require about the same fan capacity.

Using a basement fan for nighttime ventilation provides a significant benefit. At the end of the winter season, the basement remains cold because its massive concrete walls and the surrounding soil are cold. Circulating warm house air through the basement warms it up. This minimizes condensation, which causes the mildew that is notorious in basements.

A basement installation also has drawbacks. The fan intrudes visibly into the space. It is loud for anyone occupying the basement at night. If the exhaust damper is near ground level, insects can enter through the loose damper when the fan is not running, perhaps joined by mice and other critters.

Another alternative is to install a cooling fan in any wall of the house where it will not create excessive noise or become an eyesore. Such mounting is unusual, but practical. For example, you could enclose the fan in a small closet, with a louver door to draw air from the inside of the house. Install the fan at a distance from the rooms you wish to cool, to minimize noise. Select a fan that is slow and quiet. Hide the exterior opening with a trellis or other attractive visual screen.

Ventilation fans can be installed in windows, but this is not an option for your elegant home. Window fans are inefficient and noisy, and they ruin the view through the window.

Dampers and Closures

No matter where the cooling fan is located, it needs two kinds of closures. For normal operation, the fan needs a damper that closes when the fan turns off. This minimizes unwanted air leakage, and keeps insects and mice out of the house.

To completely block air leakage during the times of the year when you don't need ventilation cooling, the fan opening needs a sturdy airtight closure. This can be built in a variety of ways. Typically, a well gasketed, insulated box covers the fan assembly. The box can be hinged on one side and tipped out of the way when the fan is used.

If the fan runs with the air flow blocked, the fan motor will burn out and perhaps start a fire. To avoid this, install a contact switch that connects power to the fan only if the lid is fully open.

CIRCULATION FANS

Fans that circulate air inside a space can be a comfortable alternative to air conditioning for many hours each year. Unlike outside air ventilation fans, indoor circulation fans do not depend on the outside temperature for cooling. Therefore, they can be used even when it is warm outside.

Also, *using indoor fans in combination with air conditioning is a comfortable way to lower air conditioning cost.* Circulation fans may allow you to raise the temperature of the air conditioning thermostat by perhaps 5 °F (3 °C) or more.

Circulation fans are also effective for cooling localized outdoor spaces, especially porches.

Circulation fans work by exploiting the "wind chill" cooling effect of air flowing over the human body. Air circulation carries away body heat, and it increases the cooling of skin by perspiration. Circulation fans do not cool the room air. They must blow air over exposed skin in order to provide a benefit. *It is a waste of energy to operate a circulation fan when a space is unoccupied.*

Because the recirculated air is not cold, a fan can provide gentler cooling than air conditioning. For example, the air from an air conditioner is uncomfortably cold on exposed bodies in a bedroom, but the gentle wafting of a slow paddle fan can be ideal.

For comfortable cooling, quiet operation, and energy efficiency, a cooling fan should be *big* and *slow*. Ceiling mounted paddle fans meet these requirements best. A single ceiling fan covers a large bed or a localized activity area, such as reading chair, without wasting energy by moving air in unoccupied space. The air velocity can be adjusted over a wide range. Unlike fans that sit on the floor, ceiling fans do not pick up dust from the floor and furnishings, and they do not clutter the space.

So, we will settle on ceiling paddle fans as our preference. In warmer climates, such as Florida, ceiling fans are a universal choice for most of the rooms in a house. You can find models to fit almost any décor. Figure 4-59 is a typical indoor installation, and Figure 4-60 is a typical porch installation.

Paddle fans require little energy if they are installed and used properly. At low speed, which usually is adequate for a bedroom, a good model consumes less than 10 watts. At high speed, which is typical for a porch during warm weather, a paddle fan may use about 150 watts.

Other kinds of room air circulation fans are portable, so we don't need to deal with them in the design of your home. Anyway, there are few applications where a portable fan is more desirable than a ceiling fan.

DRW

Figure 4-59. Indoor ceiling fan installation. The length of the downrod is appropriate for the tall ceiling, which allows good air circulation.

Ceiling Height for Paddle Fans

Ceiling fans have one significant constraint, which is that they need extra ceiling height to work well and to look attractive. In Step 1, you decided which rooms will have ceiling fans and you designed the ceiling heights of those rooms accordingly.

For safety, comfort, and good appearance, paddle fans should be installed so that the blades are at least 7 feet (210 cm) above the floor. For ideal efficiency and air distribution, the blades should be installed at least 18 inches (45 cm) below the ceiling. A ceiling height of about 9 feet (270 cm) is the minimum to achieve a well balanced appearance in a formal room.

If you install a paddle fan under a slanted ceiling, the blades tips should not approach closer than about 18" (45 cm) to the ceiling at any point.

A paddle fan usually is suspended on a rod, called a "downrod," that connects the fan's hub assembly to a mounting plate on the ceiling. The height of a paddle fan can be adjusted easily by changing the length of the downrod. The downrod usually has a loose attachment at the top. This allows the fan to wobble slightly if the blades are unbalanced, avoiding stress on the rod and its ceiling mount.

DRW

Figure 4-60. Ceiling fans for a porch. Several fans are needed for good coverage. Outdoor fan cooling typically requires much more fan power than indoor cooling.

A light fixture may be installed under the hub of a paddle fan. The light fixture may hang below the hub from about 2" to 12" (5 to 30 cm). If the fan has a light fixture, raise the fan by this amount to provide adequate headroom.

For lower ceilings, such as the U.S. standard 8-foot ceiling, you can buy paddle fans that have a hub assembly that is mounted directly to the ceiling. These models are called "huggers," "flush mounted," or "low profile." They don't look as elegant as fans installed farther below the ceiling, and they sacrifice some efficiency. However, they can provide effective cooling, especially at low speed. This mounting method has the advantage of eliminating the downrod, so balancing the fan blades is less critical.

Placement and Size of Paddle Fans

Paddle fans are most effective when they are installed directly above the occupants. So, coordinate the locations of the fans with the likely layout of the room or space. You may need several fans to provide adequate coverage of a large room.

Provide a horizontal clearance of at least 18" (45 cm) between the blade tips and the nearest wall. This clearance provides better air flow near the wall and it reduces the possibility of noise when the fan runs at high speed.

Bigger fans generally are better. A bigger fan provides a more uniform breeze over a larger area, and it provides cooling at lower speeds. Lower speeds save energy and minimize noise. A large paddle fan at low speed is almost inaudible.

Common diameters for residential paddle fans range from about 42" to 54" (105 cm to 135 cm). This size range is appropriate for cooling a localized area, such as a bed or a group of chairs. Much larger sizes are available. Generally, if you want to cool a large area, use several residential-size fans and arrange them carefully.

Lighting Fixtures on Ceiling Fans

Did you ever wonder why paddle fans commonly have lights attached underneath the hub? This arrangement is needed to avoid the annoying flicker that would occur if a light fixture is mounted above the rotating blades of a fan. Since paddle fans and room light fixtures often compete for the same ceiling space, someone devised a way to install the light fixture underneath the fan, with the lamp mounting and electrical connections passing through the center of the fan motor.

Originally, incandescent bulbs were installed on stalks that extended down from the fan hub. This required a taller ceiling to lift the lamps to a satisfactory height. However, some models have lamps that are mounted in a shallow bowl in the hub, as in Figure 4-61. Fans with LED lamps may require no additional depth.

DRW

Figure 4-61. Ceiling fan with a light fixture. With a low ceiling, as in this bedroom, the light should have a shallow housing to keep it well above head level.

Some paddle fans now offer lights mounted on top of the motor housing, aimed to reflect light from the ceiling. These produce a wavering light that may be annoying.

Shopping for Ceiling Fans

Start your shopping for ceiling fans on the Energy Star Web site, which is explained at the beginning of Step 7. Energy Star-rated fans are significantly more efficient than average. The Energy Star listing states the efficiency of each fan model in terms of cubic feet per minute per watt (CFM/watt) at low, medium, and high fan speeds.

The overall quality of Energy Star certified fans is likely to be better than average, because good design of the motor, controls, fans, and lighting is needed to achieve high efficiency.

Once you have identified the most efficient models, go to the manufacturers' Web sites to see the appearance options and other features that are offered for each model.

For fans that have light fixtures, the total wattage of the lamps is stated. At the time this is being written, all Energy Star certified models with lights have compact fluorescent or LED lamps instead of incandescent lamps.

Some efficient fans models can accept a variety of light fixture styles. If you want a fan that has less efficient lamps, such as an older Victorian style with incandescent lamps on stalks, look for a fan that has a related model that is Energy Star rated.

If your paddle fans will be installed in a damp or salty environment, buy special models that resist destruction by the elements. This is important because a fan circulates moisture, salt, and corrosive pollutants over itself. Underwriters Laboratories (UL) has two ratings for fans in corrosive environments, one for "damp" locations and one for "wet" locations. For example, the former is appropriate for the inside of a house near saltwater, and the latter is appropriate for an open porch.

Efficient and User-Friendly Controls

A paddle fan should have a wide range of speeds. The low end of the speed range is most important. You will want only the gentlest air movement in bedrooms, especially after the room has cooled down. Good models have at least three speeds, and more is better. Some models may have a continuously variable speed control.

Most paddle fans can reverse the direction of rotation. This is intended for cold weather. The idea is that an upward flow of air will prevent stratification of heat. We discuss this further under the next topic.

Many models control the fan speed and the lights from pull chains that dangle from the hub. This is a convenient method of control for typical fan locations, especially over a bed. But, check the fan model. Even major fan manufacturers install the pull chains carelessly, so that they tend to jam and break.

Fans can also be controlled with wall switches. And, some models offer a remote control similar to a television control.

The most important energy-saving feature of a fan is the control that turns it off. A fan that runs in a vacant room wastes energy. So, make the switches convenient. If the fan has a light, label the switches for visitors to indicate which switch controls the fan and which the light. Occupancy sensors may be a good choice for controlling fans intended for daytime use. See *Automatic Lighting Controls*, in Step 6.

Here's an innovation to make your bedroom fans even better. The temperature drops throughout the night, so install a thermostat in the room to turn off the fan while you are asleep.

 Install a thermostat to control your ceiling fan while you sleep.

For a really deluxe bedroom installation, control the fan speed with the thermostat. This requires more complicated controls, and only a few electricians would know how to install them.

Installation Cautions

If you visit quaint tropical hangouts, you probably have seen paddle fans wobbling so badly that they seem on the verge of shaking loose. Hope it doesn't happen, because a falling piece of heavy rotating machinery would do serious damage.

You can abolish fan wobble almost completely. Good ceiling fans come with detailed installation instructions for a perfect installation. Contractors tend to disdain instructions that come with equipment, so fish the instructions out of the box and make sure that the installer follows them.

Once the fan is installed, it should not wobble at any speed. The blades are balanced prior to shipment. If the fan wobbles, either it was not installed properly or the blades are unbalanced or out of alignment.

The fan must be attached properly to a ceiling joist or other strong structural member. Most fans attach to a special electrical mounting box that should be installed before the insulation and interior sheathing. Specify this in your house drawings, along with the control wiring for the fan.

USING FANS TO REDUCE STRATIFICATION

In rooms that are very tall, temperature stratification can cause discomfort. See *Ceiling Height and Shape*, in Step 1. Fans have been used in various ways to move the warmer air in the upper part of the room down to floor level. Fans are only partially effective for this purpose.

A basic problem is that the air movement caused by the fans creates a "wind chill" that partly cancels the benefit of reducing stratification. Another penalty is the energy that is needed to operate the fans.

At present, paddle fans are the most popular type that is used to counteract stratification. To minimize the wind chill effect, the fans can be operated in reverse during cold weather. Most paddle fans have a switch that allows them to operate in reverse.

In this way, the fans blow upward toward the ceiling, rather than downward toward the occupied areas of the room. This method of operation creates a gentle upward flow of air from the floor level, while the warm air at the top of the room is forced downward along the ceiling and walls. The fans still create a wind chill effect, but it is greatly reduced.

Paddle fans prevent stratification best in well insulated rooms, where they are needed the least. They are less effective in rooms that are poorly insulated, or that have a lot of glass. In those cases, the circulation of the air over the ceiling and walls increases heat loss by conduction. Also, the downward flow of air along the walls and windows aggravates the cascading of cold air from the exterior surfaces of the room.

There is another way to use fans to reverse stratification. Install a vertical duct to transfer warm air from the ceiling to the floor level. A small, thermostatically controlled fan is located in the duct. The air discharge should be located at a convenient height close to the floor, in a location where the discharge is not annoying. Figure 4-62 shows the upper part of an installation in which the duct is located inside an interior wall.

The duct can be located anywhere that is convenient. For example, one design uses a colorful fabric tube that

DRW

Figure 4-62. The inlet for an anti-stratification fan is installed near the top of a tall slanted ceiling, where warm air from the wood stove rises. Figure 1-120 shows the room layout. The fan, which is mounted inside the wall, discharges the stratified warm air at a low level in the bedroom on the other side of the wall.

is suspended from the ceiling, with the fan located in the top of the tube.

If the floor plan includes a multi-level space, such as an atrium, similar arrangements can be used to reduce stratification between the floors. However, the only efficient way to prevent stratification between floors is to isolate each floor level, and to install a door at each stairway.

EVAPORATIVE COOLERS FOR DRY CLIMATES

Conventional air conditioning cools by the same process that is used in your refrigerator. "Evaporative cooling" is a much older kind of cooling that can be used in dry climates. It uses less energy than refrigeration cooling, and the equipment is less expensive. If you live in a dry climate, don't overlook this option.

Before we get into the details, you should know that evaporative cooling is inferior to conventional air conditioning in all respects except its lower energy cost. It is unlikely that you will want it as the primary cooling for your house. If you travel in the American Southwest, where evaporative cooling is common, you will see restaurants and bars advertise that they are "cooled by refrigeration" to reassure potential customers that they *don't* use evaporative cooling.

Even if evaporative cooling is not the best choice for the main part of your home, you may want to use it for spaces where temperature and humidity are less critical, such as a glassed-in veranda.

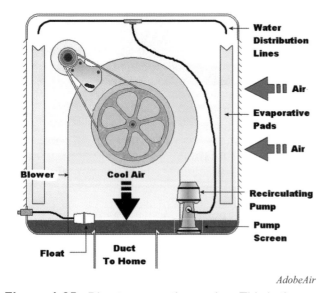

Figure 4-65. Direct evaporative cooler. This is the simplest and most common kind.

The higher humidity created inside the house by evaporative cooling can promote mildew and structural damage, and it may rust steel tools and other implements. As a rule, it is not prudent to use evaporative cooling for any part of a house that tends to remain cooler or more humid than the rest of the house. This would include basements, bathing spaces, and the laundry area.

Several kinds of evaporative coolers have been developed, but only one is presently popular for use in houses. Specialists call that kind "direct" or "single-stage." Everyone else simply calls it an "evaporative cooler" or "swamp cooler."

How Evaporative Cooling Works

The common type of evaporative cooler is mechanically very simple. Figure 4-65 shows how it operates. A fan blows outside air into the house through a large hole, which may be a window, a wall opening, or a roof opening. A wetted curtain or pad surrounds the fan intake. The outside air is pulled through the wet pad by the fan on its way into the house. A small pump circulates water over the pad to keep it wet.

The machine is packaged in a housing that is installed outside the house. Figure 4-66 shows a preferred method of installation.

Although the equipment is simple, the way it works may not be obvious. Several processes are happening at the same time:

• Entering air evaporates some of the water in the pad.

• The evaporation cools the rest of the water in the pad.

• The entering air is cooled by contact with the pad.

• The moisture that evaporates from the wet pad goes into the entering air stream, increasing its humidity.

The air is coolest where it enters the house from the evaporator. The air picks up heat and becomes warmer as it travels through the house. The air exits from the house, usually through one or more open windows.

An ordinary evaporative cooler is a once-through system. The air cannot be recycled for further cooling because its moisture content is too high. The exhaust air carries away the water that is introduced by the cooler. Also, the exhaust wastes any cooling that remains in the air.

Unlike a heat pump or air conditioner, the evaporative cooler does not take heat energy out of the entering air. Instead, *it trades temperature for humidity*. This trade can make a person comfortable only if the temperature and the humidity of the entering air are both low enough. And that depends on the climate.

The biggest disadvantage of a conventional evaporative cooler is the excessive humidity that it may create inside the house. A combination of coolness and dampness is not comfortable, and it invites mildew.

Other Kinds of Evaporative Coolers

Among engineers who work with evaporative cooling, the simple kind of evaporative cooler that we just described is called a "direct" evaporative cooler. Other designs have been developed to minimize the humidity and efficiency limitations of direct coolers.

The improved designs use a "heat exchanger." The air inside the house is recirculated through the heat exchanger, and the heat exchanger is cooled by evaporating water. In this way, no humidity enters the house, and none of the cooling effect of the evaporation is wasted. These designs have names like "indirect," "2-stage," and "hybrid."

As this is being written, these improved evaporative coolers for houses are still a rarity, and they are expensive. If they become more available, they are worth considering.

Climates for Evaporative Cooling

Evaporative cooling is limited to climates that are dry. Only dry air can evaporate water strongly enough to create the desired cooling effect.

Evaporative coolers are commonly called "swamp coolers." However, they won't work at all in a swampy climate. Instead, they may turn the inside of your home into a swamp if you operate one in weather that is not dry. In that case, the cooler simply acts as a huge humidifier, which invites indoor condensation and mildew.

The hotter the climate, the drier the outside air must be in order for evaporative cooling to work. As a realistic example, let's assume that you want to achieve an indoor temperature of 78 °F (26 °C). At this temperature, the maximum relative humidity for good comfort is about 60%. The following table shows the outside air conditions that must exist in order for an evaporative cooler to create those desired indoor conditions:

If the outside air temperature is: °F (°C)	the outside relative humidity must be less than (%):
80 (27)	50
85 (29)	38
90 (32)	29
95 (35)	23
100 (38)	16
105 (41)	11
110 (43)	8

Figure 4-66. Evaporative cooler installed through the wall of a house. This location is superior to the more common roof installation because the entering air is cooler and access for maintenance is easier. Do not install through a window.

These numbers* show that the climate must be very dry in order for an evaporative cooler to provide good comfort in a hot climate. If the climate is not dry, an evaporative cooler cannot approach the standard of comfort that is provided by mechanical air conditioning because the air will be too humid.

On the other hand, evaporative cooling may still provide a welcome improvement over no cooling at all. For example, large portable spray coolers have become popular for cooling large tents used at public events, even in climates that are not ideal for evaporative cooling.

---

* Beware of performance numbers that are published by promoters of evaporative coolers. Such sources may assume that the air inside the house is allowed to rise to 100% relative humidity. That would be very uncomfortable, and it would grow mildew. You don't want high relative humidity inside your house under any circumstances.

DRW

Figure 4-69. This is what happens to an evaporative cooler that lacks regular maintenance. The float valve is stuck, and a lot of water is being wasted in this arid location.

How can you tell if the climate is favorable for an evaporative cooler? You can search the Internet and find maps that show where evaporative coolers can be effective. For example, much of the United States that lies west of the Rocky Mountains is eligible for evaporative cooling, whereas most of the eastern U.S. is not eligible.

A good reality check is to look around the vicinity of your home site and see whether the existing houses there have evaporative coolers. If so, ask the other homeowners how well their coolers perform.

Energy Efficiency

In the best applications, evaporative cooling can cool the inside of a space using much less energy than refrigeration air conditioning. Estimates published in engineering publications state that evaporative cooling uses about one fourth as much energy.

However, this assumes that the entering air is warmed almost to room temperature before it is exhausted to the outside, that the cooled air absorbs heat in the parts of the house that most need cooling, and that the equipment is efficiently controlled. Most installations do not satisfy these conditions.

Water Requirements

Evaporative coolers use lots of water. Engineering publications estimate that typical residential evaporative coolers use about 10 gallons per hour (about 40 liters per hour) while they are operating. This water consumption can be a disadvantage in regions that suffer from drought.

As the water evaporates, contaminants that enter with the water supply are concentrated inside the unit. These will foul the machine if they are not diluted continuously. To minimize the concentration of contaminants, all evaporative coolers drain a fraction of the water. The method that wastes the most water is a continuous slow drain. A periodic flush cycle is less wasteful.

High Maintenance Requirements

Although an evaporative cooler is simpler than an air conditioner, it requires continual monitoring and maintenance. The cooler evaporates a huge amount of water, which leaves behind any minerals that are dissolved in the water. If the water supply has a high mineral content, the entire wetted interior of the unit quickly becomes caked with scale.

Most of the evaporation occurs from the pads. The deposits that form on the pads reduce the efficiency of the cooler. Therefore, replacing the pads is required at intervals ranging from one month to several months.

The water level in the unit is maintained with a float valve, similar to the float valve in a toilet. In time, scale causes the float valve to stick, at which point it must be cleaned or replaced. Scale also interferes with the operation of the drain valve and the pump that circulates water over the pads. Therefore, each unit needs a thorough cleaning on an annual basis. Figure 4-69 shows what happens if there is a lapse in maintenance.

Select the Equipment to Survive

The water that circulates through an evaporative cooler is saturated with oxygen by the entering air. As a result, it will quickly rust any exposed parts of the unit that are made of ordinary steel. Cheap evaporative coolers quickly become shabby and wasteful. So, if you want to install an evaporative cooler, search for a unit that is built to resist corrosion.

Freeze Protection

An evaporative cooler is full of water that is exposed to the outside. Hard freezing can damage the components. Therefore, make it easy to drain the unit during cold weather.

Unfortunately, desert climates often fall to freezing temperature at night, even when the daytime weather is hot.

Where to Install the Cooler

As with conventional air conditioning, you can buy "whole house" units and "window" evaporative coolers. You will want "window" units because they localize cooling to the rooms where you need it, and this limits the spread of humidity to other spaces, such as closets. The equipment is located outside the house, except for a discharge grille and a set of controls inside the room.

The best place to install an evaporative cooler is through the wall of the room that it serves, as in Figure 4-66. The location of each unit should provide good air distribution inside the room, and it should allow easy outside access for the frequent maintenance that is needed.

Don't install "window" units through windows. That wastes the windows, and it looks crude.

Don't install an evaporative cooler on a roof, even though many coolers are installed that way. A roof heats the air that enters the cooler, defeating its purpose. A roof mounted unit is difficult to maintain, and if the flushing water drains on the roof, it looks ugly and creates slime.

Instead, try to install the unit in the coolest areas outside your house. The north side usually is best.

Wherever the unit is installed, try to shade the ground and walls near the unit, using shrubbery, a fence, or other means.

Air from the cooler enters the house through a big hole. Make sure that this hole is tightly closed during cold weather. A good solution is to install an insulated, well sealed cover over the opening at times when you don't need the cooler.

Each cooler needs electrical power and a water supply pipe. You can use the water that drains from the unit to irrigate a little garden or shrubbery that shades the unit. If it is not acceptable to drain the water to the ground, you will need a drain to a sewer.

Control to Avoid Mildew

It's especially important to turn off each evaporative cooler when you don't need it. This saves energy and water, and it reduces the risk of excessive indoor humidity.

 Control evaporative cooling in a manner that saves energy and water, and that prevents mildew.

Use automatic controls as much as possible. Install a programmable thermostat or a timer to limit operation of the unit to times when the space is occupied. See *Efficient Control of HVAC*, below.

In addition, it may be prudent to install a humidistat that turns off the unit if the relative humidity inside the space becomes too high. Install the humidistat in a cool part of the house, where mildew is most likely to grow.

Some evaporative coolers may include a set of programmable controls. Check for them.

VENTILATION FOR HEALTH, SAFETY, AND HUMIDITY CONTROL

"Ventilation" generally means moving outside air into the house, and exhausting air from the house to the outside. Previously, we learned how to use outside air for cooling the house, which requires a large volume of air. Now, to maintain air quality, we are going to use much smaller quantities of outside air. Air quality ventilation includes exhausting "stale" air from the house, removing excess humidity, and exhausting fuel fumes leaked from heating equipment.

A super-efficient house minimizes leakage of outside air into the house. This fact created concern that efficient houses lack sufficient ventilation for human health. Also, moisture may accumulate inside an airtight house, causing mildew and structural damage. However, your home is designed to avoid these problems. See the sidebar.

To maintain good air quality throughout the house, remove contaminated air before it can spread to the rest of the house. The main odor sources are the kitchen and the toilet rooms. The main moisture sources are showers, baths, the kitchen, and the laundry area.

Most of your ventilation for health, safety, and humidity control is done with localized exhaust fans. Using an exhaust fan provides reliable air flow that is tailored to the application, minimizing the amount of energy that is needed to heat or cool the replacement air.

There is an important principle of ventilation that is often overlooked. You can't remove air from a space with a fan unless you allow an equal quantity of air to replace it. *Every ventilation application in your home requires an opening where the contaminated air is removed and one or more openings where the replacement air enters. The effectiveness, comfort, and energy efficiency of the ventilation depend on the locations of these openings.*

The exhaust fan usually is where the air exits the house, or close to it. (For example, exhaust for the kitchen range is provided by fan located inside the range hood.) In most houses, windows are the only entry points for the replacement air. You laid out the windows for ventilation in Step 2. You can control the direction and volume of ventilation air flow by selecting which windows you open, and by how much.

The large spaces of the house, such as the living room and bedrooms, do not require separate ventilation equipment. Contemporary standards of hygiene control body odors. Carbon dioxide and moisture from breathing are odorless and they diffuse, to be removed eventually by opening windows and doors and by the operation of the exhaust fans.

DOES ENERGY CONSERVATION CAUSE HEALTH PROBLEMS?

It's a common misunderstanding that energy conservation is responsible for bad air quality and other unhealthy conditions in houses. In reality, such conditions are caused by defects in design, construction, and equipment installation. In the past, leaky houses would relieve the effects of bad construction practice. For your home, the way to avoid air quality problems is to eliminate their causes, not to waste a lot of energy to sweep out the symptoms. The real causes and solutions for indoor air quality problems are:

- *accumulation of dirt, allergens, and other organic material in the ducts of forced air heating systems and central air conditioning systems.* The solution is to avoid ducted heating and cooling systems.
- *mold and mildew inside the walls and ceiling.* The solution is proper installation of vapor barriers and proper venting of the structure.
- *mold and mildew inside the house.* The solution is to limit inside humidity by using the various methods that we explain under *Limiting Humidity*.
- *emission of formaldehyde and other organic vapors* into the house from composite wood products and other materials. The primary solution is to avoid building materials and furnishings that emit harmful vapors. Also, an effective vapor barrier blocks vapors emitted by building materials.
- *kitchen fumes*, including combustion products from gas fueled appliances, and the smoke and fumes of cooking. The solution is to install a kitchen exhaust hood along with an adequate source of replacement air (usually, a nearby window).
- *carbon monoxide from combustion*, including operation of heating furnaces, boilers, water heaters, cooking equipment, and fireplaces. The solution is to provide adequate combustion air and to make sure that the equipment is vented properly. Select boilers, furnaces, and water heaters that have sealed combustion systems.

One of the impractical ideas that appeared recently is using a "heat exchanger" for home ventilation. The bad news is that they don't work. The good news is that you don't need them. See the sidebar, *Air Heat Recovery for Home Ventilation.*

Some harmful vapors are emitted by building materials, especially when the house is new. If you included an interior vapor barrier in Step 3, these vapors are blocked from the living space by the vapor barrier. If your home will not have a vapor barrier (usually because it is located in a warm, humid climate), be careful to avoid building materials the emit harmful vapors. These materials include chipboard, certain treated lumber, and certain foam insulation that is poured or sprayed into place.

Indoor smoking is an air quality problem that has no satisfactory solution. If your home will have smokers, Step 1 recommends creating smoking rooms that are separate from the rest of the house. Smoking rooms require their own ventilation equipment.

Now, let's design the ventilation for each application in your home.

KITCHEN VENTILATION

We covered your kitchen's ventilation layout in Step 1, under the heading, *Kitchen*. Now, let's find the best ventilation equipment.

A Better Range Hood

A range hood captures and ejects cooking fumes and moisture before they can spread into the house. Get a range hood that has a fan capacity of 500 to 800 CFM (250 to 400 L/s). The exhaust rate from a typical residential kitchen hood is only about 200 to 300 CFM (100 to 150 L/s). This is inadequate for heavy frying or other smoky cooking, which will trigger your fire alarm and leave grease on your walls. Also, a weak fan can't clear smoke from a fire.

You will use the full exhaust capacity only occasionally, and you may want to operate the hood at low flow rate for extended periods. Therefore, get a hood with a fan that has a wide range of air flow rates, down to about 20% of the maximum flow.

Your hood should also have good interior lights, with a dimmer. And, it should have an effective grease filter that is easy to clean.

Some range hoods have a temperature sensor that automatically operates the fan at full capacity in the event of a stovetop fire. This feature reduces the spread of smoke to the rest of the house, and it provides more time to respond before the fire gets out of control.

You can find range hoods with these features at reasonable cost, but you may have to search for them. Use the Internet. Find the exact model number you want, and either order it yourself or ask your contractor to order that model number.

AIR HEAT RECOVERY FOR HOME VENTILATION?

An air heat recovery unit is a simple device in which two air streams pass each other, separated by material that conducts heat. It is also called a "heat exchanger." During cold weather, the heat recovery unit salvages the heat from the air that is exhausted from the house and uses it to warm the incoming outside air. Similarly, during warm weather, the heat exchanger salvages cooling energy from the exhaust air. Heat recovery units have been used in many commercial buildings that have large ventilation requirements.

Unfortunately, heat exchangers are not practical for homes. For efficiency, air should be exhausted from the locations where odors and moisture arise, as from toilet rooms, shower rooms, the laundry area, the kitchen, and the workshop. There is no efficient or economical way to collect all that exhaust air in one place and pass it through a heat recovery unit.

In principle, you could install a heat exchanger at each exhaust fan, along with an outside air duct to feed replacement air into the space. However, such small applications are uneconomical, and the installation would be bulky and awkward. The dirty exhaust from the kitchen or workshop would clog the heat exchanger.

So, residential heat exchangers join the list of concepts that can't work well in practice. Fortunately, the design of your super-home tailors the ventilation accurately, so that heating and cooling your ventilation air won't cost much.

Some range hoods do not vent to the outside. Instead, they circulate the cooking fumes through a filter and return the air to the kitchen. Their only advantage is that they do not need a vent to the outside. Don't buy this kind of range hood. It can't clean the air adequately, it can't vent moisture, and it requires frequent cleaning.

A Better Wall Cap

The exterior wall or roof cap for the kitchen hood exhaust is important. It should be shaped to provide free air flow, and it should have a damper that resists leakage and damage from wind. This damper provides most of the resistance to air leakage, even if the range hood has an internal damper. The damper that is supplied inside the hood usually is made very loose to keep it from sticking.

In my experience, it is virtually impossible to find a good residential wall cap. One option is to buy a commercial wall cap that is intended for a larger duct

DRW

Figure 4-71. A good kitchen exhaust wall cap made by the author because of frustration with the junk on the market. The damper is open partially because the fan is operating at low speed.

size, and to use an adapter for your hood's duct size. However, an oversized wall cap is likely to be an eyesore.

So, your contractor may have to get a sheetmetal shop to make a good wall cap for you. The housing should be made of aluminum or stainless steel to resist corrosion. The flapper should be made of aluminum, so that it is light enough to open easily. Figure 4-71 shows a cap that I made for my home. It provides free discharge for the exhaust, good shielding from wind and rain, and reasonably tight closing of the damper.

VENTILATION FOR SHOWER AND BATHTUB ROOMS

A whole industry is devoted to disinfectant cleaners for showers and bathtubs, which shows how easily mildew infests these moist environments. Mildew starts to grow in a humid environment within about 24 hours. A brief period of high humidity while you are taking a shower will not allow mildew to grow, but damage will occur if the humidity lingers.

Your primary defense is effective ventilation, although ventilation alone may not suffice. Almost all shower and bathtub rooms should have exhaust fans. The only exception would be in climates that are always warm and dry, and then only if the shower or bathtub room has a window that can be opened without surrendering privacy.

While the shower or bathtub is being used, ventilation will minimize the exposure of the room surfaces to high humidity. It will minimize fogging of mirrors at adjacent washbasins, and it will deter the spread of moisture to vulnerable adjacent rooms and closets.

However, the ability of ventilation to control humidity is limited. For example, no amount of ventilation can keep a shower space dry while the shower is being used. Ventilation cannot reduce exposure of bathers to chlorine, radon, and other dangerous gases that are dissolved in the water supply.

Shower water is substantially warmer than the room surfaces. As a result, moisture has a strong tendency to condense all over the room. Ventilation becomes more effective after the shower is turned off, or after the tub is drained. The ventilation fan should continue to run as the moisture slowly evaporates from the room surfaces, towels, and mats. Therefore, the fan should have its own interval timer switch, instead of being connected to the light switch.

Typical bathroom ceiling fans have air flow capacities that range from 50 to 120 CFM (25 to 60 L/s). This is feeble. Get a larger fan capacity.

Ceiling fans may be combined with a ceiling heater, a light fixture, or both. Except for a very compact bathroom, the ventilation capacity of these combination units is inadequate. It is better to install a separate exhaust fan.

It is most effective to locate the intake for the fan inside the shower enclosure or bathtub space. Especially if you are using a larger fan, it may be necessary to install the fan remotely – typically in the attic – and connect it to the shower with a duct. This will also reduce the noise level inside the space.

The fan should exhaust to the outside, not into the attic. Attach a duct to the fan outlet to discharge the moist air to the outside. Moisture in the attic would condense on cold surfaces, including the insulation.

The ventilation air should come from inside the house. In this way, the replacement air will be warmed during cold weather. During warm weather, the interior air will be dried by the action of the air conditioning, helping to prevent mildew.

Provide a path for easy flow of ventilation air into the shower or bathtub room. Install a grille near the bottom of the door to the shower space. This will sweep the air over the floor, hastening the evaporation of water on a wet floor. Keeping the door closed during a shower will keep the moist air from dispersing into the house.

TIP: FIGHTING MILDEW IN YOUR SHOWER

Here is a trick that minimizes mildew in shower rooms and their adjacent spaces. Turn on the ceiling heater of the space during a shower. This is remarkably effective in minimizing condensation. Turn off the heater when you turn off the shower. Use this technique summer and winter. If the weather is warm, turn on the ventilation fan when you turn off the heater.

The ceiling heater uses a certain amount of energy. But, that beats scrubbing the shower room with biocide every time you take a shower.

To hasten the drying of your shower and to keep it shiny, use a squeegee to wipe down the surfaces after each shower. Attractive shower squeegees are inexpensive. You can hang one on a suction cup that attaches to the shower surface.

The weather is a dominant factor in your ability to dry out a shower or bathtub room after it is used. During cold weather, the relative humidity inside the house will be low. When that happens, the shower room can be dried simply by opening the door to the rest of the house after bathing. Under those circumstances, the escaping moisture will briefly offset winter dryness in the rest of the house.

If the climate is warm and humid, an exhaust fan alone cannot dry a shower or bath room adequately. In that case, give serious consideration to permanently installing a dehumidifier to dry the space after it is used. We will say more about this option when we cover humidity control.

VENTILATION FOR TOILET ROOMS

Ventilation for toilet rooms is important for removing odors and for removing the limited amount of humidity that originates from the toilet and the wash basin. Because the water in toilets is cooler than room temperature, it does not contribute strongly to humidity in the room. Normal use of the wash basin is brief, so it does not require much ventilation.

If the toilet room is located by itself, an ordinary ceiling exhaust fan is satisfactory. Control the fan with a switch or interval timer that is separate from the light switch. The door to the room should have a louver to admit replacement air, or the bottom of the door can be cut to provide enough clearance for ventilation.

If the climate remains warm, an outside window may provide ventilation, instead of an exhaust fan. However, this works only if the window is located so that it provides privacy and security.

If the toilet room is adjacent to a shower or bathtub room, you can use the fan in the shower room to draw air through the toilet room. The door between the toilet room and the shower requires a louver to maintain privacy when both the shower and the toilet are in use.

VENTILATION FOR THE LAUNDRY AREA

The laundry area is a significant source of moisture, especially if damp clothes are hung there. The first step in minimizing moisture problems is to locate the laundry area where it is least likely to cause trouble. We did this in Step 1.

Ventilation is effective for removing moisture only if the climate is fairly dry. If the climate is humid, ventilation is not useful. In that case, limit humidity with a dehumidifier that is installed in the laundry area. See the heading, *Using Dehumidifiers to Control Humidity*, below.

The laundry area also emits odors from soap and bleach. None of these is dangerous, and the odors dissipate fairly quickly. However, if the odors are objectionable, install a relatively small, quiet ventilation fan to exhaust the laundry area. Arrange for the replacement air to flow into the laundry area from the surrounding spaces. Install an interval timer to control the fan.

VENTILATION FOR YOUR WORKSHOP

In Step 1, you laid out your workshop for convenience, working space, and isolation of the noise and nasty fumes that originate there. Sawdust, paint fumes, welding fumes, fiberglass resins, and solvents are health hazards. Some of them are very dangerous. Protect yourself with adequate ventilation.

You want a large volume of air to carry air pollutants from the work directly to an exhaust fan, without passing over you. The appropriate air flow path is determined by the location of the exhaust fan in relation to the work area, and by the location of the replacement air sources.

The fan should have enough capacity to clear out dangerous fumes before they can spread through the shop. Typical shop work needs an exhaust rate of about 3,000 CFM (1,500 L/s). For a given air flow rate, a fan of larger diameter is quieter and more energy efficient. If the fan needs to run only occasionally, as when operating a table saw, a fan diameter of about 24" (60 cm) is appropriate. If the fan needs to run for longer periods, as with painting, a larger diameter is advisable.

The workshop needs a large supply of replacement air when the fan is running. Your layout in Step 1 should provide an efficient air flow pattern. For a workshop located inside the house, the replacement air will come through open windows, either within the workshop itself or elsewhere in the house. As a rule of thumb, the window opening should be at least as large as the fan opening.

Get a fan that has multiple speeds, with a wide speed range. Some shop work needs a strong blast of ventilation, while other work needs only a slow breeze.

To control the fan, use an interval timer switch in parallel with an ordinary toggle switch, as in Figure 4-72. This arrangement makes it easy to turn on the fan for a short period, and also to keep the fan running continuously for drying paint, etc.

Close the fan opening tightly when the fan is unused for extended periods. An exhaust fan should have a gravity damper for short term operation, but gravity dampers are leaky. To prevent air leakage during cold weather and to keep vermin from entering through the damper, design a box structure around the fan with a lid that is hinged and gasketed. This requires only a simple bit of carpentry.

If the fan runs with the air flow blocked, the fan motor will burn out and perhaps start a fire. To avoid this, install a contact switch that connects power to the fan only if the lid is fully open.

If a basement workshop is too far below grade to allow the fan to discharge through the basement wall, install a duct to discharge upward through the wall of the ground floor. The damper and the airtight closure should be installed at the wall opening. You can locate the fan on either level.

Or, install a roof-mounted fan that exhausts the workshop through a duct.

It's not a good idea to build a below-grade pit, like a window well, for the fan. Any opening below grade traps debris and rain, and it is an easy entry for vermin.

Using Your Shop Fan for Nighttime Cooling

The capacity of a shop fan typically is about the same as is needed by a nighttime cooling fan, which we covered previously. For this reason, the workshop fan may work well for night cooling ventilation. If you decide to use the workshop fan for night cooling, select a model that has a wide range of speeds. Provide the same fan controls as for a cooling fan.

DRW

Figure 4-72. Good controls for a workshop fan, including a simple on-off switch, a timer, and a fan speed switch.

ELIMINATE THE DANGER OF CARBON MONOXIDE

Carbon monoxide in homes has become a major health and safety issue, causing illness and death, along with widespread promotion of carbon monoxide detectors. Yet, despite the concern, the issue is still poorly understood by many homebuilders, so take the lead in designing your home to be free of this hazard.

First of all, carbon monoxide is not a hazard in all-electric homes, or in homes that use properly installed "sealed" combustion systems for their fuel-fired equipment.

Carbon monoxide may become a danger in homes if any fuel burning heating equipment can discharge its exhaust into the interior of the house. Under the wrong conditions, conventional boilers, furnaces, water heaters, fuel-fired space heaters, gas stoves, gas fireplaces, wood stoves, hibachis, and fireplaces can all produce dangerous amounts of carbon monoxide.

The goal is keep the combustion gas, or "flue gas," entirely outside the living space of the home. Our discussion focuses on carbon monoxide because that is usually the most dangerous component of flue gas. However, the actions that we take to eliminate the danger of carbon monoxide will also eliminate the dangers and nuisances of the other components of flue gas, including smoke, fuel odors, etc.

How Carbon Monoxide Becomes Dangerous

Any equipment that burns fuel needs a supply of oxygen for combustion. If sufficient outside air is not provided, the oxygen inside the house will be depleted. In addition to depleting oxygen for the occupants, the lack of oxygen increases the production of carbon monoxide by the flame.

The danger of air starvation has existed as long as fuel has been burned inside houses. However, older homes generally were so leaky that air leakage could replenish the oxygen consumed by the heating equipment, and carbon monoxide could escape to the outside. The danger of carbon monoxide can be greatly increased by the airtight construction of modern homes, if the combustion air supply and the combustion gas exhausts (called "flues") are not designed properly.

Most older, conventional heating equipment uses a flue that is open at the bottom, as in Figure 4-73. This kind of flue depends on convection to lift the hot exhaust gases up the flue to the outside. However, if a vacuum forms inside the house, the furnace exhaust may enter the house, rather than the flue.

What can cause a vacuum inside the house? The main causes are wind and the operation of exhaust fans. If wind that can create a downdraft in the flue, the downdraft will blow the exhaust gases into the house. For this reason, you can observe that the tops of conventional flues are cut off perfectly horizontal, and that they are elevated above the roof and any other structures that could cause a downdraft into the flue.

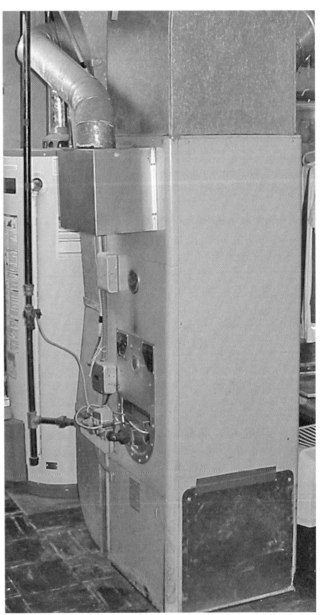

DRW

Figure 4-73. Carbon monoxide hazard. This typical furnace installation has a "draft hood" at the bottom of the flue pipe to collect the flue gas. It is open at the bottom. The open draft hood isolates the gas flow inside the furnace from pressure variations in the flue. Normally, the flue gas rises by convection into the flue pipe. However, a vacuum may be created inside the house by wind or by an exhaust fan. The vacuum can draw the exhaust gas from the furnace into the house, rather than into the flue.

Wind also creates a suction on the downwind side of a house. If there is an opening on that side, such as a fan opening with a leaky damper, the wind suction creates a vacuum inside the house. To avoid the latter problem, older houses commonly bring combustion air into the house through the attic. This works because an attic that has vents on opposite sides tends to neutralize wind pressure. The flue typically rises through the house in a "chase," which is the framed enclosure that surrounds the flue, as in Figure 3-196.

The chase extends down from the attic to the ceiling of the space where the heating equipment is located (typically the basement). Outside air from the attic can fall down to the heating equipment through the space between the chase and the flue.

Any exhaust fans, including bathroom exhaust fans, kitchen range hoods, and workshop fans, will create a vacuum in the house if proper outside air supplies are not installed for them. Exhaust fans can create a stronger indoor vacuum if they are large, or if the house structure is airtight.

Foolproof Defenses Against Carbon Monoxide

For your major heating equipment, the problems of air starvation and vacuum forming inside the house have the same solution. If you use natural gas or propane as your fuel, select high-efficiency condensing boilers and furnaces, which can completely isolate the combustion from the inside of the house. They bring combustion air directly into the heating equipment through a pipe from the outside. They also have a sealed exhaust pipe, rather than the open bottom flues of older equipment. Combustion air and exhaust gas are driven through a closed circuit by a fan that is located inside the boiler or furnace.

A sealed combustion system is immune to wind pressure. First of all, the flow inside the system is driven by a fan, which is more powerful than wind pressure. Secondly, both the combustion air intake pipe and the exhaust pipe typically pass through a nearby wall together. Both may use a common exterior wall fitting, as in Figure 4-26. With this arrangement, wind that blows on the side of the house causes the same pressure in both pipes, so that the balance of air and exhaust flow inside the system is not disturbed.

Oil-Fired Equipment is Trickier

If oil will be your fuel, preventing a carbon monoxide hazard requires more thought. Search for a reliable manufacturer who produces oil-fired equipment that has a sealed combustion system. If you can find such equipment, it will avoid the carbon monoxide hazard in the same way as gas-fired equipment that has a sealed combustion system.

The one major difference is that your oil-fired heater will need a vertical flue that rises above the roof. The flue passage through the structure will need to be sealed against air leakage, as we discussed in Step 3, under the heading, *Air Leakage Around Flues*.

If the best oil-fired equipment that is available does not offer a sealed combustion system, you will need a conventional flue.

If the house has an attic, you can draw combustion air from the attic through the flue chase, as described previously. In this case, it is important to design the attic vents so that they neutralize wind pressure.

This method allows leakage of cold outside air into the portions of the house that are below the bottom of the chase. E.g., if the chase opens to the basement, outside air will chill the basement during cold weather.

A solution to this problem is to enclose the heating equipment in a separate room that is isolated from the rest of the house and open to the outside air. For this solution to be effective, the openings in the walls of the room for pipes, ducts, and wiring must be well sealed. This is tedious, but practical.

This room is effectively outside the house. Therefore, its walls and ceiling should be insulated as for an exterior wall.

Gas Stoves and Other Equipment with Open Flames

In order to avoid a carbon monoxide hazard, all fuel fired equipment must have an adequate amount of outside air. In a house that uses a gas stove, locate an openable window near the stove, as we discussed under the heading, *Kitchen*, in Step 1. Open the window to provide combustion air while the stove is being used. Opening the window also prevents the range hood fan from creating a vacuum inside the house, which would suck exhaust into the house from other combustion equipment.

The short path between the window and the stove minimizes cooling of the space by the combustion air during cold weather. Avoiding discomfort from the cold outside air requires artful adjustment of the window opening.

With other fuel-fired equipment, such as a gas-fired space heater or a gas-fired fireplace, the vicinity of the heating equipment must be amply supplied with outside air. This requires an opening whose size is determined by the combustion air requirement of the equipment.

Select the location of the air supply so that it does not transmit wind pressure (or vacuum) into the house. This may require a duct that runs between the location of the heating equipment and a carefully situated opening in the shell of the house.

LIMITING HUMIDITY

Preventing excessive humidity is an important part of the design of any house. You need to limit humidity to prevent mildew, to stay comfortable, and to protect the structure and contents of your house from condensation damage.

Moisture in the air promotes mildew and causes physical damage only if it condenses to form liquid water, or if it is close to doing so. This will occur in any part of your house where the temperature of the surrounding air approaches the "dew point" temperature. (See the sidebar, *Why Water Vapor Condenses*, in Step 3.) Condensation will cause harm even where you don't see visible moisture forming.

Mildew is the cause of most physical damage and most of the health problems that are associated with high humidity. Mildew will grow on almost any material if moisture is available, including a microscopic layer of condensation. See the sidebar, *Defeat Mildew*.

There are two general ways to keep moisture from condensing inside your home: (1) remove moisture from the air, and (2) keep the temperature in the space above the condensation (dew point) temperature. We will use these methods in a variety of ways.

Usually we are concerned with the "relative humidity," not with the absolute amount of water vapor in the air. That's because trouble occurs when

DEFEAT MILDEW

As we design your home, we stress features that prevent mildew growth. Mildew damage is likely to occur in any climate under certain circumstances. At worst, the damage can be devastating. Mildew attacks the contents of a house, it can attack the house structure, and it can cause health problems. Many species of mildew stimulate allergies, and some are toxic. Even if the mildew is killed, its residue may be dangerous. Mildew is what causes the "musty" odor that is associated with dampness and health problems.

"Mildew" is also called "mold." It is a microscopic fungus that can grow to form large, visible colonies. The individual organism is a tiny tendril with a bud, as shown here:

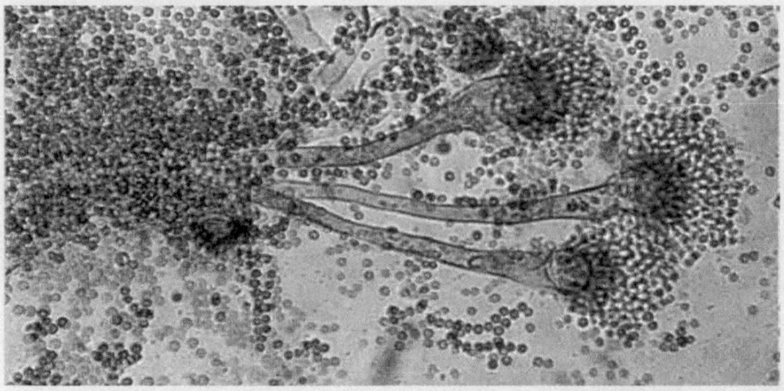

Philip R. Morey, PhD

Figure 4-74. Common *Aspergillus* mold, magnified about 1,000 times. Three parent bodies are shedding countless spores.

Mildew grows by digesting almost any organic material, including wood, paint, fabrics, carpet, and the dirt that lies on any surface. It reproduces by emitting vast numbers of microscopic spores, which are small enough to be spread by air currents. As a result, mildew spores are just about everywhere, outdoors and indoors. It's not practical to keep the spores out of the home environment. Instead, the challenge is to keep the spores from growing.

Mildew requires no light to grow. There are many species, which can grow in a wide range of temperatures. However, mildew can't grow unless it has moisture. *The main defense against mildew is preventing water leaks and condensation of moisture anywhere in the house.* That doesn't mean that you can't get your shower room steamy while you bathe, but damp spaces need to dry quickly. Mildew starts to grow in damp conditions within 24 to 48 hours.

If mildew is growing in the open, you can kill it with various commercial cleaners. Ordinary chlorine bleach is effective. The ultraviolet component of direct sunlight kills mildew. However, window glass blocks most ultraviolet light. Ventilation can inhibit mildew by wafting away local regions of high humidity within the house, but only if the ventilation air itself is relatively dry.

You can clean mildew from smooth non-porous surfaces, such as tile, metal, or plastic, by using detergent. Mildew stains in porous surfaces, such as wood and wallboard, are practically impossible to remove, even if the mildew is killed. It is generally impractical to stop mildew that is growing in thick fibrous materials, such as fabrics, carpeting, mattresses, and insulation. Such materials must be replaced if they are infested with mildew.

the relative humidity is too high. Both of the previous methods limit relative humidity, even though the second does not actually remove moisture from the air.

Protecting closets and basements from mildew damage are important special cases, so we will deal with them separately.

The relative humidity inside your home is also a major factor in comfort. Comfort requires even lower relative humidity than preventing mildew growth.*

Climate and Humidity

Humidity problems are severe in some climates, and almost absent in others. So, tailor your humidity control to the weather.

If the climate is usually dry, as in Arizona, humidity problems generally do not occur unless you have a major source of moisture inside your home.

If the climate is usually cool or cold, as in Alaska, humidity inside the house tends to remain low. This is true even if the climate is wet. The reason is that the low outside temperature condenses water vapor out of the air in the form of rain, snow, fog, or dew. Outside air is warmed when it enters the house, which lowers its relative humidity.

During cold weather, if a house has any gaps in the insulation that allow parts of the interior structure to become cold, moisture may condense on those parts of the structure. The problem is most serious in shower and bath rooms.

When the climate is warm or hot, the coolness of the shaded interior invites mildew, unless the climate is also dry.

In a hot climate, as in south Florida, using air conditioning lowers humidity effectively. However, air conditioning provides no protection when it is turned off.

If the climate is humid and warm, but not hot, air conditioning alone cannot lower humidity comfortably or efficiently. For example, houses are afflicted by mildew everywhere along the Gulf of Mexico, which bathes the adjacent land in humid air. If you have a home in such a climate, you will have to design both the structure and the HVAC to avoid moisture damage.

---

* To determine the conditions that make people comfortable indoors, HVAC engineers refer to a comfort chart that plots only two factors, temperature and relative humidity. The upper limit of relative humidity is about 60%, while the lower limit is less well defined, typically around 30%. In warm weather, the temperature limits are approximately 73 °F (23 °C) to 80 °F (27 °C). In cold weather, the temperature limits are about 68 °F (20 °C) to 75 °F (24 °C). Other factors, such as air speed and nearby surface temperatures, also affect comfort. However, those factors generally do not become important inside a well designed house.

Indoor Humidity Sources

Some of the worst mildew problems that I have observed were caused by indoor sources of moisture, usually created by the occupants. The solution is to eliminate indoor sources of humidity, or to control them effectively. We have already taken many steps in that direction. Here are the prime sources, and the main defenses against the excessive humidity they cause:

• *showers* produce prodigious amounts of water vapor because of their spraying action and the warm water temperature. You must act to dry out a shower after each use. In Step 1, you designed your shower spaces to facilitate drying and to avoid spreading moisture into the house. Under the previous heading, *Ventilation for Shower and Bathtub Rooms*, we designed ventilation to keep shower moisture out of the house.

DRW

Figure 4-75. Drying clothes on racks in the shower room caused mildew infestation throughout this apartment. The occupant does not have a vented clothes dryer and did not use an outdoor clothesline. Cleanser and bleach were used to suppress mildew on the shower room surfaces, but the unvented moisture allowed mildew to grow on wood and porous surfaces throughout the rest of the dwelling.

- *hot tubs and spas*. Keep them outdoors, as we recommended in Step 1. If you must have an indoor spa, drain it between uses and dry out the space, as for a shower.

- *air drying laundry indoors*, as in Figure 4-75. It is always risky to dry laundry by hanging it indoors, even in a dry climate. In Step 1, we designed your laundry and clothes drying spaces to keep their moisture out of the most vulnerable parts of the house.

- *using an unvented clothes dryer*. Any clothes dryer must be vented to the outside through a duct. Other alternatives, such as venting into a bucket of water, don't work.

- *evaporative coolers* can cause serious humidity problems, even though they are used in dry climates. We covered the actions needed to avoid trouble under the previous heading, *Control of Evaporative Cooling*.

- *boiling lots of water in your kitchen*. Install a range hood with ample fan capacity and use it. See the previous heading, *Kitchen Ventilation*. Keep lids on your pots and pans, as we will recommend under the heading, *Use Your Range Efficiently*, in Step 7.

- *growing plants*. If you want to grow lots of plants indoors, install a separate greenhouse and grow them there. Don't install a greenhouse against a house wall, because it will rot the wall.

- *interior plumbing leakage*. Leakage from plumbing fixtures, such as faucets or a defective shower base, can create invisible damage and raise humidity enough to promote local growth of mildew. General solutions are to design your plumbing fixtures so that leaks are visible, and to make all parts of your plumbing system accessible for inspection and repair. See *Your Water Pipes*, in Step 5.

- *water leakage into the space from the outside*. A common example is a roof leak that finds its way into a wall. Another example is a slab foundation that is not elevated above grade, allowing rain and snowmelt to penetrate between the slab and the bottom of the exterior walls. The general solution is to design every part of the structure to resist water entry.

- *humidifiers*. Unfortunately, there is no kind of humidifier that works without creating a humidity problem in the house. However, you can minimize the problems they cause, as we will explain under the following heading, *Raising Humidity*.

Toilets generally are not a major source of humidity. The water in them usually is cooler than room temperature, so it does not evaporate strongly into the surrounding space. Wash basins and sinks usually are not a problem if they are used for short periods and drained.

USING DEHUMIDIFIERS TO LOWER HUMIDITY

A dehumidifier removes moisture from the air without cooling the air. It can be located almost anywhere, requiring no connection to the outside.

A dehumidifier has the same parts as an air conditioner, but the parts are arranged differently. Air from the room passes over the cold coil, where moisture in the air condenses out. The air is then routed over the warm coil before discharging into the room. The air returns to the room at a temperature that is somewhat higher than its original temperature.

A typical residential dehumidifier is about the size of a small window air conditioner, and it makes about the same amount of noise. Dehumidifiers are inexpensive, so you can afford to install several around the house, if needed.

A dehumidifier uses less energy than an air conditioner of the same size, typically about 500 to 800 watts. Your dehumidifier should be controlled by a self-contained humidity sensor. If you build your home to keep moisture out, the average energy consumption of a dehumidifier during humid weather may be as low as 100 or 200 watts.

Residential dehumidifiers typically weigh about 40 pounds (18 kilograms). They usually have caster wheels for floor mounting, but they can be installed on a shelf, in an alcove, or anywhere else that allows free air circulation.

Where to Use Dehumidifiers

Using a dehumidifier is the most effective method of avoiding dampness and mildew in any geographic location that tends to linger at high relative humidity, such as the Gulf coast of the United States. Air conditioning can control humidity in a climate that is hot and humid, but a dehumidifier is needed for extended periods when the air conditioning is turned off.

Even in locations that do not suffer from chronic high humidity, a dehumidifier is valuable inside certain rooms that tend to be damp or cool, such as basements and shower rooms.

In drier climates, rooms that are damp for short periods, such as showers and laundry rooms, dry out quickly if they are opened to the rest of the house. But, drying must occur reliably, before mildew can take hold. If you are not sure that a space will always dry quickly, consider a dehumidifier for it.

Select a Good Model

Start your shopping on the Energy Star Web site, which we explain in Step 7. All listed Energy Star models use 10% to 20% less energy than average because they have more efficient compressors, coils, and fans.

The energy efficiency of dehumidifiers is measured by a rating called the "energy factor," which is defined as liters of water removed per kilowatt-hour (kWh) of energy consumed. (The term "energy factor" is used for other appliance ratings in different ways.)

Most dehumidifiers control their operation by sensing the relative humidity of the surrounding space. Select a model that allows you to set the desired humidity level with reasonable accuracy.

■ Minimum Operating Temperature

The biggest limitation of residential dehumidifiers has been coil freezing. This occurs when a space is cool, such as a basement in springtime, when you need dehumidification the most. In cheap units, the coil freezes when the room temperature is below about 65 °F (18 °C).

Fortunately, many newer residential dehumidifiers have automatic defrosting controls that allow operation when the room temperature is as low as 42 °F (5 °C). Be sure to select a unit that has this feature.

■ Capacity and Noise

In most cases, the size of the dehumidifier is not critical. If you have built the structure of your house to block the entry of humidity, your humidifier won't need a lot of capacity. All other things being equal, the size of the dehumidifier has minimal effect on efficiency. A larger dehumidifier will spend less time running and making noise, so it will last longer.

A good unit probably has a fan with several speeds. Lower speed provides quieter operation, while higher speed produces greater capacity.

■ Other Features

Your dehumidifier should have a relative humidity indicator. You need this to set the machine for efficient operation. Typically, you want to set the relative humidity at 55% or lower. The actual humidity level in the space increases with distance from the dehumidifier.

Your dehumidifier should also have an air filter, preferably one that is washable. If the unit does not have a filter, lint and dirt will cake on the wet dehumidifier coil, lowering efficiency and acting as a breeding site for various microorganisms that you don't want to inhale.

Some units include a time control that allows you to schedule the operation of the unit. This may be

useful if you want to limit operation to times when the noise of the unit will not be objectionable. You can achieve the same result by plugging your dehumidifier into an inexpensive timer that plugs into a wall receptacle.

A less common feature is a pause button that lets you to stop the dehumidifier for a period of time, usually to suspend the noise from the unit.

Effective Installation

Location is important. Dehumidifiers work best when they are close to the source of moisture, such as a laundry area or inside a shower room. The moist air must be able to circulate easily toward the dehumidifier. Try to locate the unit near the center of the area that you are trying to protect. Air does not circulate easily through doorways and corridors, so install the dehumidifier within the humid space.

Most dehumidifiers are designed to be set on the floor. If the floor is a slab in contact with the soil (as in a basement or on the ground floor of a house with a slab foundation) or if the floor is above an unheated space, the floor will be a cool surface that condenses moisture. For this reason, humidity and mildew tend to be worst at floor level. For this reason, placing a dehumidifier on the floor generally makes it most effective.

A dehumidifier turns water vapor into liquid water. The condensed water must be drained from the unit. Most portable dehumidifiers have a tank to collect the condensate. However, the tank may fill in less than one day during humid weather, and the unit switches

DRW

Figure 4-76. A basement dehumidifier placed where it can drain directly into the laundry sink through the green hose, bypassing the dehumidifier's internal collection tank. The white deflector above the dehumidifier distributes the air discharge into the space. In a new house, the dehumidifier could be built into the space more neatly.

Royal Sovereign

Figure 4-77. A portable dehumidifier that has a pump to drain the condensate through a small hose. This model is especially small because it does not have the usual bulky drain bucket. In this case, the condensate is being drained through a window, which is not elegant.

off automatically when the tank is full. So, you really don't want to rely on the tank.

Instead, consider installing the dehumidifier on an elevated shelf or hanger so that it can drain by gravity through its drain hose connection. You can drain the condensate to any convenient drain, such as a laundry sink, as in Figure 4-76.

A more elegant solution is to install a wall drain of the kind that is used for clothes washers. In an unfinished location, you could drain to a floor drain or sump. Or, you can make a small hole through an outside wall and drain the condensate to the outside. (This is how most air conditioners and heat pumps drain their condensate.)

 Install dehumidifiers as permanent appliances, for convenience and good appearance.

Mounting the dehumidifier at an elevated location makes it less effective for sweeping humid air from a cold floor. Therefore, be sure that the dehumidifier is installed so that it can circulate air throughout the space.

Another option is to buy a dehumidifier that includes a condensate pump, which discharges through a small hose, as in Figure 4-77. Plan how you will route the condensate hose so that it does not become a hazard or an eyesore.

Locate dehumidifiers where their noise will be least annoying. Where appropriate, install a timer to operate the dehumidifier when nobody is in the area, or buy a unit that includes a timer.

Dehumidifiers are Heaters

When a typical residential dehumidifier is operating, it blows heat into the room at the rate of about 3,000 to 5,000 BTU's per hour (about one kilowatt). This is about the same output as a small portable electric heater. About half of this heat comes from the water vapor when it condenses. The rest comes from the operation of the motor and fans in the unit.

In a well designed house, the dehumidifier operates only a small fraction of the time, so the average heat output is much lower.

By warming the air, the dehumidifier reduces its relative humidity, further helping to keep the space dry. However, this benefit is small in comparison with the removal of moisture by the dehumidifier.

Using Dehumidifiers with Air Conditioners and Ceiling Fans

In a climate that is humid, you can save energy and be more comfortable by using a dehumidifier in combination with air conditioning. Lowering the humidity allows your body to be comfortable at higher temperatures.

 Control your air conditioner, dehumidifier, and cooling fan together for optimum comfort and energy efficiency.

This is easy to control. Simply set the humidity sensor in the dehumidifier to maintain a comfortable relative humidity, typically about 60%. At the same time, set the air conditioner for a temperature that is comfortable.

When you do this, the dehumidifier will not operate as long as the air conditioner is lowering the humidity adequately. The dehumidifier takes over at lower temperatures, when the air conditioner does not operate enough to control the humidity.

Lowering the humidity greatly increases the effectiveness of ceiling fans. So, if you install ceiling fans, using a dehumidifier will reduce the need for air conditioning even more.

USING HEAT TO CONTROL HUMIDITY

Heating – by itself – is an effective way to lower relative humidity. If you raise the temperature in a space, the relative humidity falls. In fact, normal home heating during cold weather is notorious for creating excessive dryness inside homes.

For example, imagine that the temperature outside is 40 °F (4 °C) and it is raining steadily, so the outside air is saturated with moisture. If that damp outside air is brought inside the house and heated to 72 °F (22 °C), the relative humidity of the air is reduced to about 33%. Air in this condition is "dry," so the inside of the house will not suffer from dampness.

Even a small increase in temperature has a large effect on relative humidity. For example, if you raise the temperature inside a closet by 10 °F (5.5 °C), you lower the relative humidity by about 28%, which is an ample margin to prevent mildew.

For this reason, raising the temperature may be a useful method of limiting humidity in closets, occupied basements, and some other spaces.

USING AIR CONDITIONING TO CONTROL HUMIDITY

An air conditioner removes moisture from the indoor air. This is because the cooling coil is much colder than room temperature. When air is circulated through the cooling coils, moisture condenses on the coils and drains either to the outside or to a sewer connection. An air conditioner will drip a lot of water on a humid day.

It the outside temperature is much warmer than the indoor temperature, running the air conditioner usually keeps the inside of the house dry.

However, if the weather is humid, operating an air conditioner may actually worsen humidity problems in certain parts of the house. If the interior of the house or its structure is cooler than the outside air, any humid outside air that leaks into the house will condense around the points of entry and on any cold surfaces that it finds. In fact, the introduction of air conditioning is largely responsible for the proliferation of mildew damage in humid climates.

Also, operating the air conditioner for the sake of dehumidification during mild or cool weather may make the space cold and clammy. The industry has a name for this. It is called "cheap motel syndrome," and it doesn't happen just in cheap motels.

These problems of air conditioning are poorly understood by contractors, and even by engineers.

This is one reason why moisture problems are so common in mild, humid climates. Unfortunately, this limitation has become even worse in high-efficiency air conditioners. In order to gain higher SEER ratings, newer air conditioners have been designed with features that reduce their ability to remove moisture.

So, if you live in a humid climate, don't expect your air conditioners to keep the inside of your home dry enough. You will need one or more dehumidifiers for that purpose.

USING VENTILATION TO CONTROL HUMIDITY

We have already explained how to use ventilation to lower humidity in damp spaces, under the previous headings *Kitchen Ventilation*, *Ventilation for Shower and Bathtub Rooms*, *Ventilation for Toilet Rooms*, and *Ventilation for the Laundry Area*.

In summary, ventilation helps to dry out a space that is temporarily wet. But, ventilation with outside air generally is not effective for maintaining low humidity. If the outside air is dry, there will not be a humidity problem inside the house, unless an unusual amount of moisture is being generated, as in a shower.

If the outside air is warm and humid, ventilation will increase the indoor humidity. Under those weather conditions, the only way to lower the indoor humidity is to use dehumidifiers, or air conditioning (if the weather is hot), or both.

KEEPING CLOSETS DRY

In a climate that has a humid season, closets are prone to mildew if they are located in cool parts of the house. The linen closet is vulnerable because it tends to be in the path of moisture escaping from shower and bathtub rooms. The first line of defense is to locate your clothes closets and linen closet away from rooms that emit moisture, as explained in Step 1.

 An economical way to avoid mildew in closets is to install a small, safe closet heater that is controlled by a humidistat.

If the climate creates a mildew hazard throughout the house, the best protection for the closets is to install a dehumidifier in the vicinity of the closets.

An economical way to protect individual closets from mildew is to install a small heater in the closet. Raising the closet temperature by a only a few degrees is usually adequate.

You can buy special low-wattage heaters that have a very low surface temperature, so they do not create a fire hazard. One manufacturer offers models that are rated at 70 and 130 watts. They require an electrical receptacle inside the closet, so plan for this when you lay out your electrical wiring.

Another option is to install a very small electric baseboard heater inside the closet. A unit that is one foot (30 cm) wide is more than adequate for a typical closet. Install the heater along an open part of the closet floor, where air flow through the unit will not be obstructed by clothing or clutter. If the closet has an outside wall, try to install the heater on the outside wall.

 Don't use light bulbs as closet heaters! **Light bulbs are hot and fragile, so they are a fire hazard. And, they need frequent replacement.**

Now, here's the important trick: control the closet heater with a ***humidistat***, not a thermostat. Locate the humidistat on the coldest wall of the closet, but not directly above the heater. Set the humidistat to maintain about 60% relative humidity. You can buy humidistats that control the electrical power to the heater directly, avoiding the need for separate control wiring.

By controlling the closet heater with a humidistat, you will prevent the heater from operating when it is not needed. In this way, your closet heater will have a very low annual operating cost.

A heated closet should have a conventional hinged door, without louvers, to retain the heat and to limit migration of moisture into the closet. Leave a normal gap at the bottom of the door. Sliding and folding closet doors are too leaky for optimum protection against moisture.

KEEPING YOUR BASEMENT DRY

Dampness in basements is so common that we tend to think that basements must be damp. That's not true. Basements become damp for a variety of reasons, each of which has its own solution.

One cause is water penetration from wet soil outside the basement walls. Avoiding this requires good moisture protection for underground walls. We covered that in Step 3.

Dampness also occurs in basements because the floor and the underground walls are cooled by contact with the earth. When humid air enters the basement from upstairs or through leaks in the structure, it condenses on those cool surfaces.

To minimize cooling of the floor, Step 3 recommends appropriate slab insulation. To minimize cooling of the basement walls, Step 3 installs as much of the basement insulation as possible on the ***outside*** surfaces of the basement walls. It also helps to keep the basement door closed, to reduce the flow of moisture into the basement.

Another common cause of basement dampness is doing laundry there. Moisture from the washer and the laundry sink may increase basement humidity enough to cause trouble. In addition, you won't resist the temptation of hanging damp clothes in the laundry area. The ultimate solution is not to do your laundry in the basement. As you lay out your home in Step 1, create a location for the laundry room upstairs, where it will be more convenient.

If you take those steps, your basement will not be troubled by humidity as long as the outside temperature is at least a few degrees lower than the temperature inside the basement. This condition exists during the cold season.

However, the coolness of the basement still invites dampness when the weather is warm and humid. This situation is worst in spring, while the basement walls, floor, and surrounding soil remain cold, so the floor and walls can condense moisture from the increasingly humid air.

To deal with those conditions, install a dehumidifier. Most basements should have at least one. Keeping moisture out of the basement with a dehumidifier and good doors is usually the least expensive way to keep a basement dry.

When you buy the dehumidifier, select a unit that can operate at the lower temperatures of basements, as we discussed previously.

Coordinate the Dehumidifier with Heating

If the basement is occupied regularly, keeping it heated to a comfortable temperature is an effective way to minimize humidity. Use the most economical method of heating that is available, as for the rest of the house. For example, if you have hydronic heating upstairs, install it in the basement also. Insulate the basement well, and install a good door to keep the heat from escaping up the stairs.

If the humidity is still too high at the desired temperature, the basement dehumidifier should take over. Coordinating the dehumidifier with the heating requires no special effort. Set the heating thermostat to the desired temperature, and set the dehumidifier to about 60% relative humidity. Turn off the heat when the space is unoccupied, but keep the dehumidifier operating.

RAISING HUMIDITY

During cold weather, the air inside a house may become so dry that it causes discomfort or health problems. The usual relief is to operate a humidifier. Occupants who want to use a humidifier should use portable units that they can keep nearby, as in Figure 4-78. That's the only practical way to achieve high humidity where it counts, at the occupant's nostrils.

Attempting to humidify an entire room during cold weather may harm the house, and it is futile. The reason is that the coolest interior surfaces will condense moisture as fast as the humidifier adds it. Attempting to increase the humidity further will cause mildew inside the house, and perhaps, condensation damage in the structure.

The vapor barriers recommended in Step 3 are the first line of defense against this. However, high humidity inside the house will still cause condensation on portions of the structure that are not perfectly protected by the vapor barriers. These include window frames, doors and door seals, and wiring penetrations.

In your super-insulated house, the windows will be a limiting factor in the humidity that you can maintain. That is because of the relatively poor insulation value of windows, which makes them the coldest surfaces in the room. If you attempt to humidify the entire room, the windows will sweat, growing mildew on the frame and sill.

For example, on a day when the outside temperature is 20 °F (-7 °C), the temperature of the inside surface of a typical double-pane window may be 55 °F (13 °C). To avoid condensation on the windows, the relative humidity adjacent to the window would have to be lower than about 57%. You can increase the relative humidity somewhat by installing windows with greater insulation value, but your options are limited, as we saw in Step 3.

DRW

Figure 4-78. A portable humidifier located next to the user, where it is most effective.

Under these conditions, using a small portable humidifier might be able to raise the relative humidity at the occupant's nostrils to about 60%. For most people, this would be a comfortable level of humidity.

Don't install a humidifier in a central air heating or cooling system. It would cause moisture problems throughout the house, and it still won't be able to provide a high level of humidity. But, it will create enough humidity inside the ducts to grow mildew, which will then spread to the living areas. Humidifiers in central air systems regularly rust out the furnace heat exchanger and the ducts. Eventually, they form scale that clogs the humidifier, causing it to fail. (Aside from that, you should avoid central air systems. See the previous sidebar, *Why You Don't Want Central Forced-Air Heating and Cooling*.)

EFFICIENT CONTROL OF HVAC

You have designed the layout of your home's spaces and its HVAC systems to localize heating and cooling to the rooms where they are needed. Now, the final step is to turn off the heating and cooling in each room whenever it is not needed. Wherever practical, make this automatic. It is easy to leave heating, cooling, or ventilation operating unnecessarily.

For most rooms, the most effective automatic control is a programmable thermostat. Other kinds of controls are appropriate for rooms and applications that are occupied on an irregular basis. Here are the details.

Programmable Thermostats: for Rooms with Predictable Usage

A "programmable thermostat" is a thermostat combined with a timeclock. It switches from one temperature setting to another at different times. Residential models are fairly small and unobtrusive, so they won't clash with your decor. Figure 4-80 shows a typical programmable thermostat that offers a basic set of functions.

Programmable thermostats are appropriate for rooms and spaces that are occupied on a regular basis. Typical applications are bedrooms, the living room, the dining room, and the kitchen. For comfort, the programmable thermostat can be scheduled to warm or cool the room before you arrive. For energy conservation, it can be scheduled to turn off the heating or cooling shortly before you leave.

Use the *Programmable Thermostat Guide* when shopping for your programmable controls. The typical programmable thermostats for sale at hardware stores are designed for cheapness, so they may lack valuable features. To get a unit with all the features you want, you may have to do some shopping through commercial HVAC equipment catalogs. Capable units are available at modest cost.

Built-In Equipment Controls

Today, it seems that almost all kinds of HVAC equipment have some kind of electronic controls. Therefore, check out the control capabilities of the equipment before you buy. You can find the details in the user manuals that you can view on the manufacturers' Web sites.

As a rule, the flexibility of built-in controls tends to be limited, and they may be awkward to program. Use the *Programmable Thermostat Guide* as a checklist to see whether the built-in controls have all the features that you want.

If the built-in controls are inadequate, you can use a separate programmable control to turn the power to the equipment on and off.

Interval Timers: for Applications with Unpredictable Usage

An interval timer is a switch that turns on equipment for a specified time interval. The interval can be fixed or variable, depending on the type of timer. An interval timer can be a valuable method of controlling HVAC equipment that is needed on an irregular basis. For example, interval timers are commonly used to control ceiling heaters and exhaust fans in bathrooms.

Also, use interval timers to control heating, cooling, and ventilation in other irregularly used spaces, such as your workshop, sewing room, office, and recreation room.

DRW

Figure 4-80. A programmable thermostat that has a minimum set of functions. The cover is raised to show the setting instructions, which should be imprinted on the unit, as here.

PROGRAMMABLE THERMOSTAT SELECTION GUIDE

☐ Ease of Use

The best features are worthless if you don't use them. Avoid models that are difficult to program. Find a model that has large numbers in the displays, large buttons for programming, and clear instructions. You won't remember the instructions, so they should be permanently installed in the thermostat case where you can easily read them.

☐ Scheduling Flexibility

Your unit should allow you to schedule an adequate number of temperature changes during the day. For example, for heating a bedroom, a programmable thermostat should allow you to schedule at least four temperature changes daily: (1) warm up before you arise, (2) lower the temperature after you finish dressing, (3) warm up before bedtime, and (4) lower the temperature overnight.

Also, a programmable thermostat should allow you to set separate schedules for weekends and holidays. Try to find a unit that allows you to choose between different schedules easily. For example, you may want to shift to a holiday schedule during the week, without having to re-program the thermostat.

☐ Schedule Overrides

There will be times when you want to change the room temperature or to override the present schedule without having to re-program the unit. Look for the following schedule options:

(1) The thermostat's on/off switch allows you to stop all heating and cooling. This does not interfere with the preset schedules, but the HVAC must be turned on again manually. In an extreme climate, the room temperature may drift so far that it takes a long time to restore comfort. Or, water appliances may freeze.

(2) A "single-cycle override" feature allows you to simply press a button to start or stop the HVAC. The thermostat restarts the equipment at the next scheduled temperature change.

(3) A "hold" feature allows you to maintain any temperature indefinitely by pressing a button while setting the desired temperature. Pressing the button again cancels the "hold" function, returning the thermostat to its normal schedule.

☐ Stepped Temperature Settings

Some programmable thermostats reduce heating and/or cooling in steps after bedtime, such as two degrees per hour for several hours. This avoids discomfort from overheating or overcooling while you sleep.

☐ Minimum Temperature Setting

If an unoccupied room requires a minimum temperature – usually to prevent freezing of water fixtures – then the thermostat should be able to maintain the minimum temperature that is acceptable.

Unfortunately, many programmable thermostats have minimum heating temperature settings of 50 to 55 °F (10 to 13 °C). This setting is unnecessarily high for freeze protection, so it may waste heating energy during cold weather. Unless the climate is usually mild, seek a programmable thermostat that allows the temperature to be set as low as 40 °F (4 °C).

☐ Daylight Saving Time and Leap Year Reset

Check that a programmable thermostat resets the time when daylight saving time begins and ends. Also, the unit should add another day to February in leap years. But, note that daylight saving time differs between countries. Get a unit that is appropriate for your location.

☐ Optimum Start

This is an advanced feature that automatically adjusts the time that heating starts for morning warm-up based on past experience. It requires an outdoor temperature sensor. Optimum start is "nice to have," but it complicates installation and it won't save much energy in a super-efficient home.

☐ Battery Power

Most programmable thermostats are powered by their own batteries. This keeps the clock on time and preserves the schedules when external power is interrupted. Select a unit that uses inexpensive conventional batteries.

Avoid models that are powered from the control circuits of furnaces, boilers, and air conditioners, unless they also have a backup battery.

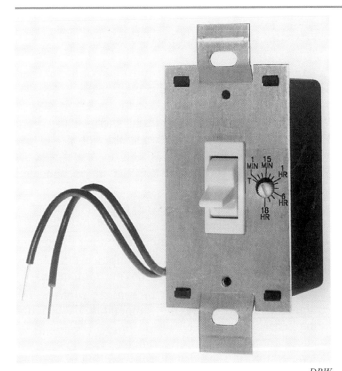

DRW

Figure 4-81. Toggle timer switch. Pressing the switch up starts the equipment for a fixed time interval. Pressing the switch down turns off the equipment. The time interval of this model can be adjusted over a wide range by removing the cover plate and setting the interval with a screwdriver.

One type of interval timer, shown previously in Figure 4-72, uses a round dial for setting the time delay. This kind is best when the application requires different time delays. If you buy a dial timer, get one that is electronic. The older mechanical type clicks annoyingly as it winds down.

Another kind of interval timer, shown in Figure 4-81, looks similar to an ordinary toggle switch. With this kind, pressing the toggle turns on the equipment for a fixed interval. If you have applications for this kind of timer, look for two important features:

- The toggle should move in two directions. Pressing the toggle in one direction turns on the equipment for a fixed interval, and pressing the toggle in the other direction turns off the equipment.

- Adjustable time delay. Get a model that has the adjustment easily accessible behind the faceplate, without the need to remove the timer from the electrical box.

Low-Limit Thermostats for Freeze Protection

If a room is vacated, the only reason to heat it is for freeze protection. Freeze protection is needed only if the space contains water pipes or water fixtures. Depending on the way that pipes and fixtures are installed, the freeze protection temperature can be as low as 40 to 45 °F (4 to 7 °C). Freeze protection

at a higher temperature is a waste of energy. Most thermostats do not have a minimum temperature setting this low, but try to find thermostats that can be set as low as 50 °F (10 °C).

If you do use heating for freeze protection in a space, install the thermostat on the coldest surface of the space. Usually, this is on an outside wall, above grade level. The thermostat should not be located within the discharge of any heating unit.

Heating a room for freeze protection is fundamentally unreliable because the protection fails if the heating fails for any reason. The only reliable freeze protection is draining the water systems, as explained in Step 5.

Hydronic heating systems can be protected by using antifreeze in the system water.

Clock Switches

Simple clock switches can be useful for controlling equipment based on the time of day. For example, if you use a dehumidifier to keep your basement dry, you don't want to hear it running at night. By controlling the power with a clock timer, you can limit operation to hours when the noise is not annoying. Figure 4-82 shows an inexpensive clock timer that plugs directly into a wall receptacle, requiring no installation effort.

If you have equipment that you want to start or stop at sunrise or sunset, you can do this with an "astronomical" time switch. This kind of timer is used primarily for control of lighting, so we cover it in Step 6.

Figure 4-82. Plug-in clock timer.

Motion Sensors

Lighting control is the primary application for motion sensors, so we discuss them in Step 6. They can also be used effectively to control cooling fans and air conditioners in response to the presence of people in the room. They are not useful for controlling primary heating, because warming up a room takes too long after the occupant enters.

Locate all controls for the convenience of the user. If a control is easy to reach, it is more likely to be used efficiently.

In addition, be careful to install thermostats where they always sense the room temperature properly. Do not install a thermostat:

- on an outside wall or on a wall with an unheated space on the other side
- in any location that is exposed to direct sunlight at any time
- in the discharge path of heating or cooling equipment
- near any heat producing equipment, such as entertainment equipment or cooking appliances.

This can fool you. With remote controls for equipment, know where the temperature is actually being sensed. It may be inside the control itself or inside the equipment. For example, see Figure 4-83. If temperature is sensed inside the heating or cooling unit, the remote control can be placed anywhere that is convenient.

DRW

Figure 4-83. Know where the actual thermostat is located. The remote control on the left is for the heat pump on the far wall. It signals the desired temperature to the heat pump. The actual thermostat is located inside the heat pump, which senses the air temperature on the wall above the fireplace. In contrast, the heating thermostat located next to the remote control, which operates a central heating system, senses the temperature where it is installed.

STEP 5

YOUR PLUMBING FIXTURES AND WATER SYSTEMS

Water is both a necessity and a luxury. If necessary, you can survive in a healthy way with only minimal water for drinking, cooking, bathing, and sanitation. On the other hand, if you water your lawn extravagantly or if you like to take long showers or if you have a swimming pool, you will use a vastly greater amount of water.

No matter how you plan to use water, we will make your water system as efficient as possible. In the U.S., water heating accounts for 24% of the natural gas used in homes, and 11% of the electricity. This makes water heating the third largest user of energy in U.S. homes. In your super-efficient home, where heating and cooling costs have been cut drastically, water heating may be your largest or second largest energy cost.

In this Step, we will start by selecting plumbing fixtures that use as little cold and hot water as possible. Then, we will maximize the efficiency of your hot water heating system. We will install filtering and other treatment that may be needed to get pure water from a contaminated local water supply. We will lay out your water pipes to avoid annoying problems, and we will minimize the risk of flooding by a failure in your water system. Throughout, we will exploit opportunities to enhance convenience, comfort, safety, and elegance.

Most of the features in this Step apply equally to a new house or to an existing house. Most of the equipment and system improvements can be installed in an existing house fairly easily. Exploit every repair as an opportunity to upgrade your water system.

EFFICIENT AND LUXURIOUS PLUMBING FIXTURES

Water systems involve two big costs, the cost of the water itself and cost of energy for heating it. In turn, the biggest factor in water heating cost is the amount of water that you use. (See the sidebar.) This makes it doubly important to design a water system that uses as little water as possible for whatever you want to do, whether it is filling a pot of water for cooking or taking a long, luxuriant shower.

Minimizing your water consumption is a matter of selecting the most efficient water using fixtures and appliances. So, we will begin by selecting your plumbing fixtures. (We will select your water using appliances in Step 7.)

SHOWER FIXTURES

In Step 1, we designed the layout of your showers. Now, let's install the faucets and shower heads.

Shower Faucets: Simplest is Best

The most efficient faucets for showers are the ordinary kind, one for hot water, one for cold water, and a diverter valve in the middle to select whether to send the water to the shower head or to a spigot near the floor. Figure 5-1 is an example. Get the kind of faucets that screw clockwise to close, and use round knobs. They are the most obvious to use. They are reliable and easy to repair. And, they are inexpensive.

Alternatively, install a single-lever faucet that controls both the temperature and water volume. Figure 5-2 is an example. The position of the lever provides a visual indication of the water temperature, but only after the hot water has flowed long enough to warm the pipes to the shower head. This kind of faucet is convenient, but it is more expensive to repair than individual faucets.

More complex faucets provide no advantages, and most of them have serious disadvantages. All non-standard types of faucets force the bather to fiddle with the faucet to adjust the temperature or the flow rate. As the bather fiddles, water is being wasted. Also, odd faucets cause the bather to select a higher flow rate than he would use with a familiar faucet.

Avoid full-flow shower faucets, which must be the stupidest idea in the history of plumbing. They have a single knob that turns on the water to full flow before allowing the bather to select the water temperature. They waste an enormous amount of water. Even with

U.S. RESIDENTIAL WATER CONSUMPTION

The U.S. Geological Survey estimated the following average household water use per individual in the United States, in gallons per day (liters per day):

toilets:	27	(100)	cold water only
laundry:	17	(60)	mixed hot & cold
showers:	14	(50)	mixed hot & cold
baths:	8	(30)	mixed hot & cold
faucets:	10	(38)	mixed hot & cold
dishwashing:	2	(8)	hot water only

These quantities vary widely among individuals, depending on gender, age, employment, social factors, and geographic location.

Homes also use a lot of water outdoors, mostly for lawns, shrubbery, and gardens. Outdoor water usage is seasonal. Variation among households is even greater than for indoor usage. Drier regions use the most outdoor water. For example, outdoor use accounts for 44% of average household water use in California, but only 7% in Pennsylvania.

DRW

Figure 5-1. This classic arrangement of shower faucets, hot and cold with the diverter valve between them, usually is best. However, there are benefits in not locating the faucets under the shower head.

DRW

Figure 5-2. If you want a single-lever shower faucet, this is the right kind. Turning it right or left adjusts the temperature. Pulling the lever in or out adjusts the flow rate. A lever gives you better control than pulling a round knob in or out. You need a separate diverter valve to send the water to a low spigot, if you have one.

a recirculating hot water system (explained later), this kind of faucet first dumps cold water on the bather, and then adds the risk of scalding while the bather struggles to set the temperature.

Don't use thermostatic shower faucets, no matter how appealing they may seem. The first slug of water coming from the hot water supply will be cold. If a thermostatic faucet is adjusted to a high temperature by a previous user, the cold water will be followed by scalding water. And, the thermostatic element will eventually fail, leaving you without a usable shower until it is repaired. Anyway, you don't need thermostatic control of your shower water because we will design your water pipes to avoid annoying fluctuations in temperature.

Shower Heads: a Compromise

Selecting your shower heads involves compromises between pleasure, convenience, water conservation, and health. Fortunately, shower heads are inexpensive and easy to replace. If you don't like one, unscrew it and try another. If you make the shower space large enough to install two shower heads, you can install two different kinds.

Expect to negotiate with your spouse about the esthetics of the water spray. Some people prefer a needle-like spray, while others want the sensation of standing under a waterfall. Unless water conservation is your overriding concern, get shower heads that allow the bather to select different spray patterns. Most adjustable shower heads adjust the spray pattern by changing the orifices or by varying the sizes of the orifices. Water consumption will vary with the setting. Figure 5-3 shows a typical adjustable unit.

Some shower heads include a pulsing spray as one of the settings. This is an esthetic feature that does not save water.

For those of European taste, shower heads are available in "telephone" style, which are installed on flexible hoses. Some people love them, others find them annoying. They are useful for parents bathing small children.

You will save water and energy if the shower head is easy to adjust. The easiest adjustment is a large butterfly knob on the side of the shower head. An adjustment ring around the perimeter of the head may be difficult to turn with wet hands. Avoid cheap units that have a knob in the center of the nozzle plate, forcing the user to reach through the spray to adjust it.

DRW

Figure 5-3. An adjustable shower head that is advertised as "water saving." Many shower heads make this claim. Select a unit that makes it easy to adjust the spray pattern with wet fingers. Make sure that the connecting pipe, or "gooseneck," is long enough to keep the shower head from dripping on the faucets below.

"High-efficiency" shower heads typically use one to two gallons per minute (4 to 8 liters per minute) in typical use, and about two to three gallons per minute (8 to 12 liters per minute) at full flow. In contrast, inefficient shower heads may pass 4 to 8 gallons per minute (16 to 32 liters per minute).

In the U.S., since 1992, shower heads have been legally limited to a maximum flow of 2.5 gallons per minute (10 liters per minute). Many other countries have similar requirements. Even so, selecting a shower head carefully may cut your shower water consumption in half.

High-efficiency shower heads limit water flow by using smaller orifices, by narrowing the spray pattern, and/or by mixing air with the water to increase the sensation of flow. They can be inexpensive because they are simple.

Shower heads with small orifices trap particles that are carried in the water. The particles eventually accumulate enough to choke the water flow. To fix this, unscrew the shower head and dump out the grit. It's easy to do.

Some shower heads include an on-off valve. This is a bad idea. In principle, once you have adjusted the faucets for the temperature you want, the water is simply turned off at the shower head. But, this keeps the faucets, the diverter valve, and the shower head itself under pressure. They will eventually leak, wasting water and perhaps doing invisible damage to the structure.

■ Don't Let Shower Heads Drip on Faucets

There is potential for trouble if a shower head is located directly above a faucet or diverter valve. All shower heads drip when they are in use, and they will drip continuously if a valve starts to leak. If water can drip on the faucets, it will work its way along the valve stem and water pipes into the wall, eventually causing damage to the wall and to the floor structure. The damage can become extensive before it becomes visible. Also, water that drips on faucets will leave an unattractive scum.

These problems occur if the bent piece of pipe that holds the shower head – called a "gooseneck" – is too short. (Figure 5-3 shows a typical gooseneck.) Therefore, make sure that your plumber installs goosenecks in your showers that are long enough so that drips from the shower head fall clear of the faucets.

Another solution is to locate the shower head so that it is not above any other plumbing fixture. There is no compelling reason why the shower head should be located directly above the faucets.

Health Concerns

If you like to take long, hot showers, here's another thing to worry about. The water in the shower contains various contaminants. If your water comes from a public system, it probably will contain chlorine, fluorine, and perhaps other water treatment chemicals. If the water comes from a well, it may contain radon. Increasingly, water supplies contain dangerous industrial pollutants, from trace amounts to high levels. And, some water supplies contain dangerous bacteria, viruses, and protozoa.

While you are in the shower, you will inhale any of those contaminants that are contained in the shower water. Unfortunately, water conserving shower heads may increase all these risks. High-efficiency shower heads commonly achieve a sensation of water flow by breaking the water stream into tiny water droplets. This action is effective in releasing dissolved gases. Also, smaller droplets (called "aerosols") can be inhaled deep into the lungs, which are particularly vulnerable to dangerous substances.

The general solution is to know your water supply and to filter your home water appropriately. We cover water filtering later in this Step.

Good ventilation of your shower room is important to prevent moisture damage. However, it won't eliminate the hazards of pollutants while you are showering.

BATHTUBS

Bathtubs are obsolete for hygiene. A tub uses a lot of water, it takes a long time to fill, and you float in your own dirt when bathing. And, as we explained in Step 1, tubs are dangerous when used as stand-up showers.

Kohler

Figure 5-4. An old style freestanding bathtub is especially easy to enter by grasping the sides of the tub. No bathtub should be used as a standing shower.

Kohler

Figure 5-5. A spa tub has a lot of plumbing for bubbles and jets. Install the tub so that the parts requiring maintenance will be easily accessible.

Bathtubs are now a luxury accessory, for taking an occasional long soak. Tubs have evolved various features, such as water jets and air bubblers, which turn them into a "spa" or "whirlpool bath." In reality, many people who install such tubs rarely use them.

If you just want to soak quietly, consider a freestanding tub of the old style that allows you to grasp both sides of the tub as you enter and emerge. This kind of tub is especially handy for bathing children. For a shower effect while sitting in the tub, you can install a "telephone" style of shower that has a flexible hose. It is mounted on a bracket attached to the tub. See Figure 5-4.

This kind of tub does not have to be built into the floor or wall, and all the parts are accessible for maintenance. Its weight is concentrated on a small area of the floor, so the floor should be especially stiff to resist cracking of the tile where the legs sit on the floor.

If you want a spa-style tub, research the catalogs and visit the showrooms. Some models allow a couple to bathe together. But, try out any model before you buy it. The appearance of the tub tells you nothing about the nature of the experience. You might not want a water jet blasting the delicate parts of your anatomy.

Spa tubs are built into the wall and floor. They need accessory pumps and electrical controls. Make sure that all the plumbing connections and electrical equipment will be accessible for maintenance once the tub is installed. See Figure 5-5.

Select any tub to be comfortable for sitting and reclining. And, select it to be safe while entering and leaving. If the tub has a wide rim, the bather can sit on the rim and swivel to get in and out.

A "walk-in" bathtub is a relatively new kind of tub that has a door in the side to allow the bather to enter and leave easily. Figure 5-6 shows an example. It has relatively tall sides, typically with a seat that provides a more upright bathing posture. Many models offer the massaging action of water jets and bubblers. In this respect, they are similar to spa tubs, and they should be installed similarly to provide access for maintenance.

The tub can be filled only after the bather has entered and the door is latched. Similarly, the bather can exit only after the tub has been drained. A "speed drain" is an option that pumps the water out of the tub more quickly. Even with this accessory, it will take a couple of minutes for a full tub to drain.

American Standard

Figure 5-6. A walk-in bathtub. The tub cannot be filled until the door is closed with the bather inside.

WASH BASINS AND SINKS

For wash basins and laundry sinks, install separate hot and cold water faucets. Install lever faucets that open fully with a quarter turn, as in Figure 5-7. These are more convenient than the older knob types that require more turning.

Most kitchens in the United States now use a single-lever mixing faucet for the sink, as in Figure 5-8. This is because the lever is a quick way of adjusting the water temperature for a variety of food preparation and rinsing activities.

Unfortunately, single-lever faucets waste hot water. They mix hot water with cold water unless the lever is in the extreme hot or cold position. Most people keep the lever somewhere near the middle position. In that

DRW

Figure 5-7. Dual lever wash basin faucets. These are the most convenient and efficient kind.

DRW

Figure 5-8. A single-lever faucet for a kitchen sink. This kind tends to waste hot water.

position, the faucet draws both hot and cold water into the line until it reaches the faucet. If you want cold water, you waste hot water. And, *vice versa*.

Therefore, it is better to use individual hot and cold water faucets. However, this choice may be overruled by the household cook. If so, try to minimize the hot water delay, using the methods that we will learn shortly.

For all sinks, select a spigot that has the water outlet as high as possible, so you can fill large pots and buckets. Also, select a spigot that is long enough to discharge near the center of the sink, so the user is not forced to lean over the sink.

For kitchen sinks and wash basins, the spigot should have a faucet aerator. This little device, which screws on to the end of the spigot, improves cleansing and conserves water. Figure 5-9 shows a typical aerator. The aerator has a matrix of passages that break up the water flow and introduce air, creating a froth. The aerator usually has a screen on the upstream side to block debris that would clog the aerator. The aerator needs to be unscrewed occasionally to dump the debris.

DRW

Figure 5-9. Typical faucet aerator.

Use good sink stoppers in all your basins so you don't have to keep the water running. Most kitchen sink drains are equipped with effective filtering stoppers. Wash basins typically use a stopper that is actuated by a rod in the faucet assembly. It must be kept clean to work properly. Pull it out occasionally and remove the hair and sludge that accumulates between the barrel of the stopper and the drain pipe. For laundry basins, use a good removable rubber stopper.

Select Basin Heights for Comfort

Injuries of the lower spinal column, or "back trouble," have become an epidemic in modern societies. Stooping over a basin is particularly aggravating to these injuries. To avoid this, increase the height of your basins so that an adult can stand upright while using them.

A good basin height for typical adults is about 36 to 38 inches (91 to 97 centimeters), which is substantially taller than the standard basin height. Cabinet manufacturers are now aware of the need for taller kitchen and washroom basins. If you can't find a standard model with adequate height, you should be able to get the height you want by special order.

 Avoid back trouble for adults by selecting wash basins that are taller than standard.

If you can't find a tall basin that pleases you, install a pedestal base under any basin or cabinet that you like. A good carpenter can make an attractive base from wood. Or, a kitchen counter fabricator can make a base from a waterproof counter material.

Children can use an adult basin by using a step stool that is designed for safety. Or, design one of your toilet rooms for use by children, with a low basin and a low toilet. Design the fixtures so that you can replace them easily with taller models when the children grow up.

TOILETS

Let's start with a toilet recommendation that works well for most homes. Install at least one pressure-flushing model for those special occasions when a conventional toilet would be overwhelmed. For the other toilet rooms, conventional siphon toilets offer a good combination of flushing performance, reliability, ease of maintenance, low noise, and low cost.

The flushing performance of conventional siphon toilets has suffered because of laws that were intended to limit water consumption. This created a surge of interest in two new types of toilets, pressure-flushing and vacuum-flushing. Meanwhile, the performance of "water saving" siphon toilets eventually improved, although they never equaled the performance of the older models.

At the same time, environmental considerations and the "green" lifestyle movement are resurrecting interest in more advanced and more primitive types of toilets. The following are your present choices.

DRW

Figure 5-10. A conventional siphon toilet. The S-trap that makes the toilet work is clearly visible.

Conventional Siphon Toilets

The siphon toilet has been the dominant type for indoor use in Europe and America since the end of the 19th century. This toilet design was a big advance because it isolates waste and odors from the inside environment of the house, and it is largely self-cleaning. Isolation from the sewer is provided by an ingeniously simple siphon (called an "S-trap") that connects the bottom of the toilet bowl to the sewer connection. In modern toilets, the siphon is molded into the porcelain body of the toilet, as shown in Figure 5-10.

The contents of the toilet are flushed into the sewer by releasing a volume of water into the bowl quickly, usually from a tank that is attached to the toilet. The increased height of water in the bowl starts a flow through the siphon. Water discharging from the outlet of the siphon into the sewer line creates a suction at the bottom of the bowl. This suction carries the waste up and over the elevated part of the trap and down into the sewer. The clean water that remains in the bottom of the bowl at the end of the flushing cycle acts as a seal between the bowl and the sewer.

(You may have noticed that the toilets in public restrooms do not have tanks. They supply water to the bowl using large water supply pipes under high pressure. This design is not suitable for most homes.)

Maintenance of siphon toilets is inexpensive and fairly easy. Repair parts have become standardized, so you can get them at any hardware store – that is, as long as you buy toilets with standard parts. Don't buy boutique toilets that have non-standard parts.

The flushing effectiveness of a toilet and the amount of water it uses are determined largely by the design of the S-trap and by the pattern of rushing water that enters the bowl. The amount of water can be reduced by making the S-trap smaller, but this will limit the size and shape of solids that can be flushed.

Long experience shows that effective flushing of conventional siphon toilets requires a certain minimum amout of water, which older toilets provided. However, in an effort to reduce water consumption, the U.S. government passed a law in 1994 that limits the water consumption of toilets to 1.6 gallons (6.4 liters) per flush. This resulted in poor flushing action. In fact, water usage may have increased because the new toilets require repeated flushes to clear heavy loads.

Newer models of water-saving siphon toilets have achieved better flushing performance, but some models are still significantly better than others. See *Consumer Reports* or other objective reviewers for their latest toilet tests.

At the present time, siphon toilets made in the U.S. are the most pleasing to use, as well as being inexpensive. They excel in self-cleaning when flushed. The Japanese, characteristically, have copied American toilets and added a variety of fancy features, such as heated seats and water jets. Toilets in Europe generally are less pleasant, seeming to be designed more for examining the contents than for flushing them.

Some siphon toilets have a "dual flushing" capability. The user can select a weaker, water saving flush for Number One, or a stronger flush for Number Two. There are different dual flushing designs, some of which are reported to be less reliable than the standard type. Figure 5-11 shows one design.

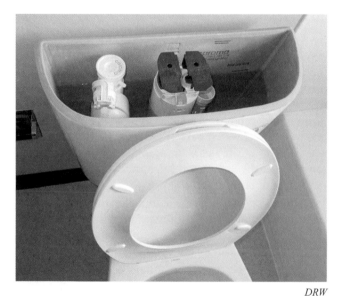

DRW

Figure 5-11. The inside of a dual flushing toilet. The user selects the flush mode by pressing one of two buttons on the top of the tank. This arrangement is awkward for a seated user.

Pressure-Flushing Toilets

Pressure-flushing toilets have several advantages, and one disadvantage. They flush significantly better than conventional toilets. Their recycling time is shorter than for conventional toilets. Flushing immediately lowers the water level in the bowl, whereas flushing a conventional toilet initially raises the level in the bowl. Therefore, a pressure-flushing toilet is less likely to wet the underside of the user with the contents of the bowl.

On the negative side, flushing is loud and abrupt. So, it is best to install your pressure-flushing toilets in toilet rooms that are located where the noise will not annoy sleepers.

The flushing water is pressurized by letting the pressure of the water supply system force the water into the bottom of a closed tank that contains air. Filling the tank compresses the air, creating pressure. Flushing the toilet releases the water from the tank.

Part of the pressurized water is aimed into the S-trap as a jet, providing a positive push that complements the suction action of the siphon. At the same time, pressurized water enters from the rim of the bowl rapidly, producing a strong swirl for cleaning the bowl surfaces and assisting the siphon action. Figures 5-12 and 5-13 compare a conventional siphon toilet to a pressure-flushing toilet.

Most pressure-flushing toilets are interchangeable with conventional siphon toilets in both appearance and plumbing connections. Thus, you are not committed to select one type or the other when you install the water and sewer pipes. You can easily upgrade from a conventional siphon toilet to a pressure-flushing model.

Pressure-flushing toilets cost about three times more than mass market siphon toilets, which still makes them one of the least expensive home appliances.

At present, the Flushmate® apparatus is used inside the pressure-flushing toilets of most manufacturers. The apparatus is enclosed inside a conventional looking ceramic tank. The Flushmate® now has a fairly long record of good performance. As a result, repair parts are fairly easy to obtain, but maybe not at your local hardware store.

Pressure-flushing toilets may malfunction if the system water pressure is too low. This may happen, for example, if there is a broken water main or if the water utility is repairing a nearby portion of the system.

Diagnosing a problem may be more difficult than with a conventional siphon toilet. Repair and adjustment is a bit finicky, but not difficult. It can be done by a homeowner who is handy enough to repair a conventional siphon toilet.

Vacuum-Assisted Toilets

Another new type that improves flushing is the vacuum-assisted toilet. It works by applying a modest vacuum to the discharge side of the siphon, pulling the contents through more strongly than the siphoning action of the S-trap alone. This requires a vacuum chamber that is installed in the drain pipe.

Vacuum-assisted toilets have one advantage, which is that they are quieter than pressure-flushing toilets. On the negative side, they have been experiencing growing pains, including poor flushing performance and difficult maintenance. If you are interested in them, check the Internet for comments about their current state of development and performance.

The cost of the toilet itself is about the same as for a pressure-flushing toilet.

At present, vacuum-assisted toilets are not directly interchangeable with conventional siphon toilets. This is a significant disadvantage. Installation may require a non-standard drain connection, so you are stuck if the toilet does not perform as well as hoped.

I doubt that vacuum-assisted toilets have much of a future in homes, unless they can be redesigned to overcome their disadvantages with respect to pressure-flushing toilets.

Toilets You Don't Want

There are various other types of toilets, but none worth considering for your home. Reliable operation and easy maintenance are the main virtues that you want, so avoid any oddball designs.

Speaking of oddball toilets, unless you are deeply committed to water conservation, avoid the various types of toilets that use no water or that use a method of flushing other than a siphon. Their esthetics range from crude to disgusting.

The least offensive are macerating toilets, like the ones used in boats and recreational vehicles. The worst are composting toilets, which are essentially outhouse toilets moved indoors. They have a seat located over an open septic tank that displays its contents quite visibly. These toilets reverse two centuries of progress in sanitary plumbing.

Toilet Convenience

The flushing handle of a toilet should be located where it is convenient for use while sitting on the toilet. The best location is at the side of the tank. Avoid toilets that have the flush handle or button located on top of the tank or on the wall behind the toilet.

American Standard

Figure 5-12. Conventional siphon toilet. The water in the bowl remains level with the top of the siphon elbow until flushing. Flushing drains the water from the tank by gravity. The water enters the bowl through the rim. The rising water level starts a siphon action, which draws the waste into the sewer.

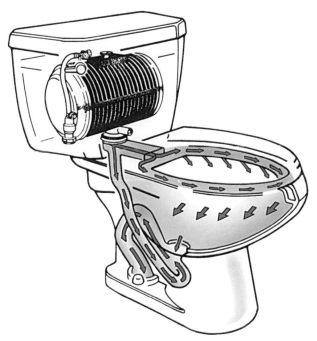

American Standard

Figure 5-13. Pressure-flushing toilet. The water for flushing is stored in a tank that is pressurized by the water system. During flushing, part of the water enters the bowl through the rim, but the rest flows through a jet that is directed into the siphon. The jet forces the waste through the siphon. The siphon action completes the discharge of waste into the sewer.

Select the height of toilets for the comfort of adults, especially for handicapped adults. You will probably be one someday. Standard toilets tend to be too low for handicapped adults, so consider a model that is somewhat taller than average.

Fortunately, a variety of seat heights are now available. Toilet bowl heights are stated from the floor to the top of the bowl rim, not including the removable seat. A good rim height for typical adults is 16 to 17 inches (40 to 43 centimeters). Some "handicap" toilets are as tall as 19 inches (48 centimeters), but these may be uncomfortable for general use. If someone in the household has an injury that makes the height critical, check the heights of various toilets to find the best height for that person.

As a temporary alternative, height extenders for toilets are available.

Children can use an adult toilet by using a step stool. Or, install a low toilet in one of your toilet rooms for use by children. Once the children have grown, it is relatively easy and inexpensive to replace the low toilet with a taller model.

BIDETS

Bidets are cultural plumbing, common in a few countries but unknown in most others. A bidet may evoke delight, puzzlement, or even indignation from your guests.

Modern bidets look somewhat like toilets. See Figure 5-14. If you live in a country where bidets are unfamiliar, distinguish yours clearly. Otherwise, a visitor may make an embarrassing mistake.

Kohler

Figure 5-14. Bidet and toilet. Be sure to use the right one.

Water usage is not a big issue with bidets, but the right location is. In cultures that take their bidets seriously, the classic location is in the bedroom, especially if the bedroom is large. Locate it where it will be easily accessible under the circumstances when it is needed, but not where it will get in the way otherwise.

Using a bidet results in some water being spilled on the adjacent floor, and the spills are not likely to be cleaned up immediately. So, create a little zone around the bidet that is resistant to water damage and that is attractive. For example, you might place the bidet behind a small screen of frosted glass that has a nice waterproof floor surface.

If you can't place a bidet in the bedroom, place it in the adjacent toilet room.

Bidets differ widely in convenience and water spillage, which depend mainly on the way that the water is projected. Since you are unlikely to find a good comparative review of bidets, you have to judge from the design of the unit.

You can buy toilets that have an added bidet function. However, this interferes with the primary function of the toilet, and *vice versa*. Such units are not a good idea. If you are going to have a bidet at all, do it right.

URINALS

Urinals are universal in men's public restrooms, and they are worth considering for a home. Urinals save water by reducing toilet flushing. It makes no sense to use six quarts (or liters) of water to flush a cup of urine. A urinal is convenient for the males in the family, and it may save a lot of water if the household includes older males who urinate frequently.

To save water, you have to select the right kind of urinal. Conventional flushing urinals don't save much water, so they have no value for homes. They use a siphon trap, like toilets, to keep sewer gases from entering the space through the urinal. The siphon requires about one gallon (4 liters) of water per flush. This is about two thirds as much water as the present U.S. standard for toilets.

There are various kinds of urinals that use little water or no water. One kind of "waterless" urinal is shown in Figure 5-15. It uses a trap that is filled with oil on the inlet side of an S-trap. The oil floats above the urine in the trap, preventing the odorous elements of the urine from evaporating into the room. Oil trap urinals require periodic replenishment of the oil and replacement of the filter cartridge. The cartridge eventually becomes clogged, usually by hair.

DRW

Figure 5-15. A waterless urinal that uses an oil trap cartridge, visible at the bottom of the enclosure. No water supply or flush valve is needed.

Waterless urinals are essentially free of odor when they are dry and clean, provided that the oil trap is properly maintained. Odor occurs primarily while the volatile components of urine are evaporating into the space from the surfaces of the bowl. This type of urinal is most appropriate for spaces where esthetics matter less, as in a workshop or outbuilding.

If your water supply has a high mineral content, scale will form slowly in drain pipes. The uric acid in undiluted urine will combine with this scale to form an especially hard compound. Therefore, be sure to install the drain pipe from a waterless urinal so that it is easily accessible for replacement at long intervals.

Another type of urinal uses a non-siphoning S-trap to isolate the urinal from the sewage system. It may use a small quantity of water to flush the surfaces of the bowl. A manual valve is located between the urinal and the trap to block the odor of urine that accumulates in the trap. A similar arrangement is used on some toilets for boats and recreational vehicles.

To select a urinal, make an Internet search for "water saving urinals" and see what is currently available from major manufacturers. As with all appliances, buy a model that has standardized components, so that you can get replacement parts far into the future.

If a urinal is to be used exclusively by adults, install it as high as practical. This will reduce splashing outside the bowl, some of which is inevitable.

Urine is somewhat corrosive, and it stains porous surfaces. Therefore, surround a urinal with surfaces that will not corrode or become disfigured by splash and bad aim.

OUTSIDE WATER TAPS

Don't forget the outside water taps. Have enough of them, and locate them for convenience. They cost little when you are building the house, and you will be glad to have them. Have one near your driveway and on each side of the house where you may do any gardening. If you will be watering your lawn, have a tap on each side of the house.

Connect the outside faucets to your water supply using large pipe. Outside applications may need high pressure and a large volume of flow.

Water that remains in outside taps will freeze as soon as the outside air drops to freezing temperature. Outside taps need reliable freeze protection, which we will cover at the end of this Step.

MAKING HOT WATER

You will need one or more hot water heaters. For most homes, selecting the best kind is easy. The most common type is likely to be your best choice. In some cases, a less common type of water heater may be appropriate. We will cover all the types that you should consider, and a couple to avoid.

Along the way, you will learn several tricks to save energy and money in your water heating. And, you will learn how to eliminate or minimize one of the biggest nuisances of home water systems, which is the delay in getting hot water to your faucets.

CONVENTIONAL STORAGE WATER HEATERS (USUALLY BEST)

The most common kind of water heater consists of a water storage tank with a heating element. This kind usually is called simply a "water heater." It is also called a "storage" water heater to distinguish it from the other kinds (although most of the other types use storage also).

This kind of water heater is probably the best choice for your home. It can provide a large volume of hot water for a long time. It needs little attention during its lifetime. The best models are energy efficient. When you buy a storage water heater, select primarily on the basis of these factors:

• the water storage capacity
• the energy source
• the energy efficiency rating
• direct-venting ability, if the water heater is fuel-fired.

Storage Capacity

A typical home should have a water storage capacity between 50 and 80 gallons (200 to 350 liters), depending on the number of people who may occupy the house. The size is not critical, unless you have frequent power outages. In case of doubt, err on the side of a larger tank.

In the event of a power outage, a well insulated water heater will keep the water hot for one or two days, and warm enough for comfortable bathing for three to five days.

The equipment label on a water heater lists a "recovery rate." This is the rate at which the heating element makes hot water, expressed in gallons or liters per hour. The recovery rate is less than the fastest rate at which you use hot water, for example, while taking a shower. That's why the storage tank is needed.

A typical gas fired water heater can heat a tank of cold water in less than one hour. An electric water heater takes longer – typically two or three hours – because of limitations on the capacity of electric circuits. Therefore, if you install an electric water heater, select a somewhat larger tank than you would select for a fuel-fired water heater.

Energy Source

The energy source may be electricity, natural gas, propane, or fuel oil. If your home will be heated with gas or oil, the same fuel usually is the best choice for a storage water heater.

If electric water heating is a candidate for your home, there are two other issues to consider. One is that you may be able to lower the cost of electric water heating by exploiting "interruptible" or "storage" electricity rates. See the sidebar, *Two Ways to Lower the Cost of Electric Water Heating*, for the details. The other issue is a concern that electric water heaters may breed harmful organisms. See the sidebar, *The Best Hot Water Temperature*, below.

If your house will be heated by wood, coal, or some other solid fuel, your decision is more complex. Consider a storage water heater that is heated by electricity or propane. Or, use one of the other types of water heaters that we will examine.

Energy Efficiency

As a matter of perspective, the heat loss from a storage water heater usually is small in relation to the amount of heat that goes down the drain when hot water is used. Nonetheless, a fuel-fired storage water heater may have two significant sources of energy waste.

One is heat loss from the water tank. Good insulation minimizes heat loss from the outside of the tank. But, fuel-fired water heaters lose considerable heat by convection through the combustion gas passage. This is a metal tube that runs from the open burner at the bottom to the flue at the top. When the burner is off, the hot water in the tank stimulates strong convection of the surrounding air through the heater.

Another inefficiency is loss of fuel energy. A "condensing" gas-fired water heater is best, typically recovering about 90% of the fuel energy. It achieves this high efficiency in the same way as a condensing hydronic boiler.

Electric water heaters have no flue, and thus no convection losses. Also, the heating element is virtually 100% efficient in converting electricity to heat.

TWO WAYS TO LOWER THE COST OF ELECTRIC WATER HEATING

If you decide to use electricity for water heating, check whether the electric utility offers a discount for water heating. Many electric utilities offer such discounts for two reasons. One is to encourage homeowners to buy electricity instead of natural gas. This incentive is disappearing as electric utilities increasingly run out of generating capacity.

However, as generating capacity becomes scarce, your water heater becomes a way for the utility to avoid the need to build new generating capacity. Because your water heater has a big tank, it is an energy storage device. So, the utility may offer you an incentive for the privilege of turning off the electricity to your water heater during peak load periods. During the power interruption, you will be limited to the hot water supply that is stored in your tank.

There are two common variations of the discount. An "interruptible" rate gives the utility the option of turning off your water heating element for a relatively short period, typically for several hours. The interruption is supposed to occur only occasionally, maybe only a few times per year.

However, be cautious about utility claims that water heating power will be interrupted "only a few times" or "only for a short while." This may be true at present, but interruptions are likely to get worse in the future, as the utility's load increases. Check the utility company's rate schedule to see how long they can interrupt your water heating, and how often. Size your water heater accordingly.

Under a "storage" rate, the utility typically turns off the water heating element for its entire period of high generating load, which may last from six to eighteen hours per day. The interruption may occur every day during certain periods, such as the summer or winter peak load months, or on weekdays. Your water heater must have a tank that is large enough to satisfy your requirements for this entire period.

If you decide to exploit a storage rate, select a water heater that is 50% to 100% larger than the usual capacity, depending on the length of the interruption that may occur. The larger tank usually can fit in the same space as a conventional tank. It is taller, and perhaps somewhat larger in diameter. The additional cost is minor, and the electric company may provide a rebate for it.

Check with your electric company to see whether it offers either type of rate. However, don't select electricity for water heating just to get the discounted rate. The utility may reduce or abandon a discount rate at any time.

In some cases, the utility offers the discount rate only for the electricity that goes to the water heater. In other cases, the utility may discount your entire electricity bill.

If you use electric water heating, exploit the biggest discount that is available. Your only risk is the possibility of running out of hot water during the interruption period. But, you can always convert to regular electric service if you later decide that you don't want the interruption. If the electric utility cancels the discount, your only disadvantage is having a somewhat oversized water heater. And, the larger tank may become desirable anyway if electricity service becomes less reliable.

Fortunately, you don't have to analyze these issues when you buy a water heater. Like most household appliances, water heaters now carry efficiency ratings. Simply select a water heater that has adequate storage capacity and that has an efficiency rating near the maximum that is available.

In the United States, the energy efficiency of a storage water heater is indicated by its "energy factor" (EF). An energy factor of 1.0 indicates perfect efficiency of energy use.

The most efficient electric storage water heaters have energy factors of about 0.95. Condensing gas-fired water heaters have energy factors as high as 0.86. Non-condensing gas-fired water heaters have maximum energy factors of about 0.67.

To find the most efficient models of water heaters, search the Internet for "water heater efficiency" or a similar phrase. At present, water heaters are not listed in the U.S. Energy Star rating system. Some organizations, such as the American Council for an Energy Efficient Economy (**www.ACEEE.org**) presently offer listings of the most efficient models of appliances.

You can reduce the energy loss from any storage water heater by lowering the hot water temperature setting. This setting is a compromise. See the sidebar.

Direct-Venting Ability

If you use natural gas or propane as the fuel for your water heater, you can build your home without a chimney, provided that none of your other heating equipment requires a chimney.

THE BEST HOT WATER TEMPERATURE

Water heaters allow you to adjust the water temperature over a wide range. For most households, 120 °F (49 °C) is a good compromise. It is warm enough for dishwashing, clothes washing, and hot showers, and it is low enough to avoid the risk of scalding. Avoiding the risk of scalding is a dominant issue if children or elderly people live in the house. On the other hand, higher water temperature provides more effective clothes washing and dishwashing.

A lower temperature setting reduces heat loss from the tank. The effect of water temperature on efficiency is small if you select a water heater with a high "energy factor" rating. However, if you install a hot water recirculation system, keep the temperature as low as possible to minimize the continuous heat loss from the hot water pipes.

Lowering the water temperature reduces the effective storage capacity of your water heater. So, buy a water heater that is big enough for your needs at the lowest temperature setting that you expect to use.

Water temperature above approximately 140 °F (60 °C) suppresses the growth of dangerous microorganisms that occur in water systems, such as the bacteria that cause Legionnaires' Disease. Unfortunately, the hazard of scalding begins at a lower temperature, in the range of 120 to 140 °F (49 to 60 °C).

All water heaters accumulate debris at the bottom of the tank that enters with the water supply. Microorganisms can feed and proliferate in this debris. In conventional fuel-fired water heaters, the flame plays on the bottom of the tank, so the water in the debris layer may be hot enough to keep it sterilized even if the water temperature is set fairly low.

However, there has been concern that electric water heaters may act as a breeding site for dangerous organisms because the heating element is located above the bottom of the tank, and stratification keeps the water in the debris layer relatively cool. How serious is this risk? Perhaps nobody really knows.

If infection from an electric water heater is a concern, you can deal with it by filtering the hot water with a type of filter that is effective for hot water. Or, install "tankless" electric water heaters for applications, such as showers, where bacteria may be a health hazard.

When you vacate the house for a few days or longer, save energy by turning the water heater off. You should always do this when you turn off the main water valve, to avoid burning out a water heater that runs dry.

DRW

Figure 5-16. A direct-vent water heater. The fan at the top of the heater draws the combustion gas through the heater and discharges it to the outside through a side wall. The exhaust gas is cool enough to be discharged through a plastic pipe.

To exploit this benefit, you need a "direct-vent" water heater. This kind of gas-fired water heater has a fan that draws the combustion gas through the heater and discharges it through an adjacent wall. Figure 5-16 shows a typical direct-venting water heater. Figure 4-26, in Step 4, shows the small outside exhaust fitting.

A direct-vent heater greatly reduces convection heat loss because it requires a fan to force the gas flow through the central heat exchanger. The fan turns off when the flame is not burning.

A direct-vent water heater cannot create a carbon monoxide hazard within the house. However, most models draw their combustion air from inside the house, in common with conventional gas-fired and oil-fired water heaters. The amount of combustion air is relatively small, but make provision for it. We covered this issue in Step 4, under the heading, *Eliminating the Danger of Carbon Monoxide.*

With present models of direct-vent water heaters, the fan makes a significant amount of noise, both inside the house and at the outside vent. The noise occurs only when the flame is burning. If the heater is located in an unoccupied space, the sound in the rest of the house is muted.

Turning the Water Heater On and Off

Turn off the water heater whenever you turn off the main water valve, which you should do whenever you vacate the house for an extended period. This is to protect the tank or the heater element from burning out if there is a leak in the house water system that empties the water heater. Also, a fire that starts in the water heater could burn down the house.

Turning off the water heater when the house is vacant also saves energy.

Most modern fuel-fired water heaters have an electric igniter that you can turn on and off with the flip of a switch. This is an important convenience.

A "pilot light" is an older kind of igniter for fuel-fired water heaters. It is a small, continuous flame that ignites the main flame. Restarting a pilot light after turning off the water heater is a tedious process that requires you to crouch down in front of the heater with a long match or a barbecue lighter. This can be almost impossible for a person who has limited mobility.

However, a water heater with a pilot light has one significant advantage: it requires no electricity. If your home loses electrical power for an extended period, a fuel-fired water heater with a pilot light will provide hot water as long as the fuel supply lasts.

Minimize Heat Loss from the Tank to the Pipes

During times when no hot water is being used, a water heater may waste energy if the hot water can escape from the tank by convection. This occurs if either the cold water supply pipe or the hot water discharge pipe is higher than the top of the water heater.

In the cold water supply pipe, the denser cold water falls into the tank, while the warmer water in the tank rises through the same pipe. This convection continues indefinitely as the escaping hot water cools in the inlet pipe. The same thing happens at the tank outlet when the water in the hot water pipes sits still and cools.

 Simple pipe loops at the water heater inlet and outlet prevent heat loss from the water heater by convection.

A simple, reliable way to avoid this energy waste is to install short descending legs in the tank's inlet and outlet pipes. The lighter hot water at the top of the tank cannot drop into the denser cold water in the descending legs. As a result, the hot water cannot move by convection into the surrounding pipes.

Figure 5-17 shows how pipe loops are installed. The descending legs can be short because the lighter hot water remains at the top. A drop of about 6" (15 cm) is ample. Pigtail loops in the inlet and outlet pipes have been used for the same purpose, and they probably work as well.

DRW

Figure 5-17. Installing descending loops at the tank inlet and outlet is a simple, foolproof method of preventing convection heat loss to the surrounding water pipes. Only the pipe near the top of the tank needs to be insulated, in most cases.

Many plumbers don't understand how these legs work, so make sure that they are installed properly. Unfortunately, the engineers who write some plumbing codes also don't understand them, so codes may require "check valves" in water heater installations. Tell your plumber to omit the check valves, and use descending pipe legs instead. See the sidebar on the next page.

HEAT PUMP WATER HEATERS (FOR WARMER CLIMATES)

A heat pump water heater is similar to a conventional storage water heater, except that it uses a heat pump as the heat source. The heat pump takes heat from the air in the surrounding space, and transfers that heat to the water in the tank. The heat pump usually is mounted on top of the tank, as in Figure 5-19.

Figure 5-19. Heat pump water heater. The heat pump on top of the tank has coils that extract heat from the surrounding air. The heat is sent to coils in the bottom of the tank. This unit also has two electric resistance heating elements, which supplement the heat pump when the air temperature is too low.

Rheem Water Heating

ANOTHER BAD IDEA: WATER HEATER CHECK VALVES

An ill-conceived method of preventing convection from idle water heaters is to install "check valves" in the cold water inlet pipe and the hot water outlet pipe. This method has no advantages. It is more complicated than using descending anti-convection legs, and it will eventually cause trouble. Unfortunately, some plumbing codes require check valves, presumably because the engineers who wrote the codes didn't understand the simpler method.

The check valves usually are located inside the pipe connections at the top of the tank. They are installed so that they open in the normal direction of flow. Each valve has a weighted disk or plug that is pushed open by system water pressure when flow is needed, but the disk is heavy enough to block flow by convection when water is not flowing into the system. Cheap plastic check valves that are provided with some water heaters may behave erratically, eventually sticking open or creating strange noises.

If a water heater uses a check valve on the *inlet* side, the system should have an expansion tank connected to the *outlet* side, as shown here. This is to absorb expansion of the water in the water heater when the heater is first turned on (after a vacation, for example). Otherwise, expansion of the water would create very high pressure in the hot water system because the check valve on the inlet side prevents the water from expanding back into the water supply. This pressure could pop the safety valve on the tank or it might create a leak in the house water system.

Check valves are a solution that is worse than the problem, requiring additional components that will eventually fail in ways that will be difficult to diagnose.

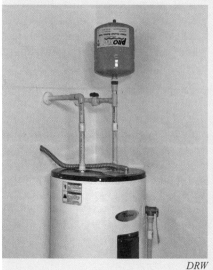

Figure 5-18. An ill-conceived solution to convective heat loss from water heaters.

DRW

A heat pump water heater is most attractive as an alternative to a conventional electric resistance water heater. In favorable applications, the heat pump typically consumes about half as much electricity as a conventional electric water heater. This is a big saving. A heat pump water heater might also offer an advantage in locations where the cost of other heating fuel is high.

As with any heat pump, the efficiency of the unit declines as the temperature difference between the output (the hot water) and input (the surrounding air) increases. Therefore, heat pump water heaters operate most efficiently (1) in a warm environment and (2) with low hot water temperatures.

Most heat pump water heaters have electric resistance heating elements to provide supplemental heating. If the heat pump cannot operate efficiently, because the surroundings are too cold or the water temperature is too high, the electric resistance heaters take over. This may cancel much of the benefit of the heat pump.

Heat pump water heaters are commercially available, but they are still unusual. Before buying one, try to find credible reviews of the available models.

Where to Install It, and Where Not to

A heat pump water heater extracts heat from the space, so it acts as a small air conditioner. This can be valuable if the climate usually is warm.

The heat pump makes noise, like a refrigerator or a room heat pump, so install it in a space where the sound is tolerable.

If the climate does not become very cold, a heat pump water heater can be installed in a garage or in a vented attic. It can also be installed in a well ventilated outdoor enclosure, preferably on the warmest side of the house. Before deciding to install the unit in a location that is exposed to outdoor temperatures, check the high and low operating temperature limits that are specified by the manufacturer.

Don't install a heat pump water heater in an indoor space if the climate has an extended cold season. In that case, extra heating would be required to cancel the cooling of the space by the heat pump.

Don't install a heat pump water heater in a space, such as a basement, that is vulnerable to mildew, because the heat pump will cool the space, increasing the risk of moisture condensation.

Don't install a heat pump water heater in a small enclosed space, such as a closet. The unit needs a large, circulating volume of air as its heat source.

TANKLESS ELECTRIC WATER HEATERS (FOR SECONDARY APPLICATIONS)

An "instant" or "tankless" water heater is an electric heating element that is installed in the water line leading to a faucet or appliance, along with an enclosure and some controls. It has no storage tank. The heater turns on automatically when hot water is needed. Tankless water heaters are popular in certain countries, especially where dwellings are small. Figure 5-20 shows a typical installation.

All tankless electric water heaters offer these benefits:

- *small size*. A tankless heater can be installed close to a faucet or appliances that it serves, such as under a sink.
- *no tank energy loss*.
- *no health hazard* from growth of harmful microorganisms inside a tank.

If tankless heaters are used to serve localized applications, such as a single wash basin, they offer these additional benefits:

- *minimal hot water delay*.
- *less hot water pipe*.

A single tankless water heater may be used to provide water for an entire house, but that generally is not a good application. Because a tankless heater provides no storage of hot water, the electric circuit that serves a whole-house tankless heater must be very large, typically about 24 kW or more. Especially in a house of medium or large size, it makes more sense to use tankless heaters for individual applications, such as wash basins. The large users of hot water in a house, such as the showers and the clothes washer, would be served by a conventional storage water heater.

No matter how they are used, electric tankless water heaters have these limitations in comparison with conventional storage water heaters:

- *temperature fluctuations*. Most tankless electric heaters can change their heating capacity only in stages. As a result, the hot water temperature fluctuates. Cheaper models have less temperature regulation, perhaps creating a scalding hazard.
- *limited water flow*. A tankless heater requires very high amperage, typically near the maximum capacity of an electric circuit. Even with this amperage, the heater has limited water heating capacity. To allow the water to reach the desired temperature, a tankless basin heater typically limits the water flow rate.
- *a separate electric circuit is required for each unit*, to ensure adequate electrical capacity for the heater.

Figure 5-20. A "tankless" electric water heater installed to serve a kitchen sink.

- *high electricity cost*. In most locations, electricity is the most expensive energy source. This is not a disadvantage in an all-electric house.
- *cannot exploit discounted electricity rates* for "storage" or "interruptible" water heating.
- *no hot water during a power outage*.

Tankless electric water heaters are most likely to be desirable if your house uses electricity as its only source of heating energy. Even if the house uses a different source of heating energy, you may want to install small electric tankless heaters at remote basins and sinks to avoid the delay in getting hot water through the pipes, especially if you need only small amounts of hot water at those locations.

TANKLESS GAS-FIRED WATER HEATERS (USUALLY UNSATISFACTORY)

To avoid suspense, I will tell you right away that it is difficult to imagine a situation where a tankless gas water heater would offer a significant advantage over a conventional water heater. That probably explains why tankless gas-fired water heaters are rare.

A tankless gas-fired water heater is essentially a large gas flame that heats the water line directly. It has a heat exchanger and various controls, but no tank. The flame burns only when hot water is needed. Figure 5-21 shows a typical installation.

A tankless gas water heater can serve an entire house. It is an alternative to a conventional gas water, and it would be installed in the home's water system in generally the same way as a conventional heater. A gas tankless heater requires the same gas supply piping and exhaust venting as any gas appliance. Therefore, tankless gas water heaters generally are not practical for localized applications, such as individual wash basins.

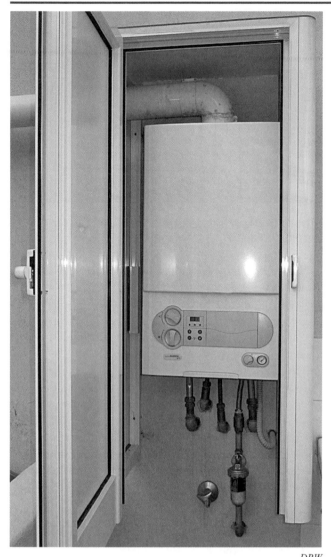

DRW

Figure 5-21. A tankless gas water heater in Italy that is used both for hydronic space heating and for domestic water heating.

In a side-by-side comparison with a conventional gas-fired water heater, the advantages of the tankless heater are:

- *unlimited hot water supply*. The flame is intense enough to maintain a constant flow of hot water, sufficient for the entire household, without being limited by tank capacity.
- *small size and weight*. A typical unit is about the size of a small suitcase. Typically, it is mounted on a wall.
- *no tank energy loss*.
- *no health hazard* from growth of harmful microorganisms inside a tank. However, this risk appears to be minimal in gas-fired water heaters, anyway.

On the other hand, some of the disadvantages of a tankless gas-fired water heaters can be crippling. The disadvantages are:

- *extreme temperature fluctuations*. With present technology, the gas flame in tankless gas heaters cannot modulate well to follow the changes in the water flow rate. The gas flame cycles on and off, or it modulates in large stages. As a result, the water temperature cycles from hot to cold. The flame does not start unless the flow exceeds a minimum, so hot water is not available at slow flow rates.
- *continuing maintenance requirement*. The intense heat of the flame maximizes the tendency of minerals to deposit on the heat exchanger, lowering capacity and creating a risk of burnout. Some units have built-in water treatment to neutralize the minerals. However, the water treatment requires periodic replacement of consumable chemicals. Even these units may require periodic treatment to remove fouling.
- *no hot water during a gas or electricity interruption*. The unit requires electricity to operate its controls.
- *additional delay in getting hot water*. It takes a few seconds for the water to reach the desired temperature, which adds to the delay caused by traveling through the pipes.

HOT WATER FROM HEATING BOILERS (ONLY FOR SOLID FUELS)

If you select hydronic heating for your home, you could heat your domestic water with your boiler instead of using a separate water heater. In this arrangement, hot water from the boiler is circulated through a heat exchanger in a separate insulated tank.

Disregard this option if your hydronic boiler uses electricity, gas, or oil. It will provide no benefit. In fact, a gas-fired water heater is more efficient than a gas-fired hydronic boiler because the colder water entering a water heater is able to extract more energy from the combustion gases.

Heating domestic water with your heating boiler may be an option of last resort if your only fuel option is a solid fuel, such as wood or coal. Many solid-fuel boilers offer a water heating option. See *Heating with Firewood and Other Solid Fuels*, in *Last Look: Energy for Pioneers*, at the end of the book.

Even in that case, you don't want to heat water from your hydronic boiler unless your climate has a long heating season. Solid fuel boilers require a lot of tending and maintenance, so you don't want to operate them just to provide water heating.

Instead, consider an electric water heater. Or, bring in propane for a gas-fired water heater. Or, if the climate is warm, consider a solar water heater.

SOLAR WATER HEATERS (ONLY FOR WARM CLIMATES)

Solar water heaters use free energy from the sun. This seems to make them an obvious choice for energy efficiency. However, that appearance is misleading because it disregards the amount of energy needed to manufacture the systems. Also, solar heaters have a dismal record of performance, caused by poor design, improper installation, inability to work during cold weather, and incompatibility with tree shading.

Still, if your home is located in a climate that stays warm and sunny, consider solar water heating as an option. See *Active Solar Heating Systems*, in *Last Look: Energy for Pioneers*, at the end of this book.

HOT WATER RECIRCULATION

When you stay in a hotel, you probably don't encounter the delay in getting hot water that occurs in your faucets at home. In the hotel, hot water must travel a long distance from the water heater to your room, so hotels are forced to take steps to eliminate a long delay. They do this by continuously circulating hot water through the supply pipes and returning it to the water heater inlet through small return pipes near each fixture.

You can use this same technique in your home. Recirculation is a time and water saver for wash basins, sinks, and showers. It improves the performance of dishwashers. It is not useful for appliances that use hot water in batches, such as clothes washers and bathtubs.

A single small pump maintains circulation through all the return lines. The pump requires a small amount of energy, typically about 100 watts. Recirculation keeps the hot water pipes warm, which increases heat loss. So, insulate all the hot water pipes that use recirculation, including the return pipes.

Recirculation is a luxury that costs a certain amount of water heating and pump energy. It saves a small amount of water by eliminating the waste of water that occurs while you are waiting for the hot water to arrive at the faucet or shower head.

A health concern is that harmful microorganisms, such as the bacteria that cause Legionnaires' Disease, may grow in the stagnant recirculation water loop when recirculation is turned off. Therefore, if you have a recirculation system, you may be committed to operating it continuously.

MINIMIZE HOT WATER DELAY

A nuisance that homeowners take for granted is the delay that occurs in getting hot water from faucets and shower heads. Hot water cools quickly as it sits in pipes. So, after you turn on the faucet, hot water has to come all the way from the heater, pushing a slug of cold water ahead of it. This wastes time, water, and heating energy.

The delay is related to the distance between the water heater and the fixture. For example, if a kitchen sink is located 50 feet (15 meters) from the water heater, it may take half a minute for hot water to appear at the faucet. In the meantime, about a gallon (four liters) of water is wasted, along with the energy that originally heated it. There are several ways to reduce or eliminate this delay.

Use the smallest practical diameter for hot water pipes that serve fixtures needing hot water quickly. This reduces the volume of cold water that has be pushed out of the pipes before the hot water arrives. Serve each hot water faucet *individually* with a small pipe that runs all the way from the water heater. Use pipe with an inside diameter of ½" (13 mm) or even smaller. Typically, limit this method to hot water pipes that serve individual basins and sinks.

Locate the water heater near fixtures that need hot water quickly. For example, if the house has a basement, install the water heater just below the kitchen, and use the shortest possible pipes to connect the water heater to the kitchen fixtures.

Install separate water heaters to serve different parts of the house, especially for a large house. Locate each heater close to users that need hot water quickly. For example, if the kitchen is located at one end of the house and several bathrooms are located at the other end, install separate water heaters to supply each group of hot water users.

If you use multiple water heaters, you can set each one for a different water temperature. If the layout permits, provide hotter water to the dishwasher and clothes washer, and perhaps to the kitchen sink and utility sink. Provide cooler water to washroom faucets and shower heads, to avoid a scalding hazard and to save energy.

Install electric "instant" or "tankless" water heaters for fixtures that need small amounts of hot water quickly. Wash basins are the typical application for tankless water heaters.

Install a recirculation system. This is an option for a large house, but it is inefficient. See the sidebar.

WATER TREATMENT: PURE WATER ANYWHERE

Water supplies are becoming increasingly polluted, to the point that many water supplies are dangerous or unpleasant to some degree. Some pollutants can be serious health hazards without being noticed. Other pollutants are primarily nuisances, creating bad taste and odor, or staining your plumbing fixtures.

Dangerous water pollutants enter your body primarily by two routes. One is by drinking the water or eating food that is prepared with the water. The other is by inhaling water droplets or gases released from water, especially in showers. Most pollutants cannot enter the body through unbroken skin, although some infections can enter through eye and nose tissues.

You can't assume that water from any public system is entirely safe. Water systems vary widely in the amount of treatment they provide, and even the best public systems may contain unsafe levels of certain pollutants. Treatment generally is done only at the water treatment plant, and various pollutants (such as lead and iron) may enter the water from the distribution pipes. Some of the water treatment chemicals used by the water utility itself may be hazardous, or they may create hazardous byproducts. And, a public water system may suffer lapses in water treatment caused by system failures or neglect.

With a private water supply, such as a well, it is likely that the water will contain other substances that are hazardous or nuisances.

To deal with hazards and nuisances in your water supply, we will learn how to test your water supply, how to select the right water treatment methods and equipment, and how to lay out your water treatment for best effectiveness and economy.

PRELIMINARY WATER TREATMENT RECOMMENDATIONS

Home water treatment is a big subject because there are many different kinds of pollutants in water supplies. Before we launch into the details, here is a shortcut set of recommendations for protecting your home water supply.

These recommendations cover the great majority of homes, plus a few important situations that occur in fewer locations. Only in isolated cases will you need to use treatment methods that are different from these.

Some of the terms in these recommendations will be unfamiliar. Don't worry. We will explain them all.

Water for Drinking and Cooking

Water for drinking and cooking is the most critical part of your water supply. In most locations, water used for these purposes should be filtered. Usually, this is easy. Install a single filtered spigot, as in Figures 5-22 and 5-23. Install the spigot on or alongside the kitchen sink, so that the spigot overhangs the sink.

Usually, the filter cartridge housing is located underneath the sink. This location makes changing the filter awkward, especially for occupants who have limited mobility. If you choose this location, install the filter housing as close to the front of the cabinet as possible.

In Step 1, we recommended installing the filter cartridge in a cabinet that is located at about chest height. If you do this, provide sufficient clearance inside the cabinet to use the filter wrench that is needed for changing most types of filters.

In most homes, all water for drinking and cooking will come from this spigot. If you want to supply drinking water in other parts of your home, such as guest bathrooms, install additional filtered taps at those locations.

Don't draw water for cooking from the hot water faucet. Instead, use water from your drinking water filter, and heat the water on the stove or in the microwave oven.

In most locations, filter your drinking water with the best available activated carbon cartridge. Typical carbon filter cartridges are rated to process from 500 to 20,000 gallons (2,000 to 75,000 liters) of water. For a given cartridge size, cartridges with smaller pore sizes have smaller filtering capacity. When limited to drinking water, even filters with the least capacity may last six months. This replacement interval is appropriate to inhibit growth of bacteria within the filter.

If your water supply has contaminants – such as lead – that are not removed by all carbon filters, be sure that your cartridges are certified to remove these pollutants. If the water supply requires treatment that carbon filters cannot provide economically, install reverse osmosis or another appropriate system for the kitchen water supply.

Don't use the cheap little filters that are installed on the ends of spigots. They are uneconomical, they have to be changed often, and they are less effective than larger filters.

Don't feed your drinking water filter from "softened" water produced by an "ion exchange" water softening system, because a carbon filter cannot remove the sodium that is added by the water softener. Instead, take the drinking water from the house water supply before it passes through the water softener.

Or, if you use softened water to avoid the bad taste that occurs when hard water is used to make hot beverages, use a reverse osmosis filter to remove the sodium from your softened water supply.

Water for Showers

In some cases, filtering shower water may be as important as filtering the water for drinking and cooking. A bather inhales fine water droplets that contain anything that is dangerous in the water supply, including radon and a wide variety of chemicals that may be carried in the water. Also, the shower atmosphere contains any gases that are released from the water.

If the hazard is radon – which is likely only with well water – treat the entire water supply for the house. Similarly, if your water supply is contaminated by dangerous levels of bacteria or organic poisons, use whole-house filtering to block such contaminants.

 For effective filtering of the water to individual showers, install separate filters for the hot and cold water supplies to each shower.

Otherwise, you can filter the water for the showers individually, using these methods:

- For the cold water to the showers, install a carbon filter in the cold water pipe that serves the showers.
- For the hot water, install a carbon filter in the cold water supply to the water heater.
- Or, if you are concerned about growth of bacteria inside the water heater, install a ceramic filter in the hot water pipe from the water heater to the showers.

To get rid of lesser nuisances, such as chlorine odor, a shower head filter may be adequate. This is a small filter that screws on to the gooseneck for the shower head, as in Figure 5-24. However, the primary filtering agent in shower filters is carbon, which is less effective for warm water than for cold water. For this reason, you probably won't find a shower head filter that meets recognized standards of filter performance.

Small shower filters are likely to be inadequate for blocking radon and many chemical contaminants. And, carbon shower filters have relatively large pore sizes in order to provide adequate flow, so they don't block bacteria effectively.

Water for Basins, Sinks, and Bathtubs

Water for basins, sinks, and bathtubs is not as critical as the water supply for drinking and showers. Fortunately, few water supplies contain pollutants that pose a hazard of absorption through skin when washing or bathing.

Protecting against microorganisms on skin is primarily a matter of dilution. Soap works primarily by flushing away microorganisms, not necessarily by killing them.

If "hardness" in the water causes excessive deposits on plumbing fixtures, the cure is to install a water softener. However, softened water imparts a soapy feel to water that is used for hand washing or bathing.

For lower levels of hardness, just clean your fixtures periodically with vinegar, lemon juice, or a commercial scum cleaner.

If your water supply contains other substances – such as iron or sulfur – that cause staining or fouling of your plumbing fixtures, install whole-house water treatment that is specific for those substances.

Water for Laundry

Laundry benefits from water treatment if the water supply contains high concentrations of hardness minerals or discoloring agents, such as iron or sulfur compounds. A water softener will remove minerals and iron. More specialized treatment methods remove iron and sulfur compounds.

If your water supply contains a significant amount of dirt, a whole-house "sediment" filter is the appropriate solution.

Water for Toilet Flushing

The only reason to filter toilet flushing water is to prevent staining of the toilets. If your water supply contains staining agents, install a whole-house filter that is specific for those pollutants.

Water for Outdoor Use

Generally, don't filter the water to your outside taps. Run your water supply directly to the outside taps, bypassing any filtering that is installed for interior uses.

Water for the Swimming Pool

If you plan to have a permanent swimming pool, it probably will have a separate filtering and treatment system. The pool has treatment requirements that are different from the rest of the house water supply. Most commonly, it involves recirculation and filtering of the pool water to remove debris. It also includes chlorination to kill dangerous microorganisms that come from the environment, especially fecal matter from animals and bathers. Do more homework about swimming pools before you design the installation for your home.

Usually, the pool can be filled from your raw water supply, either the public water system or a well. However, if the house water supply contains contaminants that require treatment for the whole house, fill the pool with water that has been treated for house usage.

Water for Hydronic Heating Systems

We covered water treatment for hydronic systems in Step 4. A hydronic heating system needs special water treatment, which is different from the water treatment that is needed to protect people.

FIRST, INVESTIGATE YOUR WATER SUPPLY

Water supplies differ greatly in the types and quantities of pollutants they contain. To design your water treatment, you need to learn what is in your water supply. Table 5-1, *Home Water Treatment*, lists the principal hazards that exist in water supplies, along with a summary of treatment methods.

Don't be overwhelmed by the many kinds of water pollutants and treatment methods that exist. Your water supply probably will contain only a few pollutants that should concern you. The majority of homes that are served by a public water system need only one simple filter, a high quality carbon filter that serves a separate drinking water spigot.

So, a large part of what follows applies to a minority of homes. If your home has some unusual contamination of its water supply, it may need more specialized treatment. Pick out what you need to know.

If your home will get its water from a public water utility, your first step is to check with the utility itself. In the U.S., public water utilities are required by law to inform customers of all contaminants in their water. The quality of this information varies from good to inadequate.

Also, do further research about the nature of water in your geographic area. The Internet is a good place to start. If your state or other locality has an environmental protection agency, check with them.

If your water will come from a private supply – such as a well, a lake, or a community reservoir – have an independent laboratory test the water from your source. This is a routine service offered by many companies. Look up "water testing" in the Yellow Pages or on the Internet. Expect to pay for this. You may be able to buy a water test kit, which consists of a container for sending a water sample to a certified testing laboratory. Hardware stores often sell these test kits, or check the Internet for a reliable laboratory.

If your water will come from a private supply, don't rely on information about the water quality of adjacent public systems. For example, if you will draw from a well, your water will be totally different from the water provided by a public system that draws from a river or reservoir.

Most water hazards and nuisances are a matter of degree. Reliable information about your water supply should include the concentrations measured over a period of time. Compare these to the official standards for safe water. Table 5-1, *Home Water Treatment*, contains typical limits for the most common hazards.

Don't believe what you are told by vendors of water treatment equipment and by water treatment companies. Many of them won't give you the best advice. They will recommend whatever they have to sell, and their level of training may be inadequate to assess the actual quality of your water.

WATER TREATMENT METHODS AND EQUIPMENT

It's not very expensive to control the most common water hazards and nuisances. On the other hand, treatment of less common contamination may be expensive and troublesome. Most pollutants can be controlled with a variety of methods. Your goal is to block all dangerous or annoying pollutants effectively, and to do so at minimum cost.

Select an appropriate capacity for each filtering or water treatment application. The capacity is expressed as the total number of gallons or liters that the cartridge or other equipment can treat. For example, a whole-house water filter should have a much larger capacity than your drinking water filter. Filters and other water treatment material must be replaced periodically to maintain their effectiveness. See the sidebar, *Replace Filters on Time*.

In filtering equipment, it is the cartridge that does all the work. Cartridges have a variety of characteristics, so you need to match the cartridges to the pollutants that you have identified in your water supply. The cartridge should be large enough to maintain its effectiveness at the maximum water flow rate, and it should be large enough so that it does not require frequent replacement. Select a filter unit that uses cartridges of standardized dimensions, which will be less expensive. And, they will be more available in the future.

"Pore size" is an important rating for filters. Pore size is stated in microns. (A micron is one millionth of a meter.) Match the pore size to the size of the particles that you need to remove, which may range in size from individual molecules to visible dirt particles. Don't make the pore size much smaller than necessary, because smaller pore size reduces the water flow rate and increases the cost of the filter.

Within each type of water treatment equipment, effectiveness may vary widely. When shopping for your equipment, check that the manufacturer recognizes the appropriate standards of NSF International, a U.S. non-profit organization that is the prime source of water treatment standards. These standards are only a starting point. The NSF certification system can be misleading, and verification is weak.

Now, let's get familiar with the water treatment equipment that you may need.

Activated Carbon Filters

"Activated carbon" filters are the main workhorse of home water filtering. They are also called "activated charcoal" filters. We will call them "carbon" filters, for short.

Carbon filters block the most common hazards and nuisances in drinking water. At the same time, they pass healthful minerals and the fluoride that is added to water to prevent tooth decay. In many locations, activated carbon is the only kind of filter that you need.

Carbon filters are similar to charcoal. The best carbon filters are made from woody material, especially coconut shells. Others are made from coal and bones. The material is subjected to a charring process that makes it highly porous. The process creates a microscopic surface area inside the material that is huge. It is estimated that one pound of good quality filter carbon has a surface area of approximately 100 acres. (In metric terms, a kilogram of filter carbon has a surface area of about 100 hectares). Figure 5-22 shows a typical carbon filter cartridge.

Carbon filters have two separate methods of trapping pollutants, *adsorption* and *pore size*. "Adsorption" is an attraction of pollutant molecules to the surface of the filter material by weak electric charges. Adsorption can trap very small particles, even the individual atoms of certain elements. Adsorption is not effective for capturing pollutants that lack electric charges on their surfaces. For example, it is not effective for capturing most minerals.

Adsorption holds pollutants weakly on the surface of the carbon, so the pollutants will hopscotch downstream to another part of the filter when the upstream part becomes loaded. As a result, the filter becomes less effective with the passage of time.

Carbon filters also block pollutants by acting as a sieve to physically block particles above a certain size. Carbon filters have pore size ratings that range from 0.5 micron to 50 microns, with a correspondingly broad range of filtering ability and cost. The passages in adsorption filters are irregular, so the pore size is nominal. Therefore, some particles that are larger than the stated pore size are likely to get through.

As a rule, the most effective carbon filters are "carbon block" cartridges. These are made of finely pulverized carbon that is tightly compressed into a solid block. This material is abbreviated "PAC," which stands for "powdered activated carbon."

"Granular" carbon filters (abbreviated "GAC") are more loosely packed, so they allow higher water flow rates. The choice depends on the application. For example, you would usually want a carbon block cartridge for your drinking water, but perhaps a granular cartridge suffices as a whole-house filter.

Carbon block (PAC) filters have the smallest pore sizes. Also, they are less likely to suffer from "channeling," which is the formation of passageways inside the filter that allow pollutants to leak through the filter material.

The smaller pore size of carbon block filters is important for blocking bacteria, protozoa, and other microorganisms. It is not very relevant for inorganic material that is trapped by adsorption.

Carbon filter systems are simple and relatively inexpensive. The equipment typically consists of one or two disposable filter cartridges, a housing for each cartridge, and water inlet and outlet connections. Figure 5-23 shows a typical under-counter installation for kitchen use.

Carbon filter cartridges usually include a pre-filter that keeps larger particles from clogging the carbon. Typically, the pre-filter is a layer of plastic fiber mesh that is wrapped around the inlet side of the cartridge. If your water supply is dirty – for example, if you get water from a cistern – install a "sediment" filter ahead of your carbon filters. Water filter packages that offer this combination are commonly available.

DRW

Figure 5-22. A typical carbon block filter cartridge. This is a good size for a household drinking water filter. On the left is the cartridge cut in half.

Table 5-1. HOME WATER TREATMENT

Water conditions are highly variable. This table includes water pollutants and treatment methods for most locations. However, some water supplies have unusual hazards. If serious contaminants exist in your water supply, investigate thoroughly before selecting your water treatment methods.

POLLUTANT	ADVERSE EFFECTS	MAXIMUM LEVEL [1]	AFFECTED WATER SOURCES	WATER USES TO FILTER	TYPICAL TREATMENT
Manmade organic compounds ("VOC's")	• Cancer	varies by type	• All water supplies	• Drinking water • Shower water	• Activated carbon • Reverse osmosis
Water treatment chemicals and their byproducts	• Cancer • Teeth staining (from fluoride)	4 mg/L, (chlorine, fluoride)	• Most public water systems and other treated water supplies	• Drinking water • Shower water	• Activated carbon Note: Carbon filters remove chlorine, but not fluoride.
Bacteria	• Infectious diseases	zero	• Untreated supplies, especially surface water	• Drinking water • Supply to water heater • Hot and cold water to showers	• Ultraviolet • Reverse osmosis • Ceramic filter • Small-pore carbon filter Note: Carbon filters breed bacteria if not replaced at proper intervals.
Viruses	• Infectious diseases	zero	• Untreated supplies contaminated by fecal material	• All human contact	• Ultraviolet
Protozoa (e.g., Giardia)	• Infectious diseases	zero	• Untreated supplies, especially surface water	• Drinking water • Supply to water heater • Hot and cold water to showers	• Activated carbon • Reverse osmosis • Ceramic filter
Radon	• Cancer	300 pCi/L	• Wells in terrain having uranium or thorium	• Drinking water • Supply to water heater • Shower water	• Aeration • Activated carbon
Sodium	• Heart disease	no standard	• Water supply from sodium-rich terrain • Ion exchange water softeners	• Drinking water	• Reverse osmosis
Hardness minerals	• Reduced laundry effectiveness • Deposits on fixtures	ca. 80-200 ppm	• Surface and well water flowing through limestone and magnesium-rich rock formations	• Supply to water heater and clothes washer • If severe, whole house, EXCEPT drinking water	• Ion exchange water softener • Reverse osmosis, for moderate hardness in limited water quantities

Contaminant	Health effects	Standard	Sources	Treatment location	Treatment
Lead	• Mental impairment • Stroke • Kidney failure • Cancer	0.015 mg/L	• Public systems with lead pipes • Older houses with lead service pipes and lead-bearing fixtures • Wells located near acid mine drainage and lead deposits	• Drinking water	• Activated carbon certified for lead removal • Reverse osmosis Note: Not all types of carbon filters remove lead.
Arsenic	• Damage to nervous system, blood vessels, skin • Cancer	0.010 mg/L	• Wells in arsenic-bearing terrain • All sources polluted by industrial arsenic	• Drinking water. • If severe, also hot and cold water to baths and showers	• With chlorinated water, reverse osmosis and activated carbon • With un-chlorinated water, oxidation pre-treatment combined with activated carbon or reverse osmosis Note: Treatment is technical, and depends on the water source.
Iron	• Staining of fixtures, crockery, and laundry • Odor • Slime • Obstruction of water system • Corrosion of iron pipe and fittings	0.3 mg/L	• Primarily wells in iron-rich terrain	• Whole house	• Activated carbon, for chlorinated water systems • Oxidation plus filtration, for non-chlorinated system • Manganese greensand filter system Note: Treatment is technical, and may be difficult for some sources.
Hydrogen sulfide	• Odor of rotten eggs • Corrosion and staining of metal fixtures	if offensive	• Wells in terrain containing hydrogen sulfide	• Whole house	• Activated carbon, for small amounts • Manganese greensand system, for moderate amounts • Chlorination system, for large amounts
Dirt & sediment	• Esthetic • Clogs filters	no standard	• Private wells and surface water supplies • Poorly maintained public systems	• If severe, whole house	• If severe, whole house sediment filter • Otherwise, pre-filters used with filters for other pollutants

Note [1]: These figures are evolving and somewhat arbitrary, depending on the sources and current knowledge.

REPLACE FILTERS ON TIME

All filters and treatment media lose effectiveness toward the end of their useful life. Some filters are replaced on the basis of time, while others are replaced on the basis of the amount of water that is filtered.

For filters where bacteria or other micro-organisms may grow – especially in carbon filters – replace the filter cartridge on the basis of time, typically every six months. If you don't, the filter itself may become a health hazard. The organisms may proliferate enough to work through the filter in large amounts long before the filter saturates with other pollutants. Select a cartridge size that is large enough to provide satisfactory filtering for this time period.

Replace earlier, rather than later. Filters are inexpensive in relation to their benefit. By the time you notice that your water has a bad taste or smell, replacing the filter is long overdue. Some dangerous water pollutants, such as lead and radon, have no taste or smell to warn you.

When you change a filter cartridge, write the date on the outside of the filter housing. Label the filter housing to indicate the type of filter cartridge. Cut the label off the filter cartridge box and tape it to the housing or inside the cabinet.

Regardless of the elapsed time or the quantity of water filtered, if the water starts to taste strange, clean out the filter housing thoroughly and replace the cartridge.

Water softeners and other water treatment devices that consume bulk material, such as salt, commonly have water meters or other methods to indicate when the media needs replacement.

Make it easy to replace filters and to refresh media. The main reason for neglect is difficult access. For example, if your kitchen drinking water filter is located under the sink, replacing the cartridges is a chore that may stop people who are not agile. So, install your water filters like your fire extinguishers, where they are easily accessible. Make it easy to clean up spilled water. Create a handy space to store spare cartridges.

Various materials can be added to carbon filters to improve their filtering of certain materials, such as lead and mercury. Specialized carbon filters typically are used in combination with ordinary carbon filters, in a housing that provides for separate cartridges. The water flows through an inexpensive filter first, then through the more expensive specialized cartridge.

■ Not for Hot Water!

Adsorption by carbon filters works well only with cold water. This is because thermal agitation of the molecules in warm water keeps pollutants from sticking to the filter surface. Water temperature approaching 140 °F (60 °C) renders adsorption almost useless.

(The carbon filter still acts as a sieve whose effectiveness depends on its pore size.)

Therefore, don't rely on carbon filters for water coming from water heaters. Instead, filter the water before it goes to the water heater. If you are concerned about bacteria that may grow in your water heater, you will need a different method to kill or remove the bacteria.

■ Bacteria Growth in Carbon Filters

Carbon filters (and other adsorption filters, such as activated alumina) introduce a hazard of their own, which is that they act as a concentrating and breeding site for microorganisms, which exist in virtually all water supplies. Bacteria are initially isolated on the upstream side of the filter, but they will eventually penetrate through the filter in large numbers.

This hazard exists even with chlorinated water supplies, which normally kill bacteria. Paradoxically, carbon filters trap chlorine effectively, so bacteria can grow in the innards of a filter where the chlorine does not penetrate.

DRW

Figure 5-23. Typical carbon filter installed under the sink. This unit serves only the drinking water spigot on the right side of the sink. This is a common location for kitchen water filters, but it is inconvenient for the needed replacement of filter cartridges. It is more convenient to install a "countertop" filter unit that has a filter size of adequate capacity or to install the filter housing in a cabinet that is located on or above the counter top.

The primary defense is timely replacement of filter cartridges, typically every six months. In fact, bacteria growth is commonly the factor that determines how often you should change carbon filters.

You may see filters that are advertised to have "silver" for the purpose of killing bacteria within the filter. Unfortunately, silver seems to have only fleeting effectiveness, so it is primarily an advertising gimmick.

■ Selecting Carbon Filters

Not all carbon filters are equal. The main differences are:

- *pore size*
- the *materials* used to make the carbon (e.g., coconut shells or coal)
- *additives* or *special manufacturing processes* that add or improve filtering of certain pollutants (e.g., lead or mercury)
- *quality*. U.S. dominance of filter manufacturing has declined, so that the market is increasingly flooded with products of dubious origin and quality. Information about such filters may be inadequate, misleading, or false.

The capability of a carbon filter is reflected in its price. A cartridge that is effective against a broad range of pollutants may cost several times more than a basic "taste and odor" filter.

For pollutants that are removed by adsorption, differences between cartridges are a matter of degree. For example, all carbon filters remove a large percentage of chlorine. For other pollutants, pore size is the main factor. For example, a pore size of 0.5 micron can block giardia cysts, but the common pore size of 10 microns is not effective against giardia.

Therefore, tailor the cartridge to each application. Go through Table 5-1, *Home Water Treatment*, along with your home water supply analysis, to identify the pollutants that you want the filter to block.

Unfortunately, you will find that most carbon cartridges do not list their effectiveness against specific pollutants, and it can be a chore to find this information.

So, what do you do? Get on the Internet and search. You may start with the NSF Web site (**www.NSF.org**), which allows you to search for all filter models that are NSF certified. The NSF site lists the specific contaminants that are certified for listed models. Unfortunately, the search function is confusing and the data appear to need updating. But at least, the NSF site lists major legitimate manufacturers.

Then, go to the Web sites of those manufacturers and search for the filter sizes that you need. For its better cartridges, the manufacturer may list the specific pollutants that the filter removes, by the percentage of removal for each pollutant.

Another approach is to make a search for filters that are targeted to specific pollutants in your water supply, such as lead, iron, or organic poisons.

Select a popular cartridge size that is adequate for each application. The capacity of a filter generally is stated as the number of gallons (or liters) that the cartridge can purify. If there are several popular sizes, favor a larger size for better filtering.

For example, the popular length of 9¾" (about 250 mm) is a good choice for drinking water, kitchen use, and showers. Figure 5-22 shows an example of this size. Some other types of filters, such as sediment filters, are also made in this size.

Avoid oddball sizes and styles, which are proliferating as water filtering becomes more common. Some manufacturers – including some of the best ones – have filters with non-standard connections, which would restrict you to that manufacturer and to its non-competitive prices.

About the only small filter that you might want is a shower head filter, which improves the smell of water, but is not reliable against serious health hazards. Figure 5-24 shows a typical example.

As you search, you will see that some filters claim that they are certified to conform to NSF Standards 53 or 42. *Such statements are meaningless by themselves*. NSF certification applies only to pollutants that are stated explicitly. Standards 53 and 42 indicate levels of effectiveness for specific pollutants, with Standard 53 being better. For example, a particular filter may be certified as meeting Standard 42 for chlorine and Standard 53 for lead.

DRW

Figure 5-24. Typical shower head filter that uses a carbon cartridge. It is not adequate for blocking serious health hazards, but it can minimize nuisances, such as chlorine.

Beware that filters coming from some countries make false claims of NSF certification and protection ability. Your best defense against false claims is to buy from well established manufacturers and vendors.

Sediment Filters

"Sediment" filters act as a simple sieve, rather than by molecular attraction or chemical action. They are available with pore sizes as small as 5 microns. They are desirable if your water supply contains a significant amount of miscellaneous dirt. They are cheaper for dirt removal than other kinds of filters.

Sediment filters are commonly used with private wells. They are also used as pre-filters for other types of water treatment that are easily clogged, such as reverse osmosis.

Inexpensive sediment filters are commonly made of tightly wound string. This material is vulnerable to channeling at high flow rates. A newer material that resists channeling is made of polypropylene fibers that are partially melted together.

There are two designs of sediment filters, "surface" filters and "depth" filters. Surface filters are simple filters that have a single pore size. Depth filters are made in layers having different pore sizes. The largest pore size is on the upstream size and deeper layers have progressively smaller pore sizes. Depth filters are intended to provide longer life when the debris in the water supply has a range of particle sizes.

DRW

Figure 5-25. Water softener. In the metal cylinder on the right, common salt replaces hardness minerals with sodium compounds. The plastic bin on the left contains salt for replenishing the unit. The sodium that is added to the water may aggravate heart disease.

Water Softeners

A "water softener" is a chemical treatment process that is designed specifically to remove "hardness" minerals from your water supply. These minerals are calcium and magnesium compounds. If they are concentrated in your water, they deposit a hard, tenacious scale or scum on your water fixtures and in your water pipes. When hard water is heated for dishwashing and laundry, the minerals precipitate in quantities that make laundry grey and stiff, and they waste detergent. The minerals make bathing unpleasant, and they also give a bad taste to hot beverages.

Water softeners are larger, more complicated, and more expensive than water filters. The apparatus typically requires about as much space as a water heater. Figure 5-25 shows a typical unit.

Most home water softeners employ a principle called "ion exchange." This process replaces the calcium or magnesium with sodium. Usually, the "hard" water is circulated through a tank of ordinary salt (sodium chloride) to convert the calcium and magnesium compounds into sodium compounds, which are much more soluble. The salt must be replenished periodically.

This method of softening water is the most common because salt is cheap. However, it is believed that increasing the amount of sodium in the water supply increases the risk of heart disease. If you use this kind of water softener, it may be prudent to install a reverse osmosis filter to remove the sodium from your drinking water.

Another disadvantage of salt-based water softeners is that they may make the water somewhat corrosive. Correcting this, if necessary, requires additional chemical treatment.

"Precipitation" is a more expensive method of softening water that avoids the problem of using salt. A combination of chemical processes is used to convert the calcium and magnesium compounds into solids that can be filtered out. The most common of these methods is the "soda-lime" process.

If you soften water for laundry, you may not want to soften the water for showers, bathing, and hand washing unless the water is very hard. Oddly, water that has been "softened" imparts a soapy feel to your skin that persists until your skin is dry.

Hardness is a matter of degree. If the hardness of your water causes only minor trouble, there are less expensive methods of dealing with it. To improve your laundry, use a detergent that contains a water softening additive, such as "aluminosilicate." Or, add packaged water softeners (which may be called "water conditioners") at the beginning of the wash and rinse cycles.

To remove superficial mineral deposits on water fixtures, wipe them with vinegar (acetic acid), lemon juice (citric acid), or a commercial cleaner for hard water deposits. If the hardness in the water makes your hot beverages taste bad, you can use bottled water to make your hot beverages.

Reverse Osmosis

Reverse osmosis uses a membrane that has extremely small pores, the size of molecules. The membrane allows water molecules to pass through, but not certain atoms or molecules, or particles of much larger size. The pore size typically is smaller than 0.001 micron.

Some of the atoms removed by reverse osmosis include sodium, fluoride, arsenic, copper, mercury, and lead. However, reverse osmosis does not block chlorine or radon. Reverse osmosis removes some larger molecules, but not all. For example, some pesticides are not blocked.

The filtering of the reverse osmosis membrane is not absolute, because microscopic flaws in the membrane allow a fraction of contaminants to pass through. Therefore, the membrane itself does not provide reliable protection against viruses, bacteria, or protozoa.

A complete reverse osmosis system includes other types of filters, so it removes most hazards from the water supply. But, reverse osmosis also removes healthful minerals and fluoride. The minerals probably are available in the foods you usually consume. You may be able to replace the fluorine by using fluoridated toothpaste.

If the water supply contains a large concentration of "hardness" minerals, reverse osmosis will remove these minerals, but they will clog the membrane quickly. If you install a water softener to remove minerals from the house water supply, a reverse osmosis filter for your drinking and cooking water will remove the harmful sodium that is added by the water softener.

To keep the membrane from becoming clogged, the filter system flushes the upstream side of the membrane. This requires additional water, which is dumped to the sewer. Typically, the flushing action requires several units of water for each unit of water that is filtered.

Significant pressure is needed to force water through the reverse osmosis membrane. In residential systems, this pressure comes from the water supply system. Typically, this pressure is barely high enough to filter a useful amount of water. Under typical conditions, a residential system may produce 10 to 50 gallons (40 to 200 liters) per day. Therefore, reverse osmosis is limited primarily to providing water for drinking and cooking. The slow trickle from the reverse osmosis membrane is stored in a small tank, typically having a capacity of about 4 gallons (16 liters).

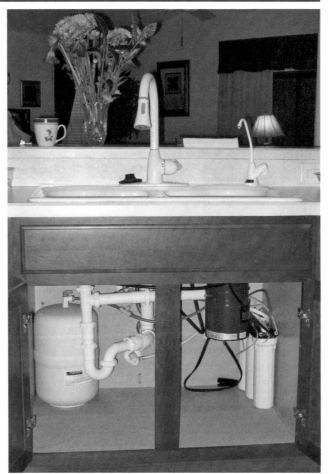

DRW

Figure 5-26. Reverse osmosis water filter under a kitchen sink. The filter membrane and two auxiliary filters are on the right in the rear of the cabinet. The storage tank is on the left. The dark item in front of the filters is a garbage grinder. This common installation makes it awkward to replace the filters. It would be better to install the filters in a cabinet above the counter.

Reverse osmosis is combined with other filters. One or two pre-filters are installed ahead of the membrane to keep the small pores of the membrane from being clogged, and typically at least one carbon filter is installed downstream to trap chlorine and organic compounds that pass through the membrane.

The membrane of the reverse osmosis system typically lasts one or two years. The other filters in the system typically need replacement every six months. Replacing all these elements is an expensive maintenance burden.

The tank and the filters usually are installed under the kitchen sink, along with the sink drains and garbage disposer, as in Figure 5-26. This makes maintenance awkward, especially for older residents. For that reason, Step 1 recommends installing kitchen water treatment equipment in a separate accessible cabinet that is located at a convenient height.

Ceramic Filters

Ceramic filters block contaminants like a sieve, strictly on the basis of pore size. They claim a reliable pore size of less than one micron, about the diameter of the smallest bacteria.

Ceramic filters have two significant advantages over carbon filters. One is that they block bacteria and other microorganisms more reliably. This is because ceramic filters have a consistently small pore size. Also, they do not block chlorine effectively, so chlorine in the water supply can kill bacteria inside the filter.

The other advantage is that ceramic filters retain their effectiveness with hot water, unlike carbon filters.

In general, ceramic filters are less effective than carbon filters for removing chemical and inorganic pollutants. However, they can be used in combination with carbon filters and other types to provide protection against a broad spectrum of pollutants.

Ceramic filters are similar to reverse osmosis filters in their range of application, their advantages, and their limitations. However, there are some differences in the specific pollutants that the two types will block.

Ceramic filters have a very slow flow rate in relation to their size. This limitation can be overcome by increasing the size and number of the filter elements, but this becomes expensive. For a given flow rate, ceramic filters are several times more expensive than good carbon filters. For this reason, ceramic filters are limited in application. They are practical primarily for filtering small quantities of water for drinking and cooking.

A specialized application is filtering hot water. This may be desirable for showers in cases where there is concern that organisms may grow inside the water heater.

Ceramic filter systems are available in a variety of configurations that are similar to those used for carbon filters. You can get systems that are installed under a counter and on the countertop. However, at the time this is written, there are only one or two manufacturers who produce a selection of ceramic filter systems for home use.

Ceramic filters are vulnerable to clogging. Their useful life is determined by the cleanliness of the water supply. The flow rate slows as pollutants accumulate on the inlet side of the filter. Unlike carbon filters, the life of a ceramic filter is not limited by growth of bacteria inside the filter.

Some ceramic filter elements can be cleaned by brushing, so they can have a very long life. However, the filter element is fragile, so it must be handled carefully to avoid cracks that could allow pollutants to penetrate through the filter.

If you do an Internet search for ceramic filters, you are likely to encounter a lot of information about "pot" filters, which are inexpensive ceramic filters that work by gravity. They typically filter about one gallon (several liters) of water per hour. This type of filter has become important in certain poor parts of the world that have disease-ridden water supplies. You can buy fancy models for home use, but they offer no advantage in a modern home.

Ultraviolet Water Treatment

Ultraviolet water treatment kills microorganisms. It has no effect on other pollutants. Ultraviolet light attacks the same groups of organisms that are controlled by chlorine, namely, viruses, bacteria, and larger single-celled microorganisms. If your water supply is not chlorinated and if it may contain harmful microorganisms, especially smaller ones, ultraviolet water treatment is probably the best way to minimize the hazard.

Ultraviolet water treatment equipment is simple and compact. Figure 5-27 shows a typical unit. It consists of an ultraviolet lamp and a transparent sleeve around the lamp through which the water flows. The only maintenance required is replacing the lamp and cleaning the housing, typically on an annual basis. The lamp consumes as much electricity as an average light bulb.

Ultraviolet light attacks the genetic material inside the organism. Therefore, ultraviolet is effective only if the organism is small enough so that the ultraviolet can penetrate into the organism. The relative effectiveness of ultraviolet for treating the different kinds of microorganisms is about the same as for chlorine, although the mechanism of action is different.

The killing power of ultraviolet light depends on its intensity and the duration of exposure. The product of these two is called the "radiation dosage." Larger and better protected organisms require a larger dosage. Bacteria, viruses, and yeasts require the lowest radiation dosage, with some exceptions. Mold spores, fungi, and algae require a considerably higher dosage. Protozoa and nematode eggs require radiation so intense that ultraviolet treatment may not be effective.

The killing action of ultraviolet light is not absolute. A fixed fraction of the remaining live organisms are killed during successive time intervals. A tiny fraction of the organisms may always survive. For this and other reasons, there are no accepted standards for ultraviolet disinfection. Also, the manufacturer may not state the actual radiation dosage provided by the equipment.

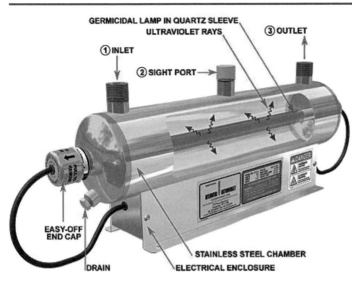

Atlantic Ultraviolet

Figure 5-27. Typical ultraviolet water treatment unit. It typically is mounted with pre-filters to keep the glass tube from being clouded by contaminants. This model is about 16" (40 cm) long.

The exposure time depends on the rate of water flow past the lamp. Therefore, most home ultraviolet water treatment is limited to the small quantities needed for drinking and cooking, and perhaps for showers. The water inlet may have a flow restrictor to slow the flow of water.

Keeping an ultraviolet unit working properly may require additional filtration. A sediment filter with a pore size of 5 microns or less usually is needed upstream of the ultraviolet unit. Its purpose is to block particles on which organisms could ride and be shielded from the radiation. Excessive hardness minerals will deposit on the transparent sleeve, so hardness should be limited to about 100 parts per million (ppm). Iron should be reduced to a concentration lower than 0.3 ppm to avoid staining the sleeve.

Activated Alumina

Activated alumina is a type of adsorption filter, somewhat similar to activated carbon. It may be desirable for some specialized applications, such as filtering arsenic and selenium from drinking water. However, it also removes fluoride.

Distillation

Distillation is a method of last resort. It removes most inorganic materials, bacteria, protozoa, and some heavy organic compounds. However, distillation is not effective for many organic compounds and some viruses. Distillation is slow and expensive. The distiller must be cleaned periodically to remove the residue from the water. Distillation generally is reserved for unusual contaminants, such as arsenic, that are difficult to remove by other means.

Acid / Alkali Treatment

If your water has unusually high or low pH, you may need to install acid or alkali treatment. Some other water treatment methods require neutral pH, or a specific range of pH, to work properly.

Other Specialized Water Treatment Methods

Some unusual situations, such as water supplies near abandoned mines, may require more specialized methods that we can't cover adequately. If you have unacceptable levels of certain unusual pollutants, such as hydrogen sulfide, you may need a treatment method that is specific for that pollutant.

If you think you need a type of water treatment that is not covered by established standards, research it thoroughly. Vendors may make wildly unrealistic claims, especially for methods that have not been well documented.

YOUR WATER PIPES

Typically, a builder routes water pipes to use the minimum amount of pipe. That's not good enough for your super-house. With a little design effort and some additional pipe, you can minimize the common annoyances of home water systems, including pressure and temperature fluctuations, delay in getting hot water to faucets, and water hammer. While you are at it, you can make your water pipes easier to repair, minimize the cost of water filtering, and minimize the risk of damage from system leaks and ruptures.

Your sophisticated pipe layout will be an innovation to your plumber, so make sure that the details are shown on your construction drawings. Be prepared to explain the reasons, so the plumber won't shortcut your design.

INSTALL THE PIPES TO BE REPLACEABLE

Contrary to intuition, the life of water pipe is only a fraction of the life of a well built house. Metal pipes corrode and plastic pipes eventually crack or disintegrate. Pipe needs repair periodically, including occasional replacement of extended lengths of the system. So, make it easy to replace the pipe. Even though you are moving into a new house, you may live long enough to be glad you did, and your heirs will admire your foresight.

Visualize how you would replace every portion of the pipe in your system. You would not want to tear open a wall or destroy an expensive floor covering to gain access to the pipe. If you must run pipe above finished ceilings and in walls, work out ways to replace the pipes without destroying the finished surfaces.

Provide access panels where pipes change direction or are connected to permanent fixtures. Design the room layout so that you can install access panels that allow long runs of pipe to be pulled out of a wall for replacement. Showers are a particularly important case, which we discussed in *Shower Rooms*, in Step 1.

Don't bury pipe in a concrete slab, because it would not be repairable. Sometimes, pipe is run through a slot in a slab to make it accessible. Don't do this either, because the slot would weaken the slab. Instead, find a way to route your pipes between ceiling joists or behind a decorative cover.

Don't install your cold water pipes alongside hot water pipes. If you do, your cold water won't be cold.

If your home will have a hydronic heating system, coordinate its pipe with your domestic water pipe. Both face the same need for periodic repair. Domestic hot water pipes can be placed alongside heating water pipes, but keep your cold water pipes away from the hot pipes.

PIPE SIZING AND LAYOUT TO AVOID INTERFERENCE BETWEEN FIXTURES

You probably had the experience of standing in a warm shower when suddenly the water pressure changes and the water gets hotter or colder. This occurs when someone else turns on a faucet, or when the clothes washer or dishwasher is operating. The cause is sloppy design of the water piping. Design your water pipes as we now recommend, and your home will be free of this annoyance.

 Eliminate annoying fluctuations in hot water temperature by using the correct pipe sizes and by routing your hot water pipes directly from the water heater to each fixture.

For cold water, use large pipes. The main pipes that carry cold water throughout the house should be the biggest. In case of doubt, make the main cold water pipes one size larger than normal. Each appliance and fixture that uses cold water should be served by a branch pipe that is one or two sizes smaller than the main pipe. This will prevent any fixture from creating an unacceptable pressure drop in other fixtures.

Use the largest pipe size to connect the water heater to the cold water supply. This will keep cold water fixtures from sapping the pressure in the hot water pipes.

In houses of average size, use pipe with an inside diameter of ¾" (19 mm) for the main cold water distribution. Use pipe with an inside diameter of ½" (12 mm) for branches that serve individual fixtures. In a large house, increase the size of the main cold water distribution pipe to 1" (25 mm).

For hot water, size the pipes and lay them out following a different set of rules. You need separate sets of pipes for hot water, depending on the application.

For fixtures and appliances where delay in getting hot water is undesirable – especially wash basins, kitchen sinks, and the dishwasher – run a separate hot water pipe to each of these fixtures directly from the water heater, keeping the pipe as short as possible. Using separate pipes for each fixture eliminates interference between different fixtures.

Make each of these pipes the smallest practical size, typically ½" (13 mm) or less. This will minimize the delay in getting hot water to the fixture. Smaller pipes accumulate less cooled water that has to be pushed out of the way before the hot water gets through. Before you lay out these pipes, refer to the other methods of reducing hot water delay that we covered previously under the heading, *Minimize Hot Water Delay*.

For fixtures and appliances that use hot water in large batches – such as the washing machine, bathtubs, and deep sinks used for filling buckets – lay out the hot water pipes like your cold water pipes. Use a large main pipe from the water heater with appropriately sized branches for the individual appliances. Make the branch pipes large enough so they don't delay filling the appliances.

PIPE LAYOUT FOR ECONOMICAL WATER FILTERING

The cost of water treatment filters and chemicals is proportional to the amount of water that you treat. For economy, arrange your water system so that each filter or treatment device is limited to the part of the water system that needs it.

Make all water treatment equipment easily accessible, and provide nearby storage for spare cartridges and other materials.

PREVENT WATER HAMMER

Water has mass, so it has kinetic energy when it flows. If you close a faucet quickly, the water comes to an abrupt stop, like a hammer hitting a nail. The great force of the abrupt stop is applied against the faucet and against the piping system upstream of the faucet. This force hammers water pipe and fittings that are attached loosely, making a noise. The hammering may also damage valves and create leaks.

Even if the occupants learn to close faucets slowly, washing machines and dishwashers have automatic valves that stop large volumes of water abruptly. When these appliances operate, you will get water hammer unless you take steps to prevent it.

Pipe movement is what causes most of the noise of water hammer. Visualize what happens to the water in a long, straight section of pipe when a downstream valve closes abruptly. The water in the straight section has a lot of mass, like a hammer head. When the valve closes, the moving water has no place to go. Its inertia wants of make it continue straight ahead. If the pipe is loose, it will move in the direction of flow. The pipe itself will jolt, and it may bang into a part of the house structure.

The general solution is to secure water pipe very snugly. The trick is to butt the ***downstream*** elbows of long pipe sections tightly against a strong part of

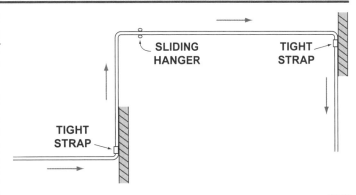

DRW

Figure 5-28. How to secure pipes to prevent water hammer. Tightly secure the downstream elbows of long pipe sections against the structure. But, between these tight attachments, loosely support a section of pipe that has a bend. The bend allows for thermal expansion and contraction.

the structure, such as a floor joist. Figure 5-28 shows the method. Use a pipe strap to hold the elbow firmly against the support. If no such part of the structure is available, attach a wood block to the structure to support the elbow.

However, you can't secure each pipe section rigidly. Between the rigid attachments, you need to have a loose section of pipe that includes a bend. The bend allows the pipe to expand and contract as the water temperature changes. Typically, this section of pipe is supported by a U-shaped hanger that is attached to a joist above the pipe.

Now that you have kept the pipe from hammering, you still have to get rid of the kinetic energy of the water. Otherwise, it will still make noise and cause

Sioux Chief

Figure 5-29. A pair of water hammer buffers installed at the hose connections to a washing machine.

damage by hammering the valves. There is a standard method of doing this, which is to install an energy absorbing buffer in the water line immediately ahead of the appliance or fixture that has valves.

The buffer is a vertical stub of pipe, as in Figure 5-29. A bubble of air is trapped in the top of the buffer. When the valve closes, the water diverts into the stub, compressing the air instead of hammering the valve. The air bubble is isolated from the water by an internal piston or diaphragm, so that the air will not dissolve into the water.

Buffers are most useful for the washing machine and the dishwasher, which have automatic valves that close abruptly. They are also advisable for manual faucets that may be slammed shut by ham-fisted occupants.

It is easy to install buffers for appliances that are connected to the house water system by removable hoses. To install buffers ahead of other valves or faucets, create removable connections for them in the water pipes.

SHOULD YOU INSULATE HOT WATER PIPES?

Contrary to intuition, it is probably uneconomical to insulate your hot water pipes. Hot water flows to each appliance for only a brief period of time, and the pipes cool quickly when the flow stops. This is because the pipes have a surface area that is large compared to their volume. No practical amount of insulation can keep your hot water pipes warm between periods of use.

If you have a conventional water heater, insulate the short sections of cold water inlet pipe and hot water discharge pipe at the top of the heater, as in Figure 5-17. This minimizes heat loss from these short pipes that is caused by convection from the tank.

There is one situation that requires insulation of all the hot water pipes. If you install a recirculating hot water system, the pipes will be warm continuously, so you should insulate them. Insulate both the supply pipes and the small recirculation pipes.

Where pipe needs to be insulated, use preformed foam insulation that is sized exactly for the pipe. Get the highest R-value that is available. Place the split in the insulation at the bottom of the pipe. Tape the joints in the insulation with long-lasting tape that is made for the purpose.

THE MAIN WATER VALVE

Your home's water system is connected to a public water system or to a well that can pump an unlimited supply of water into your home at high pressure. This makes your home vulnerable to flooding from a leak anywhere in your water system. Even a small leak may cause serious damage. If a leak occurs while the house is vacant for an extended period, the flooding can be catastrophic.

Leaks can occur in many places, including loose faucet packings, leaky gaskets, cracks in appliance hoses, pinhole corrosion of metal water pipes, and failure of plastic pipe and fittings. Freezing can break any pipe, valve, or appliance.

The main defense against damage from a leaking or ruptured water system is the valve where the water supply enters the house. It is one of your most important safety features. It is also needed for repairs to the water system.

Install the valve so that it is highly visible and readily accessible in an emergency. Install it close to the point where the water supply enters through the basement wall or through the floor slab.

Select a valve that closes in a quarter turn, rather than a conventional "globe" valve. A quarter-turn valve is easy to use, and it is less prone to leakage and breakage. Select the best quality available, because replacing it will be expensive.

To keep the main water valve from leaking, turn it from fully open to fully closed at least monthly. A leaky main water valve has limited value as a safety device, and it cannot shut off water when repairs are needed in the water system. All valves become leaky if they are not used regularly. This is because contaminants in the water supply create rough deposits on the sealing surfaces of the valve if they are not wiped off periodically by using the valve.

Make it a habit to close the main water valve whenever the house is vacated overnight. Install a permanent sign at the valve as a reminder. Include a reminder to turn off the water heater at the same time.

FREEZE PROTECTION FOR YOUR HOME WATER SYSTEM

If any part of the system that contains water can fall below freezing temperature, freezing becomes a catastrophic flooding hazard. The solution is to make sure that no part of the system is exposed to freezing temperature while it contains water. Let's look at each part of your water system, and use the appropriate protective measures.

Freeze Protection for the Water Supply Pipes

Your house water system starts either at the underground public water supply main or at a well. From that point, keep all your exterior water pipe buried well below the "frost line," which is the deepest level at which the soil freezes. Leave plenty of safety margin. The "frost line" is only an estimate based on past experience. If the climate becomes colder, frost will go deeper.

If your house has a basement, bring the water supply pipe into the basement at a safe distance below the frost line. Bring the incoming supply pipe directly into the warm interior. Don't route the incoming pipe along the foundation wall or along the rim joists.

(Figure 3-114, in Step 3, shows the incoming water pipe incorrectly installed along the foundation wall. It was later enclosed inside a framework that was erected to hold wall insulation. In this location, the pipe is not protected against freezing temperature. Instead, the pipe should have been extended inward, to the warm side of the insulation.)

If the house is built on a slab on grade, bring the water supply pipe up through the slab at a safe distance inside the edge of the slab. During cold weather, the soil around the perimeter will be much colder than the soil under the center of the slab.

Freeze Protection for the Inside Water System

Inside the house, route your water pipes away from the exterior walls, so that a local cold spot in the wall will not cause the pipe to freeze during extremely cold weather. Don't route any domestic water pipes through unheated or poorly insulated spaces, such as a garage.

In a well insulated house, the water pipes inside the house are well protected from freezing as long as the house is operating on a normal schedule. But, even in a super-insulated house, freezing of your water system is a danger if you turn off the heat when the house is vacated during cold weather. The big question is how to protect your water system reliably and without wasting energy. The answer depends on the climate and how long the house will be vacant.

If the climate can linger well below freezing temperature while the house is vacant, draining your water system is the only reliable method of freeze protection. In that case, plan your water system to make it easy to drain. The main requirements are a system shutoff valve that is located where it cannot freeze and a sewer connection at the low points of the cold and hot water systems.

A basement sink is fine for draining the system if all the water lines are installed higher than the sink. However, the main water inlet is likely to be below the sink.

If your house does not have a basement, install a drain valve immediately after the main water valve, along with an adjacent sewer drain. Put all this plumbing in a pocket below the slab, under a removable cover. This will allow you to drain the entire water system completely. This is an unusual feature, so have it drawn clearly in your construction drawings. Your plumber needs to communicate with the contractor who installs the floor slab to get this feature installed properly.

To drain the water heater, you will need an accessible drain that is located below the heater. To make this easy, install a deep, bowl shaped floor drain with a removable cover right at the heater, where it is easily accessible with a short hose from the water heater drain faucet. This is an unusual feature, so make sure that it is included in your construction drawings.

This water heater drain has other benefits. You should drain your water heater periodically to get rid of scale and other trash that accumulates at the bottom of the tank. This is messy, so people usually don't do it. If you design your water heater drain properly, the job is easy. Also, the floor drain protects the floor if the water heater or some other appliance leaks.

■ Don't Rely on the Home Heating System

Don't trust your home heating system to provide freeze protection. It won't be available if the energy supply to the house is disrupted. Winter snowstorms cause trees to fall over power lines, and hard freezes cause gas pipelines to burst. And, your heating system may fail for other reasons.

■ Don't Rely on Natural Heat

When you turn off all the heating equipment in a house, the house continues to be warmed by three heat sources: heat that is stored in the structure, solar heating through windows, and heat that rises from the earth below the house.

Can you rely on these heat sources for freeze protection? Probably not. Most of the heat that is stored in the aboveground structure will be gone within a few days, even with the best insulation. You can't rely on solar heat because winter nights are long and the daytime sunlight through an overcast sky is feeble. Anyway, an unoccupied house will have the window shades closed.

So, how about the heat that percolates up from the core of the earth? The earth temperature depends on the location. See Figure 3-111, in Step 3. In temperate climates, if the entire footprint of the house has full contact with the ground, heat from below may provide adequate protection from freezing.

On the other hand, if the deep soil temperature is below about 45 °F (7 °C), as in much of southern Canada, the margin above freezing temperature is too small to provide reliable protection. Furthermore, cold air from the upper part of a vacant house will fall to the lowest part of the house, offsetting the soil heat.

Freeze Protection for Outside Taps

Outside water faucets are directly exposed to outdoor freezing temperatures, so they need special protection. Connect each outside faucet through an isolation valve that is located within the warm part of the house. Before the start of the freezing season, close the isolation valves and crack open the outside faucets to drain them.

Install each isolation valve somewhat higher than the outside faucet, so that water in the pipe leading to the tap will drain toward the outside. Install the isolation valve at least one or two feet (about half a meter) inside the wall. This keeps the isolation valve warm enough so that it does not freeze.

Install each isolation valve where it is visible and convenient to reach, not hidden above ducts and other clutter. Mark each valve with a tag that reminds you to close the isolation valve. Drain the outside taps at the beginning of the cold season, and leave them slightly open.

Even a small air leak around the pipe where it passes through the wall may freeze adjacent pipe. Fill the gap between the pipe and the hole with durable caulking material, starting from the outside of the wall.

You can buy insulating covers for outside faucets, but they are useless. Even if they could seal tightly against the wall of the house, the temperature of the tap and the surrounding wall will quickly equalize with the outside air temperature.

Freeze Protection for Pipes in Crawl Spaces

If your house is built entirely over a crawl space, the water supply pipe must rise from underground and pass through the crawl space. Similarly, the sewer pipes must descend through the crawl space. If the weather can linger below freezing temperature, protecting the pipes in the crawl space is a challenge. The construction industry does not have a standard way of doing it reliably.

As a minimum, the pipes in the crawl space need good insulation that is sealed to prevent any outside air leaks from reaching the pipes. The insulation should extend up into the heated portion of the house and down to the frost depth in the soil. The pipes should be encased in adequate amount of foam insulation, and the insulation should have an enclosure that protects the foam from nibbling rodents and other hazards. If radon is a local hazard, the enclosure should be completely

Danfoss

Figure 5-30. Electrical heat tracing. This is an electric heating element in the form of a cable, designed to be strapped to pipe for freeze protection.

sealed by the foam insulation, so that it does not act as an entry for radon.

The degree of protection that you need depends on the climate. If freezing temperatures do not linger, insulation alone may suffice. However, if the climate has an extended cold season, you need more protection, especially for times when the house is vacated.

The only fully reliable way to avoid pipe freezing in the crawl space is to drain the water pipes down to the frost line. This requires a specialized remote valve that is located below the frost depth. The valve includes a mechanism for sucking or blowing the water out of the lines above the valve. And, the whole apparatus needs to be accessible for repair. Such an installation requires a skilled plumber who is familiar with the equipment.

"Heat tracing" is a another method of freeze protection. This is electrical heating cable that is strapped directly to exposed pipe and valves, as in Figure 5-30. The heat tracing must extend from the frost depth to the inside of the house. The pipe insulation is installed over the heat tracing, so it does not require much energy.

To avoid unnecessary operation of the heat tracing, control it thermostatically. Manufacturers of heat tracing offer various ways of doing this.

The weakness of heat tracing is that it requires a reliable electricity supply. If the electric lines are knocked down during a winter storm, heat tracing ceases to protect.

Various authorities, including some water utilities, recommend keeping the water running at a trickle to prevent freezing. Ignore such advice. It wastes a large amount of water, it wears out the faucet, and it risks flooding your home if the drain line freezes. It also requires you to keep your main water valve open, but the main valve should be closed whenever you vacate the house.

STEP 6

IDEAL LIGHTING = THE BEST LAMPS FOR EACH APPLICATION
+ THE BEST FIXTURES FOR EACH APPLICATION
+ EFFICIENT AND COMFORTABLE LIGHTING LAYOUT
+ EFFICIENT AND CONVENIENT CONTROLS

We will follow this "formula" to organize our discussion of Step 6. Good lighting is one of the most desirable features of a home. It enhances enjoyment of your activities, while poor lighting is annoying and may limit your activities. So, we will optimize the visual quality of your lighting, which means that you will be able to see well without eye strain. At the same time, we will achieve the best possible energy efficiency.

Your home depends on two kinds of lighting – daylighting and artificial lighting. We made daylighting an integral part of your home's layout in Step 2. Sunlight should be your prime lighting source during the daytime. But, parts of your home will need artificial lighting to supplement daylighting. At night, of course, you depend entirely on artificial lighting.

Your lighting design can be very creative. Lighting requirements throughout the home are diverse, and you have a vast selection of lighting equipment. You will base your design on a solid understanding of lighting principles, which you will apply to each of your rooms and activities individually.

If you are upgrading the lighting of an existing house, follow the recommendations in this Step. It is easy to replace fixtures that are installed on existing mounting boxes. If you are redecorating, select your color scheme to maximize energy efficiency and lighting quality, as we will explain.

"Scene"

Here's an important new lighting term. We will use the word "scene" to mean the area that you want to see, and that needs good illumination. The scene could be the book you are reading, or the hobby project on your workbench, or the decor of an entire room. A key to ideal lighting is to *design your lighting appropriately for each scene*.

HOW VISION WORKS

The goal of lighting is to enable you to see as well as possible. This includes the ability to see details, and to do so without discomfort, such as "eye strain." To guide your design toward this goal, let's spend a few moments to understand how human vision responds to lighting.

BRIGHTNESS, SIZE, AND CONTRAST

The most basic requirement for vision is adequate light intensity. The lens in the front of the eye focuses the light from the scene on a carpet of retinal cells located at the back of the eye. In order to see, there must be enough light coming from the scene to stimulate the retinal cells.

The amount of light coming from a scene is called its "brightness." Technically, brightness is the amount of light energy that is emitted per unit of surface area. The brightness of most scenes is determined by the amount of light that shines on the scene from the sun or from lamps. However, the brightness of some objects is determined by light that they emit themselves, as with television, computer screens, and campfires.

Increasing brightness increases your ability to see small details and small differences in color. That is why tailors, engravers, and surgeons work under high lighting intensities. Up to a point, your ability to see details increases rapidly with increasing brightness. But, beyond that point, your ability to see details increases slowly and the brightness will make you uncomfortable. After a period of exposure to excessive brightness, you will suffer "eye strain" and perhaps get a headache.

The size of details is a major factor in your ability to see, especially in dim light. If you try to read a newspaper by moonlight, you may be able to read the headlines, but probably not the small type.

Contrast is also a major factor in your ability to see. Contrast is a difference in brightness (the intensity of light) or a difference in color (the wavelength of light)

between adjacent parts of a scene. Scenes with higher contrast requires less light than scenes with lower contrast. Under dim light, black ink is easier to read on white paper than pastel ink. Similarly, it is difficult to view a photograph in dim light because much of the information consists of small differences in brightness or color.

Generally, you can't change the size or contrast of the things that you want to see. What you can control is brightness. So, design your lighting to provide sufficient brightness for the activities.

The amount of light that you need to see well increases during adulthood. Above the age of 60, the need for more light increases rapidly. Select your lamps and fixtures to provide the option of increased light for older occupants.

SHADOWS WITHIN THE SCENE

An object creates shadows that help you to perceive its size and shape. This is especially useful for seeing small objects against a background. For example, your ability to see threads in a piece of fabric comes from the small shadows cast by the threads. In fabric of a single color, you are seeing mostly the shadows of the threads, rather than the threads themselves. Although you are not aware of such small shadows, they create "texture" in the scene.

Lighting that accentuates the sharpness of shadows within a scene is called "harsh." Harsh lighting is created by small, concentrated light sources. The contrast is increased by illuminating the surfaces at a grazing angle, which lengthens the shadows. Metal engraving is an extreme example. The shadows within the cut surface make it possible for the engraver to see his work.

Lighting that subdues shadows in surfaces is called "soft." Most home lighting should be fairly soft. Soft lighting is created by light that comes from a large area, so that the shadows do not have distinct edges. For example, formal table lamps have large translucent shades to soften their lighting.

COLOR VISION

The sun emits radiation over a broad band of wavelengths. However, the sunlight that humans can see consists of a fairly narrow band of these wavelengths, which is called the "visible spectrum."* Within the visible spectrum, sunlight contains a fairly uniform distribution of light energy, as you can in Figure 2-1, in Step 2.

The perception of "color" is the ability of your eyes to distinguish between the wavelengths within this narrow band. This ability is the most interesting aspect of vision. Human beings share this ability with many insects, birds, and fish. However, many higher animals cannot distinguish colors, or they have only limited ability to see colors. Defects in color vision are fairly common among humans, but usually are limited to inability to distinguish certain specific colors.

"Cone" Cells for Color, "Rod" Cells at Night

The retina of your eye has two types of cells that sense light. These are called "cone" cells and "rods" cells because of their different shapes.

The cone cells make it possible to see colors. There are three kinds of cone cells. One kind has a peak response to yellow light, another kind to green light, and a third to blue light. The type of cone cell that responds mainly to blue wavelengths is weaker than the cone cells that peak at green and yellow. Figure 6-1 shows the response of the three types of cone cells to different wavelengths of light.

Your brain compares the response of the three types of cone cells to light that enters the eye and deduces its color from that. For example, a green light source stimulates the green-sensing cone cells more strongly than it stimulates the yellow-sensing cells, and it stimulates the blue-sensing cells only weakly. From this, the brain infers that the incoming light is green. (People who are "colorblind" generally have a deficiency in one or more of the three types of cone cells.)

Cone cells respond strongly to daylight and to normal indoor lighting, and they remain somewhat sensitive during darker twilight. But, they shut down almost completely under low nighttime light levels.

In addition to revealing colors, cone cells also allow you to see finer detail, such as you need for reading. This is because the cone cells are clustered densely near the center of your visual field. Therefore, if you are outside at early dawn, you will start to see color and you will start to be able to read at about the same time.

The rod cells enable you to see at night. They sense only light intensity, not color. But, they are much more sensitive than the cone cells. When you look at an outdoor scene that is illuminated by moonlight, only your rod cells are working. Because rod cells cannot sense differences in color, you see the world at night as black-and-white.

The "visible spectrum" is actually the sum of four separate spectra, one for each type of cone cell and one for rod cells. Together, the cone cells cover the entire visual spectrum, as shown Figure 6-1.

The rod cell response curve has approximately the same shape as the green or yellow response curves shown in Figure 6-1, but it is about 100 times more sensitive. Also, it is shifted further toward the blue colors, peaking at a wavelength toward the blue side of green. Rod cells do not respond to red colors. Therefore, anything red will appear jet black at night.

Our eyes do not have the same sensitivity for all colors. The eye is most sensitive to colors near the center of the visible spectrum. Greater light intensity is needed to reveal colors toward the blue and red ends of the spectrum. For this reason, you can see green objects in dimmer light than you can see red or blue objects.

Artificial lighting inside houses is much dimmer than direct sunlight. Typical room lighting is only a fraction of one percent of the intensity of direct sunlight. For this reason, if your decor depends on colors that lie toward the red and/or blue ends of the visible spectrum, select lamps that emit those colors strongly. Otherwise, you will need to increase the overall brightness of your lighting.

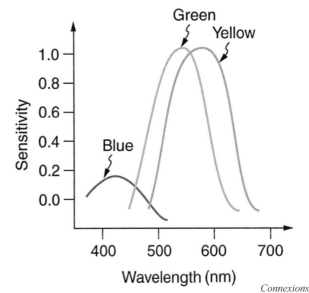

Connexions

Figure 6-1. The three types of human cone cells have their peak sensitivity at different wavelengths. This is what makes color vision possible.

---

* Light that is visible to humans lies in the narrow band of wavelengths between approximately 0.0004 and 0.0007 millimeters (0.4 and 0.7 microns). This band lies within the short wavelength end of the solar spectrum, where solar intensity is greatest. Within this range, the intensity of sunlight is fairly constant. Birds and insects can see shorter wavelengths than humans, into the ultraviolet range.

Two Ways to See Colors

The brain senses color by comparing the differences in light stimulation of the three different kinds of cone cells. For example, the color green is a specific wavelength in the visible spectrum. If you see a wavelength that is actually green, as in a rainbow, your brain will sense "green" because this wavelength stimulates the three types of cone cells in your eyes in a certain ratio.

However, there is another way to see "green," which is to see a combination of true blue light and true yellow light. This combination stimulates the cone cells in about the same ratio as true green light. Therefore, your brain is tricked into thinking that the combination of colors is "green." For example, if you mark a piece of paper with a blue highlighter pen and then mark over it with a yellow pen, you will see the illusion of "green" where the ink overlaps. The wavelength of true green is not really there.

This trick is used in many places to create the illusion of a wide spectrum of colors by using tiny dots of only three "primary" colors. For example, most color pictures in a book are printed by using dots of the three colors: cyan (blue-green), magenta (red-purple), and yellow. You can see the dots in the color photographs in this book by using a strong magnifying glass. A different combination of three primary colors – red, green, and blue – is used by most light emitting screens, such as television and computer monitors.

How Lamps Display Colors

Because sunlight has approximately equal intensity across the visible spectrum, it brings out all visible colors in a fairly uniform way. However, all the existing kinds of lamps have a very unbalanced or irregular distribution of colors. Light from incandescent lamps has strong output at the red end of the spectrum and weak output toward the blue end. Most of the other kinds of electric light have a spiky wavelength distribution, with strong output in one or more narrow bands of wavelengths.

The colors that you see in a scene depend on the colors that are emitted by the lamp. If an object has a particular color, you won't see that color unless the light from the lamp contains that same color. Figures 6-3 and 6-4 show how one object appears to have radically different color when illuminated by two common types of home lighting.

So, to achieve a good rendering of color along with energy efficiency, you need to match the color characteristics of the lamps to the decor. Lamps have two ratings that allow you to judge their color characteristics, the "color rendering index" (CRI) and the "color temperature." Both are explained in the *Lamp Selection Guide*, which follows.

The human brain strongly compensates vision to make colors seem right. The two previous photographs show adjacent bathrooms in the author's home, which both have the same wall colors. When standing inside either bathroom, the colors look normal. However, there is a doorway between the two bathrooms that makes it is possible to view both rooms simultaneously. A viewer is then able to see the strong contrast between the room colors that is caused by the differences in their lighting.

An interesting fact is that people see differences in color much more noticeably in photographs than by direct vision, as you can see by comparing Figures 6-3 and 6-4. For this reason, it is necessary to adjust your camera for the kind to lighting to make your pictures look realistic.

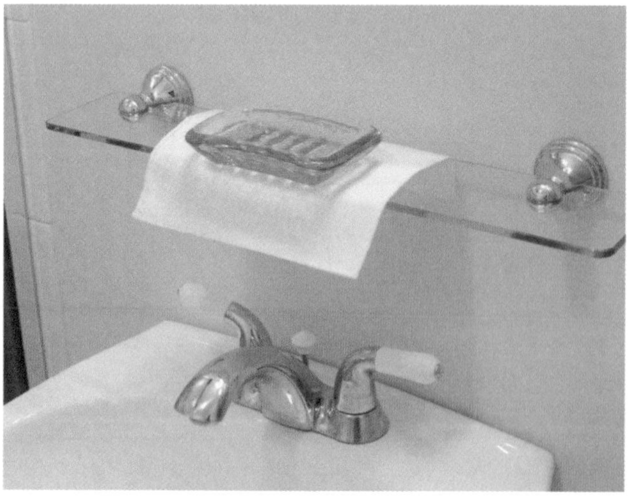

DRW

Figure 6-3. This glass soap dish is placed in a bathroom that uses incandescent light. The glass contains several metallic dyes. The incandescent light illuminates mainly the dyes that reflect a rosy tint. The incandescent light also gives the walls a "warm" appearance.

DRW

Figure 6-4. The same soap dish in a bathroom that uses fluorescent light, which illuminates mainly the dyes in the glass that reflect a blue tint. The fluorescent light also gives the walls a "cool" or bluish appearance. The wall paint is the same in both rooms.

YOUR LAMP CHOICES

There are four main types of lamps that apply to homes: *incandescent*, *LED*, *fluorescent*, and *high-intensity discharge (HID)*. Each type has important sub-types.

The lighting industry has established a variety of lamp ratings that tell you most of what you need to know about each type. These ratings are explained in the adjacent *Lamp Selection Guide*.

A different set of ratings applies to each type of lamp. The ratings that interest you the most are usually printed on the package. For example, the packages of ordinary incandescent bulbs usually state their wattage, light output, and service life. The packages of fluorescent tubes typically state their wattage, their color characteristics, and the type of starter that they need to operate properly.

For less common information, such as operating temperature limits, you need to look into the catalogs of lamp manufacturers and large dealers, which should be available on the Internet. However, that probably won't be necessary. The information that we give you here will allow you to select your lighting equipment adequately.

Now, let's get to know each type of lighting. To avoid confusion, we will say "lamp" when we mean the actual bulb that generates the light, and we will say "fixture" for the appliance that holds one or more bulbs. However, especially with incandescent lighting, it is common to use the word "lamp" to mean a fixture.*

INCANDESCENT LIGHTING

Incandescent lighting is the oldest and simplest kind of indoor electric lighting. It consists of a conducting filament that is heated by an electric current to make it glow brightly. The filament is surrounded by a glass bulb from which the air has been removed. The vacuum surrounding the filament keeps it from oxidizing and breaking, and it also insulates the filament against heat loss.

Incandescent lighting is the least energy efficient form of electric lighting, by far. And, the life of incandescent lamps is the shortest, by far. Nonetheless, incandescent lighting continues to be popular for homes because it offers several important advantages. Both the lamps and the fixtures can be inexpensive. The lamps are available in an amazing variety, suitable for many styles of lighting. They operate in all weather

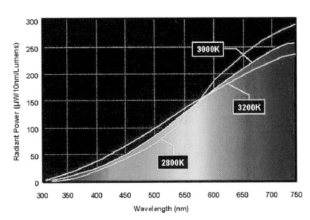

Figure 6-5. The color spectrum of an incandescent lamp. All visible colors are emitted, but the output from the red end of the spectrum is much stronger than from the blue end. The temperature of the lamp filament determines the color spectrum, with a hotter filament producing more of the blue-end colors. This is the basis of the "color temperature" rating of lamps.

conditions. Most lamps are interchangeable because they use a single style of socket, called a "medium screw base." Their light output can be adjusted over a wide range with inexpensive dimmers.

Most of these advantages can now be replicated by LED lamps, which avoid the poor energy efficiency and short life of incandescent lamps. However, at this time, LED lamps are much more expensive than incandescent lamps, and not all LED lamps can use the same inexpensive dimmers.

Incandescent lighting retains one big advantage: it illuminates all visible colors, with little discrimination between similar colors. The frequency spectrum of incandescent lamps is continuous across the entire visible spectrum, as shown in Figure 6-5. This guarantees that all colors in a scene will be revealed. However, the intensity of light output is heavily skewed toward the red end of the spectrum, with much weaker emission of light toward the blue end of the spectrum.

The slender filament of an incandescent lamp is intensely bright, much too bright to be seen without intolerable glare. To avoid the glare of the filament, most incandescent lamps have frosted bulbs, so that the bulb surface becomes the light source. However, even frosted bulbs are intensely bright. Therefore, fixtures for formal incandescent lighting, such as "table lamps," commonly use diffusing shades to increase the surface area of the light source. However, the shades absorb a substantial fraction of the light, further reducing the overall efficiency of incandescent lighting.

---

* Lighting professionals invented the word "luminaire" to explicitly indicate a "lighting fixture." This fussy language is unnecessary, so we won't use it.

LAMP SELECTION GUIDE

☐ Lumen Output

A "lumen" is the unit of visible light energy that a lamp produces. The lumen rating is the total light output of the lamp, regardless of direction. It applies to the lamp when it is new.

The lumen output of all lamps declines steadily during operation. However, the rate and amount of this "lumen degradation" varies widely. For example, conventional incandescent bulbs have rapid lumen loss, but halogen incandescent lamps have relatively slow lumen loss.

☐ Wattage

The "watt" is the basic unit of electrical power, which means it is the rate at which you put energy into the lamp. The wattage determines your energy cost.

☐ Energy Efficiency (Lumens per Watt)

Since the lumen rating tells you the light output and the wattage rating tells you the energy input, the energy efficiency of lighting is expressed as "lumens per watt." The lamp package or lighting catalog probably will not give you this figure. To get it, simply divide the "lumens" rating by the "watts" rating.

In addition to the energy used by the lamps themselves, the ballasts needed by fluorescent and HID lighting absorb energy. The lamp wattage ratings do not include the ballast energy loss, except for screw-in fluorescent fixtures.

Incandescent lighting has the lowest energy efficiency, by far. For indoor lighting, LED's and long-tube fluorescent lighting offer the highest efficiency. Compact fluorescent lamps have about half the efficiency of the best conventional fluorescent lighting.

For outdoor HID lighting, metal halide offers the highest efficiency. Other types of HID lighting have efficiencies in the same broad range as fluorescent lighting.

☐ Lamp Life

For most lamps, the package and catalog will list the lamp life in hours. This is an average, and you should take it with a grain of salt. Cheap lamps may last only a small fraction of their claimed life.

Conventional fluorescent lamps claim lives of 10,000 to 20,000 hours. The lives of HID lamps fall within the same range. Compact fluorescent lamps claim about half that range.

Conventional incandescent lamps typically last less than 1,000 hours. Halogen incandescent lamps may last twice as long.

LED lamps claim lives that are longer than for any other type, but it is too early to tell whether the claims are true. LED lamp life is sensitive to operating temperature, so it is essential for an LED fixture to provide good cooling for the lamps.

☐ Light Distribution Pattern

Information about the light distribution pattern of most lamps is not available. You have to judge it yourself by examining the lamp, and this can be tricky. Any light source that is approximately spherical, such as a frosted light bulb, emits light fairly uniformly in all directions. Any light source that is long in relation to its diameter, such as a straight fluorescent tube, emits light most strongly in a direction perpendicular to its axis.

With clear incandescent bulbs, the direction of light emission is determined by the shape of the filament. Some filament shapes emit light in very non-uniform patterns.

With HID lamps, the arc that emits the light is long and narrow, so that most light is emitted perpendicular to the axis of the lamp.

In most cases, the fixture in which the lamp is mounted will have a dominant effect on the light distribution pattern. To get efficient light distribution, the fixture should match the light emission pattern of the lamp.

Lamps with aiming reflectors, such as "PAR" (for "parabolic") lamps, emit light in a beam. "Spotlights" have a relatively narrow beam, and "floodlights" have a broad beam.

An LED lamp generally has a tiny lens that creates a relatively narrow beam. LED's are made in a variety of beam widths. To get broader light distribution, a fixture may use LED's that are aimed in different directions, or it may use an external lens to shape the beam.

☐ Candlepower

A "candlepower" rating is used only for lamps that are intended to create a beam. Such lamps usually have built-in reflectors or lenses. The candlepower is the intensity of light at the center of the beam. Most lamps for your home will not have a candlepower rating. An exception might be floodlights for outdoor use and lamps that provide accent lighting for small decorative objects.

LAMP SELECTION GUIDE

☐ Color Rendering

Human beings evolved to see colors with illumination provided by sunlight, so an ideal lamp would have the same light spectrum as sunlight, which contains all visible colors at almost equal intensity. However, there is no contemporary kind of lamp that provides such uniform illumination across the color spectrum. Furthermore, there are big differences in the color distribution of different kinds of lamps, as you can see in the light output spectra that are shown where we discuss the various lamp types.

The key point is this: in order for a lamp to reveal a particular color in a scene, the lamp must emit light of exactly that same color. If a lamp has an irregular pattern of light energy, it will reveal some colors well, and others poorly. For example, it will make a colorful plaid fabric look unbalanced and murky.

To indicate the ability of a lamp to bring out the full range of colors, the lighting industry invented a rating called the "color rendering index" ("CRI"). The CRI is a number between 0 and 100, with 100 being the best color rendering. Lamp packages usually do not list the CRI, so you have to get it from professional lighting catalogs, which major manufacturers publish on the Internet. Catalogs give CRI ratings for most fluorescent and HID lamps, but not for incandescent lamps. This is because the CRI rating of incandescent lamps is generally considered to be 100.

For your formal living spaces and anywhere that colors are important, select lamps that have a fairly high CRI. Color rendering may be less important in informal spaces, such as the garage and workshop, and for security lighting. However, don't get any lamps that have a poor CRI. They make it difficult to see, and they cause eye strain.

The CRI is an imperfect rating system, especially for comparing incandescent lighting to other types. Although the CRI of incandescent lamps is generally considered to be 100, the spectrum of incandescent lamps is tilted strongly toward the red end of the spectrum, unlike sunlight. Therefore, incandescent lamps show reddish colors much better than bluish colors, unless the scene is brightly lighted.

☐ Color Temperature

Back in the days when all indoor lighting was incandescent, the industry invented "color temperature" as a way of describing the color spectrum of lamps. As the filament of an incandescent lamp gets hotter, more of the light output spreads into the blue end of the spectrum. In incandescent lamps, this improves overall color rendering.

(Decorators and lighting professionals confuse the issue by describing reddish colors as "warm" and bluish colors as "cool," which is just the opposite of the color temperature.)

Today, color temperature is also used for fluorescent and HID lamps. These have light emission in irregular peaks, so color temperature is used to indicate the average wavelength of the light output. For such lamps, the color temperature does not indicate overall color rendering.

With LED lamps, color temperature works differently. At present, the best color rendering is achieved by starting with a blue LED and coating it with a phosphor to spread the color spectrum toward the red end of the spectrum. The more spreading, the better the color rendering. At the same time, the color temperature is lowered. Thus, *for LED's, lower color temperature implies better color rendering*. This is not true for other kinds of lamps.

Color temperature is listed as "kelvins" (abbreviated as "K"), which is the metric unit of absolute temperature. Some lamps list the color temperature on the package. For others, you need to look in a lamp catalog.

Ironically, ordinary incandescent lamps usually do not have a color temperature rating. This is because most incandescent lamps operate near the maximum temperature that the filament can tolerate. Color temperature is stated for specialized incandescent lamps that are used for photography, display lighting, and other applications where color is critical.

LAMP SELECTION GUIDE

☐ Outdoor Operating Temperature

Incandescent, LED, and HID lamps are not affected by normal outdoor temperatures. Older conventional fluorescent lamps operate properly only at indoor temperatures. Compact fluorescent lamps and some newer long-tube lamps may operate at cool outdoor temperatures, typically down to freezing temperature, but at reduced efficiency.

☐ Starting Delay

Incandescent and LED lamps reach full brightness instantly. However, the power converter used by some LED's may create a short starting delay, typically less than one second.

Conventional fluorescent lighting approaches full brightness within one or two seconds.

Most compact fluorescent lamps today are designed in a way that creates an annoying delay in reaching full brightness. This makes them inappropriate for applications that need full brightness immediately, such as lighting that is operated by a motion sensor. When operating in cooler environments, the initial brightness of the lamp is very low, and the delay in reaching full brightness may be several minutes.

All types of HID lamps have a very long delay in reaching normal brightness, typically 3 to 10 minutes. Thus, they should not be used for applications where you need light quickly. (Some special HID lamps start more quickly, but they are very inefficient.)

☐ Special Applications

If you get a big lamp catalog, it's fun to browse and discover the vast variety of lamps that are available. But, avoid selecting fixtures that require unusual lamps. In the future, the lamps may become unavailable or very expensive.

Incandescent lamps offer a cornucopia of sizes, shapes, light distribution patterns, colors, and other features. Many styles are created for decoration, such as flame-shaped bulbs for chandeliers. Others are more technical, such as an incandescent bulb with a filament shape that avoids darkening the bulb when the base is inserted upward. Low-voltage reflector lamps provide bright light, sharp focusing, and extended life. And so forth.

Fluorescent and HID lamps are available in a growing variety of sizes and shapes. This is a mixed blessing, because each type of lamp must be matched to a particular socket and ballast type. At the time this is written, there is no standardization for LED lamps or fixtures. One exception is LED fixtures that are designed to fit in standard incandescent bulb bases.

☐ Equipment Quality

There are huge differences in the quality of lamps. Good lamps last much longer than bad ones. They are more energy efficient. Their light output is better. And, they are less likely to create electrical interference and start fires.

Unfortunately, the lamp market is flooded with inferior products. To avoid trouble, buy only well established brands. All lamp manufacturers tend to exaggerate their ratings, especially for life and light output, but the major manufacturers stay closer to the truth. Pay the extra price for the best brands.

Tungsten Halogen Lamps

"Tungsten halogen" lamps are an improved version of incandescent lamps that allow the tungsten filament to survive at higher temperatures. The higher temperature provides better energy efficiency and improved light output at the blue end of the spectrum. There is a compromise between efficiency and service life, which is true of all incandescent lamps. If a halogen lamp is designed to give all the advantage to efficiency, efficiency can be improved by about 30%. If all the advantage goes to service life, life is increased by a factor of three to five.

Dimming Incandescent Lamps

Dimmers for incandescent lamps are inexpensive and easy to install. They simply replace the light switch, with no other special equipment or changes in the wiring being required.

Unfortunately, dimming greatly reduces the energy efficiency of incandescent lamps, i.e., the light output falls much faster than the energy input. Also, dimming strongly shifts colors away from the blue end of the spectrum, where incandescent lamps are already weak.

A Future for Incandescent Lighting?

If there is a future for incandescent lighting in the home, it will be limited. LED's can take over most of the lighting functions for a typical home that previously were served by incandescent lamps. However, it still makes sense to use incandescent lighting for applications that operate for only a small number of hours each year. For example, if you have a storage area that requires a bright bulb for infrequent visits, an incandescent lamp provides strong illumination with an inexpensive lamp, and the short duration of operation limits the energy cost.

Also, for applications where you want dimming over a wide range of brightness, incandescent lamps still work better than LED lamps.

L.E.D. LIGHTING

"LED" means "lighting-emitting diode." LED is the newest kind of lighting, moving into the market about as fast as Edison's incandescent light bulbs did a century ago. LED's may not replace all previous kinds of lighting, but they may soon become the best choice for most residential applications. LED lighting offers a litany of advantages over the other kinds of lighting, including:

- high energy efficiency
- longer service life than any other light source, provided that the lamps are not overheated
- less reduction in light output with age than any other lamp type
- good color rendering, if the lamp is selected properly
- light output and efficiency that are independent of the surrounding temperature
- dimming without sacrificing efficiency (But, the dimmer must be matched to the lamp.)
- small physical size
- much better resistance to physical shock than all other lamp types
- almost unlimited light distribution patterns and fixture shapes
- no reduction in life from frequent on-off cycles
- no delay in starting (Some lamps have a brief delay caused by the power converter.)
- no noise
- no electrical interference (unless created by the power converter or dimmer)
- no mercury or other materials that are hazardous to the environment.

LED lamps have been substantially more expensive than other types of lamps. However, their cost has been falling rapidly. At the same time, their efficiency has been improving steadily.

LED technology has two basic limitations. One is limited light output by individual LED cells. The other is limited color spectrum of the light output. There are various ways of overcoming these limitations, which are still evolving. LED lighting is so versatile that the variety of lamps and fixtures is virtually unlimited. To select LED lighting wisely, let's get to know its principles.

How LED's Work

LED lamps have two thin layers of semiconductor material. When a voltage is applied between the layers, electrons flow between them. As each electron moves between the layers, it undergoes a change in energy that is converted to a photon of light.

Like all other light sources, an LED converts only a fraction of the input energy into light. The rest of the energy becomes heat. Excessive temperature will destroy the LED, and operating temperature is the main factor that determines the life of an LED lamp. To keep the temperature down, the individual LED chip must be very small, as shown in Figure 6-6.

At present, individual LED's are limited to a power input ranging from a fraction of one watt to several watts. This limits the amount of light that a single LED can emit. To achieve higher light output, a lamp may use many individual LED's in a single package. By mounting the LED's in different directions, it is possible to achieve almost any desired light distribution pattern. Figure 6-7 shows an LED lamp that mimics the light distribution of a conventional light bulb.

DRW

Figure 6-6. The small yellow rectangle inside this night light is the LED chip. It consumes about one half watt. It is about eight times more efficient than the lamp in an incandescent night light.

Switch

Figure 6-7. An LED lamp that mimics an incandescent bulb. Adequate light output is achieved by mounting many individual LED's inside the bulb, facing in different directions. Electronics inside the base convert house power into the proper voltage and current for the LED's.

The individual LED chip can be encased in a tiny plastic lens to create a beam of almost any desired width. That is one reason why LED's first became popular in flashlights.

The basic LED lamp requires only a few volts of direct current. It has essentially no electrical resistance, so it will burn out instantly without a converter to lower the voltage and limit the current. The converter is a semiconductor circuit that is light and small, so the complete LED fixture can be very compact.

Color Rendering

The color of the light that is emitted by the LED chip depends on the semiconductor materials that are used. The light output of an individual LED falls within a narrow band of color. Different LED's emit colors that range across the visible spectrum and beyond. For example, the red, yellow, and green colors in most modern traffic signals are produced by three different types of LED's.

The narrow color spectrum of a basic LED makes it unsatisfactory for general lighting. Fortunately, it is possible to create a much broader spectrum of light emission. The trick is to use an LED that emits light at the extreme blue end of the spectrum. The LED is coated with phosphors that "smear out" blue light into a spectrum of longer wavelengths, as shown in Figure 6-8. (The same technique is used in fluorescent lighting.)

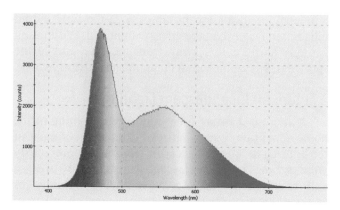

Figure 6-8. The color spectrum of a phosphor coated LED lamp. This lamp is "warm white," which means that much of the energy of the original blue light has been spread toward the red end of the spectrum.

Phosphors can produce good color rendering. So-called "warm white" LED's provide the broadest and most uniform color distribution. Unfortunately, the phosphors convert some of the light to heat, making the LED lamp less efficient.

One problem with present LED lamps is inconsistency in brightness and color. This can be very noticeable in fixtures that have several lamps in a visible row, as in some bathroom fixtures. This characteristic may improve with time, if only by sorting the lamps better before they are packaged.

Dimming LED Lamps

An LED can be dimmed efficiently by reducing the current to the lamp. Some power converters used in LED fixtures can operate with the inexpensive dimmers that are used for incandescent lighting, and others cannot.

Therefore, if you want to be able to dim an LED fixture, check whether it works with an incandescent dimmer. If not, the fixture may work with a special dimmer that is designed for that particular type of fixture.

At present, LED lamps that are designed for dimming may behave erratically, lacking a smooth change in light level. And, they may have a limited range of dimming. These are problems of quality, not limitations of technology. Buyer demand may result in better dimming performance.

The color spectrum of an LED changes when it is dimmed. The change in color is affected by the type of power converter in the fixture. Regardless, the color change probably is too subtle to be noticed in most home lighting.

FLUORESCENT LIGHTING

Fluorescent lighting has been dominant in commercial buildings for half a century, primarily because it has high energy efficiency and long lamp life. Its color rendering can be good, although it has an entirely different color spectrum than either sunlight or incandescent lighting.

Two kinds of fluorescent lighting are popular today, the original long tubes and compact fluorescent lamps (CFL's). The original style of long fluorescent tubes still has considerably better energy efficiency, lamp life, and color than the newer "compact" fluorescent lamps. The main advantage of compact fluorescent lamps is that they can substitute for incandescent bulbs.

The biggest disadvantage of fluorescent lighting is that every lamp contains mercury. The mercury in a fluorescent lamp enters the environment when the tube wears out and is broken up in the trash system.

Until LED lighting became a serious contender for indoor lighting, I would have recommended using fluorescent lighting as much as possible for your indoor lighting. However, LED lighting now appears likely to take over most residential applications for fluorescent lighting, if not all of them. Even where the long tube shape of fluorescent lighting is desirable, LED fixtures can mimic the shape and light distribution of fluorescent tubes.

Color and Color Rendering Options

Unlike incandescent lamps, fluorescent lighting does not produce a continuous spectrum of colors. To understand the color characteristics of fluorescent lighting, you need to know how a fluorescent lamp works. A fluorescent lamp consists of a glass tube with electrodes at each end. Inside the tube is a vapor of mercury. When the electric current passes through the mercury vapor, it emits mostly ultraviolet light. Ultraviolet light is dangerous and it is useless

POSSIBLE VISION HAZARD OF LED'S

The most energy efficient LED's are the ones that produce the shortest wavelengths, toward the blue end of the visible spectrum. For this reason, most plain LED's (without phosphors) produce a bluish light. Inexpensive LED flashlights are a common example.

Some experts warn that the high ratio of blue light to other colors may cause permanent damage to the retinal cells in the eye. This has been called the "blue light hazard."

Phosphors that are used to improve the color rendering of LED's mute blue light and convert much of it to longer wavelengths. This may (or may not) eliminate the blue light hazard. In particular, "warm white" LED's substantially lower the blue light output with respect to other colors.

for vision, so the inside surface of the lamp is coated with a thin layer of "phosphors," which are white and powdery. The phosphors convert the ultraviolet light to visible light by a process called "fluorescence," hence the name for this kind of lighting.

The phosphors determine the wavelengths of light that are emitted by the lamp, and hence its ability to reveal colors. Older fluorescent lamps use a single type of phosphor. The newest phosphor systems combine three different types of phosphors, each of which produces a color distribution with a different peak. Three-phosphor lamps have improved efficiency and color rendering, but they are considerably more expensive than the older types. In both the old and new types, manufacturers use different phosphors to emphasize certain ranges of colors.

The light spectrum of most fluorescent lighting has a broad background, with the narrow bands of mercury emission standing out strongly, as shown in Figure 6-9.

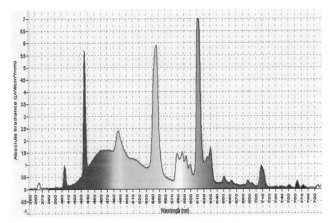

Figure 6-9. The color spectrum of a typical fluorescent lamp. The emission of individual colors and the overall color balance can be adjusted over a wide range by varying the combinations of phosphors.

Compared to incandescent lighting, fluorescent lamps can provide much better rendering of colors at the blue end of the spectrum, but they tend to be weak in the reddish colors.

The most common sizes of conventional long-tube fluorescent lamps are made in a variety of color options, each emphasizing a different part of the visual spectrum. In the past, color variations were given names such as "cool white," "warm white," or "daylight." More recently, the light output is described in terms of the "color temperature" rating. These color descriptions are printed on the lamp package, and usually on the lamp itself.

To select conventional fluorescent lamps for good color rendering, use the "color temperature" and "CRI" rating, which is explained in the *Lamp Selection Guide*.

Compact fluorescent fixtures generally do not offer color options. And, their color rendering is poorer than for the best conventional fluorescent lamps. This may be one reason why compact fluorescent lamps seem dimmer than advertised.

Long-Tube Fluorescent Lamps

The original style of fluorescent lamps have long, straight tubes. These provide the best color rendering, energy efficiency, and economy. They are four to seven times more efficient than incandescent lamps, and they last 10 to 20 times longer. They are available in many sizes.

Conventional fluorescent tubes emit light at relatively low intensity, spread over the large surface of the lamp. This reduces the glare of the lamp. Fluorescent tubes are still too bright to be viewed directly, but it is easy to install them in fixtures that avoid glare without wasting a large fraction of the light in diffusers or shades.

Light output is limited by the length of the tube to about 10 watts per foot [MF] (30 watts per meter). Some are bent in a hairpin shape to provide more light from a shorter tube. In the common sizes, you can select from a variety of lamps having different color and efficiency characteristics.

In general, straight tubes are more efficient than bent tubes. And, longer tubes are more efficient than shorter tubes. Fortunately, the most common lamp dimensions are also the most economical and the most efficient. In the United States, the most efficient lamps are straight tubes that are four feet (121 centimeters) in length.

The older types of long-tube fluorescent lamps do not operate properly when the surrounding temperature is below about 60 °F (15 °C). Below this temperature, they flicker, lose light output, and become inefficient.

At outdoor temperatures, they may not start. However, some newer types of long-tube lamps can operate down to freezing temperatures if they are powered by electronic ballasts.

You have probably noticed that long-tube fluorescent lamps are identified by a "T" designation, such as "T12." The number is the diameter of the tube in eighths of an inch. Thus, a "T12" lamp has a diameter of 1.5 inches, and a "T8" lamp has a diameter of one inch. The older tubes that dominated fluorescent lighting for a half century were mostly T12 sizes. The most recent lamps are narrower, commonly T8. The diameter alone does not tell you much about the characteristics of the lamp. However, because they are newer, T8 lamps may have better phosphors and they are more likely to be used with efficient electronic ballasts.

Long-tube fluorescent fixtures are well suited for large-area lighting in informal spaces, such as the kitchen, garage, and workshop. Also, the long tubes of conventional fluorescent lighting are well suited for illuminating wide work areas, such as kitchen counters and work benches. Long-tube lamps are also suitable for formal rooms, such as the living room, when used with valances, as we will explain.

Compact Fluorescent Lamps

Let's begin with a prediction that compact fluorescent lamps (CFL's) will be rendered obsolete by LED lighting. LED fixtures have most of the advantages of CFL's, and none of their major disadvantages. So, wherever you may have applications for CFL's, consider available LED alternatives.

There are two major classes of compact fluorescent lamps. One type has a screw base that allows it to be installed in a conventional incandescent bulb socket. This is the kind that you are most likely to use in a home. The other class of compact fluorescent lamps has various kinds of pin connections, and they require special fixtures. Figure 6-10 is a sample of both types.

Screw-in compact fluorescent "lamps" are actually complete lighting fixtures that include a fluorescent tube and a ballast. The components are mounted on standard incandescent screw bases, so they can be installed in many fixtures intended for incandescent bulbs. A large variety of configurations are available, including units with integral reflectors, various types of globes or diffusers, and various types of bases.

Screw-in fluorescent fixtures became popular because of their convenience in replacing incandescent lamps. However, even the best models are inferior to conventional fluorescent lighting in energy efficiency, color rendering, and service life. They are only about half as efficient as the best conventional fluorescent lighting because of compromises needed to achieve adequate light output with a small tube.

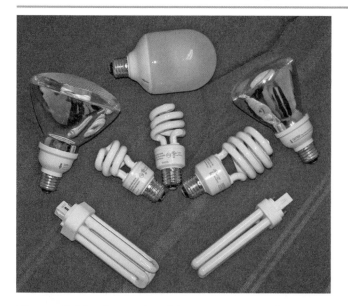

Figure 6-10. A sample of the many types of compact fluorescent lamps that are available. The ones with screw bases are complete packages that include ballasts. The other types require separate ballasts.

Screw-in fluorescent lamps are available in a range of sizes to replace the most common incandescent bulb sizes. However, don't believe the claims on the package for light output. Expect that a compact fluorescent lamp will require about one third the wattage of the incandescent lamp it replaces. For example, select a 25-watt CFL to replace a 75-watt incandescent lamp.

Compact fluorescent lamps can operate at air temperatures down to about freezing temperature. In warmer climates, you could use them for outdoor security lighting, for example.

To allow operation over a wider range of temperatures, compact fluorescent lamps mix the mercury with other metals to stabilize the mercury vapor pressure. At normal temperatures, such lamps may require more than a minute to reach full brightness as the mercury returns to a vapor state. At lower outdoor temperatures, they may require several minutes to approach full brightness.

Fluorescent Ballasts

When a fluorescent lamp is operating, it has no electrical resistance. It would burn out with a flash unless something limits the current. Therefore, all fluorescent lamps have a separate current limiting device, which is called a "ballast."

For long-tube fluorescent lamps, the ballast is built into the fixture. Commonly, a single ballast is wired to operate a pair of tubes. In screw-in CFL's, a small electronic ballast is built into the base.

There are two main types of ballasts for long-tube lamps. The older kind, called a "magnetic" ballast, is simply a coil of wire wrapped around an iron core. The newer kind, called an "electronic" ballast, uses a semiconductor circuit to convert house current into high frequency power for the lamp.

Electronic ballasts have significantly better energy efficiency. They waste little energy themselves, and they improve the efficiency of the lamps by about 10 percent, compared to operation with magnetic ballasts. Some electronic ballasts can operate lamps in much cooler environments. Also, some electronic ballasts can provide efficient dimming of fluorescent lamps, but these ballasts need special dimmers.

If you buy fixtures for long-tube lamps, select fixtures that have electronic ballasts. Magnetic ballasts no longer offer a significant cost advantage.

Fluorescent lamps and ballasts must be matched to each other to achieve good light output and energy efficiency. Therefore, be sure to buy the lamps that are specified for your long-tube fixtures.

Adjusting the Light Level of Fluorescent Lighting

Fluorescent lighting has much less flexibility in adjusting lighting levels than incandescent or LED lighting. The wattage of ordinary fluorescent tubes is fixed by the size and shape of the tube, so you can't change the light output much by swapping tubes.

 To achieve multiple lighting levels and improved energy efficiency with long-tube fluorescent fixtures, install fixtures that have multiple ballasts and switch each ballast separately.

In fixtures that contain multiple tubes, an efficient and inexpensive way to adjust light output is to provide a separate switch for each ballast in the fixture. For example, for your kitchen lighting, select 4-tube ceiling fixtures, which will have two ballasts in each fixture. Wire each ballast to a separate switch. In that way, you have the ability to turn on either two tubes or four tubes.

This option is limited by the fact that tubes usually are connected to ballasts in pairs, so it applies primarily to fixtures that have four or more tubes. Your electrician can wire the switches easily, but make sure that your construction drawings specify this.

If you are willing to spend a lot of money, you can buy special dimming systems for conventional fluorescent tubes. These require special electronic ballasts in the fixtures and special dimmer switches in the wall. This type of dimming maintains lamp efficiency and color rendering. Generally, this is too extravagant for an individual home.

Screw-in fluorescent lamps can't be used with dimmers, at least not yet. However, compact fluorescent lamps with screw bases are available in a large range of light outputs, so it is easy to change sizes. And, you can use them in fixtures that have multiple sockets that can be switched individually.

HIGH INTENSITY DISCHARGE (HID) LIGHTING

"High intensity discharge" ("HID") lighting is a family of three main types: *mercury vapor*, *metal halide*, and *high-pressure sodium*. A related type, *low-pressure sodium*, has been used for street lighting, but it has very poor color rendering.

Few homes have applications for HID lighting. An exception occurs in rural areas, where the main application is lighting large outdoor areas for extended periods. The common characteristics of all HID types are:

* high wattage
* intense light output
* long starting and restarting time
* high lamp cost.

Lamp life is about the same as for fluorescent lighting, and much longer than for incandescent lighting. Energy efficiency can be much better than for incandescent lighting, but it varies widely. Color rendering also varies widely.

A typical HID lamp is about twice the size of a large incandescent bulb. It must be installed in a fixture that has a ballast and other accessories, as in Figure 6-11.

Among the HID types, metal halide lamps provide the best color rendering, and they have excellent energy efficiency. Figure 6-12 shows a typical color spectrum of a metal halide lamp.

At the other extreme, mercury vapor and low-pressure sodium lamps have such bad color rendering that they are not worth considering.

In the middle, high-pressure sodium lamps have a moderately broad band of colors that is centered around the orange color of sodium vapor emission, as in Figure 6-13. Increasing the sodium gas pressure in

Ruud Lighting

Figure 6-11. Cutaway of a typical HID fixture. The electrical accessories are installed in a separate box at the top of fixture to protect them from the intense heat of the lamp.

the lamp broadens the color emission, but makes the lamp less energy efficient. In this lamp type, different models offer a wide range of compromise between color rendering and efficiency.

HID lamps are so bright that they will cause serious eye strain unless the fixture is mounted far above the line of sight, usually on a tall pole or high on a wall. The fixture usually has a metal reflector and/or a clear glass lens to concentrate the light where it is needed. Avoid cheap HID fixtures with plastic lenses or diffusers. The light from HID lamps contains so much ultraviolet light that it will darken a plastic diffuser, wasting light.

The biggest disadvantage of all HID lamps is long starting times, averaging about five minutes. Most lamps cannot restart until they have cooled. Therefore, they are not suitable for lighting that is needed quickly and for short periods. All HID lamps contain mercury, although sodium lamps contain less mercury than the other two types.

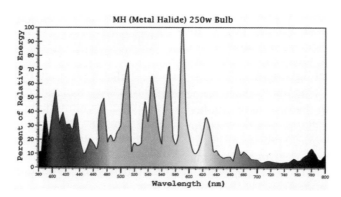

Figure 6-12. Typical spectrum of a metal halide lamp. The light consists of narrow bands of wavelengths that are emitted by the vapors of several metals. The individual bands combine to create the illusion of white light. Phosphors are used to smear out the bands into a distribution of wavelengths that cover the entire visible spectrum. Typically, emission from the red end of the spectrum is relatively weak.

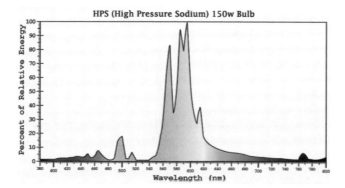

Figure 6-13. Typical spectrum of a high-pressure sodium lamp. The light emission comes mainly from sodium vapor, which has a strong orange color. There is also some mercury emission. Colors at both ends of the visible spectrum are poorly rendered by this type of lamp.

EFFICIENT AND COMFORTABLE LIGHTING LAYOUT

Effective lighting depends on the relative layout of the scene, the viewer, and the light sources. We will now learn the layout principles that will produce comfortable and energy efficient lighting.

Apply these principles separately to each scene that you need to illuminate, whether it is an individual reading chair or an entire room that is being lighted for a social gathering. These principles apply to all forms of lighting, including daylighting, electric lighting, and lighting with candles. Apply them to your built-in fixtures and to your portable fixtures.

USE LIGHT INTERIOR COLORS

One of the most effective ways to achieve high energy efficiency and good color rendering is to use light colors for the interior surfaces of the room. Light colors do not absorb much of the light that is produced by the lamps. The walls and ceiling are most important, but even the floor and the furnishings can affect room lighting.

Every colored surface is a light trap that wastes the money that you spend for lighting. When light reflects from a colored surface, it is filtered in the same way as if a colored filter were placed over the lamp. If the activities in a room are illuminated largely by light reflected from the room surfaces, this can have an adverse effect on the décor. For example, if the walls and ceiling have a pink tint, they absorb colors other than pink, so that light reflected from these surfaces suppresses other colors.

Clean white surfaces reflect about 90% of the light from your lamps. So, use white or off-white as your default color for walls and ceilings. Even tints absorb more light than you may expect. For example, a moderate pastel color absorbs about 30% the light that hits the surface. If light must reflect from the pastel surfaces three times before reaching its destination, two thirds of the light will be wasted along the way.

Colored surfaces interact differently with different kinds of lamps. For example, incandescent lamps produce light that is heavy in reddish or "warm" colors, but they are weak in bluish or "cool" colors. If the walls have a pink tint, incandescent light will make the walls look bright, but the overall room lighting will make bluish colors look dull. If fluorescent or LED light is used with pink walls, the pink tint is subdued, making the walls look dull and wasting energy.

To avoid this filtering effect, avoid uniform tints. For example, if you want to have decorated walls, use light colored wallpaper that has a pattern of many colors, and leave the ceiling white.

AVOID GLARE

"Glare" is an interference with vision and a cause of irritation that is caused by an area of excessive brightness within the field of vision. Glare is the most common flaw of lighting layout. It can occur with daylighting and with artificial lighting. In Step 2, we designed your daylighting to avoid glare. We will also eliminate glare in your artificial lighting.

Sources of Glare in Lighting

Glare occurs if a lamp or light fixture is located near normal lines of sight. Or, glare can be caused by a reflection of a lamp or fixture from a computer screen or other smooth surface. Or, a fixture may create an excessively bright visible surface, such as the wall area directly above a sconce.

The difference in brightness between a lamp and a typical scene is extreme. For example, the surface of a frosted incandescent light bulb is about 1,000 times brighter than the work surface of a typical desk. The surface of a bare fluorescent tube is about 100 times brighter than the desk. Even the surface of a fluorescent fixture diffuser is about 40 times brighter. In contrast, the scene through a window that faces toward a clear sky, away from the sun, is about four times brighter than a well lighted work surface.

The classic example of glare is exposure to a naked light bulb. However, that example is so extreme that people will take action to correct it. The more common problem is lighting that causes glare that can be endured, so that people suffer its effects for long periods.

How Glare Affects Vision

Glare interferes with vision by making eyes less able to see the details in the scene. The pupils of the eyes narrow to block the unwanted light, and the retina of the eye becomes less sensitive. Thus, glare reduces a person's ability to use the light that illuminates what you want to see. Also, the light coming from the glare source creates a halo inside the eye that tends to mask the light coming from the scene.

The adverse effects of glare increase with age, becoming severe among people over the age of 60. This is largely because the transparent components of the eye become more cloudy, increasing the masking effect of glare. Younger people can cope with glare by staring at the area of interest, looking away from the source of glare.

With mild glare, people may be unaware that their vision is impaired. Paradoxically, when the lighting layout creates glare, people may seek to improve their vision by turning on brighter lighting to compensate. They also turn on lighting fixtures throughout the room, in an attempt to make the lighting more uniform to compete with the glare source. So, glare can waste a large amount of energy.

Glare causes physical discomfort, which is commonly described as "eye strain." Mild glare leads to squinting and fatigue. More severe glare causes headaches. The discomfort increases greatly among older people.

■ Overhead Light Sources Create Less Glare

Our early ancestors lived under the light of the sun, which is the most intense light source that exists. They probably didn't have visor caps, so they evolved other ways to deal with the glare of the sun. Eyebrows shield the eyes from the blinding glare of the sun while it is overhead. Undoubtedly, humans and other creatures have neural mechanisms in their eyes and brains to compensate for the sun's glare.

These defenses against overhead glare are not absolute, but they provide considerable flexibility in selecting fixtures that are installed well above the usual lines of sight. For example, a kitchen ceiling fixture emits light from a large, highly visible surface, but its overhead location helps to avoid glare.

This effect is helped by the fact that most home activities involve a downward gaze, so that a ceiling fixture is even higher above the line of sight. This benefits reading, desk work, food preparation, workshop activity, etc.

By the same token, people are especially vulnerable to glare from light sources that are located in the lower field of vision. For example, the glare of sunlight reflected off the surface of a sea or lake is more troubling than the glare of the sun overhead. Similarly, desk lamps and other light sources that are located near eye level are likely to produce enough glare to become uncomfortable within a short time.

■ Stationary vs. Moving Activities

Glare is a function of time, as well as brightness. Activities that require looking at a scene continuously, such as reading a book or working at a desk, are vulnerable to excessive brightness within the scene. Glancing briefly at a bright object may not cause glare, because the eye does not fixate on the glare source long enough to respond to it.

Therefore, you have more latitude when designing the lighting for a room where the occupants move around or change their gaze continually. For example, bright reflections from the many metal surfaces in a kitchen usually don't bother a person who is bustling around while cooking.

For related reasons, glare does not seem to occur with very small areas of brightness, such as the reflection of a light fixture from the handle of a coffee cup. Even with a stationary activity, the eyes move too much for tiny glare sources to affect the eyes. (Lighting designers use the word "sparkle" to describe such small, harmless reflections.)

How to Avoid Glare

Now that we understand glare, let's use our knowledge to create the following guidelines for avoiding glare in your lighting layout. Apply them to each fixture and application. Some of these guidelines can avoid glare by themselves, and others may be used in combination.

- *Install fixtures far above the usual lines of sight*. Height is largely what keeps whole-room ceiling fixtures from creating glare. This is a matter of the angular distance above the line of sight, not the actual height. Most indoor activities involve looking downward, which makes ceiling fixtures acceptable even with low residential ceiling heights.

- *Select large diffusers to limit the surface brightness of fixtures*. The brightness of lamps can be reduced greatly by distributing the light emission uniformly over a large surface area.

  For example, kitchen ceiling fixtures require wide light distribution that makes them highly visible. They compensate by using diffusers that have a large surface.

  Low surface brightness is especially desirable for wash basin fixtures, which are located to illuminate the face of the user.

  All kinds of diffusers absorb a fraction of the light that is emitted by the lamps, and they scatter the light broadly.

- *Select fixtures that hide the lamps from view*. For example, "torchiere" fixtures mount the lamp in a reflecting bowl that aims the light toward the ceiling. "Sconces" emit the light upward and downward, but block a view of the lamp from eye level.

  Fixtures of this kind require the light to reflect from room surfaces repeatedly before reaching the scene. For this reason, they generally are not energy efficient for illuminating localized scenes.

- *Use reflector lamps, especially with shielding enclosures*. "PAR" lamps and other lamps with integral focusing reflectors can be effective for illuminating localized scenes. To avoid glare, install them in fixtures that have a reflective interior surface.

For example, a "downlight" can be effective for illuminating a sink. Reflector lamps installed on track lighting can illuminate various local scenes in a dressing room, such as the top of a dresser, a tie rack, and different portions of a closet.

- *Hide the lamps and the bright surfaces of the fixture by using a physical screen.* For example, valance lighting is defined by the fact that it uses a glare shield to hide the lamps.

Under-cabinet fixtures that are installed over kitchen counters are located directly in front of the viewer. Therefore, hide them completely. If the lamp is located on one side of the fixture, install the fixture so that the lamp faces the wall. Otherwise, install a valance in front of the fixtures.

- *Locate fixtures outside the normal field of vision.* This works only if the viewer is always oriented away from the fixture(s). This applies to a category of lighting that is called "task lighting," which is so important that we will devote a separate discussion to it.

- *Don't install fixtures in a way that creates excessively bright wall surfaces.* An example is wall sconces, where a bright surface is created immediately above the fixture. To avoid glare, avoid this type of fixture with lower ceiling heights, or limit the light output.

- *Arrange fixtures to keep reflections of the lamps from being visible.* This relates to another interference with vision, "veiling reflections," which we cover next.

AVOID "VEILING REFLECTIONS"

"Veiling reflection" is an interference with vision that is related to the geometry of your lighting layout. A common outdoor example is the reflection of the street scene in a storefront window, which makes it difficult to see through the window. A common indoor example is the reflection of a window or a light fixture that make it difficult to read on glossy paper or on a computer screen.

Veiling reflections are so common that you tend to ignore them, even though they may seriously interfere with your vision and cause eye strain. But, you don't have to suffer with them in your home. By understanding how veiling reflections occur, you can avoid them.

To understand veiling reflections, consider what happens when you read. Light falls on the page and penetrates into the inks, which absorb part of the light and reflect the rest. This selective reflection is what enables you to read text, as in Figure 6-14.

However, another kind of reflection also happens. With any smooth surface, a portion of the light reflects from the surface itself without penetrating into the material. All this light is reflected equally, as from a mirror. This light does not allow you to see details in the surface. In fact, it "veils" the portion of the light that shows the details. If the surface is smooth, a large fraction of the light that falls on it will be reflected in this way, as in Figure 6-15. Glossy paper, polished

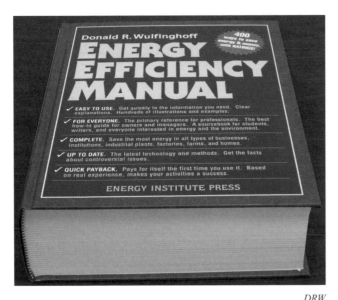

DRW

Figure 6-14. A book lying on a brown laminate tabletop. The lighting is entirely from "over the shoulder," high and to both sides of the viewer. You can read the cover easily because this geometry avoids veiling reflections.

DRW

Figure 6-15. Veiling reflections. The lighting is the same as in the previous photograph, except that a window shade has been opened directly ahead of the viewer. The reflected light from the window overwhelms the visual information that is brought out by the good lighting. The illumination level has been greatly increased, but the light coming from ahead has almost washed out your ability to read the book cover.

table tops, window surfaces, and computer screens all create strong veiling reflections.

Veiling reflections are fundamentally different from glare. Unlike glare, veiling reflections can occur without excessive brightness, and they affect people of all ages equally. Glare occurs outside the scene, whereas veiling reflections occur within the scene.

How to Avoid Veiling Reflections

You can't eliminate the veiling reflections from a smooth surface, but you can arrange your lighting layout so that veiling reflections will not reflect into your eyes. Veiling reflections are limited by geometry, like reflection from a mirror. To avoid them, arrange the layout of the light fixtures and the scene so that veiling reflections from the scene are directed away from your face.

For example, if you are reading, place the light fixture to the side, not in front of the page. It's really that simple.

Veiling reflections from television and computer screens can be very strong and annoying. To avoid them, orient the screen so that no bright area, such as a window or ceiling light fixture, is located behind you.

Veiling reflections do not occur with rough surfaces, which do not reflect like a mirror.* For this reason, you don't need to worry about veiling reflections with fabrics, carpets, common brick, and rough tile. Most newsprint paper is too rough to create an annoying amount of veiling reflections.

As with glare, veiling reflections probably won't bother you if you are moving around, such as cooking or building something in your workshop. In those situations, you can usually adjust your position to avoid the reflections.

AVOID SHADOWS ON THE SCENE

Shadows that are cast on a scene impair vision. The shadowed area may be too dark, and the contrast between the shadowed and illuminated areas may be annoying and may create glare.

Your own body, especially your hands, is the most common source of interfering shadows. For example, when you write, your hand casts a shadow on the paper. Also, your upper body can shadow your activity if the light source is located behind you.

The general way to avoid self-shadowing is to use light sources that are large in size and to arrange them to the sides of your activity, so that the viewer's body cannot block the light.

---

* If the irregularities in the surface are larger than the wavelengths of visible light, the surface cannot reflect light like a mirror. Therefore, surface roughness greater than a few microns (a few thousandths of a millimeter) will abolish most veiling reflections.

ILLUMINATE SCENES UNIFORMLY, BUT SEPARATELY

For most scenes – such as the book you are reading, the surface of your desk, or the dining room table – the illumination level should be fairly uniform. This makes the scene more pleasant to view. A good rule of thumb is to keep the illumination within different parts of a scene within a ratio of 2-to-1.

To provide uniform illumination, locate the fixtures at a greater distance from the scene than the width of the scene itself, and use fixtures that have a large effective width.

The value of uniform illumination applies to individual scenes, not to the room as a whole. For example, if you are having a party in a large room, there are many individual scenes in the rooms. Tailor the illumination level to each one. You want bright light on the buffet, medium light at the chairs, dim light on the dance floor, and very bright light on the table that holds your photo album.

It's not necessary to have uniform illumination throughout a room, unless the room is being illuminated for a single purpose (housecleaning, for example). There is no need for "background" lighting, which is a fable that was invented by lighting designers. For example, if you are sitting in your favorite chair and reading a novel, it is desirable to illuminate your book uniformly, but the rest of the room may need little or no lighting. In fact, isolated lighting for certain activities helps to provide a cozy feel.

TASK LIGHTING: GETTING IT RIGHT*

Conventional lighting wastes a large fraction of its energy by scattering light in places where it is not needed. "Task lighting" is an old concept that minimizes this energy waste by concentrating light on the limited area where it is needed. When someone first added a reflector to a candle holder, that was a major step toward task lighting.

Task lighting became a major goal of energy efficiency during the energy panic of the 1970's. Unfortunately, the task lighting of that era made a fundamental mistake by using light fixtures that were located inside the activity area, near the viewer's face. Also, they typically used small, concentrated light

---

* The task lighting configuration recommended here is a major advance in lighting efficiency and visual comfort. It has been tested extensively by the author in office and residential reading applications. The lighting fixtures and methods are covered by U.S. Patent 7,824,068, issued to the author shortly before this was written. The commercial availability of the fixtures is not yet known.

sources. The result was severe glare, veiling reflections, harsh shadows, and very uneven illumination, as in Figure 6-16. As a result, interest in task lighting withered.

We will bring back task lighting, and now we will get it right. Figure 6-17 shows how to do it. The key to comfortable and effective task lighting is to use fixtures that are designed properly and to arrange them as shown. The arrangement has these features:

- The fixtures *aim the light directly at the activity*, rather than bouncing the light from surrounding surfaces in the room.

- The fixtures *do not absorb light*. They have no shades or diffusers in the light path.

- The fixtures *emit light from a wide perimeter*, so that the light strikes the activity from many directions. This eliminates sharp shadows from the viewer's hands and improves the uniformity of illumination. The large width of the fixture also mutes any reflections of the fixture from shiny objections in the field of view.

- In each fixture, *the lamps can be aimed individually*, allowing the user to tailor the illumination to each part of the scene. For example, in Figure 6-17, separate lamps illuminate the two printers, the file trays, and the red business card file, while reducing illumination of the computer. Also, the lamps are aimed to provide crossfire that eliminates shadowing by the user's hands.

- Each fixture is *located well above the viewer's head*. This position avoids glare by exploiting the tolerance of human beings for overhead lighting.

- Each fixture is *located to the side and somewhat behind the viewer*. This position avoids veiling reflections. It further reduces the possibility of glare if the viewer turns to the side.

- There are *two fixtures, one on each side of the viewer, in approximately symmetrical positions*. The crossfire of two fixtures eliminates shadowed areas under the viewer's hands that may interfere with vision, and it provides uniform illumination across the activity. Using two fixtures is especially important if the activity area is wide, as at a desk, and if the viewer is working with his hands. If the scene is narrow, as in reading a book, a single fixture may suffice.

DRW

Figure 6-16. Bad contemporary task lighting. The visual discomfort of this arrangement is almost unbearable, so users abandoned task lighting for less efficient whole-room lighting.

 This patented lighting innovation radically improves lighting quality and energy efficiency for activities in fixed locations, such as reading and working at a desk.

This method of task lighting is novel, but it is well tested. I patented it after years of experimentation to find a fully satisfactory way of exploiting the energy efficiency benefit of task lighting, while eliminating the vision problems of earlier task lighting. For several years, I have used this task lighting for the desks in my office and for reading at home. It works really well.

Where to Use Task Lighting

The ideal task lighting that we introduce here is intended primarily for activities where a single person remains within a limited area, facing mainly in a particular direction. It is appropriate for most activities that are done while seated, such as desk work, reading, and sewing. It is also good for some standing activities, such as working at a drill press in your workshop.

DRW

Figure 6-17. Ideal task lighting using patented fixtures. All visual discomfort is eliminated. The large work area is illuminated by a total power of 29 watts. The new fixtures replace two conventional fluorescent ceiling fixtures that required a total power of 180 watts.

Protect Other Occupants from Glare

The task lighting layout in Figure 6-17 is very comfortable for the viewer, but it has the potential to cause glare for other people who may face the activity area from the front. This would be a problem if a desk,

reading chair, or other activity area faces into the occupied portion of a room. It would not be a problem if a desk faces a wall, for example.

The general solution is to break the line of sight from the bright lamps to any surrounding viewers. One method is to use task lighting fixtures that have glare shields surrounding the lamps, as in Figure 6-17. The glare shields can be completely opaque, which hides the lamps completely. Or, as in Figure 6-17, the glare shields may be partially translucent, which can provide a decorative appearance and some illumination of the ceiling and the surrouding area.

Another method is to use a separate screen to break the line of sight between the task lighting fixtures and the surrounding areas that may be occupied. The screen typically would be suspended from the ceiling, and it can be an attractive room decoration. For example, you could use a number of hangings, such as the yacht ensign in Figure 6-17. (The yacht ensign was originally installed to shield the desk from the glare of adjacent ceiling fixtures, before the task lighting fixtures were invented.)

How to Install Ideal Task Lighting

The location, the orientation, and glare shielding of the lamps in the task lighting fixtures are critical. However, the method of mounting the fixtures is entirely a matter of convenience. The fixtures can be portable or built in, depending on the application. They can be mounted on table stands, floor stands, or ceiling mounts. They can be attached to furniture or counters.

 At this point, you know more about the important principles of lighting than most professional lighting designers. You're ready to apply those principles to every part of your home. So, let's do it.

SELECTING AND PLACING YOUR LIGHTING FIXTURES

Use the *Home Lighting Worksheet*, which begins overleaf, to apply what you have learned to each room and space in your home.

Homes use two kinds of light fixtures, built-in and portable. You need to include the built-in lighting in your design. You can defer the selection of your portable lighting until after your home is built. However, have a clear idea how you will use your portable lighting, so that you can divide the lighting effectively between the two types.

WHERE TO INSTALL BUILT-IN FIXTURES

We'll start with your first big decision, which is where to install built-in fixtures, rather than portable fixtures. Portable lighting fixtures provide variety, versatility, and the option to change fixtures easily. However, built-in fixtures are a better choice for many home lighting applications. Generally, use built-in fixtures where:

• good light distribution for the scene requires a mounting location on the ceiling or high on a wall
• it is desirable to have a fixture that is large and/or heavy, e.g., a fluorescent fixture with conventional tubes
• the fixture is an element of the room's decor, e.g., a chandelier
• you want to control the lighting from a wall switch
• a portable fixture would get in the way of activities, e.g., over tables and counters
• the power cords of portable fixtures would interfere with safety or appearance
• it is awkward or dangerous to use portable fixtures, e.g., in an attic
• the lighting is outside the house.

It's Easy to Change Built-In Fixtures, But Not Their Locations

It is easy to change built-in light fixtures. Only the wiring and the electrical mounting boxes are actually built into the structure. You can change the actual fixture in a few minutes.

However, you can't change the location of the fixture, which largely determines the lighting geometry. So, use foresight in selecting the locations of the mounting boxes.

In the future, you may want to substitute a fixture that is considerably heavier than the original fixture, such as installing a formal chandelier in place of a lightweight fixture. Therefore, make sure that your electrician fastens all your mounting boxes to the structure securely.

If you think that you might install a paddle fan in place of a ceiling light fixture, install a special mounting box that is made to carry the weight and vibration of a fan.

MAKE CLEANING AND LAMP REPLACEMENT EASY

Install your built-in fixtures so that they will be accessible for cleaning and lamp replacement. If fixtures require a ladder for access, locate them so that the ladder can be set up without the need to move heavy furniture.

If you do need to install fixtures where access is awkward, avoid incandescent lamps or other lamps that have short life. Otherwise, you will become afraid to turn on the fixtures.

There is a big advantage in selecting fixtures that use the standard "medium screw base" that was originally developed for incandescent bulbs. They allow you to install a large variety of LED lamps and compact fluorescent lamps.

FAVOR LED's

At this time, LED lighting seems likely to displace the older kinds of home lighting in most applications. So, take the initiative to consider LED's for most of your home's lighting. LED fixtures behave differently from the incandescent and fluorescent fixtures that they replace, so give some forethought to the best ways to substitute LED's in your design.

Individual LED's have limited light output, so LED fixtures increase light output by mounting many LED's in large arrays. LED's emit light in a beam, which may be broad or narrow. The individual LED's in the fixture can be aimed in different directions to provide almost any desired light distribution pattern.

An LED fixture can also spread many LED's over a large surface, so that the light distribution pattern can mimic the distribution pattern of conventional fluorescent lamps or incandescent fixtures that have large diffusers.

For example, you can buy arrays of LED's that stretch to any desired length, using a common power source. These are especially useful for counter and workbench lighting.

Individual LED's are tiny and intensely bright. To avoid glare, the LED's themselves must not be visible in normal use. One solution is to mount the fixtures high overhead, aiming straight down. Another is to select fixtures that have a glare shield around the fixture or around the individual lamps.

And, another method is to use a diffuser to spread the light of many LED's over a large surface. But, all diffusers, including frosted lamp bulbs, waste energy by absorbing a fraction of the light. Milky plastic diffusers absorb about half the light of the lamps when they are new, and they darken with age. Clear "prismatic" diffusers waste less light, but they have a glinty surface appearance.

Select all your LED's to have a relatively low "color temperature," which provides better color rendering and reduces the "blue light hazard."

TRACK LIGHTING

Track lighting usually is installed on the ceiling. Individual fixtures usually can be located anywhere along the track, in any number that does not exceed the electrical capacity of the circuit. Tracks can have almost any shape, from straight lines to random curves. You can combine different kinds of fixtures on the same track, and change fixtures easily. Figure 6-18 is one of many possible configurations.

The track lighting components of different manufacturers generally are not interchangeable. So, select a family of track lighting equipment that includes all the features that you may want, now and in the future.

Electrical power is supplied at a single point in the ceiling, making installation easy. Most models allow the track to be expanded in sections, usually end-to-end. Some track systems allow you to connect sections with angle connectors and T-connectors. The track may be mounted flush to the ceiling, or it may be suspended, as in Figure 6-18.

All the fixtures installed on the track must operate together from a single switch or dimmer, so track lighting is not very energy efficient unless all the fixtures on the track are illuminating the same scene. Still, you might use track lighting for a room with diverse illumination requirements, such as a dressing room or a guest bedroom, if the room requires lighting only for short periods.

Track lighting can cause severe glare if an occupant gets into the beam of a spotlight fixture. Therefore, locate the tracks and aim spotlight fixtures to keep this from happening.

MomEndeavors.com

Figure 6-18. Typical track lighting. Electrical power requires only a single ceiling connection. The track can have almost any shape. The track may be mounted flush to the ceiling, or suspended as here. All the fixtures operate from a common switch or dimmer, which can be wasteful.

VALANCE LIGHTING, NOT COVE LIGHTING

Valance lighting consists of a valance (a decorative screen) located in front of horizontal fluorescent tubes or a horizontal row of individual lamps. The valance blocks the glare of the lamps while allowing the lamps to illuminate the walls and ceiling. Thus, valance lighting is entirely indirect. In effect, it uses the wall and ceiling as a large light fixture that provides muted illumination over a large area. Figure 6-19 shows an example that works well.

The best application for valance lighting is a formal room with a tall ceiling, where the light distribution by reflection from the ceiling and walls produces illumination that is broad and subdued. A valance should be installed well above head height to avoid glare from the brightly illuminated surfaces above and below the valances.

The energy efficiency of valance lighting is fair, at best. Every photon emitted by the lamp must bounce off a surface at least once on the way to the scene that is being illuminated. Therefore, energy efficiency and good color rendering require wall and ceiling colors that are light and fairly neutral. Also, the inside surface of the valance should be highly reflective.

The valance lighting in Figure 6-19 is a custom installation. It consists of wooden boards that are held to the wall with simple brackets. Aluminum tape covers the inside surfaces for efficient reflection. Your carpenter can easily make a similar valance from a sketch.

HOME LIGHTING WORKSHEET

☐ ALL ROOMS AND SPACES

___ Locate all fixtures to avoid glare and veiling reflections, and to provide uniform illumination of individual scenes.

___ For most applications, select fixtures that have a wide radiating surface to soften shadows in the scene.

___ Use very light interior colors, especially for walls and ceiling.

___ Match the color characteristics of the lamps to the colors of the surfaces and furnishings in the room.

___ Favor LED lamps for their instant starting, long life, and good color rendering.

___ When using LED lamps, select a low color temperature to provide good color rendering.

___ When using LED lamps in fixtures controlled by dimmers, select lamps and fixtures that provide smooth and continuous dimming over a wide range of light output.

___ Where incandescent lamps may be appropriate, install fixtures that allow later replacement of the incandescent lamps with LED lamps.

☐ BEDROOMS

___ Install one or more ceiling fixtures for cleaning and changing bedding. The same fixtures should have a dimmer for mood lighting, to accommodate sleepers, and to avoid discomfort for night-adapted vision.

___ In a climate that has a warm season, coordinate the location of ceiling fixtures with the location of a ceiling fan, which generally should be installed over the bed. Either select a fan that includes lights under its hub, or be careful to avoid interference between the fan and other light fixtures.

___ Consider track lighting or separate ceiling-mounted spotlights to illuminate wardrobes, dressers, art objects, etc.

___ Install reading lights on or near the bed(s). These may be mounted on the bed, on the adjacent wall, or on side tables. Portable wall-mounted fixtures generally work best.

☐ SPARE BEDROOMS (USED AS STORAGE ROOM, SEWING ROOM, ETC.)

___ Generally, use the same ceiling fixtures as in bedrooms.

___ Select the other fixture type(s) for the specific activities in the room.

___ Install dimming, if appropriate for the activity.

☐ DRESSING ROOMS

___ Provide individual light fixtures to highlight areas within the dressing room, such as wardrobes, dressers, tie racks, and art objects, while maintaining a lower overall mood lighting. Consider track lighting or individually mounted spotlights.

___ Install any spotlights so that occupants cannot see the lamps from any position in the room.

___ Control all the fixtures with dimmers for mood lighting, to accommodate sleepers in adjacent bedrooms, and to avoid discomfort for night-adapted vision.

___ Provide adequate lighting for cleaning, generally on the ceiling. The previous lighting may suffice. If not, install additional lighting that complements the previous lighting.

☐ TOILET ROOMS (WITHOUT SHOWER)

___ Over the basin mirror, install a fixture with large surface area and low glare. A wide fluorescent or LED fixture with a large diffuser is best. A fixture with several large globe lamps is satisfactory. Install the fixture(s) to provide good illumination of the face without being close to the line of sight into the mirror. For a small toilet room, this may be all the lighting that is needed.

━━━━ HOME LIGHTING WORKSHEET ━━━━

____ If the toilet room is used by bedroom occupants, control the basin fixture with a dimmer. This limits the fixture to incandescent or dimmable LED lamps.

____ For a larger toilet room, also install a ceiling fixture, perhaps in combination with a ceiling exhaust fan and/or ceiling heater. This fixture should use LED lamps.

____ See *Toilet Rooms*, in Step 1, for related lighting and electrical issues.

☐ TOILET ROOMS (WITH SHOWER)

____ For the basin lighting, follow the previous guidelines.

____ Also, install a ceiling fixture, perhaps in combination with a ceiling exhaust fan and/or ceiling heater. Locate it outside the shower, to illuminate the shower for cleaning and use. This fixture should use LED lamps.

☐ SHOWER ROOMS

____ See *Shower Rooms*, in Step 1, for related lighting and electrical issues.

____ Install a ceiling fixture, perhaps in combination with a ceiling exhaust fan and/or ceiling heater, in the entry area outside the shower. Locate it effectively for dressing and for illuminating the shower for cleaning and use.

____ Select a fixture that is resistant to moisture – incandescent or LED, not fluorescent.

____ Install a dimmer for the lighting.

☐ BATHTUB ROOMS

____ Install one or more ceiling fixtures, perhaps in combination with a ceiling exhaust fan and/or ceiling heater. Locate the fixture(s) for dressing, for illuminating the tub during use, and for cleaning the room.

____ Select a fixture that is resistant to moisture – incandescent or LED, not fluorescent.

____ Control the lighting with a dimmer.

☐ KITCHEN

____ Install one or more ceiling fixtures for whole room cleaning and for illumination into all cabinets. Select the fixtures to provide lateral and downward light distribution, with emphasis on lighting cabinets and counters.

____ For the ceiling fixture(s), select LED or fluorescent fixtures. For ceiling LED fixtures, select dimmable models and install a compatible dimmer. For a fluorescent fixture, install switching that selects different numbers of tubes.

____ For all counters, install separate work lighting, with separate switches. If the counter lighting is installed underneath cabinets, select long arrays of LED's. Install the fixtures so that the lamps are shielded from view. If the counter lighting is installed on the ceiling, install a row of surface-mounted LED spotlights, aimed straight down. Install all fixtures toward the front of the counters.

____ Illuminate the sink with a surface-mounted LED spotlight, aimed straight down, unless the sink is adequately illuminated by the room lighting. Install the fixture toward the front of the sink.

____ For maintenance and storage in the space under the sink and in any cabinet that contains plumbing or water treatment equipment, install a surface-mounted LED light. Install the light so that it does not create glare for the person working in the space. Control the light with a door switch or with a conveniently located manual switch.

____ Select a range hood that includes light fixtures for effective illumination of the entire range surface. For fire safety, install a range hood that is wider than the range itself.

―――― **HOME LIGHTING WORKSHEET** ――――

☐ **KITCHEN DINING AREA**

___ Install one or more ceiling-mounted fixtures directly over the center of the dining table or dining counter, with light distribution that provides uniform illumination of the dining surface.

☐ **DINING ROOM**

___ Install one or more ceiling-mounted fixtures directly over the center of the dining table.

___ Control the dining table fixtures with a dimmer.

___ If the room has major decorative accents, such as a hutch or wall decorations, install track lighting, spotlights, or low-voltage accent lighting to highlight those features. Select fixtures that can be reoriented to accommodate changes in these items. Track lighting may be the best choice. Select fixtures that hide the lamps from view. Control the fixtures with a dimmer.

☐ **LIVING ROOM**

___ All or most of the lighting for individual activities – such as reading, games, and watching television – is done with portable fixtures. Portable fixtures can tailor illumination to individual activities, and it accommodates changes in furnishings.

___ Coordinate the locations of any built-in lighting with the location of windows, clerestories, and skylights, and with the probable locations of portable lighting.

___ For whole-room lighting for cleaning and for social functions, install built-in lighting on the ceiling or along the tops of some or all of the walls.

___ For ceiling lighting in a living room with tall ceilings, consider valance lighting that uses long-tube fluorescent fixtures or long arrays of LED's.

___ For reading chairs, consider task lighting fixtures that may be mounted on the ceiling, on the walls, or on side tables. See *Task Lighting: Getting It Right*, in Step 6.

___ Install track lighting or low-voltage accent lighting for decorative accents, such as paintings, statuary, and decorative furniture. Arrange this lighting so that it does not cause glare in any part of the room.

___ Control all built-in lighting with dimmers or group switching to accommodate different room uses.

☐ **GREAT ROOM**

___ A great room is a showpiece. Unlike a living room, its functions vary, with an emphasis on large social gatherings. Decor plays a large role. So, design the lighting to accommodate a variety of uses and to highlight a variety of decor.

___ For the central portion of the room, consider one or more dramatic ceiling fixtures, such as a chandelier.

___ For the perimeter of the room, consider valance lighting that uses long-tube fluorescent fixtures or long arrays of LED's.

___ Provide separate groups of controls for each type of built-in fixture and for each area of the room. For example, provide separate control for the fixtures located where a movie screen may be installed.

___ Locate each group of controls within the area that it serves. Mark the controls to indicate the fixtures they serve.

___ Provide dimming for all the built-in lighting, except perhaps for localized accent lighting.

___ Avoid glare. Mount the fixtures that illuminate the occupied portions of the room well above the line of sight. Bright fixtures should aim straight down. Fixtures that illuminate perimeter objects should keep their lamps shielded from view.

────── HOME LIGHTING WORKSHEET ──────

___ A dead lamp will stand out, so make it easy to replace all the lamps without having to fetch a ladder or move furniture. Do not install fixtures in tall ceilings. For a chandelier mounted on a tall ceiling, include a lowering system for cleaning and lamp changing.

___ Install floor receptacles for portable lighting that may be desirable at a distance from the wall receptacles. Coordinate the location of floor receptacles with furniture and carpets.

☐ WALK-IN CLOSETS, COAT ROOMS, PANTRIES, ETC.

___ Install one or more bright ceiling lights inside the space. Select the light distribution pattern of the fixture to illuminate the entire space from the floor to the tops of shelves.

___ Control the lights with a door switch, if the door is usually closed. Or, install a convenient wall switch outside the door, on the latch side, with a telltale light in the toggle.

☐ WALL CLOSETS, LINEN CLOSETS, COAT ROOMS, PANTRIES, ETC (NOT WALK-IN)

___ If a closet door opens to a hallway, install the hallway light directly outside the closet door, if this also provides satisfactory lighting for the hallway.

___ Otherwise, install a fixture on the ceiling inside the closet, above the door.

___ Control the lights with a door switch, if the door is usually closed. Or, install a convenient wall switch outside the door, on the latch side, with a telltale light in the toggle.

☐ HALLWAYS

___ Install ceiling fixtures that have a large surface area, to minimize glare. Select a light distribution pattern that distributes light on the ceiling and walls.

___ Consider a motion sensor to control the hallway lighting. Install the sensor so that it will sense all hallway activity, but will not be triggered by activity outside the hallway.

☐ LAUNDRY ROOM

___ See *Laundry Room*, in Step 1, about laundry room layout.

___ Over the row of washer, dryer, and sink, install a long-tube fluorescent "shop light" fixture, or a row of LED fixtures of similar intensity.

___ Install similar fixtures over the sorting table and ironing board area.

☐ CLOTHESLINE AREA

___ See *Clothesline Area*, in Step 1, for possible locations for clotheslines and other laundry drying areas.

___ Position the fixture or fixtures to keep the hanging laundry from shadowing itself and other activities in the space.

___ Use LED or incandescent fixtures because of their tolerance of moisture and low temperatures.

☐ OPEN PORCH

___ People sitting on an open porch at night often prefer the darkness, or a very low level of illumination.

___ If the porch includes an entrance door, the entrance fixtures may suffice. However, the entrance fixtures should not be dimmed, and they may be too bright for porch illumination.

━━━ HOME LIGHTING WORKSHEET ━━━

_____ If other lighting is desired, install one or more ceiling fixtures that are controlled by a dimmer.

_____ If ceiling fans are installed, consider lighting that is mounted on the fans.

☐ ENCLOSED PORCH

_____ An enclosed porch may be used in the same way as an open porch at night, and should have similar lighting for that usage.

_____ An enclosed porch may also require brighter illumination for other functions, such as a buffet. For such activities, install one or more ceiling fixtures that are operated by a dimmer.

☐ WORKSHOP

_____ Paint the walls and ceiling white, even if the surfaces are unfinished.

_____ Select ceiling fixtures that have light distribution patterns appropriate for their locations in the space. Generally, select fixtures that have downward and lateral light distribution to avoid wasting light on the ceiling. To illuminate storage shelves, select ceiling fixtures that distribute light toward the shelves.

_____ Select long-tube fluorescent fixtures with electronic ballasts that can operate the lamps at lower temperatures and reach full brightness quickly.

_____ Or, select LED fixtures that have conventional screw bases, for installation in inexpensive sockets. Install the bases so that the lamps will hang vertically.

_____ Each fixture should have a pullcord switch for individual control.

_____ Where appropriate, install fixtures that resist accidental impact.

_____ For work benches and for machine tools that are fixed in position, consider task lighting. See _Task Lighting: Getting It Right_, in Step 6.

☐ GARAGE

_____ Install ceiling fixtures to illuminate the areas where people walk, not the roofs of parked vehicles. Install the fixtures to concentrate illumination at the sides of the garage and in the spaces between vehicles.

_____ Favor incandescent fixtures that offer the option to install LED lamps. These can operate efficiently at lower temperatures and reach full brightness immediately.

_____ If a portion of the garage is used as a workshop, illuminate that portion in the same way as for a workshop.

_____ If the garage is used for vehicle maintenance, install task lighting fixtures that shine into the hood area of the vehicle. See _Task Lighting: Getting It Right_, in Step 6.

☐ EQUIPMENT SPACES (HEATING, WATER HEATING, WATER TREATMENT, ETC.)

_____ Paint the walls and ceiling white, even if the surfaces are unfinished.

_____ Install fixtures to provide broad illumination of all sides of the equipment, with greatest intensity on controls, power and fuel connections, and access panels.

_____ Favor incandescent fixtures that offer the option to install LED lamps.

☐ VENTED ATTIC (VACANT OR USED FOR STORAGE)

_____ Install built-in fixtures to brightly illuminate the entire attic. This improves maintenance and insect inspections, and aids in storing items. Portable lighting is inadequate and dangerous.

_____ Use simple fixtures with screw bases, which can mount incandescent or LED lamps. They can be installed on the sides of rafters or other supports in a manner that provides good light distribution and that protects the lamps from breakage.

HOME LIGHTING WORKSHEET

___ If the attic is not used often, control all the fixtures with a single switch that is located conveniently at the attic entrance. If the attic is used for extended periods, installed multiple switches to control the fixtures in appropriate groups.

___ Install a telltale light, visible from the living space below, that indicates when the attic lights are turned on.

☐ OUTSIDE ENTRY LIGHTING (NOT IN ENCLOSED SPACE)

___ See *Outdoor Lighting*, in Step 6.

___ At each entrance, install at least one attractive fixture that has a medium screw base to accept a screw-in LED lamp. Install the fixture above head height, on the latch side of the door, so that the door locks are illuminated.

___ For greater security, install matching fixtures on both sides of the door.

___ Install a telltale light at the switch for the entry lighting. If a fixture is controlled from more than one location, install a telltale light at each location.

☐ ENCLOSED ENTRY SPACES

___ Illuminate the space as appropriate for the activities that occur there. See *Entry Spaces*, in Step 1.

___ In most cases, locate a fixture on the ceiling near the interior door. This allows occupants to identify visitors through a peephole in the door.

___ Select fixtures that have a medium screw base to accept a screw-in LED lamp.

___ For exterior (unheated) entry spaces, control the lighting with two manual switches, one inside the house and one located outside the exterior door. Or, instead of an outside manual switch, install a motion sensing switch inside the space.

☐ OUTDOOR NIGHTTIME ACTIVITIES

___ See *Outdoor Lighting*, in Step 6.

___ Install telltale lights at the indoor switches to indicate when the outdoor lighting is turned on.

☐ OUTDOOR SECURITY LIGHTING

___ See *Outdoor Lighting*, in Step 6.

___ If security lighting is triggered by motion sensors, you can increase security by using the same motion sensors to trigger an indoor alarm, telltale light, and/or video camera. However, if you do that, nocturnal animals may keep you awake all night.

☐ OUTBUILDINGS

___ Install fixtures that have light distribution patterns appropriate for the use of the building, such as storage or workshop use.

___ Select fixtures that have medium screw bases, to accept either incandescent or screw-in LED lamps. Do not use fluorescent fixtures.

___ Select fixtures that protect the lamps from accidental impact.

___ If the interior lighting cannot be seen from the house, install an entrance light or telltale light on the outside of the building that turns on with the interior lighting.

___ Provide lighting for the path between the house and the outbuilding, such as a floodlight installed high on the house.

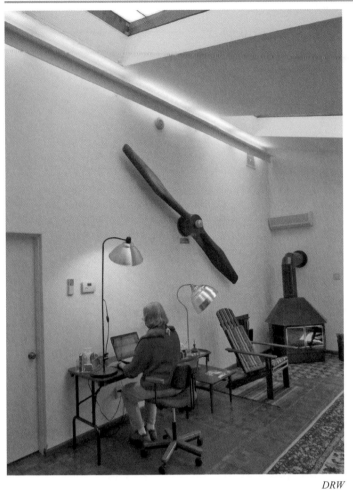

DRW

Figure 6-19. Valance lighting for a living room. This custom installation uses a line of five 4-foot (120 cm) fluorescent lamps. The valance is carefully aligned with the lamps so that the wall and ceiling surfaces are illuminated while keeping the lamps out of sight. The center lamp, the two outer lamps, and the two lamps between them are switched independently, providing a variety of light levels and illumination patterns. At night, the valance fixture illuminates the entire room. Reading lamps are used for local tasks that require brighter illumination.

You may be able to find ready-made valance fixtures. However, make sure that their geometry will produce the right light distribution on your walls and ceiling.

Today, you can use a long array of LED lamps for valance lighting. The valance can serve as the mounting for the LED strips. LED lamps emit light in focused beams, so it is easy to minimize absorption of light behind the valance. By the same token, this arrangement is less vulnerable to light loss from the dust that will accumulate on the valance.

Cove lighting is a method of ceiling illumination that looks similar to valance lighting, but it is much less efficient. The lamps are installed inside a long box structure, called a "cove," which is open to the ceiling. Coves usually are installed around the entire ceiling perimeter. The coves illuminate only the ceiling, not the walls, so they leave the wall areas relatively dark.

Cove lighting is very wasteful because light must bounce repeatedly to escape from the cove. Much of the light is absorbed by the paint and dust inside the cove. Generally, more than 90% of the light is wasted. Avoid cove lighting, even though it is a favorite of architects and interior decorators.

LOW-VOLTAGE LIGHTING

For lighting that operates at low power, such as walkway lighting and accent lighting in cabinets, you can use light fixtures that operate at low voltage. Low-voltage lighting commonly operates at 12 volts. It requires a converter to reduce the voltage from your home's primary electrical system.

The low voltage provides safety, eliminating the need for thick insulation and a ground wire. As a result, the wiring is much thinner than 120-volt or 240-volt house wiring. This makes it easy to install in furniture and cabinets. You can see numerous examples in counter and display lighting in jewelry stores and gift shops. In homes, they are used for highlighting decor, such as paintings and antiques.

For example, if you want to use LED or low-voltage incandescent lighting to highlight the items in a glass cabinet, select a system that uses a single converter to drive all the lamps. The converter is mounted on the cabinet, and the low-voltage wiring is threaded through the shelves.

For outdoor use, the safety advantage of low-voltage wiring makes it desirable for walkway lighting and other low-wattage applications.

LED lighting inherently operates at low voltage, requiring a converter. Therefore, it is naturally adaptable to low-voltage applications.

For technical reasons, the filaments of low-voltage incandescent lamps can be small and bright, making them ideal for accent lighting. Low-voltage incandescent lamps typically use a reflector to focus intense light on a small area. However, low-voltage incandescent lamps probably will soon be replaced by LED lamps.

DON'T INSTALL FIXTURES INSIDE CEILINGS

I recommend against installing any kind of light fixture inside the ceiling structure, for several reasons. The operating temperature of the lamps is increased greatly when the fixture is enclosed. This will significantly reduce the life and the energy efficiency of compact fluorescent lamps and LED's.

If the fixture is surrounded by insulation, or if a hot fixture is close to combustible materials, the fixture may become hot enough to start a fire in the ceiling. And, the high temperature will eventually degrade the wiring insulation, causing an electrical fire.

If the ceiling is also the lower surface of an attic or other space that is vented to the outside, the fixture becomes a path for air leakage. All in-ceiling fixtures are vented to limit their interior temperature, so they are inherently leakage paths. Also, it is difficult to seal the perimeter of in-ceiling fixtures to the surrounding surface.

Instead, install fixtures that mount on the ceiling surface. (You still need a small hole through the ceiling for the electrical wiring.)

INDOOR NIGHT SAFETY LIGHTING

Indoor night lighting is an important safety feature, and it costs little to install and operate. Install night lights in the areas of your home that are likely to be used at night, such as the path between your bed and the toilet room. Night light requires little energy because human vision becomes very sensitive at night, when the eye is not desensitized by bright sunlight.

Today, there is only one kind of safety lighting that you need, which is the small LED fixtures that plug into your electrical power receptacles. The receptacles are located at just the right height for illuminating the floor and the surrounding low areas of the room. Since you will have wall receptacles everywhere, it is easy to place the night lights where they can provide safe passage.

Inexpensive LED night lights may use less than one watt, and many include a sensor that turns them off whenever daylight or other lighting is present. (See Figure 6-20.) These units are so inexpensive and use so little energy that you can distribute them liberally around the house.

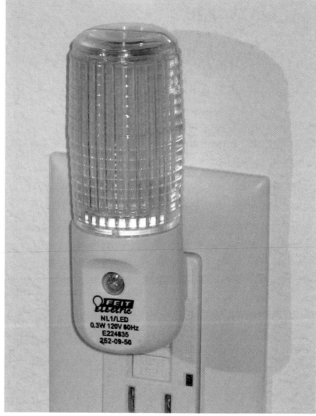

DRW

Figure 6-20. Night light. This unit claims to operate with 0.3 watts. It has a sensor that turns it off when daylight or other room light is present.

You can find plug-in night lights in a limitless variety of decorative designs at your local hardware store, at craft fairs, and elsewhere. Select units that have shades or lenses to keep your eyes from being blinded by the glare of the tiny lamps, without absorbing too much of the light output of the LED. For example, the fixture may project its light upward, illuminating the wall area above it.

In toilet rooms, wall receptacles normally are installed above basin level for convenience in connecting hair dryers, shavers, etc. A night light installed at that height would create glare if it remains on while the room is being used. Therefore, select a night light that has a sensor to turn it off when the room light is turned on.

OUTDOOR LIGHTING

Outdoor lighting has four common purposes:
* illuminating your outdoor activities
* safety and convenience in approaching your house
* revealing intruders
* showing off your home.

Optimize your lighting for each function, using the following guidelines.

Lamps for Outdoor Lighting

Select your lamps for outdoor lighting based on the climate, the length of time that the outdoor lighting operates, and the area you want to cover.

You can use incandescent, LED, and HID lamps in all climates. You can use compact fluorescent fixtures in climates that may get cool, but not cold. Don't use conventional long-tube fluorescent lamps outside.

LED lamps are replacing incandescent lamps because they offer much better efficiency and vastly longer life. Both types allow you to use dimmers, which are desirable for adapting the lighting levels to various outdoor activities.

To illuminate large outdoor areas for extended periods, HID lighting – especially metal halide – is still worth considering because of its energy efficiency and long life. Remember that HID lamps take a long time to start, and most take a long time to re-start after you turn them off. They are very bright, so they have the potential to create intense glare.

All outdoor lighting should have reasonably good color rendering to make your property and your party decorations look attractive. You want to see the colors of nature, especially the green of foliage and the colors of flowers and plants. Also, good color rendering provides better security, revealing the colorful clothing of the bad guy lurking in the shadows. Adequate color rendering for the outdoors is provided by incandescent lamps, "warm white" LED's, compact fluorescent lamps, and metal halide lamps.

Metal halide lamps operate at extremely high temperature and high internal pressure. Therefore, use them only in fixtures that protect against an explosion of the lamp.

Positioning Outdoor Fixtures

Install the outdoor fixtures where they can illuminate all your nighttime activities effectively. Mount the fixtures high to avoid glare, i.e., well above the line of sight. Where the walls of the house don't provide a good location, mount fixtures on poles, or even in trees. Mounting your fixtures high will make your security lighting difficult to sabotage by intruders.

If your home site is subject to crime, arrange your security lighting to provide direct illumination of all vulnerable entrances, including doors and ground level windows. The most energy efficient security lighting is provided by LED fixtures that are controlled by motion sensors, which we will discuss shortly.

Use reflector (PAR) lamps or focusing fixtures to concentrate light efficiently within the area that needs illumination. Incandescent, LED, and compact fluorescent lamps are available in reflector configurations. However, metal halide lamps may be limited to a fixed mounting position (base-up, base-down, or horizontal, depending on the lamp).

Your fixtures will need periodic lamp replacement. If the fixtures are located high, arrange the layout so that a ladder can be installed safely for access.

As a courtesy to your neighbors, arrange your fixtures so that your outdoor lighting does not create glare for them. Select fixtures that have shades that make the lamps invisible from your neighbors' property. Or, build baffles around your fixtures to limit their light to your property.

Decorative Outdoor Lighting

As a rule, don't use lighting to decorate your home's exterior at night. Electricity is expensive, and the resources needed to produce it are becoming scarce. Even a limited number of lamps can burn up a lot of energy if they operate all night. Think of how a small water leak can eventually flood a basement.

Okay, I relent... If you are hosting a party to show off your mansion, install some floodlights and illuminate your house like the Eiffel Tower. You built the house to impress your friends and rivals, so this is your moment. Just limit such extravagance to the hours when there are guests to impress.

If you bought a neon pink flamingo in Key West and you want to install it in your front window, go ahead. It's only a few watts. Control it with a timer that will turn it off after the bars close.

EFFICIENT LIGHTING CONTROLS

Effective control* of your lighting is vital for energy efficiency, safety, and convenience. Install controls to tailor your lighting to the places where it is needed, in the amounts needed, and at the times needed.

This part of your design is easy because efficient control usually is separate from the other aspects of your lighting. But, don't leave it to the electrician. Specify the controls for each built-in fixture in your construction drawings. Manual switches are the best controls for most of your lighting, but inexpensive automatic controls are now available to improve several kinds of home lighting.

Built-in lighting generally is controlled from built-in wall switch locations, whereas portable lighting usually is controlled with a switch at the fixture or on its electrical cord.

USE SWITCHES TO TAILOR YOUR LIGHTING

Switches are easy to install while you are building your home, but difficult to install later. So, spend some time to figure out where you will want all the switches for your built-in fixtures.

In a room with several permanently installed light fixtures, it is usually desirable to provide a separate switch for each fixture. Often, only a part of the room will require lighting. Similarly, you may want to darken part of a room so that you can view television or work on a computer.

If a fixture has several lamps, you can control the light output of the fixture by switching the individual lamps in the fixture. Your electrician can easily wire a separate switch for each lamp in an incandescent fixture, or for each ballast in a fluorescent fixture.

Locate Switches for Convenience and Safety

Install light switches so that every part of your home can be lighted before you enter it. For rooms with a single entrance, install the light switch(es) at the entrance. For rooms, corridors, stairways, and other areas that have multiple entrances, locate a switch at each entrance. Do this even if you plan to use night lighting.

Install manual switches where people expect to find them. Usually, this is on the wall at the inside of a doorway, adjacent to the doorknob but somewhat

DRW

Figure 6-21. Various ways to indicate switch functions. The telltale light on the upper switch is for an outdoor light that is not visible from inside the house. The horizontal switch orientation indicates that the light can be activated from two separate entrances. The dark switch controls a transit light in the room that can be turned on from any of three doors.

higher. One exception is switches for dark spaces, such as closets, that are entered from a lighted space. In such cases, it may be more convenient to locate the switch outside the entrance.

Switches that control equipment from a single location are called "single-pole." Other kinds of switches, called "3-way" and "4-way," are needed to control a fixture from more than one location. Be sure that your construction drawings indicate all lighting that needs to be controlled from more than one switch.

Switch Orientation

The way that switches are oriented provides an unconscious cue for using them efficiently. In the United States, people expect to push a light switch upward to turn on the lights. In many other countries, the opposite is customary. Be sure that your electrician installs the switches in the proper orientation.

This applies only to "single-pole" switches, which are switches that control a device from a single location. The "on" and "off" positions of 3-way and 4-way switches change, depending on the positions of the

---

* Among professional lighting designers, the word "control" means shaping the light distribution pattern from a fixture. We use the word "control" in the same way that we use it for other equipment, meaning to turn equipment on and off and to regulate output.

other switches controlling the same device. To avoid confusion, install 3-way and 4-way switches separately from single-pole switches.

 Provide obvious identification for switches that control fixtures from multiple locations.

To make the difference even clearer, consider installing 3-way and 4-way switches so their toggles move sideways, as in Figure 6-21.

Install Telltale Switches for Fixtures Out of Sight

Generally, install switches where you can easily see if the fixtures are on or off. However, this is not always practical. It is difficult to tell whether outdoor lighting is turned on from inside the house. Also, you can easily forget to turn off the lighting for closets and toilet rooms if the switches are located outside those rooms.

A reliable and inexpensive solution is to install telltale lights for fixtures that are out of sight. A telltale light is a small indicator light located near the switch that glows when the switch is turned on. Figure 6-21 shows an example.

If a light fixture is controlled from several locations, install a telltale light at each location.

Identify Switches Clearly

If you take advantage of your switching opportunities to tailor your lighting, some rooms will have a multitude of switches. In addition to controlling lighting, a group of switches may also control other equipment, such as an exhaust fan, a ceiling heater, or a garbage disposer. Even if you live in the house for a long time, you may have trouble remembering which switch controls which device. Guests will never figure it out.

So, if you have a batch of switches and their purposes are not obvious, label them. A fairly attractive method is installing an engraved plastic placard adjacent to the switch plate. Commercial sign makers have machines to produce these at low cost. The plastic is available in a wide range of colors. Be sure that the wording on the sign lines up with the switches.

You may be able to buy a switch plate that indicates different functions. For example, the switch plate in Figure 6-22 indicates the switches for a light fixture, an exhaust fan, and a heater. This switch plate came with a handy triple switch intended for use in shower rooms.

You can also use switches of different colors. For example, the dark toggle in Figure 6-21 indicates that the switch activates a passageway light that is operable from each of the room doors.

ANOTHER BAD IDEA: SWITCH-CONTROLLED RECEPTACLES

It is possible to control portable light fixtures with a wall switch. This is done by wiring a wall switch to control one or more wall receptacles, which may be located at the far end of the room. Portable light fixtures are plugged into those receptacles. This practice is common in bedrooms and in hotel rooms.

Usually, this is a bad idea. If someone turns off the portable fixture at its own switch, the wall switch becomes ineffective. And, the receptacle becomes annoying to use for other purposes.

If you need to turn on a room light before entering, install a wall switch at the entrance that controls a light fixture that is located anywhere in the room. If necessary for convenience, install a second wall switch to control the fixture from a location inside the room.

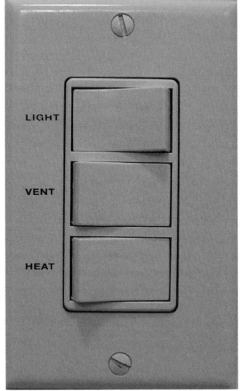

DRW

Figure 6-22. A switch plate that tells the functions of the switches. Larger type would improve legibility, requiring a separate placard installed alongside the switch plate.

To find a light switch inside a dark room, install a switch that has a lighted toggle. In bedrooms, this avoids fumbling to find the light switch at night. An alternative is to use low-wattage night lights.

AUTOMATIC LIGHTING CONTROLS

Automatic lighting controls can be a powerful aid for saving energy with certain lighting applications. They can turn lights on and off based on the time of day, the presence of daylight, the presence of people, or some combination of these. The following are the kinds of automatic lighting controls that are practical for homes.

Motion Sensors

Motion sensors are by far the most efficient way to limit lighting to times when people are present. They keep the lights turned off, except when a person or other moving object enters the area that is covered by the sensor. It's rather fun to walk through a house and have the lights turn automatically on as you enter a room or hallway.

The most common kind of motion sensor for lighting control senses the infrared heat radiation emitted by people, animals, and other objects that are warmer than the surroundings. This type of sensor responds when the warm body moves across the field of vision of the sensor. Typical outdoor infrared lighting controls have an effective range up to about 30 feet (10 meters), but the range varies with the outdoor temperature, the size of the moving object, and other factors.

Infrared motion sensors for exterior lights generally include a feature that turns the lights off during daylight.

Outdoor lighting fixtures with built-in infrared sensors have become a common item. Figure 6-23 shows a typical example. These make installation simple. It's important to install the fixture and the sensors where intruders cannot disable them.

By turning on outside lights only when you have visitors, motion sensors serve as an effective security alarm. The sudden appearance of light may also chase away deer, raccoons, and other critters who damage property.

Infrared motion sensors are vulnerable to false triggering by objects in the distance, such as pedestrians on the sidewalk in front of your house and automobile headlights in the distance. For this reason, be careful to locate and aim infrared sensors to avoid false triggering.

Motion sensors that control indoor lighting usually are installed in a conventional wall switch box, as in Figure 6-24. To avoid triggering by pets, the sensor should be selected and installed so that the lower portion of the sensor's field of vision can be blocked.

Use motion sensors only with incandescent or LED lighting. Fluorescent lamps suffer from frequent on and off cycles. Compact fluorescent lamps may require more than a minute to reach full brightness, and HID lamps have starting delays of several minutes.

Heath/Zenith

Figure 6-23. Outdoor security light, activated by an infrared motion sensor.

Figure 6-24. An infrared motion sensor that installs in a conventional electrical box on a wall. It includes a manual on-off switch on the front, which is a desirable feature.

For most applications, buy units that include a convenient manual switch that allows you to override the sensor. The manual switch should have three positions: (1) automatic control by the motion sensor, (2) always on, and (3) always off.

Search a professional electrical supplies catalog to find appropriate motion sensors. Don't leave this to your electrician. Avoid cheap hardware store units, which lack desirable features and tend to fail. Expect to spend several times the price of mass market units to get good ones.

Daylight Sensors

Daylight sensors, also called "photocells" or "photoelectric cells," switch on lights while it is dark outside. A daylight sensor is the simplest and most reliable method of control if you want security lighting during all hours of darkness. You can find many styles of outdoor lighting fixtures that include a daylight sensor. The sensor generally is so inconspicuous that it does not change the appearance of the fixture. Figure 6-25 is an example.

Commonly, a daylight sensor is combined with a motion sensor. The occupant may choose one function or the other, or a combination. For example, the fixture in Figure 6-25 has two levels of night lighting. Normally, it operates at the lower level, but the motion sensor causes it to become brighter.

You can also get indoor night safety lights that have built-in light level sensors. These turn off when there is sufficient daylight or light from other fixtures. The night light in Figure 6-20 is an example.

Heath/Zenith

Figure 6-25. Decorative outdoor lamp. The pendant at the bottom contains both a daylight sensor and a motion sensor.

Leviton

Figure 6-26. An astronomical timer that fits into a standard electrical box. The manual switch overrides the timer.

Figure 6-27. A typical plunger-type door switch. It is recessed into the hinge side of the door frame. The wiring runs inside the wall.

Astronomical Clock Timers

What if you want to operate lights for part of the night, but not all night? The easy solution is to install an "astronomical" clock timer, which is a time switch that also calculates the time of sunset and sunrise based on your location and the date. For example, you can program an astronomical timer to turn on the lights at sunset and turn them off at midnight.

Today, most astronomical timers are miniature electronic devices. Some can be plugged into a wall socket for controlling portable indoor lights. Others can be installed in a light switch box for controlling either outdoor lights or permanently installed indoor lights. Figure 6-26 is an example.

The timer should have a single-cycle override button that allows you to easily bypass the clock, either to turn on the lights or to turn them off. Alternatively, the unit may be installed in a double switch box, with a manual switch controlling power to the timer switch.

Install the timer at an obvious and accessible location, for example, next to other light switches at an entrance door.

Door Switches for Small Spaces

Door switches are an efficient and inexpensive way to control the lighting of closets, pantries, cabinets, and other small spaces that have doors that are normally kept closed. There are two main types of door switches, mechanical and magnetic.

Mechanical switches have a plunger that is depressed by the door when it is closed. Figure 6-27 shows a typical unit. For doors to walk-in spaces, a mechanical switch typically is located in the hinge side of the door frame, so that the plunger is depressed by the edge of the door. This location keeps the lights turned off even if the door is left ajar, and it minimizes the tendency of the plunger to push the door open.

Magnetic switches typically are installed on the latch side of the door frame, or on top of the door frame toward the latch side. A magnet installed on the door itself turns the switch off when the door is closed. This type of installation requires the door to be fully closed to turn off the lights.

Door switches require wiring in unusual locations. Be sure that your construction drawings show the wiring of your door switches, along with all your other switches.

STEP 7

SELECT YOUR HOUSEHOLD APPLIANCES

This is the easiest Step in the design of your super-home. There's not much doubt about which types of appliances you will want. All the information you need to select the best models is readily available. And, the sizes of major kitchen appliances are standardized, which made it easy to lay out your kitchen in Step 1.

Only in a few cases will you need to ponder whether to have a major appliance – such as a food freezer. You can defer the selection of your portable appliances, such television sets, until your home is built. But, make sure that each appliance has a well planned niche in your home.

If a particular type of appliance can use more than one energy source – for example, clothes dryers can use electricity or gas – start by deciding which energy source is best for you, guided by our review of energy sources at the beginning of Step 4.

Next, narrow your search to models that have the highest efficiencies. You can do this entirely on the Internet. We explain the appliance efficiency rating systems and how to use them.

Then, for each type of appliance, we explain the main variations, features worth considering, and any installation issues that require special attention. Finally, visit a few large appliance stores to see the styles and features that are currently available. Check the reliability and performance of current models by reading objective reviews, such as *Consumer Reports*. For more details about available features, visit manufacturers' Web sites.

Everything in this Step applies to selecting appliances for an existing home in the same way as it does for a new home.

APPLIANCE EFFICIENCY RATINGS

Selecting high-efficiency equipment is one of the Five Principles of Super-Efficiency. But until recently, it would have been practically impossible for a homeowner to do all the research needed to identify the most efficient appliances that are available. Now, selecting efficient appliances has become almost effortless. The hard work is done for you by a system of energy efficiency ratings that allow you to shop for appliances on an objective basis.

Well, almost objective. Manufacturers do their own testing, subject to test procedures that are established by industry organizations. This invites cheating. Also, the ratings for certain appliances are misleading, and we will warn you about those.

The existence of efficiency ratings has been a powerful stimulus for manufacturers to offer models with greatly improved efficiency. At the same time, inefficient models remain for the cheap end of the market. So, there is now a much greater difference between the most efficient models and the least efficient.

Efficiency ratings are continually expanding and evolving. Most appliances are now rated, but some still remain to be covered adequately. Some equipment may be covered by two or more rating systems. Some rating systems are based on others. For appliances, the following rating systems are the most important at this time.

The Energy Star Rating System

In the United States, the primary rating system for household appliances is the federal Energy Star program. Appliances that fall within the top percentage of efficiency within each type are allowed to claim Energy Star certification. The range of eligibility differs for each type of appliance.

Even more useful, the individual efficiency ratings of Energy Star certified appliances are listed on the Energy Star Web site, **www.EnergyStar.gov**. This allows you to identify the most efficient models without setting foot in a store or looking in a catalog. Searching the Energy Star Web site is now the best way to start shopping for most appliances.

Each efficiency rating is tailored to the type of appliance. Water-using equipment, including washing machines and dishwashers, are now rated for water saving as well as energy efficiency.

Energy Star is now spreading to other countries and groups of countries, including the European Union. Similar efficiency rating systems have been adopted elsewhere.

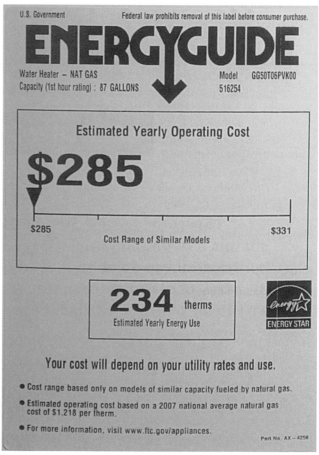

DRW

Figure 7-1. A typical appliance efficiency label.

Appliance Efficiency Labeling

The United States has another program, called *EnergyGuide*, that requires manufacturers to attach large yellow labels to all residential refrigerators, freezers, dishwashers, clothes washers, water heaters, boilers, furnaces, air conditioners, heat pumps, and pool heaters. The label on each appliance indicates the annual operating cost and/or the efficiency rating of that particular model. The label also shows how that rating compares to the lowest and highest ratings for that type of appliance. Figure 7-1 shows a typical label.

This system has a big weakness, which is that the labels give you efficiency information only for the models that are displayed in the store. *EnergyGuide* labeling has been rendered largely obsolete by Energy Star and other rating systems that can give you comprehensive efficiency rankings on the Internet before you start shopping.

YOUR MAJOR APPLIANCES

REFRIGERATORS

A refrigerator is an insulated box with built-in cooling equipment. The cooling equipment is similar to an air conditioner, except that it cools to a lower temperature. Refrigerator efficiency has improved greatly in recent years because of better insulation, more efficient cooling equipment, and better control of temperature and defrosting.

The refrigerator is usually the biggest consumer of energy in the kitchen. That's because it runs all the time. You can minimize the energy cost of your refrigerator by shopping for a high-efficiency model, by installing it properly, and by using it efficiently.

Select Your Refrigerator for Efficiency

Start your shopping on the Energy Star Web site. All models listed there use at least 15% less energy than required by current U.S. federal standards. Pick from the best of this group. (Compact models, with volumes less than 7.75 cubic feet, are listed if they use at least 20% less energy than required by current federal standards.)

The models are grouped by their configuration and major features. For each model, the Web site lists the "percent better" than U.S. federal standards. Decide on the features that you want and narrow your selection to the most efficient models in that group.

Refrigerator Options

Energy consumption increases with size, other things being equal. However, don't get a refrigerator that is too small. From experience, you will know the size that you need for your family.

Most refrigerators have a freezer section. Originally, this section was always on top. That is still the most popular configuration. Refrigerators with side-by-side freezers are less efficient, although they provide more freezer space. Some refrigerators have a freezer at the bottom, but this location is awkward.

An automatic ice maker that is located inside the freezer compartment is a desirable option. It requires a flexible connection to your cold water supply. If you install a drinking water filter for household use, connect the water supply to the ice maker from the discharge side of the water filter.

Refrigerators with chilled water dispensers and ice makers located in the door have become popular. However, it is reported that this feature increases energy use by 14% to 20%. Also, in my experience, in-door dispensers are prone to trouble.

DRW

Figure 7-2. Rust that results from condensation around the opening of a refrigerator door.

Automatic defrosting has become a standard feature. Previously, the freezer compartment would accumulate a thick layer of ice, which greatly reduced efficiency. To get rid of the ice, you had to turn off the refrigerator periodically, empty the freezer compartment, and sweep out the ice as it melted. It is a chore that you won't miss.

However, automatic defrosting approximately doubles the energy consumption of a refrigerator, compared to one that is manually defrosted on a regular basis. Especially if your climate is very dry, you might consider a manual defrost model if you want to push energy efficiency to the limit. However, if you fail to defrost regularly, you will lose your energy saving.

Sweat tends to form around the door gaskets, especially when the weather is humid. This can cause mildew and rust. (See Figure 7-2.) To avoid this sweating, some refrigerators have heating strips around the door edges. This feature consumes additional energy, but it will make your refrigerator last longer in a humid climate.

Get a refrigerator that has rollers to allow you to pull it out easily for cleaning the heat rejecting surfaces and the space behind the refrigerator.

How to Install the Refrigerator

The machinery of a refrigerator moves heat from the inside of the refrigerator into the kitchen environment. To minimize your energy cost, keep the environment around the refrigerator as cool as possible.

Most refrigerators reject heat through coils located either behind the unit or under it. The heat is carried away by convection, which is a weak force. Therefore, provide ample space around the refrigerator for the heat to escape. Since convection is upward, provide an especially large gap above the refrigerator. If you don't think that gaps around the refrigerator look pretty, get used to it. Leave even more clearance if you may want to buy a larger refrigerator later.

Install the refrigerator and freezer away from heat producing equipment, including the range, ovens, dishwasher, and water heater. Don't let direct sunlight fall on the refrigerator. If necessary, install a partition to block heat from adjacent equipment, while allowing free air circulation.

Use Your Refrigerator Efficiently

You can cut the energy cost of your refrigerator significantly by using it carefully. The big item is to minimize the time you leave the door open. Whenever the door opens, the entire volume of dense cold air inside spills out into the kitchen. If you stand there and gaze at the contents, active circulation will warm up the interior. Plan to remove all the things you need at one time.

Make a point of cleaning the heat rejecting coils or surfaces on the outside of the refrigerator every few months. Maybe stick a cleaning schedule on the side of the refrigerator.

When you receive your refrigerator, make sure that the door seals are airtight. Test for tightness by placing a slip of paper between the door frame and the gasket. Pulling out the paper should require noticeable effort, and the tightness should be equal around the door frame. If the gaskets do not seal completely, frost and mildew will form where cold air leaks out. If there are any leaks in the door gasket, return the refrigerator for replacement.

Get in the habit of thawing frozen food, especially large items, inside your refrigerator. Thawing a large item, like a pot roast, takes about one day inside the refrigerator. By planning ahead, you can save both refrigeration energy and cooking energy. This practice also reduces the risk of food poisoning because the thawing food is never exposed to room temperature.

FOOD FREEZERS

A food freezer is like a refrigerator, but it operates at lower temperature. The typical temperature inside a freezer is 0 to 5 °F (-18 to -15 °C). The lower temperature requires a freezer to use more energy, so most freezers (but not all) are optimized for energy efficiency. They are designed for less frequent access than refrigerators, and they lack frills that would compromise efficiency.

Do You Really Want a Freezer?

The first question to ask about a food freezer is whether you really want one. Your refrigerator has a freezer compartment, so why would you want more freezer space? A freezer is desirable primarily if you get food in large quantities. Do you kill your own game? Are you a rancher who sends an entire steer to the butcher for your family's own consumption? In the past, people might buy a large quantity of meat at discounted prices, but that option has largely disappeared. With large grocery stores located within short distances of most of the population, few people have a real need for a freezer.

Because the inside of a freezer is very cold, the humidity is very low. This environment quickly dries out exposed food, creating "freezer burn." (This fact is exploited in the making of freeze dried foods.) To avoid damage, frozen food must be packaged in carefully sealed wrappings. In urban environments, a food freezer often becomes a device for converting fresh food into old, dried-out food at extra cost.

Also, in the event of an electricity interruption, your freezer will warm up within hours, destroying a large amount of food. In many locations, an emergency generator is an essential accessory for a food freezer.

Select Your Freezer for Efficiency

Start your shopping on the Energy Star Web site. All models listed there use at least 10% less energy than required by current U.S. federal standards. Pick from among the best of this group. (Compact models, with volumes less than 7.75 cubic feet, are listed if they use at least 20% less energy than required by current federal standards.)

The models are grouped by their configuration and major features. For each model, the Web site lists the "percent better" than U.S. federal standards. Decide on the features that you want and narrow your selection to the most efficient models in that group.

Freezer Options

The most energy-efficient type of freezer is the classic "chest freezer." It is a big rectangular box with the door on top. When the door is opened, the dense cold air tends to remain inside the freezer. Also, the weight of the door helps to keep it tightly sealed.

A chest freezer has two main disadvantages. It has a large footprint and it is low, so that it does not use space inside the house efficiently. Also, the food is packed in depth, making it difficult to remove items that are low in the pile. As a result, food on the bottom tends to stay there a long time.

The upright freezer is a newer type that looks like a refrigerator. Access to food is more convenient, but the design is inherently less efficient. An upright freezer may be appropriate for a kitchen or pantry where you want quick access to large amounts of frozen food.

Chest freezers generally do not have automatic defrost, in keeping with their orientation toward energy efficiency. Upright models are available both with and without automatic defrost.

Where to Install a Freezer

If you install a freezer inside your kitchen, follow the same installation guidelines as for refrigerators.

If you need a food freezer primarily for long term storage, so that you won't be using it often, you can install it farther from the kitchen. Try to find a location in the house that is especially cool. In most climates, the basement is a good location for a food freezer. Basements are cooler than the rest of the house, and the operation of the freezer provides a slight useful warming to lower the relative humidity in the basement.

If the climate is usually cooler than room temperature, let nature do as much of the cooling as possible. Consider installing your freezer in the garage, on a shaded porch, or in another protected location that is not heated. Ironically, the cooling system may not function properly if the outdoor temperature becomes very cold. Check the freezer's specifications to find out the lowest external temperature that the freezer can tolerate.

Use Your Freezer Efficiently

When you receive your freezer, test the gaskets for tight sealing as we suggested for your refrigerator. If the gaskets are not entirely tight, get them fixed.

Clean the heat rejecting coils or surfaces on the outside of the freezer every few months. Put a cleaning reminder on the freezer.

Especially if you have an upright freezer, minimize the time you leave the door open.

CONVENTIONAL RANGES

Most kitchen ranges are triple appliances. They include a cooktop with burners, an oven, and a broiler. All are controlled from a single control panel. Even the more modest models now offer an array of control features. *Consumer Reports* is probably your best source for information about the features and performance of the latest models.

One choice that will have a big effect on your cooking and your energy costs is whether your range will use gas or electricity. In most cases, this decision will depend on the availability of natural gas to your home site. If you choose natural gas for your home heating, the same economics will probably favor gas for cooking. See the beginning of Step 4 to review the issues in making your energy choices.

Locate your range for efficient workflow in the kitchen, to minimize fire hazard, and to simplify the important ventilation that the range requires. We covered kitchen ventilation in Step 4, including specific recommendations for your range hood.

The components of a range are available as separate appliances. You can mount a separate cooktop in a counter, or have a portable electric cooktop. Also, your kitchen may have a separate oven/broiler. We will concentrate on the cooktop here, and cover the oven/broiler later.

Gas Ranges

Many cooks prefer gas ranges over electric ranges because a gas flame can be controlled precisely, and it distributes heat more evenly over the bottom of the pan than an electric heating element. Gas broilers provide the intense heat needed for good broiling.

There are some health concerns about natural gas itself and the combustion products of gas. Any range will leak a certain amount of unburned gas during starting, and any gas appliance is susceptible to small gas leaks. However, careful installation and an effective range hood should prevent gas from leaking into the house.

If your home site does not have gas service, you could operate a gas range with bottled propane. However, propane has a safety hazard that we explained in Step 4, especially for houses that have a basement or other space below grade.

At this time, all gas ranges have the familiar basic pattern of open gas burners. If you decide to use gas as your cooking fuel, most of your choices will be about convenience and appearance features.

Conventional gas ranges have low energy efficiency because much of the flame heats air that wafts away into the kitchen. Some sources estimate that 60% of the gas energy is wasted in this manner. However, this can vary widely. A large pot heated over a small burner at low flame will waste less heat than the same pot placed over a large burner at high flame.

Electric Ranges

Among electric ranges, the older type of spiral heating element is largely being superseded by heating elements that are hidden underneath a smooth surface. The newer types are easier to clean and they look more modern. Instead of a resistance heating element, some newer models use a tungsten halogen element (using the same principle as tungsten halogen light bulbs) to radiate heat energy to the bottom of the cookware. However, the smooth-top models are vulnerable to scratching of the cooking surface.

Electric ranges waste roughly 30% of their heating energy to the surrounding space, which is significantly less than the amount wasted by gas ranges. However, the lower heat loss of electric ranges is canceled by the energy losses that occur in generating electricity.

Use Your Range Efficiently

Kitchen ranges do not presently have efficiency ratings in the U.S. *The cook's behavior has a much bigger effect on energy consumption than differences between models.* Here are the main ways to save energy and improve cooking when using your range.

■ Skill with Pots and Pans

Keep lids on your pots and pans when you cook. This simple habit can cut your cooking energy in half, and it hastens boiling. To keep the pot from boiling over when the water reaches boiling temperature, turn the heat down to simmer, which is a slow boil. A faster boil is no hotter, it just wastes energy by making useless steam. Once boiling starts, tip the lid slightly to keep the contents from boiling over.

Use pots and pans that are larger in diameter than the burners, so that less heat will escape up the sides. Similarly, use the smallest burner on your range that will do the job.

With conventional electric ranges, use pots and pans that have very flat bottoms. This is important to provide good contact with the heating elements. Without that, the heating elements will waste energy by heating the air in the kitchen. Also, cooking time will be longer.

If your electric range has spiral heating elements, keep the reflector pans underneath the elements clean and shiny. They reflect heat from the bottom of the elements to the bottom of the pan.

The metal for pots and pans is a compromise. Aluminum has good heat conduction, and it is inexpensive, but a concern exists that aluminum may get into the food and contribute to Alzheimer's Disease. Cast iron has good heat distribution and it is inexpensive, but it is heavy. Stainless steel has poor heat conduction. Lightweight stainless cookware distributes heat poorly, and it does not lie flat. To compensate for these shortcomings, the bottoms of fancy stainless steel pans have a thick layer of aluminum or copper to distribute the heat across the pan.

Using a grease trapping lid or screen on your frying pan. It does not harm crispness, and it keeps grease from splattering over the vicinity of the range.

■ Consider a Pressure Cooker

The purpose of a pressure cooker is to allow you to cook food in water and steam that is somewhat hotter than the normal boiling temperature of water, up to about 250 °F (about 120 °C). The principle is that increased pressure increases the temperature at which water boils.

The first home pressure cookers were sold in 1938, and they quickly became popular. Since then, they have largely disappeared from modern kitchens, but they still deserve consideration.

Presto

Figure 7-6. The basic pressure cooker. The weight at the center of the lid controls the pressure. To its right is a small rubber disc that blows out of the lid and releases the steam if the pressure gets too high. Different models use a variety of safety features to prevent the lid from being removed while the cooker is under pressure.

A pressure cooker is a sealed cooking pot with a pressure regulator and a safety valve. Figure 7-6 shows a basic model. The pressure regulator is a weighted cap that sits on top of an orifice in the lid. The pressure and temperature inside the cooker are determined solely by the weight of the cap, so cooking is independent of the altitude, weather, or other factors.

A pressure cooker saves time. The higher temperature speeds cooking considerably for some foods, such as rice and meat.

The reduced cooking time also saves energy. And, because the cooker is sealed, little heat is carried away by escaping water vapor, except for a small amount of steam that escapes under the pressure regulator.

The higher temperature also helps to sterilize the food, which is why pressure cookers are used for canning. However, canning requires a special kind of pressure cooker that provides better sterilization.

If you live at a higher altitude, water in an open pot boils at temperature that may be too low for cooking meat and certain vegetables. A pressure cooker solves this problem.

If you don't need a higher temperature for cooking, you can save almost as much energy by keeping a lid on your pots and adjusting the heat to prevent overflow.

ELECTRIC INDUCTION RANGES

Induction ranges are the most recent major development in cooking, but they are a mixed blessing. Induction ranges look similar to conventional "smooth top" electric ranges, but they operate differently. High-frequency electric coils under the range surface induce electric currents in the bottom of iron or steel cookware, and these currents create heat. The ceramic range surface is not heated, and contact between the surface and the cookware is not critical.

Heat is distributed more uniformly over the bottom of the pan than with conventional electric resistance heating elements. The heat intensity is controllable instantly and over a wide range. These are benefits that caused cooks to favor gas ranges in the past, so induction cooking may shrink the market for gas ranges.

Induction heating elements are compact, so they can be mounted in many configurations. Induction cooking is available in freestanding ranges, in cooktops that can be inserted into a counter, and in small portable units. Figure 7-8 shows a typical unit. Full-sized induction ranges are similar to conventional gas and electric ranges. A lightweight portable induction cooker can serve as a portable grill.

The technology is still evolving and is still being evaluated. One big issue is the potential safety hazards of the high-frequency magnetic fields.

Electrolux

Figure 7-8. A typical induction cooktop. It looks the same as a conventional electric range. However, it needs special cookware.

Energy Efficiency

As yet, there are no efficiency standards for induction cookers. However, induction cooking is inherently efficient because the heating energy goes directly into the bottom of the pan or pot. It has better ability to capture the input energy in the cookware than other types of electric ranges, and it is much better in this regard than gas ranges.

Cookware for Induction Ranges

Induction ranges have one big limitation, compared to other kinds of ranges. They work properly only with a limited range of cookware. The cookware must capture the high-frequency magnetic field and turn the resulting electric currents into heat.

Plain or enameled cast iron cookware works well. However, the rough surfaces of cast iron may scratch the surface of the range. This makes it advisable to use a pad between the cookware and the range. The pad must be thin, non-metallic, and resistant to the highest temperatures that will occur. You can buy special pads for induction cooking, but they are a nuisance.

Ordinary stainless steel cookware will not work properly. If you want the advantages of stainless steel, you must buy special stainless cookware that is made for induction cooking. It is made from several layers of metal, including an outer layer of highly magnetic stainless steel, one or more interior layers of aluminum or copper to distribute the heat, and an inner layer of stainless steel for ease of cleaning. This cookware is expensive, especially since you need a full set of it.

For best efficiency and quickest cooking, use your pots and pans in the same way as recommended for conventional ranges.

Safety Concerns

Any new technology raises safety concerns. In the case of induction cooking, three significant concerns remain at the time this is being written.

One concern is that the magnetic field will accidentally heat the wrong metal object, such as a steel knife or spatula that is left on the cooktop. To minimize this risk, all well made induction cookers include a sensor that prevents the unit from operating unless there is a mass of iron on the surface that has about the weight of a small skillet. As a result, induction cookers don't work with very small pots or pans.

An alternating magnetic field will induce an electric current in any metal, such as a ring on your finger. However, if an iron vessel is placed on the induction element, it will draw most of the magnetic field into itself, so that your ring will not be exposed to much heating energy. When a vessel is properly placed on the surface, the heated area is limited to the region immediately above the induction element. An induction range will melt aluminum foil that is accidentally placed on top of the range.

The second major concern is whether magnetic fields in general can harm people. There have been many studies of the medical effects of magnetic fields at various frequencies. Most indicate no effect, or only questionable effects on a small fraction of susceptible subjects. Some advocates of induction ranges argue that they are safe because cell phones have proven to be safe. It's not a valid analogy. Cell phones transmit tiny amounts of power, whereas induction ranges transmit large amounts of power, literally enough to roast a turkey, for example.

The third major concern is whether the magnetic fields can interfere with the operation of medical implants, such as pacemakers and defibrillators. At the present time, some reports are waffling about this, suggesting that people should maintain a certain distance (usually stated as about one yard or one meter) from the induction element.

Microwave ovens attracted similar concerns when they were introduced, which seem to have been satisfied by the passage of time. However, this does not provide similar assurance for induction ranges. Microwave ovens achieve safety by tightly sealing the box against leakage of radiation. In contrast, the cooking surface of an induction range is wide open.

Aside from possible hazards to people, the intense magnetic field of the induction heating element can damage magnetic storage media and certain electronic instruments, such as digital cameras.

These safety concerns have not deterred a number of major manufacturers from producing induction ranges, and thereby exposing themselves to liability for injury that their products may cause. If you are considering an induction cooker and you have concerns about these issues, investigate further.

OVENS AND BROILERS

An oven cooks by creating a fairly uniform temperature environment, generally with moderate temperatures and long cooking times. The result is fairly uniform cooking, combined with the mild crust typical of baking and roasting.

In contrast, a broiler subjects the outside of the food to intensely high temperature for a short period of time. For meats, the high temperature seals the exterior and creates a tasty crust, while keeping the interior moist and flavorful. A broiler is also used for quick browning of breads, pastries, and meringues.

These two different modes of cooking are commonly performed with the same appliance, which is an insulated box that has separate heating elements for baking and broiling. The baking element is at the bottom, heating the food mainly by convection. The broiler element is at the top, and cooks the food primarily by radiation.

The oven/broiler may be combined with a range, or it may be installed separately. A separate oven can be installed at chest level, where it is more convenient than an oven located underneath a range.

Ovens and broilers can be heated with electricity or gas. Either energy source is good for baking and roasting. However, gas broilers are superior to electric broilers for producing the intense radiant heat needed for good broiling.

Convection Ovens

A convection oven is a variation of a conventional oven. The difference is that the heated air is circulated throughout the interior of the oven by a fan. Figure 7-10 shows a typical unit.

The name "convection oven" is completely wrong. Ordinary ovens, which have a heating element at the bottom, circulate heat by convection. In contrast, "convection" ovens circulate heat by using a fan. The names "fan oven" and "turbo oven" are also used for these ovens, making more sense.

Convection ovens offer improved cooking and lower energy consumption, primarily by creating a uniform temperature throughout the oven. Thus, the tops of pies, turkeys, etc. are browned as nicely as the bottoms. Also, the air circulation provides more uniform heat distribution when food is cooked at several levels inside the oven.

Convention ovens reduce cooking time, typically about 25%. This results from the better overall distribution of heat, and because the movement of the air strips away the stagnant layer of air that tends to insulate the food from the heat of the oven. By the same token, cooking temperatures can be somewhat lower than for a conventional oven.

Whirlpool

Figure 7-10. The inside of an electric convection oven. The main difference from a conventional electric oven is the large fan mounted in the rear.

Some models use a heating element in the fan discharge, instead of a heating element at the bottom of the oven. This provides even more uniform heating.

Convection ovens seem to have no disadvantages, except for a significantly higher price.

Self-Cleaning Ovens

"Self-cleaning" is a feature of some ovens that minimizes the drudgery of cleaning. It works by using prolonged high temperature to burn the greasy deposits inside the oven to an ash that is more easily removed. Ideally, the volatile components of the grease are converted to carbon dioxide and water vapor, but a certain amount of smoke is produced, requiring good ventilation during the cleaning cycle.

Typically, the cleaning cycle raises the temperature inside the oven to 900 °F (500 °C) for a period of several hours. This is much hotter than typical cooking temperature, and it creates a potential fire hazard. Therefore, self-cleaning ovens have extra insulation. As a safety feature, the oven door is automatically locked during the cleaning cycle, and it typically cannot be opened until the oven cools to a temperature of about 600 °F (300 °C).

Self-cleaning ovens use a variety of surface coatings to promote breakdown of the food deposits. Separate cleaning agents usually are not needed, but they may be recommended with some oven surfaces. The performance and durability of the surface coatings may vary, so check for independent reviews of current models in *Consumer Reports* or other reliable sources.

Energy Efficiency

There are no efficiency standards for ovens or broilers at present, at least in the U.S. The amount of insulation is an important factor, but the manufacturer may not provide enough information for you to judge the insulation quality.

Convection ovens improve energy efficiency by reducing cooking time and temperature. A saving of about 30% is commonly claimed.

A self-cleaning oven won't use much extra energy, because you won't need to use the feature often. The cost of the energy for a cleaning cycle is probably less than the cost of the cleaning materials that you would use otherwise. Also, the increased insulation in self-cleaning ovens saves energy during normal operation.

The best way to save energy with your oven/broiler is to use it efficiently. Here are a few tips:

- Keep the oven door closed. Opening the door allows the heated air that does the cooking to escape. Get an oven with a good window in the door so you know what is happening inside. If you use an oven thermometer or a meat thermometer, place it so that you can see it through the window.
- Cook all your food together, or as much as you can. Roast the potatoes along with the turkey.
- Don't preheat the oven for roasting. For baking, minimize any preheating that you may need to stabilize the temperature.
- Minimize preheating for broiling. The radiant surface should be fully hot, but it is not necessary to heat the entire inside.
- Use the self-cleaning feature as little as possible, if you have it. When you use it, start it immediately after cooking, to make use of the residual heat in the oven.

Ventilation for Your Oven

Ovens emit fumes, although the fumes are less noticeable than the steam and smoke that come from ranges. Therefore, your oven should have ventilation to the outside. If the oven is part of your range, the range hood takes care of the job. If your oven is installed separately, try to install it alongside your range. Then, you can select a fume hood that is wide enough to cover both the range and the oven.

MICROWAVE OVENS

As the name implies, a microwave oven uses high frequency radio waves to cook the food. The radiation is generated by a device called a magnetron, which was invented in World War II to generate radar waves. The radiation is tuned to a frequency that excites the molecules of water and fat in foods, so the microwave oven heats the food directly.

Every kitchen should have one or two microwave ovens. They are the most energy efficient type of cooker, they heat instantly, they save cooking time, and they create almost no mess. They have demonstrated their worth and safety over several decades of experience.

The radiation penetrates the food deeply, rather than cooking from the surface inward. However, the distribution of the radiation inside the box is somewhat spotty. Therefore, a microwave oven typically has rotating metal vanes in the path of the radiation to scatter the radiation throughout the box. Also, the oven may have a rotating food tray to expose the food to the radiation more evenly.

A microwave oven performs some cooking functions better than a range and it performs other cooking functions better than an oven, but it does not substitute for either.

Because a microwave oven does not cook from the outside, it does not create the tasty crust that is created by a conventional oven or broiler. This factor limits the kind of cooking that a microwave oven can do well.

Some microwave ovens now include a broiler or browning element to simulate the cooking of a real broiler. This is not a good compromise. A broiler inside a microwave oven cannot equal a conventional broiler, because it would create a mess inside the box. It cannot replicate the delicious contrast of textures that is produced by a good broiler. You can get good results with some dishes by cooking them part way in a microwave oven, and then finishing them in a conventional broiler.

Energy Efficiency

Microwave ovens are exceptionally energy efficient. About half the total electricity that is used by the appliance is absorbed by the food itself. Ordinary ranges and ovens waste a lot more energy by heating the surrounding air and the equipment itself.

Overall, a microwave oven is about as efficient as induction cooking, more efficient than conventional electric ranges, and still more efficient than gas ranges. (However, to balance the picture, we must repeat that a lot of energy is wasted in the generation of electricity.) Microwave ovens do not presently have efficiency ratings in the U.S. There is little efficiency difference between models.

The main way to exploit the efficiency of microwave ovens is to use them for as much of your cooking as possible. Microwave ovens don't cook everything well, but they have a wider application than most people believe. They cook most vegetables well, minimizing loss of vitamins and nutrient value. They do a fine job of baking potatoes and yams. They are quick and efficient for heating water, either a single cup or a whole pot. Get a good microwave cookbook to see the wide range of foods that can be cooked deliciously.

Use lids with your microwave-compatible cookware, or put a saucer over the cup of water that you are heating. This saves energy, saves time, and to keeps the inside of the microwave oven from being soaked or splattered.

A Matter of Timing

Control of cooking in a microwave oven is by timing and power level. Timing is the unusual aspect of microwave cooking. Because a microwave oven heats food directly, cooking time is proportional to the weight of the food being cooked. For example, baking two potatoes takes almost twice as long as baking one potato.

The power level setting cycles the magnetron on and off, allowing time for heat to flow from the warmer parts of the food to the cooler. Microwave ovens cannot heat all parts of the food to the same temperature, because water content varies in the food and because the distribution of the radiation is uneven. Using a rotating tray allows you to cook at a higher power level and save time.

Good Installation

Step 1 recommended providing space in your kitchen for two microwave ovens, one large and one medium sized. You will want to cook different foods for different times and at different power levels.

Consider installing the larger unit near your conventional oven, for preparing big feasts. For example, you can cook the vegetables in the microwave while the turkey is roasting in the oven. Install the smaller unit where it is convenient for heating quick items.

Provide a separate electric circuit for each microwave oven. A large unit draws most of the power that can be provided by a standard circuit.

Microwave ovens have the advantage of being portable devices, which makes them easy to replace or to move to a more convenient location. Don't forfeit this benefit by including a microwave oven in another appliance or by building it tightly into a cabinet. Set aside a location for your microwave oven on your countertop, or install a shelf for it at a convenient height.

The primary health hazard of microwave ovens is damage to your eyes if you stand close to a unit that leaks radiation. This can cause cataracts. Therefore, try to avoid installing a unit at eye level.

Generally, you don't need to provide ventilation for a microwave oven. Because of its high efficiency, the unit emits little heat. The cooking temperature is no higher than the boiling temperature of water, so no combustion products are created. And, the cooking occurs inside a sealed box, so there is no splatter into the surroundings.

If you use a microwave oven with a built-in broiler or browner (which I don't recommend), the high temperature will create fumes and you may need to install the unit under a ventilation hood.

DISHWASHERS

The dishwasher is another appliance that any modern home will have, unless you are keen to return to a more elemental lifestyle. Dishwashers offer a few options, some of which are worthwhile and some not.

Select Your Dishwasher for Energy and Water Efficiency

Start your shopping on the Energy Star Web site. All models listed there use at least 25% less energy than required by current U.S. federal standards. Pick from among the best of this group.

The Energy Star Web site lists the same information in two ways. One is the "energy factor." A bigger energy factor is better. The Web site also lists the "percent better" for each model, which is the percentage by which the unit exceeds U.S. federal standards.

A dishwasher uses energy in several ways. The largest part is the energy that your water heater consumes to heat the water. For this reason, the dishwasher's ability to ration water is a big factor in the efficiency rating. The dishwasher itself uses electricity to operate the motor, to operate the drying heater, and in some units, to operate a booster heater to raise the temperature of the water.

Unfortunately, the energy factor for dishwashers can be misleading. One dishwasher may have a lower energy factor simply because it offers more options, such as electric drying. So, use the efficiency rating as a starting point. If a dishwasher with a high efficiency rating doesn't have all the features you want, get a related model that has those features. The major manufacturers produce families of dishwasher models that are essentially identical, except for the auxiliary features.

Tailor the size of your dishwasher to the amount of dishwashing that you will do. A dishwasher that is too large wastes water. A dishwasher that is too small is a nuisance, requiring extra time to clean up after a big meal.

Select a dishwasher that has a choice of wash cycles so that you can tailor your energy usage to the amount of washing that your dishes and utensils require.

Use Your Dishwasher Efficiently

The best way to save energy with your dishwasher is to use it efficiently. Here are a few tips:

- Wait until your dishwasher is full, but don't overload it. The dishwasher uses the same amount of hot water regardless of the load.

- Avoid using the dishwasher for pre-rinsing the dishes and utensils, whether immediately before the washing cycle or for holding the load before washing (called "rinse-hold"). The dishwasher uses a lot of hot water for pre-rinses. Instead, scrape residue from dishes immediately after use and soak them in the sink with a little detergent. Similarly, place used utensils into a soaking pot in your sink, and flush them off before putting them into the dishwasher.

- Avoid using the drying heater. Instead, open the door at the end of the cycle and let the contents air dry. If your dishwasher has an air-dry option, use it. The drying heater is the primary means of disinfection if some food residue remains on the dishes and utensils. However, scraping and pre-soaking should allow the dishwasher to get rid of all residue.

Booster Heater?

Hotter water provides better washing. Food service establishments have dishwashers that commonly operate with water temperatures around 160 °F (70 °C). In contrast, home hot water typically has a temperature that is limited to about 120 °F (50 °C) to avoid the risk of scalding. To provide higher water temperatures for home dishwashing, some dishwashers have internal booster heaters that raise the hot water temperature by about 20 °F (10 °C).

Should you get this feature? It probably won't make much difference. Unless hot water is near boiling temperature, it does not kill bacteria. The improvement in hygiene will be minor.

The way to make your crockery and utensils sanitary is to clean them thoroughly. To avoid residual debris and water spots, scrape and soak immediately after use, and keep everything soaked in the sink until you are ready to run it through the dishwasher. Use a dishwashing detergent that is made to avoid water spots. (Water spots are patches of dissolved minerals and detergent that remain after the water evaporates during drying).

On the other hand, the amount of energy required to boost the water temperature for a dishwasher load is relatively small, about the amount of energy needed to make a pot of coffee. If the members of your household lack the discipline to pre-soak, a booster heater may be a good idea.

See the sidebar, *The Best Hot Water Temperature*, in Step 5, for more issues about setting the hot water temperature.

Isolate the Heat of the Dishwasher

A dishwasher is a large, warm object while it is running, and it gives off a lot of water vapor. Therefore, try to avoid installing it next to a refrigerator or freezer. However, this is not a big issue. Most dishwashers have some insulation on their sides. If your kitchen layout forces you to install your dishwasher next to your refrigerator, install a partition between the two.

CLOTHES WASHERS

DRW

Figure 7-15. A front loading washer and a dryer mounted on a custom stand that provides an optimum height for convenience. Units that are mounted on a tall stand should have their controls on the front.

A clothes washer consumes more energy and water than most other appliances. It has a large electric motor that does a lot of work in agitating and spinning a heavy tub of wet clothes. It uses a lot of water for washing and rinsing.

All but the cheapest models offer a large menu of control options.

Energy Efficiency and Water Efficiency

The efficiency of the best models has improved substantially in recent years. However, there is a wide range of efficiencies on the market today, so select carefully.

Start your shopping on the Energy Star Web site. All models listed there use at least 50% less energy than required by current U.S. federal standards. There are two ratings for clothes washers, one for energy efficiency and one for water consumption.

The energy efficiency of clothes washers is rated by a "modified energy factor," for which bigger numbers are better. The Energy Star site also lists the "percent better" for each model, which is the percentage by which the unit exceeds U.S. federal standards.

A clothes washer uses energy in several ways. The "modified energy factor" accounts for the energy that the water heater consumes to heat the water, the energy used by the clothes dryer, and the electricity used by the washer itself to drive the motor. To save water heating energy, efficient models use less water. To save dryer energy, washers extract more water from clothes during the spin cycle. This also reduces drying time and clothing wear.

The water usage efficiency of clothes washers is rated by a "water factor." This indicates the amount of water used in relation to the size of the washer. Unlike the energy rating, you want to select a smaller number, not a larger one.

Unfortunately, efficiency ratings for clothes washers can be misleading. A clothes washer may be penalized simply because it offers more options, such as warm water rinsing. For example, if two washing machines are identical in all respects except that one offers warm water rinsing, the latter will have a significantly lower efficiency rating. Recognizing this, manufacturers pursue higher ratings by eliminating some potentially desirable features in their most "efficient" models.

So, use the efficiency rating as a starting point. If a clothes washer with a high efficiency rating doesn't have all the features you want, get a related model that has those features. The major manufacturers produce families of clothes washer models that are essentially identical, except for the optional features.

Top Loading vs. Front Loading

Most full size residential washing machines load from the top. The popularity of this design derives primarily from its convenience in loading and unloading the clothes. In contrast, washers that load from the front offer higher efficiency.

Front loading washers require less water, less water heating energy, and less electricity for the motor. Rather than completely immersing the laundry, the front loader tumbles the laundry through a smaller volume of water. The rotation of the drum is continuous, so the motor does less work than it does in driving the oscillating agitator of a top loading washer. (Some front loaders alternate the direction of rotation periodically, which still requires less motor power than an agitator.)

Floor mounted front loaders require you to stoop to handle the laundry. That can lead to back strain, especially for older people. That's probably the main reason why front loading washers fell from popularity.

Another disadvantage of front-loading washers is that the bottom of the door opening is submerged when the unit is operating. In time, the sheetmetal around the bottom of the door becomes rusty, making it impossible to restore a tight seal by replacing the gasket.

The efficiency difference between top loaders and front loaders has been narrowing. Search for the latest efficiency ratings, and then decide whether the efficiency advantage of a front loader is worth the inconvenience and possibly shorter service life.

If you decide to buy a front loading washer, get one that offers a matching stand to raise the machine to a more comfortable level. The stand typically includes a storage drawer. So far, the stands offered for front loaders are too low, but they are better than nothing.

Even better, a competent carpenter can make a custom stand that elevates your washer and dryer to an optimum height, as in Figure 7-15. The stand should be sturdy enough to resist the shaking of an unbalanced load of clothes. If you will place your washer on a tall stand, select a model that has its controls on the front.

Other Features to Select

Efficient clothes washers are available in all residential sizes, including stacked and under-the-counter configurations.

Give yourself options. For efficiency, choose a washing machine that allows you to select the water level to fit the load, from very small loads to large loads. Some models have a small basket that can be inserted into the washer for especially small loads.

Get separate choices of washing and rinse temperatures. Models with these options will have lower efficiency ratings, which is misleading for the reasons that we explained previously.

Use Your Clothes Washer Efficiently

If you select a washing machine that gives you a full range of options, use those options wisely. Combine effective cleaning and energy efficiency by washing large loads, and by using the lowest temperatures that will provide good washing and rinsing for the articles you are washing.

Tailor the washing machine settings to the type and quantity of dirt. Underwear that you change every day can be washed in lukewarm water with a small amount of detergent. Greasy coveralls need hot water, a large slug of detergent, and a long washing cycle.

You can get better cleaning action with cold water by using detergents that are designed for cold water. Such detergents are still evolving. Check *Consumer Reports* for their current status.

Fluffing agents are lubricants that are applied to washed fabrics to allow the fibers to slide past each other. Anti-static agents disperse electric charges. The most efficient way to apply these is in the clothes dryer. However, this doesn't work for clothes that you dry on a clothesline. In that case, select a washer that adds the agent during the final rinse cycle.

CLOTHES DRYERS

Clothes dryers are not presently covered by efficiency standards, at least not in the U.S. The U.S. government asserts that all clothes dryers use about the same amount of energy. That assumption seems dubious, but we will have to wait for better guidance.

The biggest issue in buying a clothes dryer is the energy source. If the analysis at the beginning of Step 4 led you to select gas for your home heating, you probably want to use gas for your dryer. Otherwise, get an electric dryer.

Beyond that, clothes dryers now offer a number of useful options. These are the most important:

- a reliable moisture sensor that operates the dryer until the degree of dryness that you specify is reached
- a choice between drying with heat or with unheated air
- choices of drying temperature.

Drying Efficiently

A dryer uses energy primarily to evaporate the water out of the laundry. Therefore, get a washing machine that removes as much moisture as possible at the end of the wash cycle. If your clothes washer offers the options, choose a fast final spin speed or extend the time of the last spin cycle.

Let the environment do as much of the drying as possible. Doing your laundry during drier weather will save some energy, because drier air entering the clothes dryer can absorb more moisture for a given amount of heating energy.

The ultimate in exploiting dry indoor air is to operate the dryer using unheated air. In effect, the dryer becomes a clothesline with a motor.

Install Your Dryer for Convenience and Venting

Clothes dryers load from the front. The door is inconveniently low if the dryer rests on the floor. To avoid the backache, install your dryer on a pedestal that raises it to a convenient height. The pedestal should be sturdy enough to resist the shaking of the machine as the clothes tumble. Appliance manufacturers have finally recognized this need, and many models are available with optional stands that serve as storage cabinets.

 A tall stand makes your clothes dryer much easier to use, and it can provide a large storage space.

Alternatively, you can build a sturdy base that will give you even more height. Dryers do not shake as violently as washers, so they can be mounted on taller stands that provide a lot of storage capacity. See Figure 7-15, previous. If you will place your dryer on a tall stand, select a model that has its controls on the front.

The exhaust from the dryer contains water vapor and lint. To get rid of both, the dryer needs a vent pipe to the outside. Make the pipe as straight as possible. A clogged vent pipe or lint filter will cause the dryer to overheat your clothing. It may also cause a fire, which is especially dangerous because the fire is stoked by the air that is blown into the dryer.

Don't Forget the Clothesline

Step 1 recommended that you create a convenient and attractive space for installing a clothesline or other kind of hanger for drying your laundry. Remember, that's how all laundry was dried in the past. Most homes should have a powered clothes dryer, but coordinate it with your free-energy clothesline.

If your home is located in a dry climate, plan to use your clothesline for most of your drying. In other climates, a clothesline is an important supplemental method of drying.

ROOM AIR CLEANERS

The benefit of home air cleaning is controversial. In a home that is kept clean and properly ventilated, an air cleaner may provide no benefit for healthy people. It is worth noting that the U.S. Energy Star rating agency disavows any claims of health benefits from air cleaners, even though it certifies their energy efficiency. So far, it has not been possible to determine a real benefit scientifically. But, that doesn't mean that a benefit does not exist.

If the air in a house has contaminants that create discomfort or medical reactions, an air cleaner may reduce the ill effects, but may not eliminate them. Such contaminants include pet allergens, cigarette smoking, mold spores, and dust from ducted heating and cooling systems.

The best way to deal with contaminants is to eliminate the source or to localize the contaminants to selected rooms. For example, we have designed your home to avoid mildew by limiting humidity. We avoid the hazards of ducted heating and cooling systems by not using them. We isolate smoking to certain rooms that have special ventilation.

Types of Air Cleaners

There are two main classes of air cleaners, media filters and electrostatic precipitators. "Media" filters presently dominate the market. The "media" in media filters are materials that have very small pores or mesh sizes to trap particles on the surface of the media. The most effective of these are called "HEPA" filters. In principle, these can trap particles of virtually any size. Figure 7-19 shows a typical HEPA unit.

DRW

Figure 7-19. Typical room air cleaner that uses HEPA filtration. It is noisy when running.

HEPA filters require a substantial amount of fan energy to force air through the filter. For example, a typical room air cleaner that runs continuously may use as much energy as a refrigerator. Also, the fan makes a lot of noise as it works against the resistance of the media.

Electrostatic air cleaners were once popular. They work by inducing electric charges on pollutant particles in the air. The charged particles are then swept out of the air stream by electrostatic attraction. The main appeal of electrostatic units is that they create little resistance to the flow of air, and thereby minimize fan energy and noise. However, the cheap residential models became notorious for creating ozone, and they have now faded away. If good electrostatic air cleaners appear in the residential market, they probably will be expensive.

Energy Efficiency

The Energy Star efficiency rating for air cleaners is called the "clean air delivery rate per watt," abbreviated as "CADR/watt." A higher number is better.

The amount of fan energy needed by a media filter increases greatly for smaller particles. To avoid apples-and-oranges comparisons between models, the Energy Star certification requires that filters remove particles related to "dust," "tobacco smoke," and "pollen," the air pollutants most likely to be health hazard indoors.

The fan energy required is roughly proportional to the air flow rate. To save energy, filter as locally as possible. For example, if you have a favorite chair in your living room, install a smaller air cleaner near your chair.

HOME ELECTRONICS

Household electronic appliances, known in the trade as "consumer electronics," is a vast market that changes continually. It includes television, high fidelity systems, DVD players, telephones, computers, copiers, fax machines, and a stream of other electronic gadgets that range from essential to frivolous. This year's hot item is likely to be obsolete next year.

Check *Consumer Reports* and various electronic specialty magazines for the features of the latest electronic gadgets. *Consumer Reports* provides the broadest coverage, with explanations and ratings of the features that matter.

For energy efficiency ratings, check the Energy Star Web site. Electronic devices evolve so rapidly that efficiency rating systems cannot keep up with individual models. Even so, it is possible to save energy when you buy your electronic stuff. The Energy Star program establishes criteria for awarding Energy Star certification to all the common types of electronic equipment. Meeting the criteria allows the manufacturer to state that the product is Energy Star certified.

If the Energy Star Web site cannot guide you to a specific model, look for the Energy Star label on the product box when you go shopping. Figure 7-20 shows an example.

Many electronic appliances are available with a variety of control options, such as clocks and remote controls. Such appliances consume energy even when they are not operating. At present, units with Energy Star certification use less than 2 watts while in standby mode.

DRW

Figure 7-20. An Energy Star label is clustered among other labels and notices on the package of this consumer electronics item.

STEP 8

GET YOUR HOME BUILT

Congratulations! You have designed all the features of your super-house, and you are ready to get it built. This Step will cover the building process from your perspective as the owner and designer.

This book assumes that you will have your home built by a professional custom homebuilder, so we will start by establishing a good relationship with your builder. You will convey your design to the builder as a set of construction drawings, so we will explain how those drawings are made. And finally, if you desire additional design help, we will suggest how to get it.

If you are building an addition to an existing house or if you are doing a major renovation, much of this Step will apply to your project.

If you are a builder yourself, don't skip this Step. It incorporates the best construction experience of many homes. While most of it will be familiar, you will still glean some valuable ideas.

WORKING WITH YOUR BUILDER

You are the prime designer of your super-house, but we assume that you will hire a good custom home builder for the actual construction. It is the builder who will make your dream a reality, or will botch it. Working with a builder may be a profoundly satisfying experience, or it can be misery.

Your relationship with your builder probably involves more money and has a greater effect on your living conditions than any other relationship except your marriage. As in a marriage, you need to select the right partner and maintain a good relationship for the duration.

Your builder is also called a "contractor." We will use the two terms interchangeably. Let's begin by understanding who contractors are, and what they do.

WHAT CONTRACTORS DO

For building an entire house, building a major addition, or doing a major renovation, you will be dealing with a "general contractor." This is someone who brings together all the specialized skills, or "trades," of house construction – site preparation, concrete work, framing, roofing, flooring, plumbing, electrical wiring, heating, air conditioning, drywall installation, painting, and other skills. Some of the trades are independent businesses, rather than being employees of the general contractor. The general contractor thus acts as a broker and a project manager, as well as a builder.

For more limited work, such as replacing a heating system, you will deal with a contractor who has all the capabilities needed for the project. Such specialized contractors are indicated by their specialties, as for example, a "heating contractor."

The name "general contractor" (or sometimes, simply "contractor") indicates that all the work is done under a contract between the homeowner and the builder. Each of the trade specialists works for the contractor under separate contracts between themselves and the general contractor. For this reason, the specialists are called "subcontractors." The general contractor is usually where the buck stops if there is a problem with a subcontractor, so the homeowner does not need to become involved.

In most cases, the general contractor himself performs one or more of the trades. For example, the general contractor often does the carpentry work, although he might do the plumbing or electrical

work, or perhaps all three. As a rule, seek a general contractor who does a major part of the work himself. This increases the contractor's commitment to your job, improves quality control, and minimizes delays in bringing the trades to the job.

One of the main responsibilities of the general contractor is to ensure that all the requirements of the law are fulfilled. In many jurisdictions, construction practices are heavily regulated, and usually for good reason. For example, the contractor needs to make sure that clearances from boundaries are satisfied, that soil conditions are known, that building codes are satisfied, that provisions are made to prevent runoff of mud from the building site, and other responsibilities.

The contractor also gets the permits that are needed to commence construction, and to continue construction after inspections are made at several stages.

■ What Contractors Don't (or Shouldn't) Do

The best contractors are excellent organizers, supervisors, and craftsmen. But, they are not designers, engineers, or artists. Use their strengths, and don't expect them to play roles that are not theirs.

As you design your home, your potential contractor can be a valuable advisor about matters related to conventional construction. But, the design is your responsibility, not your contractor's. Your super-design will include many features that depart from conventional practice in ways that will be unfamiliar to your contractor.

Unless your contractor has an exceptional sense of style, don't look to him for guidance in the appearance or architectural aspects of your house. Many contractors – bless them! – are lacking in taste. Some of the most unattractive houses that I have encountered were built by contractors for their own families.

FINDING THE RIGHT BUILDER

An ideal homebuilder can be described by a few characteristics. He has excellent skills, including established relationships with excellent subcontractors. He has built houses that you can examine, and he has references that you can check. He has a clean business record. He is pleasant to work with. He is willing to listen, and willing to give advice. He and his subcontractors have enough available time to complete your house expeditiously.

How can you find such a builder? First of all, limit your search to builders of custom homes, not to builders of tract houses. Tract houses are mass production items, no matter how fancy they are. Don't try to make a silk purse out of a sow's ear. Getting a tract builder to modify a standard design is about like asking General Motors to build a custom car for you. It's not their kind of business.

Recommendations from previous customers are the starting point for finding your builder. To make recommendations credible, you should be able to examine the finished homes. Even better, you should be able to observe the builder at work. Fortunately, there are now a variety of Web sites and publications that provide consumer ratings of various service providers, including home builders. Check the ones that serve your geographical area.

There is one more characteristic that is essential for the builder of your super-house. The builder should not be afraid of your project because of its unusual features. He should welcome the opportunity to enhance his own reputation by advancing the state of the art.

Unless you are very lucky, you will have to interview several builders before you find the right one. Most builders are reluctant to deviate from their well practiced procedures. Don't be offended if a contractor fails to show much interest in your project. He may be a great conventional builder, but he may be uncomfortable with all the details of your super-house design. He does you a favor by opting out. Or, the timing may not be right (see the sidebar).

There may be a quicker way to find your ideal builder. As this book goes to press, we are also launching a new certification program for contractors, who will be listed in a free directory. See *Super House Certification for Designers and Contractors*, below.

When you are interviewing builders, learn about their subcontractors. You are actually selecting a team of specialists in different fields. You want a team that has a history of working together smoothly. And, you want specialists to have the necessary skills for your house. For example, if your home will have a hydronic heating system, does the builder have an HVAC subcontractor with the special skills needed to install this type of system?

Also, know the availability of the subcontractors. Does your general contractor have first claim on their services, or will he have to wait for them to become free from other jobs?

On balance, it's a good idea to find your builder as early as possible. As you communicate during the design period, the builder will see that your expectations make sense and that you won't be making unreasonable demands. By the time your design is complete, your builder will be comfortable that he can build it.

FIND YOUR BUILDER DURING AN ECONOMIC SLUMP

Don't expect to find your ideal builder during a construction boom. All builders make hay while the sun shines. They work fast, completing as many jobs as possible using rote methods. They hire temporary workers whose skills are not the best. They won't take time from the gold rush to learn the new techniques of building a super-house.

The time to meet your ideal builder is when business is slow. Then, a good builder can indulge in the satisfaction of learning new techniques. Their best subcontractors are available. Materials and labor costs are at their lowest.

Build a Good Relationship

When you find a builder you like, don't expect that he will be enthusiastic about your super-design. It will take a period of courtship for the builder to become comfortable with your innovations. By the same token, this courtship period will give you an opportunity to become certain that the builder is right for your project.

When a contractor sees something that is out of the ordinary, he views it as a potential source of trouble. If he thinks that the design is impractical or incomplete, he will fear changes, delays, and disputes. If he takes the job, he will increase his price to cover the uncertainties.

On the other hand, if the builder believes that the project will be interesting, free of trouble, and valuable to his reputation, he will lower his bid. So, make your builder love you!

If you have learned the material in this book, you know more about energy efficiency and many other important aspects of house construction than most builders. At the same time, you still know less about conventional construction. That is an unusual situation. You don't want a potential builder to see it as trouble.

First of all, don't expect any builder to believe right away that you know more than he does about any aspect of construction. Good builders take pride in their mastery of construction skills, and they may not be pleased to hear that some of their methods can be improved.

Ideally, you can eliminate this concern by presenting a fully completed set of drawings and specifications from which the builder can estimate the project cost. However, this involves a chicken-and-egg problem, because you should involve the builder in your design before the drawings are made final.

The tactful way to handle this is to clearly explain the unusual features of your house, such as the design of the walls and roof to accommodate super-insulation. If your contractor is not familiar with this book, introduce him to it.

You won't have to go through such a period of delicate courtship if you find your builder through the **SUPER HOUSE** contractor certification program, which is described below. In that case, your builder is already well versed in the principles of super-house construction and has demonstrated his commitment to them.

WORKING WITH YOUR CONTRACTOR DURING CONSTRUCTION

Plan to spend a significant amount of time at the construction site to review progress and talk to your builder. This might seem unnecessary if your drawings and specifications are perfect. But, it's not possible to foresee every construction issue, and you should not assume that the workers will carefully study all the details of your drawings.

Identify key points during construction when you should review the work with your builder. For example, you should be present during site clearing to point out which trees and shrubs to save. You should review the procedures for installing insulation immediately before that work begins. Similarly, be at the site when the vapor barrier is installed, when the hydronic system piping is installed, and so forth. More generally, be at the site to monitor every detail where we have cautioned you to take special care or to use special procedures.

Beyond that, visit the site regularly to make sure that the work advances steadily. Be tolerant of the usual delays that can occur on any construction job, but don't let your job be neglected. *The contractor should always have a competent foreman on the job*, with responsibility to keep the work going efficiently and to follow your drawings and specifications precisely.*

Be open to suggestions during construction, and consider them carefully. However, don't surrender your own judgement or violate your own preferences. If the builder wants to make any departure from the design, it should ring warning bells. Don't agree to changes unless they make the house better for you, not just easier for the builder.

If you observe mistakes or oversights, get them fixed immediately. Don't let a worker build a flaw into your perfect home. Everyone makes mistakes, and you can expect a few in your job, even if your builder is the best. Catch mistakes early, and fix them amicably.

Although you will be the expert about the super-house aspects of construction, remember that you are the customer, not the builder. Respect the contractor's chain of command. Don't create liability for yourself by giving orders to the workers. When an issue needs to be resolved, work it out at the top.

Emergencies are an exception. If you see something being done improperly, bring it to the attention of the foreman immediately. If necessary, use your authority as homeowner to stop the work. Do the same if you see an unsafe condition.

Doing Part of the Work Yourself

A sign in my car repair shop says, "Labor $50 per hour, $75 if you help."

You may want to put your own sweat equity into the house for your personal satisfaction, if not to lower your costs. It's a manly instinct, but your builder won't like it. If the homeowner works on the job, it interferes with the smooth flow of the trades. The builder has the responsibility for work flow, but he has no control over the homeowner.

Anyway, your contribution is likely to be too small to make much difference in the cost. If you want the satisfaction of handling tools, wait until your house is finished and build something else. Maybe finish the basement or build a storage building. During construction, devote your energy to monitoring the progress of the work and to making sure that all the essential details in your design are executed properly.

Shopping for Special Items

There is one worthwhile exception about involving yourself in the building process. The contractor usually is happy to let you do the shopping for items that are a matter of taste or that satisfy special technical requirements. Since you are not at the building site, you are not interfering with the work flow.

You will shop for your appliances, as we discussed in Step 7. In addition, it makes sense for you to shop for other items of personal preference, such as plumbing fixtures, light fixtures, cabinets, and door locks. You shop for them and pay for them. If the items are too heavy for you to bring to job site, the contractor will pick them up from the wholesaler at the appropriate time.

Especially if you are technically skilled, it may be best for you to buy the energy using equipment that is essential for the peak performance of your home. For example, having selected your HVAC equipment as we explained in Step 4, you may be the best person to buy the heating boiler, heat pumps, and other heating and cooling equipment. In this way, you can be sure that the equipment will have the characteristics you want.

---

* The foreman should be present and attentive to the work literally every minute. He is like the conductor of an orchestra. The workers take their cues from the foreman continually. I have seen major mistakes made by construction crews as soon as the foreman went away to get lunch.

Doing the shopping for these items can save a significant amount of money because the contractor does not have to fatten his bid to cover uncertainties in the equipment and furnishings that you will want. Also, the contractor loses less time away from the job site. But, work out this division of responsibility with your contractor before negotiating the contract.

■ Buy as a Builder

When buying equipment for your house, save money by buying it from wholesalers as an employee of your builder, not as a retail customer. Wear your work clothes and be part of the trade. Do your homework in advance by reading the catalogs, and go to the wholesaler with the correct model numbers and dimensions in hand.

Wholesale distributors usually don't have extensive showrooms, so don't expect to see samples of the equipment you want. To get familiar with equipment before you buy, go to the manufacturers' Web sites and download their technical literature. Or, go to a hardware store or other retailer and copy the model numbers. Some big wholesalers do have a limited display space for items such as bathroom fixtures.

If your builder does not have an account with a wholesaler who carries equipment you want, set up an account on behalf of the builder. Get a few of your builder's business cards for this purpose, along with his license and sales tax numbers.

THE CONSTRUCTION SCHEDULE

How long should it take to build your house? Construction cannot begin until the permits are issued. In some jurisdictions, permits may be issued on the same day. In other places, permits may take several months to issue. From that point, a well organized contractor typically can build a house of average complexity in two to four months, assuming good weather. Even the most complex and palatial house should not take longer than six to nine months to build. Add more time to begin construction if you have to build a road to a remote site, do a lot of earth moving, or bring in new utility lines.

Failing to maintain the pace of construction is a serious failing among builders, and it is common. The usual cause is that the builder spreads himself over too many jobs. Don't let this happen to you. Once the job starts, there should be major activity at your construction site on every working day, unless the work is prevented by weather. You are paying your contractor to be a project manager. It's his job to orchestrate the subcontractors so that the work proceeds smoothly and without interruption.

An unfinished house may suffer badly from the weather, especially the plywood and fabricated lumber, such as I-joists and composite beams. Any wet lumber will warp, leaving permanent distortions and stresses in your house that will cause trouble later. Therefore, the contractor should get everything under roof quickly.

Spell out the construction schedule in your contract. Don't let your contractor use your job as a fill-in for gaps in other jobs. If there is significant slippage in the schedule, especially if workers fail to appear repeatedly, you need to have a serious talk with the builder to get your job the priority it deserves.

Don't cause delay yourself. Your drawings and specs need to be complete, and you need to be available to answer any questions that the contractor may have. Have your financing arranged so that the contractor is not waiting for your bank to make progress payments.

AVOID CHANGES

The design of your house should be entirely complete before you sign the contract, down to the smallest detail that needs to be spelled out. Changing the design during construction phase is likely to create a mess. If you neglect to work out a detail during your design, it is unlikely that you will be able to work it out elegantly during construction. Instead, the builder will take a shortcut to keep the project moving, and there will be a permanent blemish in your vision of an ideal home.

The contractor will make changes that you request, but you may pay dearly for them in disappointment and in additional construction cost. Changes upset the contractor's scheduling of the trades, which may cascade into a major delay of construction.

Of course, if you become aware of a flaw in the design, or if you discover a feature that you really want to add, make the change as soon as possible.

The construction industry has developed a standard way of dealing with changes. It is the "change order," which is an addendum to your main contract that describes the additional or modified work, and the payment for it.

Change orders are undesirable because one party usually has the other party over a barrel when the change is needed. If the change is something you want, you don't have the ability to get competitive bids. If the change is desired by the contractor, the homeowner may refuse to pay for it. If a change order is needed, the only way to avoid trouble is for both parties to behave reasonably.

PAYING THE CONTRACTOR

You will pay your contractor in a series of payments. Your contract should include a schedule of these payments. Usually, payments are pegged to the completion of certain stages of the work.

Your contractor is not a bank, and you should not expect him to finance the building of your home. Expect to make an initial payment before work begins. This allows the contractor to purchase materials, pay for permits, rent equipment, and assemble his crew. The initial payment also assures the contractor that you are serious, and that you know how to write big checks.

Make your progress payments in a timely and cheerful manner. Nothing is more important to a good relationship with your builder than timely payment. His desire to get paid is just as intense as your desire to move into your house.

On the other hand, don't let the payments get ahead of the work. The need to work for the next payment is an effective motivator to keep the job on schedule.

If a problem arises that makes you hesitate to make a payment, your job may be in serious trouble. Have a meeting with the contractor, be frank, and agree how you are going to resolve the issue. Don't make the next payment until the issue is completely resolved.

Defer the last payment until the house is completed, checked, and debugged. Put this provision in your contract. Generally, you won't see the contractor again after the last payment is made. The last payment should be large enough to cover any corrective work, plus any penalties for late performance that are stated in the contract. If you don't withhold these amounts, you would have to sue for reimbursement in the event of a problem, a procedure that is usually too expensive and troublesome to be worthwhile.

Paying the Subcontractors

In most jurisdictions, you are legally responsible for payment to the subcontractors. If there is a payment dispute between the contractor and a subcontractor, you will be drawn into it. The law may allow a subcontractor to place a lien against your property if the subcontractor is not paid by the contractor.

For this reason, it is prudent to write your contract so that you pay the subcontractors directly, subject to approval of the work by the general contractor.

This method of payment may make the subcontractors more responsive to the special requirements of your super-house. However, your formal dealings with the subcontractors should be limited to payment. The general contractor is responsible for work flow and sub-contractor responsibilities. If you violate this condition, it may be difficult to hold the general contractor responsible for errors by a subcontractor.

THE CONTRACT WITH YOUR BUILDER

> NOTE: The following discussion is not intended to be legal advice, but to alert you to issues in the relationship with your builder that have legal significance. It is prudent to consult a properly qualified lawyer when dealing with legal issues.

The contract is where your expectations and those of the builder come together. You need a legal commitment that the builder will create the house that you want. The builder needs a commitment that he will be paid for his work. You and your builder make these commitments with a contract.

What is a contract? It is a legally enforceable agreement between two parties that establishes what each party will do for the other. The obligations of your builder begin and end with the wording of the contract. That's why builders are called "contractors." The contract will have a major effect on the quality of your house, it will determine the cost of your house, and it will set the tone for your relationship during construction.

As long as a few basic legal conditions are met, a contract can take any form, from a verbal agreement to a highly detailed document of many pages. For your super-house, it is prudent to use a written contract in a format that is familiar to builders of custom houses. A typical house construction contract consists of a package of documents, called "the contract documents." These consist of the drawings, any additional technical specifications, and a written document that is called "the contract" or "the agreement." The agreement will state that the drawings and specifications are to be a part of the contract.

TYPICAL PROVISIONS OF A HOME CONSTRUCTION CONTRACT

Over time, contracts for residential construction have evolved a fairly standard set of provisions or clauses that help to make the relationship between homeowner and builder run smoothly. In addition to these familiar provisions, you will want to add one or two more to highlight the special requirements of your super-house. The following are the provisions that your contract probably should have, in three groups.

The first group of provisions apply to all jobs:

- *statement of the documents that are included in the contract.* These usually include the "agreement," the drawings, and the specifications. It may include other documents that are separate, but this would be unusual. Any later change orders will become part of the contract.

- *scope of work.* This is a statement that the builder will deliver to you a house that conforms to the contract documents. It also lists other functions if it is not clear that they are an inherent part of the contractor's job. Examples are acquiring permits, grading the site, and removal of construction waste.

- *standard of performance.* This is where you insert your "super-house clause," which is described below. This provision probably will be the only unusual part of your agreement. General statements, such as saying that the house will be built "in a workmanlike manner," are too vague to be useful.

- *construction schedule*, with specified times for completion, and including provisions for weather delay, change orders, etc.

- *payment provisions*, including the total price of the work, a schedule of progress payments, and how the subcontractors will be paid. If the homeowner will pay the subcontractors directly, payments should be subject to the approval of the general contractor.

- *responsibility and authority for construction decisions*. Authority at the building site should be limited to the general contractor, subject to approval by the owner.

- *warranty*. The builder provides a warranty of his work for a stated period of time. Warranty of equipment and materials is usually the responsibility of the manufacturers.

- *handover, final payment, and release of liens*. The general contractor and subcontractors agree to abandon any claim for liens upon the handover of the house to the owner and receipt of final payment.

- *protection of the homeowner against inappropriate actions by the contractor, subcontractors, and vendors*. The contract should require appropriate licensing, insurance coverage, and perhaps bonding so that the owner is protected against injury or loss due to actions of any party under the control of the contractor.

The second group of provisions deal with unforeseen circumstances that may apply to your job. Typically, these include:

- *unexpected conditions* that require additional work or materials. An example is unexpected soil conditions that require a deeper or wider foundation. The contract should state what comprises unexpected work and how payment for it will be made.

- *change orders* originated by the owner. The contract should state what comprises a change order and how payment for it will be made.

The third group of provisions come into play only if the job gets into trouble. You hope that you won't have to use them, but they minimize the cost and interruption of construction if a dispute does arise. Also, the presence of these provisions in the contract may reduce the potential for trouble.

- *termination clause*, which states the conditions under which the homeowner or the builder may terminate the contract before completion. Typical reasons for termination include excessive delay by the builder or an owner's failure to pay.

- *how disputes will be resolved*. If you and the builder cannot resolve a problem between yourselves, your two legal alternatives are a lawsuit or arbitration. If your contract specifies arbitration, be careful. The contract should state a method of selecting the arbitrator that does not favor either party. The clause states who pays for arbitration or legal fees.

- *delay penalty*, which may be expressed as an amount of money deducted per day of delay. This is a big bludgeon, so think twice about whether to include it in your contract. The contractor will see it as a big threat in the event that uncontrollable circumstances delay the job, and he is likely to increase his price as an insurance premium.

THE SUPER-HOUSE CLAUSE

The written agreement for your super-house will look like the agreement for a conventional house in most respects. Your builder has probably seen dozens of similar agreements. This could mislead your builder into believing that your house is just another custom house.

Your explanations of the super-features of your house may not have sunk into the builder's thinking adequately by the time of negotiating the contract. A custom builder often deals with enthusiastic homeowners who are bubbling with ideas for their houses, so all your talk about the special features of your house may not seem much different. The builder will wait to see the contract, and if it looks fairly conventional, he may assume that he can build your house in the conventional way.

Deeply ingrained in the thinking of many builders is following the minimum code requirements. The notion of exceeding code requirements is alien, and might even seem illogical. So, for example, if your design triples the amount of wall insulation compared to code requirements, a builder simply may not recognize this aspect of your design.

 Add an important clause to your construction contract to ensure that you and your builder have the same understanding of your home.

Or, the builder may not take your desires seriously enough. He may understand what you want, but he may not adequately convey the special needs of your job to the workers.

Or, the builder may simply humor you, hoping to do the job in his usual way. He may figure that the courts will protect him if you make a fuss, as long as he builds your house to reasonably good conventional standards.

To defend against these possibilities, include a clause in your agreement that stipulates that your house requires special treatment. This puts the builder on notice that the special nature of your house is a legal matter. The clause should say something like this:

___. UNCONVENTIONAL CONSTRUCTION FEATURES AND STANDARDS OF WORK

It is the intent of this contract to build a house that is substantially superior to conventional construction in energy efficiency, comfort, and durability. Some of the dimensions, materials, and methods of construction differ from common practice.

In all questions regarding the methods of construction, the design documents will govern. In every part of the work where clarification or resolution is required, the builder will consult in a timely manner with the owner or the owner's agent.

For aspects of the work that are not covered specifically by the contract documents, the best conventional practice will apply, including adherence to equipment manufacturers' installation instructions.

The house will satisfy all applicable building code requirements, except when exceptions to code requirements are obtained as needed by the design documents.

HOW TO WRITE A GOOD AGREEMENT

A good contract is clear. It is written in big, easily readable type, with no fine print on the back of a form. Everything is written in plain language. It does not use obsolete legalisms (such as "whereas," "the party of the first part," etc.). It avoids superfluous words (such as "... agrees, affirms, and stipulates ..."). It is not cluttered with non-specific boilerplate.

Each party should understand and be satisfied with every word of the contract before signing it. Know that every word, number, and punctuation mark in a contract is negotiable. Don't blindly accept a contract that is drafted by someone else.

A contract always favors the person who writes it, if only because the person writing the contract has the opportunity to cover the issues that he feels are important. Then, who writes the first draft of the contract? It could be the builder, or the homeowner, or a designer hired as the owner's agent, or a lawyer who is hired by either party. Normally, one of the parties will present a contract to the other party.

As the owner of a house that will have unusual requirements, you should take the initiative to draft the contract. In writing the contract, do your homework, be smart, and be fair. It will help you to copy from good examples of residential building contracts. You can buy construction contract forms from various suppliers, and you can download a variety of free forms from the Internet. Using these materials, you can assemble a good contract.

If you have selected the right builder and if you have written a good contract, the builder should be comfortable with the agreement. If not, resolve any points of difference. But, don't forfeit any issues that you consider important.

HIRING A LAWYER TO WRITE THE CONTRACT

If you have any misgivings about your ability to write or to negotiate the contract, hire a lawyer who has experience with residential construction contracts. You are buying his experience, not his paperwork. You want the lawyer to know where potential legal trouble lurks and to steer you away from it.

Don't expect a lawyer to improve the technical content of your contract. On the contrary, the lawyer will depend on you to spell out any issues that are unusual about your project.

Before hiring a lawyer, make sure that he does not have a relationship with the builder and that he does not derive a significant part of his income in defending builders against complaints from homeowners. If a dispute with the builder arises later, you don't want your lawyer to pull his punches because he has lucrative clients on the other side of the dispute.

THE CONSTRUCTION DRAWINGS

You need to communicate your design, including all its critical details, to your builder. The standard way of doing this is with a formal set of construction drawings, perhaps supplemented by a set of written specifications. Building is a highly visual process, and the drawings convey your design in a pictorial manner. In addition, complete drawings allow your builder to estimate the cost of your job with certainty.

The better your construction drawings, the better your home will be. So, get an excellent set of construction drawings. The good news is that you have already done most of the work needed to produce them. Starting in Step 1, you created a set of working drawings and notes that record the features of your super-house. What remains now is to upgrade those working drawings to a formal set of construction drawings.

I recommend that you use a professional drafting service to do this. You could prepare the construction drawings yourself, but that would add no benefit to your design. It would take a lot of time, and it would require specialized software and equipment.

Search for "architectural drafting services" in your telephone directory or on the Internet. Find a drafting service that deals specifically with residential construction. In addition to making drawings, most drafting services can help you to fill in important details of conventional construction, such as the dimensions of floor joists and the thickness of concrete walls. Or, they can refer you to other professionals for these details. (We will discuss design helpers more generally at the end of this Step.)

THE ANATOMY OF A DRAWING SET

Construction drawings are made and organized in a standard way. Table 8-1, *Typical Construction Drawings for a Super-House*, lists the drawings in the standard sequence in which they are bound together. There are several kinds of drawings in the set. It's useful to know their names and functions because you will discuss them with your builder and with any professionals that you may use for design assistance.

A *plan* is a view that looks straight down. It is drawn to scale, providing horizontal measurements.

The first plan in your drawing set is the "site plan," which probably will be prepared by your land surveyor.

This may be followed by a landscaping plan. Before construction begins, the landscaping plan tells your builder which trees and bushes to save, and which to remove. The landscaping plan may also show the landscaping to be accomplished after construction, if you are thinking that far ahead.

The "architectural floor plans" show how the walls, windows, doors, and stairs rooms are arranged in each level of the house. Figure 8-1 is a typical floor plan. If you used a home design computer program for your floor layouts, this is similar. However, the construction floor plans are simpler because they do not include furnishings.

The architectural floor plans also serve as templates for other plans that show the plumbing, electrical, and HVAC equipment.

An *elevation* is a view looking horizontally. An "exterior elevation" shows a side of the house as it would be seen by a person standing outside the house. An elevation is flat, without perspective, so it can be scaled and marked with dimensions. Usually, there are four exterior elevations, one for each side. Figure 8-2 shows a typical exterior elevation.

An "interior elevation" shows the inside surface of a wall, as seen by a person standing inside the room and facing toward the wall. The view typically includes furnishings that are related to the wall. An interior elevation may be used to indicate the location of cabinets, to show interior trim and paint colors, and for other purposes. Interior elevations are commonly used for kitchens, as in Figure 8-3, and for toilet rooms. Most other rooms and most walls do not require interior elevations, unless the walls have special features, such as alcoves, built-in bookshelves, or fancy moldings.

A *section* is a vertical slice through the house. Sections usually are drawn to clarify structural details. For example, Figures 3-25, 3-87, and 3-107, in Step 3, are wall sections.

Sections are sometimes combined with interior elevations, showing details that are both visible and invisible in the finished house. For example, Figure 8-4 is a section drawing that shows furnishings.

This system of plans, elevations, and sections is centuries old.* The views are flat, which makes the building's true appearance somewhat difficult to visualize. These two-dimensional drawings are still the "official" format, because only the flat format can be scaled with a ruler to convey accurate dimensions.

---

* Some historians assert that the modern use of construction drawings was originated by Raffaello Sanzio da Urbino (commonly known as the painter "Raphael") around the year 1514. This was during a period when he was responsible for the construction of St. Peter's Basilica in Rome.

Table 8-1. TYPICAL CONSTRUCTION DRAWINGS FOR A SUPER-HOUSE [1]		
Name (Typical number of drawings or sheets) [2]	**Content**	**Used by:**
❑ COVER SHEET (Typ. one sheet.)	Name of project and owner. Index of drawings, schedules, and specifications. Typically has an overall view of the house, perhaps in 3-D.	All trades
❑ SITE PLAN (Typ. one sheet.)	Plan of entire property, including survey marks, compass orientation, surface contours, house footprint, pavement, water and sewer lines, location of wells and septic fields, pavement. May show grading for rain drainage, mud retention swales, etc.	Surveyor, excavator, plumber, electrician, well driller, paver
❑ LANDSCAPING PLAN (Optional, typ. one sheet.)	Landscaping, including grading, paving, and vegetation. May indicate trees and shrubbery to be saved, etc.	Excavator, landscaper
ARCHITECTURAL [3]		
❑ EXTERIOR ELEVATIONS (Typ. one drawing for each side of the house.)	Elevations that show the sides of the house from the outside. Include wall and roof finishes, windows, doors, skylights, exterior decoration, etc.	Carpenter, mason, siding contractor, roofer, gutter installer, painter
❑ FLOOR PLANS (Typ. one drawing for each floor level.)	Plans of rooms and walls, emphasizing dimensions. May show permanent fixtures, including bathroom fixtures, showers, kitchen appliances and cabinets, and fireplaces. May include floor surface designs on the main drawing or in details.	Carpenter, mason, drywall contractor, flooring installer, interior decorator
❑ REFLECTED CEILING PLAN (For rooms with complex ceilings.)	Ceiling layout, used where the ceiling has special features, including coves, ceiling tiles, ceiling light fixtures, ceiling fans, etc.	Carpenter, drywall contractor, electrician
❑ INTERIOR ELEVATIONS (For rooms with built-in wall features.)	Interior elevations of walls that have built-in features, such as alcoves and built-in shelves.	Carpenter, mason, drywall contractor, interior decorator
❑ BATHROOM & SHOWER ELEVATIONS (Typ. one drawing for each wall with features.)	Elevations of cabinets, built-in appliances, and wall fixtures. Details of wall, ceiling, and floor tiles.	Tile layer, plumber, cabinet installer, interior decorator
❑ ARCHITECTURAL DETAILS (As needed, typ. one or two sheets.)	Details related to appearance and accessories, such as brickwork detailing, gingerbread carpentry, stair details, moldings, book shelves, gutters, etc.	Carpenter, trim carpenter, mason, interior decorator, gutter installer
❑ ARCHITECTURAL SCHEDULES (Typ. one or two sheets.)	Model numbers and/or specifications of all assemblies and hardware that have special features. Includes doors, locks, windows, skylights, etc. Also, wall, ceiling, and floor finishes for each room.	Carpenter, mason, painter, flooring installer, interior decorator

Name (Typical number of drawings or sheets) [2]	Content	Used by:
❑ KITCHEN ELEVATIONS (Typ. one drawing for each wall with features.)	Elevations of cabinets, built-in appliances, and wall fixtures.	Carpenter, trim carpenter, plumber, electrician, cabinet installer, interior decorator
❑ KITCHEN EQUIPMENT SCHEDULE (May be included with kitchen elevations.)	Model numbers and/or specifications of all built-in appliances and cabinets. (Plumbing fixtures are included in plumbing equipment schedule.)	Carpenter, electrician, plumber, cabinet installer
STRUCTURAL [3]		
❑ FOUNDATION & SLAB PLAN (Typ. one sheet.)	Plans of foundation and floor slabs. Steel reinforcement. Foundation drainage. *Uses the architectural floor plans as templates.*	Excavator, concrete installer, mason
❑ FOUNDATION SECTIONS (Typ. one or two sheets.)	Sections of footings, foundation walls, slab, below-grade insulation, steel reinforcement, perimeter drainage, and backfill. Surface berms sloped to shed rain away from house.	Excavator, concrete installer, mason
❑ WALL SECTIONS (Typ. one or two sheets.)	Sections of exterior and interior walls, including masonry veneers. Shows insulation details.	Carpenter, mason
❑ STRUCTURAL DETAILS (Typ. one to three sheets.)	Details relating to the strength and integrity of the structure, including roof and floor connections, corner framing, concrete anchors, reinforcement of I-joists, steel reinforcement, framing of openings for doors, windows, and skylights, sealing of penetrations for flues, vents, and wiring. Etc.	Carpenter, mason, concrete installer
❑ WALL FRAMING ELEVATIONS (Typ. one drawing for each exterior wall.)	Elevations of wall studs, headers, sills, and major structural components.	Carpenter
❑ FLOOR FRAMING PLANS (Typ. one drawing for each frame floor.)	Plan of floor structures. Includes insulation details for insulated floors.	Carpenter
❑ ROOF FRAMING (Typ. one or two sheets.)	Plans and elevations of roof structure. Includes insulation details.	Carpenter, roofer
MECHANICAL (HVAC)		
❑ HVAC FLOOR PLANS (Typ. one drawing for each floor.)	All localized HVAC equipment, such as heat pumps and unit heaters. Distribution pipe, duct, and control wiring. *Uses the architectural floor plans and/or floor framing plans as templates.*	HVAC subcontractor, electrician
❑ HYDRONIC SYSTEM DETAILS (Typ. one sheet.)	For hydronic systems, shows the layout of the boiler, pumps, manifold, expansion tank, system filler, and connections.	HVAC subcontractor, electrician
❑ HVAC EQUIPMENT SCHEDULES (Typ. one sheet.)	Model numbers and/or specifications of all HVAC equipment that has special features. Includes auxiliary equipment, such as ceiling heaters, ceiling fans, and exhaust fans.	HVAC subcontractor, electrician

Name (Typical number of drawings or sheets) [2]	Content	Used by:
PLUMBING		
❑ **PLUMBING PLANS** (Typ. one drawing for each floor level. May be combined with HVAC plans.)	All water and sewer equipment and pipes, including water heater, filters, and water treatment. *Uses the architectural floor plans and/or floor framing plans as templates.*	Plumber, electrician, HVAC subcontractor
❑ **PLUMBING EQUIPMENT SCHEDULES** (Typ. one sheet. May be combined with HVAC schedules.)	Model numbers and/or specifications of all plumbing fixtures and equipment that has special features. Includes kitchen and bathroom plumbing fixtures.	Plumber, HVAC subcontractor
ELECTRICAL & COMMUNICATIONS		
❑ **ELECTRICAL POWER AND LIGHTING PLANS** (Typ. one drawing for each floor level.)	Electrical power system, including wiring, circuit breaker panels, and connection points for all permanently installed electrical equipment, including permanent lighting fixtures. *Uses the architectural floor plans and/or floor framing plans as templates.*	Electrician
❑ **LOW-VOLTAGE WIRING AND CABLING PLANS** (Typ. included in electrical power plans.)	All built-in equipment and wiring for intercoms, door buzzers, digital information cabling, etc. *Uses the architectural floor and/or floor framing plans as templates.*	Electrician, cable installer
❑ **ELECTRICAL EQUIPMENT SCHEDULES** (Typ. one sheet.)	Model numbers and/or specifications of all electrical system equipment that has special features. Includes permanently installed lighting fixtures.	Electrician

NOTES:

1. The number and content of the drawings in this list are typical for a super-house of average size and complexity. The list assumes wood frame construction built on a concrete foundation. Some jurisdictions have specialized requirements for drawings, such as the sheet size, issues that must be covered on the site plan, etc.

2. Several drawings may be combined on one sheet, provided that the drawings are large enough to show adequate detail.

3. Structural details often are scanty in residential drawings. When they are given, they commonly are included in the architectural drawings, or they may be divided between the architectural drawings and a separate set of structural drawings. We recommend that all structural and insulation design be presented in separate structural drawings, as in this list.

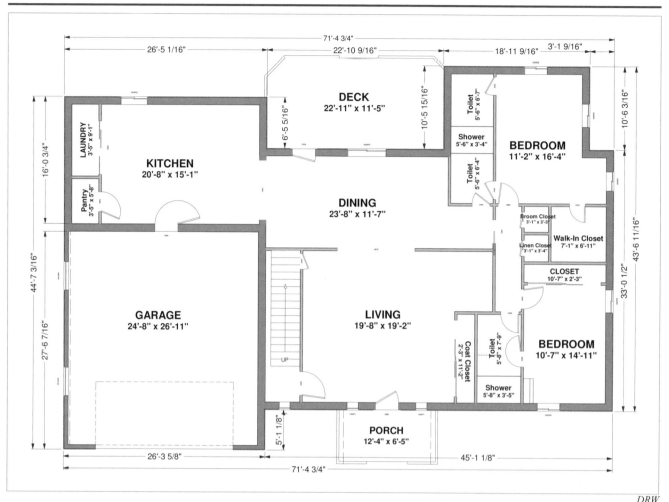

DRW

Figure 8-1. Typical "architectural floor plan." The drawing guides the building of the walls, doors, windows, and stairs. It also serves as a template for additional plans that show the plumbing, electrical, and HVAC equipment. Compare this to the much earlier drawing in Figure 1-86, which began the layout of the house.

DRW

Figure 8-2. Typical "exterior elevation."

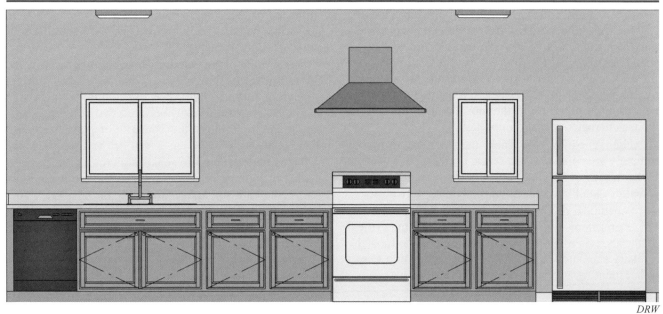

DRW

Figure 8-3. "Interior elevation" of a kitchen. It shows the locations of cabinets and appliances, and wall colors. The vee symbols on the cabinet doors are a standard method of indicating the sides where the hinges are installed.

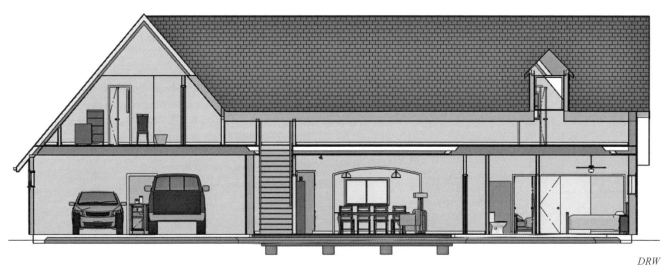

DRW

Figure 8-4. A "section" drawing that shows how furnishings and vehicles fit into the house.

Your drawings may also include a few "three-dimensional" views for orientation and to provide a more realistic sense of the actual appearance of the house. If you have been using a home design computer program, you have already created many such previews of your home.

Detail drawings are smaller drawings that supplement the main drawings at a magnified scale. They clarify... well, details. For example, many of the drawings in Step 3 are detail drawings. As we have stressed throughout your design, details make the difference between an ordinary house and a super-house, so make sure that your drawings show the details clearly.

A detail drawing may be placed on the same sheet as a primary drawing. For example, a detail drawing on the floor framing plan will show the carpenters how to reinforce the ends of the I-joists. If several detail drawings are needed for the same topic, they may be collected on a separate sheet. For example, a sheet of exterior trim details may be devoted to decorative brickwork and gingerbread carpentry.

A ***schedule*** is not a drawing, and it doesn't have anything to do with time, despite the name. It is a shopping list for the builder, presented in the form of a table. It is included with the drawings. Schedules cover items that need to be identified by special characteristics, such as size, color, model number, R-value, etc.

For example, the architectural schedules list the types, sizes, and perhaps the model numbers of the windows and doors. They also include "interior finish schedules" that list the flooring, carpet, wall paint, etc. for each room. The HVAC schedules list the sizes and model numbers of the boiler, circulating pumps, air conditioning units, room thermostats, and other items whose characteristics are important.

The schedules for each part of the drawings typically are collected on a single drawing sheet, which is the last sheet for that part. For example, the HVAC schedules are the last sheet of the HVAC drawings.

Schedules don't cover standard bulk materials or generic items, such as nails or wire. Some critical materials, such as electrical wire, are defined by industry standards or building codes, so you don't need to list them.

Drawing Sizes and Scales

If your super-house is average in size, a complete set of drawings may consist of two or three dozen sheets. A super-house will have a few more drawings than a conventional house to describe its special features and to provide better guidance to your builder.

Drawings are made in several standard *sheet sizes*, which are compromises between convenience and readability. The workers at the job site use the largest size, as in Figure 8-5. You probably will use a smaller size for convenient reference.

In the United States, the standard sheet sizes that are most commonly used for residential construction are:

- "D" size, 22" x 34". This usually is the primary size that you will use, especially for a larger house. It is good for showing floor plans and structural views of the entire house.
- "D1" size, 24" x 36", is slightly larger.
- "C" size, 17" x 22". This reduced size is more convenient at the job site, and it is practical for some of the trades. It may be appropriate as the primary size for a smaller house or apartment, or for a renovation project.
- "B" size, 11" x 17". This size is handy for reference away from the site. It is too small for the working trades.

The corresponding metric sizes are:
- "A1": 594 x 841 mm
- "A2": 420 x 594 mm
- "A3": 297 x 420 mm.

Your drafting service will have the equipment to produce all these sizes, and copies should be inexpensive. You will need copies for your general contractor, for the building permit office, for all the trades, and for yourself. As

indicated in Table 8-1, *Typical Construction Drawings for a Super-House*, different trades will need different portions of the drawing set.

The floor plans usually dictate the sheet size for the entire set of drawings. If your house has a large, sprawling footprint, you can use a smaller sheet size by dividing the floor plans between two or more sheets. For orientation, show the entire floor plan at smaller scale on a single sheet.

It is conventional to make drawings to a standard *scale*. In countries that still use English units, the most common scale for house drawings is ¼" = 1'. This means that ¼" on the drawing corresponds to one foot of actual dimension. For example, if a house is 60 feet long, the floor plan would be 15" long on the drawing. A drawing of this size would fit conveniently on a "C" size sheet, leaving room for titles, notes, etc.

Where metric units are used, the scale typically is expressed as a ratio. For example, a scale of "50:1" means that one centimeter on the drawing corresponds to 50 centimeters of actual dimension. This common scale is close to the English ¼" = 1'.

Using a standard scale minimizes the need to clutter the drawing with dimension lines. This is especially useful for the mechanical and electrical drawings, where dimension lines would be confused with pipe, electrical wiring, etc.

The lines, numerals, text, and symbols in the construction drawings should be bold enough so that they will show up clearly in the smallest drawing size that you will want. A drawing that is cluttered or difficult to read is an invitation to mistakes.

DRW

Figure 8-5. Construction drawings being used at the building site. The drawings must be absolutely clear to the builders, even in inclement weather, under muddy conditions, and with language differences.

COMPLETE YOUR WORKING DRAWINGS

Your drafting service will use the working drawings and notes that you already created as the basis for your construction drawings. So, get your drawings and notes assembled into a tidy package that will make it easy for your drafting service to work from them. Use Table 8-1, *Typical Construction Drawings for a Super-House*, as a checklist to make sure that you provide all the input needed for each sheet of the construction drawings.

You completed all the "architectural" aspects of your working drawings by the end of Step 2. If you have not already done so, make your HVAC, plumbing, and electrical working drawings by using copies of your architectural drawings as templates.

To draw piping and electrical wiring, simply draw these as heavy lines. You can use a pencil, or if you are using a home design computer program, use the line drawing capability of the program. Where pipe and wiring runs within floors, show it on the floor framing plans. Your drawings should show the wiring and pipe running through the holes that are pre-cut in the floor joists.

Similarly, you can use a pencil to draw symbols for equipment, such as a heating boiler or water softener. Or, use a convenient symbol in your home design program.

A few of the drawings in your set are prepared by specialists. For example, the site plan typically is prepared by your land surveyor. If you hire a kitchen consultant, she will prepare your kitchen drawings. Get digital versions of these drawings, if possible. Otherwise, make sure that you have clean paper copies, so that the drafting service can copy them and bind them into the complete set.

Detail Drawings Made Easy

Early in this design adventure, you learned that the difference between a super-home and an ordinary home is largely a matter of details. Those details need to be shown in your construction drawings. However, some details may be too complex for you to draw, or there may be easier ways to convey them to your drafting service. Here are some easy ways to get the details into your construction drawings.

Copy manufacturers' installation instructions. For example, if you use I-joist, get the reinforcement details from the I-joist manufacturer. Often, you can download the information from the manufacturer's Web site, and your drafting service can copy the digital file into your drawings. Or, copy the instructions in paper form on a copier.

Use photography. For example, if you want to replicate some fancy trim that you discovered on another house, include photographs of the trim in your architectural details. Your drafting service will prepare your drawings using digital technology, and they can easily include photographs that you have taken with your digital camera. Also, you can request digital photographs from manufacturers and other sources.

SPECIFICATIONS (Optional)

Some aspects of building a house are best described using words, rather than drawings. These aspects may be explained in an optional written document called "specifications," which are separate from the drawings. People in the construction business call them "specs."

Specs are not commonly used in building individual homes. In the real world, specs may not be a good way to communicate with your builder. Some good builders are poor readers. These days, many construction workers don't even speak the language of the country. In many drawings that include specs, they are poorly written boilerplate, and builders tend to ignore them.

For these reasons, I generally don't recommend using specs. Usually, it is better to convey information in the schedules or as notes on the drawings. For example, if you want custom tiles, describe them in the architectural schedules, or as a note on the relevant drawing.

However, if your home design has many specialized requirements, you may decide that specs are the best way to explain them. Where specs are used, they typically cover these kinds of issues:

- *features that cannot be well described by pictures, model numbers, or other specific identification*. For example, you might use specs to describe how certain HVAC controls should operate. Or, you may need a detailed description of custom tiles that must be procured from a particular factory.

- *procedures to be followed where conventional practice may be inadequate*. Examples are requirements for caulking and sealing, structural connections to resist wind and earth movement, backfilling materials and procedures, grading the soil around the house to keep rainwater away from the basement. Your house will have many improvements over conventional practice, and specs are one way to spell them out.

- *interactions between different construction activities*. The specifications may alert the builder to activities of other parties who perform functions such as electrical power, well drilling, and landscaping. For example, the builder is instructed not to damage trees around the house that will be kept for landscaping.

If you do use specs, write them clearly. Make the sentences short. Use large type, so that the builder can easily read the specs from a dirty copy at the job site. Bind them into the drawings, as suggested below.

You can buy residential construction specification forms, but these typically have little value. They may be fairly detailed about the architectural aspects of the design, but they typically are useless for HVAC and other vital components, especially for a super-house.

No set of specifications can be complete. That would require an encyclopedia, and it would scare away your contractor. If you use specs, limit them to specific issues that require special attention.

Since your specs will cover specialized issues, you may need a specialist or specialized expertise to write them. For example, it takes special knowledge to write the specs for concrete foundation piers that are installed in water or salty soil. You might get the necessary expertise from a specialist, from this book, or from books on specialized issues. Talk to your contractor before writing the specs, to make sure that your special requirements make sense to him.

The Best Way to Specify Equipment and Materials

Specify particular equipment or materials if one type is superior to the alternatives, or if it has features that you particularly want. This will keep the contractor from surprising you with disappointing choices.

Usually, the best way to specify equipment is to state the specific model number in the schedules. If you are not sure that the preferred model will be available, list the two or three best choices in the schedule. List them in order of preference, and state that the builder should select the highest ranking one that is available.

Don't use the term "or equal." This is a common flaw of construction specs. For example, don't specify a heat pump as "Acme Model 300 or equal." The contractor does not have the expertise or the time to judge whether one item of equipment is "equal" to another. This involves apples-and-oranges comparisons between issues like efficiency, reliability, and noise. It is your job as the designer and homeowner to make these judgments.

■ Tip: Bind the Specifications Into the Drawings

Common practice is to write the specifications on ordinary letter size paper, as a document that is separate from the drawings. This is a poor practice. Builders work primarily from drawings, and separate specs are likely to be lost.

To keep the specs from getting lost, print them on the same paper size used for the drawings. Then, bind each part of the specs behind the corresponding drawings. For example, bind the HVAC specs behind the HVAC plans and schedules. In that way, all the information related to each part of the job is coordinated and handy. Include a table of contents for the specs on the cover sheet of the drawings.

The drawings should refer to the specs where appropriate, and *vice versa*. For example, in the foundation drawings, include a boxed note with an arrow pointing to the backfill that says, "See the specifications for backfill requirements."

GETTING EXPERT HELP

By this point, you have completed the design of your super-house. Your book is worn and dog-eared. The text is covered with yellow highlighter pen. Your idea file is overflowing. You know exactly what you want, and you have produced a detailed set of drawings and specifications. You are ready to start building.

Or, maybe not …

Maybe you have just skimmed the book to this point. You are excited about the idea of designing a super-house, but you don't have the confidence that you can do it yourself. Don't worry. You will not be on your own.

As a first-time home designer, you may want personal help with your design, in addition to the detailed guidance that this book gives you. You may want an expert to guide you through the unfamiliar passages of the design process, to answer your questions, and to reassure you about your decisions. Fortunately, homebuilding is a universal human activity, so many experts are available to help you.

As we discussed previously, *your builder and subcontractors* can provide valuable instruction about conventional construction practices. And, a trusted builder can provide a candid reality check for your ideas. But please, don't expect your builder to design your home.

Also, as we discussed, your *architectural drafting service* can help you fill the blank spaces in your knowledge of conventional construction. Some drafting services have licensed professionals, and the others have access to licensed architects and engineers.

An *architect* may provide valuable design assistance, especially in defining the layout and appearance of your home. But, be careful to select an architect who is right for your project. See the following sidebar, *How About Architects?*

An *engineer* is the right expert to consult about critical structural features and soil conditions. If you need an engineer, hire one who has expertise specifically related to home construction in your local area.

Together, these experts can guide you through any of the aspects of conventional home design and construction where you may want help. And now, you know how to communicate with them about the innovative features of your home.

It gets even better. In addition to established experts about conventional home design and construction, you may soon have the assistance of designers, counselors, and contractors who are certified in the innovative methods of **SUPER HOUSE**.

SUPER HOUSE CERTIFICATION FOR DESIGNERS AND CONTRACTORS

SUPER HOUSE launches a revolution in home design. At the time this book goes to press, many aspects of your home includes improvements and innovations that are unfamiliar to builders and designers. That is why we have suggested how you can educate your builder about the super-features of your design.

It would be even better if you could choose your builder and your design helpers from a corps of professionals who have already demonstrated their desire and capability to bring your super-house into being.

 SUPER HOUSE certification makes it possible to connect with builders and design counselors who have demonstrated a knowledge of SUPER HOUSE design principles.

Therefore, at the same time that this book appears, we are also launching a certification program for **SUPER HOUSE** designers, counselors, and builders. Certification is earned by designers, counselors, and contractors who pass a thorough examination about the portions of **SUPER HOUSE** that relate to their specialties.

Design counselors, architects, and contractors who qualify for **SUPER HOUSE** certification will be listed in a directory of certified professionals and contractors on the **SUPER HOUSE** Web site, **www.MySuperHouse.com.**

SUPER HOUSE certification provides designers, counselors, and contractors with an invaluable learning opportunity, with a badge of commitment to the best home design and construction practices, and with a way to be found by homeowners who seek that commitment.

For homeowners, **SUPER HOUSE** certification provides an easy way to find designers, design counselors, and contractors who have invested their effort and reputations in learning **SUPER HOUSE** principles.

Stay in touch with the **SUPER HOUSE** Web site, **www.MySuperHouse.com**, for information about the certification program and for the directory of certified professionals.

HOW ABOUT ARCHITECTS?

A century ago, architects were skilled in all the aspects of house design. They also handled contracting, and they would supervise construction. The best work of architects was spectacular, as you can tell by looking at many beautiful houses that were built in the past. But, the practice of architecture fell into a rabbit hole of incompetence and weirdness in the 1930's, from which it has never emerged.* The important innovations in modern housing, such as the use of plywood and the development of modern heating and cooling systems, occurred outside the architect profession.

Today, an architecture student typically spends five years in school, but he may receive little practical training. Most architecture schools teach "design" in the sense of fashion design or graphics design, rather than design in the engineering sense. Much class time is spent studying art history and screwball theories. An architect today may be well versed in the superstitions of *feng shue* and Bauhaus theory, but don't assume that an architect can design windows or a heating system for efficiency and comfort.

So, what can a typical architect do for you today? The most useful thing that architects learn is making sketches and models to show space layout. With his felt tipped pen and a roll of drawing paper, an architect can quickly translate your verbal desires into sketches. This is especially valuable if you have trouble visualizing spatial relationships, especially the shape and layout portion of the design in Step 1.

---

* The strange story of architecture's decline is told in Tom Wolfe's famous little book, *From Bauhaus to Our House*.

Most architects have the equipment to produce a formal set of drawings and specifications, in the sense of putting lines on paper. But, your drawings and specs will be more detailed than anything that the architect has produced in the past, especially in showing the important features that you select in Steps 3 through 6.

If you interview a typical architect about energy efficiency, you may get a tale about "green buildings" and "sustainability." Recognize this as sales talk, which may have little scientific, engineering, or trade knowledge to back it up.

If you decide to hire an architect, the key is to find one who is excited about the opportunity to design a super-house. What matters most is the willingness of the architect to satisfy your desires, to learn from this book, and to work effectively with the builder.

A major goal of **SUPER HOUSE** is to provide architects and architecture students with their missing education in excellent home design. To stimulate that advance throughout the architect profession, the new **SUPER HOUSE** Certification program provides a special category of recognition for those exceptional architects who take the initiative to learn.

The **SUPER HOUSE** Architect Certification program is being launched as this book is published. For the latest information, visit the book's Web site, **www.MySuperHouse.com**.

That's it! You are now ready to build your ideal home. Get it built, savor its every feature, and live a long and happy life in it. I hope that you will enjoy your super-home as much as I have enjoyed working with you to make it a reality.

LAST LOOK

Energy efficiency has become a dominant issue in house design, as conventional energy sources become scarce. The same is true of water conservation. Have we done enough to prepare your house for the future?

Yes, we have. Super-efficiency is a prime goal throughout your design, in a way that is fully compatible with the other super-features of your house, including comfort, health, safety, beauty, and strength.

Still, you may have noticed that we did not include a number of conservation measures and energy sources that are enthusiastically promoted today, such as solar energy or rain barrels. That was not an oversight. The measures that we omitted are less desirable than related efficiency features that we do recommend. Or, they have serious shortcomings, including a large potential to fail.

As we progressed through the design of your ideal home, we stressed reliability and economy. If an energy conservation measure doesn't work, it doesn't save energy. Instead, it wastes energy and other resources. So, we have limited our recommendations to efficiency features that can provide energy savings with certainty.

To provide assurance that your home's design has not missed any good bets, we will take a last look around to survey other energy-saving and "green" features that you may have heard about. One purpose is to examine their promises and pitfalls. Another is to help you to improve the chance of success if you decide to include one or more of these alternatives in your home.

Some of these energy options can be made to work. But, unless you are willing to make an exceptional effort to learn about them, install them properly, and maintain them, they are certain to fail. You will be left with an expensive and unattractive mess. On the other hand, if you can afford the price and if you are willing to deal with the risks, more power to you.

How about the thrill of innovation? Most of the following energy options are no longer "innovative." They may be uncommon because they haven't worked well. It's best to think of them as high-stakes hobby projects, only rarely a best choice. Let the reliable energy-saving advances introduced in this book satisfy your appetite for innovation.

We call this extra part of the book *Energy for Pioneers*. The word "pioneer" has a double meaning. We look at some home features that were used by pioneers of the past, such as wood burning. And, we examine technology that needs further pioneering to succeed, such as geothermal heat pumps. Even if you don't use these features in your home, I hope that you will find it interesting to learn about them.

HEATING WITH FIREWOOD AND OTHER SOLID FUELS

The rationale for heating with wood and other solid fuels is that these fuels may be less expensive than conventional fuels. Or, these fuels may still be available when conventional fuels are curtailed or exhausted. From the standpoint of appearance, a stove or a fireplace can provide an elegant focus for a room, and it provides an excuse to add a fancy chimney to the exterior.

However, a super-efficient house needs only a small amount of heating, and a wood fire is a troublesome way to provide it. Wood burning requires a commitment to a different lifestyle. The delightful fireplace of your imagination will become a chore.

Starting the fire requires a significant amount of time. The fire must be tended continually. Your hands will be burned. Your clothing will get dirty. You must remove ashes every few days, and sweep the flue every year. The house will become smelly and dusty unless the installation is perfect and the draft is managed properly. Any solid fuel heater requires a large safety zone that must be kept free of combustible material.

The air pollution from wood burning has caused wood heaters to be restricted or banned in some areas. Forcing your neighborhood to breathe toxic smoke on a regular basis is not responsible.

All that being said, if you plan to build your home in a rural area, consider using an efficient wood-fired heater as a primary source of heat, perhaps in tandem with one of the modern systems covered in Step 4. If you want to burn solid fuel, there are three types of solid fuel heaters to consider:

- *heating stoves* are the least expensive option, and they have visual charm. However, they have the lowest standard of comfort. They occupy a significant amount of living space, including their safety zone. Figure LL-1 shows a typical installation.
- *solid-fuel air heating furnaces* provide better comfort than heating stoves, and they can heat multiple rooms effectively. They use a fan to circulate air through one or more rooms using ducts. Most furnaces are plain steel boxes, as in Figure LL-2, and these typically are installed in a separate furnace room where they provide no visual appeal.
- *solid-fuel hydronic boilers* provide the ability to serve multiple rooms independently. Except for the boiler, the system can be identical to the hydronic systems that we covered in Step 4, so it can provide excellent comfort and energy efficiency. The boiler

Vermont Castings

Figure LL-1. A typical wood-fired heating stove.

can be installed in a fireproof room inside the house, as in Figure LL-3, or it can be installed outside as a freestanding assembly. The same hydronic heating system can use both a solid-fuel boiler and a boiler fired by gas or oil, providing fuel versatility.

I didn't include an open fireplace among the options. A beautifully built fireplace and chimney is an expensive indulgence. Any open fireplace is very wasteful of fuel, and it is a major source of air leakage into the house. I can't recommend an open fireplace to anyone who wants an efficient home. Even so, we will discuss fireplaces in case you may want to have one in a room that can be isolated from the rest of the house.

If the visual charm of a wood fire is the primary attraction for you, a heating stove is probably your best choice. But, if your home will be heated primarily by a modern heating system, having a fireplace or heating stove is likely to waste more energy while it is idle than it saves when you use it. That's because the portion of the flue that is inside the house (even if it is hidden in a chimney) is a source of air leakage and conduction heat loss.

If you want to use solid fuel as your prime source of heating in a climate that has a cold season, a ducted furnace or a hydronic boiler is a much better choice than a heating stove.

In the following pages, we will cover all the main types of solid fuel heaters in enough detail that you will be able to select the best equipment and install it properly. But before we get to the equipment, we need to learn about the fuel.

Figure LL-2. A typical wood-fired furnace for a ducted heating system.

YOUR FUEL SUPPLY, THE DOMINANT ISSUE

The cost of fuel is not a big issue if you install a fireplace or stove only for occasional use. If you don't own a woodlot, you will simply pay the exorbitant price for an occasional bundle of firewood and enjoy the evening. Or, you can burn wax logs, or you can buy a gadget that rolls up newspapers into logs, or you can burn wood scraps from your workshop. Or whatever.

If you live in an urban or suburban area, don't expect to use your fireplace as a primary source of heat when conventional energy prices become too high in the future. Everybody else will have the same idea. Wood and other fireplace fuels will become scarce and expensive. When the Age of Petroleum ends sometime during the 21st century, wood will be an energy source that is available economically only to people who live in rural areas.

Even if you live in the country, heating with firewood is economical only if you own a woodlot or if you have a reliable long-term access to firewood. A woodlot is a stand of trees that is large enough so that the firewood grows at least as fast as you harvest it. A self-sustaining woodlot can be surprisingly small. In a mid-latitude climate, you should be able to heat a super-efficient home for a year with the wood from one typical large tree. So, a well managed stand of about 40 trees can fuel your fireplace indefinitely.

Anticipate a lot of work to prepare wood for burning. In addition to a woodlot, you will need a chain saw, log splitter, and other paraphernalia. Using this equipment is dangerous. Or, you will need to hire someone to cut your firewood every year or two.

Freshly cut wood contains a lot of water, usually more than half its weight. It takes a long time for a log to dry to a desirable moisture content of 20% or less. Expect to dry your wood for a year or more before burning it. If you burn fresh wood, it will waste a lot of its own energy to dry itself. This will reduce its heat output and greatly increase smoke and creosote deposits. And, fresh wood is a bitch to light.

Don't expect to buy firewood that has been dried properly. You will need a storage location on your property for drying your wood after you cut it or buy it. Make a shelter that keeps your firewood off the ground, shelters it from rain and snow, and allows air to circulate around it. Wood that is exposed to rain and snow will rot and lose a significant part of its fuel energy. Make your shelter large enough for at least a one-year supply of firewood.

In addition to logs, you need to maintain an ample supply of kindling to start your fires. Kindling should be very dry. You can dry and store the kindling in a decorative metal bucket inside the house. The bucket should have a lid to keep sparks from igniting the kindling.

Viessmann

Figure LL-3. A high-efficiency wood-fired boiler.

Avoid heaters that are designed to use exotic kinds of fuel, such as "pellet" fuels or corn kernels. These fuels won't be economical during future energy shortages, and more likely, they won't be available at any price.

If you will be near a source of coal, consider a heater that is designed to burn coal. You will need a coal bin, or an unattractive outside coal pile. Do more homework about coal burning before you commit to it. Coal is dirty to handle and burn, and it has special requirements.

If you interested only in decoration and your house will have natural gas service, you might install a *faux* fireplace that burns natural gas. This type eliminates all the mess. A large variety of gas fireplaces are available. But somehow…, they aren't the real thing.

THE FIRE SAFETY ZONE

Fire marshals don't like fireplaces or heating stoves. Neither do insurance companies. Fireplaces and stoves have burned down a lot of houses over the centuries. Even enclosed wood-fired boilers and furnaces increase fire danger because sparks and cinders can escape while the fuel is being added.

As a result, building codes include fire safety requirements for solid fuel heaters. But, codes are only a starting point. The only reliable way to achieve reasonable safety is to create a fire safety zone around the heater that has no combustible surfaces and that will dissipate the heat of any sparks or cinders that contact a surface. Typically, this zone will occupy 100 to 200 square feet (10 to 20 square meters). The size of the zone is the same whether you use the heater as a primary heater or only occasionally.

The fire safety zone for an solid fuel heater should protect against these hazards:

- heat radiation from the heater that may ignite the nearby walls, floor, and painted surfaces
- flying sparks that can ignite combustible material in the room
- igniting combustible material, such as newspapers, that may be left on or near the heater.

Heat radiation determines how close you can place your heater to a wall. Leave at least as much clearance as required by the instructions that come with the heater, as well as any code requirements. Beyond that, leave easy access around the heater for cleaning and maintenance.

The floor under a solid fuel heater must be fireproof in depth. The fireproof floor should surround the heater far enough to catch any sparks that fly out of the heater. Sparks can fly a long distance.

An indoor furnace or boiler normally is located on a concrete slab, either in a basement or on the ground floor of a house with a slab foundation. If practical, the space should be surrounded by a concrete wall. And, the ceiling should have a fireproof covering, such as non-flammable ceiling tiles. Most furnace rooms are not built to that standard of safety, but yours should be.

The enclosure for a furnace or boiler should be large enough to make it easy to perform the frequent cleaning that they require. Also, the space will be used to store at least a minimum supply of firewood. This creates a temptation to use the furnace room for storage, but don't succumb to it. The heater space should be maintained as a totally fireproof environment.

Consider enlarging a furnace room or boiler room so that you can store a quantity of firewood that is sufficient for a few months of heating. This will be a great convenience during cold and wet weather. Also, the heat of the furnace will help to dry the firewood. However, this makes fire safety more critical. Place a barrier between the furnace and the wood pile, so that a spark from the furnace during fueling will not ignite the wood pile. If you store wood in the furnace room, design the furnace room so that a fire in the wood pile will not spread to the house.

For a decorative wood stove installed in a formal room, a beautiful fireproof floor can be created with attractive tile. For example, see Figure 3-283. With a wooden floor structure, the tile should be installed over a base of non-combustible "concrete board."

If a heating stove has a surface that is hot enough to ignite a fire, someone will eventually leave a newspaper or other combustible material lying on the stove, where it will catch fire. The entire environment of the stove should be so fireproof that a fire on top of the stove will result in nothing worse than smoke and annoyance.

Nothing that can be ignited by a spark should be located near the fire safety zone. In a formal room, there should be no carpeting near the fireplace, nor flammable furniture. To decorate the safety zone, use metal fireplace implements and other fireproof ornaments.

If you keep a quantity of logs indoors for ready access, stow them in a special fireproof fixture, such as a brick or sheetmetal enclosure. Or, keep the logs outside. Keep your kindling in a metal can that has an overlapping lid.

HOW WOOD BURNS

Most fireplaces, heating stoves, and wood-burning boilers and furnaces are designed to burn wood in the form of logs. Wood chips, wood pellets, and other forms of wood fuel are easier to handle than logs, but all wood has the same requirements for efficient burning.

Wood is difficult to burn efficiently. It requires *high temperature*, *adequate oxygen*, and *time* to decompose the solid mass efficiently. Wood burners have big differences in performance because they differ greatly in their ability to satisfy these requirements.

Wood is composed of carbohydrates, which are compounds of carbon, hydrogen, and oxygen. Burning wood is a process of breaking apart the large carbohydrate molecules into smaller and smaller molecules, until eventually all the material has decomposed into carbon dioxide and water vapor. The carbon dioxide comes from burning the carbon in the wood. The water comes from burning the hydrogen.

The oxygen for burning must come from the atmosphere. The oxygen contained in the wood's carbohydrate molecules provides no help in burning because it has already given up its chemical energy.

Raw wood is mostly a bundle of long cellulose fibers that are glued together by lignin, a complex compound. Burning wood is difficult because this tight bundle makes most of the fuel molecules inaccessible to atmospheric oxygen. Therefore, wood must burn in stages.

In the first stage, the log must be heated to drive off moisture. Evaporating the moisture absorbs heat. To burn a cold log, this heat must come from burning other material, such as dry kindling or other logs in the fire. Even well dried firewood contains a substantial amount of moisture. Fresh or "green" wood contains so much moisture that it absorbs more heat than it can provide at first by burning.

When wood reaches a temperature of about 500 °F (260 °C), it starts to break down into smaller molecules, releasing combustible gases and vapors. Some of these vapors burn, creating heat. However, most of these gases can't ignite until they reach higher temperatures. In a cool fire, most of these valuable fuel elements are wasted, or they burn partially to create smoke and foul the flue, creating the risk of a flue fire.

Once the temperature of the volatile gases rises to 1,100 °F (600 °C) and sufficient oxygen and time are provided, the gases burn fairly completely. At this point, the fire becomes efficient.

After most of the easily decomposed matter is burned, charcoal remains. Charcoal consists of the carbon skeletons of the original carbohydrate molecules. Efficient conversion of the charcoal to carbon dioxide also requires a minimum temperature of about 1,100 °F (600 °C). (At this temperature, the solid material emits a visible glow.) A chunk of charcoal can burn only on surfaces that are exposed to air, so burning the charcoal takes a long time.

Thus, in an established fire, the fuel components include cold wood that is being heated, combustible gases that have not yet been ignited, various gases that burn at different temperatures, and charcoal that burns slowly. In order for the fire to burn efficiently, all these components must eventually burn completely. And then, the hot carbon dioxide and water vapor must transfer its heat to the surrounding space, either directly or by heating air or water.

IMPORTANT ADVANCES IN WOOD-FIRED HEATERS

One of the main challenges of burning wood is that the volatile gases, which account for about half of wood's energy, are cooked out of the wood at a much lower temperature than they will burn. If you are starting any kind of wood burner, no matter how well designed, the volatile fuel components will escape up the flue until the heater becomes hot enough to burn them.

When wood is not burned completely, the partially burned components cause trouble. They condense on the cooler surfaces of the heater and the flue in the form of so-called "creosote," forming a combustible sludge that may later fuel a dangerous flue fire. Air pollution from partial burning includes a large variety of organic compounds and particulate matter that can cause cancer and lung disease. Some of the unburned gases are outright poisons, including carbon monoxide.

In most wood heaters of the past, all the different stages of burning occurred within a single firebox. But, the stages are not all compatible. Complete combustion requires high temperature, but transfer of heat through the walls of the firebox keeps the temperature too low for efficient burning of the fuel. Similarly, loading cold logs into the firebox lowers the firebox temperature. And, when most of the fuel has burned, the temperature drops too low to burn the remainder efficiently. As a result, wood heaters of older design are both inefficient and dirty.

Recently, combustion efficiency and the efficiency of heat transfer to the space have improved dramatically in stoves, furnaces, and boilers. This was done by using separate chambers or locations within the heater to accomplish the successive phases of combustion.

In the chamber where the wood is loaded, fire first cooks the volatile gases out of the solid wood. The gases then move into a separate chamber, or to a different part of the firebox, which is heavily insulated to maintain a very high temperature. Additional air is injected into this region to completely burn the gases. An finally, the hot gases move to a third part of the heater where they give up their heat to surrounding air or water.

Because different phases of burning occur in different regions of the heater, efficiency is less sensitive to changes in burning. For example, loading cold logs lowers the temperature in the primary chamber, but the secondary chamber remains hot enough to complete the burning of the gases.

The fire needs ample air for burning, but too much air cools the fire below the critical temperature of 1,100 °F (600 °C). To minimize this problem, most efficient wood burners preheat the air before admitting it to the fire.

In the pages that follow, we will provide more detail about the present state of the art in wood stoves, wood-fired furnaces, and wood-fired boilers. Heating stoves are the oldest of the three, and their efficiency has been inching upward for two centuries. However, it appears that stove designs still do not adequately separate the combustion stages inside the metal box. Even the best stoves require an almost steady fire to maintain their claimed high efficiencies. A continuing weakness is poor transfer of heat from the stove to the room, resulting in too much of the fuel energy being wasted to the flue.

In contrast, recent improvements in wood-fired residential boilers have been phenomenal. Not long ago, most wood-fired boilers were horrendous smoke generators with poor efficiency, rapidly accumulating soot that was difficult to remove. But within the last few decades, a new class of boilers has appeared that approach the maximum theoretical efficiency of burning. Obsolete smoky boilers still dominate the market, but now you have high-efficiency options.

Improvements in wood-fired air heating furnaces have also been substantial, using technical principles that are similar to the ones used to improve hydronic boilers. However, at the time this is written, there is no satisfactory program for certifying the efficiency of wood-fired furnaces. Therefore, you are more dependent on manufacturers' claims to judge the quality of the equipment.

HEATING STOVES

Heating stoves serve two purposes, heating and decoration. These days, the great majority of heating stoves function primarily as decorations. The fact that they can provide an occasional cozy evening in winter usually is secondary.

Heating stoves are the easiest kind of solid fuel heater to install. You select your heater from a catalog, and it arrives fully assembled, or nearly so. Installing a heating stove is much easier and less expensive than building an open fireplace. Many heating stoves are now available with ratings for efficiency and air pollution.

Contemporary heating stoves are the product of five centuries of invention to avoid the discomfort, smoke, and fuel waste of open fireplaces. The development of the "airtight" stove about two centuries ago was a major advance. The stove and its flue are sealed and the flue draft maintains a suction inside of the stove that keeps smoke out of the living space. Hence, there is no need for excess air to prevent the backflow of smoke. Also, safety is greatly improved because the fire is fully enclosed (except when adding fuel).

In an airtight stove, the intensity of the fire is controlled with a damper at the air inlet, rather than with a flue damper at the outlet of the fire. The inlet damper allows effective throttling of the air, slowing its passage through the heater. This provides more time for combustion to occur and more time for the gases to give up their heat to the metal of the stove. Careful design of the air inlet guides the air through the fire for good burning efficiency.

A heating stove provides better comfort than an open fireplace because it is able to heat the air in the room by convection. Even so, a heating stove provides comfort that is primitive compared to modern heating systems. Heating is concentrated near the stove, and heat cannot be distributed effectively to more than one room. Even the best heating stoves have limited ability to regulate their output, unlike the precise temperature control of modern heating equipment. Production of carbon monoxide and flue-fouling creosote increases greatly when a stove is "idling" at low output.

Heating with a heating stove is a batch process. For the reasons that we explained earlier, the stove must maintain a hot fire to burn the fuel efficiently, and this requires a large load of fuel. Especially in a well insulated room, a wood stove either overheats the space or the fire is too cool to maintain efficient combustion. (Pellet stoves are an exception, as we will see.)

Considering all that, let's look at the details that you should consider if you decide to install a heating stove.

EPA Ratings for Heating Stoves

Since 1986, the U.S. Environmental Protection Agency (EPA) has established a certification program for heating stoves that burn wood and wood-derived fuel pellets. The ratings for all certified stoves are listed on the EPA Web site, and each certified stove has a permanent EPA rating label.

The EPA claims that certified stoves have much lower pollutant emissions and significantly higher energy efficiency than typical non-certified stoves. In order to receive EPA certification, a stove model must be tested for pollutant emission at an approved laboratory and have measured emissions that are lower than a certain limit.

There are two EPA ratings for each stove model. One is the measured particulate emissions rate, in grams per hour. This rating allows you to select one model over another for cleaner burning.

The other rating is "default efficiency," which indicates energy efficiency. The same default efficiency is assigned to each of three types of heating stove, as follows:

- catalytic stoves   72%
- non-catalytic stoves   63%
- pellet stoves   78%

A big flaw of default ratings is that they do not allow you to select between models of the same type. The energy efficiency of a stove has two components: how completely the fuel is burned, and how much of the heat of combustion is transferred into the space. The pollutant rating is an indirect guide to completeness of burning, but you have no rating to indicate how well a particular model transfers the heat of combustion into the room instead of losing it to the flue.

Beyond that, the efficiency of any stove will vary widely at different stages of burning, at different firing rates, with different moisture content of fuel, etc. For example, adding a fan kit may substantially increase heat transfer into the room, while somewhat reducing burning efficiency and increasing pollution.

Types of Heating Stoves

Heating stoves are available in several types and styles that are appropriate for serious heating. There are important differences among them. We will review the modern types, along with the features that you should consider.

■ High-Efficiency Non-Catalytic Wood Stoves

Two things must happen to make a wood stove efficient. First, the fuel must burn completely, turning into hot gases of carbon dioxide and water vapor. Then, the hot gases need to give up their heat to the surrounding space. Because the burning wood must be kept hot, these two things must occur in different parts

Morso

Figure LL-4. Contemporary version of an old stove design intended to separate the heat transfer surface of a heating stove from the firebox.

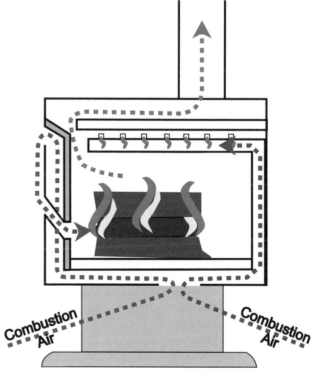

U.S. Environmental Protection Agency

Figure LL-5. Operation of a high-efficiency, non-catalytic wood stove. Two separate air supplies enter through different paths. One feeds the fuel area. The other acts as an afterburner in the gas exhaust path, completing the combustion of fuel gases and particulates. Both air supplies are pre-heated by passing through the casing. If the stove has a glass door, one air supply is routed to protect the glass.

of the stove. After leaving the combustion zone, the hot gases must come into contact with exterior surfaces of the stove long enough to extract most of their heat.

The need to separate these two functions was recognized by the 19th century. Many stoves of that era provided separate chambers for burning the fuel and then for transferring the heat from the combustion gases into the room. Figure LL-4 shows an attractive example.

Modern high-efficiency stoves commonly use an insulated firebox to maintain efficient combustion temperature. In the part of the stove where the wood is loaded, combustion is sustained by a "primary" air supply. To achieve complete burning of the fuel vapors and particulate matter, some stoves have a separate chamber in the exhaust path that is heavily insulated to maintain a high temperature. "Secondary" air is admitted to this chamber to complete the burning. Figure LL-5 shows an example of this design.

Less commonly, the stove may have a double wall, arranged so that the hot, completely burned flue gases pass between the inner and outer walls.

The primary air, and perhaps the secondary air also, are preheated by entering through passages in the hot part of the stove. In stoves that have glass to provide a view of the fire, the primary air may be circulated over the inside surface of the glass to protect the glass and keep it clean. The output of the stove is controlled, within limits, by throttling the primary air with a damper.

■ Catalytic Wood Stoves

Most catalytic stoves look similar to non-catalytic models. All legitimate models have EPA ratings for efficiency and pollutant discharge.

How do they work? As we mentioned at the beginning, reasonably complete combustion of wood is impossible without a combustion temperature of about 1,100 °F (600 °C). In a conventional heating stove, even if it is designed for high efficiency, the only way to achieve good efficiency is keep the fire hot. Such a fire may overheat the room.

It is possible to maintain high efficiency without a roaring fire by adding a catalytic combustion element in the exhaust path, as in Figure LL-6. This element is a bundle of honeycomb passages, typically having the shape of a brick. The passages are coated with a catalyst that ignites the unburned fuel in the flue gas, even at gas temperatures as low as 600 °F (320 °C). This burning raises the temperature of the catalytic element, further enhancing combustion.

Because a catalytic stove can operate efficiently at lower heat output, it can also heat much longer with a single charge of wood. This may allow the fire to continue overnight, avoiding the bother of restarting the fire in the morning.

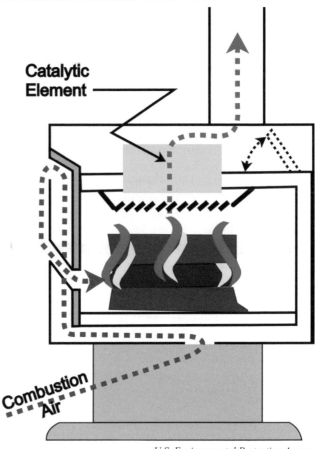

U.S. Environmental Protection Agency

Figure LL-6. Operation of a catalytic wood stove. Unburned fuel gases and particulates are burned in the catalyst, which begins to operate once the combustion gases have reached a certain temperature. Before this temperature is reached, an internal bypass damper must be opened to protect the catalyst from clogging.

Unfortunately, catalytic stoves require even more care and maintenance than non-catalytic stoves. The catalyst must be cleaned periodically to remove ash. When a fire is first started, the catalyst is bypassed with an internal damper to keep it from being clogged by the fuel vapors and smoke that are too cool for the catalyst to burn. You have to remember to close the bypass when the exhaust gas reaches the temperature where the catalyst will work. This requires a properly located thermometer. Also, you must also keep the fire from burning too hot, which would destroy the catalyst.

The EPA pollution ratings for the best catalytic stoves are better than the EPA ratings of the best non-catalytic stoves, but not by a large margin. Catalytic stoves offer the greatest pollution advantage with low, steady fires. The catalyst provides no benefit during the smoky, inefficient period when the fire is starting, because the catalyst is bypassed then.

The catalytic element is moderately expensive to replace. The active material is a thin coating of platinum or palladium, or perhaps both. The manufacturer may be tempted to skimp on them. Originally, the body of the catalytic element was made of ceramic. Now, steel elements are an option. Both are gradually destroyed in use. Manufacturers claim that the catalytic element will last for several years of heavy use. You can judge the performance of the catalyst by checking the stove thermometer.

Make sure that your stove is designed to make replacement easy. Also, consider where you will buy replacement catalysts if the stove's manufacturer goes out of business. The stove may last forever, and you don't want it to become useless because you can't get a replacement catalyst. Catalysts are made by specialized manufacturers who sell to the stove manufacturers. If you are considering a stove that is not a popular model, determine whether it uses a catalytic element that has common dimensions.

■ Pellet Stoves

"Pellet stoves" are heating stoves that are designed to burn solid fuels in the form of small pellets. Pellet stoves promise higher efficiency, less air pollution, and easier operation than heating stoves that are fueled by logs or coal. Externally, they can look similar to conventional wood stoves.

Pellets most commonly are made from wood products, either virgin timber or wood waste. Some pellet stoves may also burn corn kernels, nut shells, and other biomass or biomass products. The fuel pellets typically are about one inch (a few centimeters) in their longest dimension.

Pellets burn more efficiently than logs, primarily because their small size and large surface area allows them to reach an efficient burning temperature quickly. For the same reason, the heat output of the stove can be adjusted over a wide range. The limited size of the flame area allows the combustion air flow to be designed for efficiency and for protection of the stove's surfaces.

Pellet stoves typically have the components illustrated in Figure LL-7. The fuel pellets are stored in a hopper outside the combustion chamber. An auger or other metering device conveys the pellets to a small combustion chamber. The heat of the flame is transferred to the surrounding space through a heat exchanger. One fan is used to circulate combustion air inside the stove, and another is used to circulate the heated air to the room.

The main shortcoming of pellet stoves is their fuel supply. The stove is designed around the fuel. If the special fuel is not available, you will not be able to use the stove with ordinary wood.

Pellets made from waste products, such as sawdust, are limited in supply. They may be cheap as long as there is little demand for the waste products from which

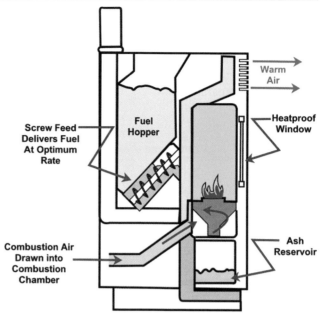

U.S. Environmental Protection Agency

Figure LL-7. Operation of a pellet stove. The specific design is closely tied to the limited range of pellet fuels that the stove can use.

they are made, but they will suddenly become scarce and expensive as soon as demand exceeds the supply.

Biomass that is grown commercially as fuel usually wastes more energy than it saves. This is because it usually takes more energy to produce a quantity of biomass fuel than the fuel will deliver when it is burned. In addition, biomass fuels contribute to soil depletion and exhaustion of fertilizer supplies. Fueling a fire with food products, such as corn kernels or soybeans, is irresponsible. Food products contain only a tiny fraction of the energy required to grow them, and they leave behind a large mass of unused biomass.

Pellet stoves need electricity to operate their accessories. If the electricity supply is interrupted, the stove will not be available for heating unless you have an emergency generator that works.

■ Coal Stoves

Coal-fired stoves are generally similar to non-catalytic wood stoves. They are available in similar styles, with similar accessories, and they have similar installation requirements. Some models are designed to burn both wood and coal, although the two fuels burn differently.

Coal stoves are uncommon today. In a situation where coal would be the preferred fuel, a coal-fired central boiler or furnace generally is a better choice.

At this time, there are no EPA ratings for heaters that burn coal only. However, there are EPA ratings for heaters that burn both wood and coal.

Heat Distribution from Heating Stoves

The main comfort limitation of heating stoves is poor heat distribution. If you plan to use a stove for serious heating, try to install it near the center of the room to minimize variations in temperature throughout the room. At the same time, don't let the stove isolate people in the room from each other. It helps to select a model that is low enough so that the occupants can look over the top of the stove while they are seated.

If you are using a fireplace or stove primarily as a decor item, don't worry too much about the efficiency of the layout. Just deal with appearance and fire safety.

Many stoves are offered with a fan kit that circulates room air over the surface of the stove. This may improve heat distribution considerably. However, unless the fan kit is carefully designed, it may suck combustion gases and smoke out of the stove and discharge them into the room. And, the fan makes noise. The only way to be sure that a fan will work well is to check with an owner of that particular model.

A heating stove distributes heat by radiation and convection, so it cannot heat more than a single space satisfactorily. Heat radiation is blocked by any surface. Convection cannot cross walls, and very little convection goes through open doors or down corridors.

A super-insulated structure helps to make a heating stove more comfortable. Because the heat loss from the room is very low, you can heat the room with a small heater. This reduces the radiation intensity and the stratification of the air temperature.

Convection from a heating stove can provide a limited amount of heat to rooms located at a higher level. Heat will rise up the stairway, if the bottom of the stairway is open to the space that has the stove. In some older houses, a grille was installed in the floor of the upstairs hallway, above the downstairs stove, to give some warmth to the upstairs rooms. You might design the living room with a mezzanine that is open to the upstairs room. However, you would have to leave the upstairs doors open, which compromises privacy.

These methods are actually more practical in a super-insulated house. The heat loss upstairs is so low that the heat from a downstairs fireplace may be able to keep the upstairs rooms warm enough for comfortable sleeping under comforters.

The Best Size for a Heating Stove

In general, select the smallest size that looks appropriate for the room and that has an adequate firebox size. If your house is super-insulated, the usual recommendations for stove size are too large. If the stove is too big for the heating requirement, the fire will be too small to keep the stove hot enough for efficient burning, despite the efficiency ratings. Also, an oversized stove will have an oversized flue, which will not operate properly at low fire.

Firebox Size

Select a stove that has a firebox that is long enough to burn logs of normal length, which is about 20" (50 cm). Shorter logs require more cutting, and you may not be able to buy them. Also, the firebox needs to be wide enough to allow you to crisscross the logs somewhat. A stack of parallel logs will not ignite easily or burn well. High-efficiency stoves tend to have smaller fireboxes, so this is a compromise.

Fueling and Ash Removal

Different models of heating stoves can be fueled from the front, sides, or top. Generally, front loading is best, especially if the front has a glass door. Loading from the front makes it easiest to place the logs properly and to adjust the pile with tongs or a poker.

Side loading can't be used if the stove is installed in a corner. Some models load from the top, but this is a bad choice. Imagine what it is like to load and adjust logs from the top of a roaring fire. In fact, one manufacturer of a top-loading stove includes a long fireproof glove with the stove.

To simplify the dirty chore of removing ashes, buy a model with a well designed ash pan. This will allow you to scrape ashes out of the firebox into the pan without spreading a lot of dust into the room. If the pan is large enough, you can scrape out the firebox several times before it is necessary to empty the pan.

Cooking Surfaces

Some stoves have a flat cooking surface, but don't take it seriously. The surface won't be hot enough for real cooking unless the stove has a roaring fire. At other times, the temperature of the surface is too high and too irregular for merely warming pots and pans.

Combustion Air for Heating Stoves

Older houses were so leaky that the leaks were sufficient to provide combustion air for a heating stove. However, an airtight house needs to include an air supply for any fuel-fired heaters. A fire that is starved for air will not burn properly, and it cannot be controlled. Smoke and carbon monoxide may back up into the room.

Some airtight stoves provide a duct connection that allows you to supply outside air directly to the stove. This avoids the need to bring the air through the house. Such connections usually are designed to provide air to the fire in the most efficient manner. This is a valuable feature. Get it if you can.

If your stove does not have an outside air connection, install an outside air source as close to it as possible. This avoids the discomfort and energy waste that results from drawing unheated outside air through the house. For example, if you install an airtight stove on legs, duct outside air to an opening underneath the stove. This opening should be larger than the combined size of the primary and secondary air openings of the stove.

The air supply from the outside should enter through a simple duct, with no fan, and the intake should be protected from wind pressure. The outside end of the air intake duct can be located in an exterior wall, with a cap like the ones used for clothes dryer vents. Or, for concealment, it can be located in a vented eave, or it can draw from a vented attic.

The outside air supply is a hole in your house. To prevent air leakage when the heater is not operating, install a tightly closing damper or stopper that can be opened and closed easily from the location of the heater. Also, provide screens to keep out insects, birds, and rodents.

DUCTED SOLID-FUEL FURNACES

A ducted forced-air heating system provides a considerable improvement in comfort and coverage compared to a heating stove. The system consists of a furnace, a fan, and ducts. It is mostly identical to the forced-air heating systems that are common in North America. The main difference is the furnace, which is fueled by wood instead of gas or oil. The best wood-fired furnaces have good fuel burning efficiency, and they make fueling and ash removal fairly easy.

If your climate has a cold season, and if you plan to use wood or another solid fuel as your primary source of heating, a ducted system is a primary candidate to consider.

Advantages

Compared to heating stoves, a wood-fired furnace is much more comfortable because all the heating occurs by warming the air to a uniform temperature, rather than heating by concentrated radiation and convection.

A single furnace can heat multiple rooms, including an entire house.

All the fueling and ash handling occurs outside the occupied area of the house, which may be a basement, a furnace room, or outdoors. Therefore, a ducted system keeps the inside of the house cleaner than using heating stoves. The warm air path is separated from the firebox and flue system by a heat exchanger, so there is less opportunity for smoke and carbon monoxide to leak into the house.

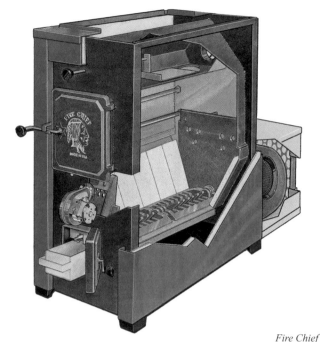

Fire Chief

Figure LL-8. Cutaway diagram of a wood-fired furnace. Efficiency features include good insulation of the firebox, a secondary combustion chamber, and a variable-speed circulation fan.

Disadvantages

A ducted system that heats multiple rooms has a number of serious disadvantages with any kind of fuel. These are summarized in the sidebar, *Why You Don't Want Central Forced-Air Heating and Cooling*, at the beginning of Step 4.

These disadvantages make a solid fuel-fired ducted system inferior to the modern heating systems recommended in Step 4. However, in comparison with heating stoves and fireplaces, a ducted system may be greatly superior in comfort.

Fuel Burning Efficiency

The energy efficiency of a furnace is the product of two factors: how completely the fuel is burned, and how much of the heat of combustion is transferred into the circulating air.

To achieve complete fuel burning, the furnace should have an insulated combustion chamber that is designed to burn both the solid and gaseous components of the fuel completely. The most efficient furnaces have two chambers. In the first, where the fuel is loaded, the fire cooks the volatile fuel gases out of the wood. In the second, very high temperature and a secondary air supply complete the burning of the fuel gases to become hot carbon dioxide and water vapor.

To capture the heat of the gases, the furnace uses a thin metal surface between the combustion gases and the air that is circulated through the house. This surface is called a "heat exchanger," and it transfers heat by conduction through the metal.

For maximum efficiency, the heat exchanger should extract as much heat as possible from the gases. This requires the heat exchanger to be large. With an efficient heat exchanger that extracts most of the heat from the combustion gases, the exhaust temperature in the flue will be relatively low, even at full fire. A typical flue temperature for a highly efficient furnace is around 400° F (200° C).

Unfortunately, there is a problem with low exhaust temperatures. The water vapor in the exhaust will combine with sulfur and other elements in the gases to form acid that can condense on the heat exchanger and corrode it. The water vapor will also condense on the heat exchanger whenever the furnace cools down.

A solution to this problem exists in high-efficiency furnaces that burn gas and oil. It is to use a stainless steel heat exchanger. However, this feature does not seem to have found its way into solid fuel furnaces.

Credible efficiency ratings for solid fuel furnaces have not yet been developed at the time this is written. However, they may appear by the time you need them. Most likely, they will be developed by the U.S. EPA, which already has ratings for wood stoves and wood-fired boilers.

In the absence of efficiency ratings, the only way you can judge the performance of a particular furnace model is to examine its features. For example, Figure LL-8 shows the features of a better quality unit. If possible, examine a unit that is operating. Measure the exhaust temperature at full fire, and look at the amount of smoke that is emitted by the flue.

Select for Easy Cleaning

The furnace should have access panels for cleaning all the surfaces that are exposed to the flue gases. Any solid fuel burner rapidly deposits soot on the heat transfer surfaces, which blocks the flow of heat into the house. This makes it necessary to clean the fireside surfaces often. This is a messy chore. Select a furnace that makes it as easy as possible.

Shaver ThermoWind

Figure LL-9. A wood-fired furnace for outdoor installation. The warm air is delivered to the house through large ducts. If the furnace is distant from the house, the ducts may run underground, as shown here.

Layout and Zoning

The best location for the furnace is a separate furnace room that has the safety features described under the previous heading, *The Fire Safety Zone*. The furnace room should have direct access to the outside, so that the occupied area of the house is isolated from the dirt of furnace maintenance and the debris of handling the fuel.

Freestanding outdoor furnaces, as in Figure LL-9, are an alternative to indoor installation. Generally, this option is desirable only for an existing house that cannot accommodate an indoor installation.

The smoke from an outdoor furnace may dirty the house and property. The only way to avoid this is to extend the flue to a height above the top of the house roof.

To minimize energy waste and to improve temperature control, tailor the layout of the ducts to the room layout that you designed into Step 1. The main ducts should serve at least the "day cluster" of rooms that we defined in Step 1. Extend the ducts to the bedrooms if it is practical to do so.

For a large "independent room" that is used only occasionally, such as a great room, consider installing a separate heating stove in that room.

Ducts, Dampers, and Fan Speeds

To achieve reasonably uniform temperatures in the spaces served by a furnace, the ducts should allow the air to move easily. The ducts should be large, they should have few bends, and the bends should be well rounded.

Locate all air ducts entirely within the insulated shell of the house, not in an attic or crawl space. Therefore, the interior framing of the house needs to include ample space to run the ducts both horizontally and vertically. If the furnace is located in a basement, ducts generally run horizontally along the basement ceiling, and then rise to individual rooms above. On upper floors, horizontal ducts normally run in an enclosure along the ceiling. Consider raising the ceiling height to accommodate horizontal duct enclosures.

If the furnace serves more than one room, efficient dampers are needed to adjust air flow to each room, and to shut off heating to idle rooms. Make an effort to get good dampers, and to install them so they are easily accessible for adjustment and maintenance. You can buy automatic dampers that are thermostatically controlled by the room temperature.

The air needs a path to return from the heated rooms back to the furnace. The easiest and cheapest method is to route the returning air through the corridors and common areas, to an opening in the wall of the furnace room. This requires a louver of adequate size in the door or wall of each of the heated rooms.

If you shut off part of the air flow with dampers, you need to reduce the intensity of the fire proportionally. Otherwise, the furnace and ducts will overheat. The heat exchanger in the furnace may fail, allowing smoke and carbon monoxide to enter the air stream. The ducts may become hot enough to start a fire in the structure. To guard against overheating, buy a furnace that controls the combustion air supply with a thermostatic damper that senses the air supply temperature. The damper should adjust the air slowly and continuously to avoid sudden changes in the fire. Also, the furnace should have a separate temperature alarm that warns if the air supply becomes dangerously hot.

If you reduce the air flow with dampers, you need to reduce the speed of the air circulating fan. Otherwise, the air flow to heated rooms will become too cool, the fan will be noisy, and the fan will waste energy. Make sure that your furnace fan can reduce air flow over a wide range, down to perhaps one fourth of maximum air flow. Such a wide range requires a special kind of fan and speed control.

WOOD- AND COAL-FIRED BOILERS FOR HYDRONIC HEATING

The most comfortable and efficient way to heat a house with solid fuel is to install a hydronic heating system. We covered modern hydronic heating in Step 4. The significant difference here is that the boiler is fired with solid fuel, rather than with gas or oil.

With a solid fuel, the boiler requires major continuing effort to operate and maintain. You will get dirty operating it. You have to refuel the boiler daily or more often. You have to haul away the ashes every few days. And, to maintain efficiency, you need to clean a solid-fuel boiler fairly often. Burning wood creates a lot of soot and "creosote," which sticks to the heating surfaces. This must be cleaned out periodically, or it will severely reduce the efficiency of the boiler, overheat the steel, and corrode the boiler. Cleaning any kind of solid-fuel boiler is a messy job.

You can use a solid-fuel boiler in combination with a conventional boiler that is fueled by propane, fuel oil, or even electricity. The wood-fired boiler would be your primary boiler, and the conventional boiler would serve as a backup for times when you don't want to burn wood. For reliability and ease of repair, both boilers should be entirely independent of each other, including separate flues.

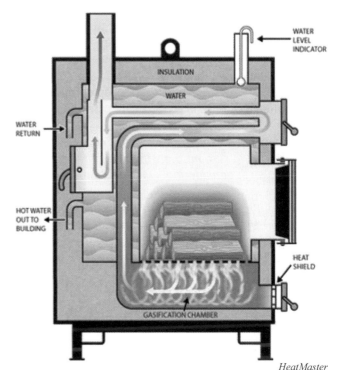

HeatMaster

Figure LL-10. Diagram of a "gasification" boiler. The secondary gas burning chamber is located below the firebox. This design yields much higher fuel burning efficiency and much lower pollution emission than is possible with old-style single-chamber boilers.

Or, you may be able to find a solid fuel boiler that includes a separate oil or gas burner. This arrangement is more compact. But, a dual-fuel boiler is less efficient for burning conventional fuels than a boiler that is dedicated to a single conventional fuel.

"Gasification" Boilers: the New Paradigm

Most wood-fired boilers have been notoriously smoky and inefficient. The reason is that the combustion chambers in cheap boilers are surrounded by the water. The cold surfaces keep the wood vapors from igniting and burning completely, so efficiency is poor and smoke is heavy. Also, wood-fired boilers tend to operate at a low average output, which keeps the fire from getting hot enough for good combustion.

The earlier heading, *Important Advances in Wood-Fired Heaters*, explained recent improvements that have radically improved efficiency and reduced pollution in wood-fired stoves, furnaces, and boilers. The most aggressive of these improvements have occurred in wood-fired boilers

The improvement in boilers is achieved primarily by separating the combustion and heat transfer processes in three different parts of the boiler. In the chamber where the logs are loaded, the combustible gases are cooked out of the wood at relatively low temperature and with limited air. The gases are then routed to a second insulated chamber where they are burned with additional air at very high temperature, reducing the gases entirely to carbon dioxide and water vapor. The fully burned gases are then routed through tubes to heat the water in the boiler. Figure LL-10 is a diagram that shows the separate regions of the boiler.

In order to distinguish the new, more efficient type of boiler, their manufacturers adopted the term "gasification boiler" to describe them. The new name will help you to find an efficient boiler.

If you plan to heat your home with a wood-fueled hydronic system, a gasification boiler is the only type worth considering. The fact that the gases are burned in a separate insulated chamber tends to maintain high efficiency even when cold logs are loaded into the first chamber. Once the fire is well established, burning is so complete that little visible smoke is emitted.

Efficiency Ratings for Wood-Fired Boilers

Until recently, only a small number of manufacturers made efficient wood-fired boilers. But now, the U.S. Environmental Protection Agency (EPA) has established a certification program for wood-fired boilers. This has spurred a growing number of manufacturers to offer wood-fired boilers with greatly improved efficiency and greatly reduced air pollution. As this is being written, the EPA has commenced

Wallnoefer Walltherm

Figure LL-11. A gasification boiler installed in a formal room. This model radiates about 30% of its heat output into the room. The remaining 70% is used for hydronic heating for the rest of the house, requiring a separate water storage tank. This promotional photo does not show an ample fire safety zone, and the nearby light-colored decor is incompatible with the grime that accompanies fueling and ash handling.

Pro-Fab Empyre

Figure LL-12. A wood-fired boiler that is designed for outdoor installation is being placed on a concrete pad.

"Phase 2" certification, which replaces an earlier, less stringent certification program.

To find manufacturers and models that meet the EPA Phase 2 requirements, search the Internet for "EPA Phase 2 wood boilers."

Select for Easy Cleaning

Regular cleaning is essential to keep the boiler efficient. Soot must be brushed out of the heat transfer surfaces and the flue. Select a boiler that has access panels that allow the easiest possible cleaning of the tubes and other surfaces that are exposed to the flue gases.

If the boiler is located inside an enclosed space, design the space so that you can easily use the brushes and other tools that you will need to clean the boiler.

Where to Locate the Boiler

A solid fuel boiler may be installed inside the house or as a freestanding unit outside the house. If you are designing a new house, most of the arguments favor installing the boiler inside the house. Nobody wants to trek outside repeatedly to refuel the boiler, especially during cold or muddy weather. For an indoor installation, the main installation issues are fire safety, convenience of fueling, and ease of maintenance. The earlier heading, *The Fire Safety Zone*, covers these issues.

Generally, the boiler should be located in its own space to keep dirt and wood debris out of the living space when handling the fuel, and to keep soot outside the living space when cleaning the boiler. However, some German manufacturers are introducing fancy gasification boilers for installation in formal rooms. These function as decor items because they have glass windows in the front to allow occupants to see the flames. Figure LL-11 shows an example.

In the past, wood-fired boilers generally were installed outside the house. However, there no longer seems to be much justification for outside installation, except for an existing house that does not have adequate space for an inside installation. For outdoor installation, boilers are delivered to the home site as freestanding units, as in Figure LL-12. These require only a small concrete pad for installation. They have a plain metal roof, and they don't look pretty.

For a better appearance, a wood-fired boiler may be installed in an enclosure about the size of a child's playhouse. The enclosure can be decorated as attractively as your imagination allows. In any event, the boiler itself is much smaller than the wood pile that feeds it.

Even the best wood-fired boiler will produce enough smoke to make a house and property grimy unless the smoke is discharged above the roof level of the house. If you install the boiler inside your house, it will have a conventional flue that rises above the roof, usually by a minimum distance that is specified in the building code.

If you install the boiler outdoors, the flue that is provided with the boiler will be too low to protect the house from the smoke. In that case, installing the boiler at a distance from the house is the usual form of protection that is used. This solution is unreliable because smoke can still blow toward the house when the wind is unfavorable.

Also, this approach to avoiding smoke requires a long run of well-insulated underground pipes to carry the heated water to the house and back. Good insulated pipe and proper installation are expensive. Doing the job well requires special knowledge that many heating contractors don't have.

You can install an outside boiler close to the house and keep the house clean if a very tall flue is installed on the boiler, as in Figure LL-13.

Greenwood

Figure LL-13. This outdoor boiler installation avoids dirtying the house by using a flue that is tall enough to clear the top of the roof. The appearance is rural.

OPEN FIREPLACES

A thousand years ago, most people heated their dwellings with fires that were located near the center of an earthen floor, away from the combustible parts of the structure. The main disadvantage of this arrangement was the smoke from the fire, which was unhealthy for the occupants and made everything sooty. The smoke was exhausted through a hole in the roof, but this did not keep the smoke out of the living space.

Around the 14th century, European peoples started using stone fire enclosures that included chimneys to channel the smoke directly to the outside. During the following centuries, these open fireplaces were mostly built into walls, because they are easier to build that way and because a fireplace in the wall takes up less of the living space. Special brick and masonry were developed to withstand the heat of the fire.

The chimney did keep most of the smoke out of the living space, but this important advance in smoke removal came at the cost of radically increased fuel consumption. The chimney creates a strong suction, or "draft," that draws heated air out of the house. In addition to sucking the warm air out of the house, the chimney also discards most of the heat of the fire itself. The open fireplace captures little heat from the combustion gases. Even the heat absorbed by the chimney is largely lost through the chimney's outdoor surface. Open fireplaces are so inefficient that forests near cities were stripped to provide firewood, even with the smaller populations of earlier centuries.

To minimize excessive draft and heat loss, a damper was added in the flue. But, the effectiveness of a flue damper is limited by the fact that it is installed at the outlet of the fire. Closing the damper tends to cause smoke to back into the room. So, occupants respond by keeping the damper wide open. As a result, the primary benefit of the damper is to minimize air leakage through the flue when the fireplace is not operating.

Open fireplaces emit heat into the house almost entirely by radiation from the hot surfaces of the burning logs and from the hot brickwork that lines the visible part of the fire space. Radiation does not heat air. This makes the heating from an open fireplace uncomfortable. People are warmed on the side of their bodies facing the fire, but the other side receives no heat and is exposed to the unheated air in the room. Remember when you were sitting around a camp fire on a cold night? You were baked on one side and frozen on the other. It might have been fun for one night, but it wasn't comfortable.

The flue damper fits very loosely. It cannot block air leakage into the house through the chimney when the fire is not burning. Therefore, an open fireplace is a major hole in the airtight structure of the house.

The conclusion is that *no type of open fireplace can be either efficient or comfortable*. An open fireplace can be beautiful, but it can't be practical. If you install an open fireplace in your house, it will be entirely as a decoration, including the rare times when you will actually light a fire in it.

Certainly, a fireplace can be an object of great beauty if it is designed with a strong sense of style. The stonework and brickwork of the fireplace and the chimney, mantels of stone or wood, and accessories such as andirons provide many opportunities to create an impressive visual presence, as in Figure LL-14.

But, this beauty comes at a high cost. The interior masonry and stonework and the exterior chimney structure require special taste and skill. Both must be large and well proportioned. The chimney will complicate the carpentry of the house, making it difficult to seal air leaks.

So, if you want to give your house distinction on a limited budget, spend your money on features other than an open fireplace. However, if you really must have an open fireplace, we will summarize the main points.

Air Pollution from Open Fireplaces

Open fireplaces are unfriendly to the environment. The main problem isn't the occasional tree that you cut for fuel. It's the smoke. All fireplaces and heating stoves burn fuel incompletely, creating combustion products that cause cancer and other lung ailments. From an environmental standpoint, the best of fireplaces is much worse than even a mediocre heating stove.

An open fireplace cannot act as the hot combustion chamber needed for efficient wood combustion. The

DRW

Figure LL-14. An attractive open fireplace that was once the primary source of heating for this 18th century house. It continues to be a focal point of the decor, even though more modern heating is now used. The chimney has been closed to prevent heat loss.

volatile gases that are cooked out of the wood will be sucked into the chimney before they are able to burn completely, so that a wood fire from a fireplace produces mostly smoke and dangerous air pollutants, rather than clean combustion products.

The Size of the Fireplace and Chimney

An open fireplace heats the room almost entirely by radiation. Therefore, the fire chamber should be small enough so that a relatively small fire will heat the firebrick enough to radiate heat well. Also, you can't get a good fire going in an open fireplace if the surrounding surfaces are cold.

Unfortunately, an open fireplace that is sized for effective heating is likely to look too small for the room. Since you would be installing a fireplace primarily as a decoration, heating effectiveness will not be an issue, anyhow. If you decide to have an open fireplace, design it to be as attractive as possible. You can make the surrounding masonry and trim as big as you want, while keeping the fire chamber as small as practical.

The exterior chimney structure has a strong influence on the exterior appearance of your house. Unfortunately, small chimneys don't look good. Since an open fireplace performs only a decorative function, either have a suitably large and fancy chimney, or no fireplace at all.

Building a Fireplace In Frame Construction

Chimneys are a danger to frame construction. Visualize a creosote fire in the chimney, causing the flue liner to crack and allowing hot gas to escape through cracks in the chimney and ignite the frame structure. It is difficult to isolate the chimney from the frame structure in a way that reliably prevents this. A metal flue inside the chimney is about the only method, so the chimney itself serves only as a decorative covering for the metal flue.

Air leakage is another problem of chimneys in frame construction. There is relative motion between the chimney and the frame wall, caused by different rates of expansion and contraction as the temperature changes. Also, wood shrinks and warps, whereas masonry does not. To minimize the leakage, design both the chimney structure and the frame wall so that the gap between the two can be well insulated and sealed from air leakage.

The masonry of a fireplace has minimal insulation value, so the fireplace is a major path for conduction heat loss. To minimize this, build the chimney structure outside the insulated wall. If you will have a large masonry structure surrounding the hearth, build it inside the insulated wall. In this way, only the hearth itself penetrates the insulated wall.

DRW

Figure LL-15. A fancy freestanding fireplace. It actually burns wood, but mainly as a decor item. This type has all the disadvantages of any open fireplace.

Fireplaces with Heat Exchangers

By the 1700's, it was realized that the gases produced by a fire contain a large fraction of the fire's heat. About the same time, iron foundries had developed the ability to produce complex castings. During that period, various individuals (including the ever ingenious Benjamin Franklin) devised heat exchangers for open fireplaces. Air from the room passes through the heat exchanger without being polluted by the fire. In most fireplaces, the room air is drawn through the heat exchanger by convection, although some later variations use fans.

Such heat exchangers can work reasonably well, but they provide only a modest improvement for a fundamentally inefficient type of heater. They improve comfort by heating the air in the room directly. Some heat exchanger assemblies also include a passage to feed outside air directly to the fire, so that cold air does not have to be drawn through the room.

The heat exchanger must be large in order to work well, with the room air entry and discharge grilles alongside the hearth. Therefore, the fireplace, the chimney, and the surrounding masonry must be built around it. Fireplace heat exchangers are a gamble because they are not standard items. They may increase the efficiency and comfort of an open fireplace, but you probably won't be able to predict their actual performance.

DRW

Figure LL-16. Enclosed fireplace. This unit has a damper to control combustion air, which enters the bottom of the brass front along with air to be heated. Heated air enters the room through a grille at the top of the brass front.

Freestanding Fireplaces

An open fireplace does not have to be built into a wall. It can be built anywhere in a room. A fireplace located away from a wall can be open on all sides, making the fire highly visible and improving the radiation of heat into the space.

To limit weight and avoid the need for a separate foundation, freestanding fireplaces usually are made of steel, although they can be decorated with a veneer of brick or stone. They are available in a great variety of styles, limited only by the imagination of the manufacturers. Typically, a steel pipe flue rises straight up through the roof, as in Figure LL-15.

Having the flue inside the exterior walls avoids the heat loss of an exterior chimney, but overall, freestanding fireplaces are as wasteful as other open fireplaces. They are just as prone to smoking, they suck warm air out of the building, and they are equally vulnerable to chimney fires.

Combustion Air for Fireplaces

An open fireplace needs a large supply of air to maintain an adequate draft through the flue. The amount of air needed for the draft is much greater than the amount of air needed for combustion. Even leaky old houses did not provide enough draft to avoid smoky fires, so homeowners learned to open windows to provide draft air for fireplaces. That was an inefficient and uncomfortable solution.

If you decide to install an open fireplace, you can buy a fireplace assembly that includes a direct outside air connection as well as a heat exchanger to improve recovery of heat from the fire. This may be worthwhile

if it is well designed. Scrutinize the design to be sure that it will serve its purpose effectively.

If your fireplace does not have an outside air connection, install an outside air source as close to the fireplace as possible, to minimize the discomfort and energy waste that results from drawing unheated outside air through the house.

The air supply from the outside should enter through a simple duct, with no fan. The outside end of the air intake duct can be located in an exterior wall, with a screened cap of adequate size. Or, for concealment, the outside air opening can be located in a vented eave, or it can draw from an attic.

For a fireplace of typical size, the air supply duct should be about 6 inches (15 centimeters) in diameter. This is a big hole in your house. To prevent air leakage when the fireplace is not being used, install a tightly closing damper or stopper in the duct that can be opened and closed easily. Also, provide screens to keep out insects, birds, and rodents.

ENCLOSED FIREPLACES

An enclosed fireplace is a hybrid of a heating stove and an open fireplace. It is like an open fireplace, except that it has an airtight glass front and an inlet air damper. Figure LL-16 shows a typical example.

The enclosed front eliminates the large amount of excess air that is needed to keep smoke from backing into the room. The inlet air damper provides effective throttling of the fire that is not possible with a flue damper. Also, when the fireplace is idle, the glass front blocks leakage of outside air from the flue into the house.

Because enclosed fireplaces are built into a wall, they cannot provide effective heating of the room air by convection. Some models do include a heat exchanger to provide a certain amount of convective air heating, but this emits only a fraction of the heat that would be provided by a cast iron heater located inside the room.

Also, the glass front of the fireplace absorbs most of the heat radiation from the fire. Therefore, an enclosed fireplace is less effective as a radiant heater than an open fireplace. Most models offer the option of leaving the glass doors open, substituting a screen to keep larger sparks from flying into the room. However, this turns the unit into an open fireplace, with all its risks and limitations.

Enclosed fireplaces retain the other liabilities of open fireplaces. They are just as difficult and expensive to install. With frame construction, they impose the same difficulty of creating a tight, safe seal between the masonry structure of the fireplace and the wooden structure of the house.

FIREPLACE INSERTS

What if you buy a house that has an open fireplace, and you want to burn wood without the enormous energy waste of an open fireplace? The answer is to install a heating stove in the fireplace.

The insert stove should have a tightly sealed flue connection to the original chimney. This avoids sucking air out of the house when the fire is burning, and it blocks cold air from entering through the chimney when the fire is out.

The simplest approach, and probably the best, is to buy a good conventional heating stove (catalytic or non-catalytic) and connect it to the chimney through the fireplace. If the fireplace is large enough, install the stove inside the fireplace, as in Figure LL-17.

In a typical fireplace, a great deal of heat loss occurs through the brickwork of the firebox. You can reduce this heat loss by installing the wood stove in front of the original fireplace. Install an insulated panel to cover the fireplace opening, and pass the heating stove flue through the panel. The mantel and the decorative stonework around the fireplace remain visible. This is your only option if the wood stove is too large to fit inside the fireplace.

Shutterstock

Figure LL-17. A modern wood stove installed in the fireplace of a restored old house. It is important to make a tight seal between the stove's flue and the original chimney.

FLUES FOR SOLID FUELS

Any burner for wood or other solid fuel needs a special kind of flue. The flue has two important functions. It removes smoke and other products of combustion, including dangerous gases such as carbon monoxide. And, it creates a suction (or "draft") that draws combustion air through the fire.

A "chimney" is a fireproof structure, usually made of masonry, that surrounds and supports a flue. With masonry fireplaces, the chimney usually is an extension of the fireplace structure.

Heating stoves and metal freestanding fireplaces usually have uninsulated bare flue pipes inside the house (which provide some additional heat). The pipe outside the living space may have several designs. If it runs inside a masonry chimney, it may have a single wall, wrapped with fireproof insulation. If the pipe is exposed to the outside or to a frame structure, it may have a double or triple wall. Exterior pipe may be bare or it may be enclosed for the sake of appearance.

If a fireplace or stove performs badly, the fault usually lies with the flue. The flue itself is simple, but its design is critical. The design of the flue for a heating stove or a fireplace is more demanding than the design of a flue for a modern boiler or furnace. An improperly installed flue will force smoke into the room and make your fireplace a nuisance instead of a pleasure.

From the standpoint of energy efficiency, the flue is the Achilles heel of solid-fuel heating equipment, wasting energy even when the equipment is idle. With present flues, there is no way to avoid a significant amount of air leakage and conductive heat loss.

The flue also creates a safety hazard. A properly designed flue will provide more suction than is needed while the fire is burning actively. However, at the end of the burn, when the fire cools and produces little flue gas, the flow in the flue may reverse. This is dangerous because the smoldering fire produces a large amount of carbon monoxide. If the reversal occurs while the fire is still smoldering, carbon monoxide will flow into the house.

Flues have always been a hit-or-miss feature of house construction. Building code requirements for flues are only a starting point. If you plan to install a solid fuel heater, do more homework about flues. These are the main points.

Creating a Good Draft

A flue acts as a pump that sucks the gases from the fire to the outside. It works because the top of the flue is higher than the air inlet at the heater. The flue gases expand and become lighter as they are heated. The cold surrounding atmosphere is heavier than the light gases inside the flue, so it pushes the combustion gases up and out of the flue.

The strength of the draft is proportional to the height difference between the top of the flue and air inlet to the heater. In a house of normal height, this distance is adequate if the exhaust gases are able to flow easily. The convection force of the draft is weak, so the flue should be free of obstructions, such as sharp bends or long horizontal runs. To get the best draft, install the flue straight up through the roof, if practical. If bends are required to go through a wall, make them rounded. Keep any horizontal run short, and tilt it slightly upward. Install a well designed chimney cap that deflects downdrafts from wind while minimizing resistance to exhaust.

Design the flue to prevent backdraft. This is a flow of cold outside air down into the flue, even as exhaust gases are rising through the flue. The two streams pushing past each other make the draft irregular, causing an unstable fire and pushing smoke and carbon monoxide into the room. To avoid backdraft, make it easy for the flue gases to rise. Also, avoid oversizing the inside diameter of the flue. In an oversized flue, the exhaust flows so slowly that outside air can spill into the top of the flue, especially at low fire. In general, use a flue of the same diameter as the flue collar on the stove.

The flue for an airtight stove needs to be only a fraction of the size of the flue for a fireplace. The flue for an open fireplace needs to pass a large amount of excess air to keep smoke from entering the room. If you succumb to an urge to have an open fireplace, seek flue size recommendations from expert sources, such as books or Web sites devoted to fireplaces.

Use round flue pipe, even inside a chimney. In rectangular flues, it is easy for outside air to backflow down the corners of the flue while the hot gases travel up the center. Also, the colder corners of the tile encourage creosote deposits, which are difficult to remove from the corners.

Protecting Against Flue Fires

Protecting your house against flue fires is a dominant issue in the design of a flue. The smoke from wood fires contains a large volume of soot and "creosote," which is a general name for sticky combustible material that cooks out of the fuel without burning completely. A lot of this material is produced when a fire first starts. It collects on the inside wall of the flue. If this material is not removed from the flue periodically, it will accumulate enough to fuel a fire inside the flue. The fire can be hot enough to crack the flue, allowing the hot gases to leak out. Or, the heat from the hot flue can ignite any combustible material in the surrounding structure.

Periodic sweeping with a special brush is needed to prevent this. To make cleaning easy, use round flue pipe, even in a ceramic chimney. Avoid bends or connections that make it difficult to pass the flue brush. Make the top and bottom of the flue accessible for the chimney sweep. The bottom of each vertical section of pipe should have a cleanout cap, if it does not end at the stove.

Expect that chimney cleaning will be overlooked at some point during the life of the house. Therefore, design the flue to isolate a flue fire from the structure of the house. Design your flue conservatively, with multiple layers of separation between the flue gases and the combustible house structure. Also, maintain a separation between the flue and any combustible structure.

If a flue fire occurs, it probably will be necessary to replace the flue pipe or flue liner. Therefore, while you are designing the flue for ease of cleaning, also design it for ease of replacing the pipe.

A flue fire may be invisible, so you may not know that you have a damaged and dangerous flue. Therefore, the flue should be inspected every time it is cleaned.

Metal Flues

The best kind of exterior or hidden flue for any type of solid fuel heater is a specially fabricated metal pipe with two or three concentric walls. Insulation may be installed between two of the walls. The inner wall of the best pipes is stainless steel, and the outer walls are usually galvanized steel. Flues of this kind can be purchased in various lengths, with all necessary installation accessories, such as bends, top caps, bottom supports, and cleanout openings. Plan the flue to make installation as easy as possible.

The multi-wall pipe provides fire protection. The outer pipe is isolated from the hot gases, reducing the chance that the flue will start a fire in the surrounding structure. If a flue fire cracks the inner pipe, the space between the pipes provides a path for the flues gases to vent and cool.

The multiple walls and the insulation reduce heat loss, keeping the inside surface warmer. This reduces the amount of creosote and soot that collects in the flue. The warmer flue also reduces the tendency of cold outside air to backflow along the inner wall of the pipe.

The exterior metal flue looks too industrial for an elegant house, so you will probably hide it inside some sort of enclosure. For example, see Figure 1-183, in Step 1. For a classic masonry fireplace, you can enclose a metal flue in a traditional looking masonry chimney.

With heating stoves and some fireplaces, a portion of the flue is visible inside the house. This length of pipe is a decorative item that can be enameled in colors to match the stove, if desired. Typically, the visible pipe has only a single wall, so it can become quite hot. The pipe itself contributes significantly to heating the space. By the same token, this section of pipe can become quite cold when the stove is not firing. Special care is needed to seal the joints in single-wall pipe against air leakage into the space.

Clay Tile Flues are Obsolete

In the past, the best masonry fireplaces were built with a masonry chimney that encloses a flue made of special clay flue liner tiles. The tiles are rectangular in cross section to fit the shape of the chimney. They are stacked on top of each other with mortar joints.

If the chimney is built properly (many are not), the flue tiles are separated from the chimney by a gap of an inch or so (several centimeters). The gap insulates the tiles from the outside, allowing the tiles to get hotter. This improves the draft and slows the deposit of creosote.

Consider this method of construction to be obsolete. Flue tile may be cracked by a flue fire, creating the risk of a house fire. Broken tile allows hot gases to heat the outer chimney, which is in contact with the structure of your house. Cracked flue tile is practically impossible to repair properly.

The rectangular shape of the flue passage is undesirable, for reasons that we stated previously. If you want to have a brick chimney for the sake of appearance, consider using a round metal flue liner instead of ceramic flue tiles. You can make the outer chimney as big as you want for the sake of appearance, while sizing the flue passage to provide good draft. Design the chimney to make the pipe easy to clean and to replace.

The Flue Damper, an Unsolved Problem

Earlier, we explained the purpose of a flue damper in controlling the draft in an open fireplace. In the best airtight stoves, the draft is controlled by a damper located at the inlet of the stove itself. In addition, most heating stoves have a flue damper located in the section of pipe just above the stove.

When the heater is not firing, the flue damper is supposed to block the flow of cold outside air into the house. However, typical flue dampers are not able to do this. In fact, the flue damper typically is undersized or it has a hole in it to ensure a minimum of venting for safety. If you use your fire only occasionally, this safety feature is likely to cost you more money in heat loss than the fireplace or stove will save.

For easy access, flue dampers usually are positioned near the bottom of the flue. This location allows the entire flue above the damper to fill with dense, cold outside air. The weight of this air column forces it past the loose damper, through the connections in the flue pipes, through any joints in the stove, and around the door of the stove. In addition, the cold air keeps the surfaces of the flue and the stove cold.

To prevent all this heat loss, you would like to plug the flue tightly at that point where it passes through the roof or wall of the house. To the best of my knowledge, a safe, reliable, and easily usable flue damper of this kind is not yet available as a proven product.

Air Leakage Around Flue Penetrations

If you use a metal flue pipe, the space between the outside of the flue and the wall or roof is a major air leakage path. Step 3 explains how to seal this large gap in a way that protects the structure from the high temperature of the flue.

MOVABLE INSULATION FOR WINDOWS

We have learned how to achieve outstanding energy efficiency in almost every part of your home. However, windows continue to be a nagging exception. That's why we devoted Step 2 to achieving the best compromise between the important functions of glass and its poor energy efficiency.

The basic problem is the lack of a practical transparent material that has good insulation value. There has been a great deal of effort since the 1970's to develop windows with reduced heat loss, but this effort has yielded only limited gains. The best windows still have about ten times more heat loss per unit of area than well-insulated walls. As a result, if your house is located in a cold climate, your primary method of minimizing heat loss is to keep your windows as small as possible.

Another possible method is to cover the windows with some kind of insulation during the hours of darkness. Since the insulation is not transparent, it must be removed every day. For that reason, this concept is called "movable insulation." Or, "thermal shutters."

In principle, movable insulation can greatly reduce window heat loss. During cold weather, the hours of darkness outnumber hours of daylight, and the lowest temperatures occur at night. During the day, when the insulation is removed, entering sunlight usually offsets the heat loss, especially if the windows are oriented as recommended in Step 2.

During the 1970's, several types of movable insulation were popular, but they all vanished. Some had fundamental flaws, while others were just too awkward. Acceptable types of movable insulation are not commercially available at this time, so we can't recommend it for your house. Still, the concept continues to hold promise.

Perhaps, acceptable products will be available by the time you read this. Or, you may want to design movable insulation for your windows on a custom basis, especially if your house is located in a climate where the winters are long and cold. To help you select movable insulation – or even to make your own – we will outline the main issues to consider.

CHARACTERISTICS OF GOOD MOVABLE INSULATION

Whether you buy movable insulation or make your own, it should have these characteristics:

- *High insulation value*. The insulation value should be at least several times the insulation value of the window. More insulation is better, even if it is not practical to match the insulation value of the wall.

- *Tight air sealing*. Movable insulation should seal tightly against the window structure, to prevent heat loss by air leakage into the space between the insulation and the glazing. Also, the design should make it easy to block air leaks where electrical wiring or mechanical actuators for movable insulation pass through the structure of the house.

- *Prevention of condensation*. Any water vapor that leaks from the inside of the house encounters colder surfaces as it travels outward. If the vapor condenses, the moisture will damage the structure or the insulation. To prevent this, the movable insulation system should use the same techniques that we explained in Step 3 for protecting walls from moisture damage.

- *Durability*. All the critical components, including the insulation itself, gaskets, hinges, etc., should last for many years. External components should resist damage from sunlight, rain, ice, and extreme temperatures.

- *Ease of maintenance*. Components that wear, such as hinges and seals, should be easily replaceable. The design should not include any specially manufactured components that will become unavailable within the life of the house.

- *Convenience*. Thermal shutters must be opened and closed on a daily basis, so operating them should be easy, or perhaps automatic.

- *Good appearance*. Movable insulation is a highly visible element, so it shouldn't be ugly. It should be unobtrusive or easy to decorate, or both. Mechanical actuators should be hidden or unobtrusive.

Movable insulation may be located inside the glass, outside the glass, or between the panes of multiple-glazed windows. Each of the three locations has its own challenges. Let's examine all three.

MOVABLE INSULATION INSIDE THE GLAZING

During the 1970's, interior insulating blankets for windows were popular. They came in various styles that placed a layer of insulation between the inside of the room and the window. Some were made in the form of heavily insulated shades that fit snugly against the window frame, as in Figure LL-20. Others were removable foam rubber plugs, cut to fit the window opening and encased in decorative fabric, like crib mattresses. These designs were inexpensive, reasonably attractive, and easy to install and use.

This type of movable insulation has largely vanished because it can cause serious condensation damage. The insulation blanket keeps heat from escaping to the window, so the inside surface of the window becomes almost as cold as the outside air. Water vapor in the air leaks around the edges of blanket and condenses on the glass and frame, causing mildew, rot, and rust.

DRW

Figure LL-20. A window quilt, in raised position, installed in the bedroom of a Wyoming ranch house. The dry climate keeps condensation from forming on the window when the quilt is lowered. Still, it is inadvisable to lower the window quilt for longer than overnight.

Even one night of condensation can damage the trim around a window. If a window blanket is left in place for the duration of a vacation, the owners may return to find a mildewed mess around the entire window structure.

Unfortunately, condensation would be even worse in your super-insulated house than in a conventional house. Your house will have a highly effective vapor barrier that makes it possible to maintain higher relative humidity inside the house during cold weather. This a comfort asset, but it tends to increase condensation on the windows.

MOVABLE INSULATION OUTSIDE THE GLAZING

One way to avoid condensation damage is to install the insulation on the outside of a window or skylight. Because the entire window assembly is kept warm by the outer insulation, moisture does not condense on the window. External thermal shutters can employ plastic foam insulation to exploit its high R-value and to reduce the thickness required.

A challenge of exterior movable insulation is surviving outdoor conditions, including wind, rain, snow, sunlight, temperature extremes, and physical impact. Wind is the biggest threat, exerting a large force on the shutter, especially when it is in the open or partially open position. This requires strong mounting to the wall structure and strong mechanisms to move and hold the shutters. Protection from rain and snow for window thermal shutters can be provided by wide roof overhangs or by other structures that overhang the shutters.

Figure LL-21 shows external thermal covers that I installed for two large passive solar skylights on my house. The installation was thermally successful, but failed because I could not devise satisfactory automatic actuators for the large covers, each of which is the size of an airplane wing.

(Failure can be instructive, but we don't want you to have any failures. The lesson here is not to build any feature into your home until you have fully worked out the details.)

An external thermal shutter for windows probably would be built like an insulated entrance door, with gaskets or weatherstripping on all sides. The shutters might fold back alongside the window, like conventional shutters. Or, they might lift upward, like an awning.

If the glazing is vertical, as in most windows and clerestories, it is a challenge to keep the shutter sealed against air leakage when it is closed. Some kind of reliable clasp is needed to hold the shutter tightly all around its edge. (Refrigerator doors use magnetic seals that stick to the metal body of the refrigerator. Something similar might be adapted to outdoor use.)

Exterior thermal shutters need a practical actuator that allows you to open and close them from inside the house. As a minimum, it should be possible to operate and lock the shutters by opening the window and reaching through it. In a climate that can be very cold, the shutters should have an actuator that allows the windows to remain closed.

Designing the actuators is a bigger hurdle than the shutters themselves. A good carpenter could make an effective set of exterior thermal shutters, including the necessary gaskets. However, the actuators require skills and equipment that are more industrial in nature. This is not a job for the typical home designer.

DRW

Figure LL-21. Exterior insulating covers for two large skylights that were designed to provide passive solar heating. The cover on the left is open, the one on the right is closed. The shutters had good insulation value, and their weight kept them well sealed when closed. However, they were eventually abandoned because a satisfactory mechanical actuator could not be devised without creating an industrial appearance.

MOVABLE INSULATION BETWEEN THE PANES

Let's consider another possibility. If movable insulation poses a risk of moisture damage when placed on the inside, and if it requires a lot of engineering when placed on the outside, how about avoiding both problems by using movable insulation between the panes of glass?

That concept enticed inventors throughout the 1970's, and several types of inside-the-window movable insulation were offered for sale. Unfortunately, none worked well. It proved to be difficult to get the insulation in and out of the gap between the panes, to seal against convection currents between the insulation and the glass, and to stow the insulation material when it is removed from the window.

One briefly popular technique was blowing foam beads into the window at night. It worked pretty well in terms of moving most of the insulation, but electrostatic charge caused beads to stick to much of the glass area.

A further difficulty of placing insulation between the panes is that the optimum spacing between window panes is about one half inch or less (about one centimeter). Wider spacing to accommodate the insulation allows increased convection inside the window. Also, the gap between the panes cannot be sealed and cannot be filled with special energy-saving gases. Thus, heat loss through the window during the daytime, when the insulation is removed, would be much higher than for a conventional window.

ACTIVE SOLAR HEATING SYSTEMS

"Active" solar heating systems collect the heat of sunlight using collectors that are installed outside the insulated shell of the house. Most active systems operate by circulating water between the collectors and a storage tank. Some systems have been designed to heat air with external collectors of various kinds.

The name "active" distinguishes these systems from "passive" systems, which admit sunlight directly into the house without any moving parts or fluids.

Active solar systems are designed either for space heating or for domestic water heating. Domestic water heating systems are simpler, smaller, more efficient, and more economical than space heating systems.

Solar heating seems almost ideal in its lack of direct adverse effects on the environment. It is quiet, it emits nothing into the surroundings, and it requires nothing from the surroundings, except perhaps for a small amount of electricity to operate pumps and/or fans.

The main environmental cost of solar systems is the energy and materials required to produce them. Unfortunately, the amount of energy that is required to manufacture an active solar system is a large fraction of the amount of energy that the system can collect during its service life. This makes the economics poor. Realistic payback periods exceed ten years for water heating systems, and they exceed twenty years for space heating systems.

The technology has been static for decades. The principles are well known, and commercial equipment is available. Maintenance requirements are modest. One fundamental problem – getting rid of excess solar heat – does not yet have a fully satisfactory solution.

Many thousands of solar collector systems were installed from the 1960's to the 1980's, but hardly any systems of that era remain today. They failed primarily because of poor design and stupid installation. That does not mean that solar heating cannot work well, but it is a warning that solar heating requires more attention than it was given.

Systems that use conventional flat-plate collectors have a fundamental climate limitation. With low outside air temperatures, even if there is strong sunshine, the collectors cannot heat water to a temperature that is high enough to be useful. This limitation is especially severe with space heating systems, which require a relatively high water temperature to operate.

For these reasons, I do not recommend an active solar system for space heating. Instead, put your money into making your house super-efficient, and pocket the difference.

If you live in a climate that is always mild or warm and if energy costs are high, you might want to install a solar system for heating your domestic water. Solar water heating systems are relatively small and they can be simple to install. They are more expensive than a conventional water heater, but they require little or no energy to operate. Simple, packaged domestic water heating systems are presently popular in some warmer climates, such as the lands that border the Mediterranean Sea.

Solar collector systems operate much better in summer than in winter. The average air temperature surrounding the collectors is higher, reducing heat loss. The sun shines on the collectors for a larger fraction of daily hours, and the sun is higher in the sky and less likely to be obstructed.

THE SOLAR COLLECTORS

The collectors of an active solar system are a prominent feature of the house's exterior. They typically are mounted on the roof, but they could be mounted anywhere that has a direct view of the sun for most of the day.

Most collectors use the "flat plate" design, which consists of a shallow sealed box with a glass cover facing the sun. Figure LL-24 shows typical flat plate collectors that are used in both water heating and space heating systems.

DRW
Figure LL-24. Typical flat plate collectors used for water heating on an Italian island.

Figure LL-25. Focusing solar collectors. Parabolic mirrors focus a large amount of sunlight on a small tube, creating very high water temperatures. The cost and the temperatures are too high for residential applications.

Inside the box, sunlight is captured by circulating water through a heat collecting plate that has a black, highly absorbing surface. Insulation is installed behind the heat collectors to reduce heat loss from the rear of the enclosure. The glass cover is needed to keep the surrounding atmosphere from cooling the heat absorbing surfaces.

Flat plate collectors have a dark and somewhat blotchy appearance. However, everyone has seen solar collectors by now, so they don't seem strange.

When water is circulating through the collectors, the maximum temperatures range from 120 °F to 170 °F (50 °C to 80 °C) on sunny days. This is satisfactory for bathing and laundry. However, these relatively low temperatures make flat plate collectors inefficient heat sources for home heating. Interior heating equipment must be powered by fans because the temperatures are too low for convective heating units, such as baseboard convectors.

For economy, flat plate collectors are almost always mounted on a fixed frame. With this mounting, they should face almost true south and upward toward an elevation in the sky where the sun travels during the winter months. Deviations from these orientations greater than about 20 degrees will significantly reduce heat collection.

To provide higher water temperatures, some collectors use parabolic reflectors to focus sunlight on heat collecting tubes, as in Figure LL-25. The reflectors track the sun across the sky. Focusing collectors are disabled by cloud cover or haze. They are much more expensive than flat plate collectors, so they typically cannot repay their cost in a reasonable period of time. Because of these limitations, they have been used only for specialized applications in sunny climates.

Big Decision Factor: Access to Sunlight

In order for an active system to be useful, the collectors must be exposed to direct sunlight for most of the day. This requirement is more challenging than it may seem. The sun travels through a large part of the sky, and most of this must be open to view by the collectors. One of the most common flaws of solar systems has been shading of the collectors by trees, terrain, other buildings, and even by parts of the same building.

Most critically, space heating systems must be able to see the winter sun when it remains low in the sky. This requires a commitment to clearing all obstructions that would shade the collectors, and then to keeping them cleared in the future. In most locations, such a commitment will seriously affect the appearance of your property.

Problems of Roof Installation

At present, solar collectors usually are installed on the roof. This location offers the advantage of using space that is not useful for other purposes. However, it incurs several problems.

In a warm climate, one of the most effective methods of keeping your home cool is to shade the house and surrounding property with trees, as Step 2 explains. Unfortunately, effective tree shading is likely to interfere with solar collectors that are mounted on the house. Mounting the collectors on the roof also interferes with routine replacement of the roof surface.

A possible solution to these problems is to locate the collectors in a sunny location away from the shaded parts of the house. If such a location is available, the penalty is a greater length of pipe and somewhat increased pump energy.

Try to make the exterior components accessible for inspection and maintenance. Well installed collectors do not require much maintenance, but they should be inspected regularly, primarily to reveal any leaks that may occur. Washing grime off the collectors will maintain their efficiency and slow corrosion of the metal box.

SOLAR DOMESTIC WATER HEATING SYSTEMS

The simplest practical kind of solar domestic water heater is shown in Figure LL-26. It consists of a hot water storage tank that is located above one or more solar collector panels. A mixture of water and antifreeze circulates by convection between the collectors and a heat exchanger inside the water tank. Cold domestic water is fed into the bottom of the tank, where it is heated by the heat exchanger. The heated water is withdrawn from the top of the tank.

This system is entirely external. It requires no pumps or controls, and no energy to operate. If it is well designed and if the environment is benign, it can last about as long as a conventional fuel-fired heater.

Typically, there is no control of the water storage temperature. The tank temperature is allowed to rise to maximize heat storage. As a result, a scalding hazard is a feature of most simple solar hot water systems

The solar collector is protected from freezing by the antifreeze. The hot water storage tank is protected from freezing by the mass of the water in the tank, by insulation surrounding the tank, and by circulation of water through the tank. As long as the outside temperature rises above freezing temperature during the daytime, the tank is unlikely to freeze.

This kind of solar water heater is popular around the Mediterranean Sea, where it is commonly installed as a packaged system on the flat roofs of masonry buildings. With a different mounting, it could be installed on any roof, on a wall, or on the ground. For example, the tank could be installed in an attic, and the collectors could be mounted on a wall below the attic.

The sun can warm fixed collectors for about ten hours per day, or less during winter. This assumes that the collector is not shaded during any part of this period. At the end of the period, the tank contains all the solar heated water that will be available for the next fourteen hours or so. An electric heater may be installed inside the water tank as a backup during cooler weather, and to provide freeze protection. Or, the water from the solar tank may be sent to a conventional water heater inside the house for additional warming.

In climates where an exterior storage tank might freeze, the tank is installed inside the house. If the tank is located below the collectors, the antifreeze mixture must be circulated through the system with a pump. The indoor tank will have its own source of heat, either electricity or fossil fuel, that is used when solar heating is insufficient.

DRW

Figure LL-26. A type of solar water heater that is common around the Mediterranean Sea. Antifreeze solution is heated by sunlight in the collectors and rises by convection to a heat exchanger in the water storage tank. Hot water is tapped from the top of the tank and is replaced at the bottom. The system requires no pumps. An electric heater may be installed in the tank to heat the water during cold or cloudy weather.

SOLAR SPACE HEATING SYSTEMS

An active solar space heating system is a hydronic system that uses solar collectors to heat the system water, instead of a boiler. The collectors are the same as for domestic water heating systems. In addition, the system needs a huge tank to store the heating water for use at night and during cloudy weather.

Solar space heating systems have two fundamental problems that have kept them from being practical. One is the inability of flat plate collectors, during cold weather, to produce water temperatures that are high enough for space heating. The other is the size and weight of the water storage tank.

Water has limited heat storage capacity that must be compensated by using an enormous volume of it. To be useful, the storage tank must be big, heavy, and expensive. Even so, a day or two of overcast skies will deplete the heat in the tank during cold weather.

Because of these limitations, solar space heating systems need a backup source of heat, such as a fuel-fired high efficiency hydronic boiler. Unfortunately, except in warm climates, experience has shown that much of the heating will be provided by the supplemental boiler, rather than by the sun.

SYSTEM SIZE, SPACE, AND WEIGHT

The main decisions in designing a solar system are the total area of the collectors and the size of the water tank. These are judgment calls. Larger collectors can heat more water. A larger tank can store more heat to cover longer periods. A location that has a lot of cloudy weather will require substantially larger collectors and a larger tank than a location that usually has clear skies.

For domestic water heating in a warm climate, a collector area of about 30 to 60 square feet (3 to 6 square meters) is common. A warm-weather system of the kind shown in Figure LL-26 typically has a tank capacity of about 50 to 90 gallons (180 to 330 liters).

For colder climates, the collector area typically is much larger, typically exceeding 100 square feet (10 square meters). In such climates, the system typically has two indoor tanks. The solar heated tank typically holds about 100 gallons (400 liters). It must be large enough to store hot water through long nights and cloudy weather. The conventional water heater that is used for supplemental heating has a tank of conventional capacity, typically about 50 gallons (200 liters) in size.

A solar space heating system for a super-efficient house of typical size might have collectors that range in size from 150 to 400 square feet (15 to 40 square meters).

The water storage tank for a space heating system for a well insulated house typically would have a capacity ranging from 500 to 1,500 gallons (2,000 to 6,000 liters). It would weigh, respectively, about 5,000 to 14,000 pounds (2,000 to 6,000 kilograms). Because of its weight, the tank should be installed on a reinforced foundation, typically in a basement.

FREEZE PROTECTION

Because the exterior components of the system are filled with water, they need freeze protection. Most systems rely on antifreeze in the water that circulates through the collectors.

The most common antifreeze for domestic water heating systems is propylene glycol. If it leaks into the water supply in small quantities, it is harmless. In fact, it is used as an additive in foods and medicines. A less expensive antifreeze may be used in space heating systems.

Another method of freeze protection is to drain the collectors and other external equipment to an indoor holding tank if the outside temperature approaches freezing. Such "draindown" systems are probably too complicated to be reliable for the life of the house.

GETTING RID OF EXCESS HEAT

At times when the solar system collects more heat than is needed, where does the excess heat go? As of now, there is no satisfactory answer to this question. This issue has been a major factor in system failure and reduced collector life.

When no heat is taken from the collectors, their temperature rises until the heat loss from the collector surface equals the solar heat input. This equilibrium temperature is called the "stagnation temperature." Even though the working temperature of a collector system may be well below the boiling point of water, the stagnation temperature may be much higher than the boiling point.

To keep parts of the system from exploding or blowing out if the temperature rises too high, collector systems have pressure-relief valves. A common source of failure is leakage of water and antifreeze through these valves during hot weather. The system refills automatically, but antifreeze is not added. Then, during cold weather, the system freezes and is destroyed.

With flat plate collectors, various methods are used to keep collector temperature within limits. None of them is entirely satisfactory. One method is installing an external heat rejection coil to vent excess heat from the system. This requires pump and fan energy to be expended during periods when heating is not needed. Movable shading for the collectors would be more efficient, and it would reduce weathering of the collectors during idle periods, but practical shades for collectors have not yet appeared.

ALL-AIR SOLAR HEATING SYSTEMS

Attempts have been made to heat air directly with sunlight, without using water and antifreeze as a collection and storage medium. The basic idea is to let sunlight warm the interior of a glazed enclosure, and to circulate air through the enclosure to warm the house.

Perhaps the most common attempt of this kind is to build a greenhouse against the south wall of the house, and to circulate air through the greenhouse.

A variation of this is a "Trombe wall," which is glazing that is placed over a sunlit wall, with an air space between the glazing and the wall.

Still another approach is to use air heating solar collectors, which mimic the appearance of water heating solar collectors. Figure LL-27 shows a typical rooftop air heating collector.

To store the collected heat for times when it is needed, the air can be circulated through a bed of massive material, such as a bin of rocks or a matrix of concrete blocks. However, the air passages and storage bins are bulky, and the house has to be built around them.

Such "all-air" systems have not proven to be practical. The basic problem is that useful quantities of air cannot be heated during cold weather to a temperature that is high enough for heating the house.

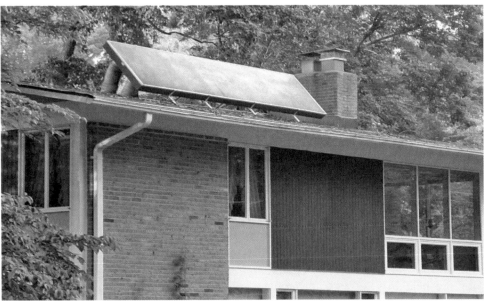

DRW

Figure LL-27. An air heating solar collector. This is a box with a transparent cover in which sunlight heats a dark interior. Air from inside the house is circulated through the box. The inlet and outlet air ducts are visible on the left side of the collector.

PASSIVE SOLAR HEATING

"Passive" solar heating is heating by direct radiation of sunlight into the house through the windows and other glazing. A "passive solar house" is one that is designed to collect a large amount of solar heat in this way. The original concept of passive solar systems was to substantially enlarge the area of glass facing the sun, so that sunlight could satisfy all or most of the heating requirement of the house. Figure LL-30 is an example of a house built in accordance with this concept.

Figure LL-30. Passive solar house.

Solar heating can occur only during hours of sunshine, so the passive solar concept generally includes some form of heat storage to capture sunlight during the day and to release it into the house at night.

Interest in passive solar systems blossomed in the 1970's, when it was visualized as a simpler and cheaper alternative to active solar heating systems. The passive solar concept was not originally related to super-insulation, so the glass was greatly enlarged to compensate for the heat loss through inadequate insulation.

To date, the promise of passive solar heating has not been fulfilled. Virtually all houses that rely on passive solar heating have suffered from problems that few homeowners would consider acceptable. The large glass area of passive solar houses makes them cold and drafty during winter, even when the sun is shining. During warm weather, glass that is not shaded properly causes overheating and extreme glare. Hardly any "solar house" can claim to be attractive, and many are outright ugly.

Passive solar heating is a prime example of a viscerally appealing energy conservation concept whose numbers don't add up. Even if you are willing to take a major risk for the sake of energy efficiency, this is not a good risk to take.

At least, not yet. The development of glazing that has greatly improved insulation value, if it ever occurs, might turn passive solar heating from a failure into a desirable method of heating a home or parts of a home.

Designing the glass in a home involves a fairly large number of issues, which Step 2 covers. Passive solar heating affects all of them, which would make a successful passive solar design very complex.

THE APPEAL OF PASSIVE SOLAR

The logic of passive solar heating is seductively simple. When a window is exposed to direct sunlight, it admits many times more heat than it loses by conduction, even if the weather is very cold.

For example, visualize a cold day in winter. The temperature is 10 °F (-12 °C), the sky is clear, and the sun is 30° above the horizon at noon. If a high-quality double-glazed window is facing south, the amount of solar energy entering the window is about 200 BTU's per hour per square foot (620 watts per square meter). At the same time, the heat loss from the same window by conduction is only about 25 BTU's per hour per square foot (78 watts per square meter).

In this optimum situation, sunlight through the windows is adding heat to the house eight times faster than heat is being lost by conduction. In the middle latitudes, even though winter days are shorter than winter nights, the average amount of energy admitted by the glass may still exceed the amount of heat that is lost. Therefore, it seems that glazing alone can provide all or most of the heating requirement for a house.

THE SHORTCOMINGS OF PASSIVE SOLAR

And now, the reality check.

The ideal conditions that make passive solar heating so appealing exist for relatively few hours each year. During cold weather, nighttime hours greatly exceed daylight hours. Even during the daytime, the intensity of sunlight may be feeble for a large fraction of the time because of cloud cover and masking of the sun by surrounding horizon clutter.

The underlying factor that makes passive solar impractical is the **high conduction heat loss of glass**, which leaks away the heat that is collected from the sun.

Conduction heat loss makes the interior surface of the glass cold, even when direct sunlight is entering. If the glass area is large, this produces serious **discomfort during cold weather**. The cold surface chills the room air, which washes down from the glass and creates uncomfortable drafts. Also, the cold surface absorbs heat that is radiated from skin and clothing, creating a "negative campfire" effect.

Large room temperature variations occur during the heating season. Room temperature rises when direct sunlight enters the glass, then falls as internal heat leaks out through of the glass. Thermal storage has only a limited ability to moderate the temperature cycles.

For similar reasons, **warmer temperatures are available only in rooms having glass that faces the sun**, and then only from a few hours after sunrise to a few hours after sunset. Other rooms will have substantially lower temperatures.

Blocking excessive sunlight is necessary during warmer weather. For effective control, the glazing should be shaded from the outside. However, no equipment exists for external variable shading that is reliable, economical, attractive, and strong enough to resist wind.

Visual glare occurs in the rooms where the glazing is installed. Any shading that you install to control the glare will dominate the appearance of the room, and it is likely to be awkward.

The **house orientation, floor plan, roof design, and location must be adapted** to passive heating, complicating the design and perhaps compromising other desired features.

The **external appearance** of a passive solar house is difficult to make attractive.

You probably won't solve all these problems, which have confounded many designers and enthusiasts. Don't let a desire for passive solar heating distract you from the really good energy saving opportunities of super-house design, which make passive solar heating largely unnecessary.

ACCESS TO WINTER SUN

The sun is a radiant heater. It delivers energy by line of sight. If you want to heat your house with sunlight, sunlight must be able to shine directly through the glass. Indirect sunlight is too weak to provide a net heat gain.

During winter, the sun remains low throughout the day. And, it travels in an arc, rising in the southeast and setting in the southwest. This low arc of travel makes sunlight vulnerable to obstruction by the objects that commonly surround a home site. These include trees and tall shrubbery, rising terrain toward the south, and other houses toward the south, including houses that may be built in the future.

Therefore, passive solar heating requires you to select a home site that will guarantee a direct view of the winter sun during most daylight hours. And, you must keep that view of the sun clear of trees and other obstructions. This is a major commitment, which can be achieved at relatively few home sites.

Geographic Limitations

The greatest potential of passive solar is in the middle latitudes, where the winter sun is strong enough to be useful for heating and the climate is cold enough to need it. At these latitudes, winter sunlight enters vertical glass at an angle that is most effective for heat collection.

At higher latitudes, winter has few hours of sunlight, so energy efficiency strongly favors minimizing the glass area. Also, the sun is so low in the sky that it is likely to be obstructed for much of the day.

At lower latitudes, even in the high mountains of Mexico and South America, climates are usually warm enough so that passive heating offers little benefit in a well insulated house. Also, the sun travels too high in the sky to allow efficient heat collection by vertical glass.

In general, passive solar requires a clear sky for a large fraction of daylight hours during cold weather. In any location that tends to be cloudy during cold weather, there is no practical way for the heating benefit to overcome the heat losses.

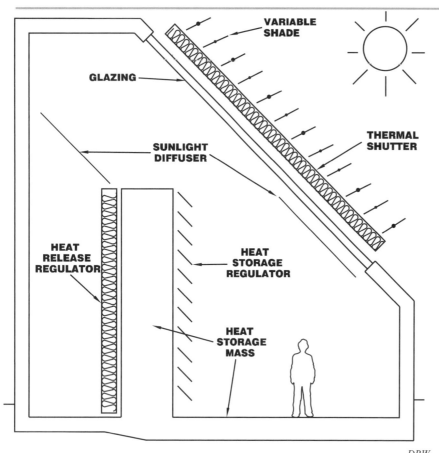

DRW

Figure LL-31. The elements of a passive solar house. This conceptual drawing symbolizes all the features that a successful passive solar heating system would need. Any passive heating system is also a daylighting system, and the design must perform well in both roles. Some of these elements have not yet been developed successfully.

HEAT INPUT, STORAGE, AND RELEASE

When the sun shines directly through the glass, heat pours into the house. At all other times, heat drains rapidly out of the house through the same glass. This cycling between heat gain and heat loss creates large swings in room temperature. To reduce these fluctuations, passive solar designs usually include some form of heat storage to absorb excess solar heat during the daytime and to release it at night.

Controlling the input, storage, and release of solar heat are functions that have not yet been successfully managed. Figure LL-31 sketches the elements of a passive solar design that would be needed to achieve reasonably successful performance.

In systems that are strictly "passive," heat storage consists of a stationary mass inside the house that is exposed to the incoming sunlight. A large amount of mass is needed to absorb the amount of heat that is needed to keep the home warm overnight. For example, in Figure LL-31, the house is designed so

that sunlight entering through the living room windows during winter falls on a thick interior masonry wall.

Another design uses a thickened concrete floor slab as the storage mass, with windows located low in the wall so that sunlight falls on the floor. Other designs use tanks filled with water.

The fraction of sunlight that is absorbed by the storage mass is determined by its surface color and texture. By selecting these, you can tailor the fraction of sunlight that goes into storage. (Most heat enters the storage mass by direct absorption of the sunlight, which is independent of the room air temperature. Relatively little heat is absorbed by conduction from the room air.)

Sunlight is converted to heat in the surface of the storage mass. The heat then goes in two directions. A fraction of the heat immediately warms the air at the surface by conduction, and the rest of the heat moves deeper into the storage mass. Penetration of heat into a thick mass of masonry is slow, typically requiring several hours. This delay is what makes mass useful for storage.

If the storage mass is located between two rooms, the room on the sunlighted side will be warmed sooner and to a higher temperature than the room on the other side. For example, in Figure LL-31, sunlight is absorbed on the living room side of the interior masonry wall. This surface is warmed immediately, and it warms the air in the living room. In addition, heat travels slowly through the masonry and emerges into the bedroom. If the delay in traveling through the wall is several hours, peak heating of the bedroom will occur in the evening, and warming of both the living room and the bedroom will continue through the middle of the night.

In this example, the living room surface of the masonry wall may be heated to a peak temperature of 95 °F (35 °C). The living room air is heated by conduction from all the surfaces in the room that absorb sunlight. Most of the heat input to the living room is needed to offset the heat loss from the glass. In contrast, the bedroom side of the masonry wall may be heated to a peak temperature of only 77 °F (25 °C), which provides feeble heating. However, if the house walls are super-insulated and if the bedroom windows are small, a thick comforter may allow cozy sleeping.

Passive Heat Storage: a Big Challenge

When sunlight strikes the heat storage mass, it can be reflected into the room or it can be absorbed into the storage mass. You can adjust the ratio of the two over a wide range by selecting the color and texture of the sunlighted surface.

You can adjust the heat storage capacity by selecting the type and quantity of storage material.

You can adjust the time delay by selecting the thickness of the storage material.

However, these characteristics remain fixed. In order to adapt to changing weather conditions, the system needs variable control of heat storage and heat release, as shown in Figure LL-31. That is possible, but I am not aware of any installations in which such regulation has been used successfully.

As a practical matter, heat storage cannot prevent large variations in room temperature from day to night. By morning, the entire house is cold, and it will be hours before sunlight can restore a comfortable temperature. What is worse, the absorption of incoming solar heat by the storage mass during the morning slows the heating of the house.

At the end of daylight, heat continues to diffuse into the storage mass, so the temperature at the surface of the storage mass drops. This lowers heat output when it is needed the most.

The ultimate limitation of passive heat storage is that no practical amount of storage mass can absorb enough heat from sunlight to satisfy the heating requirements of the house. In order to drive enough heat into the mass, the surface of the storage mass would have to be much hotter than room temperature, making the interior temperature intolerable during hours of sunlight. It would be like living inside a solar panel.

In contrast, an active solar heating system can control the indoor temperature precisely as long as the water storage tank still contains sufficient heat.

PASSIVE SOLAR VS. SUPER-INSULATION

Your primary method of minimizing heating cost should be super-insulation, which minimizes heat loss. Passive solar requires glass – which has very large heat loss. So, as long as glass has poor insulation value, passive solar heating is self-defeating.

Under most conditions, the glass area in each room should be determined by the room's needs for daylighting, view, and ventilation. Do not increase the glass area further for the sake of passive solar heating.

In contrast to passive solar heating, super-insulation is practical, inexpensive, and free of unpleasant side effects. Exploit solar heating only to the extent that you can do it without compromising super-insulation and the other desirable features of your home.

SOLAR ELECTRICITY GENERATION

One of the major breakthroughs of the semiconductor revolution was direct generation of electricity from sunlight. This type of electricity generation uses "photovoltaic" (PV) cells. These can be seen everywhere, powering small calculators, navigational aids on waterways, spacecraft, and many other small applications. Any number of PV cells can be mounted on large panels to increase their total power output.

Photovoltaic generation seems almost too good to be true. It has no moving parts, requires little maintenance, makes no noise, requires no input of water or other substances from the environment, and produces no pollution (except in the manufacturing process). It is not especially ugly. And, unlike wind generators, photovoltaic generation does not interfere with communications or endanger birds.

At present, the big obstacle to photovoltaic generation is the high cost of the systems. This is a reflection of the amount of energy required to make and install the materials. Everyone is hoping that the cost can be reduced drastically by future developments.

A fundamental issue for home design is whether it makes sense for each house to generate its own electricity. Usually, the answer is no. The only exception is building in a location where access to a public utility network is not available. You may also want to install a PV system to take advantage of tax credits or utility rebates. However, such artificial economic incentives do not save energy or help the environment.

Here are the highlights of PV systems, which will help you decide whether you want to become involved with them.

HOW PHOTOVOLTAIC CELLS WORK

A photovoltaic cell is astonishingly simple. It consists of a semiconductor material (silicon, germanium, or some less common materials) that is made in two microscopically thin layers. One layer is "doped" with a small concentration of another material. This causes the boundary between the two layers to act as a one-way gate for electrons.*

When sunlight falls on the semiconductor material, the photons of energy in the sunlight knock electrons from one layer to the other, but they can't get back across the boundary. As the electrons pile up on one side, they create a voltage. The voltage can force the electrons through a circuit as an electric current.

At the present time, two kinds of semiconductor material are used to make photovoltaic cells. One type consists of pure, specially treated crystals of certain materials, usually silicon. Cells made in this manner have the best efficiency, but they are expensive. A second kind of semiconductor is called "amorphous" (which means "not crystalline"). Amorphous semiconductors are less expensive, but they are substantially less efficient and they lose efficiency as they age.

The best hope is that efficient photovoltaic material can be made in large sheets, without the need to connect arrays of individual small cells. Effort in this direction continues, but a fundamental breakthrough is needed to achieve a combination of cost and efficiency that can make photovoltaic generation suitable for widespread application.

ENERGY OUTPUT

The energy output of a PV system is limited by the low energy content of sunlight. At the earth's surface, the maximum power of solar energy is somewhat less than one kilowatt per square meter of collecting area. And, most of the time, only a fraction of that amount is available.

Let's calculate the average output for a collector panel of one square meter (about 10 square feet). A cell efficiency of 20% yields a maximum output of about 190 watts. An average of 12 hours of daylight reduces this to about 95 watts. If the collector panel is fixed, i.e., it does not track the sun, the output is reduced to about 60 watts. Atmospheric losses and shading at low sun altitude reduces this to about 50 watts. Average sky clarity of 70% lowers this to 35 watts. If the effective coverage of the panel area by the semiconductor material is 80%, the panel output is down to 28 watts.

Thus, a good contemporary fixed solar panel, installed in a favorable location, has an average power output of about 28 watts per square meter, or about 2.6 watts per square foot. That's not much.

The energy output in terms of weight is much more favorable. The photovoltaic material itself is almost weightless. Most of the weight of a typical system is in the structure that holds the PV material. The weight and cost of the structure is determined primarily by the need to keep wind from blowing the solar cells away. This has prompted ideas for eliminating the support structure, for example, by making the photovoltaic material part of a roof or wall surface.

---

* The semiconductor materials for PV cells and LED chips are similar. An LED light is essentially a PV cell operating in reverse.

DRW

Figure LL-34. The photovoltaic panels for a Wyoming ranch house electrical system. They are installed on mounts that allow them to track the sun.

PHOTOVOLTAIC SYSTEMS

In the past, photovoltaic systems were limited to isolated applications that could not be served economically by a public utility system. For example, Figures LL-34 through LL-36 show a photovoltaic system for a remote cattle ranch.

The photovoltaic cells produce direct-current electricity when the sun shines. This electricity is used to charge conventional batteries, similar to automobile batteries. Another device, called an "inverter," converts the electricity from the batteries to alternating current at the proper voltage for the house.

The system also needs a conventional fuel powered generator to cover extended periods of cloudy skies or occasional periods of high power consumption.

The batteries and the fuel powered backup generator are major costs. Batteries have a limited number of storage cycles, so they must be replaced periodically. They pollute the environment when they are discarded or recycled. For safety, the batteries should be located in an isolated room or structure that is well ventilated. To minimize the noise of the backup generator, the equipment usually is installed at some distance from the house.

More recently, photovoltaic systems have been installed on individual houses in locations where electricity is readily available from public utilities. In home systems, the collectors commonly are installed on the roof, as in Figure LL-37. Photovoltaic collector arrays are not attractive, but they are not ugly either.

Photovoltaic systems of this kind typically do not have batteries or a backup generator. Instead, electricity is produced in tandem with a connection to the public utility. If the house system cannot produce as much electricity as the house needs, additional electricity is purchased from the public utility. If the house system produces more electricity than needed, the utility typically is required to buy the excess from the homeowner.

DRW

Figure LL-35. The back of a photovoltaic panel, which is thin and light.

DRW

Figure LL-36. The inside of the equipment building, which contains the needed batteries, battery chargers, controls, and switchgear. Not shown is the diesel generator, which operates whenever a larger amount of power is needed.

In areas where houses are served by reliable public electric utilities, this kind of system – consisting only of PV panels and the circuitry needed to make them operate in parallel with the public utility – is the only kind worth considering.

DOES HOME-BASED PV MAKE SENSE?

One of the biggest mistakes in current energy policy is confusing energy efficiency in homes with energy supply for homes. There is no inherent reason why an individual homeowner should produce the electricity for his home, any more than it makes sense for an individual automobile owner to drill for oil and refine his own fuel. Still, connecting home-based PV systems to the electric utility network does offer some significant advantages, both for the homeowner and for the public utility system.

All photovoltaic systems require storage capacity and/or backup generation, because the sun shines only during the daytime, and then often at reduced intensity. By connecting to an electricity grid, the home-based system achieves unlimited backup capacity, eliminating the need for either backup or storage in the home system itself.

Furthermore, a large electricity network can blend the output of home-based PV systems with the output of different generator types, including wind, hydro, nuclear, conventional fuels, etc. For example, wind generators can produce electricity at night, when PV systems cannot.

Home-based PV systems offer two advantages for a utility network that wants to add PV generators to its other generators. One is that the house is already connected to the utility grid, so extra transmission costs are avoided. And, the house provides the space for the collectors, so that the public utility does not have to find space to install them.

In effect, the individual homeowner provides the utility with mounting space for a limited amount of PV generating capacity. It's like growing food in many backyard garden plots, instead of on large farms.

DRW

Figure LL-37. A house in Maryland whose south-facing roof is covered with photovoltaic panels. The panels are connected to the public electric utility.

If a utility network includes home-based PV systems that are distributed over a large area, another benefit is averaging the availability of sunlight. When a cloud passes over one home-based PV system, electricity production by that system almost ceases. However, if the cloud cover is partial, the total electricity production of all the home-based systems may still be significant.

On the negative side of the ledger, all forms of energy production benefit from economies of scale. Small systems are inherently more expensive, and usually less efficient, than large systems.

Home-based PV systems need special equipment to protect the public power system from failures in the home systems. Public utilities consider such small systems to be a nuisance, because amateurs are hooking into their intricate, professionally operated system, and they may jeopardize the entire utility network. In some jurisdictions, the public utility may charge homeowners a fee for protecting their system.

Unfortunately, many countries have enacted utility regulations that obscure the true economics of home PV systems. Governments typically require public utilities to serve as a backup for home-based systems. As a result, the utility must duplicate the capacity of the home systems, which wastes equipment and the energy that is required to make the duplicate equipment.

In addition, governments commonly require public utilities to purchase excess electricity produced by home systems at rates that are much higher than market value. To recover these added costs, public utilities must pass the cost of serving home generators to the rest of their customers.

CONFLICT WITH SHADING AND ROOF MAINTENANCE

By coincidence, the amount of PV cell area that is needed to power a house is roughly equal to the roof area of the house. (Solar heating systems, which we covered previously, require much less area.) For this reason, it seems natural to use the roof to support the PV panels.

However, roof mounting incurs several problems. One is that the roof may not have surfaces that are oriented for efficient collection of sunlight. Another is conflict with using trees and tall shrubbery to shade the house.

Roof mounted PV panels make it expensive to replace the shingles or other weather surface of the roof. One solution being considered is to use the PV panels themselves as the weather surface of the roof, replacing shingles, tiles, and other conventional roofing materials. That concept started to become reality around 2012, but it is too early to tell how well it will work in practice.

One way to avoid conflicts with the roof is to mount the PV panels somewhere else, typically on a ground supported structure. This requires an equivalent area of ground that has clear access to sunlight throughout the day and throughout the year. This solution restricts the shading and landscaping of the property. To keep the ground usable, the panels might be mounted on a large framework that serves as a canopy or pavilion for outdoor activities.

WIND ENERGY

We'll be quick about this. Wind energy has no application for individual housing unless (1) your home does not have access to a public electricity supply *and* (2) your home site is consistently windy, with a prevailing wind speed of at least 18 miles per hour (29 kilometers per hour). Only a tiny fraction of humanity lives in such locations. I wouldn't even mention wind energy, except for the fact that wind generators for individual homes continue to excite unrealistic hopes.

Decades of experience and analysis make it clear that wind generators must be very big to be economical. Wind generators having a capacity of more than one million watts are now recognized as the most economical size. Even such large machines need to be clustered in "wind farms" of many generators. For example, see Figure LL-40. Such a wind farm generates electricity for thousands of homes, and it requires a professional utility system to manage it.

Noise is a problem of on-site wind generators. Newer models have become much quieter, but they still become a torment after a while.

Well, how about your retirement home in an isolated, windy location, such as the Bahamas Out Islands? In a location that has both wind and sun, experience indicates that a photovoltaic system is preferable to a wind generator, primarily because the photovoltaic system is silent.

If you want to live in an isolated location that is windy and dark, seek counseling.

DRW

Figure LL-40. A small portion of a wind farm in New Mexico. Each generator has a maximum output of 1.5 megawatts. The house is abandoned, which tends to happen near wind farms.

"ZERO ENERGY" HOUSES AND "GOING OFF THE GRID"

A "zero-energy" house is one that requires no purchase of energy sources after the house is built. That is, the house includes equipment to generate all its own energy needs. In most cases, electricity is generated with photovoltaic or wind generators. Locally cut wood commonly is used as a heating and cooking fuel.

Since the house requires no external source of power, it does not need a connection to a public utility system, so it may "go off the grid." This is an extreme form of dependence on solar energy, wind, wood, local hydropower, or other local energy sources.

"Zero energy" houses and "going off the grid" are romantic notions without real merit, unless public power is unavailable or unreliable. It makes no sense to create an independent utility system to serve an individual house if a public utility grid is available.

Alternative sources of electricity may become important, but they generally belong on the grid of a large electric utility, not on your roof. The reason is that all sources of electricity, whether modern or old fashioned, have large economies of scale.

Furthermore, photovoltaic systems produce electricity only when the sun shines, and wind generators produce electricity only when the wind blows briskly. Their electrical output is badly matched to the energy requirement of an individual house, which occurs in spurts. A large utility system can average the output of many generators and the energy needs of many houses, making up the difference with a variety of generators and storage systems.

To serve a single house with solar or wind generators, you have to size the equipment for your heaviest energy usage, so much of the equipment capacity is wasted. In addition, you would need a large array of batteries to match the availability of sunshine or wind to your energy usage. Batteries are expensive, they need periodic replacement, and they pollute the environment when they are recycled or discarded.

Even with a lot of batteries, a house that is off the grid still needs a backup generator, which typically is a portable gasoline generator purchased at the hardware store. This is not a particularly efficient machine, and most of its cost is wasted as it sits idle.

The public electric power grid has extremely high reliability because it is connected to many generators and it has alternative distribution paths. A large system can afford to keep maintenance crews on duty around the clock. You can't compete with a tiny system of your own. So, leave alternative energy sources to the utility companies, and instead, design your house to require as little energy as possible.

"Going off the grid" is like having a big, expensive model railroad. Only, instead of running a toy railroad, you are running a toy utility system. If that hobby interests you, go for it. Just be aware that you won't be helping the environment, and you certainly won't save any money.

Geothermal Heat Pumps and Air Conditioners

First, let's be clear about the name of this technology. "Geothermal" heat pumps are heat pumps that use the underground soil or a body of water as a source of heat or as a place to dump heat. Such systems were originally called "ground source" or "earth-coupled." Promoters stole the name "geothermal" from an entirely different energy source, namely, heat created in the earth by volcanic activity or radioactive decay. In the residential sector, the name "geothermal" has stuck, so we will use it.

Engineers who deal with commercial applications commonly use the terms "ground source heat pumps" or "geoexchange."

Here's the bottom line: geothermal heat pumps have a theoretical potential to extend the range of heat pumps to much colder climates, and to operate more efficiently in all climates. However, exchanging heat with soil is limited by serious problems that have not been solved in ways that are practical for houses. Furthermore, your super-efficient house will require so little energy for heating and cooling that an earth-coupled heat pump can't be economical, even if it works properly. Therefore, I can't recommend a soil-buried geothermal system.

Geothermal systems that exchange heat with bodies of water can be more reliable, but they are not very efficient for heating in cold climates. They are more advantageous for cooling in warm climates.

As we saw in Step 4, conventional split-system heat pumps that can operate comfortably in cold climates have recently become available. However, they cannot offer the promised efficiency advantage of earth-coupled heat pumps.

You may savor the challenge of making an earth-coupled heat pump work efficiently. In that case, enjoy yourself. However, recognize that you are indulging in an expensive technical hobby that won't help the environment.

If you do decide to install a geothermal heat pump, you have more homework to do. The following pages explain the main points of each type of system. This will help you to decide whether you want to take the plunge. If you do, this discussion will help you to minimize the adverse effects of the unsolved problems.

This overview will enable you to speak intelligently with engineers who design these systems, with contractors who install them, and with the vendors who sell the equipment. Be aware that the geothermal industry avoids discussing the limitations of the technology. In the residential market, vendors generally pretend that the problems don't exist. Sadly,

geothermal today is largely a market for suckers who are enthralled by technology that they don't understand.

The following applies both to geothermal heat pumps and to geothermal air conditioners. An air conditioner is simply a heat pump that operates only to provide cooling. To save words, we will simply say "heat pumps" instead of "heat pumps and air conditioners." Similarly, we will usually say "heat source" as shorthand for "heat source and/or heat sink."

THE MAIN POINTS

Step 4 explained that the maximum efficiency of any heat pump depends on the difference between the inside temperature and the outside temperature. The efficiency of ordinary heat pumps drops drastically as the weather gets colder. In fact, ordinary heat pumps must cease operating and rely on an auxiliary heat source when the outside air falls below a certain temperature.

Conventional ("air-source") heat pumps suffer from these limitations because they use the outside atmosphere as their source of heat. In principle, we can get better performance by using the deep soil around the house as the heat source. This promises an improvement because the deep soil is considerably warmer than winter air temperatures and considerably cooler than summer air temperatures. Heat pump systems exploiting this principle were first promoted during the 1970's as a way of expanding the market for heat pumps into colder climates where air-source heat pumps can't work well.

In addition to using deep soil as the heat source, geothermal heat pumps may also use underground water (a water well) or a body of surface water (a lake or river) as a heat source.

In addition to improving the efficiency of heating, the geothermal concept can improve the efficiency of cooling by using the same soil or bodies of water to discard heat. (Places where heat is discarded are called "heat sinks.") Because soil and bodies of water are cooler than the surrounding air during hot weather, they absorb heat more easily, lowering cooling cost.

The basic principles of earth-coupled heat pumps are the same as for conventional heat pumps. The big practical difference is the "heat exchanger," the part of the system that collects heat from the ground or discharges heat into the ground. Each type of heat exchanger involves a specialized set of issues. Each type is expensive, and each type trades performance against cost.

Unfortunately, at the present time, earth-coupled heat exchangers have serious installation limitations that prevent them from adequately exploiting the potential of the concept. Overcoming these limitations, using present methods, is prohibitively expensive. Therefore, we have to await better methods of installing earth-coupled heat exchangers.

Most geothermal heat pump systems use water to move heat to and from the environment. Therefore, the heat pumps are designed to heat and cool water. Such heat pumps are called "water-source" heat pumps.

If the heat source is soil or a body of water, the water used for heat transfer usually flows in a closed system of pipes. If the heat source is a water well, the water may come directly from the well, or a heat exchanger may be used to provide isolation from contaminants in the well water.

Most of the refrigerants used in heat pumps create toxic chemicals if they come into contact with water. To protect the environment, the heat pump is connected to the water source with a double-wall heat exchanger. This reduces the efficiency of the heat pump by a small amount. Other methods of isolation have a higher efficiency penalty.

USING SOIL AS THE HEAT SOURCE

In principle, using the earth as the heat source for a heat pump promises the greatest efficiency improvement. However, the characteristics of soil are highly variable from one location to another, and it is expensive to place a heat exchanger in soil at an efficient depth. The following are the main issues in using soil as a heat source.

Soil Temperature and Depth

The temperature of soil at a distance below the surface varies much less than the temperature of the atmosphere. At a depth of 30 feet (10 meters), the soil temperature in most locations is essentially constant. See Figure 3-111, in Step 3, which shows that deep soil is considerably warmer than average winter air temperatures, especially in colder climates. Figure 3-111 also shows that deep soil is considerably cooler than average summer air temperatures.

Closer to the surface, the soil temperature varies significantly with the time of year. At a depth of 6 feet (2 meters), the soil temperature typically varies by about half of the seasonal difference in average surface temperatures.

The seasonal cycle of soil temperature lags the seasonal cycle of air temperature. At a depth of 6 feet (2 meters), the lag is about one month. At a depth of 12 feet (4 meters), the lag is about three months. The lag improves the efficiency of earth-coupled heat pumps early in the heating and cooling seasons, but it becomes a liability late in the seasons.

A fundamental problem is that the operation of a soil-coupled heat pump changes the long-term temperature of the soil. For example, when a heat pump is providing heating, it takes heat from the soil. This makes the soil colder, which reduces efficiency. If the system takes more heat from the soil during cold weather than it rejects during warm weather, the decrease in soil temperature will carry over from year to year. Eventually, the soil temperature may become low enough to cancel most of the benefit of the original soil temperature.

Available data on this issue are still sketchy, and geothermal advocates don't like to talk about it. The importance of this effect depends on soil type and water content, the heat exchanger size, and the system operating schedule.

Soil Heat Exchangers

To extract heat from the ground (or to discard heat into it), a great length of pipe is buried in the soil. Some systems circulate the refrigerant directly through the pipe, which is most efficient in principle. However, this poses a risk of refrigerant contamination of the ground water if the pipe leaks, which is almost certain to happen eventually. For this reason, the usual practice is to circulate water through the pipe, perhaps with an antifreeze additive. An indoor heat exchanger connects the water pipes to the heat pumps.

The pipe must be able to resist soil conditions, such as acidity, for many years. For direct circulation of refrigerant, specialized copper alloy tubing is used. If water is used as a heat transfer medium, the pipe usually is a particular type of plastic. It must be compatible with any antifreeze material that is used. Plastic pipe has experienced failures, including unreliable joints.

Nobody seriously claims that the expensive underground heat exchanger will survive for more than a small fraction of the life of a well built house.

The pipe may be buried in two ways, either as a horizontal grid near the surface, or as deep vertical hairpin loops. With both types of fields, the largest cost of a soil-coupled heat exchanger is burying the pipe. Equipment is needed to dig holes in the ground, and labor is needed to insert the pipe and to make the connections. These costs vary greatly from one location to another. Cost may favor one type of heat exchanger in one location, and a different type in a different location.

■ Horizontal Soil Fields

With horizontal fields, the goal is to lay a grid of heat exchanger pipe at an efficient depth. Horizontal fields need a large amount of surface area, so one challenge is to bury the pipe so that it makes best use of the land area. Another challenge is to minimize the number of pipe connections, which are a significant labor cost and a potential source of leakage.

The original method of burying a horizontal field was to lay the pipe in slit trenches spaced three to six feet (one to two meters) apart. This requires a large amount of trenching and many pipe joints. In addition, because of soil collapse, it was virtually impossible to dig slit trenches deep enough to reach efficient soil temperatures.

A newer alternative is to excavate a large area, lay the pipe grid, and backfill over the pipe. This requires moving a lot of soil. Figure LL-42 shows a currently popular variation of this method.

Wikipedia Commons

Figure LL-42. "Slinky loop" geothermal heat exchanger in a horizontal field. Much soil must be moved. This method lays the pipe quickly, but wastes material. It requires considerable pump energy.

Horizontal fields have fallen out of favor because they need a large amount of land area. The ground cannot be used for other purposes that might endanger the heat exchanger. Leaks in the system are difficult to find and expensive to repair.

A universal failing of horizontal fields is that contractors do not bury them deeply enough to provide the benefit that is expected. The cost of burying the pipe increases with depth, so installers typically bury horizontal fields too shallow for good efficiency.

A promised improvement for horizontal fields is the use of a laser guided borer to make tunnels for the heat exchanger pipe entirely underground. As this is written, it is too early to tell how well this will work.

■ Vertical Loops

Vertical pipe fields minimize land requirements. Using ordinary well drilling methods, as in Figure LL-43, one or more hairpin loops is buried in holes that range in depth from 100 to 500 feet (30 to 150 meters). Because each loop has buried connections only at the bottom, leaks are less likely. If a loop does leak underground, the offending loop must be isolated at the surface and abandoned.

Vertical fields have a big unsolved efficiency problem, called "crosstalk." Both the supply and return sides of the hairpin loop must be inserted into a

Depositphotos

Figure LL-43. Drilling for a vertical loop geothermal heat exchanger.

narrow hole. As a result, there is a substantial amount of heat conduction from the warmer side of the loop to cooler side. This short circuiting occurs strongly in the upper part of the loop, where the temperature difference between the sides of the loop is greatest.

Below a certain depth, crosstalk eliminates the temperature difference between the loop and the soil, making the lower portion of the loop useless. As a result, the system will not have the efficiency that is expected from the amount of pipe that is buried. A partial solution is to increase the number of loops and limit their depth. However, this increases land requirements and installation cost.

The holes must be filled with a special material to maintain thermal contact between the pipes and the soil, and to allow for expansion and contraction of the pipes. This material is called "grout." Typical grout materials are bentonite clay and various kinds of concrete. Grout is a potential source of trouble. The material must be matched to the geology of the hole, which may vary from top to bottom. The contractor may select the wrong grout material, or the grout may fail. Depending on the location, some grout material must be kept damp indefinitely.

The geology of the soil has a big effect on the recommended depth for a vertical loop, the type of drilling needed, and the method of grouting the pipe. Since earth consists of strata, the only way to determine the geology of the hole is to make a full-depth test bore and conduct measurements of the soil properties at each depth. This is expensive, and usually is done only for larger commercial projects. So, for residential applications, the design of vertical loop heat exchangers is done with guesswork, generally tending toward cheapness and sacrificing efficiency.

USING A WATER WELL AS THE HEAT SOURCE

"Ground water" is a water source that is underground. An underground body of water is called an "aquifer." If your house is located in an area that has a useful amount of ground water, you may be able to use the ground water as a heat source for your heat pumps. The temperature of ground water is determined by the deep soil temperature (see Figure 3-111), which is favorable for both heating and cooling.

The ground water is extracted through a well and is piped to the heat pumps. The largest cost of this type of system is well drilling. This cost varies widely, depending on the depth, the nature of the ground, the need for reinjection, and other factors. The system cost is reduced if you would be drilling a well anyway for your home's water supply.

Some jurisdictions may require that you inject the water back into the aquifer. (Otherwise, the water would be dumped into a stream, sewer, lawn sprinkler, etc.) This requires two wells. One draws water out of an aquifer at one depth, and the other returns the water to a different aquifer at a different depth. It may be possible to use a single bore hole to reach both aquifers with a coaxial pipe.

The energy needed to pump the water through the system subtracts from the overall energy efficiency of the system. A deep well pump may require so much energy that it cancels the benefit of the system. In any event, it is important to control the operation of the pump or pumps to minimize this penalty.

The flow of water from a well is not constant. The amount of water in the aquifer may diminish as the aquifer is exploited by others. If you foresee increased use of the aquifer by later development in your area, consider whether the aquifer will be able to continue serving your heat pumps in the future.

Ground water usually is saturated with minerals. When ground water is used as a heat source, it is cooled in the heat exchanger of the heat pump, and becomes less able to dissolve minerals. As a result, the minerals are deposited in the heat exchanger, which requires periodic cleaning. Failure to clean the heat exchanger will seriously degrade the performance of the system.

USING SURFACE WATER AS THE HEAT SOURCE

"Surface water" is any substantial body of water that is exposed to the surface, such as lakes, rivers, and streams. If a satisfactory body of surface water is available, it is relatively easy to exploit it for use with a geothermal heat pump.

Surface water is the least expensive geothermal source. It requires no well drilling or extensive earth moving. The heat exchanger is simply a length of plastic pipe that is submerged in the water, as in Figure LL-44.

Wikipedia Commons

Figure LL-44. A pond water heat exchanger. Plastic pipe is attached to a grid, with concrete blocks as anchors. The empty pipes are keeping the assembly afloat. When the pipes are filled with the heat exchange fluid, the assembly sinks to the bottom of the pond.

Heat transfer with the surrounding water is efficient, minimizing the amount of pipe that is needed. The pipe can be wound in a coil for convenience. The heat exchanger is connected to the heat pumps through a closed water circuit.

Typically, the heat exchanger requires no routine maintenance. If the heat pump is located above the surface of the water, the hydrostatic pressure inside the loop provides pressure that keeps dirt from entering the system if there is a leak.

Generally, it is not practical to pump the surface water directly through the heat pumps. Surface water contains a substantial amount of dirt, so filtration would be difficult. Also, surface water is corrosive because exposure to the atmosphere keeps it saturated with oxygen, and it may be acidic because of acid rain. And, the water may be saturated with minerals, some of which would deposit inside the heat exchanger.

The Temperature of Surface Water

Surface water originates from rain, melting snow, or underground springs. The source determines the original temperature of surface water. For example, a river that is fed by melting snow starts out very cold. The temperature changes downstream as the water exchanges heat with the earth and with the atmosphere.

Surface water is cooled by evaporation and by radiation into the night sky. (See the sidebar, *The Sky is Cold*, in Step 2.) These effects, plus contact with earth, tend to keep surface water cooler than the atmosphere during warm weather. On the other hand, dirty water absorbs solar heat during the day. A dirty shallow pond may be substantially warmer than a clear pond.

These factors can combine in different ways, yielding large differences in the temperature of the water source. For example, a deep lake that is fed primarily by snow melting will remain cold all year. On the other hand, a rapidly flowing stream or river tends to approach the "wet bulb" temperature* of the air. So, if you have access to a body of water that may serve as a heat source or heat sink, be sure that you understand its temperature characteristics during the seasons when you would use it.

The temperature of surface water generally is excellent for a heat pump that is cooling. The temperature of the water during the heat of the day is substantially lower than the air temperature.

However, surface water is much less profitable as a source of heat for heating. In a moderate climate, the winter temperature of surface water may be just as cold as the average air temperature, or even colder, so a surface water source provides little or no advantage for heating.

As we saw, several factors tend to keep surface water cool. The ultimate limitation is that surface water freezes at 32 °F (0 °C). The water source must exceed this temperature by 5 °F to 10 °F (3 °C to 6 °C) so that it will not freeze on the outside of the heat exchanger. (The water inside the loop is protected from freezing by antifreeze.)

A quirk of nature helps to prevent freezing when the heat source is a lake or other stationary body of surface water. Water is most dense at a temperature of 39 °F (4 °C). If the surface of the lake freezes, the water in the lake will stratify so that the temperature remains near 39 °F (4 °C) toward the bottom. The earth temperature under the lake tends to keep the lake from freezing all the way to the bottom. As long as the lake does not freeze entirely, it will maintain a bottom temperature near 39 °F (4 °C) throughout a cold winter.

INSIDE THE HOUSE: EFFICIENT HEAT PUMP LAYOUT

Step 4 recommends installing heat pumps so that they can serve each room or zone individually. The same principle applies to earth-coupled systems. Each zone has a water-source heat pump, which takes or rejects heat from a water loop that goes to the heat exchanger.

The water loop should feed the heat pumps in parallel, so that each unit receives the warmest water when heating, and the coldest water when cooling.

To minimize pump energy, the simplest and most reliable approach is to provide a separate water pump for each heat pump. Each water pump circulates water between the heat pump and the water loop. Each water pump is controlled so that it runs only when the heat pump that it serves is operating.

In addition, a separate pump circulates water in the loop between the house and the heat exchanger. This is similar to the "primary-secondary" pumping for hydronic systems that is explained in Step 4.

Step 4 also recommends split-system heat pumps in which a single outside unit is able to serve a number of inside units. A similar arrangement for water-source heat pumps would save cost and simplify the loop piping. If you contemplate a geothermal system, find out whether water-source heat pumps with this feature are available.

---

* If you wrap a wet cloth around the bulb of a thermometer and blow air on it, the thermometer will register a temperature that is lower than the temperature of the surrounding air. This is because evaporation of the water cools the bulb. Engineers call this lower temperature the "wet bulb temperature." Less humidity in the surrounding air results in faster evaporation and lower wet bulb temperatures.

HEAT RECOVERY APPLIANCES

Air conditioners and heat pumps (when they are cooling) remove heat from the inside of your house and discard it to the outside. A lot of heat is moved this way. Similarly, refrigerators and food freezers remove heat from the inside of the box and discard it to the surroundings (usually the inside of the house). Many people have had the idea of recovering this discarded heat for some useful purpose, rather than throwing it away.

A fundamental limitation is the relatively low temperature at which the heat is discarded. In order to make cooling equipment as efficient as possible, it is designed to reject heat at the lowest possible temperature. Typically, this temperature is only about 10 to 15 °F (6 to 8 °C) higher than the surrounding air temperature.

In most homes, the only possible application for recovered heat at such a low temperature is preheating domestic hot water. Incoming cold water typically has a temperature that ranges from 50 °F (10 °C) to 75 °F (24 °C), depending on the source of the water and the time of the year. Homes typically heat domestic water to temperatures between 120 °F (49 °C) and 140 °F (60 °C). On the basis of these temperatures, the heat rejected from efficient cooling units can be used to accomplish about two thirds of the heating of domestic hot water.

But, there is a time limitation. You can recover heat from a cooling unit only during periods when cooling is being done. Preheated water can be stored in a tank until it is needed, but the practical time limit for storing warm water is about one to three days.

Various manufacturers have offered appliances that combine cooling with water heating. However, there are several reasons not to recommend them.

Most advanced countries now have laws that require the manufacturers of common appliances to meet high standards of efficiency. These requirements generally are not applied to combination appliances. Thus, a standard model of air conditioner or heat pump may be significantly more efficient than a heat recovery model.

Step 4 recommends multiple split-system air conditioners and heat pumps. These locate the compressor and heat rejection coil outside the house. It would be awkward to route the heat into the house for water heating.

You could adapt "geothermal" heat pumps for heat recovery, because they reject heat through a water loop that could be routed for water heating fairly easily. However, this would be a further complication on a system that is already too risky and expensive to be desirable for most homes.

Similar considerations apply to refrigerators and freezers, except that they remove heat from the inside of an insulated box and throw it into the house. This is a form of heat recovery, whether you want it or not. The recovered heat may be useful during cold weather, but not during warm weather. But in any event, the amount of heat to be recovered from refrigerators and freezers is small. The heat that is discharged into the room is largely offset by heat that is leaking from the room back into the cold interior of the unit.

In summary, a heat recovery appliance won't save much energy or money, and you probably won't be able to find anyone to repair it. But, it may be a source of amusement if you like to tinker.

EARTH-SHELTERED CONSTRUCTION

In earth-sheltered construction, most of a house is covered with soil. This can be done in two ways. One is to build the structure mostly above grade, then build up soil around the walls, and perhaps cover the roof with soil. Figure LL-47 is an example of this method.

The other method is to dig a hole in the ground, build the house in the hole, and backfill the soil to cover the house.

Why would anyone want to do such a thing? Right away, there is the question of esthetics. From the inside, an earth-sheltered house has a seriously limited view of the outside world. And from the outside, an earth-sheltered house looks like, well… a mound of dirt.

Fieldstone Suite

Figure LL-47. An earth-sheltered guest house near Ithaca, New York. Contact with the outside is through the south face, which is flanked by retaining walls that are properly inclined to resist soil pressure.

Burying homes in the ground or in hillsides has been done by various cultures through the ages. The concept re-emerged during the frenzied days of the 1970's energy crises, when the concept of dirt was appealing to many in the Sixties Generation. The logic was vague, but eventually three justifications emerged.

The first justification was to use soil as an insulating material because it is cheap. Soil can be considered a poor grade of insulation. Its only advantage is that the material itself is dirt cheap. Soil is heavy. A strong and expensive structure is needed to withstand the pressure of soil on the walls or roof. The structure is similar to a bomb shelter.

Because soil is porous, there needs to be a waterproof barrier between the soil and the outer structure of the house, and the barrier needs to provide drainage away from the structure. If the structure is above grade, this part of the design is feasible. However, if the house is buried below grade, ground water will turn the house into a submarine, with comparable difficulty in keeping the water outside. Consider the difficulty of dealing with a damp basement (covered in Step 3), and expect to spend even more effort to keep an entirely buried house dry.

So, the expectation of low cost gives way to the opposite reality of exceptionally high cost to achieve reasonable comfort and protection from dampness.

The second attraction of earth-sheltered construction is to exploit the thermal mass of soil. The thermal mass of a thick layer of soil – at least several feet (one meter) in thickness – averages the outside temperature when it cycles from too hot in the daytime to too cold at night, creating a moderate indoor temperature. (See the sidebar, *Can Your House Benefit from Thermal Lag?*, in Step 3.) The needed average temperature is limited to certain locations and certain seasons.

The third advantage claimed for earth-sheltered construction is to exploit the fact that underground soil temperatures are milder and more stable than the temperatures near the surface. This is true. However, this benefit is limited primarily to the portions of the building that are deeply buried. Lesser benefit applies to the roof and to the higher portions of the walls that are covered by shallower soil.

In summary, advocates of earth-sheltered houses envision a house that is shielded from the temperature extremes of the outdoor world, surrounded by a blanket of soil that is somewhat cooler than the indoor temperature. The heat generated within the house by appliances and people is expected to warm the inside of the house to a comfortable room temperature. Also, internal heat would lower the relative humidity without any further energy input. *Voila!*, the perfectly comfortable and energy-efficient house.

Unfortunately, this vision may be far from reality. What you may get – in the absence of elaborate and expensive measures – is a damp cave. Unlike a house whose walls are above grade, the moisture inside a buried house cannot diffuse outward into the atmosphere. If the soil contains any water – and most soil does – the outside of the buried walls will remain at a relative humidity of 100%. The moisture in the soil will diffuse toward the inside. This is the same situation that causes basements to be damp. If the roof of the house is covered with soil, the situation is even worse because rain falling on the roof flows through the soil and adds to the burden of moisture surrounding the house.

The overhead soil requires a slope, as does any roof. Therefore, it must be planted with vegetation that has a dense root system, to keep the soil cover from washing away. All kinds of plants take root on slopes, but don't expect a nice carpet of grass unless you can cover the building with soil that is only moderately sloped. Steep soil requires vegetation similar to that used by highway departments to cover road cuts. It will have a definitely wild appearance. On the positive side, this taller vegetation adds significant shading to temper a hot climate.

Finally, there is another problem that may be worse than any of the previous. If radon exists in the soil of your building site, earth-sheltered construction becomes suicidal. Refer to our discussion of radon in Step 3.

So, even for the most adventurous homebuilder, earth-sheltered construction offers little appeal. Unless…, your priority is excellent protection from windstorms and nuclear attack.

UNUSUAL STRUCTURES

This book shows how to build the best possible house, at the lowest possible cost, and with a minimum of risks and difficulties. To provide these benefits, we have selected common materials, common methods of construction, and a basically rectangular shape for rooms and structures.

There are many other ways to build a house, but none of them provides an equally good combination of comfort, energy efficiency, economy of construction, and reliability. Most unusual house designs offer no benefit other than novelty. Unusual designs don't age well. Build such a house, and you are likely to be left with a white elephant that has little market value.

DRW

Figure LL-50. A geodesic dome house. The main portion is two stories tall. The hexagonal window provides daylight for the upper floor.

THE SHAPE OF THE HOUSE

Most houses have a basically rectangular shape, and they enclose rectangular spaces. The reason is that rectangles accommodate people and furnishings efficiently. Domes, A-frames, and other shapes do not. Furthermore, it is easier and less expensive to build a rectangular box than to build other shapes.

Perhaps the most popular non-rectangular building shape in recent history has been the geodesic dome, which was promoted by the eccentric visionary Buckminster Fuller. Figure LL-50 shows an example. The original idea was to save energy and construction cost by minimizing the surface area of the exterior.

Kits for geodesic houses are still offered. Typically, they include a prefabricated lumber frame that holds blocks of insulating foam. The outside can be covered with a plastic stucco-like material or with plywood and shingles. Other kits consist of formed blocks of insulation that are covered with concrete.

UNUSUAL CONSTRUCTION MATERIALS

Beware of unusual construction materials. Many types of construction materials have been used for houses, but unusual ones are likely to give you nasty surprises.

Thousands of years of history have shown which materials are the most durable for buildings. Masonry – stone, brick, or concrete – can last for millennia if it is set on a firm foundation and loaded properly. Wood lasts for many centuries if it is kept dry and protected from vermin. Thick steel components, such as the I-beams used in basements, will endure for the life of the house, if they are kept dry. Aluminum has a long life if it is protected with a good enamel and if it is used in appropriate non-structural applications, such as window frames and siding.

But, avoid organic construction materials, such as plastics and adhesives. They rarely provide a significant advantage, other than initial cheapness. Contrary to popular opinion, plastics and adhesives do not survive for a long time. Even the most durable will last for only a fraction of the life of a well designed house. You certainly don't want to use them for any part of your house that carries a load or that will be difficult to replace.

An important exception is plywood, a composite material made with adhesives. We can gamble on it because the plywood in a finished house is held together in the long term primarily by the nails that attach it, rather than by the adhesives between the layers.

Log houses periodically become popular in parts of the world where straight timber is plentiful. Aside from offering a rustic appearance that waxes and wanes in popularity, log houses provide little actual benefit.

Logs have mediocre insulation value, typically about one third the R-value of glass fiber insulation. A house that is built from logs will develop major air leaks because of the way that timber warps and splits as it dries. The corners are difficult or impossible to seal reliably.

So, a log house cannot be super-efficient by itself. To make it super-efficient, you would have to build a super-efficient structure inside it, taking great care to plug air leakage paths. Also, log construction makes it difficult to do a lot of things that would be easy otherwise, such as increasing insulation value, installing electrical wiring, etc.

A variety of dubious construction concepts stem from a desire to use materials that have a "natural" flavor. Straw bale houses are an example. Figure LL-51 shows an especially attractive example. Straw has moderately good insulating value*, but no other advantages as a construction material. Straw rots, it burns, and it is food for vermin. Straw seems cheap only until you calculate the cost of building with it.

Sod roofs are an anachronism. Yes, pioneers in arid Western states used them on their adobe houses, but damp sod will destroy the structure of a house that is built in a climate with appreciable rainfall. Sod requires dense, low-height vegetation with a strong root system to hold it together. Pioneers settled for cactus or grass. Okay, you don't want cactus, so how are you going to get the lawn mower on the roof?

Another itch that people want to scratch is using lightweight concrete structures. Concrete has minimal insulation value, causing people to invent various structures that combine concrete and plastic foam insulation. In most such combinations, the materials fail to compensate for each other's weaknesses. The concrete usually is too thin, so it crumbles. Making the concrete thick enough for strength provides heat paths through the wall that negate the high insulation value of the foam insulation.

To sum up, common building materials allow you a virtually unlimited range of good design options for your house. Use conventional materials wisely, and you won't need to risk the hazards of unproven methods and materials.

Wikipedia Commons

Figure LL-51. A house with straw bale construction. A great deal of effort has been devoted to make the house attractive. Its survival will depend on the ability of the structure to completely protect the straw from vermin and moisture.

---

* The insulation value of straw bale walls has been measured by several organizations, yielding wildly different results. Thus far, it appears that a carefully built straw bale wall will yield an insulation value of about R-2 per inch (RSI 0.15 per centimeter). The straw itself should be installed perpendicular to the direction of heat flow, or in other words, parallel to the wall. An important step is to remove all the straps from the bales and to fill the gaps between them. These requirements make it difficult to install the straw properly.

RAINWATER RECOVERY

At first glance, collecting rainwater from your roof and storing it in a cistern or rain barrels seems like a simple way to provide water for your home and to reduce the load on public water resources. But usually, it isn't. Like many conservation concepts, rain harvesting is an appealing delusion that fades in the face of basic calculations and practical difficulties.

Municipal water systems are one of the most important developments of civilization because individual collection of rainwater is unreliable and unhealthy. If your home site lies within the jurisdiction of a public water system, you should almost certainly get your home water from the public system.

If you are outside the reach of a public water system, a water well probably will be your best water supply. Well water is essentially filtered water from a source that does not support biological contamination. Some well water does contain noxious contaminants, and it should be treated as we recommend in Step 5.

In a limited range of situations, the best water source may be an open body of water, such as a river or lake. However, water wells usually are available near such bodies of water, and they are preferable to the open water.

If your home site is one of those rare places where rainwater recovery is worth considering, these are the main issues.

HOW MUCH RAIN CAN YOU COLLECT?

If you expect rain to be your primary source of water, then the average rainfall at your location must exceed your average water usage. If rainwater harvesting is to supplement other sources of water, there should be enough rain to make collecting it economical and worth the bother.

If you determine that the total yearly amount of rainfall is adequate for your needs, here is the next thing that you need to understand: *the longer the intervals between rainfall, the larger your water storage needs to be*.

Rain collection enthusiasts typically think in terms of recovering rainwater from the roof. This is done with a rain barrel that is filled from the house's gutters, as in Figure LL-53. When rainfall first begins, the rain barrel is bypassed to flush out the dirt coming from the roof and gutters. Then, a diverter is adjusted to direct the rain into the barrel.

U.S. EPA

Figure LL-53. A typical rain barrel installation. The adjacent gutter downspout has a diverter that can direct roof drainage into the barrel or can bypass it. This barrel has two bottom outlets, one fixed and one connected to a hose.

Unfortunately, if your roof is your rain collector, it probably won't collect enough water to run a household, or even major applications such as toilet flushing. Your roof area is competing with the entire land area of the region that feeds a public water supply, and that is no contest.

A roof collection system might serve a household if the climate is rainy all year, as in Ketchikan, Alaska. Indeed, a roof collection system might be your prime choice if your home in a wet climate is not served by a public water system.

In a climate with more normal rainfall, if the land area of your property is fairly large, and if it is graded toward a low point, you can use your acreage to collect rainwater in a pond. Unless the climate will reliably keep the pond filled, you will need to transfer the water to a cistern or tank as soon as it is collected.

HOW CLEAN IS RAINWATER?

We tend to assume that rainwater is pure. Unfortunately, it isn't. As rain falls, it collects dust and pollutants from the atmosphere, including some dangerous microorganisms (such as the bacteria that cause Legionnaires' Disease) that ride on dust particles. On the positive side, rainwater is "soft" in terms of dissolved minerals and it is free of many dangerous pollutants (such as radon, arsenic, and organic poisons) that reside in the ground.

Rain is further polluted by whatever lies on your roof and in the gutters used to channel the rainwater to the cistern. Take a look at a typical roof in your area and inside the gutters. You will find rotting vegetation, earthworms, bird droppings, small animal carcasses, an oily film from the asphalt in shingles, etc.

If you collect rainwater in a pond, it will contain an even greater variety of undesirable contaminants. Any river or reservoir that feeds a public water supply also contains those things, but they are removed by large filtration plants. Large water treatment plants clean water much more economically than you can clean the water for an individual home.

If you use your roof to collect rainwater, you can use rainfall to flush your roof and gutters before putting water into storage. However, such flushing eliminates only a fraction of the bad stuff on your roof and in the gutters. And, it wastes a large part of the rainfall.

APPLICATIONS FOR RAINWATER

At present, the primary application for small scale rainwater recovery appears to be gardening, along with limited irrigation of lawns and shrubbery. However, rain irrigates these applications directly. Storing rainwater would make sense only if you have periods of heavy rain separated by long intervals of drought. In that case, you would need a very large storage capacity.

In principle, the water treatment methods of Step 5 can be used to clean a rainwater supply for all your household applications, including drinking, cooking, and washing. But, this requires continuing monitoring and maintenance. A rainwater supply potentially contains many dangerous organisms and materials, so a lapse of maintenance could cause a tragedy.

Using rainwater for indoor applications requires a separate water system, in addition to a primary system that is served by a public water supply or by a well. The primary system must back up the rainwater system. This complicates the piping.

Usually, the only safe indoor application for rainwater is toilet flushing. Toilet flushing is the largest indoor user of water, estimated to account for 40% of U.S. residential indoor use, so using rainwater for toilet flushing might seem like a good idea. However, in a water starved location, you won't collect nearly enough rainwater to serve typical toilet usage.

RECYCLING HOUSEHOLD SEWAGE

In modern homes, everything that drains to the sewer is sent either to a public sewage system or to an individual septic system. Advocates of water conservation have long suggested that the water in the sewage should be recovered for further use on site.

In brief, forget about it, unless you are a dedicated enthusiast.

The sources of sewage in a home commonly are classified as "black water" and "grey water." Black water is any water that contains human waste, generally from toilets, urinals, and bidets. Grey water is every other source of sewage, including the discharge from showers, sinks, and washing machines.

Black water is a primary carrier of certain deadly epidemic diseases, such as cholera and typhoid fever. It requires treatment to kill the disease causing organisms, or it requires disposal in a manner that leads to natural degradation or isolation of the organisms. Attempting to recover black water within your home is courting disaster.

(In centuries past, certain cultures routinely used human waste as fertilizer, but that practice has largely disappeared. Human waste is sometimes treated to create a sanitary commercial fertilizer, such as Milorganite®, but this requires an industrial scale process.)

Recycling grey water in individual homes or small communities is a fad that rarely survives scrutiny. Usually, the only indoor application for grey water is toilet flushing. This requires a separate set of drain pipes from the grey water sources to a storage tank, and thence to the toilets. The grey water cannot be allowed to stagnate in a tank, or it will breed an ecosystem that you would not want inside your home.

The usual outdoor application for grey water is irrigation. However, grey water contains detergents, salts, and pathogens that make it undesirable for this application without some form of treatment that would not be economical on a small scale.

INDEX

200-Year Rule 243

A

Addition to Existing House
15, 93–97
  adding stairs 95
  adding upper floors 94–95
  expanding at same level 95
  expanding upward and outward
    97

Adhesives. *See also* **Sealants**
  cautions 283
  functions 283

A-frame 117, 317–318, 672

Air Binding (in hydronic heating)
447

Air Cleaner 600–601

Air Conditioners 469–470
  See also **Heat Pumps**
  central, avoid 416, 470
  compared to heat pumps 469
  ductless 469
  energy efficiency ratings 463
  how they work 456–457
  split-system 469
  window-type 469–470

Air Filters 478

Air Leakage
  around doors
    231, 374–375, 378, 379
  around flue 334–335, 645
  around plumbing vents 334–335
  around windows 231. *See
    also* **Windows, Installation**
  holes & gaps, minimize sizes
    232
  prevention, with house wrap 237
  prevention, with overlapping
    joints 233

  prevention, with sealants
    233–236. *See also* **Sealants**
  prevention, with wall sheathing
    194, 233, 295–296
  through fireplace 640
  through flue damper 643, 645
  through interior of structure 231
  through leaky windows 231
  through penetrations 231
  through structural joints 231
  through wiring holes 348

Air Quality
  & airtight construction 231, 490
  ventilation. *See* **Ventilation, for
    Air Quality**

Airtight Construction.
  See **Air Leaage;**
  See **Air Quality;**
  See **Health**

Aluminum Siding 104

Anchor Bolts 200, 239, 286

Appliances 587–601
  efficiency ratings 588
  features. *See* **name of appliance**
  heat recovery appliances 669
  shopping for 587
  ▶ air cleaner 600–601
  ▶ clothes dryer 599–600
  ▶ clothes washer 598–599
  ▶ convection oven 594–595
  ▶ dishwasher 597–598
  ▶ electronic appliances 601
  ▶ food freezer 590–591
  ▶ microwave oven 594–595
  ▶ oven & broiler 594–595
  ▶ pressure cooker 592–593
  ▶ range, conventional 591–593
  ▶ range, induction 593–594
  ▶ refrigerator 589–590

Architect. *See* **Design Assistance**

Architectural Style 98–99
  alternatives to blank walls
    112–114
  alternatives to excessive glass
    area 112–114
  decoration. *See* **Decoration**
  defining features 98
  energy efficiency, effect on 99
  roof. *See* **Roof Styles**
  when to select 98

Attic
  access 30–31, 239
  cooling. *See* **Roof, Cool**
  fan. *See* **Fans, Cooling;**
    See **Roof, Cool**
  insulation. *See* **Insulation of
    Roof**
  moisture venting 325–327
  storage space 30–31, 78–79

Awnings 161–162

B

Balcony 56–57
  as entrance cover 55
  for shading 161

Balloon Frame Construction 201

Basement
  block radon entry 273–275
    See also **Radon Mitigation**
  block water entry 273–275
  decision to build 77
  foundation drainage 274–277
  ground water, as hindrance to
    246
  insulation. *See* **Insulation of
    Basement**
  moisture venting 277–278
  walls. *See* **Walls, Basement**

Bathrooms. *See* **Bathtub Rooms;**
  See **Shower Rooms;**
  See **Toilet Rooms**

Bathtub 514–515
  hazard of falls 32, 37, 514
  hot tub. *See* **Hot Tub**
  room for. *See* **Bathtub Room**
  spa 515
  walk-in 515
  weight on floor 37

Bathtub Rooms 37

Beam Roof. *See* **Roof, Beam**

Bedrock 246–247.
  See also **Foundation**

Bedroom Clusters 68–69
  See also **Floor Plan**

Bedrooms 26–27

Beds, Types 26–27

Bidet 520

Blue Light Hazard (LED) 559

Board-and-Batten Siding 104

Boiler, Heating 434–438
  air supply, combustion 444–445
  condensing 434–436
  control, time 438
  control, water temperature reset 437
  flue 444–445. *See also* **Flue**
  fueled with natural gas 434–436
  fueled with oil 436–437
  fueled with propane or LPG 436
  fueled with solid fuels 436
  fueled with wood 626, 629–630,
    637–639. *See also* **Heating**
    with Firewood
  leak detection 438, 451.
    See also **System Feeder,**
    Hydronic
  select, how to 437
  sizing 437
  space for 51–52

Breakfast Room 43. *See*
  also **Dining Areas, Informal**

Brick
  arches 108–109
  brick-and-block 106, 202,
    310–311
  brick shelf 87, 280, 309
  brick veneer 87, 98–99, 106,
    201, 309–310
  decoration of 99, 103, 107–108
  embodied energy 89
  firebrick 640–641, 645
  kinds of 106–107
  over wide openings 397–398
  paving, for patio 57
  thermal lag 92

Builder. *See* **Contractor**

Building Codes 205–206
  explanation 205–206
  International Residential Code
  205

Butler Pantry 41

C

Capillary Break (for foundation)
254

Carbon Monoxide Hazard
495–496

Carpentry, Ornamental 131–134

Carpet 406, 407. *See also* **Rugs**

Carport 50–51
  as entrance 54

Caulking. *See* **Sealants**

Ceiling
  height 84–85
  shapes 84–85
  surfaces. *See* **Interior Surfaces**

Certification, Super House
621–622. *See also* **Contractor;**
  See also **Design Assistance**

Chair Lift 72. *See also* **Elevator**

Chimney
  as decoration 112, 626
  definition 643
  fire hazard 641
  for fireplace 640–641

Clapboard Siding 104

Clerestory 168–171
  comparison to other glazing 142
  daylighting with 168–171
  solar heating with 151–152. *See*
    also **Solar Heating, Passive**

Closet Heater, Humidity
Controlled 502–503

Closets, Broom 28

Closets, Clothes 27

Closets, Coat 28–29

Closets, Linen 28

Clothes Dryer 599–600

Clothesline Area 48

Clothes Washer 598–599

Coal 417
  See also **Energy Sources**
  cost comparison.
    See **Energy Cost**
  for boilers 436, 637–639
  for heating stoves 631, 633
  handling 628
  synthetic gas, from 418
  synthetic oil, from 419

Cold Weather Refuge Rooms 46

Color
  color vision 551–552
  for exterior decoration 111–112
  for interior surfaces 564
  lamp color output. *See* **Lamps**

Comfort
  effect of glass
    36, 49, 149–150, 655
  effect of insulation
    306, 345, 413

of cooling fans.
See **Fans, Cooling**
of evaporative coolers **486–487**
of heating stoves **626, 630, 634**
of heat pumps **454–455**
of hydronic heating. *See*
Heating System, Hydronic
of room heating equipment.
See **Heating Equipment,**
Room Heaters
related to air flow. *See* **Ventil-**
ation, for Comfort Cooling
related to humidity **498**
related to temperature **498**

Computer Program, Home
Design 62–63

Concrete Block
foundation **186, 255**
radon hazard **244**
walls **202**

Concrete, Poured
foundation **186–192, 250–254**
steel reinforcement **252–254**
structure **202**

Condensation
from air conditioners **465**
from condensing boilers &
furnaces **435**
from dehumidifiers **500–501**
from heat pumps **465**
how water vapor condenses
224–225
in house structure **224–225**.
See also **Condensation**
Damage in Structure,
Preventing
on below-grade openings **74**

Condensation Damage in
Structure, Preventing 224–230
condensation damage, explained
224–225
damage prevention strategy **226**
in cold & moderate climate **228**
in humid sub-tropical climate
229
in tropical climate **230**
mildew damage **229**

snow & ice damage **328**
with vapor barrier **226–230**.
See also **Vapor Barrier**
with venting **226, 228–230**.
See also **Venting, Moisture**

Condensing Boilers & Furnaces
435, 436.
See also **Boiler, Heating;**
See also **Furnace, Forced-Air**

Construction. *See* **House**
Construction

Contract for Construction
609–611
clauses **609–610**
definition of contract **609**
how to write **611**
lawyer, hiring to write **611**
payments **608**
Super House clause **610–611**

Contractor 604–608. *See*
also **Contract for Construction**
certification. *See* **Certification,**
Super House
contract. *See* **Contract for**
Construction
finding good contractor
604–606. *See also*
Certification, Super House
payment **608, 609**
subcontractors **604, 608**
what they do **604**
what they don't do **604**
working with **606–607**

Convection Oven 594–595

Cooling
comfort
See **Air Conditioners;**
See **Evaporative Cooler;**
See **Fans, Cooling;**
See **Heat Pumps;**
See **Shading, for Cooling**
food. *See* **Food Freezer;**
See **Refrigerator**
roof. *See* **Roof, Cool**

Cooling Capacity
calculations **458–459**

Cool Roof. *See* **Roof, Cool**

Corridor
width recommendations **70**

Cost
frame vs. masonry construction
92
how to lower construction cost
86–88
of energy sources. *See* **Energy**
Cost; *See* **Energy Sources**
of equipment.
See **name of equipment**
of house **86–88**
of Super House **15**

Cove Lighting 571

Crawl Space 266–269
accessibility **268**
floor above **266**
freeze protection for pipes
268, 546
moisture from ground, block
267
radon protection **267–268**
See also **Radon Mitigation**

Curtains 165–166

D

Day Cluster (of rooms) 67
See also **Floor Plan**

Daylighting 140, 167–175
glare, avoiding **167**
with clerestories **168–171**
with light pipes **174–175**
with skylights **172–174**
with windows **167–168**

Deck (outdoor platform) 57
as entrance cover **55**

Decoration.
See also **Architectural Style**
of brick surfaces. *See* **Brick**
of floors. *See* **Floor Surfaces**
of roof. *See* **Roof Styles**
of walls
See **Wall Surfaces, Exterior**
of windows
See **Windows, Applications**

with color, exterior 111–112

with color, interior 564

with foliage
See **Foliage**;
See **Landscaping**

with ornamental carpentry
See **Ornamental Carpentry**

Degree-Days. *See also* **Insulation, Amounts**

base temperatures for 210

explained 210

limitations 210

of geographic locations 211–212

Dehumidifiers

See also **Humidity, Lowering**;
See also **Mildew**

coordinate with air conditioning 501

coordinate with cooling fans 501

draining 500–501

in laundry area 47

in shower room 37

installation 500–501

selection 500

where to use 499

Den 44

Design Assistance 621–622

architect 621–622
See also **Certification, Super House**

architectural drafting service 621

certified designer. *See* **Certification, Super House**

contractor 621. *See also* **Certification, Super House**

engineer 621

Design, Home. *See* **Table of Contents**

aids 62–63

assistance.
See **Design Assistance**

certification, Super House 621–622

computer program 62–63

outline of 14

Dimensions. *See also* **Size**

exploit standard dimensions 64

in this book 64

metric, nominal 62

of drawings 618

used in drawings 618

Dining Areas, Informal 42–43

Dining Room 43

Dishwasher 597–598

Door Locks 380–384

cylinders & keys 382

keyed-alike locks 382

knobs & handles 382

lock, biometric 382

lock, deadbolt 381

lock, keypad 382

lock, latching 380

lock, Segal deadbolt 381

strike plate, reinforced 383

Doors, Entrance 374–384
See also **Entrance Spaces**

▸ Entrance Door Selection Guide 376–378

frame molding 379

glazing 377–378

hinges, reinforced 384

location 74
See also **Floor Plan**

locks. *See* **Door Locks**

materials 376–377

opening style 376

pre-fabricated assembly 378–379

reinforcement 382–384

R-value 376–377

size 376

storm door, avoid 379

strength 239, 377

threshold 374–375

weatherstripping 375, 378

Doors, Garage & Larger 389–399

▸ Large Door Selection Guide 390–393

air leakage 390

appearance 390–391

counterbalances 392

door, bi-fold 396

door, hydraulic 395

door, roll-up 394

door, sectional 389

door, side-hinged 394

door, single-panel 395

door, sliding 395

door, tilt-up 394

durability 391

insulation 390

openers, powered 393

resistance to intrusion 392

resistance to wind damage 239, 392

safety features 393

screen, garage door 48–49

size limits 390

wall opening 397–399

windows 393

Doors, Interior 385–388

door, accordion 388

door, closet 387–388

door, folding 388

door, French 385–388

door, hinged 385–388

door, louvered 386

door, pocket 386

door, sliding 386–387

width recommendations 70

Dormer

framing 318

interior appearance 123

styles 117, 121–123

Double-Wall Construction 291

Drainage, Surface 248, 260, 275

Drains

floor drains 52, 279, 444

for condensing boilers & furnaces 435

for dehumidifier 500–501

for heat pump condensate 465

sewer, during construction 189–190

sewer, in floor plan 69–70

Drawings, Construction 612–620
  detail drawings, made easy **619**
  scale & sizes **618**
  specifications **619–620**
  typical drawing set **613–615**
  working drawings
    See **Drawings, Working**

Drawings, Working (by reader)
61–64, 612, 619

Dressing Rooms 27–28

Drywall. *See* **Gypsum Board**

Ductless Air Conditioners 469

Ductless Heat Pumps 459–462

E

Earth-Coupled Heat Pump.
  See **Geothermal Heat Pump**

Earthquakes
  locations of **243**
  resistance to **242–243**

Earth-Sheltered Construction
670–671

Electricity
  See also **Energy Sources**
  characteristics **417**
  cost comparison
    See **Energy Cost**
  electrical wiring
    See **Wiring & Cable**

Electric Resistance Heaters
471–474. *See also* **Heating**
Equipment, Room Heaters
  energy efficiency **471**

Elevator 70–72
  See also **Chair Lift**

Embodied Energy 89–90

Emergency Exit
  from emergency shelter **59-60**
  from upper level rooms **181**

Emergency Shelter 46, 58–60

Energy Cost 419–421
  ▶ Energy Cost Worksheet
  419–421
  energy cost comparison **419–421**
  energy prices, sources **421**

Energy Efficiency
  effect of architectural style **99**
  effect of size of house **89–90**
  Five Principles **15**
  need for **14, 625**
  of equipment
    See **name of equipment**
  of glazing. *See* **Glazing,**
    Efficiency Enhancement
  of insulating materials
    See **Insulation, Amounts**;
    See **Insulation, Materials**
  of Super House **14**
  ratings. *See* **Ratings**

Energy Factor (water heater) 523

Energy Sources 417–421
  coal **417**. *See also* **Coal**
  comparison of energy sources
    417–421
  cost of. *See* **Energy Cost**
  electricity **417**
  for specific equipment
    See **name of equipment**
  fuel oil **418–419**
  natural gas **418**
  pellet fuels **628, 633**
  propane & LPG **418**
  solar energy, for electricity
    generation. *See* **Solar**
    Electricity Generation
  solar energy, for heating
    151–152.
    See also **Solar Heating,**
      Active Systems;
    See also **Solar Heating,**
      Passive
  wind energy **662**
  wood
    See **Heating with Firewood**

Energy Star. *See* **Ratings**

Entrance Spaces 52–55, 74.
  See also **Doors, Entrance**
  alcove **54**
  below grade, avoid **74–75**
  canopy **54**
  carport **54**
  foyer **52–55**
  mud room **52–55**
  porch **54**
  recessed **54**
  roof overhang **55**
  vestibule **52–55**

Equipment Space 51–52

Evaporative Cooler 486–490
  2-stage **487**
  climates for **487**
  comfort limitations **486–487**
  energy efficiency **488**
  explained **486–487**
  indirect **487**
  installation **488–489**
  maintenance burden **488**
  mildew, avoiding **489**
  water requirements **488–489**

Expansion Rooms 67
  See also **Floor Plan**

F

Fans
  anti-stratification **485**
  bathroom **492**
  ceiling. *See* **Fans, Cooling**
  comfort cooling. *See* **Fans,**
    Cooling
  paddle. *See* **Fans, Cooling**
  roof cooling. *See* **Roof, Cool**
  ventilation. *See* **Ventilation**

Fans, Cooling
  attic fan **480–481**
  ceiling fans **482–484**
  outside air (night cooling) fan
    481–482
  roof cooling fans **341–342**
  workshop fan, for cooling **494**

686

Faucets
    basin & sink 516
    outside 521
    shower 512–513

Filters
    air 478, 600–601
    water. *See* **Water Treatment**

Fire Safety
    emergency exit 181
    insulation of structure for 345
    of chimney 641, 645
    of fireplace 628, 641
    of flue 643–645. *See also* **Flue**
    of fuels. *See* **name of fuel**
    of heating stove 628
    of insulation materials.
        See **Insulation, Materials**
    of kitchen 40–41

Fireplace
    air leakage 643
    air pollution 640
    air supply 642
    comfort limitations 640
    damper 640
    design issues 641–642
    efficiency limitation 626, 640
    enclosed 642
    fireplace insert 643.
        See also **Heating Stoves**
    fire safety zone 628
    flue 643–645
    freestanding 641–642
    gas-fired 479
    surrounding space 52, 628

Flat Roof
  See **Roof Structure, Flat**

Flood Plain 249

Floor Heating
    electric 473
    hydronic 431–434, 443

Floor, Overhanging
    for living space 76–77
    for shading 161

Floor Plan 61–75
    bedroom clusters 68–69
    corridors 70
    day cluster 67
    doors, exterior 74
    independent rooms 69
    load-bearing walls 65–66
    orient to neighbors 74
    orient to street 73
    orient to the sun 75. *See*
        also **Solar Heating, Passive**;
        See also **Step 2**
    orient to view 73
    room groups 66–67
    wet walls 69–70

Floor Structure, Wooden
  193–197, 282–288
    above crawl space 266, 287
    above wet ground 269, 287
    connection to foundation
      200, 286
    insulation
        See **Insulation of Floor**
    joist dimensions 285
    joists 193–197, 200, 282–285.
      See also **I-Joist**
    joist spacing 285
    rim joists 193–197
    subfloor 194, 197, 200, 233,
      285–286

Floor Surfaces 405–410
    ▶ Floor Surface Comparison
      (table) 406
    carpet, wall-to-wall 406, 407
    ceramic floor tile 406, 407–408
    composition floor tile 406, 407
    concrete paint 406, 409
    hardwood parquet 406, 407
    hardwood strip 405–407
    rugs 406
    sheet flooring 406, 407–408
    terrazzo 406, 409

Floor Tile 406, 408–409

Flooring. *See* **Floor Surfaces**

Flue
    air leakage around 334–335, 645
    air leakage through 643
    airtight flue. *See* **Sealed**
      Combustion System
    carbon monoxide hazard
      495–496
    chimney. *See* **Chimney**
    damper 640, 645
    for oil-fired equipment 496
    for solid fuels 643–645

Foliage
    ▶ Tree & Shrub Selection Guide
      156–157
    for exterior decoration 113–114
    for shading 153–158
    plan for growth 157–158
    preserve before construction 135

Food Freezer 590–591

Foundation 250–269
    bedrock 246–247
    capillary break 254
    comparison of types 251
    drainage 275–277
    footing 254
    foundation type
      See **Foundation, (Type)**
    frost heaving 247–248
    gravity drain 276
    height above grade 260
    poured concrete 252–253
    soil strength to support 247
    steel reinforcement 252–253
    sump pump 277

Foundation, Concrete Block
  186, 251, 255

Foundation, Floating Slab
  251, 255–259
    cracking, prevention 258
    explained 255–256
    frost heaving, prevention
      256–257
    height above grade 260

Foundation, Friction Piling
  250–251

Foundation, Pier 251, 259

Foundation, Shear Wall 250–255
basement wall 250
dimensions 250
explained 250
footing 254
partial-height 254–255
poured concrete 252
reinforcing steel 252–253

Foundation, Stem Wall 266–268

Foundation, Stone 186, 251, 255

Foyer 52–55

Frame Construction
balloon frame construction 201
basics 193–201
compared to masonry
construction 91–92
condensation protection
See **Condensation Damage
in Structure, Preventing**
floors. *See* **Floor Structure,
Wooden**
moisture venting
See **Venting, Moisture**
platform construction 193–200
post-and-beam construction 201
roof. *See* **Roof**
walls. *See* **Walls, Frame**

Freeze Protection
crawl space 268.
See also **Water Pipes**

Frost Depth 247–248

Frost Heaving 247–248

Fuel Oil
See also **Energy Sources**
characteristics 418–419
cost comparison
See **Energy Cost**
leakage 475

Furnace Filters 478

Furnace, Forced-Air 477–478
See also **Heating System,
Forced-Air**
as space heater 477
condensing. *See* **Condensing
Boilers & Furnaces**
filters 478
wood-burning
626, 629–630, 635–637

G

Gable
end wall reinforcement
314–315, 319
end wall vents 340
styles. *See* **Roof Styles**

Gambrel Roof
See **Roof Structure, Gambrel**

Garage 49–50
as entrance 54
clothes drying in 48
door opening 398–400

Garage Door
See **Doors, Garage & Larger**

Gas
See **Natural Gas**;
See **Propane & LPG**

Geodesic Dome 672

Geothermal Heat Pump 664–668
basics 664–665
heat source: soil 665–667
heat source: surface water
667–668
heat source: water well 667
interior system, design 668
unsolved problems 664–666

Gingerbread (decoration)
See **Ornamental Carpentry**

Glare
definition 167
from clerestories 171
from lamps, fluorescent 560
from lamps, incandescent 553

from lamps, LED 571
from light pipes 174
from low sunlight 56
from night lighting 579
from outdoor lighting 580
from roof surfaces 339
from skylights 173–174
from sunlight 167, 171, 654–655
from task lighting 567–568
from toilet room lighting 31–32
from track lighting 571
from water & snow 73, 178
from windows 168
from window shades 164–166
in passive solar house 654–655
protection from clerestory glare
171
protection from light fixture
glare 564–566
protection from skylight glare
173–174
protection from solar glare
153–166, 167

Glazing, Applications
▶ Glazing Comparison (table)
142–143
five functions of 140
for appearance enhancement
140.
See also **Architectural Style**
for daylighting. *See* **Daylighting**
for solar heating 151–152. *See
also* **Solar Heating, Passive**
for ventilation 140, 179–180
for view 140. *See also* **View**
heat loss, minimize 149, 153,
182–183
in clerestories. *See* **Clerestories**
in doors 377–378
in light pipes 174–175
in skylights. *See* **Skylights**
in windows.
See **Windows, Applications**
shading of glazing.
See **Shading, for Cooling**

Glazing, Efficiency Enhancement
frame thermal break **364**
insulating gases **361**
low-E coating **359**
minimize glazing area **149–150**
movable insulation (thermal shutters) **150, 646–648**
number of panes **361**
storm window **373**
tandem windows **371–372**

Glazing, Materials
coating, heat filtering **360**
coating, low-E **359**
energy efficiency. *See* **Glazing, Efficiency Enhancement**
glass, darkening **358**
glass, decorative **358**
glass, diffusing **357**
glass, general **357**
glass, impact-resistant **357**
glass, mirror **358**
glass, obscuring **358**
glass, tinted **358**
glazing, plastic **357**

Grade Beam 260

Great Room 44–45

Grey Water Recycling 676

Ground Water
at building site **246**
basement, hindrance to **246**

Gutter Installation
to keep foundation dry **260, 275**

Gypsum Board 308
noise reduction **345**

H

Half-Timbered Walls 110

Hallway. *See* **Corridor**

Handicap Access
between floors **72**
chair lift **72**
elevator **72**

Hardwood Flooring 405–407

Header
in frame wall. *See* **Walls, Frame**
over wide door. *See* **Doors, Garage & Larger**

Health. *See also* **Safety**
air quality.
See **Air Quality**; *See* **Ventilation, for Air Quality**
mildew. *See* **Mildew**
radon hazard. *See* **Radon**
shower hazards **514**
smoking hazards **72–73, 491**
ventilation. *See* **Ventilation, for Air Quality**
water supply
See **Water Treatment**

Heat Pumps 454–468.
See also **Air Conditioners**
advantages & disadvantages **454–455**
air discharge temperature **454**
air distribution **454, 465**
best climates for **455**
cold weather models **455**
comfort limitations **454–455**
condensate drainage **465**
control features **464**
cooling capacity, calculation **458–459**
ductless **459–462**
energy efficiency **454–455**
energy efficiency, decline with outside temperature **454–455**
energy efficiency, ratings **463–464**
geothermal
See **Geothermal Heat Pump**
heating capacity, calculation **458**
heating capacity, decline with outside temperature **454**
how they work **456–457**
inside units, types **460–462**
installation **465–468**
noise ratings **464**
refrigerant pipes **414, 465, 467–468**

selection of **459–463**
split-system **459–462**
supplemental heaters **462**
water heater **525–526**
zones, heating & cooling, defining **458**

Heat Radiation Barrier
explained **337, 343–344**
installation **318, 327, 343–344**

Heat Recovery
appliances **669**
from ventilation air **491**

Heating Capacity
calculations **458**
of equipment
See **name of equipment**

Heating Equipment, Room Heaters
baseboard convector, electric **472**
baseboard convector, hydronic **425–429.** *See also* **Heating System, Hydronic**
ceiling heater, fan-forced **471**
ceiling heating, radiant **473**
fan-coil unit, hydronic **431**
See also **Heating System, Hydronic**
fireplace, gas fired **479**
fireplace, gas-fired
See **Fireplace**
floor heating, electric **473**
floor heating, hydronic **431–434, 443.** *See also* **Heating System, Hydronic**
furnce, forced-air **477–478**
heating stove
See **Heating Stoves**
heat lamp **474**
portable electric heater **474**
radiant heater, electric **474**
radiant heater, gas-fired **479**
radiator, electric **473**
radiator, hydronic **430**
See also **Heating System, Hydronic**
unit heater, electric **474**

unit heater, gas-fired 478

unvented heaters 475

venting gas-fired heaters 475, 477

wall heater, fan-forced, electric 472–473

wall heater, gas-fired 476–477

Heating Recommendations

avoid central forced-air heating 416

heating equipment comparison (table) 415

recommended primary systems 414, 417

Heating Stoves 626, 629–635

air supply 634–635

catalytic wood stoves 631–632

coal stoves 631

comfort limitations 626, 630, 634

efficiency improvements 629–630

fireplace insert 643

fire safety 643

fire safety zone 628

flue 643–645

heating limitations 634

non-catalytic wood stoves 631–632

pellet stoves 631, 633

ratings, efficiency 631

ratings, pollution 631

selection issues 634–635

surrounding space 52, 628

Heating System, Forced-Air 416

Heating System, Hydronic 422–453

air binding 447

air, removing from system 445–448

air separator 448

air vent 448

boiler. *See* **Boiler, Heating**

Builder's Hydronic System Checklist 440–441

check valves 451

components of 444

contractor skill is critical 422

expansion/pressurization tank 448–450

filling 453

freeze protection 452

heating capacities, calculating 423–425

heating zones, defining 423

insulation 452

leak detection 438, 451

location of equipment 51–52

pipes, routing & installing 451

prefabricate loop components 445

pressure setting 449–451

primary-secondary pumping 442

pumps 451

purging 453

room heating equipment, comparison (table) 427

room heating equipment, types 425–434. *See also* **Heating Equipment, Room Heaters**

system feeder
See **System Feeder**

system layout, for floor heating 443

system layout, for most homes 438–442

water treatment 452

Heating with Firewood 626–645

fuel supply 627–628

how wood burns 629

in boiler, wood-fired 626–627, 629–630, 637–639
See also **Boiler, Heating**

in fireplace. *See* **Fireplace**

in furnace, wood-fired 626–627, 630–631, 635–637
See also **Furnace, Forced-Air**

in heating stove
See **Heating Stoves**

Hip Roof. *See* **Roof Styles**

Home Activities Worksheet 19–25

Home Site Selection

bedrock 246–247

eroding cliff, on 249

eroding shoreline, on 249

flood plain 249

frost depth 247–248

glare from water view 178

ground water 246

radon 244–245

sinkholes 248

soil strength 247, 249

surface water drainage 248
See also **Drainage, Surface**

view. *See* **View**

volcano, near 249

wet ground 269

Hot Tub 137. *See also* **Bathtub**

Hot Water. *See* **Water Heating**

House Construction

basics (primer) 186–205

by homeowner 606–607

changes 607, 610
See also **Contract for Construction**

contract. *See* **Contract for Construction**

contractor. *See* **Contractor**

design. *See* **Design, Home**

design assistance
See **Design Assistance**

drawings. *See* **Drawings, Construction**

frame vs. masonry 91–92

home site. *See* **Home Site Selection**

masonry construction
See **Masonry Construction**

materials, unusual 672–673

schedule 607, 609
See also **Contract for Construction**

shape of house 672–673

structure 185–408

House Wrap 237

Humidifiers 504

Humidity, Lowering 497–503
See also **Mildew**
  causes of humidity problems 498–499
  in basement 503
  in closets 502–503
  with air conditioner 502
  with dehumidifiers
    See **Dehumidifiers**
  with heating 502
  with ventilation 502
    See also **Ventilation, for Humidity Control**

Humidity, Raising 504

Hurricanes
  emergency shelter 58–60
  locations of 241
  protection against. *See* **Wind Damage, Preventing**

Hurricane Straps 239, 312–315, 319

HVAC 413–508
  definition 413
  equipment. *See* **name of equipment**

Hydronic Heating
  See **Heating System, Hydronic**

I

Ice Dam 328. *See also* **Snow & Ice Protection**

I-Joist 193–197, 282–285
  as rafters 319
  cautions 283–285, 319

Independent Rooms 69
  See also **Floor Plan**

Innovations
  ▶ in Super House 14–15
  ▶ Innovation symbol 14
  air leakage around wiring, preventing 348–349
  attic access 30–31
  attic storage space 30–31, 78–79
  certification of designers & contractors 621

clerestories for daylighting 168–171
closet heater, humidity controlled 502–503
clothes dryer stand 600
cold weather refuge rooms 46
combined control of air conditioner, dehumidifier & cooling fan 501
construction contract, Super House clause 610
cool roof 336–344
corners, strong 294
dehumidifier, built-in 501
dehumidifier in laundry area 47
dehumidifier in shower area 37
efficient glazed space 182
electric receptacle convenience 347
evaporative cooler, effective control 489
fluorescent fixture ballast switching 561
heat pumps for cold weather 455
home activities inventory 19
hydronic system feeder 450
insulation of existing walls 306
insulation of interior walls, floors & ceilings 345
insulation workmanship 223, 348
joists, precut holes in 284
kitchen fire safety 40–41
kitchen water filter enclosure 39
light switch identification 582
roof access 124
roof deck rot protection 330
roof, heat radiation barrier 343
roof overhang framing 121
roof truss, strengthening 316
roof truss, walkways 322
room clusters 66
sealants, proper use 233
shading combinations 166
shading for cooling 153
shower curb drainage 36
shower fixture mounting 34
shower water treatment 531

specifications, bind in drawings 620
steel reinforcement, better 252
storage room 29
strong room 29
sun shading, effective 153–167
super-insulation 207
task lighting 568
thermostatic control of ceiling fans 484
thermostatic control of outside air cooling 481
wall sheathing, strong attachment 297
wall sheathing to block air leakage 296
wall studs for super-insulation 291
wall studs, wiring notches 290
wash basin, comfortable height 517
water heater, reducing convection loss 525
water pipe, layout to avoid interference between fixtures 542
window security 367
window sill height for privacy 177
windows, replacement ease 368
windows, tandem installation 371

Instant Water Heater
  electric 527
  gas-fired 527–528

Insulation, Amounts
  ▶ Insulation Worksheet 213–217
  Conduction Heat Loss formula 207
  degree-days. *See* **Degree-Days**
  R-value, calculation procedure 209–217
  R-value, definition 207
  R-values, of materials (table) 208
  RSI (metric R-value), definition 208
  super-insulation 207

Insulation, Materials 218–223
▸ insulation, explained 218
beadboard 222
cellulose, loose 221
cellulose, wet sprayed 222
fiber, glass 218–220
fiber, mineral 218–220
foam board 222
perlite 223
plastic foam beads 223
plastic foam, sprayed 223
polyisocyanurate 222
polystyrene, expanded 222
polystyrene, extruded 222
polyurethane 222
soil 223
straw 223
urea formaldehyde 223
vermiculite 223

Insulation of Basement 277–281
See also **Insulation of Foundation**
floor slab insulation 279–280
R-value
See **Insulation, Amounts**
wall insulation, exterior 278–279
wall insulation, interior 280–281

Insulation of Floor 287–288
overhanging floor 287–288
over vented space 288.
See also **Crawl Space**

Insulation of Foundation. *See also* **Insulation of Basement**
floating slab foundation 256–259

Insulation of Glazing
See **Glazing, Efficiency Enhancement**

Insulation of Interior Walls, Floors & Ceilings 345–346
for energy conservation 345
for fire safety 345
for noise reduction 346

Insulation of Roof 320–324
attic 321–323
beam roof 320–321
concrete roof 323–324
flat roof 323–324
R-value
See **Insulation, Amounts**
space for insulation 124
triangle-frame roof 320–321
truss roof 321–322

Insulation of Walls, Frame
existing walls, adding to 305–307
exterior walls 297–298
installation, correct 297–298
R-value
See **Insulation, Amounts**
vapor barrier
See **Vapor Barrier**
with cellulose 298
with fiber batts 200, 297

Insulation of Walls, Masonry 301–304
existing walls, adding to 306–307
exterior insulation 302–304
interior insulation 301–302
R-value
See **Insulation, Amounts**
vapor barrier, for interior insulation 302

Insulation of Water Pipes
See **Heating System, Hydronic;**
See **Water Pipes**

Insulation, Workmanship 223, 297–298, 347–348
conflict with wiring, avoid 347–348

Insulation Worksheet 213–217

Interior Surfaces 200, 308
color 564
floor. *See* **Floor Surfaces**
gypsum board 308
tile 289, 308, 406, 408–409

J

Joists
See **Floor Structure, Wooden;**
See **I-Joist**

K

Kitchen 38–41
eat-in 42. *See also* **Dining Areas, Informal**
features 38–39
fire safety 40–41, 491
range hood 491
ventilation 39–40, 491–492

Knee Wall 81, 318

L

Lamps 553–563
▸ Lamp Selection Guide 554–556
ballasts, fluorescent 561
color rendering 555
color temperature 555
compact fluorescent 554–556, 559–561
energy efficiency 554
fluorescent 554–556, 559–562
halogen 557
incandescent 553–557
LED 554–556, 557–559, 570–571
light distribution pattern 554
lumens 554
mercury vapor 554–556, 562
metal halide 554–556, 562
outdoor operating temperature 556
service life 554
sodium vapor 554–556, 562
starting delay 556

Landscaping
See also **Drainage, Surface;**
See also **Foliage**
preserve original trees & shrubs 135

Last Look: Energy for Pioneers
625–676

Latitude
definition 144
effect on climate 146–147
effect on shading 153, 160, 171
effect on sun's position & timing
144–148

Laundry Area 46–47
See also **Appliances;**
See also **Clothesline Area**

Laundry Chute 48

Layout, Interior. *See* **Floor Plan**

Light
infrared 141
of lamps. *See* **Lamps**
of sun. *See* **Sunlight**
ultraviolet 141
visible 140–141

Light Pipe 174–175
comparison to other glazing 142
for daylighting 174–175.
See also **Daylighting**

Lighting 549–584
See also **Daylighting**
▶ Home Lighting Worksheet
572–577
arrangement
See **Lighting Layout**
controls. *See* **Lighting Controls**
fixtures. *See* **Lighting Fixtures**
formula for ideal lighting 549
glare. *See* **Glare**
lamps. *See* **Lamps**
light intensity. *See* **Sunlight;**
See **Vision, Human**
recommendations 572–577
task lighting 567–569
veiling reflections 566
visual quality
See **Vision, Human**

Lighting Controls 581–584

astronomical timers 584
daylight sensors 584
door switches 584
manual switches 581–582
motion sensors 583
switch identification 581–582

Lighting Fixtures 570–580
built-in fixtures, where to install
570
cove lighting 578
low-voltage lighting 578
night safety lights 579
outdoor fixtures 580
portable fixtures 570
recommendations 572–577
switches. *See* **Lighting Controls**
task lighting 567–569
track lighting 571
valance fixtures 571, 578

Lighting Layout
▶ Home Lighting Worksheet
572–577
glare, to avoid 564–566
light interior colors, use 564
shadows on scene, to avoid 567
task lighting 567–569
veiling reflections, to avoid 566

Lintel. *See also* **Header**
definition 398

Living Room 44

Load-Bearing Walls
See **Walls, Interior;**
See **Floor Plan**

Log House 672–673

Lumens (lighting) 554

M

Mansard Roof
See **Roof Structure, Mansard**

Masonry Construction
See also **Masonry, Materials**
basics 201–204
comparison to frame
construction 91–92
concrete frame 202
foundation. *See* **Foundation**
steel reinforcement 252–254
thermal lag 92
walls. *See* **Walls, Masonry**
wall surfaces
See **Wall Surfaces, Exterior**

Masonry, Materials
See also **Masonry Construction**
brick. *See* **Brick**
concrete block.
See **Concrete Block**
concrete, poured
See **Concrete, Poured**
filler blocks 202–204
stone. *See* **Stone**
strength characteristics 201–202

Microwave Oven 594–595

Mildew
causes of 498–499
cleaning 497
explained 497
in basement 503
in closets 502–503
in shower 493
in structure
See **Condensation Damge in
Structure, Preventing**
prevention with
dehumidifiers 499–501
See also **Dehumidifiers**
prevention with heating 499
prevention with ventilation 499
See also **Ventilation, for
Humidity Control**

Mold. *See* **Mildew**

Motion Sensors 508

Movable Insulation (for glazing) 646–648

Mud Room 52–55

Multi-Story House
adding upper floor 94–95, 97
decision to build 76–77
relative cost 76, 87
stairs. *See* Stairs
temperature stratification 71

N

Natural Gas
See also Energy Sources
characterisitics 418
cost comparison
See Energy Cost
equipment using. *See* name of equipment
leakage to interior 475

Noise
absorbing materials
See Gypsum Board
insulation to absorb 346
interior doors, to block 385–388
of equipment
See name of equipment

O

Office (room type) 44

Off the Grid, Living 663

Oil, Heating. *See* Fuel Oil

Ornamental Carpentry 131–134

Outdoor Amenities 135–137
See also Landscaping
coordination with floor plan 73–74
hot tub 137
in Home Activities Worksheet 25
outbuildings 135
swimming pool 135–137

Ovens & Broilers 594–595

Overhanging Floor
See Floor, Overhanging

P

Pantry 41–42

Parlor 45

Parquet (floor) 406–407

Passive Solar Heating
See Solar Heating, Passive

Patio 56–57

Pellet Stoves 631, 633

Perm Rating 226–227

Photovoltaic System
See Solar Electricity Generation

Pipes
flue. *See* Flue
natural gas 189
refrigerant. *See* Heat Pumps
sewer. *See* Drains
underground 189–190
water. *See* Water Pipes

Plans Books 61

Platform Construction 193–199
See also Frame Construction

Plumbing
drains. *See* Drains
fixtures. *See* name of fixture
freeze protection
See Water Pipes
hot water. *See* Water Heating
pipes. *See* Water Pipes
vents, air leakage around 334–335

Plywood
adhesives in 283
inferior substitutes 285–286
permeability, to moisture 225–228
roof deck. *See* Roof Deck
R-value (RSI) 208

subfloor
See Floor Structure, Wooden
underlayment
See Floor Structure, Wooden
wall sheathing
See Wall Sheathing, Exterior

Pocket Doors 386

Porch 55–56
as appearance enhancement 98, 112
as entrance cover 55
as entrance space 54, 55
for clothes drying 48
for protection against sliding snow & ice 125
for shading 161
privacy 56
screened 56
sun porch 56
See also Sunroom

Post-and-Beam Construction 201

Pots & Pans 592, 593

Pressure Cooker 592–593

Privacy. *See also* Security
by interior doors 385–388
by interior shading fixtures 153, 164–166
dressing room for 27
glazing materials for 358
porch, for 56
toilet room design for 33
window design for 36, 149, 176–178

Propane & LPG
See also Energy Sources
characterisitics 418
cost comparison
See Energy Cost
leakage to interior 475

Purlins (roof component) 331–332

Q

R

R-value (RSI)
    See **Insulation, Amounts**

Radiators. *See* **Heating Equipment, Room Heaters**

Radon
    basics 244–245
    dangers 244–245
    entry from crawl space 245
        See also **Crawl Space**
    entry from soil 244–245
    entry from water supply 245
    in crawl spaces 267–268, 546
    in showers 245, 514, 531
    protection from
        See **Radon Mitigation**;
        See **Water Treatment**
    testing for 245

Radon Mitigation 261–268
    backdrafting, avoid 265
    basics 261–263
    for crawl spaces 267–268
    monitoring 264
    sizes, pipe and fan 263–265
    sump pump system 265–266
    system protection 264–265
    under foundations 261–266

Rainwater Recovery 674–675

Range, Conventional 591–593

Range Hood (kitchen)
39–41, 424, 491, 595

Range, Induction 593–594

Ratings
    air conditioner efficiency
        (SEER) 469
    appliance efficiency ratings 588
    boiler efficiency (AFUE) 437
    boiler, wood-fired 638
    clothes washer (energy efficiency) 598
    clothes washer (water consumption) 598
    doors (NFRC) 374
    Energy Star rating system 588
    heating stove (default efficiency) 631
    heating stove (pollution) 631
    heat pump cooling efficiency (SEER) 463
    heat pump heating efficiency (HSPF) 463–464
    heat pump noise (sone) 464
    home electronics efficiency 601
    insulation (R-value) 207–209
    lamp color (color temperature) 552, 555
    lamp color rendering (CRI) 552, 555
    lamp energy efficiency 554
    moisture permeability (perm) 226–228
    skylight (NFRC) 400
    water filter (NSF) 533, 537–538
    water filter (pore size) 532–533
    water heater (energy factor) 523
    window (NFRC) 351, 368

Rebar (steel) 252–254

Refrigerant 456–457

Refrigerator 589–590

Reverse Osmosis (water filter)
530–531, 534–535, 539

Ridge Vents 341

Roller Shades 164–165
    See also **Shading Fixtures, Interior**

Roof 312–344
    access to rooftop 124
    appearance. *See* **Roof Styles**
    cooling fans 341–342
    cool roof. *See* **Roof, Cool**
    heat radiation barrier
        See **Roof, Cool**
    insulation
        See **Insulation of Roof**
    leaks 332
    living space in 77–83
    overhang. *See* **Roof Overhang**
    shapes & styles (gallery) 116–125
    slope 115
    snow & ice protection
        See **Snow & Ice Protection**
    structures, by type
        See **Roof Structure, (Type)**
    styles. *See* **Roof Styles**
    surfaces. *See* **Roof Surfaces**
    underlayment 332–333
    ventilation, for cooling 340–343
    vents 340–341
    weak shapes 124
    wind damage, resistance 312–315

Roof, Cool 336–344
    components of 336–337
    cooling by ventilation 340–343
    cooling fans 341–342
    cool surfaces 337–339
        See also **Roof Surfaces**
    heat radiation barrier 343–344
    roof depth, extra 124
    solar heating of surfaces 337–338

Roof Deck 319, 330–332

Roof Overhang
    benefits 115
    for entrance cover 55
    for shading 159. *See also* **Shading Fixtures, Exterior**
    framing, strong 316–317

Roof Structure, A-Frame 117, 317–318, 672

Roof Structure, Beam
    defined 80
    designs 80–81
    insulation 320–321
    moisture venting 327
    rafter depth 318
    secure both ends 319

Roof Structure, Collar Beam 319–320

Roof Structure, Flat 83
  concrete deck 332
  insulation 323–324

Roof Structure, Gambrel 82, 118

Roof Structure, Mansard 82–83, 118

Roof Structure, Triangle-Frame
  connections, strong 317–318
  description 81
  insulation 320–321
  moisture venting 327
  rafter depth 318

Roof Structure, Truss
  advantages 78–79
  defined 78
  designs 78–79
  disadvantage 79
  insulation 321–322
  moisture venting 325–327
  trusses, strengthen 315–316

Roof Styles
  ▶ style gallery 116–123
  A-frame 117, 672
  dormer. *See* **Dormer**
  Dutch hip 118
  flat 120
  gable 116–117, 121
    See also **Gable**
  gambrel 118
  half hip 118
  hip 117
  mansard 118
  overlapping shed 119
  pagoda 119
  pyramid 119
  saltbox 118
  shed 119

Roof Surfaces
  ▶ Roof Surface Comparison (table) 127
  ceramic tiles 128–129
  cool 337–339
  installation 334
  metal panel 128–129
  metal shingles and tiles 129–130

  shingles, asphalt 126–127
  shingles, wood 130
  slate 130
  sod 130, 671, 673
  solar heating of (table) 337–338
  thatch 130
  types 126–130
  underlayment 332–333

Rooms
  See also **name of room**
  arrangement. *See* **Floor Plan**
  bedroom clusters 68–69
  day cluster 67
  design, by type 26–60
  expansion rooms 67
  independent rooms 69
  room groups 66–69

Rugs 406, 410. *See also* **Carpet**

S

Safety
  See also **Security;**
  See also **Health**
  bathtub 32, 37
  building codes 205–206
  carbon monoxide 495–496
  emergency exit 181
  emergency shelter 58–60
  fire safety. *See* **Fire Safety**
  floor surfaces, slippery
    See **Floor Surfaces**
  fuels. *See* **name of fuel**
  intrusion, resisting. *See* **Security**
  lighting, night safety.
    See **Lighting Fixtures**
  radon. *See* **Radon;**
    See **Radon Mitigation**
  roof access, safe 124
  roof collapse
    See **Roof Structure, Collar Beam;**
    See **Roof Structure, Gambrel;**
    See **Roof Structure, Triangle-Frame;**
    See **Roof Structure, Truss**
  snow & ice, falling from roof
    See **Snow & Ice Protection**

  stairs. *See* **Stairs**
  windstorms
    See **Wind Damage, Preventing**

Scene (lighting term) 550

Screened Porch 56

Sealants
  application, proper 233–234
  materials 234–236
  protection of 236

Sealed Combustion System
  See also **Flue**
  avoids carbon monoxide hazard 496
  for boiler 444–445
  for gas-fired room heaters 476

Security
  See also **Safety**
  See also **Privacy**
  door locks. *See* **Door Locks**
  doors, reinforcement 382–384
  garage door, reinforced 391–392
  lighting. *See* **Lighting Fixtures**
  strong room 29–30
  windows, intrusion-resistant 366–367

SEER (cooling efficiency) 463–464

Sewing Room 44

Shading Fixtures, Exterior 158–163
  awnings 161–162
  balcony 161
  design of 158
  false eaves 161
  gable end overhangs 159–161
  lourvers, fixed 163
  louvered shutters 162
  louver panels 162
  overhanging floor 161
  porch 161
  roof overhangs 159
  south-facing glazing, for 159–160
  trees & shrubs. *See* **Foliage**

Shading Fixtures, Interior
164–166
curtains & draperies 165–166
roller shades 164–165
venetian blinds 165

Shading, for Cooling 153–166
with exterior fixtures
See **Shading Fixtures,**
Exterior
with foliage 153–158
with interior shading devices
See **Shading Fixtures,**
Interior

Sheetrock. *See* **Gypsum Board**

Shingles, Roofing
asphalt 126–127
metal 129–130
wood 130

Shower
faucets 512–513
heads 513–514
health hazards 514
water treatment
See **Water Treatment**

Shower Rooms 32–37

Sill Plate 193, 195, 286, 292

Sinkholes 248

Sinks 516

Size. *See also* **Dimensions**
exploit standard sizes 64
metric real vs. nominal 64
of corridors 70
of doors 70
of drawings 618
of glazing 149–150, 153
of house 86–90
of rooms, to fit furnishings 65
of stairs 71

Sky Temperature 180

Skylight 174–176, 400–404
▶ Skylight Selection Guide
401–404
appearance 180
comparison to windows,
clerestories & light pipes
(table) 142–143
condensation damage 403–404
for daylighting 172–174
See also **Daylighting**
frame construction 403
glazing 402, 404
See also **Glazing, Materials**
heat loss 403
installation 400, 402
leakage 400, 402
openable 403
ratings 400
shading devices, integral 404
size 401
types 401

Smoking Room 72–73

Snow & Ice Protection
▶ Snow & Ice Protection
Checklist 125
condensation damage 328
ice dams 328
roof shape 329
safety under eaves 125
snow fences, avoid 125, 329

Sod Roof 671, 673

Soil
as heat source
See **Geothermal Heat Pump**
as insulation 670
earth-sheltered house 670–671
frost depth 247–248
pressure 270–273
See also **Walls, Basement**
radon in 244–245
See also **Radon**
strength, to support foundation
247
temperature of deep soil 278
thermal lag 92, 670
water in 246

Solar Collectors
air heating. *See* **Solar Heating,**
Active Systems
photovoltaic. *See* **Solar**
Electricity Generation
water heating. *See* **Solar**
Heating, Active Systems

Solar Electricity Generation
658–661
access to sunlight 661
conflict with roof maintenance
661
energy output 658
how it works 658
system arrangements 659–661

Solar Heating, Active Systems
649–653
access to sunlight 650
all-air systems 653
dimensions 652
excess heat problem 652
freeze protection 652
solar collectors 649–651
space heating systems 651
water heating systems 651

Solar Heating, Passive 654–657
See also **Glazing, Applications**
access to winter sunlight 655
appeal of 654
design issues 656–657
problems of 654–655
with clerestories
See **Clerestories**
with windows 151–152

Spa. *See* **Bathtub;** *See* **Hot Tub**

Specifications (construction)
619–620

Split-System Air Conditioners
469

Split-System Heat Pumps
459–462

Stairs
dimensions **71**
handicap access **72**
preventing stratification **71**
safety **71**
where to locate **70, 95**

Steel
concrete reinforcement **252–254**
rebar, improved **253**

Stem Wall 260, 266–268
See also **Foundation**

Stone
foundation
See **Foundation, Stone**
stone veneer **99, 109–110**
thermal lag **92**
walls. *See* **Walls, Stone**

Storage Rooms 29

Storm Door 379

Storm Windows 373

Stratification, Temperature
between floors **70-71**
fans to prevent **485**
stair isolation **71**
tall ceilings, with **85**

Straw Bale House 673

Strong Room 29–30

Stucco 105

Studs, Wall. *See* **Wall Studs**

Style. *See* **Architectural Style**

Subfloor
See **Floor Structure, Wooden**

Sump Pump 277
radon removal system **265–266**

Sun, Motion of 141–148
orient floor plan to **75**

Sun Position Charts 144–148

Sun & View Survey 147–148

Sunlight
components of **140–141**
glare from. *See* **Glare**
infrared **141**
intensity of **167**
ultraviolet **141**
visible **140–141**

Sunroom 49, 182–183

Super-Insulation
amount of. *See* **Insulation, Amounts**
as design principle **15, 207**
of basement
See **Insulation of Basement**
of floors
See **Insulation of Floor**
of foundation
See **Insulation of Foundation**
of roof. *See* **Insulation of Roof**
of walls, frame. *See* **Insulation of Walls, Frame**
of walls, masonry. *See* **Insulation of Walls, Masonry**

Swamp Cooler
See **Evaporative Cooler**

Swimming Pool 135–137

System Feeder (hydronic system) 450–451
for draining system **450–451**
for leak protection **438, 451, 452**
for purging system **453**
for system pressurization **449, 450–451**
for system water treatment **450, 452**
location in system **439, 444**

T

Tandem Windows 371–372

Task Lighting 567–569

Terrazzo 406, 409

Thermal Lag 92

Thermal Shutters (glazing) 646–648

Thermostats
▶ Programmable Thermostat Selection Guide **506**
freeze protection **507**
programmable **505–506**
proper location **508**

Tile
floor **408–409**
interior surfaces **308**
roof **129–130**

Time Controls
clock switches **507**
interval timers **505, 507**

Toilet Rooms 31–32

Toilets 517–520
convenience **519–520**
conventional (siphon) toilets **517–518**
pressure-flushing **517, 518**
primitive & disgusting **519**
recommended types **517**
vacuum-assisted **519**

Tongue-and-Groove Decking 332

Tornadoes
emergency shelter **58–60**
locations of **241–242**
protection against. *See* **Wind Damage, Preventing**

Track Lighting 571

Trees & Shrubs. *See* **Foliage**

Triangle-Frame Roof. *See* **Roof Structure, Triangle-Frame**

Tubular Skylights. *See* **Light Pipe**

Turbine Ventilators 342

U

Underlayment
floor. *See* **Floor Structure, Wooden**
roof surface **332–333**

Urinal 520–521

V

Valance Lighting 571

Vapor Barrier
explained **226–228**
for frame walls & ceilings **299–300**
for masonry walls **302**
perm rating, explained **226**
perm ratings of materials (table) **227**

Veiling Reflections 566–567

Venetian Blinds 165. *See also* **Shading Fixtures, Interior**

Ventilation, for Air Quality 490–494
by openable glazing **179**
by range hood. *See* **Range Hood**
of kitchen **39, 491–492**
of toilet rooms **493**
of workshop **493–494**

Ventilation, for Combustion Air.
See also **Flue**
for equipment with open flames **496.**
See also **Kitchen**
through chase from attic **496**
through openable glazing
See **Clerestories**;
See **Skylights**;
See **Windows**
through sealed combustion system. *See* **Sealed Combustion System**

Ventilation, for Comfort Cooling
by fans. *See* **Fans, Cooling**
by openable glazing **179**
See also **Clerestories**;
See also **Skylights**;
See also **Windows**

Ventilation, for Humidity Control
See also **Venting, Moisture**;
See also **Mildew**
by openable glazing
See **Clerestories**;
See **Skylights**;
See **Windows**
limitations **502**
of bathtub room **492–493**
of crawl space
See **Crawl Space**
of kitchen **491–492**
of laundry space **493**
of shower **492–493**
of toilet rooms **493**

Ventilation, for Roof Cooling 336–337, 340–343

Venting, Combustion Gas
See **Flue**;
See **Heating Equipment, Room Heaters**;
See **Sealed Combustion System**

Venting, Moisture
See also **Ventilation, for Humidity Control**;
See also **Condensation Damage in Structure, Preventing**
basement **277–278**
insulation above roof **327**
roof **323–326**
walls, frame **300**
walls, masonry **302**

Vestibule 52–55

View
glare from water & snow **178**
orient house toward **73**
window design for **176–178**

Vinyl Siding 104

Vision, Human 550–552
color vision **551–552**
effect of age **550**
effect of contrast **550**
effect of glare **564–566**
effect of light intensity **550**
effect of veiling reflections **566–567**

W

Wall Sheathing, Exterior
▶ description **194, 198–200, 295–298**
as air leakage barrier **194, 295**
as base for exterior fixtures **295**
as base for exterior surfaces **194, 295–296**
as structural component **194, 239, 295**
installation **194, 199, 297**
materials **194, 295–296**
moisture permeability **227**
See also **Condensation Damage in Structure, Preventing**
thickness **296**

Wall Studs
described **194, 197, 200**
dimensions **289**
fabricated (thicker walls) **290–292**
solid (thinner walls) **290**
spacing **289, 290**
strength requirements **290**
wiring passages **290–291**

Wall Surfaces, Exterior 308–311
aluminum siding **104**
appearance **104–114**
blank walls, avoiding **112–114**
board-and-batten **104**
brick **106–108, 309–310, 398**
clapboard **104**
decoration with foliage **113**
decoration with ornaments **113**
half-timbered **110**
lightweight surfaces **104–106, 308**
painted **104, 111–112**
plastic (vinyl) siding **104**
shingles **104**
stone **109–110**
stone veneer **311, 398**
stucco **104**

Walls, Basement 270–281
See also **Foundation**
  design for strength 271–273
  insulation 278–279, 280–281
  soil pressure 270–273

Walls, Frame
  condensation, prevention
    299–300. *See also*
    **Condensation Damage in
    Structure, Preventing**
  corners, strong 294–295
  double-wall 291
  headers 194, 197, 292–293
  insulation. *See* **Insulation of
    Walls, Frame**
  moisture venting 300
    See also **Venting, Moisture**
  openings 197
  openings for doors & windows
    194, 197, 293–294
  plate, bottom 292
  plate, sole 292
  plate, top 292
  sheathing, exterior. *See* **Wall
    Sheathing, Exterior**
  sheathing, interior
    See **Interior Surfaces**
  studs. *See* **Wall Studs**
  vapor barrier 299–300
    See also **Vapor Barrier**

Walls, Interior
  insulation.
    See **Insulation of Interior
    Walls, Floors & Ceilings**
  load-bearing 65–66, 189, 191
  wet walls 69–70

Walls, Masonry
  basement. *See* **Walls, Basement**
  brick-and-block 310
  concrete block 202
  concrete frame 202
  filler blocks 202–204
  insulation. *See* **Insulation of
    Walls, Masonry**
  interior surfaces. *See* **Interior
    Surfaces**
  moisture venting 302, 304.
    See also **Venting, Moisture**

  stone-on-block 311
  stone walls 109–110, 201–202
  vapor barrier 302. *See
    also* **Vapor Barrier**

Walls, Stone 109–110, 201–202

Wash Basins 516
  faucets 516
  height 517

Water
  consumption, by use 512
  faucets. *See* **Faucets**
  filters. *See* **Water Treatment**
  heaters. *See* **Water Heating**
  in soil. *See* **Ground Water**
  pipes. *See* **Water Pipes**
  rainwater recovery 674–675
  treatment. *See* **Water
    Treatment**
  waste water recovery 676
  well water.
    See **Water Treatment**;
    See **Well Water**

Water Hammer 543–544

Water Heating 522–529
  delay at faucet, minimizing 529
  electricity cost, lowering 523
  energy sources for 522
  energy use for 511
  hot water recirculation 529
  pipe heat loss, reducing 525
  space for water heater 51–52
  temperature setting 524
  water heater, conventional
    (storage) 522–525
  water heater, direct-venting
    523–524
  water heater, heat pump
    525–526
  water heater, solar. *See* **Solar
    Heating, Active Systems**
  water heater, space heating
    boiler as 528
  water heater, tankless, electric
    527
  water heater, tankless, gas-fired
    527–528

Water Pipes 542–546
  ease of repair 542
  freeze protection 544–546
  insulation 544
  layout, for water treatment 543
  layout, to avoid interference
    between fixtures 542–543
  layout, to minimize hot water
    delay 529
  main water valve 544
  water hammer, preventing
    543–544

Water Softener
  534–535, 536–537, 538–539

Water Treatment 530–541
  ▶ methods & equipment (table)
    534–535
  ▶ recommendations, by usage
    530–532
  filter, carbon
    533, 534–535, 536–538
  filter, ceramic 534–535, 540
  filter, reverse osmosis
    534–535, 539
  filters, sediment 534–535, 536
  filter, ultraviolet
    534–535, 540–541
  for hydronic heating system 452
  pollutants (table) 534–535
  testing water supply 532
  water softener
    See **Water Softener**
  well water. *See* **Well Water**

Well Water
  as heat source & sink. *See*
    Geothermal Heat Pump
  radon hazard 245
    See also **Radon**
  treatment
    See **Water Treatment**

Wet Walls 69–70
See also **Floor Plan**

700

Wind Damage, Preventing
▸ Wind Protection Checklist **239**
hurricanes **241**
roof design for **312–315**
tornadoes **241–242**

Wind Energy 662

Window Sills, Fancy
103, 289, 368, 371

Window Terminology 353

Windows, Applications
See also **Glazing, Applications**
comparison to clerestories, skylights & light pipes **142–143**
for appearance enhancement **100–103, 140, 180**
for daylighting **167–168**
See also **Daylighting**
for emergency exit **181**
for solar heating **151–152**
See also **Glazing, Applications**;
See also **Solar Heating, Passive**
for ventilation **179**
See also **Ventilation**
for view **176–178**
See also **View**
in shower rooms **36**
in toilet rooms **32**
privacy, design for **176–178**
See also **Privacy**
shading
See **Shading, for Cooling**
sizing, to reduce heat loss **149–150**

Windows, Installation
finned windows, easy replacement **368–370**
mounting features **364–365**
tandem windows **371–372**
unframed glass **370**
windows without finned frame **370**

Windows, Materials & Components
frame materials **362–364**
glazing edge seals **362**
glazing materials
See **Glazing, Materials**
insulating fill gases **361**
number of panes **361**
spacing between panes **361–362**
thermal break (metal frames) **364**
weatherstripping **365–366**

Windows, Selection Factors
▸ Window Selection Guide **352–367**
▸ recommendations **350–351**
ability to replace glazing **366**
ability to replace weatherstripping **366**
cleaning, ease **352**
fixed or openable **352**
mounting method **364–365**
openable windows, styles **353–356**. *See also* **Windows, Types of Opening**
ratings, NFRC **351, 368**
resistance to intrusion **366–367**
resistance to storm damage **239, 366–367**
service life **350**
shape **352**
size **352**

Windows, Types of Opening 354–356
awning **355**
casement, inward swinging **355**
casement, outward swinging **355**
combination hinged (tilt-turn) **356**
double-hung **354–356**
hopper **356**
jalousie (louver) **356**
slider, horizontal (glider) **354–356**
slider, vertical (single-hung) **354–356**
storm windows **373**

Wiring & Cable
air leakage around, prevent **348–349**
convenience features **347**
insulation interference, avoid **347–348**
passages in joists **284**
passages in wall studs **290–291**
underground **189–190**

Wood
as heating fuel **627–628, 629**
fireplace. *See* **Fireplace**
floor structure. *See* **Floor Structure, Wooden**
floor surfaces
See **Floor Surfaces**
house construction
See **Frame Construction**
pellet fuels **631, 633**
roof. *See* **Roof**
walls. *See* **Walls, Frame**
wood-fired heating equipment
See **Heating with Firewood**

Workshop 51
in garage. *See* **Garage**
ventilation **493–494**

X, Y

Z

Zero-Energy House 663